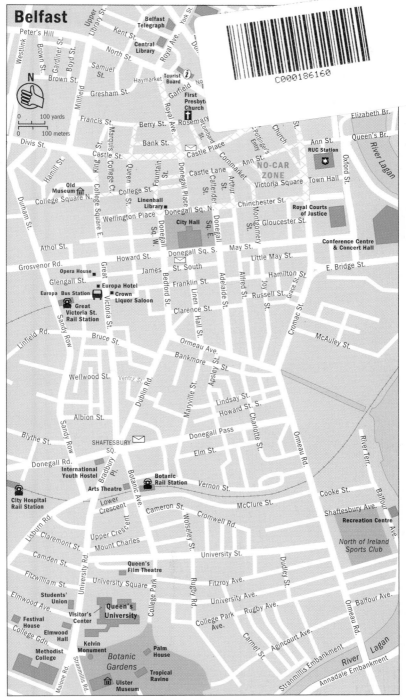

Belfast

50p

C000186160

Dublin

TO ✈ St. George's ✝

Mountjoy Sq.

North Great George's St.
Charles St. Great
Rutland St. Upr.
Summer St. N.
N. Circular Rd.
William St. N.
Dunne St.
Portland Row

Temple St. N.
Gardiner Pl.
Hill St.
Gardiner St. Middle
Gardiner Ln.
Summerhill Rd.
Rutland St. Lwr.
Buckingham St. Upr.
Empress Pl.
Killarney St.
Amiens St.

Blessington St.
Wellington St. Lwr.
Dorset St. Upper

Dublin Writers Museum 🏛
Hugh Lane Gallery 🏛
N'l Wax Museum 🏛
Abbey Presbyterian ✝

Denmark St. Great
James Joyce Center

Sean Mac Dermott St.
Railway St.

Connolly Station 🚗

Parnell Sq. N.
Garden of Remembrance
Parnell Sq.
Parnell Sq. W.
Parnell Sq. E.
Gate Theatre

Sheriff St. Lwr.

Dominick St. Lower
Parnell St.
Rotunda Hospital ✝
Parnell Sq. S.

Foley St.

Inner Dock

Moore Ln.
Moore St. Upper
O'Connell St. Upper
Marlborough St.

Tyrone House ✝

Corporation St.
Store St.
Talbot Ln.
Amiens St.

Financial Services Center

George's Dock

Commons St.

Moore St. Market
Earl St. N.
Talbot St.

Jervis St.
Mary St.
Henry St.
Liffey St. Upr.
General Post Office 📭
Prince's St. N.
O'Connell St. Lower
Abbey St. Lower
Liberty Hall

Busaras 🚌
Beresford St.
Memorial Rd.

Custom House

St. Mary's Church ✝
Abbey St. Upper
Abbey St. Middle
Hot Press
Global Internet Cafe
Eden Quay
Custom House Quay
North Wall

Liffey St. Lwr.
Lotts Row

Strand St. Great
Ormond Quay
Bachelors Walk
O'Connell Bridge
Burgh Quay
George's Quay
City Quay
River Liffey

Ha'Penny Footbridge
Aston Quay
Fleet St.
Poolbeg
Tara St. Station 🚗
Gloucester St.
Princes St.
Creighton St.

Wellington Quay
S. Temple Bar
Stock Exchange
Bank of Ireland
D'Olier St.
Westmoreland St.
Tara St.
Luke St.
Moss St.
Townsend St.
Lombard St. E.
Sandwith St. Lwr.

Essex St. E.
Sycamore St.
Eustace St.
Temple Ln. S.
Anglesea St.
Cope St.
Dame St.
College Green
Pearse St.
✝

Town Hall
Dublin Castle

Westland Row
Pearse Station 🚗
✝
Boyne St.

S. Great Georges St.
🏛 (i)
Wicklow St.
Suffolk St.
Nassau St.
Lincoln Pl.
Sandwith St. Upr.

Trinity College

American Express
Central Cybercafé
Drury St.
William St. S.
Clarendon St.
Grafton St.
Duke St.
Anne St. S.
Frederick Ln.
Frederick St.

Fenian St.
Denzille Ln.
Holles St.

Planet Cyber Cafe
Great St. Upr.
Stephen St. Lwr.
Longford St. Gt.
Chatham St.
Molesworth St.

National Gallery 🏛

National Library 🏛
Mansion House
Leinster House 🏛

Merrion Sq.

Adelaide Hospital
Mercer St. Upr.
Aungier St.
Peter Row
York St.
St. Stephen's Green W
St. Stephen's Green N
Dawson St.
Kildare St.
National Museums 🏛
Government Buildings
Merrion Row
Merrion St. Upper
Fitzwilliam La.
Mount St. Lwr.

Wexford St.
Harcourt St.
St. Stephen's Green E

St. Stephen's Green

St. Stephen's Green S
Hume St.
Ely Pl.
Baggot St. Lower
Mount St. Upr.

Camden Row
Sants St.

University College Dublin
National Concert Hall

Earlsfort Ter.
Leeson St. Lwr.
Quinn's Ln.
Pembroke St. Upr.

Fitzwilliam Sq.

Number 29
Bank of Ireland

Fitzwilliam St. Upr.
Fitzwilliam St. Lwr.
James's St. E.
Lad Ln.

Cork and Galway

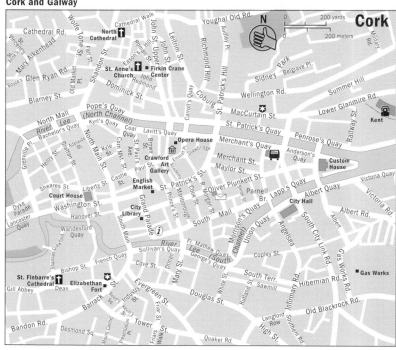

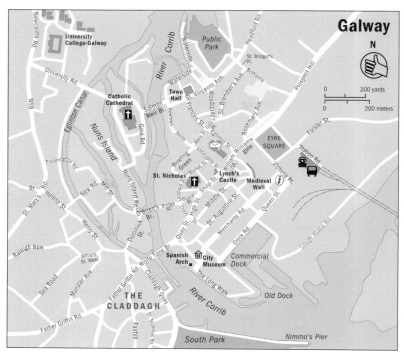

◼ Let's Go writers travel on your budget.

"Guides that penetrate the veneer of the holiday brochures and mine the grit of real life."

—*The Economist*

"The writers seem to have experienced every rooster-packed bus and lunar-surfaced mattress about which they write."

—*The New York Times*

"All the dirt, dirt cheap."

—*People*

◼ Great for independent travelers.

"The guides are aimed not only at young budget travelers but at the independent traveler; a sort of streetwise cookbook for traveling alone."

—*The New York Times*

"Flush with candor and irreverence, chock full of budget travel advice."

—*The Des Moines Register*

"An indispensible resource, *Let's Go*'s practical information can be used by every traveler."

—*The Chattanooga Free Press*

◼ Let's Go is completely revised each year.

"Only *Let's Go* has the zeal to annually update every title on its list."

—*The Boston Globe*

"Unbeatable: good sightseeing advice; up-to-date info on restaurants, hotels, and inns; a commitment to money-saving travel; and a wry style that brightens nearly every page."

—*The Washington Post*

◼ All the important information you need.

"*Let's Go* authors provide a comedic element while still providing concise information and thorough coverage of the country. Anything you need to know about budget traveling is detailed in this book."

—*The Chicago Sun-Times*

"Value-packed, unbeatable, accurate, and comprehensive."

—*Los Angeles Times*

Let's Go Publications

Let's Go: Alaska & the Pacific Northwest 2000
Let's Go: Australia 2000
Let's Go: Austria & Switzerland 2000
Let's Go: Britain & Ireland 2000
Let's Go: California 2000
Let's Go: Central America 2000
Let's Go: China 2000 **New Title!**
Let's Go: Eastern Europe 2000
Let's Go: Europe 2000
Let's Go: France 2000
Let's Go: Germany 2000
Let's Go: Greece 2000
Let's Go: India & Nepal 2000
Let's Go: Ireland 2000
Let's Go: Israel 2000 **New Title!**
Let's Go: Italy 2000
Let's Go: Mexico 2000
Let's Go: Middle East 2000 **New Title!**
Let's Go: New York City 2000
Let's Go: New Zealand 2000
Let's Go: Paris 2000
Let's Go: Perú & Ecuador 2000 **New Title!**
Let's Go: Rome 2000
Let's Go: South Africa 2000
Let's Go: Southeast Asia 2000
Let's Go: Spain & Portugal 2000
Let's Go: Turkey 2000
Let's Go: USA 2000
Let's Go: Washington, D.C. 2000

Let's Go *Map Guides*

Amsterdam	New Orleans
Berlin	New York City
Boston	Paris
Chicago	Prague
Florence	Rome
London	San Francisco
Los Angeles	Seattle
Madrid	Washington, D.C.

Coming Soon: *Sydney* and *Hong Kong*

Let's Go

2000

IRELAND

Deirdre O'Dwyer
Editor
Lillian Lew-Hailer
Associate Editor

Researcher-Writers:
Susan Biancani
Steve Hely
Oliver Lewis
Jessica Tardy

Macmillan

HELPING LET'S GO If you want to share your discoveries, suggestions, or corrections, please drop us a line. We read every piece of correspondence, whether a postcard, a 10-page email, or a coconut. Please note that mail received after May 2000 may be too late for the 2001 book, but will be kept for future editions. **Address mail to:**

Let's Go: Ireland
67 Mount Auburn Street
Cambridge, MA 02138
USA

Visit Let's Go at **http://www.letsgo.com,** or send email to:

feedback@letsgo.com
Subject: "Let's Go: Ireland"

In addition to the invaluable travel advice our readers share with us, many are kind enough to offer their services as researchers or editors. Unfortunately, our charter enables us to employ only currently enrolled Harvard-Radcliffe students.

Published in Great Britain 2000 by Macmillan, an imprint of Macmillan Publishers Ltd, 25 Eccleston Place, London, SW1W 9NF, Basingstoke and Oxford
Associated companies throughout the world
www.macmillan.co.uk

Maps by David Lindroth copyright © 2000, 1999, 1998, 1997, 1996, 1995, 1994, 1993, 1992, 1991, 1990, 1989, 1988 by St. Martin's Press

Published in the United States of America by St. Martin's Press

ISBN: 0 333 77979 7

First edition
10 9 8 7 6 5 4 3 2 1

Let's Go: Ireland is written by Let's Go Publications, 67 Mount Auburn Street, Cambridge, MA 02138, USA.

Let's Go® and the thumb logo are trademarks of Let's Go, Inc.
Printed in the USA on recycled paper with biodegradable soy ink.

ABOUT LET'S GO

FORTY YEARS OF WISDOM

As a new millennium arrives, *Let's Go: Europe*, now in its 40th edition and translated into seven languages, reigns as the world's bestselling international travel guide. For four decades, travelers criss-crossing the Continent have relied on *Let's Go* for inside information on the hippest backstreet cafes, the most pristine secluded beaches, and the best routes from border to border. In the last 20 years, our rugged researchers have stretched the frontiers of backpacking and expanded our coverage into Asia, Africa, Australia, and the Americas. We're celebrating our 40th birthday with the release of *Let's Go: China*, blazing the traveler's trail from the Forbidden City to the Tibetan frontier; *Let's Go: Perú & Ecuador*, spanning the lands of the ancient Inca Empire; *Let's Go: Middle East*, with coverage from Istanbul to the Persian Gulf; and the maiden edition of *Let's Go: Israel*.

It all started in 1960 when a handful of well-traveled students at Harvard University handed out a 20-page mimeographed pamphlet offering a collection of their tips on budget travel to passengers on student charter flights to Europe. The following year, in response to the instant popularity of the first volume, students traveling to Europe researched the first full-fledged edition of *Let's Go: Europe*, a pocket-sized book featuring honest, practical advice, witty writing, and a decidedly youthful slant on the world. Throughout the 60s and 70s, our guides reflected the times. In 1969 we taught travelers how to get from Paris to Prague on "no dollars a day" by singing in the street. In the 80s and 90s, we looked beyond Europe and North America and set off to all corners of the earth. Meanwhile, we focused in on the world's most exciting urban areas to produce in-depth, fold-out map guides. Our new guides bring the total number of titles to 48, each infused with the spirit of adventure and voice of opinion that travelers around the world have come to count on. But some things never change: our guides are still researched, written, and produced entirely by students who know first-hand how to see the world on the cheap.

HOW WE DO IT

Each guide is completely revised and thoroughly updated every year by a well-traveled set of over 250 students. Every spring, we recruit over 180 researchers and 70 editors to overhaul every book. After several months of training, researcher-writers hit the road for seven weeks of exploration, from Anchorage to Adelaide, Estonia to El Salvador, Iceland to Indonesia. Hired for their rare combination of budget travel sense, writing ability, stamina, and courage, these adventurous travelers know that train strikes, stolen luggage, food poisoning, and marriage proposals are all part of a day's work. Back at our offices, editors work from spring to fall, massaging copy written on Himalayan bus rides into witty, informative prose. A student staff of typesetters, cartographers, publicists, and managers keeps our lively team together. In September, the collected efforts of the summer are delivered to our printer, which turns them into books in record time, so that you have the most up-to-date information available for your vacation. Even as you read this, work on next year's editions is well underway.

WHY WE DO IT

We don't think of budget travel as the last recourse of the destitute; we believe that it's the only way to travel. Living cheaply and simply brings you closer to the people and places you've been saving up to visit. Our books will ease your anxieties and answer your questions about the basics—so you can get off the beaten track and explore. Once you learn the ropes, we encourage you to put *Let's Go* down now and then to strike out on your own. You know as well as we that the best discoveries are often those you make yourself. When you find something worth sharing, please drop us a line. We're Let's Go Publications, 67 Mount Auburn St., Cambridge, MA 02138, USA (email: feedback@letsgo.com). For more info, visit our website, http://www.letsgo.com.

v

HOW TO USE THIS BOOK

Welcome, gentle Reader, to *Let's Go: Ireland 2000*, a multi-splendored yet tasty little book intended to bring out the best *bodhrán*-banging, Guinness-guzzling, sheep-loving budget traveler in you.

As we begin our collective journey, let us, for a moment, take time out from the high-speed thrills of travel and get to know one another. Let us attempt to escape the dry, businesslike relationship most often achieved between book and reader. Let us have a drink. After all, what is *Let's Go* but a publican of sorts, that clear, reliable, identifiable figure who serves you what you want when you want it. No frills—ok, a few frills—but we're here to answer crucial questions with accuracy, honesty, and precision. Stout, lager, whiskey, whatever your preferred method of getting drunk off Irish culture, our pub is stacked and waiting for you to explore its cozy snugs, its hearty grub, and its odd cast of characters.

Of course, as we pour your pint and wait for it to settle, we'll take the opportunity to ask you some questions, to see just what kind of a drinker you are, to see how much and in what way you will cherish the creamy goodness of "the blonde in the black skirt." Are you Reader enough to make your own way along one of the suggested itineraries in our **Discover Ireland** introduction? Are you Reader enough to deal with our hints for beating the travel industry that are included in our **Essentials** chapter? Are you Reader enough to cope with a country that includes both Peatland Park and Peatland World? We cover 'em both if you're ready, and, even better, in our **Life and Times** section, we attempt to make sense of the history and culture of the country that finds them meaningful. Are you Reader enough to hike the 89,000 miles of hiking trails we include? Are you Reader enough to quaff Guinness from jam jars, part of our extensive pub coverage that includes carefully plotted pub crawl maps in Dublin (p. 107) and Belfast (p. 411)? Are you Reader enough to deal with the worldly ways of London, which we considerately include as a convenience to aid your travel?

Before the dark stuff gets to your head, you might want to familiarize yourself with some organizational tactics. At the start of each chapters, we provide a list of **Regional Highlights** that should help you prioritize your travels. In cities and larger towns, an **Orientation** section provides a rudimentary verbal map, laying out the city and the relative locations of key points. **Practical Information** provides hard data on things like transportation, tourist offices, financial services, emergency contacts, internet access, and telephone info. **Accommodations, Food,** and **Pubs** listings feature ranked entries; those establishments we feel provide the highest quality at the lowest price can be found at the top with a thumbs up icon at their side. **Sights** and **Entertainment** name the places we recommend you visit and the festivals we recommend you debauch.

Well, we hope that you've enjoyed the first of many sweet pints. Remember that a good drink becomes ever so much tastier when shared among a community of friends, fools, and fellow travelers. So drain the dregs of our cumulative wisdom and let us go to your head, dear Reader. Go forth and enjoy.

Sliánte!

A NOTE TO OUR READERS The information for this book was gathered by *Let's Go*'s researchers from May through August. Each listing is derived from the assigned researcher's opinion based upon his or her visit at a particular time. The opinions are expressed in a candid and forthright manner. Those traveling at a different time may have different experiences since prices, dates, hours, and conditions are always subject to change. You are urged to check beforehand to avoid inconvenience and surprises. Travel always involves a certain degree of risk, especially in low-cost areas. When traveling, especially on a budget, always take particular care to ensure your safety.

CONTENTS

MAPS

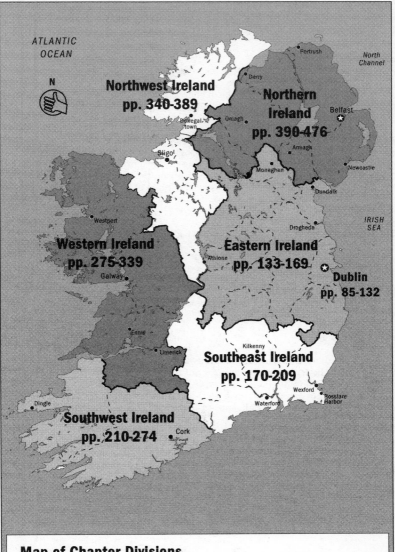

ATLANTIC
OCEAN

N

**Northwest Ireland
pp. 340-389**

Portrush

North
Channel

Derry

**Northern
Ireland
pp. 390-476**

Belfast

Donegal
town

Omagh

Armagh

Sligo

Newcastle

Monaghan

Dundalk

IRISH
SEA

Westport

Drogheda

**Western Ireland
pp. 275-339**

Athlone

**Eastern Ireland
pp. 133-169**

Galway

**Dublin
pp. 85-132**

Ennis

Kilkenny

Limerick

**Southeast Ireland
pp. 170-209**

Wexford

Rosslare
Harbor

Dingle

Waterford

**Southwest Ireland
pp. 210-274**

Cork

Map of Chapter Divisions

Eastern Ireland
Counties: Monaghan, Cavan, Louth, Meath, Longford, Westmeath, Offaly, Laois, Kildare, and Wicklow.

Southeast Ireland
Counties: Tipperary, Kilkenny, Carlow, Wexford, and Waterford.

Southwest Ireland
Counties: Cork and Kerry.

Western Ireland
Counties: Limerick, Clare, Galway, and Mayo.

Northwest Ireland
Counties: Roscommon, Leitrim, Sligo and Donegal.

Northern Ireland
Counties: Derry, Antrim, Tyrone, Fermanagh, Armagh, and Down.

RESEARCHER-WRITERS

Susan Biancani *Counties Antrim, Derry, Donegal, Down, Louth*
Susan came to Ireland like the reincarnation of the Hound of Ulster—everything from bus schedules to speeding cars bounced off her thick skin. Susan's softer side surfaced in her improved coverage of cheese, cheese, and cheese. After some long, strenuous days of biking, Susan still found energy to seek out Donegal wool and fix herself a fine meal. Keep on smiling, kid. *Comhghairdeas!*

Steve Hely *Counties Cork, Kerry, Limerick, Tipperary, Waterford*
Steve received the most fan mail, ate the most chocolate cake, and sent home the most tabloids. He overcame the most daunting of transport challenges and made friends with all manners of creature, from hippy musicians, to virile goats, to a Posh Spice. Steve is a storehouse of ideas for the future of the series, including the upcoming *Let's Go Illustrated*, complete with lemurs, archeological oddities, and converted schoolhouses. *Go n-éire an t-ádh leat!*

Ollie Lewis *Counties Carlow, Dublin, Kildare, Kilkenny, Longford,*
Meath, Waterford, Westmeath, Wexford, Wicklow
Super-sleuth Ollie did it all—urban, suburban, and rural—with style, humor, and unbeatable detail. Nothing was spared the scrutiny of his discerning eye, not even British *Cosmo*. His unfailing dedication improved Dublin but left his feet to fall into rack and ruin, much like many an ancient sight on his route. Ollie's charm made him likely the first RW to ever travel onboard an Alpha Romeo, and certainly the most deserving. *Máith thú!*

Jessica Temple Tardy *Counties Armagh, Cavan, Clare, Fermanagh, Galway, Leitrim,*
Mayo, Monaghan, Roscommon, Sligo, Tyrone
Jess won over the locals with her fabulous red hair and soulful crooning. She bravely tackled the technological wizardry of the job and investigated the finer points of Ireland's infants, B&Bs, and wide beds. Among her most memorable adventures were a remarkably long drive through the Sperrins, a horseback ride for two, and an intensive hands-on study of Irish medical care. Thumbs up, lassie. *Go n-éire an bothar leat!*

Laura Beth Deason *Editor, London*

Claire Lewis *London*
Yvonne Tsang *London*
Lano Williams *London*

ACKNOWLEDGMENTS

These books don't just put themselves together, you know.

TEAM IRELAND THANKS: Thanks a million to our little R(ub)-a-dub-dubs. Mr. Beepers, you kept us laughing, and swept up all our commas along the way. Thanks to darlin' Daryl "The-Wonderboy-and-encyclopedic-master-of-all-knowledge-plus-he's-a-really-swell-guy" Sng, who helped us lots. Alex, without you, the devil would have stayed down in the hole. Christian who we suspect cared more than he let on. Melissa R., Matt D., Adam, Jon S., Laura Beth, and Alice F. for smoothing out our rough edges. Anne Chisholm for taking care of everyone and everything. Dr. O'Dwyer, our *idirgalachtach scoláire*. Vanessa, Monica, and Elena. Pete, Anna, Sarah, James, Tom, Alice D, Marshal, and everyone to the right.

DEIRDRE THANKS: Thanks to Lilli, the world's most perfect co-worker. Run Lilli! Run! but not too far. For sheer brilliance in all things Irish, and endless support, thanks to my father. Fondest regards to the rests of the family as well, from Dublin to San Francisco. Brenna, thanks for listening, thanks for having me, and thanks for all that's ahead.

LILLI THANKS: Deirdre, editor-extraordinaire, all around great gal, and my general savior. Mom, Dad, and Kevin, whom I love dearly. Hitomi, Wendy, Markella, Cristy, Caroline, and Jon who all managed to live with me. The Seattle crew, the inventor of bowling, and the kickball kids.

Editor
Deirdre O'Dwyer
Associate Editor
Lillian Lew-Hailer
Managing Editor
Benjamin Paloff

Publishing Director
Benjamin Wilkinson
Editor-in-Chief
Bentsion Harder
Production Manager
Christian Lorentzen
Cartography Manager
Daniel J. Luskin
Design Managers
Matthew Daniels, Melissa Rudolph
Editorial Managers
Brendan Gibbon, Benjamin Paloff,
Kaya Stone, Taya Weiss
Financial Manager
Kathy Lu
Personnel Manager
Adam Stein
Publicity & Marketing Managers
Sonesh Chainani,
Alexandra Leichtman
New Media Manager
Maryanthe Malliaris
Map Editors
Kurt Mueller, Jon Stein
Production Associates
Steven Aponte, John Fiore
Office Coordinators
Elena Schneider, Vanessa Bertozzi,
Monica Henderson

Director of Advertising Sales
Marta Szabo
Associate Sales Executives
Tamas Eisenberger, Li Ran

President
Noble M. Hansen III
General Managers
Blair Brown, Robert B. Rombauer
Assistant General Manager
Anne E. Chisholm

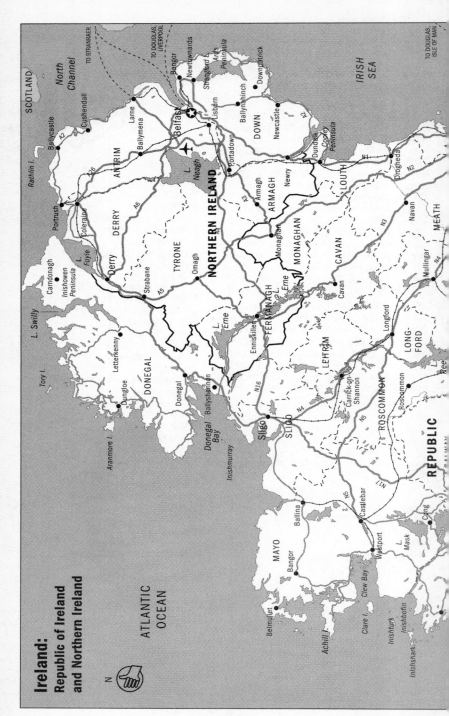

Ireland:
Republic of Ireland
and Northern Ireland

N

ATLANTIC
OCEAN

SCOTLAND

North
Channel

IRISH
SEA

TO STRANRAER

TO DOUGLAS,
LIVERPOOL

TO DOUGLAS,
ISLE OF MAN

Rathlin I.

Ballycastle

Cushendall

Portrush

Coleraine

DERRY

Larne

Ballymena

ANTRIM

Belfast

Lisburn

Bangor

Newtownards

Ards
Peninsula

Strangford L.

Ballynahinch

Downpatrick

DOWN

Newcastle

Portadown

Armagh

ARMAGH

Newry

Dundalk

Copley
Peninsula

L.
Neagh

NORTHERN IRELAND

Monaghan

MONAGHAN

LOUTH

N1

Drogheda

N2

Tory I.

L. Swilly

Candonagh

Inishowen
Peninsula

Letterkenny

Dungloe

DONEGAL

Donegal

Ballyshannon

Donegal
Bay

Inishmurray

Derry

Strabane

L.
Foyle

Omagh

TYRONE

Enniskillen

L.
Erne

FERMANAGH

L. Erne

CAVAN

Cavan

Longford

LONG-
FORD

Navan

MEATH

Mullingar

N4

N3

Arannore I.

Aughill I.

Belmullet

Inishkea

Bangor

MAYO

Clare I.

Inishturk

Inishbofin

Inishshark

Ballina

Castlebar

Westport

L.
Mask

Clew Bay

Sligo

SLIGO

N16

LEITRIM

Carrick-on-
Shannon

ROSCOMMON

Roscommon

N5

Cong

REPUBLIC

XII

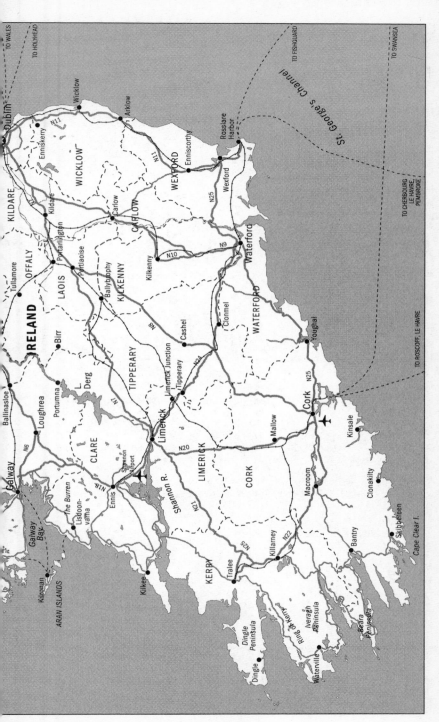

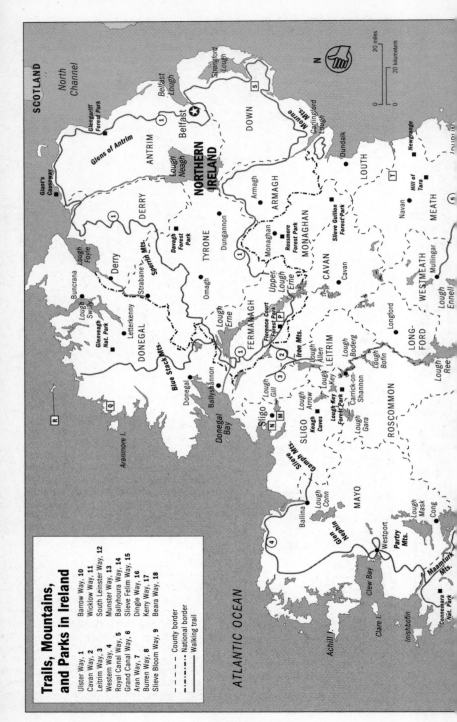

Trails, Mountains, and Parks in Ireland

Ulster Way, 1
Cavan Way, 2
Leitrim Way, 3
Western Way, 4
Royal Canal Way, 5
Grand Canal Way, 6
Aran Way, 7
Burren Way, 8
Slieve Bloom Way, 9

Barrow Way, 10
Wicklow Way, 11
South Leinster Way, 12
Munster Way, 13
Ballyhoura Way, 14
Slieve Felim Way, 15
Dingle Way, 16
Kerry Way, 17
Beara Way, 18

- - - - County border
-·-·-·- National border
———— Walking trail

ATLANTIC OCEAN

SCOTLAND

North Channel

Giant's Causeway

Glenariff Forest Park

Belfast Lough

Glens of Antrim

Belfast

ANTRIM

DOWN

NORTHERN IRELAND

Mourne Mts.

Strangford Lough

Carlingford Lough

Lough Foyle

Buncrana

Lough Swilly

Letterkenny

DERRY

Derry

Sperrin Mts.

Strabane

Davagh Forest Park

TYRONE

Omagh

Dungannon

Lough Neagh

Armagh

ARMAGH

Monaghan

MONAGHAN

Rossmore Forest Park

Slieve Gullion Forest Park

Dundalk

LOUTH

Newgrange

Hill of Tara

MEATH

Navan

Glenveagh Nat. Park

DONEGAL

Blue Stack Mts.

Donegal

Ballyshannon

Lough Erne

Upper Lough Erne

Florence Court Forest Park

FERMANAGH

Lower Lough Erne

CAVAN

Cavan

Mullingar

WESTMEATH

Lough Ennell

LONG-FORD

Longford

Lough Ree

Araínmore I.

Donegal Bay

Lough Gill

Sligo

SLIGO

Lough Gill

Lough Arrow

Keash Caves

Iron Mts.

Lough Allen

Lough Key Forest Park

LEITRIM

Carrick-on-Shannon

Lough Boderg

Lough Bofin

ROSCOMMON

Slieve Gamph Mts.

Ballina

Lough Gara

Lough Conn

MAYO

Glen Nephin

Lough Mask

Partry Mts.

Cong

Westport

Clew Bay

Achill I.

Clare I.

Inishbofin

Maamturk Mts.

Connemara Nat. Park

XIV

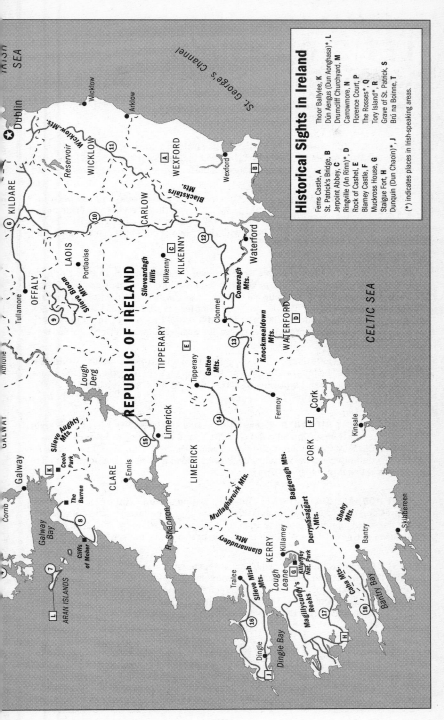

Historical Sights in Ireland

Fenns Castle, **A**
St. Patrick's Bridge, **B**
Jerpoint Abbey, **C**
Ringville (An Rinn)*, **D**
Rock of Cashel, **E**
Blarney Castle, **F**
Muckross House, **G**
Staigue Fort, **H**
Dunquin (Dun Chaoin)*, **J**

Thoor Ballylee, **K**
Dún Aengus (Dun Aonghasa)*, **L**
Drumcliff Churchyard, **M**
Carrowmore, **N**
Florence Court, **P**
The Rosses*, **Q**
Tory Island*, **R**
Grave of St. Patrick, **S**
Brú na Bóinne, **T**

(*) indicates places in Irish-speaking areas.

IRISH SEA

St. George's Channel

CELTIC SEA

★ Dublin

Wicklow

Arklow

Wexford

Reservoir

WICKLOW

Wicklow Mts.

KILDARE

OFFALY

LAOIS

Tullamore

Portlaoise

Athlone

Lough Derg

REPUBLIC OF IRELAND

Slieve Bloom Mts.

CARLOW

KILKENNY

Kilkenny

Slieveardagh Hills

Waterford

WATERFORD

Clonmel

Comeragh Mts.

Blackstairs Mts.

WEXFORD

TIPPERARY

Tipperary

Galtee Mts.

Knockmealdown Mts.

Fermoy

Cork

Kinsale

Limerick

LIMERICK

CORK

GALWAY

Galway

Galway Bay

Corrib

Slieve Aughty Mts.

Coole Park

The Burren

CLARE

Ennis

R. Shannon

Mullaghareirk Mts.

Baggeragh Mts.

Shehy Mts.

Bantry

Skibbereen

Cliffs of Moher

ARAN ISLANDS

KERRY

Killarney

Killarney Nat. Park

Glanaruddery Mts.

Derrynasaggart Mts.

Tralee

Slieve Mish Mts.

Dingle

Dingle Bay

Lough Leane

Magillycuddy's Reeks

Caha Mts.

Bantry Bay

XV

LET'S GO PICKS

BEST PUBS: The Stag's Head, Dublin, has well pulled pints and a chatty clientele (p. 106). In Belfast, everyone from bikers to teenyboppers heads to **Lavery's Gin Palace** (p. 410). The future of trad looks rosy at **Roisín Dubh** in Galway (p. 312). **An Droichead Beag** keeps Dingle tipsy and toe-tapping (p. 266).

BEST MUSIC: In Westport, **Matt Malloy's** has Ireland's musicians stopping by at all hours (p. 330). **McGrory's,** in Culdaff, boasts big name trad groups and local songsters (p. 385). **Dolan's** in Limerick plays the perfect tune for a great crowd (p. 280).

BEST LEGENDARY LANDSCAPES: The spurge is poisonous, so gaze but don't graze at the **Poison Glenn,** Donegal (p. 371). Take in the lake views at **Glendalough,** which St. Kevin preferred to women (p. 139). **Navan Fort** (a.k.a. *Emain Macha*), near Armagh, is home to twins, men with the pangs of childbirth, and a fascinating archeological site (p. 439).

BEST PLACES TO STAY: Maria's Schoolhouse, Union Hall, has the best and the brightest of everything (p. 232). Pull your caboose into the **Corcreggan Mill Cottage Hostel,** Dunfanaghy, where railroad cars serve as dorms. Live like the Earl of Cork at **Ballintaggart Hostel** in Dingle, but watch out for his wife (p. 265). Abandon technology and relax inside gas-lamp-lit **Flax Mill Hostel** in the Sperrin Mountains (p. 475). Get spoiled in Georgian splendor at **The Saddler's House** in Derry (p. 460).

BEST VIEWS: Yeats still can't get enough of the views from **Drumcliff** towards **Ben Bulben** (p. 347). The hike, waterfall, and lake sum up to perfection at **Pedlar's Lake,** Connor Pass (p. 269). The valley of **Port** affords an appropriately private view of the devil's nether regions (p. 365).

BEST LITERARY HIDEOUTS: Escape the *fatwa* in the safety of Howth's **lighthouse,** just as Salman Rushdie did (p. 126). Claim the throne of literary genius at **Synge's Chair** on Inishmaan in the Aran Islands (p. 304). Dubliners take pause for poetic contemplation beside a bronze Patrick Kavanagh on his memorial bench by the **Grand Canal** (p. 114).

BEST ODDBALL COLLECTIONS: The Irish National Stud, Kildare, is a hilarious expression of personal whim and whimsy (p. 145). The bizarre little collection in Sneem's **sculpture park** includes an homage to pro wrestling (p. 263). The **Ceim Hill Museum** in Union Hall has a mix-and-match take on eras and artifacts (p. 232).

BEST CRITTERS: Knocknarea's **bilingual sheep** win for the third year in a row (p. 346). The Fota Island **lemurs** make a strong debut (p. 223), along with the one and only **king's cow** of Tory Island (p. 372). Technically not a critter anymore, the **Great Irish Elk** in Dublin's Natural History Museum is still super cool (p. 112). Rounding out the picks are the ice cream-producing **goats** of Cape Clear Island (p. 235).

DISCOVER IRELAND

Who will go with Fergus now,
And pierce the deep wood's woven shade,
And dance upon the level shore?
Young man, lift up your russet brow,
And lift your tender eyelids, maid,
And brood on hopes and fear no more.

And no more turn aside and brood
Upon love's bitter mystery;
For Fergus rules the brazen cars,
And rules the shadows of the wood,
And the white breast of the dim sea
And all the dishevelled wandering stars.

W.B. Yeats, 1893

Literary imaginations have immortalized Ireland's natural scenery since the ancient times of Celtic bards. Travelers who come to Ireland with this poetic imagery in mind won't be disappointed: this largely agricultural and sparsely populated island has experienced little physical change over thousands of centuries. Spectacular, windswept scenery wraps around the coast, and small mountain chains punctuate interior expanses of bogland. Pockets of civilization dot the landscape, ranging in size from one-street villages to small market towns to a handful of cities. Dublin and Belfast have flowered into cosmopolitan urban centers, suffusing sophistication into all in their orbits. While some fear that the encroachment of international influences signifies the extinction of native folkways, the survival of traditional music, dance, storytelling, and pub culture in both rural and urban areas proves otherwise. The Irish language lives on in small, secluded areas known as *gaeltacht*, as well as on road signs, in national publications, and in a growing body of modern literary works. For international visitors, today's Ireland promises an old-world welcome along with the edge of urban counter-cultures.

Although the chapters in *Let's Go: Ireland* do not mirror these divisions, it's useful to know that Ireland is traditionally divided into four provinces: **Leinster,** the east and southeast; **Munster,** the southwest; **Connacht,** the province west of the river Shannon; and **Ulster,** the north. Six of Ulster's nine counties make up Northern Ireland, part of the United Kingdom. Under the 1998 Northern Ireland Peace Agreement, residents of Northern Ireland may choose whether to individually identify as Irish or British, but word choice can still be sticky. "Ireland" can mean the whole island or the Republic of Ireland, depending on who's listening. "Ulster" is a term used almost exclusively by Protestants in Northern Ireland. It's best to refer to "Northern Ireland" or "the North" and "the Republic" or "the South." "Southern Ireland" is not a viable term.

DISCOVER

FACTS AND FIGURES

■ **Capitals:** Dublin and Belfast.
■ **Populations:** 3,619,480 people live in the Republic. 1,642,000 people live in Northern Ireland.
■ **Population Distribution:** More than 35% of the population lives within 60 mi. of Dublin.
■ **Emigration Rate:** 1 person per 1000.

■ **Land Area:** 70,280 sq km
■ **Land Use:** Arable land 13%, permanent pastures 68%, forests and woodlands 5%, other 14%.
■ **Natural Resources:** Zinc, lead, natural gas, barite, copper, gypsum, limestone, dolomite, peat, silver.

THINGS TO DO

Ireland's small area is well-stocked with activities to suit the whims of hikers, bikers, esthetes, poets, birdwatchers, musicians, drinkers, and come what may. The following is a brief summary of popular activities, destinations, and cultural phenomena. For more specific regional attractions, see the **Highlights of the Region** section at the beginning of each chapter.

NATURAL WONDERS AND HIKING

The west coast is spread with a gorgeous and dense concentration of natural wonders, including the limestone moonscape of **The Burren** (p. 295) and the **Cliffs of Moher** (p. 293), which soar 700 ft. above the sea. The **Ring of Kerry** (p. 256) encircles a peninsula speckled with mountains and glens, waterfalls and lakes, and beaches and cliffs; its natural phenomena are most densely packaged in **Killarney National Park** (p. 253), at the gateway to the peninsula. In the remote Co. Donegal, the Slieve League mountain-pass is fronted by the highest seacliffs in Europe. Donegal's **Glenveagh National Park** (p. 373) contains salt-and-peppered **Mount Errigal**, close to the bewitching **Poison Glen** (p. 370). The bizarre honeycomb columns of **Giant's Causeway** (p. 453) spill out from the Antrim Coast, a long strip of rocky crags and white beaches. Several developed paths allow hikers to spend any number of days exploring Ireland's various mountain chains: the **Wicklow Way** passes through the **Wicklow Mountains** (p. 142) in Dublin's backyard, the **Ulster Way** treks through the **Sperrin Mountains** (p. 475), and the **Dingle Way** (p. 263) courses along the bumps of one of the island's prettiest stretches.

ANCIENT AND MEDIEVAL RUINS

The ancient peoples of Ireland had a taste for heavy rocks and underground chambers, resulting in structures that the passage of time has done little to demolish. In Co. Meath, the 5000-year-old passage-grave at **Newgrange** (p. 148) is an architectural feat that stumps present-day engineers. The nearby **Hill of Tara** (p. 149) has been the symbolic throne of sorts for Irish bigwigs from pre-Christian rulers, to St. Patrick, to 19th-century nationalists. On the west coast, the **Poulnebrane Dolmen** (p. 297) marks a group grave site with a 25-ton capstone atop two standing rocks. On the limestone **Rock of Cashel** (p. 179), a mish-mosh of early Christian structures pop up across the skyline, including a medieval cathedral and a celtic cross. **Glendalough** (p. 139) is the picturesque home of St. Kevin's 6th-century monastery and 100 ft. round tower.

LITERARY LANDMARKS

Ireland's natural beauty and urban grime have inspired many centuries of superb literary output. Dublin has endured the caustic wit of **Jonathan Swift, Oscar Wilde, George Bernard Shaw, James Joyce, Sean O'Casey, Samuel Beckett, Brendan Behan, Flann O'Brien,** and **Roddy Doyle,** to name but a few. **W.B. Yeats** scattered his poetic settings throughout the island, but he chose Co. Sligo for his gravesite. **John Millington Synge** found literary greatness by depicting the domestic squabbles of Aran Islanders. **Seamus Heaney** has compared the bogland's fossilized remains of pre-Christian sacrifices to The Troubles of present-day Northern Ireland. In Belfast,

Brian Moore and Paul Muldoon illustrate the everyday life of individuals in a city that receives world recognition only for its extraordinary events. Brian Friel's plays bring to life the wilds and folkways of County Donegal. Limerick has had a successful facelift since the poverty-stricken days described by Frank McCourt in his childhood memoirs. Ireland's ancient mythology is the most pervasive of all its literary forms; virtually every nook and cranny on the island is accountable to fairies, giants, gods, and even the occasional leprechaun.

ISLANDS

Ireland's island status has helped it preserve unique traditional customs that separate it from the rest of Europe; its satellite islands play the same role in relation to the mainland. The people of the Aran Islands (p. 300) still live much like the rest of Ireland did at the turn of the century: they speak Irish; eke out their living fishing in *curraghs*, ancient cloth-covered rowboats; and have numerous quirky superstitions, including one that prevents fishermen from learning to swim. Off the Dingle Peninsula, the now depopulated Blasket Islands (p. 268) were once the home of several impoverished memoirists who prophesized "after us there will be no more." Today the island provides little talk but great walks around exquisite natural scenery and haunting village ruins. Tory Island's (p. 372) counter-culture is undoubtedly Ireland's strangest: this island of 160 individuals elects its own king, sponsors its own school of painters, remembers having descended from pirates and *poitín* smugglers, and refers to the mainland as "the country."

BREWERIES AND DISTILLERIES

The Irish claim that stout is good for you, and whiskey is the water of life; it follows that the island's breweries and distilleries are its holy wells. The Guinness Hopstore (p. 115) provides only a handful of clues about how to concoct the dark stuff. Smithwicks stores its blonder brew in a former monastery in Kilkenny (p. 170). Dublin's Jameson Distillery (p. 118) makes a slightly sweeter version of whiskey than that stored in barrels at Bushmills Distillery (p. 454) in Co. Antrim.

FESTIVALS

Ireland celebrates its warmer months with festivals galore—virtually every small village finds reason to gather its sheep for show, pull pints, and tune its fiddles. In late April, Galway gathers international bards for its Poetry and Literature Festival (p. 306). Mid-May brings Armagh's Apple Blossom Festival (p. 436). Joycean scholars take part on an 18-hour ramble through Dublin's streets every year on June 16, Bloomsday (p. 121). Early August brings all types of musicians, artists, and merrymakers to Waterford's Spraoi festival (p. 202). He-goats compete for the title of alpha-male in Killorglin's Puck Fair (p. 256) in mid-August. The Connemara Pony Show (p. 320) brings its colts to Clifden in late August. Around the same time, every set in Ireland tunes in to the nationally televised Rose of Tralee Festival and Pageant (p. 270). Cape Clear Island spins yarns at the International Storytelling Festival (p. 235), also in late August. Many return home happy from the Lisdoonavarna Matchmaking Festival (p. 296) in early September.

SUGGESTED ITINERARIES

THE BEST OF IRELAND (3½ WEEKS)

Land in Dublin (p. 86) and spend several days exploring this thousand-year-old city that's a bastion of literary history and, these days, the stomping-ground of international hipsters. Take the train up to Belfast (p. 399). Belfast's complex history is spectacularly illustrated in the murals that decorate its sectarian neighborhoods. Catch the bus to Giant's Causeway (p. 453), a strange formation of octagonal rocks that some call the earth's eighth natural wonder. Before you head back into the Republic, stop in at Derry (p. 458). A city that wears its strife-ridden past on its sleeve, Derry provides a hopeful forecast for the possibility of reconciliation among Northern communities.

Suggested Itineraries

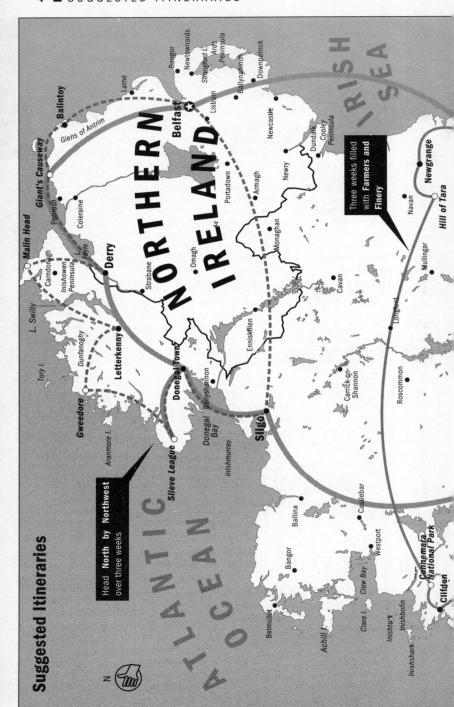

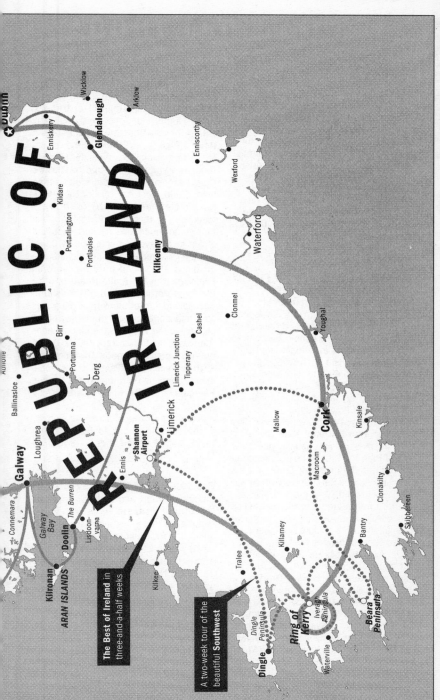

REPUBLIC OF IRELAND

The Best of Ireland in three-and-a-half weeks

A two-week tour of the beautiful **Southwest**

Ride the bus to **Donegal Town** (p. 356), spend a night at the pub, and head out the next morning to climb **Slieve League** (p. 361), the tallest seacliffs in Europe. Next up is **Sligo** (p. 340), once the beloved home of W.B. Yeats. From there, head to **Galway** (p. 306), an artsy student town that draws the best musicians on the island to its pubs. Catch up on sleep on the ride to the **Ring of Kerry** (p. 256). This peninsula contains picture-postcard villages and **Killarney National Park** (p. 253), an area with exquisite mountains, lakes, and wildlife. Return to civilization in the relaxed city of **Cork** (p. 212). On your way back to Dublin, take a detour to **Kilkenny** (p. 170), where a former monastery is now the Smithwick's brewery, Ireland's oldest.

IRELAND'S FARMERS AND FINERY (3 WEEKS) Get a taste of both urban and rural Ireland. Arrive in **Dublin** (p. 86), hit the National museums by day, spend the evening on a literary pub crawl, and finish off the night in Temple Bar, one of the trendiest spots in Europe. From Dublin, take a daytrip to **Newgrange** (p. 148), a neolithic burial site with some dandy engineering behind it; nearby **Hill of Tara** (p. 149) was the seat of Irish rulers from pre-Christian times to just several hundred years ago. Go cross-country to **Connemara National Park** (p. 324). Connemara is an Irish-speaking peninsula with **Clifden** (p. 320) as its accommodating capital. Wind along Connemara's breathtaking coastal road to **Galway** (p. 306). This friendly city plays spokesperson for rural Ireland's traditional music and crafts, entertaining thousands of international visitors in its small pedestrianized streets. Take the boat from Galway to the **Aran Islands** (p. 300) and check out ancient ring forts and recently knit Aran sweaters. Return via **Doolin** (p. 293). This superbly musical village sits beside the **Burren** (p. 295), a rocky bed of ancient fossils and unique vegetation. South of Doolin, waves smash pathetically against the looming **Cliffs of Moher** (p. 293). Return to Dublin via the **Wicklow Mountains** (p. 139). The Wicklow Way offers several days of hiking through "The Garden of Ireland."

NORTH BY NORTHWEST (3 WEEKS) Step off the plane in **Belfast** (p. 399) and hop into a Black Cab for a fascinating tour of the Golden Mile, sectarian murals, and the peace wall of this famous but little understood city. Take the Antrim Coaster bus north along the waterfront past the glorious **Glens of Antrim** (p. 441). Farther along the coast, Ballintoy village lies beside the **Carrick-a-rede Rope Bridge** (p. 452), a fishermen's construction that provides thrills for landlubbers. The volcanic spillage of **Giant's Causeway** (p. 453) is the stuff of Irish legend and most any tour of the North. From there, head to **Derry** (p. 458), a medieval city that competes with Dublin for historic importance. It's just a hop and a skip across the border to County Donegal, the most remote and untouched area on the island. Head up the Inishowen Peninsula to reach **Malin Head** (p. 386) the most northerly point of the island. Back inland, **Letterkenny** (p. 378) serves as a transportation hub to the rest of the county. To the west lies the mountainous **Glenveagh National Park** (p. 373) and the Irish-speaking area of **Gweedore** (p. 370), a source of brilliant Irish traditional music. Continue on to the **Slieve League Penisula** (p. 359), where soaring seacliffs are a bus ride away from the conveniences of **Donegal Town** (p. 356). Before heading back to Belfast, tour Yeats Country around **Sligo** (p. 340).

THE SOUTHWEST (2 WEEKS) Land at Shannon Airport and make your way to the **Dingle Pensula** (p. 263), where mountains, beaches, and Irish-speakers abound. Next, circle the **Ring of Kerry** (p. 256), southeast of Dingle. Home to magnificent **Killarney National Park** (p. 253), this highly touristed peninsula provides access to the mostly bypassed **Valentia Island** (p. 259) and **Skellig Rocks** (p. 260). Don't miss a third finger of land—the **Beara Peninsula** (p. 239), the most remote and, arguably, most splendid of the three. Stop in to **Cork City** (p. 212) on the way back to the airport to reacclimate to a busier pace of life and enjoy a final pint.

LIFE AND TIMES

HISTORY

PRE-CHRISTIAN IRELAND (TO AD 450)

What little knowledge historians have of ancient Irish culture they have ascertained from the fragile and spotty remains of its stone structures, landscaping, and metalware. Ireland's first settlers came from Britain in about 7000 BC. These Neolithic mound-builders founded an agrarian civilization. They left behind various structures that may be identified today on the Irish landscape. **Dolmens,** arrangements of enormous stones to create table-like form, were probably created as shrines (see **Poulnabrane Dolmen,** p. 297). **Passage graves** are ornamented, underground stone hallways and chambers containing corpses and cinerary urns (see **Newgrange,** p. 148). **Stone circles** are rings of pint-sized gravestones most likely marking spots of religious importance, including passage graves.

Bronze blazed into Ireland circa 2000 BC; over the next 700 years, the agrarian society restructured itself to form a warrior aristocracy. In the first two centuries of the **Bronze Age** (900-700 BC), known as the Irish Golden Age, Irish culture flowered, due in part to the central position held by warrior nobles in Atlantic trade routes between Gibraltar and Sweden. During this period, the past era's stone structures evolved to create new types: **ring forts** (see **Dún Aengus,** p. 303), which are protective walls that circled encampments and villages; **souterrains,** or underground hideouts for storing loot and escaping from marauders; and **clochans,** which are mortarless beehive-shaped stone huts. Remains of these structures are scattered across Ireland and many of its islands.

The **Celts** began migrating to Ireland from central Europe around 600 BC, and kept coming for the next 600 years. The Romans were too busy conquering Germanic tribes on the continent and in England to ever make it to Ireland. The Celts prospered on the peaceful isle, speaking Old Irish and living in small farming communities organized under regional chieftains. In the new power structure, chieftains ruled over territories called *tuath*, while provincial kings ruled over several *tuatha*. The **Uliad of Ulster,** chariot warriors and the most famous chieftains, dominated the La Tene culture from their capital near Armagh. These kings organized raids on Britain, established settlements in Scotland and Wales, and inspired the mythic heroism prominent in the *Tain* and other Irish epics (see **Legends and Folktales,** p. 20).

EARLY CHRISTIANS AND VIKINGS (450–1200)

Ireland was Christianized in a piecemeal fashion by a series of hopeful missionaries starting with **St. Patrick** in the 5th century. According to legend, St. Patrick was born in England and kidnapped as a boy into Irish slavery, from which he escaped to return to England. He later returned to Ireland at the command of a prophetic vision, but without the church's sanction, most likely landing in southeast Co. Down (see **Saul,** p. 430) and proselytizing to the northwestern parts of the island.

Missionaries and monks entering Ireland after the 5th century brought a new culture along with them. They recorded what they found in Latin, including a description of a system of writing already present on the island. They found this script on **ogham stones,** large obelisks engraved with a non-Latin script of dots and slashes that marked property. These monuments recorded the name of a man and his father, and are still present in the Burren (see p. 295), at the Hill of Tara (see p. 149), and at Bruna Boinne in Co. Meath (see p. 148). Missionaries also introduced a new architectural style to Ireland that included the Viking-inspired **round tower.**

These towers were built as fortifications against invaders; their sturdy form survives in the dozens today. A few now charge admission, but most are just sitting in fields and forests, in various states of disrepair. **High crosses,** or Celtic crosses, are a hybridization of Christian and Celtic esthetics: their form combined the cross with a circle to win the devotion of the native sun-worshipping pagans. These stone crucifixes can be large enough to dwarf a person and have elaborate carvings on their sides, sometimes illustrating Bible stories or legends of saints.

As barbarians overran the continent safety-seeking monks began arriving in Ireland in mass numbers. The enormous **monastic cities** of the 6th to 8th centuries earned Ireland its reputation as the "land of saints and scholars." From their bases in Armagh (see p. 439), Glendalough (see p. 139), Derry (see p. 458), Kells (see p. 151), Clonmacnoise (see p. 166), and elsewhere, the monastics of the Early Irish Church recorded the old epics, wrote long religious and legal poems in Old Irish and Latin, and illuminated gospels. The 7th century **Book of Durrow,** the earliest surviving illuminated manuscript, and the early 9th century **Book of Kells,** are now exhibited at Trinity College (see p. 111). The efforts of Irish missionaries converted (and reconverted) much of Europe to Christianity, although the Early Irish Church remained decidedly independent of Rome. Instead, monastic cities allied themselves with up-and-coming chieftains; Armagh, an important religious center, owed its prominence in part to the **Uí Néill** (O'Neill) clan, whose jurisdiction gradually spread from Meath to central Ulster.

The golden age of Irish scholasticism was interrupted by Viking invasions in the 9th and 10th centuries. Their raidings were most frequent along the southern coast, where they founded permanent settlements at Limerick, Waterford, and Dublin. They built Ireland's first castles, allied themselves with the equally fierce chieftains, and left the southeast littered with Viking-derived place names.

In the first decade of the new millennium, strife broke out amongst the chieftains: High King **Brian Boru** and his warlike **Dal Cais** clan of Clare, challenged the Ui Neill clan for control of Ireland with the capture of Armagh in 1002. In the following years, the clans of Ireland fought ferociously amongst themselves. The Dal Cais won a phyrric victory in the epic **Battle of Clontarf,** fought near Dublin in 1014, in which Brian Boru was lost. Ireland was then divided between chieftains **Rory O'Connor** and **Dermot MacMurrough,** who continued fighting for the crown of High King. Dermot made the mistake of seeking the assistance of English Norman nobles in reconquering Leinster. Richard de Clare, known popularly as **Strongbow,** was all too willing to help. Strongbow and his Anglo-Normans arrived in 1169 and cut a bloody swath through south Leinster. Strongbow married Dermot's daughter **Aoife** after Dermot's death in 1171, and seemed ready to proclaim an independent Norman kingdom in Ireland. Instead, he affirmed his loyalty to King Henry II and generously offered to govern Leinster on England's behalf.

FEUDALISM (1200–1607)

Thus began English hold over Irish land. The following feudal period saw constant power struggles between Gaelic and Norman-descended English lords. Norman strongholds, concentrated in Leinster, had more towns, including the **Pale,** a fortified domain around Dublin, and more trade, while Gaelic Connacht and Ulster remained agrarian. Yet, the two sides were hardly divided culturally: old English and Irish fiefdoms built similar castles, ate similar foods, appreciated the same poets, and hired the same mercenaries. Overseas, the crown fretted over this cultural cross-pollination, and in 1366 it sponsored the notorious **Statutes of Kilkenny.** These decrees banned English colonists (dubbed "more Irish than the Irish themselves") from speaking Irish, wearing Irish styles of dress, or marrying native Irish, and forbade the Irish from entering walled cities (like Derry). The harsh statutes had little effect, especially in the face of the Gaelic lords' increased success in reclaiming their territorial inheritance. Feudal skirmishes and economic decline plagued the English lords until the rise of the "Geraldine Earls," two branches of the FitzGerald family who fought for control of south Leinster. The victors, the

Earls of Kildare, ruled Ireland fairly unhindered from 1470 to 1534, to such an extent that the English crown grew fearful of their independence. In 1494, **Poynings' Law** limited their authority, and that of subsequent leaders, by declaring that the Irish Parliament could convene only with the consent of England and that any laws passed must meet the approval of the Crown.

The English Crown increased its control over Ireland throughout the next century. When Henry VIII broke with the Catholic Church to create the Church of England, a newly convened Dublin Parliament passed the 1537 **Irish Supremacy Act,** which declared Henry head of the Protestant **Church of Ireland,** and effectively made the island property of the Crown. The Church of Ireland held a privileged position over Irish Catholicism, even though the English neither articulated any substantive difference between the two religious outlooks nor attempted to convert the Irish masses. The lords of Ireland, however, both English and Gaelic, wished to remain loyal both to Catholicism and to the Crown—a near impossible order to fill. Bold **Thomas FitzGerald** of Kildare sent a missive to Henry VIII stating this position. In response, Henry destroyed his power. A reactionary FitzGerald uprising in Munster in 1579 planted in English heads the idea that Irish land had to be directly controlled by Protestants if it were to be considered safe and loyal. In defiance of the crown, **Hugh O'Neill,** an Ulster earl, raised an army of thousands in open rebellion in the late 1590s. Gaelic lords supported him, but the Old English lords were divided. The King of Spain promised naval assistance; his Armada arrived in Kinsale Harbour in 1601 but sat inactive as armies from England demolished O'Neill's forces. Their power broken, O'Neill and the rest of the major Gaelic lords soared out of Ireland in 1607 in what came to be known as the **Flight of the Earls.** They promised to return with assistance from the forces of Catholic rulers on the continent, but never achieved this aim. The English took control of the land, and parceled it out to Protestants.

PLANTATION AND CROMWELL (1607–1688)

The English project of dispossessing Catholics of their land and "planting" Ireland with Protestants was most successful in Ulster. Scottish Presbyterian tenants and laborers (themselves displaced by the English) joined the expected mix of adventurers, ne'er-do-wells, and ex-soldiers. The project in the North became known as the **Ulster Plantation.** King Charles's representative in Ireland, Lord Wentworth, pursued a policy with few supporters outside England that closed off the South to the Scots and continued confiscating more land than there were Protestant takers. The now landless Irish revolted in Ulster in 1641 under a loose group of Gaelic-Irish leaders. **Owen Roe O'Neill,** of the next O'Neill generation, returned from the Continent to lead the insurrection; the uprising even received the backing of the Catholic Church. The rebels advanced south, and in 1642 formed the **Confederation of Kilkenny,** an uneasy alliance of the Church and Irish and Old English lords. Some English lords considered themselves to be rebelling against treasonous viceroy, while still acting loyal to the King; thus, the concurrent English Civil War complicated their already tangled interests. Negotiations between the Confederation and King Charles ended with **Oliver Cromwell's** victory in England and his arrival in Ireland at the head of a Puritan army.

Cromwell's army destroyed anything they did not occupy, and then some. Catholics were massacred and whole towns razed as the Confederation dwindled away. Entire tracts of land were confiscated and handed out to soldiers and Protestant adventurers. The native Irish landowners had the options of going "to hell or to Connacht," the desolate and infertile region in Ireland's west. Some of the richest landowners found (paid for) ways to stay, while smaller farmers were displaced. By 1660, the vast majority of Irish land was owned, maintained, and policed by Protestant immigrants. After Cromwellian forces were deposed in the Restoration, Charles II passed the 1665 **Act of Explanation;** it required the Protestant newcomers to relinquish one-third of their land to the "innocent papists." In actuality, Catholics received scant compensation.

LIFE AND TIMES

THE PROTESTANT ASCENDANCY (1688–1801)

Thirty years after the English Civil War, English political disruption again resulted in Irish bloodshed. Catholic **James II,** driven from England by the "Glorious Revolution" of 1688, came to Ireland with his army, intending to gather military support to reclaim his throne. Jacobites (James's supporters) and Williamites (supporters of new Protestant King William III) fought each other in battles that had far-reaching political and symbolic consequences throughout Ireland. The battle between the two kings has since been mythologized to represent the subjugation of Irish Catholics under their Protestant superiors. In 1689, James attempted to take the northern city of Derry, where a young band of **Apprentice Boys,** closed the gates at his approach. The ensuing **Seige of Derry** lasted 105 days. The Apprentice Boys have since becomes Loyalist icons (see p. 458). The war between William and James ended on July 12, 1690 at the **Battle of the Boyne,** with James's defeat and exile. The battle is still celebrated by many Northern Protestants, in marches that take place on July 12, Orange Day (named for William of Orange). The war's end delivered the **Treaty of Limerick,** that ambiguously promised Catholics undelivered civil rights. Instead, the **Penal Laws,** enacted at the turn of the 18th century, further limited Catholics economically, and banned the public practice of their religion at a time when Catholics comprised 90 percent of the island's population.

The newly secure Anglo-Irish elite built their own culture in Dublin and the Pale with garden parties, gossip, and architecture second only to London. The term **"Ascendancy"** was coined to describe a social elite whose distinction depended upon Anglicanism. Within this exclusive social structure, such thinkers as **Bishop George Berkeley** and **Edmund Burke** rose to prominence. **Trinity College** flourished as the quintessential institution of the Ascendancy. Despite their cultural ties, many of these aristocrats felt little political allegiance to England. **Jonathan Swift** campaigned against dependency upon England, tirelessly pamphleteering on behalf of both the Protestant Church and the rights of the Irish people. Swift was an early proponent of the Irish Parliamentary patriots who advocated an Anglo-Irish state free from the authority of the English Parliament, yet owing allegiance to the King and excluding Catholics. Meanwhile, displaced peasants filled Dublin's poorer quarters, creating the horrific slums that led Swift to write "A Modest Proposal" (see **Literature 1600-1880,** p. 22).

Away from the Pale and Ulster, the Catholic merchant class continued to grow in cites like Galway and Tralee. Early in the 18th century, Catholics practiced their religion furtively, using large, hidden, flat rocks—appropriately dubbed **Mass rocks**—when altars were unavailable. Denied official education, Gaelic-Irish teens learned literature and religion in **hedge schools,** hidden assemblies with teachers who were often fugitive priests. The hedge schools became a powerful symbol of dispossessed Irish in the 18th century. Landlords were typically Anglo-Irish Protestants and their tenants Gaelic-Irish Catholics—a cultural divide that made brutal rents and eviction policies easier for landlords to adopt. Meanwhile secret agrarian societies, like the **Defenders,** formed to defend peasant holdings.

REBELLION, UNION, REACTION (1775–1848)

The American and French Revolutions inspired notions of independence in small political organizations such as the **United Irishmen,** which began as a radical Ulster debating society. When war between England and Napoleon's France seemed likely, the United Irishmen were outlawed. They managed to reorganize themselves as a secret society. Their Protestant leader, **Theobald Wolfe Tone,** hoped that a general uprising would create an independent, non-sectarian Ireland. A bloody uprising of peasants and priests erupted in May 1798. The rebels made their last stand at **Vinegar Hill,** near Enniscorthy in Co. Wexford (see p. 187); they fell in the thousands. A month into the battle, French troops arrived and managed to hold territory there for about a month before meeting utter destruction. French soldiers were held as prisoners of war and shipped home; Irish soldiers were executed.

TRINITY COLLEGE CHRONOLOGY

Through the late 16th century, the English toyed with the idea of an Irish university. In 1592, a small group of Dubliners took education into their own hands and obtained a charter from Queen Elizabeth to found Trinity College. The city granted the new foundation the lands and run-down buildings of a monastery just southeast of the city walls. The late 17th century brought turmoil to its hallowed halls: the Provost fled in 1641, the college had to pawn its plate in 1643, and all fellows and students were expelled in order to turn the college into barracks for James II's soldiers in 1689.

Trinity was up and running again by the beginning of the 18th century with the construction of the library underway. Trinity, the university of the Protestant Ascendancy, met few disturbances save the small number of boisterous Jacobites who unsuccessfully tried to introduce radical politics into this burgeoning intellectual aristocracy. In 1793, Trinity admitted its first Roman Catholic students. In the late 19th century, the tumultuous political climate finally seeped into the college grounds. The government made numerous attempts to incorporate Trinity into a federated university with several other Irish academic institutions; the college vehemently and ultimately successfully opposed such threats to its independence. It began admitting women in 1904, and they comprised 16% of the student population only ten years later. World War I and the creation of the Republic left Trinity without resources or strength in a divided Ireland, while newer universities in the U.K. quickly gained prestige. With the help of a long-needed annual state grant, finally secured in 1947, Trinity has continued to prosper through its fourth century. (See **Dublin**, p. 111.)

The Battle of Vinegar Hill embedded in the Nationalist imagination as an episode of unrestrained English brutality.

Any hopes England had held of making Irish society less volatile by relaxing anti-Catholic laws were canceled by the rebels' actions in Co. Wexford. The British abolished Irish "self-government" altogether. The 1801 **Act of Union** dissolved the Dublin Parliament and created "The United Kingdom of Great Britain and Ireland;" the Church of Ireland was subsumed by the "United Church of England and Ireland." Wolfe Tone committed suicide in captivity, while other United Irishmen escaped to France, building a secret network that would eventually link up with the Fenians (see **The Famine**, below).

Dublin's mad gaiety vanished. The Anglo-Irish gentry collapsed as agrarian violence escalated. English and Continental visitors to Ireland were aghast at its rural poverty. Meanwhile, the Napoleonic Wars raged in Europe, and many feared that Napoleon would set his sights on discontented Ireland. Paranoid generals constructed short, thick, cylindrical structures named **Martello towers** along the Irish coast, but the assault that never came. The British copied the form of these towers from examples they saw on Cape Mortella in Corsica. (The British, apparently, felt free to improve on the name.)

Union meant Irish representatives now held seats in the British parliament. Electoral reforms of the 1810s and 20s lowered the property qualifications for voting, allowing many Catholic farmers the vote. They elected Catholic **Daniel O'Connell** to Parliament in 1829, essentially forcing Westminster to repeal the remaining anti-Catholic laws that would have barred him from taking his seat. O'Connell acquired the nickname "The Liberator," and his efforts within Parliament allotted money to improve Irish living conditions, health care, and trade. When unsympathetic Tories took power, O'Connell convened huge rallies in Ireland, showing popular support for repealing the Act of Union. Romantic Nationalism, imported from Germany and Italy, pervaded the intellectual air, and some felt O'Connell had not gone far enough. "Young Ireland" poets and journalists led by John Mitchel (whom Yeats quoted: "Send war in our time, O Lord") saw violence as the necessary means to independence. They tried to revolt in 1848, but much of Ireland was starving and their efforts went unnoticed.

From this political enthusiasm arose unprecedented social reform. The 1830s brought the passage of the **Irish Poor Law Act,** which established workhouses to provide in-kind services for impoverished citizens. In 1836, the police force was centralized and professionalized under the title **Royal Irish Constabulary,** which later became the model for the British Empire's colonial police forces.

THE FAMINE (1845-1870)

In the first half of the 19th century, the potato was the only crop capable of providing enough nutrients per acre to support the Irish population. This reliance had devastating effects when the potato, along with most other crops, fell prey to fungal disease between 1845 and 1847. The **Great Famine,** which was far harsher than any small blight or crop failure of the early 19th century, lasted roughly from 1847-1851. In that short period of time, an estimated two to three million people died. Another million emigrated to Liverpool, London, Australia, and America. Depopulation in Connacht, in the west, was particularly severe.

While the Irish were eating grass, the British shipped thousands of pounds of grain from the island. British authorities often forcibly exchanged what few decent potatoes peasants could find with inedible grain. Catholic peasants who accepted British soup in exchange for their conversion to Protestantism earned the disdainful title "Soupers," a slur that stuck with families for decades. In future decades, Nationalists interpreted British insensitivity to the starvation of the Irish masses as ethnic cleansing. In analyzing the Famine, contemporary English economists adopted the rhetoric of a "Malthusian apocalypse." Two Irish economists' understanding of the tragedy advanced political and economic thought. **Isaac Butt,** founder of the Irish Home Rule Party (see **Parnell's Cultural Nationalism,** below) argued that it was hypocritical of the British to claim political unity while refusing to provide economic aid. **John Elliot Cairnes** blasted the idea of *laissez faire,* which he claimed was only applicable to those countries whose economic organization and division of land imitated the English system.

After the famine, the societal structure of surviving Irish peasants completely reorganized itself: the bottom layer of truly penniless farmers had been eliminated; men married late; and eldest sons inherited whole farms, while unskilled younger sons often left Ireland. The depopulation of the island continued after the 1840s as **emigration** became an Irish way of life. The **Encumbered Estates Act** began the 50-year process of removing the landlord class—a process which was continued by a series of Land Acts and the Congested Districts Board, which converted Ireland, with the exception of Dublin and northeast Ulster, into a nation of conservative, culturally uniform, Catholic smallholders. Rural standards of living improved with the extension of railroads into a system farther reaching than today's.

British injustice fueled the formation of more angry, young nationalist groups. In 1858, James Stephens, who had previously worked with the Young Ireland movement, founded the Irish Republican Brotherhood (IRB), commonly known as the **Fenians.** The Fenians was a secret society aimed at the violent removal of the British. In 1867, Fenian violence made William Gladstone, among others, notice the Irish discontent, and a year later he became Britain's Prime Minister under the slogan "Justice for Ireland." Gladstone's justice consisted of diminishing the minority Protestant Church of Ireland and battling for land reform. Combining agrarian thinkers, Fenians, and Charles Stewart Parnell, the **Land League** of the 1870s pushed for reforms with O'Connell-style mass meetings.

PARNELL'S CULTURAL NATIONALISM (1870-1914)

In 1870, Isaac Butt (see **the Famine,** above) founded the **Irish Home Rule Party**. Its several dozen members adopted obstructionist tactics: making long, dull speeches, introducing endless amendments, and generally trying to keep the rest of Parliament angry, bored, and ineffective until they saw fit to grant Ireland autonomy. Home Ruler **Charles Stewart Parnell** was a charismatic Protestant aristocrat with an American mother and a hatred for everything English. Backed by Parnell's invigorated Irish party, Gladstone introduced a **Home Rule Bill,** which was defeated. Parnell found redemption in the public eye when letters linking him to the **Phoenix Park Murders,** an infamous Fenian crime, turned out to be forgeries. In 1890, however, allegations that Parnell was having an extra-marital affair were proven true; the scandal split all of Ireland into Parnellites and anti-Parnellites. The moral divide also ran through the Home rulers, leaving their political ideals to fall by the wayside.

While the parliamentary movement split, civil society grew ambitious. The **Irish Women's Suffrage Federation** was established in 1911, following the lead of the British and American suffragettes. Marxist **James Connolly** led strikes in Belfast. In Dublin, **James Larkin** spearheaded an enormous general strike in 1913, a short-term defeat that nevertheless established large trade unions in Ireland. Conservatives, attempting to "kill Home Rule by kindness," also pushed for social reform. Most important of their efforts was the **Wyndham Land Purchase Act** of 1903, which provided huge incentives for landlords to sell their estates to the government so that ownership might be transferred to the tenants.

Meanwhile, various groups tried to revive what they took to be essential "Gaelic" culture, unpolluted by foreign influence. The **Gaelic Athletic Association** (see **Sports**, p. 30) worked to replace English sports with hurling, camogie, and Gaelic football. The **Gaelic League** (see **The Irish Language**, p. 19) spread the use of the Irish language. A side effect of these organizations' work was that the word "Gaelic" became synonymous with "Catholic." In addition, cultural developments rapidly merged with political movements. The Fenians actively involved themselves in the Gaelic cultural organizations as an opportunity to disseminate their ideas. Arthur Griffith, who advocated Irish abstention from British politics, began a tiny movement and little-read newspaper both of which went by the name **Sinn Féin** (SHIN FAYN), meaning "Ourselves Alone." As the Home Rule movement grew, so did resistance to it. Between 1910 and 1913, thousands of Northern Protestants opposing Home Rule joined mass rallies, signed a covenant, and organized into a quasi-militia named the **Ulster Volunteer Force (UVF).** Nationalists led by **Eoin MacNeill** in Dublin responded in 1913 by creating the **Irish Volunteers,** which the Fenians correctly saw as a potentially revolutionary force.

THE EASTER RISING (1914–1918)

In the summer of 1914, Irish Home Rule seemed imminent and Ulster ready to go up in flames, but neither happened—World War I did. British Prime Minister Henry Asquith passed a **Home Rule Bill** on the condition that the Irish Volunteer and Home Rule parties would recruit Irishmen for the British army. Asquith followed with a Suspensory Act, which delayed home rule until peace returned to Ulster; meanwhile, 170,000 Irish Volunteers and 600,000 other Irishmen enlisted on the Allied side. An 11,000-member armed guard, the remnants of the Volunteers, remained in Ireland. They were officially led by MacNeill, who knew nothing of the revolt that the Fenians were planning. If an architect can be ascribed to the ensuing mayhem, it was poet and schoolteacher **Padraig Pearse,** who won his co-conspirators over to an ideology of "blood sacrifice." Pearse believed that if a small cache of committed men died publicly and violently as martyrs for Ireland, then the entire population of the island would join in the struggle for independence.

The Volunteers conducted a series of unarmed maneuvers and parades throughout 1915 and 1916. The government at Dublin Castle was convinced of their harmlessness. Fenian leaders were meanwhile planning to receive a shipment of German arms for use in a nationwide revolt on **Easter Sunday, 1916**. The arms arrived a day too early and were never picked up. The British captured and hanged **Roger Casement,** the man who was to meet the shipment. Fenian leaders, however, continued planning their rebellion, and mustering support from the Volunteers. They told MacNeill about the arms shipments, and provided "evidence" of Dublin Castle's intention to suppress the Volunteers. Fearing the destruction of the Volunteers, MacNeill gave orders for mobilization on Easter Sunday. On Saturday he learned that the Castle order had been forged and the arms had been captured. He then inserted in the Sunday papers a plea ordering all Volunteers *not* to mobilize.

MacNeill and most Fenian leaders had been thinking in terms of military success, which at that point was clearly impossible, but Pearse's followers wanted martyrdom. On Sunday the Pearse group met and decided to have the uprising on the following Monday, April 24, in Dublin. Pearse, James Connolly, and about one thousand others seized the **General Post Office** on O'Connell St. (see p. 116), read aloud a "Proclamation of the Republic of Ireland," and held out through five days of fighting in downtown Dublin. Dubliners initially saw the Easter rebels as criminals, since their only tangible accomplishment was massive property damage.

The harsh reaction of the British martial-law administration to Easter Sunday transformed turned popular opinion on its head. Over ten days in May, fifteen "ringleaders" received the death sentence, among them Pearse, Pearse's brother (executed primarily for being Pearse's brother), and James Connolly, who was shot while tied to a chair because his wounds prevented him from standing. **Éamon de Valera** was spared because the British wrongly thought him an American citizen. **Kilmainham Gaol,** the site of the executions, became a shrine of martyrdom. By June Pearse's prophecy proved true: the public had grown sympathetic to the martyrs and increasingly anti-British. In 1917, the Volunteers reorganized under master spy and Fenian bigwig **Michael Collins.** The Sinn Féin party, falsely associated with the Rising, became the political voice of military Nationalism. Collins brought the Volunteers to Sinn Féin, and de Valera became the party president. When, in 1918, the British tried to introduce a military draft in Ireland, the public turned overwhelmingly to Sinn Féin, repudiating the nonviolence of the Home Rule party.

INDEPENDENCE AND CIVIL WAR (1919–1922)

Extremist Irish Volunteers became known as the **Irish Republican Army (IRA),** which functioned as the military arm of the Sinn Féin government. The new government fought the **War of Independence** against the British, who reinforced their police with **Black and Tans**—demobilized soldiers whose nickname referred to their patched-together uniforms. Both the IRA's guerrillas and the Black and Tans were notorious for committing atrocities. In 1920 British Prime Minister Lloyd George, supported by U.S. President Woodrow Wilson, passed the **Government of Ireland Act**, which divided the island into Northern Ireland and Southern Ireland, two partially self-governing areas within the U.K. After the general elections for Parliament, Lloyd George felt compelled to open negotiations with de Valera, a nearly impossible feat when both sides refused to recognize the other's legality. Finally, hurried negotiations produced the **Anglo-Irish Treaty,** which created a 26-county Irish Free State while recognizing British rule over the northern counties. The treaty also imposed on Irish officials a tortuous oath of allegiance to the King of England but not to the British government. Lloyd George pushed the treaty forward by threatening war if it was rejected.

Sinn Féin, the IRA, and the population each split on whether to accept the treaty. Collins said yes; de Valera said no. When the representative parliament voted yes, de Valera resigned from the presidency and Arthur Griffith assumed the position. The capable Collins government began the business of setting up a nation, with treasury, tax collection, a foreign ministry, and an unarmed police force called the *Garda Siochana* (GUARD-a SHEE-a-khahn). A portion of the IRA, led by **General Rory O'Connor,** opposed the treaty; this faction was also thought to be behind the assassination of Sir Henry Wilson, the newly appointed military advisor to the government of Northern Ireland. O'Connor's Republicans occupied the Four Courts in Dublin, took a pro-treaty Army general hostage, and were attacked by the forces of Collins's government. Two years of **civil war** followed, tearing up the countryside and dividing the population. The pro-treaty government won, but Griffith died suddenly from the strain of the struggle and Collins was assassinated before the end of 1922. The dwindling minority of anti-treaty IRA officers went into hiding. The disillusioned Sinn Féin denied the legitimacy of the free state government, and resisted referring to the Republic by its official name of Éire, calling it instead "the 26-county state" or "the Dublin Government."

THE HISTORY OF THE REPUBLIC OF IRELAND

Seventy-eight years of Republican independence has created a modern civic society with a flowering culture that infuses modernity with centuries-old practices. Strong regional distinctions and accents combine with a gaping urban-rural divide to enliven the national character. The social role of government, along with its unique relation to the church, are complicated by the increasing secularization of this traditionally pious society. Poverty and unemployment have historically been widespread, but the Republic's membership in the European Union has proven enormously beneficial to its economic infrastructure and development; in recent years, the media has dubbed Ireland the "Celtic Tiger." In the face of change, the lifestyle of the Irish goes unspoiled, continuing to center itself around music, sports, a laid-back attitude, and the pub.

THE DE VALERA ERA (1922–1960)

The new 26-county Irish Free State emerged from civil war having lost its most prominent leaders, and needing to protect those ministers who remained. The Anglo-Irish Treaty required the newly elected Dáil to frame a constitution by December 6, 1922. With time running out, **W.T. Cosgrave** was elected prime minister and passed a preliminary constitution in haste. Under the guidance of **Éamon de Valera,** the government ended armed resistance by May 1923, imprisoned Republican insurgents, and executed 77 of them. Cosgrave and his party Cumann na nGaedheal (which evolved into today's **Fine Gael** party) headed the first stable Free State administration until 1932. His government restored civil order, granted suffrage to women in 1923, and brought **electrical power** to much of the West by damming the Shannon River. In the first elections of the newly-formed Republic, the anti-treaty voters supported abstentionist Sinn Féin (see p. 12). Then in 1927 de Valera broke with Sinn Féin and the IRA and founded his own political party, **Fianna Fáil,** in order to participate in government and oppose the treaty nonviolently. Fianna Fáil won the 1932 election, and de Valera held power for much of the next 20 years. In line with de Valera's vision of Ireland as a nation of Catholic small farmers, Fianna Fáil broke up the remaining large landholdings and imposed high tariffs, producing a trade war with Britain that battered the Irish economy until 1938. Meanwhile IRA hard-liners trickled out of jails in the early 30s, resumed violence, and saw their party outlawed in 1936.

"In the name of the most Holy Trinity," de Valera and the voters approved the permanent Irish Constitution in 1937. It declares the state's name to be Éire, and establishes the country's legislative structure, which consists of two chambers, both with five year terms. The **Dáil** (DAHL), the powerful lower house, is composed of 166 seats directly elected in proportional representation. The less important upper house, the **Seanad** (SHA-nud), has 60 members who are chosen by electoral colleges. The **Taoiseach** (TEE-shuch; Prime Minister) and **Tánaiste** (tah-NESH-tuh; Deputy Prime Minister) lead a Cabinet, while the **President** is the ceremonial head of state, elected to a seven-year term. The constitution originally contained a "special position" clause concerning the **Catholic Church** in Ireland, but the clause was deleted by a constitutional amendment in 1972.

Ireland maintained neutrality during WWII, despite German Air raids on Dublin and pressure from U.S. President Franklin Roosevelt. Despite their neutral status, many Irish citizens identified with the Allies, and around 50,000 served in the British army. **The Emergency,** as the war was known, meant strict rationing of basic foodstuffs and severe censorship of newspapers and letters. While the young government lacked the monetary and military strength to have a large effect on the war, Éire's expression of neutrality effectively assisted the Allies. For example, downed American or British airmen were shipped north to Belfast, while downed German pilots were detained in P.O.W. camps. When the Germans firebombed Belfast in 1941 for its involvement in the war, Dublin's fire brigade came to the city's rescue. De Valera, in an exaggerated show of neutrality, was the world's only head of government to deliver official condolences to the German ambassador on the death of Hitler.

A Fine Gael government under **John Costello** in 1948 had the honor of officially proclaiming "the Republic of Ireland," and ending supposed British Commonwealth membership. Britain recognized the Republic in 1949 but declared that the U.K. would maintain control over Ulster until the Parliament of Northern Ireland consented to join the Republic. Costello's government was plagued with problems. There were many disagreements between the new coalition government and the church, exemplified by proposed reforms to the health care plan. Dr. Noel Browne, appointed Minister of Health to the Dáil, proposed a "Mother and Child Scheme" to improve a previous health bill passed by the Fianna Fáil in 1947. Browne's suggestions included free maternity care to all mothers, childcare up to the age of 16, and an education plan. The plan was criticized as being reminiscent of the socialized British National Health Service, and by the Catholic Church for running counter to church teachings.

The last de Valera government, in office from 1951 to 1959, and its successor, under **Sean Lemass,** finally boosted the Irish economy by ditching protectionism in favor of attempts to attract foreign investment. In place of verbal and military skirmishes over constitutional issues, which had dominated the 20s, Irish politics became a contest between two ideologically similar parties. Fianna Fáil and Fine Gael vied against each other to provide local benefits and constituent services.

RECENT HISTORY (1960–1998)

By reaching out Ireland has kept its young people in. In the 1960s, increased contact with the rest of the world meant slowed emigration and accelerated economic growth, resulting in increased national confidence. In 1967, the government introduced free secondary education, including state grants for privately owned schools; in 1968, it introduced free university education for those below a certain income level. Tourism became a major industry; Bord Fáilte has expanded tremendously to create a major source of employment. In 1969, the Troubles in the North disturbed citizens but the Republic's political and economic trends remained stable. While politicians still expressed nationalist sentiments, few people cast votes based on Northern events (see p. 392).

Ireland entered the European Economic Community, now the **European Union** (EU), in 1973. EU membership and an increased number of international visitors helped introduce the process of secularization in Ireland. **Garret FitzGerald** revamped the Fine Gael partly under a secular banner; during the late 70s and early 80s, he and **Charlie Haughey,** a Fianna Fáil leader, alternated as Taoiseach. Flip-flopping between parties produced a bewildering set of economic programs and initiatives, which were periodically interrupted by internal corruption. EU membership and funds continued to be crucial to Ireland's economy, helping it to pull out of mid-80s recession. Greater involvement in the Continent's culture and economy offered Ireland an alternative to dependence on the United Kingdom. In 1985 FitzGerald signed the **Anglo-Irish agreement,** which granted Éire an official, though not legal, role in Northern negotiations.

In 1990 the Republic broke progressive social and political ground when it elected its first female president, **Mary Robinson.** Social reform made further gains when the small, leftist **Labor Party** enjoyed enormous and unexpected success in the 1992 elections. In September of 1993, a coalition between the Labor Party and Fianna Fáil was elected. The new Taoiseach, **Albert Reynolds,** declared that his top priority was to stop violence in Northern Ireland. In August 1994 he announced the nearly miraculous cease-fire agreement with Sinn Féin and the IRA.

Reynolds was forced to resign in December, 1994, following a scandal involving his appointee for President of the High Court Attorney General **Harry Whelehan.**

Whelehan had been heavily criticized for his lack of action in a case involving a pedophilic priest, **Father Brendan Smyth.** Other scandals in the Church indicated that the conservative government had been protecting priests from legal charges of sexual misconduct and abuse, and that the Church was no longer beyond reproach in Ireland. During the week following Whelehan's appointment, Fine Gael, led by **John Bruton,** introduced a no-confidence motion against the government. After Reynold's resignation, the Labour Party formed a new coalition with Fine Gael, and Bruton became Taoiseach.

In June 1997, Fianna Fáil won the general election, making **Bertie Ahern,** the 45-year-old party leader, the youngest Taoiseach in the history of the state. Ahern joined the peace talks that produced the **Northern Ireland Peace Agreement** in April of 1998 (see p. 392). On May 22, 1998, in the first island-wide election since 1918, an overwhelming 94% of voters in the Republic voted for the enactment of the Agreement. Among other things, the historic Agreement created a North-South Ministerial Council, a cross-border authority focussing on such issues as education, transportation, urban planning, environmental protection, tourism, and EU programs. (For the recent status of the Peace Agreement, see p. 397.)

FURTHER READING ON IRISH HISTORY

Let's Go provides only a very condensed account of Irish history. For more intensive reading, Mark Tierney's *Modern Ireland* is a clear and comprehensive narrative covering the period from 1850 to 1968; *The Oxford History of Ireland* is a good source on earlier periods; Thomas Cahill's *How the Irish Saved Civilization* is an eye-opening account of monastic Ireland; and R.F. Foster's hefty tome *Modern Ireland: 1600-1972* is authoritative and interesting if you know a little already. For a history of Northern Ireland since Republican independence, see **Northern Ireland,** p. 392. The locals will do their best to fill you in on what you can't learn ahead of time.

CURRENT ISSUES

As Ireland becomes more active in the global economy, the nation struggles to balance its traditionally conservative values with increasingly liberal international standards. The Republic's progressive liberal movement gained ground in 1990 with the election of President Mary Robinson. A forward-looking activist, Robinson worked vigorously to elevate her office above the purely ceremonial role it traditionally played. With the greater involvement of women in public life, the **women's movement** has emerged from its position as a subsidiary of general political activism.

CHARLES HAUGHY served as the Fianna Fáil Irish Prime Minister (Taoiseach) off and on between 1979 and 1992. These days his name still appears in Irish front-page headlines, but they inevitably concern criminal, rather than civic, behaviors. Since his rise to political fame in the 1960s, Haughey's unaccountably extravagant lifestyle has captured the public eye. Haughey has faced investigations concerning tax evasion, the mishandling of political funds, gun smuggling, and taking bribes from Ben Dunne, heir to the Dunnes Stores fortune. In late 1999, the Moriarty Tribunal heard testimony on the ex-Taoiseach's finances, including allegations that money intended for an aide's liver transplant was diverted to Haughey's son Ciaran. Meanwhile, author Kevin O'Connor chronicled Haughey's romantic indescretions in the book *Sweetie.* The book claims that, in addition to a 20 year affair, a severe roughing-up that Haughey publicly blamed on a horse-riding accident was in fact the bruising a group of brothers gave him after finding him in a stable with their sister. Yet, the scandal-plagued Haughey remains a tenacious public figure, proudly defending himself and suing O'Connor for libel, and to whom the Fianna Fáil are indebted.

In November 1995, the closest vote in Irish history—50.3% to 49.7%—legalized divorce. The **Divorce Bill** allows divorce if spouses have lived apart for four years with "no reasonable prospect of a reconciliation."

Equally encouraging to progressives and disturbing to the Catholic Church is the **gay and lesbian rights** movement, which is slowly gaining legal ground. In 1980, the first legal challenge to laws against homosexuality was brought before the High Court. Lawyer Mary Robinson (later to be President) represented David Norris, a gay lecturer at Trinity College, in his challenge of the tacit discriminatory laws. Their challenge lost in both the High and Supreme Court of Ireland. In 1988, Norris won an appeal to the European Court of Human Rights in Strasbourg, and Ireland was required to change its laws. In June 1993, the age of consent between gay men was set at age 17. A large and relatively open gay scene has developed in Dublin, and colleges are becoming more aware of gay issues. A pamphlet offering advice to third-level students about "coming out" at college was recently distributed nationwide, and many campuses support gay student groups. The recent public "coming out" by the lead singer of Boyzone, one of Ireland's favorite pop groups, is sure to increase awareness and acceptance of the gay lifestyle.

Abortion policies have changed little over the decades. In 1983, voters approved a constitutional amendment securing "the right to life of the unborn." In February of 1992, the High Court horrified much of the public by ruling that a 14-year-old girl (called X in court papers), who said she had been raped, could not leave the country to obtain an abortion. In November 1992, voters passed a measure allowing the "right to information"; in May 1995, the High Court made it legal for centers to give advice on where to go abroad. Voters, however, still reject motions to legalize abortion. Current President **Mary McAleese**, a law professor and the first Northern resident to hold her office, was elected in 1997, claiming that she would rather resign from the presidency than sign into law a bill liberalizing abortion policies.

Ireland's economy is booming, in large part due to increased foreign investment over the past decade. Relatively few regulations and huge incentives have drawn foreign investors, strengthening the currency and boosting Ireland's economy at one of Europe's fastest rates. Industry has been expanding at an unprecedented pace and tourism remains one of the most profitable portions of the Republic's economy. Unemployment is comparatively low. After the fiscally fantastic years of 1996 and 1997, EU funding appeared so successful that the organization drastically reduced the quantity of its aid to Ireland. In 1998, however, the inflation rate reached 3.2%, a three year high, placing it well above that of the rest of the EU. There is some concern about economic overheating, and the effects of converting to the **euro** (see p. 41), the new EU currency that came into non-cash existence in 1999. The transition will be tempered by dual (euro and punt) currency, price listing, and exchange rates until January 1, 2002.

According to a report completed in 1999, the unemployment rate should be reduced to three percent by the year 2005. This is indicative of a drastic change in Ireland's pattern of emigration. Since the time of the famine, emigration had become a way of life for young Irish seeking work. 1999 was the first year in recent history in which the rate of immigration to Ireland surpassed the rate of emigration away from the island. The Republic has opened its borders to thousands of refugees, who are greatly aided by the Church and economic upswing.

As more young Irish spend time abroad and more international travelers spend time in Ireland, the culture's conservatism slowly cracks. The short-term result is a growing generation gap and disparity between rural and urban areas. The majority of the Republic remains safe and sober, but Dubliners endure the problems of all large cities, including crime and drugs. While the Irish are eager to dispel the picturesque stereotype of the "land of saints and scholars" (and poverty and drunkenness), they hope to retain the safety afforded by their religious and family-oriented past.

LITERARY TRADITIONS

HISTORY OF THE IRISH LANGUAGE

Irish is the corpse that sits up and talks back.

Nuala Ní Dhomhnaill

The constitution declares Irish to be the national language of the Republic. Yet, only 60,000 individuals compose the exclusively Irish speaking community, or **gaeltacht** (GAYL-tacht). The larger *gaeltacht* is composed of small settlements scattered about the most remote regions of the island. The most prominent *gaeltacht* are located in Connemara in Co. Galway (see p. 317), in patches of Co. Donegal (see p. 370), on the Dingle Peninsula (see p. 263), on Cape Clear Island (see p. 235), and in the Aran Islands (see p. 300). These geographically disparate communities are further divided by three different dialects: Donegal Irish, Connemara Irish, and Munster Irish in the South. Donegal's Irish, like its traditional music, retains traces of past contact with Scotland and Scottish Gaelic. The transformation of Ireland into an English speaking island began in the 17th century with the arrival of the English merchant and professional class. Everyone in contemporary Ireland speaks English, but the purest form of Celtic culture survives in the gaeltacht's centuries-old traditions such as storytelling and singing. The oldest vernacular literature and the largest collection of folklore in Europe are in Irish.

Irish is a Celtic language that shares its Indo-European origin with Scottish Gaelic and Manx, and more distantly with Breton, Welsh, and Cornish. The Irish language is called *Gaeilge* by its speakers; the English word "Gaelic" refers to the Scottish language. The Celtic language arrived in Ireland in about the third century B.C. The earliest written records of Irish remain on **ogham** stones (see p. 7), in a script composed of variously angled strokes. The Latin alphabet took over soon after, and Irish scholastic writing flourished between 600 and 900 A.D., when monastic scholarship flowered. This blessed bliss was interrupted by the start of Viking raids in the 8th century. Even so, the Viking settlers learned to speak Irish. In 1600 there were as many speakers of Irish worldwide as of English. The Anglophones, however, had more money and better armies; over the next 250 years, Irish speakers had to learn English to conduct business and their children grew up speaking only English. Irish became the language of the disenfranchised. In the mid 19th century, the British introduced systematic schooling in rural areas, and required that pupils receive their education in English. The Famine hit Irish-speaking areas hardest, and the number of Irish speakers continued to decline.

Irish re-entered the lives of the privileged classes with the advent of the Gaelic Revival. In 1893, **Douglas Hyde** (who later became the first president of Éire) founded the **Gaelic League** in order to inspire enthusiasm for Irish among people who didn't grow up speaking it. Writers who were bilingual from birth enjoyed Douglas Hyde's famous mispronunciations, while native English-speakers excitedly took up his cause. W.B. Yeats and Lady Gregory count among Hyde's admirers; they founded the Abbey theater in Dublin for the promotion of Irish playwrights. The League aimed to spread the everyday use of Irish as part of a project to de-Anglicize the island, just as the Gaelic Athletic Association aimed to overpower English sports. Placing political importance in cultural nationalism, Hyde believed that cultural change was more important than political revolution, but many Gaelic Leaguers disagreed. Eventually, Hyde resigned from presidency of the Gaelic League because of its development into a separatist organization. The nationalistic enthusiasm of Hyde's entourage was later satirized in such works as Flann O'Brien's *An Béal Bocht* ("the poor mouth," see p. 24), written in 1941.

The revolutionaries of 1916 and the political leaders of the 20s were almost without exception excited about reinvigorating the Irish language, and they tried to use the government to strengthen it: the civil service exam included an Irish test, and Irish became a compulsory subject in school. Preoccupied with economic development, the people and governments of the postwar Republic resented these policies. Today, several civil service positions still require a language examination, but a leaving certificate in Irish is no longer needed to attend university. As Irish has lost its compulsory stigma, it has grown in popularity with native English speakers. The last 15 years have seen a renewed interest in all things Celtic and more controversy over the fate of Irish. Adults who hated Irish in their youth regret having let it atrophy and now attend classes. All schoolchildren are still required to take extensive Irish courses, and many parents are sending their children to *gaelscoileanna* (GAYL-kol-AH-nuh), Irish immersion schools located in the *gaeltacht*). The modern Irish-literature community, which produces dozens of novels, poetry collections, and critical essays every year, has finally begun to influence the Irish language curriculum, once filled only with antiquated traditional novels.

Late 20th century authors have returned to writing in Irish. **Michael Hartnett** writes solely in Irish. **Nuala ní Dhomhnaill** composes poetry in Irish, while her public readings are generally bilingual. In contrast to the archaic subject matter non-speakers associate with the Irish language, her work brings refrigerators, feminism, and smart bombs into proximity with the banshee. The younger poet **Biddy Jenkinson** refuses to authorize any translation of her work into English, although it has been translated into French. The preeminent Irish-language novel is **Maírtín Ó Cadhain's** *Cré na Cille* (Churchyard Clay), a dialogue among corpses in a graveyard. Seamus Heaney is best known for his poems in English, but much of his scholarly work involves translating poems from Irish. Heaney and others have thus revived interest in the works of itinerant poets of past centuries, such as the masterful **Rafferty.**

All the same, the area of the *gaeltacht* continues to shrink. Long-term trends in most *gaeltachta* still point to depopulation and dispersal, as Ireland's strengthening economy brings improvements in roads and communications to the previously isolated Irish-speaking regions. The government continues its efforts to preserve, if not promote, the language. A Connemara-based Irish radio station and a new Irish language television station, *Telifís na Gaelige* (T na G [TEE NUH JEE] to locals), expand Irish-hearing opportunities. While most Irish do not want to see their language die, some see the appropriation of money to Irish programs as a waste.

Peruse the **Glossary** (p. 493) for a list of Irish words and phrases.

LEGENDS AND FOLKTALES

In early Irish society, language was equal to action. What the bard (directly from the Irish *baird*) sang about battles, valor, and lineage was the only record a chieftain had by which to make decisions. Poetry and politics of the Druidic tradition were so intertwined that the *fili*, trained poets, and *breitheamh* (BREH-huv), judges of the Brehon Laws, were often the same people. The poet-patron relationship was symbiotic—the poet sang long praise poems about his lord in return for food and shelter.

Scholars have been arguing for decades about the conflation of fact and fiction in Ireland's epic mythology. The vast repertoire includes romances, war stories, revenge tales, and many instances of cattle raiding. (Cattle was the ancient Celtic men's most marketable commodity—slaves and women were valued in cows.) Long sagas were passed down orally through many generations. They survive today in written form thanks to the scholastic diligence of medieval monks. Manuscripts compile bits and pieces of different narrative versions. The less fortunate aspect of the monks' work is that they sometimes altered details to propagate Christianity; they manufactured tales of historical saints by appropriating stories of pre-Christian heroes and gods. Despite the many hands through which these tales fell, they still provide essential clues to reconstructing Ireland's ancient past. They reveal much about the lifestyles of its patriarchal culture, as well as the rituals that informed today's archeological remains.

MEN IN LABOR There was a young woman who took up with a very wealthy, but lonely, landlord in Ulster. She cooked, swept, kept him clothed, and soon became pregnant with his child. One day they went to a local fair. The landlord grew boastful and claimed that his wife could outrun the king's chariot. The woman pleaded with him and then the crowd to pardon her from the race since she was with child. She found no sympathy, and as she began the race she cursed the whole of Ulster. She tied with the chariot. Upon crossing the finish line, she let out a terrible scream as she gave birth to twins. The nearby area was named Emain Macha (the twins of Macha) after the twins. The men who had heard her scream, as well as nine generations of their families, were cursed with the pangs of childbirth in their most desperate times. That is how Queen Macha cursed Ulster, how the men of Ulster came to have labor pains for five nights and four days, and why they were unable to protect their famous bull from Queen Medbh in the Cattle Raid of Cooley. Cúchulainn was exempt from this curse.

The long, famous **Book of Invasions** (*Leabhar Gabhála*; LOWR GA-vah-lah) is a record of the pre-Christian cultures and armies that have invaded Ireland, from Noah's daughter Cesair, up to the Celts. These tales locate the Irish peoples' ancestry in the Greek islands, where Nemed, a Scythian, became lost at sea after pursuing a mysterious tower of gold that rose out of the waves. After a year and a half of wandering, he and his ships landed safely in Ireland, until the next wave of settlers arrived...and the next, and the next, including the **Fir Bolg,** meaning "bag men." They were soon defeated by the **Túatha de Danann** (TOO-uh DAY dah-NAN), invaders from northern lands. The Túatha were a god-like race associated with light, but prone to human foibles. The Túatha de Danann battled the evil, dark, and ugly **Formorian** race, but eventually met their equal in the **Milesians,** the forefathers of the Celts. The Milesians drove the Túatha de Danann into the ground, where they were reduced to what are known simply as *fairies*. Many people in Ireland today still believe that fairies emerge occasionally to aid or fight with mortals, and seduce (or abduct) mortal beauties. When the Túatha de Danann retreated to the other world, the Celts acquired some of their ways and skills.

Poets living in the chieftains' households invented the art of verse satire. These poets had the power to curse and lay a *geis*, a magic compulsion or prohibition. Several "cycles," or collections, of tales narrate the life stories of a set of heroes and villains. The most extensive is the **Ulster Cycle,** which includes the adventures of King Conchobar, or Conor, of Ulster and his clan, the **Ulaid,** and his archenemy, his ex-wife Queen Medbh of Connacht. Ulster's champion is **Cúchulainn** (COO-khull-yun), the king's nephew, an athlete extraordinare known as the Hound of Ulster whose adventures begin at the age of five. The Amazonian warrior Scathach taught him the arts of war and how to wield the Gae Bolga, the sun-god's destructive spear. The central tale of the Ulster Cycle is the **Táin bo Cuailnge** (Cattle Raid of Cooley), in which Queen Medbh (MAVA) decides first to borrow, and then to steal, the most famous bull in the country, the Donn of Cooley. She assembles an army to capture the bull and invades Ulster when all the Ulster warriors are disabled by the curse of Queen Macha. Only the 17-year-old Cúchulainn is immune, and he single-handedly defeats Medbh's soldiers over a season-long period. The cycle also includes the story of Deirdre, Queen of Sorrow, who King Conor courted, coveted, and cursed to make Ireland's version of the Helen of Troy story.

Other cycles include **Tales of the Traditional Kings** and the **Cycles of Finn,** and **Ossian.** Finn McCool (Fionn MacCumaill), a strongman with smarts, leads a group of heroes that includes his son, Ossian, and his grandson, Oscar. In some stories, he is a king or a giant with supernatural powers who saves Ireland from monsters. In others, he is more or less a mercenary.

Toward the end of the first millennium, the oral tradition of the bards ceded some ground to the monastic penchant for writing it all down. The monastic settlements of pre-Norman Ireland compiled enormous annals of myth, legend, and history. An established pagan tradition and the introduction of Christianity created a tension in Irish literature between recalling old bardic forms and incorporating a new world-view. Resentment of the church's high-handedness is apparent in **Sweeney Astray,** the story of a pagan king turned into a bird by a monk's curse. The relevance of the tale to the continued interference of the church in Irish literary imagination is evidenced by Seamus Heaney's translation of the poem in the 1980s.

Literati have periodically compiled Ireland's **folktales.** These tales include other-worldly creatures like **banshees,** that are still believed to forecast an imminent death when they are heard wailing outside the house of an ailing individual, and descendants of the Túatha de Danann. **Leprechauns** are a late, degenerate conflagration of Ireland's mythic creatures, mainly embraced by foreign cultures. For more myths and tales, try *Folktales of Ireland*, edited by Sean O'Sullivan; W.B. Yeats's *Fairy Folk Tales of Ireland* and *A Treasury of Irish Myth, Legend, and Folklore*; or *Irish Myths and Legends* by Yeats and Lady Augusta Gregory.

1600-1880

After the English succinctly dispossessed the local Irish chieftains in the Battle of Kinsale in 1601 (see p. 8), most Irish writers predicted the imminent collapse of Irish language and culture. The new English lords sought to maintain their power by forcing the native Irish tenants to speak English and convert to the Church of Ireland. As the bards of the Irish courts lost their high status, they carried on their work amongst the peasant classes, so that Ireland developed a vernacular literary culture. The majority of the works written in Irish at this time lament the state of Ireland as a land under cultural attack; a leitmotif in poetry of the time is the metaphor of Ireland as a captive woman. Perhaps the most famous of these poems is **Roisin Dubh,** which describes Ireland a beautiful dark woman, or "black rose."

In long-colonized Dublin, **Jonathan Swift** (1667-1745) wrote some of the most sophisticated, misanthropic, and marvelous satire in the English language. Swift served for decades as the Dean of St. Patrick's Cathedral, and towered above his Anglo-Irish contemporaries with his mix of moral indignation, bitterness, and wit. Like writers throughout the island, Swift felt compelled to write about the sad condition of starving Irish peasants. Besides his masterpiece *Gulliver's Travels*, Swift wrote political pamphlets and essays decrying English cruelty to the native Irish, while defending the Protestant Church of Ireland. "A Modest Proposal" (1729) suggests that the overpopulated and hungry native Irish sell their children as food.

In the mid-19th century, the famine hit, and folk-culture fell by the wayside in the face of destitution; while the peasants starved, the Industrial Revolution passed by Ireland. Cosmopolitan Dublin managed to breed talent, but talented young writers moved on from Trinity to London to make their names. **Oscar Wilde** (1856-1900) moved to London and set up as a cultivated aesthete to write one novel and many sparklingly witty plays, including *The Importance of Being Earnest* (1895). His work critiqued society and propriety while fetishizing it; he personally challenged Irish clichés and Victorian determinism by perfecting a stylish demeanor more English than the English themselves. Prolific playwright **George Bernard Shaw** (1856-1950) was also born in Dublin but moved to London in 1876, where he became an active socialist. *John Bull's Other Island* (1904) depicts the increasing hardships of the Irish peasant laborer. Shaw himself identified much of his writing as Irish, in form if not always in content: "When I say I am an Irishman I mean that my language is the English of Swift and not the unspeakable drivel of the mid-19th century newspapers." Shaw won the Nobel Prize for Literature in 1925 for a body of work that includes *Arms and the Man (1932)*, *Candida (1905)*, *Man and Superman (1931)*, and *Pygmalion (1938)*.

THE IRISH LITERARY REVIVAL

Towards the end of the nineteenth century, a portion of Ireland's crop of young writers no longer turned to London to cultivate their talent. Rather, a vigorous and enduring effort known today as the **Irish Literary Revival** took over the scene. Members of this movement turned to Irish culture, from its ancient mythology to contemporary folktales, for inspiration. Writers such as W.B. Yeats, Lady Gregory, and A.E. overturned the assumption that the indigenous culture was less sophisticated than that of England. The task of literature was now to discover the real Ireland, whether Gaelic or Anglicized (or both). Interest in the Irish language suddenly revived. The memoirs of Irish speakers were discovered and embraced. The most famous of them is *Peig*, the autobiography of **Peig Sayers**; it is a mournful book about a girl growing up on the Blaskets (see p. 268), that is still read in schools today. This memoir, and others like it, led readers to mourn the decline of Gaelic culture and language. The Gaelic League was founded by Douglas Hyde to teach Irish to English-speaking adults (see **The Irish Language**, p. 19).

The Irish Literary Revival was hardly a nostalgic movement; it recognized the Anglo-Irish perspective as a practical reality, so that many authors continued to write in English, the most commonly understood language on the island by that time. Yeats and Lady Gregory recorded and published mythology and folktales in English. **Lady Augusta Gregory** (1852-1932), wrote 40 plays as well as a number of translations, poems, and essays. She began her career by collecting the folktales and legends of Galway's poor residents and later discovered her own skill as a writer of dialogue, creating mainly comedic plays with a staunch nationalism. The revival also looked to ancient mythology and fairytales to find personal meaning, a strain that is exhibited in the works of the mystic George Russel, who went by the pseudonym **A.E.** The early poems of **William Butler Yeats** (1865-1939) create a dreamily rural Ireland of loss and legend. His early work, from *Crossways* (1889) to *In the Seven Woods* (1904), won Yeats worldwide fame thanks to the appeal of his mystic vision of picturesque Ireland. Yeat's vision changed remarkably after he realized the role of the Gaelic Revival in promoting the nationalism that led to the violence of the Irish Civil War. "Easter 1916" described the sudden transformation that the Easter rebels brought to the Irish national self-image: "All changed, changed utterly / A terrible beauty is born." Yeats later bought and renovated a stone tower, Thoor Ballylee (see p. 300), in which he lived with his family in isolation. The tower became a part of the idiosyncratic symbolism that appears in the last two decades of his poems, from *The Tower* (1928) to the posthumous *Last Poems* (1939). In 1923, he became the first Irishman to win the Nobel Prize.

In 1904, Yeats and Lady Gregory founded the **Abbey Theater** in Dublin (see p. 120), in order to "build up a Celtic and Irish school of dramatic literature." But conflict almost immediately arose between various contributors. Was this new body of drama to be written in verse or prose, in the realistic or the fantastic and heroic mode? In theory, the plays would be written in Irish, but in practice they needed to be written in English. A sort of compromise was found in the work of **John Millington Synge** (1871-1909), whose English plays were perfectly Irish in essence. A multi-faceted man who "wished to be at once Shakespeare, Beethoven, and Darwin," he spent much of his early years traveling and living in Paris. During one of his many stays in Ireland, Synge met Yeats, who advised that he look for inspiration on the Aran Islands. This advice, which Synge followed in 1898, led him to write *The Aran Islands*, a documentary of life on the islands (see p. 300). His experiences also gave him the subject matter for writing his black comedy *The Playboy of the Western World* (1907), which destroys the pastoral myth about Irish peasantry and portrays a rural society divided into classes. The play's first production instigated riots. **Sean O'Casey** (1880-1964) also caused rioting at the Abbey with the premier in 1926 of *The*

Plough and Star, which depicted the Easter Rebellion without mythologizing its leaders. In general, however, his plays were well received by Dublin's middle class, as they were the first portrayals of gritty urban life in their fair city; examples of his work are *Juno and the Paycock* (1924) and *The Shadow of a Gunman* (1923).

After the heroism of the Civil War and Republicanism, Ireland had suddenly become conservative. In this atmosphere, the Irish Ireland movement, provincial and Catholic in its beliefs, brought about the **Censorship of Publications Act** in 1929. This act severely restricted the development of Irish literature. In the journal which he edited, the poet A.E. fought against such repression. He envisioned a broad cultural synthesis that would include various cultures and religions, not just those that Ireland's new government accepted.

MODERNISM

Many authors still found Ireland too small and insular an island to suit their literary aspirations. The most famous of Ireland's expatriates is **James Joyce** (1882-1941); his novels are recognized as some of the seminal works of Modernism. Joyce was born and educated in Dublin, but he left Ireland forever in 1904, because of the following sentiment: "How sick, sick, sick, I am of Dublin! It is the city of failure, of rancour and of unhappiness. I long to be out of it." All the same, Joyce's writing never did leave Ireland, as his novels and stories exclusively describe the lives of Dubliners, and obsessively detail the city's geography and establishments. Joyce's most accesible writing is the collection of short stories titled *Dubliners* (1914). His first novel, *A Portrait of the Artist as a Young Man* (1914), uses the protagonist Stephen Daedalus to describe Joyce's own youth in Dublin, and his decision to leave his country, religion, and family behind him. Stephen Daedalus reappears in *Ulysses*, Joyce's revolutionary novel of 1922. *Ulysses* chronicles one day in the life of the antihero, Leopold Bloom, a middle-class Jewish man living his life in a stagnating Dublin. The novel's structure follows that of Homer's *Odyssey*—hence the title. It was first published in serial form in a small American magazine in 1918 and banned for obscenity by a U.S. Court in 1920. In 1922, Sylvia Beach's Paris-based Shakespeare and Co. published the first full edition. In his last book, *Finnegans Wake* (1939), Joyce falls into a reverie of allusion, puns, and onomatopoeia that defies all attempts at light reading, but sounds fantastic.

Samuel Beckett (1906-89) served as Joyce's personal assistant in his twenties, admiring him so much that he's said to have modeled his personal costume after Joyce. Like Joyce, Beckett fled to Paris to pursue his writing career; unlike Joyce, he left most of vernacular Ireland behind him. He wrote most of his work in French. His three novels (*Molloy, Malone Dies*, and *The Unnameable*), world-famous plays (*Waiting for Godot, Endgame*) (all written 1946-1950), and bleak prose poems convey a deathly pessimism about language, society, and life. Beckett won the Nobel Prize in 1969, but did not accept it on the grounds that Joyce had never received it.

Other authors felt the influence of Modernism, without needing to turn their back on Ireland. **Flann O'Brien** (1912-66), who also wrote under the pseudonym Myles Na gCopaleen, let loose an unrestricted literary inventiveness that earned him an international reputation. O'Brien represents a trend of the 1940s, when the short story was becoming a popular, successful, and sophisticated art form in Ireland. These stories frequently took the common lives of Irish people as their theme, depicting individual liberty and energy as victims of oppressive provincialism. O'Brien tried to provide a comic answer to Joyce and set himself in opposition to a cultural and linguistic lethargy. His most celebrated novel, *At Swim Two Birds* (1939), is a comedy combing ancient Irish mythology with the fantasies of a foppish university student in early 20th century Dublin.

POEMS, PLAYS, AND PLOTS IN THE 20TH CENTURY

Censorship remained an overwhelming force through most of this century, banning writers from Edna O'Brien to F. Scott Fitzgerald. Should a citizen's complaint prove a book to be indecent, obscene, or advocating unnatural forms of birth control, the censorship board would outlaw the book indefinitely. Even classic Irish language works came under scrutiny, although *Ulysses* had escaped attack in the Republic despite being banned in the U.S.

After the 1940s, Irish poetry was once again commanding widespread appreciation. Living in the backwash of the Revival and the Civil War, these new Irish poets questioned their cultural inheritance, finding a new version of Ireland that was a parody of the old one. **Patrick Kavanaugh** (1906-67) debunked a mythical Ireland in such poems as "The Great Hunger" (1945), which was banned for its obscenities, prompting the Irish police to visit Kavanaugh's house and seize the manuscript. The works of both **Thomas Kinsella** and **John Montague** display a keen awareness of the history of Irish poetry with a sensitivity to mid-nineteenth century civil strife, at the same time as they created intensely introspective poetry. **Derek Mahon** saw the poet as anthropologist rather than student of Irish inheritance or of Republicanism. He tried to focus on the common elements that people of all cultures share. Although some poets are directly political and almost propagandistic, much of contemporary poetry is intensely private. Most poets treat the political issue from a distant, everyday perspective. Contemporary poet **Frank Ornsby** writes poetry devoid of political conflict that celebrates the rituals of domestic life. **Paul Muldoon** adds quirk and confusion to the humdrum existence of today's Ireland. **Eavan Boland** is one of the few modern Irish writers who have attempted to capture the experience of middle-class Irish women and reached public recognition.

The dirt of Dublin continues to provide fodder for generations of writers beyond O'Casey and Joyce. Notorious wit, playwright, poet, and terrorist **Brendan Behan** created semi-autobiographical works about delinquent life such as his play *The Quare Fellow* (1954). The mild-mannered schoolteacher **Roddy Doyle** wrote the well-known Barrytown Trilogy about family good times in down and out Dublin (see **Film**, p. 29), as well as the acclaimed *The Woman Who Walked Into Doors* (1996). Doyle won the Booker Prize in 1994 for *Paddy Clarke Ha Ha Ha*.

Poetry and the novel are the dominant strains of Irish literature in this century, but other types of authorship have also produced fine results. Native playwrights include politically conscious **Frank McGuinness** and **Brian Friel**. Friel's *Dancing at Lughnasa* (1990) was a Broadway hit. Important critics and essayists include **Conor Cruise O'Brien,** a former diplomat who writes about most everything—history, literature, culture, politics; **Denis Donoghue,** whose *We Irish* is a vigorous, skeptical lit-crit grab-bag; and the provocative **Declan Kiberd,** whose Ireland is a postcolonial society more like India than like England.

BEHAN Northern Catholic playwright Brendan Behan was born in 1923 and, at the age of 16, was arrested in Liverpool for carrying explosives for the IRA. He was sentenced to Borstal (the juvenile prison) for 18 months, an experience that provided the basis for his 1958 novel *Borstal Boy*. After his release, he returned to the IRA; four years later he was arrested again for shooting a policeman. A tiny 1956 Dublin production of his play, *The Quare Fellow*, brought him instant acclaim, and a production in London soon thereafter brought him critical success. In addition to his plays, he often published stories in the *Irish Times* and the *Irish Press*. In the late 50s he moved to Paris, where he spent his time writing pornography and drinking heavily. He developed a reputation for his drunken performances at productions of his own plays. While Behan was in New York, comedian Jackie Gleason became his drinking buddy. Behan passed away in 1964.

A pair of brothers who grew up in Limerick and emigrated to New York have recently achieved international best-seller stardom. **Frank McCourt** won the Pulitzer Prize for his 1996 memoir about his poverty-stricken childhood, *Angela's Ashes* (1996). His brother **Malachy McCourt** recently published his equally popular memoir, *A Monk Swimming* (1999).

MODERN WRITERS IN NORTHERN IRELAND

The literature of Northern Ireland describes two culturally divided groups, Catholics and Protestants. Many Northern writers attempt to create works of relevance to members of both communities. Protestant poet **Louis MacNeice** (1907-63) infused his lyric poems with a Modernist concern for struggle and social upheaval, but he took no part in the sectarian politics. His *Valediction* masterfully attacks an idealized Ireland. Novelist **Brian Moore's** *The Emperor of Ice Cream* (1965) is a coming-of-age story set in wartime Belfast. Born in rural Co. Derry, **Seamus Heaney,** won the Nobel Prize for Literature in 1995, and is the most prominent living Irish poet. His subject matter ranges from bogs to bombings to archeological remains. While his tone is often highly lyrical, Heaney writes in an anti-pastoral mode. His fourth book, *North* (1975), tackles the Troubles head-on. He was part of the **Field Day movement,** led by Derry poet and critic **Seamus Deane,** which produced what was billed as the definitive anthology of Irish writing, although it's recently come under heavy fire for its relative lack of women writers. One of Heaney's contemporaries, **Paul Muldoon,** occupies himself with self-skepticism and an ear for weird rhymes, rather than politics.

MUSIC

TRADITIONAL AND FOLK MUSIC

Irish traditional music is alive and kicking. Commonly called "trad", it is the centuries-old array of dance rhythms, cyclic melodies, and embellishments that has been passed down through generations of musicians. These tunes can be written down, but that's not their primary means of transmission. Indeed, a traditional musician's training consists largely of listening to and innovating from the work of others. Any music session in a pub will sample from a variety of types, including reels, jigs, hornpipes, and slow airs. These are the skeletons around which the players in a trad session build the music. The same tune will produce a different result every session.

Irish traditional music may be heard in two ways: recordings, and impromptu evening pub sessions. Best-selling recording artists include **Altan, De Danann,** and the **Chieftains.** Other excellent groups that are available on compact discs are the **Bothy Band** and **Planxty** of the 1970s, and, more recently, **Nomos, Solas, Dervish,** and **Deanta.** These bands have brought Irish music into international prominence, starting with the early recordings of the Chieftains and their mentor **Sean O'Rioda,** who, in the 1950s, fostered the resurrection of trad from near extinction to national art form. While recording bands perform regularly at concerts, most traditional musicians are accustomed to playing before smaller, more intimate audiences of locals at a pub. A session takes place when independent musicians gather at the pub to play together; as such, sessions are an excellent way to witness the real, amorphous identity of Irish traditional tunes. *Let's Go* lists many pubs with regular trad sessions, but you'll find the best music by asking local trad enthusiasts. Pubs in Counties Clare, Kerry, Galway, Sligo, and Donegal are especially strong. If you want a guarantee that you'll hear lots of traditional music, find a **fleadh** (FLAH), a musical festival at which musicians' officially scheduled sessions often spill over into nearby pubs. **Comhaltas Ceoltóirí Éireann,** the national traditional music association, organizes *fleadhs.* Write or call them at 32 Belgrave Sq., Monkstown, Co. Dublin (tel. (01) 280 0295; www.mayo-ireland.ie/CCE.htm).

The techniques of trad have little in common with those of European classical music; it's often said that training in one is an impediment to playing the other. The instruments with which Irish trad music is most frequently played are the fiddle, the wooden flute, the button accordion or smaller concertina, the tin whistle, and the *uilleann* pipes (elbow pipes). These pipes appear similar to the Scottish bag-pipes, but are played significantly differently: the bellows are held under the arm and pumped thus. The resulting sound is far more melodic than the Scottish instrument, resembling a sweet fiddle rather than a war instrument. The unwieldy harp, Ireland's national symbol, is rarely encountered in live trad music now but is frequently heard in recordings. The *bodhrán* (BAU-ron), a hand-held drum, wasn't seen as a legitimate instrument until the 60s, when **Sean Ó Riada** introduced it in an effort to drive rock and jazz drumming out. Today, the *bodhrán* has skillful specialists. It is played either with both ends of a stick or with the bare hand. Less common percussion instruments include the spoons and the bones, which are played by clicking two sheep ribs together. Irish music has benefited from the recent introduction of instruments from other cultures, so that a session might feature anything from a guitar or banjo to a jew's harp or didgeridoo.

Purists get in heated arguments about what constitutes "traditional" singing. A style of unaccompanied vocals called *sean-nós* ("old-time") is definitely the oldest form on the island. This style of nasal singing descends from keening, an ancient practice of wailing lamentation. It requires the vocalist to sing each verse of a song differently, by peppering the tune with syllabic embellishments and tonal variations. More common than *sean-nos* is folk singing, which refers to guitar- or mandolin-accompanied ballads. Sessions in pubs typically alternate between fast-paced traditional instrumental music and folk songs. Ireland's favorite traditional songsters include **Dominick Behan, The Dubliners, Christy Moore,** and **Sean Tyrell.** The Irish also appreciate international crooners, so that sessions will likely feature a Joni Mitchell tune.

For the atonal, dance provides a means of participating in traditional Irish culture. Indeed, hard-shoe dancing involves creating a percussion accompaniment by pounding the floor with foot-loose fury. Individual **step-dancing** and group **set-dancing** are centuries-old practices, but the spontaneous and innovative streak in each is fading fast. Today, traditional dancing follows the regimentation of formal competitions where traditional dancers compete according to rote standards of perfection. *Céilís,* at which attendants participate in traditional Irish set-dancing, still take place in most Irish towns. The world-sweeping spectacles of *Riverdance* and *Lord of the Dance* offer loose interpretations of Irish dance, breathing (entirely) new life into the form.

ROCK, PUNK, AND POP

Music is one of Ireland's national resources, meaning that most everyone has some sort of audible talent. Concurrently, the Irish have a wide-ranging musical appreciation. Along with their vastly successful exportation of trad, the Irish have developed a taste for outside forms of music, and often times adapt them. This cross-pollination produces musicians who draw on traditional and eclectic elements. The first commercially successful artist to do so was **John McCormack** of Athlone, one of the finest tenors of the early 20th century. While he was known internationally for opera, he endeared audiences to the Irish folk songs he invariably included in his recitals.

Bridging the gap between traditional folk ballads and contemporary Ireland to great popular acclaim is **Christy Moore,** who has been called the Bob Dylan of Ireland. The ballads and anthems that Moore made popular now form something of a pub sing-along canon—hardly a late-night session goes by without someone's moving rendition of "Ride On," "City of Chicago," or the lament "Irish Ways and Irish Laws." His younger brother **Luka Bloom** takes a few steps further along the road to pop sensibility, but still sings the confessionals of a proud young Irishman. **Horslips** became hugely popular in the 70s by trying to merge trad and rock forms but wound up shuffling uneasily between the two. **Van Morrison'** early inspirations included American soul and blues, which he submerged into Celtic "soul." The London-based **Pogues** also felt the desire to fuse rock and trad, to far different effect. Their lead singer Sean MacGowan named the Dubliners' Luke Kelly and Jimi Hendrix as his idols. In albums such as *Rum, Sodomy, and the Lash*, they whipped out reel and jigs of drunken, punk-damaged revelry, accompanied by MacGowan's poetic descriptions of Irish emigrant sorrows, and the horrors of sectarian violence.

Another outlet for trad in modernity is the synthesizer. Enya used Irish lyricism and electronics to create a style of pervasive tunes you hear before Aer Lingus in-flight movies. The rest of her immediate family makes up the members of Clannad, who sound much like Enya, with the infusion of several wooden and winded instruments. More recently, the Afro-Celt Sound System have achieved popular and critical success with their fusion of traditional Celtic and African sounds with manic rhythms of drum and bass.

Irish musicians have dabbled in practically every genre of pure-bred rock. In the 70s, **Thin Lizzy** produced early heavy metal laced with a sensitivity to Irish literary greatness. Around the same time, the worldwide punk rock explosion spawned brilliance in Belfast, where **Stiff Little Fingers** spat forth three years of excellent anthems. Throughout the North, punk became an outlet for the youth culture trying to escape the conflicts and bigotries of its parents. The most successful of these groups were Derry's **Undertones,** which eventually evolved into the garage rock of That Petrol Emotion. Punk was also creating a ruckus down in late 70s Dublin. The **Boomtown Rats** sold well, and made a star of their frontman Bob Geldoff who went on to found Live Aid. Slightly afterwards, the **Virgin Prunes** did their best to live up to their name, which is Dublinese for "freak" or "outcast." Their lead singer **Gavin Friday** continues to create cabaret-style alternative rock. In the 90s, punk's grunge legacy has made waves in both Northern Ireland and the Republic. **Ash** heralded a 90s revival of the Belfast punk aesthetic; their album *1977* reached number one on the UK charts. The presently defunct **My Bloody Valentine** weaved shimmering distortions to land them in the outskirts of grunge.

Ireland's musicians have also set their sights on mainstream super-stardom, and achieved that goal often enough. **U2** is Ireland's biggest rock export. From the adrenaline-soaked promise of the 1980 *Boy*, the band slowly ascended into the rock stratosphere, culminating in world-wide fame with *The Joshua Tree* (1987). The band found new vitality in *Achtung Baby* (1991) and *Pop* (1997), and while fans wondered if the band had sold out or was only pretending to, the music spoke for itself. **Sinéad O'Connor** stood her own as an independent female rockstar with attitude long before the lauded American phenomenon of the late 1990s. The low-ercase **cranberries** and the sibling-based **Coors** have cornered the international soft rock market. The boy-group **Boyzone** has conquered the UK charts and the hearts of millions of pre-adolescent girls; similar black magic is practiced on the opposite sex by their sisters in the girl-group **Bewitched**.

POPULAR MEDIA

FILM

The deceivingly luscious soil that devastated the lives of the native Irish for so many centuries is finally turning a profit thanks to Ireland's burgeoning movie industry. The island's expanses of green, its picturesque villages, and comparatively low labor costs are a filmmaker's dream. Hollywood discovered Ireland in John Wayne's 1952 film *The Quiet Man*, giving an international audience of millions their first view of the island's beauty. Aside from the garish green of Hollywood technicolor vision, art-filmmakers have also found Ireland. Robert Flaherty created cinematic Realism in *Man of Aran*. Alfred Hitchcock filmed Sean

O'Casey's *Juno and the Paycock* with the Abbey Theatre Players in 1930. American director John Huston, who eventually made Ireland his home, made numerous films there; his last work *The Dead* (1987) is the film version of James Joyce's story from *Dubliners.*

In the last ten-odd years, however, the Irish government has begun to encourage a truly Irish film industry. An excellent art cinema has opened in Temple Bar in Dublin, and there's an office two blocks away to encourage budding moviemakers. These recent efforts have resulted in a less idealistic but, most times, equally loving vision of Ireland. Based on the novels of the Barrytown Trilogy by Roddy Doyle, **The Commitments** (1991), **The Snapper** (1993), and **The Van** (1996) followed a family from the depressed North Side of Dublin as its members variously form a soul band, have a kid, and get off the dole by running a chipper. Another Dublin saga, **The General** (1998; see p. 143), by the English director John Boorman, describes the true rise and fall of one of the most notorious criminals in recent Irish history. Dublin-native **Neil Jordan** has become a much sought-after director thanks to the success of **The Crying Game** (1992), **Michael Collins** (1996), and **The Butcher Boy** (1998). More recently, **Jim Sheridan** has worked along with actor Daniel Day Lewis in two films that take a humanitarian approach to the lives of Catholics and Protestants in the Troubles **In the Name of the Father** (1993) and **The Boxer** (1997). The Ireland of fairytales is captured with exquisite cinematography in **The Secret of Roan Inish** (1995) and **Into the West** (1993). In 1999, the popularity of Irish scenery and accents was attested to by the profitable production of two highly Irish sounding and looking films by non-Irish filmmakers: Hollywood produced a film version of Donegal playwright Brien Friel's **Dancing at Lughnasa,** the government of the Isle of Man sponsored **Waking Ned Devine,** which describes the crazy antics of a village of rustic eccentrics. Numerous Irish actors and actresses have reached international super-stardom; among them, are Gabriel Byrne, Aidan Quinn, and Liam Neeson, who won an Academy Award for his leading role in *Schindler's List* (1993.)

The **Galway Film Fleadh** is Ireland's version of Cannes, appropriately reduced in scale but still featuring a week's worth of quality films. The **Dublin Film Festival** runs for a week in the middle of April. The month-long **Dublin Lesbian and Gay Film Festival,** occupies all of August. Dublin also hosts the **Junior Dublin Film Festival** during the last week of November and the first week of December, showing the world's best children's films. In Northern Ireland, the **Foyle Film Festival** takes place in Derry during the last week in April.

NEWSPAPERS AND OTHER MEDIA

The Republic and Northern Ireland together support eight national **dailies** with a combined circulation of around 1.5 million. The largest of these papers in the Republic are the *Irish Times* and the *Irish Independent* (www.irish-times.com and www.independent.ie). The *Times* takes a liberal voice, and is renowned worldwide for its excellent coverage of international affairs. The *Independent* is more internally focused, and often times maintains a chatty writing-style. *The Herald* is an evening daily that hovers somewhere in the middle. Neither the *Times* nor the *Independent* comes out with a Sunday paper, but their readership is generally satisfied with an Irish version of *The London Times.* The best selling paper in the North is the *Belfast Telegraph* (www.belfasttelegraph.co.uk). The sectarian community is represented by two mainstream newspapers: Unionists read the *Belfast Newsletter,* while Nationalists turn to the *Irish News.* **Tabloids** like the *Daily Mirror,* the *Irish Sun,* the *Irish Star,* and the *Sporting News* offer low-level coverage with an emphasis on stars, scandals, and sports, and the occasional topless picture. A large number of regional papers offer more in-depth local news; the largest is the *The Cork Examiner.* British papers are sold throughout the Republic and Northern Ireland.

BBC brought radio to the Irish island when it established a station in Belfast in 1924; two years later, the Irish Free State started the radio station 2RN in Dublin. Television struck when BBC began TV broadcasts from Belfast in 1953. Ulster Television, the island's first independent channel, was established in 1959. In 1961, the Republic's national radio service made its first television broadcast, renaming itself **Radio Telefís Éireann (RTE).** Most of the island now has cable service with access to the BBC and other independent British channels, the most popular of which is Rupert Murdoch's SKY Television. The Irish government's most recent developments include the start of Irish language radio and TV stations, called Telifis na Gaelige (see **The Irish Language,** p. 19) These efforts are aimed at combatting the contribution of modern media forms to the distinction of the Irish language.

Computers have infected Ireland—viruses, Y2K concerns and all. Most of the major international manufacturers are represented, and local companies make personalized computers (some, such as the Celtic computer, are even proud of their heritage). Software is a huge industry in Ireland, the world's second largest exporter of the stuff. While email has yet to overrun the Trinity campus, access is becoming easier to find in cafes and hostels. The tourism industry is also becoming internet commerce savvy; many towns and accommodations have their own web sites and email accounts.

SPORTS

The Irish take enormous pride in their two native sports: hurling and Gaelic football. For many Irish, these games are the reason that spring changes into summer. Many a day would be wasted trying to find a farmer, business executive, or sheep unaware of his or her county's progress. Regional divisions are most obvious in county allegiances. Be warned of (and recommended to) the hysteria of any Irish sporting event, when hordes of fans bedecked in their county colors bring bedlam to Irish city streets. Attending a pub the day of that county's game will leave you happy, deaf, drunk, and counting down the days to the next round.

Most traditional Irish sports are modern developments of contests fought between whole clans or parishes across expanses of countryside. In 1884, the **Gaelic Athletic Association (GAA)** was founded to establish official rules and regulations for hurling, Gaelic football, and other ancient Irish recreations. A secondary function of their efforts was to promote a non-British identity on the island. The organization's first patron was Archbishop Croke of Cashel and Emly; his name later came to adorn Croke Park in Dublin, Ireland's biggest Gaelic games stadium. The GAA divided the island on a club-county-province level, in which the club teams organized mostly according to parish lines. Arranged according to the four provinces Connacht, Munster, Leinster, and Ulster, all 32 counties of the island compete in the knockout rounds of the two sports' "All Ireland" Championships, but only two make it to the finals in September. Despite the fervent nationalism of its beginnings, the GAA has always included the Northern Ireland teams in these leagues. Sectarian politics plague today's GAA, leaving its fate uncertain.

According to the GAA, "played well, **Gaelic football** is a fast, skillful game striking to the eye. Played badly, it is an unimpressive spectacle of dragging and pulling!" Gaelic football seems like a cross between soccer and rugby, although it predates both of them. The ball is shorter and fatter than a rugby ball. Players may run holding the ball for no more than four paces, after which they must bounce, kick, or punch it in any direction. At each end of the field is a set of goalposts, and below the crossbar there is a net resembling a soccer net. One point is scored for putting the goal over the crossbar between the posts, three for netting it. The game is played by both men and women in teams of 15, for two 30-minute periods. Charging is within the rules.

As fans like to say, if football is a game, then **hurling** is an art. This fast and dangerous-looking game was first played in the 13th century. Perhaps best imagined as a blend of lacrosse and field hockey, the game is named after the stick with which it is played, the *caman* or "hurley." The hurley—like a hockey stick with a shorter and wider blade—is used to hit the ball along the ground or overhead. Players may also kick the ball, or hit it with the flat of their hands. The ball, or *sliothar*, is leather-covered and can be caught for hitting, or carried along on the stick. Teams of 15 players each try to score a point by hitting the ball over the eight-foot-high crossbar of the goalposts. A goal is worth three points and is scored by hitting the ball under the crossbar. The female version of hurling is called camogie, and permits only twelve team members but considerably more protective ware.

Soccer, commonly called **football**, enjoys an equally fanatical, if less patriotic, following as hurling and gaelic football. The Irish dream of international stardom in this sport, and came closer to achieving it when they reached the quarter-finals of the 1994 World Cup. The Irish are also fiercely devoted to the football clubs of England. Rugby achieves a strong fan base in both the Republic and Northern Ireland. Horse racing maintains a devoted following in the Republic, thanks to Co. Kildare's well appreciated place as a breeding ground for champion racehorses. Watersports like surfing and sailing are popular hobbies, particularly along the Western and Northwestern coasts.

FOOD AND DRINK

SOLIDS

Food in Ireland can be fairly expensive, especially in restaurants. The basics—and that's what you'll get—are simple and filling. The restaurant business is a fairly recent phenomenon in Ireland: up until the economy took off about 20 years ago, only a few restaurants graced the streets of even Dublin. Today, eateries clutter the streets of Ireland's mini-metropolises, many of which specialize in international fares. The rural byways of the island still remain limited in their culinary offerings. A quick and greasy staple everywhere are "chippers" (fish and chips shops), and "take-aways" (take-outs). At chippers, "fish" is a whitefish, usually cod, and chips are served with salt and vinegar; ketchup sometimes costs extra. Fried food delicacies include chips with gravy, potato cakes (flat pancakes made of potato flakes), or the infamous spiceburger (a fried patty of spiced breadcrumbs). Most pubs serve food as well as drink, and **pub grub** is a good option for a substantial and inexpensive meal. Typical pub grub includes Irish stew (meat, potatoes, carrots, and onions), burgers, soup, and sandwiches.

Most Irish meals are based on a simple formula: meat, potatoes, and greens. Preparation usually involves frying or boiling. *Colcannon* (a potato, onion, and cabbage dish), "ploughman's lunch," and Irish stew are Irish specialties. Loud and long will the Irish bards sing the praises of the Clonakilty man who first concocted **black pudding.** This delicacy was invented during a shortage and makes the most of the bits of the pig not usually eaten. Black pudding is, as one local butcher put it, "some pork, a good deal of blood, and grains and things—all wrapped up in a tube." White pudding is a similar dish that uses milk instead of blood. **Irish breakfasts,** often served all day and a given at any B&B, include eggs, sausage, white or black pudding, porridge, rashers (a more thickly sliced version of American bacon), a fried tomato, brown bread, and toast.

The culinary merit of the Irish resides in their bread. Most famous is **soda bread,** a heavy white bread sweetened by raisins, and especially yummy when fried. Most common are **brown bread** and **batch loaves.** Brown bread is thick and grainy, while batch loaves are square-shaped white bread ideal for sandwiches. Another indigenous bread is **barm brack**; perfect for holidays, it is a spicy mixture of dried fruits and molasses mixed to a lead-like density. Sandwiches are often served on a **bap,** a round, white bun. All of these breads are excellent in combination with locally produced cheeses, which make up a small industry in the Southwest.

Seafood can be a real bargain in smaller towns; mussels and oysters are splendid when marinated in Guinness. In addition to the widespread fried fish, smoked mackerel is splendid year-round and Atlantic salmon is freshest around July. Regional specialties include **crubeen** (tasty pigs' feet) in Cork, **coddle** (boiled sausages and bacon with potatoes) in Dublin, and **blaa** (sausage rolls) in Waterford. Wexford berries in the Southeast are luscious May through July. **Tea** accompanies most meals; it has come to signify more than just that which quenches thirst or politely washes down unwanted cabbage. If the Irish drink Guinness for strength, they drink tea for everything else.

In the North, an Irish Breakfast is called an **Ulster Fry**. Aside from that, food in the North is much the same as that in the Republic. Throughout the island, breakfast is the first meal of the day, followed by "dinner" at midday, and then an evening "tea" accompanied by a light meal fare.

LIQIUDS: PUBS AND PINTS

A study released in the summer of 1998 found that Irish students spend roughly £80 a month on drinks, which is no wonder considering the centrality of pubs in Irish culture. More so in the Republic than in the North, the pub is, in a sense, the living room of the Irish household. Locals of all ages from every social milieu head to the public house for conversation, food, singing and dancing, and **craic** (crack), an Irish word meaning "a good time." Although the clientele of the average public house is predominantly male, women feel comfortable here, especially on the weekends in urban areas when students swarm the town. People aren't normally looking for much other than communal talk and drink. In the evening, some pubs host traditional music. Local and traveling musicians toting fiddles, guitars, *bodhráns* (a shallow, one-sided drum), and tin whistles, drop in around 9:30pm to start impromptu trad sessions (see Music, p. 26). In rural pubs, there's also the chance that a *seanachaí* (SHAN-ukh-ee), or travelling storyteller, might demand an audience.

Pubs in the Republic are generally open Monday through Saturday from 10:30am to 11:30pm (11pm in winter) and Sunday from 12:30 to 2pm and 4 to 11pm (closed 2-4pm due to the Holy hour). Pubs are now able to obtain late hours licenses that allow them to stay open until midnight-2am. These later hours are becoming increasingly common in Dublin. Some pubs, especially ones catering to a clientele of fishermen, have been granted special "early" licenses, which allow them to open at 7:30am and require an act of Parliament to revoke. Pubs almost never charge a cover price or require a drink minimum. Pubs in the North tend to be open Monday through Saturday from 11:30am to 11pm, and Sunday from 12:30 to 2:30pm and 7 to 10pm. Some pubs close for a few hours on weekday afternoons as well, particularly in rural areas. Pub lunches are usually served from Monday to Saturday, 12:30 to 2:30pm, while soup, soda bread, and sandwiches are served all day. Children are often not allowed in pubs after 7pm. The legal drinking age in Ireland and Northern Ireland is 18.

Beer wins a landslide victory as the drink of choice in Irish pubs. Cocktails are an oddity found mainly in American-style bars and discos, and most pubs stock only a few bottles of wine. Beer comes in two basic varieties, **lagers** (blond, fizzy brews served cold, a bit weaker than ales or stouts) and **ales** (slightly darker, more bitter, and sometimes served a bit warmer than lagers). **Stout,** a type of ale, is thick, dark-ruby colored, and made from roasted barley to impart an almost meaty flavor. Guinness stout inspires a reverence otherwise reserved for the Holy Trinity. Known variously as "the dark stuff," "the blonde in the black skirt," or simply "I'll have a pint, please," it's a rich, dark brew with a head thick enough to stand a match in. It's also far better in Ireland than anywhere else. For a sweeter taste, try it with blackcurrant or cider. **Murphy's** is a similar, slightly creamier stout brewed in Cork. Cork also produces **Beamish**, a tasty "economy" stout. Stout takes a while to pour properly (usually 3-4min.); it should be drunk in slow measure, as well. **Smithwicks** is a hoppy, English-style bitter commonly perceived of as of as an old man's drink. Two more popular domestic lagers are **Kilkenny** and **Harp**. You'll likely be surprised by the many pubs serving Budweiser or Heineken here and by the number of young people quaffing such imported lagers. In general, the indigenous brews are far worthier. Beer is served in imperial **pint glasses** (about 20oz.) or half-pints (called a "glass"). Ordering a beer by name will bring you a full pint, so be loud and clear if you can only stay for a half (or just take the pint and drink faster). A pint of Guinness usually costs between IR£2-3, with prices rising steeply in urban settings. **Never tip the barman.**

Irish whiskey, which Queen Elizabeth once claimed was her only true Irish friend, is sweeter than its Scotch counterpart, spelled "whisky" (see p. 225). Irish monks invented whiskey, calling it *uisce beatha*, meaning "water of life." In Ireland, whiskey is served in larger measures than you might be used to. **Jameson** is popular everywhere. Dubliners are partial to **Powers and Sons. Bushmills,** distilled near Portstewart, is the favorite in the North. Drinkers in Cork enjoy **Paddy's. Irish coffee** is sweetened with brown sugar and whipped cream and laced with whiskey. It's been more popular with the tourists than the natives ever since its alleged invention at Shannon Airport by a desperate bartender looking to appease cranky travelers on a layover. (Others place the drink's origin in San Francisco.) **Hot whiskey** (spiced up with lemon, cloves, and brown sugar) can provide a cozy buzz. In the west, you may hear some locals praise "mountain dew," a euphemism for poitín (put-CHEEN), an illegal distillation sometimes given to cows in labor that ranges in strength from 115 to 140 proof. *Poitín* makes after-hour appearances in pubs throughout the island, but be warned that *poitín* is a highly toxic substance. While most alcoholic drinks are based on ethanol, *poitín* uses lethal methanol.

ESSENTIALS

FACTS FOR THE TRAVELER

WHEN TO GO

Timing is everything. Traveling during the low or off season (mid-Sept. to May) has its benefits: airfares are less expensive, and you won't have to fend off flocks of fellow tourists. The flip side is that many attractions, hostels, bed and breakfasts (B&Bs), and tourist offices close in winter, and in some rural areas of western Ireland, local transportation drops off significantly or shuts down altogether. Most unfortunate are the short daylight hours in the winter, when the sun goes down at around 5pm.

Although festivities increase with the population during the summer, Ireland's calendar of events is continually jam-packed. A thriving music scene fills pubs year-round, with increased performances in the summer. The acclaimed theater productions of Dublin and Belfast occur mostly during fall and winter. Countless music, film, arts, and, above all, region-specific festivals spring up practically every week; a visit during a town festival will meet an explosive display of excitement, community, and beer consumption. Although different festivals occur throughout the year, the summer months bear a high concentration of them. See **Appendix** for a complete 2000 festivals calendar.

The infamous rainy Irish weather is subject to frequent changes but relatively constant temperatures. The east and south coasts are the driest and sunniest, while western Ireland is wetter and cloudier. Spring is the driest season in Ireland, especially on the east coast. May and June are the sunniest months, particularly in the south and southeast, and July and August are the warmest. December and January have the worst weather of the year: wet, cold, and cloudy.

Average Temperature	low	°F	high	low	°C	high
Summer (°F/°C)	60		65	15		18
Winter (°F/°C)	40		45	4		7

GOVERNMENT INFORMATION OFFICES

Irish Tourist Board (Bord Fáilte): Tel. (1850) 230 330 from Ireland; (020) 7493 3201 from the U.K.; (353) 666 1258 from elsewhere); www.ireland.travel.ie. **Australia:** Level 5, 36 Carrington St., Sydney NSW 2000 (tel. (02) 9299 6177; fax 9299 6323). **Canada:** 2 Bloor St. W., Toronto ON M4W3E2 (tel. (416) 925 6368; fax 961 2175). **U.S.:** 345 Park Ave., New York, NY 10154 (tel. (800) 223 6470 or (212) 418 0800; fax 371 9052). **New Zealand:** Dingwall Building, 87 Queen St., Auckland (tel. (00649) 379 3708; fax 302 2420). **South Africa:** Everite House, 20 De Korte St., Braamfontein, Johannesburg (tel. (002711) 339 4865; fax 339 2474). **U.K.:** 150 New Bond St., London W1Y 0AQ (tel. (020) 7493 3201; fax 493 9065).

Northern Ireland Tourist Board: Head Office: 59 North St., **Belfast**, BT1 1NB, Northern Ireland (tel. (01232) 246609; fax 240960; www.ni-tourisim.com). **Dublin:** 16 Nassau St., Dublin 2 (tel. (01) 679 1977; CallSave (1850) 230230; fax (01) 677 1587. **Canada:** 2 Bloor St. W., Toronto ON M4W3E2 (tel. (416) 925 6368; fax 925 6033). **U.K.:** British Travel Centre, 12 Lower Regent St., London SW1Y 4PQ (tel. (020) 7839 8417). From elsewhere overseas, contact any British Tourist Office. Tourist boards should have free brochures as well as *Where to Stay in Northern Ireland 1999,* a list of all B&Bs and campgrounds (UK£4). #701, New York, NY 10176 (tel. (800) 326 0036 or (212) 922 0101; fax 922 0099).

DOCUMENTS AND FORMALITIES

> **ENTRANCE REQUIREMENTS.**
> **Passport** (p. 37). Required for citizens of Australia, Canada, New Zealand, South Africa, the EU, and the U.S.
> **Visa** (p. 38). Not required for short term travel from EU, Commonwealth, and North American countries.
> **Work Permit** (p. 39). Required for all foreigners planning to work in Ireland.
> **Driving Permit** (p. 70). Required for all those planning to drive.

IRISH EMBASSIES AND CONSULATES IN...

Australia and New Zealand: 20 Arkana St., Yarralumla ACT 2600 (tel. (02) 62 73 30 22; fax 62 73 37 41).

Canada: 130 Albert St., Ste. 1105, Ottawa, Ontario K1P 5G4 (tel. (613) 233 62 81; fax 233 58 35).

South Africa: Tubach Centre, 1234 Church St., 0083 Colbyn, Pretoria (tel. (012) 342 50 62; fax 342 45 72).

U.K.: 17 Grosvenor Pl., London SW1X 7HR (tel. (020) 72 35 21 71; fax 72 45 69 61).

U.S.: Irish Embassy, 2234 Massachusetts Ave. NW, Washington, D.C. 20008 (tel. (202) 462 3939; fax 232 5993). Consulates: 345 Park Ave., 17th floor, New York, NY 10154 (tel. (212) 319 2555); Rm. 911, 400 N. Michigan Ave., Chicago, IL 60611 (tel. (312) 337 1868); 44 Montgomery St., #3830, San Francisco, CA 94104 (tel. (415) 392 4214); 535 Boylston St., Boston, MA 02116 (tel. (617) 267 9330).

U.K. EMBASSIES AND CONSULATES IN...

For addresses of embassies in countries not listed here, check the Foreign and Commonwealth Office website at www.fco.gov.uk/directory/posts.asp.

Australia: British High Commission, Commonwealth Ave., Yarralumla, Canberra, ACT 2600 (tel. (02) 6270 6666; fax (02) 6273 3236).

Canada: British Consulate-General, 777 Bay St., Suite 2800, Toronto, Ont. M5G 2G2 (tel. (416) 593 1290; fax (416) 593 1299).

France: British Consulate, 9 Ave Hoche, 8é, Paris (tel. (01) 42 66 38 10).

Ireland: British Embassy, 29 Merrion Rd., Ballsbridge, Dublin 4 (tel. (01) 205 3700; fax 205 3885).

New Zealand: British High Commission, 44 Hill St., Thorndon, Wellington (tel. (04) 472 6049; fax (04) 473 4982; www.brithighcomm.org.nz). Also at 151 Queen St., Auckland 1 (tel. (09) 309 2973).

South Africa: British High Commission, Greystoke, 255 Hill St., Acadia, Pretoria (tel. 012 483 1200; fax 012 483 1302).

U.S.: British Consulate, 19 Observatory Circle NW, Washington, D.C. 20008 (tel. (202) 588-7800; fax (202) 588-7850 (visa), (202) 588-7892 (passport); www.britain-info.org). British Embassy, 3100 Massachusetts Ave. NW, Washington, D.C. 20008 (tel. (202) 462-1340). Local consulates can also be found in many cities, including Atlanta, Boston, Chicago, Houston, Los Angeles, New York, and San Francisco: call the Consulate in D.C. for contact details.

EMBASSIES AND CONSULATES IN IRELAND

Australia: The Republic, Fitzwilton House, Wilton Terr., Dublin 2 (tel. (01) 676 1517; fax 678 5185).

Canada: The Republic, Canadian Embassy, Canada House, 65 St. Stephen's Green, Dublin 2 (tel. (01) 478 1988; fax 478 1285). **U.K.,** Canadian High Commission, McDonald House, 1 Grosvenor Sq., London W1X 0AB (tel. (0171) 258 6600; fax 258 6506).

New Zealand: The Republic, New Zealand Consulate General, 46 Upper Mount Joy St., Dublin 2 (tel. (01) 676 2464; fax 676 2489). **U.K.,** New Zealand Embassy, New Zealand House, 80 Haymarket, London SW1Y 4QT (tel. (0171) 930 8422).

South Africa: The Republic, South Africa Embassy, Alexandra House, Earlsford Terr. (tel. (01) 661 5553; fax 661 5590), Dublin 2. **U.K.,** South African High Commission, South Africa House, Trafalgar Sq., London WC2N 5DP (tel. (0171) 930 4488; fax 451 930 1510).

United Kingdom: The Republic, British Embassy, 29 Merrion Rd., Dublin 4 (tel. (01) 269 5211; fax. 205 3885).

United States: The Republic, American Embassy, 42 Elgin Rd., Ballsbridge, Dublin 4 (tel. (01) 668 7122; fax 668 9946). **Northern Ireland** Consulate General, Queen's House, 14 Queen St., Belfast BT1 6EQ (tel. (01232) 328239; fax 248482).

PASSPORTS

REQUIREMENTS. Citizens of Australia, Canada, New Zealand, South Africa, the EU, and the U.S. need valid passports to enter Ireland and to re-enter their own country. Citizens of the U.K. do not need their passport, but may want to bring it. Ireland does not allow entrance if the holder's passport expires in under six months; returning home with an expired passport is illegal and may result in a fine.

PHOTOCOPIES. It is a good idea to photocopy the page of your passport that contains your photograph, passport number, and other identifying information, along with other important documents such as visas, travel insurance policies, airplane tickets, and traveler's check serial numbers, in case you lose anything. Carry one set of copies in a safe place apart from the originals and leave another set at home. Consulates also recommend that you carry an expired passport or an official copy of your birth certificate in a part of your baggage separate from other documents.

LOST PASSPORTS. If you lose your passport, immediately notify the local police and the nearest embassy or consulate of your home government. To expedite its replacement, you will need to know all information previously recorded and show identification and proof of citizenship. In some cases, a replacement may take weeks to process, and it may be valid only for a limited time. Any visas stamped in your old passport will be irretrievably lost. In an emergency, ask for immediate temporary traveling papers that will permit you to re-enter your home country. Your passport is a public document belonging to your nation's government. You may have to surrender it to a foreign government official, but if you don't get it back in a reasonable amount of time, inform the nearest mission of your home country.

NEW PASSPORTS. All applications for new passports or renewals should be filed several weeks or months in advance of your planned departure date. Most passport offices do offer emergency passport services for an extra charge. Citizens residing abroad who need a passport or renewal should contact their nearest embassy or consulate.

Australia: Citizens must apply for a passport in person at a post office, a passport office, or an Australian diplomatic mission overseas. Passport offices are located in Adelaide, Brisbane, Canberra, Darwin, Hobart, Melbourne, Newcastle, Perth, and Sydney. New adult passports cost AUS$126 (for a 32-page passport) or AUS$188 (64-page), and a child's AUS$63 (32-page) or AUS$94 (64-page). Adult passports are valid for 10 years and child passports for 5 years. For more info, call toll-free (in Australia) 13 12 32, or visit www.dfat.gov.au/passports.

Canada: Application forms are available at all passport offices, Canadian missions, many travel agencies, and Northern Stores in northern communities. Passports cost CDN$60, plus a CDN$25 consular fee, are valid for 5 years, and are not renewable. For additional info, contact the Canadian Passport Office, Department of Foreign Affairs and International Trade, Ottawa, ON, K1A 0G3 (tel. (613) 994-3500; www.dfait-maeci.gc.ca/passport). Travelers may also call 800-567-6868 (24hr.); in Toronto, (416) 973-3251; in Vancouver, (604) 586-2500; in Montreal, (514) 283-2152.

Ireland: Citizens can apply for a passport by mail to either the Department of Foreign Affairs, Passport Office, Setanta Centre, Molesworth St., Dublin 2 (tel. (01) 671 1633; fax 671 1092; www.irlgov.ie/iveagh), or the Passport Office, Irish Life Building, 1A South Mall, Cork (tel. (021) 27 25 25). Obtain an application at a local Garda station or post office, or request one from a passport office. Passports cost IR£45 and are valid for 10 years. Citizens under 18 or over 65 can request a 3-year passport that costs IR£10.

New Zealand: Application forms for passports are available in New Zealand from most travel agents. Applications may be forwarded to the Passport Office, P.O. Box 10526, Wellington, New Zealand (tel. 0800 22 50 50; www.govt.nz/agency_info/forms.shtml). Standard processing time in New Zealand is 10 working days for correct applications. The fees are adult NZ$80, and child NZ$40. Children's names can no longer be endorsed on a parent's passport—they must apply for their own, which are valid for up to 5 years. An adult's passport is valid for up to 10 years.

South Africa: South African passports are issued only in Pretoria. However, all applications must still be submitted or forwarded to the applicable office of a South African consulate. Tourist passports, valid for 10 years, cost around SAR80. Children under 16 must be issued their own passports, valid for 5 years, which cost around SAR60. Time for the completion of an application is normally 3 months or more from the time of submission. For further information, contact the nearest Department of Home Affairs Office (www.southafrica-newyork.net/passport.htm).

United Kingdom: Full passports are valid for 10 years (5 years if under 16). Application forms are available at passport offices, main post offices, and many travel agents. Apply by mail or in person to one of the passport offices, located in London, Liverpool, Newport, Peterborough, Glasgow, or Belfast. The fee is UK£31, UK£11 for children under 16. The process takes about four weeks, but the London office offers a five-day, walk-in rush service; arrive early. The U.K. Passport Agency can be reached by phone at (0870) 521 04 10, and more information is available at www.open.gov.uk/ukpass/ukpass.htm.

United States: Citizens may apply for a passport at any federal or state courthouse or post office authorized to accept passport applications, or at a U.S. Passport Agency, located in most major cities. Refer to the "U.S. Government, State Department" section of the telephone directory or the local post office for addresses. Passports are valid for 10 years (5 years if under 18) and cost US$60 (under 18 US$40). Passports may be renewed by mail or in person for US$40. Processing takes 3-4 weeks. For more info, contact the U.S. Passport Information's 24-hour recorded message (tel. (202) 647-0518) or look on the web at http://travel.state.gov/passport_services.html.

VISAS, INVITATIONS, AND WORK PERMITS

VISAS. Citizens of most countries, including Australia, Canada, European Union countries, New Zealand, South Africa, the United Kingdom, and the United States, do not need visas to visit Ireland. If in doubt, or if your home country does not appear on the above list, check with your embassy.

WORK PERMITS. Admission as a visitor does not include the right to work, which is authorized only by a work permit, and entering Ireland to study requires a special visa. For more information, see **Alternatives to Tourism,** p. 45.

IDENTIFICATION

When you travel, always carry two or more forms of identification on your person, including at least one photo ID. A passport combined with a driver's license or birth certificate usually serves as adequate proof of your identity and citizenship. Many establishments, especially banks, require several IDs before cashing traveler's checks. Never carry all your forms of ID together, however; you risk being left entirely without ID or funds in case of theft or loss. It is useful to carry extra passport-size photos to affix to the various IDs or railpasses you may acquire.

STUDENT AND TEACHER IDENTIFICATION. The **International Student Identity Card (ISIC)** is the most widely accepted form of student identification. Flashing this card can procure you discounts for sights, theaters, museums, accommodations, meals, train, ferry, bus, and airplane transportation, and other services. Present the card wherever you go, and ask about discounts even when none are advertised. The international identification cards are preferable to institution-specific cards because the tourism personnel in Ireland are taught to recognize the former. For U.S. cardholders traveling in Ireland, the ISIC also provides insurance benefits, including US$100 per day of in-hospital sickness for a maximum of 60 days, and US$3000 accident-related medical reimbursement for each accident (see **Insurance,** p. 55). In addition, cardholders have access to a toll-free 24hr. ISIC helpline whose multilingual staff can provide assistance in medical, legal, and financial emergencies overseas (tel. 800-626-2427 in the U.S. and Canada; elsewhere call collect (181) 666 90 25).

Many student travel agencies around the world issue ISICs, including STA Travel in Australia and New Zealand; Travel CUTS in Canada; USIT in Ireland and Northern Ireland; SASTS in South Africa; Campus Travel and STA Travel in the U.K.; Council Travel, STA Travel, and via the web (www.counciltravel.com/idcards/index.htm) in the U.S.; and any other travel agency with a student focus. When you apply for the card, request a copy of the *International Student Identity Card Handbook*, which lists some of the available discounts in Ireland. You can also write to Council for a copy. The card is valid from September of one year to December of the following year and costs AUS$15, CDN$15, or US$20. Applicants must be at least 12 years old and degree-seeking students of a secondary or post-secondary school. Because of the proliferation of phony ISICs, many airlines and some other services require additional proof of student identity, such as a signed letter from the registrar attesting to your student status that is stamped with the school seal or your school ID card. The **International Teacher Identity Card (ITIC)** offers the same insurance coverage, and similar but limited discounts. The fee is AUS$13, UK£5, or US$20. For more information on these cards, contact the **International Student Travel Confederation (ISTC),** Herengracht 479, 1017 BS Amsterdam, Netherlands (from abroad, call 31 20 421 28 00; fax 421 28 10; email istcinfo@istc.org; www.istc.org).

The **TravelSave stamp,** available for £8 at any **usit** (see p. 61) in Ireland, is an addition to your ISIC card, which cuts fares almost in half on national rail and will let you break your journey to visit at any stop on the way to your final destination (valid for 1 month). It also provides 15% discounts on bus fares (except on fares less than £1).

YOUTH IDENTIFICATION. The International Student Travel Confederation also issues a discount card to travelers who are 25 years old or younger but not students. Known as the International Youth Travel Card (IYTC; formerly the GO25 Card), this one-year card offers many of the same benefits as the ISIC, and most organizations that sell the ISIC also sell the IYTC. A brochure that lists discounts is free when you purchase the card. To apply, you will need either a passport, valid driver's license, or copy of a birth certificate, and a passport-sized photo with your name printed on the back. The fee is US$20.

CUSTOMS

Upon entering Ireland, you must declare certain items from abroad and pay a duty on the value of those articles that exceed the allowance established by Irish customs service. Keeping receipts for purchases made abroad will help establish values when you return (see Value Added Tax, below). It is wise to make a list, including serial numbers, of any valuables that you carry with you from home; if you register this list with customs before your departure and have an official stamp it, you will avoid import duty charges and ensure an easy passage upon your return. Be especially careful to document items manufactured abroad.

Upon returning home, you must declare all articles acquired abroad and pay a **duty** on the value of articles that exceed the allowance established by your country's customs service. Goods and gifts purchased at **duty-free** shops abroad are not exempt from duty or sales tax at your point of return; you must declare these items as well. "Duty-free" merely means that you need not pay a tax in the country of purchase. For more specific information on customs requirements, contact the following information centers:

Australia: Australian Customs National Information Line 1 300 363; www.customs.gov.au.

Canada: Canadian Customs, 2265 St. Laurent Blvd., Ottawa, ON K1G 4K3 (tel. (613) 993-0534 or 24hr. automated service 800-461-9999; www.revcan.ca).

Ireland: The Collector of Customs and Excise, The Custom House, Dublin 1 (tel. (01) 679 27 77; fax 671 20 21; email taxes@revenue.iol.ie; www.revenue.ie/customs.htm).

New Zealand: New Zealand Customhouse, 17-21 Whitmore St., Box 2218, Welington (tel. (04) 473 6099; fax 473 7370; www.customs.govt.nz).

South Africa: Commissioner for Customs and Excise, Private Bag X47, Pretoria 0001 (tel. 012 314 99 11; fax 328 64 78).

United Kingdom: Her Majesty's Customs and Excise, Custom House, Nettleton Road, Heathrow Airport, Hounslow, Middlesex TW6 2LA (tel. (020) 8910 36 02/35 66; fax 910 37 65; www.hmce.gov.uk).

United States: U.S. Customs Service, Box 7407, Washington D.C. 20044 (tel. (202) 927-6724; www.customs.ustreas.gov).

VAT (VALUE-ADDED TAX)

Both Ireland and Northern Ireland charge value-added tax (VAT), a national sales tax on most goods and some services. In Ireland, the VAT ranges from 0% on food and children's clothing to 17% in restaurants to 21% on other items, such as jewelry, clothing, cameras, and appliances; the VAT is usually included in listed prices. The British rate, applicable to Northern Ireland, is 17.5% on many services (such as hairdressers, hotels, restaurants, and car rental agencies) and on all goods (except books, medicine, and food). Prices stated in *Let's Go* include VAT. **Refunds** are available only to non-EU citizens and only for goods taken out of the country, not services. In Ireland, VAT refunds are available on goods purchased in stores displaying a "Cashback" sticker (ask if you don't see one). Ask for a voucher with your purchase, which you must fill out and present at the Cashback service desk in Dublin or Shannon airports. Purchases greater than ₤200 must be approved at the customs desk first. Your money can also be refunded by mail, which takes six to eight weeks. Visitors to Northern Ireland and the Isle of Man can get a **VAT refund** on goods taken out of the country through the **Retail Export Scheme.** Look for signs like "Tax Free Shopping" or "Tax Free for Tourists" and ask the shopkeeper about minimum purchases (usually ₤50-100) as well as for the appropriate form. Keep purchases in carry-on luggage so a customs officer can inspect the goods and validate refund forms. To receive a refund, mail the stamped forms back to the store in the envelope provided. Refunds can take up to three months to be processed. In order to use this scheme, you must export the goods within three months of purchase.

MONEY

If you stay in hostels and prepare your own food, expect to spend anywhere from US$18-30 per person per day. **Accommodations** start at about £8 -10 per night for a single bed while the cost for a basic sit-down **meal** begins around £6. Transport and beer will increase your daily budget significantly. Carrying cash with you, even in a money belt, is risky but necessary; personal checks from home are usually not accepted and even traveler's checks may not be accepted in a few locations.

CURRENCY AND EXCHANGE

Legal tender in the Republic of Ireland is the Irish pound (or "punt"), denoted £. It comes in the same denominations as the British pound (which is called "sterling" in Ireland) but has been worth a bit less recently. British small change is no longer accepted in the Republic of Ireland. The Irish punt is difficult to convert abroad.

Legal tender in Northern Ireland is the British pound. Northern Ireland has its own bank notes, which are identical in value to English, Scottish, or Manx notes of the same denominations. Although all of these notes are accepted in Northern Ireland, Northern Ireland bank notes are not accepted across the water. U.K. coins now come in logical denominations of 1p, 2p, 5p, 10p, 20p, 50p, and £1. An old "shilling" coin is worth 5p, a "florin" 10p. "Quid," popular slang for pounds sterling, derives from *cuid*, which serves as both the singular and plural in Irish. Therefore the plural of quid is "quid," not "quids."

Most banks are closed on Saturday, Sunday and all public holidays. The majority of Irish towns have 24-hour ATMs. Most businesses close on "bank holidays," which occur several times a year in both countries. Banks in Ireland are usually open Monday to Friday 9am to 4pm. Usual bank hours in Northern Ireland are Monday to Friday 9:30am to 4:30pm. In both the Republic and the North, some close for lunch and many close early or late one day per week.

The currency chart below is based on published exchange rates from August 1999. For U.K. exchange rates, applicable to Northern Ireland, see p. 390.

THE IRISH POUND

US$1 = £0.76	IR£1 = US$1.32
CDN$1 =£0.52	= CDN$1.94
UK£1 =£1.20	= UK£0.83
AUS$1 =£0.50	= AUS$2.00
NZ$1 =£0.41	= NZ$2.48
SAR1=£0.13	= SAR7.96
ECU1 = £0.79	= ECU1.27

 THE EURO. On January 1, 1999, Ireland accepted the euro (ECU) as its common currency. The punt (£) will continue to be accepted in Ireland until January 1, 2002, when the euro will become the only accepted currency. *Let's Go* lists all prices in punts, as these will still be most relevant in 2000. Updated information on the euro can be found on the EU's website at www.europa.eu.int/.

As a general rule, it's cheaper to convert money in Ireland. It's good to bring enough foreign currency to last for the first 24-72hr. of a trip to avoid being penniless after banking hours or on a holiday. Travelers living in the U.S. can get foreign currency from the comfort of their home; **Capital Foreign Exchange** (tel. 888-842-

Money From Home In Minutes.

If you're stuck for cash on your travels, don't panic. Millions of people trust Western Union to transfer money in minutes to 165 countries and over 50,000 locations worldwide. Our record of safety and reliability is second to none. For more information, call Western Union: USA 1-800-325-6000, Canada 1-800-235-0000. Wherever you are, you're never far from home.

www.westernunion.com

WESTERN UNION | MONEY TRANSFER

The fastest way to send money worldwide:

0880) or **International Currency Express** (tel. 888-278-6628) will deliver foreign currency (for over 120 countries) or traveler's checks overnight (US$15) or second-day (US$12) at competitive exchange rates.

Watch out for commission rates and check newspapers for the standard rate of exchange. Banks generally have the best rates. A good rule of thumb is only to go to banks or bureaux de change that have at most a 5% margin between their buy and sell prices. Since you lose money with each transaction, convert in large sums (unless the currency is depreciating rapidly). Also, using an ATM card or a credit card (see p. 44) will often get you the best possible rates.

If you use traveler's checks or bills, carry some in small denominations (US$50 or less), especially for times when you are forced to exchange money at disadvantageous rates. However, it is good to carry a range of denominations since charges may be levied per check cashed.

TRAVELER'S CHECKS

Traveler's checks are one of the safest and least troublesome means of carrying funds, since they can be refunded if stolen. Several agencies and banks sell them, usually for face value plus a small percentage commission. (Members of the American Automobile Association, and some banks and credit unions, can get American Express checks commission-free; see **Driving Permits and Insurance,** p. 70). **American Express** and **Visa** are the most widely recognized. If you're ordering checks, do so well in advance, especially if you are requesting large sums.

Each agency provides refunds if your checks are lost or stolen, and many provide additional services, such as toll-free refund hotlines in the countries you're visiting, emergency message services, and stolen credit card assistance. In order to collect a **refund for lost or stolen checks,** keep your check receipts separate from your checks and store them in a safe place or with a traveling companion. Record check numbers when you cash them, leave a list of check numbers with someone at home, and ask for a list of refund centers when you buy your checks. Never countersign your checks until you are ready to cash them, and always bring your passport with you when you plan to use the checks.

American Express: Call 800 251 902 in Australia; in New Zealand 0800 441 068; in the U.K. (0800) 521 313; in the U.S. and Canada 800-221-7282. Elsewhere, call U.S. collect 1-801-964-6665; www.aexp.com. The Dublin office can be reached at (3531) 679 9000 or (3531) 605 7709. Checks can be purchased for a small fee (1-4%) at American Express Travel Service Offices, banks, and American Automobile Association offices. AAA members (see p. 70) can buy the checks commission-free. American Express offices cash their checks commission-free (except where prohibited by national governments), but often at slightly worse rates than banks. *Cheques for Two* can be signed by either of two people traveling together. The booklet *Traveler's Companion* lists travel office addresses and stolen check hotlines for each European country. The hotline number in Ireland is (800) 626 000.

Citicorp: Call 800-645-6556 in the U.S. and Canada; in Europe, the Middle East, or Africa, call the London office at 44 (20) 7508 7007; from elsewhere, call U.S. collect 1-813-623-1709. Traveler's checks in 7 currencies. Commission 1-2%. Guaranteed hand-delivery of traveler's checks when a refund location is not convenient. Call 24hr.

Thomas Cook MasterCard: From the U.S., Canada, or Caribbean call 800-223-7373; from the U.K. call (0800) 622 101; from elsewhere, call 44 1733 318 950 collect. Checks available in 13 currencies. Commission 2%. Thomas Cook offices cash checks commission-free. Allied Irish Bank and th National Irish Bank are Thomas Cook affiliates in the Republic.

Visa: Call 800-227-6811 in the U.S.; in the U.K. (0800) 895 078; from elsewhere, call 44 1733 318 950 and reverse the charges. Any of the above numbers can tell you the location of their nearest office.

CREDIT CARDS

Credit cards are generally accepted in all but the smallest businesses in Ireland. Major credit cards—**MasterCard** and **Visa** are welcomed most often—can be used to extract cash advances in Irish pounds from associated banks and teller machines throughout Ireland. Credit card companies get the wholesale exchange rate, which is generally 5% better than the retail rate used by banks and other currency exchange establishments. **American Express** cards also work in some ATMs, as well as at AmEx offices and major airports. All such machines require a **Personal Identification Number (PIN)**. You must ask your credit card company for a PIN before you leave; without it, you will be unable to withdraw cash with your credit card outside your home country. If you already have a PIN, check with the company to make sure it will work in Ireland.

Credit cards often offer an array of other services, from insurance to emergency assistance. Check with your company to find out what is covered.

CREDIT CARD COMPANIES. Visa (U.S. tel. 800-336-8472) and **MasterCard** (U.S. tel. 800-307-7309) are issued in cooperation with individual banks and some other organizations. **American Express** (U.S. tel. 800-843-2273) has an annual fee of up to US$55, depending on the card. Cardholder services include the option of cashing personal checks at AmEx offices, a 24-hour hotline with medical and legal assistance in emergencies (tel. 800-554-2639 in U.S. and Canada; from abroad call U.S. collect 1-202-554-2639), and the American Express Travel Service. Benefits include assistance in changing airline, hotel, and car rental reservations, baggage loss and flight insurance, sending mailgrams and international cables, and holding your mail at one of the more than 1700 AmEx offices around the world.

CASH CARDS

Cash cards—popularly called ATM (Automated Teller Machine) cards—are widespread in Ireland, though some small towns still do without. Depending on the system that your home bank uses, you can probably access your own personal bank account whenever you need money. ATMs get the same wholesale exchange rate as credit cards. Despite these perks, do some research before relying too heavily on automation. Your bank may charge an additional fee and there is often a limit on the amount of money you can withdraw per day (usually about US$500, depending on the type of card and account). Computer networks are also known to fail. If you're traveling from the U.S. or Canada, memorize your PIN code in numeral form since machines elsewhere often don't have letters on their keys. Also, if your PIN is longer than four digits, ask your bank whether the first four digits will work, or whether you need a new number.

The two major international money networks are **Cirrus** (U.S. tel. 800-4-CIRRUS (424-7787) and **PLUS** (U.S. tel. 800-843-7587 for the "Voice Response Unit Locator"). To locate ATMs around the world, use www.visa.com/pd/atm or www.mastercard.com/atm.

GETTING MONEY FROM HOME

AMERICAN EXPRESS. Cardholders can withdraw cash from their checking accounts at any of AmEx's major offices and many of its representatives' offices, up to US$1000 every 21 days (no service charge, no interest). AmEx also offers Express Cash at any of their ATMs in Ireland. Express Cash withdrawals are automatically debited from the Cardmember's checking account or line of credit. Green card holders may withdraw up to US$1000 in a seven day period. There is a 2% transaction fee for each cash withdrawal, with a US$2.50 minimum/$20 maximum. To enroll in Express Cash, Cardmembers may call 800-CASH NOW (227-4669) in the U.S.; outside the U.S. call collect 1-336-668-5041. The AmEx national number in Ireland is (800) 626 000.

WESTERN UNION. Travelers from the U.S., Canada, and the U.K. can wire money abroad through Western Union's international money transfer services. In the U.S., call 800 325 6000; in the U.K., call (0800) 833 833; in Canada, call (800) 235 0000; in Ireland, call (800) 395 395. The rates for sending cash are generally US$10-11 cheaper than with a credit card, and the money is usually available at the place you're sending it to within an hour.

U.S. STATE DEPARTMENT (U.S. CITIZENS ONLY). In emergencies, U.S. citizens can have money sent via the State Department. For US$15, they will forward money within hours to the nearest consular office, which will disburse it according to instructions. The office serves only Americans in the direst of straits abroad; non-American travelers should contact their embassies for information on wiring cash. Check with the State Department or the nearest U.S. embassy or consulate for the quickest way to have the money sent. Contact the Overseas Citizens Service, American Citizens Services, Consular Affairs, Room 4811, U.S. Department of State, Washington, D.C. 20520 (tel. (202) 647-5225; nights, Sundays, and holidays 647-4000; fax (on demand only) 647-3000; travel.state.gov).

ALTERNATIVES TO TOURISM

STUDY

It's not difficult to spend a summer, a term, or a year studying in Ireland or Northern Ireland. Each of the major regions in Ireland has a university and smaller, *gaeltacht* communities support Irish language programs. Enrolling as a full-time student is more difficult. The requirements for admission can be hard to meet unless you attended an EU secondary school. American students must pay full fees; EU students go free, so Americans are a welcome source of funds, but places are few, especially in Ireland. Local libraries and bookstores are helpful sources for current information on study abroad, and the Internet has a study abroad web site at www.studyabroad.com. **Council** sponsors over 40 study abroad programs throughout the world. Contact them for more information (see **Travel Agencies,** p. 61).

UNIVERSITIES. Most American undergraduates enroll in programs sponsored by U.S. universities. However, good local universities can be much cheaper than an American university program, though it may be more difficult to receive academic credit. Schools that offer study abroad programs to foreigners are listed below.

Trinity College Dublin: Offers a 1-year program of high-quality, academically prestigious undergraduate courses for visiting students. Graduates can also register as one-year students not reading for a degree. Write to The Office of International Student Affairs, Arts and Social Sciences Bldg., Trinity College, Dublin 2, Ireland (tel. (01) 608 1396; email scoyle@tcd.ie). **Irish Studies Summer School** at Usit NOW, 19-21 Aston Quay, Dublin 2, Ireland (tel. (01) 602 1741; email lyclarke@usit.ie; www.usitnow.ie) is a seven week long program offering courses in Irish culture and history. From North America, contact Irish Studies Summer School, usit, New York Student Centre, 895 Amsterdam Ave., New York, NY 10025 (tel. (212) 663 5435; email usitny@aol.com). usit also administrates the summer program **Ireland in Europe,** 2 weeks of courses about Irish civilization.

University College Dublin: Its **International Summer School**, Newman House, 86 St. Stephen's Green, Dublin 2, Ireland (tel. (01) 475 2004; email summer.school@ucd.ie; hermes.ucd.ie/summerschool) offers a 2½-week course in July on Irish tradition and contemporary culture for students over 17.

University College Cork: International Education Office, West Wing, Main Quad, Western Rd., University College, Cork, Ireland (tel. (021) 902 543).

University College Galway: International Office, Galway, Ireland (tel. (091) 750 304; email intloffice@mis.ucg.ie). Offers year and semester opportunities for junior-year students who meet the college's entry requirements. **Summer school** courses offered July-Aug. include Irish Studies, Education, and Creative Writing.

Queen's University Belfast: Study Abroad for a semester or year. There is also a new 4-week **Introduction to Northern Ireland** program in January that studies the political, social, and economic questions unique to the North. Contact the International Liaison Office, Queen's University Belfast, Belfast BT7 1NN, UK (tel. (028) 9033 5415; email ilo@qub.ac.uk).

American Institute for Foreign Study, College Division, 102 Greenwich Ave., Greenwich, CT 06830 (tel. (800) 727-2437; www.aifs.com). Organizes programs for high school and college study in universities in Ireland. Summer, fall, spring, and year-long programs available. Scholarships available. Contact Dana Maggio with questions at dmaggio@aifs.com.

Beaver College Center for Education Abroad, 450 S. Easton Rd., Glenside, PA 19038-3295 (tel. 800-755-5607 or 888-BEAVER9; fax (215) 572-2174; email cea@beaver. edu; www.beaver.edu/cea). Operates summer-, semester- and year-long programs in Ireland. Applicants preferably should have completed three full semesters at an accredited university. Programs run anywhere from US$1900 for a summer program to US$20,000 for a full year abroad.

Experiment in International Living, Summer Programs (tel. 800-345-2929; fax 802-258-3428; email eil@worldlearning.org). Founded in 1932, it offers cross-cultural, educational homestays, community service, ecological adventure, and language training in Ireland. Programs are 3-5 weeks long and run from US$1800-$5000. Positions as group leaders are available world-wide for college graduates with strong in-country experienced language skills for the host country and experience working with high school students.

Council on International Educational Exchange (CIEE), 205 East 42nd St., New York, NY 10017 (tel. 888-COUNCIL (268-6245); fax 212-822-2699; www.ciee.org) sponsors work, volunteer, academic, internship, and professional study abroad programs in Ireland.

International Association for the Exchange of Students for Technical Experience (IAESTE), 10400 Little Patuxent Pkwy. #250, Columbia, MD 21044-3510 (tel. 410-997-3068; fax 410-997-5186; email iaste@aipt.org; www.aipt.org). Operates 8- to 12-week programs in Ireland for college students who have completed 2 years of study in a technical field. Non-refundable US$50 application fee; apply by Dec. 16 for summer placement.

LANGUAGE SCHOOLS. Programs are run by independent local organizations, and generally include food and lodging. Homestays are also a possibility.

Oideas Gael: Glencolmcille, Co. Donegal, Ireland (tel. (073) 30248; email oidsgael@iol.ie; www.Oideas-Gael.com). Offers week-long Irish language and culture courses from Easter until Aug. in various activities including bilingual hillwalking, set-dancing, painting, archaeology, and weaving.

FURTHER READING

Academic Year Abroad. Institute of International Education Books (US$45).

Vacation Study Abroad. Institute of International Education Books (US$40).

Peterson's Study Abroad Guide. Peterson's (US$30).

Vacation Work's Overseas Summer Jobs, Work Your Way Around the World, and *Council's Work Abroad* list working options by country for every country.

Vacation Work's International Directory of Voluntary Work lists programs in Ireland.

WORK

Ireland's recent economic boom means that for the first time in centuries, more people are coming to work in Ireland than leaving it. Even so, the unemployment rate in Ireland is high for an EU country. Travellers are most likely to find work in touristed urban centers such as Dublin, Glaway, or Cork. Aside from semi-skilled labor, the recent investments of software companies in Ireland favor computer-savvy types. European Union citizens can work in any EU country, and if your parents were born in an EU country, you may be able to claim dual citizenship with Ireland, or at least the right to a work permit. Commonwealth residents with a parent or grandparent born in the U.K. do not need a work permit to work in Northern Ireland. Contact your British Consulate or High Commission for details before you go and the Department of Employment when you arrive. If you do not fit into any of these categories, you must apply for a **work permit** to be considered for paid employment in the Republic or Northern Ireland. Your prospective employer must obtain this document, usually demonstrating that you have skills that locals lack.

If you are a full-time student at a U.S. university, the simplest way to get a job abroad in Ireland is through work permit programs run by **Council on International Educational Exchange (Council)** and its member organizations. For a US$225 application fee, Council can procure three- to six-month work permits and a handbook to help you find work and housing.

AU PAIR
interExchange, 161 Sixth Ave., New York, NY 10013 (tel. (212) 924 0446; fax 924 0575; email interex@earthlink.net), provides information on international work, au pair programs, and au pair positions in Ireland.

AGRICULTURE
Willing Workers on Organic Farms (WWOOF), PO Box 2675, Lewes, U.K., BN7 1RB (email fairtours@gn.apc.org; www.phdcc.com/sites/wwoof). Membership (US$10) in WWOOF allows you to receive room and board at a variety of organic farms in Ireland in exchange for your help on the farm.

ARCHAEOLOGICAL DIGS
Archaeological Institute of America, 656 Beacon St., Boston, MA 02215-2010 (tel. (617) 353-9361; fax 353-6550; email aia@bu.edu; www.archaeological.org), puts out the *Archaeological Fieldwork Opportunities Bulletin* (US$16 for non members), which lists field sites in Ireland. This can be purchased from Kendall/Hunt Publishing, 4050 Westmark Dr., Dubuque, Iowa 52002 (tel. 800-228-0810).

VOLUNTEER

Volunteer jobs are readily available almost everywhere. You may receive room and board in exchange for your labor. You can sometimes avoid the high application fees charged by the organizations that arrange placement by contacting the individual workcamps directly; check with the organizations.

Service Civil International Voluntary Service (SCI-VS), 814 NE 40th St., Seattle, WA 98105 (tel./fax (206) 545-6585; email sciivsusa@igc.apc.org). Arranges placement in workcamps in Ireland for those age 18 and over. Local organizations sponsor groups for physical or social work. Registration fees US$50-250, depending on the camp location.

Volunteers for Peace, 1034 Tiffany Rd., Belmont, VT 05730 (tel. (802) 259-2759; fax 259-2922; email vfp@vfp.org; www.vfp.org). A nonprofit organization that arranges speedy placement in 2- to 3-week workcamps in Ireland comprising 10-15 people. Most complete and up-to-date listings provided in the annual *International Workcamp Directory* (US$15). Registration fee US$195. Free newsletter.

FURTHER READING

International Jobs: Where they Are, How to Get Them, Eric Kocher and Nina Segal. Perseus Books (US$16).

How to Get a Job in Europe, Robert Sanborn. Surrey Books (US$22).

The Alternative Travel Directory, Clayton Hubbs. Transitions Abroad (US$20).

Work Abroad, Clayton Hubbs. Transitions Abroad (US$16).

International Directory of Voluntary Work, Victoria Pybus. Vacation Work Publications (US$16).

Teaching English Abroad, Susan Griffin. Vacation Work (US$17).

Overseas Summer Jobs 1999, Work Your Way Around the World, and *Directory of Jobs and Careers Abroad.* Peterson's (US$17-18 each).

OTHER RESOURCES

TRAVEL BOOKSTORES

Check local listings for travel bookstores near you. You can also contact the following travel bookstores for comprehensive catalogues of titles, maps, and accessories.

Adventurous Traveler Bookstore, 245 S. Champlain St., Burlington, VT 05401 (tel. 800-282-3963; (802) 860-6776; fax 860-6667; www.adventuroustraveler.com). You can browse and buy titles at their website.

Bon Voyage!, 2069 W. Bullard Ave., Fresno, CA 93711-1200 (tel. 800-995-9716, from abroad (209) 447-8441; fax (209) 266-6460; www.bon-voyage-travel.com). They specialize in Europe but have titles pertaining to other regions, as well. A free catalogue is available, order by phone.

Travel Books & Language Center, Inc., 4437 Wisconsin Ave. NW, Washington, D.C. 20016 (tel. 800-220-2665 or (202) 237-1322; fax 237-6022; www.bookweb.org/bookstore/travelbks). You can find over 60,000 titles from around the world with the help of friendly sales staff, but cannot order on the web.

THE WORLD WIDE WEB

Ireland's National Tourism Database (www.touchtel.ie) has extensive information on hostels, camping, castles, car rentals, and more; accessible by county and region. Also includes some information on Northern Ireland.

Official Guide to Northern Ireland (www.interknowledge.com/northern-ireland) provides information on sights, accommodations, transportation, and other travel tips for Northern Ireland, arranged by city and county.

City.Net Ireland (www.city.net/countries/ireland) provides links of interest to travelers, divided into subject categories.

Microsoft Expedia (expedia.msn.com) has everything you'd ever need to make travel plans on the web; you can compare flight fares, look at maps, and make reservations. FareTracker, a free service, sends you monthly mailings about the cheapest fares to any destination.

Shoestring Travel (www.stratpub.com), an alternative to Microsoft's monolithic site, is budget travel e-zine that features listings of home exchanges, links, and accommodations information.

Let's Go (www.letsgo.com) is where you can find our newsletter, information about our books, up-to-the-minute links, and more.

FURTHER READING

How to Plan Your Dream Vacation Using the Web. Elizabeth Dempsey. Coriolis Group (US$25).

Nettravel: How Travelers Use the Internet, Michael Shapiro. O'Reilly & Associates (US$25).

Travel Planning Online for Dummies, Noah Vadnai. IDG Books (US$25).

SAFETY AND SECURITY

Ireland and Northern Ireland are safer for the traveler than most other European countries, but theft and harassment do happen, especially in urban centers.

BLENDING IN. Tourists are particularly vulnerable to crime because they often carry large amounts of cash and are not as street savvy as locals. To avoid unwanted attention, try to blend in as much as possible. The gawking camera-toter is a more obvious target than the low-profile traveler. Familiarize yourself with your surroundings before setting out; if you must check a map on the street, duck into a pub or shop. Also, carry yourself with confidence; an obviously bewildered bodybuilder is more likely to be harassed than a stern and confident 98-pound weakling. If you are traveling alone, be sure that someone at home knows your itinerary, and **never admit that you're traveling alone.**

EXPLORING. Extra vigilance is always wise, but there is no need for panic when exploring a new city or region. Find out about unsafe areas from tourist offices, from the manager of your hotel or hostel, or from a local whom you trust. You may want to carry a **whistle** to scare off attackers or attract attention. The **emergency number** in both the Republic and the North is 999; no coins are required. When walking at night, stick to busy, well-lit streets and avoid dark alleyways. Do not attempt to cross through parks, parking lots or other large, deserted areas. Buildings in disrepair, vacant lots, and unpopulated areas are all bad signs. The distribution of people can reveal a great deal about the relative safety of the area; look for children playing, women walking in the open, and other signs of an active community. Keep in mind that a district can change character drastically between blocks. If you feel uncomfortable, leave as quickly and directly as you can, but don't allow fear of the unknown to turn you into a hermit. Careful, persistent exploration will build confidence and make your stay in an area more rewarding.

GETTING AROUND. If you are using a **car,** learn local driving signals and wear a seatbelt. Children under 40 lbs. should ride only in a specially-designed carseat, available for a small fee from most car rental agencies. The main concern for most drivers is getting used to driving on the left-hand side of the road, which holds for both the Republic and Northern Ireland. Study route maps before you hit the road; some roads have poor (or nonexistent) shoulders, few gas stations, and roaming animals. In many regions, road conditions necessitate driving more slowly and more cautiously than you would at home. If you plan on spending a lot of time on the road, you may want to bring spare parts. For long drives in desolate areas invest in a cellular phone and a roadside assistance program (see p. 70). Be sure to park your vehicle in a garage or well-traveled area, and use a steering wheel locking device in larger cities. **Sleeping in your car** is one of the most dangerous (and often illegal) ways to get your rest. If your car breaks down, wait for the police to assist you. If you must sleep in your car, do so as close to a police station as possible. Drive with extra caution at night, when drunk drivers hit the roads.

Let's Go does not recommend **hitchhiking** under any circumstances, particularly for women (see **Getting Around,** p. 68).

ESSENTIALS

ESSENTIALS

SELF-DEFENSE. There is no sure-fire set of precautions that will protect you from all of the situations you might encounter when you travel. A good self-defense course will give you more concrete ways to react to different types of aggression. **Impact, Prepare,** and **Model Mugging** can refer you to local self-defense courses in the United States (tel. 800-345-5425) and Vancouver, Canada (tel. (604) 878-3838). Workshop (2-3 hours) start at US$50, and full courses run US$350-500. Both women and men are welcome.

FURTHER INFORMATION

The following government offices provide travel information and advisories by telephone or on their websites:

Australian Department of Foreign Affairs and Trade. Tel. (2) 6261 1111. www.dfat.gov.au.

Canadian Department of Foreign Affairs and International Trade (DFAIT). Tel. 800-267-8376 or (613) 944-4000 from Ottawa. www.dfait-maeci.gc.ca. Call for their free booklet, *Bon Voyage...But.*

United Kingdom Foreign and Commonwealth Office. Tel. (0171) 238 4503. www.fco.gov.uk.

United States Department of State. Tel. (202) 647-5225. travel.state.gov. For their publication *A Safe Trip Abroad,* call (202) 512-1800.

FINANCIAL SECURITY

PROTECTING YOUR VALUABLES. To prevent easy theft, don't keep all your valuables (money, important documents) in one place. **Photocopies** of important documents allow you to recover them in case they are lost or filched. Carry one copy separate from the documents and leave another copy at home. Label every piece of luggage both inside and out. **Don't put a wallet with money in your back pocket**. Never count your money in public and carry as little as possible. If you carry a purse, buy a sturdy one with a secure clasp, and carry it crosswise on the side, away from the street with the clasp against you. Secure packs with small combination padlocks which slip through the two zippers. A **money belt** is the best way to carry cash; you can buy one at most camping supply stores. A nylon, zippered pouch with a belt that sits inside the waist of your pants or skirt combines convenience and security. A **neck pouch** is equally safe, although far less accessible. Refrain from pulling out your neck pouch in public; if you must, be very discreet. Avoid keeping anything precious in a fanny-pack (even if it's worn on your stomach): your valuables will be highly visible and easy to steal. Keep some money separate from the rest to use in an emergency or in case of theft.

CON ARTISTS AND PICKPOCKETS. Among the more colorful aspects of large cities are **con artists.** Con artists and hustlers often work in groups, and children are among the most effective. They possess an innumerable range of ruses. Beware of certain classics: sob stories that require money, rolls of bills "found" on the street, mustard spilled (or saliva spit) onto your shoulder distracting you for enough time to snatch your bag. Be especially suspicious in unexpected situations. Do not respond or make eye contact, walk quickly away, and keep a solid grip on your belongings. Contact the police if a hustler is particularly aggressive.

In city crowds and especially on public transportation, **pickpockets** are amazingly deft at their craft. Also, be alert in public telephone booths. If you must say your calling card number, do so very quietly; if you punch it in, make sure no one can look over your shoulder.

ACCOMMODATIONS AND TRANSPORTATION. Never leave your belongings unattended; crime occurs in even the most demure-looking hostel or hotel. If you feel unsafe, look for places with either a curfew or a night attendant. *Let's Go* lists locker availability in hostels and train stations, but you'll need your own **padlock.** Lockers are useful if you plan on sleeping outdoors or don't want to lug everything with you, but don't store valuables in them. Most hotels also provide lock boxes free or for a minimal fee.

Be particularly careful on **buses,** carry your backpack in front of you where you can see it, don't check baggage on trains, and don't trust anyone to "watch your bag for a second." Thieves thrive on **trains;** professionals wait for tourists to fall asleep and then carry off everything they can. When traveling in pairs, sleep in alternating shifts; when alone, use good judgement in selecting a train compartment: never stay in an empty one, and use a lock to secure your pack to the luggage rack. Keep important documents and other valuables on your person and try to sleep on top bunks with your luggage stored above you (if not in bed with you).

If you travel by **car,** try not to leave valuable possessions—such as radios or luggage—in it while you are away. If your tape deck or radio is removeable, hide it in the trunk or take it with you. If it isn't, at least conceal it under something else. Similarly, hide baggage in the trunk—although savvy thieves can tell if a car is heavily loaded by the way it sits on its tires.

TIPPING AND BARGAINING

Some restaurants in Ireland figure a service charge into the bill; some even calculate it into the cost of the dishes themselves. The menu often indicates whether or not service is included (ask if you're not sure). For those restaurants that do not include a tip in the bill, more common in cities, customers should leave 10-15%. The exact amount should truly depend upon the quality of the service. For waiter service in a bar or lounge, 20p will do. Tipping is less common for other services, especially in rural areas, but is always very welcome. Porters, parking-lot attendants, waitstaff, and hairdressers are usually tipped. Cab drivers are usually tipped 10%. Hotel housekeepers will welcome a gratuity, but owners of establishments, including B&Bs, may be insulted by a tip. Above all, **never tip the barman.**

DRUGS AND ALCOHOL

A meek "I didn't know it was illegal" will not suffice. Remember that you are subject to the laws of the country in which you travel, not to those of your home country, and it is your responsibility to familiarize yourself with these laws before leaving. If you carry **prescription drugs** while you travel, it is vital to have a copy of the prescription and a note from a doctor, readily accessible at country borders.

Avoid public drunkenness; it is against the law in many countries. It can also jeopardize your safety and earn the disdain of locals.

HEALTH

Common sense is the simplest prescription for good health while you travel. Travelers complain most often about their feet and their gut, so take precautionary measures: drink lots of fluids to prevent dehydration and constipation, wear sturdy, broken-in shoes and clean socks, and use talcum powder to keep your feet dry. To minimize the effects of jet lag, "reset" your body's clock by adopting the time of your destination as soon as you board the plane.

BEFORE YOU GO

Preparation can help minimize the likelihood of contracting a disease and maximize the chances of receiving effective health care in the event of an emergency.

For minor health problems, bring a compact **first-aid kit,** including bandages, aspirin or other pain killer, antibiotic cream, a thermometer, a Swiss Army knife with tweezers, moleskin, decongestant for colds, motion sickness remedy, medicine for diarrhea or stomach problems, sunscreen, burn ointment, and a syringe for emergency medical purposes (get a letter of explanation from your doctor). **Contact lens** wearers should bring an extra pair, a copy of the prescription, a pair of glasses, plenty of solution, and eyedrops.

In your **passport,** write the names of any people you wish to be contacted in case of a medical emergency, and also list any **allergies** or medical conditions you would want doctors to be aware of. Allergy sufferers might want to obtain a full supply of any necessary medication before the trip. Matching a prescription to a foreign equivalent is not always easy, safe, or possible. Carry up-to-date, legible prescriptions or a statement from your doctor stating the medication's trade name, manufacturer, chemical name, and dosage. While traveling, be sure to keep all medication with you in your carry-on luggage.

IMMUNIZATIONS

Take a look at your immunization records before you go. Travelers over two years old should be sure that the following vaccines are up to date: MMR (for measles, mumps, and rubella); DTaP or Td (for diptheria, tetanus, and pertussis); OPV (for polio); HbCV (for haemophilus influenza B); and HBV (for hepatitis B). Check with a doctor for guidance through this maze of injections.

USEFUL ORGANIZATIONS

The U.S. **Centers for Disease Control and Prevention (CDC)** (tel. 888-232-3299; www.cdc.gov) is an excellent source of information for travelers around the world and maintains an international fax information service for travelers. The CDC also publishes the booklet "Health Information for International Travelers" (US$20), an annual global rundown of disease, immunization, and general health advice, including risks in particular countries. This book may be purchased by sending a check or money order to the Superintendent of Documents, U.S. Government Printing Office, P.O. Box 371954, Pittsburgh, PA, 15250-7954. Orders can be made by phone (tel. (202) 512-1800) with a major credit card (Visa, MasterCard, or Discover).

The **United States State Department** (http://travel.state.gov) compiles Consular Information Sheets on health, entry requirements, and other issues for all countries of the world. For quick information on travel warnings, call the **Overseas Citizens' Services** (tel. (202) 647-5225; after-hours 647-4000). To receive the same Consular Information Sheets by fax, dial (202) 647-3000 directly from a fax machine and follow the recorded instructions. The State Department's regional passport agencies in the U.S., field offices of the U.S. Chamber of Commerce, and U.S. embassies and consulates abroad provide the same data, or send a self-addressed, stamped envelope to the Overseas Citizens' Services, Bureau of Consular Affairs, #4811, U.S. Department of State, Washington, D.C. 20520.

FURTHER READING

For detailed information and tips on travel health, including a country-by-country overview of diseases, check out the **International Travel Health Guide,** Stuart Rose, MD (Travel Medicine, $20). Information is also available at Travel Medicine's website (www.travmed.com).

For general health information, contact the **American Red Cross.** The ARC publishes *First-Aid and Safety Handbook* (US$5) available for purchase by calling or writing to the American Red Cross, 285 Columbus Ave., Boston, MA 02116-5114 (tel. 800-564-1234, M-F 8:30am-4:30pm).

MEDICAL ASSISTANCE ON THE ROAD

In the event of sudden illness or an accident, dial **999,** the general **emergency** number for the Republic of Ireland and Northern Ireland. It's a free call from any payphone to an operator who will connect you to the local police, hospital, or fire brigade. EU citizens receive health care; others must have medical insurance or pay upfront. Doctors in Ireland are well trained and English speaking; hospitals are fairly well spread and listed in Practical Information sections. Accomodation owners should know a local doctor and directions to the nearest hospital.

If your regular **insurance** policy does not cover travel abroad, you may wish to purchase additional coverage, particularly for traveling in Europe. With the exception of Medicare, most health insurance plans cover members' medical emergencies during trips abroad; check with your insurance carrier to be sure. For more information on, see **Insurance,** p. 55).

MEDICAL CONDITIONS

Those with medical conditions (e.g., diabetes, allergies to antibiotics, epilepsy, heart conditions) may want to obtain a stainless steel **Medic Alert** identification tag (US$35 the first year, and US$15 annually thereafter), which identifies the condition and gives a 24hr. collect-call information number. Contact the Medic Alert Foundation, 2323 Colorado Ave., Turlock, CA 95382 (tel. 800-825-3785; www.medicalert.org). Diabetics can contact the **American Diabetes Association**, 1660 Duke St., Alexandria, VA 22314 (tel. 800-232-3472), to receive copies of the article "Travel and Diabetes" and a diabetic ID card, which carries messages in 18 languages explaining the carrier's diabetic status.

If you are **HIV** positive, contact the Bureau of Consular Affairs, #4811, Department of State, Washington, D.C. 20520 (tel. (202) 647-1488).

ENVIRONMENTAL HAZARDS

SUNBURN. It rains a lot in Ireland, but the sun also shines. If you're prone to sunburn, bring sunscreen with you, and apply it liberally and often to avoid burns and risk of skin cancer. If you are planning on spending time near water, you are at risk of getting burned, even through clouds. Protect your eyes with good sunglasses, since ultraviolet rays can damage the retina of the eye after too much exposure. If you get sunburned, drink more fluids than usual and apply Calamine or an aloe-based lotion.

PREVENTING DISEASE

FOOD- AND WATER-BORNE DISEASES. Prevention is the best cure: be sure that everything you eat is cooked properly and that the water you drink is clean. Tap water in Ireland is generally safe. River, streams, and lakes, however, may carry bacteria and water from them should always be purified. To purify your own water, bring it to a rolling boil or treat it with **iodine tablets,** available at any camping goods store. As in all parts of the world raw shellfish, unpasteurized milk, and sauces containing raw eggs may also have harmful bacteria. Always wash your hands before eating, or bring a quick-drying purifying liquid hand cleaner like Purell. Your bowels will thank you.

Traveler's diarrhea results from drinking untreated water or eating uncooked foods. It is usually an indication of your body's temporary reaction to the bacteria in unfamiliar food ingredients. It can last three to seven days. Symptoms include nausea, bloating, urgency, and malaise. If the nasties hit you, have quick-energy, non-sugary foods with protein and carbohydrates to keep your strength up. Over-the-counter remedies (such as Pepto-Bismol or Immodium) may counteract the problems, but they can complicate serious infections. Avoid anti-diarrheals if you suspect that you are risk for other diseases. The most dangerous side effect of diarrhea is dehydration; the simplest and most effective anti-dehydration formula is 8 oz. of (clean) water with a ½ tsp. of sugar or honey and a pinch of salt. Soft drinks without caffeine and salted crackers are also good. Down several of these remedies a day, rest, and wait for the disease to run its course. If you feel the illness is serious and lingering, the best course is to see a doctor.

Parasites such as microbes and tapeworms also hide in unsafe water and food. **Giardia,** for example, is acquired by drinking untreated water from streams or lakes all over the world, including Western Europe. Symptoms of parasitic infections in general include swollen glands or lymph nodes, fever, digestive problems, and anemia. Boil your water, wear shoes, avoid bugs, and eat only cooked food.

OTHER INFECTIOUS DISEASES

Rabies is transmitted through the saliva of infected animals. It is fatal if untreated. Avoid contact with animals, especially strays. If you are bitten, wash the wound thoroughly and seek immediate medical care. Once you begin to show symptoms (thirst and muscle spasms), the disease is in its terminal stage. If possible, try to locate the animal that bit you to determine whether it does indeed have rabies. A rabies vaccine is available but is only semi-effective. Three shots must be administered over one year.

Hepatitis B is a viral infection of the liver transmitted through the transfer of bodily fluids, by sharing needles, or by having unprotected sex. Its incubation period varies and can be much longer than the 30-day incubation period of Hepatitis A. A person may not begin to show symptoms until many years after infection. The CDC recommends the Hepatitis B vaccination for health-care workers, sexually active travelers, and anyone planning to seek medical treatment abroad. Vaccination consists of a 3-shot series given over a period of time, and should begin 6 months before traveling.

Hepatitis C is like Hepatitis B, but the modes of transmission are different. Intravenous drug users, those with occupational exposure to blood, hemodialysis patients, or recipients of blood transfusions are at the highest risk, but the disease can also be spread through sexual contact and sharing items like razors and toothbrushes, which may have traces of blood on them.

AIDS, HIV, AND STDS

Acquired Immune Deficiency Syndrome (AIDS) is a growing problem around the world. The World Health Organization estimates that there are around 30 million people infected with the HIV virus, and women represent 40% of all new HIV infections.

The easiest mode of HIV transmission is through direct blood-to-blood contact with an HIV-positive person; *never* share intravenous drug, tattooing, or other needles. The most common mode of transmission is sexual intercourse. Health professionals recommend the use of latex condoms. Since it isn't always easy to buy condoms when traveling, take a supply with you before you depart for your trip. Some countries screen incoming travelers, primarily those planning extended visits for work or study, and deny entrance to HIV-positive people. Contact the consulate for information about this policy.

For more information on AIDS, call the **U.S. Centers for Disease Control**'s 24-hour hotline at 800-342-2437. In Europe, contact the **World Health Organization,** Attn: Global Program on AIDS, Avenue Appia 20, 1211 Geneva 27, Switzerland (tel. 44 22 791 21 11; fax 791 31 11), for statistical material on AIDS internationally. Council's brochure *Travel Safe: AIDS and International Travel* is available at all Council Travel offices and at their website (www.ciee.org/study/safety/travelsafe.htm).

Sexually transmitted diseases (STDs) such as gonorrhea, chlamydia, genital warts, syphilis, and herpes are easier to catch than HIV, and some can be just as deadly. **Hepatitis B and C** are also serious sexually-transmitted diseases (see **Other Infectious Diseases,** above). It's a wise idea to actually look at your partner's genitals before you have sex. Warning signs for STDs include swelling, sores, bumps, or blisters on sex organs, rectum, or mouth; burning and pain during urination and bowel movements; itching around sex organs; swelling or redness in the throat, flu-like symptoms with fever, chills, and aches. If these symptoms develop, see a doctor immediately. When having sex, condoms may protect you from certain STDs, but oral or even tactile contact can lead to transmission.

WOMEN'S HEALTH

Women traveling in unsanitary conditions are vulnerable to **urinary tract** and **bladder infections,** common and severely uncomfortable bacterial diseases that cause a burning sensation and painful and sometimes frequent urination. To avoid these infections, drink plenty of vitamin-C-rich juice and plenty of clean water, and urinate frequently, especially after intercourse. Untreated, these infections can lead to kidney infections, sterility, and even death. If symptoms persist, see a doctor.

Women are also susceptible to **vaginal yeast infections,** a treatable but uncomfortable illness. Wearing loosely fitting trousers or a skirt and cotton underwear will help. Yeast infections can be treated with an over-the-counter remedy like Monostat or Gynelotrimin. Bring supplies from home if you are prone to infection, as they may be difficult to find on the road. Some travelers opt for a natural alternative such as plain yogurt and lemon juice douche if other remedies are unavailable.

Tampons and **pads** are sometimes hard to find when traveling, and your preferred brands may not be available, so it may be advisable to take supplies along. **Reliable contraceptive devices** may also be difficult to find. Women on the pill should bring enough to allow for possible loss or extended stays. Bring a prescription, since forms of the pill vary a good deal. Women who use a diaphragm should bring enough contraceptive jelly. Though condoms are increasingly available, you might want to bring your favorite brand before you go, as availability and quality vary.

Abortion is illegal in Ireland. Women who need an **abortion** while abroad should contact the **International Planned Parenthood Federation,** European Regional Office, Regent's College Inner Circle, Regent's Park, London NW1 4NS (tel. 44 171 487 7900; fax 487 7950), for more information.

For more information, check out *Handbook for Women Travellers* by Maggie and Gemma Moss (Piatkus Books, US$15).

INSURANCE

Travel insurance generally covers four basic areas: medical/health problems, property loss, trip cancellation/interruption, and emergency evacuation.

Medical insurance (especially university policies) often covers costs incurred abroad; check with your provider. **Medicare does not cover foreign travel.** Canadians are protected by their home province's health insurance plan for up to 90 days after leaving the country; check with the provincial Ministry of Health or Health Plan Headquarters for details. Australians traveling in the U.K. are entitled to many of the services that they would receive at home as part of the Reciprocal Health Care Agreement. **Homeowners' insurance** (or your family's coverage) often covers theft during travel and loss of travel documents (passport, plane ticket, rail-pass, etc.) up to US$500.

ISIC and **ITIC** provide basic insurance benefits, including US$100 per day of in-hospital sickness for a maximum of 60 days, US$3000 of accident-related medical reimbursement, and US$25,000 for emergency medical transport (see **Identification,** p. 39). Cardholders have access to a toll-free 24-hour helpline whose multilingual staff can provide assistance in medical, legal, and financial emergencies overseas (tel. 800-626-2427 in the U.S. and Canada; elsewhere call the U.S. collect 1-713-267-2525. **American Express** (tel. 800-528-4800) grants most cardholders automatic car rental insurance (collision and theft, but not liability) and ground travel accident coverage of US$100,000 on flight purchases made with the card.

Prices for travel insurance purchased separately generally run about US$50 per week for full coverage, while trip cancellation/interruption may be purchased separately at a rate of about US$5.50 per US$100 of coverage.

INSURANCE PROVIDERS. Council and **STA** (see p. 64 for complete listings) offer a range of plans that can supplement your basic insurance coverage. Other private insurance providers in the **U.S. and Canada** include: **Access America** (tel. 800-284-8300; fax 804-673-1491); **Berkely Group/Carefree Travel Insurance** (tel. 800-323-3149 or (516) 294-0220; fax 294-1095; info@berkely.com; www.berkely.com); **Globalcare Travel Insurance** (tel. 800-821-2488; fax (781) 592-7720; www.globalcare-cocco.com); and **Travel Assistance International** (tel. 800-821-2828 or (202) 828-5894; fax 828-5896; email wassist@aol.com; www.worldwide-assistance.com). Providers in the **U.K.** include **Campus Travel** (tel. (01865) 258 000; fax 792 378) and **Columbus Travel Insurance** (tel. (0171) 375 0011; fax (02) 375 0022). In **Australia** try **CIC Insurance** (tel. 9202 8000; fax 9202 8220).

PACKING

Pack according to the extremes of climate you may experience and the type of travel you'll be doing. **Pack light:** a good rule is to lay out only what you absolutely need, then take half the clothes and twice the money. The less you have, the less you have to lose (or store, or carry on your back). Don't forget the obvious things: no matter when you're traveling, it's always a good idea to bring a rain jacket (Gore-Tex is a miracle fabric that's both waterproof and breathable), a warm jacket or wool sweater, and sturdy shoes and thick socks. You may also want to add one outfit beyond the jeans and t-shirt uniform, and maybe a nicer pair of shoes if you have the room. Remember that wool will keep you warm even when soaked through, whereas wet cotton is colder than wearing nothing at all. If you plan to be doing a lot of hiking, see **Outdoors,** p. 78.

LUGGAGE. If you plan to cover most of your itinerary by foot, a sturdy **frame backpack** is unbeatable. **Internal-frame packs** mold better to your back, keep a lower center of gravity, and can flex adequately on difficult hikes that require a lot of bending and maneuvering. **External-frame packs** are more comfortable for long hikes over even terrain—like city streets—since they keep the weight higher and distribute it more evenly. Look for a pack with a strong, padded hip belt to transfer weight from your shoulders to your hips. Good packs cost anywhere from US$150 to US$500. Before you leave, pack your bag, strap it on, and imagine yourself walking uphill on hot asphalt for three hours; this should give you a sense of how important it is to pack lightly. Organizations that sell packs through mail-order are listed on p. 78.

Toting a **suitcase** is fine if you plan to live in one or two cities and explore from there, but a very bad idea if you're going to be moving around a lot. Make sure suitcases have wheels and consider how much they weigh even when empty. Hard-sided luggage is more durable but more weighty and cumbersome. Soft-sided luggage should have a PVC frame, a strong lining to resist bad weather and rough handling, and its seams should be triple-stitched for durability.

In addition to your main vessel, a small backpack, rucksack, or courier bag may be useful as a **daypack** for sight-seeing expeditions; it doubles as an airplane **carry-on.** An empty, lightweight **duffel bag** packed inside your luggage may also be useful. Once abroad you can fill your luggage with purchases and keep dirty clothes in the duffel.

SLEEPSACKS. Some youth hostels require that you have your own sleepsack or rent one of theirs. If you plan to stay in hostels you can avoid linen charges by making the requisite sleepsack yourself: fold a full size sheet in half the long way, then sew it closed along the open long side and one of the short sides. Sleepsacks can also be bought at any Hostelling International outlet store.

WASHING CLOTHES. *Let's Go* attempts to provide information on launderettes in the **Practical Information** listings for towns and cities. Many hostels also have self-service laundry facilities, availbale for £2-4.

ELECTRIC CURRENT. In Ireland, electricity is 220 volts AC, enough to fry any 110V North American appliance. 220V Electrical appliances don't like 110V current, either. Visit a hardware store for an adapter (which changes the shape of the plug) and a converter (which changes the voltage). Don't make the mistake of using only an adapter (unless appliance instructions explicitly state otherwise).

CONTACT LENSES. Machines which heat-disinfect contact lenses will require a small converter (about US$20) to 220V. Consider switching temporarily to a chemical disinfection system, but check with your lens dispenser to see if it's safe to switch; some lenses may be damaged by a chemical system. Contact lens supplies may be expensive and difficult to find; bring enough saline and cleaner for your entire vacation.

FILM. Your best bet is to bring film with you. It may be more expensive, difficult to find, and of a different brand in Ireland. If you're not a serious photographer, you might want to consider bringing a **disposable camera**. Despite disclaimers, airport security X-rays *can* fog film, so ask the security to hand inspect it. Always pack it in your carry-on luggage, since higher-intensity X-rays are used on checked luggage.

OTHER USEFUL ITEMS. No matter how you're traveling, it's always a good idea to carry a first-aid kit including sunscreen, insect repellent, and vitamins (see **Health,** p. 51). Other useful items include: an umbrella; sealable plastic bags (for damp clothes, soap, food, shampoo, and other spillables); an alarm clock; sun hat; moleskin (for blisters); needle and thread; safety pins; sunglasses; pocketknife; plastic water bottle; compass; string (makeshift clothesline and lashing material); towel; padlock; whistle; rubber bands; flashlight; soap; earplugs; electrical tape (for patching tears); tweezers; a small calculator for currency conversion; a pair of flip-flops for the shower; a money-belt for carrying valuables; deodorant; razors; tampons; and condoms (see **AIDS, HIV, and STDs,** p. 54).

FURTHER READING
The Packing Book, Judith Gilford. Ten Speed Press ($9).
Backpacking One Step at a Time, Harvey Manning. Vintage ($15).

SPECIFIC CONCERNS
WOMEN TRAVELERS

Women exploring on their own inevitably face some additional safety concerns, but it's easy to be adventurous without taking undue risks. In general, Ireland is an extremely safe place to travel. If you are concerned, you might consider staying in hostels which offer single rooms that lock from the inside or that offer rooms for women only. Communal showers in some hostels are safer than others; check them before settling in. Stick to centrally located accommodations and avoid solitary late-night treks or metro rides.

When traveling, always carry extra money for a phone call, bus, or taxi. **Hitching** is never safe for lone women, or even for two women traveling together. Look as if you know where you're going (even when you don't) and consider approaching older women or couples for directions if you're lost or feel uncomfortable.

Cities in Ireland are safe by city standards; however, harrassment may be more common in urban areas. Your best answer to verbal harassment is no answer at all; feigned deafness, sitting motionless and staring straight ahead at nothing in particular will do a world of good that reactions usually don't achieve. The extremely persistent can sometimes be dissuaded by a firm, loud, and very public "Go away!"

Don't hesitate to seek out a police officer or a passerby if you are being harassed. *Let's Go: Ireland* lists emergency numbers (including rape crisis lines) in the Practical Information listings of most cities. Memorize the emergency numbers in the places you visit. Carry a **whistle** or an airhorn on your keychain, and don't hesitate to use it in an emergency. An **IMPACT Model Mugging** self-defense course will not only prepare you for a potential attack, but will also raise your level of awareness of your surroundings as well as your confidence (see **Self Defense,** p. 50). Women also face some specific health concerns when traveling (see **Women's Health,** p. 54).

FURTHER READING: WOMEN TRAVELERS
A Journey of One's Own: Uncommon Advice for the Independent Woman Traveler, Thalia Zepatos. Eighth Mountain Press (US$17).
Adventures in Good Company: The Complete Guide to Women's Tours and Outdoor Trips, Thalia Zepatos. Eighth Mountain Press (US$7).
Travelers' Tales: Gutsy Women, Travel Tips and Wisdom for the Road, Marybeth Bond. Traveler's Tales (US$8).
A Foxy Old Woman's Guide to Traveling Alone, Jay Ben-Lesser. Crossing Press (US$11).

TRAVELING ALONE

There are many benefits to traveling alone, among them greater independence and challenge. Traveling alone in Ireland is remarkably safe; hostel and B&B owners are welcoming to solo travelers. As a lone traveler, you will have greater opportunity to interact with the residents of the region you're visiting.

On the other hand, any solo traveler is a more vulnerable target of harassment and street theft. Lone travelers need to be well-organized and look confident at all times. If questioned, never admit that you are traveling alone. Maintain regular contact with someone at home who knows your itinerary.

A number of organizations supply information for solo travelers, and others find travel companions for those who don't want to go alone. Two are listed here.

Connecting: Solo Traveler Network, P.O. Box 29088, 1996 W. Broadway, Vancouver, BC V6J 5C2, Canada (tel. (604) 737-7791; email info@cstn.org; www.cstn.org). Bi-monthly newsletter features going solo tips, single-friendly tips and travel companion ads. Annual directory lists holiday suppliers that avoid single supplement charges. Advice and lodging exchanges facilitated between members. Membership US$25-35.

Travel Companion Exchange, P.O. Box 833, Amityville, NY 11701 (tel. (516) 454-0880 or 800-392-1256; www.travelalone.com). Publishes the pamphlet *Foiling Pickpockets & Bag Snatchers* (US$4) and *Travel Companions*, a bi-monthly newsletter for single travelers seeking a travel partner (subscription US$48).

FURTHER READING

Traveling Solo, Eleanor Berman. Globe Pequot (US$17).

The Single Traveler Newsletter, P.O. Box 682, Ross, CA 94957 (tel. (415) 389-0227). 6 issues US$29.

OLDER TRAVELERS

Senior citizens are eligible for a wide range of discounts on transportation, museums, theaters, concerts, restaurants, and accommodations. If you don't see a senior citizen price listed, ask, and you may be delightfully surprised.

Agencies for senior group travel are growing in enrollment and popularity. These are only a few:

ElderTreks, 597 Markham St., Toronto, ON, Canada, M6G 2L7 (tel. 800-741-7956 or (416) 588-5000; fax 588-9839; email passages@inforamp.net; www.eldertreks.com).

Elderhostel, 75 Federal St., Boston, MA 02110-1941 (tel. (617) 426-7788 or (877) 426-8056; email registration@elderhostel.org; www.elderhostel.org). Programs at colleges, universities, and other learning centers in Ireland on varied subjects lasting 1-4 weeks. Must be 55 or over (spouse can be of any age).

The Mature Traveler, P.O. Box 50400, Reno, NV 89513 (tel. (775) 786-7419 or 800-460-6676). Has soft-adventure tours for seniors. Subscription US$30.

Walking the World, P.O. Box 1186, Fort Collins, CO 80522 (tel. (970) 498-0500; fax 498-9100; email walktworld@aol.com; www.walkingtheworld.com), sends trips to Ireland.

FURTHER READING

No Problem! Worldwise Tips for Mature Adventurers, Janice Kenyon. Orca Book Publishers (US$16).

A Senior's Guide to Healthy Travel, Donald L. Sullivan. Career Press (US$15).

Unbelievably Good Deals and Great Adventures That You Absolutely Can't Get Unless You're Over 50, Joan Rattner Heilman. Contemporary Books (US$13).

BISEXUAL, GAY, AND LESBIAN TRAVELERS

Ireland is more tolerant of homosexuality than one might expect. As is true elsewhere, people in rural areas may not be as accepting as those in cities, whose attitudes have noticeably changed since the decriminalization of homosexuality in the Republic in 1993. Dublin now supports a gay community, with growing student societies at Trinity and UCD, a gay youth group that has doubled its size over the last five years, and a growing array of pubs and clubs. Belfast and, to a lesser degree, Cork also have increasingly open gay scenes. *Gay Community News* covers mostly Irish gay-related news, and its listings page covers most gay locales in all of Ireland. *Let's Go: Ireland* has gay pub and nightlife listings as well as phone numbers for gay information in Dublin, Belfast, Cork, and elsewhere. Clubs tend to be frequented by both sexes but with a larger male contingent. Below are a few resources for the BGL traveler:

Ireland's Pink Pages (http://indigo.ie/~outhouse/). Ireland's web-based BGL directory. Regional info, including the Republic and the North. Helpful links.

Gay's the Word, 66 Marchmont St., London WC1N 1AB (tel. (0171) 278 7654; email gays.theword@virgin.net; www.gaystheword.co.uk). The largest gay and lesbian bookshop in the U.K. Mail-order service available. No catalogue of listings, but they will provide a list of titles on a given subject.

Giovanni's Room, 345 S. 12th St., Philadelphia, PA 19107 (tel. (215) 923-2960; fax 923-0813; email giophilp@netaxs.com). An international feminist, lesbian, and gay bookstore with mail-order service which carries the publications listed here.

International Gay and Lesbian Travel Association, 4331 N. Federal Hwy., Suite 304, Fort Lauderdale, FL 33308 (tel. (954) 776-2626 or 800-448-8550; fax (954) 776-3303; email IGLTA@aol.com; www.iglta.com). An organization of over 1350 companies serving gay and lesbian travelers worldwide. Call for lists of travel agents, accommodations, and events.

International Lesbian and Gay Association (ILGA), 81 rue Marché-au-Charbon, B-1000 Brussels, Belgium (tel./fax 32 2 502 24 71; email ilga@ilga.org; www.ilga.org). Not a travel service. Provides political information, such as homosexuality laws of individual countries.

FURTHER READING

Spartacus International Gay Guide. Bruno Gmunder Verlag. (US$33).

Ferrari Guides' Gay Travel A to Z, Ferrari Guides' Men's Travel in Your Pocket, Ferrari Guides' Women's Travel in Your Pocket, and *Ferrari Guides' Inn Places.* Ferrari Guides (US$14-16). For more information, call (602) 863-2408 or 800-962-2912 or check their website (www.q-net.com).

The Gay Vacation Guide: The Best Trips and How to Plan Them, Mark Chesnut. Citadel Press (US$15).

TRAVELERS WITH DISABILITIES

Ireland is not particularly wheelchair accessible. Ramps, wide doors, and accessible bathrooms are less common than in the U.S., even in cities such as Dublin. *Let's Go: Ireland* lists and indexes wheelchair-accessible hostels. Guide dogs are always conveyed free, but both the U.K. and Ireland impose a six-month quarantine on all animals entering the country and require that the owner obtain an import license. Write to the British Tourist Authority or Bord Fáilte for free handbooks and access guides.

Those with disabilities should inform airlines and hotels of their disabilities when making arrangements for travel; some time may be needed to prepare special accommodations. Advance booking is strongly recommended; if you notify a bus company of your plans ahead of time, they will have staff ready to assist you. Call ahead to restaurants, hotels, parks, and other facilities to find out about the existence of ramps, the widths of doors, the dimensions of elevators, etc.

Rail is probably the most convenient form of travel for disabled travelers in Ireland. Not all train stations are wheelchair accessible. Large stations in Britain are equipped with wheelchair facilities, and the Hertz, Avis, and National car rental agencies have hand-controlled vehicles at some locations.

The following organizations provide information or publications that might be of assistance:

DTour (http://www.iol.ie/infograf/dtour) is a web-based visitors' guide to Ireland for people with disabilities. Index of accommodation and transportation facilities, with links to other resources in Ireland.

Access Department, The National Rehabilitation Board, 25 Clyde Rd., Dublin 4. Offers a county-by-county fact sheet about accommodations facilities.

Mobility International USA (MIUSA), P.O. Box 10767, Eugene, OR 97440 (tel. (541) 343-1284 voice and TDD; fax 343-6812; email info@miusa.org; www.miusa.org). Sells *A World of Options: A Guide to International Educational Exchange, Community Service, and Travel for Persons with Disabilities* (US$35).

Moss Rehab Hospital Travel Information Service (tel. (215) 456-9600; www.mossresourcenet.org). A telephone and internet information resource center on international travel accessibility and other travel-related concerns for those with disabilities.

The following organizations arrange tours or trips for disabled travelers:

Directions Unlimited, 720 N. Bedford Rd., Bedford Hills, NY 10507 (tel. 800-533-5343; in NY (914) 241-1700; fax 241-0243; email cruisesusa@aol.com). Specializes in arranging individual and group vacations, tours, and cruises for the physically disabled. Group tours for blind travelers.

The Guided Tour Inc., 7900 Old York Rd., Suite 114B, Elkins Park, PA 19027-2339 (tel. 800-783-5841 or (215) 782-1370; email gtour400@aol.com; www.guidedtour.com). Organizes travel programs for persons with developmental and physical challenges around Ireland.

FURTHER READING

Resource Directory for the Disabled, Richard Neil Shrout. Facts on file (US$45).

Wheelchair Through Europe, Annie Mackin. Graphic Language Press ((760) 944 9594; email niteowl@cts.com) (US$13).

Global Access (www.geocities.com/Paris/1502/disabilitylinks.html) has links for disabled travelers in Ireland.

MINORITY TRAVELERS

The majority of Ireland's 5 million people are white and Christian (largely Catholic in the Republic, mixed Catholic and Protestant in the North). While a growing Malaysian, Indian, and Pakistani population resides mainly in and around Dublin, on the whole, the Irish have never had to address racial diversity on a large scale. Darker-skinned travelers may be the subjects of unusual attention, especially in rural areas, but comments or stares are more likely to be motivated by curiosity than ill will. Ireland has a Jewish community of 1800 people, concentrated in Dublin, that experiences little anti-Semitism.

For further reading, see *Go Girl! The Black Woman's Book of Travel and Adventure,* by Elaine Lee (Eighth Mountain Press, US$18).

TRAVELERS WITH CHILDREN

Family vacations often require that you slow your pace, and always require that you plan ahead. When deciding where to stay, remember the special needs of young children; call ahead to hostels and B&Bs to make sure they are child-friendly. If you rent a car, make sure the rental company provides a car seat for younger children. Consider using a papoose-style device to carry a baby on walking trips. Be sure that your child carries some sort of ID in case of an emergency or he or she gets lost, and arrange a reunion spot in case of separation when sight-seeing.

Virtually all museums and tourist attractions also have a children's rate. Children under two generally fly for 10% of the adult airfare on international flights (this does not necessarily include a seat). International fares are usually discounted 25% for children from two to 11. Finding a private place for **breast feeding** is often a problem while traveling, so pack accordingly.

FURTHER READING

Take Your Kids to Europe, Cynthia W. Harriman. Globe Pequot (US$17).

How to take Great Trips with Your Kids, Sanford and Jane Portnoy. Harvard Common Press (US $10).

Adventuring with Children: An Inspirational Guide to World Travel and the Outdoors, Nan Jeffrey. Avalon House Publishing ($15).

Trouble Free Travel with Children, Vicki Lansky. Book Peddlers (US$9).

DIETARY CONCERNS

Let's Go lists restaurants with vegetarian options when we find them. You're not likely to find pub grub without meat, but in almost every town at least one restaurant will have something for vegetarians. Morning baked goods are especially good. Vegans will have more of a challenge and may frequently need to cook for themselves. For more information about vegetarian travel, contact:

North American Vegetarian Society, P.O. Box 72, Dolgeville, NY 13329 (tel. (518) 568-7970; email navs@telenet.com; www.cyberveg.org/navs/). Publishes Transformative Adventures, a guide to vacations and retreats (US$15).

Travelers who keep kosher should contact synagogues in larger cities for information on kosher restaurants; your own synagogue or college Hillel should have access to lists of Jewish institutions across the nation. Kosher is not a common term or practice in Ireland; if you are strict in your observance, you will have to prepare your own food on the road.

The Jewish Travel Guide lists synagogues, kosher restaurants, and Jewish institutions in over 80 countries. Available from Vallentine-Mitchell Publishers, Newbury House 890-900, Eastern Ave., Newbury Park, Ilford, Essex, U.K. IG2 7HH (tel. (0181) 599 88 66; fax 599 09 84). It is available in the U.S. ($16) from ISBS, 5804 NE Hassallo St., Portland, OR 97213-3644 (tel. 800-944-6190).

FURTHER READING

The Vegan Travel Guide: U.K. and Southern Ireland. Book Publishing Co. (US$15).

The Vegetarian Traveler: Where to Stay if You're Vegetarian, Jed Civic. Larson Pub. (US$16).

Europe on 10 Salads a Day, Greg and Mary Jane Edwards. Mustang Pub. (US$10).

GETTING THERE

BUDGET AND STUDENT TRAVEL AGENCIES

A knowledgeable agent specializing in flights to Ireland can make your life easy and help you save, too, but agents may not spend the time to find you the lowest possible fare — they get paid on commission. Students and under-26ers holding **ISIC and IYTC cards** (see **Identification,** p. 39), respectively, qualify for big discounts from student travel agencies. Most flights from budget agencies are on major airlines, but in peak season some may sell seats on less reliable chartered aircraft.

Campus/Usit Youth and Student Travel (www.usitcampus.co.uk). In the U.K. call (0870) 240 10 10; in North America call 44 171 730 21 01; worldwide call 44 171 730 81 11. Offices include: 19-21 Aston Quay, O'Connell Bridge, **Dublin** 2 (tel. (01) 677 8117; fax 679 8833); 52 Grosvenor Gardens, **London** SW1W 0AG; New York Student Center, 895 Amsterdam Ave., **New York,** NY, 10025 (tel. (212) 663-5435; email usitny@aol.com). Additional offices in Cork, Galway, Limerick, Waterford, Coleraine, Derry, Belfast, and Greece.

Council Travel (www.counciltravel.com). U.S. offices include: Emory Village, 1561 N. Decatur Rd., **Atlanta,** GA 30307 (tel. (404) 377-9997); 273 Newbury St., **Boston,** MA 02116 (tel. (617) 266-1926); 1160 N. State St., **Chicago,** IL 60610 (tel. (312) 951-0585); 10904 Lindbrook Dr., **Los Angeles,** CA 90024 (tel. (310) 208-3551); 205 E. 42nd St., **New York,** NY 10017 (tel. (212) 822-2700); 530 Bush St., **San Francisco,** CA 94108 (tel. (415) 421-3473); 1314 NE 43rd St. #210, **Seattle,** WA 98105 (tel. (206) 632-2448); 3300 M St. NW, **Washington, D.C.** 20007 (tel. (202) 337-6464). **For U.S. cities not listed,** call 800-2-COUNCIL (226-8624). Also 28A Poland St. (Oxford Circus), **London,** W1V 3DB (tel. (0171) 287 3337), **Paris** (tel. 01 44 41 89 89), and **Munich** (tel. 089 39 50 22).

CTS Travel, U.K: 44 Goodge St., London W1 (tel. (0171) 636 00 31; fax 637 53 28; email ctsinfo@ctstravel.com.uk).

Educational Travel Center (ETC), 438 North Frances Street., Madison, WI 53703 (tel. (800) 747 5551; fax (608) 256 2042; email edtrav@execpc.com; www.edtrav.com). Flight information; HI-AYH cards, Eurail, and regional passes. Write for their free pamphlet *Taking Off.* Student and budget airfares.

Rail Europe Inc., 226 Westchester Ave., White Plains, NY 10604 (tel. (800-438-7245; fax 800-432-1329; www.raileurope.com). Sells all Eurail products and passes, national railpasses including Brit Rail, and point-to-point tickets. Up-to-date information on all rail travel in Europe, including Eurostar and the English Channel train.

STA Travel, 6560 Scottsdale Rd. #F100, Scottsdale, AZ 85253 (tel. 800-777-0112; fax (602) 922-0793; www.sta-travel.com). A student and youth travel organization with over 150 offices worldwide. Ticket booking, travel insurance, railpasses, and more. U.S. offices include: 297 Newbury Street, **Boston,** MA 02115 (tel. (617) 266-6014); 429 S. Dearborn St., **Chicago,** IL 60605 (tel. (312) 786-9050); 7202 Melrose Ave., **Los Angeles,** CA 90046 (tel. (323) 934-8722); 10 Downing St., **New York,** NY 10014 (tel. (212) 627-3111); 4341 University Way NE, **Seattle,** WA 98105 (tel. (206) 633-5000); 2401 Pennsylvania Ave., Ste. G, **Washington, D.C.** 20037 (tel. (202) 887-0912); 51 Grant Ave., **San Francisco,** CA 94108 (tel. (415) 391-8407). In the U.K., 6 Wrights Ln., **London** W8 6TA (tel. (0171) 938 47 11 for North American travel). In New Zealand, 10 High St., **Auckland** (tel. (09) 309 04 58). In Australia, 222 Faraday St., **Melbourne** VIC 3053 (tel. (03) 9349 2411).

Students Flights Inc., 5010 East Shea Blvd., #A104, Scottsdale, AZ 85254 (tel. 800-255-8000 or (408) 951-1177; fax 951-1216; email info@isecard.com; isecard.com). Also sells Eurail and Europasses and ISIC cards.

Travel CUTS (Canadian Universities Travel Services Limited), 187 College St., **Toronto,** Ont. M5T 1P7 (tel. (416) 979-2406; fax 979-8167; www.travelcuts.com). 40 offices across Canada. Also in the U.K., 295-A Regent St., **London** W1R 7YA (tel. (0171) 255 19 44).

Unitravel, 1173 Administration Dr., Suite 120, **St. Louis,** MO 63146 (tel. 800-325-2222 or (314) 569-2501; fax 569-2503). Offers discounted airfares on major scheduled airlines.

usit Youth and Student Travel, 19-21 Aston Quay, O'Connell Bridge, **Dublin** 2 (tel. (01) 602 1777; fax 679 8833). In the U.S.: New York Student Center, 895 Amsterdam Ave., **New York,** NY 10025 (tel. (212) 663-5435; email usitny@aol.com). Additional offices in **Cork, Galway, Limerick, Waterford, Maynooth, Coleraine, Derry, Athlone,** and **Belfast.** Specializes in youth and student travel. Offers low-cost tickets and flexible travel arrangements all over the world. Supplies ISIC and FIYTO-GO 25 cards in Ireland only.

Wasteels, Victoria Station, London, U.K. SW1V 1JT (tel. (0171) 834 70 66; fax 630 76 28; www.wasteels.dk/uk). A huge chain in Europe, with 203 locations. Sells the Wasteels BIJ tickets, which are discounted (30-45% off regular fare) 2nd class international point-to-point train tickets with unlimited stopovers (must be under 26); sold only in Europe.

Other organizations that specialize in finding cheap fares include:

Cheap Tickets (tel. 800-377-1000) flies worldwide to and from the U.S.

Travel Avenue (tel. 800-333-3335) rebates commercial fares to or from the U.S. and offers low fares for flights anywhere in the world. They also offer package deals, which include car rental and hotel reservations, to many destinations.

BY PLANE

When it comes to airfare, a little effort can save you a bundle. If your plans are flexible enough to deal with the restrictions, courier fares are the cheapest. Tickets bought from consolidators and standby seating are also good deals, but last-minute specials, airfare wars, and charter flights often beat these fares. The key is to hunt around, to be flexible, and to persistently ask about discounts. Finding a cheap airfare will be easier if you understand the airlines' systems. Call every toll-free number and don't be afraid to ask about discounts; if you don't ask, it's unlikely they'll be volunteered. Have knowledgeable travel agents guide you; better yet, have an agent who specializes in the British Isles to guide you. An agent whose clients fly mostly to Nassau or Miami will not be the best person to hunt down a bargain flight to Dublin. Travel agents may not want to spend time finding the cheapest fares (for which they receive the lowest commissions), but if you travel often, you should definitely find an agent who will cater to your needs and track down deals in exchange for your frequent business.

Students and others under 26 should never pay full price for a ticket. Seniors can also get great deals; many airlines offer senior traveler clubs or airline passes with few restrictions and discounts for their companions as well. Sunday newspapers often have travel sections that list bargain fares. Australians can consult the Saturday travel section of the *Sydney Morning Herald*.

DETAILS AND TIPS

Timing: Airfares to Ireland peak between early June and late August, and holidays are also expensive periods in which to travel. Midweek (M-Th morning) round-trip flights run US$40-50 cheaper than weekend flights, but the latter are generally less crowded and more likely to permit frequent-flier upgrades. Return-date flexibility is usually not an option for the budget traveler; traveling with an "open return" ticket can be pricier than fixing a return date when buying the ticket and paying later to change it.

Route: Round-trip flights are by far the cheapest; "open-jaw" (arriving in and departing from different cities) and round-the-world, or RTW, flights are pricier but reasonable alternatives. Patching one-way flights together is the least economical way to travel. Flights between capital cities or regional hubs will offer the most competitive fares. Since Ireland is mostly smaller cities, you might find it cheaper to take the plane to London and ferry across the Irish Sea (see By Ferry, p. 10). Major Irish destinations are Shannon, Dublin, Cork, and Belfast. Shannon is often cheaper for transatlantic flights, as many stop there anyway en route to other airports (until recently, airlines were required by law to do so); Cork and Belfast tend to be the most expensive destinations.

Boarding: Whenever flying internationally, pick up tickets for international flights well in advance of the departure date, and confirm by phone within 72 hours of departure. Most airlines require that passengers arrive at the airport at least two hours before departure. One carry-on item and two pieces of checked baggage is the norm for non-courier flights. Consult the airline for weight allowances.

Fares: Round-trip fares to Western Europe from the U.S. range from US$150-400 (during the off-season). Budget tickets to Dublin range from US$160-$400 depending on the time of the year.

COMMERCIAL AIRLINES

The commercial airlines' lowest regular offer is the **APEX** (Advance Purchase Excursion) fare, which provides confirmed reservations and allows "open-jaw" tickets. Generally, reservations must be made 7 to 21 days in advance, with 7- to 14-day minimum and up to 90-day maximum-stay limits, and hefty cancellation and change penalties (fees rise in summer). Book peak-season APEX fares early, since by May you will have a hard time getting the departure date you want.

Although APEX fares are probably not the cheapest possible fares, they will give you a sense of the average commercial price, from which to measure other bargains. Specials advertised in newspapers may be cheaper but have more restrictions and fewer available seats. A popular carriers to Ireland is its national airline **Aer Lingus** (tel. (800) 474 7424; www.aerlingus.ie), has direct flights to the U.S., service to South Africa, and constant flights to London and Paris. If another airline doesn't fly directly to one of the airports in Ireland, it can almost certainly get you to London. For connections to Ireland from London, see **Flights from Britain,** below.

OTHER CHEAP ALTERNATIVES

TICKET CONSOLIDATORS. Ticket consolidators, or **"bucket shops,"** buy unsold tickets in bulk from commercial airlines and sell them at discounted rates. Consolidator flights are the best deals if you are traveling on short notice (you bypass advance purchase requirements, since you aren't tangled in airline bureaucracy); on a high-priced trip; or in the peak season, when published fares are jacked way up. Fares sold by consolidators are generally much cheaper; a 30-40% price reduction is not uncommon. There are rarely age constraints or stay limitations, but unlike tickets bought through an airline, you won't be able to use your tickets on another flight if you miss yours, and you will have to go back to the consolidator to get a refund, rather than the airline. Keep in mind that these tickets are often for coach seats on connecting (not direct) flights on foreign airlines, and that frequent-flyer miles may not be credited. Decide what you can and can't live with before shopping.

The best place to look is in the Sunday travel section of any major newspaper, where many bucket shops place tiny ads. Call quickly, as availability is typically extremely limited. Not all bucket shops are reliable establishments, so insist on a receipt that gives full details of restrictions, refunds, and tickets, and pay by credit card. For more information, check the website **Consolidators FAQ** (www.travel-library.com/air-travel/consolidators.html) or the book *Consolidators: Air Travel's Bargain Basement,* by Kelly Monaghan (Intrepid Traveler, US$8). In London, a call to the **Air Travel Advisory Bureau** (tel. (0171) 636 50 00) can provide names of reliable consolidators and discount flight specialists.

It pays to be a smart shopper. Among the many reputable and trustworthy companies are, unfortunately, some shady wheeler-dealers. Contact the local Better Business Bureau to find out how long the company has been in business and its track record. It is preferable to deal with consolidators close to home so you can visit in person, if necessary. Ask to receive your tickets as quickly as possible so you have time to fix any problems. It may be worth paying with a credit card (despite the 2-5% fee) so you can stop payment if you never receive your tickets. Beware the "bait and switch" gag; shyster firms will advertise a super-low fare and then tell a caller that it has been sold. Although this is a viable excuse, if they can't offer you a price near the advertised fare on *any* date, it is a scam to lure in customers—report them to the Better Business Bureau. Also ask about accommodations and car rental discounts; some consolidators have fingers in many pies. Mmmm, pie.

For destinations worldwide, try **Airfare Busters,** Houston, TX (tel. 800-232-8783; www.afbuster.com); **Pennsylvania Travel,** Paoli, PA (tel. 800-331-0947; www.patravel.com); **Cheap Tickets,** with offices in Los Angeles, San Francisco, Honolulu, Seattle, and New York (tel. 800-377-1000); **Interworld** (tel. 800-468-3796; fax 443-0351; www.interworldtravel.com); **Travac** (tel. 800-872-8800; fax (212) 714-9083; email mail@travac.com; www.travac.com). **NOW Voyager,** 74 Varick St. #307, New York, NY 10013 (tel. (212) 431-1616; fax 334-5243; email info@nowvoyager-travel.com; www.nowvoyagertravel.com), acts as a consolidator and books discounted international flights, mostly from New York, as well as courier flights (see **Courier Companies and Freighters** below), for an annual fee of US$50. For a processing fee, depending on the number of travelers and the itinerary, **Travel Avenue,** Chicago, IL (tel. 800-333-3335; fax 800-838-4376; email webmaster@travelavenue.com; www.travelavenue.com), will search for the lowest international airfare available, including consolidated prices, and will even give you a 5% rebate on fares over US$350. **Rebel Tours,** 25050 Avenue Kearny, Suite 215, Valencia, CA 91355 (tel. 800-227-3235; fax 805-294-0981; email travel@rebeltours.com; www.rebeltours.com) also books flights to Europe.

CHARTER FLIGHTS. Charters are flights contracted by a tour operator to fly extra loads of passengers during peak season. Charters are often considerably cheaper than flights on scheduled airlines, some operate nonstop, and restrictions on minimum advance-purchase and minimum stay are more lenient. However, charter flights fly less frequently than major airlines, make refunds particularly difficult, and are almost always fully booked. Schedules and itineraries may also change or be cancelled at the last moment (as late as 48 hours before the trip, and without a full refund), and check-in, boarding, and baggage claim are often much slower. As always, pay with a credit card if you can, and consider traveler's insurance against trip interruption.

Discount clubs and **fare brokers** offer members savings on last-minute charter and tour deals. Study their contracts closely. **Travelers Advantage,** Stamford, CT (tel. 800-548-1116; www.travelersadvantage.com; US$60 annual fee includes discounts, newsletters, and cheap flight directories) specializes in European tour packages.

STANDBY FLIGHTS. To travel standby, you will need considerable flexibility in the dates and cities of your arrival and departure. Companies that specialize in standby flights don't sell tickets but rather the promise that you will get to your destination (or near your destination) within a certain window of time (anywhere from 1-5 days). You may only receive a monetary refund if all available flights which depart within your date-range from the specified region are full, but future travel credit is always available.

Carefully read agreements with any company offering standby flights, as tricky fine print can leave you in the lurch. To check on a company's service record, call the Better Business Bureau of New York City (tel. (212) 533-6200). It is difficult to receive refunds, and clients' vouchers will not be honored when an airline fails to receive payment in time.

Airhitch, 2641 Broadway, 3rd Fl., **New York,** NY 10025 (tel. 800-326-2009 or (212) 864-2000; fax 864-5489; www.airhitch.org) and **Los Angeles,** CA (tel. (310) 726-5000). In Europe, the flagship office is in **Paris** (tel. 0147 00 16 30) and the other one is in **Amsterdam** (tel. (020) 626 32 20). Flights to Europe cost US$159 each way when departing from the Northeast, US$239 from the West Coast or Northwest, US$209 from the Midwest, and US$189 from the Southeast. Travel within the USA and Europe is also possible, with rates ranging from US$79-$139.

AirTech.Com, 588 Broadway #204, New York, NY 10012 (tel. (212) 219-7000, fax 219-0066; email fly@airtech.com; www.airtech.com). Rates to Europe (continually updated, so call and verify) from the Northeast start at US$169; from the West Coast US$229; from the Midwest/Southeast US$199. AirTech.Com also arranges courier flights and regular confirmed-reserved flights at discount rates.

AIR COURIER FLIGHTS. Couriers help transport cargo on international flights by guaranteeing delivery of the baggage claim slips from the company to a representative overseas. Generally, couriers must travel light (carry-ons only) and deal with complex restrictions on their flight. You will probably never see the cargo you are transporting—the company handles it all—and airport officials know that couriers are not responsible for the baggage checked for them. Most flights are round-trip only with short fixed-length stays (usually one week) and a limit of a single ticket per issue. Most of these flights also operate only out of the biggest cities, like New York. Generally, you must be over 21 (in some cases 18), have a valid passport, and procure your own visa, if necessary. Groups such as the **Air Courier Association** (tel. 800-282-1202; www.aircourier.org) and the **International Association of Air Travel Couriers,** 220 South Dixie Hwy., P.O. Box 1349, Lake Worth, FL 33460 (tel. (561) 582-8320; email iaatc@courier.org; www.courier.org) provide their members with lists of opportunities and courier brokers worldwide for an annual fee. For more information, consult *Air Courier Bargains* by Kelly Monaghan (The Intrepid Traveler, US$15) or the *Courier Air Travel Handbook* by Mark Field (Perpetual Press, US$10).

FURTHER READING

The Worldwide Guide to Cheap Airfare, Michael McColl. Insider Publications (US$15).

Discount Airfares: The Insider's Guide, George Hobart. Priceless Publications (US$14).

Travelocity (www.travelocity.com). A searchable online database of published airfares. Online reservations.

Air Traveler's Handbook (www.cs.cmu.edu/afs/cs.cmu.edu/user/mkant/Public/Travel/airfare.html).

TravelHUB (www.travelhub.com). A directory of travel agents that includes a searchable database of fares from over 500 consolidators.

FLIGHTS FROM BRITAIN

Airplanes fly between Dublin, Shannon, Cork, Kerry, Galway, Knock, Sligo, and Waterford (in Ireland); Belfast and Derry (in Northern Ireland); Gatwick, Stansted, Heathrow, Luton, Manchester, Birmingham, Liverpool, and Glasgow airports; and Ronaldsway on the Isle of Man. Flying to London and connecting to Ireland is often easier and cheaper. Aer Lingus (see p. 64) and several other carriers offer service on these routes. **British Midland Airways** (in the U.K. (0870) 607 0555; in the Republic (01) 283 0700; www.iflybritishmidland.com/) flies about seven times per day to London Heathrow. **British Airways** (in the U.K. (0345) 222111; in the Republic (800) 626747; in the U.S. (800) AIRWAYS or 247 9297; www.british-airways.com), flies about five times per day Monday through Friday, Saturday and Sunday six per day. Prices range from UK£70-150 return but can drop from time to time. Call and inquire about specials. **Ryanair** (in the U.K. (0870) 333 1250; in the Republic (01) 609 7800) connects Kerry, Cork, and Knock to London and nine other destinations in England and Scotland. Flights from London to Dublin or Belfast generally take 1¼hr. The **Air Travel Advisory Bureau,** 28 Charles Sq., London N16HT, England (tel. (0171) 636 50 00; fax 251 88 77; www.atab.co.uk) will put you in touch with the cheapest carriers out of London for free.

BY FERRY

Ferries are popular and usually more economical if considerably more time-consuming form of transportation than airplanes. Boats run from Pembroke Dock in South Wales to Rosslare Harbour in southeast Ireland; from Holyhead in North Wales to Dún Laoghaire (dun LEER-ee), a suburb of Dublin; from Swansea in South Wales to Cork; and from Stranraer, Scotland, to Belfast and Larne, Northern Ireland. Almost all sailings in June, July, and August are "controlled sailings," which means that you must book the crossing ahead of time (a few days in advance is usually sufficient). Low season on ferry prices runs March to May and October to December; mid-season is June to mid-July and September; high season is mid-July to August.

Fares vary tremendously depending on time of year, time of day, and type of boat. Traveling mid-week and during the night promises the cheapest fares. Adult single tickets usually range from £20 to £35, and a world of discount rates is out there waiting to be explored. Some people ask car drivers to let them travel as one of four free passengers that a set of wheels gets. Students, seniors, families, and youth traveling alone should almost never pay full fare. Children under 5 almost always travel free, and bikes can usually brought on for no extra charge. **An Óige (HI) members** receive up to a 20% discount on fares from Irish Ferries and Stena Sealink. **ISIC cardholders** with the **Travel Stamp** (see p. 61) receive a 15% discount from Irish Ferries and an average 17% discount (variable among four routes) on StenaLine ferries. Ferry passengers from the Republic are taxed an additional IR£5 when travelling from England to Éire.

BRITAIN AND FRANCE TO IRELAND

Assorted bus tickets that include ferry connections between Britain and Ireland are also available as package deals through ferry companies, travel agents, and USIT offices. Contact Bus Éireann for information (see **By Bus,** p. 67).

Irish Ferries sails from Holyhead, North Wales, to Dublin (3½hr.) and from Pembroke, Wales, to Rosslare Harbour (4hr.). Also sails from Cherbourg and Roscoff, France to Cork and Rosslare Harbour (about 22hr.); Eurailpasses grant passage on ferries from France. For specific schedules and fares contact them at: 2-4 Merrion Row, **Dublin** 2 (reservations tel. (01) 638 3333, fax 661 0743); St. Patrick's Bridge, **Cork** (tel. (021) 551 995; fax 504 651); **Rosslare Harbour** (tel. (053) 33158); **Holyhead,** Wales (tel. (0990) 329 129); and **Pembroke, Wales** (tel. (0990) 329543). Their after-hours information line in Ireland is (01) 661 0715. Email info@irishferries.ie; www.irishferries.ie.

Stena Line ferries go from Holyhead, North Wales, to Dún Laoghaire (3½hr. on the Superferry); from Fishguard, South Wales, and Pembroke, Wales to Rosslare Harbour (3½-3¾hr.); and from Stanraer, Scotland, to Belfast (90min. on the Stena Line, 3hr. on the SeaCat). Offers package deals that include train service from London. Contact them at: Charter House, Park St., Ashford, Kent TN24 8EX, England (tel. (0990) 707 070; fax (01233) 202 241); **Dun Laoghaire Travel Centre** (tel. (01) 204 7777); **Rosslare Harbour** (tel. (053) 33115); Tourist Office, **Cork** (tel. (021) 272 965); Tourist Office, Arthurs Quay, **Limerick** (tel. (061) 316 259). For 24hr. recorded information, contact **Ferry Check** (tel. (01) 204 7799; email david@seaview.co.uk; www.seaview.co.uk/Stena.html).

Cork-Swansea Ferries sails between Swansea, South Wales, and Cork (10hr.). Contact them at 52 South Mall, Cork (tel. (021) 271166; fax 275061; email scs.iol.ie).

Hoverspeed SeaCat sails from Stranraer to Belfast (1hr.), and the **SuperSeaCat Ferry** sails from Liverpool, England to Dublin (4hr.). These SeaCat trips are faster than ferries but considerably pricier. For information and bookings, contact them at U.K. tel. (0990) 523 523 or in the Republic (1800) 551 743.

BY BUS

Bus Éireann (the Irish national bus company) reaches Britain and even the continent by working in conjunction with ferry services and the bus company **Eurolines** (UK tel. (01582) 404 511; www.eurolines.com). To get to Ireland from Britain, there are connecting services from Bristol and London to Cork, Waterford, Tralee, Killarney, Ennis, and Limerick, and from Cardiff and Birmingham to Cork, Waterford, Ennis, and Limerick. Prices range from IR£10 to £25. Tickets can be booked through USIT, any Bus Éireann office, Irish Ferries, Stena Line, or any Eurolines (or National Express office in Britain (tel. (0990) 808 080). Inconvenient arrival and departure times mean you won't be sleeping very well. The immense **Eurolines** network connects with many European destinations. Take an **express bus** to Dublin through London from over 400 destinations in Europe with Eurolines (U.K.) Ltd., 52 Grosvenor Gardens, London SW1W OAU (tel. (01582) 404 511); London to Dublin UK£15, return £29; London to Paris UK£34, return £44. Contact the Bus Éireann General Inquiries desk in Dublin (tel. (01) 836 6111) or a travel agent.

ONCE THERE

GETTING AROUND

Fares on all modes of transportation are either "single" (one-way) or "return" (round-trip). "Period returns" require you to return within a specific number of days; "day return" means you must return on the same day. Unless stated otherwise, *Let's Go* always lists single fares. Round-trip fares on trains and buses are rarely more than 30% above the one-way fare.

Roads between Irish cities and towns have official letters and numbers ("N" and "R" in the Republic; "M," "A," and "B" in the North), but most locals refer to them by destination ("Kerry Rd.," "Tralee Rd."). Signs and printed directions sometimes give only the numbered and lettered designations, sometimes only the destination. Most signs are in English and Irish; destination signs in the *gaeltachta* are most often only in Irish. Old black and white road signs give distances in miles; new green and white signs are in kilometers. Speed limit signs are in miles per hour.

BY BUS

Buses in the Republic of Ireland reach many more destinations and are less expensive than trains. The national bus company, **Bus Éireann** (email info.buseireann.ie; www.buseireann.ie), operates both long-distance **Expressway** buses, which link larger cities, and **Local** buses, which serve the countryside and smaller towns. Timetables for bus services are most easily accessed by visiting local bus stations, or Bus Eireann's website. The invaluable bus timetable book (£1) is hugely difficult to obtain for personal ownership, although it should be available for purchase at Busáras Station in Dublin as well as the occasional tourist offices. A myriad of **private bus services** are faster and cheaper than Bus Éireann. *Let's Go* lists these private companies in areas they service. Most of these services link Dublin to one or two towns in the west. In Donegal, private bus providers take the place of Bus Éireann's nearly nonexistent local service. Expressway buses allow passengers to store luggage in the bus's undercarriage, or carry hand-luggage on board. Bicycles may be stored for a £5 fee in the udercarriage, provided there's room.

Return tickets are always a great value. For students, purchasing a Travel Stamp along with your ISIC card affords huge discounts on bus travel (see p. 39). Bus Éireann's discount **Rambler** tickets mostly aren't worth buying; individual tickets often provide better value. The Rambler ticket offers unlimited bus travel within Ireland for three of eight consecutive days (£28; £14 child), eight of 15 consecutive days (£68; £34 child), or 15 of 30 consecutive days (£98; £49 child). A combined **Irish Explorer Rail/Bus** ticket allows unlimited travel eight of 15 consecutive days on rail and bus lines (£100; £50 child). Purchase these tickets from Bus Éireann at their main bus station in Dublin, Store St., Dublin 1 (tel. (01) 836 6111), or at their Travel Centres in Cork (tel. (021) 508188), Waterford (tel. (051) 879000), Galway (tel. (091) 562000), Limerick (te. (061) 313333), and other transportation hubs. Contact the **Irish Rail** information office at 35 Lower Abbey St., Dublin 1 (tel. (01) 836 6222).

Ulsterbus, Laganside, Belfast (tel. (01232) 333000; email feedback@ulsterbus.co.uk; www.ulsterbus.co.uk), the North's version of Bus Éireann, runs extensive and reliable routes throughout Northern Ireland, where there are no private bus services. Coverage expands in summer, when several buses running a purely coastal route, and full- and half-day tours leave for key tourist spots from Belfast. Pick up a regional timetable free at any station. Again, the bus discount passes won't save you much money: a **Freedom of Northern Ireland** bus and rail pass offers unlimited travel for one day (UK£10), or several consecutive days (3-day pass £25; 7-day pass £37).

The **Irish Rover** pass covers both Bus Éireann and Ulsterbus services. It sounds ideal for vistors intending to travel in both the Republic and Northern Ireland, but unless you're planning to spend lots of time on the bus, its actual economic benefits are debatable (unlimited travel for 3 of 8 days £36, £18 child; for 8 of 15 days £85, £43 child; for 15 of 30 £130, £65 child). The **Emerald Card** offers unlimited travel on on Ulsterbus; Northern Ireland Railways; Bus Éireann Expressway, Local, and City services in Dublin, Cork, Limerick, Galway, and Waterford; and intercity, DART, and suburban rail Iarnród Éireann services. The card works for eight out of 15 consecutive days (£115, £58 child) or 15 out of 30 consecutive days (£200, £100 child).

BY TRAIN

Iarnród Éireann (Irish Rail) is useful only for travel to urban areas, from which you'll need to find another form of transporation to reach Ireland's picturesque villages and wilds. Trains from Dublin's Heuston Station chug towards Cork, Tralee, Limerick, Ennis, Galway, Westport, Ballina, and Waterford; others leave from Dublin's Connolly Station to head for Belfast, Sligo, Wexford and Rosslare. Trains also make connections between these various cities. For schedule information, pick up an InterCity Rail Travellers Guide (50p), available at most train stations. The **TravelSave** stamp, available for £8 at any USIT if you have an ISIC card, cuts fares by thirty to fifty percent on national rail. (It also provides 15% discounts on bus fares above £1). A **Faircard** (£8) can get anyone age 16 to 26 up to 50% off the price of any InterCity trip. Those over 26 can get the less potent **Weekender card** (£10; up to a third off, valid F-Tu only). Both are valid through the end of the year. The **Rambler** rail ticket allows unlimited train travel on five days within a fifteen day travel period (£67). For combined bus and train travel passes, see **By Bus**, p. 67. Information is available from Irish Rail information office, 35 Lower Abbey St., Dublin 1 (tel. (01) 836 3333; email INFO@irishrail.ie; www.irishrail.ie). Unlike bus tickets, train tickets sometimes allow travelers to break a journey into stages yet still pay the price of a single-phase trip. Bikes may be carried on most trains for a fee of £2-6, depending on its weight; check at the station for the restrictions of specific trains.

While the **Eurailpass** is not accepted in Northern Ireland, it *is* accepted on trains (but not buses) in The Republic. A range of youth and family passes are also available, but Eurailpasses are generally cost-effective only if you plan to travel to the Continent as well. The BritRail pass does not cover travel in Northern Ireland, but the month-long **BritRail+Ireland** works in both the North and the Republic with rail options and round-trip ferry service between Britain and Ireland (US$408-770). Great value resides in the youth passes for inidividuals under the age of 26. You'll find it easiest to buy a Eurailpass before you arrive in Europe; contact Council Travel, Travel CUTS, Let's Go Travel (see p. 64), or any of many other travel agents. The **Rail Europe Group,** 500 Mamaroneck Ave., Harrison, NY 10528 (tel. (800) 438 7245; fax (800) 432 1329 in the U.S.; and tel. (800) 361 7245; fax (905) 602 4198 in Canada; www.raileurope.com), also sells point-to-point tickets.

Northern Ireland Railways (Belfast tel. (01232) 899411; www.nirailways.co.uk) is not extensive but covers the northeastern coastal region well. The major line connects Dublin to Belfast (2hr., M-Sa 8 per day, Su 5 per day, UK£17, £26 on weekends; student rates available). When it reaches Belfast, this line splits, with one branch ending at Bangor and one at Larne. There is also rail service from Belfast and Lisburn west to Derry and Portrush, stopping at three towns between Antrim and the coast. British Rail passes are not valid here, but Northern Ireland Railways offers its own discounts. A valid **Northern Ireland Travelsave** stamp (UK£7, affixed to back of ISIC) will get you 50% off all trains and 15% discounts on bus fares over UK£1 within Northern Ireland. The **Freedom of Northern Ireland** ticket allows unlimited travel by train and Ulsterbus and can be purchased for seven consecutive days (UK£37), three consecutive days (£25), or a single day (£10).

BY CAR

DRIVING PERMITS AND CAR INSURANCE. The advantages of car travel speak for themselves. Disadvantages include high gasoline prices, the unfamiliar laws and habits associated with driving in foreign lands, and, for Americans and most other nationalities, the fact that in Ireland, as in Britain, **you drive on the left.** Be particularly cautious at roundabouts (rotary interchanges)—give way to traffic from the right. Irish drivers speed along narrow, twisting, pot-holed, poorly lit back roads. You will need to drive rather slowly and cautiously, especially at night. The **Association for Safe International Road Travel (ASIRT)** can provide more specific information about road conditions. It is located at 5413 West Cedar Lane 103C, Bethesda, MD 20814 (tel. (301) 983-5252; fax 983-3663; email asirt@erols.com; www.asirt.org). ASIRT considers road travel (by car or bus) to be relatively safe in Ireland.

Irish law requires drivers and passengers to wear seat belts—these laws are enforced. In Ireland, children under 12 are not allowed to sit in the front seat of a car. Children under 40 lbs. should ride only in a specially designed carseat, which can be obtained for a small fee from most car rental agencies.

In the Republic of Ireland, roads numbered below N50 are "primary routes," which connect all the major towns; roads numbered N50 and above are "secondary routes," not as well trafficked but still well signposted. Regional "R-roads" are rarely referred to by number. Instead, the road takes the name of its destination. The general speed limit is 55 mph (90km per hr.) on the open road and either 30 mph (50km per hr.) or 40 mph (65km per hr.) in town. There are no major highways.

Northern Ireland possesses exactly two major highways (M-roads or motorways) connecting Belfast with the rest of the province. The M-roads are supplemented by a web of "A-roads" and "B-roads." Speed limits are 60 mph (97km per hr.) on single carriageways (non-divided highways), 70 mph (113km per hr.) on motorways (highways) and dual carriageways (divided highways), and usually 30 mph (48km per hr.) in urban areas. Speed limits are always marked at the beginning of town areas. Upon leaving, you'll see a circular sign with a slash through it, signaling the end of the speed restriction. Speed limits aren't rabidly enforced; remember, though, that many of these roads are sinuous and single-track—use common sense.

Renting (hiring) an automobile is the least expensive option if you plan to drive for a month or less, but the initial cost of renting a car and the price of gas will astound you in Ireland. People under 21 cannot rent, and those under 23 often encounter difficulties. Major rental companies include **Alamo, Avis, Budget Rent-A-Car, Murrays Europcar, Hertz, Kenning, McCausland,** and **Swan National.** Prices range from IR£100 to IR£300 (plus VAT) per week with insurance and unlimited mileage. For insurance reasons, most companies require renters to be over 23 and under 70. Some plans require sizable deposits unless you're paying by credit card. Make sure you understand the insurance agreement before you rent; some require you to pay for damages that you may not have caused. Automatics are around 40% more expensive to rent than manuals (stickshifts). Rental agencies convenient to major airports are **Budget Rent-A-Car,** 151 Lower Drumcondra Rd., Dublin 9 (tel. (01) 837 9611; £45 per day), or **Thrifty** (tel. (061) 472 649) at the Shannon Airport (£35 per day).

INTERNATIONAL DRIVING PERMIT (IDP). If you plan to drive a car while in Ireland for longer than a 3 month period, you must have an International Driving Permit (IDP). If you intend to drive for longer than one year, you'll need to get an Irish driver's license.

Your IDP, valid for one year, must be issued in your own country before you depart; AAA affiliates cannot issue IDPs valid in their own country. You must be 18 years old to receive the IDP. A valid driver's license from your home country must always accompany the IDP. An application for an IDP usually needs to include one or two photos, a current local license, an additional form of identification, and a fee.

Australia: Contact your local Royal Automobile Club (RAC) or the National Royal Motorist Association (NRMA) if in NSW or the ACT (tel. (08) 9421 4298; www.rac.com.au/travel). Permits AUS$15.

Canada: Contact any Canadian Automobile Association (CAA) branch office in Canada, or write to CAA, 1145 Hunt Club Rd., Suite 200, K1V 0Y3 Canada. (tel. (613) 247-0117; fax 247-0118; www.caa.ca/CAAInternet/travelservices/internationaldocumentation/idptravel.htm). Permits CDN$10.

Ireland: Contact the nearest Automobile Association (AA) office, or write to the U.K. address: The Automobile Association, International Documents, Fanum House, Erskine, Renfrewshire PA8 6BW UK. (tel. 44 990 500 600). Permits IR£4. The Irish Automobile Association (tel. (01) 677 9481) is on 23 Suffolk St., Rockhill, Blackrock, Co. Dublin. They honor most foreign automobile memberships (24hr. breakdown and road service tel. 800 667 788; toll-free in Ireland).

New Zealand: Contact your local Automobile Association (AA) or their main office at Auckland Central, 99 Albert St. (tel. (09) 377 4660; fax 302 2037; www.nzaa.co.nz). Permits NZ$8.

South Africa: Contact your local Automobile Association of South Africa office or the head office at P.O. Box 596, 2000 Johannesburg (tel. (011) 799 1000; fax 799 1010). Permits SAR28.50.

U.K.: Visit your local AA Shop. To find the nearest location that issues the IDP, call (0990) 500 600. More information available at www.theaa.co.uk/motoring/idp.asp. Permits UK£4.

U.S.: Visit any American Automobile Association (AAA) office or write to AAA Florida, Travel Related Services, 1000 AAA Drive (mail stop 100), Heathrow, FL 32746 (tel. (407) 444-7000; fax 444-7380). Sells the International Driving Permit (IDP). You do not have to be a member of AAA to receive an (IDP/IADP). Permits US$10.

American Automobile Association (AAA) Travel Related Services, 1000 AAA Dr. (mail stop 100), Heathrow, FL 32746 (tel. 800-222-4357). Provides road maps and many travel guides free to members. Offers emergency road services (for members), travel services, and auto insurance. The IDP is available for purchase from local AAA offices. To obtain an IDP in the U.K., contact the **Automobile Association Headquarters** (tel. (0990) 44 88 66).

CAR INSURANCE. Most credit cards cover standard insurance. If you rent, lease, or borrow a car, you will need a **green card,** or **International Insurance Certificate,** to prove that you have liability insurance. Obtain it through the car rental agency; most include coverage in their prices. If you lease a car, you can obtain a green card from the dealer. Some travel agents offer the card; it may also be available at border crossings. Verify whether your auto insurance applies abroad; even if it does, you will still need a green card to certify this to foreign officials. If you have a collision abroad, the accident will show up on your domestic records if you report it to your insurance company. Rental agencies may require you to purchase theft insurance in countries that they consider to have a high risk of auto theft. Ask your rental agency about Ireland.

BY MOPED AND MOTORCYCLE

Motorized bikes don't use much gas, can be put on trains and ferries, and are a good compromise between the high cost of car travel and the limited range of bicycles. However, they're uncomfortable for long distances, dangerous in the rain, and unpredictable on rough roads and gravel. Always wear a helmet, and never ride with a backpack. If you've never been on a moped before, the winding Wicklow Mountains are not the place to start.

BY BICYCLE

Much of Ireland's and Northern Ireland's countrysides are well suited for cycling by daylight; many roads are not heavily traveled. Single-digit N roads in the Republic, and M roads in the North, are more busily trafficked; try to avoid them. Begin your trip in the south or west to take advantage of prevailing winds.

Many airlines will count your bike as your second free piece of luggage, and a few charge extra. The additional fee runs about US$60-110 each way. Bikes must be packed in a cardboard box with the pedals and front wheel detached; airlines sell bike boxes at the airport (US$10). Most ferries let you take your bike for free or for a nominal fee. You can always ship your bike on trains, but the cost varies.

Riding a bike with a frame pack strapped on it or your back is about as safe as pedaling blindfolded over a sheet of ice; panniers are essential. The first thing to buy, however, is a suitable **bike helmet** (US$25-50). U-shaped **Citadel** or **Kryptonite locks** are expensive (starting at US$30), but the companies insure their locks against theft of your bike for one to two years. For mail order equipment, **Bike Nashbar,** 4111 Simon Rd., Youngstown, OH 44512 (tel. 800-627-4227; www.nashbar.com), beats all competitors' offers and ships anywhere in the U.S. or Canada.

Bikes can go on some trains but not all: inquire at the information desk. You'll have better luck getting your bike on a bus if you depart from a terminal, not a wayside stop. Bikes are allowed on Bus Éireann at the driver's discretion (if the bus isn't crowded) for a fee of £3-5, but this fee isn't always enforced; the fee for taking a bike on the train is at between £2-6, depending on the weight of the bike. It's a pain to bring a bike on an airplane, and each airline has different rules. *Let's Go* lists bike shops and bike rental establishments wherever we can find them. The cash deposit may often be waived if you pay for the rental with a credit card.

Irish Cycle Hire, Mayoralty St., Drogheda, Co. Louth (tel. (041) 984 1067, 984 3982, or 984 2338; fax 983 5369; email irch@iol.ie), has offices in Dublin, Cork, Killarney, Dingle, Galway, Westport, Ennis, and Donegal. The Drogheda office, which is the office to contact with any questions, is open daily from 9am to 5:30pm. Most other offices are open from May to October daily 9:30am to 6pm; some offices are closed on Sundays, although their depots stay open. All charge IR£6 per day, £30 per week, with £30 deposit. Bikes come with lock pump and repair kit. One-way rental (renting in one location and dropping off in another) is possible for IR£10. Students with ID get a 10% discount.

Rent-A-Bike, 58 Lower Gardiner St., Dublin (tel. (01) 872 5399), rents 21-speed cross-country and mountain bikes for £40 per week, plus £40 deposit. The shops will equip you with locks and repair kits. Used bikes, which you can sell back up to four months later for half price, are sometimes available in September or October at the Dublin shop. All bookings should be made through the head office in Dublin. (Open daily 9am-5pm.)

Raleigh Rent-A-Bike rents for IR£10 per day, £40 per week, plus £50 deposit. The shops will equip you with locks, patch kits, and pumps, and for longer journeys, pannier bags (IR£10 per week). Their **One-Way Rental** plan allows you to rent a bike at one shop and drop it off at another for a flat charge of IR£15. Reservations should be made through the main office at 8 Botanic Road, Galssnevin, Dublin 9 (tel./fax (01) 873 3622; www.trackbikes.com). A list of Raleigh dealers is available at most tourist offices and bike shops. You might also contact **Raleigh Ireland Limited** (tel. (01) 626 1333), 10 Raleigh House, Kylemore Rd., Dublin 10. In West Cork, the **Wheel Escapes** program provides one-way rental to a series of hostels.

Many small local dealers and hostels also rent bikes; rates are usually IR£6 to £9 per day and £25 to £35 per week. Tourist offices can direct you to bike rental establishments and distribute leaflets on local biking routes, as well as providing the extensive *Cycle Touring Ireland* (£7). If you plan to do much long-distance riding, you might also check a travel bookstore for other Irish cycling guides. Mountaineers Books (tel. (800) 553 4453; bear@mountaineers.org; www.mountaineers.org) sells *Ireland by Bike: 21 Tours* for US$15 (plus US$3 shipping). Write to them at 1001 SW Klickitat Way, Suite 201, Seattle, WA 98134. If you are nervous about striking out on your own, **CBT Tours** (tel. (800) 736 2453 or (312) 475 0625; fax 475 0627; www.cbttours.com) in the U.S. and Canada offer bicycle tours through the U.K. and Ireland that are geared toward the travelers on a tight budget. Ten-day tours pass through the greatest hits of the Southwest to the West coast of Ireland for US$139 per day, including accommodations and some meals. CBT also arranges discounted airfares for their participants. Adequate **maps** are a necessity; Ordnance Survey maps (£4.50) or Bartholomew maps are available in most bookstores in Ireland and the U.K., and in good ones in the U.S.

BY FOOT

Ireland's mountains, fields, and heather-covered hills make walking and hiking an arduous joy. The **Wicklow Way,** a popular trail through mountainous Co. Wicklow, has hostels designed for hikers within a day's walk of each other. The best hill-walking maps are the Ordnance Survey series (IR£4.50 each). There are many other trails all over the island; consult Bord Fáilte for more information and free pamphlets.

The **Ulster Way** encircles Northern Ireland with 560 mi. of marked trails. Less industrious trekkers are accommodated by frequent subdivisions. Plentiful information is available on the numerous paths that lace Northern Ireland. For the booklet The *Ulster Way* (free), contact the **Sports Council for Northern Ireland,** House of Sport, Upper Malone Rd., Belfast BT9 5LA (tel. (028) 9038 1222). If you're planning a hike through the Mourne Mountains, contact the **Mourne Heritage Center,** 87 Central Promenade, Newcastle, Co. Down BT33 OHH (tel. (028) 4372 4059).

For guided backpacking tours, you can try **Tír na nÓg Tours,** 57 Lower Gardiner St., Dublin 1 (tel. (01) 836 4684). Six-day tours zip across the south and and north of the island, while three- and four-day tours cover the same ground along with the Southwest. The price includes transportation, breakfast, admission to visitors centers, and accommodations along the way. Three- and six-day tours leave one to two times per week throughout the year (3-day £89; 6-day IR£169). Four-day tours run weekly March to October (IR£119).

BY THUMB

 Let's Go strongly urges you to consider seriously the risks before you choose to hitch. We do not recommend hitching as a safe means of transportation, and none of the information presented here is intended to do so.

No one should hitch without careful consideration of the risks involved. Not everyone can be an airplane pilot, but almost any bozo or lunatic can drive a car, especially in Ireland. Hitching means entrusting your life to a random person who happens to stop beside you on the road and risking theft, assault, sexual harassment, and unsafe driving. Hitching in Ireland has a glowing reputation, but it does have sobering risks—the past few years have seen several instances of violence against hitchers. There has been a recent backlash against hitching in both parts of Ireland; the percentage of travelers hitching has declined drastically. Locals in Northern Ireland do not recommend hitching there.

In spite of these disadvantages, some find the gains are many. Favorable hitching experiences allow you to meet local people and get where you're going, especially in rural areas, where public transportation is less reliable. While we don't endorse hitchhiking, we'll tell you some ways to make it safer and how to do it right.

The decision to pick up a hitcher can be a difficult one for a driver, so a smart hitcher will do everything possible to make it easier. Your success as a hitcher will depend partly on **what you look like.** Successful hitchers travel light and stack their belongings in a compact but visible cluster. Most Europeans signal with an open hand, rather than a thumb; many write their destination on a sign in large, bold letters and draw a smiley-face under it. Drivers prefer hitchers who are neat and wholesome. No one stops for anyone wearing sunglasses. **Where you stand** is vital. Experienced hitchers stand where drivers can stop, have time to look over potential passengers as they approach, and return to the road without causing an accident. Hitching on hills or curves is hazardous and largely unsuccessful; traffic circles and access roads to highways are better. In the **Practical Information** section of many cities, we list the bus lines that take travelers to strategic points for further hitching.

You can get a sense of the amount of traffic a road sees by its letter and number: in the Republic, single-digit N-roads (A-roads in the North) are as close as Ireland gets to highways, double-digit N-roads see some intercity traffic, R-roads (B-roads in the North) generally only carry local traffic but are easy hitches, and non-lettered roads are a **hitcher's purgatory.** In Northern Ireland, hitching (or even standing) on motorways (M-roads) is illegal: you may only thumb at the entrance ramps—*in front* of the nifty blue and white superhighway pictograph (a bridge over a road).

Safety issues are always imperative, even for those who are not hitching alone. If you're a woman traveling alone, don't hitch. A man and a woman are a safer combination, two men will have a harder time, and three will go nowhere. Hitchhiking at night can be particularly dangerous; experienced hitchers stand in well-lit places and expect drivers to be leery of nocturnal thumbers. Safety-minded hitchers avoid getting in the back of a two-door car and never let go of their backpacks. They will not get into a car that they can't get out of again in a hurry. If they ever feel threatened, they insist on being let off, regardless of where they are. Acting as if they are going to open the car door or vomit on the upholstery usually gets a driver to stop.

If you are hitching a **long distance** or to a remote spot with an intervening town between your present and desired location, you would do well to make your sign for the intervening town rather than your final destination. Shorter lifts are easier to pick up because it's easier for the driver and because more cars will be going to the nearby spot than to the distant one. If the driver is not going the entire way, then you've at least covered some of the distance and probably put yourself in a better location for hitching the rest of the way.

ACCOMMODATIONS

Bord Fáilte (bored FAHL-tshah; meaning "welcome board") is the Republic of Ireland's tourism authority. Actually a government department (and a fairly important one), its system for approving accommodations involves a more-or-less frequent inspection and a fee. Approved accommodations get to use Bord Fáilte's national booking system and display its icon, a green shamrock on a white field. Approved campgrounds and bed and breakfasts are listed with prices in the *Caravan and Camping Ireland* and *Bed and Breakfast Ireland* guides, respectively, available from any Bord Fáilte office. Bord Fáilte's standards are very specific and, in some cases, far higher than what hostelers and other budget travelers expect or require. Unapproved accommodations can be better and cheaper than their approved neighbors, though some unapproved places are, of course, real dumps. Most official tourist offices in Ireland will refer *only* to approved accommodations; some offices won't even tell you how to get to an unapproved hostel, B&B, or campground. Most tourist offices will book a room for a £1-3 fee, plus a 10% deposit. **Credit card reservations** can be made through Dublin Tourism (tel. (1800) 6686 6866). Approval by the **Northern Ireland Tourist Board** is legally required of all accomodations in the North. Their tourists offices can therefore provide you with all the contact information you'll need to find a night's lodging.

HOSTELS

A HOSTELER'S BILL OF RIGHTS. There are certain standard features that we do not include in our hostel listings. Unless we state otherwise, you can expect that every hostel has: no lockout, no curfew, a kitchen, free hot showers, secure luggage storage, and no key deposit.

For those looking to make friends and for a unique experience minus the expense, hostels are the place. Hostels are generally dorm-style accommodations, often in single-sex large rooms with bunk beds, although some hostels do offer private rooms for families and couples. They sometimes have storage space for your use, bike rentals, and laundry facilities. There can be drawbacks: some hostels close during certain daytime "lock-out" hours, have a curfew, don't accept reservations, or impose a maximum stay. In Ireland, a bed in a hostel will usually fall in the range £7-10.

In Ireland more than anywhere else, senior travelers and families are invariably welcome. Some hostels are strikingly beautiful (a few are even housed in castles), but others are little more than run-down barracks. You can expect every Irish hostel to provide blankets, although you may have to pay extra for sheets (see **Packing,** p. 56). Hostels listed are chosen based on location, price, quality, and facilities.

For the various services and lower rates offered at member hostels, hostelling associations, especially **Hostelling International (HI),** can definitely be worth joining. A membership in any national HI affiliate allows you to stay in HI hostels in any country. Nonmembers may ask at hostels for an "International Guest Card." HI hostels are scattered throughout Ireland, and many accept reservations via the International Booking Network (tel. (02) 9261 1111 from Australia, 800-663-5777 from Canada, (01629) 581 418 from the U.K., (01) 301 766 from Ireland, (09) 379 4224 from New Zealand, 800-909-4776 from U.S.; www.hiayh.org/ushostel/reserva/ ibn3.htm) for a nominal fee. HI's umbrella organization's web page (www.iyhf.org) lists the web addresses and phone numbers of all national associations and can be a great place to begin researching hostelling in a specific region. Hosteling membership is rarely necessary in Ireland, although there are sometimes member discounts. For non-members, an overnight fee plus one-sixth of the annual membership charge buys one stamp; a card with six stamps is proof of full HI membership. In Ireland, the HI affiliate is **An Óige** (an OYJ), which operates 37 hostels countrywide. Many An Óige hostels are in remote areas or small villages and were designed mostly to serve hikers, long-distance bicyclists, anglers, and others who want to see nature rather than meet people. The North's HI affiliate is **YHANI** (Youth Hostel Association of Northern Ireland). It operates only nine hostels, all comfortable. Some HI hostels operate only from March to November, April to October, or May to September.

A number of hostels in Ireland belong to the **Independent Holiday Hostels (IHH).** The 150 IHH hostels have no lockout or curfew (with a few exceptions), accept all ages, require no membership card, and have a comfortable atmosphere; all are Bord Fáilte-approved. Pick up a free booklet with complete descriptions of each at any IHH hostel. Contact IHH at the IHH Office, 57 Lower Gardiner St., Dublin (tel. (01) 836 4700). The **Independent Hostel Organization (IHO)** is a recently formed group of a even more hostels.

Lastly, if you have Internet access, check out the **Internet Guide to Hostelling** (www.hostels.com), which includes hostels from around the world in addition to oodles of information about hostelling and backpacking worldwide. Reservations for over 300 **Hostelling International (HI)** hostels (see listing below) may be made via the International Booking Network (IBN; U.S. tel. (202) 783 6161), a computerized system that allows you make reservations months in advance for a nominal fee. Credit card bookings may be made over the phone; contact An Óige or YHANI. Other comprehensive hostelling websites include www.hostels.com and www.eurotrip.com/ accommodation. To join HI, contact one of the following organizations:

Australian Youth Hostels Association (AYHA), 422 Kent St., Sydney NSW 2000 (tel. (02) 9261 1111; fax 9261 1969; email yha@yhansw.org.au; www.yha.org.au). One-year membership AUS$44, under 18 AUS$13.50.

Hostelling International-Canada (HI-C), 400-205 Catherine St., Ottawa, ON K2P 1C3 (tel. 800-663-5777 or (613) 237-7884; fax 237-7868; email info@hostellingintl.ca; www.hostellingintl.ca). One-year membership CDN$25, under 18 CAN$12; 2-yr. CAN$35.

An Óige (Irish Youth Hostel Association), 61 Mountjoy St., Dublin 7 (tel. (01) 830 4555; fax 830 5808; email anoige@iol.ie; www.irelandyha.org). One-year membership IR£10, under 18 IR£4, families IR£20.

Youth Hostels Association of New Zealand (YHANZ), P.O. Box 436, 173 Cashel St., Christchurch 1 (tel. (03) 379 9970; fax 365 4476; email info@yha.org.nz; www.yha.org.nz). One-year membership NZ$24, ages 15-17 NZ$12, under 15 free.

Hostelling International South Africa, P.O. Box 4402, Cape Town 8000 (tel. (021) 24 2511; fax 24 4119; email info@hisa.org.za; www.hisa.org.za). One-year membership SAR50, under 18 SAR25, lifetime SAR250.

Scottish Youth Hostels Association (SYHA), 7 Glebe Crescent, Stirling FK8 2JA (tel. (01786) 891 400; fax 891 333; email info@syha.org.uk; www.syha.org.uk). Membership UK£6, under 18 UK£2.50.

Youth Hostels Association of England and Wales (YHA), 8 St. Stephen's Hill, St. Albans, Hertfordshire AL1 2DY, England (tel. (01727) 855 215 or 845 047; fax 844 126; email yhacustomerservices@compuserve.com; www.yha.org.uk). One-year membership UK£11, under 18 UK£5.50, families UK£22.

Hostelling International Northern Ireland (HINI), 22-32 Donegall Rd., Belfast BT12 5JN, Northern Ireland (tel. (01232) 324 733 or 315 435; fax 439 699; email info@hini.org.uk; www.hini.org.uk). One-year membership UK£7, under 18 UK£3, families UK£14.

Hostelling International-American Youth Hostels (HI-AYH), 733 15th St. NW, Suite 840, Washington, D.C. 20005 (tel. (202) 783-6161 ext. 136; fax 783-6171; email hiayhserv@hiayh.org; www.hiayh.org). One-year membership US$25, over 54 US$15, under 18 free.

BED AND BREAKFASTS

For a cozy alternative to impersonal hotel rooms, B&Bs (private homes with rooms available to travelers) range from the acceptable to the sublime. Hosts will sometimes go out of their way to be accommodating by accepting travelers with pets, giving personalized tours, or offering home-cooked meals. "Full Irish breakfasts"—eggs, bacon, bread, sometimes black or white pudding, fried vegetables, cereal, orange juice, and coffee or tea—are often filling enough to get you through until dinner. Singles run about £15-25, doubles £20-36. On the other hand, many B&Bs do not provide phones, TVs, or private bathrooms.

B&Bs displaying a shamrock are officially approved by Bord Fáilte. For accommodations in Northern Ireland, check the Northern Ireland Tourist Board's annual *Where to Stay in Northern Ireland* (UK£4), available at most tourist offices. Be aware that Bord Fáilte meets at the end of the year and decides how much prices should increase in the Republic of Ireland. As our prices were researched in the summer of 1999, they may have increased since publication.

UNIVERSITY DORMS

Many colleges and universities open their residence halls to travelers when school is not in session—some do so even during term-time. These dorms are often close to student areas—good sources for information on things to do—and are usually very clean. Getting a room may take a couple of phone calls and require advance planning, but rates tend to be low, and many offer free local calls. For appropriate cities, including Dublin and Belfast, *Let's Go* lists colleges that rent dorm rooms among the accommodations.

HOME EXCHANGE AND RENTALS

Home exchange offers the traveler various types of homes (houses, apartments, condominiums, villas), plus the opportunity to live like a native and to cut down dramatically on accommodation fees—usually only an administration fee is paid to the matching service. Once you join or contact one of the exchange services listed below, it is then up to you to decide with whom you would like to exchange homes. Most companies have pictures of member's homes and information about the owners. A great site listing many exchange companies can be found at www.aitec.edu.au/~bwechner/Documents/Travel/Lists/HomeExchangeClubs.html. Home rentals, as opposed to exchanges, are much more expensive. However, they can be cheaper than comparably-serviced hotels. Both home exchanges and rentals can be ideal for families with children, or travelers with special dietary needs as you often get your own kitchen, maid service, TV, and telephones.

HomeExchange, P.O. Box 30085, Santa Barbara, CA 93130 (tel. (805) 898-9660; email admin@HomeExchange.com; www.homeexchange.com.

Intervac International Home Exchange, Phillipstown, Ballymakenny Rd., Drogheda, Ireland. (tel. 353-41-309 30; fax 353-41-309 29; email fkelly@intervac.ie; www.intervac.com).

The Invented City: International Home Exchange, 41 Sutter St., Suite 1090, San Francisco, CA 94104 (tel. 800-788-2489 in the U.S. or (415) 252-1141 elsewhere; fax 252-1171; email invented@aol.com; www.invented_city.com). For US$75, you get your offer listed in 1 catalog and unlimited access to the club's database containing thousands of homes for exchange.

FURTHER READING

Campus Lodging Guide (18th Ed.). B&J Publications (US$15).

The Complete Guide to Bed and Breakfasts, Inns and Guesthouses in the U.S., Canada, and Worldwide, Pamela Lanier. Ten Speed Press (US$17).

CAMPING AND THE OUTDOORS

Camping brings you closest to the land, the water, the insects, and continued financial solvency. Ireland is well endowed with sites and not at all endowed with snakes. Most campsites are open from April to October, although some stay open year-round. Youth hostels often have camping facilities (the charge is usually half the hostel charge), which is fortunate for many backpackers as many campsites are designed for people with caravans (RVs) rather than people with tents. You can legally set up camp only in specifically marked areas unless you get permission from the person on whose land you plan to squat. It is legal to cross private land by **public rights of way;** any other use of private land without permission is considered trespassing. Remember, bogs catch **fire** extremely easily.

Camping in State Forests and National Parks is not allowed in Ireland, nor is camping on public land if there is an official campsite in the area. It is also illegal to light fires within 2km of these forests and parks. Designated caravan and camping parks provide all the accoutrements of bourgeois civilization: toilets, running water, showers, garbage cans, and sometimes shops, kitchens, laundry facilities, restaurants, and game rooms. In addition, many have several caravans for hire at the site. Northern Ireland treats its campers royally; there are well-equipped campsites throughout, and spectacular parks often house equally mouthwatering sites.

USEFUL PUBLICATIONS AND WEB RESOURCES

A variety of publishing companies offer hiking guidebooks to meet the educational needs of novice or expert. For information about camping, hiking, and biking, write or call the publishers listed below to receive a free catalogue.

ESSENTIALS

Automobile Association, A.A. Publishing. Orders and enquiries to TBS Frating Distribution Centre, Colchester, Essex, CO7 7DW, U.K. (tel. (01206) 25 56 78; www.theaa.co.uk). Publishes *Camping and Caravanning: Britain & Ireland* (UK£8).

The Caravan Club, East Grinstead House, East Grinstead, West Sussex, RH19 1UA, U.K. (tel. (01342) 326 944; www.caravanclub.co.uk). Members receive a 700-page directory and handbook, discounts and a monthly magazine (£27.50).

Family Campers and RVers/National Campers and Hikers Association, Inc., 4804 Transit Rd., Bldg. #2, Depew, NY 14043 (tel./fax (716) 668-6242). Membership fee (US$25) includes their publication *Camping Today.*

The Mountaineers Books, 1001 SW Klickitat Way, #201, Seattle, WA 98134 (tel. 800 553-4453 or (206) 223-6303; email alans@mountaineers.org; www.mountaineers.org). Over 400 titles on hiking (the *100 Hikes* series), biking, mountaineering, natural history, and conservation.

Stanfords Ltd., 12-14 Long Acre, London, WC2E 9LP, U.K. (tel (0171) 836 2260; fax 379 4776), supplies maps of just about anywhere, especially the British Isles.

Sierra Club Books, 85 Second St. 2nd Fl., San Francisco, CA 94105-3441 (tel. 800- 935-1056 or (415) 977-5500; www.sierraclub.org/books). Books include *Wild Ireland* ($16).

CAMPING AND HIKING EQUIPMENT

Good camping equipment is both sturdy and light. Camping equipment is generally more expensive in Australia, New Zealand, and the U.K. than in North America.

Sleeping Bag: Most good sleeping bags are rated by "season," or the lowest outdoor temperature at which they will keep you warm ("summer" means 30-40°F at night and "four-season" or "winter" often means below 0°F). Sleeping bags are made either of down (warmer and lighter, but more expensive, and miserable when wet) or of synthetic material (heavier, more durable, and warmer when wet). Prices range from US$80-210 for a summer synthetic to US$250-300 for a good down winter bag. **Sleeping bag pads,** including foam pads (US$10-20) and air mattresses (US$15-50) cushion your back and neck and insulate you from the ground. Bring a **"stuff sack"** or plastic bag to store your sleeping bag and keep it dry.

Tent: The best tents are free-standing, with their own frames and suspension systems; they set up quickly and only require staking in high winds. Low-profile dome tents are the best all-around. When pitched their internal space is almost entirely usable, which means little unnecessary bulk. Tent sizes can be somewhat misleading: two people *can* fit in a two-person tent, but will find life more pleasant in a four-person. If you're traveling by car, go for the bigger tent, but if you're hiking, stick with a smaller tent that weighs no more than 5-6 lbs (2-3kg). Good two-person tents start at US$90, four-person tents at US$300. Seal the seams of your tent with waterproofer, and make sure it has a rain fly. Other tent accessories include a **battery-operated lantern,** a **plastic groundcloth,** and a **nylon tarp.**

Backpack: If you intend to do a lot of hiking, you should have a frame backpack. **Internal-frame packs** mold better to your back, keep a lower center of gravity, and can flex adequately to allow you to hike difficult trails that require a lot of bending and maneuvering. **External-frame packs** are more comfortable for long hikes over even terrain since they keep the weight higher and distribute it more evenly. Whichever you choose, make sure your pack has a strong, padded hip belt, which transfers the weight from the shoulders to the legs. Any serious backpacking requires a pack of at least 4000 cubic inches (16,000cc). Allow an additional 500 cubic inches for your sleeping bag in internal-frame packs. Sturdy backpacks cost anywhere from US$125-420. This is one area where it doesn't pay to economize—cheaper packs may be less comfortable, and the straps are more likely to fray or rip. Before you buy any pack, try it on, insist on filling it with something heavy and walking around the store to get a sense of how it distributes weight before committing to buy it. A **waterproof backpack cover** will prove invaluable. Otherwise, plan to store all of your belongings in plastic bags inside your backpack.

Boots: Be sure to wear hiking boots with good **ankle support** which are appropriate for the terrain you plan to hike. Your boots should fit snugly and comfortably over one or two wool socks and a thin liner sock. Breaking in boots properly before setting out requires wearing them for several weeks; doing so will spare you from painful and debilitating blisters.

Other Necessities: Raingear in two pieces, a top and pants, is far superior to a poncho. **Synthetics,** like polypropylene tops, socks, and long underwear, along with a pile jacket, will keep you warm even when wet. When camping in autumn, winter, or spring, bring along a **"space blanket,"** which helps you to retain your body heat and doubles as a groundcloth (US$5-15). Plastic **canteens** or water bottles keep water cooler than metal ones do, and are virtually shatter- and leak-proof. Large, collapsible **water sacks** will significantly improve your lot in primitive campgrounds and weigh practically nothing when empty, though they are bulky and heavy when full. Bring **water-purification tablets,** or shell out money for a portable water-purification system, for when you can't boil water. Though most campgrounds provide campfire sites, you may want to bring a small **metal grate** or **grill** of your own. For those places that forbid fires or the gathering of firewood, you'll need a **camp stove.** The classic Coleman stove starts at about US$40. You will need to purchase a **fuel bottle** and fill it with propanet. A **first aid kit, swiss army knife, insect repellent, calamine lotion,** and **waterproof matches** or a **lighter** are other essential camping items.

The mail-order/online companies listed below offer lower prices than many retail stores, but a visit to a local camping or outdoors store will give you a good sense of items' look and weight.

Campmor, P.O. Box 700, Upper Saddle River, NJ 07458-0700 (U.S. tel. (888) 226 7667, outside U.S., call (201) 825-8300; email customer-service@campmor.com; www.campmor.com).

Discount Camping, 880 Main North Rd., Pooraka, South Australia 5095, Australia (tel. (08) 8262 3399; fax 8260 6240; www.discountcamping.com.au).

Eastern Mountain Sports (EMS), 327 Jaffrey Rd., Peterborough, NH 03458 (tel. (888) 463 6367 or (603) 924 7231; www.emsonline.com; email emsmail@emsonline.com) Call the above number for the branch nearest you.

Mountain Designs, P.O. Box 1472, Fortitude Valley, Queensland 4006, Australia (tel. (07) 3252 8894; fax 3252 4569; www.mountaindesign.com.au).

Recreational Equipment, Inc. (REI), Sumner, WA 98352 (tel. (800) 426 4840 or (253) 891 2500; www.rei.com).

YHA Adventure Shop, 14 Southampton St., London, WC2E 7HA, U.K. (tel. (020) 7836 8541). The main branch of one of Britain's largest outdoor equipment suppliers.

WILDERNESS SAFETY

Stay warm, stay dry, and stay hydrated. The vast majority of life-threatening wilderness situations result from a breach of this simple dictum. On any hike, however brief, you should pack enough equipment to keep you alive should disaster befall. This includes **raingear, hat** and **mittens,** a **first-aid kit,** a **reflector,** a **whistle, high energy food,** and extra **water.** Dress in warm layers of **synthetic materials** designed for the outdoors, or **wool.** Pile fleece jackets and Gore-Tex raingear are excellent choices. Never rely on **cotton** for warmth. This "death cloth" will be absolutely useless should it get wet. Make sure to check all equipment for any defects before setting out, and see **Camping and Hiking Equipment,** above, for more information.

Check **weather forecasts** and pay attention to the skies when hiking. Weather patterns can change suddenly. Let someone know when and where you are going hiking, either a friend, your hostel, a park ranger, or a local hiking organization. Do not attempt a hike beyond your ability—you may be endangering your life. See **Health,** p. 51 for information about outdoor ailments such as hypothermia, giardia, rabies, and insects, as well as basic medical concerns and first-aid.

ENVIRONMENTALLY RESPONSIBLE TOURISM. The idea behind responsible tourism is to leave no trace of human presence behind. A campstove is the safer (and more efficient) way to cook than using vegetation, but if you must make a fire, keep it small and use only dead branches or brush rather than cutting vegetation. Make sure your campsite is at least 150 ft. (50m) from water supplies or bodies of water. If there are no toilet facilities, bury human waste (but not paper) at least four inches (10cm) deep and above the high-water line, and 150 feet or more from any water supplies and campsites. Always pack your trash in a plastic bag and carry it with you until you reach the next trash can. If you would like more information on these issues, contact one of the organizations listed below.

Earthwatch, 680 Mt. Auburn St., Box 403, Watertown, MA 02272 (tel. (617) 776-0188; fax 926-8532; email info@earthwatch.org; www.earthwatch.org).

Ecotourism Society, P.O. Box 755, North Bennington, VT 05257-0755 (tel. (802) 447-2121; email ecomail@ecotourism.org; www.ecotourism.org/tes-info.html).

EcoTravel Center: www.ecotour.com.

National Audobon Society, Nature Odysseys, 700 Broadway, New York, NY 10003 (tel. (212) 979-3066; email travel@audobon.org; www.audobon.org).

Tourism Concern, Stapleton House, 277-281 Holloway Rd., London N7 8HN, England (tel. (0170) 753 3330; www.gn.apc.org/tourismconcern).

Don't leave food or other scented items (trash, toiletries, the clothes that you cooked in) near your tent. **Bear-bagging**—hanging edibles and other good-smelling objects from a tree out of reach of hungry paws—is the best way to keep your toothpaste from becoming a condiment. Bears are also attracted to any **perfume,** as are bugs, so cologne, scented soap, deodorant, and hairspray should stay at home.

For further reading, look over *How to Stay Alive in the Woods* by Bradford Angier (Macmillan, US$8).

CAMPERS AND RVS. Renting an RV, called a caravan in Ireland, will always be more expensive than tenting or hostelling, but the costs compare favorably with the price of staying in hotels and renting a car (see **Rental Cars,** p. 84), and the convenience of bringing along your own bedroom, bathroom, and kitchen makes it an attractive option, especially for older travelers and families with children.

Rates vary widely by region, season (July and August are the most expensive months), and type of RV. It always pays to contact several different companies to compare vehicles and prices.

FURTHER READING

Camping Your Way through Europe, Carol Mickelsen. Affordable Press (US$15).

Exploring Europe by RV, Dennis and Tina Jaffe. Globe Pequot (US$15).

Great Outdoor Recreation Pages, www.gorp.com.

KEEPING IN TOUCH

MAIL

SENDING MAIL TO AND RECEIVING MAIL IN IRELAND. Airmail letters under 1 oz. between North America and Ireland take six to nine days and cost US$.90 or CDN$.95. Allow at least five to seven days from Australia (postage AUS$1.20 for up to 20 grams) and 2-3 from Britain (postage 30p for up to 20g). Envelopes should be marked "air mail" or "par avion" to avoid having letters sent by sea. There are several ways to arrange pick-up of letters sent to you by friends and relatives while you are abroad.

General Delivery: Mail can be sent to Ireland through **Poste Restante** (the international phrase for General Delivery) to almost any city or town with a post office. Address *Poste Restante* letters to: Luke KELLY, Poste Restante, Enniscorthy, Co. Wexford, Ireland." The mail will go to a special desk in the central post office, unless you specify a post office by street address or postal code. As a rule, it is best to use the largest post office in the area, and mail may be sent there regardless of what is written on the envelope. When possible, it is usually safer and quicker to send mail express or registered. When picking up your mail, bring a form of photo ID, preferably a passport. There is generally no surcharge; if there is a charge, it generally does not exceed the cost of domestic postage. If the clerks insist that there is nothing for you, have them check under your first name as well. *Let's Go* lists post offices in the **Practical Information** section for each city and most towns.

American Express: AmEx's travel offices throughout the world will act as a mail service for cardholders if you contact them in advance. Under this free **Client Letter Service,** they will hold mail for up to 30 days and forward upon request. Address the letter in the same way shown above. Some offices will offer these services to non-cardholders (especially those who have purchased AmEx Travelers Cheques), but you must call ahead to make sure. Check the **Practical Information** section of the countries you plan to visit; Let's Go lists AmEx office locations for most large cities. A complete list is available free from AmEx (tel. (800) 528 4800).

If regular airmail is too slow, **Federal Express** (tel. 13 26 10 in Australia; Ireland tel. 800 535 800; New Zealand tel. 0800 733 339; South Africa tel. 021 551 7610; U.K. tel. 0800 123 800; the U.S. and Canada tel. 800-463-3339; for other countries,call the U.S. tel. for international operator 800-247-4747) can get a letter from New York to Dublin in two days for a whopping US$25.50; rates among non-U.S. locations are prohibitively expensive (London to Dublin, for example, costs upwards of US$40). By **U.S. Express Mail,** a letter from New York would arrive in Dublin within four days and would cost US$5. From Australia, EMS can get a letter to Ireland in three to four working days for AUS$27.

Surface mail is by far the cheapest and slowest way to send mail. It takes one to three months to cross the Atlantic and two to four to cross the Pacific—appropriate for sending large quantities of items you won't need to see for a while. When ordering books and materials from abroad, always include one or two **International Reply Coupons (IRCs)**—a way of providing the postage to cover delivery. IRCs should be available from your local post office and those abroad (US$1.05).

SENDING MAIL IN IRELAND. Aerogrammes, printed sheets that fold into envelopes and travel via airmail, are available at post offices. It helps to mark "airmail" if possible, though "par avion" is universally understood. Most post offices will charge exorbitant fees or simply refuse to send aerogrammes with enclosures. Airmail from Ireland to the U.S. averages five to six days; to Europe its averages three to four days. Times are less predictable from smaller towns.

To send a postcard to an international destination within Europe costs 32p and to any other international destination via airmail costs 45p. Domestically, postcards require 30p. To send a letter (up to 25g) to another European country costs 32p and to anywhere else in the world via airmail costs 45p.

TELEPHONES

CALLING IRELAND FROM HOME
To call Ireland direct from home, dial:

1. The **international access code** of your home country. International access codes include: Australia 0011; Ireland 00; New Zealand 00; South Africa 09; U.K. 00; U.S. 011.
2. The **country code** of the region you're calling. Country codes include: 353 to reach the Republic of Ireland; 44 to reach Northern Ireland and Britain; 08 to reach Northern Ireland from the Republic.

3. **The city code.** City codes are usually listed with a 0 at their start (for example, Dublin's city code is 01). This zero is dropped when dialing. *Let's Go* lists telephone codes in **Practical Information** sections, except when covering rural areas where more than one telephone code may apply, where we list the area code before the number. The city code is 028 throughout the north.

4. **The local number.** Regional telephone codes range from two to five digits, and local telephone numbers range from five to seven digits.

CALLING HOME FROM IRELAND

A **calling card** is probably your best and cheapest bet. Calls are billed either collect or to your account. **MCI WorldPhone** also provides access to MCI's Traveler's Assist, which gives legal and medical advice, exchange rate information, and translation services. Other phone companies provide similar services to travelers. **To obtain a calling card** from your national telecommunications service before you leave home, contact the appropriate company below.

USA: AT&T (tel. 888-288-4685); **Sprint** (tel. 800-877-4646); or **MCI** (tel. 800-444-4141; from abroad dial the country's MCI access number).

Canada: Bell Canada **Canada Direct** (tel. 800-565-4708).

U.K.: British Telecom **BT Direct** (tel. (0800) 34 51 44).

Ireland: Telecom Éireann **Ireland Direct** (tel. 800 250 250).

Australia: Telstra **Australia Direct** (tel. 13 22 00).

New Zealand: Telecom New Zealand (tel. (0800) 000 000).

South Africa: Telkom South Africa (tel. 09 03).

To call home with a calling card, contact the Ireland operator for your service provider by dialing:

AT&T: Tel. 1 800 550 000.

Sprint: Tel. 1 800 552 001.

MCI WorldPhone Direct: Tel. 1 800 551 001.

Canada Direct: Tel. 800 565 4708.

BT Direct: Tel. 800 34 51 44.

Ireland Direct: Tel. 800 250 250.

Australia Direct: Tel. 13 22 00.

Telecom New Zealand Direct: Tel. 800 000 000.

Telkom South Africa Direct: Tel. 09 03.

Wherever possible, use a calling card for international phone calls, as the long-distance rates for national phone services are often exorbitant. You can usually make direct international calls from pay phones, but if you aren't using a calling card you may need to drop your coins as quickly as your words. Where available, prepaid phone cards and occasionally major credit cards can be used for direct international calls, but they are still less cost-efficient. Look for pay phones in public areas, especially train stations, as private pay phones are often more expensive. Although incredibly convenient, in-room hotel calls invariably include an arbitrary and sky-high surcharge (as much as US$10).

If you do dial direct, dial 00 (the international access code in both the Republic and Northern Ireland), and then dial the country code and number of your home. **Country codes** include: Australia 61; New Zealand 64; South Africa 27; U.K. 44; U.S. and Canada 1. Alternatively, you can access an Irish international operator at 114. Note that to call the North from the Republic, you dial 08 plus the regional phone code (*without* dropping the initial zero) plus the number. Phone rates tend to be highest in the morning, lower in the evening, and lowest on Sunday and late at night. International calls from the Republic are cheapest during **economy periods.** The low-rate period to North America is Monday through Friday 10pm to 8am and Saturday and Sunday all day; to EU countries it's Monday through Friday 6pm to 8am and Saturday and Sunday all day; to Australia and New Zealand call Monday through Friday 2 to 8pm and midnight to 8am and Saturday and Sunday all day. There are no economy rates to the rest of the world. Long distance calls within the Republic are also cheapest Monday through Friday 6pm to 8am and Saturday and Sunday all day.

The expensive alternative to dialing direct or using a calling card is using an international operator to place a **collect call.** An English-speaking operator from your home nation can be reached by dialing the appropriate service provider listed above, and they will typically place a collect call even if you don't possess one of their phone cards.

CALLING HOME FROM THE REPUBLIC OF IRELAND
Operator (not available from card phones): 10.
Directory inquiries (for the Republic and the North): 1190.
International directory inquiries: 1197.
Telecom Éireann information number: (1800) 330 330.
International operator: 114.
International access code: 00.

CALLING WITHIN IRELAND
The simplest way to call within the country is to use a coin-operated phone. Using Irish pay phones can be tricky. Public phones come in two varieties: **coin phones** and **card phones.** Public coin phones will sometimes make change (it depends on the order in which you insert coins) but private pay phones (called "one-armed bandits") in hotels and restaurants do not—once you plunk in your change, you can kiss it good-bye. In any pay phone, do not insert money until you are asked to, or until your call goes through. The frightening pip, pip noise that the phone makes as you wait for it to start ringing is normal and can last up to 10 seconds. Local calls cost 20p on standard pay phones; "one-armed bandits" can charge 30p or whatever they please. Local calls are not unlimited—one unit pays for four minutes.

The smart option for non-local calls is buying a **prepaid phone card,** which carries a certain amount of phone time depending on the card's denomination. The time is measured in minutes or talk units (e.g. one unit/one minute), and the card usually has a toll-free access telephone number and a personal identification number (PIN). Most cards contain the pin on the card itself. To make a phone call, you dial the access number, enter your PIN, and at the voice prompt, enter the phone number of the party you're trying to reach. A computer tells you how much time or how many units you have left on your card. Phone rates tend to be highest in the morning, lower in the evening, and lowest on Sunday and late at night. News agents sell phone cards in denominations of £2, £8, or £15. For calls direct-dialed to the U.S. during the cheapest hours, one unit lasts eight seconds, so a 100-unit (£15) card lasts for 13.3 minutes. Talk fast. Card phones have a digital display that ticks off the perilous plunge your units are taking. When the unit number starts flashing, you may push the eject button on the card phone; you can then pull out your expired calling card and replace it with a fresh one. If you try to wait until your card's units fall to zero, you'll be disconnected. Eject your card early and use that last remaining unit or two for a local call.

CALLING WITHIN AND FROM NORTHERN IRELAND AND LONDON
Operator: 100.
Directory inquiries: 192.
International operator: 155.
International directory assistance: 153.
International access code: 00.

Pay phones in Northern Ireland initially charge 10p for local calls; most calls cost 20p. A series of harsh beeps warns you to insert more money when your time is up. The digital display ticks off your credit in 1p increments so you can watch your pence in suspense. Unused coins are returned are only sometimes returned. You may use all remaining credit on a second call by pressing the "follow on call" button (often marked "FC"). Phones don't accept 1p, 2p, or 5p coins. The dial tone is a continuous purring sound; a repeated double-purr means the line is ringing. Northern **Phonecards,** in denominations of £2, £5, £10, and £20, are sold at post offices and newsstands. The £5 and higher denominations provide extra credit. Phone booths that take cards (the majority) are marked by yellow signs; coin booths are marked with white signs. In Belfast, British Telecom card phones, labeled in green and blue, take phonecards, credit cards (Visa or MasterCard/Access), and change.

Reduced rates for most international calls from the UK apply Monday through Friday 8pm to 8am, and weekends all day. Rates are highest Monday through Friday 3 to 5pm. The low-rate period to Australia and New Zealand is daily midnight to 7am and 2:30 to 7:30pm. Rates to the Republic of Ireland go down Monday through Friday 6pm to 8am and weekends.

EMAIL AND INTERNET

Let's Go lists and indexes **internet access,** which is steadily increasing in Ireland. **Electronic mail (email)** is an attractive option of staying in touch. With a minimum of computer knowledge and a little planning, you can beam messages anywhere for no per-message charges. For information on internet accessibility world-wide, contact cyber-star.com, cybercaptive.com, netcafeguide.com, which lista host of connections to sites supplying further internet information on any country.

Internet access is available in Irish cities in privately owned cafes and occassionally in libraries. Thirty minutes of access costs £3-5. One strategy is to befriend college students as you go and use their email accounts. Other free, web-based email providers include Hotmail (www.hotmail.com), RocketMail (www.rocketmail.com), and Yahoo! Mail (www.yahoo.com). Many free email providers are funded by advertising and some may require subscribers to fill out a questionnaire. Almost every internet search engine has a free email service.

Travelers who have the luxury of a laptop with them can use a **modem** to call an internet service provider. Long-distance phone cards specifically intended for such calls can defray normally high phone charges. Check with your long-distance phone provider to see if they offer this option.

COUNTY DUBLIN

Dublin and its suburbs form a single economic and commercial unit, the majority of which can be reached by DART (Dublin Area Rapid Transit), suburban rail, or Dublin buses. On weekends, the city center teems with suburbanites, tourists, and international hipsters looking for a good time. Despite the homogenizing effects of a booming economy and sprawling development, Dublin's suburbs offer a competitive, less polluted alternative to the city; at the same time, they host far too many crowds to fit the bill of Ireland's romanticized rural villages. County Dublin boasts beautiful beaches, literary history attractions, imposing castles, and monastic ruins, but the chief impression of most visitors is that this jet-setting metropolis has left the relaxed, agricultural lifestyle of the rest of the island far behind.

HIGHLIGHTS OF COUNTY DUBLIN

- Explore Ireland's **National Museums** (p. 113), taking in Celtic Goldwork, a Carravagio, and the skeleton of an ancient Irish Elkhorn.
- Window shop on **Grafton Street** (p. 112), then head around the corner to **Temple Bar** (p. 114) for a night of tomfoolery in its pubs and clubs.
- The late 16th-century campus of **Trinity College** shelters the **Book of Kells** (p. 111), a four-volume medieval edition of the Gospels with gold illumination.
- Follow the footsteps of Joyce from his **Martello Tower** (p. 129) at Dún Laoghaire and along **O'Connell St.** (p. 116), making stops at pubs that hosted such literary giants as Samuel Beckett, Brendan Behan, Bernard Shaw, and Flann O'Brien.
- Check out the blond in the black skirt at the **Guinness Hopstore** (p. 115).
- Get a glimpse into the rebellion of Easter 1916 at **Kilmainham Gaol** (p. 116).
- Escape the city and head to **Howth** (p. 125) for a breath of fresh sea air.

▐ GETTING AROUND THE COUNTY

Rail lines, bus lines (both state-run and private), and the national highway system radiate from Ireland's capital. Major highways **N5** and **N6** lead to **N4**, **N8**, **N9**, and **N10** all feed into **N7**, dumping buses and cars into Dublin's vehicular sphere. Because inter-city transport is so Dublin-centric, you may find it more convenient in the long run to arrange your travel in other parts of the Republic while you're in the capital. Students may wish to get a TravelSave stamp for bus and rail discounts (see **Practical Information,** p. 94); for more information on national and international transportation, see **Essentials,** p. 66.

BY BUS

The lime-green **Dublin Buses'** service to the entire county is extensive. The buses, which come in a variety of shapes and sizes all sporting "db" logos, run from 5am to 11:30pm and comprehensively cover the city and its suburbs: north to **Howth, Balbriggan,** and **Malahide;** west to **Rathcoole, Maynooth,** and **Celbridge;** and south to **Blessington, Enniskerry, Dún Laoghaire,** and **Bray.** Buses are cheap (£0.55-1.10), and most frequent between 8am and 6pm (generally every 8-20min., other times every 30-45min.). Most bus routes end or begin at the city center, at stops located near Christ Church, the Trinity College facade, St. Stephen's Green, O'Connell St., or Parnell St. Bus stands along the quays post timetables detailing routes around the city center and their termini. It's easiest to figure out bus routes by using the *Map of Greater Dublin* (£4.10) in conjunction with the *Dublin Bus Timetable* (£1.50). Both are available from newsagents and the **Dublin Bus Office** at 59 Upper O'Connell St., where free handouts about individual routes are also available (see **Getting Around the City,** p. 92). Dublin Bus runs the **NiteLink** service to the suburbs (Th-Sa nights at 12:30am, 1:30am, 2:30am, and 3:30am; £2.50, no passes valid). Tickets for the NiteLink are sold at the Dublin Bus Office, by Nitelink bus drivers, and from a van parked on the corner of Westmoreland and College St. next to the Trinity College entrance. Some city center shops also carry tickets; look for the NiteLink sign in windows. The **Airlink** service (#747 and 748) connects **Dublin airport** to the Central Bus Station (£3) and Heuston Station (£3.50), with stops including O'Connell St. (every 10-15min., 6:30am-11:45pm). **Wheelchair-accessible buses** are limited: the only options are the **OmniLink** service (#300), which cruises around Clontarf (60p), and the #3 bus from Whitehall to Sandymount (via O'Connell St.).

Travel passes were not designed for the casual traveler; each pass has a time limit that requires several trips a day to validate its price. **Travel Wide** passes offer unlimited rides for a day or a week. (Day £3.30; week £13, students with Travel-Save stamp £10.) Be warned, though, that a Dublin Bus week runs from Sunday to Saturday inclusive, no matter when you purchase the pass. In other words, a weekly pass bought Friday night will expire after only one day. Dublin Bus months, similarly, are calendar months. Other tickets allow for both bus and suburban rail/DART travel. (Adult one-day **short hop** £4.50, weekly £16, monthly £44.) For most travelers, the only worthwhile prepaid ticket might be the **2 Easy Range**, which gives two bus rides within a month and potentially more hassle than savings. (£1.10-2.50, depending on the distance to be covered.) All special tickets are available at the bus office and at roughly 250 newsagents around the city; an ISIC card is required for student rates.

THE COUNTY BY TRAIN

Co. Dublin's suburban rail network reaches a sizable range of outlying areas. The electric **DART** trains run frequently up and down the coast, serving the suburbs on both the north and south sides. The trains put buses to shame in terms of cost and speed, but only reach a limited number of destinations. Fortunately, that number will continue to increase over the next couple years. From **Connolly, Pearse,** and **Tara St.** stations in the city center, the DART shoots all the way south past **Bray** and north to **Howth.** The DART runs every 10-15min. from roughly 6:30am to 11:30pm; a ride costs £0.55-1.10. Tickets are sold in the station and usually must be presented at the end of the trip. The orange trains of the **suburban rail** network continue north to **Malahide, Donabate,** and **Drogheda;** south to **Wicklow** and **Arklow;** and west to **Maynooth** and **Mullingar.** These trains all leave from Connolly Station. All but the line west stop at Tara St. and Pearse Stations as well. Trains to **Kildare** leave from Heuston Station. Trains are frequent every day (roughly 30 per day) except Sundays. Complete DART/suburban rail timetables are available at many stations (50p). **Bicycles** are never permitted on DART trains, sometimes on suburban rail lines (ask first), and usually on mainline trains for a small fee (£6 single, £12 return). Special rail and bus/rail tickets are generally cost-effective only for those with a transport addiction.

DUBLIN

In a country known for its relaxed pace of life and rural sanctity, Dublin stands out for its international style and boundless energy. The city's offerings have expanded enormously with the booming Irish economy. The Irish who live outside of Dublin worry that it has taken on the characteristics of big cities everywhere: crime, rapid social change, and a weakness for short-lived trends. Yet, while Dublin may seem harsh by Irish standards, it's still as friendly a major city as you'll find. While not cosmopolitan in the sense of London or New York, Dublin feels more European than either. It boasts vibrant theater, music, and literary productions. A new generation of pubs need not fight with their elders—there's plenty of business to go around, for now at least. New accommodations, museums, concert venues, and construction projects litter the city.

Ireland is changing at a startling pace, and Dublin, with close to a third of the country's population in its environs, is at the forefront of those changes. Fueled by

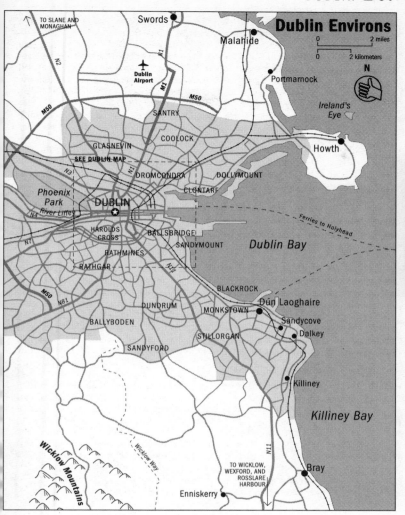

Dublin Environs

0   2 miles
0   2 kilometers

N

TO SLANE AND MONAGHAN

Swords

Malahide

Portmarnock

Dublin Airport

Ireland's Eye

SANTRY

COOLOCK

Howth

GLASNEVIN

SEE DUBLIN MAP

DROMCONDRA

DOLLYMOUNT

CLONTARF

Phoenix Park

DUBLIN

River Liffey

Ferries to Holyhead

HAROLDS CROSS

BALLSBRIDGE

Dublin Bay

SANDYMOUNT

RATHMINES

RATHGAR

BLACKROCK

Dún Laoghaire

DUNDRUM

MONKSTOWN

Sandycove

BALLYBODEN

Dalkey

STILLORGAN

SANDYFORD

Killiney

Killiney Bay

Wicklow Mountains

Wicklow Way

TO WICKLOW, WEXFORD, AND ROSSLARE HARBOUR

Bray

Enniskerry

the EU and international and rural immigration, the city's zooming cultural and economic growth has led to the rocketship success of Temple Bar as the new nightlife hub. Smithfields, west across the River Liffey, is undergoing development to make it the next cultural center. Despite all the change, the image of old Ireland persists in the castles, cathedrals, and fine pubs that saturate the city.

The first record of human settlement around Dublin is a map made by the Greek scholar Ptolemy, who called the site Eblana. After years of visiting, the Vikings eventually set up a permanent town, Dubh Linn ("Black Pool"), around the modern College Green. The Viking Thingmote, or hill of assembly, stood there as the administrative center for both Viking powers and the Norman Pale until William III's 1690 victory at the Battle of the Boyne. During the ensuing Protestant Ascendancy (see p. 10), the Irish Parliament House sprang up near the old Viking center. The period's Protestant English culture remains evident today in the architecture of Dublin's tidy Georgian squares.

Dublin

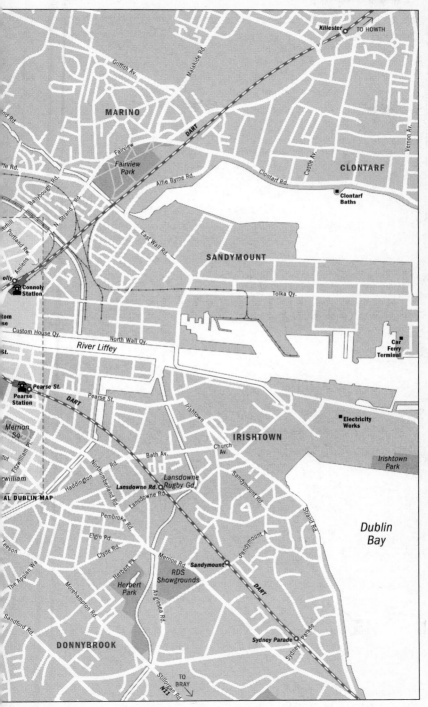

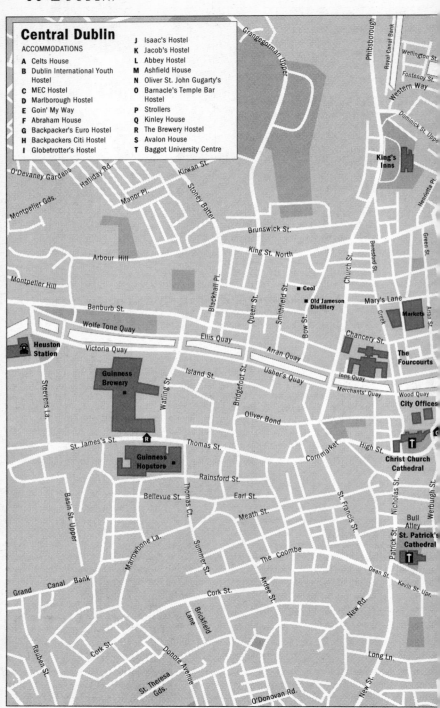

Central Dublin

ACCOMMODATIONS

A Celts House
B Dublin International Youth
   Hostel
C MEC Hostel
D Marlborough Hostel
E Goin' My Way
F Abraham House
G Backpacker's Euro Hostel
H Backpackers Citi Hostel
I Globetrotter's Hostel

J Isaac's Hostel
K Jacob's Hostel
L Abbey Hostel
M Ashfield House
N Oliver St. John Gugarty's
O Barnacle's Temple Bar
   Hostel
P Strollers
Q Kinley House
R The Brewery Hostel
S Avalon House
T Baggot University Centre

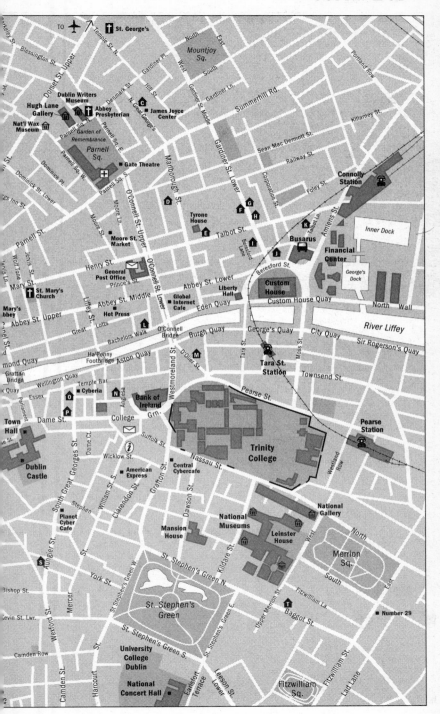

The capital of Ireland since the late 17th century, Dublin's blend of cultures has occasioned extraordinary intellectual and literary communities. From Swift and Burke to Joyce and Beckett, Dublin has produced so many great writers that nearly every street contains a literary landmark. Pubs continue to shelter much of Dublin's public life and world-renowned music scene. Dublin may not look like the "Emerald Isle" that the tourist brochures promote, but its people still embody the notorious charm and warmth of the Irish.

▣ GETTING AROUND THE CITY

For more on national and international transportation, see **Essentials,** p. 66.

COUNTY DUBLIN

Airport: Dublin Airport (tel. 844 4900). **Dublin buses** #41, 41B, and 41C run to Eden Quay in the city center with stops along the way (every 20min., £1.10). The **Airlink shuttle** runs non-stop directly to Busáras Central Bus Station and O'Connell St. (30-40min., every 10-15min., £3) and on to Heuston Station (50min., £3.50), but it's hardly worth the price in comparison to the #41 line. **Airport Express buses** (tel. 844 4265) go to Busáras and O'Connell St. (30min.; M-Sa 6:30am-10:50pm, Su 7:10am-11pm; departs every 15-30min.; £2.50). A **taxi** from the airport to the city center costs roughly £12-15. Wheelchair-accessible cabs may be available; call ahead (see **Taxis**).

Trains: Irish Rail, Iarnród Éireann (EER-ann-road AIR-ann) has a travel center at 35 Lower Abbey St. (tel. 836 6222). Its information desks and booking windows at all three of the city's major stations may have longer lines. You can purchase a ticket in advance at the center, or buy one at a station 20min. before departure time. The travel center also spews data on DART, suburban trains, international train tickets, and cross-channel ferries. Open M-F 9am-5pm, Sa 9am-1pm. For specific routes, you can also call the 24hr. "talking timetables," which recite schedules of trains to Belfast (tel. 855 4477), Cork (tel. 855 4400), Galway/Westport (tel. 855 4422), Killarney/Tralee (tel. 855 4466), Limerick (tel. 855 4411), Sligo (tel. 855 4455), Waterford (tel. 855 4433), and Wexford/Rosslare (tel. 855 4488). Two train stations have nighttime phone lines as well: Connolly Station (tel. 703 2358, M-Sa 5:30-9pm and Su 4:30-8:30pm) and Heuston Station (tel. 703 2131, M-Sa 5:30-8pm and 9-10pm, Sa 7:30am-8pm and 9-10pm, Su 8am-10pm). **Connolly Station**, Amiens St. (tel. 836 3333), is north of the Liffey and close to Busáras Bus Station. Buses #20, 20A, and 90 at the station head south of the river, and the DART runs to Tara on the south quay, but it's faster to walk. Trains to **Belfast** (2¼hr.; 8 per day, Su 5 per day; £17), **Wexford** via **Rosslare** (3hr.; 3 per day, Su 2 per day; £10.50), and **Sligo** (3½hr.; 3 per day, F 4 per day, Su 3 per day; £13.50). **Heuston Station** (tel. 703 2132) is south of Victoria Quay, well west of the city center, a 25min. walk from Trinity College. Buses #26, 51, and 79 go from Heuston to the city center. Trains to **Limerick** (2¼hr., 9 per day, £25), **Galway** (2½hr.; 5 per day, Su 4 per day; £15, F and Su £21), **Waterford** (2½hr.; 4 per day, Su 3 per day; £12), **Cork** (3½hr.; 8 per day, F 11 per day, Su 6 per day; £32), and **Tralee** (4½hr.; 6 per day, F 7 per day, Su 4 per day; £33.50). Any of the Dublin buses heading east will take you into the city. **Pearse Station,** just east of Trinity College on Pearse St. and Westland Row, receives southbound trains from Connolly Station. Bus #90 (every 10min., 60p) makes the circuit of Connolly, Heuston, and Pearse Stations and Busáras. Connolly and Pearse are also **DART** stations serving the north and south coasts (see **Getting Around the County,** p. 85).

Buses: Info available at the **Dublin Bus Office,** 59 O'Connell St. (tel. 873 4222 or 872 0000); the Bus Éireann window is open M-F 9am-5pm, Sa 9am-1pm. Inter-city buses to Dublin arrive at **Busáras Central Bus Station,** Store St. (tel. 836 6111), directly behind the Customs House and next to Connolly Station. Bus Éireann runs to **Waterford** (2¾hr.; 7 per day, Su 5 per day; £7), **Wexford** (2¾hr.; 10 per day, Su 7 per day; £7), **Belfast** (3hr.; 7 per day, Su 4 per day; £10.50), **Rosslare Harbour** (3hr.; 10 per day, Su 7 per day; £9), **Limerick** (3¼hr.; 13 per day, Su 7 per day; £10), **Sligo** (4hr., 3 per day, £8.50), **Galway** (4hr.; 14 per day, Su 4 per day; £8), **Derry** (4¼hr.; 4 per day, F 5 per day, Su 4 per day; £10.50), **Donegal Town** (4¼hr.; 5 per day, F 6 per day, Su 3 per day; £10), **Shannon Airport** via a shuttle connection every ½hr. from Limerick (4½hr., 13 per day, £14), **Cork** (4½hr.; 4 per day, Su 3 per day; £12), **Westport** (5hr.; 3 per day, Su 1 per day; £10), **Tralee** (5½hr.; 8 per day, Su 9 per day; £14), and **Killarney** (6½hr., 5 per day, £14). For more information on inter- and intra-city buses, see **Getting Around the County,** p. 85. New anti-monopoly legislation has increased the number of private bus companies. If the tourist office is not yet allowed to help you out here, it's possible that **PAMBO** (Private Association of Motor Bus Owners), 32 Lower Abbey St. (tel. 878 8422), can provide the names and numbers of private bus companies serving particular destinations. Open M-F 10am-5pm.

Ferries: Bookings in **Irish Rail office** (above). **Stena Line** ferries arrive from **Holyhead** at the **Dún Laoghaire** (p. 132) ferry terminal (tel. 204 7777), from which the **DART** shuttles passengers to Connolly Station, Pearse Station, or Tara St. Station in the city center (£1.30). **Buses** #7, 7A, and 8 go from Georges St. in Dún Laoghaire to Eden Quay (£1.30), though the DART is the easier way to go. **Irish Ferries** (24hr. tel. (1890) 313 131; www.irishferries.ie) arrive from Holyhead at the **Dublin Port** (tel. 607 5665), from which buses #53 and 53A run every hour to Busáras (80p); to get to the ferryport, Dublin Bus also runs connection buses timed to fit the ferry schedule (£2-2.50). **Merchant Ferries** also docks at the Dublin ferryport and runs a route to **Liverpool** (8hr.; 2 per day; £40, car £150-170); booking for Merchant is only available from **Gerry Feeney,** 19 Eden Quay (tel. 819 2999). **The Isle of Man Steam Packet Company** (tel. 44 (1800) 551 743) also docks at Dublin Port, and runs services to its own country.

Local Transportation: Dublin Bus, 59 O'Connell St. (tel 873 4222 or 872 0000). Open M 8:30am-5:30pm, Tu-F 9am-5:30pm, Sa 9am-1pm. See **Getting Around the County,** p. 85.

Taxis: National Radio Cabs, 40 James St. (tel. 677 2222 or 836 5555). **Blue Cabs** (tel. 676 1111), **ABC** (tel. 285 5444), and **City Group Taxi** (tel. 872 7272) have wheelchair-accessible taxis (call in advance). All 24hr. £2.20 plus 90p per mi.; 80p call-in charge. It's easiest to pick up cabs at numerous taxi stands around the city, including in front of Trinity, and on Lower Abbey St. at the bus station, and on Parnell St.

Car Rental: Budget, 151 Lower Drumcondra Rd. (tel. 837 9611), and at the airport. Summer from £35 per day, £165 per week; winter £30, £140. Ages 23-75. **Argus,** 59 Terenure Rd. East (tel. 490 4444; fax 490 6328). Also in the tourist office on Suffolk St. and the airport. Summer from £45 per day, £230 per week; winter £140 per week. Ages 26-70; seasonable prices by special arrangement for ages 23-26. **Alamo,** Dublin Airport (tel. 844 4086). Summer from £35 per day, £195 per week; winter £30, £175. Ages 21-75; additional insurance cost for ages 21-24. If booked early enough, many rental agencies offer free pickup or delivery.

Bike Rental: see **By Bicycle,** p. 72. **Raleigh Rent-A-Bike,** Kylemore Rd. (tel. 626 1333). Limited one-way rental system (£10 surcharge). £10 per day; £40 per week; deposit £50. Raleigh dealers close to city center are **MacDonald Cycles,** 38 Wexford St. (tel. 475 2586), and **Cycle Ways,** 185-6 Parnell St. (tel. 873 4748). The cheaper **Irish Cycle Hire** (tel. (041) 41067) runs out of the An Óige youth hostel. £6-7 per day, £30-35 per week; deposit £30. Open daily 9:30am-6pm. **Dublin Bike Tours** (tel. 679 0889), behind the Kinlay House hostel on Lord Edward St., also rents and provides advice on route planning. £10 per day, students £8; per week £40, £35; ID deposit.

Bike Repair and Storage: Square Wheel Cycleworks, Temple Lane South (tel. 679 0838), off Dame St. Excellent advice on bicycle touring and expert repair; storage 30p per half-day, 60p per day, £2.50 per week. Open M-F 8:30am-6:30pm. **Dublin Bike Tours** (see **bike rental;** tel. 679 0889) has a smaller storage space, roughly £5 per week. **Cycle Ways** (see **bike rental;** tel. 873 4748), will do same-day repairs.

Hitchhiking: Since Co. Dublin is well served by bus and rail, there is no good reason to hitch, and *Let's Go* does not recommend it. Hitchers coming to Dublin generally ask drivers to drop them off at one of the myriad bus and DART stops outside the city. Those leaving Dublin ride a bus to the city outskirts where the motorways begin. Buses #25, 25A, 66, 66A, 67, and 67A from Middle Abbey St. travel to Lucan Rd., which turns into N4 (to Galway and the West). To find a ride to Cork, Waterford, and Limerick (N7), hitchers usually take bus #51, 51B, 68, or 69 from Fleet St. to Aston Quay to Naas Rd. (pronounced "nace"). N11 (to Wicklow, Wexford, and Rosslare) can be reached by buses #46 and 84 from Eden Quay, or #46A from Fleet St. toward Stillorgan Rd. N3 (to Donegal and Sligo) can be reached on buses #38 from Lower Abbey St. or #39 from Middle Abbey St. to Navan Rd. Buses #33, 41, and 41A from Eden Quay toward Swords send hitchers on their way to N1 (Belfast and Dundalk).

◆ ORIENTATION

The **River Liffey** is the natural divide between Dublin's North and South Sides. The more famous sights, posh stores, excellent restaurants, and Heuston Station are on the **South Side**. The majority of hostels, the bus station, and Connolly Station sprout up on the **North Side**. Over all, Dublin is refreshingly compact, if complicated by the abundance of names each street adopts during its passage though town. Buying a map with a street index is a great idea and time saver. Collins publishes the invaluable, color-coded *Handy Map of Dublin* (£4.64), available at the tourist office and most book stores. For less handiness but more detail, get the *Ordinance Survey Dublin Street Map* (£4.50); its hefty street index is in a separate booklet. The streets running alongside the Liffey are called **quays** ("keys"); their names change every block. Each bridge over the river also has its own name, and streets change names as they cross. If a street is split into "Upper" and "Lower," then the "Lower" is always the part of the street closer to the mouth of the Liffey.

The core of Dublin is circumscribed by **North** and **South Circular Rd.**, which have their own assortment of name changes. Almost all sights are located within this area, and you can walk from one end to the other in about 40min. **O'Connell St.**, three blocks west of the Busáras Central Bus Station, is the primary link between north and south Dublin. South of the Liffey, O'Connell St. becomes **Westmoreland St.**, passes **Fleet St.** on the right, curves around Trinity College Dublin on the left, and then becomes **Grafton St.** One block south of the Liffey, **Fleet St.** becomes **Temple Bar.** While Temple Bar is the name of a street, it usually applies to the area as a whole, which has ballooned in the last decade with batallions of students and tourists hitting its pubs nightly. During the day, its eclectic array of funky restaurants and assortment of art museums and workshops attract better behaved crowds. **Dame St.** runs parallel to Temple Bar with Trinity College as its terminus, and defines the southern edge of the district. **Trinity College** functions as the nerve center of Dublin's cultural activity, drawing legions of bookshops and student-oriented pubs into its orbit. The college touches the northern end of **Grafton St.**, where street entertainers and world-class shoppers appreciate each other. Grafton's southern end opens onto **St. Stephen's Green**, a sizable public park.

Merchandise and services on the north side of the Liffey tend to be more affordable than their southern counterparts. **Henry St.** and **Mary St.** comprise a pedestrian shopping zone that intersects with O'Connell just after the **General Post Office (GPO)**, two blocks from the Liffey. The North Side has the reputation of being a rougher area, especially after sunset. This reputation may not be wholly deserved; avoid walking in unfamiliar areas on either side of the Liffey at night, especially if you're alone. Phoenix Park should definitely be avoided at night.

⑦ PRACTICAL INFORMATION

TOURIST AND FINANCIAL SERVICES

Tourist Information: Main Office, Dublin Tourist Centre, Suffolk St. (tel. (1850) 230 330 in Ireland, (0171) 493 3201 in the U.K., (066) 979 2083 from outside both; email information@dublintoursim.ie; www.visitdublin.com). From Connolly Train Station, walk left down Amiens St., take a right onto Lower Abbey St., pass Busáras, and continue until you come to O'Connell St. Turn left, cross the bridge, and walk past Trinity College; Suffolk St. will be on your right. The Centre is in a converted church. Accommodation service with £1 booking fee and 10% non-refundable deposit; £2 charge to book outside Dublin. Credit card bookings by phone (tel. (0800) 6686 6866; email reservations@dublintourism.ie). **American Express** maintains a branch office with currency exchange here (tel. 605 7709). **Bus Éireann** and **Irish Ferries** have representatives on hand to provide info and tickets. Irish Ferries desk open all year M-F 9am-5:30pm. **Argus Rent a Car** (tel. 490 4444; fax 490 6328; email info@argus-rentacar.com; www.argus-rentacar.com) has a desk here (tel. 607 7701). Argus desk open M-Sa 9am-5pm. A list of car rental agencies is also available from the Bord Fáilte folk. Office open July-Aug. M-Sa 9am-7pm, Su 10:30am-2:30pm; Sept.-June M-Sa 9am-6pm. Reservation desks close one hour early.

Branch Tourist Offices: Dublin Airport. Open daily 8am-10pm; July and Aug. daily 8am-1:30pm. **Dún Laoghaire Harbour,** Ferry Terminal Building. Open daily 10am-6pm (subject to ferry arrivals). **Tallaght,** The Square. Open M-Sa 9:30am-noon and 12:30pm-5pm. **Baggot St.** Open M-Sa 9:30am-12:30pm and 1-5pm. **13 Upper O'Connell St.** Open M-Sa 10am-1:30pm and 2-5:30pm. The latter four branches are well-stocked and less crowded than the airport and Suffolk St. branches. All telephone inquiries handled by the central office.

Northern Ireland Tourist Board: 16 Nassau St. (tel. 679 1977 or (1850) 230 230). Books accommodations in the North. Open M-F 9am-5:30pm, Sa 10am-5pm.

Temple Bar Information Centre: 18 Eustace St. (tel. (1850) 260 027). Heading away from Trinity College, make a right off Dame St. where it intersects both Eustace and Great Georges St. Lots of brochures about the area's frequent outdoor events, and other topics, such as *Where to Go, Eat, Shop, Drink, and Stay* in Temple Bar. Open June-Sept. M-F 9am-6pm, Sa 11am-4pm, Su noon-4pm; Oct.-May M-F 9am-6pm, Sa noon-6pm.

Community and Youth Information Centre: Sackville Pl. (tel. 878 6844), on Marlborough St. Library with a wealth of resources on careers, culture, outings, travel, and tourist information, hostels (no bookings), camping, roommates, sporting events, counseling, and referrals. Info on youth and special-needs groups. Open M-W 9:30am-1pm and 2-6pm, Th-Sa 9:30am-1pm and 2-5pm.

Budget Travel: usit NOW (Irish student travel agency), 19-21 Aston Quay (tel. 679 8833), near O'Connell Bridge. The place to seek Irish travel discounts. ISIC, HI, and EYC cards; TravelSave stamps £8. Photo booths £3. Big discounts, especially for people under 26 and ISIC cardholders. They will book you into Kinlay House (see **Hostels**), a hostel run by usit, for a £1 deposit. Internet access £1 per 15min., £2.50 per 45min. with ISIC card. Open M-W and F 9am-6pm, Th 9am-8pm, Sa 10am-5:30pm. **Dust Travel** (tel. 677 5076), located inside Trinity College, also specializes in student travel. Turn left inside the main gate. Open M-F 9:30-10:30am and noon-5pm.

An Óige Head Office (Irish Youth Hostel Association/HI), 61 Mountjoy St. (tel. 830 4555), at Wellington St. Follow O'Connell St. north, continuing through all its name changes. Mountjoy St. is on the left, about 20min. from O'Connell Bridge. Book and pay for HI hostels here. Also sells package bike and rail tours. The *An Óige Handbook* lists all HI hostels in Ireland and Northern Ireland. Membership £10, under 18 £4. Open M-F 9:30am-5:30pm, Sa 10am-12:30pm.

Embassies: Australia, 2nd fl., Fitzwilton House, Wilton Terr. (tel. 676 1517; fax 678 5185). Open M-Th 8:30am-12:30pm and 1:30-4:30pm, F 9am-noon. **Canada,** 65 St. Stephen's Green South (tel. 478 1988). Open M-F 9am-1pm and 2-4:30pm. **New Zealand** embassy in London: New Zealand House, 80 Haymarket, London SW1Y 4TQ. From Ireland, dial 00 44 (171) 930 8422. **South Africa,** 2nd fl., Alexandra House, Earlsfort Centre (tel. 661 5553; email saembdub@iol.ie). Open M-F 8:30am-5pm. **U.K.,** 29 Merrion Rd. (tel. 269 5211). Open M-F 9am-5pm. **U.S.,** 42 Elgin Rd., Ballsbridge (tel. 668 8777). Open M-F 8:30am-5pm.

Banks: Bank of Ireland, AIB, and **TSB** branches with bureaux de change and **24hr. ATMs** cluster on Lower O'Connell St., Grafton St., and in the Suffolk and Dame St. areas. Most bank branches are open M-F 10am-4pm. Bureaux de change also found in the General Post Office and in the tourist office main branch.

American Express: 61-3 South William St. (tel. 677 5555; fax 677 5577), at the back of Grafton St. Traveler's check refunds (tel. 618 5588). Currency exchange; no commission for AmEx Traveler's Checks. Client mail held. Open M-F 9am-5:30pm. Smaller branches inside the tourist center on Suffolk St. and at 43 Nassau St.

LOCAL SERVICES

Luggage Storage: Connolly Station. £2 per item. Open M-Sa 7:40am-9:15pm, Su 9:10am-9:45pm. **Heuston Station.** £1.50, £2.50, or £3.50 per item, depending on size. Open daily 6:30am-10:30pm. **Busáras.** £2 per item, backpacks £3. Open M-Sa 8am-7:45pm, Su 10am-5:45pm.

Lost Property: Connolly Station (tel. 703 2363), **Heuston Station** (tel. 703 2102), **Busáras** (tel. 703 2489), and **Dublin Bus** (tel. 703 3055).

Library: Dublin Corporation Central Library, Henry and Moore St. (tel. 873 4333), in the ILAC Centre. Video and listening facilities and a children's library. Telephone directories on shelves for EU countries and on microfilm for U.S. and Canada. Open M-Th 10am-8pm, F-Sa 10am-5pm.

Women's Resources: Women's Aid helpline (tel. (1800) 341 900) staffed 10am-10pm. Info on legal matters, and support groups. **Dublin Well Woman Centre,** 35 Lower Liffey St. (tel. 872 8051) is a private health center for women; it also runs a **clinic** (tel. 668 3714) at 67 Pembroke Rd.

Gay, Lesbian, and Bisexual Information: See p. 123.

Ticket Agencies: HMV record stores and **TicketMaster** have something of a marriage; head to the HMV on Grafton St., the HMV ticket desk at the Suffolk St. tourist office, or call 817 0592.

Laundry: The Laundry Shop, 191 Parnell St. (tel. 872 3541). Closest to Busáras and the North Side hostels. Wash and dry £4.20-5. Open M-F 8am-7pm, Sa 9am-6pm. **All-American Launderette,** 40 South Great Georges St. (tel. 677 2779). Wash and dry £4, serviced £4.60. Powder 50p. Open M-Sa 8:30am-7pm, Su 10am-6pm.

EMERGENCY AND COMMUNICATIONS

Emergency: Dial 999; no coins required.

Garda: Dublin Metro Headquarters, Harcourt Sq. (tel. 478 5295), Store St. Station (tel. 855 7761), Fitzgibbon St. Station (tel. 836 3113). **Garda Confidential Report Line:** Tel. (1800) 666 111.

Counseling and Support: Tourist Victim Support, Parliament St. (tel. 478 5295). If you are robbed, this organization will help you find accommodations and put you in contact with your Embassy or family; a loss or crime report must first be filed with a Garda station. **Samaritans,** 112 Marlborough St. (tel. (1850) 609 090 or 872 7700), for the depressed, or suicidal. 24hr. **Rape Crisis Centre,** 70 Lower Leeson St. (24hr. hotline tel. (1800) 778 888; office tel. 661 4911). Office open M-F 8:30am-7pm, Sa 9am-3pm. **Cura,** 30 South Anne St. (tel. 671 0598), Catholic-funded support for women with unplanned pregnancies. The **Dublin AIDS Alliance,** 53 Parnell Sq. (tel. 873 3799), offers information, and various community support resources. The **AIDS Helpline** (tel. 872 4277) is manned M-F 7-9pm, Sa 3-5pm. **Alcoholics Anonymous,** 109 South Circular Rd. (tel. 453 8998). Office staffed M-Th 9:30am-1pm and 2-5:30pm, F 9:30am-1pm and 2-4:30pm. After-hours (tel. 679 5967). Open M-F 6:30-10pm and Sa-Su 10am-10pm. **Narcotics Anonymous** (tel. 830 0944), 24hr. phone service.

Pharmacy: O'Connell's, 55 Lower O'Connell St. (tel. 873 0427). Convenient to city bus routes. Open M-Sa 8:30am-10pm, Su 10am-10pm. Other branches are scattered around the city center, including Grafton St.

Hospital: St. James's Hospital, James St. (tel. 453 7941). Served by bus #123. **Mater Misericordiae Hospital,** Eccles St. (tel. 830 1122 or 830 8788), off Lower Dorset St. Served by buses #10, 11, 13, 16, 121, and 122. **Beaumont Hospital,** Beaumont Rd. (tel. 837 7755 or 809 3000). Served by buses #27B, 51A, 101, 103, and 300. The conglomerate **Tallaght Hospital** (tel. 414 2000), farther south, is served by buses #49, 49A, 50, 54A, 65, 65B, 75, 76, 77, 77A, 201, 202.

Post Office: General Post Office (GPO), O'Connell St. (tel. 705 7000). Dublin is the only city in Ireland with postal codes. Even-numbered postal codes are for areas south of the Liffey, odd-numbered are for the north. *Poste Restante* pick-up at the bureau de change window. Open M-Sa 8am-8pm, Su 10am-6:30pm. **Postal code:** Dublin 1.

Internet Access: Free Internet research (not email) is available at the **central library** (see **Local Services,** above), and you can pay for access at many hostels and some shops. Specialized Internet cafes tend to be busiest in the afternoon; mornings and late evenings have shorter waits. **Global Internet Cafe,** 8 Lower O'Connell St. (tel. 878 0295), a block north of the Liffey and on the right. The widest array of services, but the wait can be up to 30min. £1.25 per 15min., students £1. Open M-Sa 10am-11pm, Su noon-10pm. **Central Cybercafe,** 6 Grafton St. (tel. 677 8298), the newest. £1.25 per 15min., students £1. **The Planet Cyber Cafe,** 23 South Great Georges St. (tel. 679 0583). The most science-fictiony; tasty nibblies, too. £1.50 per 15min. Open Su-W 10am-10pm, Th-Sa 10am-midnight. **Cyberia Cafe,** Temple Ln. South (tel. 679 7607). The smokiest. £1.50 per 15min., students £1.25. Open daily 10am-11pm.

Phones: Telecom Éireann inquiries tel. 1904, phonecard refunds tel. (1850) 337 337. Public payphones on almost every corner. For more info, see **Keeping in Touch,** p. 80.

Directory Inquiries: Tel. 1190 for all of Ireland. No charge.

PHONE CODE:	Dear, dirty 01.

■ ACCOMMODATIONS

Dublin has a handful of marvelous accommodations, but the ever-flowing glut of visitors ensures that real dumps stay open as well. Reserve as early as possible, particularly around Easter weekend, bank holiday weekends (in either Ireland or England), sporting weekends, St. Patrick's Day, around New Years, and from July through August. Private hostel rooms and B&B singles are especially hard to come by. The tourist offices books local accommodations for £1, but they only deal in Bord Fáilte-approved B&Bs and hostels, which aren't necessarily better than unapproved ones. Dublin hostels that pay the fee to be plugged into Bord Fáilte's system are Abraham House, Abbey Hostel, Avalon House, An Óige, Barnacle's Temple Bar House, the Brewery Hostel, Celts House, Globetrotter's Tourist Hostel, Goin' My Way, Isaac's, Jacob's Inn, Kinlay House, the Marlborough Hostel, Oliver St. John Gogarty's, Morehampton House, and Mount Eccles Court.

Phoenix Park may tempt the desperate, but camping there is a terrible idea. If the Garda or park rangers don't get you to leave, the threat of thieves and drug dealers should. If the accommodations listed below are full, consult Dublin Tourism's annually updated *Dublin Accommodation Guide* (£3), or ask hostel and B&B staff for referrals.

HOSTELS

To deal with the large crowds, Dublin's hostels lean toward the institutional, especially in comparison to their more personable country cousins. The beds south of the river fill up fastest, as they are closest to the city's sights and nightlife; they also tend to be more expensive than their northern counterparts. Dorm prices range from £7 to £15 per night. Always **reserve ahead** in the summer and on weekends throughout the year, especially for private rooms. Call as early as possible, even if it's a few hours before you'll arrive. The hostels in **Dún Laoghaire** (see p. 127), only a DART ride away, are an alternative to city life. All listed hostels have 24hr. reception unless otherwise noted.

■ **Barnacle's Temple Bar House,** Temple Ln. (tel. 671 6277; email templeba@barnacles.iol.ie). "The burning hot center of everything." A new, well-kept hostel right in Temple Bar. All rooms with bath and excellent security. June-Sept. 10-bed dorms £11, 6-bed dorms £13, 4-bed dorms £15, doubles and twins £20; Mar.-May and Oct. about £1 cheaper; Nov.-Feb. about £2-3 cheaper. Small continental breakfast included.

▨ **The Brewery Hostel,** 22-23 Thomas St. (tel. 453 8600; fax 453 8616; email breweryh@indigo.ie). Follow Dame St. past Christ Church through its name changes, or take bus #123. Next to Guinness and a 20min. walk to Temple Bar. The only hostel in Dublin to combine excellent facilities with a personable, community feel. Barbeque patio and a comfy lounge make it easy to meet other hostelers. Rooms are a bit snug but the beds are good. The distinct odors of Guinness production waft through the whole neighborhood, which, unfortunately, isn't the safest. All rooms with bath. Free carpark. Kitchen and small dining area open 24hr. 8-10 bedded dorms £10-12, quads £15 per person, doubles £22 per person, singles £28 per person. Continental breakfast included. Free luggage storage. Laundry £3.50.

Avalon House (IHH), 55 Aungier St. (tel. 475 0001; fax 475 0303; email info@avalon. ie). Turn off Dame St. onto Great Georges St.; the hostel is a 10min. walk down on your right. Temple Bar is within stumbling distance. Completely refurbished in 1998, and continually improving. Avalon boasts a new kitchen, email access, and top-notch security. Co-ed showers, toilets, and dorms. Dorms provide privacy with a split-level setup. This is your best bet near the city center. Bike rack. Internet access. In-house cafe with meals under £5; open noon-10pm. June-Sept. large dorms £11, 4-bed dorms £13.50, doubles £32; Mar.-May and Oct. £9, £12.50, £30; Nov.-Feb. £8, £11.50, £28. Rooms with bath add about £1. Singles also available. Small continental breakfast included; full Irish £3. Free luggage storage opened every 2hr., or get a personal luggage cage (£1). Towels £1 with £5 deposit. Non-smoking. Wheelchair accessible.

Abbey Hostel, 29 Bachelor's Walk, O'Connell Bridge (tel. 878 0700 or (1800) 306 070; email info@abbey-hostel.ie; www.indigo.ie/~abbeyhos). From O'Connell Bridge, turn left to face this emphatic yellow addition to Dublin's hostel scene. A little pricey, but it's clean, comfy, and well kept. All rooms with bath. Great location. £6 dinner; served 6-9pm. Internet access £1 per 7min. Big dorms June-Sept. £14, 6-bed dorms £16, 4-bed dorms £17; Oct. and Mar.-May £10, £13, £15; Nov.-Feb. £8, £11, £13. Doubles £40-60. Some prices higher on weekends. Free luggage storage, or super-security (whether you're staying at the hostel or not) for £2.50.

Abraham House, 82-3 Gardiner St. Lower (tel. 855 0600; tel./fax 855 0598; email abraham@indigo.ie). A well-kept hostel with clean rooms and good bathrooms. Bureau de change. Internet access. Kitchen open until 10pm. June-Sept. 12-bed dorms £8.50, 6-bed £11, 4-bed £12.50, doubles £30; Mar.-May and Oct. £8, £9, £11, £22.50; Nov.-Feb. £7.50, £8, £9.50, £22.50; rooms with bath available for several pounds more. Light breakfast and towels included. Laundry £4.

Jacobs Inn, 21-28 Talbot Pl. (tel. 855 5660; fax 855 5664; email jacob@indigo.ie). Two blocks north of the Customs House, Talbot Pl. stretches from the back of the bus station up to Talbot St. Rooms, all with bath, are on the nicer end of the standard hostel issue; kitchen and TV room aren't. The pub next door pours abnormally cheap pints. Apr.-Oct. 6- to 8-bed dorms £10.95, 4-bed dorms £15.50, 3-bed dorms £16.50, doubles £39; Nov.-Mar. £2 cheaper per person. Luggage storage accessible every 30min. Towels £1. Laundry £5. Bed lockout 11am-3pm. Wheelchair accessible.

Globetrotter's Tourist Hostel (IHH), 46-7 Lower Gardiner St. (tel. 873 5893; fax 878 8787; email gtrotter@indigo.ie; www.iol.ie/globetrotters). Comfortable beds are packed close but separated by partitions. Excellent bathrooms and superb showers. Internet access. July to mid-Sept. dorms £15, mid-Sept. to June £12. Great breakfast included. Free luggage storage. Safety deposit boxes £1.50. Towels 50p.

Celts House, 32 Blessington St. (tel. 830 0657; email res@celtshouse.iol.ie). 38 comfy, solid wooden bunk beds in a brightly painted, friendly atmosphere. The bedrooms are nicer than the bathrooms, and it's all a 15min. walk from the city center. Internet access. Dorms £9, 4-bed £10.50; double £32. Key deposit £5. Sheets £1.50. Caretaker is sleeping, but available 11pm-9am.

Mount Eccles Court (M.E.C.), 42 North Great Georges St. (tel. 878 0071; fax 874 6472; email meccles@iol.ie). Walk up O'Connell to Parnell St., turn right, then take the first left. The hostel is three-fourths of a block down on the right. A former convent, this boxy Georgian edifice seems impossibly large inside. Dorms have lots of beds but even more room. En suite rooms have nicer bathrooms. Nice lawn in back, and the street is restfully quiet. Apr.-Sept. 16-bed dorms £8.50, 10-bed £10.50, 6-bed £11.50, twin £16 per person; Oct.-Mar. £7.50, £8, £9, £14; with bath add 50p-£1. Small continental breakfast included. Free luggage storage and car park available. Towels £1.

Morehampton House Tourist Hostel, 78 Morehampton Rd., Donnybrook (tel. 668 8866; fax 668 8794), at the intersection with Marlborough Rd. and Herbert Pk. On buses #10 and 46A (10min. bus ride, 20min. walk from city center). Though out of the way, this refurbished Victorian building provides accommodations that are clean, cheerful, and comfy, if a bit cramped. Bike park and garden. 16-bed dorms £8, 10-bed dorms £13, 6- to 8-bed dorms £13-14, doubles £35; Oct.-May £1-2 cheaper; add about £2 for rooms with bath. Free luggage storage.

Marlborough Hostel (IHH), 81-82 Marlborough St. (tel. 874 7629; fax 874 5172; email marlboro@internet-ireland.ie), between O'Connell and Gardiner St. Large rooms, and a nice barbeque patio in back. Less nice are the single-sex communal showers. Bike shed. July-Sept. 4- to 10-bed dorms £8.50-10; twin £15; Oct.-Jun. dorms £7.50-8.50, twin £13. Small continental breakfast included. Sheets 50p. Check-out 10:30am.

Dublin International Youth Hostel (An Óige/HI), 61 Mountjoy St. (tel. 830 1766; fax 830 1600; email anoige@iol.ie; www.irelandyha.org). O'Connell St. changes names 3 times before reaching the left turn onto Mountjoy St. Welcome to the mothership. A convent converted into a 365-bed hostel, with phone booths that were once confessionals. Large rooms, squeaky bunks. Security's okay, but watch your belongings. Bureau de change. Internet access. Cafe has cheap meals (£3.50) and packed lunches (£2). Shuttles to Temple Bar. Big dorms £10, 4- to 6-bed dorms £11, double £26; Oct.-May £1-2 cheaper. Breakfast included. Luggage storage 50p. Sheets £1.50. Towels £1. Self-service laundry £4. Carpark. Wheelchair accessible.

Baggot University Centre, 114 Baggot St. (tel. 661 8860), by the intersection with Fitzwilliam St. The facilities would benefit from refurbishment and some rooms can get crowded, but Sean and Moira Fitzgerald make up for it with a personal touch unparalleled in the city. Free coffee, tea, bread, and fruit available at all times. They'll also drive you to and from the ferryport. Carpark and bike storage. 5- to 8-bed dorms £12; doubles £30. Key deposit £2. Free luggage storage.

Strollers, 29 Eustace St. (tel./fax 677 5614; email strollers29@hotmail.com). In the middle of Temple Bar action, this smaller hostel has a friendly staff, but the beds, common area, and security could use some improvement. Dorms £12.50-14.50, doubles £35. Free towels and small breakfast.

Isaacs Hostel, 2-5 Frenchman's Ln. (tel. 855 6215 or 855 6574; email isaacs@indigo.ie), off the lower end of Gardiner St. behind the Customs House. The most basic of a biblical chain that includes plusher Jacob's nearby. Rooms are comfortable enough. Heavy timber ceilings and a split log-furnished common area give a rough-hewn feel. Cafe. Internet access £4 per hr. Dorms £8-9.25, triples £16.50, doubles £16, singles £18.95; Nov.-Mar. £1 cheaper per person. Towels £1. Laundry £5. Bed lockout 11am-2:30pm.

Kinlay House (IHH), 2-12 Lord Edward St. (tel. 679 6644; fax 679 7437; email kindub@usit.ie), the continuation of Dame St. Country boys who came to work in the city once slid down the beautifully carved oak banisters in the lofty entrance hall. Today, tired backpackers trudge upstairs to collapse on mediocre beds. You can gaze out at Christ Church Cathedral across the street from the soft couches in the TV room. Bureau de change. Internet access. Wake-up calls. 10-bed dorms £9.50; 4- to 6-bed dorms £13; doubles £28, with bath £32; singles £18. Oct.-June prices £1 less. Breakfast and towel included. Lockers 50p. Free luggage storage. Laundry £5.

Oliver St. John Gogarty's Temple Bar Hostel, 18-21 Anglesea St. (tel. 671 1822; fax 671 7637). A dim entry hall leads to average rooms. The kitchen is adequate. The location's unbeatable if you're looking to frolic in Temple Bar. June-Sept. dorms £16, triples £17, twins £21 per person; Mar.-May and Oct. £14, £16, £18; Nov.-Feb. £12-13, £14, £16; weekends always £1 more. £5 key deposit. Internet access. Laundry £2.

Goin' My Way (Cardijn House), 15 Talbot St. (tel. 878 8484). Cheap beds in non-smoking rooms. Internet access. Dorms £9, quads £48, twins £28. Towels and a continental breakfast included. Midnight curfew.

Backpackers Citi Hostel, 61-62 Lower Gardiner St. (tel. 855 0035). Wiry, squishy beds and beat-up showers seem to value history over cleanliness, but they don't take reservations, so if you're in a pinch there's almost always a bed free. Internet access. Dorms £8-10. Bed lockout 11am-3pm.

Backpackers Euro Hostel, 80-81 Lower Gardiner St. (tel. 836 4900). Same as its sister Citi Hostel, but the dorms have 12 beds instead of 8 and the bathrooms are in further disrepair. Again, no reservations, so you're likely to find a wiry bed here. Weekdays May-Sept. dorms £8, Apr.-Oct. £7; weekends always £10. Bed lockout 11am-5pm.

Other budget options exist. **Ashfield House,** 19-20 D'Olier St. (tel. 679 7734; fax 679 0852; email ashfield@indigo.ie) has just jumped one rung up from a nice hostel to a budget hotel, but they may still have some good deals.

Also worth considering is university housing, available during the summer months (roughly mid-June to mid/late-Sept.). It's student housing, so don't expect anything fancy, but the prices are only a fraction more expensive than those of hostels. **Dublin City University,** Glasnevin (tel. 704 5736), can be reached on bus #11, 11A, 11B, 13, or 19A from the city center. (Singles with bath around £23, doubles with bath around £34.) Other options are through **usit** (see p. 94), which operates **University College Dublin** dorms in Belfield (tel. 269 7111; £24 single in an apartment of four), and **University of Dublin** dorms in Rathmines (tel. 497 1772; £32 per person).

BED AND BREAKFASTS

A blanket of quality B&Bs covers Dublin and the surrounding suburbs. Those with a green shamrock sign out front are registered, occasionally checked, and approved by Bord Fáilte. B&Bs without the shamrock haven't been inspected but may be cheaper and better located; with a good location, B&Bs often find that Bord Fáilte's advertising is unnecessary. General housing costs have skyrocketed in Dublin, dragging B&B prices along with them. Prices range from £16 at the very lowest to well upwards of £30 per person sharing. On the North Side, B&Bs cluster along **Upper** and **Lower Gardiner St.,** on **Sheriff St.,** and near **Parnell Sq.** Exercise caution when walking through this inner-city area at night. The B&Bs listed below are warm and welcoming standouts in this neighborhood.

Suburban B&Bs are often spare rooms in houses emptied of children. With everything in Dublin so compact, they tend to be close to the city center. **Clonliffe Rd., Sandymount,** and **Clontarf** are no more than a 15min. bus ride from Eden Quay. Suburban chances for decent B&Bs are greater, especially for those without a reservation. B&Bs in **Howth** (see p. 125) and **Dún Laoghaire** (see p. 127) are just as accessible (by DART) from Dublin. **Maynooth** (see p. 144) and **Malahide** (see p. 126), accessible by suburban rail, are also good places to stay. Aside from the regions covered below, you can find large numbers of B&Bs within the city limits in **Rathgar** (Dublin 6), **Drumcondra** (Dublin 9), **Templeogue** (Dublin 6W), and **Santry Rd.** (Dublin 9, close to the airport). Dublin Tourism's annually updated *Dublin Accommodation Guide* (£3) lists the locations and rates of all approved B&Bs.

NEAR O'CONNELL STREET:
PARNELL SQUARE AND GARDINER STREET

The B&Bs in this area can be a budget traveler's hell. Many travelers arrive late at night by bus or train and, knowing no better, are plundered here. Fleabags abound, tucked between quality guesthouses with exorbitant rates. Plan ahead, or choose a suburban B&B. Gardiner St. runs parallel to O'Connell St. and leads to the Custom House; Parnell Sq. sits at the top of Upper Gardiner St. Both Lower and Upper Gardiner St. are within walking distance of Busáras and Connolly; buses #41, 41A, 41B, and 41C from Eden Quay will take you to the farthest reaches of the road.

Parkway Guest House, 5 Gardiner Pl. (tel. 874 0469). Rooms are plain but high-ceilinged and immaculate, and the location just off Gardiner St. is excellent. Run by a mother-and-son team. The son offers discerning advice on the city's restaurants and pubs, and could talk for hours about Irish sports—his hurling scars brand him an authority. Singles £21; doubles £35, with bath £44.

Charles Stewart Budget Accommodation, 5-6 Parnell Sq. (tel. 878 0350 or 878 1767; email cstuart@iol.ie; www.iol.ie/~cstuart). Continue up O'Connell St. past Parnell St. and look on your right. Technically a hostel but much more like a guesthouse. Single £20, £37 with bath; twin bunks £40; double £50. Rates 10% lower in winter. Full Irish breakfast included. Laundry £3. Wheelchair accessible.

Glen Court, 67 Gardiner St. Lower (tel. 836 4022), 1 block west of Busáras, 2 blocks east of O'Connell. A Georgian house that's showing its age. The rooms are tiny. For the location you can't beat the price. Singles £16, doubles £30, triples £42, quads £52.

Marian B&B, 21 Upper Gardiner St. (tel. 874 4129). Brendan and Cathrine McElroy provide lovely rooms, at a better price than comparable neighborhood accommodations. Singles £20, doubles £40.

Carmel House, 16 Upper Gardiner St. (tel. 874 1639; fax 878 6903). An elegant breakfast room and a generally high comfort factor are fairly priced, given the skyrocketing rates in the area. Rooms from £18-20 per person, £22.50-30 with bath.

CLONLIFFE ROAD

This modest, respectable neighborhood has a few friendly empty-nests-turned-B&Bs. The neighborhood is an ideal place to stay if you're planning to attend an event at **Croke Park,** or if you want to listen to the concerts there for free. Take bus #51A from Lower Abbey St., or make the 20 min. walk from the city center up O'Connell St., right on Dorset St., across the Royal Canal, and right onto Clonliffe Rd. Buses #41A, 41B, and 41C all serve the area from the airport.

Mona B&B, 148 Clonliffe Rd. (tel. 837 6723). Firm beds in rooms kept tidy by a proprietress who offers tea and cakes upon arrival. Singles £17, doubles £32. Open May-Oct.

St. Aidan's B&B, 150 Clonliffe Rd. (tel. 837 6750). Good beds, non-smoking rooms, and friendly proprietor create a relaxing atmosphere. Singles £17; doubles £34, with bath £40. Open Apr.-Sept.

Clonliffe B&B, 94 Clonliffe Rd. (tel. 837 9656). Hospitable owners pamper you in this sunny spot. Singles £23 with breakfast, £20 without; doubles £40, £32.

Mrs. Molly Ryan, 10 Distillery Rd. (tel. 837 4147), off Clonliffe Rd., on the left if you're coming from the city center. A yellow house attached to #11. The unsinkable Molly Ryan, in her countless years, has never marked the B&B with a sign. Small rooms, small prices. Singles £16, doubles £28.

SANDYMOUNT

Sandymount is a peaceful neighborhood near **Dublin Port,** 1¾ mi. south of city center, and famous for its Joycean associations. Take bus #3 from Clery's on O'Connell St. or the DART to **Landsdowne Rd.** or Sandymount stops (10min.).

Rita and Jim Casey, Villa Jude, 2 Church Ave. (tel. 668 4982), off Beach Rd. Bus #3 to the first stop on Tritonville Rd; Church Ave. is back a few yards. Call for directions from the Lansdowne Rd. DART stop. Mrs. Casey has nourished 7 children and countless others with her homemade bread and strapping Irish breakfasts. Not a very quiet street by day. Singles £17, doubles £30.

Mrs. Dolores Abbot-Murphy, 14 Castle Park (tel. 269 8413). Ask the bus #3 driver to drop you at Sandymount Green; continue past Browne's Deli and take the first left. 5min. walk from Sandymount DART stop. Cheerful rooms look onto a peaceful cul-de-sac with flowers bloomin' everywhere. The dining room adds elegance to every meal. Singles £20, with bath £25; doubles £38, with bath £44.

COUNTY DUBLIN

Mrs. Bermingham, 8 Dromard Terr. (tel. 668 3861), on Dromard Ave. Take the #3 bus to the next stop after Sandymount Village. Mrs. Bermingham's red brick house is covered with ivy. One room has a lovely bay window overlooking the garden. Soft beds with fluffy comforters. Most rooms without bath. Singles £17, doubles £32.

CLONTARF

Clontarf Rd. runs north from the city along Dublin Bay, to the neighborhood that shares its name. The view along it includes coastal grass, the harbor, some industrial smokestacks of the **Dublin Port** facility, and the impressive **Dublin Mountains** in the backdrop. Sea breezes are more pleasant than the harbor traffic; some B&Bs are inland a few blocks and avoid both. Make arrangements ahead of time, since many B&Bs in Clontarf go unmarked. Bus #130 runs from Lower Abbey St. to Clontarf Rd. (15min.).

The White House, 125 Clontarf Rd. (tel. 833 3196). Sink into your bed and look out at pristine rose gardens. Singles £25, off-season £20; doubles £36, with bath £40.

Bayview, 98 Clontarf Rd. (tel. 833 3950). The Barry family provides fresh, airy rooms, with every sort of wallpaper imaginable. Singles £20, doubles £40.

Mrs. Geary, 69 Hampton Ct. (tel. 833 1199). Hampton Ct. is a cul-de-sac development built just past where Vernon Ave. bends left as you come up from Clontarf Rd. Bus #130 heads right up Vernon Ave. from Lower Abbey St. Spacious and relaxing once you find it. Singles £25, doubles £38. Open Apr.-Sept.

CAMPING

Most campsites are far from the city center, but camping equipment is available in the heart of the city. **The Great Outdoors,** Chatham St. (tel. 679 4293), off the top of Grafton St., has an excellent selection of tents, backpacks, and cookware. (10% discount for An Óige/HI members. Open M-W and F-Sa 9:30am-5:30pm, Th 9:30am-8pm.) **O'Meara's Camping,** 4-6 Bridgefoot St. (tel. 670 8639), off Thomas St. near the Guinness brewery, sells camping equipment and rents tents. (4-person tent £29 per week. Open Jan.-Sept. M-Sa 10am-6pm, Su 2:30-5:20pm; Oct.-Dec. M-Sa 10am-6pm.) **Phoenix Park** is not safe for camping.

Camac Valley Tourist Caravan & Camping Park, Naas Rd., Clondalkin (tel. 464 0644; email camacmorriscastle@tinet.ie), near Corkagh Park. Accessible by bus #69 (35min. from city center, £1.10). Food shop and kitchen facilities. Showers 50p. Tents £3-4 plus £1 per adult, 50p per child. Laundry £3.50. Wheelchair accessible.

Shankill Caravan and Camping Park (tel. 282 0011; fax 282 0108). The DART and buses #45 and 84 from Eden Quay run to Shankill, as does bus #45A from the Dun Laoghaire ferryport. Middle-aged tourists in caravans alternate with shrubs and tents. £4.50-5 per tent plus £1 per adult, 50p per child. Showers 50p.

North Beach Caravan and Camping Park (tel./fax 843 7131), in Rush. Bus #33 from Eden Quay (50min., 23 per day) and the suburban train come here. Peaceful, beachside location in a quiet town just outside Dublin's sphere of urbanity. Kitchen. £4 per person, children £2. Electricity £1. Showers 50p. Open Mar.-Oct.

LONG-TERM STAYS

Visitors expecting to spend several weeks in Dublin may want to consider a bedsit or sublet. Longer stays are often most economical when sharing the cost of renting a house or apartment with others. Rooms in locations outside the city center, like Marino and Rathmines, fetch about £32-50 per week (ask whether electricity, phone, and water are included). B&Bs sometimes give reduced rates for long-term stays but are very reluctant to do it in the summer. There are a number of sources for finding roommates and possible sublets; Dublin's countless university students are often looking for them, usually for the summer but also on a weekly basis. The most up-to-date, comprehensive postings of vacancies are at **usit,** 19-21 Aston

Quay (see **Tourist Services,** p. 94). Supermarket noticeboards are another source. **Trinity College** has two spots worth checking out: the noticeboard near the guard's desk in the Student Union, and by the main gate. Also check out the tourist office's comprehensive *Dublin Accommodation Guide* (£3), and classified ads in the *Irish Independent,* the *Irish Times,* and, most useful, the *Evening Herald.*

If you want someone else to do the legwork, **Dublin Central Reservations,** 3 Sandholes, Castleknock (tel. 820 0394; email bookings@dcr.ie), can arrange for short or long stays in both humble and super-snazzy accommodations, for as low as £150 per week, with no finder's fee. (Open M-F 9am-7pm, Sa 11am-5:30pm.)

⬛ FOOD

Dublin's many **open-air markets** sell fresh and cheap fixings. Vendors with thick Dublin accents hawk fruit, fresh Irish strawberries, flowers, and smelly fish from their pushcarts. The later in the week, the more lively the market. Actors head to **Moore St. Market** to try to perfect a Dublin guttural accent, and get fresh veggies to boot. (Open M-Sa 7am-5pm.) Moore St. runs between Henry and Parnell St. The **Thomas St. Market,** along the continuation of Dame St., is a calmer alternative for fruit and vegetable shopping. (Open M-Sa 9am-5pm.) On Saturdays, a gourmet open-air market takes place at **Temple Bar.** The cheapest **supermarkets** around Dublin are in the **Dunnes Stores** chain, with branches at St. Stephen's Green Shopping Centre, the ILAC Centre off Henry St., and on North Earl St. off O'Connell. (All open M-W and F-Sa 9am-6pm, Th 9am-8pm.) **Quinnsworth** supermarkets, gradually changing names to **Tesco,** are also widespread. The **Runner Bean,** 4 Nassau St. (tel. 679 4833), vends wholefoods, homemade breads, veggies, fruits, and nuts for the squirrel in you. (Open M-Sa 8am-6pm.) **Down to Earth,** 73 South Great Georges St. (tel. 671 9702), stocks health foods, herbal medicines, and a dozen varieties of granola. (Open M-Sa 8:30am-6:30pm.) Health food is also available around the city at various branches of **Nature's Way;** the biggest is at the St. Stephen's Green shopping center (tel. 478 0165).

TEMPLE BAR

This neighborhood is ready to implode from the proliferation of creative eateries catering to every budget. Temple Bar has more ethnic diversity in its restaurants than the combined counties of Louth, Meath, Wicklow, and Longford (and probably Offaly, too). The **Temple Bar Passport** is a coupon book available to guests at certain accommodations; of the hostels, only Gogarty's Hostel stocks it.

🔲 **Cafe Irie,** Fownes St. (tel. 672 5090), above the colorful Sé Sí Progressive. Probably the best value in Temple Bar. Lip-smackingly good sandwich concoctions under £3. Even vegans can get what they want. Open M-Sa 9am-8pm, Su noon-5:30pm.

La Mezza Luna, 1 Temple Ln. (tel. 671 2840), corner of Dame St. Celestial food. Roast pepper and chicken crepe £8.50. Daily lunch specials £5; served noon-3pm. Delicious desserts £3.50. Open M-Th noon-11pm, F-Sa noon-11:30pm, Su noon-10:30pm.

Bad Ass Cafe, Crown Alley (tel. 671 2596), off Temple Bar. Burned down in 1994 but, like phoenixes, Bad Asses rise from the ashes. American food in a gimmicky, touristy atmosphere. Sinéad O'Connor once worked here. Lunch £4-7. Medium pizza £5.15-7.75. Student discount with ISIC card. Open daily 9am until "late" (past midnight).

Poco Loco, 32 Parliament St. (tel. 679 1950), between Grattan Bridge and City Hall. Cheap Mexican foodstuffs. Enchiladas, burritos, chimichangas, and tacos £5.75. Vegetarian friendly. Open M-Tu 5-11pm, W-Th 5-11:30pm, F-Sa 5pm-midnight, Su 5-10pm.

Eliza Blues, 23-4 Wellington Quay (tel. 671 9114), by Eustace St. Enjoy your meal while gazing out at the Liffey. Chicken stuffed with salmon £6.75. Open daily 7:30am-11pm.

Botticelli, 3 Temple Bar (tel. 672 7289). Don't expect flowers on the tables or a lot of attention from the waitstaff. This bustling Italian joint is all about quality food. Pasta or pizza £6, Moët champagne £45. Open daily 10am-midnight.

GRAFTON STREET AND SOUTH GREAT GEORGES STREET

■ **Cornucopia,** 19 Wicklow St. (tel. 677 7583). This vegetarian horn of plenty spills huge portions onto your plate. If you can find a seat, sit down for a rich meal (about £5) or just a snack (about £1.50). Take-away. Open M-W and F-Sa 9am-8pm, Th 9am-9pm.

Chez Jules, 16a D'Olier St. (tel. 677 0499). Specializes in seafood dishes. Veggie dish of the day £7; special 2-course lunch £5.90. Open M-F noon-3pm and 6pm-11pm, Sa 1-3:30pm and 6-11pm, Su 5-10pm.

Wed Wose Cafe, 18 Exchequer St. (tel. 672 7323), off South Great Georges St., near the red brick market. Lovely breakfasts served all day in Dublin's slickest greasy spoon. Irish breakfast £3; sandwiches £1.50. Open M-Sa 8am-5pm, Su 10am-4pm.

Metro Cafe, 43 S. William St. (tel. 679 4515). New wave cafe with a fine coffee selection and homemade breads. Simple but scrumptious. Sandwiches £3.50. Open M-Tu and F 8am-8pm, W 8am-9pm, Th 8am-10pm, Sa 9am-7pm, Su 10:30am-6pm.

Leo Burdock's, 2 Werburgh St. (tel. 454 0306), uphill from Christ Church Cathedral. Take-away only. Eating Burdock's fish and chips is a religious experience that's a regular pilgrimage for many Dubliners. All sorts of fish £3; large chips £1.20. Open M-Sa noon-midnight, Su 4pm-midnight.

Harrison's, Westmoreland St. (tel. 679 9373). Romance that special someone without spending a fortune. While the mellow music wafts about, catch the lunch specials (£3.50-5.50) or the candlelit 4-course dinner (£10 M-Th, £11 F-Sa; 5-7pm). Open daily noon-10:30pm.

NORTH OF THE LIFFEY

Eateries here are less interesting than their counterparts on the South Side. **O'Connell St.** sports blocks of neon fast-food chains, and side streets overflow with fish-and-chips shops and newsagents hawking overpriced groceries.

Flanagan's, 61 O'Connell St. (tel. 873 1388). "A well-regarded establishment whose tourist trade occasionally suffers from being too close to a McDonald's," describes Tom Clancy in *Patriot Games*. Veggie dishes £6; calzone £4.90. Cheaper eats and leopard-print seats at the pizza-pasta joint upstairs. Open daily 8am-11pm.

The Winding Stair Bookshop and Cafe, 40 Lower Ormond Quay (tel. 873 3292), near the Ha'penny Bridge. Cafe overlooking the river shares 2 floors with bookshelves. Contemporary Irish writing, periodicals, and soothing music decrease the pace. Salads around £4; sandwiches £2. Open M-Sa 10:30am-5:30pm, Su 1-6pm.

Clifton Court Hotel, Eden Quay (tel. 874 3535). Excellent pub grub served with cigars in a convivial atmosphere. Chef's, vegetarian, and seafood specials daily £6. Food served daily noon-9pm. Trad music nightly at 9pm.

O'Shea's Hotel, 19 Talbot St. (tel. 836 5670), at Lower Gardiner St. Good pub grub until 9pm nightly. Very convenient to the north side accommodations that cluster nearby.

THE BEST OF THE REST

Bewley's Cafes. A Dublin institution. Dark wood paneling, marble table tops, and mirrored walls complete the "oriental" look, apparently. Decadent pastries (£1) and outstanding, rabid coffee. Meals are plain but inexpensive. 3 branches: 78 Grafton St. (635 5470), was recently renovated to its disimprovement, but the room for its most famous patron, James Joyce, still charms (open daily 7:30am-11pm, weekends may go later); 12 Westmoreland St. (tel. 677 6761; open M-Sa 7:30am-7:30pm, Su 9:30am-8pm); 13 South Great Georges St. (open M-Sa 7:45am-6pm); and on Mary St., past Henry St. (open M-W 7am-9pm, Th-Sa 7am-2am, Su 10am-10pm).

Beshoff's. A dream-chipper named after the cook in *Battleship Potemkin*. Branches at 6 Lower O'Connell St. (open 10am-10pm daily) and 14 Westmoreland St. (open Su-Th 11am-11pm, F-Sa 11am-3am).

☑ PUBS

James Joyce once proposed that a "good puzzle would be to cross Dublin without passing a pub." A local radio station once offered £100 to the first person to solve the puzzle. The winner explained that you could take any route—you'd just have to visit them all on the way. Dublin's pubs come in all shapes, sizes, specialties, and subcultures. Dublin is the place to hear Irish rock and, on occasion, trad. Ask around or check *In Dublin, Hot Press,* or *Event Guide* for pub music listings. Normal pub hours in Ireland end at 11:30pm, but the laws that dictate these hours are rapidly changing. An increasing number of Dublin pubs have permits for late hours, at least on some nights; drink prices at these watering holes tend to rise around 11pm, in order to cover the permit's cost (so they claim). Bars will post their closing time as "late," meaning after midnight and, sometimes, after their legal limit. ID-checking is more enforced in Dublin than in most of Ireland. Carding almost always takes place at the door, rather than at the bar.

Many heated debates stem from the postulate that Guinness tastes slightly different from every tap. In-depth *Let's Go* research continues to fuel the rivalry between two pouring heavyweights. Multiple trips and dozens of tastings have failed to pick out a clear-cut winner. The **Guinness Hop Store** (see p. 115), behemoth of stout production, shares its pedestal with **Mulligan's** (see **Pubs,** p. 106). Honorable mention goes to **The Stag's Head** (see p. 106) and **Brogan's Bar.**

The **Let's Go Dublin Pub Crawl** aids in discovering the city and researching the best pint of Guinness. We recommend that you begin your crawl at the gates of Trinity College, then stroll up Grafton St., teeter to Camden St., stumble to South Great Georges St., and triumphantly drag your soused self to Temple Bar. Start early (say, noon).

GRAFTON STREET AND VICINITY

Sinnott's, South King St. (tel. 478 4698). Classy crowd of 20-somethings gather in this basement pub with wooden beam rafters. Portrays itself as a pub for readers and writers, but let's be honest, it's for drinkers. Chart music packs the dancefloor until 2am.

McDaid's, 3 Harry St. (tel. 679 4395), off Grafton St. across from Anne St. The center of Ireland's literary scene in the 50s. Book-adorned walls, packs in a yuppie crowd downstairs and a more sedate set above. W blues; Su blues and jazzier tunes.

Café en Seine, 40 Dawson St. (tel. 677 4369). Built to impress. A chic cafe with dainty pastries in front, while a very long bar undulates through a high-ceilinged hall with a super-nouveau decor. A large crowd of mixed ages packs in, apparently indifferent to the fact that the Seine is not at all nearby. Late bar W-Sa until 2am; Su jazz 1-3:30pm.

M. J. O'Neills, Suffolk St. (tel. 679 3614), across from the tourist office. The maze of staircases is quiet by day, but a fun, young crowd meets here at night. Sports screen. Late closing Th-F 12:30am, Sa midnight.

Davy Byrne's, 21 Duke St. (tel. 677 5217), off Grafton St. A lively, middle-aged crowd throngs at the pub that Joyce chose as the setting for the Cyclops chapter in Ulysses. The images of Joyce himself on the walls hint at some redecorating since then.

The International Bar, 23 Wicklow St. (tel. 677 9250), on the corner of South William St. Excellent improv comedy M, stand-up W and Th (cover £5). All other nights, and Su afternoon, blues and trad (cover £5).

The Pavilion, Trinity College (tel. 608 1000), head to the far right corner of campus from the main gate. During the summer, watch a cricket match and wax philosophical over Guinness at the Pav. Open all year, daily noon-11pm. From October to May, you can also join the Trinity students under the vaults of **The Buttery,** located in a basement to the left as you enter campus. Open M-F 2-11pm.

HARCOURT AND CAMDEN ST.

The Bleeding Horse, 24 Upper Camden St. (tel. 475 2705). You can't beat it, 'cause it ain't dead yet. All sorts of little nooks for private affairs. Late bar with DJ Th-Sa.

The Odeon, the Old Harcourt Train Station (tel. 478 2088)). The Odeon has a columned facade, and the second longest bar in Ireland (after the one at the Galway races). Everything here is gargantuan. The upstairs is cozier (i.e. still huge). DJ on Sa. Late bar Th-Sa.

The Chocolate Bar, Harcourt St. (tel. 478 0225), in the Old Harcourt Railway Station. Young clubbers drink here until **The Pod,** the attached nightclub, opens (see p. 108).

WEXFORD ST. AND SOUTH GREAT GEORGES

✦ **The Stag's Head,** 1 Dame Ct. (tel. 679 3701). The subtle and ancient entrance is marked by a mosaic of a stag's head on the sidewalk. Beautiful Victorian pub with stained glass, mirrors, and yes, a stag's head. The crowd dons everything from t-shirts to tuxes and spills out into the alleys. Truly excellent grub. Entrees around £5-7; served M-F 12:30-3:30pm and 5:30-7:30pm, Sa 12:30-2:30pm. Late bar Th-F till 12:30am.

✦ **Whelan's,** 25 Wexford St. (tel. 478 0766). Continue down South Great Georges St. The stage venue in back hosts big-name trad and rock groups. Cover £5-8. Gigs followed Th-Su by pop and dance music. Open Th-Su until 1:30am.

The Mean Fiddler, 26 Wexford St., next door to Whelan's. Live music regularly for a hip crowd. Think electric fiddle. Bar open Su-W from 5pm, Th-Sa from 4pm. At 11pm the gates of the attached nightclub open. Cover £4.

The Globe, 11 South Great Georges St. (tel. 671 1220). Pretentious clientele? "Wankers," the barman corrects, "not pretentious. Arty farty wannabe artists." Maybe so, but it's a fine spot for relaxing with a Guinness or frothy cappuccinos. Meet the regular cast of amicable if somewhat freakish characters—if your hair's not dyed, you might want to bleach it. Rí Rá nightclub attached (see p. 108).

Hogan's, 35 South Great Georges St. (tel. 677 5904). Attracts a trendy crowd despite its basic name and bizarre decor. Su DJ from 4pm. Late bar Th-Sa until 1:30am.

The Long Hall, South Great St. Georges, next door to Hogan's. Lots of mirrors for primping, pints for chatting, and an authentic old world feel to please youngsters.

TEMPLE BAR

✦ **The Palace,** 21 Fleet St. (tel. 677 9290), behind Aston Quay. This classic, neighborly Dublin pub has old-fashioned wood paneling and close quarters; head for the comfy seats in the skylit back room. The favorite of many a Dubliner.

Oliver St. John Gogarty (tel. 671 1822), at Fleet and Anglesea St. Lively and convivial atmosphere in a traditionally decorated pub. Named for Joyce's nemesis and onetime roommate, who appears in *Ulysses* as Buck Mulligan (see p. 129). Trad sessions daily from 2:30pm on. Open M-F until 1:30am, Sa until midnight, Su until 1am.

The Foggy Dew, Fownes St. (tel. 677 9328). Like a friendly, mellow neighborhood pub, but twice as big. The Foggy Dew makes a great spot for a pint or two without the artsy flash of other Temple Bar pubs. Live rock Sunday nights.

The Porter House, 16-18 Parliament St. (tel. 679 8847). The largest selection of world beers in the country, and 8 self-brewed kinds of porter, stout, and ale. If you're up for it, try An Brainblásta—7% alcohol by volume. Their excellent sampler tray includes a sip of ale brewed with oysters and other oddities (£6). Late bar Th-F to 1:30am, Sa to midnight. Occasional trad, blues, and rock gigs.

Brogan's Bar, 75 Dame St. (tel. 679 9570). An unassuming little place, largely ignored by tourists in spite of its location. An impressive collection of Guinness paraphernalia.

Messrs. Maguire, Burgh Quay. You'll still find new rooms here after hours inside, especially if you've been quaffing the homemade microbrews. Late bar W-Sa. Trad Su-Tu.

Buskers, Fleet St. (tel. 677 3333 ext. 2145). Large, industrial bar with a small dance floor in the back. Dance to DJ hits as you swill your pint. Late bar Th-F until 1am.

THE BEST OF THE REST

✦ **Mulligan's,** 8 Poolbeg St. (tel. 677 5582), behind Burgh Quay off Tara St. Upholds its reputation as one of the best pint pourers in Dublin. The crowd consists mainly of middle-aged men. A taste of the typical Irish pub: low key and nothing fancy. Really.

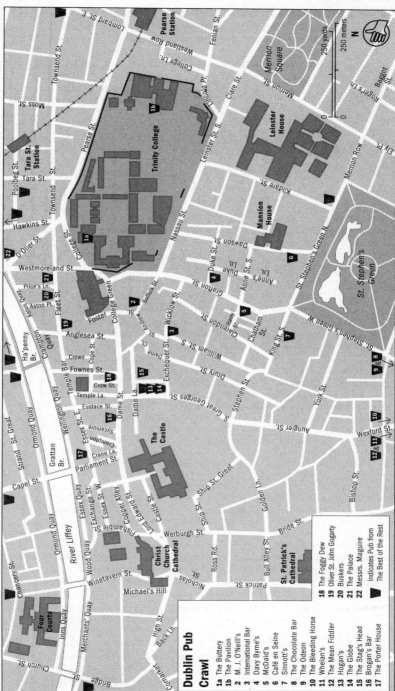

COUNTY DUBLIN

Dublin Pub Crawl

1a The Buttery
1b The Pavilion
2 M. J. O'Neill's
3 International Bar
4 Davy Byrne's
5 McDaid's
6 Café en Seine
7 Sinnott's
8 The Chocolate Bar
9 The Odeon
10 The Bleeding Horse
11 Whelan's
12 The Mean Fiddler
13 Hogan's
14 The Globe
15 The Stag's Head
16 Brogan's Bar
17 The Porter House
18 The Foggy Dew
19 Oliver St. John Gogarty
20 Buskers
21 The Palace
22 Messrs. Maguire

▶ Indicates Pub from The Best of the Rest

The Brazen Head, 20 North Bridge St. (tel. 679 5816), off Merchant's Quay. Dublin's oldest pub, established in 1198 as the first stop after the bridge on the way into the city. The courtyard is quite the pickup scene on summer nights. Nightly Irish music, weekend late bar until 12:30am.

The Shelbourne Bar, the Shelbourne Hotel (tel. 676 6471), at the corner of Kildare St. and St. Stephen's Green North. The best place for cocktails in Dublin. Also the center of Ireland's media culture—political cartoons decorate the walls, and journalists chat it up. The hotel's other bar, the **Horseshoe Bar,** attracts the bigwig politicians, who gripe about the journalists. Open M-Sa.

Lanigans, Clifton Court Hotel, Eden Quay (tel. 874 3535). Imagine a pub with Irish singers that actually attracts more Dubliners than tourists: this happy pub is it. Live music nightly at 9pm breaks down generational barriers and breaks into Irish dancing M-Th.

Zanzibar, (tel. 878 7212), at the Ha'Penny Bridge. Indefinite North African decorative theme. If you can worm your way down the long hall to the dance floor, it's all pop favorites. Quite the hot spot. Late bar past 1am nightly. DJ M-Th from 10pm, F-Sa from 9pm.

Slattery's, 129-31 Capel St. (tel. 872 7971). Trad and pop nightly downstairs. Upstairs rock and blues Th-Su (£3-4 cover).

Hughes, 19 Chancery St. (tel. 872 6540), behind the Four Courts. A delightful venue for trad (nightly) and set dancing (M, W, and Th around 9:30pm).

The Wind Jammer, Townsend St. (tel. 677 2576), at East Lombard St. For mornings when you need a pint with your muesli, this "early house" opens at 7:30am every day.

Pravda, (tel. 874 0090), at the north side of the Ha'penny Bridge. The Russian late bar and Russian DJ action lasts until a Russian 1:30am. Actually there's nothing Russian about the place other than the Cyrilic on the wall murals. This theme bar is trendy, popular, and gay-friendly. Probably Russian-friendly, too.

Life, Lower Abbey St. (tel. 878 1032), behind the Salvation Army. The young and the beautiful head here after work to talk about important things, like image. Late bar Th-F until 1:30am, Sa until midnight.

⚑ CLUBLIN

In recent years, clubs have displaced rock venues at pubs as the hippest source of Dublin's nightlife, though the pubs are fighting back with later hours. As a rule, clubs open at 10:30 or 11pm, but the action only starts up after 11:30pm when the pubs close. Clubbing is an expensive way to end the night, since covers run £4-10 and pints are a steep £3. The last four clubs listed are a bit cheaper, but can't provide a full night's entertainment. **Concessions** provide discounts with varying restrictions. A good place to get them is Stag's Head (see **Pubs,** p. 106) around 11pm, though any nightclub attached to a bar will distribute in the home bar. There are a handful of smaller clubs on **Harcourt** and **Leeson St.** that can be fun, if austere. Most clubs close between 1:30am and 3am, but a few have been known to last until daybreak. To get home after 11:30pm when Dublin Bus stops running, dancing fiends take the **NiteLink bus** (1 per hour, Th-Sa 12:30-3:30am, £2.50), which runs designated routes from the corner of Westmoreland and College St. to Dublin's suburbs. **Taxi** stands are located in front of Trinity, the top of Grafton St. by St. Stephen's Green, and on Abbey St. Lower. Be prepared to wait 30 to 45min. on Friday and Saturday nights. For further listings, see **Gay and Lesbian Dublin,** p. 123.

The Kitchen, The Clarence Hotel (tel. 677 6635), Wellington Quay, Temple Bar. With 2 bars and a dance floor, this U2-owned club is exceptionally well designed and the coolest spot in town. Half of it is impossible to get into on most nights because it's filled with "VIPs." Dress as a rocker or a model. Cover £8-10, students £3-4 on Tu.

Rí-Rá, 1 Exchequer St. (tel. 677 4835), in the back of the Globe (see **Pubs,** p. 106). Generally good music that steers clear of pop and house extremes. 2 floors, several bars, and more nooks and crannies than a crumpet. Open daily 11pm-2:30am. Cover £6.

POD, 35 Harcourt St. (tel. 478 0225). Spanish-style decor meets hardcore dance music. As trendy as The Kitchen. The truly brave venture upstairs to **The Red Box** (tel. 478 0225), a separate, more intense club with a warehouse atmosphere, brain-crushing music, and an 8-person-deep crowd at the bar to winnow out the weak. Cover £8-10; Th ladies free before midnight; Th and Sa £5 with ISIC card. Start the evening at the Chocolate Bar or the Odeon, which also share the building (see **Pubs,** p. 105).

Club M, Blooms Hotel, Anglesea St. (tel. 671 5485), Temple Bar. One of Dublin's largest clubs, attracting a crowd of diverse ages and styles, with multiple stairways and a few bars in the back. Run up and down the charts all night, and end up with a nice headache from the lightshow. Cover around £6.

Velvet, 60 Harcourt St. (tel. 478 3677). A smaller venue, usually blasting house and glam-girly sounds; looks up to the POD and Kitchen crowd. Open nightly. Cover Th £6, F-Sa £8, W student night £3 or free.

The Funnel, 24 City Quay (tel. 677 5304). A smokey, mixed crowd grooves under the military netting to psychedelic techno, funk, house, and garage. Occasional live acts. Cover hovers around £7, before 11pm £5.

Boomerang, Temple Bar Hotel, Fleet St. (tel. 677 3333). Poppy danceables played for a broad dance pit under a low basement ceiling. Open Th-Su until 2:30am. Cover M-Sa £5-8, Su free. Concessions available in Busker's upstairs (see **Pubs,** p. 106).

Republica, Kildare St., in the bottom of the Kildare Hotel. A funny little place that plays charts, is relatively cheap, and has a variety of good drink deals. Cover £4-5.

Club Aquarium (Fibber's), 80-82 Parnell St. (tel. 872 2575). No charts here; mostly indie. Houses Ireland's only metal club. Occasional goth nights. Weekend cover £3-5.

Klub ZaZu, 21-5 Eustace St. (tel. 670 7655). The only 18+ club in Temple Bar, so the crowd's a bit younger here. Cover W-Th £5, F £6, Sa £7.

The Palace Niteclub, Camden St., in the Camden de Luxe Hotel (tel. 478 0808). A meat market for a large, drunk, mostly under-20 crowd. Pop faves blast under a huge barrel-vaulted ceiling. Free every night until 10pm; W students £3, Th-F cover £5, Sa £6. The legal age for consent in Ireland is 17.

The Turk's Head (tel. 679 2606), beneath the bar on Parliament St. A selection of 70s and 80s classics. Open nightly 10:30pm-2am. No cover.

◉ TOURS

SELF-GUIDED WALKING TOURS

Dublin is definitely a walking city. Most major sights lie within a mile of O'Connell Bridge. The tourist office sells *Dublin's Top Visitor Attractions* (£2.50), which lists the main sights, essential info about them, and directions. Several signposted walks wind through the city. The first three walking tours listed are in *Heritage Trails: Signpost Walking Tours of Dublin,* available at the tourist office (£2.50).

THE CULTURAL TRAIL. Starring James Joyce and Sean O'Casey, this route zips past the important sights on the North Side: the Four Courts, the Custom House and King's Inns, the Municipal Gallery, and the Dublin Writers' Museum.

THE OLD CITY TRAIL. This walk begins on College Green and weaves its way through the Liberties and the markets, ending in Temple Bar. Ironically, the Old City trail hits some of the city's newest, most garish exhibits, including Dublinia and the Dublin Viking Adventure.

GEORGIAN HERITAGE TRAIL. This path covers the best-preserved Georgian streets, terraces, and public buildings south of the Liffey, which no visitor to Dublin should deprive themselves the pleasure of viewing.

ULYSSES MAP OF DUBLIN. A tourist office brochure (£1) charts Leopold Bloom's haunts and retraces his poetic actions, beginning with kidneys for breakfast. The entire walk takes 18 hours (including drinking and debauching).

ROCK 'N' STROLL TRAIL. The disturbingly worshipful brochure sold at the tourist office (£2.50) makes a circuit of significant sights in Dublin's recent musical history. It provides the grim details of Sinéad O'Connor's waitressing job at the Bad Ass Cafe and U2's Windmill Lane Studios.

GUIDED WALKING TOURS

If you lack the discipline to follow a self-guided walking tour in its entirety, you might consider a guided one. Tours generally last about 2hr., but entertaining anecdotes and continuous movement preclude boredom.

HISTORICAL WALKING TOUR. Provides a 2hr. crash course in Dublin's history from the Celts to the present, stopping at nine points of historical interest and laying great emphasis on the "gritty" lives of ordinary Dubliners. *(Meet at Trinity's front gate. Tel. 878 0227; email tours@historicalinsights.ie; www.historicalinsights.ie. May-Sept. M-F 11am and 3pm, Sa-Su 11am, noon, 3pm; Oct.-Apr. F-Su noon. £5, students £4.)*

TRINITY COLLEGE WALKING TOUR. Moderately irreverent and hugely pretentious, it concentrates on University lore, while glimpsing Dublin's history. *(Leaves roughly every 45min. from the info booth inside the front gate. Tel. 608 1000. 30min. £5, students £4; includes admission to the Old Library and the Book of Kells.)*

DUBLIN FOOTSTEPS. Treads the beaten path of Irish literary greats past the Georgian architecture that housed them. *(Meet upstairs at the Grafton St. Bewley's. Tel. 496 0641 or 490 9341. 2hr. M, W, F, and Sa 10:30am. £5. Free coffee at the end.)*

1916 REBELLION WALKING TOUR. The creation of the Republic began with the 1916 Rebellion (see **Easter Rising,** p. 13), which took place solely in Dublin. This tour shows you the scars it left and the state it created. *(Meet at the International Bar, 23 Wicklow St. Tel. 676 2493. 2hr. Mid-May to Aug. Tu-Sa 11:30am. £6, students and seniors £5.)*

AUDIO WALKING TOUR OF DUBLIN. This comprehensive guide will please those who don't ask questions. *(Aston Quay. Tel. 670 5266. Open daily 10am-5pm. Half-day £6, students £4.50; full day £8; deposit required.)*

GUIDED PUB CRAWLS

THE DUBLIN LITERARY PUB CRAWL. The tour traces Dublin's liquid history in reference to its literary history, spewing snatches of history between delivering entrancing monologues. *(Meet at The Duke, 2 Duke St. Tel. 670 5602; email colm@dublinpubcrawl.com; www.dublinpubcrawl.com. Easter-Oct. M-Sa 7:30pm, Su noon and 7:30pm; Nov.-Easter Th-Sa 7:30pm, Su noon and 7:30pm. £6.50, students £5.50. Book at the door or at the Suffolk St. tourist office for 15p extra.)*

MUSICAL PUB CRAWL. An enjoyable jaunt led by two musicians and their instruments, who'll teach you how to differentiate between one session and another by the end. *(Show up a little early upstairs at Oliver St. John Gogarty's, on the corner of Fleet and Anglesea St. Tel. 478 0193; email musical.pub.crawl@officelink.eunet.ie. May-Oct. daily 7:30pm, Nov. and Feb.-Apr. F-Sa 7:30pm. £6, students and seniors £5.)*

GUIDED BICYCLE TOURS

DUBLIN BIKE TOURS. If you want to get more exercise and cover more ground, rent a bike and take a tour. Guides lead you past a mix of cultural and historical sights while taking advantage of quieter back streets. *(Meet 15min. early at the front gate of Christ Church. Tel. 679 0899. 3hr. Apr.-Oct. daily 10am and 2pm; Dublin at Dawn Tour Sa 6am. £15 includes bike and insurance, concession £12. Booking ahead is advised.)*

BUS TOURS

Dublin Bus runs a number of tours through and around the city, including the first three listings below. All three depart from the Dublin Bus office, 59 O'Connell St. (Tel. 873 4222. Open M-Sa 9am-7pm.)

THE GRAND DUBLIN TOUR. Parades non-stop around all the major sights and every corner of the city. Take photographs from an open-top bus, or a normal double-decker in the rare event of Irish rain. *(3hr. Daily 10:15am and 2:15pm. £10.)*

THE DUBLIN CITY HOP-ON HOP-OFF. This tour lets you thoroughly explore Dublin's major sights, including the Writers Museum, Trinity, and the Guinness Brewery. You can exit and board the bus at your leisure. *(Roughly 1¼hr. Departs Apr.-Sept. daily nearly every 10min. 9:30am-5pm, then every ½hr until 7pm. £7.)*

THE GHOSTBUS TOUR. The "world's only Ghostbus" lets you see the dead and undead aspects of the city. *(2¼hr. Tu-F 7:30pm, and Sa 7, 7:30, and 9:30pm. £12.)*

GUIDE FRIDAY. Hear the perspective of a private bus line, with open-top buses and full hop-on/hop-off privileges, not to mention discounts at a number of sights. *(Trips depart from O'Connell St. Tel. 676 5377. Buses run frequently mid-July to Aug. 9:30am-7:30pm; Oct.-Mar. 9:30am-4:30pm; Sept. and Apr. to mid-July 9:30am-5:30pm. £8, students and seniors £7, children £3.)*

◉ SIGHTS

SOUTH SIDE

TRINITY COLLEGE AND NEARBY

TRINITY COLLEGE. Ancient walls contain Trinity's sprawling expanse of stone buildings, cobblestone walks, and green grounds. The British built Trinity in 1592 as a Protestant religious seminary that would "civilize the Irish and cure them of Popery" (see **Trinity College Chronology,** p. 11). The college became part of the accepted path that members of the Anglo-Irish elite tread on their way to high government and social positions. The Catholic Jacobites who briefly held Dublin in 1689 used the campus as a barracks and prison (see **The Protestant Ascendancy,** p. 10). Jonathan Swift, Robert Emmett, Thomas Moore, Edmund Burke, Oscar Wilde, and Samuel Beckett are just a few of the famous Irishmen who studied here. Bullet holes from the Easter 1916 uprising scar the stone entrance. Until the 1960s, the Catholic church deemed it a cardinal sin to attend Trinity; once the church lifted the ban, the size of the student body more than tripled. *(Between Westmoreland and Grafton St. in the very center of Dublin, the main entrance fronts the block-long traffic circle now called College Green. Pearse St. runs along the north edge of the college, Nassau St. to its south. Tel. 608 1000. Grounds always open. Free.)*

THE OLD LIBRARY. This 1712 chamber holds an invaluable collection of ancient manuscripts including the magnificent **Book of Kells.** Around AD 800, four Irish monks squeezed multicolored ink from bugs and plants to illuminate this four-volume edition of the Gospels. Each page holds a dizzyingly intricate latticework of Celtic designs, into which images of animals and Latin text are interwoven. In 1007 the books were unearthed at Kells, where thieves had apparently buried them. For preservation purposes, the display is limited to two volumes, of which one page is turned each month. A new exhibit elegantly details the history of book's illumination, as well as describing the library's other prize holdings. The **Book of Durrow,** Ireland's oldest manuscript (see **Pre-Christian Ireland,** p. 7), is also on display here periodically. Upstairs, the library's **Long Room** contains "Ireland's oldest harp," the so-called **Brian Ború Harp** (the design model for Irish coins), and one of the few remaining 1916 proclamations of the Republic of Ireland. The room's towering shelves hold thousands of obsolete tomes. *(From the main gate, go straight; the library is on the southern side of Library Square. Open June-Sept. M-Sa 9:30am-5pm, Su noon-4:30pm; Oct.-May M-Sa 9:30am-5pm, Su noon-4:30pm. £4.50, students and seniors £4.)*

THE PHIL Founded in 1684, Trinity College's University Philosophical Society is the oldest undergraduate student society in the world. With a current membership of 2000 students, "the Phil" counts Jonathan Swift, Oscar Wilde, Bram Stoker, and Samuel Beckett among its alumni. Throughout the past three centuries, the Society has held debates and read papers every Thursday evening at 7:30pm, even through times of trouble. Perhaps its most famous feat began as a humble protest against a young dean with a penchant for Draconian discipline. Three or four students in 1734 threw rocks at the window of the teacher, Edward Ford. He responded by shooting a gun vaguely in their direction. The students, in heightened anger, returned to their own rooms and loaded up on the pistols that, being responsible students, they kept there. In the ensuing shoot-out, Ford was mortally wounded and died within hours. The students were promptly expelled from Trinity, but they avoided incarceration because the judge deemed the event merely a student prank that got out of hand.

OTHER SIGHTS WITHIN TRINITY. In Trinity's Davis Theater, the **Dublin Experience** audiovisual show takes visitors on a 45min. historical tour of Dublin, reminiscent of grade-school educational films. (Daily 10am-5pm, on the hour. £3, students and seniors £2.50; combination ticket to Library and Dublin Experience £6, students £5.) **The Douglas Hyde Gallery,** on the south side of campus, exhibits the works of contemporary artists. (Open M-Sa 10am-5pm. Free.) During the academic year, Trinity pulses with events, which are listed on bulletin boards under the front arch and by the Nassau St. entrance. Upwards of 50 concerts and plays are posted.

BANK OF IRELAND. Staring down Trinity from across College Green is the monolithic Bank of Ireland. Built in 1729, the building originally housed the 18th-century **Irish Parliament,** a body that represented the Anglo-Irish landowning class. Its members envisioned a semi-independent Irish "nation" under the British crown made up of the privileged Protestants of the Pale. After the Act of Union (see p. 10), the British sold the building to the bank on the condition that the bank blot out any material evidence of the parliament. Enormous curved walls and pillars were erected around the original structure to make the whole thing look more impressive; the bank inside is actually much smaller. Tourists can still visit the former chamber of the **House of Lords,** which contains a huge 1780s chandelier and Maundy Money—special coins once given to the poor on the Thursday before Easter and legal tender only for that day. (Tel. 677 6801. Open M-W and F 10am-4pm, Th 10am-5pm. 45min. guided talks Tu 10:30am, 11:30am, and 1:45pm. Free.)

GRAFTON STREET. The few blocks South of College Green are off-limits to cars and ground zero for shopping tourists and residents alike. Grafton Street's **street performers** range from string octets to jive limboists. Upstairs at the Grafton St. branch of Bewley's is the **Bewley's Museum,** located inside the coffee chain's former chocolate factory. Tea-tasting machines, corporate history, and a display on Bewley's Quaker heritage are among the curiosities. (Open during cafe hours. Free.)

THE DUBLIN CIVIC MUSEUM. This pint-size, two-story townhouse holds photos, antiquities, and knick-knacks relating to the whole range of Dublin life, from the accessories of the Vikings to the shoes of Patrick Cotter, the 8'6" "giant of Ireland." (58 South William St. Tel. 679 4260. Open Tu-Sa 10am-6pm, Su 11am-2pm. Free.)

KILDARE STREET

The block bordered by Kildare St., Merrion St. (the continuation of Nassau St.), and St. Stephen's Green is loaded with national buildings.

THE NATIONAL MUSEUM. The largest of Dublin's museums contains a number of beautiful artifacts spanning the last two millennia. The museum contains extraordinary artifacts of ancient Ireland. One room gleams with the **Tara Brooch, Ardagh Hoard** (including the great chalice), and other Celtic goldwork. Another section is devoted to the Republic's founding years, and shows off the bloody vest of nation-

It's a **big world.**

And **we've got** the **network** to cover it.

Use **AT&T Direct**® Service
when you're out exploring the world.

AT&T
direct
service

Exploring the corners of the earth? We're with you. With the world's most powerful network, **AT&T Direct®** Service gives you fast, clear connections from more countries than anyone,* and the option of an English-speaking operator. All it takes is your AT&T Calling Card. And the planet is yours.

For a list of AT&T Access Numbers, take the attached wallet guide.

*Comparison to major U.S.-based carriers.

AT&T Access Numbers

Austria ●	0800-200-288	Egypt ●(Cairo)	510-0200
Albania ●	00-800-0010	(Outside Cairo)	02-510-0200
Armenia ●▲	8♦10111	Estonia	800-800-1001
Bahrain	800-000	Finland ●	9800-100-10
Belgium ●	0-800-100-10	France	0-800-99-0011
Bulgaria ▲	00-800-0010	Germany	0800-2255-288
Croatia	0800-220111	Greece ●	00-800-1311
Czech Rep. ▲	00-42-000-101	Hungary ●	00-800-01111
Cyprus ●	080-90010	Ireland ✓	1-800-550-000
Denmark	8001-0010	Israel	1-800-94-94-949

Italy ●	172-1011	Russia ●▲	
Luxembourg†	0-800-0111	(Moscow)▶	755-5042
Macedonia, F.Y.R. of ○		(St. Petersburg)▶	325-5042
	99-800-4288	Saudi Arabia ◇	1-800-10
Malta	0800-890-110	South Africa	0-800-99-0123
Monaco ●	800-90-288	Spain	900-99-00-11
Morocco	002-11-0011	Sweden	020-799-111
Netherlands ●	0800-022-9111	Switzerland ●	0-800-89-0011
Norway	800-190-11	Turkey ●	00-800-12277
Poland ●▲	00-800-111-1111	U.K. ▲✧	0800-89-0011
Portugal ▲	0800-800-128	U.K. ▲✧	0500-89-0011
Romania ●	01-800-4288	U.A. Emirates ●	800-121

FOR EASY CALLING WORLDWIDE
1. Just dial the AT&T Access Number for the country you are calling from. *2.* Dial the phone number you're calling. *3.* Dial your card number.

For access numbers not listed ask any operator for **AT&T Direct®** Service. In the U.S. call 1-800-331-1140 for a wallet guide listing all worldwide AT&T Access Numbers.
Visit our Web site at: www.att.com/traveler
Bold-faced countries permit country-to-country calling outside the U.S.
- ● Public phones require coin or card deposit.
- ▲ May not be available from every phone/payphone.
- ▶ Additional charges apply outside the city.
- ◇ Calling available to most countries.
- ✓ Await second dial tone.
- ✓ Use U.K. access number in N. Ireland.
- ✧ If call does not complete, use 0800-013-0011.
- † Collect calling from public phones.
- ○ Public phones require local coin payment through the call duration.

When placing an international call *from* the U.S., dial 1 800 CALL ATT.

©1999 AT&T

alist hero **James Connolly.** Much of the Republican presentation has been moved to the recent offshoot **National Museum, Collins Barracks,** off Wolfe Tone Quay on the west end of town (see p. 118). *(Kildare St., adjacent to Leinster House. Tel. 677 7444. Open Tu-Sa 10am-5pm, Su 2-5pm. Free. Guided tours at 2:15, 3:15, and 4:15pm. £1.)*

THE NATIONAL GALLERY. A collection of over 2400 canvases includes paintings by Brueghel, Goya, Carravaggio, Vermeer, Rembrandt, and El Greco. Works by 19th-century Irish artists compose a major part of the collection; of special interest are the works of **Jack Yeats,** the brother of William. Portraits of Lady Gregory, James Joyce, and George Bernard Shaw complete the display. *(Merrion Square West. Tel. 661 5133. Open M-Sa 10am-5:30pm, Th 10am-8:30pm, Su 2-5pm. Free guided tours Sa 3pm, Su 3 and 4pm. Free.)*

THE NATURAL HISTORY MUSEUM. Tightly packed galleries contain dead animals in menacing poses. The collection of Irish wildlife ranges from the extinct Great Irish Elk to leeches and tapeworms. *(Merrion Square West. Open M-W and F-Sa 10am-5:30pm, Th 10am-8:30pm, Su 2-5pm. Free.)*

LEINSTER HOUSE. The Duke of Leinster built his home on Kildare Street back in 1745, when most of the urban upper-crust lived north of the Liffey. By erecting his house so far south, where land was cheaper, he was able to front it with an enormous lawn. Now Leinster House provides chambers for the **Irish parliament,** or An tOireachtas (on tir-OCH-tas). It holds both the **Dáil** (DOIL), which does most of the government work, and the **Seanad** (SHAN-ad), the less-powerful upper house. The Dáil meets, very roughly, from October to Easter (with lots of breaks), Tuesday and Wednesday 3-9pm, and Thursday 10am-3pm. When the Dáil is in session, visitors can view the proceedings by contacting the Captain of the Guard, who conducts some **tours** of the Dáil's galleries. *(Tel. 678 9911. Passport necessary for identification. Tours meet hourly on Saturdays in the adjacent National Gallery.)*

THE NATIONAL LIBRARY. Chronicles Irish history and exhibits literary objects in its entrance room. *(Kildare St, adjacent to Leinster House. Tel. 661 2523. Open M-W 10am-9pm, Th-F 10am-5pm, Sa 10am-1pm. Free. Academic reason required to obtain a library card and entrance to the reading room; usually just "being a student" is enough.)*

ST. STEPHEN'S GREEN AND MERRION SQUARE

ST. STEPHEN'S GREEN. The 22-acre park was a private estate until the Guinness clan bequeathed it to the city. Today the park is a hotbed of activity, crowded with arched bridges, an artificial lake, flowerbeds, fountains, gazebos, punks, couples, strollers, swans, a waterfall, and a Henry Moore statue. During the summer, all enjoy the outdoor musical and theatrical productions near the old bandstand. *(Kildare, Dawson, and Grafton St. all lead to it. Open M-Sa 8am-dusk, Su 10am-dusk.)*

MERRION SQUARE. The square and adjacent **Fitzwilliam Street** visually stimulate with Georgian buildings fronted by elaborate doorways. W.B. Yeats moved from 18 Fitzwilliam St. to 82 Merrion Sq. Farther south on **Harcourt St.,** playwright George Bernard Shaw and Dracula's creator, Bram Stoker, were once neighbors at #61 and #16, respectively. **#29 Lower Fitzwilliam Street** gives tourists an impression of late 18th-century Dublin domestic life. *(Tel. 702 6165. Open Tu-Sa 10am-5pm, Su 2-5pm. 1hr. guided tour. £2.50, students and seniors £1.)* The prim Georgian townhouses continue up **Dawson Street,** which connects St. Stephen's Green to Trinity College one block west of Leinster House. Dawson street has the honour of providing an address to the **Mansion House,** home of the Lord Mayors of Dublin since 1715. The house's eclectic facade exhibits the styles of several eras. The Irish state declared its independence here in 1919; the Anglo-Irish truce was signed here in 1921.

NEWMAN HOUSE. A fully restored building that was once the seat of **University College Dublin,** the Catholic answer to Trinity (see p. 111). Joyce's years here are chronicled in *Portrait of the Artist as a Young Man.* The poet Gerard Manley Hopkins spent the last years of his life teaching classics at the college. *(85-86 St. Stephen's Green South. Tel. 706 7422. Open June-Sept. Tu-F noon-5pm, Sa 2-5pm, Su 11am-2pm. £2, students and seniors £1.)*

COUNTY DUBLIN

THE SHAW BIRTHPLACE. Suitable for viewing as either a period piece or a glimpse into the childhood of George Bernard Shaw. Mrs. Shaw held recitals here, sparking little George's interest in music, and kept a lovely Victorian garden, sparking George's interest in landscape painting. So how did he get into socialism in London? (*33 Synge St. Tel. 475 0854. Between Grantham and Harrington St. off Camden Rd. near the Grand Canal Bridge. Convenient to buses #16, 19, or 122 from O'Connell St. Open May-Oct. M-Sa 10am-5pm, Su 11am-5pm. £2.60, students and seniors £2.10; joint ticket with Dublin Writers Museum £4.60, or the Writers Museum and the James Joyce Museum £6.50.*) Nearby is the **Grand Canal**, where a statue of the poet **Patrick Kavanagh** sits on his favourite bench by the water.

THE IRISH JEWISH MUSEUM. A restored former synagogue houses a large collection of artifacts, documents, and photographs chronicling the history of the small Jewish community in Ireland from 1079 (five arrived and were sent away) through later waves of European migration. The most famous Dublin Jew covered is, predictably, Leopold Bloom, hero of *Ulysses*. (*3-4 Walworth Rd., off Victoria St. South Circular Rd. runs to Victoria St.; from there the museum is signposted; buses #16, 20, or any others to South Circular Rd. will take you there. Tel. 676 0737. Open May-Sept. Tu, Th, and Su 11am-3:30pm, Oct.-Apr. Su 10:30am-2:30pm. Access at other times is fairly easily arranged.*)

TEMPLE BAR

West of Trinity between Dame St. and the Liffey, the Temple Bar neighborhood wriggles with activity. Narrow cobblestone streets link cheap cafes, hole-in-the-wall theaters, rock venues, and used clothing and record stores. In the early 1980s, the Irish transport authority intended to replace the neighborhood with a seven-acre transportation center and short-term leased the land while acquiring all the necessary property. The artists and transient types who lived around Temple Bar started a brouhaha about being forced into homelessness. In 1985 they circulated petitions and saved their homes and businesses from the rapacious transit project. Temple Bar then grew at lightning speed into one of the hottest spots for nightlife in Europe. To steer the growth to ends more cultural than alcoholic, the government-sponsored Temple Bar Properties has since spent over £30 million to build a whole flock of arts-related tourist attractions, with independent ones sprouting up alongside.

CULTURAL CENTERS AND GALLERIES. Among Temple Bar's most inviting are: **The Irish Film Centre** (see **Cinema,** p. 121), featuring specialty and art house film (6 Eustace St.; tel. 679 5744; email ifc@iol.ie; iftn.ie/ifc); **The Temple Bar Music Centre** (see p. 119), with events and concerts virtually every night (Curved St.; tel. 670 9202; email tbmusic@indigo.ie; www.indigo.ie/~tbmusic); **The Ark,** a cultural center aimed at seven- to fourteen-year-olds (Eustace St.; tel. 670 7788); Ireland's only **Gallery of Photography** (Meeting House Sq.; tel. 671 4654; email gallery@irish-photography.com); and the sizeable **Temple Bar Gallery & Studios** (5-9 Temple Bar; tel. 671 0073; email tbgs@indigo.ie; www.paddynet.ie/tbgs).

DAME STREET AND THE CATHEDRALS

DUBLIN CASTLE. Norman King John built the castle in 1204 on top of the first Viking settlement of Dubh Linn; more recently, a series of structures from various eras have covered the site, dating mostly from the 18th and 19th centuries and culminating in a rather uninspired 20th-century office complex. For 700 years after its construction, Dublin Castle was the seat of British rule in Ireland. Fifty insurgents died at the castle's walls on Easter Monday, 1916 (see **Easter Rising,** p. 13). Since 1938, the presidents of Ireland have been inaugurated here. The **State Apartments,** once home to English viceroys, now entertain EU representatives and foreign heads of state. Next door, the **Dublin City Hall,** designed as the Royal Exchange in 1779, boasts an intricate inner dome and statues of national heroes like Daniel O'Connell. (*Dame St., at the intersection of Parliament and Castle St. Tel. 677 7129. State Apartments open M-F 10am-5pm, Sa–Su and holidays 2-5pm, except during official functions. £3, students and seniors £2. Grounds free.*)

CHRIST CHURCH CATHEDRAL. Dublin's cathedrals are considered works of art more than centers of worship in the 20th century. Built centuries ago for Catholic worship, they were forced to convert to the Church of Ireland in the 16th century (see p. 8). Sitric Silkenbeard, King of the Dublin Norsemen, built a wooden church on this site around 1038, and Strongbow rebuilt it in stone in 1169. Further additions were made in the following century and in the 1870s. Stained glass sparkles above the raised crypts, one of which supposedly belongs to Strongbow. The cavernous crypt once held shops and drinking houses, but now cobwebs hang down from the ceiling, fragments of ancient pillars lie about like bleached bones, and a mummified cat is caught in the act of chasing a mummified mouse. *(At the end of Dame St., uphill and across from the Castle. Tel. 677 8099. Take buses #50 from Eden Quay or 78A from Aston Quay. Open daily 10am-5:30pm except during services. Donation of £2 strongly encouraged, concessions £1.)*

DUBLINIA. This recent appendage to **Christ Church Cathedral** recreates medieval Dublin, with life-size reconstructions. It's informative, if a little underwhelming. Wholey uncharming is the buboe-covered mannequin in the Black Death display. *(Adjacent to Christ Church Cathedral. Tel. 679 4611. Open Apr.-Oct. daily 10am-5pm; Sept.-Mar. 11am-4pm. £4, students and children £3, includes admission to Christ Church.)*

ST. PATRICK'S CATHEDRAL. The body of the church dates to the 12th century, although Sir Benjamin Guinness remodeled much of the church in 1864. Measuring 300 ft. from stem to stern, it's Ireland's largest cathedral. St. Patrick allegedly baptized converts in the park next door. Artifacts and relics from the Order of St. Patrick show up inside. Jonathan Swift spent his last years as Dean of St. Patrick's; his crypt rises above the south nave. *(From Christ Church, Nicholas St. runs south and downhill, becoming Patrick St. Take bus #49, 49A, 50, 54A, 56A, 65, 65B, 77, or 77A from Eden Quay. Tel. 475 4817. Open Apr.-Sept. daily 9:30-11am, 12:45-3pm, and 4:15-5pm; Oct.-Mar. 10-11am and 12:45-3pm. £2, concessions £1.)* Beside the cathedral, **Marsh's Library** is Ireland's oldest public library. A peek inside reveals its elegant wire alcoves, and an extensive collection of early maps. *(St. Patrick's Close. Tel. 454 3511. Open M and W-F 10am-12:45pm and 2-5pm, Sa 10:30am-12:45pm. £1 donation expected.)*

ST. AUDOEN'S CHURCH. The Normans founded Dublin's oldest parish church. It's not to be confused with the more modern, Catholic St. Audoen's. Papal Bulls were read aloud here during the Middle Ages. *(High St. Open Sa-Su 2:30-5pm.)* **St. Audoen's Arch,** built in 1215 next to the church and now obscured by a narrow alley, is the only gate that survives from Dublin's medieval **city walls.** During the 16th century, the walls ran from Parliament St. to Dublin Castle, along the castle walls to Little Ship St., along Francis St. to Bridge St., and then along the Liffey.

DUBLIN'S VIKING ADVENTURE. Walk through the Dublin of the 9th and 10th centuries, and talk with Dubliners of that time. For added fun, try to get the actors to break character. *(Essex St. West. Tel. 679 6040. Take buses #51, 51A, 51B, 79, and 90 from Aston Quay. Open Tu-Sa 10am-4:30pm; closed Nov.-Feb. 1-2pm. £5, students and seniors £4.)*

GUINNESS BREWERY AND KILMAINHAM

GUINNESS HOPSTORE. Guiness brews its black magic on Crane St. off James St., and perpetuates the legend of the world's best stout at its Hopstore. The building still smells from the hops that were stored there for 200 years. Farsighted Arthur Guinness signed a 9000-year lease at the original 1759 brewery nearby. The Hopstore has displays on the historical and modern processes of brewing and a short promotional film. Best of all is the bar, where visitors get two complimentary glasses of dark and creamy goodness. Some believe this glass to be the best Guinness in Dublin and, as such, the world's best beer. Don't even ask if it's "good for you." Drink, silly tourist, drink. *(St. James's Gate. From Christ Church Cathedral, follow High St. west (away from downtown) through its name changes—Cornmarket, Thomas, and James. Take bus #51B or 78A from Aston Quay or bus #123 from O'Connell St. Tel. 408 4800; www.guinness.ie. Open Apr.-Sept. M-Sa 9:30am-5pm, Su 10:30am-4:30pm; Oct.-Mar. M-Sa 9:30am-4pm, Su noon-4pm. £5, students and seniors £4, under 12 £1.)*

KILMAINHAM GAOL. Almost all of the rebels who fought in Ireland's struggle for independence from 1792 to 1921 spent time here. "The cause for which I die has been rebaptized during this past week by the blood of as good men as ever trod God's earth," wrote Sean MacDiarmada in a letter from Kilmainham to his family while he awaited execution for participation in the 1916 Easter Rising (see p. 13). The jail's last occupant was **Éamon de Valera,** the future Éire leader. Today the former prison is a museum that traces the history of penal practices over the last two centuries. Tours, which lasts about an hour, begin in the prison chapel. *(Inchicore Road. Take bus #51 from Aston Quay, #51A from Lower Abbey St., or #79 from Aston Quay. Tel. 453 5984. Open Apr.-Sept. daily 9:30am-4:45pm; Oct.-Mar. M-F 9:30am-4pm, Su 10am-4:45pm. £3, seniors £2, students and children £1.25.)*

THE ROYAL HOSPITAL KILMAINHAM. It was built in 1679 as a hospice for retired or disabled soldiers. Today the compound houses the **Irish Museum of Modern Art.** The facade and courtyard copy those of Les Invalides in Paris; the baroque chapel is quite a sight, too. Museum curators took some heat over the avant-garde use of this historic space. Modern Irish artists are intermixed with others as the gallery builds up a permanent collection in its unfortunately shaped galleries. *(Military Road. Tel. 612 9900; email info@modernart.ie. Museum and building open Tu-Sa 10am-5:30pm, Su noon-5:30pm. Free. Guided tours W and F 2:30pm, Su 12:15pm. Call for events.)*

NORTH SIDE
O'CONNELL ST. AND PARNELL SQUARE

O'CONNELL STREET. Dublin's biggest shopping thoroughfare starts at the Liffey and leads to Parnell Square. At 150 ft., it was once the widest street in Europe, though it's hard to imagine anyone traveling to Madrid in 1749 with a yardstick to compare. In its pre-Joycean heyday, it was known as Sackville St.; later the name was changed in honor of "The Liberator" (see p. 14). The center traffic islands contain monuments to Irish leaders Parnell, O'Connell, and James Larkin, who organized the heroic Dublin general strike of 1913 (see p. 13). **O'Connell's statue** faces the Liffey and O'Connell Bridge; the winged women aren't angels but Winged Victories, although one has a bullet hole from 1916 in a rather inglorious place. At the other end of the street, **Parnell's statue** points towards nearby Mooney's pub while Parnell's famous words "Thus far and no further" are engraved below his feet. A block up O'Connell street, where Cathedral St. intersects on the right, the 1988 statue of a woman lounging in water is officially named the Spirit of the Liffey or **"Anna Livia,"** unofficially and scathingly called "the floozy in the jacuzzi," "the whore in the sewer" (in Dublin, that rhymes, too), or "Anna Rexia." Newer statue of **Molly Malone** of ballad fame, on Grafton St., gets called "the tart with the cart" and "the dish with the fish." One monument you won't see is **Nelson's Pillar,** a free-standing column that commemorated Trafalgar and stood outside the GPO for 150 years. The IRA blew it up in 1966 in commemoration of the 50th anniversary of the Easter Rising. Nelson's English head rests safely in the Dublin Civic Museum.

THE GENERAL POST OFFICE. Not just a fine place to send a letter, the Post Office was the nerve center of the 1916 Easter Rising (see p. 13). Patrick Pearse read the Proclamation of Irish Independence from its steps. When British troops closed in, mailbags became barricades. Outside, a number of bullet nicks are visible. *(O'Connell Street. Tel 705 7000. Open M-Sa 8am-8pm, Su 10am-6:30pm.)*

HUGH LANE MUNICIPAL GALLERY OF MODERN ART. A small but impressive collection hangs in **Georgian Charlemont House.** When American painter Lane offered to donate his collection of French Impressionist paintings to the city, he did so on the condition that the people of Dublin contribute to the gallery's construction. Because his collection and the architect chosen to build the gallery were foreign, Dubliners refused to lend their support; Yeats lamented their provincial attitudes in a string of poems. Lane's death aboard the *Lusitania* in 1915 raised decades of disputes over his will, resolved by a plan to share the collection between the gallery in Dublin and the Tate Gallery in London. *(Parnell Sq. North. Tel. 874 1903. Open Tu-Th 9:30am-6pm, F-Sa 9:30am-5pm, Su 11am-5pm. Free.)*

COUNTY DUBLIN

DUBLINESE Mastering the Dublin dialect has been a persistent challenge to writers and thespians of the 20th century. James Joyce, Brendan Behan, and Roddy Doyle are just a few ambitious characters who have tried to capture the nuances of this gritty and superbly witty city. The following is a short introduction to Dubliners' favorite phrases.

NAMES FOR OUTSIDERS:
The rivalry between Dubliners and their country cousins is fierce. For Dubliners, all counties outside their own blur into one indiscriminate wasteland populated with "culchies," "plonkers," "turf-gobblers," and "muck-savages."

IN TIMES OF DIFFICULTY:
Dublinese is expeditious in keeping others in line. Idiots are rebuked as "eejits"; in dire situations, they are called "head-the-ball." Total exasperation calls for "shite and onions." When all is restored to order, it's said that "the job's oxo and the ship's name is murphy."

AFFECTIONATE NICKNAMES FOR CIVIC LANDMARKS:
Over the past couple decades, the government has graced the city with several public art works that personify the Irish spirit in the female form. Dubliners have responded with poetic rhetoric. Off Grafton St., the statue of the fetching fishmongress Molly Malone is commonly referred to as "the tart with the cart." The goddess of the River Liffy sits in a fountain on O'Connell St. and is popularly heralded as the "floozy in the jacuzzi" and even "the whore in the sewer" (pronounced WHEW-er).

THE DUBLIN WRITERS' MUSEUM. Read your way through placards and placards describing the city's rich literary heritage, or listen to it on an audio headset tour. Rare editions, manuscripts, and memorabilia of Swift, Shaw, Wilde, Yeats, Beckett, Brendan Behan, Patrick Kavanagh, and Sean O'Casey blend with caricatures, paintings, and an incongruous Zen Garden. *(18 Parnell Sq. North. Tel. 872 2077. Open June-Aug. M-F 10am-6pm, Sa 10am-5pm; Sept.-May M-Sa 10am-5pm. £3, students and seniors £2.55. Combined ticket with either Shaw birthplace or James Joyce Centre £4.60.)* Adjacent to the museum, the **Irish Writer's Centre**, is the center of Ireland's living writing community, providing a working space for today's aspiring Joyces. Frequent poetry and fiction readings present current writings to the public. The center is not a museum, but if you ring the doorbell you can get information about Dublin's literary happenings. *(19 Parnell Sq. North. Tel. 872 1302. Open M-F 9am-5pm.)*

JAMES JOYCE CENTER. This new museum features Joyceana ranging from portraits of individuals who inspired his characters, to the more arcane delights of Joyce's nephew, who runs the place. Feel free to mull over Joyce's works in the library or the tearoom. Call for info on lectures, walking tours, and Bloomsday events. *(35 North Great Georges St. Up Marlborough St., and past Parnell St. Tel. 873 1984; email joycecen@iol.ie. Open M-Sa 9:30am-5pm, Su 12:30-5pm; Jul.-Aug. extra Su hours 11am-5pm. £2.75, students and seniors £2.)*

HOT PRESS IRISH MUSIC HALL OF FAME. Dublin's sparkling new anthem to its musical wonders found a great location. A headset tour takes you through memorabilia-laden displays on the history of Irish music from bards to the modern studio, heaping lavish praise on such stars as Van Morrison, U2, and, uh, Boyzone. The concert venue **HQ** is attached (see Entertainment, p. 119). *(57 Middle Abbey St. Tel. 878 3345; www.irishmusichof.com. Open daily 10am-6pm last entry. £6; students, seniors, and children £4.)*

OTHER SIGHTS. Just past Parnell Sq., the **Garden of Remembrance** eulogizes the martyrs who took the GPO. A cross-shaped pool is visually anchored at one end by a statue representing the mythical Children of Lir, who turned from humans into swans. They proclaim, in Irish, their faith in a vision of freedom: "In the winter of bondage we saw a vision. We melted the snows of lethargy and the river of resurrection flowed from it." *(Open until dusk.)* Turn right on Cathedral St., to find the inconspicuous **Dublin Pro-Cathedral,** the city's center of Catholic worship, where tens of thousands once gathered for Daniel O'Connell's memorial service. "Pro" means "provisional"—many Dublin Catholics want Christ Church Cathedral returned (see p. 114). On Granby Row, the **National Wax Museum** has life-size replicas of everyone from Hitler to the Teletubbies, including the Pope (and his Popemobile) and a life-size rendering of Da Vinci's "Last Supper." *(Tel. 872 6340. Open M-Sa 10am-5:30pm; Su noon-5:30. £3.50, students £2.50, children £2.)*

ALONG THE QUAYS

THE CUSTOM HOUSE. Dublin's greatest architectural triumph, the Custom House was designed and built in the 1780s by James Gandon, who gave up the chance to be St. Petersburg's state architect to settle in Dublin. The building's expanse of columns and domes suggests the mixture of Rome and Venice that the 18th-century Anglo-Irish wanted their city to become. Carved heads along the frieze represent the rivers of Ireland; the Liffey is the only girl in the bunch. *(East of O'Connell St. at Custom House Quay, where Gardiner St. meets the river. Tel. 878 7660. Visitor's Centre open mid-Mar. to Nov. M-F 10am-5pm, Sa-Su 2-5pm; Nov. to mid-Mar. W-F 10am-5pm, Su 2-5pm.)*

FOUR COURTS. Another of Gandon's works, the building appears monumentally impressive from the front, but the back and sides reveal 20th-century ballast. On April 14, 1922, General Rory O'Connor seized the Four Courts on behalf of the anti-Treaty IRA; two months later, the Free State government of Griffith and Collins attacked the Four Courts garrison, starting the Irish Civil War (see p. 14). The building now houses the highest court in Ireland. *(Inn's Quay, several quays to the west of the Custom House.)*

ST. MICHAN'S CHURCH. The dry atmosphere has preserved the corpses in the vaults, which inspired Bram Stoker's *Dracula.* Of particular interest in this creepy place is a 6 ft. 6 in. crusader (dead) and the hanged, drawn, and quartered bodies of two of the 1798 rebels (very dead). *(Church St. Open Mar.-Oct. M-F 10am-12:45pm and 2-4:45pm, Sa 10am-12:45pm; Nov.-Feb. M-F 12:30-3:30pm, Sa 10am-12:45pm. £2, students and seniors £1.50, under 16 50p. Church of Ireland services Su 10am.)*

SMITHFIELD

Dublin is trying to turn this neighborhood by the quays into the next Temple Bar, but with an emphasis on culture rather than nightlife.

OLD JAMESON DISTILLERY. Learn how science, grain, and tradition come together to create the golden fluid called whiskey. A film recounts the rise, fall, and spiritual renaissance of Ireland's favorite spirit; the subsequent tour walks you through the actual creation of the drink. More entertaining and less commercial than the Guinness Brewery tour, the experience ends with a glass of the Irish whiskey of your choice; be quick to volunteer in the beginning and you'll get to sample a whole tray of different whiskeys. Feel the burn. *(Bow St. From O'Connell St., turn onto Henry St. and continue straight as the street dwindles to Mary St., then Mary Ln., then May Ln.; the warehouse is on a cobblestone street on the left. Tel. 807 2355. Tours daily 9:30am-5pm. £3.95, students and seniors £3.)*

CEOL IRISH TRADITIONAL MUSIC CENTRE. Just because the content's traditional doesn't mean the presentation is. Computers and interactive media provide extensive demonstrations of the various instruments, songs, and dances that make up trad as we now know it. A 20min. 180-degree film concludes the exhibit. *(Next door to Jameson, at the base of the large chimney between North King St. and Arran Quay. Tel. 817 3820; email info@ceol.ie; www.ceol.ie. Open M-Sa 9:30am-6pm, Su 10:30am-6pm. £3.92, students and seniors £3.50, children £3.)*

DISTANT SIGHTS

PHOENIX PARK. Europe's largest enclosed public park is most famous for the "Phoenix Park murders" of 1882. The Invincibles, a tiny nationalist splinter group, stabbed the Chief Secretary of Ireland, Lord Cavendish, and his Under-Secretary 200 yd. from the Phoenix Column. A British Unionist journalist forged a series of letters linking Parnell to the murderers (see p. 12). The **Phoenix Column,** a Corinthian column capped with a phoenix rising from flames, is something of a pun—the park's name actually comes from the Irish *Fionn Uisce,* "clean water." The 1760-acre park incorporates the President's residence *(Áras an Uachtaraín),* the U.S. Ambassador's residence, cricket pitches, polo grounds, cattle, and grazing red deer. The deer are quite tame and not to be missed; they usually graze in the thickets near Castleknock Gate. The park is usually peaceful during daylight hours but unsafe at night. *(Take bus #10 from O'Connell St. or #25 or 26 from Middle Abbey St. west along the river. Free.)* **Dublin Zoo,** one of the world's oldest zoos and Europe's largest, is in the park. It contains 700 animals and a discovery center that features the world's biggest egg. *(Bus #10 from O'Connell St. passes the zoo. Tel. 677 1425. Open M-Sa 9:30am-6pm, Su 10:30am-5pm. £6, children and seniors £3.50, families £17.50-22.)*

CASINO MARINO. It's an architectural gem and house of tricks. You can certainly gambol here, but you can't gamble; it's a casino only in the sense of "small house," built for the Earl of Charlemont in 1758 as a seaside villa. Funeral urns on the roof are chimneys, the columns are hollow and serve as drains, the casino has secret tunnels and trick doors, and the lions standing guard are actually made of stone. *(Off Malahide Rd. Take bus #123 from O'Connell St. or #27 or 42 from the quays by Busáras. Tel. 833 1618. Open daily June-Sept. 9:30am-6:30pm, May and Oct. 10am-5pm, Nov. W and Su noon-4pm, Feb.-Apr. Th and Su noon-4pm. Admission by guided tour only. £2, seniors £1.50, students and children £1.)*

GAA MUSEUM. Those interested in or mystified by Irish athletics—hurling, gaelic football, camogie, and handball—will appreciate this establishment at **Croke Park.** The Gaelic Athletic Association presents the rules, history, and heroes of its national sports, with the help of touchscreens, audio-visual shows, and a bit of do-it-yourself. *(Tel. 855 8176. Open May-Sept. daily 9:30am-5pm, Oct.-Apr. Tu-Sa 10am-5pm, Su noon-5pm; last admission 4:30pm; admission on game days to ticket holders only. £3, students and seniors £2, under 12 £1.50.)*

▣ ENTERTAINMENT

Be it poetry or punk you fancy, Dublin is equipped to entertain you. The *Event Guide* (free) is available at the tourist office, Temple Bar restaurants, and the Temple Bar Info center. It comes out every other Friday with ads in the back, fawning reviews in the front, and reasonably complete listings of museums and literary, musical, and theatrical events in between. The glossier *In Dublin* (£1.95) comes out every two weeks with feature articles and listings for music, theater, art exhibitions, comedy shows, clubs, museums, gay venues, and movie theaters. *Events of the Week* is a much smaller, free booklet, and also jammed with ads, but there's good info buried in it. Additionally, hostel staff are often good, if biased, sources of information.

MUSIC

Dublin's music world attracts performers from all over the country. Pubs are the scene of much of the musical action, since they provide musicians with free beer and a venue. There is often a cover charge of £3-4 on better-known acts. *Hot Press* (£1.50) has the most up-to-date music listings, particularly for rock. Its commentaries on the musical scene are usually insightful, and its left-leaning editorials give a clear impression of what the Dublin artistic community is thinking. Tower Records on Wicklow St. has reams of leaflets. Bills posted all over the city also inform of coming attractions. Scheduled concerts tend to start at 9pm, impromptu ones later.

Traditional music (trad) is not a tourist gimmick but a vibrant and important element of the Dublin music scene. Some pubs in the city center have trad sessions nightly, others nearly so: **Hughes', Slattery's, Oliver St. John Gogarty,** and **McDaid's** are all good choices (see **Pubs,** p. 105). The best small venue for live music, from rock to folk, is **Whelan's,** 25 Wexford St. (tel. 478 0766), the continuation of South Great Georges St., with music nightly. Covers vary. Next door, **The Mean Fiddler,** Wexford St., has rollicking shows. Big deal bands frequent the **Baggot Inn,** 143 Baggot St. (tel. 676 1430). U2 played here in the early 80s; some people are still talking about it. **The Temple Bar Music Centre,** Curved St. (tel. 670 9202), has events and concerts virtually every night. The **National Concert Hall,** Earlsfort Terr. (tel. 671 1533), provides a venue for classical concerts and performances. July and August bring nightly shows. (Tickets £6-12, students half-price.) A summer lunchtime series makes a nice break from work on occasional Tuesdays and Fridays. (Tickets £3-6.) Programs for the **National Symphony** and smaller local groups are available at classical music stores and the tourist office. Sunday afternoon jazz is a common phenomenon at such places as the **Café en Seine** (see **Pubs,** p. 105). **Isaac Butt** on Store St. and the **Life** bar (see **Pubs,** p. 106) have periodic jazz as well. The new **HQ** venue (tel. 878 3345), in the Hot Press Hall of Fame on Middle Abbey St. (see **Sights,** p. 116), considers itself one of the nicest venues in Europe. Big acts play at the 1600-capacity **Olympia,** 72 Dame St. (tel. 677 7744), and **Vicar St.,** 99 Vicar St., off Thomas St. (tel. 454 6656). Superstar acts play to huge crowds at **Tivoli Theatre,** 135-138 Francis St. (tel. 454 4472). The very biggest names in music play at **Croke Park,** Clonliffe Rd. (tel. 836 3152), and the **R.D.S.** (tel. 668 0866) in Ballsbridge.

THEATER

Dublin's curtains rise on a full range of mainstream productions and experimental theater. Showtime is generally 8pm. Off Dame St. and Temple Bar, smaller theater companies thrive, presenting new plays and innovative interpretations of the classics. Box office hours are usually for phone reservations; box offices stay open until curtain on performance nights.

◼ **Abbey Theatre,** 26 Lower Abbey St. (tel. 878 7222), was founded by Yeats and his collaborator Lady Gregory in 1904 to promote Irish cultural revival and modernist theater, which turned out to be a bit like promoting corned beef and soy burgers—most people wanted one or the other. J.M. Synge's *Playboy of the Western World* was first performed here in 1907. The production occasioned storms of protest and yet another of Yeats' political poems (see **The Irish Literary Revival,** p. 23). Today the Abbey, like Synge, has become quite respectable as the National Theatre. Tickets £10-16, matinees Sa 2:30 £8, student rate M-Th £8. Box office open M-Sa 10:30am-7pm.

Peacock Theatre, 26 Lower Abbey St. (tel. 878 7222), the more experimental studio theater downstairs from the Abbey. The usual evening shows plus occasional lunchtime plays, concerts, and poetry. Lunch events £8, students £5; theater tickets £8-10, matinee £6. Box office open M-Sa at 7:30pm, 8:15pm curtain; Sa matinees 2:45pm.

Gate Theatre, 1 Cavendish Row (tel. 874 4045), specializes in international period drama. Tickets £13-15; M-Th student discount at curtain with ID £6, subject to availability. Box office open M-Sa 10am-7pm.

Project Arts Centre, 39 East Essex St. (tel. (1850) 260 027). Sets its sights on being avante-garde, and presents every imaginable sort of artistic presentation. Tickets under £10; student concessions available. Box office open daily 11am-10pm. The gallery hosts rotating visual arts exhibitions. Open same time as box office. Free.

Gaiety, South King St. (tel. 677 1717), provides space for modern drama, ballet, music, and the Opera Ireland Society. Tickets £10-16. Box office open M-Sa 10am-8pm.

Andrews Lane Theatre, Andrews Ln. (tel. 679 5720), off Dame St. Every sort of drama on two stages; the studio stage is usually more experimental. Main stage tickets £8-13, studio £5-8. Box office open daily 10:30am-7pm.

City Arts Centre, 23-25 Moss St. (tel. 677 0643), parallel to Tara St. off Georges Quay. Avant-garde exploration of political and sexual issues. Tickets £6, students £4. Box office open daily 9:15am-5pm.

Samuel Beckett Theatre, Trinity College (tel. 608 1000). Inside the campus. Hosts anything it happens by, including scores of student shows.

CINEMA

Ireland's well-supported film industry got a kick in the pants with the arrival of the **Irish Film Centre,** 6 Eustace St. (tel. 679 3477; email fii@ifc.ie; www.iftn.ie/ifc), Temple Bar. The IFC mounts tributes and festivals, including a French film festival in October and a gay and lesbian film festival in early August. A variety of classic and European art house films appear throughout the year. You must be a "member" to buy tickets. (Weekly membership £1; yearly membership £10, students £7.50. Membership must be purchased at least 15min. before start of show; each member can buy only 4 tickets per screening. Matinees £2; 5pm showing £2.50; after 7pm £4, students £3. 18 and older.) **The Screen,** D'Olier St. (tel. 672 5500), also runs artsy reels. First-run movie houses cluster on O'Connell St., the quays, and Middle Abbey St. The **Savoy,** O'Connell St. (tel. 874 6000), and **Virgin,** Parnell St. (tel. 872 8400), offer a wide selection of major releases. If their screens aren't big enough for you, head to the **Sheridan IMAX,** Parnell Center, Parnell St. (tel. 817 4200).

SPORTS AND RECREATION

Dubliners aren't as sports-crazy as their country cousins tend to be, but that's not saying much. Sports are still a serious business, especially since most final games take place here. The season for **Gaelic football** and **hurling** (see **Sports,** p. 30) runs from mid-February to November. Action-packed and often brutal, these games are entertaining for any sports-lover. Provincial finals take place in July, national semifinals on Sundays in August (hurling the first week, football the 2nd and 3rd weeks), and All-Ireland Finals in either late August or early September. Games are played in **Croke Park** and on **Phibsborough Rd.** Tickets are theoretically available at the turnstiles, but they tend to sell out quickly; All-Ireland Finals tickets sell out immediately. Your best bet is to hit the Dublin pubs on game day and see who's selling. Home games of the Irish **rugby** team are played in **Lansdowne Road Stadium,** with the peak of the season spanning from February to early April. **Camogie** (women's hurling) finals also occur in September. For sports information, check the Friday papers or contact the Gaelic Athletic Association (tel. 836 3232). **Greyhound racing** continues all year. (W, Th, and Sa at 8pm at Shelbourne Park; tel. 668 3502. M, Tu, and F at 8pm at Harold's Cross; tel. 497 1081.) **Horse racing** runs and bets at Leopardstown Racetrack, Foxrock, Dublin 18 (tel. 289 2888). At the beginning of August the **Royal Dublin Horse Show** takes place at the RDS in Ballsbridge.

FESTIVALS AND EVENTS

The tourist office's annual *Calendar of Events* (£1) offers info on events throughout Ireland, including Dublin's many festivals, antique and craft fairs, flower marts, horse shows, and the like. The biweekly *Events Guide* or *In Dublin* (£1.95) are also good sources.

BLOOMSDAY. Dublin returns to 1904 each year on June 16, the day on which the 24hr. journey of Joyce's *Ulysses* takes place. Festivities are held all week long, starting before the big day and (to a lesser extent) continuing after it. The James Joyce Cultural Centre (see p. 116) sponsors a reenactment of the funeral and wake, a lunch at Davy Byrne's, and a breakfast with Guinness. *(Tel. 873 1984.)* On the day itself, a Messenger Bike Rally culminates in St. Stephen's Green with drink and food. Many bookstores have readings from *Ulysses.* Some of the better ones are Hodges Figgis and Waterstone's (see **Literary Shopping,** below).

MUSIC FESTIVALS. The **Festival of Music in Great Irish Houses,** held during the second and third weeks of June, organizes concerts of period music in 18th-century homes across the country, including ones in the city. *(Tel. 278 1528.)* The **Feis Ceoil** music festival goes trad in mid-March. *(Tel. 676 7365.)* The **Dublin International Organ and Choral Festival** lifts every voice in Christ Church Cathedral. *(Tel. 677 3066 ext. 416; email organs@diocf.iol.ie.)* The **Guinness Blues Festival** is a three-day extravaganza in mid-July, getting bigger and broader each year. *(Tel. 497 0381; www.guinessbluesfest.com.)* Ask at the tourist office about *fleadhs* (FLAHS), traditional day-long music festivals that pop up periodically.

ST. PATRICK'S DAY. The half-week leading up to it occasions a city-wide carnival of concerts, fireworks, street theater, and intoxicated madness. Many pubs offer special promotions, contests, and extended hours. *(Mar. 17. Tel. 676 3205; email info@paddyfest.ie; www.paddyfest.ie.)*

THE DUBLIN THEATRE FESTIVAL. This premier cultural event, held the first two weeks of October, is a spree of about 20 works of theater from Ireland and around the world. Tickets may be purchased all year at participating theaters, and, as the festival draws near, at the Festival Booking Office. *(47 Nassau St. Tel. 677 8439. Tickets £10-16, student discounts vary by venue.)*

THE DUBLIN FILM FESTIVAL. Irish and international movies make up nearly two weeks of screenings, with a panoply of seminars in tow. *(March. Tel. 679 2937; email dff@iol.ie; www.iol.ie/dff.)*

SHOPPING

Dublin is not really a center for international trade, and consumer goods are generally expensive. Your time may be better spent in pubs and castles. That said, if something is made anywhere in Ireland, you can probably find it in Dublin. Stores are usually open Monday through Saturday from 9am to 6pm, with later hours on Thursdays (until 7-8pm). Tiny shops pop up everywhere along the streets both north and south of the Liffey, but Dublin's major shopping is on **Grafton** and **Henry St.** On pedestrianized Grafton St., well-dressed consumers crowd into boutiques and restaurants, while sidewalk buskers lay down their caps for money. Teens and barely-twenties buy their used clothes and punk discs in the **Temple Bar.** Across the river, **Henry St.** and **Talbot St.** sport shops for those on a tighter budget. On **Moore St.,** street vendors sell fresh produce at very low prices. (M-Sa 7am-5pm.) **Clery's,** Upper O'Connell St. (tel. 878 6000), is Dublin's principal department store. (Open M-W and Sa 9am-6:30pm, Th 9am-9pm, F 9am-8pm.)

At the top of Grafton St., **St. Stephen's Green Shopping Centre** is, well, a mall. Two more shopping malls are planted near O'Connell Street: **ILAC,** off Mary St., and the **Jervis Shopping Center,** up by Parnell St. Nearby, Lord Powerscourt's 200-year-old townhouse on Clarendon St. has been converted into the **Powerscourt Townhouse Centre**—a string of chic boutiques carrying Irish crafts. GenX shoppers should head to **Georges St. Market Arcade** on South Great Georges St. near Dame St. The arcade includes a number of vintage clothing, jewelry, and used record stalls as well as a fortune-teller. (Open M-Sa 10am-6pm, Th 8am-7pm.)

DUBLIN'S LITERARY SHOPPING

Eason, 80 Middle Abbey St. (tel. 873 3811), off O'Connell St. A floorspace bohemoth. Lots of serious tomes and an extensive "Irish interest" section. Wide selection of local and foreign magazines and newspapers. Their bargain shelves are in the cleverly named **Bargain Books,** and reside diagonally across Abbey St. Open M-W and Sa 8:30am-6:45pm, Th 8:30am-8:45pm, F 8:30am-7:45pm, Su 1:45-5:45pm.

Winding Stair Bookstore, 40 Ormond Quay (tel. 873 3292), on the North Side. 3 atmospheric floors of good tunes, great views, and cheap food. New and used books, contemporary Irish literature, and literary periodicals. Open M-Sa 10am-6pm, Su 1-6pm.

Fred Hanna's, 27-29 Nassau St. (tel. 677 1255), across from Trinity College at Dawson St. An intelligent staff answers all questions about contemporary Irish writing. Open M-Sa 9am-6pm, Th till 8pm.

Books Upstairs, 36 College Green (tel. 679 6687), across from Trinity Gate. Dublin's pioneer alternative bookshop. Extensive sections on gay literature and women's studies. The principal distributor for *Gay Community News.* Open M-F 10am-7pm, Sa 10am-6pm, Su 1-6pm.

Hodges Figgis, 56-58 Dawson St. (tel. 677 4754). Part of an English chain, this large bookstore has a good selection for eclectic tastes. Open M-F 9am-7pm, Sa 9am-6:30pm, Su noon-6pm.

Waterstone's, 7 Dawson St. (tel. 679 1415), off Nassau St. 5 floors of well-stacked books and an informed reference staff. Open M-W and F 9am-8pm, Th 9am-8:30pm, Sa 9am-7pm, Su 11am-6pm.

An Siopa Leabhar, 6 Harcourt St. (an SHUP-a LAU-er; tel. 478 3814). Varied selection of Irish historical and political books, as well as tapes and books on traditional music. Specializes in literature and resources in Irish. Open M-F 9:30am-5:30pm, Sa 10am-1:30pm and 2-4pm.

RECORDS, TAPES, AND CDS

Megastores sit around Grafton St. and the quays.

Claddagh Records, 2 Cecilia St. (tel. 677 0262), Temple Bar, between Temple Ln. and Crow St. Best selection of trad and a variety of music from other countries. Open M-F 10:30am-5:30pm, Sa noon-5:30pm.

Celtic Note, 14-15 Nassau St. (tel. 670 4157). Specializes in traditional Irish music. Open M-W and F-Sa 9:30am-6:30pm, Th 9:30am-8pm, Su 11am-6pm.

Freebird Records, 1 Eden Quay (tel. 873 1250), on the North Side facing the river. Crowded basement shop tucked below a newsstand proves its name with Dublin's best selection of indie rock. Open M-W and Sa 10:30am-6pm, Th-F 10:30am-7:30pm.

Comet Records, 5 Cope St. (tel. 671 8592), Temple Bar. Much like Freebird, but smaller and open later. More info on current groups and gigs. Lots of vinyl and indie CDs. Punk, metal, techno, and t-shirts, too. Open M-Sa 10am-6:30pm, Th-F 10am-7:30pm.

Smile, 59 South Great Georges St. (tel. 478 2005). Good selection of American soul and jazz. A wall of used books, some of which expound on rock. Open M-Sa 10am-6pm.

GAY, LESBIAN, AND BISEXUAL DUBLIN

Dublin's progressive thinking fosters PRIDE, an annual, week-long festival in July celebrating gay identity. **Gay Community News (GCN),** 6 South William St. (tel. 671 0939 or 671 9076; email gcn@tnet.ie), is free and comes out monthly, offering the most comprehensive and up-to-date information on gay life and nightlife in Dublin. It's available at Books Upstairs (see **Literary Shopping**), Cornucopia, the George, and venues around Temple Bar. *GCN* has extensive listings of support groups and other organizations in the back. *Sceneout* magazine is a periodic supplement to *GCN* that focuses on nightlife and prints classifieds. The "queer" pages of *In Dublin* list pubs, dance clubs, saunas, gay-friendly restaurants, bookshops, hotlines, and organizations. Since gay Dublin seems to be in a particularly constant state of flux, the listings are comprehensive but sometimes outdated. Books Upstairs was Dublin's first bookstore to have a gay literature shelf, and it's still got the best selection. Eason is another source of gay periodicals.

Gay Switchboard Dublin is a good resource for events and updates, and sponsors a hotline (tel. 872 1055; Su-F 8-10pm). **The National Gay and Lesbian Federation,** Hirschfield Centre, 10 Fownes St. (tel. 671 0939), in Temple Bar, offers counseling on legal concerns. The lesbian community meets at **Lesbians Organizing Together (LOT),** 5 Capel St. (tel. 872 7770). The drop-in resource center and library is open Tuesdays through Thursdays 10am to 5pm. **Outhouse,** 65 William St. (tel. 670 6377), is a queer community resource center, offering a library, cafe, info, and advice. Outhouse organizes all sorts of social groups, support groups, seminars, and information sessions for gays, lesbians, teenagers, alcoholics, combinations of the above, and everyone else. **Gay Information Ireland** has a website at www.geocities.com/WestHollywood/9105. Tune into local radio for gay community talk shows: **Innuendo** is broadcast on 104.9FM (Tu 2-3pm); 103.8FM has **Out in the Open** (Tu 9-10pm); and **Equality** airs on 101.6FM (Th 4:30pm).

GAY-FRIENDLY BARS AND NIGHTCLUBS

The gay nightclub scene is particularly thriving, with gay venues (usually clubs rented out) just about every night. Keep up-to-date by checking out the various entertainment publications around town. Pubs that haven't advertised as gay or gay-friendly are an assortment of good and bad apples.

The George, 89 South Great Georges St. (tel. 478 2983). This throbbing, purple man o' war is Dublin's first and most prominent gay bar. A mixed-age crowd gathers throughout the day to chat and sip. The attached nightclub opens W-Su. Su night Bingo is accompanied by so much entertainment that sometimes the bingo never happens. Cover £4-7 after 10pm. Look spiffy—no effort, no entry. Frequent theme nights.

Out on the Liffey, 27 Upper Ormond Quay (tel. 872 2480). Ireland's second gay bar; its name plays on the more traditional Inn on the Liffey a few doors down. Comfortably small. The short hike from the city center ensures a more local crowd on most nights. Late bar W until 12:30am, F until 1:30am, and Sa until midnight. F-Su nights filled with music and a variety of live acts and dancing. Cover £2-3.

The Front Lounge, Parliament St. (tel. 670-4112). The velvet seats of this gay-friendly bar are popular with a very mixed, trendy crowd.

WEEKLY GAY ENTERTAINMENT

Sundays: Playground at Republica, Earl of Kildare Hotel, Kildare St. (tel. 679 4388). 11pm-late. Cover £4-5. **Lollipop** at Velvet, 60 Harcourt St, spins the charts. 11pm-late. Cover £4-5.

Mondays: Freedom at ZaZu, 21-5 Eustace St. (tel. 670 7655). It's been around for a while, and draws trendy crowds. 11pm-late, cover £4.

Tuesdays: Tag & Shag at Republica, Earl of Kildare Hotel, Kildare St. (tel. 679 4388). Sometimes just called "Shag"—the name says it all. Cover £3-4.

Fridays: HAM, at the POD, 35 Harcourt St. (tel. 478 0225), in the Old Harcourt St. Railway Station. One of the oldest, most established, and most widely known gay clubs. Cover £6-8, before 11pm £5. Every other week, HAM is preceded by **Gristle,** a sit-down cabaret. 9-11pm. £5 includes HAM entry.

DUBLIN'S SUBURBS

Strung along the Irish Sea from Donabate in the north to Bray in the south, Dublin's suburbs offer a calm alternative to the voracious human tide on Grafton Street. Two regions that stand out from the uniform suburban sprawl are the tranquil Howth Peninsula to the north and the cluster of suburbs around the port of Dún Laoghaire south of Dublin Bay. North of Dublin, castles and factories are surrounded by planned housing developments, all clamoring for a view of the rocky shore. The Velvet Strand in Malahide, a plush stretch of rock and water, is Dublin's best beach (see p. 126). Dublin's southern suburbs tend to be tidy and fairly well-off. The coastal yuppie towns from Dún Laoghaire to Killiney form a nearly unbroken chain of snazzy houses and bright surf.

The DART, suburban rail, and buses make the region accessible. Any of these suburbs north or south of Dublin can be seen in an afternoon, and all share Dublin's **phone code:** 01, the loneliest you'll ever dial.

HOWTH

The affluent peninsula of Howth (rhymes with "both") dangles from the mainland in edenic isolation, less than 10 mi. from the center of Dublin. Howth offers a brief look-in at many of Ireland's highlights: rolling hills, pubs, a literary landscape, and a castle. The town's sprawl is densest near the harbor, where the fishing industry sometimes makes the air less edenic. Man-made structures from various millennia dot the rest of the island, connected by quiet paths around hills of heather and stunning cliffs.

PRACTICAL INFORMATION

The easiest way to reach Howth is by **DART.** Take a northbound train to the end of the line (30min., 6 per hr., £1.15). **Buses** bound for Howth leave from Dublin's Lower Abbey St.: #31 runs every hour to the center of Howth, near the DART station, and #31B adds a loop that climbs Howth Summit. Turn left out of the station to get to the harbor and the **tourist office,** in the Old Courthouse on Harbour Rd. It provides free, xeroxed maps and glossier, more comprehensive map-and-book packs (£4). (Open May-Aug. M-Tu and Th-F 11am-5pm, W 11am-1pm.) When the tourist office is closed, head for the hand-drawn map of the peninsula posted at the harbor entrance across from the St. Lawrence Hotel.

There is an **ATM** at the **Bank of Ireland** (tel. 839 0271), on Main St. (Open M-F 10am-4pm, Th 10am-5pm.) Down the street is **C.S. McDermott's Pharmacy,** 5 Main St. (Tel. 832 2069. Open M-Sa 9am-6pm, Su 10:30am-1pm.) The **post office** is at 27 Abbey St. (tel. 831 8210).

ACCOMMODATIONS

Howth's B&Bs concentrate around Thormanby Rd., which forks off upper Main St. and heads for the Summit; bus #31B heads up the hill hourly. Howth B&Bs attach a high price to their quiet.

Gleann na Smól (tel. 832 2936), on the left at the end of Nashville Rd. off Thormanby Rd. The closest affordable option to the harbor. Firm beds for the weary; MTV and CNN for the post-literate; and a generous supply of books to suit wormier guests. Singles £25, doubles £36-40. Ask about ISIC discounts.

Hazelwood (tel. 839 1391), at the end of the cul-de-sac in the Thormanby Woods estate, 1 mi. up Thormanby Rd. Mrs. Rosaleen Hobbs serves breakfast around a single large table for the paying guests. The non-paying ones—foxes, birds, and other wildlife in the backyard—also get their feed. Top-notch beds on the most silent of streets. Bus #31B runs up Thormanby Rd., or call from the DART station for a lift. Singles £30, doubles £42; all rooms with bath.

Highfield (tel 832 3936), 1 mi. up Thormanby Rd. Highfield's sign is obscured by its hedges; it's on the left as you go up the hill. Toys and playsets litter the lawn, but inside are tidy, floral-covered bedrooms. Singles £35, doubles £42; all rooms with bath.

FOOD AND PUBS

Quash your monstrous traveler's appetite with fabulous pizza and sundaes at **Porto Fino's** (tel. 839 3054), on Harbour Rd. (Open M-F 5pm-midnight, Sa-Su noon-midnight.) **Caffe Caira** (tel. 839 3823), at Harbour Rd. and Abbey St., is an above average chipper. The takeaway window serves the same fare as the restaurant for a fraction of the price. (Burgers or fish £1.50, chips £1.10. Restaurant open daily noon-9:30pm; take-away open noon-1am.) Hungry shoppers run to **Spar Supermarket,** St. Laurence Rd. (tel. 832 6496), off Abbey St. (Open M-Sa 8am-10pm, Su 8:30am-9:30pm.) The **St. Lawrence Hotel** (tel. 832 2643) drops trad in the Anchor Bar during the summer months. (Music M-F from 9pm.) For more local flavor, join the fishermen at the **Lighthouse,** Church St. (tel. 832 2827), and relax with a pint and frequent trad. (Sessions Su, M, W, and F from about 9pm.)

SIGHTS

Maud Gonne, winner of Yeats' unyielding devotion, described her childhood in Howth in *A Servant of the Queen:* "After I was grown up I have often slept all night in that friendly heather... From deep down in it one looks up at the stars in a wonderful security and falls asleep to wake up only with the call of the sea birds looking for their breakfasts." A 3hr. **cliff walk** rings the peninsula and passes heather and thousands of seabird nests. The trail is well tread, but narrow. The best section of the walk is a hike (1hr.) that runs between the harbor and the lighthouse at the southeast tip of the peninsula. At the harbor end, **Puck's Rock** marks the spot where the devil fell when St. Nessan shook a Bible at him. The nearby **lighthouse,** surrounded by tremendous cliffs, housed Salman Rushdie for a night during the height of the fatwa against him. To get to the trailhead from town, turn left at the DART and bus station and follow Harbour Rd. around the coast for about 20min. From the lighthouse, hike downhill. Bus #31B from Lower Abbey St. in Dublin makes it to the cliffs; from the bus stop make your way to the lower path, or stay in the parking lot and admire the magnificent view: on a clear day you can see the Mourne Mountains in Northern Ireland.

In town, the relatively intact ruins of 14th-century **St. Mary's Abbey** stand peacefully surrounded by a cemetery at the bend in Church St. Get the key to the courtyard from the caretaker, Mrs. O'Rourke, at 13 Church St.

Several sights cluster in the middle of the peninsula, to the right as you exit the DART station and then left after ¼ mi. at the entrance to the Deer Park Hotel. Up this road lies the private **Howth Castle,** an awkwardly charming patchwork of different materials, styles, and degrees of upkeep. At the end of the driveway to the side of the castle, the **National Transport Museum** fills a barn with a dusty graveyard of tired, green buses. You can't even climb on them or toot their horns. (Tel. 848 0831. Open June-Aug. M-Sa 10am-5pm, Su 2-5pm; Sept.-May Sa-Su 2-5pm. £1.60, seniors and children 80p.) Farther up the hill, an uncertain path leads around the right side of the Deer Park Hotel to the fabulous **Rhododendron Gardens,** in which Molly remembers romance (and such) at the end of Joyce's *Ulysses.* (Always open. Free.) At the top of the forested path, you emerge into an astounding floral panorama overlooking Howth and Dublin to the south. The flowers bloom in June and July. Turn right as soon as you enter the gardens (or cut beforehand through the golf course to tee 4) to see a collapsed **portal dolmen** (see **Pre-Christian Ireland,** p. 7) with a 90-ton capstone that marks the grave of someone much more important in 2500 BC than now.

Just offshore, **Ireland's Eye** once provided both religious sanctuary and strategic advantage for monks, whose former presence is notable in the ruins of **St. Nessan's Church,** and one of the coast's many **Martello towers** (see **Rebellion, Union, Reaction,** p. 10). The monks eventually abandoned their island refuge when pirate raids became too frequent. The island's long beach is now primarily a bird haven. **Frank Doyle & Sons** (tel. 831 4200) jets passengers across the water (15min.; every 30min. weather permitting; £5 return, children £2.50). Their office is on the East Pier, toward the lighthouse. For a taste of one of the oldest trades on earth, **Fingal Traditional Sailing** (tel. 843 0340) can boat you around Lambay Island in a traditional vessel. (Half-day and full-day hooker trips available from Howth, Rush, Skerries, and Malahide.)

MALAHIDE

Eight miles north of Dublin, rows of prim and proper shops smugly line the main street in Malahide. The gorgeous parkland around historic **Malahide Castle,** and the gorgeous furnishings inside, help justify the town's pride. The National Gallery has loaned furnishings and portraits from various periods between the 14th and 19th centuries. The dark carved panelling of the oak room and the great hall are magnificent. (Tel. 846 2184. Open Apr.-Oct. M-Sa 10am-5pm, Su 11am-6pm; Nov.-Mar. M-F 10am-5pm, Sa-Su 2-5pm. Admission by tour only; no tours 12:45-

AMAZING GRACE Howth Castle is a private residence, belonging to the St. Lawrence family, which has occupied it for four centuries, but you might try knocking if your surname is O'Malley. In 1575, the pirate queen Grace O'Malley (see **Clare Island,** p. 331) paid a social call but was refused entrance on the grounds that the family was eating. Not one to take an insult lightly, Grace abducted the St. Lawrence heir and refused to hand him back until she had word that the gate would always be open to all O'Malleys at mealtimes.

2pm. £3.10; students and seniors £2.60.) The adjacent **Talbot Botanic Gardens** are abloom and open only from May to September. (Open daily 2-5pm. £2.) If you do get a craving for wintry twigs, though, the 250 acre **park** of the castle desmesne keeps its densely foliated paths open all year. (Open daily June-Aug. 10am-9pm, May and Sept. 10am-8pm, Apr. and Oct. 10am-7pm, Nov.-Jan. 10am-5pm, Feb.-Mar. 10am-6pm. Free.) Next to the castle, you can also choo-choo-choose to see the **Fry Model Railway,** a 2,500 sq. ft. working model with frighteningly detailed renderings of all your favorite Dublin landmarks. (Tel. 846 3779. Open Apr.-Sept. M-Sa 10am-1pm and 2-5pm, Su 2-6pm; Apr.-May and Sept. closed F; Oct.-Mar. Sa-Su 2-5pm. £2.85, seniors and under 18 £2.15; combined rates available with castle tour.) If you're in town, make sure to hit Malahide's gorgeous **beach**; continue slightly farther towards neighboring Portmarnock for the even softer, more luxurious **Velvet Strand.**

With the expansion of the DART line to Malahide scheduled to start in summer 2000, getting there should become easier than ever. The less frequent suburban rail will continue to swing through town as always, as will buses #42 (from Beresford Place, behind the Custom House), 32A (from Lower Abbey St.), and 230 (from Dublin airport). All forms of transport to Dublin (except the 32A) run at least once an hour, usually more, and cost around £1.10. From the **train/DART station** on Main St. (tel. 845 0422), turn right to reach the nearby castle desmesne, or turn left to reach the equally nearby **Diamond,** the central intersection of town. The friendly folks at the **Citizens Information Centre,** Main St., in the parking lot behind the library, provide free maps and info about Malahide, its sights, its B&Bs, and unexpected pregnancies. (Open M-F 10am-noon and 2:30-4pm.) Continue straight on Main St. for 10min. (it becomes Coast Rd.) to reach the B&Bs of Biscayne, a cul-de-sac development to the right. Betty O'Brien will chat your ears off over breakfast at **Pegasus,** 56 Biscayne. (Tel. 845 1506. June-Aug. singles £30, doubles £38-40; Mar.-May and Sept.-Oct. singles £25, doubles £36-38.) Its neighbor **Aishling,** 59 Biscayne (tel. 845 2292), offers tea facilities, hairdryers, and lots of pink in all rooms. (Doubles £36, with bath £38. Open Apr.-Oct.) Lots of restaurants in town demand lots of ducats, but a few pubs serve cheaper grub. **Smyth's** (tel. 845 0960), on New St., by The Diamond, serves up burgers till 9:45pm and trad afterward. (Burgers £5-6. Trad M-Th.) **Duffy's,** Main St. (tel. 845 0735), serves cheap and delicious sandwiches (£2-3).

DÚN LAOGHAIRE AND VICINITY

As Dublin's major out-of-city ferry port, Dún Laoghaire (dun-LEER-ee) is the first peek at Ireland for many tourists. Fortunately, it makes a good spot to begin a ramble along the coast south of Dublin. The surrounding towns, from north to south, are: Blackrock, Monkstown, Dún Laoghaire, Dalkey, and Killiney; they are connected by a series of paths called the "Dún Laoghaire Way," "Dalkey Way," and so on. Getting from one town to the next is quick and simple if you stay within a few blocks of the sea. For those who don't want to invest the shoe leather, the DART also makes for great (if brief) coastal views between Dalkey and Bray. An entertaining ramble would begin with a ride on bus #59 from the Dún Laoghaire DART station to the top of Killiney Hill and proceed along the path through the park and down into Dalkey. Summer evenings are the best time to visit, when couples stroll down the waterfront and the whole town turns out for weekly sailboat races.

■ PRACTICAL INFORMATION

Reach Dún Laoghaire by **DART** from Dublin (£1.10), or southbound **buses** #7, 7A, 8 or (on a longer, inland route) 46A from Eden Quay. From the ferry port, **Marine Rd.** climbs up to the center of town. **George's St.**, at the top of Marine Rd., holds most of Dún Laoghaire's shops, many right at the intersection in the **Dún Laoghaire Shopping Centre.** (Open M-W and Sa 9am-6pm, Th-F 9am-9pm, Su 12-6pm.) **Patrick St.**, which continues Marine Rd.'s path uphill on the other side of George's St., offers cheap eateries. The **tourist office** (tel. 280 6600), in the ferry terminal, is accustomed to dealing with delirious travelers and equipped with copious maps and pamphlets on the whole area up to Dublin. (Open M-Sa 10am-6pm.) Ferry travelers can change money at the terminal's bureau de change. (Tel. 667 1856. Open M-Sa 9am-5pm, Su 10am-5pm.) Less immediate exchange can be made at the **Bank of Ireland**, 101 Upper George's St. (Open M-W and F 10am-4pm, Th 10am-5pm. **24hr. ATM**). **Bike hire** is only available at the hostels.

■ ACCOMMODATIONS

As the port for the Stena ferries and a convenient DART stop on the way to Dublin, Dún Laoghaire is prime breeding ground for B&Bs, only a portion of which are modestly priced. Three hostels are also within walking distance.

Belgrave Hall, 34 Belgrave Sq. (tel. 284 2106; email info@dublinhostel.com; www.dublinhostel.com). From the Seapoint DART station, head left down the coast, then zigzag right, left, right, left at each intersection to Belgrave Sq. A top-tier hostel that feels old but not run-down: high ceilings with plaster ornament, wood and marble floors, and a collection of old furniture complete the look. Small continental breakfast and very large wolfhounds included. Internet access. Summer F-Sa 10-bed dorm £13, 4-6 bed £15, Su-Th all rooms £12; winter £10-12, or £55 per week. Laundry £3-6. **Bike rental** £10 per day. Free parking.

Marina House, 7 Old Dunleary Rd. (tel. 284 1524; www.marinahouse.com). Head left out of Salthill and Monkstown DART station; it's next to the Purty Kitchen. Too new to have any dirt yet, just rough raw wood and the most solid, comfy beds you'll find. Owners Donagh and Mike will join you for drinks out back at night and then get up early to bake *pain au chocolat* for your breakfast. Laid-back and trusting atmosphere. Internet access. Dorms summer £12, winter £10. Non-smoking bedrooms.

Old School House Hostel (IHH), Elbana Ave. (tel. 280 8777; osh@iol.ie), right off Marine Rd. A new staff has let this old gem tarnish a bit. It's got more beds and tighter security than the two others nearby, but not many other advantages. 6-bed dorms £8, quads £44, doubles £26-30. Add 50p for rooms with bath. Sheets included. Towels £1. Laundry £3. Bureau de change. **Bike rental.** Wheelchair accessible.

Marleen, 9 Marine Rd. (tel. 280 2456). Fall off the DART or ferry, and you'll be here. Great location, just west of the harbor. 200 years old and an undulating floor to prove it. Friendly owners; TV and tea facilities in every room. Singles £36, doubles £36.

Avondale, 3 Northumberland Ave. (tel. 280 9628), next to Dunnes Stores. A crimson carpet and darling cocker spaniel lead guests to big beds. Singles £25, doubles £37.

🍴📭 FOOD, PUBS, AND ENTERTAINMENT

Stock up on provisions at **Tesco Supermarket** (tel. 280 0668), downstairs in the Dún Laoghaire shopping center. (Open M-W and Sa 8:30am-7pm, Th-F 8:30am-9pm, Su 11am-6pm.) Fast-food restaurants and inexpensive coffee shops line George's St. **Bits and Pizzas,** 15 Patrick St., gets thumbs up from the locals for good value. (Lunch special of pizza, cole slaw, and tea £4. Open M-Sa noon-midnight.) **La Strada,** 2-3 Cumberland St. (tel. 280 2333), near the Marina hostel on the continuation of George's St., is worth the journey for reasonably priced Italian dishes.

For the best collection of pubs, head north to Monkstown. If you insist on staying south, have no shame and head to **Farrell's** (tel. 284 6595), upstairs in the Dún Laoghaire Shopping Centre; the panoramic coastal view looks fine through a pint glass. Next door to the Marina Hostel, the **Purty Kitchen** pub (tel. 284 3576) opens its loft for a purty little nightclub with darn poppy music and jazz on Wednesdays. (No cover Th and Su; W and F-Sa £5.) The best *craic*, though, is at the **Cultúrlann na hÉireann** (tel. 280 0295), next door to the Belgrave Hall hostel. The headquarters of Comhaltas Ceoltóirí Eireann, a massive international organization for Irish traditional music, the Cultúrlann houses bona fide, non-tourist oriented trad sessions, as well as *céilí* dancing. It's as much a community center as a pub. (Mid-June-Sept. M-Th sit-down performances at 9pm, tickets £6; year-round F *céilí* £4.50, Sa sessions £2.)

👁 SIGHTS

The **harbor** itself is a sight, filled with yachts, boat tours, car ferries, and fishermen. Frequent summer evening boat races draw much of the town. On a clear day, head down to the piers—the setting for Samuel Beckett's *Krapp's Last Tape*—to soak up the sun, or brood.

For more organized sightseeing, try the **National Maritime Museum,** Haigh Terr. From the ferry port, turn left on Queen's Rd. to the stone steps that lead up to Haigh Terr. The museum is in the Mariners' Church. The massive lens from the Bailey Lighthouse in Howth rotates majestically in front of a large stained-glass window. Other exhibits include a longboat (like a rowboat, but better) sent by revolutionary France to support the United Irishmen in 1796, and a piece of the first transatlantic cable, laid by a local captain. (Tel. 280 0969. Open May-Sept. Tu-Su 1-5pm; Apr. and Oct. Sa-Su 1-5pm. £1.50, children 80p.)

■**James Joyce Tower,** in the Martello tower in Sandycove, is a fascinating retreat, especially for tourists with a specific interest. From the Sandycove DART station, go left at either the green house or Eagle House down to the coast, turn right and continue to the Martello tower; or take bus #8 from Burgh Quay in Dublin to Sandycove Ave. James Joyce stayed in the tower for a tense six days in August 1904 as a guest of Oliver St. John Gogarty, a Dublin surgeon, poetic wit, man-about-town, and the first civilian tenant of the tower. Unfortunately, Gogarty's other guest was an excitable Englishman with a severe sleepwalking problem. One night, as the foreigner paced about dreaming of a terrible panther, Gogarty shouted "leave him to me!" and fired his shotgun overhead into a row of saucepans that fell onto Joyce. Joyce left that morning, and infamized Gogarty in Chapter One of *Ulysses*. The novel is partially set in and around the tower, with Gogarty transformed into Buck Mulligan, the Englishman into "an Englishman," and Joyce into Stephen Daedalus, who meditates on the "snot-green" sea from the gun platform at the top of the tower. Sylvia Beach, Joyce's publisher, opened the tower as a museum in 1962. The two-room museum contains Joyce's death mask, his bookshelves, some of his correspondence, clippings of Ezra Pound's rave reviews, and lots of editions of *Ulysses*, including one illustrated by Henri Matisse. One letter to Italo Svevo mentions a briefcase "the color of a nun's belly." Genius! Upstairs, the Round Room reconstructs Joyce's bedroom; even if you haven't read any Joyce, you'll enjoy views from the gun platform of "many crests, every ninth, breaking, plashing, from far, from farther out, waves and waves." (Tel. 872 2077. Open Apr.-Oct. M-Sa 10am-1pm and 2-5pm, Su 2-6pm; Nov.-Mar. by appointment. ₤2.60, seniors and students ₤2.10.)

At the foot of the tower lies the infamous **Forty Foot Men's Bathing Place,** also of Joycean fame. A wholesome crowd with plenty of toddlers splashes in the shallow pool facing the road. But behind a wall, on the rocks below the battery and adjacent to the Martello Tower, men traditionally skinny-dip year-round; apparently, they don't mind that they're a tourist attraction. The pool rarely contains 40 men, and even more rarely 40 ft. men; instead, the name derives from the Fortieth Regiment of British foot soldiers, who made it their semi-private swimming hole. Joyce's host, Oliver St. John Gogarty, once took the plunge here with a reluctant George Bernard Shaw in tow.

Heading further south from Dún Laoghaire, Killiney (kill-EYE-nee), Dublin's poshest suburb, has a gorgeous beach. Pick up the Heritage map of Dún Laoghaire for details on seven area walks that hit Killiney. To reach the twin summits of **Killiney Hill Park,** start on Castle St., take a left onto Dalkey Ave. and climb Dalkey Hill. From the top, the views are breathtaking—that dark smudge on the horizon is called Wales. A commemorative obelisk tops the western summit, with the **wishing steps** nearby. Walk around each level of the steps from base to top, turn to face Dalkey Island, and make a wish: it's bound to come true. Beware that this process only works if you walk in a clockwise direction; in earlier times, women wishing to acquire the power of witchcraft walked naked in a counter-clockwise direction. The Heritage guide states that "visitors should not do this on Killiney Hill!" Slip down the path to Torca Rd., where **Shaw's Cottage,** up the road on the left, was home to young George Bernard Shaw (see **Literature 1600-1880,** p. 22). Steps descend from Torca Rd. to coastal Vico Rd., which runs to Dalkey. Killiney itself has a bonny beach with good swimming.

BRAY

Despite its official location in Co. Wicklow, Bray functions as suburb of Dublin: cityfolk flock to its beach, and it's the final stop for southbound DART trains. Well-tended gardens set against a somewhat overdeveloped seafront are demonstrative of Bray's compromising position between urban and rural Ireland. Bray's transport to both is extremely handy.

⑦ PRACTICAL INFORMATION. To reach **Main St.** from the DART station, head out either **Quinsborough Rd.** or **Florence Rd.** which run perpendicular to the tracks. Bray is a 45min. **DART** ride from Connolly Station (₤2.60 return), and buses #45 and #84 arrive from Eden Quay. Bray has good connections to **Enniskerry,** Co. Wicklow: from the Bray DART station, bus #85 runs to Enniskerry (₤1), competing with **Alpine Coaches** (tel. 286 2547), which runs to Enniskerry, Powerscourt Gardens, Powerscourt Waterfall, and Glencree (May-Sept.; see the tourist office for a schedule). **St. Kevin's Bus Service** (tel. 281 8119) shuttles from the town hall on Main St. to **Glendalough** (1hr., 2 per day, ₤5). The **tourist office** (tel. 286 7128) is the first stop south of Dublin that can give you info on Co. Wicklow. (Open June-Sept. M-Sa 9am-4:45pm, Oct.-May M-Sa 9:30am-4:30pm.) The office, which supplies a handy town map (free), shares a building with the Heritage Centre, downhill on Main St. next to the Royal Hotel. **Bray Sports,** 8 Main St. (tel. 286 3046), **rents bikes.** (₤10 per day, ₤50 per week; deposit ₤50.) The **Cyber Left,** 89 Main St. (tel. 205 0003), has email and internet access (₤5 per hr.) as well as games (₤3 per hr.). Friendly management lets you help yourself to coffee or snacks as you write home. (Open M-Sa 10am-10pm, Su 1-10pm.) The **post office** (tel. 286 2554) perches on Main St.

▐▛▐▓ ACCOMMODATIONS, FOOD, AND PUBS. Seafront **B&Bs** line the Strand. The cheaper ones are on Sidmonton Ave., off the Strand, and Meath Rd., parallel to the Strand and one block inland. Mary Wafer provides a good value at **Bayview,** Meath Rd. (tel. 286 0887), a small B&B whose three rooms have high ceilings, TVs, and no trace of smoke. (Singles £20, doubles £33.) Across the street, **Shoreline** (tel. 286 6063) has been splendidly overhauled by new owners. (Doubles £36.)

The shelves overflow with groceries at **SuperQuinn** (tel. 286 7779) on Castle St., the continuation of Main St. downhill and across the bridge from the tourist center. (Open M-T 8:30am-8pm, W-F 8:30am-9pm, Sa 8:30am-7pm.) The surrounding shopping center also houses fruit stands and sandwich shops. At the other end of Main St., the historic **town hall** now houses the prettiest little McDonald's you'll ever see. If it's good food, not history, you want, the best meal in town is waiting at **Escape,** Albert Ave. (tel. 286 6755), at the intersection with the Strand. Heaping portions of creative vegetarian dishes please any appetite. A new menu appears daily. (Lunches around £4.75, dinners about £8. Open M-Sa 11am-10:30pm, Su noon-8:45pm.) **Pizzas 'n' Cream,** Albert Walk (tel. 286 1606), serves crepes, too (under £6). The liveliest pub action takes place along the Strand, on huge patios lined with picnic benches when the weather cooperates. The **Porter House** (tel. 286 0668) boasts a near endless list of beers and microbrews. (Food served till 9pm. Music W.)

▣ SIGHTS. Bray's history since the Neolithic Age is on display in the small but well-designed **Heritage Centre,** Main St., in the same building as the tourist office. The late Joe Loughman, local historian and phone repairman, gathered the center's artifacts by exchanging them with the local populace for working phones. The floor shows a giant map of Bray. (Tel. 286 7128. Same hours as tourist office. Donations requested.) Along the beachfront, grim amusement palaces cater to a dwindling crowd of Dublin beachgoers. Low-confidence gamblers can try 2p slot machines in the **Fun Palace.** If those stakes are still too high, opt for the kiddie rides, dodgems, or video games. (Open 10am-late.) Halfway down the strand, the new **Natural Sea Life Center** marks the dawning of the age of aquariums, when love will steer the starfish. New wave music, dark passages, and fish of all sizes make for a mellow time, as long as you don't confuse the touchpools with the manta ray tank. (Tel. 286 6939. Open M-F 11am-5:30pm, Sa-Su 11am-6pm. £5.50, seniors £4.50, students £4, children £3.95. Wheelchair accessible.)

If the neon's bugging you and you need a breath of fresh air, head to the summit of **Bray Head,** looming high above the south end of the strand. The trailhead is easy to find; walk along the coast, and cut uphill when you reach steps up the hill. For further direction, check out the crude mural of a map on the snack shed of the golf course to the right of the steps. **Raheenacluig,** in the middle of the golf course, is what's left of a 13th-century Augustinian Church. Various trails wind their way to Bray Head's summit with varying directness; as long as you aim for the cross on top you can't go wrong. The hike up takes a good 30min.; the views over town and sea are well worth it.

NEAR BRAY
POWERSCOURT ESTATE AND WATERFALL

Five miles east of Bray, the grand **Powerscourt Estate** perches by Enniskerry in County Wicklow. Built in the 1730s, the house developed into an architectural landmark, designed in part by a man who measured the length of his workday with a bottle of sherry. Unfortunately, the house was gutted by flames in 1974. Work has recently commenced to gradually fix up the lost interior; for now, an exhibition about the house's history is the main attraction of its interior. The terraced gardens out back justify their high admission cost. Landscaping of every sort, from formal Italian vistas to Japanese paths, surround the house while the pointed Sugar Loaf mountain admires from the distance. Beasts rest in peace under the headstones of the pet cemetery in the back. To reach the estate, take a **bus** from Bray (#85 or the private Alpine line) or from Dublin directly (#45). The estate is a few hundred yards up the left fork as you face the town clock. (Tel. (01) 204 6000. Open daily 9:30am-5:30pm. Gardens and house $5, seniors and students $4.50; gardens only $3.50, $3.20.)

The famed **Powerscourt Waterfall** is 5km outside Enniskerry, County Wicklow. It's Ireland's highest at 398 ft. A couple of Alpine buses from Bray head there daily, and hikers along the Wicklow Way (see p. 142) pass close by. Otherwise, follow the somewhat cryptic signs from Enniskerry. The waterfall is most impressive in late spring and after heavy rains. (Open summer 9:30am-7pm, winter 10:30am to dusk. $2, students and seniors $1.50.)

EASTERN IRELAND

Woe to the unfortunate tourists whose exposure to eastern Ireland is limited to what they see out of the window on a bus headed from Dublin to the West. Eastern towns are the sources of many a marvel. The monastic city at Clonmacnoise and the ruins in Co. Meath, which are older than the pyramids, continue to mystify archaeologists. The mountains of Wicklow offer spectacular views, and tired hikers can head downhill to relax on the beach. The tiny lakeland towns of Co. Monaghan, really a part of the Fermanagh Lake District in the North (see p. 467), harbor the warmest waters in the northern half of Ireland. And where else but Kildare can you find a horse farm run according to the laws of metaphysics or a theme-park based on bogs? Counties Meath, Louth, Wicklow, and Kildare all hold delights fit for daytrips from Dublin.

HIGHLIGHTS OF EASTERN IRELAND

■ A vision from God told St. Kevin to build his monastery at **Glendalough (p. 139)**, the most blessed spot on the island.
■ The **Wicklow Mountains** (p. 139) please hikers with the 76 mi. long **Wicklow Way,** while drivers enjoy the scenic **Mountain Rd.**
■ **Brú na Bóinne** (p. 148) is a spread of impressive pre-Christian monuments: **Newgrange, Knowth** and **Dowth,** and the **Hill of Tara.**

COUNTY WICKLOW

Mountainous Co. Wicklow allows wilderness fans to lose themselves on deserted back roads, zoom down seesaw ridges by bicycle, and still be back in Dublin by nightfall. Wild as parts of it are, the whole county is in the capital's backyard. Its major sights are accessible by buses from downtown Dublin, but moving about within the county is often best done by bike or car. The Wicklow Way hiking trail is an excellent reason to forsake urban amenities and rough it for a week.

Co. Wicklow was once rich in gold, but Bronze-age peoples exhausted the source. Later, 9th century Vikings used present-day Wicklow and Arklow as bases from which to raid Glendalough and other monasteries. Norman invaders in the 1100s followed the same pattern, building defenses on the coast while leaving the mountains to the Gaelic O'Toole and O'Byrne clans. English control was not fully established until the 1798 rebellion, when military roads and barracks were built through the interior so that the British Army could hunt down the remaining guerrillas (see **History,** p. 10). The mountains later produced a mining industry in the southern part of the county. Bray is in Co. Wicklow, but since it's on the DART, *Let's Go* covers it as a suburb of Dublin (see p. 132).

WICKLOW COAST

The uncrowded towns of the Wicklow coast seem a world away from nearby, jet-setting Dublin. As an entranceway to the southeast coast, it lacks the heavy-hitting historical sites of the inland route through Glendalough and Kilkenny, but it is also faster by any means of transport. For those interested catching a glimpse of Dublin, these towns aren't *too* outrageously far to make a cheaper home base.

WICKLOW TOWN

Wicklow Town is touted for both its coastal pleasures and its usefulness as a departure point into the Wicklow Mountains. Wicklow has a wider selection of restaurants than the surrounding area and plenty of accommodations within walking distance of the pubs. While an abundance of low-end shops make the town itself a little drab, a few hours spent hiking or biking along the nearby coastal road can pleasantly occupy an afternoon.

P **PRACTICAL INFORMATION.** Long, skinny **Abbey St.** snakes past the Grand Hotel to the grassy triangle of **Fitzwilliam Square** (by the tourist office), then continues as **Main St.** to its terminus in **Market Square. Trains** run to **Dublin's** Connolly Station (1¼hr.; M-Sa 4 per day, Su 3 per day; £7.50) and to **Rosslare Harbour** via **Wexford** (2hr., 3 per day, £15). The station is a 15min. walk east of town on Church St; head out Main St. past the Grand Hotel and turn right at the Statoil garage. **Bus Éireann** leaves for Dublin from the gaol and the Grand Hotel at the other end of Main St. (1½hr.; M-Sa 9 per day, Su 6 per day; £4.40). **Wicklow Tours** (tel. 67671) runs a somewhat reliable van to **Glendalough** (£6) via **Rathdrum,** picking up from the hostel, the Bridge Tavern, and the Grand Hotel (June-Aug. 2 daily). The **tourist office,** Main St., Fitzwilliam Sq. (tel. 69117), provides free maps of town and county, and can fill you in on the Wicklow Way and other nearby attractions. (Open June-Sept. M-F 9am-6pm, Sa 9:30am-6:30pm; Oct.-May M-F 9:30am-5:30pm; always closed for lunch 1-2pm.) An **AIB,** with a **24hr. ATM,** conducts business on Main St. (Open M 10am-5pm, Tu-F 10am-4pm.) **Wicklow Hiring,** Abbey St. (tel. 68149), **rents bikes.** (£6 per day, £30 per week; deposit £30. Open M-Sa 8:30am-1pm and 2-5:30pm.) The **post office** (tel. 67474) sits on Main St. (Open M-F 9am-5:30pm, Sa 9:30am-12:50pm and 2:10-5:30pm.) Wicklow's **phone code** is 0404 once in my life.

▏ **ACCOMMODATIONS.** The lovely **Wicklow Bay Hostel,** The Murrough (tel. 69213, email wicklowbayhostel@tinet.ie). sports good beds, clean rooms, and amazing sea views. From Fitzwilliam Sq., walk toward the river, cross the bridge, and head left until you see the big building called "Marine House." (Dorms £8-8.50, private rooms £10 per person. Open Feb. to mid-Nov.) Travelers will also be content in almost any of the many B&Bs on Patrick Rd., uphill from Main St. and past the church. It takes a bit of energy to hike the 15min. up to friendly Helen Gorman's **Thomond House,** Upper Patrick Rd. (tel. 67940), but the splendid panoramic views and superbly comfortable rooms justify it. Phone for a pick-up. (Singles £22; doubles £34, with bath £38. Open Apr.-Oct.) Though directly across from the old gaol, Ann O'Reilly's **The Warrens,** Kilmantin Hill (tel. 69899), hasn't copied its design, offering instead mellow, comfy bedrooms with TVs and small baths. (Singles £21, doubles £34.) Several campgrounds are scattered around the area. **Webster's Caravan and Camping Park** (tel. 67615), 2½ mi. south of town on the coastal road at Silver Strand (see **Sights**), will let you pitch a tent. (One-person tent £3.50, two-person £6. Showers 50p. Open June-Aug.) In Redcross, 7 mi. down N11, **River Valley** (tel. 41647) offers greater luxuries. (£5 for a tent plus £1 per person. Showers 50p. Open Mar.-Sept.)

▐▐ **FOOD AND PUBS.** Main St. is lined with greasy take-aways alongside fresh produce shops. The new **SuperValu,** Wentworth Pl. (tel. 61888), just off Church St., offers a DIY selection. **Quinnsworth,** out on Dublin Rd., offers an even wider selection of nutriments. **The Old Court Inn,** Market Sq. (tel. 67680), serves a good plate of grub daily until 9pm, specializing, as the entire Wicklow coast does, in fish. Plant yourself in **Pizza del Forno,** Main St. (tel. 67075), to enjoy a variety of non-Italian foods. (Full breakfast £4, lunch specials with tea or coffee £4.50, unique desserts £1.70-4. Open M-Sa 10am-8:30pm, Su 10am-9:30pm.) **Philip Healy's,** Fitzwilliam Sq. (tel 67380), serves food all day but wins

Eastern Ireland

EASTERN IRELAND

fans as a lively, welcoming hotspot at night. The **Bridge Tavern,** Bridge St. (tel. 67718), reverberates occasionally with music (T trad) and is known to have informal concertina sessions on summer nights to complement the snooker.

⌖ **SIGHTS.** The premier attraction in town is **Wicklow's Historic Gaol,** up the hill from Market Sq., which you can now inspect without leading a rebellion or stealing a loaf. The newly opened museum fills up nearly 40 cells with tableaux, audio clips, displays, and activities about the gaol, its history, and convict transportation to Australia. If the recorded wails and moans seem a bit overdone, the live actors keep things grounded and entertaining. Blow your nose at an improper time and you might get two days of bread and water. (Tel. 61599; www.wicklow.ie/gaol. Open daily Apr.-Sept. 10am-5pm, Mar. and Oct. 10am-4pm. Tours leave every 10min., excepting 1-2pm. $3.75, students and seniors $3, children $2.) The first left past Market Sq. leads to **Black Castle.** The Normans built the castle in 1178; the local Irish lords immediately started attacking and finally destroyed it in 1301. Since then, numerous other attacks and changes in ownership have left only a few wind-worn heaps of stones, though the promontory on which it was built is a great vantage point above the sea and meadows. The staircase cut into the seaward side of the remains reputedly accesses a tunnel to the nearby convent. At the other end of Main St., the crumbs of a 13th century **Franciscan Friary** hide behind a small gate and a run-down hut. The Friary was founded at the same time as Black Castle and fell along with it. It was subsequently rebuilt and became a place of retirement for both Normans and native Irish, who considered it neutral ground.

A cliff trail provides smashing views en route to **St. Bride's Head** (a.k.a. Wicklow Head), where St. Patrick landed on Travilahawk Strand in 432. The local population greeted him by knocking the teeth out of one of his companions (Mantan, "the toothless one" or "gubby"), who was later assigned to convert the local residents. Either cut through the golf course from Black Castle or head out the coastal road past the golf club and meet the trailhead in the parking lot on the left; hiking to St. Bride's Head takes over an hour. At Market Sq., Main St. becomes Summer Hill and then Dunbur Rd., the coastal road, from which beaches extend south to Arklow. From Wicklow, the closest strips of sun and sand are **Silver Strand** and **Jack's Hole,** though most people head to the larger stretch of **Brittas Bay,** midway between Wicklow and Arklow. Starting in the last week of July, Wicklow hosts its **Regatta Festival,** the oldest such celebration in Ireland. The two-week festival features hard-core skiff racing and, on the lighter side, a race of whimsically homemade barges; join the spectators on the bridge and let loose with eggs and tomatoes! At night, amicable pub rivalries foster singing competitions and general merriment. Contact the tourist office for more information.

NEAR WICKLOW: AVONDALE HOUSE

Avondale House, the birthplace and main residence of political leader **Charles Stewart Parnell,** is now a Parnell museum where restorers have turned the clocks back to the 1850s. The walls are plastered with transcriptions of Parnell's love letters to his mistress Kitty O'Shea. The 20-minute biographical video is a well-produced, illuminating glimpse into Parnell's life and his role in the development of Irish independence. (Tel. 46111. Open daily mid-Mar.-Oct. 11am-6pm. $3, students and seniors $2.50.) Flora fanatics will fawn over several hundred acres of **forest** and parkland that surround the house and spread along the west bank of the Avonmore River. (Always open.) Diverse tree species stretch out over Avondale's grounds and blossom along the **Great Ride,** a meandering grassy expanse that was once an avenue for horse riding.

Avondale House is on the road from Wicklow Town to Avoca, one mile after Rathdrum (see below) and before the Meeting of the Waters. From Rathdrum, take Main St. heading toward Avoca and follow the signs. **Buses** arrive in Rath-

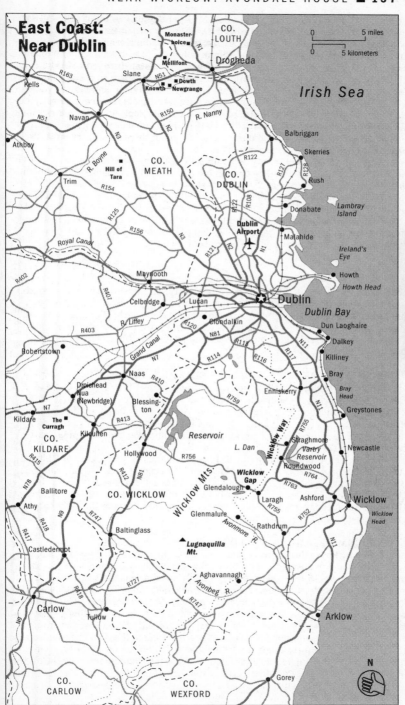

**East Coast:
Near Dublin**

0 _____ 5 miles
0 _____ 5 kilometers

Irish Sea

CO. LOUTH

Monaster-boice
Mellifont
Drogheda
Slane
Knowth · Dowth
Newgrange
Kells
R163
Navan
N51
Athboy
N3
R. Boyne
Hill of Tara
Trim
R154
CO. MEATH
R. Nanny
Balbriggan
Skerries
R122
R127
R128
Rush
CO. DUBLIN
R125
R156
R121
R108
R122
N2
Donabate
Lambray Island
Dublin Airport
Malahide
Ireland's Eye
Howth
Howth Head
Royal Canal
R402
Maynooth
R407
Celbridge
Lucan
N3
Dublin
Dublin Bay
Dun Laoghaire
R. Liffey
R120
Clondalkin
N81
Dalkey
Robertstown
R403
R114
R113
R116
R117
N11
Killiney
Grand Canal
N7
Bray
Bray Head
Naas
R410
Droichead Nua (Newbridge)
Blessington
R759
Enniskerry
Greystones
N7
Kildare
The Curragh
R413
CO. KILDARE
Kilcullen
Hollywood
Reservoir
R756
L. Dan
Wicklow Way
Straghmore
Vartry Reservoir
Roundwood
Newcastle
R415
R412
N81
Wicklow Gap
Glendalough
R764
R763
Ballitore
N9
CO. WICKLOW
Wicklow Mts.
Laragh
Ashford
Wicklow
Athy
R418
Glenmalure
Glenmure
R755
R752
Wicklow Head
R417
Baltinglass
Avonmore R.
Rathdrum
Castledermot
▲ Lugnaquilla Mt.
Aghavannagh
Avonbeg R.
R727
R418
R747
Carlow
Tullow
Arklow
N9
CO. CARLOW
CO. WEXFORD
Gorey
N

drum from **Dublin** (2¾hr., M-Sa 2 per day, Su 1 per day), as do **trains** (1hr., M-F 4 per day). The **tourist office** (tel./fax 46262), in the square at the center of town, will help you locate one of the many B&Bs around Rathdrum should you wish to stay. (Open Sept.-May M-F 9:30am-5:30pm; July-Aug. M-F 9:30am-5:30pm, Sa-Su 1-6pm.) The cheapest option is **The Old Presbytery Hostel (IHH),** (tel. 46930; fax 46604; email hostel@hotmail.com), a fairly luxurious setup in a 200-year-old former monastery, with everything from laundry machines to an exercise room. To find it, continue past the tourist office, turn left after the grocery store, and then right at the top of the hill. (Up to 6-bed dorms £9; Sept.-Apr. £8; singles £10. Wheelchair accessible.) The **post office** (tel. 46211) is concealed within "Smith's Fancy Goods" on the square, and the Bank of Ireland there has a **24hr. ATM.** The **phone code** is 0404 goodness sakes!

Rathdrum now serves primarily as a hub for excursions outside the town, most notably to Avondale House. The **Cartoon Inn** (tel. 46774), on Main St., a pub with wacky cartooned walls, refers to the International Cartoon Festival that Rathdrum held until recently. The festival may be revived for the millenium; call ahead for details. If you need to kill time until the bus comes, check out the **Woolpack Pub** (tel. 46574) in the square, for scrumptious servings (main courses £4-7), home-made desserts, and discos on weekend nights (no cover). Hollywood groupies might recognize the upstairs as one of the settings for the film *Michael Collins*.

ARKLOW

When St. Kevin visited Arklow in the 5th century, he blessed the town's fishermen and guaranteed prosperity. The Anglo-Irish gentry bestowed a more tangible blessing in the 18th century by building a modern harbor, and Arklow has since blossomed into a strapping and well-known port and shipbuilding center. The town is an increasingly popular weekend spot for Dubliners craving a break from the city.

◪ ORIENTATION AND PRACTICAL INFORMATION. Arklow is 40 mi. south of Dublin on N11 (Dublin/Wexford Rd.). The town spans the mouth of the Avoca River, with a harbor, beaches, and potteries along the quays, and most of the shops up the hill along Main St. **Trains** run to Arklow from **Dublin** on their way to **Rosslare** (M-Sa 4 per day, Su 2 per day). **Bus Éireann** runs local service to Arklow and also passes through on its way to **Rosslare** and **Wexford,** stopping by the bridge and at The Chocolate Shop on Main St. (M-Sa 7-8 per day, Su 6 per day, £6.50). The Arklow **tourist office** (tel. 32484) lies on the hill, in the kink in Main St. (Open May-Sept. daily 9:30am-6pm.) The **Bank of Ireland** (tel. 32004) and **AIB** (tel. 32529) on Main St. both have 24-hour **ATMs. Black's Cycle Center,** Wexford Rd. (tel. 31898), is a **bike rental** agency off of Main St., to the left of the rotarary. (Open in summer M-Sa 9:30am-6pm, winter hours vary. £10 per day.) The **phone code** is a fishy 0402.

◪◪ ACCOMMODATIONS AND FOOD. The cheapest stay in Arklow is the new **Avonmore House Hostel,** Ferrybank (tel. 32825; fax 33772). Follow the road up from the bridge on the north bank (not Main St.) and look on your left. Whether you stay in a six- to eight-bed dorm (£8-9.50) or camp on the back lawn (£5), you'll have access to sparkling showers, kitchen, and cable TV. (Breakfast £2; £3 key deposit.) The hostel is only open from April to October, and recommends reservations in July and August, so you might stay in one of Arklow's slew of B&Bs instead. **Vale View,** Coolgrevaney Rd. (tel./fax 32622), boasts glass-roofed suites on the top floor, great for star-gazing or listening to the patter of raindrops (£18); to find it, continue straight past the roundabout on Main St., which changes names to Coolgreaney Rd. If you go left at the roundabout (past the bike shop), you'll find a bevy of other B&B options.

The Riverwalk Restaurant (tel. 31657), down from Main St. on the Avoca River, serves hearty fare at good prices. (Meals around £4.50. Open daily 9am-9pm.) Main St. offers a number of cheap eats as well; try the **Parlour Café** (tel. 91299) for all-day breakfast (£1-3), the **New Dehli** (tel. 32002) for a lunchtime sandwich (£1.50), and just about any of the pubs for dinner. Though she doesn't serve food, **Mary B** on Lower Main St. (tel. 32788) offers a lounge bar with a smorgasbord of live music on weekend nights in the summer starting at around 9pm.

⚅ SIGHTS. Smeared across Arklow's sea coast are several swimmable **beaches,** miles of turf for roaming, and a small **wildlife reserve.** The walk along the muddy **Avoca River** is lovely, but why walk when you can paddle? **Paddle-boats, rowboats,** and **canoes** can sometimes be hired next door to the Riverwalk Restaurant (£2 per person for 30min.). For those into pottery and glassware, the Arklow and Wicklow Vale **pottery shops** at the end of the south quay sell a large selection straight from the kilns. If you prefer model ships to real ones, head away from the harbour and set sail for the **Arklow Maritime Museum,** which froths on St. Mary's Rd. between the train station and Main St. (Open M-F 9:30am-1pm and 2-5pm, Sa 10am-1pm and 2-5pm in summer; Oct.-Apr. closed on Sa. £2, students £1.) This two-room museum displays nearly all that remains of Arklow's maritime past. The highlights of the collection include a piece of the first transatlantic cable, laid by an Arklow captain, and a video on the history of the town.

WICKLOW MOUNTAINS

Over 2000 ft. high, covered by heather, and pleated by rivers, the Wicklow summits are home to grazing sheep and a few villagers. Glendalough, a lush, blessed valley in the draws a steady summertime stream of coach tours from Dublin. Visitors in the know make it a point to see Ireland's largest waterfall, the Powerscourt Waterfall, in Enniskerry (see p. 131). Public transportation is severely limited, so driving is the easiest way to connect the scattered sights and towns. The climbs can be rough for hikers, but their efforts are rewarded by the most well-kept trail in Ireland, the Wicklow Way, and hostels catering to their interests. Stop by the tourist offices at Bray, Wicklow Town, Arklow, and Rathdrum for advice and free, colorful maps.

GLENDALOUGH

In the 6th century, a vision told St. Kevin to give up his life of ascetic isolation and found a monastery. Reasoning that if you've got to be a monk, you'd might as well be a monk in one of the most spectacularly beautiful valleys in Ireland, he founded Glendalough (GLEN-da-lock, "glen of two lakes"). During the great age of Irish monasteries—563 to 1152—monastic schools were Ireland's religious and cultural centers, attracting pilgrims from all over Europe to the "land of saints and scholars." Supported by lesser monks who farmed and traded, the privileged brothers inscribed religious texts and collected jewels and relics for the glory of God. Today the valley is known for its monastic ruins, excellent hikes, and swarms of tourists. Glendalough consists of just St. Kevin's habitat, a hostel, and an overpriced hotel and restaurant; for more affordable food, B&Bs, and groceries, travelers should head to Laragh (LAR-a), a village 1 mi. up the road (sign posted; 10min. walk from the Wicklow Way; 15 mi. from Powerscourt, 7 mi. from Roundwood). On Sundays, the 2km drive to Laragh can take up to 15min. due to traffic.

EASTERN IRELAND

■ PRACTICAL INFORMATION. Aside from the countless charter bus tours, most pilgrims to Glendalough come by car; a few hike the Wicklow Way into town; and the rest take buses run by the private **St. Kevin's Bus Service** (tel. (01) 281 8119). The buses run from St. Stephen's Green West, Dublin (M-Sa at 11:30am and 6pm, Su 11:30am and 7pm; £6, £10 return). They also leave from Bray, just past the Town Hall-cum-McDonald's (M-Sa 12:10pm and 6:30pm, Su 12:10pm and 7:30pm; £6 return). Buses return from the glen in the evening (M-F 7:15am and 4:15pm, Sa 9:45am and 4:15pm, Su 9:45am and 5:30pm; 9:45am departure F year-round and daily July-Aug.). **Bus Éireann** (tel. (01) 836 6111 to book) also runs **tours** to Glendalough and through the mountains, with the driver as tour guide (daily Apr.-Oct.; depart Busáras Station in Dublin 10:30am, return by 5:45pm; £17, children £9). **Wicklow Tours** (tel. 67671) runs a fairly reliable van to **Rathdrum** (Avondale) and **Wicklow** (departs from Glendalough Hotel daily June-Aug., £4 return). **Hitching** to Glendalough is fairly easy from Co. Wicklow towns, though from Dublin much of the Glendalough-bound traffic is bus tours. Hitchers starting at the beginning of N11 in southwest Dublin hop to the juncture of N11 with Glendalough's R755. *Let's Go* does not recommend hitchhiking.

Various vendors offer tourist information. The Board Fáilte **tourist office** (tel. 45688), across from the Glendalough Hotel, provides info about the area and Dublin, and can book accommodations. (Open mid-June to Sept. Tu 11am-1pm and 2-6pm, W-Su 10am-1pm and 2-6pm.) The **Glendalough Visitor Centre** (see **Sights**) picks up the slack when the tourist office is closed. The **National Park Information Office** (tel. 45425), between the two lakes, is the best source for hiking information in the region. (Open May-Aug. daily 10am-6pm, Apr. and Sept. Sa-Su 10am-6pm. When closed, call the **ranger office,** tel. 45338 or 45561.) **Bike rental** is available at the Glendaloch hostel. (£7 per day, £35 per week; £30 deposit.) **Laragh IT** (tel. 45600), in the parking lot next to Lynham's pub, has **internet access.** (£5 per hour.) The **phone code** wakes for matins at 0404.

■ ACCOMMODATIONS, FOOD, AND PUBS. The **Glendaloch Hostel (An Óige/HI)** (tel. 45342) is a 5min. walk up the road past the Glendalough visitors center. An Óige opened up this new beauty last year after £1.3 million renovations. Prices are high, but with good beds, excellent security, and an in-house cafe, it's the best option in the area. (6- and 8-bed dorms £11, quads £12.50, doubles £30; subtract £1-2 per person in off season. Breakfast £2.25, £4.50 full Irish; dinners £5. Towels 50p. Laundry £4. Internet access. **Bike rental.** Wheelchair accessible.) In nearby Laragh, the **Wicklow Way Hostel** (tel. 45398) offers a less comfortable and less expensive stay. The private rooms are cleaner and more agreeable. The attached cafe serves inexpensive breakfasts. (Dorms £7, twins £12.50 per person.) The **Old Mill Hostel** (tel. 45156), a 10min. hike down the road across from Lynham's Pub, has closed its dorm accommodations, but you can probably still get private and barren doubles and singles. (£16.50 per person, includes breakfast. Midnight curfew. **Camping** £4 per person. Showers free. No kitchen.)

B&Bs abound in Laragh. One of the most welcoming is **Gleann Albhe** (tel. 45236), next to the post office. Bathrooms, TVs, and tea facilities found in every room, and you can look out a spectacular bay window while you choose your breakfast option. (Singles £25, doubles £36-40.) Part of the view is **Oakview B&B** (tel. 45453), down the driveway by the Wicklow Heather, where excellent, flowered rooms await. (Doubles £32, with bath £38; single £24. Open Mar.-Oct.)

The **Wicklow Heather** (tel. 45157), 75m up the road toward Glendalough, serves divine concoctions, especially for well-behaved vegetarians. (Open daily 8:30am-10pm. Breakfast £4.25, most entrees under £8.) **Lynham's** (tel. 45345) also piles plates high with hot edibles. (Entrees £7-10. Open daily 12:30-3:30pm and 5:30-9pm.) Attached **Lynham's Pub** attracts travelers with its cover bands and rock sessions most weekend nights.

⊞ SIGHTS. Glendalough is a single, multifold sight. Smooth glacial valleys embrace the two lakes and the monastic ruins, where the **Visitor Centre** presents everything that's known about them. The admission charge covers an exhibition, a 17min. audiovisual show on the history of Irish monasteries in general, and a tour of the ruins. (Tel. 45324. Center open daily June-Aug. 9am-6:30pm, Sept. to mid-Oct. 9:30am-6pm, mid-Oct. to mid-Mar. 9:30am-5pm, mid-Mar. to May 9:30am-6:30pm. Tours every 30min. on peak days. £2, students and children £1. Wheelchair accessible.) The ruins themselves, next to the hotel, are free and always open.

The present ruins were only a small part of the monastery in its heyday, when wooden huts for low-status laborer monks were plentiful. The centerpiece is **St. Kevin's Tower,** a 100 ft. round tower with a mere 3 ft. foundation, built in the 10th century as a watchtower, belltower, and retreat. The entrance is 12 ft. from the ground: when Vikings approached, the monks would climb the inside of the tower floor by floor, drawing up the ladders behind them. The **Cathedral,** constructed in a combination of Greek and Roman architectural styles, was once the largest in the country. In its shadow is **St. Kevin's Cross,** an unadorned, early high cross. It was carved before the monks had tools to cut holes clean through the stone (see **Early Christians and Vikings,** p. 7). The 11th century **St. Kevin's Church,** with an intact stone roof, acquired the misnomer "St. Kevin's Kitchen" because of its chimney-like tower. After use as a church for 500 years, it lay derelict until the 19th century, when locals revived its use for a brief period.

The **Upper and Lower Lakes,** across the bridge and to the right, are a rewarding side-trip from the monastic site. Hikers and bikers can cross the bridge at the far side of the monastery and head right on the paved path for 5min. to reach the serene **Lower Lake.** 25min. farther, the path hits the National Park Information Office (see **Practical Information**) and the magnificent **Upper Lake.** Drivers should continue past the hotel and park in the lot by the Upper Lake. The trail continues along the lakeside, looking across to **St. Kevin's Bed,** the cave where he prayed. Legend says that when St. Kevin prayed, his words ascended in a vortex of flame and light that burned over the Upper Lake's dark waters with such intensity that none but the most righteous monks could witness it without going blind. Further along the trail are the burial grounds of local chieftains.

EASTERN IRELAND

CLIMBING A STAIRWAY TO KEVIN

In Glendalough lived an old saint
Renowned for his learning and piety.
His good manners he wouldn't taint
To be mixing with female society...

St. Kevin was apparently an angelically beautiful man who wasn't interested in women. A lascivious local lass named Kathleen made advances on Kevin, forcing him to retreat to his hermitage in Glendalough. So smitten was she that she followed him there, and he withdrew to his cave near the Upper Lake. Kathleen scoured the area until Kevin's dog gave him away. When she followed the dog to Kevin's cave, she found him asleep and began to take advantage of the situation. Kevin awoke and angrily flung her from the rocky ledge now called "Lady's Leap" into the lake, where she drowned. Kevin felt guilty, lived a life of atonement, and prayed that none might ever drown in the lake again. Despite his lack of interest in women, St. Kevin was known for his kindness to the local animals.

... He gave the old creature a shake,
I wish that the garda had caught him,
For he threw her right into the lake
And begorah! she sank to the bottom.
Dublin Street Ballad

THE WICKLOW WAY

Founded in 1981, Ireland's oldest marked hiking trail is also its most spectacular. Stretching from Marlay Park at the border of Dublin to Clonegal, Co. Carlow, the 76 mi. Wicklow Way meanders south through Ireland's largest highland expanse. Yellow arrows and signs keep the trail well-marked along various footpaths, dirt roads, and even paved roads that weave over heathered summits and through steep glacial valleys. Civilization is rarely more than 3km away, but appropriate wilderness precautions should still be taken. Bring warm, windproof layers and raingear for the exposed summits, and while the terrain never gets frighteningly rugged, sturdy footwear is still a must (see **Wilderness Safety,** p. 79). Water is best taken from farmhouses (with permission), not streams. Open fires are illegal within a mile of the forest and should be monitored vigilantly. Most tourist offices in the county sell the invaluable *Wicklow Way Map Guide* ($4.50), which is the best source for information about the trail and sights along the way.

Six days of hiking for seven to eight hours will carry you from one end to the other, though shorter routes proliferate. Numerous side trails around the Way make excellent day hikes; *Wicklow Way Walks* ($4.50) outlines a number of these loops. The northern 44 mi. of the Way, from Dublin to Aghavannagh, attract the most people with the best scenery and all of the hostels; An Óige publishes a pamphlet detailing 4-5hr. hostel-to-hostel walks. (Available at An Óige hostels in Co. Wicklow and Dublin.) A trip hitting the highlights of the Way would run from the Powerscourt Waterfall near Enniskerry (see p. 131) to Glendalough (about 20 mi.), passing the stupendous **Lough Dan,** and the even more stupendous **Lough Tay,** with views as far as Wales.

In order to avoid devastating trail erosion, bikes are only allowed on forest tracks and paved sections of the Way, but plenty of off-Way roads provide for equal beauty. For a particularly scenic route, ride or drive take R759 to **Sally Gap,** west of the Way near Lough Tay, and then head south on R115 past **Glenmacnass Waterfall** to Glendalough (roughly 15 mi.).

Several bus companies can drop you off at various spots in the mountains. **Dublin Bus** (tel. (01) 873 4222) runs frequently to Marlay Park in Rathfarnham (#47B and 48A) and Enniskerry (#44, or 85 from Bray), and less frequently to Glencullen (#44B). **Bus Éireann** (tel. (01) 836 6111) comes somewhat near the Way farther south, with infrequent service from Busáras to Aughrim, Tinahely, Shillelagh, and Hackettstown. **St. Kevin's** (tel. (01) 281 8119) runs two shuttles daily between St. Stephen's Green West (in Dublin), Roundwood, and Glendalough ($6, return $10). For further information about the Way, contact the **National Park Information Office** (tel. (01) 45425) between Glendalough's lakes (see **Glendalough,** p. 139); if they're closed try the **ranger station** nearby (tel. 45338 or 45561). Forestry lands are governed by **Coillte** (KWEEL-chuh, tel. (01) 286 7751), though much of the Way is simply on a right-of-way through private lands.

◣ ACCOMMODATIONS

Camping is feasible along the Way but generally requires planning ahead. Many local farmhouses will let you pitch a tent on their land if you ask. National Park lands are fine for short-term, low-impact camping; pitching a tent in state forest plantations is prohibited. An Óige runs a cluster of hostels, most of which lie quite close to the Way itself; with the exception of the Glendaloch Hostel, all bookings are handled through the An Óige head office in Dublin (tel. (01) 830 4555), email anoige@iol.ie). Hostels line the Wicklow Way from north to south in the following order:

Glencree (An Óige/HI), Stone House, Enniskerry (tel. (01) 286 4037). From Enniskerry, 12km out on the Glencree Rd. 3½km off the Way and a bit too remote. Dorms June-Sept. £6.50, Oct.-May £5.50.

Knockree (An Óige/HI), Lacken House, Enniskerry (tel. (01) 286 4036), on the Way. A reconstructed farmhouse 4 mi. from the village and 2 mi. from Powerscourt Waterfall. From Enniskerry, take the right fork road leading uphill from the village green, take a left at Buttercups Newsagent, and begin a steep walk, following signs for Glencree Dr. Fireplace in the dining area. Dorms June-Sept. £6.50, Oct.-May £5.50. Sheets £1. Lockout 10:30am-5:30pm (unless it's raining).

Tiglin (An Óige/HI), a.k.a. **Devil's Glen,** Ashford (tel. 0404 40259), 5 mi. from the Way by the Tiglin Adventure Centre. From Ashford, follow Roundwood Rd. for 3 mi., then follow the signs for the Tiglin turnoff and R763 on the right; a hilly 8 mi. from Powerscourt. 50 beds in basic, single-sex dorms; mattresses are droopy, but sleepable. June-Sept. £7, Oct.-May £6. Towels 50p. 11pm curfew.

Wicklow Way Hostel (tel. (0404) 45398), beside the Way in Laragh. Dorms £7. See **Glendalough**, p. 139.

Old Mill Hostel (tel. 45156). 10min. down the road from the Wicklow Way Hostel, and nearly straddling the Way. Some doubles, singles available; see **Glendalough,** p. 139

Glendaloch (An Óige/HI) (tel. (0404) 45342), A stone's throw from the Way, by the monastic ruins. Dorms £11, quads £12.50 per person. See **Glendalough,** p. 139.

Glenmalure (An Óige/HI), Glenmalure. At the end of a dead-end road, 12km south along the Way from Glendalough. On the roads, head from Glendalough to Laragh and take every major right turn. Basically just a roof over 16 beds; not even connected by telephone. Wake up with a cold shower. June-Sept. £6.50, Oct.-May £5.50.

A number of B&Bs along the Way offer camping and pick-up, if you call ahead. The *Wicklow Way Map Guide* comes with a sheet that lists about twenty. The following few will both allow camping and pick-up hikers if necessary. **Coolakay House,** (tel. (01) 286 2423) is 2½ mi. outside Enniskerry. (£22 per person.) In Knockananna, **Hillview B&B,** Tinahely (tel. (0508) 71195), sits a mile from the Way. (Single £16, double £30. **Camping** £3-5 per person.) **Rosbane Farmhouse,** Rosbane (tel. (0402) 38100), is a 7min. walk from the Way, near the summit of Garryhoe. (£17 per person. **Camping** £4 per tent.) **Orchard House,** Tinahely (tel. (0402) 38264), is within earshot of the trail. (Singles £22-24, doubles £36-40. **Camping** £10 per tent.)

WESTERN WICKLOW

Squatter, lumpier, and less traveled than the rest of the county, western Wicklow offers scenic hikes for misanthropes. You won't find picnicking families from the suburbs here. It's possible to hike between western Wicklow and the Wicklow Way, but turn around if you see a red flag—Communists! Actually, the straight-shooting Irish Army maintains a few shooting ranges in the region. Hiking is safe in areas without flags. To reach **Ballinclea Hostel (An Óige/HI)** (tel. (045) 404 657), hike 2.5km uphill to Donard (well-signposted), and then follow the hostel signs for another 2.5km uphill. Clean, simple, and well off the beaten path, Ballinclea offers good access to hikes in the region. (Dorms £6.50. Sheets £1. Lockout 10am-5:30pm. Open Mar.-Nov. daily; Dec.-Feb. F-Sa.) More beds exist in Blessington.

BLESSINGTON

Blessington lies beside the reservoir of the Liffy, close to the intersection of the N81 from Dublin and the R410 from Naas. Hikers come to rest here after exploring the western Wicklow Mountains, while cultured types make the daytrip from Dublin to check out the world-class art at Russborough House. To reach Blessington, the easiest option is to take the hourly #65 **bus** from Eden Quay in Dublin (£1.25). **Bus Éireann** also passes through town on its Dublin-Waterford route (M-W and Sa 2 per day, Th and Su 3 per day, F 4 per day); peculiarly, only southbound buses will pick up passengers, while northbound buses drop them off. Turn to the Blessington **tourist office** (tel. 865 850), in the town square, for ideas on outdoor pursuits. (Open mid-June to Aug. M-F 10am-6pm, Sa 10am-5pm, Su erratically; Sept. to mid-June M-F 10am-2pm.) **Ulster Bank,** Main St. (tel. 865 125), has a bureau de change and an **ATM. Hillcrest Hire,** Main St. (tel. 865 066), **rents bikes.** (£7 per day, £30 per week; £20 deposit.) The **phone code** is 045.

Five miles out on the road to Valleymount, **Baltyboys (An Óige/HI)** (tel. 867 266), known simply as the Blessington Lake Hostel, has excellent views and a warden who will bend over backwards to help you out. (June-Sept. dorms £6.50, Oct.-May £5.50; students £5, £4.50. Sheets 85p. Laundry £1. Lockout 10am-5pm. Open daily Mar.-Nov.; Dec.-Feb. Th-Su.)

Russborough House (tel. 865 239) spreads its Palladian grandeur 3km south on the N81, toward Baltinglass. Richard Cassells, who also designed Dublin's Leinster House and much of Trinity College, built the house in 1741 for Joseph Leeson, a member of the Anglo-Irish parliament. Russborough now houses an impressive collection of paintings, sculpture, furniture, and baroque plasterwork. In 1986, a Dublin gangster known as the General orchestrated the theft of the 17 most valuable paintings, including works by Goya, Vermeer, and Velasquez; all but one have since been recovered. The best pieces are now in the National Gallery in Dublin, but a few excellent ones remain, among them a Rubens. Unfortunately, the tour is little more than a soporific catalog of each room's contents. (Open Easter-Apr. and Oct. Su 10:30am-5:30pm, May-Sept. daily 10:30am-5:30pm. Admission by hourly 45min. tours only. £4, seniors and students £3, children £2.)

COUNTY KILDARE

The towns immediately west of Dublin in Co. Kildare are still well within the city's orbit; the best sights—Kildare's horses and Lullymore Heritage Park—make easy daytrips. The county is linked to Dublin by more highways: half of Kildare was included in the Pale, the region of English dominance centered around Dublin. From the 13th to the 16th century, the FitzGerald Earls of Kildare controlled all of eastern Ireland. Today, mansions and the big-money Irish Derby evoke Kildare's former prominence, and it remains an international hotspot of the horse world.

MAYNOOTH

A growing Catholic seminary and university makes Maynooth (ma-NOOTH) the town of saints and scholars. In 1795, King George III was concerned that priests educated in Revolutionary France would acquire dangerous notions of independence. He granted permission for St. Patrick's College, the first Catholic seminary in Ireland, to open. He later said that opening St. Patrick's "cost me more pain than the loss of the colonies." The Maynooth Seminary was the only site for training Irish Catholic priests during much of the 19th century. Although other centers exist today, many priests are still ordained here.

🛪 **PRACTICAL INFORMATION.** Maynooth is 15 mi. west of Dublin on the M4. Suburban **trains** run from Connolly Station in **Dublin** (20min.; M-Sa 15 per day, Su 3 per day; £1.60). **Bus** #66 runs directly to Maynooth, and #67A gets there via **Celbridge** (both about 1hr.; roughly twice an hour; £1.65 from Middle Abbey St. or £1.10 from the quays by Heuston Station). **Hitchers** from Dublin stand on Chapelizod Rd., between Phoenix Park and the Liffey, or even farther west where Chapelizod becomes Lucan Rd. *Let's Go* does not recommend hitchhiking. The **Citizens Information Centre** (tel. 628 5477), upstairs on Main St., is a volunteer-staffed center that answers questions about the area and hands out xeroxed maps. (Open M-F 9:30am-4:30pm.) **usit** (tel. 628 9289) has a budget travel office on Main St., specializing in student travel and discounts. (Open M-F 9:30am-5:30pm, Sa 10am-1pm.) The St. Patrick's visitor's center (see **Sights**) also provides helpful information about the town and area. Check your email at the **Cyber X Internet Cafe** (tel. 629 1747) in the Glenroyal shopping center off Celbridge Rd. (Open daily noon-midnight. £4 per hr., students £2.50). 01 walks the Path of **Phone Codes.**

▛▜▟ ACCOMMODATIONS, FOOD, AND PUBS. St. Patrick's College rents out student apartments during the summer; the fee includes access to the college sports facilities. (Singles £15-17, with breakfast £20-22; doubles from £26, with breakfast £35. Available mid-June to Sept. Contact Bill Tinley at the conference center, tel. 708 3726.) The **Leinster Arms,** Main St. (tel. 628 6323), is mainly a food-serving pub, but it's also a great B&B value for groups since guests pay a flat £30 per room. Reserve ahead in summer; some rooms have bath and kitchen. (Food served 10:30am-10pm.) Enjoy light fare at **Elite Confectionery,** Main St. (Tel. 628 5521. £2-3. Open M-Sa 8:30am-6:30pm.)

▣ SIGHTS. The powerful Fitzgerald family controlled its vast domain from **Maynooth Castle,** built in 1176. Since being dismantled in 1647, the castle has crumbled, leaving only the ruins of a few block-like towers, which nevertheless cast a stately shadow over the beer can-strewn lot on Main St. Hundreds of birds will take off when you climb the staircase to the roofless Great Hall and become the sole, if temporary, resident of the castle. (Pick up key from Mrs. Bernadette Foy, 10 Parson St., on the road across from the castle.) Beside the castle sits **St. Patrick's College,** whose sculpted gardens and austere architecture put students in the right frame of mind to study Catholic dogma. The impressive **College Chapel,** ornamented from top to toe, dates from the late 19th century Gothic revival. In the courtyard garden next to it, walk the Path of Saints or the Path of Sinners, past Fonts of Faith, Understanding, and Pain, or gaze meditatively at a carving of the Apocalypse in 5000-year-old bog wood. Behind that courtyard, follow the building around to the left to reach a cathedral nave of interwoven trees, leading to a small cemetery that spans centuries. The **Visitor Centre,** under the left arch in front of you as you enter the college grounds, provides a campus map, and Christian paraphernalia displays. Their tours of the college, given on demand, are worth your while. (Tel. 708 3576. Open M-F 11am-5pm, Sa-Su 2-6pm. Tours £3, students £2.) The college's **Ecclesiastical Museum** combines Catholic ritualistic props with 19th century scientific equipment.

NEAR MAYNOOTH: CELBRIDGE

The *raison d'être* of Celbridge (SELL-bridge) is **Castletown House,** the magnificent home of sometime Speaker of the Irish House of Commons, William Connolly. The richest man in 1720s Ireland, Connolly built himself this magnificent home and touched off a nationwide fad for Palladian architecture. After major refurbishing, the castle opened for public tours last summer and has since been trying to reclaim the sumptuous original furniture from disparate corners of the world. At this point the rooms are pretty bare. What does survive is worth seeing; the print room, with Ireland's only surviving cut-out wall decorations, and the garish Venetian chandeliers in the Long Gallery are particularly fantastic. (Tel. (01) 628 8252. Open Apr.-May Su 1-6pm; June-Sept. M-F 10am-6pm, Sa-Su 1-6pm; Oct. M-F 10am-5pm, Su 1-5pm; Nov. Su 1-5pm. Last tours 1¼hr. before closing. Admission by guided tour only; tours should start on the hour. £2.50, seniors £1.75, children and students £1.) Instead of donating money to charity, Conolly's widow built an obelisk 2 mi. behind the estate to employ famine-starved locals in 1740. Known as **Conolly's Folly,** its unruly stack of arches were copied and enlarged for the original plans of the Washington Monument. At the other end of Main St., the grounds of **Celbridge Abbey** harken back to a rich girl's enigmatic relationship with Jonathan Swift around 1700. Elegant gardens and walks make for fine picnicking. (Tel. 627 5508. Open M-Sa 10am-6pm, Su noon-6pm. £2.50, seniors and children £1.50.)

Buses #67 and 67A run to Celbridge from Middle Abbey St., **Dublin.** (₤1.65; #67A also goes to Maynooth.) The **Arrow** suburban rail also arrives roughly every hour at the Hazelhatch & Celbridge stop from Dublin's Heuston Station (₤6). A shuttle bus runs the sizeable distance between the station and town during peak hours; otherwise it's a ₤3 taxi.

KILDARE

Kildare is Ireland's horse-racing mecca. Carefully bred, raised, and raced here, purebloods are the lifeblood of the town. Kildare's past was more influenced by Christianity; it grew up around a church founded here around 480 by St. Brigid. The sacred lass chose a site next to an oak tree that she saw in a vision, giving the town its original name *Cill Dara*, meaning "Church of the Oak." The center of town is a triangular Square scarred, unlike its calmer equine periphery, by the unceasing trucking traffic of the N7.

◪ **PRACTICAL INFORMATION.** Kildare saddles the busy, harrowing N7 (Dublin-Limerick) and is well connected by **train** to **Dublin's** Heuston Station (40min.; M-Th 12 per day, F 14 per day, Su 11 per day; ₤7.50). Head straight out of the train station for several blocks to reach The Square. **Bus Éireann** hits big, bad **Dublin** (1½hr.; M-F 14 per day, Sa 13 per day, Su 7 per day; ₤5.50), and if you place your money right you may even land in **Cork** (3½hr.; 3 per day, Su 2 per day; ₤12) or **Limerick** (2½hr., 14 per day). **Rapid Express Coaches** (tel. (01) 679 1549) offers a cheaper service between Middle Abbey St. (Dublin) and Kildare (4-6 per day, ₤2.50). The Kildare **tourist office** (tel. 522 696), The Square, offers basic information and free maps. (Open June-Sept. M-Sa 10am-1pm and 2-6pm.) The **Bank of Ireland** (tel. 521 276), The Square, has a **24hr. ATM.** (Open M 10am-5pm, Tu-F 10am-4pm.) If you can't ride a horse, **bike rental** is dirt cheap at **Bikes and Bits** (tel. 521 457) on Claregate St. (Open M-Sa 9am-6pm.) The **post office** is on Dublin St., near The Square. (Open M and W-F 9am-5:30pm, Tu 9:30am-5:30pm, Sa 10am-1pm.) The **phone code,** 045, won in a photo-finish.

◪◪◪ **ACCOMMODATIONS, FOOD, AND PUBS.** Accommodations in Kildare are neither handsome or sleek. A short walk from The Square, **Fremont,** Tully Rd. (tel. 521 604), sets up its rooms in a quasi-rural setting, en route to the Stud Farm and Japanese Gardens. (Singles ₤22, doubles ₤34.) 5 mi. out of town, in the middle of nowhere, Julie and Colm Keane run the new **Eagle Hill B&B** (tel. 526 097) on a working sheep farm. As you approach the town southbound, take the left before Kildare and follow the Eagle Hill signs to top-notch beds, showers, and morning meals. Call for pick-up.

Pubs are plentiful, and most serve food. **The Silken Thomas,** The Square (tel. 522 232), has locally renowned meals, ranging from sandwiches (₤2-3) to bar lunches (lamb with mint sauce ₤5.25) to pricey entrees. (Food served 12:30-10pm.) The pub's name isn't a euphemism, but a reference to "Silken Thomas" FitzGerald, who raised a revolt against the British in Dublin in 1534. **Li'l Flanagan's,** in back of The Silken Thomas (tel. 522 232), is a small, delightfully scruffy, old-time pub with dark, low ceilings and open peat fires. (Trad or rock W-M.) **Nolan's,** The Square (tel. 521 528), is a low-key pub that was once a hardware store. The saws are gone, but Nolan's compensates with trad most nights.

◪ **SIGHTS.** The 10th century **Round Tower,** just off The Square, is one of the few in Ireland that visitors can actually enter and climb up; most of the others have no floors inside. (Open M-Sa 10am-1pm and 2-5pm, Su 2-5pm. ₤2, children 50p.) Recently restored **St. Brigid's,** a Church of Ireland cathedral that has weathered over 200 derelict years, lies in the shadow of the tower. The cathedral dates from the 12th and 13th centuries, and sits on the site of a church founded by St. Brigid in 480. She was one of the first and only powerful women in the Catholic Church.

(Open May-Oct. M-Sa 10am-1pm and 2-5pm, Su 2-5pm.) Next to the church is **St. Brigid's Fire Temple,** a pagan ritual site that Brigid repossessed for Christianity. Only female virgins were allowed to tend the fire, which burned continually for 1000 years. (Archbishop George Browne of Dublin ended it by extinguishing the flames, not the virginity.)

More exciting is **The Irish National Stud and Japanese Gardens,** "where strength and beauty live as one." Colonel William Hall-Walker, the mastermind behind the 1900 creation of the Stud, was nothing short of a freak. The mystical son of a Scottish brewer, he would cast a foal's horoscope at its birth; if unfavorable, the foal would be sold, regardless of its lineage. The stables have skylights, since, of course, the stars dictate destiny. The small **Irish Horse Museum** tells the history of the horse with a few displays and the skeleton of Arkle, a quite dead champion. **The Japanese Gardens** tell the allegory of the "life of man" through a beautiful, semi-narrative trail. From the cave of birth to the hill of mourning, visitors experience learning, disappointment, and marriage in the mediums of caves, hills, and bridges. Hall Walker designed it, and while he was clearly a nut, it makes a worthy game. The newest addition to the Stud grounds is the 4 acre **St. Fiachra's Garden,** that opened just last year for the new millennium. St. Fiachra's strives for uniqueness, with quiet lakes, huts, and a pit of Waterford Crystal. (1 mi. from The Square out Tully Rd. and well sign-posted. Tel. 521 617. Open daily mid-Feb. to mid-Nov. 9:30am-6pm; last admission 5pm. 35min. guided tours of the National Stud leave on the hour beginning at 11am. £6, students and seniors £4.50.)

NEAR KILDARE TOWN: THE CURRAGH

Entertainment in Kildare is understandably equinocentric. Between Newbridge and Kildare on the M7 lies **The Curragh,** 5000 acres of perhaps the greenest fields in Ireland. Thoroughbred horses graze and train, hoping one day to earn fame and fortune at the **Curragh Racecourse** (tel. (045) 441 205), which hosts the **Irish Derby** (DAR-bee) on the first Sunday in July. The Derby is Ireland's premier sporting and social event, and one of the most prestigious races in the world. Other races are held from late March through October, roughly every third weekend (Sa and Su only). The Irish Rail timetable lists dates, and trains stop at The Curragh on race days. (Train £14 from Heuston Station, includes admission. Admission generally £8-10, but up to £35 for the Derby; students and seniors half-price.) Bus Éireann also serves the Curragh on race days (leaves 1½hr. before races from Dublin, £9). Hit the Curragh as early as 7:30am, and watch scores of horses take their daily training run on one of the five gallops, each 1-1½ mi. long. Driving off-road is acceptable within reason, but horses always have the right of way.

PEATLAND WORLD AND LULLYMORE

When times get tough in the bogs, the boglanders know who to turn to: their friend, peat. Ten miles from Kildare in Lullymore, **Peatland World** explains this phenomenon. Located on a mineral island in the immense Bog of Allen, Peatland World features a museum and natural history gallery. On display are bog-preserved prehistoric artifacts, a model of an Irish cottage with a turf fire, and trophies from turf-cutting competitions. (Tel. (045) 860 133. Open Apr.-Oct. M-F 9:30am-5pm, Sa-Su 2-6pm; Nov.-Mar. M-F 9:30am-5pm. £3, students £2.50.) Two miles toward Allentown, the **Lullymore Heritage & Discovery Park** shows what life in the boglands was like from the Mesolithic era to the 1798 rebellion to the famine. To reach Lullymore from Kildare, take Rathangan Rd. to Rathangan, and then Allentown Rd. from there. (Tel. (045) 870 238. Open Apr.-Oct. daily 8:30am-6pm, Nov.-Mar. M-F 8:30am-4:30pm; other times by appointment. 1½hr. tour. 3 tours per afternoon daily in summer. £3.50, students £3.) Buses drive to Allenwood, a few miles north of Lullymore, from Dublin (1hr; M-Sa 8 per day, Su 3 per day; £4.40).

EASTERN IRELAND

COUNTY MEATH

Meath is a quiet, peaceful county, with ancient crypts lurking in its hills. The nearby Hill of Tara was Ireland's political and spiritual center in pre-historic times, and retains its mystique. In pre-Norman times, Meath was considered Ireland's fifth province. Vikings made their mark at Drogheda, beside the Boyne River.

BOYNE VALLEY

The thinly populated Boyne Valley safeguards Ireland's greatest archeological treasures, and is just a short bus ride away from Dublin. Massive passage tombs like Newgrange create subtle bumps in the landscape that hardly sign the cavernous underground chambers they cover. They are older than the pyramids and at least as puzzling: virtually nothing is known about the rituals and design on which they are based. The Celtic High Kings once ruled from atop the Hill of Tara, leaving a wake of mysterious folklore. The Hill's enduring symbolic significance and 360-degree views attract visitors a-plenty, as do the well-preserved Norman fortifications in the town of Trim. Every so often, farmers plow up artifacts from the 1690 Battle of the Boyne (see **Drogheda**, p. 153), which are filed away in a small information center and a view of the landscape.

BRÚ NA BÓINNE: NEWGRANGE, KNOWTH, AND DOWTH

Along the curves of the river between Slane and Drogheda sprawls Brú na Bóinne (broo na BO-in-yeh, "homestead of the Boyne"). The 10 sq. km landscape swells with no fewer than 40 passage tombs from around the 4th millenium BC. The mind-boggling engineering talents of their Neolithic farming architects constructed Newgrange, Dowth, and Knowth in proximity to one another in the valley.

One explanation of their existnce proposes that improvements in farming gave folks some extra time to build structures that would remain intact and even waterproof some 5,000 years down the road. The larger mounds took a good half-century to build, by men with only 30 yr. lifespans. Hundreds of enormous kerbstones were moved by raw manpower from 10km away (each took 80 men four days), and countless smaller rocks were boated in from 80km away in Wickow. Passage tombs are hardly limited to the Boyne Valley, but the world's largest and finest tombs are here. The purpose of passage tombs remain a mystery that excavations continue to try to solve.

The most impressive of the three, for archaeologists if not for visitors, is **Knowth** (rhymes with "mouth"). Evidence exists of a hunter-gatherer settlement on the site (4000 B.C.), and also of an extraordinary number of more recent dwellers: the Stone Age brainiacs who built the mound you see today; mysterious Bronze Age "beaker people," named for their distinctive urns; Iron Age Celts, whose many burials include two headless men with their gaming dice; and Christians as late as the 12th century. The enormous passage tomb houses an unusual *two* burial chambers, back to back, with separate entrances to the east and west. Long-term excavations, and the demands of preservation, prevent visitors from actually entering the tomb, but the visitor's centers tour offers a peek.

Newgrange regained an umpteenth of its ancient prominence in the 1960s when a roof box was discovered over the passage entrance. At dawn on the shortest day of the year (December 21), and for two days to either side, seventeen minutes of golden sunlight reach straight to the back of the 19 m. passageway and irradiate the burial chamber. The calendar alignment, while impressive, is quite common in passage tombs; Newgrange is unique in having a separate entrance exclusively for the worshipped golden orb. Because the passage is shorter and a little wider than Knowth, you can actually enter into the cool bowels of the 1 acre mound and see two-thirds of all the Neolithic art in Western Europe. Amidst the intricately carved patterns, diamonds, and spirals, you can read graffiti from 18th century visitors who clearly didn't have the brains of their distant ancestors. The highlight of the tour is a simulation of the golden winter solstice.

Dowth (rhymes with "Knowth") has been closed to the public for several years, because of ongoing excavations. To gain admission, get a PhD in archaeology. To access Knowth and Newgrange, it's necessary to pay admission into the ■**Brú na Bóinne Visitor Centre**, located near Donore on the south side of the River Boyne, across from the tombs themselves. Do not try to make your way directly to the sites—a guard minds the gate. Instead, head to the visitor center and immediatly book a tour. The place is mobbed every day in the summer, and Sundays are simply manic; from June through August, you'll most likely be turned away if you get there after 2:30pm, since the tours have limited sizes. While you wait for your tour, check out the center's excellent exhibit on how gifted and talented stone agers lived. A nifty film on the winter solstice runs every 15min. (Tel. (041) 988 0300. Open Mar.-Apr. 9:30am-5:30pm, May 9am-6:30pm, June to mid-Sept. 9am-7pm, the rest of Sept. 9am-6:30pm, Oct. 9:30am-5:30pm, Nov.-Feb. 9:30am-5pm. Admission to center only £2, seniors £1.50, students and children £1; center and Newgrange tour £3, £2, £1.25; center and Knowth £2, £1.50, £1; center, Newgrange, and Knowth £5, £3.50, £2.25. Tours last 1hr. and start every 30min. until 90min. before closing. Last admission to center 45min. before closing.) Downstairs, a **tourist office** (tel. (041) 80305) can give you a free area map. (Open daily 9am-7pm.)

To reach the center from Drogheda, turn left by the bus station and head straight on the uphill road. It's a pleasant 5 mi. bike ride, and hitchers report successful journeys. **Bus Éireann** shuttles to the visitor center from **Dublin** (1½hr.; 5 per day, Sa-Su 4 per day; £7 return), stopping at **Drogheda** (10min., £2 return). Several guided bus tours from Dublin include admission to the sights. Bus Éireann (tel. (01) 836 6111) covers Newgrange and either Tara/Trim or Mellifont/Monasterboice (Sa-Th, £17). Just down the road from the Newgrange site, **Newgrange Farm** has a coffee shop and a petting zoo for the kids. Willie Redgrave will charm kids and parents alike with his tractor tour of the farm, including a smaller passage tomb, a bit of wildlife, agitated bulls, and plenty of tooth faeries. (Tel. (041) 24119. Open daily Easter-Aug. 10am-6pm; last admission 5pm. 30min. tour leaves Su at 3 and 4pm, or whenever there's enough interest. £1.50.)

HILL OF TARA

From prehistoric times until at least the 10th century, Tara was the political and often religious center of Ireland. Three of the seventy sites strewn around the hill have been excavated, leaving archaeologists and tourists with a fistful of questions. They do know that ancient peoples built a Stone Age tomb and an Iron Age fort here. Later it was the seat of the powerful Uí Néill family, when control of Tara theoretically entitled a warlord to be High King. Ownership of the hill was disputed until the 10th century, but the arrival of St. Patrick around 400 deposed Tara from its position as the Jerusalem of Ireland. In modern times, the hill's aura persists: Daniel O'Connor gathered "a million" people here for a Home Rule rally in 1843. A cult destroyed one site a century ago in their fervent search for the Arc of the Covenant. Five thousand years of history have left a strong legacy of myth and legend, much of which is refuted by archaelogical findings—the interest of the site lies in choosing which side to believe.

The enormous site is about 5 mi. east of Navan on the N3. Take any local (not express) bus from Dublin to **Navan** (1hr.; M-Sa 15 per day, Su 7 per day; £5.50) and ask the driver to let you off at the turnoff. The site is about a mile straight uphill. The actual buildings—largely wattle, wood, and earthwork—have long been buried or destroyed; what you'll see are grassy, windswept dunes forming concentric rings as if from a pebble in a pond. They are always open for exploration, but to make any sense of them you have to hit the visitors center, in an old church at the site. The center displays aerial photos of Tara, and shows a good 20min. slideshow about Tara's history. After the film, your ticket entitles you to an excellent guided tour (35min.) that circles the site. The full site encompasses 100 acres of many smaller mounds and ring forts, though the tour usually covers only the sites at the top of the hill. (Tel. (046) 25903. Center open daily early-May to mid-June and mid-Sept. to Oct. 10am-5pm, mid-June to mid-Sept. 9:30am-6:30pm. £1.50, seniors £1, students and children 60p.)

TRIM

A flock of enormous, well-preserved Norman castles and abbeys overlook this charming heritage town on the River Boyne. Jaded travelers should treat themselves to this daytrip from Dublin.

⚑ PRACTICAL INFORMATION. Castle St. intersects the central **Market St.**, which has most of the town's shops, then crosses the **River Boyne** under the psuedonym **Bridge St.** and curves uphill on the far side as **High St.** before splitting into **Haggard St.** and the road to the nearby Newtown ruins. **Bus Éireann** stops on Castle St. in front of the castle en route to **Dublin** (1½hr.; M-Sa 8 per day, Su 3 per day; £5). Trim's **tourist office,** Mill St. (tel. 37111), has a useful self-guided walking tour of Trim (£1.95) and meaty information on Meath. (Open daily 10am-1pm and 2-5pm; longer summer hours.) The **Bank of Ireland** (tel. 31230) surveys Market St. (Open M 10am-5pm, Tu-F 10am-4pm.) The **post office** collects stamps up the street. Trim's **phone code,** 046, is undergoing continual renovations.

▟▛▟ ACCOMMODATIONS, FOOD, AND PUBS. The Bridge House Tourist Hostel (tel. 31848), perched next to the tourist office, on the River Boyne, offers a mixed bag of coed rooms: they range from cramped to luxurious. The nifty TV lounge is a converted medieval wine cellar. (4-bed dorms £10, doubles £25; all with bath. Free towels.) Trim's B&B options are, on the whole, excellent. The **White Lodge B&B** is 10min. walk from the bus stop. Cross the bridge and follow signs for Newtown, or call for a pick-up. (Single £20-25; double £32-36; £2 cheaper per person with continental breakfast, £3 cheaper without any breakfast. Non-smoking.) In the heart of town, **Brogan's,** High St. (tel. 31237), offers cramped but otherwise top-notch rooms with TV, bath, and telephones in all. (Singles £25; doubles £40.)

Get your groceries at **SuperValu** (tel. 31505), at the top of Haggard St. (Open M-W and Sa 8am-7:30pm, Th-F 8am-9pm, Su 8am-6pm.) **The Pastry Kitchen,** Market St. (tel. 36166), is a greasy spoon that serves a decent meal. (Sandwiches £1.50. Open M-Sa 7:30am-6pm, Su 10am-2pm.) For lunch, head to **The Abbey Lodge,** Market St. (tel. 31285), for a huge plate of standard pub fare. (Meals £4-5. Lunch served 12:30-2:30pm.) The **Emmet Tavern** (tel. 31378), on Emmet St. (left as you face the post office), has boisterous customers. Bring your fiddle to the old-fashioned **The Bounty** (tel. 31640), across the street from the hostel.

⚙ SIGHTS. Norman invader Hugh de Lacy first built **Trim Castle** in 1172 to intimidate the natives. The unruly O'Connors of Connacht trashed the place a year later. A new castle was then constructed in the 1190s; Mel Gibson sacked it 800 years later for a scene in *Braveheart*. For a few centuries in between, the enormous castle—the largest Norman one in Ireland, with walls up to 12 ft. thick—was an important fortification for all of Meath. It defended a walled town with separate gates and battlements. When Norman power here collapsed, the castle lost nearly all its strategic importance and therefore survived relatively untouched. Tourism conquers all, however, and the Heritage Service renovations have kept most of the castle closed for the past several years, adding floors, paths, and a small exhibition space for tourists. Work crews are hustling to re-open the castle by (hopefully) June 2000, and access to the main keep will probably be by guided tour only (potentially £2-3).

Across the river stands what's left of the 12th century **Yellow Steeple,** a belltower named for its twilight gleam; the gleam left with the lichen that was removed during restoration. In its shadow, **Talbot's Castle** was adapted from the steeple's original abbey and lived in by a Shakespearean character, Jonathan Swift, and the undefeated Duke of Wellington at various points. Despite the "private house" sign, the current owner often provides tours of its motley interior upon request. To get there, take the first right after crossing the bridge; a right-of-way through the driveway leads to the Yellow Steeple and the **Sheep Gate,** the only surviving medieval gate of the once walled town. Ten minutes out Dublin Rd. in the direction opposite the castle, you can hear your own glorious voice bouncing off cathedral ruins across the river from **Echo Gate.** The cathedral grounds contain a tomb with two figures mistakenly called the **Jealous Man and Woman.** The name comes from the sword between them, which conventionally signified not resentment but chastity. Put a pin between the two figures; when the pin rusts (which shouldn't take long in this damp country) your warts should disappear. For more spicy history, **Trim Visitor's Centre,** next to the tourist office on Mill St., educates and frightens with a multimedia presentation and an excellent, dramatic slideshow. Displays describe decapitations, the lecherous behavior of sinewy, hairy Hugh de Lacy, and hideous plague rats—maybe Trim isn't so prim and proper after all. (Tel. 37227. Open M-F 10:30am-5pm, Su 1:30-5pm. Closed for lunch 12:30-1:30pm. Admission for the 35min. shows every 45min. £2, students and seniors £1.25.) Greenthumbs will enjoy the **Butterstream Gardens,** a 15min. walk past the SuperValu and left of the off-license. The several acres of paths, flowers, and pools are especially beautiful in late June. (Tel. 36017. Open daily Apr.-Sept. 11am-6pm. £3.)

For one week each June (usually the last), the **Scurlogstown Olympiad Town Festival** fills Trim with animal shows, carnival rides, and traditional music concerts.

BEYOND THE VALLEY OF THE BOYNE

KELLS (CEANANNAS MÓR)

Kells is internationally famous thanks to a book that neither began nor ended up there. The monastery at Kells was founded by St. Columcille (also known as St. Columba) in 559, before he went on to found the more important settlement of Iona on an island west of Scotland. It was at Iona that the famous *Book of Kells*, an elaborately decorated Latin version of the gospel, was begun. It came to Kells in some form of development in 804, when the Columbans fled Iona. In 1007, the book was stolen, its gold cover ripped off, and the pages buried in the bog, from which they were rescued two months later. It remained in Kells until 1661, when Cromwell carted it off to Trinity College, where it is now recovering. Kells is trying to get the book back, which Trinity finds amusing.

Even without the book, Kells boasts some of Ireland's best-preserved monastic ruins, including an oratory, a round tower, and four high crosses. The fifth and largest cross, Market Cross, stood for a millennium with relatively little mishap before it was knocked off its pedestal two years ago by a school bus driver. The discombobulated cross has been moved to Trim.

■ **PRACTICAL INFORMATION. Bus Éireann** stops outside the tourist office en route to Dublin (1hr.; M-Sa hourly, Su 12 per day; £6.30). The **tourist office** (tel. 49336), housed inconspicuously in the town hall on Headfort Pl., provides town maps and a handy heritage trail booklet (both free). **AIB** bank (tel. 40610) has an **ATM** on John St. (Open M 10am-5pm, Tu-F 10am-4pm.) The **post office** (tel. 40127) sits on Farrel St. (Open M-Sa 9am-5:30pm.) Kells' **phone code,** 046, hasn't been swiped or toppled. Yet.

■ ■ ■ **ACCOMMODATIONS, FOOD, AND PUBS. Kells Hostel** (tel. 49995; email hostels.iol.ie) sports a big kitchen, a friendly staff, and decent facilities; renovations to the common areas should finish in time for the high-season of 2000. From the center of town, head uphill on Carrick St.; the bus from Dublin will stop across the street from the hostel. Hostelers can use the attached gym for £3. (June to mid-Sept. coed 7-bed dorms £7.50, private 2-4 bed rooms £10 per person; mid-Sept. to Dec. and Mar.-June £7, £9. Laundry £4.50. Limited email access. Open Mar.-Dec.) B&Bs in town are pricey but excellent. **White Gables,** Headfort Pl. (tel. 40322 or 49672; email kelltic@tinet.ie), is just down the hill from the tourist office on the left. The rooms are top-notch, and your eggs will be cooked by a former chef. (Singles £25, doubles £40.)

SuperValu is smack-dab across from the hostel. (Open M-W and S 8am-7:30pm, Th-F 8am-9pm, Su 9am-6:30pm.) **Pebbles,** Newmarket St. (tel. 49229), is the most popular coffee shop in Kells, serving up a light fare. (Lasagne £1.50, lunch specials around £4. Open M-Sa 8am-5:30pm.) The **Round Tower,** Farrell St. (tel. 40144), offers a sizeable menu of grub within a wide price range. (Food served until 9pm.) Get a hell of a meal at **Dante's,** Market St. (tel. 41630), which serves up pasta and pizza in abundance. (Entrees around £8. Open noon-3pm and 6-11pm.) **O'Shaughnessy's,** Market St. (tel. 41110), has good pub grub (£4.50) and a variety of live music Friday through Sunday evenings. The **Blackwater Inn,** Farrell St. (tel. 40386), offers trad most Mondays and live rock on Wednesdays and Fridays. Black water? They must mean Guinness.

◎ SIGHTS. As part of its centuries-long position as a center of Christian learning, the monastery at Kells was a favorite target of rival monasteries. The current structure, with the exception of the 12th century belltower, dates back only as far as the 1700s. Inside **St. Columba's Church** (tel. 40151), there's a replica of *The Book of Kells,* and copies of selected pages enlarged for your viewing pleasure. The door should be open during daylight hours; if not, ask at the gate outside. Four large **high crosses** covered with biblical scenes sprinkle the south and west side of the church. The north cross is little more than a stump, but the east cross remains intact and depicts the making of crosses. A 12th century wall successfully encircled the church until 1997, when the County Council began building a path alongside it that undermined its foundations and caused it to topple. The nearby 100 ft. round tower failed to serve any protective function: its monks were torched, its book and saintly relics were stolen, and the would-be High King Murchadh Mac Flainn was murdered in it in 1076. If you hoist yourself up into its doorway and look in, the resident pigeons will probably poop on you.

Fortune reserved her smile for **St. Columcille's House,** across Church Ln., an awe-inspiring oratory where the *Book of Kells* may have been completed. Pick up the key from Mrs. Carpenter in a beige house at 10 Church Ln., and head 200 yd. uphill to the unmistakable oratory. The place looks almost exactly as it would have in St. Columcille's day, except that the current doorway enters into the basement, which was originally connected by a secret tunnel to the church. In centuries past, the three tiny attic rooms housed large relics and larger families.

Two miles down Oldcastle Rd., within the People's Park, is the **Spire of Loyd,** a 150 ft. viewing tower erected by the old Headfort landlords. Constructed as a work project for the poor, its ostensible purpose was to allow the Headfort women to watch the hunt comfortably and safely. Next to the spire is the recently restored **Graveyard of the Poor,** where the area's huge pauper population buried its dead in mass graves during the Famine.

LOUTH, MONAGHAN, AND CAVAN

County Louth's Cooley Peninsula boasts hills and seacoasts that hold a position of high esteem in the minds of hikers, bikers, and ancient bards. The tiny villages of Co. Cavan and Co. Monaghan make convenient, even pleasing rest-stops on journeys to the Northwest. Belturbet of Co. Cavan is covered under the Fermanagh Lake District in Northern Ireland.

ANALYZING INSECURE CASTLES When you're scampering around the half-ruins of Ireland's medieval castles, take a minute to think about the stairs. Even in castles designed to be homesteads, stairs could be a significant form of defense. Most obvious is the occasional absence of them: a number of castles had their doorways on the second (Irish "first") floor, so that access was only possible through a ladder that could be raised. And if attackers made it past the moat, gate, and walls, the staircases inside could still favor the owner. The distances between steps are often awkwardly inconsistent, not from poor construction but rather to trip any strangers running up. And the twists in the spirals are significant, too: some steps curve up to the left—making ascending assaulters attack as southpaws, while defenders descending could fight with the right. In a culture where left-handedness was suppressed as a sign of the devil, fighting right-handed was practically universal. Sometimes, castles were built with stairs curving right, favoring the invader; in such instances, the owner was so often away from his castle that reclaiming it from rogues was expected to be a regular affair.

DROGHEDA

Drogheda (DRA-hed-a) perches on steep slopes that look onto the Boyne river. Its drab and industrial waterfront is counteracted by inland streets lined with cheerful pubs. Drogheda's Viking past lingers in the crumbling walls and gates that surround the city. Most sights in Co. Meath make a pleasant bike ride from Drogheda.

EASTERN IRELAND

▐ TRANSPORTATION

Trains: Tel. 983 8749, east of town on the Dublin road. Follow John St. south of the river. To **Dublin** (1hr., express 30min.; M-Sa 20 per day, Su 7 per day; £7.50) and **Belfast** (2hr.; M-Sa 7 per day, Su 4 per day; £12.50).

Buses: Station on John St. (tel. 983 5023), at Donore Rd. Inquiries desk and **luggage storage** open M-F 9am-6:15pm, Sa 8:30am-1:30pm. To **Dundalk** (40min.; M-Sa 13 per day, Su 10 per day; £4.40), **Dublin** (50min.; M-F 24 per day, Sa 17 per day, Su 9 per day; £4.80), **Belfast** (2hr.; M-Sa 7 per day, Su 3 per day; £8.60), **Mullingar** (2hr.; M-Th and Sa 1 per day, F 2 per day, Su 1 per day; £4.80), **Athlone** (2½hr.; M-Th and Sa 1 per day, F 2 per day, Su 1 per day; £9), and **Galway** (4hr.; M-Th and Sa 1 per day, F 2 per day, Su 1 per day; £14).

Bike Rental: Quay Cycles, 11 North Quay (tel. 983 4526). £8 per day, £5 with *Let's Go* or ISIC, £30 per week; ID deposit. Helmet included. Open M-Sa 9am-6pm.

▐ PRACTICAL INFORMATION

Tourist Offices: (tel. 983 7070), in the bus station. Offers the *Drogheda Town Map* (£1), which identifies all Drogheda's sights as well as a map of the region. Open M-Sa 9:30am-6pm, Su 11:45am-5pm. A far superior, second tourist office in Millimount (tel. 984 5684) has more time and desire to help. Head up towards the Martello Tower to find it. Open M-F 9:30am-1pm and 2-5pm.

Banks: Numerous banks line West St. **AIB,** (tel. 983 6523) and **TSB** (tel. 983 8703) have **ATMs.** Both open M-W and F 9:30am-5pm, Th 9:30am-7pm.

Emergency: Dial 999; no coins required. **Garda:** West Gate (tel. 983 8777).

Hospital: Our Lady of Lourdes, Cross Lanes (tel. 983 7601).

Laundry: FM Laundrette, 13 North Quay (tel. 983 6837). Self-service £4.30, full service from £4. Open M-Sa 9am-6pm.

Post Office: West St. (tel. 983 8157). Open M-Sa 9am-5:30pm; Tu late opening 9:30am.

PHONE CODE: Sings silly camp songs at 041.

ACCOMMODATIONS

The **Green Door Hostel**, 47 John St. (tel. 983 4422), recently opened a block up from the bus station, offering top-notch beds in a friendly atmosphere that compensates for cramped living quarters. (June-Sept. 10-bed dorms £10, private rooms £13; Oct.-May £8, £10. Limited laundry and internet facilities. Bike and car park.) Drogheda's older hostel, **Harpur House (IHO)**, William St. (tel. 983 2736), is cheap but ranks far behind the Green Door in terms of quality. Follow Shop St. from the bridge up the hill, continue up Peter St. and take a right onto William St.; the hostel is the last house on the right. (10-bed dorms £8, private rooms £12. Full Irish breakfast £4. Free towels.) Well-kept and backpacker-friendly, **Abbey View House**, Mill Lane (tel. 983 1470), defines B&B courtesy. From the bus station, head north on the Belfast Rd. (N1) over the bridge and take the first left and the first left again. Sitting pretty on the River Boyne, the house has parking, big rooms with patchwork quilts, and an alleged tunnel to Monasterboice. (Single £20, double £30.) Likable Dennis Dineen at the **Roseville Lodge B&B**, Georges St. (tel. 983 4046), offers motel-like rooms, all with bath. (Singles £20, doubles £35.)

FOOD AND PUBS

An **open-air market** has been held in Bolton Square every Saturday since 1317. **Dunnes Stores** (tel. 983 7063) and **Quinnsworth/Tesco** (tel. 983 7209) on West St. have groceries every day. (Both open M-Tu and Sa 9am-6:30pm, W-F 9am-9pm; Dunnes also opens Su noon-6pm.) **La Pizzeria**, 38 Peter St. (tel. 983 4208), cooks all kinds of Italian specialities. It's also very popular, so make reservations or arrive before 9pm if you want a seat. (Pasta £5.50, pizza around £6. Open M-Tu and Th-Su 6-11pm.) For breakfast or a tasty sandwich creation, **Go Bananas** (tel. 983 8975) on West St. (Sandwiches £1.60-£2.50. Open M-Sa 9am-6pm.) **Bridie Mac's,** West St. (tel. 983 0965), supplies everything from snacks (£3) to full meals (£7) to live music. (Bar food served daily 3-8pm. Music Th-Sa.)

As the largest town in the area, Drogheda has a pretty active nightlife. Dark wood engulfs **Peter Matthews**, 9 Laurence St. (tel. 983 7371), better known as **McPhail's,** a very old, very likable pub. (Live rock, blues, jazz, and Latin Th-Su nights.) **The Weavers,** West St. (tel. 983 2816), is renowned for its carvery lunch and dinner grub, but the crowd really comes for cover bands and top 40 DJs on weekends. (No cover.) Sessions in the poster-plastered confines of **Cairbre (Carberry's),** Back Strand, stand out among the town's sparse trad offerings.

When the pubs close, Drogheda keeps on running like a syndicated cartoon. **The Earth,** in back of the Westcourt Hotel on West St. (tel. 983 0969), resembles a Flintstones pub, with fossils embedded in the walls and bar, rock-themed bathrooms, and not a single straight wall. (Open Th-Su from 11pm. Cover £5; less with concession available at Bridie Mac's.) George and Jane Jetson, in contrast, whizz around the corner to **Number 4,** Stockwell Ln. (tel. 984 5044), for the sleekest and trendiest of late bars. (Open past 2am. DJ Th-Su, live bands F. Cover £2-5 Th-Sa.) Leave Pebbles and Elroy at home—Number 4 is 21 and over, and the Earth is 23 and over.

SIGHTS

Walking Tours of Historical Drogheda (tel. 984 5684) provide a good introduction to town. (1½hr. Tours leave Tu-Sa at 10:20am from the bus station tourist office and 2:20pm from Millimount. £1.50, seniors £1.) Better still is doing the walk on your own under the guidance of either the *Drogheda Heritage Route* pamphlet or the *Local Story* booklet, both available at the Millimount tourist office.

Drogheda has two **St. Peter's Churches**, both worth visiting. Stare face to face with a blackened, shriveled head in the imposing, neo-Gothic St. Peter's Church on West St. Built in the 1880s, St. Peter's safeguards what's left of the martyred saint Oliver Plunkett. A handful of his bones are on display, as is the door of his London prison cell. (Open daily 8:30am-8:30pm.) The other **St. Peter's Church** (Church of

Ireland) hoards bad luck up at the top of Peter St. The original timber structure was destroyed in a 1548 storm. Another timber structure replaced it, only to be torched (with refugees inside) by Cromwell in 1649. The present church dates to 1753. Mounted on the wall of the cemetery's back left corner are **cadaver tombs,** with brutally realistic carvings of the half-decayed bodies of a man and woman. Dating from 1520, they are two of only nineteen such tombs left in the world. At the end of West St. stand the four-story twin towers of **St. Laurence's Gate,** a 13th century outer gate that is no less impressive for never having faced a serious attack. At the top of the hill on Peter St., the 14th century **Magdalen Tower,** covered with tufts of grass, is all that remains of the Dominican Friary that once stood on the spot. Old Abbey, south of West St., collects urban refuse under the few remaining arches of the 5th century **Abbey of St. Mary d'Urso.**

Across the river, the newly reconstructed Martello tower dominates the skyline. Inside, the **Millmount Museum** displays artifacts from the Civil War period, antique household appliances, and a geological collection. (Tel. 983 3097. Open Apr.-Oct. M-Sa 10am-5:30pm, Nov.-Mar. W and Sa-Su 2-5pm. £2.50, student £2, seniors and children £1.50.) Behind it, on Mary St., a new **heritage center** is planned to take over the old Church of Ireland St. Mary's Church (again, not to be confused with its Catholic doppelganger St. Mary's).

The Battle of the Boyne raged at **Oldbridge,** 3 mi. west of Drogheda on the Slane Rd. In 1690, William of Orange's momentous victory over James II secured for Protestants the English Crown and at least the eastern half of Ireland (see **The Protestant Ascendancy,** p. 10). A small information trailer parks there now, providing historical and genealogical information about the battle. You can climb some steps for a view of the battle site, but there's little to see. (Tel. 984 1644. Open all year M-F 9:30am-5pm, May-Sept. additionally Sa-Su 10am-5pm. £1.)

During the second week of July, locals swagger through the streets to the Latin rhythms of the **Samba Festival.**

MONASTERBOICE AND MELLIFONT ABBEY

What were once two of the most important monasteries in Ireland now crumble 5 mi. north of Drogheda. The grounds of **Monasterboice** (MON-uh-ster-boyce) hold a round tower and some of the most spectacular high crosses in existence. The monastery was one of Ireland's most wealthy from its founding around 520 until the Vikings sacked it in 1097. (Always open. Free.) **Muireadach's Cross,** the first high cross you'll see upon entering, sports an array of Biblical scenes and Celtic designs. On one side, Satan sneakily pulls down his side of the Judgment scales and then kicks 14 poor souls to hell. At a height of nearly 7 yd., the **West Cross** is the tallest High Cross in Ireland.

THE SIEGE OF DROGHEDA Cromwell's two day siege of Drogheda in 1649 was the first time in the town's illustrious history that its walls were breached. Originally twin towns separated by the Boyne, Drogheda was well-entrenched on both sides, and only a retractable drawbridge connected the two halves. So how did a warty man like Cromwell win so quickly? He was a lying, lucky bastard. One of the Drogheda captains had a wooden leg, so Cromwell sparked a rumor that the limb was full of gold. (His troops must not have been too bright, since no one could possibly walk with that sort of weight.) The rumor worked: Cromwell's men tracked down the poor captain faster than you can say "greed," and immediately ripped off his prosthesis. Disappointed that a wooden leg is in fact merely wood, they consoled themselves by beating the captain to death with his own limb—no doubt one of the more unique deaths in military history. If Cromwell's troups were gullible, though, the Drogheda citizens were just plain clueless. Retreating from Cromwell's bloody charge, once the walls were breached, the Droghedans all crossed from the south side of the river to the north—and forgot to raise the drawbridge behind them. Cromwell proceeded to flame-broil the town, churches and all.

As the monastery at Monasterboice fell, the Cistercians planted their first foothold for Rome just a few miles away. **Mellifont Abbey** quickly grew from its 1142 founding to become one of Ireland's wealthiest monastic settlements, playing host to a number of tragedies en route. The 1152 Senate of Mellifont weakened the independent Irish monastic system, and sent their traditions of scholarship into decline. Three years later Cistercian Pope Adrian IV issued a bill giving the English King authorization to "correct" Ireland, which served as approval for the Norman invasion of the 1170s. In 1603, the last of the O'Neills, who had once ruled Ulster, surrendered to the English here and then fled Ireland for the Continent (see **Feudalism, p. 8**). The ruins lack grandeur as well as basic substance, since most of the site's stones were plundered between 1727 and 1880 for use in nearby buildings. The romanesque octagon of the **lavabo,** where monks once cleansed themselves of sins and grime, offers a sense of the original structure's impressiveness. A small visitor center offers a tour of the site. (Tel. (041) 982 6459. Open daily May to mid-June 10am-5pm, mid-June to mid-Sept. 9:30am-6:30pm, mid-Sept. to Oct. 10am-5pm. £1.50, seniors £1, students 60p. After hours the site is free.)

Both sets of ruins are well-signposted off the Drogheda-Collon Rd. The best route for cyclists heads 5 mi. north on the wide shoulder of the N1 (Belfast Rd.) until the Dunleer exit; at the bottom of the ramp, turn left and follow the Monasterboice signs. When that road ends, turn right and veer left when you meet the larger Drogheda-Collon Rd. to get to Mellifont and eventually return to Drogheda. The Mellifont visitor center has a free hand-drawn map of the area.

DUNDALK

The home of the Harp brewery, Dundalk is located at the mouth of Dundalk Bay. Recently, Dundalk has made efforts to establish itself in the tourism industry as a source of knowledge about the history and mythology of the Cooley Peninsula. The town has a more long-standing reputation as a nightlife hub for locals throughout the Eastern counties.

◪ **ORIENTATION AND PRACTICAL INFORMATION.** The main street in Dundalk is **Clanbrassil St.,** with **Park St.** as the runner-up. Dundalk's streets change names often; Clanbrassil becomes **Market Square,** then **Earl St.** as it heads south. Earl St. intersects **Park St.,** which becomes **Francis St.,** then **Roden Pl.,** then **Jocelyn St.** if you head left from Earl St. To the right, Earl St. becomes **Dublin St.** The N1 highway zips south to Dublin and north to Belfast, becoming A1 at the border. The **train station** is on **Carrickmacross Rd.** From Clanbrassil St., turn right on Park St. then right on Anne St., which becomes Carrickmacross. Trains run to **Belfast** (1hr.; M-Sa 7 per day; Su 4 per day; £9) and **Dublin** (1hr.; M-Th 10 per day, F 11 per day, Sa 12 per day, Su 5 per day; £11). **Buses** stop at the Bus Éireann station (tel. 933 4075) on Long Walk, which is parallel to Clanbrassil, and run to **Belfast** via **Newry** (1½hr.; M-Sa 9 per day, Su 3 per day; £7), and **Dublin** (1½hr.; M-F 16 per day, Sa 13 per day, Su 7 per day; £7). The **tourist office,** Jocelyn St. (tel. 933 5484), hands out the free *Dundalk Town Guide,* which includes maps marked with the city's sights. From the bus stop, take Clanbrassil St. down to Park and turn left to reach Jocelyn St.; the office is on the right after the cathedral. (Open June-mid-Sept. M-F 9am-6pm, Sa 9:30am-1pm and 2-5:30pm; mid-Sept.-May M-F 9:30am-1pm and 2-5:30pm, Sa 10am-1pm and 2-6pm.) **Banks,** including the **AIB, Bank of Ireland,** and **Ulster Bank,** are scattered within a block of each other on Clanbrassil St.; most have **24hr. ATMs.** FonaCab, Francis St. (tel. 937 4777), has 24hr. **taxi** service for club kids. Additionally, many taxis stand in the square (tel. 932 6666). The **post office** (tel. 933 4444) is on Clanbrassil St. (Open M and W-Sa 9am-5:30pm, Tu 9:30am-5:30pm.) Life, the universe, and the **phone code** sum to 042.

ACCOMMODATIONS, FOOD, AND PUBS. Glen Gat House, 18-19 The Crescent (tel. 933 7938; glengat@indigo.ie), rests around the corner from Dublin St. near the train station. Its award-winning garden and quality accommodations justify the splurge. (£18.) In town, **Oriel House,** 63 Dublin St. (tel. 933 1347), is well located and inexpensive. Its dim rooms lack any accoutrement, though the proprietress is lovely. (Singles £12, doubles £20.)

Restaurants and late-night fast food cluster on the main streets in town. The sign hanging in the window of **Deli Lites** on Clanbrassil St. challenges passersby with "Try our delicious sandwiches, no one likes a coward." The lion-hearted will be pleased with gourmet sandwiches (£2-3). Fashionable types go to **Cafe Metz,** Francis St. You, too, can afford to be seen at this art deco dining hall if you order from the low-priced yet filling sandwich menu. (Sandwiches around £3. Open M-Sa 8:30am-6pm, dinner 7pm, Su 9:30am-8:30pm.)

Only the trepidatious will need guidance in seeking out Dundalk's pub scene, but here are a few picks. The miniature buggy in its front window and the antiques inhabiting its cabinets lend **M. Courtneys,** 43-44 Park St. (tel. 932 6652), the air of a converted carriage house. Hitch up here for a night of good *craic* and, perhaps an impromptu session of trad. The **Windsor Bar,** Dublin St. (tel. 933 8146), is convenient to Oriel House and serves particularly tasty pub grub. (Full meals £4-5, sandwiches £2; food served noon-3pm.) **Mr. Ridleys,** 92 Park St. (tel. 933 3329), welcomes patrons with live music and a nightclub running almost nightly. (Cover £2-6, concessions 40% for pub-goers.) **Jockey's** (tel. 933 4621), on Anne St., tempts pedestrians with its alluring front, and serves good, cheap pub grub during the day. (Breakfast daily 10am, lunch noon-2:30pm. Trad F 10pm.) For pints and dancing, head to one of the spacious bars in the **Imperial Hotel** (tel. 933 2241): **Rockwell's,** a gilt-and-mirrored pub, or the **Arc Nightclub,** a late-night disco. (Bar open daily 11:30am-11:30pm. Club open Th-Su 10:30pm-2:15am. Cover varies.)

SIGHTS. The gothic **St. Patrick's Cathedral,** Francis St., was modeled after King's College Chapel in Cambridge. (Tel. 933 4648. Open daily 7:30am-5pm.) Next door to the tourist office, the **County Museum** caters to those with a particular interest in "Louth's industrial legacy"—perfect for that research paper on Louth's tractors. It's real draw, however, is upstairs on two newly opened floors exhibiting the archaeology, mythology, and history of the county. Other gems include reproductions of a prehistoric cave dwelling and modern Irish living room. (Tel. 932 6578. Open Tu-Sa 10:30am-5:30pm, Su 2-6pm. £2, students and seniors £1, children 60p.) In the far northwest corner of town off Mount Ave., the 12th-century **Cúchulainn's Castle** supposedly stands on the birthplace of Cúchulainn, the hero of the **Ulster Cycle** of myths (see **Literary Traditions,** p. 19). The seven-story high **Seatown Windmill** was once one of the largest in Ireland, but the wind was taken out of its sails when they were removed in 1885. Beaches beckon from **Blackrock,** 3 mi. south on R172.

COOLEY PENINSULA

The numerous trails in the mountains that surround the Cooley Peninsula are a hiker's paradise, and Carlingford Lough has the warmest waters in the northern half of the island. Several ancient Irish myths are set in this dramatic landscape, among them the epic *Táin bo Cuailnge,* or "The Cattle Raid of Cooley" (see **Literary Traditions,** p. 19). Remarkably well preserved stone remnants of medieval settlements are scattered throughout the peninsula. Cooley's **phone code** is a dastardly cow thief named 042.

CARLINGFORD

Situated at the foot of Slieve Foy, the highest of the Cooley Mountains, the coastal village of Carlingford has hardly grown in size since it hit its mercantile heyday in the 14th to 16th centuries. Today, its narrow alleys and tidy buildings house numerous craft shops and closet-sized art galleries. The village is a little pile-up of buildings and ruins was recently named "Tidiest Town" by Board Fáilte.

🔟 PRACTICAL INFORMATION. Buses (tel. 933 4075) stop along the waterfront on their way to **Newry** (30min., M-Sa 2 per day) and **Dundalk** (50min., M-Sa 5 per day, £3.20). **Teach Eoalais** (CHOCK OAL us), Old Quay Ln. (tel. 937 3888), next to PJ's Anchor Bar, offers **tourist information.** (Open mid-June-Aug. daily 9:30am-7pm; Sept.-mid-June M-F 9:30am-5pm.) From the bus stop, walk half a block inland and half a block to the left. An **AIB** bank (tel. 937 3105) is on Newry St. (Open Tu and Th 10:30am-12:30pm and 1:30-2:30pm.) For **taxi** service call **Gally Cabs** (tel. 937 3777).

🔟🔟🔟 ACCOMMODATIONS, FOOD, AND PUBS. At the **Carlingford Adventure Centre and Hostel (IHH),** Tholsel St. (tel. 937 3100), the friendly staff leads adventurers down long cement-block corridors to small, dark rooms with wooden bunks. The hostel is often filled with groups of school children; call ahead in May and June. (8-bed dorms £8.50, 4-bed dorms £9.50, bunked doubles £10.50. Open Feb.-Nov., all year for groups. Wheelchair accessible.) **B&Bs** in Carlingford tend to be posh and expensive. **Murphy House,** Dundalk St. (tel. 937 3735), offers small but charming rooms in a converted 18th century cottage. (Singles £25 during the week, £28 weekends; doubles £36.) You can dance the hora all the way to the **Shalom B&B,** Ghan Rd. (tel. 937 3151), signposted from the waterfront. (Singles £24.50, doubles £36.) **Viewpoint,** Omeath Rd. (tel. 73149), just off the waterfront beyond King John's castle, provides motel-style rooms with baths, private entrances, and incredible views of the mountains and the lough. (£20.)

Carlingford contains a handful of pubs and eateries, and their offerings range from traditional Irish hospitality to supernatural phenomena. Particularly good *craic* is on tap at **Carlingford Arms,** Newry St. (tel. 73418). The pub serves hearty meals. (Entrees around £5, food served 12:30-9:30pm. Folk music Sa after 9:30pm.) Fronted by **H. O'Hares Family Grocery** and located across the street from the hostel, **PJ Anchor's Bar** (tel. 937 3106), is barely larger than a breadbox, but tight quarters make for close friendships. During good weather, the backyard provides a refreshing alternative location to devour soup and sandwiches (less than £2) and locally caught oysters (£3.50 for six). The real magic is inside where the publicans proudly display the clothes of a leprechaun caught in the nearby hills several years ago (see **Sights**). Homemade sweets and light lunches are there for the taking at **Georgina's Bakehouse** (tel. 937 3346), located atop Castle Hill. (Soup, sandwich, desert £1.75 each. Open daily 10:30am-6pm.)

🔟 SIGHTS. The **Holy Trinity Heritage Centre** is housed in a renovated medieval church squeezed between several recent centuries' worth of buildings. The centre's staff educates visitors on the history and local lore of Carlingford from the 9th century to the present. (Church Yard Rd. Tel. 937 3454. Open Sa-Su and bank holidays noon-5pm. £1, children 50p.) Nearby, the ruins of the **Dominican Friary** are open for exploration. You can pretend that you're a Dominican friar and Cromwell is oppressing you. Carlingford's three other surviving medieval buildings provide interesting scenery for a stroll through town, but their interiors are closed to visitors. **King John's Castle,** by the waterfront, is the largest and most foreboding of Carlingford's medieval remains. Built in the 1190s and named for King John, who visited briefly in 1210, the castle is now locked as renovations are taking place. **Taaffe's Castle,** toward town along the quay, was built in the 16th century as a merchant house on what was then the waterfront, and it contains classic Norman defensive features. In a tiny alley off Market Square, the turret-laden 16th-century **Mint** is fenestrated with five ornate limestone windows. At the end of the street, one of the old 15th-century town gates, the **Tholsel** (TAH sehl), makes a narrow passageway for cars entering town. The **Adventure Centre** (see **Accommodations**), Tholsel St. (tel. 937 3100), gives instruction in **canoeing, windsurfing, kayaking, currach building,** and **sailing.** (All activities £28 per day, children £16.)

For those seeking more group-oriented (or booze-oriented) recreation, Carlingford hosts several festivals during the year. In late September, a **medieval banqueting weekend** brings parades, costumes, and indigestion, and a weekend-long **folk festival** draws musicians from all over the Republic.

THE LEPRECHAUN OF SLIEVE FOY One misty morn about a decade ago, PJ (the late owner of PJ's Anchor Bar) was going about his usual morning work—painting murals over the windows of abandoned houses—when he heard a high-pitched yell. On his way to investigate the source of the noise, he met a school teacher who had also heard the scream. The men's keen ears soon led them to the place where the yell had originated. About halfway up Slieve Foy was a "fairy ring" of trampled grass with bones and a wee leprechaun suit at its center. The men picked up the leprechaun's remains and returned to Carlingford with their amazing discovery in hand. Further investigation determined that the bones were from a sheep. However, as PJ later commented, everyone knows that leprechauns are changelings, and this one had probably turned into a sheep on the men's approach. The story soon reached the ears of national and international reporters, and for a short time afterwards, Carlingford was known worldwide as the town that had seen a leprechaun.

MONAGHAN

Monaghan (MOH-nah-han) is a busy market town with a population of 6000 that's encircled by minor, egg-shaped hills called drumlins. Its inland location means most tourists fly by it on their way from Dublin to coasts north and west. While not many look in at Monaghan, it still looks out, and boasts a thriving, eclectic music scene—you're as likely to hear a harmonica in a pub as you are a *bodhrán* or even a saxophone. Surprisingly, the town is relatively tourist-free, but that just means the *craic* is less polluted.

◪ PRACTICAL INFORMATION. The **bus depot** (tel. 82377) is north of Market Sq. (Open M-Sa 8:30am-8pm; additional phone hours Su 10am-2pm and 4-8:30pm.) Buses run to **Belfast** (1½hr.; M-Sa 5 per day, Su 2 per day; £5.50) and **Dublin** (2hr.; M-Sa 7 per day, Su 3 per day; £6). From Church Square, walk up the Market St. hill to find the **tourist office.** (Tel. 81122. Open June-Sept. M-Sa 9am-6pm, Su 10am-2pm. Call for winter hours.) **AIB**, The Diamond, has an **ATM. Tommy's** (tel. 84205) runs **taxis,** and you might be able to **rent bikes** at **Clerkin's** (tel. 81113) on Park St. (£5 per day. Open M-W and F-Sa 9am-1pm and 2-6pm.) The **post office** (tel. 82131) lies just north of Church Square on Mill St. (Open M-Sa 9am-6pm). **Spyderbyte**, off The Diamond, is the most convenient cafe with internet access between Dublin and Belfast. (Open M-F 11am-11pm, Sa 11am-8pm, Su 2-10pm. £3 per 30min., cheaper after 6pm.) To call the **hospital,** dial 81811; for the **Garda,** call 82222. The **phone code** is a rascally redhead singing the blues to 047.

◪▣▣ ACCOMMODATIONS, FOOD, AND PUBS. Monaghan has no hostels, but **Ashleigh House**, 37 Dublin St. (tel. 81227), has rosy rooms and "whatever you want" for breakfast. (£16, with bath £20.) Two doors down, **Argus Court**, 32 Dublin St. (tel. 81794), provides a no-frills B&B upstairs from your basic pub. (Singles £18, doubles £32.) If all else fails, call Monaghan's **Ancestor Research Center** (tel. 82304) and stay with a distant relative.

There's a **SuperValu** supermarket (tel. 81344) on Church Square. (Open M-Th 9am-7pm, F 9am-9pm, Sa 9am-6pm.) **Pizza D'Or,** 23 Market St. (tel. 84777), behind the tourist office, is a town institution. It stays open until after the pubs close, and your *Let's Go* book gets you a £1 discount on a pizza. (Pizzas from £3.50. Open M-F 5pm-1am, Sa-Su 5pm-3am.) **Tommy's** (tel. 81772), around the corner from the Squealing Pig, has burgers and grease. The diner furniture was new in the fifties and hasn't died yet and, yes, they serve pizza. (12 in. pies from £3. Open M-Sa 10am-8pm.) For classier surroundings at low-brow prices, **Mediterraneo** on Main St. makes decadent pasta dishes and gourmet pizzas. (Margherita pizza £6.95. Open M-Sa 6pm-11pm, Su 6pm-10pm.)

Pubs cluster off Church Sq. and down Dublin St. from The Diamond. **The Squealing Pig,** The Diamond (tel. 84562), with its barn-like wooden floor and large-screen TV, gets the vote for the most popular pub in town. (21 and up.) **McKenna's Pub,** Dublin St. (tel. 81616), books mostly blues acts for its upstairs stage. (Music Th-Sa.) The floor, dating from 1934, is far newer than the tables, which were once distillery barrels. **Patrick Kavanaugh's,** off Church Square (tel. 81950), is an intimate old kitchen that was converted into a pub well before anyone can remember. It draws a young crowd with trad Wednesday and Sunday evenings. **Jimmy's** (tel. 81694), a classy 1950s pub on Mill St. off Church Sq., serves up trad on Thursdays and jazz on Sunday mornings.

🎫 **SIGHTS.** In the center of town, the **Monaghan County Museum,** Hill St., across from the tourist office, painstakingly chronicles Co. Monaghan's history. (Tel. 82928. Open Tu-Sa 11am-1pm and 2-5pm. Free.) The 14th century **Cross of Clogher** looks on. The comprehensive and detailed **St. Louis Heritage Centre,** Market Rd., which traces the St. Louis Order of nuns, occupies a red-brick building in the convent school grounds. (Tel. 83529. Open M-Tu and Th-F 10am-noon and 2:30-4:30pm., Sa-Su 2:30-4:30pm. £1, children 50p. Wheelchair accessible.) Past sisters' hairshirts and cutlery are on display, while chaste Barbie dolls model the evolution of nun fashion. The 1895 **St. Macartan's Cathedral,** on the south side of town is Monaghan's most impressive building and offers panoramic views of the town. The Monaghan pub scene goes into overdrive during the first weekend in September with the **Jazz and Blues Festival.** (Contact Somhairle McChongaille, tel. 82928, for details.) Acts from Delta to Dublin land in Monaghan to shake the little town right to its rafters.

CASTLEBLAYNEY

Twenty miles southeast of Monaghan on the bus route to Dublin, Castle-blayney specializes in fun and games: it has an adventure center, a main street crammed with funky pubs, and a karaoke bar. Nearby, **Lough Muckno Leisure Park** has 900 acres of forest; **Lough Muckno** ("Lake of the Swimming Pig") is where large numbers of perch, trout, and pike live until caught. The **Adventure Centre** offers all manner of land and water sport to the energetic. (Open June-Sept. Tu-F 2-7pm, Sa-Su noon-7pm. **Windsurfing** £20 per 4hr., **tennis** £2 per hr.) If you liked summer camp, you'll love **Castleblayney's Hostel (IHH)** (tel. (042) 46256), in the same building as the adventure center. (Dorms £10, with continental breakfast £12, with full breakfast £15. Open Apr.-Oct.). **Camping** space is available. (£4 per tent plus £1 per person. Open St. Patrick's Day to mid-Oct.) The **White House B&B** (tel. (042) 46242) outside the park, has bright rooms and a garden for lounging in the sun. (Singles £18; doubles £16, with bath £17.50.)

Pack a picnic at **Spar** supermarket (tel. (042) 40137), on the way to the park. (Open M-Sa 8am-10pm, Su 9am-10pm.) **Barney's,** Main St. (tel. (042) 40120), fries fast food and is the cheapest of the town's offerings. (Open M-Sa noon-1am, Su 3pm-1am.) The best desserts are at **Deirdre's Home Bakery** (tel. (042) 49588) two doors down. The town's a wee bit hipper since the **Hale-Bopp Night-club** (tel. (042) 49550) opened above **The Comet Bar** in 1998, two decades after space funk imploded. (Cover £5.) Enlarge your liver with some pints from **Tiny's** (tel. (042) 40510), Main St. Karaoke fever strikes at **The Conabury Inn** (tel. (042) 40047) on most Wednesdays and Saturdays in the summer. During the rest of the week, the place is just your average, smoky pub.

WESTMEATH, OFFALY, LAOIS, AND LONGFORD

These central counties are often passageways rather than destinations. The nineteen lakes of Co. Westmeath have earned it the nickname "Land of Lakes and Legends." Farther south in famously soggy Co. Offaly, small towns and the impressive ruins of Clonmacnoise civilize the peatland. The Slieve Bloom Mountains, between Mountrath, Kinitty, and Roscrea, are splendid and underappreciated. Co. Longford is calm and collected, but hardly exciting.

MULLINGAR

Mullingar is planted in the center of Co. Westmeath and serves most travelers as a transportation stop between Dublin and the west coast. Discos at night and the nearby sights during the day might occupy travelers spending the night in town.

7 **PRACTICAL INFORMATION.** From the train station, follow the road and turn right onto **Dominick St.**, which runs through the town center and various names (Dominick, **Oliver Plunkett, Pearse,** and **Austin Friars St.**). The station is open 6am-9pm and charges a minimum of £1 for **luggage storage. Trains** (tel. 48274) chug to **Dublin** (1¼hr.; M-Th 4 per day, F 5 per day, Sa-Su 3 per day; £8.50) and **Sligo** (2hr.; M-Th and Sa-Su 3 per day, F 4 per day; £10.50). **Bus Éireann** stops variously at the train station, Kilroy's on Austin Friars St., and the Belvedere Gift Shop on Castle St., on its way to **Athlone** (1hr., 1-2 per day, £4.80), **Dublin** (1½hr.; M-Sa 6 per day, Su 3 per day; £7), **Sligo** (2½hr., 3 per day, £4.80), and **Galway** (2¾hr., 1-2 per day, £4.80). **O'Brien's Bus Co.** (tel. 48977) sends buses to **Dublin** (M-Sa 5 per day, Su 3 per day) from in front of the post office on Dominick St.

The **tourist office** (tel. 48650), in Market Sq. at the corner of Pearse and Mount St., offers a free county guide with an area map, a good £1 town map, and plenty of info about nearby sights and activities. (Open all year M-F 9am-6pm, plus May-Oct. Sa 10am-1pm and 2-6pm.) Every major bank has a branch, most with **ATMs**, along the main drag; **TSB**, Oliver Plunkett St., has the longest hours. (Open M-W and F 9:30am-5pm, Th 9:30am-7pm.) Escape from thoughts of Mullingar at the Wry Mill **internet cafe** (tel. 48635), on Oliver Plunkett St. (£4 per hr. Open daily 8am-9pm.) The **post office** (tel. 48393) is on Dominick St. (Open M-Sa 9am-5:30pm.) The **phone code** is on a losing streak with a record of 044.

■☆▣ **ACCOMMODATIONS, FOOD, AND PUBS.** The **Newbury Hotel,** Dominick St. (tel. 42888), offers the best B&B value in town, with clean, well-equipped rooms just up from the train station. (Singles £15, with bath £25; doubles £50.) Across the road, the **Railway House B&B,** Dominick St. (tel. 41142) offers decent rooms with TV and tea. (Singles £23, doubles £40.) **John Daly's** pub, 2 Oliver Plunkett St. (tel. 42724), offers B&B upstairs on Market Sq. (Singles £25, doubles £40.)

The Wry Mill Cafe, Oliver Plunkett St., offers simple, fat sandwiches (£2.50) and entrees (£4-5.50). **The Kitchen Fare Deli,** Mount St. (tel. 41294), is a great place to lunch on delicious specials (£4) and fruit scones. (Open M-Sa 8:30am-6pm.) The lines are understandably long at the **Greville Arms Hotel,** Pearse St. (tel. 48563); the restaurant is a bit pricey, but the carvery gives excellent bloat for your buck. (M and Th trad.) Candlelit trad sessions draw big crowds on Wednesday nights at **Hughes Corner House** (tel. 48237), on the corner of Pearse and Castle St. **The Final Fence,** Oliver Plunkett St. (tel. 48688), hosts a nightclub with disco, top 40, and techno on weekend nights. (Cover £5, concessions available in pubs.)

🎦 🎭 SIGHTS AND ENTERTAINMENT. Crowned with two spires, the **Cathedral of Christ the King** towers over Mary St. Inside, an **ecclesiastical museum** fills display cases with all sorts of items, from the vestments of St. Oliver Plunkett, Ireland's most recently canonized saint, to a model of the cathedral made from 68,750 matchsticks. (Tel. 48338. Museum open Th and Sa-Su 3-4pm or by appointment. £1.) The **Military Museum**, Columb Barracks (tel. 48391), is on the south side of the canal bridge; take an immediate right, and then left. (Open by appointment. Free.) Plays keep the new **Mullingar Arts Center** on Mount St. busy. (Tickets from £8, students and seniors from £6. Box office tel. 47777; open 9:30am-9pm.)

The tourist office can provide all the info you need about **fishing** for trout, bream, carp, pike, rudd, and roach on the many nearby lakes, including equipment and boat rentals. The best fishing in town actually takes place in mid-July at the **Mullingar International Bachelor Competition** (tel. 44044), the culmination of a week-long festival supposedly geared toward family-oriented activities.

NEAR MULLINGAR

Heading north of Mullingar, the Fore Trail first follows N4 to Coole, then turns east onto R395, and finally swoops back down to Mullingar on R394 through Fore. The Belvedere Trail, which covers the area south of Mullingar, follows N52 to N6 and then takes Kilbeggan Rd. back to Mullingar. The trails are designed with car drivers in mind, but both are perfectly bikable as well.

THE FORE TRAIL

The first stop on the Fore Trail is the little village of **Multyfarnham**, 6 mi. along the way. At a 15th century **Franciscan friary**, life-size figures in a peaceful garden depict the stations of the cross. Tommy Newman (tel. (044) 71111) rents out **boats** (£25 per day), and hiking trails lace the area. Four miles farther, the N4 runs between the town of **Coole** and **Turbotstown House**, a 200-year-old Georgian mansion that's privately owned. (Open May-Sept.) Two miles east on the R395, toward Castlepollard, are the Gothic Revival towers of romantic **Tullynally Castle**. The surrounding 30 acres of gardens include a pond inhabited by black Australian swans. (Tel. (044) 61159. Tours of castle Sept. 1-15 and mid-June to July 2-6pm. Gardens open daily May-Sept. 2-6pm. Castle and gardens £4.50, children £2.50.)

With a little marketing, the ruins of **Fore** could be the next Glendalough (see p. 139). The most extensive Benedictine ruins in Ireland, Fore is widely known for its seven wonders: water that flows uphill, water that won't boil, a tree that won't burn, a monastery that should have sunk into the bogs, a mill without a source of water to turn its wheel, a stone lifted by prayer alone, and a saint encased in stone. **Fore Abbey** was founded around 630 by St. Fechin and rebuilt 12 times after fires. Additions to the site date from the 11th, 13th, and 15th centuries. **St. Fechin's Church**, in the graveyard, is the oldest standing building. Up the hill, the tiny **Anchorite's Church** housed hermits well into the 17th century; get the key at the Seven Wonders pub nearby. The abbey is on the **Shamrock Experience** tour (tel. (046) 40127), based in Kells (see p. 151).

A smart detour from the Fore Trail heads 8 mi. out Oldcastle Rd. (R335) to the **Loughcrew Cairns** (Slieve na Calliagh, meaning "Witch Hill"). Similiar to Newgrange (see p. 148), Loughcrew is a collection of passage tombs dating to 3000 BC; unlike Newgrange, Loughcrew is undertouristed and cheap. The largest of the thirty scattered tombs, the creatively named **Cairn T** features some fine carving and the famous **Hag's Chair**, thought to have been used first for a royal seat and much later for a clandestine Christian altar. From May to October, a trailer (tel. (049) 854 2009) at the base of the hill provides the key to let you poke around inside the tomb. Bring a flashlight. (£1, seniors 70p, students 40p.) From the trailer, it's a 20min. hike up to the tomb.

The Fore Trail continues along the R395 to the R394, where it turns south to reach **Collinstown**. Another detour leads out the R395 to **Delvin**, where the ruins of a 12th century castle mark the onetime western boundary of the British-controlled

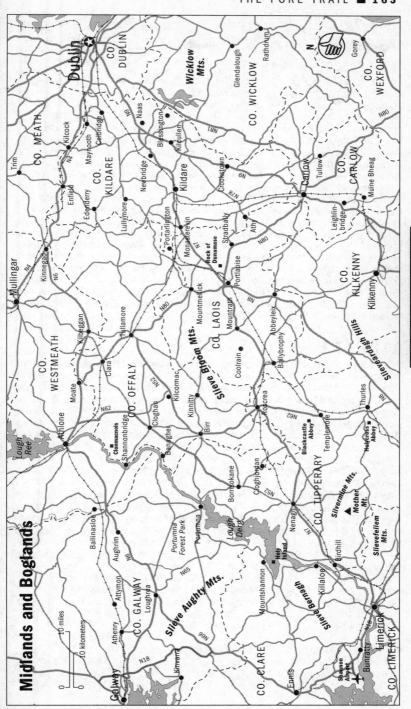

Midlands and Boglands

Pale. Back in Collinstown, the trail carries on to **Crookedwood,** where a well-preserved 14th century church sits in front of a ring fort. (Key at the nearby house.) The trail continues south and returns to Mullingar.

THE BELVEDERE TRAIL

Four miles south of Mullingar, the 18th century **Belvedere House and Gardens** pompously promenade along the shore of Lough Ennel. The house strives for imperial grandeur, with Roman gods frescoed along the ceiling. Robert Rochford, Lord Belvedere, for whom the house was built, also commissioned the fake "ruins" of a nonexistent abbey in order to obstruct his view of his brother's superior rose garden. The ruin is now called the **Jealous Wall** to his disgrace. (Tel. (044) 42820. Open daily July-Aug. noon-6pm; Easter-June and Sept. noon-5pm. £1, students 50p.)

Turning off the N52 and onto the N6, the trail continues to the small town of **Kilbeggan** at the next major intersection west. **Locke's Distillery,** a former firewater factory, has been converted into a museum. The zany anecdotes about workers' experiences on the job make the tour worthwhile. (Tel. (0506) 32134. Open daily Apr.-Oct. 9am-6pm; Nov.-Mar. 10am-4pm. £3; students, seniors, and children £2.50.) From Kilbeggan, the trail turns right, heading northeast toward **Lough Ennell,** a major bird sanctuary favored by trout fishermen. To fish yourself, you may need a permit from a local tackle shop. (Pike fishing is free; permit needed for trout. £5 per day.) On the shore of the lough sits **Lilliput House,** sadly life-size, and **Jonathan Swift Park,** with trails, fishing piers, and a good beach for swimming. Swift supposedly conceived *Gulliver's Travels* during a visit to Lough Ennell in the 1720s, and the surrounding area was renamed Lilliput shortly after the book's publication in 1726. The Belvedere Trail returns to Mullingar along the N52.

ATHLONE

Set amongst the flat lands of Roscommon and Westmeath, Athlone is the center of everything in the middle of nowhere. Positioned at the intersection of the Shannon River and the Dublin-Galway road, the city is a transportation hub, with cars, truck, trains, and buses charging through town on cross-country trips. The 13th-century Norman castle that dominates the waterfront attests to former Athlone's past strategic importance. Visitors spending the night in Athlone might best spend their day at sights outside of town, either along the scenic Shannon or at the monastic ruins at nearby Clonmacnois.

⚐ PRACTICAL INFORMATION. Athlone's **train** and **bus depot** (tel. 73322) is on **Southern Station Rd.,** which runs parallel to **Church St.** (Ticket window staffed M-Sa 9am-5:30pm.) **Trains** leave for **Galway** (1¼hr.; 8-9 per day; M-Th and Sa £7.50, F and Su £11), and **Dublin** (1¾hr.; M-Sa 11 per day, Su 9 per day; M-Th and Sa £9.50, F and Su £12.50). **Buses** shuttle in from **Dublin** on route to **Galway** (14-15 per day, £7), **Kilkenny** (1 per day, £11), **Cork** (1 per day, £13), **Limerick** (M-Sa 3 per day, Su 1 per day; £9.70), and **Killarney** (M-Sa 3 per day, Su 1 per day; £14). A private bus line, **Nestor Buses** (tel. (091) 797 244), also serves the region; for their routes and schedules, call Nestor or stop by the Royal Hotel. The **tourist office** (tel. 94630), in the castle, has free maps and the *Athlone and District Visitors Guide*. (Open Easter-Oct. M-Sa 9am-6pm, Su 10am-5pm.) **Bank of Ireland** (tel. 75111) and **AIB** (tel. 72089), on Church St., have **24hr. ATMs.** (Both open M 10am-5pm, Tu-F 10am-4pm.) The **post office** (tel. 83550) is on Barrack St., by the castle. (Open M and W-Su 9am-5:30pm, T 9:30am-5:30pm.) Athlone's **phone code** is 0902.

⚑ ACCOMMODATIONS. The **Lough Ree Lodge,** Dublin Rd. (tel. 76738; fax 76477; email loughreelodge@tiniet.ie), is the sole hostel in the area. Walk out Church St. past the shopping center, take the right fork; keep going, over the bridge, until the college. A city bus shuttles between the Esso station near the hostel and the

Golden Island shopping mall (50p, roughly every 30min. M-Sa 9am-6pm). Located a good 35min. hike from the castle, Lough Ree is called a hostel but the "s" is silent: all rooms are small, private, and furnished. (Singles £14, doubles £24; all with bath. Continental breakfast included. Laundry £2. Wheelchair accessible.)

B&Bs line the route to the hostel. Closer to town, you can get a cozy room for a nice price at **Shannon View**, 3 Shannon Villas (tel. 78411), a few blocks up Church St. from the church. (£15.) **The Thatch** (tel. 94981), opposite the castle, has palatial rooms and a good deal of noise from the bars below; quieter rooms are pricier. (Singles £25, £38-50 doubles.) The closest camping is at **Lough Ree East Caravan and Camping Park** (tel. 78561 or 74414), staked out 3 mi. northeast on N55 (Longford Rd.). Follow signs for Lough Ree. (Tent £3. Showers 50p. Open May-Sept.)

⌂▨ FOOD AND PUBS. Head downstairs at **Dunnes Stores** (tel. 75212) on Irishtown Rd. for your multiple grocery needs. (Open M-W and Sa 9am-6:30pm, Th-F 9am-9pm, Su noon-6m.) **loaves & fishes bistro** (tel. (087) 290 9370), tucked away by the fork in Church St., may not be great at capitalization, but its dishes are miraculously tasty, especially for vegetarians. (Entrees around £4.50. Open M-W 9:30am-6pm, Th-Sa 9:30am-8pm.) **Bradbury's**, across from the church on Church St., is where locals go for cheap, delicious breakfast and lunch. (Sandwiches from £1.50, entrees under £5. Open M-Sa 8:30am-6pm, in summer also Su 8:30am-6pm.) Next door, the **Bonne Bouche** (tel. 72112) serves a small variety of dishes that will fill your plate and please your palate. (Entrees £6. Open roughly 10am-8pm daily.)

Sean's Bar (tel. 92358), behind the castle on Main St., may be Ireland's oldest inn, but the building stands up to raucous trad five nights a week. She went through a phase as The Hooker, but now **Gertie Brown's**, the Strand (tel. 74848), found her old self and entertains more regulars than ever. (M trad sessions). The crowd at the **Palace Bar**, Market Sq. (tel. 92229), crosses all generational lines, and enjoys occasional live music. Two clubs vie for late-night attention. At **BoZo's**, in Conlon's on Dublingate St., kids have a clownishly good time boogying to chart music. (£3-5 cover. Open Th-Su 11:15pm-2am.) At **Ginkel's 2000,** the 19-24 crowd spiffs up for the trendy leopardskin decor. (W-Sa cover around £5.) *The Westmeath Independent* has entertainment listings.

◐ SIGHTS. Athlone's national fame comes from a single, crushing defeat. Williamite forces besieged **Athlone Castle** in 1691. With the help of extra beer rations and 12,000 cannonballs, they didn't take long to cross the river and sweep up. The defending Jacobites, unskilled soldiers at best, suffered massive casualties; the attackers, in contrast, lost fewer than 100 of their 25,000 strong (see **The Protestant Ascendancy**, p. 10). The castle is now free for all to wander around, providing some grand Shannon views. (Open May-Sept. daily 9:30am-6pm.) Inside, the **Athlone Castle Visitor Centre** tells the story play-by-bloody-play in a 45min. audio-visual show that sides heavily with the losers. The museum inside the visitor center has gramophones, uniforms from the Civil War, and other oddities. (Tel. 94630. Open May-Sept. daily 10am-4:30pm. £2.60, seniors and students £1.80; museum only, half-price.) You can watch the master at work in the small **Athlone Crystal Factory**, 29-31 Pearse St., then covet the glistening products in the small factory shop. (Tel. 92867. Open M-Sa 10am-1pm and 2-6pm.) **Viking Tours,** 1-2 Gleeson St. (tel. 73833; mobile (086) 262 1136), departs from the strand across the river from the castle and sails a replica Viking ship up the Shannon to Lough Ree and Clonmacnois. (1½-4hr.; 2 or more per day. £6, students and children £3.)

The last week in June brings the **Athlone Festival,** which includes parades, exhibits, and free concerts. Aspiring singers head to Athlone in late autumn for the **John McCormack Golden Voice** opera competition, named for Athlone's most famous tenor (see **Music,** p. 26). Contact the Athlone Chamber of Commerce (tel. 73173).

CLONMACNOIS

Isolated 14 mi. southwest of Athlone, the monastic ruins of Clonmacnois (clonmuk-NOYS) watch over the Shannon's boglands. St. Ciaran (KEER-on) founded the monastery in 548; his settlement grew into a city and important scholastic center. Monks wrote the precious **Book of the Dun Cow** at Clonmacnois around 1100, on vellum supposedly from St. Ciaran's cow. The holy cow traveled everywhere with the saint, and miraculously produced enough milk for the whole monastery. More recently, Seamus Heaney's *Seeing Things* retells a vision of manned ships passing through the air above the city in 748, described in the monastery's *Annals*. If you have a car, the easiest way to reach Clonmacnois from Athlone or Birr is to take N62 to Ballynahoun, then follow the signs. Clonmacnois is accessible by bike, but it involves 14 mi. of hilly terrain. Hitchers first get a lift to Ballynahoun on heavily trafficked N62, then get a ride from there to Clonmacnois. *Let's Go* does not recommend hitchhiking.

Nowadays, the ships stay in the Shannon and the cows speckling the landscape have ordinary udders, but the grandiosity of the site still incites the imagination. The **cathedral** shows evidence of having endured countless attacks in its day; the current structure dates from about 909. One of its doorways is known as the **whispering arch;** even quiet sounds will travel audibly up one side over to the other. Various stories explain the arch: perhaps priests didn't want to get too close to plague-riddled confessors, or perhaps it allowed young lovers to maintain all the proper appearances of prayer while actually having private conversations. The cathedral is the final resting place, after a number of less reliable resting places, of the body of Rory O'Connor, the last High King of Ireland (died 1198). **O'Connor's Church,** built in the 12th century, has Church of Ireland services at 4pm on Sundays in July and August. Peaceful **Nun's Church** is beyond the modern graveyard behind the main site, about a ¼ mi. away down the path. Its finely detailed chancel and doorways are some of the best Romanesque architecture in Ireland.

Access to Clonmacnois is through the **visitors center** with displays that include a 23min. audio-visual show. (Tel. (0905) 74195. Open mid-Mar.-May and mid-Sept.-Oct. daily 10am-6pm, June-early-Sept. daily 9am-7pm, Nov.-mid-Mar. daily 10am-5pm. £3, seniors £2, students £1.25. Wheelchair accessible.) The **tourist office** (tel. (0905) 74134), at the entrance to the Clonmacnois car park, gives local information and sells various guides to the monastic city. (Open Mar.-Nov. daily 10am-6pm.) **Paddy Kavanaugh** (tel. (0902) 74839 or (087) 240 7706) runs a minibus tour that hits the monastery, a local pub (Paddy might down a Guinness while you have lunch), the Clonmacnois, and **West Offaly Railway** (tel. (0905) 74114), a train tour through a peat bog. Paddy's blue van departs daily at 11am from Athlone Castle, pauses at the train station, and will make stops elsewhere with advance notice; tours return around 4pm. (Runs Apr.-Oct., or by arrangement. £17, students £13.)

Mr. and Mrs. Augustin Claffey's B&B, Shannonbridge Rd. (tel. (0905) 74149), near the ruins, is a restored cottage dating from 1843. Two double beds, a lambskin rug, and a peat fire are complemented by modern, self-catering conveniences. Reservations are highly recommended. (£12. No heat, so only open Apr.-Oct.) Another option is **Kajon House,** Shannonbridge Rd., (tel. (0905) 74191), a few hundred yards past the Claffeys. The splendid Mrs. Kate Harte will pick you up in Athlone if you call ahead. She'll also make a dinner for any budget. (Single £21-23; doubles with bath £32-36.) The area's camping is 3 mi. east, at the **Glebe Touring Caravan and Camping Park.** (Tel. (0902) 30277. Tents £3. Laundry £3. Open Easter-Oct.)

BIRR

William Petty labelled Birr *"Umbilicus Hiberniae,"* the belly button of Ireland. Who knows why; it's not the center of Ireland—maybe he'd had a pint too many at the pub. The highlight of the town, and well worth a visit, is **Birr Castle,** which developed into a hotbed of scientific discovery in the 19th century. The rest of Birr is pleasant if unremarkable, and makes a good starting point for exploring the **Slieve Bloom Mountains**. The mountains don't actually start until **Kinnitty,** 9 mi. east;

if you don't have a car, your best bet is to bike there. Too few cars go by to make hitching practical, and hitchhiking is frowned upon by *Let's Go*.

⚡ ORIENTATION AND PRACTICAL INFORMATION. The *umbilicus* of Birr is **Emmet Sq.** Most shops and pubs are in The Square, or south down **O'Connell St.** The areas north and west of the square down **Emmet St.** and **Green St.** are primarily residential. Buses stop at the post office in The Square. **Bus Éireann** runs to **Athlone** (50min., 1 per day, £5), **Cahir** (2hr., 1 per day, £8.80), and **Dublin** (2½hr., M-Sa 4 per day, £6-7). **Kearns Coaches** offer better fares to **Dublin** (2-3 per day) and **Galway** (1¾hr., every other day); get a schedule at Square News in Emmet Sq. To reach the sleek **tourist office** (tel. 20110) from Emmet Sq., walk down O'Connell and Main St. and then make a right onto Castle St.; the office is on the right. (Open May-Sept. daily 9:30am-1pm and 2-5:30pm.) They have some maps of the Slieve Blooms and can put you in touch with guides. **P.L. Polan,** Main St. (tel. 20006), **rents bikes.** (£7 per day, £30 per week; deposit £40. Open M-W and F-Sa 9:30am-6:30pm.) The **Bank of Ireland** (tel. 20092) has an **ATM** in Emmet Sq. The **phone code** is a chilly 0509.

📷🏠 ACCOMMODATIONS, FOOD, AND PUBS. Kay Kelly's B&B (tel. 21128) rests atop her toy store on Main St. and boasts comfortable rooms with a playground out back. (£17.50, all with bath.) **Spinners Town House,** Castle St. (tel. 21673), offers a crisp decor and spacious rooms; framed documents from Birr's past sprinkle the walls. In addition, there's a charming bistro downstairs, and breakfast options include scrambled eggs with smoked salmon. (£17.50-20 per person sharing, additional £5 for a single. All rooms with bath.) Locals will point you to **Kong Lam,** Main St. (tel. 21253), for a cheap Chinese meal that you can eat in or take out. (Entrees £5-6. Open Su-Th 5pm-12:30am, F-Sa 5pm-1am.) Spend a few more pence on lunch at the **Coachhouse Lounge** (tel. 20032) in Dooly's Hotel on the square. The liveliest pub is **Whelehan's,** Connaught St. (tel. 21349), owned by three members of the stellar Offaly hurling team.

🔭 SIGHTS. You're welcome to tread on the Earl of Rosse's turf at **Birr Castle,** which, unusually, remains his private home. The 120-acre demesne contains babbling brooks and the tallest box hedges in the world. The new **Historic Science Centre,** inside, has some good exhibits on the 19th century residents' pioneering work in photography and astronomy. The Third Earl of Rosse discovered the Whirlpool Nebula with the Leviathan, an immense telescope whose 72 in. mirror was the world's largest for 72 years. The fourth Earl measured the heat of the moon. When the weather cooperates, you can observe the Leviathan in action. (Tel. 20336; www.birrcastle.com. Castle open daily 9am-6pm. £5, seniors and students £3.50, children £2.50. Leviathan tours daily 2:30pm. Wheelchair accessible.)

During **Birr Vintage Week,** in mid-August, people across the town celebrate their Georgian heritage: they wear vintage clothes, create vintage store windows, drive vintage cars, watch a vintage air show, and drink till the night is old.

◪ SLIEVE BLOOM MOUNTAINS

Though not even 2000 ft. at their highest, the Slieve Bloom Mountains seem to burst from the rolling plains between Birr, Rosscrea, Portlaois, and Tullamore. A combination of bogland (no smoking—it's highly flammable!) and primarily managed forest, the Slieve Blooms are best seen while hiking along the 48 mi. circle of the **Slieve Bloom Way.** The best asset of the Slieve Blooms, contrary to what a tourist office might tell you, is precisely their lack of tourist-oriented activity—there's nothing to do but relax, as well you should. The towns around the mountains are bastions of rural Ireland's highly local, small-town lifestyle.

Transportation is the tricky part. Drivers should have no problem. Some of the best towns for entry to the mountains are **Kinnitty,** to the northwest, and **Mountrath,** to the south; getting from one to the other makes a reasonable driving route. Travelers reliant on public transportation are considerably handicapped. The most important thing is to talk to people; ask how to get places, where to go, and who else to talk to. The **tourist offices** of the surrounding towns are good starting points; the Portlaoise office (tel. (050) 221 178) can provide a very handy list of Co. Laois residents who have recently trained as tourist guides. Noreen Murphy (tel. (050) 32727) is a mountain specialist. Marguerite Sheeran runs the **Slieve Bloom Bike Hire** (tel. (050) 235 277) out of Coolrain, to the south of the mountains, and can provide routes, maps, and multi-day route-planning as needed; what she can't do is flatten the hills. Call to arrange pick-up, if needed, from any nearby town. (£7 per day, £30 per week, £40 deposit. Raleigh one-way rental available.)

The owners of the **Farren House** hostel (tel. (0502) 34032) can give you a lift out to their place from **Ballacolla,** a town accessible by two buses a day from Portlaoise. The hostel rooms are large and comfy, and the sculptures made of old farm junk in the driveway will force a smile. (Dorms £9. Continental breakfast £2.50, full Irish £3.50. Laundry service £3-4. Wheelchair accessible.)

The *craic* can be mighty in these villages if your timing's right. When the town pubs have trad sessions, it's not to draw tourists. On Thursday nights the **Thatched Village Inn** (tel.(0502) 35277) in Coolrain gets the locals together for some contagiously fun set dancing. If you'd rather have your set dancing outside, in a bog, and on a mountain, the **Fraughan Festival** is the event for you: ten days of music and dancing inspired by Lughnasa (sounds curiously like "lunacy"), a pagan sun-worshipping fete. (Late July or August. Contact Micheál Lalor, tel. (0502) 32323.)

ROSCREA

Picturesque Roscrea (ross-CRAY), actually in Co. Tipperary, poses 10 mi. south of Birr and to the southwest of the Slieve Blooms. On Castle St., a 13th century castle with a fine vaulted ceiling provides the setting for **Damer House,** the best-preserved example of Queen Anne architecture in Ireland. The house doesn't have much of interest other than its spectacular **Bog Butter,** a 1000-year-old chunk of dairy heroically rescued from the bog. A small **tourist office** in Damer House has the useful and free *Roscrea Heritage Walk* map. (Open daily June-Aug. 9:30am-5pm. Last admission 5:45pm.) Across the courtyard, the **Heritage Center** provides access to the castle and tours on demand. (Tel. (050) 521 850. Open daily from mid-May-Sept. 9:30am-6:30pm; last admission 5:45pm. £2.50, seniors £1.75, students £1.)

Bus Éireann stops at Christy Maher's pub on Castle St., just downhill from the castle. Buses go to and from **Athlone** (1½hr., 1 per day), **Limerick** (1½hr., 13 per day), **Dublin** (2hr., 13 per day), and **Cork** (3hr., 1 per day). **Rapid Express Coaches** (tel. (056) 31106) leave from the Rosemary Quare fountain to follow similar routes at better prices (M-Sa 6 per day, Su 4 per day). **Bank of Ireland** (tel. (050) 521 877) on Castle St. sports a **24hr. ATM.** (Open M-W and F 10am-4pm, Th 10am-5pm.) Mrs. Fogarty will take good care of you in the elegant rooms of the **White House,** Castle St. (tel. (050) 521 516); look for a building painted lavender and lime green. (£15, £20 with bath.) Groceries abound at **Tesco,** Castle St. (tel. (050) 522 777), in the Roscrea Shopping Center. (Open M-W and Sa 8:30am-7pm, Th-F 8:30am-10pm, Su 10am-6pm.) **Mick Delahunty's,** Main St. (tel. (050) 522 139), offers pub grub and music on Tuesday and Saturday nights. (Burgers £2.50. Food served 10:30am-9pm.)

PORTLAOISE

Ask the folks at the tourist office what there is to do in the town of Portlaoise (port-LEESH), and it's a safe bet that they'll direct you exclusively to things outside it. The one worthwhile sight within close range is the **Rock of Dunamase.** Take Stradbally Rd. eastwards 4 mi., and follow the sign at the big red church to Athy/Carlow, and the rock is on your left. The truly ancient fortress, recorded by Ptolemy, was the definition of impregnability until Cromwellian technology impregnated it with balls of iron. It sits upon a meager hill that provides an excellent lookout point for viewing the Slieve Bloom Mountains and beyond.

Lawlor Ave. runs parallel to **Main St.** The **train station** (tel. 21303) is in a quirky gray house at the curve on Railway St. (Open daily 6:45am-6:30pm.) **Trains** run to **Dublin** and points south (1hr.; 9-11 per day, Su 5 per day; £10.50). **Bus Éireann** stops at Egan's Hostelry on Main St. and on Lawlor Ave. (the highway) on the way to **Dublin** (1½hr., 13 per day, £6). **Rapid Express** (tel. (067) 26266) also serves **Dublin** from Lawlor Ave. (5-6 per day). The **tourist office,** Lawlor Ave. (tel. 21178), provides information on the Slieve Blooms and the Midlands. (Open July-Aug. M-Sa 10am-1pm and 2-5:30pm; Sept.-June M-F 10am-1pm and 2-6pm.) **AIB** (tel. 21349) graces Lawlor Ave. with a **24hr. ATM.** There's a **laundromat** (tel. 62088) in the mini-mall across from the public library. (Wash and dry £4-5. Open M-Sa 8:30am-6pm.) The regional **post office** (tel. 74219) is inside the shopping court on Lawlor Ave. (Open M-F 9am-5:30pm, Sa 10am-1pm and 2-5pm.) The **phone code,** 0502, rhymes with snort quiche.

Affordable accommodations in town are limited. **Donoghue's B&B,** 1 Kellyville Park (tel. 21353), is in a large, beautifully kept house with flower gardens and a friendly proprietor. (Singles £25, doubles £36.) **Kirwan's Caravan and Camping Park** (tel. 21688) will let you pitch a tent 1km from town out Mountrath Road R445. (Tent £3. Showers 50p. Kitchen, TV room, and laundry available. Open Apr.-Oct.) For loony groceries, head to **CrazyPrices** (tel. 21730), inside the shopping mall on Lawlor Ave. (Open M-Tu, and Sa 9am-7pm, W-F 9am-9pm.) **Dowlings** (tel. 22770), half way up Main St. on the left, offers the best deal on a quick bite. (Entrees £3-4. Open M-Sa 9am-6pm.) The sparkling new **Dunamaise Theatre and Arts Center** (tel. 63355), on Church Rd., schedules a steady flow of dance, theater, and visual arts.

SOUTHEAST IRELAND

Historically the power base of the Vikings and then the Normans, the influence of the Celts is faintest in southeast Ireland. Town and street names in this region are likely derived from Viking, Norman, and Anglo-Saxon origins. Beaches are the most fruitful of the Southeast's tourist attractions, drawing mostly native Irish admirers to the coastline that runs from Kilmore Quay to tidy Ardmore. Wexford is a charismatic town, packed with historic sites and convenient to many of the Southeast's finest attractions, while Waterford has the resources, nightlife, and grit of a real city. Cashel boasts a superbly preserved cathedral complex. Continue your hunt for raging nightlife south from Dublin through Carlow, Kilkenny, and Waterford; alternatively, the daylight hours are most enjoyably spent exploring the pretty paths through Glendalough, the Wicklow Mountains, Enniscorthy, and Wexford. Continental and British travelers stuff themselves into cars speeding to and from Europe via Rosslare Harbour on the southeastern tip of the island.

HIGHLIGHTS OF SOUTHEAST IRELAND

■ Kilkenny (p. 170) dazzles in its medieval costume, accessorizing with a castle (p. 175) and Jerpoint Abbey's Cistercian ruins (p. 176).

■ **Cashel** (p. 179) proudly points the way to nearby natural wonders: the looming Rock of Cashel, the Galty Mountains, and the Mitchelstown Caves.

■ Follow the 43 mi. East Munster Way through the bumpy **Comeragh** and **Knockmealdown Mountains** (p. 185).

KILKENNY AND CARLOW

Northwest of Wexford and Waterford, and east of the Irish metropolis of Dublin, the counties of Kilkenny and Carlow consist of lightly populated hills and plains characterized by small farming villages and the occasional medieval ruin. Kilkenny City is the bustling exception to the seemingly endless string of provincial towns; it's a popular destination for both international tourists and young Irish on the move. The town of Carlow, though much smaller, buzzes on weekend nights.

KILKENNY

As the economy of the Celtic Tiger roars, the best-preserved medieval town in Ireland has launched a historical preservation campaign to draw more visitors and net a few more Tidy Town awards. Kilkenny's handsome streets, nine churches, and 78 pubs are all cloaked in the architecture of past eras. Kilkenny storefronts have done away with tacky neon, and now even fastfood joints have hand-painted facades. These efforts are reaping their just reward: the town's population of 25,000 doubles during the high season.

TRANSPORTATION

Trains: Kilkenny Station, Dublin Rd. (tel. 22024). Open M-Sa 8am-9:30pm, Su 10am 10:30pm. Always staffed, although the ticket window is open only around departure times. Kilkenny is on the main **Dublin-Waterford** rail route (M-Sa 4-5 per day, Su 3-4 per day). To **Thomastown** (15min., £4.50), **Waterford** (45min., £5), and **Dublin** (2hr., £11). Connections to western Ireland can be made at **Kildare Station,** 1hr. north on the Dublin-Waterford line.

Southeast Ireland

SOUTHEAST IRELAND

St. George's Channel

N

WICKLOW
Wicklow
Arklow
Arklow Head

KILDARE
Athy
N78
6N
N9N
N81

WEXFORD
Ferns
Enniscorthy
N11
N80
Wexford
Wexford Harbour
Rosslare
Rosslare Harbour
N25
Kilmore Quay
Saltee Islands

CARLOW
Carlow
N80
N9

LAOIS
Portlaoise
N80
N8
Barrow
N7
River

KILKENNY
Kilkenny
N10
N9
Thomastown
Kells
R. Nore
New Ross
Arthurstown
Duncannon
Waterford Harbour
Passage East
Dunmore East
N9
N25

OFFALY
Birr
N52
N62
N52

TIPPERARY
Roscrea
Thurles
N75
N8
Cashel
Clonmel
Tipperary
Nenagh
N7
N24

WATERFORD
Waterford
Carrick-on-Suir
Tramore
Tramore Bay
N24
R683
Dungarvan
Dungarvan Harbour
Ringville
Ardmore
N25
N72
Cahir
Lismore
N8

GALWAY
N65
N6
N18

CLARE
Killaloe
Ennis
N18
Shannon Airport
River Shannon
N19
N67
N68

LIMERICK
Limerick
Newcastle West
N24
N20
N21
N69

CORK
Mallow
Cork
Youghal
Youghal Bay
Blackwater River
N20
N8
N73
N72
N25

KERRY
Killarney
N21
N22
N23
N72

MUNSTER

LEINSTER

0   20 miles
0   20 kilometers

Buses: Kilkenny Station, Dublin Rd. (tel. 64933), and on Patrick St. in the city center. Buses leave for **Clonmel** (90min.; Su-F 5 per day, Sa 6 per day; £5), **Waterford** (90min.; M-Sa 2 per day, Su 1 per day; £5), **Rosslare Harbour** via Waterford (2hr.; M-Sa 5-6 per day, Su 3 per day), **Dublin** (2hr.; Sa-Th 5 per day, F 6 per day; £7), **Limerick** via Clonmel (2½hr.; M-Sa 5 per day, Su 1 per day), **Cork** (3hr.; M-Sa 3 per day, Su 2 per day; £9), and **Galway** via Athlone (5hr.; daily mid-June-mid-Sept.; £12). **Buggy's Coaches** (tel. 41264) run from Kilkenny to **Ballyragget** (30min., M-Sa 2 per day) and to **Castlecomer** (15min., M-Sa 5 per day, £1) with stops at **Dunmore Cave** (20min.) and the An Óige hostel (15min.). **J.J. Kavanagh's Rapid Express** (tel. 31106) has routes in the area with prices that routinely beat Bus Éireann's (**Dublin** M-Sa 5 per day, Su 1 per day).

Taxi: All the companies now have a £4 minimum, plus an additional £1.20 per mile after 3-4 miles. **Kevin Barry** (tel. 63017). **Kilkenny Cabs** (tel. 52000).

Car Rental: Barry Pender, Dublin Rd. (tel. 65777 or 63839), rents to anyone 23 or older. Compact car £50 per day, £250 per week. Open M-F 9am-5:30pm, Sa 9am-1pm.

Bike Rental: The cheapest is **J.J. Wall Cycle,** Maudlin St. (tel. 21236). £6 per sentimental day, £35 per effusive week. Tear-jerking ID deposit. Open M-Sa 9am-6pm. Or head to hassle-free **Kilkenny Cycles,** Michael St. (tel. 64374). £7 per day, £35 per week. £50 or passport deposit. Open M-Sa 9am-6pm.

☑ ORIENTATION AND PRACTICAL INFORMATION

From Kilkenny Station, turn left on **John St.** and continue downhill to reach a large intersection with **High St.** and **The Parade,** dominated by the castle on your left. Most activity takes place in the triangle formed by **Rose Inn, High,** and **Kieran St.** Hitchhikers take N10 south to Waterford, Freshford Rd. to N8 toward Cashel, and N10 past the train station toward Dublin. Patience is required of hitchhikers, of whom *Let's Go* does not approve.

Tourist Office: Rose Inn St. (tel. 51500; fax 63955). On the second floor of a 16th century pauper house. Free town maps. Open Oct.-Mar. M-Sa 9am-5pm, Apr.-Sept. M-Sa 9am-6pm, July-Aug. M-Sa 9am-8pm, May-Sept. also Su 11am-1pm and 2-5pm.

Banks: Bank of Ireland, Parliament St. (tel. 21155), has an **ATM,** while the High St.-Parade intersection has 5 more at 4 banks. All banks open M 10am-5pm, Tu-F 10am-4pm.

Laundry: Brett's Launderette, Michael St. (tel. 63200). Wash and dry £5.70. Open M-Sa 8:30am-8pm; last wash 6:30pm.

Pharmacy: Several sit on High St. All open M-Sa 9am-6pm; Sunday rotation system.

Emergency: Dial 999; no coins required. **Garda:** Dominic St. (tel. 22222).

Hospital: St. Luke's, Freshford Rd. (tel. 51133). Continue down Parliament St. to St. Canice's Cathedral, then turn right and veer left onto Vicars St., then left again onto Freshford Rd. The hospital is down on the right.

Post Office: High St. (tel. 21833). Open M-Tu, Th-Sa 9am-5:30pm, W 9:30am-5:30pm.

Internet Access: Compustore (tel. 71200), in the Market Cross shopping center off High St. £2 per 15min., £3 per 30min., £5 per hour. Open M-W and Sa 10am-6pm, Th-F 10am-8pm. Same prices at **Cyberworld** (tel. 51882), upstairs at the Ormonde hostel. Open daily 10am-10pm.

| PHONE CODE | Oh my god, 056 killed Kenny! You bastards! |

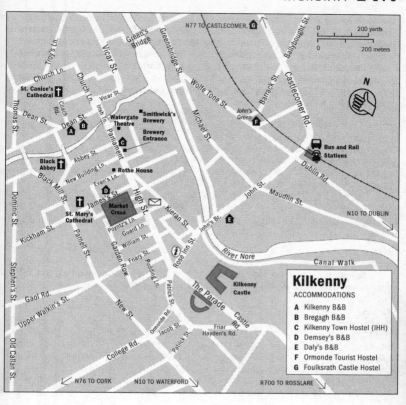

ACCOMMODATIONS

B&Bs average £19, but some places will hike prices up to £25 on weekends, when the town is packed. Call ahead in summer, especially on weekends. Waterford Rd. and more remote Castlecomer Rd. have the highest concentration of beds.

Foulksrath Castle (An Óige/HI), Jenkinstown (tel. 67674). 8 mi. north of town on N77 (Durrow Rd.). Turn right off N77 at signs for Connahy; it's ¼ mi. down on the left. Buggy's Buses (tel. 41264) run from The Parade to the hostel M-Sa at midday and 5:30pm and leave the hostel for Kilkenny shortly after 8:25am and around 3pm (20min., £1; call the hostel for exact times). Housed in a 16th century castle, it's one of the nicest hostels in Ireland. Dorms £5.50-7.50. Continental breakfast £2.50. Sheets £1. Laundry £4. Kitchen open 8am-10pm.

Kilkenny Tourist Hostel (IHH), 35 Parliament St. (tel. 63541; kilkennyhostel@tiniet.ie). Directly across from popular pubs and next to the Smithwicks brewery. Always brimming with activity as people bustle about in the kitchen, lounge on couches, and sip Guinness on the front steps. If it's not luxurious, at least it's fun. Great town info posted in front hall, from train schedules to trad sessions to cyclist maps. Non-smoking. 6- to 8-bed dorms £7, doubles £20; add £1 May-Sept.; Sept.-June 50p discount to *Let's Go* users. Laundry £3. Kitchen open 7am-11pm with microwave. Check-out 10:30am.

Ormonde Tourist Hostel, Johns Green (tel. 52733), opposite the train station. This former hospital is a 10-15min. walk from the best nightlife and attractions in town. It's hardly altered to fit its new purpose: hard surfaces and fluorescent lights abound. At least the rooms are plenty big. Dorms around £8.50-9.50, doubles £22. Laundry £4. Kitchen open until 10pm. Check out 10:30am. Curfew 3am.

Demsey's B&B, 26 James's St. (tel. 21954). A little old house by the Superquinn, off High St. Spacious, well-decorated rooms with TVs and friendly proprietors nearby. Single £20, double with bath £36.

Bregagh House B&B, Dean St. (tel. 22315). Pristine rooms with handsome wood furniture and firm beds. Singles £18-25, doubles with bath £36-44; Nov.-May £34.

Kilkenny B&B, Dean St. (tel. 64040). Basic, clean rooms. A sign warns that the house is guarded by an attack housewife, but don't worry, she's actually rather charming. It's worth a try to charm the prices down; their range can be huge and arbitrary. Weekends especially high. Singles £15-25, doubles £32-50.

Daly's B&B, 82 Johns St. (tel. 62866). Immaculately non-descript rooms. Single £23, double £40; reduced prices in the off season. Breakfast £2 per person.

Tree Grove Caravan and Camping Park (tel. 70302). 1 mi. past the castle on the New Ross road (R700). 2-person tent £6. Free showers.

Nore Valley Park (tel. 27229; 27748). 7 mi. south of Kilkenny between Bennetsbridge and Stonyford, signposted from Kilkenny: Take the R700 to Bennetsbridge; just before the actual bridge take the signposted right. A class act, with free hot showers, a TV room, and a play-area for children. 2-person tent £6.50. Laundry £4.50. Open Mar.-Oct.

FOOD

The biggest grocery selection is at **Superquinn** (tel. 52444), in the Market Cross shopping center off High St. (Open M-Tu and Sa 9am-7pm, W-F 9am-9pm.) **Dunnes Supermarket** (tel. 61655) sells housewares and food on Kieran St. (Open M-Tu and Sa 8:30am-7pm, W-F 8:30am-10pm, Su and bank holidays 10am-6pm.) Everything in Kilkenny's restaurants is great except the prices, which all hover in the lower stratosphere. Here are some reasonable options, or you might try one of the pubs.

Langton's, 69 John St. (tel. 65133). An eccentric owner has earned a host of awards for his ever-changing pub. Bar food with succulent sauces? Didn't know it existed. Lunch £5, served daily noon-6pm. Dinner menu in the double digits, served daily 6-10:30pm.

Pordylo's, Butterslip Ln., between Kieran and High St. Zesty dinners from across the globe, many of which love vegetarians. Some meals under £8. Open nightly 6-11pm.

Ml. Dore, High St. (tel. 63374). Near Kieran St. Come to Dore's trendy atmosphere to smoke, smoke, and smoke some more. Sandwiches £2, light entrees £5-6. Open M-Sa 8am-10pm, Su 9am-9pm.

Ristorante Rinuccini, 1 The Parade. (tel. 61575), opposite the castle. Couples enjoy mood lighting and romantic music while sucking face. Lunch £5-6, served noon-2:30pm; dinner £7-9, served 6-10:30pm; early evening specials 6-7:30pm for £6-7.

Italian Connection, 38 Parliament St. (tel. 64225). Italian food, mahogany, carnations, and still it's not fancy. Lunch specials daily noon-3pm, £5-6. Open daily noon-11pm.

Lautrec's, 9 St. Kieran St. (tel. 62720). A well-trained chef makes quick, mostly Italian lunches for £5-6. Dinners are pricier. Food served noon-10:30pm.

PUBS

Kilkenny is known as the "oasis of Ireland." Enough said.

Maggie's, St. Kieran St. (tel. 62273). Crowds bury themselves in this superb, aged wine cellar. Trad most nights of the week, rock on summer weekends.

The Pump House, 26 Parliament St. (tel. 63924). Remains a favorite among locals and many hostelers. Loud, conveniently located, and generally packed. Trad M-Th in the summer, Su rock and blues.

Matt the Miller's, 1 John St. (tel. 61696), at the bridge. Huge, thronged, and magnetic. It'll suck you in and force you to dance to silly Euro pop. M cover £2 for rock music and late bar hours.

Caisleán Uí Cuain (cash-LAWN ee COO-an), 2 High St. (tel. 65406), at The Parade. A local crowd settles in for pints and all types of music on all sorts of nights.

Cleere's, 28 Parliament St. (tel. 62573). Thespians from the theatre across the street converge here during intermission for a pint (and to watch *Monty Python* rather than the game). There's even an ex-theater in back. Trad Mondays.

Ryan's (tel. 62881), on Friary St. just off High St. No frills, just a pub with a good crowd and frequent trad.

Kyteler's Inn, St. Kieran St. (tel 21064). The 1324 house of Alice Kyteler, Kilkenny's witch, whose four husbands had in common a knack for getting poisoned on their first anniversaries. Nowadays the food and drink are safer, and trad fills the air two nights a week. Late night F-Su, shimmy next door at **Nero's,** a nightclub that's burning down the house. Cover £5-7. Open 11pm-2am.

Quay's, John St. (tel. 70844). Across from Matt the Miller's, with a deliciously aged feel. Trad W and F, and Su morning jazz.

⦿ SIGHTS

Kilkenny itself is a sight, since the government preserved (or recreated) most of the buildings' medieval good looks. The belle of the ball is 13th century **Kilkenny Castle,** The Parade. It housed the Earls of Ormonde from the 1300s until 1932. Many rooms have been restored to their former opulence. Ogle the Long Room, reminiscent of a Viking ship, which displays the portraits of English bigwigs. The basement houses the **Butler Gallery,** which hangs modern art exhibitions. This level also houses a cafe in the castle's kitchen, home to the castle's ghost. (Tel. 21450. Castle and gallery open June-Sept. daily 10am-7pm; Oct.-Mar. Tu-Sa 10:30am-12:45pm and 2-5pm, Su 11am-12:45pm and 2-5pm; Apr.-May daily 10:30am-5:30pm. Castle access by guided tour only. £3, students £1.50.) The 52-acre landscaped **park** adjoining the castle provides excellent scenery for an afternoon jaunt. (Open daily 10am-8:30pm. Free.) Across the street, the internationally known **Kilkenny Design Centre** fills the castle's old stables with expensive Irish crafts. (Tel. 22118. Open Apr.-Dec. M-Sa 9am-6pm, Su 10am-6pm; Jan.-Mar. M-Sa 9am-6pm.) For the down-and-dirty on Kilkenny's folkloric tradition, and an introduction to other sights in the town, take the **Tynan Walking Tours** (tel. 65929). Besides conjuring some animated lore, the tour is the only way to see the old city jail. Tours depart from the tourist office on Rose Inn St. (Tours Mar.-Oct. M-Sa 6 per day, Su 4 per day; Nov.-Feb. Tu-Sa 3 per day. About 1hr. £3, students and seniors £2.)

13th century **St. Canice's Cathedral** sits up the hill off Dean St. The name "Kilkenny" itself is derived from the Irish Cill Chainnigh, "Church of St. Canice." The thin, 100 ft. tower next to the cathedral was somehow built without scaffolding, in pre-Norman times, and somehow still stands on its 3 ft. foundations. £1 and a bit of faith let you climb the series of six steep ladders inside to reach a panoramic view of the town and its surroundings. (Tel. 64971. Open Easter-Sept. M-Sa 9am-1pm and 2-6pm, Su 2-6pm. Donation requested.) The **Black Abbey,** off Abbey St., was founded in 1225 and got its name from the habits of its Dominican friars. Outside, you'll see a row of stone coffins used to contain bodies struck by the Black Death. Inside, a non-period restoration job and heavy silence reign. Nearby you can gaze up at the dark heights of **St. Mary's Cathedral,** constructed during even the darkest years of the famine. **Rothe House,** Parliament St., a Tudor merchant house built in 1594, is now a small museum of local archaeological finds and Kilkennian curiosities. (Tel. 22893. Open Apr.-Oct. M-Sa 10:30am-5pm, Su 3-5pm; Nov.-Mar. M-Sa 1-5pm, Su 3-5pm. £2, students £1.50.)

It is rumored that crafty 14th century monks brewed a light ale in the St. Francis Abbey on Parliament St.; the abbey is in ruins but its industry survives in the abbey's yard at the **Smithwicks Brewery.** Commercial use started in 1710, making it the oldest brewery in Ireland (Guinness started up nearly 50 years later). Unfortunately, the company profanes the abbey by brewing Budweiser as well. Show up at 3pm outside the green doors on Parliament St. for a free audiovisual tour and ale tasting. (Tours July-Aug. M-F.)

🎵 ENTERTAINMENT

The tourist office can provide a bimonthly guide to the town's happenings, and *The Kilkenny People* (£1) is a good newsstand source for arts and music listings. **The Watergate Theatre,** Parliament St. (tel. 61674), stages shows year-round. (Tickets usually £6-7, student discounts available. Booking office open M-F 11am-7pm, Sa 2-6pm, Su 1hr. before curtain.) During the second or third week of August, Kilkenny holds its annual **Arts Festival** (tel. 63663), which has a daily program of theater, concerts, recitals, and readings by famous European and Irish artists. (Event tickets free-£12; student and senior discounts vary by venue. Tickets sold at 92 High St., or by phone.) Kilkenny's population increases by over 10,000 in early June for the **Cat Laughs** (tel. 51254), a weekend festival featuring international comedy acts. The cat in question is the Kilkenny mascot of nursery rhyme fame:

> There once were two cats from Kilkenny.
> Each thought there was one cat too many.
> So they fought and they fit,
> And they scratched and they bit,
> 'Til excepting their nails and the tips of their tails
> Instead of two cats there weren't any.

NEAR KILKENNY: THOMASTOWN AND JERPOINT ABBEY

The eerie Dunmore Caves to the north and Jerpoint Abbey to the south of Kilkenny provide worthy excuses to flee town for an afternoon. Thomastown, a tiny community perched on the Nore River, is the gateway to the impressive **Jerpoint Abbey,** 1½ mi. away. Founded around 1160, the abbey is one of the most beautiful Cistercian ruins in Ireland, with remarkable etchings and tombs. Free tours, given on request, will clue you in to the archaeological detective work that's been done on the motley assortment of carved artistry. (Tel. (056) 24623. Open daily Mar.-Apr. 10am-5pm; May 9:30am-5:30pm; June-Aug. 9:30am-6:30pm; Sept. 10am-5:30pm. £2, seniors £1.50, students £1.) In town, at one end of Market St. rests the remains of **Thomastown Church,** built in the early 13th century. Three curiosities lie amongst the church's gravestones: an ancient ogham stone (see **History of the Irish Language,** p. 19), part of a Celtic cross, and a weathered 13th century effigy.

Bus Éireann stops at the Jerpoint Inn in Thomastown between **Waterford** and **Kilkenny** (M-Sa 7 per day, Su 4 per day). The folks at the **Jerpoint Inn,** across the street, can provide a schedule for the **Rapid Express** (tel. (056) 31106), a private bus service running between Dublin and Tramore. Those in need of cash should head to the **Bank of Ireland** (tel. (056) 24213) and its **ATM. Simon Treacy Hardware** (tel. (056) 24291) **rents bikes** (£5 per day, £25 per week; deposit £20), and can put you in touch with horse manure distributors (£2 per bag; open M-Sa 9am-6pm).

The serene **Watergarden,** Ladywell St. (tel. (056) 24690), serves an amazing lunch. Members of **Camphill Community,** an organization that supports and employs the mentally handicapped, serve primarily vegetarian and organic delectables in a cozy cafe with lovely gardens out back. (Sandwiches and small entrees £3-4. Open Tu-F 10am-5pm, Su noon-5pm.) **O'Hara's** pub (tel. (056) 24597) has 200 year old walls and fireplaces.

DUNMORE CAVE

On the road to Castlecomer 10km north of Kilkenny lurks the massive Dunmore Cave (tel. (056) 67726). Known fondly as "the darkest place in Ireland," the cave is bedecked with fascinating limestone formations. Recently unearthed human bones show that roughly 100 people died underground here in 928, probably while hiding from Viking marauders. (Open mid-Mar. to mid-Sept. daily 10am-7pm; mid-Sept. to Nov. daily 10am-6pm; Nov.-mid-Mar. Sa-Su and holidays 10am-5pm; last admission 45min. before close. £3, children free.) **Coaches** (tel. (056) 41264) runs a bus between Kilkenny and Castlecomer; the driver will stop 1km from the site on request. From the drop-off point, the route is well-signposted (20min., M-Sa 5 per day, £1). If you're driving, take N78 (Dublin-Castlecomer Rd.) from Kilkenny; the turn-off for the cave is on the right after the split with N77 (Durrow Rd.).

CARLOW

A small, busy town, Carlow sits on the eastern side of the River Barrow on N9 (Dublin-Waterford). Seamlessly placid today, in past centuries Carlow hosted several of the most gruesome historic battles between Gael and Pale. During the 1798 Rising (see **Rebellion, Union, Reaction,** p. 10), 640 Irish insurgents were ambushed in the streets of Carlow; they were buried across the River Barrow in the gravel pits of Graiguecullen (greg-KULL-en). A part of the gallows from which they were hanged is now displayed in the county museum. Carlow's surprisingly good nightlife routinely attracts a disproportionate crowd from all over.

🖬 PRACTICAL INFORMATION. Trains run through Carlow from Heuston Station in **Dublin** on their way to **Waterford** (1¼hr.; M-Th and Sa 5 per day, F and Su 3 per day; £12). From the train station, it's a 15min. walk to the center of town; head straight out of the station down **Railway Rd.,** turn left onto **Dublin Rd.,** and make another left at the Court House onto **College St.** The cheapest **buses** to **Dublin** depart from Doyle's by the Shamrock D.I.Y.—you can go to the Custom House for as little as £4 return. **Bus Éireann** bounces from Carlow to **Waterford** (1¼hr.; M-Sa 8 per day, Su 5 per day; £5), **Dublin** (1¾hr.; M-Sa 7 per day, Su 4 per day; £6), and **Athlone** (2¼hr., 1 per day, £9.70). **Rapid Express Coaches,** Barrack St. (tel. 43081), runs a bus through **Tramore-Waterford-Carlow-Dublin** and back (M-Sa 8-10 per day, Su 7-8 per day); stop by their office to pick up timetables. The Carlow **tourist office,** Kennedy Ave. (tel. 31554), tucked in the car park by the Dinn Rí, hands out *A Guide to County Carlow,* which includes a town map. (Open M-Sa 9:30am-1pm and 2-5:30pm.) **Rent bikes** from **Coleman Cycle,** 19 Dublin St. (Tel. 31273. £5 per day, £25 per week; deposit £40. Open M-Sa 8:30am-7pm.) The **post office** mails your post or posts your mail from the corner of Kennedy Ave. and Burrin St. (Open M and W-Sa 9am-5:30pm, Tu 9:30am-5:30pm.) **Internet access** awaits at **Communicate Now** (tel. 43700) in the Carlow Shopping Centre between Tullow St. and Kennedy Ave. (First 20min. £2, each subsequent 10min. £1. Open M-W and Sa 10am-6pm, Th-F 10am-9pm.) The **phone code** is 0503.

🖍 ACCOMMODATIONS. The **Otterholt Riverside Lodge** (tel. 30404; fax 30200), a hostel near the banks of the River Barrow, is by far the best place to stay in Carlow. The 200 year old Georgian residence provides sturdy beds in clean, colorful rooms. It's a half-mile from the center of town on Kilkenny Rd.; the bus to Kilkenny will stop in front of it upon request. (Dorms £8, doubles £20. **Camping** £4. Wash and dry clothes for £3. Saturday nights tend to fill up, so reserve ahead.) The **Redsetter Guesthouse,** 14 Dublin Rd. (tel. 42837 or 41848), next to the Royal Hotel in the center of town, offers spacious rooms with phones, TVs, and bath. (Single £17, with bath £22; doubles £40.)

SOUTHEAST IRELAND

■■ **FOOD AND PUBS. Superquinn** (tel. 30077), in the Carlow Shopping Centre, supplies groceries and fresh fruit. (Open M-Tu and Sa 8:30am-7pm, W-F 8:30am-9pm.) **Scragg's Alley,** 12 Tullow St. (tel. 42233), fills you with cheap, hearty lunches in an old Irish kitchen; get to the pub through an arched tunnel. (Food served daily noon-2:30pm.) At **Bradbury's,** 144 Tullow St. (tel. 43307), you can buy both cheap, good food and pricey, bad art. (Open M-Sa 8:30am-6pm.) **Teach Dolmain** (CHOCK DOL-men), 76 Tullow St. (tel. 31235), sets a good price for a plate that's teach full of award-winning grub; it's a pretty happening pub at night, too. (Food served daily noon-9pm.)

The hippest spot in town is the **Dinn Rí** (tel. 33111), a super-pub that spans the entire block between Tullow St. and Kennedy Ave. It's been named one of Ireland's best pubs for the past two years, and its two nightclubs combine on Saturday nights to admit 2000. (Nightclub open F-Su until 2am. Cover F and Su ₤5, Sa ₤6.) Carlow grooves to live rock and tributes at **Scragg's Alley,** Tullow St. (Music W, F, and Su). Saturday and most Friday nights, the music continues upstairs at the **Nexus Nightclub.** (Cover F ₤5, Sa ₤6.) **Tully's,** 149 Tullow St. (tel. 31862), has a crowd of beautiful people and occasional live music. **O'Loughlin's,** 53 Dublin St. (tel. 32205), is dark and velvety with typewriters strewn about. There's no music, but a chatty, young crowd tries desperately to be bohemian.

■ **SIGHTS.** In the middle of a field about a 10min. drive from Carlow lies the **Brownshill Dolmen,** marking the site of an ancient burial and possibly human sacrifice. The granite capstone is somewhat large, sort of the way Mama Cass was somewhat large. It is, in fact, the largest of its kind in Europe, tipping the scales at no less than 150 tons. How it was lifted, five millennia ago, is a total mystery. Follow Tullow St. through the traffic light and straight through the roundabout; the dolmen is 2 mi. away in a field on the right. **The Carlow Museum,** just off Centaur St., looks like somebody's attic. Current plans are to move the assortment of artifacts to the old library on Dublin St. and restore the vacated building to its proper form as a concert hall and stage. (Tel. 40730. Open Tu-F 11am-5pm, Sa and Su 2-5pm. ₤1.50, students 75p.) **Carlow Castle** lurks behind the storefronts on Castle St. Sadly, the castle ruins are closed to the public. The castle's current condition can be blamed on one Dr. Middleton, who intended to convert the castle into an asylum that would require larger windows and thinner walls. To make his modifications, he used the delicate touch of dynamite—explosives are fickle.

The best time to visit Carlow is during the first two weeks of June, when the town hosts **Éigse** (AIG-sha, "gathering"), a 10-day festival of the arts. Artists from all over Ireland come to present visual, musical, and theatrical works; some events require tickets. Check in at the Eigse Festival office for more information (tel. 40491; www.itc-carlow.ie/eigse).

COUNTY TIPPERARY

In south Tipperary, the towns of Clonmel, Cahir, and Cashel are enveloped in a sprawl of medieval ruins and idyllic countryside. North Tipperary is far from the beaten tourist track, and for good reason: the fertile region has more spud farmers than visitor centers. South of the Cahir-Cashel-Tipperary triangle stretch the Comeragh, Galty, and Knockmealdown Mountains. Although Lismore is located in Co. Waterford, it is covered under Co. Tipperary with the Knockmealdowns.

TIPPERARY TOWN

> Good-bye to Piccadilly/Farewell to Leicester Square.
> It's a long way to Tipperary/And my heart lies there.

This celebrated town is perhaps less exciting for today's travelers than the World War I marching song would imply. In fact, the song was written in 1912 by an Englishman who had never been to Tipperary. "Tipp Town," as it's affectionately known, is primarily a market town for the fertile Golden Vale farming region. Compared with the soft rolling hills of the surrounding area and the much acclaimed **Glen of Aherlow** to the south, Tipp Town doesn't tend to impress. The **tourist office,** James St. (tel. 51457; www.iol.ie/tipp), just off Main St., is a useful resource for trips into the glen and the nearby mountains. Glen of Aherlow trail maps sell for 50p. (Open mid-Mar.-Oct. M-Sa 9am-7pm.) An **AIB** is on Main St., along with its rival **Bank of Ireland.** Each offers the convenience of an **ATM.** (Both open M-W and F 10am-4pm, Th 10am-5pm.) The **post office** hides on Davis St. (Open M-F 9am-5:30pm, Sa 9am-noon and 1-5:30pm.) The **phone code** is 062 and tipsy.

The aptly named **Central House B&B,** 45 Main St. (tel. 51117), has a welcoming owner and spacious twins and doubles. (£18 per person.) Other B&Bs are on Emly Rd. about a half-mile west of town off Main St. Tipp features a full-scale **SuperValu** on Main St. (Open M-W and Sa 9am-6pm, Th and F 9am-9pm.) For simple bistro fare, you're sure to get lucky at the **Shamrog,** Davis St. (Open M-W 9am-8pm, Th-Sa 9am-9pm.) **The Brown Trout,** Abbey St. (tel. 51912), one block down Bridge St. from Main St., is well-regarded. (Meals £5-8. Open daily 12:30-3pm and 6-9:30pm.) A pool table and music on weekend nights draw a young crowd to **The Underground Tavern,** James St. (tel. 33965), in a converted wine cellar. Tipp's oldest tavern, **Corny's Pub** (tel. 33036), on Davitt St., often hosts trad. The town becomes as lively as London annually with mid-July's **Pride of Tipperary Festival,** featuring bands, sporting events, and old-fashioned fun.

CASHEL

The town of Cashel lies halfway between Limerick and Waterford, tucked between a series of mountain ranges on N8. Legend has it that the devil furiously hurled a rock from high above the Tipperary plains when he discovered a church being built in Cashel. The airborne assault failed to thwart the plucky citizens, and today the town sprawls at the foot of the commanding 300 ft. **Rock of Cashel.** With two splendid hostels and a convenient location, Cashel is as fitting a base for the backpacker as it was for the medieval religious orders that scattered the region with ruins. **Bus Éireann** (tel. 62121) leaves from Bianconi's Bistro on Main St., serving **Cahir** (15min., 4 per day, £2.40), **Cork** (1½hr.; M-Sa 3 per day, Su 2; £8), **Limerick** (4 per day, £8.80), and **Dublin** (3hr., 4 per day, £9). Bus transport to **Waterford** is available via Cahir. Hitching to Cork or Dublin along N8 is a common occurrence, and thumbing west to Tipp and Limerick on N74 is also feasible. *Let's Go* does not recommend this sort of transport. Cashel's efficient **tourist office** (tel. 61333) shares space with the Heritage Centre in the recently renovated Cashel City Hall on Main St. (Open daily May-June and Aug.-Sept. 9:30am-5pm, July 9:30am-6pm.) **McInerney's,** Main St. (tel. 61225), next to SuperValu, **rents bikes.** (£7 per day, £30 per week. Open M-Sa 9:30am-6pm.) **AIB,** Main St., has a bureau de change and an **ATM.** (Open M-W and F 10am-12:30pm and 1:30-4pm, Th 10am-12:30pm and 1:30-5pm.) The **post office** (tel. 61418) is also on Main St. (Open M and W-F 9am-1pm and 2-5:30pm, Tu 9:30am-1pm and 2-5:30pm, Sa 9am-1pm). The **phone code** rocks the Cashel at 062.

⬛ ACCOMMODATIONS. A few hundred yards from the ruins of Hore Abbey lies the stunning ⬛**O'Brien's Farm House Hostel** (tel. 61003). A 5min. walk from Cashel on Dundrum Rd., the hostel has an incredible view of the Rock and cheerful rooms. (6-bed dorms £8.50, private rooms £10-12.50. **Camping** £3.50. Serviced laundry £5.) Back in town, the plush **Cashel Holiday Hostel (IHH),** 6 John St. (tel. 62330,;email cashel@iol.ie), just off Main St., has a gorgeous kitchen crowned with a glass pyramid skylight. Spacious bedrooms are named after Irish heroes—there's something thrilling about sleeping in "King Cormac's Room." (4- to 8-bed dorms £7.50, 4-bed dorms with bath £9, private rooms £10 per person, singles £12.50. Laundry £3.50. Key deposit £3. Internet access.) The high quality and high prices of local B&Bs reflect the number of tourists drawn to the Rock. Just steps from the Rock on Moor Lance is **Rockville House** (tel. 61760), a fantastic bargain with elegant and fully equipped bedrooms; turn past the tourist office and pass the model village museum. (Doubles and triples £16 per person, singles £20.)

🗂️🗺️ **FOOD AND PUBS. The Bake House** (tel. 61680), across from the Heritage Centre on Main St., is the town's best spot for scones, coffee, and light meals with pseudo-elegant upstairs seating. (Open M-Sa 8am-9pm, Su 9am-9pm.) Superior pub grub is served up at **O'Sullivan's** on Main St. (Tel. 61858. £4.50-5.50; food served M-Sa noon-3pm.) Mediterranean fare draws customers to the **Spearman Restaurant** (tel. 61143), on Main St. (Lunches £6-9, dinner from £8. Open M-Sa 12:30-2:30pm and 5:30-9pm, Su 12:30-2:30pm and 6-9pm.) Ostentatiously orange **Pasta Milano**, Lady's Well St. (tel. 62729), has extensive and affordable cuisine and wines. (Pasta £7-11, pizza £5.50-9. Open M-Th noon-11am, F-Su noon-midnight.) **SuperValu Supermarket**, Main St. (tel. 61555), offers the biggest selection of groceries. (Open Su-W 8am-6pm, Th-Sa 8am-9pm.) **Centra Supermarket**, Friar St., is open daily 7am-11pm.

The *craic* is nightly, the trad 3-4 times a week, and the atmosphere timeless at **Feehan's**, Main St. (tel. 61929). The bartenders at well-appointed **Dowling's**, 46 Main St. (tel. 62130), make it their one and only business to pour the best pint in town. Innocuous-looking **Ryan's**, Main St. (tel. 61431), hides a mighty multilevel beer garden that alternates trad and rock several nights a week. **Moor Lane Tavern**, Main St. (tel. 62080), excites young locals with cocktails and tunes on the weekends.

🏛️ **SIGHTS. The Rock of Cashel** (also called **St. Patrick's Rock**) is a huge limestone outcropping topped by medieval buildings. The Rock itself is attached to a number of legends, some historically substantiated, others more dubious. Almost certainly St. Patrick baptized the king of Munster here around AD 450; whether or not he accidently stabbed the king's feet in the process is debatable. Periodic guided tours are informative if a bit dry; a less erudite but equally awe-inspiring option is to explore the rock's buildings yourself. (Rock open daily mid-June to mid-Sept. 9am-7:30pm, mid-Sept. to mid-Mar. 9:30am-4:30pm, mid-Mar. to mid-June 9:30am-5:30pm. Last admission 45min. before closing. £3, students £1.25.) Two-towered **Cormac's Chapel**, consecrated in 1134, holds semi-restored Romanesque paintings, disintegrating stone-carved arches, and a barely visible, ornate sarcophagus once thought to be in the tomb of King Cormac. A highlight of Cashel's illustrious history was the reported burning of the cathedral by the Earl of Kildare in 1495; when Henry VII demanded an explanation, the Earl replied, "I thought the Archbishop was in it." Henry made him Lord Deputy. The 13th century **Cashel Cathedral** survived the Earl and today's visitors can inspect its vaulted Gothic arches. Next to the cathedral, a 90 ft. **round tower**, built just after 1101, is the oldest part of the Rock. The **museum** (tel. 61437), at the entrance to the castle complex, preserves the 12th century **St. Patrick's Cross**. A stirringly narrated film on medieval religious structures is shown every hour or so. Down the cow path from the Rock lie the ruins of **Hore Abbey**, built by Cistercian monks who were fond of arches, and presently inhabited by nonchalant sheep. (Always open. Free.)

The small **Heritage Centre** (tel. 35362), in the same building as the tourist office on Main St., features permanent exhibitions, including "The Rock: From 4th to 11th Century" and its sequel, "The Rock: 12th-18th Century," as well as temporary exhibitions on such themes as Hore Abbey, Cashel Palace, and life in Cashel. (Open May-Sept. daily 9:30am-5:30pm, Oct.-Apr. M-F 9:30am-5:30pm. £1, students 50p.) The **GPA-Bolton Library**, John St. (tel. 61944), past the hostel, displays a musty collection of books and silver that formerly belonged to an Anglican archbishop of Cashel, Theophilus Bolton. The collection harbors ecclesiastical texts and rare manuscripts, including a 1550 edition of Machiavelli's *Il Principe*, the first English translation of *Don Quixote*, and what is locally reputed to be the smallest book in the world. (Open July-Aug. Tu-Su 10am-6pm, Sept.-Dec. and Mar.-June M-F 9:30am-5:30pm. £1.50, students and seniors £1.) The **Brú Ború Heritage Centre** (tel. 61122), at the base of the Rock, performs Irish traditional music, song, and dance to international acclaim. (Performances mid-June to mid-Sept. Tu-Sa at 9pm. £8, £27 with dinner.) In the town of **Golden**, 5 mi. west of Cashel on Tipperary Rd., stand the ruins of lovely **Althassel Abbey**, a 12th century Augustinian priory founded by the Red Earl of Dunster.

CAHIR

Cahir (CARE) maintains a delicate balance of commerce and tourism—a massive concrete grain depot looms over the well-preserved castle that is the town's pride and joy. It's worth an afternoon's visit, but the only hostels are in the surrounding countryside and a long trek to the limited food and pub options in town.

⁊ PRACTICAL INFORMATION. **Trains** leave from the station off Cashel Rd., just past the church, for **Limerick** and **Waterford** (M-Sa, 1 per day). **Bus Éireann** runs from the tourist office to **Cashel** (15min., ₤2.50), **Limerick** via **Tipperary** (1hr.; M-Th and Sa 4 per day, F 5 per day; ₤7.30), **Waterford** (1¼hr.; M-Th and Sa 5 per day, F 6 per day; ₤7.70), **Cork** (1½hr., 4 per day, ₤7), and **Dublin** (3hr., 4 per day, ₤10). **Hitchers** to Dublin or Cork position themselves on N8, a 20min. hike from the center of town. Those hoping to hitch to Limerick or Waterford wait just outside of town on N24, which passes through the town square. In either case, *Let's Go* does not recommend hitchhiking. The centrally located **tourist office,** Castle St. (tel. 41453), gives out free town maps but can't provide much advice about the mountains. (Open daily July-Aug. 10am-6pm, mid-Apr.-June and Sept. M-Sa 9:30am-6pm.) Backpackers can stow their bags free for a time at the **Crock O' Gold,** across from the tourist office. **AIB,** just up the street from the tourist office, has a trusty **ATM.** (Open M-Tu and Th-F 10am-4pm, W 10am-5pm.) The **phone code** is a cahiring and nurturing 052.

⌨⌗▤ ACCOMMODATIONS, FOOD, AND PUBS. There are two hostels in the countryside relatively close to Cahir. **Lisakyle Hostel (IHH)** (tel. 41963), 1 mi. south on Ardfinnan Rd., is the more accessible of the two. If coming from the bus station, walk up the hill and make a right at Cahir House. The exterior is bedecked with flowers, and the rooms are basic but reasonable resting places. Reserve a bed with the hostel's courteous owners at **Condon's Shop,** Church St., across from the post office, who will also arrange lifts to the hostel from town. (6- to 8-bed dorms ₤7, private rooms ₤8.50 per person. Sheets 50p. **Camping** ₤4.) The **Kilcoran Farm Hostel (IHH)** (tel. 41906 or (088) 539 185) promises to be an education in rural living— the vocal sheep out back are garrulous hosts. From Cahir, take Cork Rd. for 4 mi., turn left at the Top Petrol Station, and then, after a quarter mile, veer right at the T-shaped junction. Call for pickup from town. (Private rooms ₤7.50 per person.) One of the closest B&Bs to Cahir is **The Rectory,** Cashel Rd. (tel. 41406; email faheyr@tinet.ie), which provides enormous, old-fashioned rooms. (Doubles and twins ₤17-18 per person. Open Apr.-Oct.) **Tinsley House** (tel. 41947), above a small shop in the square, has TV- and bath-equipped rooms, and the proprietor is an encyclopedia of local history. (Singles ₤20, doubles and twins ₤18 per person.)

The best bet for groceries is **SuperValu Supermarket,** Bridge St. (tel. 41515), across the bridge from the castle. (Open M-Th 8am-6pm, F 8am-8pm, Sa 8am-9pm.) **Castle Arms,** Castle St. (tel. 42506), serves up cheap grub in an atmosphere that could only be called "pub." (Hot entrees ₤3.50-4.50.) A local favorite is the **Galtee Inn,** The Square (tel. 41247), where lunch is reasonable, though dinners swell in size and price. (Lunch ₤5.50; served daily noon-3pm.) Cannons once aimed towards the castle from the site of **J. Morrissey's,** Castle. St. (tel. 42123), but these days more peaceful invaders reign. Mr. and Mrs. Knight won the pub in a Guinness promotion. **Galtee Inn,** and the **Castle Arms,** Castle St. (tel. 42506), are quieter locales for a civilized drink.

◎ SIGHTS. Cahir is often defined by **Cahir Castle,** one of the larger and better preserved castles in Ireland. It is exactly what every tourist envisions a castle to be—heavy, lots of battlements, and gray. Built in the 13th century to be all but impregnable to conventional military attack, the castle's defenses were rendered obsolete by the advent of the age of artillery. In 1599, the Earl of Essex forced its surrender by tossing some cannonballs its way, one of which is still visibly stuck in the wall. Note the 11,000-year-old preserved head of the long-extinct Irish Elk; the noble beast's antlers span nearly an entire wall. Climb the towers for an unparalleled view of the tourist office and parking lot. There is a free, hour-long tour of the castle. (Tel. 41011. Open daily mid-June to mid-Sept. 9am-7:30pm, mid-Mar. to mid-June and mid-Sept. to mid-Oct. 9:30am-5:30pm, mid-Oct. to mid-Mar. 9:30am-4:30pm. £2, seniors £1.50, students £1. Last admission 30min. before closing.)

The broad River Suir that flows into Waterford Harbour is still a mere stream in Cahir. The wildly green **river walk** starts at the tourist office and leads past the 19th century **Swiss Cottage,** a 30min. walk from town. A charming jumble of architectural styles, the cottage was built so that the occupants of Cahir Castle could fish, hunt, and pretend to be peasants. Gorgeously restored, it is a delight for anyone who fancies building, decorating, and being rich. (Tel. 41144. Access by 30min. guided tour only. Last admission 45min. before closing. Open May-Sept. daily 10am-6pm, Apr. Tu-Su 10am-1pm and 2-5pm, Mar. and Oct.-Nov. Tu-Su 10am-1pm and 2-4:30pm. £2, seniors £1.50, students £1.) **Fishing** opportunities line the river walk past the Swiss Cottage. Fishing licenses are required, and can be obtained at the Heritage cornerstone on Church St. (Tel. 42730. Open daily 7am-11pm.)

The **Mitchelstown Caves** drip 8 mi. off the Cahir-Cork road in the hamlet of **Burncourt,** about halfway between Cahir and Mitchelstown. A 30min. tour takes you deep into a series of gooey, rippled subterranean chambers filled with fantastic mineral formations. (Tel. 67246. Open daily 10am-6pm; last tour 5:30pm. £3.)

NEAR CAHIR: GALTY MOUNTAINS AND GLEN OF AHERLOW

South of Tipperary Town, the river Aherlow cuts a rich and scenic valley. West of Cahir, along the south edge of the glen, the Galty Mountains rise abruptly. This purplish and lake-dotted range boasts **Galtymore,** Ireland's third-highest peak at 3018 ft. The Glen and mountains are idyllic surroundings for a picnic-based daytrip or a full-fledged trek. Serious hikers should invest in sheets 66 and 74 of the *Ordnance Survey,* available at local tourist offices and bookstores in Tipperary and Cahir (£4.20). The Tipp Town tourist office sells a series of trail maps, each containing written directions detailing a "classic" and a less strenuous "family walk" (50p). The walks wind through the **Glen of Aherlow, Lake Muskry, Lake Borheen, Glencush, Lake Curra,** and **Duntry League Hill. Glenbarra** is also a popular base camp, reached by driving west from Cahir toward Mitchelstown.

The **Glen of Aherlow (Ballydavid Wood) Youth Hostel (An Óige/HI)** (tel. (062) 54148), 6 mi. northwest of Cahir off Limerick Rd. is a renovated old hunting lodge that makes a good start for cavorting around the Galtees. (June-Sept. dorms £7, Mar.-May and Oct. £6.) On occasion, dedicated hikers make the 10 mi. trek across the mountains to the **Mountain Lodge (An Óige/HI),** Burncourt (tel. (052) 67277), a gaslit Georgian hunting lodge in the middle of the woods. From Cahir, follow the Mitchelstown Rd. (N8) 8 mi., then turn right at the sign for another 2 mi. on an unpaved path. (Dorms June-Sept. £6.50, Mar.-May £5.50.) The **Kilcoran Farm Hostel** (tel. (052) 41906) is a convenient stop on the hike back (see **Cahir**). The campsite in the Glen of Aherlow, **Ballinacourty House** (tel. (062) 56230), is excellent, and the staff provides detailed information on the Glen. (£8 per tent, off-season £7; additional £1 per person. Meals and cooking facilities available. Open Apr.-mid-Sept.) They also operate a pleasant **B&B** and restaurant. (Doubles with bath £18 per person). To reach Ballinacourty House, take R663 off the Cahir-Tipperary road (N24) in Bansha and follow the road for 8 mi. to the sign-posted turnoff.

CLONMEL (CLUAIN MEALA)

Clonmel (pop. 17,000) derives its name from the Irish phrase for "the honey meadow." This medieval town on the banks of the River Suir (SURE) turns sweet about it in the fall, when locally produced Bulmer's Cider fills the air with apple scents. As Co. Tipperary's economic hub, Clonmel has all the comforts of modern life and offers pubs and accommodations after a day spent exploring the nearby Comeragh Mountains.

▐ TRANSPORTATION

Trains: Prior Park Rd. (tel. 21982), about 1 mi. north of the town center. Trains chug from here to **Limerick** (50min., M-Sa 2 per day, £9) and **Waterford** on the way to **Rosslare Harbour** (1¼ hr., M-Sa 1 per day, £11).

Buses: Bus information is available at **Rafferty Travel,** Gladstone St. (tel. 22622). Open M-Sa 9am-6pm. Buses leave from in front of the train station to **Waterford** (1hr.; M-Sa 7 per day, Su 5 per day; £5.90), **Kilkenny** via **Carrick-on-Suir** (M-Sa 4 per day, Su 3 per day; £3.50), **Limerick** via **Tipperary** (5 per day, £8.80), **Cork** (2hr., 3 per day, £9), **Dublin** (3¼hr., 3 per day, £8), **Rosslare** (3½hr.; M-Sa 3 per day, Su 2 per day; £10), and **Galway** (3¾hr.; M-F 5 per day, Su 3 per day; £12). **Rapid Express** (tel. 29292) runs their own bus to **Dublin** via **Kilkenny** (3hr.; M-Sa 3 per day, Su 2 per day; £5).

▐ ORIENTATION AND PRACTICAL INFORMATION

Clonmel's central street runs parallel to the **Suir River.** From the station, follow **Prior Park Rd.** straight into town. Prior Park Rd. becomes businesslike **Gladstone St.,** which intersects the main drag, known successively as **O'Connell St., Mitchell St., Parnell St.,** and **Irishtown. Sarsfield St.** and **Abbey St.** run off the main street toward the riverside quays.

Tourist Office: Sarsfield St. (tel. 22960), across from the Clonmel Arms Hotel. Pick up the 6 self-guided walking tours of Clonmel and the Nire Valley (50p), and the free Heritage Trail map of town. Open June-Aug. daily 9:30am-5:30pm, Sept.-May M-F 9:30am-5:30pm.

Bank: AIB (tel. 22500) and **Bank of Ireland,** both with **ATMs,** are neighbors on O'Connell St. Both open M 10am-5pm, Tu-F 10am-4pm.

Pharmacy: Joy's, 68 O'Connell St. (tel. 29314), within Superquinn off Emmett St. Open M-W and Sa 9am-6pm, Th-F 9am-9pm.

Emergency: Dial 999; no coins required. **Garda:** Emmet St. (tel. 22222).

Hospital: St. Joseph's/St. Michael's, Western Rd. (tel. 21900).

Post Office: Emmet St. (tel. 21164), parallel to Gladstone St. Open M-F 9am-5pm, Sa 9am-1pm.

PHONE CODE:	Sweet nectar of Bulmer's youth, 052.

▐ ACCOMMODATIONS

Not the most backpacker-friendly town in Ireland, Clonmel caters more to the hotel and B&B crowd. The only hostel, ▧**Powers-the-Pot Hostel and Caravan Park,** Harney's Cross (tel. 23085), is well outside of town. To reach the hostel, follow Parnell St. east out of town, turn right at the first traffic light (not N24), cross the Suir, and continue straight for 5½ mi. of arduous mountain road to the signposted turnoff. The 19th century house is supposedly the highest in Ireland, and holds fluffy beds and a bar/restaurant under a thatched roof. (Breakfast £4.50, dinners £7.50-10.) Owners Niall and Jo can answer all your hillwalking questions and provide maps and guides for the Munster Way. (Dorms £7, private rooms £8. **Camping** £3.50 per person. Laundry £2. Freezing and smoking facilities for anglers. Open May- mid-Oct.)

In Clonmel, the area past Irishtown along the Cahir Rd. is scattered with **B&Bs.** If you're willing to walk a mile or two to town, your options are relatively extensive. Closer to downtown, guests watch playful swans from the windows of their large rooms at the **Riverside House** (tel. 25781), on New Quay overlooking the Suir. (£17.50 per person.)

⬛⬛ FOOD AND PUBS

The local outpost of the **Tesco** (tel. 27797) supermarket empire is on Gladstone St. (Open M-Tu and Sa 8:30am-7pm, W-F 8:30am-9pm; Su 11am-6pm.) **The Honey Pot**, 14 Abbey St. (tel. 21457), sells health foods and bulk grains, and hosts an organic vegetable market on Saturday mornings. (Open M-Sa 9:30am-6pm.)

Angela's Wholefood Cafe, Abbey St. (tel. 26899), off Mitchell St. Exquisitely fresh and creative vegetarian and meat dishes served on country pine tables. Salads, specials £5-6. Open M-F 9am-5:30pm, Sa 9am-5pm.

Catalpa, Sarsfield St. (tel. 26821), next to the tourist office. Italian feasts served in a former bank vault. Popular with the locals. Call ahead for reservations. Pasta £5-7; pizza £4.20-5; meat dishes £7-13. Open Tu-Su 12:30-2:30pm and 6:30-11pm.

Tom Skinny's Pizza Parlor, 4 Gladstone St. (tel. 26006). Pizza made fresh right before your eyes. Most pizzas £4-8. Open daily noon-midnight.

Niamh's (NEEVS), Mitchell St. (tel. 25698). Specialty coffees, hot lunches, sandwiches, and all-day breakfasts served up in a relaxing deli-style restaurant. Whopping vegetarian pita £3.75. Open M-F 9am-5:45pm, Sa 9am-5pm.

John Allen's (tel. 20928), next to the church in Irishtown, is surprisingly bright, luring a jolly crowd of all ages with trad once a week. Enormous, elaborate **Mulcahy's**, 47 Gladstone (tel. 25054), displays a curious combination of decorative themes. (Trad weekend nights.) Thursday through Sunday, the pub also hosts **Danno's**, an over 18 disco. (Cover £5.) **Barry's**, O'Connell St. (tel. 25505), counters with a nightclub of their own, **Goodfellas**, mobbed by young groovers Thursday through Sunday. (Cover £3-5.) Check the *Nationalist* for entertainment listings.

👁 SIGHTS

Clonmel might win the best-signposted tourist-trail award, but certainly not the content or eloquence portions of the pageant. Pick up the Heritage Trail map in the tourist office (free). Stops along the way include the **West Gate** at the west end of O'Connell St., an 1831 reproduction of the medieval gate that separated Irishtown from the more prosperous Anglo-Norman area. The 84 ft. octagonal tower of **Old St. Mary's Church**, Mary St., stands near the remnants of the town wall that failed to keep Cromwell's armies out in 1650. Just inside the door of the **Franciscan Friary**, Abbey St., are the 15th century tomb effigies of a knight and lady of the Butler family of Cahir. Clonmel's history as a transportation center is remembered at the **Museum of Transport** in a converted mill off Emmett St. Antique cars and accessories form the bulk of the collection. (Tel. 29727. Open June-Sept. M-Sa 10am-6pm, Su 2:30-6:30pm; Oct.-May closed Su. £2.50.)

The **Tipperary S.R. County Museum** hosts small traveling art exhibitions. The well-documented but inexplicable upstairs gallery concentrates on esoteric facets of local history, including a 1000 lb. skull of the long-extinct giant Irish elk. (Parnell St. Tel. 25399. Open Tu-Sa 10am-1pm and 2-5pm. Free.) Several walks in the area and nearby Nire Valley are described in the tourist office's glossy leaflets *Clonmel Walk #1* and *#2* (50p each). See **Comeragh Mountains** (below) for day hike info.

THE EAST MUNSTER WAY

The East Munster Way footpath starts in Carrick-on-Suir, hits Clonmel, skirts the Comeragh Mountains, and runs full-force into the Knockmealdowns, ending 43 mi. later in Clogheen. From there, connections can be made through the Druhallow Way to the Kerry Way. The best maps to use are sheets 74 and 75 of the *1:50,000 Ordnance Survey* series. In addition, the *East Munster Way Map Guide* (£4), available at the tourist office and at Powers-the-Pot Hostel, in Clonmel, provides a written guide and an accurate but less detailed map (as an added bonus, it points out all the pubs along the way). The route contact is the Tipperary Co. Council in Clonmel (tel. (052) 25399), but Powers-the-Pot is the best information center on hiking in the Comeragh and Knockmealdown Mountains. For more wilderness advice, see **Camping**, p. 77.

COMERAGH MOUNTAINS

The Comeragh "mountains" are more like large hills; not even the highest peaks are very steep. The ground is almost always soft and wet; most of the terrain is manageable in sneakers. *Nire Valley Walk #1* to *12* (50p each, at the Clonmel tourist office and Powers-the-Pot Hostel) are excellent waterproof maps illustrating day hikes from Clonmel. For more extensive hikes, begin from **Powers-the-Pot Hostel**, ½ mi. off the Munster Way (see **Clonmel**, p. 182). The best map of the Comeraghs is sheet 75 of the *Ordnance Series*. With a map in hand, head east from Powers-the-Pot and follow the ridges south. The land is mostly open and in good weather it's relatively hard to get lost, but make sure that someone knows you're out there. Guided walking is also available; inquire with Niall at **Powers-the-Pot** (tel. (052) 23085). You might also consider doing the Comeragh Mountains on horseback. (Call **Melody's** in Ballymacarbry, tel. (052) 36147. £10 per hour.) The technical term for the mountain hollows so common in the mild Comeraghs is "cwms" (KOOMS). Borrowed from the Welsh, it's the only word in the English language without a vowel.

KNOCKMEALDOWN MOUNTAINS

Straddling the Tipperary-Waterford border 12 mi. south of Cahir, the Knockmealdown Mountains are roughly contoured, like the inside of an Aero bar. *Knockmealdown Walks 1* to *4* (50p) are available at local tourist offices, including those in Clonmel and Clogheen. All four start at Clogheen; walks 2 and 4 assume transportation to nearby carparks. As an alternative, many hikers prefer to begin in the town of **Newcastle,** where tiny but locally renowned **Nugent's Pub** stands. For guided **tours,** contact Helen McGrath (tel. (052) 36359). Tours depart at noon on Sundays from the Newcastle Car Park. (£5, other days available by request.) Sights to head for include the spectacular **Vee Road** south from Clogheen, which erupts with purple rhododendrons on its way to the **Knockmealdown Gap.** Just before the **Vee,** in the town of **Graigue,** thirsty pilgrims can stop in at **Ryan's Pub,** a charming little thatched building in the middle of a farm yard. At the pass of the Knockmealdown Gap, about two-thirds of the way to the top of the gap, the pines give way to heather and bracken, and a parking lot marks the path up to the top of **Sugarloaf Hill.** The walk takes about an hour and on a clear day it affords a panorama of patchwork fields. From there, you can continue on to the **Knockmealdown Peak** (2609 ft.), the highest in the range. Beautiful (and supposedly bottomless) **Bay Loch,** on the road down to Lismore, is the stuff of legend. The affable and decidedly unofficious **tourist office** in Clogheen (tel. (052) 65258; across from the Vee Rd. turnoff) is generous with local maps and lore. (Open M-Sa 9am-5pm.) 5min. from the village on Cahir Rd., **Parsons Green** (tel. (052) 65290), part garden and part **campsite,** offers river walks, boat rides, and pony rides. (£6 per 2-person tent. Kitchen. Laundry £4.) The **Kilmorna Farm Hostel** (tel. (058) 54315) in Lismore is a more luxurious, less convenient base for hiking in the range (see Lismore, below).

LISMORE

The disproportionate grandeur of Lismore's castle and cathedral reminds visitors that this sleepy little town was once a thriving monastic center. Nestled against the Blackwater River at the end of Vee Rd., Lismore is actually in Co. Waterford, but makes a convenient base for exploring Tipperary's Knockmealdown Mountains.

THE FALL OF THE HOUSE OF USSHER Rather

Keily was the notoriously mean landlord who owned property around Lismore. During the mid-19th century, his most common management technique was forcing successful tenant farmers to abandon their land, then moving them higher in the mountains to enrich yet-unworked soil. When he married, his wife wanted a castle as elegant as the one at Lismore. Keily, or rather, Keily Ussher (he added the second name for an aristocratic ring) started to build a grand castle several miles from Lismore. Poor planning soon got the best of Keily Ussher, and he built only the grand entrance arch before exhausting his funds.

🛈 PRACTICAL INFORMATION. **Bus Éireann** stops across from the tourist office and runs to **Dungarvan** (½hr., 1-2 per day), **Waterford** (1¼hr., F and Sa 1 per day), and **Cork** (1¼hr., F 1 per day). The best way to get to Lismore is by foot or bike on the Vee Rd. or along the Blackwater River. Hitching to Dungarvan is common, but not recommended by *Let's Go*. To get to Cork, hitchers first ride east to Fermoy, then head south on N8. Lismore's extremely helpful **tourist office** (tel. 54975) shares the old courthouse building with the **heritage center.** (Open June-Aug. M-Sa 9:30am-5:30pm, Su noon-5:30pm; Apr.-May and Sept.-Oct. M-Sa 9:30am-5:30pm, Su noon-5:30pm.) The **phone code** is resigned to fate at 058.

🛏🍴🍺 ACCOMMODATIONS, FOOD, AND PUBS. One mile from Lismore, barnyard sounds fill the rooms at the **Kilmorna Farm Hostel** (tel. 54315). From town, walk up Chapel St. to the left of the Interpretive Center, take the first left at the Catholic church, and follow the signs (or call for a lift). The 18th century coach house is completed by gingham curtains and beds built by a local craftsman. The working farm supports cows, chickens, horses, six dogs, and a TV. (3- to 6-bed dorms ₤8, doubles ₤19. Continental breakfast ₤4. Laundry ₤4.) Basic hardwood dorms are tucked above the bar at the **Red House Inn** (tel. 54248) across from the Interpretive Center on Main St. (₤16 per person.)

Lismore is less impressive on the restaurant front than on the hostel one. **Super-Save** (tel. 54122) has groceries on East Main St. (Open M-W 9am-6pm, Th 9am-7:30pm, F 9am-8pm, Sa 9:30am-8:30pm.) **Eamonn's Place,** East Main St. (tel. 54025), serves Irish meals in their gorgeous beer garden. (Lunch entrees from ₤5, served M-F 12:30-2pm; dinners ₤7-8, served M-Su 6-9pm.) **Madden's Bar,** East Main St. (tel. 54148), serves surprisingly refined lunches at reasonable prices (₤4-6) and many a pint in their renovated pub. The **Red House Inn** (tel. (058) 54248) has periodic bursts of trad on weekend nights.

☎ SIGHTS. Swathed in foliage and looming grandly over the Blackwater River, **Lismore Castle** is stunning. Once a medieval fort and bishop's residence, the castle was extensively remodeled in the 19th century with great imagination but little historical insight. In 1814, the Lismore Crozier and the *Book of Lismore,* priceless artifacts thought to have been lost forever, were found hidden in the castle walls. The castle was once the home of Sir Walter Raleigh, and also the birthplace of 17th century scientist Robert Boyle (of PV=nRT fame). The castle is privately owned by the English Duke of Devonshire, who occasionally accommodates guests at an estimated ₤7,000 per week. Admire the castle from the bridge over the Blackwater River, because its **gardens** are not worth their admission fee. (Tel. 54424. Open mid-Apr. to Sept. daily 1:45-4:45pm. ₤3, under 16 ₤1.50.) The bridge is also the starting point for the shady and peaceful **Lady Louisa's Walk** along the tree-lined Blackwater.

Locals whisper that a secret passage connects the castle to **St. Carthage's Cathedral,** Deanery Hill. Outside the cathedral, a large number of tombs are sealed with stone slabs in the ancient graveyard. The graves are a relic of Lismore's infamous past as a center for body-snatching; the slabs ensured that stiffs wouldn't be stolen. The cathedral did better at retaining historical markers: a collection of 9th and 10th century engraved commemorative stones are set into one wall of the cathedral.

Lismore's **Heritage Center** (tel. 54975), in the town square, includes a 30min. video presentation and a cursory exhibit highlighting the 1000-year-old *Book of Lismore*. (Open June-Aug. M-Sa 9:30am-6pm, Su noon-5:30pm; Apr.-May and Sept.-Oct. M-Sa 9:30am-5:30pm, Su noon-5:30pm. £3, students £2.50.) The center also runs guided tours of town (£3) and sells self-guided tour booklets (£1). Those seeking to vary their Guinness diet should stop in at the **West Waterford Vineyards**, 5 mi. from Lismore off Dungarvan Rd. The Vineyard produces a dry white wine in addition to seasonal fruit wines like pear and strawberry and will send you on your way armed with any local information you wish. (Tel. 54283. Open daily 10am-8pm; call ahead for wine tastings.) Two miles from Lismore is a car park for the locally beloved **Towerswalk**. From the castle, cross the bridge back and make a left. The towers and entrance gate to a grand castle were begun by Keily-Ussher, a local landlord, in the mid-19th century (see **The Fall of the House of Ussher,** below). Today there is a woodsy walk to "the Folly." (1hr.).

WEXFORD AND WATERFORD

Geography makes Co. Wexford's oceanfront the entrance to Ireland for many visitors coming from France, Wales, or England. Ireland's invaders—from Vikings to Normans, Christians to modern backpackers—have begun their island-conquering here. Naturally, with so many people passing through, Wexford has been particularly prone to foreign influences. Away from the salty pubs and crowded streets of Wexford town, thin beaches stretch from dismal, highly-trafficked Rosslare Harbour and pop up again at the county's southwest edge, along idyllic Waterford Harbour and Tramore. Co. Waterford is dedicated to the production of industrial and agricultural goods. Waterford City is the commercial and cultural core of the Southeast, where thriving crystal and other, sootier, industries create an urban environment that is worlds apart from the sheep-speckled fields of the inner county. New Ross, with its fine hostels and urban amenities, is a good base for exploring the Southeast.

Slí Charman (SHLEE KAR-man), usually referred to as "An Slí," is a pathway that runs 135 mi. along Wexford's coast from the Co. Wicklow border through Wexford and Rosslare to Waterford Harbour. The relatively close Wicklow Way provides more invigorating hikes. Maps of both hang at major Bord Fáilte offices in Wexford and Waterford. Major roads in the region are the east-west N25 (Rosslare-Wexford-New Ross-Waterford), the north-south N11 (Wexford-Enniscorthy-Arklow-Dublin), and the N79 from Enniscorthy to New Ross.

ENNISCORTHY

The handsome town of Enniscorthy perches 14 mi. north of Wexford on the hills that straddle the River Slaney. The town is exceptionally conscious of its part in the history of Irish nationalism: mention the year '98 to a local, and he'll assume you mean the **Rebellion of 1798** against the British. In that year, a local priest led an uprising that held the British at bay for 12 days at nearby Vinegar Hill, where the rebels were eventually defeated (see **Rebellion, Union, and Reaction,** p. 10). In the 20th century, Enniscorthy was one of the only towns to join Dublin's 1916 Easter Rising, and the last to surrender (see **The Easter Rising,** p. 13). Today Enniscorthy's booms are attributable to the economy rather than cannons: large amounts of recent construction have produced a sparkling new 1789 museum and a new hostel. Older sites complement the new, including a highly eclectic museum housed in a 13th century Norman castle. While the history lesson on Ireland's political conflicts may be a sobering experience, Enniscorthy's 20 or so pubs greatly diminish the chances of that—especially during one of the town's many summer festivals.

🔁 **ORIENTATION AND PRACTICAL INFORMATION.** The N11 motorway passes straight through Enniscorthy, heading north toward Arklow, Wicklow, and Dublin and south toward Wexford. **Trains** connect Enniscorthy to **Rosslare** (50min., £7) in one direction and **Dublin** (2¼hr., £10) in the other (3 per day each direction). From the railway station, cross the river at the **Slaney Dr. bridge,** then take a left to reach **Abbey Square,** one of the main shopping areas, or keep heading uphill to hit the other, **Market Square. Buses** stop outside the Bus Stop Shop on **Templeshannon Quay,** between the two bridges and across the river from the squares, then run south to **Wexford** (M-Sa 8 per day, Su 6, £3.50) and **Waterford** (3 per day, £7.50), and north through **Ferns** (10min.) to **Dublin** (M-Sa 6-7 per day, Su 5 per day, £7). The moderately informed **tourist office** (tel. 34699) is in the castle off Castle Hill. (Open M-Sa 10am-6pm, Su 2-6pm; winter hours are shorter.) Use the info-center to get a map of the town and other handouts; for intensive advice, though, the fabulous **Maura Flannery** in the souvenir shop across the street is your woman (tel. 36800 or (086) 816 2301, fax 36628). A number of banks offer **24hr. ATMs: AIB** (tel. 33184; open M 10am-5pm, Tu-F 10am-4pm); the **Irish Permanent Bank,** Market Sq. (tel. 35700; open M-Tu and Th-F 9:30am-5pm, W 10:15am-5pm); and the **Bank of Ireland** on the roundabout at Abbey Sq. (tel. 33158; open M 10am-5pm, Tu-F 10am-4pm). **Kenny for Bikes,** on the river at Slaney St. (tel. 33255 or (087) 232 1137; email kennysfb@iol.ie), will rent bikes (£8 per day, less for extended rentals) even for one-way trips to other cities, or arrange multi-day bike tours of the Southeast. If you'd rather take a taxi call 37222, 33975, 36666, or 37888. One **post office** (tel. 33226) is located by the Abbey Sq. roundabout, and another is across the street from the cathedral. The **phone code** is 054.

🛏️🍴🍺 **ACCOMMODATIONS, FOOD, AND PUBS. Platform 1,** Railway Sq. (tel. 37766; fax 37769; email plat@indigo.ie), is a shimmering new hostel right by the train station that should provide all the space and security you could desire, and a shower in the billiard room in case things get really heated (dorm £8, twin £30, quad £45, off-season prices may be lower; handicapped accessible). B&B options are numerous, and some of the best easily justify a 15-minute walk (or £2 taxi) from Main St. At **Adelmar,** Summerhill (tel. 33668), Mrs. Agnes Barry's hospitality and delightful company do the trick. Turn right past Murphy's Hotel then left on Bohreen Hill and follow the signs. (£15. Open June-Sept.) **Don Carr House,** on Bohreen Hill (tel. 33458), has a homey feel and a sumptuous sunroom (£16, with bath £18). If you want to stay closer to the action, **P. J. Murphy's B&B,** 9 Main St. (tel. 33522)—not to be confused with Murphy's Hotel—is directly above it; Murphy's Pub fills the ground floor of the building, which is just steps away from Market Square. (£16; with bath £17.)

Food eagerly awaits you at various pubs or at the **L&N Supervalu** (tel. 34541) in the shopping center on Mill Park Rd. off of Abbey Sq. (Open M-Tu, and Sa 8am-8pm, W 8am-9pm, Th-F 8am-10pm.) Vegetarians or those seeking home-baked goodies should head to **The Baked Potato,** 18 Rafter St. (tel. 34085), for cheap, hot food. (Open M-Sa 8am-6pm.) The baked goods are especially tasty across the street at **Karen's Kitchen,** 11 Rafter St. (Tel. 36488. Bakery items around £1; most entrees £2.50-4.50. Open M-Sa 9am-6pm.) **Rackards,** 23 Rafter St. (tel. 33747), with a little more room and weekly trad sessions, is among the hippest spots in Enniscorthy. Zesty lunch is served here from noon to 3pm (prawns in rich Marie Rose dressing with chips £4.95). Twice-awarded Wexford County "pub of the year," **The Antique Tavern,** 14 Slaney St. (tel. 33428), is crammed with artifacts from Enniscorthy's role in the Rebellion of 1798, plus a gas mask. The sign out front of this cozy spot explicitly forbids "three card tricksters" and bandits (you know who you are).

🏛️ **SIGHTS.** The new **National 1798 Visitor Centre,** a five-minute walk away from town on Mill Park Rd., is an impressive multimedia barrage of information about the Vinegar Hill battle. One room presents the conflict as a chess problem with larger-than-life pieces; there's also a 14-minute film with all the battle stabbing you

N
N10
N9
CO. CARLOW
Muine Bheag
Thomastown
Graiguena-managh
R. Nore
CO. KILKENNY
Blackstairs Mts.
N80
N79
New Ross
N25
N9
N25
Waterford
Passage East
Ferry
Tramore
Dunmore East
Tramore Bay
Waterford Harbor
The Hook
John F. Kennedy Memorial Forest Park
Dunbrody Abbey
Ballyhack
Duncannon
Hook Head
CO. WEXFORD
N11
Ferns
Enniscorthy
N11
Gorey
Courtown
Ballycanew
Kilmuckridge
Blackwater
Curracloe
North Bay
The Slobs
Wexford Harbor
Wexford
South Bay
Rosslare Strand
Rosslare Harbor
Leaning Tower Ruins
St. George's Channel
TO FISHGUARD
TO PEMBROKE
TO LE HAVRE
TO CHERBOURG
Ballyteige Bay
Kilmore Quay
Saltee Islands
0   5 miles
0   5 kilometers

Southeast Coast

SOUTHEAST IRELAND

could want. The visually sharp exhibits drive home the magnitude of 20,000 patriotic deaths. If you're up for a 4km walk (or drive), head across the river to the summit of **Vinegar Hill** itself; the battle site gives a fantastic view of the town below. For a more intimate perspective, Maura Flannery's **Walking Tour of Enniscorthy** can't be beat. The one-hour tour reveals the dirty little secrets of the town's prestigious past. Find out about the time in 1649 that Enniscorthy women got Cromwell's soldiers drunk and killed them, or how John P. Holland, a native son, invented the submarine—kind of the way Da Vinci did. (Information available at the tourist office. Tours in English or French leave on the hour starting at 10am from the craft shop; call ahead to reserve a place; five person minimum. £3, children £1.50; ask for senior discounts; mention *Let's Go* for further savings.)

The Norman castle houses the tourist office, but the **Wexford County Museum** (tel. 35926) fills the bulk of the building. (Open M-Sa 10am-6pm, Su 2-6pm; shorter hours in the off-season. £3, seniors and students £2, children 50p.) The museum chronicles Co. Wexford's collective stream of consciousness, providing a unique take on your customary historical narrative. Initially a 13-object display in 1960, curators have stuffed the castle from dungeon to eaves with such odd bits as ship figureheads and a collection of international police patches. The museum's highlights include the original letters and belongings of the principle players of the 1798 and 1916 rebellions.

St. Aiden's Cathedral, Cathedral St., uphill from Murphy's Hotel, was started in 1843 under the close supervision of architect Augustus Pugin, who littered his Gothic Revival creations across the whole of Ireland. Its location on an incline required St. Aiden's to take on an unusually long and narrow form. In Market Sq., a statue commemorates **Father Murphy,** who led the town in rebellion in 1798. The priest had been something of a Loyalist before an angry mob threatened to burn down his church. He responded with instantaneous revolutionary zeal, and promptly put himself at the head of the rowdy crowd.

If you're around in late June, check out the annual **Strawberry Fair.** Ten days of festivities and fructose mean you can paint the town red. Pubs host theater performances that draw literati, while music plays on well past sunset. The **Blues Festival** in mid-September features three days of entertainment by locally and internationally renowned musicians. Contact Maura Flannery (tel. 36800) for information.

WEXFORD

Gaels, Vikings, and Normans all worked together—well, against each other—to create the winding, narrow streets of modern Wexford. The sidewalks are so small that cars along Main St. (technically but not practically closed to traffic) must yield to the flocks of mothers pushing baby carriages down its middle. The town's main attraction for visitors is undoubtedly its abundance of quality pubs and restaurants. Excellent pubs and restaurants now fill the stone passageways built in the 12th century when the Normans conquered the Viking settlement of Waesfjord. Conquest after bloody conquest has left the town with an interesting tale to tell—as the Heritage Center puts it, the "ability to recover from trauma" is central to Wexford. The prominent Bull Ring and surrounding Norman ruins remain visual reminders of the history that features the likes of Henry II and Oliver Cromwell. The Twin Churches punctuate the skyline of the huddled harbor city.

▶ TRANSPORTATION

Trains: O'Hanranhan (North) Station, Redmond Sq. (tel. 22522), a 5min. walk along the quays from Crescent Quay. If the booking office is closed, you can buy tickets on the train. Information available from 7am until last departure. Trains hustle to **Rosslare Harbour** (30min., 3 daily, £2) and to Connolly Station in **Dublin** (2¾hr., 3 daily, £10.50, Friday £13.50).

Buses: Stop at the train station. If the station office is closed, hit the Station Cafe (tel. 24056) across street for info. Buses run to **Rosslare Harbour** (20min., M-Sa 10 per day, Su 9 per day, £2.50) and to **Dublin** (2½hr., M 8 per day, T-Sa 7 per day, Su 4 per day, £7). Buses to and from **Limerick** (4 daily) connect with Irish Ferries and Stena-Sealink sailings. From mid-July to Aug., buses run directly to **Galway** (6hr.) and other western points via **Waterford** (1hr.) and **Limerick** (3½hr.).

Taxi: Walsh Cabs (tel. 41449; mobile (088) 567 489); **Noel Ryan** (tel. 24056).

Bike Rental: The cheapest rentals are from the **Bike Shop,** North Main St. (tel. 22514; email gordon@iol.ie), £8 per day, £30 per week; £40 deposit; £12 extra to drop off elsewhere in the country. Open M-Sa 9am-6pm. **Hayes Cycle Shop,** 108 South Main St. (tel. 22462), leases Raleigh touring bikes for £10 per day, £40 per week; £50 or ID deposit. Open M-Sa 9am-6pm; bikes available by arrangement on Su.

Hitchhiking: The odds of getting a ride are highest around noon or from 5-7pm. Hitchhikers to Dublin (via N11) reportedly stand by the Wexford Bridge off the quays; those bound for Rosslare want to head south along the quays to Trinity St., just past the Talbot Hotel. Hitchers heading to Cork, New Ross, or Waterford continue down Westgate and turn left onto Hill St. then right onto Upper John St. (N25). N11 and N25 merge near the city, so savvy hitchers make a point of specifying either the Dublin Rd. (N11) or the Waterford Rd. (N25). *Let's Go* does not recommend hitchhiking.

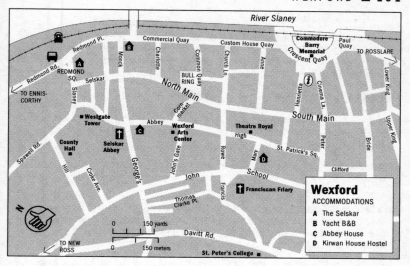

Wexford

ACCOMMODATIONS

A The Selskar
B Yacht B&B
C Abbey House
D Kirwan House Hostel

ORIENTATION AND PRACTICAL INFORMATION

In the year 2000, construction should be complete on the town's new marina, located by the **Crescent Quay** in the center of the waterfront. Most of the town's action takes place one block inland and uphill, along the twists and turns of **Main St.** A plaza called the **Bullring** is near the center of town, a few short blocks from where North Main St. changes to South. Another plaza, **Redmond Square,** sits at the north end of the quays, near the train and bus station. The two steeples that define the town's skyline are a less prominent pair to viewers within its narrow streets, but other towers help as landmarks, including the **Franciscan Friary** perched at the top of the hill.

Tourist Office: Crescent Quay (tel. 23111). Scars on the windowsills attest to the centuries of sailors who have sharpened their knives on them. The free, ad-packed *Wexford: Front Door to Ireland* and *Welcome to Wexford* include maps. Open Apr.-Oct. M-Sa 9am-6pm; July-Aug. M-Sa 9am-6pm, Su 11am-5pm; Nov.-Mar. M-F 9:30am-5:30pm.

Banks: 24hr. ATMs are available at, among other places: **AIB,** South Main St. (tel. 22444; open M 10am-5pm, Tu-F 10am-4pm); the **Bank of Ireland** at the Bullring (tel. 23022; open M 10am-5pm, Tu-F 10am-4pm); and **TSB,** 73-75 Main St. (tel. 41922; open M-W and F 9:30am-5pm, Th 9:30am-7pm).

Laundry: My Beautiful Launderette, St. Peter's Sq. (tel. 24317), up Peters St. from South Main St. Full- or self-service; pickup and delivery available. Wash £1.85, dry 80p, soap 40p. Open M-Sa 9:30am-6pm. **Pádraig's Launderette,** 4 Mary St. (tel. 24677), next to the hostel. No self-service drying available. Open M-F 9:30am-6:30pm, Sa 9am-9pm.

Pharmacy: A gaggle of pharmacies along Main St. rotate Sunday, late, and lunchtime hours. All open M-Sa 9am-1pm and 2-6pm.

Emergency: Dial 999; no coins required. **Garda:** Roches Rd. (tel. 22333).

Hospital: Wexford General Hospital, New Town Rd. (tel. 42233), on N25/N11.

Post Office: Anne St. (tel. 22123). Open M and W-Sa 9am-5:30pm, Tu 9:30am-5:30pm. Smaller offices on South Main St. and near the intersection of Main and Monck St.

PHONE CODE	053.

ACCOMMODATIONS

If the hostels and B&Bs listed are full, ask the proprietors for recommendations or look along N25 in either direction (Rosslare Rd. or New Town Rd.). If you're planning to be in town during the opera festival (see **Entertainment**), book as far in advance as possible; some rooms are reserved a year ahead of time.

Kirwan House Hostel (IHH), 3 Mary St. (tel. 21208; email kirwanhostel@tinet.ie). Short of communal space, but not communal good feeling. Kirwan is a refurbished 200-year-old house right in the heart of town with some slants and creaks in its wooden floors. Launderette next door. Internet access £1.50 for 20min. **Bike rental** £6 per day. Dorms £7.50-8.50; doubles £19-22.

Abbey House, 34 Abbey St. (tel. 24408), flaunts a fantastic location and comfy quarters. Definitely call ahead, as the owner is often out. £20 single, doubles with bath and TV £32.

The Selskar (tel. 23349), corner of North Main and Selskar St. No frills but a great location. Construction for significant expansion should finish soon; for now, a double and twin on each floor share a bathroom, kitchen, and sitting area with TV. Continental breakfast only. Call ahead or ask at the bar downstairs. £30.

The Yacht B&B, 2 Monck St. (tel. 22338), lets rooms above the Yacht Pub, overlooking the River Slaney. Singles £20; doubles £30. Reservations encouraged.

Carraig Donn, New Town Ct. (tel. 42046), off New Town Rd. (Waterford Rd.) just before the hospital. Call from town for pick-up, or trek 15min. along Main St., and over the hill. Large rooms and a cheerfully dated decor. Singles £17; doubles £16 per person. Wheelchair accessible.

Ferrybank Caravan and Camping Park, (tel. 44378). On the eastern edge of town, across from Dublin Rd. Take the bridge and continue straight to the camping site. Beautiful ocean view, clean area. £5 per 1-person tent; £7 per 2-person tent. Showers 75p. Laundry £1.50. Open Easter-Oct.

FOOD

The **Dunnes Store,** Redmond Sq. (tel. 45688), has everything from food to clothes to lampshades. (Open M-Tu and Sa 9am-7pm, W-F 9am-9pm, Su 11am-6pm.) **L&N Supervalu,** Custom House Quay (tel. 22290; open M-Tu and Sa 9am-7pm, W-F 9am-9pm, Su 9am-6pm), and **CrazyValue,** Crescent Quay (tel. 24788; open M-Tu 9am-7pm, W-F 9am-9pm, Sa 9am-6pm), are large supermarkets. In general, restaurant prices increase after 6pm, but there's definitely good grub to be found before then:

The Sky and the Ground, 112 S. Main St. (tel. 21273). Until about 6pm, scaled-down versions of the pricier fare served by the late-night upstairs restaurant **Heavens Above.** Most main courses in the pub £5-7. Music Su-Th, usually trad.

Greenacres, 56 N. Main St. (tel. 21788), is Wexford's gourmet grocery, with a gem of a cafe in back. It's an extra special find for vegetarians, although their chicken, honey, and mustard casserole (£4.25) is a triumph. Cafe open M-Sa 9am-5:30pm.

The Tack Room, 38 N. Main St. (21669), right by the Bullring. Nothing too fancy, but it's done well and will stick to your ribs. Entrees around £5. Food served until 8:30pm.

Tim's Tavern, 51 South Main St. (tel. 23861), offers only the finest pub grub, having won national awards for dishes like honey roast duck, stuffed loin of pork, and bacon and cabbage—all served with vegetables and potatoes. Lunch entrees £5-6. Similar food (more veggies, more sauces, more expensive) for dinner. Lunch served daily noon-6pm, dinner 6-10pm. Occasional trad sessions.

SOUTHEAST IRELAND

PUBS AND CLUBS

Wexford's pubs run the gamut from traditional to trendy, oftentimes combining the two under one roof. Music, whether it be acoustic or electronic, is a staple.

Mooney's Lounge, Commercial Quay (tel. 24483), by the bridge. Newly expanded into the building next door (though only connected by the kitchen), the two halves of Mooney's comprise *the* late-night hot spot in Wexford. All sorts of live music Th-Su, in one half or the other. Signs requesting well-dressed and 21+ crowds seem unenforced on both counts. Separate entrances for the lounge and concert areas. Occasional cover charge for larger gigs.

The Centenary Stores, Charlotte St. (tel. 24424). A classy crowd of twenty-somethings flocks to the Stores, a pub and dance club housed within a former warehouse. Excellent trad on Sunday mornings as well as Monday and Wednesday nights. Blues and folk on Tuesday nights. A DJ spins techno and top 40 on a black-lit dance floor from 11pm-2am on weekends running from Thursday to Sunday night. Cover £5 for the nightclub, sometimes £3 if you're already in the pub.

The Tackroom, 38 N. Main St. (21669), by the Bullring. Soft pine walls absorb the musings of a mellow crowd. Open till 11:30pm M-W, all other nights 12:30am.

O'Faolain's (oh FWAY lans), 11 Monck St. (tel. 23877). A bar for all generations, with live music almost every night. A nightclub spins from F-Su nights, with DJ, dance floor, and all. In case you have one too many and lose your sense of direction, there's a signpost inside directing you to all nearby towns. Cover £5 for the nightclub; you can get in for £3 if you're chillin' in the pub before 11pm. Pub open M-Th until 11:30pm; nightclub open until 1:30am.

 SIGHTS

The historical society (tel. 22311) runs free evening **walking tours** upon request. Tours depend on weather and interest—it's best to call after 5pm for availability. *Welcome to Wexford* (free at the tourist office) details a 45min. self-guided walking tour. The remains of the Norman **city wall** run the length of High St. **Westgate Tower,** near the intersection of Abbey and Slaney St., is the only one of the wall's six original gates that still stands. The tower gate now holds the **Westgate Heritage Centre,** where an excellent 27min. audio-visual show recounts the history of Wexford; you'll walk out thinking Wexford's the most important place in Ireland. (Tel. 46506. Open M-F 10am-4pm. £1.50, children 50p.) Next door, the peaceful ruins of **Selskar Abbey**—site of Henry II's extended penance for his role in Thomas Becket's murder—act as a flowerbed for glorious weeds. (Same hours as the center. Free.) Enter through the wicket gate to the left of the Centre.

An open area between North and South Main St. marks the Bull Ring. Bull baiting was inaugurated in 1621 by the town's butcher guild as a promotional device. The mayor got the hide while the poor got the meat. **The Pikeman,** a statue of a stalwart peasant fearlessly brandishing a sharp instrument, commemorates the 1798 uprising (see **Rebellion, Union, Reaction,** p. 10). Facing the sea stands the statue of Commodore John Barry, Wexford-born founder of the U.S. Navy. The **Friary Church** in the Franciscan Friary, School St., houses the "Little Saint" in the back corner of the nave. This wax effigy of young St. Adjutor shows the bloody gash inflicted by the martyr's Roman father. Franciscan monks have lived in town since 1230—keep a lookout for peaceful fellows in brown robes.

 ENTERTAINMENT

Many of the pubs in town offer music nightly. For more detailed information, check *The Wexford People* (85p in newsstands, or leaf through it in a pub), which lists events for all of Co. Wexford. The funky **Wexford Arts Centre,** Cornmarket (tel. 23764; fax 24544), presents free visual arts and crafts exhibitions; evening performances of music, dance, and drama also take place in the center throughout the year (generally £5-6). On Wednesday nights between June and August, take part in an open trad session, or pay £2 to watch. (Centre open M-Sa 10am-6pm). The **Theatre Royal**, High St. (tel. 22400; box office tel. 22144; box office fax 47438), produces performances throughout the year, culminating in the internationally acclaimed **Wexford Festival Opera** (www.wexfordopera.com), which in 2000 will run from Oct. 19 to Nov. 5. For these festivities, three obscure but deserving operas are rescued from the artistic attic and performed in an intimate setting. (Box office open May-Sept. M-F 9:30am-5:30pm and during performances; Oct. daily 9:30am-11pm. Opera tickets £42-52, available from early June.) A fringe festival fills afternoons and late-nights with cheaper options, from about £5.

THE IRISH NATIONAL HERITAGE PARK AND THE SLOBS

Wexford worked hard to get its **Slobs,** and they're a sight to see. "Slob" is the term for the cultivated mudflats to the north and south of Wexford Harbour that are protected from flooding rivers by dikes. The Slobs are renowned for the rare geese who winter there at the **Wexford Wildfowl Reserve.** Ten thousand of Greenland's white-fronted geese (one-third of the world population) descend on the Slobs from October to April, cohabiting with other rare geese, some from as far away as Siberia and Iceland. Resident Irish birds arrive in the summer to mate along the channels. The **Reserve Centre** will help visitors spot specific species. The Reserve is on the North Slob, 2 mi. north of Wexford town. Take Castlebridge/Gorey Rd. to well-signposted Ardcavan Ln. (a £3.50 cab ride), or hike through the Ferrybank caravan park and along the increasingly sandy beach (40min.). If you keep hiking along the coast, you'll reach Curracloe Beach, 6 mi. north of town, where Steven Spielberg filmed the D-Day landings in *Saving Private Ryan*. (Tel. (053) 23129. Open daily mid-Apr. -Sept. 9am-6pm; Oct.-Apr. 10am-5pm. Free.)

The **Irish National Heritage Park,** lets you stroll through 9000 years of Irish history in just a few hours. From a Stone Age campsite to an early Norman tower, check out replicas of houses, tombs, and fortifications that archaeologists have discovered across Ireland. The park is 3 mi. outside Wexford, on the N11; some cab companies offers a discount rate of £3.50. (Tel. (053) 20733; email info@inhp.com; www.inhp.com. Open daily 9:30am-6:30pm. £5, students £4. Restaurant open 12:30-5:30pm, entrees around £6. Wheelchair accessible.)

ROSSLARE HARBOUR

Rosslare Harbour is an over-equipped seaside village from which the ferries to France and Wales depart; it is not to be confused with Rosslare, the less important town between Rosslare Harbour and Wexford on N25. Rosslare Harbour's primary purpose is to receive or bid farewell to Ireland's visitors and voyagers, and it is best seen from the porthole of a departing ferry. Ferries from Rosslare Harbour run daily to Britain and every other day to France. To get from the ferry port to the town, climb either the ramp or the steps up the cliff.

▮ TRANSPORTATION

Trains: The train office (tel. 33114 or 33592) is open daily 6am-9:30pm. Trains run from the ferry port to **Wexford** (20min., 3 per day, £2), **Waterford** (1¼hr., same line as Limerick, £6), **Limerick** (2.5hr., M-F 2 per day, Sa-Su 1 per day, £12), and **Dublin** (3hr., 3 per day, £10.50).

Buses: Buses run out of the same office as the trains (tel. 33592) and stop in front of J. Pitt's Convenience Store by the ferry port in Kilrane, as well as the Catholic church in Rosslare Harbour. They run to **Wexford** (20min., M 11 per day, T-Sa 10 per day, Su 9 per day, £2.50), **Waterford** (M-Su 4 per day, Su 3 per day, £8.80), **Dublin** (3hr., M 10 per day, T-Sa 9 per day, Su 7 per day, £9), **Cork** (M-Sa 4 per day, £13), **Killarney** (£15), **Tralee** (£16), **Limerick** (M-Sa 2 per day, Su 3 per day, £13), and **Galway** via **Waterford** (2 per day, £16).

Ferries: The terminal is open daily 6:30am-9:30pm. **Stena Line** (tel. 33115, recorded info 33330) and **Irish Ferries** (tel. 33158; fax 33544; www.irishferries.com) serve the ferry port, which also houses a bureau de change. Open daily 7am-10pm. For info on ferries from Rosslare Harbour to England and France, see **By Ferry**, p. 66. **Trains** and **buses** often connect with the ferries. Bus Éireann and Irish Rail have desks in the terminal (tel. 33592).

Car Rental: An office in the ferry terminal offers **Europcar** (tel. 33634 or 22122), **Hertz** (33238), and **Budget** (33318) rentals; competitive prices hover around £90-96 for three days (includes £10.50 per day for insurance), £154-175 for a week. Drivers aged 21-22 must pay £10 extra per day.

Taxis: To get to B&Bs outside of town, call **Dermot O'Hagan** (tel. 33777), or **Jimmy Ferguson** (tel. 33355).

Hitchhiking: Rides are hard to come by, as neither locals surfeited with tourists nor a foreign family of four in an overstuffed car are likely to pick you up. *Let's Go* does not recommend hitchhiking.

▐ PRACTICAL INFORMATION

The mediocre Rosslare-Kilrane **tourist office** (tel. 33622 or 33232) is 1 mi. from the harbor on Wexford Rd. in Kilrane, and better for souvenirs than information. (Open daily 10:15am-5pm and 5:30-8pm.) If you need help in the ferry terminal, head to the port authority desk (tel. 33114). Currency can be exchanged at the **Bank of Ireland** (tel. 33304), on Kilrane Rd. past the supermarket. (Open M-F 10am-12:30pm and 1:30-4pm; **ATM.**) **Emergency**: Dial 999; no coins required. The **post office** (tel. 33201), in the **SuperValu supermarket,** has a bureau de change. (Open M-F 9am-1pm and 2-5:30pm, Sa 9am-1pm.) **Phone Code**: 053.

▐ ACCOMMODATIONS

The nature and function of Rosslare Harbour makes accommodations here convenient but inevitably mercenary. Exhausted ferry passengers take what they can get in town, while the better places to stay in Wexford and Kilmore Quay go untenanted. B&Bs swamp N25 just outside of Rosslare Harbour. There is a noticeable difference between approved and non-approved B&Bs on N25; in Rosslare, more than anywhere in Ireland, take the Bord Fáilte shamrock as a measure of quality.

▨ **Mrs. O'Leary's Farmhouse,** Killilane (tel. 33134), off N25 in Kilrane, a 15min. drive from town. Set on a glorious 100-acre farm, Mrs. O'Leary's place is a holiday unto itself. A grassy lane leads past dunes of wildflowers to a secluded beach. Call for pickup from town. £16, with bath £18.

Marianella B&B (tel. 33139), off N25 across from the pharmacy. Sue Carty's house lacks a great view, but she welcomes you with tea and cookies. Singles £17; doubles £32, with bath £36. Spacious family room available.

Clifford House, Michael Delaney (tel. 33226; email cliffordhouse@tinet.ie), Barryville. Turn left at the top of the cliff and head for the last house down. Nestled on a quiet cul-de-sac, Clifford's boasts bright, comfortable rooms at a convenient location. As you sip your tea, watch the ferries arrive and depart. £17, with bath £18.

Rosslare Harbour Youth Hostel (An Óige/HI), Goulding St. (tel. 33399; fax 33626). Take a right at the top of the cliff, then head left around the far corner of the Hotel Rosslare; the hostel is past the supermarket to the left. Offers decent showers, cramped bunks, cinderblock walls, and a collection of continental youth. Marta, the wacky Alpine manager, is currently painting up a color storm to hide the industrial feel. June-Aug. dorms £7.50; Sept.-May £6.50. Sheets £1.50. Midnight curfew. Summertime bike rental £6.50 per day.

◐ FOOD

The restaurants in Rosslare Harbour tend to be expensive. The **SuperValu supermarket** (tel. 33107), has a a substantive selection; it's to your right on your way to the hostel. (Open M-F 8am-7pm, Sa 8am-6pm, Su 9am-1pm.) The **Portholes** (tel. 33110) matches meals with a mini maritime museum. (Entrees £6-9; served noon-2:30pm and 6-9:45pm, soup and sandwiches available in between.) The pub in the **Devereux Hotel** (tel. 33216), just up from the ferry terminal, has good pub grub for decent prices. A large lunch costs about £4; the dinner menu entrees jump to £8-12.50.

KILMORE QUAY AND THE SALTEE ISLANDS

Thirteen miles southwest of Rosslare Harbour on Forlorn Point, the small fishing village of Kilmore Quay charms visitors with its beautiful beaches, thatched roofs, and whitewashed seaside cottages. This is the place to come for getting away from it all. There's not much in town, which is all the more reason to come. Two streets diverge from the harbour: **Wexford Rd.** and the **"Back Rd."** Information is available at the **Stella Maris Community Centre** on Wexford Rd., which also has private showers (£1.50), a game room, and a wonderful coffee shop with huge meals for about £3.50. (Tel. 29922. Open daily 9am-5pm; center open M-Sa 9am-10pm, Su 9am-9pm.) The village berths its **Maritime Museum** in the lightship *Guillemot*, once anchored near the harbor, now cemented into it. The tour, offered in English, French, and German, encompasses Irish naval history and the history of the town. (Tel. 29655. Open June-Aug. daily noon-6pm; May and Sept. Sa-Su noon-6pm. £2, students, seniors, and children £1.) **Dick Hayes** (tel. 29704; mobile (087) 254 9111) offers to bring you aboard for deep-sea angling and reef-fishing; call ahead to arrange a time and ask about renting equipment. The **Kilmore Seafood Festival** runs for 10 days in mid-July with loads of cheap seafood, music, and games.

To reach Kilmore Quay from Rosslare Harbour, take Wexford Rd. to Tagoat and turn left; from Wexford, take Rosslare Rd., turn right on the R739 near Piercetown, and continue 4 mi. to town. **Bus Éireann** runs between Wexford and Kilmore Quay (W and Su 2 per day, £4 return); the rest of the week, go with the local **Viking** bus service (tel. 21053) that runs between the two towns and will stop for you many places en route (M-Sa 2 per day, £4 return). **Doyle's Hackney & Bus Hire** (tel. 29624; mobile (087) 472 959) runs a shuttle into Wexford leaving at 11am and returning at 2pm (Tu, Th, F). He is also available for hackney service 24hr. (A hackney is similar to a taxi; see **Getting Around**, p. 68.) **Bike rental** is available at **Kilmore Quay Bike Hire** (tel. 29781), out of the Quay House guesthouse on Wexford Rd. past the post office. (£8 per day, £30 per week.) The **post office** (tel. 29641) does its business. (open M-F 9am-1pm, Th 9am-1pm) in **Murphy's food store** (tel. 29641, open 8am-8pm daily) on Wexford Rd. The **phone code** is 053.

The Haven (tel. 29979), 100 yd. down from the first right after the post office, has a water view, several kinds of tea and coffee, and an elegant and friendly proprietor, Betty Walsh. (Doubles £30, with bath £32.) Mrs. Deirdre Brady's **Castle View** (tel. 29765) has friendly and bright surroundings right on Wexford Rd. and is within a stone's throw of a random castle that was plopped down here in the 15th century. (Singles £18, doubles £32.) The budget traveler dead set on passing up wonderful B&Bs might want to try the **Kilturk Independent Hostel** (tel. 29883), 1.5 mi. from town on Wexford Rd., between Kilmore Quay and Kilmore Town. The buses between Wexford and Kilmore Quay will stop at the hostel by request, or call for a pickup. Spacious common areas and a new restaurant provide plenty to do outside the rainbow-colored rooms. (Dorms £7; private room £9. Sheets £1. Open May-Sept.) For the freshest of fresh seafood, take yourself to the **Silver Fox**, across from the Maritime Museum (tel. 29888; open M-Sa 12:30-9:30pm, Su 12:30-9pm; lunch specials 12:30-2:30pm).

Kilmore Quay sends boat trips out to the two **Saltee Islands**, formerly pagan pilgrimage sites and now Ireland's largest bird sanctuary, with a winged population nearing 50,000. These islands are home to puffins, razorbills, and grey seals, but owned by the absentee landlord Prince Michael Salteens (no relation to the cracker). A narrow ridge of rock is thought to have connected the smaller island to the mainland in ancient times. This land bridge, called **St. Patrick's Causeway,** was used for driving cattle to the island for pasture. Due to natural erosion, the land bridge is now submerged. Weather permitting, boats leave the mainland each morning, stranding you for picnics and ornithology. **Declan Bates** (tel. 29684; mobile (087) 252 9736) makes the half-hour trip daily at around 11am, to return at 4:30pm (£12).

NEW ROSS

New Ross is an ideal rest stop on a tour of Ireland's southeast corner. Waterford, the Hook, Wexford, and Kilkenny all lie within easy reach. The town also has a tidy list of sights to tick off, most involving the Irish exodus and beloved great-grandson John F. Kennedy. The Dunbrody, a coffin ship replica from the famine era, is a must-see.

🚩 ORIENTATION AND PRACTICAL INFORMATION. Most of New Ross' activity takes place on the strip of waterfront known simply as **The Quay.** Other major thoroughfares are **Mary St.,** which extends uphill from the bridge, and **South St.** which runs parallel to The Quay one block inland (and changes its name to **North St.** once it crosses Mary St.). New Ross is on the N25 (to Wexford and Waterford) and the N30 (to Enniscorthy). Hitchers can find plenty of rides on either, especially in the morning and late afternoon. *Let's Go* does not recommend hitching at any time of day. **Bus Éireann** runs from The Mariners Inn, The Quay, to **Waterford** (25min., M-F 11 per day, Sa 10 per day, Su 5 per day, £3), **Rosslare Harbour** (1hr., M-F 5-6 per day, Sa 4-5 per day, Su 3 per day, £7), and **Dublin** (3hr., M-Sa 3 per day, Su 4 per day, £7). **Kavanagh's** (tel. 0563 1189) runs a shuttle to Dublin and back (M-Sa, £7). **Budget** (tel. 421 550), located on The Quay in a gas station a few blocks from the tourist office, will **rent cars** to anyone 23 or older (£45 per day, £180 per week). The New Ross **tourist office,** on The Quay (tel. 421 857; www.newrosschamber.ie), just down the street from the SuperValu, is small but informative and offers useful maps in the free *New Ross Town and Area Guide* and *A Guide to New Ross.* (Open May-Sept. M-Sa 9am-1pm and 2-8pm, Su noon-1pm and 2-6pm.) Banks with **24hr. ATMs** abound: the **Bank of Ireland,** The Quay (tel. 421 267), is just steps away from the bus stop and tourist office; the **AIB** (tel. 421 319) and **TSB** (tel. 422 060) are across from each other on South St. (All banks open M 10am-5pm, T-F 10am-4pm.) The **post office** (tel. 421 261) delivers on Charles St., just off the Quay. (Open M-F 9am-5:30pm, Sa 10am-4pm.) The **phone code,** 051, is a sixth-cousin-twice-removed of the Kennedys.

🖐🗎🖼 ACCOMMODATIONS, FOOD, AND PUBS. **Mac Murrough Farm Hostel** (tel. 421 383; email machostel@tinet.ie) is a good enough reason to be in (well, near) New Ross. Follow Mary St. uphill to its end, turn left, then take the first right. Pass the cross and take a left at the supermarket, then a right at the Statoil Station; the remaining mile to the hostel is well-marked with signs. Call for pick-up. Delightfully down-to-earth owners make this the place to stay. The sheep give a rowdy greeting, and with a dog named Floozie, you can't go wrong. (Dorms £7, double £9 per person.) For a bed in town and a bigger dent in your wallet, **Riversdale House,** William St. (tel. 422 515), is the nicest of the B&Bs. Follow South St. all the way to William St., then turn left up the hill. Friendly owners take pride in the commanding view of town from their snazzy rooms. (Singles £26, doubles £19 per person.) **Inishross House,** 96 Mary St. (tel. 21335), is closer still and a good deal cheaper, though the ancient house and furnishings feel a little stale. (Singles £19, doubles £16 per person.) The tourist office can provide a list of other B&Bs, if these are booked.

    L&N SuperValu, The Quay (tel. 421 392), is your generic grocer. (Open M-W and Sa 9am-6pm, Th-F 9am-9pm.) **The Sweeney,** 1 Mary St. (tel. 421 963), serves all-day breakfast (£2-3), sandwiches (£1.50), and larger entrees (£3-7) in a room forested with palm trees. (Open T-Sa 9am-6pm.) Bright and airy **John V's,** 5 The Quay (tel. 425 188), will serve you a hefty portion of pub grub at reasonable cost. (Lunch around £5, served daily noon-2:30pm; dinner £6-8, served daily 5-9pm.) Enjoy a meal in sightseeing transit on board **The Galley** (tel. 421 723), which runs daily restaurant cruises from New Ross into Waterford Harbour. Choose your meal: lunch (2hr.; 12:30pm; £13, £6 for cruise only), tea (2hr.; 3pm; £6, £5 for cruise only), or dinner (2-3hr.; 6 or 7pm; £20-24, £10 for cruise only).

🔲 **SIGHTS.** New Ross's sights are as modest as the town itself, but a flashier profile may lie in the town's future upon the completion of **Dunbrody,** an exact replica of a New Ross ship that carried thousands of famine-struck emigrants to North America in the mid-19th century. The cargo ship's deck packed as many as 300 passengers; remarkably, there was never a death en route. The work is still unfinished due to a shortage of funds, leaving the Dunbrody dry-docked. Builders hope to complete the project by the summer of 2000. It will then sail to harbors across the world, with New Ross as its permanent home-base. (Open July-Aug. 10am-7pm, Oct.-Mar. noon-5pm, other months 10am-4:30pm.) For landlubbers, there's **St. Mary's Church,** off Mary St., built by Strongbow's grandson in the early 13th century. Mrs. Culleton, four doors down at 6 Church St., can provide the key and a booklet detailing the significance of the stone structures inside the building. Outside of town, the **John F. Kennedy Arboretum** blooms with life—nearly 6000 species of it. Stroll around 623 beautiful acres dedicated to the memory of Ireland's favorite U.S. President, and learn that the lineage of Camelot traces back to Co. Wexford. A small cafe doubles as a gift shop. (Tel. 388 171. 7 mi. south of New Ross on the R783 Ballyhack Rd. Open daily May-Aug. 10am-8pm; Apr. and Sept. 10am-6:30pm; Oct.-Mar. 10am-5pm. Last admission 45min. before closing. £2, seniors £1.50, children £1.)

THE HOOK

Southeast of New Ross, the Hook is a peaceful peninsula noted for its historic abbeys, forts, and lighthouses. Sunny coastlines draw deep-sea anglers to Waterford Harbour and Tramore Bay, while the pubs on the oceanfront keep the midnight oil burning till god knows when. The peninsula may be approached by an inland route from New Ross (see p. 197), or by crossing the Waterford Harbour on the Ballyhack-Passage East **ferry** (see p. 200). Interesting scenery makes for challenging bike rides. The Hook is perhaps best explored with a car; hitching short rides is generally quite easy, although *Let's Go* does not recommend hitchhiking. Don't rely on tourist offices, you can plan ahead by checking out the following websites: www.thehook-wexford.com, and hookinfo@iol.ie.

ON THE ROAD TO BALLYHACK: DUNBRODY ABBEY

Two miles from Ballyhack on New Ross Rd., is Dunbrody Abbey, a magnificent Cistercian ruin dating back to the late 12th century. Almost wholly intact, this abbey lets you wander up staircases and through little rooms with such freedom that you might even play a short game of medieval hide-and-seek. Get the key and brochures across the road at the visitor's center that sits among the ruins of a castle once associated with the abbey. The center features a doll-house replica of what the castle would have looked like fully furnished and intact. An impressive hedge-row maze, planted in 1992, began with 2 ft. high yew trees which confounded only Lilliputians. They're now about 5½ ft. tall, and expected to reach 15 ft. (Tel. 388 603. Centre open July-Aug. 10am-7pm; May-June and Sept. 10am-6pm. Abbey admission £1.50, children £1. Maze and castle admission £1.50, children £1.)

BALLYHACK AND ARTHURSTOWN

The profile that Ballyhack shows its cross-channel neighbor, Passage East, is dominated by 15th century **Ballyhack Castle.** Built by the Crusading Order of the

Knights Hospitallers in the 1450s, the castle was recently restored and now offers a few small displays and some general info about the Hook area. The tour of the castle is pithy, but it does offer some keen tidbits: the repulsive gargoyle on the seaward-wall is locally known as Cromwell's face. (Tel. 389 468. Open mid-June-Sept. M-F 10am-1pm and 2-6pm, Sa-Su 10am-6pm. £1, students 40p.)

If you're hungry in this vicinity, either go for broke at one of the high-end restaurants, or head to **Byrne's** (tel. 389 107), a small food store and pub right by Ballyhack's ferry port. The pub offers only sandwiches (under £2), but the store can supply you with more. (Store open M-Sa 9:30am-9:30pm, Su noon-2pm and 4-7pm.) If you need a taxi, call **M&T Cabs** (tel. 388 577; mobile (087) 465 961). For accommodations, head to nearby **Arthurstown.** Take a right from the landing area of the Ballyhack ferry port and follow the Slí Charman (SHLEE KAR-man) coastal path. The village lies a few minutes walk up this trail, which continues to wrap around the entire coastline of Co. Wexford. **Arthurstown** has opulent ocean views and a pub, but hardly a bite to eat, so get your grub back at Ballyhack. The first left coming from Ballyhack is the driveway to the **Arthurstown Youth Hostel (An Óige/HI)** (tel. 389 441), housed in a building that was built to the uncompromising specifications of the English coast guard two centuries ago. The warden is a walking encyclopedia with high cleanliness standards. (Dorms £7, under 18 £4.50, private rooms add £1. Sheets £1. Curfew 10:30pm. Lockout 10:30am-5pm. Open June-Sept.) You might treat yourself to **Glendine House B&B** (tel. 389 258; email glendine-house@tinet.ie), a large, Georgian manor up Duncannon Hill. It's hard to miss: look for the horses munching on the front lawn. The rooms are huge, beautifully decorated, and grandly comfortable—you'll be tempted to move in. (Singles £20; doubles £40. Internet access.)

DUNCANNON TO HOOK HEAD

South of Arthurstown, the scenic Hook Head Peninsula begins. The weather can be ferocious in the winter—just look at the windblown slant to the trees. The area's serene by summer, making for pleasant jaunts around the bizarre assortment of medieval ruins and new bungalows that clutters the landscape. The peninsula's circuit is best covered by car, but brave bikers can handle it if they've planned ahead. The nearest bike rental is back in Waterford (see p. 202). From Arthurstown, head east on Duncannon Rd. and keep an eye out for the sharp right turn with a sign for "Duncannon." The town lies one mile down that road.

Duncannon Fort (tel. 389 454 or 389 188) perches on the cliffs at the edge of the village. The fort has long failed to meet public expectations. From the moment it was built in the 1580s, people complained that it was too easy to conquer by land. In the 17th century, it surrendered to both Cromwell and William of Orange. Tours are given by request. A small cafe provides shelter from the wind and an assortment of hot and cold eats (£4). (Open daily June-mid-Sept. 10am-5:30pm., mid-May to Oct. daily 10am-5:30pm. £1.50, seniors £1.)

Geared towards families, the **Duncannon Festival,** the first week in July, offers a variety of food and activities. Call Eileen Roche (tel. 389 188) for details. The **Strand Stores** (tel. 389 216), also in Duncannon, sells groceries. (Open daily 9am-10pm.) Across the street, the **Strand Tavern** (tel. 389 109) serves some bar food in front of a tranquil ocean view. (Some entrees £5-8; bar food 12:30-6:30pm.)

Stuck halfway between Duncannon and the tip of the peninsula at **Hook Head, Templetown** has little to offer, other than **Templar's Inn** (tel. (051) 397 162), a great pub that's the best feeding hole on the peninsula. Bedecked with road signs, Templar's serves gargantuan portions of bar food from noon to 9pm, and the cheery pub keeps running long past its official closing time of 11:30pm. There's little else to do in town, although urgent road signs along the coast sound pretty exciting: "GREAT CARE MUST BE TAKEN NEAR THE WATERS EDGE ALONG THE CLIFFS FREAK WAVES SLIPPERY ROCKS." The **Hook Lighthouse,** a stout medieval tower founded by St. Dubhan, is the oldest beacon in the British Isles. On the eastern side of the peninsula is Ireland's own **Tintern Abbey,** founded in the 13th century and three miles from the Ballycullane stop on the Waterford-Rosslare train line. (Wander freely; tours ₤1.50.) Call the tourist office (tel. 397 502) in nearby **Fethard** for more info on the abbey and on the entire Hook region. (Open Sept.-June M-F 9:30am-5:30pm; July-Aug. M-F 9:30am-5:30pm, Sa-Su 11am-3pm.)

WATERFORD HARBOUR

East of Waterford City, Waterford Harbour straddles the Waterford-Wexford county line. It is here that Oliver Cromwell coined the phrase "by hook or by crook": he had plotted to take Waterford City from either Hook Head or the opposite side of the harbor at Crooke. Both sides of the harbor are host to historic ruins, friendly fishing villages, and stunning ocean views. In most of the region, travelers should expect peace and quiet, not convenience. To cross the harbor, either drive for 37 mi. up and around through New Ross or take the **Passage East Car Ferry** (tel. 382 480 or 382 488) between Ballyhack and Passage East. (Continuous sailings Apr.-Sept. M-Sa 7am-10pm, Su and holidays 9:30am-10pm; Oct.-Mar. M-Sa 7am-8pm, Su and holidays 9:30am-8pm. Pedestrians 80p, ₤1 return; cyclists ₤1.50, ₤2 return; car ₤4, ₤6 return.) Unless you're looking for complete rest and relaxation, **Passage East** is best passed through. The journey to Passage East from Waterford and then around the Hook is great by bike, but be warned that there's no place to rent a bike in the harbor area other than Waterford (see p. 202). The road between Passage East and Dunmore East is a bit hilly and should be used only by those looking to increase their heart rate significantly. From Wexford, follow signs for Ballyhack to reach the ferry, though from that distance, driving through New Ross might be faster. The **phone code** for the region is 051.

DUNMORE EAST

Vacationing Irish families have made the small town of Dunmore East their summertime mecca. If the weather's good, be careful not to squish one of the small children swarming on the wee beaches. When you're not looking out for kids underfoot, look out to sea—the calm harbor, stunning cliffs, and distant Hook compose a spectacular view. In general, the summer is busy while the winter months are desolate.

The town is spread along two areas, the strand and **Dock Rd.,** which leads up the hill and to the docks. There's **no ATM** in Dunmore, but any of the small groceries along Dock Rd. should have a bureau de change, including **Dingley's** (tel. 383 372; open 8am-10pm). The **Suirway** bus service (tel. 382 209; 24hr. timetable tel. 382 422) runs the 9½ mi. from Waterford to Dunmore East (30min., M-Sa 3-4 per day, ₤1.80). Wait for it outside the Bay Cafe, or just flag it down anywhere on its route.

The elegant **Dunmore Harbour House (IHH),** Dock Rd. (tel. 383 218), offers convenient rooms and new hostel accommodations, some with an ocean view. (Dorms ₤9-13.50.) **Carraig Liath B&B,** Dock Rd. (tel. 383 273), near the strand, provides clean, bright rooms, and a garden patio overlooking the harbor. (Doubles ₤38-44. Open Apr.-Oct.) In the off season, **Church Villa** (tel. 383 390) is just about the only B&B open. The 150 year old house is small but pleasant, with a relaxing sun room. (Singles ₤20-24.50, doubles ₤36.) Down by the strand, the **Queally's Caravan and Camping Park** (tel. 383 001) will let you squeeze a tent among its trailers. (₤8-10.)

Groceries are plentiful at **Londis Supermarket,** Dock Rd. (Open M-Th 8:30am-9pm, F-Su 9am-10pm; shorter hours in winter.) The **Bay Cafe,** also on Dock Rd. (tel. 383 900), serves homemade food for sit-down or take-away meals. (Sandwiches ₤1.50, entrees ₤4-5.50. Open daily 9am-6pm.) Farther along the road, the **Ocean Hotel Restaurant** (tel. 383 136) has an assortment of curry, steak, and veggie dishes. (Meals from ₤6. Open M-Sa 10am-10pm, Su 12:30-2pm and 4-9pm.) In the evenings, Dunmore citizens gather at the **Anchor** (tel. 383 133) to enjoy live music.

Swimming is good at Dunmore's **beaches,** especially at several points where trails descend to isolated coves below, offering more seclusion. Kittiwakes (small gulls) throng the coastline, building their nests in cliff faces unusually close to human habitation. On the cliffs of **Badger's Cove,** especially, you'll see hundreds of them. Less fowled cliffs are accessible by the dirt road past Dock Rd.; the waves crashing into the rocks here are mesmerizing. To leave shore, head to the docks, where the **Dunmore East Adventure Centre** (tel. 383 783) will teach you to **snorkel, surf, kayak, canoe,** and a variety of other activities. Bring a towel and swimsuit; they provide the equipment. Space fills quickly, so call ahead to reserve a spot. (July-Aug. ₤15 per half-day; Sept.-June ₤14.) **Mooring Marine** (tel. 383 647), next door, will rent you a boat or take you **diving** and **angling.** (Prices start at ₤15 per hr.)

TRAMORE

Trá Mór means "big beach" in Gaelic; those crazy Celts had an eye for the obvious. Tramore (stress on the second syllable) draws an enormous number of tourists to its smooth 3 mi. strand. In the summer, the beach and boardwalk bustle with bathers and music. Despite tacky amusements that can be found at seaside resorts the world over, Tramore retains its small-town character. The cliffs that rise above the beach offer great places to stay and amazing ocean views.

⊠ PRACTICAL INFORMATION. Tramore can be a maze to get around, since few streets keep their names for more than a block. The bus station is on **Waterford Rd.** (technically **Turkey Rd.**), a block from the intersection of **Strand St.** (which becomes **Main St.** and then **Summer Hill**) and **Gallwey's Hill** (which joins **Church Rd.** up the cliff). All sorts of buses connect Tramore to **Waterford,** 15 minutes away. **Bus Éireann** runs both local and express routes, stopping both at the station and at various other points around town (at least 1 per hr., ₤4). **Rapid Express Coaches** (tel. 872 142) also sends buses from the station every 2hr. The **tourist office** (tel. 381 572) moves all over town, and was last seen across the street from the bus station. (Open June-mid-Sept. M-Sa 9am-1pm and 2-6pm.) An **AIB** is around the corner on Strand St., and the **Bank of Ireland** lies farther up; both have **24hr. ATMs. Pedal Power Cycles,** on Market St. just off Main St. (tel. 381 252), **rents bikes,** but the town is so darn hilly that you'll want to head straight for the somewhat easier countryside. (₤10 per day, ₤50 per week; deposit required.) Tramore's **phone code** is a beachin' 051.

⊠ ACCOMMODATIONS. The Cliff, Church St. (tel. 381 363), owned by the YWCA, probably has the best view in Tramore. More a guest house than a hostel, the Cliff provides bed, breakfast, and, for a little extra, an evening meal. (Singles ₤13-18, doubles ₤40-48.) Tramore is bursting with B&Bs, with the cheapest along Waterford Rd. and the best along Church Rd. **Venezia,** Church Road Grove (tel. 381 412), sign posted off Church Rd., is immaculate and glossy, with top-notch beds. (Singles ₤18, doubles ₤36.) **Turret House,** Church Rd. (tel. 386 342), has huge rooms with huge windows, some with ocean views and bath (Singles ₤17-25 and up, doubles ₤36-40; ₤2 less per person without bath.) Turn sharply right at the top of Gallwey's Hill to find it. If you can live without the ocean view, **Church Villa,** Church Rd. (tel. 381 547) fills its windows with church spires and a cemetery. The rooms are small, clean, and cheap. (₤13, ₤15 with bath.) **Ard More House,** Doneraile Dr. (tel. 381 716), looks over rooftops and a pretty garden to the water. Head up Church Rd. and take your first left. (₤18-18.50 per person. Open Apr.-Sept.) Located 1½ mi. out Dungarvan Coast Rd., between the golf course and the Metal Man monument to shipwreck victims, the family-style **Newtown Caravan and Camping Park** (tel. 381 979) is the best of several nearby campsites. (Tents ₤3.50-10 per person, depending on the season and your method of transport. Showers 50p. Open Easter-Sept.)

⊠⊠ FOOD, PUBS, AND ENTERTAINMENT. Tourist traps line the beach and the amusement park; walk inland instead for regionally famous **Cunningham's Fish and Chips,** Main St. (Fish and chips ₤3.40. Open daily 5pm-midnight.) **The Sea Horse,** Strand St. (tel. 386 091), has great pub grub, fancy coffee, and a friendly atmosphere. (Entrees ₤5; food served noon-9pm.) **An Chistin** (tel. 391 416), newly opened on Main St., serves tasty sandwiches (₤2) and entrees (₤4-4.50) to carnivores and vegetarians alike. (Open daily 9:30am-7pm.) Further up Main St., **Londis** (tel. 381 217) just renovated its large grocery store. (Open daily 8am-10pm.) As for watering holes, locals love to be hip and abbreviate their faves. The three floors of **The Victoria House ("The Vic"),** Queens St. (tel. 390 338), get younger, louder, and more crowded as you descend. The younger crowd also packs **The Hibernian** or **"Hi B"** (tel. 386 396), at the intersection of Gallwey's Hill and Strand St. After the nightly live music at the bar ends, everyone hops to the Hi B disco next door, where chart music blasts for a packed floor. (Disco W-Su. £5 cover. Doors close at 1am.) Seeking tamer fun, most locals congregate in the plush environs of **O'Neill's** (tel. 381 088) on Summer Hill.

The promenade on the waterfront provides all sorts of entertainment, such as the **Splashworld** indoor water park, an assortment of white-knuckle rides and specialized pools. (Tel. 390 176. Open Mar.-Oct. daily 11am-8pm; Nov.-Feb. M-F noon-8pm, Sa-Su 11am-6pm. £5, students £3.25.) Just outside of town, the cliffs are undoubtedly more spectacular. Follow the red-figure icons along the **Doneraile Walk,** a path stemming off Church Rd. that leads to fabulous cliffs and sea views. About a mile out, you can dive and swim in **Guillamene Cove,** or spy from the cliff tops 80 ft. up. Ignore the "MEN ONLY" sign; a smaller one underneath explains that it's been "retained merely as a relic of the past."

WATERFORD

Huge metal silos and harbor cranes greet the first-time visitor to Waterford. Fortunately, behind this industrial facade lies a city with ten centuries of history. The grandson of the Viking Ivor the Boneless founded Vadrafjord around AD 914 to harbor his longships, making it the oldest city in Ireland. Long considered mere brutes, the Vikings have recently gained recognition as suave contributors to the development of this mercantile hub, along with the Angles and Normans that followed. Traces of the Viking settlement persist in Waterford's streets, despite the massive freighters that have since replaced the longships. Scores of pubs and shops make Waterford an indulgent break from touring the small towns that dot the rest of the county.

▐ TRANSPORTATION

Airport: Tel. 875 589. Served by **British Airways.** Follow The Quay, turn right at Reginald's Tower, then left at the sign. 20min. from town. No city buses head that way, so take a taxi if you aren't driving.

Trains: Plunkett Station, across the bridge from The Quay. For information, call M-F 9am-6pm (tel. 317 889; 24hr. recorded timetable tel. 876 243). Train station staffed M-Sa 9am-6pm, Su at departure times. JFK's ancestors grew up in Waterford, and the city is still well-connected. Trains chug to **Kilkenny** (40min.; M 5 per day, T-Sa 4 per day, Su 3 per day; £5), **Rosslare Harbour** (1hr., M-Sa 2 per day, £6), **Limerick** (2¼hr., M-Sa 2 per day, £10), and **Dublin** (2½hr.; M and F 5 per day, T-Sa 4 per day, Su 3 per day; £12, F £15).

Buses: Tel. 879 000. The station sits on the Quay, near the bridge. Office open M-Sa 8:15am-6pm. To **Kilkenny** (1hr.; M-Sa 2 per day, Su 1 per day; £5), **Rosslare Harbour** (1¼hr.; 4 per day, Su 3 per day; £8.80), **Limerick** (2½hr.; 4 per day, F 5 per day, Su 5 per day; £9.70), **Cork** (2½hr.; M-Sa 8 per day, Su 5 per day; £9), **Dublin** (2¾hr.; M-Sa 7 per day, Su 4 per day; £7), and **Galway** (4¾hr.; M-Sa 8per day, Su 5 per day; £13).

Local Transportation: City buses leave from the Clock Tower on The Quay. 75p for trips within the city, mostly around Cork Rd. The **City Imp** minibuses (70p) also cruise the town. Check the tourist office for details.

Bike Rental: Wright's Cycles, Henrietta St. (tel. 874 411), for Raleigh rentals. £10 per day, £40 per week; £50 deposit, £15 charge for one-way rental. Open T-Th 9:30am-6pm, F 9:30am-9pm, Sa 9:30am-5:30pm, except closed every day for lunch 1-2pm. Cheaper rentals at **Spokes,** 20 Patrick St. (tel. 841 800). £7 per day, £25 per week; deposit £40. Open M-Th 9am-6pm, F 9am-8:30pm, Sa 9am-5:30pm.

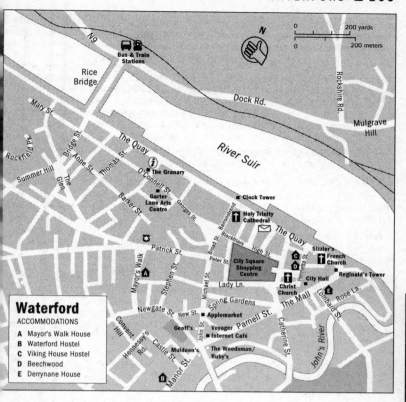

Waterford

ACCOMMODATIONS

A Mayor's Walk House
B Waterford Hostel
C Viking House Hostel
D Beechwood
E Derrynane House

Taxis: A piece of cake to find, 24hr. a day. Either go to the **cab stand** on Broad St., or think of a catchy name and dial it: **7 Cabs** (tel. 877 777); **Five-O Cabs** (tel. 850 000).

Car Rental: Enterprise (tel. 304 804) will rent to anyone 25 or older. £35 per day.

Hitching: The rare hitchers place themselves on the main routes, away from the tangled city center. To reach N24 (Cahir, Limerick), N10 (Kilkenny, Dublin), or N25 (New Ross, Wexford, Rosslare), they head over the bridge toward the train station. For the N25 to Cork, they continue down Parnell St.; others take a city bus out to the Waterford Crystal Factory before they stick out a thumb. *Let's Go* does not recommend hitching.

🛈 ORIENTATION AND PRACTICAL INFORMATION

Waterford is a mix of narrow Viking streets and broad English thoroughfares. The quays on the **River Suir** and **Barranstrand St.** (through its many name changes) form a crooked T-shaped city center.

Budget Travel: USIT, 36-37 Georges St. (tel. 872601; fax 871 723). Near the corner of Gladstone St., 1 block west of Barronstrand St. ISICs, **Travelsave** stamps, student deals for daily flights and bus/ferry packages from Waterford to London (see **Getting There,** p. 61). Open M-F 9:30am-5:30pm, Sa 11am-4pm.

Banks: 24hr. ATMs abound all along major roads. On the Quay, they're at **AIB** (tel. 876 607), by the clock tower; and the **Bank of Ireland** (tel. 872 074). Both are open M 10am-5pm, Tu-F 10am-4pm.

Luggage Storage: Plunkett Station. £1 per item. Open M-Sa 7:15am-9pm.

Laundry: Duds'n Suds, Parnell St. (tel. 841 168). Self wash and dry £3.50 per load. Service available. Open M-Sa 7:30am-9pm.

Emergency: Dial 999; no coins required. **Garda:** Patrick St. (tel. 874 888).

Counseling and Support: Samaritans, 16 Beau St. (tel. 872 114). 24hr. listening service. **Rape Crisis Centre** (tel. 873 362). Call M-F 9-11:30am, plus T 2-4pm and Th 8:30-10pm. **Youth Information Centre:** 130 The Quay (tel. 877 328; email wyic@io.ie). Information on work, travel, health, and on a variety of support groups (including gay and lesbian support groups). Photocopy, fax service, and internet access. Open to all, M-F 9:30am-5:30pm.

Hospital: Waterford Regional Hospital (tel. 873 321). Follow The Quay east to the Tower Hotel; turn left, then follow signs straight ahead to the hospital.

Pharmacy: The Broad St. Pharmacy (tel. 878 103). Open M-Sa 8:30am-10pm, Su 10am-7pm.

Post Office: The Quay (tel. 874 321), the largest of several. Open M and W-F 9am-5:30pm, T 9:30am-5:30pm, Sa 9am-1pm.

Internet Access: Voyager Internet Cafe, Parnell Court, Parnell St. (tel. 843 843). At the intersection of Parnell and John St., in a shopping center. No food, no drink, just computers. £1.50 per 15min. Open M-W 8:30am-12:15am, Th-Su 8:30am-3:30am.

PHONE CODE	Alpha Romeos stop for Agent 051.

ACCOMMODATIONS

Most B&Bs in the city are nothing special; those outside town on the Cork Rd. are better; the hostels are best of all.

Barnacle's Viking House (IHH), Coffee House Ln., Greyfriars, The Quay (tel. 853 827; email viking@barnacles.iol.ie). Follow The Quay east past the Clock Tower and post office; the hostel is the mango-colored building on the right, tucked behind other buildings. Spacious quarters; even 12-bed dorms can feel private. Large comfy common room, top-notch security, and a small breakfast to top it off. Dorms £7.50-8.50; double with bath £13.50-15.50; plenty of options in between. Laundry service £4 per load. Luggage storage 50p per day. Lounge and kitchen accessible 6am-midnight. Wheelchair accessible.

Waterford Hostel (IHO), 70 Manor St. (tel. 850 163). From the Quay, walk down John St. and turn right onto Manor St. The hostel is on your right before the traffic lights. Clean and comfortable. Real bathrooms (not stalls) make up for the small lounge and kitchen. Key deposit £2. Dorms Su-Th £9, F-Sa £10.

Mayor's Walk House, 12 Mayor's Walk (tel. 855 427). A 15min. prestigious walk from the train station. Quiet rooms at a simple price. The Ryders offer advice, biscuits, and a bottomless pot of tea. Singles £16, doubles £30; with continental breakfast only £13.50. Open Feb.-Nov.

Beechwood, 7 Cathedral Sq. (tel. 876 677). From the Quay, go up Henrietta St. Mrs. Ryan invites you into her charming home, located on a silent pedestrian street. Look out the window at Christ Church Cathedral. Singles £19; doubles £32.

FOOD

Despite an overwhelming presence of fast food chains, Waterford has some bonafide restaurants with fair prices. You might want to try Waterford's contribution to Irish cuisine, the *blaa* ("blah"), a floury white sausage roll of Huguenot origins. Besides the *blaa*, Waterford gave the world the modern process of bacon curing. To satisfy your pork cravings (and pick up some cheap groceries while you're at it), visit **Dunnes Stores** (tel. 853 100) in the City Square Mall. (Open M-W 9am-7pm, Th-F 9am-9pm, Sa 9am-6pm, and Su noon-6pm.) **Treacy's,** on The Quay near the Granville Hotel, has a large selection for a late-night grocery, and even a small deli. (Open daily 9am-11pm.)

Gino's, John St. (tel. 879 513), at the Apple Market. A busy family restaurant serves pizza made right before your eyes. Reservations recommended on F-Sa nights, or call in an order to go. Individual pizza £2.50 plus 55p per topping. Open daily till 10:45pm (for seating) or 11pm (for take-out).

Cafe Luna, 53 John St. (tel. 843 539), offers cheap food with a trendy touch. Open M-W until 12:15am, Th-Su until 3:30am.

Haricot's Wholefood Restaurant, 11 O'Connell St. (tel. 841 299). Vegetarians and the carnivores live in harmony with Haricot's tasty, innovative dishes; if the harmony doesn't incite conversation, they can reach for the stack of newspapers. Most entrees £5-7. Open M-F 9:30am-8pm, Sa 9:30am-6pm.

Sizzlers, on The Quay toward Reginald's Tower (tel. 852 100). Always open, always popular. The best greasy spoon you can find (entrees £2-6), but no salad bar.

The Pantry, 61 The Quay (tel. 871 142). Hidden right next to the Granville Hotel. Home fare served in a friendly, casual atmosphere. Sandwiches under £5. Open M-Sa 8:30am-5:30pm.

The Reginald, 2-3 The Mall (tel. 855 087). A faux castle facade nestled behind the real Reginald's Tower. This bar, restaurant, and "Knight Club" serves rich, delicious food in a classy environment. Dinner's expensive, but lunch is reasonable. Carvery lunch daily noon-3pm, bar menu 3-7:30pm, dinner 6-10:30pm.

Bewley's (tel. 870 506), at the intersection of Broad and Patrick St. A national chain, or rather institution, their food is savory and their coffee topped with frothing milk. Open M-Th and Sa 7:30am-5:30pm, F 7:30am-6:30pm.

▥ PUBS AND CLUBS

The Quays are loaded with pubs; even more reside on John St. A number run discos on weekend nights, so there's always somewhere open late.

T&H Doolan's, George's St. (tel. 841 504). In a fantastic building, Doolan's has been serving crowds for 300 years now. Especially popular with out-of-towners. Trad nightly. Open until 11:30pm, Su 11.

Geoff's, 9 John St. (tel. 874 787). Most locals will tell you that Geoff's is the place to see and be seen. Bring a cell phone to chat on around the table, while slurping your pint and laughing a bit too loudly.

Muldoon's, John St. (tel. 873 693). Starts humming when the other places close. Although it has a generic sports bar feel and a loud crowd of older 20- and 30-somethings, the late hours (last call 1:30am) and free snacks (after 11:30) provide incentive to stop by. There's no room for a dance floor, but no one seems to notice.

The Woodman, at Parnell and John St. (tel. 858 130). Late bar hours on M and W keep the downstairs busy with a mixture of drinkers. Ruby's Nightclub spins a variety of music and opens both floors for people to mill around on Tu and Th-Su nights.

Mullane's, 15 Newgate St. (tel. 873 854), off New St. It's necessary to go a bit out of your way to come across sessions this hard core. A sprinkling of the young, a dash of tourists, and older regulars result in the perfect mix. Call ahead for session times; the pub is almost empty when there isn't one.

Granville Hotel Bar, The Quay (tel. 305 555). Slip inside Waterford's four-star hotel and treat yourself to the plush environs of its bar. A mellow place to chat and pretend you're not staying in a hostel—and it's not as though the Guinness costs more.

SIGHTS

You can cover all of Waterford's sights in a day, but only if you move quickly. The **Waterford Crystal Factory,** 1 mi. out on N25 (Cork Rd.), is the city's gem of sorts. Witness master craftsmen transform molten goo into sparkling crystal—an impressive process to say the least. Admire the finished products, and their astronomical prices, in the gallery. (Tel. 373 311 or 332 500. 1hr. tours every 15min., audio-visual shows on demand. Apr.-Oct. tours daily 8:30am-4pm, showroom open 8:30am-6pm; Nov.-Mar. tours daily 9am-3:15pm, showroom open 9am-5pm; Jan.-Feb. showroom only, open 9am-5pm. Tours £3.50, students £2. Wheelchair accessible.) City bus #1 (Kilbarry-Ballybeg) leaves across from the Clock Tower every 30 min. and passes the factory (75p), or catch the City Imp (a red-and-yellow minibus) along Parnell St. and request a stop at the factory (70p, runs every 15-20min.).

In the same building as the tourist office, the exhibit of **Waterford Treasures at the Granary** recently replaced the old heritage center. Thanks to a little help from the EU, this £4.5 million project lets you go at your own pace through a sleek presentation of the city's history. The artifacts, such as the town's written charters, make quite an impressive show; the glitzier exhibits, like the Viking boat simulation with mechanically rocking seats, are worth skipping. (Tel. 304 500; email mail@waterfordtreasures.com; www.waterfordtreasures.com. Open daily June-Aug. 9:30am-9pm, Sept.-May 10am-5pm. £3, students and seniors £2.50.)

Most of Waterford's historical structures have been converted into retail space. Because the town has hardly expanded outward since 1790, buildings of several eras—Viking, Victorian, and modern—are piled on top of each other. One excellent way to sort things out is the **Walking Tour of Historic Waterford** (tel. 873 711 or 851 043). These one-hour tours depart from the Granville Hotel on the Quay and provide a thorough introduction to Waterford's mongrel history. (Mar.-Oct. daily at noon and 2pm. £3.) The tour also hits a number of the city's big sights, some of which are worth further investigation. **Reginald's Tower,** at the end of The Quay, has guarded the entrance to the city since the 12th century. (Tel. 304 220. Tours on demand. Open daily 10am-6pm, last tour 5:15pm. £1.50, seniors £1, students 60p.) Its virtually impenetrable 10 ft. thick Viking walls have housed a prison, a mint, and the wedding reception of Strongbow and Aoife (see **Early Christians and Vikings,** p. 7). You can see remnants of the old **city walls,** both Viking and medieval, surrounding the city center. The biggest blocks are behind the Theatre Royal on Spring Garden and Patrick St., extending to Bachelor's Walk.

Many of Waterford's more recent monumental buildings were the brainchildren of 18th century architect John Roberts. The **Theatre Royal** and **City Hall,** both on The Mall, are his secular masterpieces. He also designed both the Roman Catholic **Holy Trinity Cathedral** on Barronstrand St., and the Church of Ireland **Christ Church Cathedral** in Cathedral Square (up Henrietta St. from the Quay), making Waterford the only European city to have Catholics and Protestants worship in buildings united by a common architect. Christ Church Cathedral has the rather gruesome cadaver-motif tomb of Bishop Rice, complete with vermin chewing on his corpse.

🎵 **ENTERTAINMENT**

The tourist office can provide an annual list of major events in town, and any of the local newspapers, including the free *Waterford Today,* should have more specific entertainment listings. Keep your eyes peeled for posters as well. The **Waterford Show** (tel. 358 397 or 875 788; mobile (087) 681 7191) at City Hall is an entertaining performance of Irish music, stories, and dance. A ticket costs £7, but that also gets you glasses of Baileys or wine. (May-Sept. Tu, Th, and Sa at 9pm. July-Aug. also W at 9 pm. Safest to call for reservations or make them at the tourist office.) The **Garter Lane Arts Centre**, 22a O'Connell St. (tel. 855 038), supports all different forms of art in its old Georgian building. Visual exhibits constantly grace the walls and are usually free; musical concerts cost £10 at most; and dance and theater grace its stage year round. (Box office open M-Sa 10am-6pm and until 9pm on performance nights. Student and senior prices available.) Waterford's largest festival is the **Spraoi** (SPREE; tel. 841 808; spraoi@voyager.ie), on the early August bank holiday weekend. A celebration of life in general, the Spraoi attracts bands from around the globe and culminates in a sizeable parade.

DUNGARVAN

Filled with fishermen and market-goers, Dungarvan is more endearing than most transportation hubs. There isn't too much to see, but ocean winds and a vibrant pub scene make the town a pleasant stop-over for travelers on the south coast.

🛈 ORIENTATION AND PRACTICAL INFORMATION. Main St., also called **O'Connell St.**, runs through the central square; **Emmet St.**, or **Mitchell St.**, runs parallel to Main St. one block uphill and is home to the hostel and a number of B&Bs. The road to Cork veers off Emmet St. at the Garda station. **Buses** (tel. (051) 79000) run from Davitt's Quay east to **Waterford** (1hr., daily 11 per day, £5), west to **Cork** (M-Sa 7 per day, Su 5 per day; £7), and north to **Lismore** (daily, usually in the evening). From **Waterford** buses run through to **Dublin** and **Rosslare**. The helpful **tourist office** (tel. 41741) on The Square dispenses free maps and keeps music listings for area pubs. (Open June-Aug. M-Sa 9am-9pm, Su 9am-6pm; Sept.-May M-Sa 9am-6pm.) The best villages in West Waterford are inaccessible by bus; bike rental is available at **O'Mahoney's Cycles**, (tel. 43346), across the bridge and past the traffic lights in Abbeyside, a 10min. walk from The Square. (£5 per day. Call ahead.) **Bank of Ireland**, The Square, has a **24hr. ATM** that accepts all major cash networks, as does **AIB**, just steps away on Meagher St. (Both open M 10am-5pm, Tu-F 10am-4pm.) The **post office** (tel. 41210) sits on Bridge St., just outside The Square. (Open M-F 9am-5:30pm, Sa 9am-3pm.) The southern-styled **phone code** is 058.

🛉🍴🍺 ACCOMMODATIONS, FOOD, AND PUBS. The **Dungarvan Holiday Hostel (IHH)**, Youghal Rd. (tel. 44340), just off Emmet St., opposite the Garda Station, is housed in a former Christian Brothers Friary, and still hasn't shaken off the cold monastic feel. (8- to 10-bed dorms £7.50, private rooms £8.50 per person. **Bike rental** £6 per day. Wheelchair accessible.) On Mitchell St. across from St. Mary's Church, **Santa Antoni** (tel. 42923), and its gregarious owner offer bright rooms. (Singles £13, doubles £12 per person; £2-3 less without breakfast.) Two doors down the road, **Amron** (tel. 43337) nearly bursts with the energetic hospitality of its proprietress, who lets small but pleasant doubles and twins (£15, £16 with bath), and fluffy beds in the skylit loft (£10-12).

The immense **Supervalu** (tel. 92150) is on Main St. (Open M-W 9am-7pm, Th and Sa 9am-8pm, F 9am-9pm, Su 10am-6pm.) Laid-back **Ormond's Cafe**, The Square (tel. 41153), a few doors down from the tourist office, serves outstanding desserts, and meals to precede them, in its stone-walled, skylit cafe. (Sandwiches £2-3, hot meals £4-5. Open M-Sa 8am-6pm.) Settle into bizarre wood furniture for finely prepared meals, desserts, and coffee at **Interlude** (tel. 45898) in Davitt's Quay next to the castle. (Most meals £4.95-7.95. Open Tu-W 10:30am-9pm, Th-Sa 10:30am-9:30pm, Su 10:30am-7:30pm.)

The *Events and Activities Guide*, available free at the tourist office, has a pub music directory. The **Gows**, 13 Main St. (tel. 41149), is probably the best pub in town, even though their sign is upside-down. (Trad 4-5 nights a week.) **Davitt's Pub**, Davitt's Quay (tel. 44900), is huge and usually packed. (Disco Th-Su 11:30pm-2:15am. Cover £5. Occasional live acts.) **The Lady Belle** (tel. 44222) on The Square, has peerless maritime decor and 2-3 nights of trad a week. The regulars at **The Enterprise** (tel. 41327), across The Square, sometimes work themselves into a trad frenzy. In true seaside form, Dungarvan has an **Anchor Bar** (tel. 41249), on Davitt's Quay, where rock and trad bands perform on weekends. Small but sprightly **Bridie Dee's,** 18 Mary St. (tel. 44588), has trad from Thursday to Sunday night.

■ **SIGHTS.** The tourist office offers **walking tours** of medieval and Georgian Dungarvan. (1hr., £1.50.) They also arrange 2hr. bus tours of town (£3), and give out free Tourist Trail maps, highlighting Dungarvan's seven or eight sights. **King John's Castle,** presiding over Davitt's Quay, fell into disrepair at the beginning of the 14th century. The IRA didn't help matters much when they set the place on fire in 1922. It's not open to the public, but the Office of Public Works has its hands on it, so it's bound to end up a heritage center some day.

There's not much else to see in Dungarvan itself, but the deep-sea **fishing** is excellent. The nearby waters have a reputation for sharks. Capt. John Tynan leads expeditions on "The Avoca." (£30 with rod and tackle; inquire at The Enterprise, tel. 24657.) The "Chaser V" can also be chartered at a similar price (tel. 41358). **Baumann's Jewellers,** 6 St. Mary St. (tel. 41395), dispenses tackle, licenses, and a wealth of inside information.

Dungarvan is home to several annual festivals. **Féile na nDéise** packs the Square with free concerts during the first weekend in May. The **Motorsport Weekend** pulls in vintage and race car enthusiasts in mid-July.

ARDMORE

Devotees of beaches and St. Declan flock to Ardmore in equal measure. The monk christianized the town in the 4th century; ruins back the town's claim to be the oldest Christian settlement in Ireland. Pilgrims come to town on July 24 for the Feast of St. Declan, but droves of more casual tourists bask in the mild waters off the sandy beach and jagged cliffs throughout the summer.

■ **PRACTICAL INFORMATION. Buses** run to **Cork** (1½hr.; M-Sa 3 per day, July-Aug. M-Sa 5 per day, Su 3 per day; £7.30), and **Waterford** via **Dungarvan** (2hr.; July-Aug. M-Th 2 per day, F 4 per day; Sept.-June F 1 per day, Sa 2 per day; £7.70). The **tourist office** (tel. 94444), in the carpark by the beach, is housed in what appears to be a demonic sandcastle. The office dispenses information about the local beaches as well as an excellent leaflet outlining a **walking tour** of town. (Open daily June-Aug. 11am-1pm and 2-5pm.) Ardmore is a 3 mi. detour off Cork-Waterford Rd. (N25). **Hitching** from the junction can be slow, and is not recommended by *Let's Go.* God's gift to the **phone code** is 024.

■ **ACCOMMODATIONS, FOOD, AND PUBS.** A hop, skip, and a jump away from the beach are the simple comforts of the **Ardmore Beach Hostel,** Main St. (tel. 94501), including back-patio beach access. (Dorms June-Aug. £8, Sept.-May £7; private rooms £12.50 per person. Sheets £1.) **Byron Lodge,** Middle Rd. (tel. 94157), has literary aspirations and rooms with sunny alcoves. From Main St., take the street that runs uphill between the town's two thatched cottages. Georgian items vie with more recent additions for furnishing supremacy. (Singles with bath £21. Doubles £16 per person, £18 with bath. Open Easter-Sept.) Beach-front **camping** at **Healy's** (tel. 94181) usually requires a reservation months ahead, but there are rumors that a new campsite is on its way (call the tourist office).

Ardmore's food offerings are not extensive but tasty nonetheless. **Quinn's Foodstore** (tel. 94250), is in the town center. (Open daily 8am-9pm.) The local favorite is **Cup and Saucer,** Main St. (tel. 94501), which has a delightful flower garden out back for sunny days. (Open daily 10am-8pm.) Vast **Paddy Mac's,** Main St. (tel. 94166), has pub grub on reserve, and a variety of music near-nightly. **Keever's Bar,** Main St. (tel. 94141), is another favorite of the older Ardmore crowd.

SIGHTS. The all-encompassing must-do in Ardmore is the **cliffwalk,** a windy 3 mi. path with great views of the ocean and stops at all of Ardmore's historic sites. The free map and guide pamphlet are available at the tourist office and the hostel. At one end of the walk is the **cathedral,** built piecemeal between 800 and 1400, on the site of St. Declan's monastery. He is said to be buried here, and the faithful avow that soil from the saint's grave cures diseases. The cathedral houses 2 ogham stones in addition to its own carvings. The cathedral and its graveyard are marked by a 97 ft. high **round tower,** whose door is a monk-protecting 12 ft. above the ground. **St. Declan's Stone** is perched at the water's edge, on the right from Main St. along the shore. The stone allegedly floated from Wales after the saint's visit there. Devotees sometimes wedge themselves underneath the stone on "Pattern Day," the saint's feast. Down past the Cliff House hotel at the other end of the cliffwalk is **St. Declan's Well,** which contains water that is said to cure all afflictions. Despite an abundance of old Coast Guard stations on the cliff, the shore has seen the end of many vessels. Ardmore is one end of the 56 mi. **St. Declan's Way,** which runs up to Cahir in Co. Tipperary.

SOUTHWEST IRELAND

With it's natural drama and beauty, it's not surprising that Southwest Ireland has produced some of the country's greatest storytellers. The astonishing landscape, from ocean-battered cliffs to mystic stretches of lakes and mountains are matched by a momentous history. Outlaws and rebels once lurked in hidden coves and glens now frequented by visitors and ruled over by publicans. The grand architecture of Cork City (pop. 150,00) tells of the areas gradual growth and constant rebuilding. A day's drive away, rural villages move to an ancient rhythm. There are good reasons why tourist buses chug to majestic Killarney and the Ring of Kerry. Nowhere in Ireland has signs in as many languages as Killarney, all of them screaming "buy me." Indeed, the land in west Cork is steadily being bought by investors and the occasional movie star. If the tourist mayhem is too much for you, it's easy to retreat to the more quiet stretches along the Dingle Peninsula and Cork's southern coast.

HIGHLIGHTS OF SOUTHWEST IRELAND

■ Run the **Ring of Kerry** circuit (p. 256), taking in exquisite mountains, lakes, and forests in **Killarney National Park** (p. 253). Trek out to the tip of the peninsula and catch a boat to **Valentia Island** (p. 259) and the **Skellig Rocks** (p. 260).

■ Wave at Fungi the Dolphin from the beach at **Dingle** (p. 264), then explore the coastline of this Irish-speaking peninsula by bike.

■ Forsake civilization and embrace the wild on a hike through the Miskish Mountains of the **Beara Peninsula** (p. 239).

■ Check out a hurling game at the Blackrock stadium and then head to one of **Cork's** (p. 212) pubs to discuss the results.

COUNTY CORK

Historically, eastern Cork's superb harbors made it a prosperous trading center. Its distance from Dublin and the Pale gave the English less leverage over it. Perhaps as a result, Cork was a center of patriotic activity during the 19th and early 20th centuries. Headquarters of the "Munster Republic" controlled by the anti-Treaty forces during the Civil War, the county produced patriot Michael Collins, as well as the man who assassinated him in 1922 (see **Independence and Civil War,** p. 14). The energies of today's Cork City are directed toward industry and culture, while the sea towns of Kinsale and Cobh gaily entertain tall ships and stooped backpackers. West Cork, the southwestern third of the county, was once the "badlands" of Ireland; its ruggedness and isolation rendered it lawless and largely uninhabitable. Ex-hippies and antiquated fishermen have replaced the outlaws; they do their best to make the villages ultra-hospitable to tourists. Roaringwater Bay and wave-whipped Mizen Head mark Ireland's land's end. The lonely beauty here is a stately solitude unmarred by the Kelly-green shamrocks planted prominently in other parts of Ireland. Ireland's rich archaeological history is particularly visible in Cork. Celtic ring forts, mysterious stone circles, and long-ruined abbeys dot the sheep-speckled hills.

The **Wheel Escapes** program provides an excellent way to traverse the wilds of West Cork while burning off that extra pint. You can rent a bike at any of the hostels listed below and drop it off at any other hostel on the list. (£7 per day, £35 per

Southwest Ireland

SOUTHWEST IRELAND

N

20 miles

20 kilometers

0

0

TIPPERARY

Templemore

N62

N73

N8

Thurles

Cashel

N62

N74

Cahir

Tipperary

N24

N8

Comeragh Mts.

Monavullagh Mts.

Clonmel

Carrick-on-Suir

N76

Knockmealdown Mts.

Galty Mts.

WATERFORD

Dungarvan

N72

Dungarvan Harbour

N25

Youghal

Youghal Bay

Knockadoon Head

LIMERICK

Limerick

Shannon Airport

N19

N18

N69

N21

Newcastle West

N20

N24

Mitchelstown

N73

Fermoy

N72

N8

M U N S T E R

River Shannon

Mouth of the Shannon

Tarbert

N69

Listowel

Castleisland

N21

N20

C O R K

Kanturk

N72

Rathmore

Mallow

N20

Blarney

Ballincollig

Cork

Cork Harbour

Midleton

N25

Fota

Cobh

Great Island

Power Head

Kinsale

Kinsale Harbour

Old Head of Kinsale

▲ Musheramore

Boggeragh Mts.

Macroom

River Lee

N22

Bandon

N71

Courtmacsherry Bay

Glanaruddery Mts.

Tralee

N21

N23

N22

Killarney

Killorglin

K E R R Y

IVERAGH PENINSULA

Crohane Mt. ▲

Mangerton Mt. ▲

Macgillycuddy's Reeks

Killarney National Park

Dartmoygart **Mts.**

Slieve Mish Mts.

Caherconree Mt. ▲

Ballyvourney

Ballingeary

Shehy Mts.

Dunmanway

R586

Leap

Clonakilty

Rosscarbery

Timoleague

Glandore

Unionhall

Clonakilty Bay

Galley Head

Seven Heads

Dingle Bay

Killorglin

N70

Cahersiveen

Waterville

Caherdaniel

Kenmare River

Sneem

N70

Kenmare

N71

Glengarriff

Caha Mts.

Eyeries

Allihies

Castletownbere

Bantry Bay

Bantry

N71

Glengarriff

Schull

Skibbereen

Baltimore

Castletownshend

Toe Head

Sheep's Head

Dunmanus Bay

Mizen Head

Goleen

Crookhaven

Cape Clear Island

Sherkin Island

Dursey Head

Dursey Island

Bere Island

Bull's Head

Cod's Head

Lamb's Head

Dingle Peninsula

Dingle Bay

Brandon Head

▲ Brandon Mt.

Stradbally Mt.

Cloghane

Stradbally

Dingle

Ventry

DINGLE PENINSULA

N86

Castlegregory

Tralee

Tralee Bay

Rough Point

Kerry Head

Ardfert

Ballydavid Head

Ballyquin

Sybil Head

Ballyferriter

Dunquin

Slea Head

Doulus Head

Great Blasket I.

Valencia Island

Bray Head

Bolus Head

Skellig Michael

Hog's Head

ATLANTIC OCEAN

week, helmet, lock, tool bag, and panniers included.) For more info, call one of the following participating hostels: Maria's Schoolhouse, Union Hall; Russagh Mill Hostel and Adventure Center, Skibbereen; Rolf's Hostel, Baltimore; Schull Backpacker's Lodge, Schull; Bantry Independent Hostel, Bantry; Shiplake Mountain Hostel, Dunmanway; and Murphy's Village Hostel.

CORK

As Ireland's second-largest city, Cork (pop. 150,000) is the center of the southwest's sports, music, and arts. Strolls along the pub-lined streets and river quays reveal grand and grimy architecture, as well as more recent commercial and industrial development, evidence of Cork's history of ruin and reconstruction. Indeed, what older charms industry has not blackened, the English have blighted. The old city burned down in 1622, Cromwell expelled half its citizens in the 1640s, the English Duke of Marlborough laid siege to Cork in 1690, and the city was torched again in 1920 during the Irish War of Independence. Wise visitors will more politely exploit the city's resources and use Cork as a place to eat, drink, shop, and sleep while exploring the exquisite scenery of the surrounding countryside. Within the city limits, time is best filled by taking in the vibrant street scene, or meandering across the pastoral campus of University College of Cork.

✦ ORIENTATION

Downtown Cork is the tip of an arrow-shaped island in the **River Lee.** Many central north-south streets were once Venice-style canals, but in the 1700s, Cork discovered pavement. The river still runs through the present-day city, with the center lying on the island, the southern side filled with quiet avenues, and the north side dominated by the sight-filled **Shandon** district. Downtown action concentrates on **Oliver Plunkett St., Saint Patrick St., Paul St.,** and the north-south streets that connect them. Heading west from the Grand Parade, **Washington St.** becomes **Western Rd.** and then the N22 to Killarney; to the north of the Lee, **MacCurtain St.** flows east into **Lower Glanmire Rd.,** which becomes N8 and N25. Cork is compact and pedestrian-friendly. City buses criss-cross the city and its suburbs. From downtown, catch the buses (and their schedules) at the bus station on **Merchant's Quay** or on St. Patrick St., across from the Father Matthew statue.

▣ TRANSPORTATION

Airport: Cork Airport (tel. 313 131), 5 mi. south of Cork on Kinsale Rd. **Aer Lingus** (tel. 327 155), **British Airways** (tel. (800) 626 747), and **Ryanair** (tel. (061) 097 800) connect Cork to Dublin, various English cities, and Paris. A taxi (£7-8) or bus (16-18 per day, £2.50) will deliver you from the airport to the bus station on Parnell Place.

Trains: Kent Station, Lower Glanmire Rd. (tel. 506 766), across the river from the city center in the northeast part of town. Open M-Sa 7am-8:30pm, Su 7am-8pm. Train connections to **Limerick** (1½hr., M-Sa 5 per day, Su 4 per day, £15.50), **Killarney** (2hr., M-Sa 6 per day, Su 4 per day, £15.50), and **Tralee** (2½hr., M-Sa 6 per day, Su 4 per day, £15.50), and **Dublin** (3hr., M-Sa 11 per day, Su 6 per day, £32). Best prices with advance booking.

Buses: Parnell Pl. (tel. 508 188), 2 blocks east of Patrick's Bridge on Merchants' Quay. Inquiries desk open Oct.-Apr. M-Sa 9am-6pm, Su 12-6pm; May-Sept. daily 9am-6pm. Bus Éireann goes to all major cities: **Bantry** (2hr., M-Sa 3 per day, Su 2 per day, £8.80), **Killarney** (2hr., M-Sa 7 per day, Su 5 per day, £8.80), **Limerick** (2hr., M-Sa 6 per day, Su 5 per day, £9), **Rosslare Harbour** (4hr., M-Sa 3 per day, Su 2 per day, £13), **Tralee** (2½hr., M-Sa 7 per day, Su 5 per day, £9.70), **Waterford** (2¼hr., M-Sa 8 per day, Sun 6 per day, £9), **Galway** (4hr., M-Sa 5 per day, Su 4 per day, £12), **Dublin** (4½hr., M-Sa 4 per day, Su 3 per day, £12), **Sligo** (7hr., 3 per day, £16), **Belfast** (7½hr., M-Sa 3 per day, Su 2 per day, £17), and **Donegal Town** (9hr., 1 per day, £17).

Ferries: Ringaskiddy Terminal (tel. 275 061), 8mi. south of the city, shoves one ferry off for Swansen, England daily (£44-64, prices increase June-Aug.). For 24hr. ferry information, call (01) 661 0715; tickets can be bought on Bridge St. at the **Irish Ferries** office (tel. 551 995; open M-F 9am-5pm, Sa 9:15am-12:45pm). The terminal is a 30min. bus ride from the bus station in Cork (£3). See **By Ferry,** p. 66.

Local Transportation: Downtown **buses** run every 10 to 30min. from about 7:30am-11:15pm M-Sa, with reduced service on Su from 10am-11:15pm. Fares from 70p. The main bus station at Parnell Pl. offers free timetables (tel. 508 188).

Car Rental: Great Island Car Rentals, 47 MacCurtain St. (tel. 503 536). £40 per day, £115 for 3 days, £160 per week for subcompact standard. Min. age 23. **Budget Rent-a-Car,** Tourist Office, Grand Parade (tel. 274 755). £33 per day, £90 for 3 days, £165 per week. Min. age 23.

Bike Rental: The Bike Shop, 68 Shandon St. (tel. 304 144) rents bikes for £7 per day, £30 per week. The Raleigh Rent-a-Bike program at **Cycle Scene,** 396 Blarney St. (tel. 301 183) rents bikes that can be returned at the other Raleigh locations across Ireland. £10 per day, £40 per week. £50 deposit.

Hitching: Hitchhikers headed for West Cork and County Kerry walk down Western Rd. past both the An Óige hostel and the dog track to the Crow's Nest Pub, or take bus #8. Those hoping to hitch a ride to Dublin or Waterford should stand on the hill next to the train station on the Lower Glanmire Rd. *Let's Go* does not recommend hitching as a safe means of transportation.

◪ PRACTICAL INFORMATION

TOURIST AND FINANCIAL SERVICES

Tourist Office: Tourist House, Grand Parade (tel. 273 251), near the corner of South Mall and Grand Parade downtown across from the National Monument, offers a Cork city guide and map (£1.50), booking, car rentals, and advice. Open June M-Sa 9am-6pm; July-Aug. M-Sa 9am-7pm, Su 10am-5pm; Sept.-May M-Sa 9:30am-5pm.

Budget Travel Office: USIT, 10 Market Parade (tel. 270 900), in the Arcade off Patrick St. This large, helpful travel office sells **TravelSave** stamps, Rambler tickets, and Eurotrain tickets. Open M-F 9:30am-5:30pm, Sa 10am-2pm. A second office (tel. 273 901) is at University College across from Boole Library. Open M-F 9:30am-5:30pm. **SAYIT,** Grand Parade (tel. 279 188) specializes in similar offerings.

Banks: TSB, 4-5 Princes St. (tel. 275 221). Open M-W and F 9:30am-5pm, Th 9:30am-7pm. **Bank of Ireland,** 70 Patrick St. (tel. 277 177). Open M 10am-5pm, Tu-F 10am-4pm. Most banks in Cork have **24hr. ATMs.**

LOCAL SERVICES

Luggage Storage: Lockers £1 at the **train station.** Storage at the **bus station** £1.30 per item, 80p each additional day. Open M-F 8:35am-6:15pm, Sa 9:30am-6:15pm.

Bookstores: Waterstone's, 69 Patrick St. (tel. 276 522). Monstrously huge. Open M-Th 9am-8pm, F 9am-9pm, Sa 9am-7pm, Su noon-7pm. **Mercier Bookstore,** 18 Academy St. (tel. 275 040), off Patrick St. Specializes in Irish interest books. Open M-F 9:30am-6pm, Sa 9:30am-5:30pm. **Cork Bookshop,** Carey Lane (tel. 271 346). Easily browsable selection. Open M-F 9am-6pm.

Camping Supplies: Outside World and the Tent Shop, Parnell Pl. (tel. 278 833), next to the bus station. 2-person nylon tent £17 per week; deposit £10. Extensive stock of camping supplies, including boots and clothing. Open M-Sa 9:30am-6pm. Backpacks and other gear are available for purchase, along with free advice, at **Hillwalking** (tel. 271 643), also next to the bus station. Open M-Sa 9am-5:30pm.

Bisexual, Gay, and Lesbian Information: The Other Place, 8 South Main St. (tel. 278 470), is a resource center for gay and lesbian concerns in Cork; it hosts a gay coffeehouse (open M-Sa 10am-6pm), as well as a gay bar (see **Clubs**). **The Other Side Bookshop** (tel. 278 470), upstairs, sells new and used gay and lesbian publications. Open

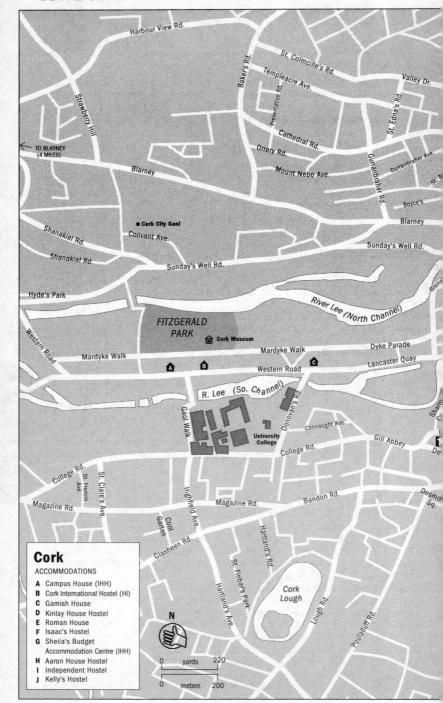

Cork

ACCOMMODATIONS

A Campus House (IHH)
B Cork International Hostel (HI)
C Gamish House
D Kinlay House Hostel
E Roman House
F Isaac's Hostel
G Sheila's Budget
  Accommodation Centre (IHH)
H Aaron House Hostel
I Independent Hostel
J Kelly's Hostel

N

0   yards   220
0   meters   200

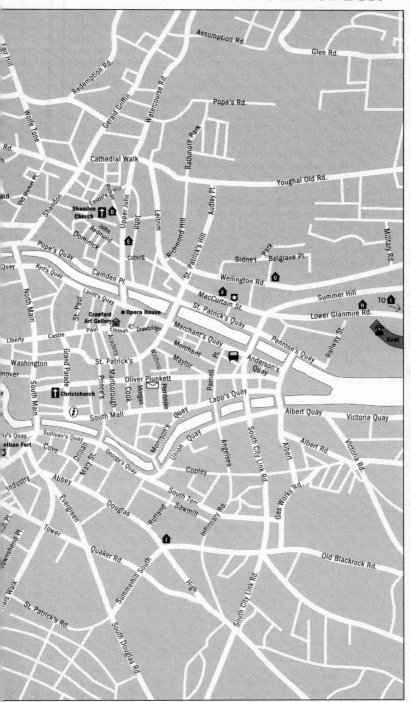

M-Sa 10am-5:30pm. **Gay Information Cork** (tel. 271 087) offers a telephone help-line W 7-9pm and Sa 3-5pm. Lesbian line Th 8-10pm. The second weekend of May is **Cork Women's Fun** weekend. Contact The Other Place for info.

Laundry: Duds 'n Suds, Douglas St. (tel. 314 799), around the corner from Kelly's Hostel. Provides dry-cleaning services, TV, and even a small snack bar. Wash £1.50, dry £1.80. Open M-F 8am-9pm, Sa 8am-8pm. **Clifton Launderette,** Western Rd. (tel. 251 886), by the University. Large load, full service £5.20. Open M and F 9:30am-8pm, Tu-Th and Sa 9:30am-6:30pm.

EMERGENCY AND COMMUNICATIONS

Emergency: Dial 999; no coins required. **Garda:** Anglesea St. (tel. 522 000).

Crisis and Support: Rape Crisis Centre, 5 Camden Pl. (tel. (800) 496 496). 24hr. counseling. **AIDS Hotline,** Cork AIDS Alliance, 16 Peter St. (tel. 276 676). Open M-F 10am-5pm. **Samaritans** (tel. 271 323 or (800) 609 090) offers a 24hr. support line for depression.

Hospital: Mercy Hospital, Grenville Pl. (tel. 271 971). £20 fee for access to emergency room. **Cork Regional Hospital,** Wilton St. (tel. 546 400), on bus #8.

Pharmacies: Regional Late Night Pharmacy, Wilton Rd. (tel. 344 575), opposite the Regional Hospital on bus #8. Open M-F 9am-10pm, Sa-Su 10am-10pm. **Phelan's Late Night,** 9 Patrick St. (tel. 272 511). Open M-Sa 9am-10pm, Su 10am-10pm. **Boots,** 71 Patrick St. (tel. 270 977). Open M-Th and Sa 9am-6pm, F 9am-8pm.

Post Office: Oliver Plunkett St. (tel. 272 000). Open M-Sa 9am-1pm and 2-5:30pm.

Internet Access: The Favourite, 122 Patrick St. (tel. 272 646), at the top of Patrick St. near Merchant Quay. Internet access in video-game-like stalls at the rear of the store. Bring £1 coins. Open daily 9am-10:30pm. **The Victoria Sporting Club** (tel. 504 749) on St. Patrick's Quay. Internet Access £6 per hour. Open M-Sa 10am-11pm.

PHONE CODE	021.

◤ ACCOMMODATIONS

Cork's nine hostels range from drearily adequate to wonderfully welcoming. B&Bs are clustered along Western Rd. near University College. The other concentration of accommodations is in the slightly more central area along MacCurtain St. and Lower Glanmire Rd., near the bus and train stations.

HOSTELS

Sheila's Budget Accommodation Centre (IHH), 3 Belgrave Pl. (tel. 505 562), by the intersection of Wellington Rd. and York St. The staff's smiling faces welcome guests to a large, perk-filled and comfortable hostel. Centrally located, Sheila's offers a big kitchen and summertime barbecues in a secluded backyard. Internet access (£2 per 20 min.), video rental (£1), sauna (£1.50 for 40 min.). The 24hr. reception desk doubles as a general store and offers breakfast (£1.50). All rooms non-smoking. 6-bed dorms £7; 4-bed dorms £8.50; doubles £21. Rooms available with bath. Free luggage storage. Sheets 50p. Key deposit £5. Check-out 10:30am. **Bike rental** £6.

The Cork City Independent Hostel, 100 Lower Glanmire Rd. (tel. 509 089). From the train station, turn right and walk 100 yd.; the hostel is on the left. The friendly guests, staff, and long-time residents relax together in the courtyard and a common room filled with snazzy pop-art. Comfortable rooms and a laid-back atmosphere add to the convenience of this cheerful hostel. Dorms £7; doubles £17. Laundry £3.50. Key deposit £3.

Cork International Hostel (An Óige/HI), 1-2 Redclyffe, Western Rd. (tel. 543 289), a 15min. walk from the Grand Parade. Bus #8 stops across the street if you ask the driver to let you off there. Immaculate but barren bunk rooms in a stately brick Victorian townhouse. **Currency exchange.** Dorms £8 July-Aug., £7.50 June, £6.50 Oct.-May; doubles £12.50. Reduced prices for youths under 18. All rooms with bath. Continental breakfast £2. Check-in 8am-midnight. **Bike rental** £5 per day, £30 per week.

Aaron House, Lower Glanmire Rd. (tel. 551 566). From the train station, turn right and walk 75 yd.; a bright painted sign marks the hostel on the left. A casual atmosphere adds to the comfortable rooms and convenient location. Dorms £7. Doubles £17. Continental breakfast included. **Bike rental** £6 per day.

Isaac's (IHH), 48 MacCurtain St. (tel. 508 388; www.ibi.ie/isaacs). From the bus stop, cross the nearby bridge and take the second left onto MacCurtain St. This hugely modern institution is conveniently located near the bus and train stations. Cafe open for breakfast and lunch. 11- to 16-bed dorms £7.95; 4- to 8-bed dorms £9.25. Continental breakfast £2.25, Irish £3.25. 24hr. reception. Dorm lockout 11am-3pm.

Kinlay House (IHH), Bob and Joan Walk (tel. 508 966; kincork@usit.com), down the alley to the right of Shandon Church. Located in less-than-posh but convenient Shandon, Kinlay House is large and clean, if motel-like. Each of the modern rooms has a locker and wash basin. Video library and game room. 10- to 14-bed dorms £8; doubles £25; singles £15. 10% discount with ISIC. Continental breakfast included. Laundry £3.60. Internet access £1.50 per 15min. 50p key deposit. Free parking.

Kelly's Hostel, 25 Summerhill South (tel. 315 612; kellyshostel@hotmail.com). From the bus station, go down Abgelson St. across the South Channel, turn left on Old Blackrock Road, and look for the sign with a weary Garfield. This hostel sits far from Cork's major attractions, but it still draws plenty of devoted occupants. Each room is named after a famous Irish poet, and hand-inscribed poems share the walls with intricate decorations. Lockers in every room, but you'll need your own padlock. Cable TV and videos. Free coffee and tea. No smoking. Dorms £7; triples with bath £10 per person. Laundry £3.50.

Campus House (IHH), 3 Woodland View, Western Rd. (tel. 343 531). From the Grand Parade turn onto Washington St. (which later becomes Western Rd.) and continue for 15min., or take bus #8. Adequate and clean, with a touch of motherly warmth. Dorms £6.50-7.50. Sheets 50p. Reception daily 9am-10pm.

BED AND BREAKFASTS

Garnish House, Western Rd. (tel. 275 111). Prepare to be pampered. Gorgeous rooms, fluffy comforters, fruit, and flowers. Fresh tea and scones when you arrive. The breakfast menu features 30 choices. Singles from £25; doubles from £40, with jacuzzi from £50. Free laundry service.

Roman House, St. John's Terrace, Upper John St. (tel. 503 606). Cross the North Channel by the Opera House, make a left on John Redmond St., and then bear right onto Upper John St. Cork's only B&B catering specifically to gay and lesbian travelers, Roman House is decorated decadently. Vegetarian breakfast option. Washbasins, TVs, oversized armchairs, and tea and coffee-making facilities in every room. Singles from £20; doubles £36.

☑ FOOD

Don't explore Cork's city center on an empty stomach; delicious restaurants and cafes abound. Particularly appealing are the lanes connecting Patrick St., Paul St., and Oliver Plunkett St. The **English Market,** accessible from Grand Parade, Patrick St., and Prince St., displays a wide variety of meats, fish, cheeses, and fruits. Pastries soar to the heavens in the second-floor **Farmgate Cafe.** (Market and cafe open M-Sa 9am-5pm.) Cork's historic role as a meat-shipping center meant that Corkonians often got stuck eating leftovers: feet, snouts, and other delectable goodies. Cork's local specialties include *crubeen* (pig's feet), *drisheen* (blood sausage; its texture is a hybrid of liver and Jell-O), and Clonakilty black pudding (an intriguing mixture of blood, grain, and spice). For the less carnivorous, there's a scone around every corner, and many restaurants have vegetarian options. **Tesco,** Paul St. (tel. 270 791), is the biggest grocery store in town. (Open M-W and Sa 8:30am-8pm, Th-F 8:30am-10pm.)

◩ **Scoozi,** in the alley just off Winthrop Ave. (tel. 275 077). Follow the tomato signs to this expansive, brick-and-wood-lined establishment. It's the perfect spot for enjoying burgers, pizza, grilled chicken, and pasta with wild abandon amongst crowds. Pesto chicken breast on a bun with fries and coleslaw £6.85. Open M-Sa 9am-11pm, Su noon-10pm.

Polo's Gourmet Cafe, Washington St. (tel. 277 099). You'll admire yourself as well as the food in the wall-long mirror of this sparkling eatery. Polo offers a particularly Irish selection of sandwiches and all-day breakfast. Open M-W 8am-midnight, Th-Su 8am-4am.

The Gingerbread House, Paul St. (tel. 276 411). Huge windows, cool jazz, and heavenly breads, pastries, and quiche. Open M-W, Sa 8:15am-7pm, Th-F 8:15am-9pm, Su 8:15am-6pm.

Truffles Restaurant, 6 Princes St. (tel. 270 251). A cozy little bistro right off Patrick St. that serves traditional Irish fare with a creative twist, like Clonakilty chicken wrapped in smoked bacon (£6). Small, intimate tables on the second floor look over the busy shopping street below. 3-course lunch special £5. Open summer daily 10am-10pm, winter daily 10am-6:30pm.

Quay Co-op, 24 Sullivan's Quay (tel. 317 660). A cow's delight: nary a creature was sacrificed for the scrumptious vegetarian dishes served in this classy establishment. Excellent soups and an inexpensive wine list. Daily specials around £5. Veggie burger £4. Open M-Sa 9am-9pm. The store downstairs caters to all organic and vegan needs. Store open M-Sa 9am-6:15pm.

Bully's, 40 Paul St. Enjoy fine Italian specials while sitting at candlelit tables and gazing at sketches of warmer lands. Pizza from £4.50. Lasagna £5. Extensive wine list. Open M-Sa noon-11:30pm, Su 1-11pm. Call ahead for reservations.

Gino's, 7 Winthrop St. (tel. 274 485), between Patrick and Oliver Plunkett St. Super fresh pizza draws crowds. Cork's best ice cream has them staying for desert. Lunch special includes pizza and ice cream (£4.50.) Open M-Sa noon-11pm, Su 1-11pm.

The Delhi Palace, 6 Washington St. (tel. 276 227). Consume like a maharajah. Vegetarian dishes £6.50-£12, meat dishes from £6. Dinner daily 5:30pm-midnight.

◪ PUBS

Cork's pubs have all the variety of music and atmosphere you'd expect to find in Ireland's second-largest city. Along Oliver Plunkett St., Union Quay, and South Main St., there are more pubs than you can shake a stick at. Cork is the proud home of **Murphy's,** a thick, creamy stout that some say, and especially in Cork, tastes as good as Guinness. The cheaper stout, **Beamish,** is also brewed here. Nearly all pubs stop serving at 11:30pm.

◩ **The Western Star,** Western Rd. (tel. 543 047). Packed with a student crowd, this pub grooves to pop and dance music despite a nearly suburban location. If you're staying nearby in summer, enjoy the outdoors bar on the patio by the Lee River. Free barbecue F-Sa. Sandwiches £1.80.

An Spailpín Fanac, (uhn spal-PEEN FAW-nuhk), 28 South Main St. (tel. 277 949), across from the Beamish brewery. One of Cork's most popular pubs and about as old as they get—it opened in 1790. The name means "the wandering potato picker," but the largely tourist crowd is less likely to stray. Come nightfall, all are safely tucked into the brick-walled, wood-trimmed nooks for conversation. Live trad complements the decor most nights. Pub grub (Irish stew £3.75) served M-F noon-3pm.

The Lobby, 1 Union Quay (tel. 319 307). The largest of the Quay pubs and arguably the most famous venue in Cork, the Lobby has given some of Ireland's biggest folk acts their start. Live music nightly at 9:30pm, ranging from trad to acid jazz. Two floors overlook the river. Occasional cover £4.

Gallaghers, MacCurtain St. A traditional pub conveniently located to welcome tourists, especially on "Backpacker Nights" (M-Tu), when a three-pint pitcher sells for £6. Also featuring an array of filling pub grub. Most meals around £4.50.

Charlie's, Union Quay (tel. 965 272). Art by local student artists decks the walls of the smallest of the Quay pubs. Gaggles of locals and tourists pack in for live trad nightly in the summer, and 3-4 sessions per week during the rest of the year.

Rosie O'Grady's, N. Main St. (tel. 278 253). Brace yourself. A wild, swelling crowd and pulsing trad render the Rosie's experience one of Cork's liveliest.

The Black Bush, Oliver Plunkett St. (tel. 270 870). Cork's late-night bar, the Bush is open until 2am, drawing all types to the relaxing atmosphere fostered by its traditional interior and frequent live music.

John Reardon and Son, Washington St. (tel. 271 969). Lively and popular with a late-twenties local crowd in its pseudo-medieval interior. Open until 2am Th-Su. Over 23yrs. only.

An Phoenix, 3 Union Quay (tel. 964 275). Punk, rock, and indie bands attract a young crowd upstairs, while all ages hold court in the lower level. Call for schedule.

The Thirsty Scholar, Western Rd. (tel. 276 209), across the street from Jury's Hotel. Steps from campus, this congenial pub is proof that students will walk no farther for a pint than they have to. Live summer trad sessions.

Loafer's, 26 Douglas St. (tel. 311 612). Cork's gay and lesbian pub fills up nightly with all age groups. Lively conversation and live bands contribute to this cozy spot.

🎵 MUSIC AND CLUBS

Cork fosters a prolific number of aspiring young bands, but the turnover rate is high—what is hip one week can be passé the next. To keep on top of the scene, check out *List Cork,* a free bi-weekly schedule of music available at local stores. The **Lobby** (see **Pubs**) and **Nancy Spain's,** 48 Barrack St. (tel. 314 452), are consistently sound choices for live music. **Fred Zepplins** on Parliament St., and **An Phoenix** (see **Pubs**) host alternative, punk, and indie bands. (Call for live music schedule. Cover $3-8.) Cork is also full of trendy nightclubs that suck up the sloshed and swaying student population once the pubs have closed. Before you fork over your $3-5 cover charge, remember that clubs close at 2am.

Garbys, Oliver Plunkett St. (tel. 270 074). Track lighting illuminates young groovers grinding. The £2-5 cover allows access to the lower dance floor and the retro-flavored upstairs.

Sir Henry's, South Main St. (tel. 274 391). Arguably the most popular club in Cork, and also the most intense. Prepare to wedge yourself between sweaty, semi-conscious bodies. Cover £2-11.

City Limits, Coburg St. (tel. 501 206). A pleasant, mixed-age crowd. DJs spin anything from the 60s to the 90s Th and Su 11pm-2am. Comedy nights F-Sa 9pm. Cover £3-5.

Club FX and **Grapevine,** Gravel Ln. (tel. 271 120). From Washington St., make a right on Little Hangover St. and then a left onto Gravel Ln. Club FX features two levels with plenty of pulsating lights, while the Grapevine sports a Mediterranean decorative scheme and a young, self-conscious crowd. Open W-Su 10:30pm-2am. Cover £3-5.

Temple of Sound (tel. 271 632), at the corner of Crane and Phoenix St. From S. Mall, turn onto Crane just past Pembroke St. to worship at the temple of house, dance-pop, and techno. Formerly Surfers Beach Club, the aquatic theme still rides well with the young dudes. £5-7 cover.

Cubans, Hanover St. (tel. 279 250). The wall-paintings of Cork's newest club insist ancient Roman is where it's at. Even a cover charge hovering around £5 and a long wait in line can't cramp the style of local patrons breaking down to 90s dance hits.

The Other Place, in a lane off of South Main St. (tel. 278 470). Cork's gay and lesbian disco rocks every Friday and Saturday 11:30pm-2am. Dance floor and a bar/cafe upstairs. Highly appreciated by Cork's gay population, especially the younger set, on weekend nights. The first Friday of the month is ladies' night. Cover £4.

◉ SIGHTS

Cork's sights are loosely divided into several districts: the Old City, the South Bank, the Shandon neighborhood, and the university. All can be reached by foot, which is perhaps the best choice in this pedestrian-friendly city. For guidance, pick up *The Cork Area City Guide* at the tourist office (£1.50).

THE OLD CITY

Cork's major sights are located in the oldest part of the city that sits on the island created by the passage of the River Lee through the center of town.

TRISKEL ARTS CENTER. The small but dynamic Triskel Arts Centre maintains two small galleries with rotating contemporary exhibits. It also organizes a wide variety of cultural events, including music, film, literature, theater, and the visual arts. *(Tobin St. Tel. 272 022; triskel@iol.ie. Open M-Sa 10am-5:30pm. Free. Cafe open M-F 8am-5:30pm, Sa 9am-5:30pm.)*

KEYSER HILL. On a nice day, you can get a decent view of Cork (and much too good a view of Beamish Brewery) from Keyser Hill. At the top of the stairs leading up the hill is **Elizabethan Fort,** a star-shaped, ivy-covered remnant of English rule in Cork. In true Cork fashion, the fort has been destroyed three times since its completion in 1603, most recently by anti-treaty IRA forces in 1922. In these peaceful times, the fort houses the Garda station. To access the fort's strategically valuable view, climb the stairs just inside the main gate. *(Follow South Main St. away from Washington St., cross the South Gate Bridge, and turn right onto Proby's Quay and then left onto obscure Keyser Hill. Always open. Free.)*

ST. FINBARR'S CATHEDRAL, on Proby's Quay, is a testament to the Victorian love of Gothic bombast. St. Finbarr allegedly founded his "School of Cork" here in 606, but no trace of the early foundation remains. The present cathedral was built between 1735 and 1870. *(Bishop St. Tel. 963 387. Open Apr.-Sept. M-Sa, 10am-5:30pm, Oct.-Mar. 10am-5pm. £2 donation requested.)*

CHRIST CHURCH, in the center of the city, is an emblem of the persistence of Catholicism in Cork; it has been burned to the ground three times since its 1270 consecration but was rebuilt promptly each time, most recently in 1729. Surrounding the church is an eclectic collection of sculptures, making the church grounds a pleasant resting spot on a stroll through the city. *(Off the Grand Parade just north of Bishop Lucey Park. Walk down the Christ Church Lane (keeping the park on your left) to emerge on South Main St., once the city's main drag. To the right is the steepleless Christ Church, now the Cork City Archives (closed to tourists). Always open. Free.)*

SHANDON AND EMMET PLACE

On the other side of the Lee, North Main St. becomes Shandon St., heart of the Shandon neighborhood. Shandon lacks affluence, but has plenty of pride.

ST. ANN'S CHURCH. Commonly called **Shandon Church,** after its steeple, Shandon Tower. The now barely visible red-and-white (sandstone and limestone) strips on the steeple inspired the "Rebel" flag, still ubiquitous throughout Cork; the salmon on top of the church spire represents the River Lee. Like most of Cork, the original church was ravaged by 17th century pyromaniacal English armies; construction of the current church began in 1722. Four clocks grace the four sides of Shandon's tower. Notoriously out of sync with each other, the clocks have been held responsible for many an Irishman's tardy arrival at work and have earned the church its endearing nickname, "the four-faced liar." Admission to the tower favors the non-claustrophobic with the option of climbing up the tower's extremely narrow passage to reach a spectacular view. Visitors can also subject the city to their experiments in bell-ringing (sheet music provided, 8-5-2-1-1-1-8 reportedly a good tune). *(Walk up Shandon St., take a right down unmarked Church St., and go straight towards the tower. Tel. 505 906. Open in summer M-Sa 9:30am-5:30pm. £3 adults, £2.50 students and seniors.)*

OTHER SIGHTS. Crawford Municipal Art Gallery is housed within an elegant 18th century customs house, the gallery specializes in the paintings of Irish masters like James Barry and Jack Yeats, along with contemporary work by aspiring artists of all nationalities. Adjacent is the monstrous, cement Opera House, erected 20 years ago after the older, more elegant opera house went down in flames. *(Emmet Place. Over the hill from Shandon Church, across the north fork of the Lee. Tel. 273 377. Gallery open M-Sa 10am-5pm. Free.)* **Cork Butter Museum** comes closer than one might think to making Cork's commerce history and preserved butter interesting. *(Church St. Tel. 300 600. Open M-Sa 10am-5pm. £2.50, students and seniors £2.)* At the **Shandon Craft Centre,** potters, basket-weavers, and other artisans ply their trade and sell their wares. *(Church St. Across from the Church.)*

WESTERN CORK

Cork's other major sights are on the western edge of the city. From Grand Parade, walk down Washington St., which soon becomes Western Rd.

CORK CITY GAOL. If time's tight in Cork, go directly to the Cork City Gaol. The museum is a reconstruction of the gaol as it appeared in the 1800s. Visitors are equipped with audio-cassette tours that bring to life the squabbles of the plastic prisoners and guards that fill the gaol's cells. Descriptions of Cork's social history accompany tidbits about miserable punishments, like the "human treadmill" used to grind grain. The tour culminates with a film that presents views of the gaol from both sides of the law. *(Sunday's Well Rd. From Fitzgerald Park, cross the footbridge at the western end of the park, turn right onto Sunday's Well Rd., and follow the signs. Tel. 305 022. Open daily Mar.-Oct. 9:30am-6pm, Nov.-Feb. 10am-5pm. Last admission one hour before closing. £4.50, students and seniors £3. Admission includes audio-tape tour.)* The same building houses the **Radio Museum,** which chronicles the history of radio in Ireland and the world. A shortwave station allows visitors to listen in on static-clouded broadcasts. *(Open daily Mar.-Oct. 9:30am-6pm, Nov.-Feb. 10am-5pm. £3.50, students and seniors £2.50. Combined admission to Gaol and museum £7, students and seniors £4.50.)*

UNIVERSITY COLLEGE CORK (UCC). Built in 1845, the campus is a collection of gothic buildings, manicured lawns, and sculpture speckled grounds, all of which make for a fine, secluded afternoon walk or picnic along the Lee. One of the newer buildings, **Boole Library,** celebrates the mathematician George Boole, the mastermind behind Boolean logic. Sir Arthur Conan Doyle used Boole as the model for his character Prof. James Moriarty, Sherlock Holmes's nemesis. *(Main gate on Western Rd. Tel. 90300. Always open. Free.)*

CORK PUBLIC MUSEUM. Enclosed within the splendid floral surroundings of **Fitzgerald Park,** the museum's astoundingly esoteric exhibits feature such varied goodies as 17th and 18th century toothbrushes and the 1907 costume worn by James Dwyer, chief sheriff of Cork. *(Across the street from UCC on Western Rd. Tel. 270 679. Open M-F 11am-1pm, 2:15-5pm, Su 3-5pm. M-Sa free; Su 75p, students free.)*

🎵 ENTERTAINMENT

The always lively streets of Cork make finding entertainment easy. If you tire of drinking, take advantage of Cork's music venues, dance clubs, theaters, and sports arenas, or just explore the innumerable cafés and bookshops.

THEATER AND FILM

Everyman's Theatre (a.k.a. "the Palace"), MacCurtain St. (tel. 501 673), stages big-name musicals, plays, operas, and concerts. (Tickets $8-15. Box office open M-Sa 10am-5pm, 7pm on show dates.) The **Opera House,** Emmet Pl. (tel. 270 022), next to the river, presents an extensive program of dance and performance art. (Tickets from $10. Open M-Sa 9am-5:30pm.) The **Granary,** Mardyke Quay (tel. 904 275), stages performances of new scripts by local and visiting theater companies. **Triskel Arts Centre,** Tobin St. (tel. 272 022), simmers with avant-garde theater and performance art and hosts regular concert and film series. The **Irish Gay and Lesbian Film Festival** happens in mid-October (call The Other Place for details, see **Clubs**). For a fix of mainstream American celluloid and the occasional Irish or art-house flick, head to the **Capitol Cineplex** (tel. 272 216), at Grand Parade and Washington St. (£4.50; before 6pm students can purchase tickets for £3.50; matinees £3.)

SPORTS

Cork is sporting-mad. Its soccer, hurling, and Gaelic football teams are perennial contenders for national titles (see **Sports**, p. 30). **Hurling** and **Gaelic football** take place every Sunday afternoon at 3pm from June to September; for additional details, call the GAA (tel. 963 311) or consult *The Cork Examiner*. Be cautious when venturing into the streets on soccer game days (especially during championships), where screaming, jubilant fans will either bowl you down or, better, force you to take part in the revelry. Tickets to big games are £13-15 and scarce, but Saturday, Sunday, and Wednesday evening matches are cheap (£1-4), or free. You can buy tickets to these local games at the **Pairc Uí Chaoimh** (park EE KWEEV), the Gaelic Athletic Association stadium. To get there, take the #2 bus to Blackrock, and ask the driver to let you off at the stadium. Indoor-athletes might head **The Leisureplex,** 1 MacCurtain St. (tel. 505 155), where 24hr. pool, bowling, video games, and laser tag offer an escape from the Irish rain.

FESTIVALS

See big-name musicians for free in local pubs during the three-day **Guinness Jazz Festival** (tel. 273 946) in October. Anyone in town during that weekend needs to book well ahead at hostels. Also popular is the week-long **International Film Festival** (tel. 271 711), in early October at the Opera House and the Triskel Arts Centre. Documentaries and shorts vie for prizes. During the first week in May, the **International Cork Choral Festival** (tel. 308 308) fills City Hall, churches, and outdoor venues with singing groups from across the globe. The **Sense of Cork Festival** (tel. 310 597), a cornucopia of local crafts, theater, and music, is held the last week in June.

NEAR CORK

Love, tragedy, and free drinks await you just outside Cork City. A kiss is no longer just a kiss at the Blarney Stone, the ultimate Irish tourist attraction. Aficionados of maritime tragedy can get their fix at Cobh, the final stop for the Titanic and numerous immigrant "coffin ships." Head to Fota for beastly adventures; you can frolic with scimitar-horned oryx and screeching mandrils. Sweet, sweet Jameson is distilled in Midleton, where visitors learn themselves why Queen Elizabeth once called Irish whiskey her one true Irish friend.

BLARNEY (AN BHLARNA)

Whether you're in the mood to admire the idyllic Irish countryside or simply dying to stand in a damp castle passageway, **Blarney Castle,** with its **Blarney Stone,** is the quintessential tourist spot. The prevailing myth of the stone's origin holds that it is a chip of the Scottish Stone of Scone that was presented to the King of Munster in gratitude for support during a rebellion in 1314. Today it stands as just another slab of limestone among so many others in the castle wall. Still, with everyone else doing it, you might just find yourself bending over backwards to kiss the stone in hopes of acquiring the legendary eloquence bestowed on those who smooch it. The term "blarney" refers to the supposedly Irish talent of stretching, or even obstructing, the truth. Queen Elizabeth I allegedly coined it during her long and tiring negotiations over control of the castle. The owner, Cormac McCarthy, Earl of Blarney, followed the rules of 16th century diplomacy, writing grandiose letters in praise of the Queen, but he never relinquished the land. Ruffling her royal feathers, the Queen was heard to say, "This is all blarney—he never says what he means!" The Irish consider the whole thing a bunch of blarney; they're more concerned with the sanitary implication of so many people kissing the same rock. More impressive than the stone is the castle itself, built in 1446. (Tel. 385 252. Open June-Aug. 9am-7pm, Su 9:30am-5:30pm; Sept. M-Sa 9am-6:30pm, Su 9:30am-sundown; Oct.-Apr. M-Sa 9am-sundown, Su 9:30am-sundown; May M-Sa 9am-6:30pm, Su 9:30am-5:30pm. £3.50, seniors and students £2.50, children £1.)

Adjacent to the castle lies the **Rock Close,** an extensive and impressive rock-and-plant garden created by Druids to mark their sacred grounds. In contrast to the ever-crowded castle, the Rock Close and adjacent fields are usually unpopulated. The limestone cave and dungeons near the castle are inviting for those who enjoy exploring the dark and dank (remember to bring a flashlight). The **Blarney Woolen Mills** (tel. 385 280), across from the castle, are the other main attraction of Blarney. The Mills, a one-stop Irish tourist shop, offer all kinds of goods, from home-spun sweaters to mass-produced sweatshirts. (Open M-Sa 9am-6pm.)

Bus Éireann runs buses from **Cork** to Blarney (M-Sa 16 per day, Su 10 per day, £2.50 return). From June 1 to Sept. 4, they also offer an **Open Top Tour,** which winds its way from the Cork bus station through the city and on to Blarney Castle, where it stops for sight-seeing and shopping, and then heads back to Cork (2 per day; 3 hr.; buses leave at 10:30am and 2:45pm; £6; advanced booking recommended). The **phone code** in Blarney is a rock-solid 021.

Blarney is a short and pleasant bike ride from Cork, or 25 minutes by bus, so there is no reason, practical or otherwise, to stay overnight. Should you fall madly in love with the Blarney Stone after giving it a wet-lickery one, you can rent functional beds at the **Blarney Tourist Hostel** (tel. 385 580 or 381 430), 2 mi. from town on the Killarney Rd. in a converted farmhouse. (Dorms £7.) Closer to town but more expensive, the **Rosemount B&B** offers comfortable beds just up the hilly lane from the bus stop. (£15, with bath £17.) **Blarney Camping and Caravan Park** (tel. 385 167), is located on Stoneview Rd. near Blarney Castle. (Tents £6, £2 per person. Free showers.) **The Blarney Stone** (tel. 385 482), cooks up Irish specialties for crowds of tourists. (Meals £3.50-7. Open M-Sa 9am-10:30pm, Su 11am-9:30pm.) Pub fare is served at the **Muskerry Arms** (tel. 385 066), along with trad and cabaret. (Music nightly 9:30-11:30pm.)

COBH AND FOTA ISLAND

Little more than a slumbering harbor village today, Cobh (KOVE) was Ireland's main transatlantic port until the 1960s. For many of the emigrants who left between 1848 and 1950, the steep hillside and multi-colored houses were their final glimpse of Ireland. In keeping with Irish tradition, Cobh has some sad stories to tell. Cobh was the *Titanic's* last port of call four days before the "unsinkable" ship went down. Later, when the Germans torpedoed the *Lusitania* during World War I, most survivors and some of the dead were taken back to Cobh in lifeboats. There is a Lusitania Memorial in Casement Square; a cemetery outside of town contains a mass grave of 150 of the fallen. Cobh is best reached by **rail** from **Cork** (25min., M-Sa 19 per day, Su 8 per day, £2.50 return). The **phone code** docks at 021.

In remembrance of its eminent but tragic history, Cobh recently established a museum called **The Queenstown Story,** adjacent to the Cobh railway station. The museum's flashy multimedia exhibits trace the port's history, with sections devoted to emigration, the *Lusitania,* the *Titanic,* and the peak of transatlantic travel. In June 1995, the Cork-Cobh train ran into the museum, hurtling through two walls and the ceiling—not an auspicious start in this accident-prone town. (Tel. 813 591. Open daily 10am-6pm, last admission 5pm. £3.50, students £2.50.) **St. Colman's Cathedral** towers over Cobh. (Open daily 7am-8pm. Free.) Its ornate Gothic spire dominates the town's architectural landscape. The spire is closed to visitors, who will have to content themselves with the view of the harbor from the hill. Completed in 1915, the cathedral boasts the largest carillon, or harmonized bell system, in Ireland, consisting of 47 bells weighing over 7700 pounds. The small **Cobh Museum,** housed inside the Scots Church on High Rd., up the stairs by the train station, deals almost exclusively with Cobh's maritime history. (Tel. 813 591. Open M-Sa 11am-1pm, 2-6pm, Su. 3-6pm. £1.)

Cobh revels in its aquatic heritage. The **tourist office** (tel. 813 301; www.cobhharbourchamber.ie) occupies the recently restored site of the Royal Cork Yacht Club, built in 1854 and reputed to be the world's first yacht club. Located on the water up the hill from the train station, the office gives out free maps, guides and advice. (Open M-Sa 9:30am-5:30pm, Su 11am-5pm.) Visitors interested in creating their own ocean adventure can contact **International Sailing** (tel. 811 237). Based on East Beach, lessons are available, as are canoes ($8 per 3hr.), sailing dinghies (from $24 per 3hr.), and windsurfing equipment ($18 per 3hr.; open daily 9:30am-6pm.) Those who prefer to learn the past before they repeat it can take a guided tour on the **Titanic Trail** (tel. 815 211 for information; daily at 3pm from the Commodore Hotel; $3.50). The second week in July brings **Seisiún Cois Cuan Festival,** a celebration of traditional Irish music and storytelling. During the second week of August, the **Cobh People's Regatta** draws many cruise liners to the harbour, including the QE2.

Should you decide to anchor in Cobh, join the family at **Beechmont House Hostel** (tel. 812 177). Their home sits at the top of a steep climb up Bond St. ($8 includes breakfast. Call ahead.) Pubs, restaurants, and B&Bs face Cobh's harbor from Beach St. **The River Room,** on West Beach (tel. 813 293), grills "ciabattas," large sandwiches on tasty bread ($3.25), and lunchtime quiche. (Open daily 9am-6pm.) **The Queenstown Restaurant** (tel. 813 591) will offer you a sandwich ($2.95), pastries, or a daily special while you mull over the town's disasters in the pretty entrance hall to the Queenstown Story Heritage Center. (Open daily 9:30am-5pm.) Alternatively, buy a picnic at **SuperValu** supermarket (tel. 811 586) on West Beach and eat it at John F. Kennedy Park on the waterfront. (Open M-W 9am-6pm, Th-F 9am-9pm.) Cobh holds its own in the pub count. The DJs and rock acts at the **Voyager** (tel. 814 161) pack in a young horde nightly. The **Ship's Bell** (tel. 811 272) attracts a more seasoned, local crowd for pub grub and live trad on weeknights.

Ten minutes from Cobh by rail lies **Fota Island**, where penguins, peacocks, cheetahs, and giraffes roam, largely free of cages, in the **Fota Wildlife Park.** This may well be the closest you'll ever come to a ring-tailed lemur. The 70 acre park houses 70 species of animals from South America, Africa, Asia, and Australia. (Tel. (021) 812 678. Open Apr.-Oct. M-Sa 10am-6pm, Su 11am-6pm. Last admission 5pm. $4.40, students $3.50.) The **Fota Arboretum,** a kilometer from the station, but adjacent to the park, boasts a range of plants and trees as diverse and exotic as the beasts next door. (Gates close at 5:30pm. Free.) Fota is an intermediate stop on the **train** from Cork to Cobh; if you buy a ticket from Cork to Cobh or vice versa, you can get off at Fota and re-board for free.

MIDLETON

A short drive or bus ride from Cork or Cobh on the main Cork-Waterford highway (N25), Midleton beckons pilgrims of the water of life (Irish for whiskey) to the **Jameson Heritage Centre.** (Tel. 613 594. Open Mar.-Nov. daily 10am-6pm. $3.95, students and seniors $3.50, children $1.50.) The center rolls visitors through a one-hour tour detailing the craft and history of whiskey production. Better yet, they give you a glass of the potent stuff at the end—for demonstration, of course. After all, "the story of whiskey is the story of Ireland." The highlight of Midleton (aside from the whiskey, of course) is its hostel, **An Stór (IHH)** (tel. 633 106). From Main St., turn onto Connolly St. and then take your first left. The hostel's name means "the treasure" in Irish. Bright, clean, and covered with blooming window boxes, the hostel teaches its guests some elementary though useless Irish by naming its rooms after indigenous bird species. Fortunately, they are also listed in English so that you can find your room if you have a drop too much at the Heritage tour. The friendly proprietors can advise you on local attractions ranging from castle visits to scenic bike rides. (Dorms $7; doubles and twins $10 per person. Laundry $2.) Hearty Irish food to help soak up the whiskey can be found at **Finin's** (tel. 631 878), on Main St. **La Trattoria,** 48 Main St. (tel. 631 341) has a lengthy menu of solid meals from $4.50, and a short wine list. Head to **The Meeting Place,** Connolly St. (tel. 631 928), for a pint and excellent live music on Tuesday nights (occasional $2.50 cover). **The Town Hall Bar,** inside Walis and Sons at 74 Main St. (tel. 631 155), is another excellent live music venue.

KNOW YOUR WHISKEY

KNOW YOUR WHISKEY Anyone who drinks his whiskey as it's meant to be drunk—"neat," or straight—can tell you that there's a huge difference between Irish whiskeys (Bushmills, Jameson, Power and Son, and the like), Scotch whiskys (spelled without an e), and American whiskeys. But what makes an Irish whiskey *Irish?* The basic ingredients in whiskey—water, barley (which becomes malt once processed), and heat from a fuel source—are always the same. It's the quality of these ingredients, the way in which they're combined, and the manner in which the combination is stored that gives each product its distinct flavor. The different types of whiskey derive from slight differences in this production process. American whiskey is distilled once and is often stored in oak, bourbon is made only in Kentucky, scotch uses peat-smoked barley, and Irish whiskey is triple distilled. After this basic breakdown, individual distilleries will claim that their further variations on the theme make their product the best of its class. The best way to understand the distinctions between brands is to taste the various labels in close succession to one another. Line up those shot glasses, sniff and then taste each one (roll the whiskey in your mouth like a real pro), and have a sip of water between each brand.

YOUGHAL

Thirty miles east of Cork on N25, beach-blessed Youghal (YAWL, or "Y'all" for Southerners) can be a stopover on the way to Waterford and points east. If you've seen the movie *Moby Dick* with Gregory Peck, you've seen Youghal—it was filmed here in 1954. A popular, tacky beach and the narrow streets of what claims to have once been "Europe's leading walled port" keep Youghal interesting even after its brief brush with fame.

⚑ PRACTICAL INFORMATION. Buses stop in front of the public toilets on Main St., across from Dempsey's Bar, and travel to **Cork** (50min.; M-Sa 13 per day, Su 9 per day; £5.50) and **Waterford** via **Dungarvan** (1½-2hr.; M-Sa 13 per day, Su 5 per day; £8.80). **Hitching** to Cork or Waterford along N25 is possible but discouraged by *Let's Go.* The helpful **tourist office**, Market Sq. (tel. 92390), on the waterfront behind the clocktower, distributes a useful "tourist trail" booklet (free) and can steer you to trad sessions in town. (Open July-Aug. M-F 9am-7pm, Sa-Su 10am-6pm; June and Sept. M-Sa 10am-6pm; Oct.-May M-F 9:30am-5:30pm.) Call me **phone code** 024.

▊▊▊ ACCOMMODATIONS, FOOD, AND PUBS. The **Stella Mara** hostel (tel. 91820) has a simple, sterile feel and a few rooms with a view. (6- to 12-bed dorms £8. Doubles and twins £10 per person with bath. Sheets £1. Key deposit £5.) Majestic **Avonmore House** (tel. 92617) on South Abbey, boasts fully equipped rooms kept tidy by a professional staff. (Singles £25, doubles and twins £18-20 per person.)

Youghal may have more chip fryers per capita than any other town in Co. Cork; luckily, it also has a few less grease-oriented establishments. The **Coffee Pot,** 77 North Main St. (tel. 92523), is extremely popular among locals, serving pastries, soup, and light meals. (Entrees £4-6. Open M-F 9:30am-7:30pm, Sa 9:30am-6pm, Su 7am-11pm.) The **Tower Restaurant** (tel. 91869) at the base of its namesake, grills up omelettes and baguettes at lunchtime (£3-5), and more extensive meals, including vegetarian options, at dinner. (Dinners around £7.50. Open M noon-4pm, Tu-Sa noon-4pm and 7-10pm, Su 1-5pm and 7-9pm.) Should Youghal not tempt the taste-buds, head to **SuperValu** (tel. 92150) in the town center on Main St. (Open M-W 9am-7pm, Th and Sa 9am-8pm, F 9am-9pm, Su 10am-6pm.)

Traditional crannies fill with music twice weekly at the popular **Nook Pub** (tel. 92225). Young'uns flock to **The Clock Tavern**, South Main St. (tel. 93052), where the dark recesses are filled with the sounds of frequent rock acts, particularly on weekends. A more sedate atmosphere prevails at the **Central Star** (tel. 92419),

North Main St., dedicated to darts and hurling discussions. Tourists grip seaside pints at **Moby Dick's** (tel. 92099), across from the tourist office, filled with nautical murals and weekend trad.

◪ **SIGHTS.** Enjoyably informative historical **walking tours** of Youghal leave from the tourist office. (1½hr. June-Aug. M-F 11am and 3pm, Sa 11am. £2.75, students £2.) The huge **Clockgate,** built in 1777, straddles narrow, crowded Main St. Visible from the site are the old city walls, built on the hill sometime between the 13th and 17th centuries. The tower served as a prison and low-budget gallows (prisoners were hanged from the windows). On Church St., **St. Mary's Church** and **Myrtle Grove** stand side-by-side. St. Mary's Church is possibly the oldest operating church in Ireland; parts of it remain from the original Danish-built church constructed in 1020. One corner of the church holds the elaborate grave of Robert Boyle, first Earl of Cork. **Myrtle Grove** was the residence of Sir Walter Raleigh when he served as mayor here in 1588-89. Though privately owned and closed to the public, you can gawk or groan, according to your taste, at the window where Raleigh's buddy Edmund Spencer is said to have finished his hefty epic poem *The Faerie Queen*. For an encapsulated version of Youghal's history since the 9th century, drop by the tourist office's **Heritage Centre.** (Same phone and hours as the tourist office. £1.) The center focuses on Youghal's history as a seaport; Cromwell left Ireland from the harbor after he'd finished making a mess of things throughout the country. Across the street from the tourist office and up a little alley, the **Fox's Lane Folk Museum** is the place to investigate the history of razor blades and sewing machines. (Open Tu-Sa 10am-1pm and 2-6pm. Last admission 5:30pm. £2.)

On the first weekend in August, the streets of Youghal fill with music, theater, and food for the annual **Busking Festival.** Throughout August, the **Fairies Festival** brings Celtic art, music, and storytelling to town. **Ceolta Sí** (KYOL-ta SHEE; "fairy music") reaps the talent of local youth in an enjoyable, semi-professional program of traditional dance, music, and storytelling throughout the summer at the Walter Raleigh Hotel. (July-Aug. Th 8:30pm. £2.50.)

WEST CORK

From Cork City, there are two routes to Skibbereen and West Cork: an inland route and a coastal route through Kinsale. Two major **bus routes** begin in Cork City and serve West Cork. A coastal bus runs from Cork to **Skibbereen,** stopping in **Bandon, Clonakilty,** and **Rosscarbery** (M-Sa 3 per day, Su 2 per day). An inland bus travels from Cork to **Bantry,** stopping in **Bandon** and **Dunmanway** (M-Sa 3 per day, Su 2 per day). **Hitchers** are reported to have few problems in these parts. *Let's Go* does not recommend hitching.

THE INLAND ROUTE

Cyclists and drivers wishing to save time or avoid crowds should consider one of the inland routes from Cork to Skibbereen, Bantry, the Beara, or Killarney. Popular routes are Cork-Macroom-Killarney, Cork-Macroom-Ballingeary-Bantry/Glengarriff, and Cork-Dunmanway-Bantry/Skibbereen. The rocky face of the Shehy Mountains is forested with some of Ireland's best-preserved wilds. The attraction of the area is its abundance of interesting walks and bike rides.

DUNMANWAY AND BALLINGEARY

South of Macroom on R587, **Dunmanway** is less a town than a single busy main square. **Bus Éireann** voyages to Dunmanway from **Cork** (4 per day, Su 2 per day, £6.30) and from Dunmanway to **Glengarriff** via **Bantry** (3 per day, Su 2 per day). Buses stop in front of the News Basket on The Square. The best place to stay, and one of the best reasons to come to Dunmanway, is the ▓**Shiplake Mountain Hostel (IHH)** (tel. (023) 45750), nestled in the hills 3 mi. from town. Visitors are welcome

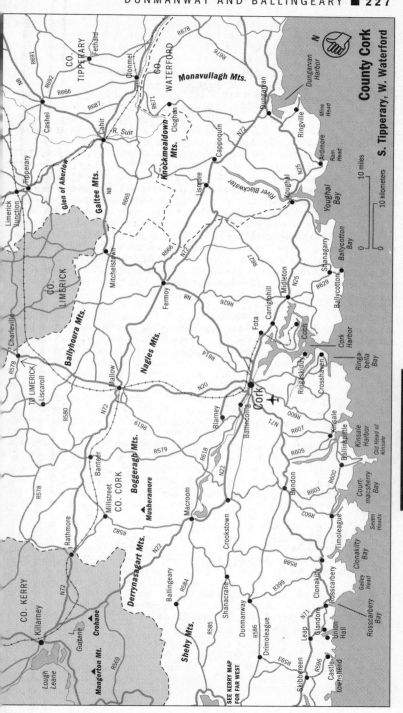

to call for a ride from Dunmanway, or follow Castle St. (next to Gatsby's Night-club) out of town toward Castle Donovan and then turn right at the hostel sign. Shiplake is an ideal base for hikers and bikers looking to explore the area's lakes, castles, and countryside. The proprietors have heaps of information and contagious enthusiasm for this spectacular area. They **rent bicycles** (£7 per day, part of the Wheel Escapes program), and cook what is perhaps the best hostel food in Ireland. A caravan of cozy, refurbished trailers painted in bright colors accommodates couples or families in addition to pleasant dorms. (Dorms £7, caravan £8 per person. **Camping** £4 per person. Wholefood groceries available. Vegetarian meals and healthy breakfasts £2.50-6.) Dunmanway's 8500 people support 23 pubs. The **Shamrock**, (tel. (023) 45142), dating from 1750, has a traditional atmosphere and occasional music to match. **An Toisín**, Main St. (tel. (023) 45954), fills the square with diverse music on weekend nights. **The Arch Bar**, (tel. (023) 45155) often fills with locals, as does **Gatsby's**, the disco upstairs that attracts the young and funky.

Over the mountains to the northwest of Dunmanway on R584, quiet **Ballingeary** is the failing heart of one of West Cork's declining *gaeltachts*, and holds the entrance to the **Gougane Barra Forest.** (Admission £1 for hikers and bikers, £3 for cars.) From the road though the forest, visitors can see the River Lee's pure source streams flow together. A church marking the site of St. Finbarre's monastery lies at the base of the mountains, next to a lake. Sweeping views reward those willing to climb the wooded trails to the ridgeline. The quiet, very basic **Tig Barra Hostel (IHH)** (tel. (026) 47016) makes a good base for exploring all this nature. (Dorms £8. **Camping** £3 per person. Lock-out 10pm-5am. Open mid-Mar.-Sept.)

COASTAL ROUTE

From Kinsale, southerly R600 stands watch over farming valleys before skirting the coast on the way to Clonakilty. From Cork, N71 stretches its tough asphalt skin all the way to Clonakilty via Bandon. Past Clonakilty, the population begins to thin out. Inland, mountains rise, rocky ridges replace smooth hills, and sunset-laden shoals proliferate as Ireland's southern coast starts to look like its western one. Crossroads along N71 link mellow tourist towns and hardworking fishing villages. "Blow-ins," ex-patriots from America and Northern Europe, have settled in the area by the hundreds, replacing the area's dwindling Irish population. These kick-back expats appreciate the leisurely pace and extraordinary scenery of the southwest but have shaped its culture to their own tastes. Trad thrives in these small towns, attracting long-time locals and artsy foreigners alike.

The islands in the stretch of ocean between Baltimore and Schull may be the wildest, remotest human habitations in all of southern Ireland. High cliffs plunge into the sea, creating a parcel of local shipwrecking tales. The O'Driscoll clan of pirates informally ruled the bay for centuries, sallying into the Atlantic for raids, off-loading brandy from Spanish galleons, then speeding home through secret channels between the islands.

KINSALE

Upscale Kinsale (Cionn tSáile) is mobbed with people and money every summer, when its population temporarily quintuples. Visitors come to swim, fish, and eat at Kinsale's famed "Good Food Circle" (of 12 expensive restaurants). Luckily, Kinsale's best attractions—its pubs, forts, and pretty seaside location—can be enjoyed on a budget. Kinsale's pleasant present hardly suggests the grimmer role the town has played in history. In the 1601 **Battle of Kinsale,** Elizabethan English armies destroyed the native Irish followers of Ulster chieftain Hugh O'Neill, while O'Neill's blockaded allies from Spain watched the action from ships stationed nearby. (See **History,** p. 7.) For almost two centuries after the English victory, Kinsale was legally closed to the Gaelic Irish. In 1688, the freshly deposed King James II of England, trying to gather Catholic Irish support for a Jacobite invasion of Scotland, entered Ireland at this very spot. The attention of the outside world turned here again in 1915, when the *Lusitania* was torpedoed and sank just off the Old Head of Kinsale.

◱ ORIENTATION AND PRACTICAL INFORMATION. Kinsale is a 30-minute drive southwest of Cork on R600. The city lies at the base of a U-shaped inlet. Facing the water, **Charles Fort** and the **Scilly Walk** (pronounced "silly") are to the left; the piers, **Compass Hill,** and **James Fort** are to the right; the town center is behind you. **Buses** to and from **Cork** stop at the Esso station on the Pier (40 min., M-F 9 per day, Sa 10 per day, Su 3 per day, £3.80 return). The **tourist office,** Emmet Pl. (tel. 772 234), in the black-and-red building on the waterfront, gives out free maps. (Open Mar.-Nov. daily 9am-6pm.) **Bank of Ireland,** Pearse St. (tel. 772 521), has a **24hr. ATM.** (Open M 10am-5pm, Tu-F 10am-4pm). **Rent bikes** (£6 per day, £2 per hour) and fishing poles (£10 per day, tackle included) at **Deco's** (tel. 774 884) on Main St. (Open June-Aug. M-Sa 9am-6pm, Su 10am-6pm; Sept.-May M-Sa 9am-6pm.) The **phone code** is a barnacle-encrusted 021.

▛ ACCOMMODATIONS. Although Kinsale's hotels and plush B&Bs cater to an affluent tourist crowd, there are two hostels nearby. The **Castlepark Marina Centre (IHH),** (tel. 774 959) sits across the harbor, a 40min. walk from town. From the bus depot, walk along the pier away from town for 10min., turn left to cross large Duggan Bridge, and then take another left just past the bridge; follow this road back toward the harbor. **Ferries** leave the Trident Marina for the hostel June through August (typically on the hour, call the hostel for a schedule, £1). This stone-fronted building stands just below the James Fort and offers marvelous views of Kinsale. Rooms are large, airy, and bright. Some have beach access and bay windows that open out onto the harbor. (Dorms £9, off season £8; doubles £10 per person, off season £9. Laundry £2. Safe-deposit box 50p. Wheelchair accessible. Open mid-Mar.-Dec.) The hostel's **restaurant** features a gourmet menu (salmon with lime and tarragon crème fraisch £9.25). Closer to town, **Dempsey's Hostel (IHH),** Cork Rd. (tel. 772124), is a 2min. walk from town on Cork Rd., next to the Texaco station. It's made up of clean, pleasant rooms and an industrial kitchen. (Dorms £6; doubles £8 per person. Sheets £1. Shower 50p. Check-in by 5pm.) **Camping** is another option here. (£3.) **O'Donovan's B&B,** Guardwell Rd. (tel. 772 428), has comfortable and reasonably priced accommodations. (£14, with bath £16.) There's **camping** outside of town at **Garrettstown House Holiday Park** (tel. 778156), 6 mi. west of Kinsale on R600 in Ballinspittle. (2-person tent with car £8. Open May-Sept.)

◱▨ FOOD AND PUBS. Kinsale is Ireland's gourmet food capital—locals claim it's the only town in Ireland with more restaurants than pubs. The **Good Food Circle** has 12 restaurants that uphold both Kinsale's well-deserved culinary reputation and its notoriety for tourist-scalping expense. The budget-conscious fill their baskets at the **SuperValu** (tel. 772 843) on Pearse St. (Open M-Sa 8:30am-9pm, Su 10am-7pm.) **Cafe Palermo,** Pearse St. (tel. 774 143), serves delicious Italian food, fresh salads, and rich desserts. (Lunch about £5. Open daily 10am-11pm.) **1601,** Pearse St. (tel. 772 529), cooks up high-quality pub grub. (Soup £2.50, burgers £6.25.)

On a weekend night, a stroll through Kinsale's small maze of streets will magically lead you to great trad. **1601** fiddles four nights a week. Harder to hear from a distance, but worth stepping into, **The Spaniard** (tel. 772 436) rules over the Kinsale pub scene from the hill on the Scilly Peninsula (follow the signs to Charles Fort for ¼mi.). It has stone walls, dark wood paneling, low-beamed ceilings, a bar the length of the Shannon, and trad several nights a week. Downhill from The Spaniard and farther on the Scilly Walk, **The Spinnaker** (tel. 772 098) presides over the harbor with a nautical theme and a variety of music, including American rock for the expats. Those who make the hike to Charles Fort are rewarded at the inviting **Bulman Bar** (tel. 772 131), a picturesque spot for downing a pint of Ireland's own black gold. Just remember you'll have to take the long Sobriety Walk back to town.

▣ **SIGHTS.** The half-hour trek up **Compass Hill,** south of Main St., rewards with a view of the town and its watery surroundings. More impressive is the view from **Charles Fort,** a classic 17th century star-shaped fort that remained a British naval base until 1921. The fort's battlements and buildings, overlooking the water, are an inviting and nearly limitless chance to climb and explore. Reach Charles Fort by following Scilly Walk, a sylvan path along the coast at the end of Pearse St. (30min.). (Tel. 772 263. Sack the fort mid-June to mid-Sept. daily 9am-6pm; mid-Apr. to mid-June and mid-Sept. to mid-Oct. M-Sa 9am-5pm, Su 9:30am-5:30pm. £2, students and children £1. Guided tours on request.) Across the harbor from Charles Fort, the ruins of star-shaped **James Fort,** now heavily grass covered, delight casual explorers with secret passageways and panoramic views of Kinsale. To reach the fort, follow the pier away from town, cross the Duggan bridge, then turn left. After exploring the ruins and the rolling heath, descend to Castlepark's hidden arc of beach behind the hostel. (Always open. Free.)

Desmond Castle, Cork St., a 15th century custom house, served as an arsenal during the 100-day Spanish occupation in 1601, and a naval prison during the 18th century. Exhibits on salty French and American prisoners accompany ones on the role of Kinsale as wine port, culminating in a world map made out of corks. (Open June-Sept. daily 9am-5pm. £3, students £1.50.)

In 1915, the British ocean liner *Lusitania* sank off the Old Head of Kinsale, a promontory south of the town; over 1000 civilians died. A German torpedo was to blame, and the resulting furor helped propel the United States into World War I. Hearings on the *Lusitania* case took place in the Kinsale Courthouse, Market Sq. The courthouse now contains a regional museum expected to reopen in the summer of 2000 after extensive renovations. In town, up the hill from Market Square, the restored west tower of the 12th century **Church of St. Multose,** patron saint of Kinsale, is worth peaking your head into. Its ancient graveyard bewitches visitors, though nearby construction projects can upset the tranquility of both visitor's and residents. (Tel. 772 220. Church open until dusk. Graveyard always open. Free.)

If forts and museums aren't adventure enough for you, the **Kinsale Outdoor Education Centre** (tel. 772 896) rents windsurfing equipment, kayaks, and dinghies. Full-day deep-sea fishing trips and scuba diving excursions can be arranged at **Castlepark Marina** (tel. 774 959) arranges full-day deep-sea fishing trips. (Boats from £10 per hour, fishing from £25, rod rental £5.)

CLONAKILTY

Once a linen-making town with a workforce of over 10,000 people, Clonakilty ("Clon," pop. 5000) lies between Bandon and Skibbereen on N71. Henry Ford was born nearby, but residents take more pride in the 1890 birth of military leader, spy, and organizational genius **Michael Collins.** During the Civil War Collins returned to his home, incorrectly believing "they surely won't kill me in my own country." He was ambushed and killed 25 miles from town (see **Independence and Civil War,** p. 14). The area is peppered with monuments to national heroes who met bitter ends. Most visitors, however, are more interested in relaxing than causing a stir, so they head to the nearby **Inchydoney Beach.** Come nightfall, Clonakilty's streets reverberate with vibrant pubs and live music. During the second week of July, Clon is especially lively with the **Black and White (Pudding) Festival,** when prizes are given out for best recipe and most pudding consumed. Not for the faint of heart, or stomach (see **Food,** p. 31).

🔃 **ORIENTATION AND PRACTICAL INFORMATION.** Clonakilty's main streets jut out from the statue of the axe-wielding rebel **Tadgh an Astna. Pearse St.** runs inland and turns into **Western Rd.** To the rear of the statue Rossa St. passes the **Wheel of Fortune Water Pump** and runs into **Connelly.** Astna St. and **Wolfe Tone St.** angle off the statue towards the harbor, making a triangle with **Clark St.**

Buses from **Skibbereen** (2-3 per day, £4.30) and **Cork** (4 per day, £5.90) stop in front of Lehane's Supermarket on Pearse St. The new **tourist office,** Wolfe Tone St. (tel. 33226), hands out maps and advice. (Open May-Dec. 9am-6pm.) **AIB** and **Bank of Ireland** cash in on Pearse St.; both have an **ATM.** The **post office** addresses town from a Gothic building on Patrick St. (Open M-F 9am-5:30pm, Sa. 10am-4pm.) You can walk the 3 mi. to Inchydoney or rent a **bike** at **MTM Cycles** (tel. 33584) on Ashe St. (£8 per day, £35 per week.) The **phone code** is a bit of blood and 023 shoved into an intestine and fried up.

█ ACCOMMODATIONS. The sparklingly clean **Old Brewery Hostel,** Emmet Sq. (tel. 33525), also known as the Clonakilty Hostel, sports a super kitchen, comfortable new beds, and a slightly dour atmosphere. Coming from Lehane's, head down Pearse St., make a left at the Roman Catholic church, then a right at the park in Emmet Sq. (Dorms £7, doubles £20. Wheelchair accessible.) Just east of town is Mrs. McMahon's **Nordav,** 70 Western Rd. (tel. 33655), a right turn after the museum. Set back from the road behind a well-groomed lawn and splendid rose gardens, this B&B features gloriously huge three-room suites and smaller, but still lovely, double rooms (£18-25 per person). **Desert House Camping Park** (tel. 33331) is connected to a dairy farm, a half mile southeast of town on Ring Road. (£6 per family tent, 50p per person; £5 per small tent. Showers 50p. Open May-Sept.)

█ FOOD AND PUBS. Clonakilty is famous (or infamous) for its style of **black pudding,** a sausage-like concoction made from beef, blood, and grains (see **Food and Drink,** p. 31). For those eager to try it, or the white variety (made with pork and no blood) pull up a chair at **Twomey's** (tel. 33365; open M-Sa 9am-6pm), or head to any local market. Luckily, Clonakilty offers other culinary options. **Fionnuala's Little Italian Restaurant,** 30 Ashe St. (tel. 34355), has commendable food and a wide variety of wines in an old Irish house. (Meals from £5.50. Open daily 6pm-10pm.) **Betty Brosnan,** 58 Pearse St. (tel. 34011), specializes in homemade baked goods, lasagna, and sandwiches. (£2-5. Open daily 9am-6pm.) Brown-bag it at **Lehane's Supermarket** (tel. 33359) on Pearse St. (Open M-Th 8am-6:30pm, F 8am-9pm, Sa 8am-7pm, Su 9am-1:30pm.)

There's music aplenty in Clonakilty. The hugely popular **De Barra's** on Pearse St. (tel. 33381), has folk and trad nightly all year. Though the pub is enormous (3 rooms, 2 bars, and a beer garden), you'll be feeling claustrophobic by 8:30pm. Four nights a week, trad bounces off the walls of **O'Brien's,** Rossa St. (tel. 35570), and into its beer garden. Around the corner from De Barra's, **Shanley's,** 11 Connolly St. (tel. 33790), juggles folk, rock, and the occasional nationally known star. Nightly music, pool, and darts, keep **Bernie's Bar,** Rossa St. (tel. 33567), filled from wall to poster-covered wall.

█ SIGHTS. To fill the hours before the pubs pick up, join the locals and birds at **Inchydoney Beach,** billed as one of the nicest beaches east of Malibu. On Inchydoney Rd., you'll pass the **West Cork Model Railway Village,** where the towns of Kinsale, Bandon, and Clonakilty, all along the former West Cork Railway, are replicated in miniature circa 1940. (Tel. 33224. Open daily Feb.-Oct. 11am-5pm, Sa-Su 1-5pm. £3, students £2.) Back in town, the **West Cork Museum,** Western Rd., displays an early 20th century beer pouring machine, the christening shawl of patriot O'Donovan Rossa, and other assorted historical Clon minutiae. (Open May-Oct. M-Sa 10:30am-5:30pm, Su 2:30-5:30pm. £1.50, students 50p.) Tours of various sites relating to the life and death of **Michael Collins** can be arranged through the tourist office or Timothy Crowley (tel. 46107). The **Lios na gCon Ring Fort,** 2 mi. east, has been "fully restored" based on excavators' clues. It is still undergoing some construction; inquire at the tourist office about the date of its completion.

UNION HALL AND CASTLETOWNSHEND

In the land that lies between Clonakilty and Skibbereen, pastures and rolling hills give way to forests as the landscape gets too rocky for farming. Sleepy towns dot the hills, each with a few rows of pastel houses, a couple of B&Bs, and at least a few pubs. Just across the water from the picturesque but unexciting hamlet of Glandore sits the fishing village of **Union Hall**, once a hangout for **Jonathan Swift** and family. Now it's home to the legendary ☒**Maria's Schoolhouse (IHH)** (tel. (028) 33002). Formerly the Union Hall National School, Maria's hostel is resplendently a redecorated and refitted with a cathedral ceiling and an enormous window in the huge common room, big skylights in the dorm, and a healthy breakfast spread. This hostel is reason enough for a detour en route to Skibbereen. (Dorms £8, doubles £20-30. Hot breakfast £5, continental £3; 3-course dinner with the off-chance of musical accompaniment £15. Laundry £4. **Bike rental** £7 per day. **Canoeing** lessons £15 per 2hr. Wheelchair accessible.) Maria's also houses **Atlantic Sea Kayaking** (tel. 33002), which offers a variety of kayaking lessons and expeditions. (2hr. lesson £15, 3hr. £25, 6hr. £35.) To get to Maria's, turn right in the center of Union Hall, left at the church, and straight for half a mile, or call Maria for a lift. Back in town, **Dinty's Bar** (tel. (028) 33373) serves up huge portions of seafood-geared grub. (Dinners from £5.50; food served 12:30-2:30pm and 6-9pm.) **Nolan's Bar** (tel. (028) 33758) supplies a few bites and spirited trad on Wednesday and Friday nights. **Casey's Bar** (tel. (028) 33590) provides a waterside-patio beer garden on which to enjoy your fresh seafood or less expensive pub grub. (Food served daily noon-8:30pm.) **Mahoney's** (tel. (028) 33610) jovial atmosphere and billiard tables draw a young crowd.

Pterodactyl teeth, dinosaur droppings, stone age calendars, and rifles from the Easter Rising draw scholars from across the world to the **Ceim Hill Museum,** about 3 mi. outside town. From Maria's Schoolhouse, head right, keeping the lake to your left. The steep road up Ceim Hill is to the right, past a set of farm buildings. The museum's proprietress, who is possibly older and more interesting than most of her exhibited items, found many of these prehistoric artifacts in her backyard. (Tel. (028) 36280. Open daily 10am-6:30pm. £2.)

Travelers passing along the Skibbereen Road toward Union Hall may want to pause in the shady seaside groves of **Rennin Forest**. Further on, signs point out **Castletownshend,** the point of hasty escape for many defeated rebels after the **Battle of Kinsale.** Visitors with time to pause in this hamlet by the sea, can pop into **Mary Ann's Bar and Restaurant** (tel. (028) 36146) for cream- and seafood-oriented pub grub. (Food served noon-2:30pm and 6-9pm.) **Knockdrum Fort,** just west of town, is a typical example of what becomes of an Iron Age Celtic fort over the centuries.

SKIBBEREEN

The biggest town in West Cork, Skibbereen (pop. 2100) is a convenient stop for travelers roaming through the more gorgeous wilds of Co. Cork. When Algerian pirates sacked Baltimore in 1631, the survivors moved inland, establishing Skibbereen as a sizable settlement. The town suffered particularly during the Famine; a popular post-famine folk ballad litanizes the "cruel reasons" that led many residents to "leave old Skibbereen." Recently, however, the town has seen happier days, evolving into a market town for Cork's farmers. Friday is the best day to visit, when farmers tote in plants, fresh produce, and pies for sale on Bridge St. (early afternoon). Or treat yourself to a new heifer at the cattle market on Wednesdays, also on Bridge St. (11am-4pm.) Many stores in Skibbereen close on Thursday at around noon to recover between busy market days.

🚩 **ORIENTATION AND PRACTICAL INFORMATION.** Skibbereen is L-shaped, with **North St.** standing as the base and **Main St.** and **Bridge St.** comprising the height (Main St. turns into Bridge St. at the small bridge). The clock tower, post office, and stately "Maid of Erin" statue are at the elbow. Hitchers typically stay on

N71 to go east or west but switch to R595 to go south. **Buses** stop in front of Cala-hane's Bar, Bridge St. and run to Baltimore (June-Sept. M-Sa 5 per day, Oct.-May 4 per day; £2.10), Cork (M-Sa 3 per day, Su 2 per day; £8.80), Clonakilty (M-F 3 per day, Sa 2 per day; £4.40), and Killarney (1 per day, £11). The **tourist office** (tel. 21766) is housed in the Town Hall, North St. (Open in summer M-F 9:15am-5:30pm.) **AIB,** 9 Bridge St. (tel. 21388), and **Bank of Ireland,** Market St. (tel. 21700), are both open M-Tu and Th-F 10am-4pm, W 10am-5pm. **Roycroft Stores** (tel. 21810), Ilen St. off Bridge St. **rent bikes.** (£8.50-10 per day, includes helmet; £40 deposit. Raleigh's One-Way Rent-A-Bike; call for details. Open M-Sa 9:15am-6pm.) Scrub those duds at **Hourihane's Launderette,** Ilen St. (tel. 22697), behind the Busy Bee. (£3.50 per load. Open daily 10am-10pm.) The **post office** can be found in The Square. Open M-Sa 9am-5:30pm. Skib's **phone code** is 028.

▌ ACCOMMODATIONS. **Russagh Mill Hostel and Adventure Center (IHH,)** grinds to a halt about 1mi. out of town on Castletownshend Rd. (tel. 22451). This renovated 200-year-old mill regularly hosts groups of hikers and rock climbers, along with taking in a few hostelers on the side. (Dorms £8, private rooms £12 per person. Check-out 10:30am.) The proprietress of **Bridge House,** Bridge St. (tel. 21273), could be a set designer for Victorian period films. Bridge House is a visual experi-ence, with lavish canopy beds in ornate satin-laced rooms, and the biggest bathtub in Cork. (£17, with bath £18.) **Ivanhoe** on North St. (tel. 21749), has big beds and bathrooms, and tasty breakfast. (Singles £20; doubles Jun.-Aug. £18 per person, Sept.-May £15 per person.) The **Hideaway Campground,** Castletownshend St. (tel. 22254), just outside of town keeps the concrete walls within view. (2-person tent £8. Showers 50p.)

▐▊ FOOD AND PUBS. Along Main and North St. a handful of inviting options exist in the cluster of cafés. Skib's **SuperValu** supermarket (tel. 21400) does its stuff on Main St. (Open M-Sa 9am-6:30pm). **◪The Wine Vaults',** Bridge St. (tel. 23112), delicious and inexpensive pizzas, sandwiches, and salads transcend the term "pub grub." (Food served daily noon-9pm.) At **Kalbo's Bistro,** 48 North St. (tel. 21515), cool jazz and innovative meals go hand in hand. The desserts are a must. (Lunch £4.50-6.50, dinner from £7. Open M-Sa 11:30am-4:30pm, 6:30-9:30pm, Su noon-2:30pm, 6:30-9:30pm.) Wake up well with **The Stove's,** Main St. (tel. 22500), morning scones and hearty breakfasts. Drop by later in the day for Irish specialties. (Meals £4-5. Open M-Sa 8am-6pm.) **Bernard's,** on Main St. (tel. 21772), behind O'Brien's Off License, serves above-average pub grub and baked goods in a large, beautiful bar/restaurant. (Meals £7-10; food served 9am-9pm.) The **Elton Hotel Bistro,** Bridge St. (tel. 22000), claims that Michael Collins ate his last meal here. Supposing things haven't changed since 1922, he had a good variety to choose from, including vege-tarian options. (Meals £6-13. Open 8am-9pm.)

Find live blues and folk and a young crowd at the **Wine Vaults,** where locals and tourists mingle jovially. The most comfortable digs are at **Bernard's,** all the better to converse in. **Seán Óg's,** Market St. (tel. 21573), hosts contemporary folk and blues several nights a week, a Tuesday night trad session, and an outdoor beer gar-den nightly. **Kearney's Well,** 52-53 North St. (tel. 21350), attracts lively locals, while the **Cellar Bar,** Main St. (tel. 21329), has boisterous chatter to accompany the clat-ter of billiards. On Fridays and Saturdays, the Cellar opens up Skibbereen's only disco, **DF's Nite Club.** (Disco 11:30pm-2am. Cover £5.)

▨ SIGHTS. The **West Cork Arts Centre,** North St., across from the town library, shows changing exhibits of Irish art and a permanent collection of Cork crafts. (Tel. 22090. Gallery open M-Sa 10am-6pm. Free.) It also schedules poetry readings, concerts, dance performances, and other cultural events. Get wired into the local arts scene with a free copy of *Art Beat*, a guide to the arts in Cork, available at the Centre. The **gardens** at **Liss Ard Experience,** down Castletownshend Rd. toward the hostel, promise to "induce new perceptions of light and sky." Created as a unique attempt at conservation, the nonprofit organization's 50 acres include a waterfall garden, a wildflower meadow (with over 100 species of butterflies), and the surreal "Irish sky garden," designed by American artist James Turrell. (Tel. 22368. Open May-Sept. M-F 9am-6pm, Su noon-6pm. £3, students £2.) Three and a half miles west of town on the Baltimore Rd., the well-maintained **Creagh Gardens** contrast with their woodland setting. (Tel. 22121. Open daily 10am-6pm. £3, children £1.50.) During the end of July, Skibbereen celebrates **Welcome Home Week,** which features street entertainment and live bands.

BALTIMORE

Once a seaside base for pirates, the tiny fishing village of Baltimore (pop. 200) now serves as a point of departure for **Sherkin Island** and **Cape Clear Island.** The watery graves offshore hold scores of **shipwrecks,** making Baltimore a diver's hunting grounds. On land, the stone remains of **Dún na Sead, "The Fort of the Jewels,"** one of nine 16th century O'Driscoll castles stand in the center of town. Even today, your best bet at stopping a man in the street is to shout, "Mr. O'Driscoll!" O'Driscoll family members from near and far congregate here every June to elect a chieftain and to stage a family gathering, complete with live music, jammed pubs, and inebriation. Artists and tourists come here with equal enthusiasm to enjoy bright, dramatic seascapes.

⌖ ORIENTATION AND PRACTICAL INFORMATION. Baltimore's main road runs about a mile and a half through town and out to the **Beacon,** a lighthouse perched on a magnificent cliff with views over the ocean and across to **Sherkin Island.** The window of the post office has a full schedule of the **buses** running to and from Skibbereen (M-Sa 3-4 per day). Information about **ferry service** is available from the ferry offices at the Sherkin Islands (tel. 20125) and **Cape Clear Island** (tel. 39119). The **tourist office** (tel. 20441), halfway up the steps from the ferry depot, is non-Bord Fáilte and keeps sporadic hours. Next door, **Islands Craft** (tel. 20347) dispenses helpful information on Sherkin and Cape Clear, including ferry schedules and historical accounts of the islands, but has sporadic hours. All crafts in the shop are handmade on one of the islands. (Open Jul.-Aug. M-Sa 11am-5:30pm, Su 12:30-5:30pm.) The **post office** is inside the small general store above the craft shop. (Open M-F 9am-5:30pm, Sa 9am-1pm.) The **phone code** is a pillaging 028.

⌂⌕⌷ ACCOMMODATIONS, FOOD, AND PUBS. A visit to Baltimore requires a stay at **Rolf's Hostel (IHH),** Skibbereen Rd. (tel. 20289). A delightful German family runs this 300-year-old complex of stone farmhouses a 10-minute walk up the turnoff immediately before the village. Comfortable pine beds (brass in the private rooms) and a dining room with stunning views and delicious food are hard to resist. (Dorms £7-8; doubles £25. **Camping** £3.50 per person. Laundry £4. **Bike rental** £7 per day, part of the Wheel Escapes program, see p. 210.) Rolf's also runs **Cafe Art,** where guests can choose from an extensive, if expensive, menu. (Main courses £9-11.50.) The **Lifeboat Restaurant** (tel. 20143), in the post office building, serves cheap soup, sandwiches, quiche, and pastries, in a glass room on the harbor's edge. (Entrees £3-5. Open daily 10am-5:30pm.) Stock up on food for the islands at **Cotter's** (tel. 20106), on the main road facing the harbor. (Open M-Sa 9:30am-8pm, Su 10:30am-8pm.) All of Baltimore's pubs offer food. **Declan McCarthy's,** just above the pier (tel. 20159), is the liveliest pub, with trad and folk (often big name) bands three to four nights a week in summer. (Occasional cover £3-6.) The comfortable stools and tables outside **Bushe's Bar** (tel. 20125) are prime spots for scoping out the harbor. Just around the corner, the cozy **Algiers Inn** (tel. 20145), lures many a tourist to its comfortable interior. (Food served M-Sa 5:30-9:30pm.)

◨ SIGHTS. Much to the woe of landlubbers, many of Baltimore's best sights are under water. Wrecks of U-boats and galleons await the amphibious. To arrange dives or rentals, contact the **Baltimore Diving & Watersports Centre** (tel.

20300), on the pier near the ferry dock. (3hr. dive, including equipment from £45; course and dive for the inexperienced £30; sea angling trips from £30 per day.) The tourist office casts out information on deep sea angling and sailing trips. **Atlantic Boating Service** (tel. 22734), located at the end of the pier, offers water-skiing (starting at £20 per 30min.) and boat rental (summer £15 per hour, off-season £10 per hour). Explorers equipped with bicycles or cars head east to circle **Lough Ine** (EYEN, sometimes spelled Hyne), Northern Europe's only saltwater lake, where clear rapids change direction with the tide. The lough, originally a freshwater lake, was inundated when sea levels rose after the last Ice Age. It is now a stomping ground for marine biologists, who search out the dozens of subtropical species it shelters. Trails thread through the woods around the lake, with the steeper climbs affording incredible views.

SHERKIN ISLAND

Just an hour away by ferry from Baltimore, Sherkin Island (pop. 100) offers sandy, cliff-enclosed beaches, wind-swept heath, an over-abundance of cows, and absence of people. **Ferries** come from **Baltimore** (in summer 8 per day, in winter 3 per day, £4 return). Ferry schedules are posted outside the Island Craft office in Baltimore (see above), and **Vincent O'Driscoll** (tel. 20125) can provide information. Ferries also run from **Schull** (1hr., July-Aug. 3 per day, June and Sept. 2 per day, £6 return). For information, call Kieran Molloy (tel. 28138).

Spending the night on Sherkin Island is a tranquil treat at **Cuina House** (tel. 20384) where every spacious, wood-floored room offers an ocean view. To reach the B&B, take the road behind the Jolly Roger. (£16, with bath £18. Evening meals £8.) **Murphy's Bar** (tel. 20116), close to the ferry landing and next to Dún-na-Long ruins, has mean pints and expansive views. (Food served 12:30-7pm.) The **Islander Restaurant** (tel. 20116) next door offers an informal atmosphere and a fine view of the harbor. (Dinner served 6-9:30pm. Open June-Sept.) The amiable **Jolly Roger** (tel. 20379) across the street has sessions nearly every night in summer, and quite dependable pub grub until late. The **Abbey** (tel. 20181), on the main road, is the only food store on the island and stocks only the basics. (Open in summer M-Sa 9am-6pm, Su noon-6pm.)

The first thing you'll encounter off the ferry, are the ruins of a 15th century **Franciscan abbey** founded by Fineen O'Driscoll. Vengeful troops from Waterford sacked the abbey in 1537 to get back at the O'Driscolls for stealing Waterford's wine. The ruins are currently undergoing renovation, and may be open to the public by summer of 2000. Unimpressive **Dún-na-Long Castle** ("fort of the ships"), also built by the buccaneer clan and sacked in the same raid, lies in ruins north of the abbey behind Murphy's Bar. (Castle always open. Free.) Stay straight on the main road from the ferry dock and you'll pass the blue-green **Kinnish Harbour** and Sherkin's yellow one-room schoolhouse, where the island educates its children. The beaches on Sherkin are sandy, gradually sloped, and great for swimming. **Trabawn Strand, Cow Strand,** and the long **Silver Strand** are all on the west side of the island (follow the main road and sign posts). The defunct **lighthouse** on **Horseshoe Harbour** stares across the channel toward her sister in Baltimore.

CAPE CLEAR ISLAND (OILEÁN CHLÉIRE)

The rugged landscape seen from the bumpy ferry docking at Cape Clear Island seems incapable of providing for its sparse population of 150 individuals. But the island swells in capacity every summer with the arrival secondary school students who come here to brush up on their Irish. The main industry of this wild and beautiful island, however, is still farming; the landscape of patchwork fields separated by low stone walls hasn't changed much since the Spanish galleons stopped calling here hundreds of years ago. The density of the hills in the terrain invites only the most enduring of bike riders. Life is leisurely and hours are approximate; the island's stores and pubs keep flexible hours, and B&Bs rise and decline according to the residents' inclination to host guests. For an updated version of opening hours and general island information, head to the **Co-op office** (tel. 39119), where they hand out free maps, or check the bulletin board at the end of the pier. **Ferries** run to and from **Baltimore** (June and Sept. 2 per day; July-Aug. M-Sa 3 per day, Su 4 per day; Oct.-Apr. M-Th and Sa-Su 1 per day, F 2 per day; May M-F 2 per day, Sa-Su 1 per day; £8 return). Call Capt. Conchúr O'Driscoll (tel. 39135) for more information. Ferries to the island from **Schull** leave daily in June at 5:30pm and in July and August at 10am, 2:30pm, and 4:30pm.

⌐ ACCOMMODATIONS. Cléire Lasmuigh (An Óige/HI) (tel. 39144), the Cape Clear Island Adventure Centre and Hostel, is about a 10-minute walk from the pier (keep to the left on the main road). The hostel often fills up with Irish students in the summer, so those eager to enjoy its comfy dorms and harbor views should call ahead. (June-Sept. £7, Oct.-May £6.) The **Roaringwater Bay Centre** (tel. 39198) runs **sea kayaking** and **diving** trips out of the hostel, luring armies of adventurers to the picturesque stone building. (Kayaking from £35, diving from £25.) The proprietors of Ciarán Danny Mike's (see **Food and Pubs**) run the hospitable **Cluain Mara B&B** (tel. 39153) in the house adjacent to their pub. (£15, with bath £16; self-catering apartment across the road £25.) Further along the road, up the steep hill past the hostel, **Ard Na Ganthe** (tel. 39160) has spacious doubles and family rooms (£16 per person). **Cuas an Uisce campsite** (tel. 39136), on the south harbor, is a five-minute walk from the harbor: go up the main road, turn right past the motley-colored houses, then bear left. Campers get a glorious view of the hostel across the lovely harbour. (Open June-Sept. £2.70 per person. Tent rental £10. Showers 50p.)

⌐⎍ FOOD AND PUBS. The one grocery store, **An Siopa Beag** (tel. 39119), stocks the essentials, like ice cream, in a white building a few hundred yards down the pier to the right (open Jun.- Aug. M-Sa 9:30am-1:30pm, 2:30-6pm; Sept.-May 9:30am-4pm). The island **craft shop** sells everything from used books to warm sweaters, and gives out information for free. (Open Sept.-June daily 9:30am-1:30pm, July 2:30-6pm, Aug. 7:30am-8:30pm.) Food options on Cape Clear are limited. **Cistin Chéire** (tel. 39145) serves sandwiches, soup, and pastries harborside. (Sandwiches from £2.25. Open May-Sept. daily noon-6pm, 7:30-9pm.) **Ciarán Danny Mike's** (tel. 39172) is the southern-most pub in Ireland.

What the Cape Clear pub scene lacks in variety it makes up for in stamina. The island has no resident authorities to regulate after-hours drinking. The island's 150 people support three pubs. **The Night Jar's** (tel. 39102) boisterous atmosphere makes up for its bare interior, while **Club Chléire** (tel. 39184), above the café, has live sessions most weekend nights, often lasting until 4am or later. Those feeling spontaneous should bring their ukuleles to **Ciarán Danny Mike's** for good spirits, song, and billiards.

⌘ SIGHTS. About a 25min. walk up a steep hill from the pier is the island's **Heritage Centre,** half a room containing everything from an O'Driscoll family tree to a deck chair from the equally ubiquitous *Lusitania*. Since over half of the exhibits are in Irish, it's a quick trip for the Irish-challenged. (Open June-Aug. daily 2-5:30pm. £1.50, students £1, under 18 50p.) On the road to the center, **Cleire Goats** (tel. 39126) is home to the best bred goats in Ireland, if not the world. For 75p you can test the owners claim that goat's milk ice cream is richer than the cow kind. Cleire Goats also runs half-day to 8-week goat-keeping courses that promise to blend "theory and practice." A right turn past the heritage center leads to the **windmills** that until recently generated three-quarters of the island's electricity. From the island's many hills, you can gaze out at the ruins of an O'Driscoll castle (near the North Harbor) and the old lighthouse (to the south, beyond the hostel). Neither building, or what remains of them, can be explored, however, for both are private property. Offshore 3 mi. to the east, is **Fasnet Lighthouse.** Cape Clear also shelters gulls, stormy petrels, cormorants, and ornithologists. The **bird observatory,** the white farmhouse on North Harbour, is one of the most important in Europe. Get a hefty dose of island lore at Cape Clear's annual **International Storytelling Festival** (tel. 39157) in early September, featuring puppet workshops, music sessions, and a weekend's worth of memorable tales. (£6 per event, £24 for the festival.)

THE MIZEN HEAD PENINSULA

If you've made the mistake of skipping Cape Clear Island, you'll have to take the land route to Schull, Crookhaven, and Mizen Head. Whatever route you choose, you'll end up at the windswept, beach-laden, and gloriously unspoiled southwest tip of Ireland. The **phone code** masts the Mizen at 028.

SCHULL

A seaside hamlet 45min. by ferry from Cape Clear and 4 mi. west of Ballydehob on R592, Schull (SKULL) is the last glimpse of culture and commerce on the peninsula. With its one busy street, a great hostel, and excellent eateries, it's the best base for exploring the **Mizen Head Peninsula.** Be warned that many travelers are wise to Schull's charms; holiday cottages and B&Bs draw droves of vacationers during the summer months.

⊠ PRACTICAL INFORMATION. Buses to Cork (M-Sa 3 per day, Su 1 per day; £13 return) and **Goleen** (2 per day, 1 on Sundays) stop in front of the AIB building on Main St. From June to September, there is also bus service between Schull and **Killarney** (1 per day). Check the schedule posted in the window of the library on Main St., and at the Bunratty Inn, the local Bus Éireann agent. **Ferries** connect Schull to **Cape Clear** and **Sherkin** (June and Sept. 1 per day, July-Aug. 3 per day, £8 return) and to Baltimore (June-mid-Sept. 3 per day, £6 return). Contact Capt. O'Driscoll (tel. 39135) for more information. Pick up the prosaic and lengthy *Schull Guide*, which has particularly good suggestions for walks and bike rides in the area, in any store (£1.50). Either sing on a street corner or get cash at the **24hr. ATM** at **AIB** (tel. 28132) on Upper Main St. (Open M-F 10am-12:30pm and 1:30-4pm.) Although many of Schull's attractions are aquatic, terrestrial types can **rent bikes** at **Freewheelin'**, Cotter's Yard (tel. 28165), off Main St. (£8 per day, £45 per week. Open M-Sa 10am-noon.) A cheaper and more convenient option is the Wheels Escapes program (see p. 210), available at the hostel in Schull. The **post office**, Main St. (tel. 28110), shares shutter space with a photography shop.

▛▟▟ ACCOMMODATIONS, FOOD, PUBS. Schull's appeal for budget travelers is immeasurably enhanced by the presence of the **Schull Backpackers' Lodge (IHH),** Colla Rd. (tel. 28681). From the Pier head right towards town, then bear left at the fork, turn left at the church; the way is well marked. The wooden lodge is bright and immaculate, with fluffy comforters, and some of the best showers in West Cork. (High-season dorms £8; quads £8; doubles £24, with bath £26. Laundry £3. **Bike rental** £7 per day, £35 per week.) **Adele's B&B,** Main St. (tel. 28459), warms you up with small fireplaces and dark wooden floors. (£14.50, includes continental breakfast.) Three miles from town on the way to Goleen, **Jenny's Farmhouse** (tel. 28205) offers a quiet place to crash. (£10, with breakfast £12-14. Ideal for drivers and bicyclists; call for possible pick-up from Schull.)

Schull is known for its upscale shopping and eateries. The town is a treat for scone and brown bread connoisseurs. **Adele's Restaurant** (tel. 28459) bakes decadent cakes and pastries, and dishes up tasty soups, salads, and sandwiches in a proper tea room. She opens again in the evening for scrumptious, if pricey, meals. (Dinner £8-10. Lunch and tea served Tu-Su 9:30am-6pm, dinner Th-Su 6-10pm. Open May-Oct.) Not to be outdone, the multi-talented **Courtyard** (tel. 28390) down the street bakes eight types of bread (85p-£1) and sells a variety of gourmet wholefoods, soups, and sandwiches. (Store open M-Sa 10am-4pm. Fish, pasta, and meat dinners served daily 6:30-9:30pm.) On Mondays, Fridays, and some Sundays, the adjacent **pub** features trad, jazz, and blues. The **Bunratty Inn** (tel. 28341), up the hill on Main St., prepares, as proclaimed on a sign outside, some of West Cork's finest pub fare. (Meals from £6; food served M-Sa noon-8pm.) The **Bunratty Inn** and **An Tigín** (tel. 28830) both host live folk and rock one night a week during the summer. **The Galley Inn** (tel. 28733) concocts a mean bowl of soup and pricey meat and fish dinners as well as rollicking tunes twice a week and during some long weekends. (Food served noon-3pm and 5:30-8:30pm.) Before leaving, stock up for Mizen forays at one of Schull's **grocery stores** on Main St.: **Spar Market** (tel. 28236; open M-Sa 7am-9pm, Su 8am-8pm) or smaller **Hegarty's Centra** (tel. 28520) across the street (open daily 7:30am-10:30pm).

☎ **SIGHTS.** Schull is a great spot from which to explore the **walking** and **biking** trails that snake along the water and up the nearby hills. Inquire at the Backpacker's Lodge for maps and information. The Republic's only planetarium, the **Schull Planetarium**, Colla Rd., offers extraterrestrial diversions for rainy days. (Tel. 28552. £1. 54min. star shows at 4pm or 8pm; £3.) A calm harbor and numerous shipwrecks make Schull a diver's paradise. The **Watersports Centre** (tel. 28554) on the pier **rents dinghies, sailboards, wet-suits,** and **scuba tanks.** (Open M-Sa 9:30am-8:30pm. Dinghies £25 half day, windsurfing £10 half day.)

CROOKHAVEN AND MIZEN HEAD

The Mizen becomes more scenic and less populated the farther west one goes from Schull. The peninsula continues to lose its native population, with reinforcements coming in the form of European house-buyers. Accordingly, the Mizen is mobbed during peak-season weekends, as water-worshippers pack sandy beaches. The most reliable transit is **Betty's Bus Hire** (tel. 28410), which will take you on a tour of the Mizen via the scenic coast road (£5). The tour includes bits of local history and runs to the **Mizen Vision** (see below). Betty leaves from Schull at 11am on Tuesdays and Thursdays in June, July, and August; other times can be arranged. **Bus Éireann** only goes as far as **Goleen** (2 per day; inquire in Schull or Ballydehob for schedule). **Hitching,** which is not recommended by *Let's Go*, is convenient in the peak-season, with hitchers often perching at the crossroads on Goleen Rd. outside of town. Confident **cyclists** can make a daytrip to Mizen Head (36mi. return from Schull).

The block-long town of **Goleen** seems to move at half-pace with only half-charm. Just up the hill from town is **The Ewe** (tel. 35492), a surprising and wonderfully eccentric "art retreat." For £2, visitors can stroll the eclectically decorated garden, and may be enticed to stay for a week long pottery class (from £125, including spacious accommodation). Recluses wishing to stay the night can treat themselves to **Heron's Cove B&B** (tel. 35225), down the hill from Goleen on the water (£18.50-25). The **restaurant** downstairs serves excellent seafood, although catching the fish out back yourself would be a good deal cheaper (sandwiches from £4).

Slightly longer than the main road, and tremendously worthwhile, the coast road winds to Barley Cove Beach and Mizen Head. Tiny **Crookhaven** (pop. 37), a 1 mi. detour off this road, is perched at the end of its own peninsula. You can meet half of the population at work in **O'Sullivan's** (tel. 35319), which serves sandwiches, soups, desserts, and cold pints on the water's edge (food served noon-8:30pm); and the **Crookhaven Inn** (tel. 35309), which provides similar fare in a lovely outdoor cafe overlooking the bay. (Sandwiches £1.70, meals £5-7; food served daily noon-8pm.) **Barley Cove Caravan Park** (tel. 35302), 1½ mi. from Crookhaven, offers camping on the edge of the wind-swept peninsula. (£9 per tent. Mini-market and laundry. Open Easter-Sept. **Bike rental** £5 per ½-day, £8 per day; deposit £40.) Campers have a short walk to the warm, shallow waters of **Barley Cove Beach,** a sandy retreat for those bathers not ready to brave the frigid sea.

Three miles past Barley Cove, Ireland ends at spectacular **Mizen Head,** whose cliffs rise to 700 ft. **Mizen Head Lighthouse,** built in 1909, was recently automated and electrified, and the buildings nearby were turned into a small museum, the **Mizen Vision.** To get to the museum, you'll have to cross a suspension bridge only slightly less harrowing than the rendering of a shipwreck that is its centerpiece. The museum also assembles lighthouse paraphernalia and illuminates the solitary lives of lighthouse keepers. Its small, very windy viewing platform is the most southwesterly point in Ireland. (Tel. 35115. Open June-Sept. daily 10am-6pm; Apr.-May and Oct. 10:30am-5pm; Nov.-Mar. Sa-Su 11am-4pm. £250, students £1.75.)

BEARA PENINSULA

The wild and majestic scenery of the Beara is combined with a profound sense of tranquility. Fortunately, the hordes of tourists circling the nearby Ring of Kerry usually skip the Beara altogether. For unspoiled scenery and solitude the Beara is superb; if you're looking for pubs, people, and other signs of civilization, you might be happier on the Iveragh or Dingle Peninsulas.The spectacular **Caha** and **Slieve Miskish Mountains** march down the center of the peninsula, separating the Beara's rocky southern coast from its lush northern coast. West Beara remains remote—travelers traverse treacherous single-track roads along the stark Atlantic coastline, picking their way past mountains, rocky outcrops, and the occasional herd of sheep. The dearth of cars west of Glengarriff makes **cycling** the Beara a joy (weather permitting), but for **hitchhikers,** the town marks the point at which they'll find themselves admiring the same views for longer than their sanity can bear.

BANTRY

According to the *Book of Invasions*, Ireland's first human inhabitants landed just a mile from Bantry (see **Legends and Folktales,** p. 20). Invading Bantry quickly became a fad, with English settlers arriving in the bay and driving the Irish out in the 17th century. Wolfe Tone and a band of Irish patriots tried to return the favor with the help of an ill-fated French Armada in 1796. Today's invaders come in the form of tourists eager to sample Bantry's elegance and relive its history, or to start off on a trek to the more remote areas westward.

⌇ PRACTICAL INFORMATION. Bantry sits at the east end of **Bantry Bay.** If your back is to the water, the road leading out of **Wolf Tone Square** to the right is **New St.,** which becomes **Bridge St. Williams St.** branches off New St. to the right. **Barrack St.** intersects New St. a bit farther up. **Sheep's Head** stretches due west and the Beara Peninsula is northwest. Cars, cyclists, and hitchers stay on N71 to get in or out of town. *Let's Go* does not recommend hitchhiking.

Buses stop outside of Julie's Takeaway in Wolfe Tone Sq., several doors from the tourist office toward the pier. **Bus Éireann** heads to **Glengarriff** (M-Sa 3 per day, Su 2 per day, £2.25), and **Cork** and **Bandon** (M-Sa 3 per day, Su 2 per day, £8.80). June-Sept. only, buses go to **Skibbereen** (2 per day), **Killarney** via **Kenmare** (2 per day), and **Schull** (1 per day). **Berehaven Bus Service** (tel. 70007) stops in Bantry on the way to and from **Cork.** The **tourist office** in Wolfe Tone Sq. (tel. 50229) has a bureau de change and maps of Bantry and Sheep's Head for sale. (Open Mar.-Oct. M-Sa 9am-6pm.) A Sheep's Head information kit (£4.95), including a map and well-illustrated book, is sold at the **Craft Shop** (tel. 50003) on Glengarriff Rd. (Open M-Sa 9:30am-6pm.) **AIB,** Wolfe Tone Sq. (tel. 50008) has an **ATM,** unlike **Bank of Ireland,** Wolf Tone Sq. (tel. 51377). (Both open M-W and F 10am-4pm, Th 10am-5pm.) **Rent bikes** from **Kramer's** (tel. 50278) on Glengarriff Rd., Newtown. (£8 per day, £40 per week; deposit credit card, license, or passport. Open M-Sa 9am-6pm.) **Coen's Pharmacy** (tel. 50531) dispenses cures on Wolfe Tone Sq. (Open M-Tu and Th-Sa 9:30am-1pm and 2-6pm, W 9:30am-1pm.) Find the **garda** Wolfe Tone Sq. (tel. 50045), and **St. Joseph's Bantry Hospital,** on Dromleigh (tel. 50133), a quarter-mile past the library. The **post office** (tel. 50050) is at 2 William St. (Open M-Sa 9am-5:30pm.) Bantry's **phone code** banters away at 027.

📐 ACCOMMODATIONS. Bantry Independent Hostel (IHH), Bishop Lucey Pl. (tel. 51050), not to be confused with the "small independent hostel" on the square, is the more comfortable and relaxed of Bantry's two hostels. Head away from town on Glengarriff Rd. (Marino St.), take the left fork, and walk a quarter mile. It has decent bunks, a pretty common room, and a secluded setting. (6-bed dorms £7; private rooms £10 per person. Key deposit £1. Laundry £4. Open mid-Mar.-Oct.) **Harbour View Hostel** (Small Independent Hostel), Harbour View (tel. 51140), to the left of the fire station along the water, provides basic, cramped accommodations. (Dorms £7; private rooms £7.50 per person). Four miles from town in Ballylickey, the **Eagle Point Camping and Caravan Park,** Glengarriff Rd. (tel. 50630), has private beach and tennis courts, a TV room, and free showers. (£4 per person. Laundry £3. Open May-Sept.)

📷🍴 FOOD AND PUBS. SuperValu supermarket is on New St. (Open M-Th 8:30am-7pm, F 8:30am-9pm, Sa 8:30am-6:30pm.) **Organico,** Glengarriff Rd. (tel. 51391), stocks health food. Bantry has a number of inexpensive restaurants. **O'Siochain,** Bridge St. (tel. 51339), serves well-prepared food in a comfy, kitschy coffeehouse. (Sandwiches £1.50, pizza and entrees from £5. Open daily 9am-10pm.) Vegetarians need not apply at **Peter's Steak House** (tel. 50025) on New St. (Most entrees £6-12. Open daily 10am-midnight.) Large and tasty portions of pizza and pasta can be had inexpensively at the **Brick Oven** (tel. 52500) in Wolfe Tone Sq. (Open M-Sa 11:30am-12:30am, Su 2pm-12:30am.)

Filling grub and rollicking good times can be found in Bantry's pubs. Bantry nightlife has kicked into overdrive thanks to **1796** (The Bantry Folk Club; tel. 52396), Wolfe Tone Sq. They host live music ranging from nationally known musicians to impromptu sessions and serve food. (Pasta £4-5, meat dishes £10; served daily noon-9pm.) Aside from being an exceedingly popular pub, **The Snug,** Wolf Tone Sq. (tel. 50051), also serves up grub at great prices (burgers £4-6) and occasional bursts of trad and folk. As any good seaside town should, Bantry sports its **Anchor Bar,** New St. (tel. 50012). Drop yours next to their miniature lighthouse and listen to folk or rock on Thursdays. **The Schooner,** off New St. (tel. 52115), carries a cargo of mixed music on weekends. Lonely Yankees should stop by the **Kilgoban Pub** on the way to the hostel—it was won by an American couple in the Guiness "win your own pub in Ireland" contest.

👁 SIGHTS. Bantry's biggest tourist attraction is **Bantry House,** a Georgian manor with an imposing garden overlooking Bantry Bay. The long and shaded driveway to the house is a 10min. walk from town on Cork Rd. The ornate interior is decorated with impressive art and furnishings, that matches the elaborate grounds. The former seat of the four Earls of Bantry (and the current residence of the same, though now less wealthy, family), the house was transformed into a hospital during Ireland's Civil War and again during the Emergency (neutral Éire's term for World War II). (Tel. 50047. Open mid-Mar.-Oct. daily 9am-6pm. House and garden £6, students £4. Garden £2.)

The same earls, however, had a bit of scrambling to do when Irish rebel **Theodore Wolfe Tone** successfully borrowed a bit of France's anti-English sentiment for his own anti-English insurrection (see **Rebellion, Union, Reaction, p. 10**). Wolfe Tone's idea and campaign, as well as the 1970s discovery of one Armada ship that had been scuttled in the harbor, is thoroughly and interestingly documented in the museum of the **1796 Bantry French Armada Exhibition Centre.** Enjoy the irony of its location next to Bantry House, the home of Richard White, who mobilized British resistance to Wolfe Tone's invasion. (Tel. 51796. Open Mar.-Nov. daily 10am-6pm. £3, students £1.75.) **Sea trips** (tel. 50310) circumnavigate the harbor or drop you at **Whiddy Island,** a blend of quiet beaches and crude oil depositories that attracts birds and their watchers. (Trips depart every hr. July-Sept. daily 10am-7pm. £4 return.)

County Kerry and West Cork

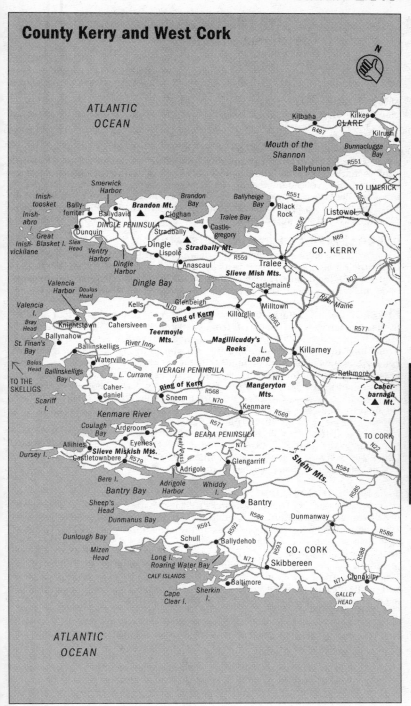

ATLANTIC OCEAN

ATLANTIC OCEAN

CLARE
Kilbaha
Kilkee
Kilrush
R487
Bunnaclugga Bay
Mouth of the Shannon
Ballybunion
R551
TO LIMERICK
Ballyheige Bay
Black Rock
Listowel
R556
CO. KERRY
N69
Smerwick Harbor
Brandon Bay
Inishtooskel
Ballyferriter
Brandon Mt.
Ballydavid
Cloghan
Tralee Bay
Castlegregory
Inishabro
DINGLE PENINSULA
Stradbally
Inishvickilane
Great Blasket I.
Dunquin
Dingle
Stradbally Mt.
Slea Head
Lispole
Ventry Harbor
Anascaul
Tralee
Dingle Harbor
Slieve Mish Mts.
N23
Castlemaine
R559
Dingle Bay
Valencia Harbor
Doulus Head
Kells
Glenbeigh
Milltown
River Maine
R577
Valencia I.
N70
Ring of Kerry
Killorglin
Bray Head
Knightstown
Cahersiveen
Teermoyle Mts.
Magillicuddy's Reeks
L. Leane
R563
Killarney
St. Finan's Bay
Ballynahow
Ballinskelligs
River Inny
Waterville
Rathmore
Bolus Head
Ballinskelligs Bay
L. Currane
IVERAGH PENINSULA
Mangerton Mts.
N71
Caherbarnagh Mt.
TO THE SKELLIGS
Caherdaniel
Ring of Kerry
R568
Sneem
N70
Kenmare
R569
TO CORK
Scariff I.
Kenmare River
R571
BEARA PENINSULA
N22
Coulagh Bay
Ardgroom
Eyeries
N71
Shehy Mts.
R584
Dursey I.
Allihies
Slieve Miskish Mts.
Castletownbere
R579
Adrigole
Glengarriff
R585
Bere I.
Adrigole Harbor
Whiddy I.
Bantry Bay
Sheep's Head
Bantry
Dunmanway
R586
Dunmanus Bay
R591
R592
R586
Dunlough Bay
Schull
Ballydehob
R593
CO. CORK
R588
Mizen Head
Long I.
N71
Skibbereen
Roaring Water Bay
CALF ISLANDS
Clonakilty
Baltimore
N71
Cape Clear I.
Sherkin I.
GALLEY HEAD

Bantry is home to the **West Cork Chamber Music Festival** (tel. 61576) during the last week of June. The heart of the festival is the **RTE Vanburgh String Quartet,** who are joined by scores of other international performers.

SHEEP'S HEAD

Largely ignored by tourists passing through Skibbereen, Bantry, and Glengarriff, narrow Sheep's Head makes a pleasant daytrip by bike or on foot. The **Sheep's Head Way** across the middle of the peninsula affords great mountain views. The **Craft Shop** in Bantry has a book and map detailing the walk (see above). Hitchers may find it difficult to get a ride to or from the peninsula, since it's the least populated part of West Cork. **Cyclists** head west along the cove-filled southern shore and return by the barren and windswept northern road, while **hikers** explore the spine of hills down the middle. Sheep's Head itself is marked by its lighthouse and spectacular, untouristed cliff top vistas. If you're lucky, you might see the tide change in Bantry Bay, where incoming breakers meet the outgoing tide to create a mini-maelstrom. For a snack on the way out, try the **Tin Pub** in **Ahakista,** on the southern road; the corrugated iron "shack" serves gratifying sandwiches.

GLENGARRIFF AND GARINISH ISLAND

Glengarriff is a choice gateway to the Beara Peninsula, with a handful of pubs and restaurants. A short ferry ride away, the bizarre gardens at Garinish Island contrast with the familiarly Irish scenery on the mainland. Glengarriff's popularity as an entrance way results in a town with more Aran sweaters than natives.

⚆ PRACTICAL INFORMATION. Buses stop in front of Casey's Hotel on Main St. **Bus Éireann** runs to Glengarriff from **Castletownbere** (£2.25), **Bantry** (25min., M-Sa 3-5 per day, Su 2-3 per day, £2.25), and **Skibbereen** (1½hr., 2 per day). From June to mid-September one Bus Éireann route runs along a string of gems twice a day: **Kenmare** (45min.), **Killarney** (1¾hr.), and **Tralee** (3hr.). **Berehaven Bus Service** (tel. 70007) serves **Cork** (2¾hr.; M-Sa 3 per day, Su 2 per day; £7) and **Bantry** (M 2 per day, Tu and Th-Sa 1 per day; £3). Glengarriff is graced with two friendly **tourist offices.** The Bord Fáilte office (tel. 63084) is on Bantry Rd. next to the Eccles Hotel, and has more hiking maps than a forest has trees. (Open June-Sept. M-Sa 10am-1pm and 2:15-6pm.) The large, privately run office is next to the public bathrooms and offers typical shamrock schlock. (Open daily 9am-6pm.) The **AIB,** Main St. (tel. 63220), has a steady cash flow. (Open M-F 9:30am-3:30pm.) The **post office** (tel. 62001) is inside O'Shea's Market on Main St. The **phone code** is fun dialin' 027.

▮▮▮ ACCOMMODATIONS, FOOD, AND PUBS. The best place to stay in Glengarriff is the very friendly ▨**Murphy's Village Hostel** (tel. 63555), in the middle of the village on Main St. Munch one of Mrs. Murphy's banana muffins while perusing readily available maps and information in the cafe downstairs as a great start to your Beara trek. (Dorms £7.50-8, private rooms £11 per person. Laundry £4.50.) Murphy's also **rents bikes** as part of the Wheel Escapes program. (£7 per day, £35 per week.) The **Hummingbird Rest** (tel. 63195), a 10min. walk from town along Kenmare Rd., has slightly crowded dorms (£6) and the best **camping** (£3) in town. In the center of town, behind the craftshop, **Maureen's B&B,** Main St. (tel. 63201), offers comfortable rooms. (From £14.) Two **campsites** are neighbors on Castletownbere Rd. 1½ mi. from town: **Dowling's** (tel. 63154) and **O'Shea's** (tel. 63140). (Both £6-8 per tent. Open mid-Mar.-Oct.) **The Coffee Shop,** Main St. (tel. 63073) has cake, sandwiches, and hot meals (£2-5), while **Johnny Barry's** (tel. 63315) and **The Blue Loo** (tel. 63167), also on Main St., serve standard pub grub. Johnny Barry's has live folk and cover bands Monday through Saturday; the Blue Loo covers a wide musical spectrum most nights of the week during the summer.

Glengarriff's best feature is its proximity to the lush **Glengarriff National Nature Reserve and Ancient Oak Forest,** where trails allow you to hike through giant rhododendrons and moss-strewn evergreens. Walking trails area range from pebbled paths for curious, scone-snarfing pedestrians to rugged climbs for serious, granola-munching hikers. *Walking Around Glengarriff,* available at hostels in town and at the tourist office, outlines several walks in the park; more detailed maps are available for those with a good pair of boots and a yearning for thrills from hills. Glengarriff is also a good starting point for the 125 mi. **Beara Way** walking path.

The town's popularity, however, really comes from **Garinish Island,** a small island in Glengarriff Harbour. Garinish was a rocky outcrop inhabited by gorse bushes until 1900, when financier Annan Bryce dreamed up a fairyland for his family; a million hours of labor and countless boatloads of topsoil later, he had his garden and mansion. The Bryce family bequeathed their blooming island to the Irish people in 1953. Three companies along the main Glengarriff Rd. run **ferries** to the island (£4-5 return); you'll likely catch a glimpse of seals on the 8min. journey. (Tel. 63040. Open July-Aug. daily 10am-6pm; June and Sept. M-Sa 10am-6pm, Su 1-6pm; Mar.-Apr. and Oct. M-Sa 10am-4pm, Su 1-6pm. Last landing 1hr. before closing. £2.50, students £1.) Bountiful lakes, rivers, and inlets around Glengarriff treat fishermen well. Try to wrap you tongue around the name of **Lake Eekenohoolikeaghaun** while you wait for a nibble on your line. Upper and Lower Lough Avaul are also well stocked with brown and rainbow trout, but you need a fishing permit to catch them. **Barley Lake,** nearby rivers, and the ocean do not require permits. For more details, pick up the free *Fishing in Glengarriff.* (Call the regional Fisheries Board, tel. (026) 41222; or ask around at the piers.)

The breathtakingly handsome **Healy Pass** branches north off R572 near Adrigole; it's a narrow, winding road that takes you through the green and rocky **Caha Mountains** to **Lauragh** (see **Eyeries and Ardgroom,** p. 246). On the south side of the pass, along the Castletownbere Rd. in Adrigole, the **Hungry Hill Hostel** offers bright new dorms (£7.50-8), as well as **bike rental** and internet access. (Bikes £5 per day. Internet £2.50 per 30min.) Adventurers can tackle the 2245 ft. **Hungry Hill,** where, on rainy days, a mountaintop lake overflows to create Ireland's tallest waterfall.

CASTLETOWNBERE

A stroll along the waterfront shipyards of Castletownbere, one of Ireland's largest fishing ports, is an informal education in marine biology. The largest town on the Beara Peninsula grows even busier during the summer when long-distance cyclists speed through it, leaving rows of peaceful fishing boats in their wake. In winter, the boats get busy plucking the fruits of the sea. Castletownbere is a gateway to the silent coastal villages further along the peninsula and on Beara Island. This reluctant hub has energetic downtown pubs and flavorful restaurants to revitalize weary trekkers on their way to and from the Beara.

☎ PRACTICAL INFORMATION. Bus Éireann offers service to **Cork** (9-11 daily, 3hr., £14), and summer service between Castletownbere and **Killarney** via **Kenmare** (June 26-Sept. 2 M-Sa 2 per day, £8.80). **Berehaven Bus Service** (tel. 70007) leaves from the parking lot next to O'Donoghue's and heads to **Bantry** via **Glengarriff** (M 2 per day, Tu-Sa 1 per day; Glengarriff 45min., £2.70; Bantry 1½hr., £4) and to **Cork** (3hr., Th only, £8). Two **minibus** services leave **Cork** for Castletownbere (M-Sa 6pm, Su 8pm) and will take groups on tours of the Beara; phone **Harrington's** (tel. 74003) or **O'Sullivan's** (tel. 74168) for mandatory reservations (Cork £8, £14 return; tours £18-25). The closet-sized **tourist office** (tel. 70054), behind O'Donoghue's by the harbor, gives away heaps of maps. (Open June-Sept. M-F 10:30am-5pm.) The **AIB,** Main St. (tel. 70015), has an **ATM.** (Open M 10am-12:30pm and 1:30-5pm, Tu-F 10am-12:30pm and 1:30-4pm.) **Bike hire** is possible but not promised during summer months at **Spar,** Main St. (Tel. 70020. £7 per day, deposit £20. Open M-Sa 8am-10pm, Su 9am-10pm.) The **phone code** triangle is 027.

■■■ ACCOMMODATIONS, FOOD, AND PUBS. Two miles west of town on Allihies Rd., just past the fork to Dunboy Castle, the **Beara Hostel** (tel. 70184) has decent rooms and hands out "welcome cakes" upon arrival, but be warned that the rural location may involve more of an outdoorsy experience than you bargained for. (Dorms £7; private rooms £8.50 per person, £9.50 with bathroom. **Camping** £4 per person. **Bike rental** £8 per day, £35 per week; passport deposit.) Six miles west of Castletownbere is the euphoria-inducing **Garranes Farmhouse Hostel (IHH)** (tel. 73147). Stay on the Allihies Rd. and look for the sign; a taxi from Castletownbere costs £7. This luxurious and intimate cottage perched above the sea has a view worthy of a pilgrimage. Phone ahead to confirm that all the space hasn't been absorbed by the Buddhist center next door (see **Sights**). (Dorms £7; doubles £18. Laundry £4.) Just over a mile from town towards Glengarriff, the friendly and knowledgeable Black family runs the **Seapoint B&B** (tel. 70292), with spacious rooms and sea views. They welcome vegetarians, gay and lesbian travelers, and everyone else. (Singles £20, doubles £32. Laundry £5.) **Castletown House,** Main St. (tel. 70252), above the Old Bank Seafood Restaurant, offers lovely rooms and lots of advice. (£15, with bath £17. Prices change often.)

SuperValu, Main St. (tel. 70020), sells the largest selection of foodstuffs. (Open M-Sa 8am-9pm, Su 9am-9pm.) Seafood spawns in almost all of Castletownbere's restaurants. One exception is **The Old Bakery,** Main St. (tel. 70901), which serves piping-hot pizzas and an extensive menu of top-quality curries, sandwiches, and pasta (£4-6) in a charming building that was, unsurprisingly, once a bakery. It is now a great spot to sit on a rainy day. (Open M-Sa 9am-9pm, Su 10am-9pm.) **Jack Patrick's,** Main St. (tel. 70319), serves enormous fish platters, and is affordable at lunchtime. (Entrees around £4.25. Open M-Sa 11am-9pm, Su 12:30-9pm.) For the less gourmet, the **Cronin's Hideaway,** Main St. (tel. 70386), serves reasonable food fast and fresh. (Entrees £3-7.50. Open M-Tu 12:30pm-3pm, W-Sa 5pm-12:30 am, Su 12:30pm-12:30am.) **MacCarthy's,** Main St. (tel. 70014), the most popular pub in town and a well-stocked grocery, serves food all day. (Sandwiches under £2. Trad and ballads on the weekends.) **O'Donoghue's** pub, Main St. (tel. 70007), on The Square, lures a younger throng with its pool table, sunny (or starry) tables outside, and occasional music. Trad on summer Fridays keeps feet tapping at **Twiney's Ivy Bar**, Main St. (tel. 70114).

■ SIGHTS. Castletownbere's seat at the foot of hefty **Hungry Hill** (2245ft.) makes it a fine launch pad for daytrips up the mountain. (Inquire at the tourist office; see **Hungry Hill Hostel,** p. 243.) In addition, the huge harbor is a joy for watersports enthusiasts. **Beara Watersports** (tel. 70692) rents **dinghies, kayaks,** and **canoes.** Call for bookings. Two miles southwest of Castletownbere on the Allihies Rd., a 50p fee buys you admission to the two separate ruins of **Dunboy Castle.** Cows graze the grounds of the eerie and enormous crumbling Gothic-style halls of its 19th century mansion. A quarter of a mile past the mansion, the ruins of the 14th century fortress **O'Sullivan Bere** lie in far worse shape. The original owner accidentally blew the fort up in 1594, and English armies ruthlessly finished the job eight years later. The road that runs past the castle becomes a shady trail that passes a number of sheltered coves perfect for quiet beach walks. Six miles west of town, the **Dzogchen Buddhist Centre** (tel. 73032) is perched on the same cliff top as the Garranes Hostel. The views from the meditation room are inspiration in themselves. A very respected Tibetan Buddhist teaching site, the center offers a daily program with meditation and compassion exercises.

NEAR CASTLETOWNBERE: BERE ISLAND

Bere Island provides views of the Beara Peninsula that stretches out across the water from it. The spectacular ferry ride to this fishing community makes a quiet daytrip. Two **ferries** chug to Bere Island. **Murphy's Ferry Service** (tel. 75014) leaves from the pontoon 3 mi. east of Castletownbere off the Glengarriff Rd., but lands you much closer to the island's "center," at **Rerrin Village** (6 per day, £4 return). The other company, **Bere Island Ferry** (tel. 75009), leaves from the center of Castletown-bere but drops you inconveniently on the western end of the island (June 21-Sept. 7 per day, Su 5 per day; £3). Off-season return times can be uncertain; you may want to discuss your plans with the driver.

Bere Island used to be a British naval base; forts and military remnants are still scattered around the island. The Irish Army now uses the island for training. If you plan to stay the night, you can check out the island's **self-catering accommodation** (tel. 75028) or dock at **Mrs. O'Sullivan's Harbour View B&B** (tel. 75011), a half-hour walk from the Bere Island Ferry on the west end of the island. (£14, with bath £16.) **Kitty Murphy's Cafe** (tel. 75004), next to the Murphy ferry landing or a 4 mi. walk from the Bere Island ferry, is a pretty little cafe that serves the only affordable food on the island. Gaze at the maps or chat with a local at **Desmond O'Sullivan's** pub next door. Across the harbor from Rerrin, the masts of a fishing ship protrude from the sea like giant iron toothpicks. The ship mysteriously burned in 1982 after her owner ran out of money to pay the crew.

DURSEY ISLAND

The best scenery on the Beara is on Dursey Island, reached by Ireland's only cable car (tel. (027) 73017). The cables begin 5 mi. out from Allihies, off the Casteltown-bere Rd., and stretch across the water. Inside the car, a small copy of the 91st Psalm adorns the wall, and you may just find yourself calling upon "the Lord your defender" as you dangle above the Atlantic. (Car runs, based on demand, M-Sa 9-11am, 2:30-5pm, and 7-8pm; Su hours vary depending on which church has mass that morning; £2.50 return.) The 10min. aerial trip is the most exciting aspect of Dursey. Walks around the island expose you to a stark combination of sea, sky, land, and sheep. The English army laid waste to Dursey Fort in 1602 after raiding the unarmed garrison and callously tossing soldiers over the cliffs to their doom. A trip to the western tip provides a stunning view over sea cliffs and a chance to observe the island's much-vaunted migrant bird flocks. There are no accommoda-tions on the island, but camping is legal. Besides, the island's seven residents could use the company.

Food and rest for the Dursey-bound is dispensed at the **Windy Point House** (tel. (027) 73017). Located near the base of the cable car, Windy Point provides a full midday menu, comfortable accommodations, and sweeping views of Dursey Sound. (Sandwiches under £2. Food served 11am-6pm. B&B £17 with bath.)

NORTHERN BEARA PENINSULA

Past Castletownbere, the Beara Peninsula stretches out into the Atlantic, extend-ing through craggy knolls, cliff-lined coasts, and desolate villages. A striking dearth of trees makes apparent the harshness of life on the peninsula. The stark isolation of this part of the Ring of Kerry is both an attraction and a frustration for hitchers, who report success only during the mid-afternoon beach traffic in July and August; *Let's Go* does not recommend hitchhiking. Despite some steep hills and barren stretches, biking is the way to go.

ALLIHIES

Set between the **Slieve Mts.** and the sea, abandoned cottages nearly outnumber inhabitants in Allihies. Fenced off mine shafts, empty buildings, and a carved up hillside testify to the once booming copper-mining industry in the area. Even **Bally-donegan Strand** is a by-product of the mines: the sand is the ground-up extracts of the mountains. More pristine and secluded are the white sands of **Garnish Strand,** which lies a few miles down the road toward **Dursey** (follow the signs to the right at the fork). The road to the Dursey cable car, off the Castletownbere Rd., passes by **Lehanmore Ring Fort**, still an impressive remnant, though its crumbling walls can barely keep the cows out these days. Some might call Allihies desolate, while oth-ers might delight in the sunset at its metallic beaches.

Those planning to stay can find a warm welcome and warmer showers at **The Village Hostel (IHH)**, Main St. (tel. (027) 73107) next to the very red O'Neill's pub. (Dorms £8, private rooms £9 per person. Laundry £3.50. Open May-Oct.) A mile south of the village (and well marked by signs) lies the **Allihies Youth Hostel (An Óige/HI)** (tel. (027) 73014), which, despite remarkable views, is so institutional it threatens to compound the sense of isolation in Allihies. (Dorms £6.50, under 18 £5. Sheets 50p. Reception 9-11am and 4-7pm. Open June-Sept.) **Anthony's** (tel. (027) 73002) is well-equipped for **camping**, with showers and scenery. (£6 per tent.) Take the road towards the beach, turn right at the beach, and look for signs that say "Campground." **O'Sullivan's** (tel. (027) 73004) can fill your shopping bag or picnic basket and **rents bikes**. (£6 per day. Open daily 9am-9pm.) Allihies's four pubs cater mostly to locals. Usually one pub—seemingly chosen by tacit consensus among the villagers—is lively each night. **O'Neill's** (tel. (027) 73008) is a safe bet, usually hosting trad and ballads on Wednesdays. It's also the best bet for a prepared meal. (Sandwiches £1.50-5; hot food £5-8; evening menu from £7, served daily 6-9pm.) **The Lighthouse** is a popular spot on Fridays, as are the **Oak Bar** and **O'Sullivans**. All have occasional trad sessions.

EYERIES AND ARDGROOM

Cross some of the most barren land in Ireland to reach the colorful hamlet of Eyeries. Once there, loafers can rest at the **beach,** while those intent on heading farther afield should examine several mysterious ancient sites. The pamphlet, *Eyeries and Ardgroom on the Ring of Beara*, available at the hostel and several stores in the area, can direct you to **Ballycrovane,** where the tallest *ogham* stone (see **Early Christians and Vikings,** p. 7) in Ireland stands. This 17 ft. stone is on private property, but well sign-posted; the landowners collect £1 from each visitor. Further on in Kilcatherine sits the **Hag of Beara,** a bizarre rock formation that legend holds is the petrified remains of an ancient woman. Nearby, off the Allihies Rd., lies one of Ireland's oldest churches and a **Mass Rock,** which was used as an alter by Catholics during periods of repression (see **The Protestant Ascendancy,** p. 10). Five minutes east of the village, the **Ard Na Mara Hostel** (tel. (027) 74271) makes the best base for explorations. Ocean views combine with a friendly staff to make for a soothing stay. (Dorms £7, private rooms £8. **Camping** £3.50.)

The only other thing to see on the northern side of the Beara (except for more mountains, more forests, and more sea) are the **Derreen Gardens,** half a mile north of **Lauragh** (LAH-rog) on the coast road, where you can lose yourself in the mossy tunnels that run through evergreens and massive rhododendrons. These rhododendrons, taller than most buildings in Ireland and ambitious growers, originally occupied almost the entire garden. (Tel. (064) 83103. Open Apr.-Sept. daily 11am-6pm. £3.) The **Glanmore Lake Youth Hostel (An Óige/HI)** (tel. (064) 83181) makes a good base for hiking or fishing in the little-explored mountains near Lauragh. The prim and immaculate hostel is housed in a stately former schoolhouse with great mountain views. Follow signs from town; it is located 3 mi. from Lauragh on a dead-end road. (Dorms £6. Open Apr.-mid-Oct.) Heading east past Eyeries, you pass through **Ardgroom** (a-GROOM), a small village with a good pub. **The Holly Bar** (tel. (027) 74082) hosts live trad on most Tuesdays, Fridays, and Sundays in July and August, and serves up a mean bowl of seafood chowder (£3.50).

COUNTY KERRY

The wee villages, mountainous landscape, and the dramatic seacoast of County Kerry fit the bill of what many tourists expect to see in Ireland. Residents know that as the Celtic Tiger roars throughout the rest of the island, their idyllic countryside is becoming a thing of the past. While Kerry's economy relies on tourism, the county hangs on to its cultural isolation. In (relatively large) Dingle, townspeople talk of things being brought in from the outside—usually meaning Tralee, only 30 mi. away. Fortunately, importing bus loads of foreign vacationers has hardly polluted the Irish language and folk ways long since abandoned elsewhere in Ireland.

The Iveragh Peninsula, commonly equated with the Ring of Kerry road, has the mountainous Killarney National Park at its base and the Skelligs far off its western shore. Noxious tour buses often hog the roads, but the views are incomparable. The Dingle Peninsula is rapidly growing in popularity, but narrow roads help preserve the ancient sights and traditional feel of Slea Head, the West Dingle *gaeltacht*, and the Blasket Islands. Urban Tralee serves as a transportation center to more rural regions to the south and west. Summer bus transport is readily available to most areas of the country, though public transportation dries up, particularly along coastal routes, in the off-season.

KENMARE

A bridge between the Ring of Kerry and Beara, Kenmare has adapted to a continuous stream of visitors. Everything to be seen in a classic Irish town is here, from colorful houses to misty mountain views. Busloads of tourists can dilute Kenmare's appeal, but services and pleasant surroundings overshadow the sweater stalls and postcard stands.

▐ TRANSPORTATION

Buses: Leave from Brennan's Pub on Main St. for **Sneem** (35min., June-Sept. M-F 2 per day) and **Killarney** (1hr., M-Sa 3 per day, Su 2 per day), where connections to Cork and Tralee can be made.

Bike Rental: Finnegan's (tel. 41083), on the corner of Henry and Shelbourne St. £8 per day, £40 per week. Open M-Sa 9:30am-6:30pm.

▌ ORIENTATION AND PRACTICAL INFORMATION

Kenmare's streets form a triangle: **Henry St.** is the lively base, while **Main** and **Shelbourne St.** connect on either side. The intersection of Henry and Main St. forms **The Square,** which contains a small park and the tourist office. Main St. then becomes N71 heading towards **Moll's Gap** and **Killarney**; N70 to **Sneem** and the **Ring of Kerry** also branches off this road. From Kenmare, cunning travelers take N70 west (not N71 north) to do the Ring clockwise and avoid tour bus traffic.

Tourist Office: The Square (tel. 41233). Open daily April-Oct. 9am-6pm.

Bank: AIB, 9 Main St. (tel. 41010). Open M-Tu and Th-F 10am-4pm and W 10am-5pm. **ATM** takes all major cards.

Laundry: O'Sheas, Main St. (tel. 41394). Wash and dry £5. Open M-F 8:30am-6pm, Sa 9:30am-6pm.

Pharmacy: Sheahan's, Main St. (tel. 41354). Open M-Sa 9am-6pm. **Brosnan's,** Henry St. (tel. 41318). Open M-Sa 9:30am-6:30pm, Su 12:30-1:15pm.

Emergency: Dial 999; no coins required. **Garda:** Shelbourne St. (tel. 41177).

Hospital: Old Killarney Rd. (tel. 41088). Follow Henry St. past The Square.

Post Office: Henry St. (tel. 41490), at the corner of Shelbourne St. Open M-F 9am-1pm and 2-5:30pm, Sa 9am-1pm.

Internet: Bean and Leaf, Rock St., (tel. 42019), off Main St. £1.50 for 15min. Fantastic coffee, cakes, and pastries also available. Open Mar.-Nov. M-F 9:30am-6:30pm, Sa-Su 10am-6:30pm.

| PHONE CODE: | 064 has a great view of chocolate cake. |

ACCOMMODATIONS

Kenmare satisfies its steady stream of visitors with convenient, if less than gorgeous accommodations.

Fáilte Hostel (IHH), corner of Henry and Shelbourne St. (tel. 42333). Not the white building that says "private hostel," but the one across the street. The proprietors make certain that the only thing loud about this hostel is its 70s decor. Dependable beds in a stately if somewhat worn house. Common room with a VCR for rainy days. Dorms £7.50, doubles £20, private rooms with at least 3 beds £8.50 per person. 1am curfew.

Keal Na Gower House B&B, The Square (tel. 41202). Sleep comfortably in this small B&B within earshot of a brook. One room has bathtub; the other two have brook views. Doubles and twins £18 per person.

The Coachman B&B, Henry St. (tel. 41311). Decent twin and triple rooms above the bar. £12-15 per person, £20 with bath.

Ring of Kerry Caravan and Camping Park, Sneem Rd. (tel. 41648), 3 mi. west of Kenmare. Overlooks mountains and a bay. Equiped with a kitchen, TV room, and small shop. £4 per person. Open May-Sept.

FOOD AND PUBS

Good food is plentiful, if pricey, in Kenmare. Smaller cafes are good for a scone or a snack, while pubs offer cheap lunches. **SuperValu** (tel. 41037) is on Main St. (Open M-Th 8am-8pm, F 8am-9pm, Sa 8am-7pm, Su 9am-5pm.) **The Pantry,** Henry St. (tel. 42233), sells wholefoods and organic produce. (Open M-Sa 9:30am-6pm.)

The New Delight. All the veggies you couldn't find in Ireland, a few at unbeatable prices. Just don't ask for meat or a cola. Nut burger and hemp seed £4.50. Open daily June-Nov. 10am-8pm.

An Leath Phingin, 35 Main St. (tel. 41559). Italian masterpieces served up on two floors of an old stone townhouse. They even make their own pasta and smoke their own salmon. Most pizzas £6.95-7.50. Open Th-Tu 6-10pm.

Mickey Ned's, Henry St. (tel. 41591). Lunch-time crowds come for sandwiches (from £1.60) and ice cream (cones 85p). Open M-Sa 9am-5:30pm.

Cafe Indigo, The Square (tel. 42356). Art deco interior and funky blue lighting make this a snazzy refuge. Grilled marinated tiger prawn skewer £8.50. Food served daily 7-10:30pm. M-F and Su late bar open until 1am.

Kenmare's pubs attract a hefty contingent of tourists. Native Guinness guzzlers, however, hear too much good music to quibble over "Kiss me, I'm a leprechaun" hats. **Ó Donnabháin's,** Henry St. (tel. 42106), is a favorite among natives, with a pleasant beer garden out back. Huge **Murty's,** New Rd. (tel. 41453), just off Henry St., features live bands (W, F-Sa) and disco (Th, Su). **Brennan's,** Main St. (tel. 41011), serves pub grub and biweekly live music. Smart tourists mob nightly music performances at **The Square Pint. Crowley's,** Henry St. (tel. 41472), asks: "When you've got frequent trad sessions, why bother with interior decorating?"

SIGHTS

There are plenty of good hikes in the country around Kenmare, but few sights in the town itself. The ancient **stone circle,** a two-minute walk from The Square down Market St., is the largest of its kind in southwest Ireland (55ft. diameter), but it ain't no Stonehenge. (Always open. £1.) The stone circle is one stop on Kenmare's **tourist trail** (maps at the tourist office), a well-marked route that leads visitors over historic bridges and past a small tower known as **Hutchin's Folly.** The new **Kenmare Heritage Centre,** in the same building as the tourist office, has a model of the stone circle and historical exhibits, as well as puzzling attempts to connect the town to Margaret Thatcher and Confederate general P.G.T. Beauregard. (Same hours as the tourist office. Cassette self-tour £2, students £1.50.) The **Kenmare Lace Centre** has demonstrations of the Kenmare lace-making technique, invented in 1862 by nuns at the Kenmare convent and once on the cutting edge of lace. Local artisans are currently resurrecting the craft. (Open M-Sa 10am-1pm and 2-5:30pm. Free.)

Seafari Cruises (tel. 83171) explores Kenmare Bay and its colonies of otters, seals, and whales. (3 per day. £10, students £8.) The cruises depart from the pier; follow Glengarriff Rd. and turn right just before the bridge. **Kenmare Bay Sea Sports** (tel. 42255), based at the Dromquinna Manor Hotel, 3 mi. from town on the Sneem Rd., launches **kayaking, waterskiing, windsurfing,** and **tube rides.** (£6-12 per person.)

KILLARNEY

With something for everyone, Killarney seems to have just about everyone at once. Just a short walk away from some of Ireland's most extraordinary scenery, Killarney's economy celebrates tourism. You'll find all you need in town, plus lots of trinkets to weigh down your pack, but all that fades to dust in the face of the glorious national park outside of town.

▐ TRANSPORTATION

Trains: Killarney Station (tel. 31067, recorded info tel. (066) 26555), off East Avenue Rd. near the intersection with Park Rd. Open M-Sa 7:30am-10pm, Su 30min. before train departures. Trains run to **Cork** (2hr., 5 per day, £9.50), **Limerick** (3hr.; M-Sa 4 per day, Su 3 per day; £15), and **Dublin** (3½hr., 4 per day, £33.50).

Buses: Park Rd. (tel. 34777), in a trailer next to the outlet mall. Open M-Sa 8:30am-5pm. Buses rumble to **Cork** (2hr., 3-5 per day, £8.50), **Dingle** (2hr., 3-6 per day, £8.50), **Limerick** (2hr., 4-5 per day, £9.30), **Shannon** (3hr., 3-4 per day, £10), **Dublin** (6hr., 3-4 per day, £14), **Galway** (7hr., 5-7 per day, £13), and **Sligo** (7½hr., 2-3 per day, £15.50). Buses leave daily June-Sept. for the **Ring of Kerry Circuit,** with stops in **Killorglin, Glenbeigh, Kells, Cahersiveen, Waterville, Caherdaniel, Sneem,** and **Moll's Gap.** £8 if booked from a hostel; £12 return with 1-night stop for students. **Bus Éireann** also runs a no-frills Ring of Kerry circuit in the summer (2 per day; see **Ring of Kerry,** p. 256). The June-mid-Sept. **Dingle/Slea Head** tour (M-Sa 2 per day) stops in **Inch, Anascaul, Dingle, Ventry, Slea Head, Dunquin,** and **Ballyferriter** (£9.70).

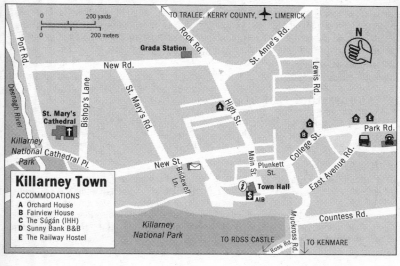

Killarney Town

ACCOMMODATIONS
A Orchard House
B Fairview House
C The Súgán (IHH)
D Sunny Bank B&B
E The Railway Hostel

🛂 ORIENTATION AND PRACTICAL INFORMATION

Killarney packs into three crowded major streets. **Main St.,** in the center of town, begins at the Town Hall, then becomes **High St. New St.** and **Plunkett St.** both intersect Main St., each heading in different directions. New St. heads west toward Killorglin. Plunkett St. becomes **College St.** and then **Park Rd.** on its way east to the bus and train stations. **East Avenue Rd.** connects the train station back to town hall before becoming Muckross Rd. on its way to the Muckross Estate and Kenmare.

Tourist Office: Beech St. (tel. 31633), off New St. Exceptionally helpful and deservedly popular. Open July-Aug. M-Sa 9am-8pm, Su 9am-1pm and 2:15-6pm; June and Sept. M-Sa 9am-6pm, Su 10am-6pm; Oct.-May M-Sa 9:15am-5:30pm, Sa 9:15am-1pm.

Banks: AIB, Main St. (tel. 31047), next to the town hall on Main St. Open M-Tu and Th-F 10am-4pm, W 10am-5pm. **TSB,** 23-24 New St. (tel. 33666). Open M-W and F 9:30am-5pm, Th 9:30am-7pm. **Bank of Ireland,** New St. (tel. 31050). Open M-Tu and Th-F 9am-4pm, W 9am-5pm. All three have **ATMs.**

Bike Rental: O'Sullivans, Bishop's Ln. (tel. 31282), next to Neptune's Hostel. £6 per day, £30 per week. Free panniers, locks, and park maps. Open daily 8:30am-6:30pm. **Killarney Rent-a-Bike,** with locations at the An Súgán hostel and Market Cross, Main St. (tel. 32578). £6 per day, £30 per week, free maps, locks, and panniers.

American Express: East Avenue Rd. (tel. 35722). Moneygrams, traveler's checks, card and traveler's check replacement, and client mail service. Open May-Sept. M-F 8am-7:30pm, Sa 9am-6pm, Su in July in Aug. 9am-7pm; Feb.-Apr. M-F 9am-5pm.

Laundry: J. Gleeson's Launderette (tel. 33877), next to Spar Market on College St. £4.50 per load. Open M-W and Sa 9am-6pm, Th-F 9am-8pm.

Pharmacy: Sewell's Pharmacy (tel. 31027), corner of Main and New St. Open Sept.-June M-Sa 9:30am-6:30pm, July-Aug. M-Sa 9:30am-9:30pm. No snake-bite kits, but that's usually not a problem around here.

Emergency: Dial 999; no coins required. **Garda:** New Rd. (tel. 31222).

Hospital: District Hospital, St. Margaret's Rd. (tel. 31076). Follow High St. 1 mi. from the town center. Nearest emergency facilities are in Tralee.

Post Office: New St. (tel. 31288). Open M and W-Sa 9am-5:30pm, Tu 9:30am-5:30pm, Sa 9am-1pm.

Internet Access: PC Assist (tel. 37288), at the corner of High St. and New Rd. (not New St.). £1.50 per 15min., £5 per hr. Open M-Sa 9am-6pm. **Cafe Internet,** New St. (tel. 36741). £1.50 for 15min.; ½hr. of access with sandwich and drink £5. Open M-Th 9:30am-8pm, F 9:30am-7pm, Sa 10am-7pm.

PHONE CODE:	064 owns a small t-shirt store.

🏚 ACCOMMODATIONS

With every other house a B&B, it's easy to find cushy digs in Killarney, though you may want to call ahead to the 3 hostels in town during summer months. Camping is not allowed in the National Park, but there are excellent campgrounds nearby.

IN TOWN

The Súgán (IHH), Lewis Rd. (tel. 33104), 2min. from the bus or train station. Make a left onto College St.; Lewis Rd. is the first right. Somewhat cramped quarters are well compensated for by the exuberant management, and impromptu storytelling and music around the fire-lit stone common room. Small, ship-like bunk rooms blur the distinction between intimacy and claustrophobia. 4- to 8-bed dorms £9. **Bike rental** £5 per day, £30 per week, helmet included.

Neptune's (IHH), Bishop's Ln. (tel. 35255), the first walkway off New St. on the right. Immense and clean with good showers, solid mattresses, and numerous amenities. The staff is friendly and professional. 8-bed dorms £7.50; 4- to 6-bed dorms £8.50; doubles £10 per person; 10% ISIC discount. Breakfast £1.50-3.50. Free luggage storage; £5 locker deposit. Laundry £5. Internet access £2 for 15min. **Tour booking:** Dingle tour £12, Ring of Kerry £8. **Bike rental** £6 per day.

The Railway Hostel (IHH), Park Rd. (tel. 35299), across the street from the train station. Big, bright building with skylights, a modern kitchen, and a pool table. Friendly staffers tread on new hardwood floors at this recently renovated hostel. 4- to 8-bed dorms £8-8.50, doubles £12 per person. Breakfast £2-3. 3am curfew. **Bike rental** £6 per day.

Orchard House, Fleming's Ln. (tel. 31879), off High St. Make yourself at home in the center of town. This friendly and immaculate place is hard to beat. Singles £18; doubles £16-17 per person. Most rooms with bath.

Sunny Bank B&B (tel. 34109). A 5min. walk from the town center on Park Rd. directly across from the bus station. Cheerful and downright luxurious with bath and TV in all rooms. Specially modified showers with serious water pressure. Twins and doubles June-Sept. £20, Oct.-May £16-17.

Fairview House, College St. (tel. 34164), next to An Súgán. Treat yourself right with a fluffy bed and TV in this spotless B&B. £17-22.50 per person.

OUTSIDE TOWN

Peacock Farms Hostel (IHH), (tel. 33557). Take Muckross Rd. out of town and turn left just before the Muckross post office. Take that road 2 mi. and follow the signposts—if you think you're nearly there, you haven't gone far enough. A less taxing alternative is to call for a ride from the bus station. Overlooking Lough Guitane and surrounded by Killarney's slopes, this hostel is home to a friendly family of peacocks and a collection of homing pigeons. Skylights, hand-painted showers, and comfy rooms. Daily bus to town. 8-bed dorms £6, twins £7 per person. Open Apr.-Sept. Wheelchair accessible.

Bunrower House (IHH), Ross Rd. (tel. 33914). Follow Muckross Rd. out of town and take a right at the Esso station onto Ross Rd. The hostel is about ¾ mi. down the road on the left. Call for a ride from the train or bus station. Located just a few hundred yards from Ross Castle, the "Bun" has a common room with wood fire, spacious bunk rooms, sky-lit toilets, and outstanding showers. 4-6 bed dorms £7-8, doubles £9 per person. **Camping** in the quiet yard is the closest you can legally get to sleeping in the National Park (£3.50). **Bike rental** £6.

Aghadoe Hostel (An Óige/HI) (tel. 31240). In Aghadoe, 3 mi. west of town on the Killorglin Rd. Call for free van ride to and from bus and train stations. A grandiose and well-equipped hostel in a stone mansion surrounded by forests. Occasional music, barbecues, and talks on local history. Dorms June-Sept. £7.50, Oct.-May £6.50. Sheets £1. Continental breakfast £2; cafe food £1.50-3.50. Laundry £4. Internet access £2 per 30min. Reception 7:30am-midnight. **Bike rental** £6 per day.

Black Valley Hostel (An Óige/HI) (tel. 34712), 1 mi. from town on Gap of Dunloe Rd. This spare but spotless hostel, one of the last places in Ireland to receive electricity, is conveniently located on the Kerry Way. Buy food in town or eat at the hostel. Dorms £6.50, off-season £6. Sheets 80p. Midnight curfew.

Fossa Caravan and Camping Park (tel. 31497), 3½ mi. west of town on the Killorglin Rd. Kitchen, laundromat, tennis courts, shop, and restaurant. July-Aug. £4 per person, mid-Mar.-June and Sept.-Oct. £3.50. Showers 50p. Wash £1.50, dry 50p per 20min. Open mid-Mar.-Oct. **Bike rental** £6.

Flesk Caravan and Camping (tel. 31704), 1 mi. from town on Muckross Rd. by the Texaco station. £3.50 per person. Laundry £3.50. Showers 20p. Open Mar.-Oct.

⬢ FOOD

Food in Killarney is affordable at lunchtime, but prices skyrocket in the evening. **Quinnsworth,** in an arcade off New St., is the town's largest grocer. (Open M-W and Sa 8am-8pm, Th-F 8am-10pm, Su 10am-6pm.) A number of fast-food joints and take-aways stay open until 2-3am nightly to satisfy the post-Guinness munchies.

Teo's, 13 New St. (tel. 36344). The taste and atmosphere of the Mediterranean in the heart of Shamrock country. Vegetarian options Meals around £7. Open noon-10:30pm.

Celtic Cauldron, 27 Plunkett St. (tel. 36821). The best bet for the adventurous. Feast on traditionally prepared foods of the ancient Celts, then wash it all down with a tall glass of mead. Bacon, seaweed and cockle crepe made in the medieval Welsh style £5.75. Open mid-Mar.-Nov. daily 6-10pm.

Mac's, 6 Main St. (tel. 35213). Filling fried breakfasts and cheap lunches £1.50-4.50. Killarney's best selection of ice cream as well. Open M-F 9:30am-6pm, Sa 9:30am-9:30pm, Su noon-9:30pm.

Greens, Bridewell Ln. (tel. 33083), on the left off New St. Fresh and creative vegetarian dishes with an international flair. Lunch £4-6. Dinner entrees £8-10. Open Mar.-Dec. Tu-Sa noon-2:30pm and 6:30-9:30pm, Su 5:30-9:30pm.

O'Meara's Restaurant, 12 High St. (tel. 36744), above O'Meara's bar. Lunch or dine on eclectic and high-quality cuisine from around the world. Lunch £6-8; 3-course early bird dinner 6-7:30pm £12. Open Tu-Su noon-10pm.

Robertino's, 9 High St. (tel. 34966). Eat Italian food in the company of plaster Greco-Roman goddesses. Most dinners £6.95-9.65. Open daily 12:30-3pm and 4-10pm.

▟ PUBS AND CLUBS

Battalions of jig-seeking tourists have influenced Killarney's pubs, making your drinking narrow and noisy. Trad is a staple of the summer nights.

Yer Mans, Plunkett St. (tel. 32688). Locals and a few well-informed tourists (pat yourself on the back), come here for jazz and blues 3-4 nights a week. Yer Man's is the only pub in the world licensed to serve Guinness in jam jars (£1.25, upon request).

Buckley's Bar, College St. (tel. 31037). Tranquil trad fans gather under the skylight for nightly sessions during July and Aug.

O'Connor's Traditional Pub, 7 High St. (tel. 32496). Tourists and locals mingle in this upbeat, comfortable pub. Trad Mondays and Thursdays.

Fáilte Bar, College St. (tel. 33404). A large, relaxed crowd gathers at this dark and woody pub. Disco beats F-Sa are relieved on Su by trad.

Several **nightclubs** simmer from 10:30pm until 1:30-2am. Most charge £3-5 cover, but often offer discounts before 11pm. **The Crypt,** College St. (tel. 31038), next to the Killarney Towers Hotel, looks gothic but attracts neatly dressed trendy types. (Mixed dance music nightly; over 23.) **Alchemy,** (tel. 31640), next to Danny Mann's, attempts to funkify a young crowd with three bars, and a thumping dance floor into pure funk. (Varied music and frequent theme nights.) Smallish **Rudy's Nightclub** (tel. 32688), above Yer Mans on Plunkett St., pounds out dance hits and occasional live alternative music. (Th-Su. Cover £3-5 for live bands.) Check the *Killarney Advertiser* (free) and the *Kingdom* (70p) for town and county events.

◉ ♫ SIGHTS AND ENTERTAINMENT

Congested with bureaux de change, souvenir shops, and disoriented foreigners, Killarney town's charm is elusive at best. Divine glory, on the other hand, awaits in the National Park just beyond city limits. The neo-Gothic **St. Mary's Cathedral** on

New St., with three huge altars, seats 1400 in its rough limestone structure. (Always open. Free.) You're in luck if you hit town during one of Killarney's festivals; locals take them quite seriously and come out en masse. In mid-March, Killarney hosts the **Guinness Roaring 1920s Festival,** for which pubs, restaurants, and hostels bust out in jazz, barbershop singing, and flapper regalia. In mid-May and mid-July, horses gallop in the **Killarney Races** at the racecourse on Ross Rd. (Tickets available at gate, £3-5.) The **Killarney Regatta,** the oldest regatta in Ireland, draws rowers and spectators to Lough Leane in early to mid-July. (Tickets £5.) The Killarney area has excellent salmon and trout **fishing,** especially in late summer and September. Unhindered trout fishing is allowed in nearly all of Killarney's lakes, but fishing in rivers and Barfinnihy Lake requires a permit. (Permits £3 per day.) Contact **O'Neill's Fishing Shop,** Plunkett St. (tel. 31970) for details. **Hiking and Biking Outdoor Centre,** 12 College St. (tel. 35153) rents rods for £6 per day.

KILLARNEY NATIONAL PARK

Ice Age glaciers sliced up the Killarney region, scooping out a series of lakes and glens and scattering silk-smooth rocks and precarious boulders. The resulting landscape is a dazzling marvel to hike, bike, or climb. The 37 sq. mi. park, stretching west and south of Killarney toward Kenmare, incorporates a string of forested mountains and the famous **Lakes of Killarney: huge Lough Leane (Lower Lake),** medium-sized **Middle (Muckross) Lake,** and small **Upper Lake,** 2 mi. southwest and connected by a canal. An indigenous herd of 850 elusive red deer roam the glens that surround the lakes.

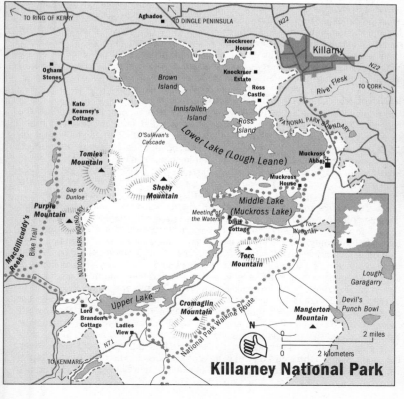

Killarney National Park

Kenmare Rd. curves along the southeastern shores of the lakes between park sites but misses some woodland paths. With many more tourists than Irish driving these sections, hitching can be difficult. *Let's Go* does not recommend hitchhiking. Biking is a great way to explore, and **bike rentals** are readily available in town (see **Practical Information**, p. 249). Walkers can't travel as far in a day, but they have more freedom to climb off-road trails. Unfortunately for both bikers and hikers, many tourists admire the woods from horse-drawn carriages ($20-24), which leave the roads strewn with *cac capall* (Irish for the substance whose smell may be your constant companion). The park's size demands a map, available at the Killarney tourist office or the **Information Centre** behind Muckross House. (Tel. 31440. Open daily June-Sept. 9am-7pm.)

The most frequented destinations are the **Ross Castle** and **Lough Leane** area, **Muckross House** on Middle Lake, and the **Gap of Dunloe** just west of the park area, bordered on the southwest by **Macgillycuddy's Reeks,** Ireland's highest mountain range (most of the peaks are under 3000ft.). The Gap of Dunloe is a full-day excursion. The others can be managed in several hours, or stretched out over a full day, depending on your mode of transport. Hikers and bikers should take the necessary precautions and watch out for traffic as well (see **Camping,** p. 78).

The best way to see almost all of the park in one day is to bike to the Gap of Dunloe (see **Gap of Dunloe,** p. 255). If the idea of a 14 mi. bike excursion fills you with trepidation, there are several short, well-marked, and well-paved walking trails closer to the Killarney side of the park. The park is also a perfect starting point for those who plan to walk the 129 mi. **Kerry Way**—essentially the Ring of Kerry on foot. Do not attempt the Kerry Way from October to March, when rains make the uneven terrain dangerous. The **Old Kenmare Road,** the first (or last) leg of the walk, passes through the spectacular Torc and Mangerton Mountains and can be managed in one day. From Killarney, follow the Kenmare Rd. 4 mi. and turn left just beyond the main entrance to Muckross House—the path leaves from the carpark on this side road. The Killarney tourist office sells a *Kerry Way* guide, with topographic maps of the Way. The excellent 1:50,000 Ordnance Survey maps (unfortunately, far from waterproof) of the Iveragh include minor roads, trails, and archaeological points of interest ($4.60).

ROSS CASTLE AND LOUGH LEANE

From town, **Knockreer Estate** is a short walk down New St. past the Cathedral. The original mansion housed Catholic Earls of Kenmare and, later, the Grosvenor family of long *National Geographic* fame. The current building, dating only from the 1950s, is unimpressive and not open to the public, but nearby nature trails afford great views of the hills, mountains, and roaming deer. You can drive or walk out to **Ross Castle,** a right on Ross Rd. off Muckross Rd. 2 mi. from Killarney, but the numerous footpaths from Knockreer are more scenic (15min. walk). The castle, built by the O'Donoghue chieftains in the 14th century, was the last in Munster to fall to Cromwell's army (see **Feudalism,** p. 8). In the last two decades, the castle has been completely renovated and refurbished in 15th century style. Tales of a dreary castle life may be strangely soothing to haggard travelers. (Tel. 35851. Admission by guided tour only. Open daily June-Aug. 9am-6:30pm, May-Sept. 10am-6pm; Oct. 9am-5pm. Last admission 45min. before closing. $2.50, students $1.) Past the castle, paths lead to the wooded and relatively secluded **Ross Island**—not an island at all, but a peninsula shaped like a lobster claw that stretches out into Lough Leane. Green colored pools testify to thousands of years of copper mining.

The view of Lough Leane and its mountains from Ross Island is magnificent, but the best way to see the area is from the water. Two **waterbus services,** Pride of the Lakes (tel. 32638) and Lily of Killarney (tel. 31068), leave from behind the castle for lake cruises (5-6 per day in summer, $5). You can hire rowboats by the castle ($2 per hr.), or take a **motorboat trip** (tel. 34351) to Innisfallen Island ($3), the Meeting of the Waters through Lough Leane and Muckross Lake ($5), or the Gap of Dunloe through Lough Leane, Muckross Lake, and Upper Lake ($7.50, $10 return). Bringing your bike by boat to the Gap saves time.

On Innisfallen Island sit the stoic remains of **Innisfallen Abbey,** founded by St. Finian the Leper around AD 600. The abbey was eventually transformed into a university during the Middle Ages. The *Annals of Innisfallen,* now entombed at Oxford, recount world and Irish history. The annals were written in Irish and Latin by 39 monastic scribes and supposedly finished in 1326. At the abbey's center is a yew tree; yew and oak groves were sacred to the Druids, so abbeys were often built among and around them. The separate Augustinian abbey is so ruined it's barely recognizable.

MUCKROSS AND THE MEETING OF THE WATERS

The remains of **Muckross Abbey,** built in 1448, lie 3 mi. south of Killarney on Kenmare Rd. Cromwell tried to burn it down, but enough still stands to demonstrate the grace of the part-Norman, part-Gothic cloisters. The abbey's grounds contain a modern graveyard filled with expired locals and lively tourists. (Always open. Free.) From the abbey, signs direct you to **Muckross House,** a massive 19th century manor whose garden blooms brilliantly in early summer. The grand and proper house, completed in 1843, reeks of aristocracy and commands a regal view of the lakes and mountains. It's elaborate furnishings and decorations include justifiably angry-looking deer mounted on the walls. Upon first visiting Muckross House, the philosopher George Berkeley proclaimed: "Another Louis XIV may make another Versailles, but only the hand of the Deity can make another Muckross." (Tel. 31440. Open daily July-Aug. 9am-7pm, Sept.-June 9am-6pm. House and farms each £3.80, students £1.62; joint tickets £5.50, students £2.75.) Outside the house lie the **Muckross Traditional Farms,** a living history museum designed to recreate rural life in early 20th century Kerry. Whip up traditional Kerry dishes or crafts in the farm's classes or just lounge on the expansive lawns.

A path leads along the water from Muckross House towards the 60 ft. drop of **Torc Waterfall.** Well worth braving piles of horse manure, the waterfall is also a starting point for several short trails along **Ford Mountain.** Walks along the moss-jacketed trees afford some of Killarney's best views. In the opposite direction from Muckross House, it's a 2 mi. stroll to the **Meeting of the Waters;** walk straight down the front lawn and follow the signs. The paved path is nice, while the dirt trail through the **Yew Woods** is more secluded and not accessible to bikes. **The Meeting of the Waters** is a quiet sight where channels connecting Upper Lough introduce themselves to Middle Lough, which then gives a watery handshake to Lower Lough. The weary, however, will be more happy at meeting a cold drink and sandwich at **Dinis Cottage.** (Tel. 31954. Open mid-May-Sept. daily 10:30am-6pm.)

There's no direct route from the Muckross sights to Ross Castle; those wishing to do both in one day have to go back through Killarney, for a total trip of 10 mi.

GAP OF DUNLOE

A pilgrimage to the Gap of Dunloe guarantees misty mountain vistas and significant calorie expenditure. There are plenty of organized trips to the Gap that can be booked from the Killarney tourist office. These trips, designed to be combination walking tour and boat-trip, shuttle visitors to the foot of the Gap, effectively cutting the 7 mi. from Killarney. (Around £13.) Foresighted travelers will pack a lunch, though a warm meal or a cold pint may be hard to resist. After walking over the Gap and down to **Lord Brandon's Cottage,** trippers pause for a bite (sandwiches £2-3.50) and meet a boat, which takes them across the lake to **Ross Castle.** (Open June-Sept. daily 9am-6pm.) A bus returns them to Killarney. Walking the Gap in this direction, however, is a trek up the long side of the mountain. Far better, and potentially less expensive, is to attack the Gap by bike from the opposite direction. Bring your bike on the **motorboat** trip to the head of the Gap from Ross Castle (£7, book ahead at the tourist office, bikes permitted on board). From Lord Brandon's Cottage on the Gap, turn left over the stone bridge and continue for about 2 mi. to the hostel and church. A right turn up a road with hairpin turns will bring you to the top of the Gap a breathtaking 1½ mi. later. Beyond is a well-deserved 7 mi. downhill coast through the park's most breathtaking scenery.

SOUTHWEST IRELAND

At the foot of the Gap, you'll pass **Kate Kearney's Cottage.** Kate Kearney was an independent mountain-dwelling woman famous for brewing the near-poisonous *poitín.* Now her former home is a pub and restaurant that sucks in droves of tourists. (Tel. 44116. Open daily 9am-11pm; restaurant open until 9pm. Occasional live trad.) The 8 mi. ride back to Killarney passes the entirely ruined **Dunloe Castle,** an Anglo-Norman stronghold demolished by Cromwell's armies. Bear right after Kate's, turn left on the road to Fossa, and turn right on Killorglin Rd. There is also a set of *ogham* stones from about AD 300 (see **History of the Irish Language,** p. 19).

RING OF KERRY

The Southwest's most celebrated peninsula holds picturesque villages, fabled ancient forts, religious monuments, and rough romantic scenery often perceived as representative of Ireland itself. The majestic views of the Iveragh Peninsula rarely disappoint the droves of tourists who cruise through the region in private buses with megaphone-touting tour guides. Greater rewards await travelers who take the time to explore the rugged landscape on foot or by bike. A lucky few spend weeks on the peninsula soaking up the sea spray and grand views that tour buses can't access.

The term "Ring of Kerry" is generally used to describe the entire Iveragh Peninsula, but it more correctly refers to a set of roads: N71 from Kenmare to Killarney, R562 from Killarney to Killorglin, and the long loop of N70 west and back to Kenmare. If you don't like the prepackaged private bus tours based out of Killarney, **Bus Éireann** runs a regular summer circuit through all the major towns on the Ring (2 per day), allowing you to get off anywhere and anytime you like. Riders have the option of paying the round-trip fare, getting off the first bus at a suitable spot, and then using the same ticket on a later bus, as long as it's all done in one day. Buses travel around the Ring counterclockwise, from Killarney to Killorglin, west along Dingle Bay, east along Kenmare River, and north from Kenmare back to Killarney. In summer, other buses also travel clockwise from Waterville back to Killarney (2 per day). Bikers may find themselves jammed between buses and cliffs on the narrow roads, though traffic can often be avoided by doing the Ring clockwise. Drivers are forced to choose between lurching behind large tour buses or meeting them face-to-face on narrow roads.

The Ring of Kerry traditionally commences in Killorglin. If you are traveling clockwise around the Ring on N70, stop at the **Quarry in Kells** (tel. 77601), a restaurant, craft shop, and convenience store with magnificent views. The shop is particularly inviting to haggard bikers cycling against hurricane-like winds. (Open Easter-Oct. daily 10am-5:30pm.)

KILLORGLIN

Killorglin sits placidly beside the river Laune in the shadow of Iveragh's mountain spine, 13 mi. west of Killarney. Tourists pass through on their way to more spectacular scenery further west. Killorglin makes up for what it lacks in sights with festivities dedicated to he-goats. From August 10-12, the streets fill up for the riotous Puck Fair, a celebration of the crowning of a particularly virile goat as King Puck. Pubs stay open until 3am, then close for an hour or so to allow publicans to rest their pint-pulling arms. Be forewarned that the town's hostel and B&Bs often book up as early as a year in advance of the revelry. During the rest of the year, residents entertain the Ring crowd. Sights are generally a few miles from town and best reached by car or bike.

7 ORIENTATION AND PRACTICAL INFORMATION. Killorglin's **Main St.** runs uphill from the water and widens to form **The Square.** At the top of The Square to the right, **Upper Bridge St.** climbs to the tourist office at the intersection of **Iveragh Rd.** The Ring of Kerry **bus** stops in Killorglin just past the tourist office (**Cahersiveen** 50min., £5; **Waterville** 1¼hr., £5.90; **Sneem** 3hr.; June-Sept. 2 per day). The eastbound bus from Cahersiveen goes more directly to **Killarney** (Sept.-June M-Sa 1 per day, July-Aug. M-Sa 2-4 per day). The spiffy, octagonal **tourist office** (tel. 976 1451) hands out armfuls of relevant information. (Open May-Sept. M-F 9:30am-5:30pm, Sa 9am-6pm, Su 10am-3pm.) **AIB** (tel. 976 1134) is at the corner of Main St. and New Line Rd. (Open M and W-F 10am-4pm, Tu 10am-5pm. **ATM.**) **O'Shea's** (tel. 976 1919) on Main St. **rents bikes.** (£7.50 per day, £40 per week. Open M-Sa 9am-6pm.) Clothes sparkle at **Starlite Cleaners,** Langford St. (tel. 976 1296), to the left from the top of The Square. (£5 per load. Open M-Sa 9am-6pm.) The **post office** (tel. 976 1101) is on Main St. (Open M-F 9am-5:30pm, Sa 9am-1pm.) The **phone code,** 066, is a particularly lustful he-goat.

■■■ **ACCOMMODATIONS, FOOD, AND PUBS.** Laune Valley Farm Hostel **(IHH)** (tel. 976 1488), 1½ mi. from town off Tralee Rd., is bright and bucolic and hosts a local population of cows, chickens, dogs, and ducks—save your table scraps. Fresh milk and eggs from the farm are for sale. (8-bed dorms £7; doubles £10 per person, £12.50 with bath. **Camping** £3 per person. Wheelchair accessible.) **Orglan House** (tel. 976 1540), a 3min. walk from town up a steep hill on Killarney Rd., has grand views from immaculate rooms and relieves you from brown bread delirium with its delicious, individually tailored breakfasts. (£16-18.) Pleasant **Laune Bridge House** (tel. 976 1161) is a few doors down from Orglan. (Singles £25, £18 per person with bath.) Sleep in the fresh Kerry air at **West's Caravan and Camping Park** (tel. 976 1240), a mile east of town on Killarney Rd. (July 9-Aug. 20 £3.50, Aug. 21-July 8 £3. Showers 50p. Laundry £4. Open Easter to late Oct.)

Fortify yourself at **Bunker's** (tel. 976 1381), a red-faced restaurant and take-away across from the tourist office. (Open daily 9:30am-9:30pm.) Their regal purple pub lies next door, where occasional live music is performed. Across from the tourist office, the **Far East** (tel. 976 2588) fries up elegant Chinese meals. (Meals £7.50-9.50; takeaway £5-6. Open M-F 6-11:30pm, Sa-Su 6pm-midnight.) Budget food comes at the expense of ambience at the **Starlite Diner,** The Square (tel. 976 1296). Take your food upstairs for a more dignified dining experience. (Burgers £3.50; all-day breakfast is £4. Open daily 9:30am-11pm.) Young locals satisfy all their Guinness needs at **Old Forge,** Main St. (tel. 976 1231), a lively stone pub. (Trad M-W, occasional disco nights.) An older and more subdued crowd watches football at the **Laune Bar,** Lower Main St. (tel. 976 1158), on the water. The Laune Rangers football club was founded here in 1888. (Th night trad.) DJs and cocktails lure a young mob to **The Shamrock,** Main St. (tel. 976 2277).

■ **SIGHTS.** Killorglin hides its only major sight in **The Basement Museum,** down Mill Rd. past the church. The museum's exhibits focus on the Puck Fair and circus visits. (Tel. 976 1353. Sporadic hours, call ahead.) Five miles from town off Killarney Rd. sits the 16th century **Ballymalis Castle** on the banks of the Laune in view of Macgillycuddy's Reeks. **Cromane Beach** lies 4 mi. west of town; follow New Line Rd., which branches off Main St. south of The Square. **Cappanalea Outdoor Education Centre** (tel. 976 9244), 7 mi. southwest of Killorglin off the Ring of Kerry Rd., offers **canoeing, rock-climbing, windsurfing, sailing, hill walking,** and **fishing.** (£10 per half-day, £18.50 per day. Open daily 10am-5pm. Book a few days in advance.)

CAHERSIVEEN

Best known in Ireland as the birthplace of patriot Daniel O'Connell (see p. 10), even those immune to history lessons will enjoy Cahersiveen's (CARS-veen) coastal location. Its two hostels are excellent bases for exploring the nearby beach and historical sites, or for longer excursions to Valentia Island or the Skelligs. There's no shortage of nightlife—while Cahersiveen's 30 pubs may seem like a more than generous helping, older residents wistfully recollect when there were 52.

⚡ PRACTICAL INFORMATION. The Ring of Kerry **bus** stops in front of Banks Store on Main St. (June-Sept. 2 per day) and continues on to **Waterville** (25min., £2.70), **Caherdaniel** (1½hr., £3.10), **Sneem** (2hr., £6.30), and **Killarney** (2½hr., £9). One route heads directly east to **Killarney** (M-Sa 1-2 per day). Cahersiveen's official **tourist office** (tel. 947 2589) is housed in former barracks on the road to Ballycarbery Castle. (Open May to mid-Sept. M-Sa 10am-6pm, Su 1-6pm.) The **Old Oratory craftshop** (tel. 947 2996) on Main St. is another good source of local information. (Open June-Sept. M-Sa 10am-6pm, July-Aug. also open Su noon-6pm.) Main St. is home to an **AIB** (tel. 947 2022) with an **ATM**. (Open M 10am-5pm, Tu-F 10am-3pm.) **Casey's**, Main St. (tel. 947 2474), **rents bikes**. (£7 per day, £35 per week; helmet and lock included. Open daily 9am-6pm.) The **post office** (tel. 947 2010) is a final stop on Main St. (Open M-F 9:30am-1pm and 2-5:30pm, Sa 9:30am-1pm.) Cahersiveen's **phone code** gets its kicks with 066.

🏠🍴🍺 ACCOMMODATIONS, FOOD, AND PUBS. The **Sive Hostel (IHH)**, 15 East End, Main St. (tel. 947 2717), has a welcoming and well-informed staff, comfortable beds, and a third floor balcony that overlooks the castle across the river. (8-bed dorms £7, doubles £18. Sheets 50p. **Camping** £4 per person. Wash £2, dry £2. Internet access £5 per hr.) Behind its charming bay window and flowerpot facade, **Mortimer's Hostel**, Main St. (tel. 947 2338), competes with the Sive in friendliness. Mortimer's features a large, comfortable common room and a great garden. (Dorms £6.) Mortimer himself is unsurpassed in local knowledge. He also runs the **Mannix Point Caravan and Camping Park** (tel. 947 2806), located at the west end of town. One of the best campsites in the country, the site adjoins a waterfront nature reserve and faces across the water toward the romantic ruins of Ballycarbery Castle. Mannix Point's common area comes complete with a turf fire. (£3.40 per person. Kitchen. Free Showers. Open mid-Mar. to mid-Oct.)

Grudle's, Main St. (tel. 947 3177), has carefully prepared pizza, pastas, and other Mediterranean fare at reasonable prices, plus suspiciously good cakes and pastries. (Most meals £4.95-7.50. Open daily noon-10pm.) The casual **Cupan Éile**, Main St. (tel. 947 3200), meets all your sandwich needs (£1.60-3.50) and fires up a filling breakfast (£3.75-4, vegetarian option). Hearty pub grub is served up at **The Town House**, Main St. (tel. 947 2531), with most meals £5-7. (Open M-Sa 12:30-8:30pm, Su 12:30-2pm and 4-9pm.) A 3 mi. trip to **O'Neill's Point Bar**, Reenard Pier (tel. 947 2165), gets you famously good seafood. (Meals £5-9. Open mid-Mar.-Nov. M-Sa noon-12:15pm and 6:30-9:30pm, Su 6-9:30pm.)

Cahersiveen's long Main St. still has several pubs of the early 20th century variety: these establishments are both watering holes and the proprietor's "main" business, whether it be general store, blacksmith, leather shop, or farm goods retail. The **Anchor Bar** (tel. 947 2049), toward the west end of Main St., sells Guinness alongside fishing tackle. Don't come before 10pm, and take your drink into the kitchen for friendly conversation. **Mike Murt's** (tel. 947 2396) brims with Irish character. Be prepared to tell your life story to the entire pint-clutching ensemble. **The Shebeen** (tel. 947 2361) has trad nearly every night in the summer. Modern times have hit **Fertha Bar**, where trendy rock bands frequently appear on weekends. Locals speak lovingly of **Sceilig Rock** (tel. 947 2305), where pop and trad take turns shaking the wooden floor.

🏛 SIGHTS. **O'Connell's Church** in town is the only one in Ireland named for a layperson. "The Liberator" and other aspects of Irish history are celebrated at the **Old Barracks Heritage Centre**, in the tourist office. (Tel. 947 2589. Open M-Sa 10am-6pm, Su 1-6pm. £2.50.) Though the center's exhibits are well-presented, the appearance of the building will hold your interest longer. Its bizarre architecture inspired a local rumor that confused officials had accidentally built a colonial outpost, while a proper barracks was erected somewhere in India. Across the bridge past the barracks, a wealth of fortifications huddle together. Turn left past the bridge, then left off the Main Rd. to reach the ruins of the 15th century **Ballycarbery Castle**, once held by O'Connell's ancestors. Two hundred yards past the castle turnoff, two of Ireland's best-preserved stone forts spread over a small stretch of land. You can walk atop the 10 ft. thick walls of **Cahergall Fort,** or visit the small stone dwellings of **Leacanabuaile Fort.** A few minutes walk beyond the second fort is **Cuas Crom** beach, known as the best swimming spot in the area. The first weekend in August, Cahersiveen hosts the **Celtic Music Weekend,** featuring street entertainment, fireworks, pub sessions, and numerous free concerts.

VALENTIA ISLAND

Shady country roads thread across Valentia Island, linking beehive huts, ogham stones, and small ruins. The island's stupendous views of the mountainous mainland are reason enough to come to Ireland. Bridge and ferry connections to the mainland are at opposite ends of the island; regardless of which route you choose, be sure to bring along your bike. The first transatlantic telegraph cable connected Valentia to Newfoundland.

⚐ PRACTICAL INFORMATION. The comically short **car ferry** trip departs from **Reenard Point,** 3 mi. west of Cahersiveen off the Ring of Kerry Rd. Passing cars make the walk to the Point slightly difficult; a taxi from Cahersiveen runs about £4. The ferry drops you off at **Knightstown,** the island's population center. (Ferries depart every 10min. daily 8:15am-19:30pm. Cars £5 return, pedestrians £1.50, cyclists £3.) The bridge connecting Valentia to the mainland starts at **Portmagee,** 10 mi. west of Cahersiveen. To get to Portmagee, go south from Cahersiveen or north from Waterville (a longer trip), then west on R565. Hitching to Portmagee is difficult and not recommended by *Let's Go.* Enthusiastic bikers can should follow the "loop" (Waterville to Ballinskelligs, Portmagee to Knightstown to Cahersiveen). Serious site-seekers can get free maps from the Cahersiveen **tourist office.**

⚐☐ ACCOMMODATIONS AND FOOD. Should you choose to spend the night on Valentia, the island's best budget accommodations are just outside of town at ▧**Coombe Bank House** (tel. 947 6111). Follow the main road and turn right just past the Pitch & Putt. This hostel and B&B occupies a grand stone house with a fine interior. (Dorms £10, continental breakfast £4; B&B £18. Free use of laundry facilities.) 1½ mi. down the main road from Knightstown lies tiny **Chapeltown,** home to the **Ring Lyne Hostel** (tel. 947 6103), which has basic double and triple rooms above a pub. (£8-9.) The large **Royal Pier Hostel (IHH)** (tel. 947 6144) in Knightstown once hosted Queen Victoria; though the paint may be peeling and the dorms a bit crowded, it still maintains some grandeur. (8-bed dorms £8.50, private rooms £10 per person, B&B £20. Laundry £4.) A few blocks up the hill from the pier, **Altzamuth House** (tel. 947 6300) has basic, pretty rooms and a sunny breakfast room. (£16, with bath £17.) **Spring Acre** (tel. 947 6141) across from the pier, has bedrooms with huge waterfront windows. (£17 with bath.) **Boston's** (tel. 94 76140), on the main road out of Knightstown, has seafood salads (£5.50) and sandwiches (£3.50-4.95; food served daily 11am-9pm).

☐ SIGHTS. The road from town to the **old slate quarry** offers some of Valentia's best views across Dingle Bay. Slate from the massive quarry roofed the Paris Opera House and the British Parliament; the hollowed-out cliffside now houses a "sacred grotto." At the opposite end of the island, you can hike up to the ruins of a Napoleonic lookout tower with views to the Skelligs at **Bray Head.** On the way there from Knightstown, you'll pass the turnoff for **Glanleam Subtropical Gardens,** which feature such luminaries as the 50 ft. tall Chilean Fire Bush. (Tel. 947 6176. Open daily mid-Sept.-May 11am-5pm. £2.50, students £2.)

SOUTHWEST IRELAND

YOUR IRISH ANCESTORS Your grandparents might not have come from Clonakilty, but if you go back far enough, you've got an Irish relative. In 1992 Swiss geologist Ivan Stossel discovered a track of small footprints on the rocky shore of Valentia Island. After analyzing layers of volcanic ash in the groove-like prints, scientists concluded that they were made 385 million years ago, making them the oldest fossilized footprints in the Northern Hemisphere. The prints are believed to be those of a "Devonian tetrapod," a four-legged creature that predates the dinosaurs. The prints are currently unmarked and unprotected, although the government is taking steps to preserve this and other important archeological sites. For now, locals can direct you to the obscure prints.

THE SKELLIG ROCKS

The Skellig Rocks are a stunning mass of natural rubble about 8 mi. off the shore of the Iveragh Peninsula. As your boat bounces by **Little Skellig,** the rock pinnacles appear to be snow-capped; increased proximity reveals that the peaks are actually covered with 22,000 crooning, nest-wetting gannets. Boats dock at the larger **Skellig Michael.** Climb the vertigo-inducing 650 steps past puffins, kittiwakes, gannets, and petrels to reach a **monastery.** 6th century Christian monks carved out an austere community along the craggy faces of the 714 ft. high rock. Their beehive-like dwellings are still intact and fascinatingly explained by guides from the Irish heritage service, though the dark interiors and stark surroundings speak for themselves of the monks' spiritual lives. There is no toilet or shelter on the rock, but you're welcome to picnic on the steep faces that George Bernard Shaw declared "not after the fashion of this world."

The fantastic and stomach-churning **ferry voyage** takes 45 to 90min., depending on conditions, point of departure, and boat. Both hostels and the campsite in Cahersiveen will arrange trips that include a ride to the dock for £20. Joe Roddy (tel. 947 4268) and Sean Feehan (tel. 947 9182) depart from **Ballinskelligs** (£20), and Michael O'Sullivan (tel. 947 4255) and Mr. Casey (tel. 947 2437) leave from **Portmagee** (£20). Seanie Murphy picks up passengers in Reenard and Portmagee (tel. 947 6214). Roddy and O'Sullivan will give you a lift from **Waterville,** and Casey will pick you up from your hostel in **Cahersiveen.** The boats run mid-March to October, depending on the weather; phone ahead for reservations and to confirm that the boats are operating. They usually leave between 9:30am and noon and land for at least 2hr. on the island. The grass-roofed **Skellig Experience** visitor center is just across the Portmagee Bridge on Valentia Island. Videos and models engulf visitors in virtual Skellig, and for an extra (steep) charge you can sail from the center to the islands themselves, although the boats do not dock. The video is a relaxing diversion, provided you ignore the dramatic rhetorical questions. (Tel. 947 6306. Open daily Apr.-Sept. 9:30am-6pm. £3, with cruise £15; students £2.70, £13.50.)

WATERVILLE

The main strip of Waterville is wedged between the waters of Lough Cussane and crashing Atlantic waves. Lined with hotels built for wealthy English vacationers, Charlie Chaplin among them, Waterville's tourist traffic comes mostly from tour bus groups discharged for a seaside lunch before rumbling on to more sensational destinations. The meditative traveler is left to quietly walk along the shore.

🔋 **PRACTICAL INFORMATION.** The Ring of Kerry **bus** stops in Waterville in front of the Bay View Hotel on Main St. (June-Sept. 2 per day), with service to **Caherdaniel** (20min., £2.20), **Sneem** (50min., £4.30), and **Killarney** (2hr., £8.60). **Bus Éireann** travels to **Cahersiveen** once per day. The **tourist office** (tel. 947 4646) soaks up sea spray across from Butler Arms Hotel on the beach. (Open June-Sept. daily 9am-6pm.) The **phone code** is 066.

▐▛▟ ACCOMMODATIONS, FOOD, AND PUBS. Firm mattress fanatics will rejoice in the unyielding beds at **Peter's Place** (tel. 947 4608). Though construction keeps the house a bit hectic, an oceanside location and brown bread compensate. Peter himself is an energetic and friendly host, as well as a savvy sheep-shearing expert. (Sept.-May 6-bed dorms £6, June-Aug. £7. **Camping** £3.50.) A mile out of town on the Cahersiveen road, campers get an ocean view at **Waterville Caravan and Camping Park** (tel. 947 4191; tents £7-8.50; showers 50p). If you're tracking down more luxurious accommodations, aim for **The Huntsman** (tel. 947 4124) next to the tourist office, with pleasant rooms above a pub. (Twins £18-22 per person.)

An Corcán (tel. 947 4711), across from the Butler Arms Hotel, feeds the weary affordable meals. (Breakfast £3-5, lunch and dinner entrees £4-7. Open daily 8am-9:30pm.) Up the hill from the tourist office, the **Beach Cove Cafe** (tel. 947 4733) offers take-away cuisine. This quasi-fast food joint nearly overlooks your wallet. (Entrees £2-4. Open M-Th 11:30am-10pm, F-Su 11:30-4am.) The **Lobster Bar and Restaurant,** Main St. (tel. 947 4255), is worth a visit just to see the icon outside—a giant lobster clutching a Guinness—but stay for the food. (Seafood-sprinkled pub grub around £5.) The Lobster stays lively into the evening, with a pool table and alternating disco and trad most summer nights. Gaelic football legend **Mike O'Dwyer** (tel. 947 4248) lends his name to a pub and nightclub at the Strand Hotel down the road. ("Piper 2000" nightclub W and Sa-Su. Cover £4.) **The Bay View Hotel** (tel. 947 4122) throws down a Friday night disco (cover £4); either of its two bars is good for drinking. **The Fishermen's Bar** (tel. 947 4144) poured pints for Charlie Chaplin.

▨ SIGHTS. Lough Currane's waters lie about 2 mi. inland from town; follow the lake road with the ocean to your right and turn left, or just head inland along smaller roads. Locals claim that a submerged castle can be seen in times of low water, but visitors are more likely to see the ruins of a monastery on Church Island. **Waterville Boats** (tel. 947 2455), based at the Lobster Bar, rents motorboats (£25 per day) and organizes sea and lake fishing trips (£20-60 per day).

The Irish-speaking hamlet of **Ballinskelligs** between Waterville and Bolus Head isn't worth a special trip, but if you're there to catch a Skellig-bound boat, check out the ruins of **Ballinskelligs Monastery,** near the pier. It was here that the monks moved from their lofty heights after 11th century storms made journeys to the island increasingly treacherous. The quiet **Prior House Youth Hostel (An Óige/HI)** (tel. 947 9229) overlooks the bay and offers basic hostel accommodations. (Dorms £7. Open Apr.-Oct.) Two miles south of Ballinskelligs, **Bolus Head** affords great views of the Skelligs and bay on clear days.

CAHERDANIEL

There's delightfully little in the village of Caherdaniel to attract the Ring's drove of travel coaches, but this hamlet (two pubs, a grocer, a restaurant, and a take-away) has the advantage of proximity to one of Ireland's best beaches and one of the region's finest hostels. Derrynane Strand, 2 mi. of gorgeous beach ringed by picture perfect dunes, is 1½ mi. from Caherdaniel in Derrynane National Park.

▐ PRACTICAL INFORMATION. The **bus** stops in Caherdaniel twice a day at the junction of the Ring of Kerry Rd. and Main St. picking up passengers for **Sneem** (½hr., June-Sept. 2 per day, £2.90) and **Killarney** (1½hr., June-Sept. 2 per day, £7.30). The new **tourist office** is a mile east of town at the Wave Crest Camping Park. (Open May-Sept. daily 8am-10pm.) Information is also dispensed at **Mathius Adams Junk Shop** (tel. 947 5167) in the town center. (Open daily 10am-5pm.) Caherdaniel's **phone code** is 066.

█▐█ ACCOMMODATIONS, FOOD, AND PUBS. Guests have the run of the house at ▐The Travellers' Rest Hostel (tel. 947 5175). A relaxed sitting room with a fireplace and small dorms make the house look and feel more like a B&B. (July-Aug. 4- to 6-bed dorms £8, Sept.-June £7.50; Jul.-Aug. private rooms £9.50 per person, Sept.-Aug. £9. Continental breakfast £2.50.) The **Caherdaniel Village Hostel** (tel. 947 5277), across the street from Skellig Aquatics, resides in the first English police building to be deserted in the Civil War (see p. 14). The hostel offers basic comforts and a sky-lit common room. The managers can also arrange climbing trips and diving holidays; see Skellig Aquatics listing for rates. (8-bed dorms £8. Open Mar.-Nov.) A mile west of town on the Ring of Kerry road is the intimate seven-bed **Carrigbeg Hostel** (tel. 947 5229), which features expansive views of the surrounding hills and bay; call for pick-up from Caherdaniel. (Jul.-Aug. 6- to 8-bed dorms £8, Sept.-June £7.50; July-Aug. triples £9.50., Sept.-Aug. £9. Laundry £3.50.) Campers get their beauty sleep 1 mi. east of town on the Ring of Kerry road at **Wave Crest Camping Park** (tel. 947 5188), overlooking the beach. The well-stocked shop (open 8am-10pm) and self-service laundry (£4 per load) are handy. (£3.25 per person. Showers 50p. Open mid-Mar.-Sept.)

The **Courthouse Cafe** (tel. 947 5005), which serves the most affordable food in town, has both sit-down and take-away menus. (Sandwiches under £2. Open daily 5-11:30pm.) **Freddy's Bar** (tel. 947 5400) sells groceries and serves pints to locals. The **Blind Piper** (tel. 947 5126) is a popular local meeting place with outdoor tables by a stream. Occasional folk and trad drown out the bubbling water.

▨ SIGHTS. Derrynane House, sign-posted just up from the beach, was the residence of Irish patriot Daniel "The Liberator" O'Connell, who won Catholic representation in Parliament in 1829 (see **Rebellion, Union, Reaction,** p. 7). Inside the house, you can check out the dueling pistol that O'Connell used to kill challenger John d'Esterre, as well as the black glove he wore to church for years afterwards to mourn his victim. The 30min. film on O'Connell presents an engrossing and refreshingly multi-faceted image of the acerbic barrister. A few trails lead from the house through dunes and gardens. A stylized picture of the house, alongside a portrait of its most famous resident, is on the £20 note. (Tel. 947 5113. Open May-Sept. M-Sa 9am-6pm, Su 11am-7pm; Apr. and Oct. Tu-Su 1-5pm; Nov.-Mar. Sa-Su 1-5pm. Last admission 45min. before closing. £2, students and children £1.)

If you're up to 6 mi. of uphill hiking or pedaling, the pre-Christian **Staigue Fort,** west of town, will make you feel tall and powerful. The largest stone fort in Ireland, Staigue Fort stands high on a hill overlooking the sea, and protects you from Pictish invaders. Skip the **heritage center** devoted to the fort, which runs the danger of being an over-hyped tourist attraction. (Tel. 947 5288. Fort always open. Free. Heritage center open Easter-Oct. daily 10am-10pm. £2, students £1.50.)

For a close look at undersea life, contact **Skellig Aquatics** (tel. 947 5277; half-day dive £30). **Derrynane Sea Sports** (tel. 947 5266) handles the watersporting in this area. (**Sailing** £15 per hr., **windsurfing** £8 per hr., **waterskiing** £12 per hr.)

SNEEM

Tourists make Sneem their first or last stop along the Ring, and the town is prepared to receive them. Canned Irish music rolls out of the Irish music shop on the South Square, amongst the clutter of postcard stands. Two public squares and a unique sculpture collection give Sneem a quirky charm worth exploring.

▐ PRACTICAL INFORMATION. The Ring of Kerry **bus** travels to **Killarney** via **Kenmare** (1hr., June-Sept. 2 per day, £5.50). Sneem's **tourist information center** (tel. 45270) is housed in the Joli Coeur Shop near the bus stop. (Open mid-Mar.-Nov. daily 10:30am-5:30pm.) Helpful advice is also dispensed at the **post office** (tel. 45110) a few doors down. (Open M-F 9am-1pm, 2-5:30pm, Sa 9am-1pm.) Bike rental is available at **M. Burns' Bike Hire** (tel 45140), on The North Sq. (£6 per day, £33 per week. Open M-Sa 9:30am-7pm.) If Sneem's **phone code** took out a personal, it would read "attractive 064 likes long walks, leather, and Sneem."

⚑⚐✉ ACCOMMODATIONS, FOOD, AND PUBS. The **Harbour View Hostel** (tel. 45276), a ¼ mi. from town on Kenmare Rd., used to be a motel and still looks like one, with ranch-style units in a gravel lot. The dorms are crowded and involve walk-throughs. (4-bed dorms £8, doubles or twins £10 per person, singles £15. **Camping** £5. Sheets 50p. Laundry £5.) Sneem's oldest and arguably nicest B&B is **The Bank House,** North Sq. (tel. 45226; www.sneem.com/bankhouse.html). The friendly owners giggle with enthusiasm for the region. (£17-18 per person. Open Mar.-Nov.) **Old Convent House,** Pier Rd. (tel. 45181), a right off The South Sq. just after Erin Co. Knitwear, has rooms with mountain views. (£18 per person. Laundry £4.) Near the town center, **Goosey Island Campsite** (tel. 45577) is ideally located for sculpture park exploration. (£4 per person. Showers 50p. Open Apr.-mid-Oct.)

Check out the **Riverain Restaurant** (tel. 45245) for vegetarian meals and a view of the river. (Lunches £2-6, most evening meals £7-9. Open May-Aug. 12:30-4pm and 5-9:30pm.) Massive pub meals are served at **The Blue Bull** (tel. 45382), by the post office. Stick around for occasional ballad sessions. On the north side of town, **The Village Kitchen** (tel. 45281) serves seafood and sandwiches in a comfortable cafe setting. (Sandwiches under £2; entrees £5-6.50. Open 9:30am-8:30pm.) Gallop down to the **Hungry Knight** (tel. 45237) for cheap fast food or a game of pool with young Sneemers. (Open June-Sept. M-Sa 11-3:30am.) At the **Fisherman's Knot** (tel. 45224), across the bridge on Caherdaniel Rd., locals tap their toes to trad a few nights a week. **O'Shea's** reverberates with frequent, old-fashioned sessions.

◉ SIGHTS. When Charles de Gaulle visited Sneem in 1969, the town was so honored that its people erected a monument to commemorate the event: a bronze sculpture of de Gaulle's head mounted on a boulder of local stone. Thus, a tradition was born. Today, Sneem's **sculpture park** celebrates the late President Cearbhaill O'Dalaigh, the Egyptian Goddess Isis, wrestling champ "Crusher" Casey, and the terribly strange set of cave buildings on the banks of the river. It's difficult to decide whether the sculptures or their collective name—"The Way the Fairies Went"—is more bizarre. Pick up the *Sneem Guide* in the tourist office for an abbreviated tour (25p). Jackie O'Shea (tel. 45369) runs **deep-sea angling** trips from Rossdohan Pier, 5 mi. from town on the Kenmore Rd. (From £25.)

DINGLE PENINSULA

For decades, the Dingle Peninsula was the under-touristed counterpart to the Ring of Kerry. Word has finally gotten out, and the Killarney and Ring of Kerry tourist blitz has recently begun to encroach upon this scenic, Irish-speaking peninsula. Slieve Mish and the flat farming country of East Dingle are not as convenient for backpackers as Dingle Town, the charming, if increasingly pricey, regional center.

Spectacular cliffs and sweeping beaches rim the Dingle Peninsula, which still remains more congested with ancient sites than tourbuses. A *gaeltacht* to the west of Dingle Town preserves the heritage that local storytellers have kept alive for centuries. Locating a grocery store among Irish signs may be a challenge, but, thankfully, Guinness signs still mark the pubs. Dingle's *bohareens* (side roads) are best explored by bike: the entire western circuit, from Dingle out to Slea Head, up to Ballydavid, and back, is only a daytrip, while the mountainous northern regions are more arduous excursions. The Cloghane/Brandon area in the north remains most free of foreigners; Slea Head, Dunquin, and the Blasket Islands are the most other-worldly spots. Maps available in area tourist offices describe The Dingle Way, a 95 mi. walking trail that circles the peninsula. A Dingle Peninsula website offers details (www.dingle-peninsula.ie).

While Dingle Town is well connected to Killarney and Tralee, public transport within the peninsula is scarce. Buses to towns in South Dingle run daily in July and August, but only two or three times a week during the rest of the year. There is no direct bus service to villages north of Dingle Town. For detailed bus information, call the Tralee station (tel. (066) 23566). Summertime hitchers often get lifts through the Connor Pass. The **phone code** for the entire peninsula is 066.

DINGLE

Though the *craic* in Dingle is still home-grown, increasing armadas of tourists cloy the docks, pubs, and smart pubs of this bayside town. Visitors are indulged with music sessions, fantastic hostels, and the gregarious dolphin, Fungi, who charms the whole town from his permanent residence in Dingle Bay. After scouring the deserted parts of the peninsula for vistas and ogham stones, you can return to town in the evening for music and quality time with your publican.

▐ TRANSPORTATION

Buses: Buses stop on Ring Rd. by the harbor, behind Garvey's SuperValu. Bus information is available from the Tralee bus station (tel. (066) 712 3566). **Bus Éireann** runs to **Ballydavid** (Tu and F 3 per day, £3.15 return), **Dunquin** and **Ballyferriter** (summer M and Th 4 per day, Tu-W and F-Sa 2 per day, Su 1 per day; £2.30), **Tralee** (1¼hr.; June-Sept. 6 per day, Su 5 per day, Oct.-May 6 per day, Su 4 per day; £5.90), and **Killarney** (1½hr.; June-Sept. 3 per day, Su 2 per day; £7.30). From June-Sept. additional buses tour the south of the peninsula from Dingle (M-Sa 2 per day).

Bike Rental: Paddy's Bike Shop, Dykegate St. (tel. 915 2311), rents the best bikes in town. £5 per day, £25 per week. Open daily 9am-7pm.

▐ ORIENTATION AND PRACTICAL INFORMATION

Dingle dangles in the middle of the southern coast of Dingle Peninsula. R559 heads east to Killarney and Tralee, and west to Ventry, Dunquin, and Slea Head. A narrow road running north through the Connor Pass leads to Stradbally and Castlegregory. The streets of downtown Dingle approximate a grid pattern. **Strand St.** runs next to the harbor along the marina; **Main St.** is its parallel counterpart further uphill. **The Mall, Dykegate St.,** and **Green St.** connect the two, running perpendicular to the water. On the eastern edge of town, Strand St., The Mall, and **Tralee Rd.** converge in a roundabout.

Tourist Office: Corner of Main and Dykegate St. (tel. 915 1188). You'll be vying for attention with scores of confused tourists. Open June-Aug. M-Sa 9am-6pm, Su 10am-6pm; Sept.-Oct. and mid-Mar.-May M-Sa 9am-5pm.

Banks: AiB, Main St. (tel. 915 1400). Open M 10am-12:30pm and 1:30-5pm, Tu-F 10am-12:30pm and 1:30-4pm. **Bank of Ireland,** Main St. (tel. 915 1100). Same hours. Both have multi-card tolerant **ATMs.**

Camping Equipment: The Mountain Man, Strand St. (tel. 915 2400). Open daily July-Aug. 9am-9pm, Sept.-June 9am-6pm. No tent rental. Offers 2½hr. bus tours to Connor Pass and Slea Head (£8), and a shuttle to the Blasket ferry (£6), in addition to the very informative *Guide to the Dingle Peninsula*, which includes a walking map (£5).

Laundry: Níolann an Daingin, Green St. (tel. 915 1837), behind El Toro. Wash and dry from £5.50. Open M-Sa 9am-5:30pm.

Pharmacy: O'Keefe's Pharmacy Ltd. (tel. 915 1310). Open M-W and F-Sa 9:30am-6pm, Th 9:30am-1pm, Su 9:30am-12:30pm.

Emergency: Dial 999; no coins required. **Garda:** The Holy Ground (tel. 915 1522).

Post Office: Upper Main St. (tel. 915 1661). Just the place for mailing Fungi postcards. Open M-F 9am-1pm and 2-5:30pm, Sa 9am-1pm.

Internet Access: Dingleweb, Main St. (tel. 915 2477). £1.50 per min., £5 per hour.

PHONE CODE:	Friendly 066 frolics in Dingle Harbour.

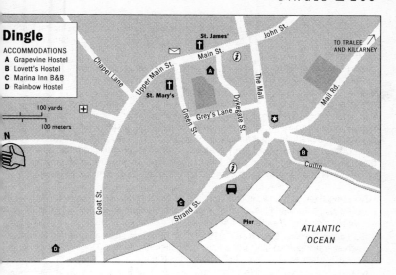

Dingle

ACCOMMODATIONS
A Grapevine Hostel
B Lovett's Hostel
C Marina Inn B&B
D Rainbow Hostel

ACCOMMODATIONS

here are great hostels in Dingle, although some are a long walk from town. Many stel owners vie for your business as the buses empty. B&Bs along Dykegate and rand St. and hostels in town tend to fill up fast in the summer; call ahead.

Ballintaggart Hostel (IHH) (tel. 915 1454), a 25min. walk east of town on Tralee Rd. Ballintaggart is set in the grand stone mansion where the Earl of Cork strangled his wife after a poisoning attempt went awry. Her ghost supposedly haunts the enormous bunk rooms, enclosed cobblestone courtyard, and elegant, fire-heated common rooms. Free shuttle to town. 12-bed dorms £7, 8- to 10-bed dorms £8, 4-bed £10, twins and doubles £14 per person; off-season prices £1-2 cheaper. **Camping** £3.50 per person. Breakfast £2-4. Laundry service £4. **Bike hire** £7 per day, £4 per 3hr.

Rainbow Hostel (tel. 915 1044; email info@net-rainbow.com; www.rainbow.com), 15min. west of town on Strand Rd. Bear right and inland at the corner of Dunquin Rd. One of Ireland's largest and best-decorated hostels. Free lifts to and from town. 6-bed dorms £8, doubles £10 per person. **Camping** £4. Laundry £4. **Bike rental** £6 per day.

Grapevine Hostel, Dykegate St. (tel. 915 1434), off Main St. Smack in the middle of town and just a short stagger from Dingle's finest pubs. The friendly folks at the Grapevine welcome you to close but comfy bunk rooms and the music-filled common room with its dangerously cushy chairs. 4- to 8-bed dorms £7-8.50.

An Caladh Spáinneach (un KULL-uh SPINE-uck; the Spanish Pier), Strand St. (tel. 915 2160). No frills, but reasonable beds and a great waterfront location. Dorms £7-8; doubles £10 per person. Open May-Oct.

Lovett's Hostel, Cooleen Rd. (tel. 915 1903). Turn opposite the Esso Station past the roundabout, right on the bay. This small hostel perches on the outskirts of town, away from most of the hustle and bustle. Dorms £7-8, doubles £18, triples £24.

Old Mill House, Dykegate St. (tel. 915 1120; verhoul@iol.ie; www.iol.ie/~verhoul). The comfortable pine beds in this bright house are outdone only by its vivacious owner. You can save a few pounds by passing on breakfast, but the amazing crepes are well worth it. Singles £15-22, doubles and triples from £16 per person.

SOUTHWEST IRELAND

Kirrary House (tel. 915 1606), across from Old Mill House. With good cheer and pride Mrs. Collins puts guests up in her delightful rooms. Book your archaeological tours here with *Sciuird* Tours, offered by Mr. Collins (see **Sights**). £18-19 per person with bath. **Bike rental** £6 per day.

Sleeping Giant, Green St. (tel. 915 2666). Small, well-located house has soft beds a decent prices. 4- to 6-bed dorms £9, triples £33, doubles and twins with bath £26.

◗ FOOD

Dingle is home to all sorts of eateries, from gourmet seafood restaurants to dough nut stands. **SuperValu supermarket,** The Holy Ground (tel. 915 1397), stocks a Supe Selection of groceries and juicy tabloids. (Open M-Sa 8am-9pm, Su 9am-6pm.) ▲ **Grianán,** Dykegate St. (tel. 915 1090), near the Grapevine Hostel, has crunch wholefoods and organic vegetables. (Open M-F 9:30am-6pm, Sa 10am-6pm.)

The Oven Door, The Holy Ground (tel. 915 1056), across from SuperValu. Crispy pizza (£4-7), spectacular sundaes (£3), and incredible cakes draw droves to this wood an stone cafe. Open Mar.-Christmas daily 10am-10pm.

The Forge, The Holy Ground (tel. 915 2590). This large green-and-red family restaura serves lunches from £5, and pricier but delightful dinners. Open Mar.-Oct. M, W-S noon-2:30pm and 6-10pm, Su 2-3pm and 6-10pm.

Danno's, Strand St. (tel. 915 1855). The railroad theme may send some folks chuggin away, but this popular pub can't be beat for hearty burgers and cold pints. Burgers £ 7, other entrees £5-9. Food served M-Sa noon-2:30pm and 6-9pm.

The Global Village, Main St. (tel. 915 2325). Fantastic variety of meals from around th world, including several vegetarian options. Swap travel stories with the owner, who co lected many of the recipes himself. Lunch £4-6, most dinners £8-11. Open mid-Ma Oct. M-Sa 9:30am-10pm, Su 19am-10pm.

An Café Liteartha, Dykegate St. (tel. 915 1388), across the street from the Grapevin This cafe and bookstore was one of the first Irish-language cafes in the Republic, a many an Irish *cómbra* can still be heard. Don't bring your full appetite. Open M-F 10a 5:30pm, Sa-Su 11am-5:30pm. Bookstore open until 6pm.

◪ PUBS

Dingle has 52 pubs for 1500 people. Many pubs are beginning to cater to tourist but the town still produces copious *craic*.

An Droichead Beag (The Small Bridge), Lower Main St. (tel. 915 1723). The most pop lar pub in town unleashes the best trad around—401 sessions a year.

O'Flaherty's Pub, The Holy Ground (tel. 915 18130), a few doors up from the traffic c cle. Trad masters have the pub filled by 9pm.

An Conair, off Main St. on Conor Pass Rd. (tel. 915 2011). Lusty Irish singing resonat through the beer garden several nights a week. M night set dancing.

M. Nelligans, Main St. (tel. 915 1723). Not as lively as some of her neighbors, b encapsulates all the features of a traditional pub. Trad nightly.

Dick Mack's, Green St. (tel. 915 1960), opposite the church. At "Dick Mack's Bar, Bo Store, and Leather Shop," the proprietor leaps between the bar and his leather-tooli bench. Shoeboxes and whiskey bottles line the walls. Though heavily touristed, th strong local following frequently bursts into song.

Murphy's, Strand St. (tel. 915 1450). Nightly ballads boom out of this classic, crowde pub by the marina.

Marie De Baras, Strand St. (tel. 915 1215), draws a mixed age and largely tourist crov to hear great folk and trad with a modern twist.

SIGHTS

Fungi the Dolphin swam into Dingle Bay one day in 1983 with his mother, and the pair immediately became local celebrities. Dolphins had visited the bay before, but Fungi took to it like a fish to water, cavorting with sailors and swimmers, flirting with TV cameras, and jumping in and out of the water for applause. Mom has gone on to the great tuna can in the sky, but egomaniacal Fungi remains fond of humans. Wetsuited tourists incessantly swarm around him. **Boat trips** to see the dolphin leave from the pier constantly in summer. (Most around £6.) A free alternative is to watch the antics from the shore east of town. To get there, walk 2min. down Tralee Rd., turn right at the Skellig Hotel, and then follow the beach away from town for about 10min. The small beach on the other side of a stone tower is often crowded with Fungi-seekers. Anti-dolphinites can be lured along by the promise of great views on the walk. The best times to see him are 8-10am and 6-8pm. You can rent a **wetsuit** from **Flannery's** (tel. 51967), just east of town off Tralee Rd. (£14 per 2hr., £22 overnight.) **Dingle Eco-Tours** (tel. (087) 285 8802) give a broader view of the harbor's life and cruise past Dunbey Fut as well. **Deep-sea angling** trips (tel. (087) 461 591), leave daily in the summer. (£14, equipment included.) Perhaps the closest look at sea creatures is available at **Dingle Ocean World,** Strand St. The aquarium is a great option for a rainy day. Observe swimming fish in an underwater tunnel, and pet and prod skates and rays in the touch tank. (Tel. 915 2111. Open daily July-Aug. 9am-9:30pm; Apr.-July and Aug.-Sept. 10am-6pm; Oct.-Mar. 10am-5pm. £4.50, students £3.50.)

The information office at the Mountain Man sells *The Easy Guide to the Dingle Peninsula* (£5), which details walking tours, cycling tours, and local history, and includes a map. **Sciúird Archaeology tours** (tel. 915 1606) take you from the pier on a 3hr. whirlwind bus tour of the area's ancient spots (2 per day, £8; book ahead). Summer festivals periodically bring the carnival to town. The **Dingle Regatta** hauls in the salty mariners on the third Sunday in August. In early September, the **Dingle Music Festival** lures big-name trad groups and other performers from across the musical spectrum (tel. 915 2477; www.iol.ie/~dingmus).

SLEA HEAD AND DUNQUIN

Glorious **Slea Head** impresses with jagged cliffs and plunging waves. Green hills, interrupted by rough stone walls and occasional sheep, suddenly break off into the foam-flecked sea. *Ryan's Daughter* and parts of *Far and Away* were filmed around here, indicative of the scenery's tendency towards the highly dramatic. By far the best way to see Slea Head and Dunquin in a day or less is to bike along the predominantly flat **Slea Head Drive.**

Past Dingle Town towards Slea Head sits the village of **Ventry** (Ceann Trá), home to a sandy beach and the brand-new **Ballybeag Hostel** (tel. 915 9876; email balybeag@iol.ie). The hostel sits on an inland turn just past the beach. Huge beds, soothing sitting rooms, and regular shuttle buses into downtown Dingle make it ideal shelter for explorers of both Slea Head and Dingle. (4-bed dorms May-Oct. £9, off-season £7.50. **Bike rental** £2.50-5 per day. Laundry £4.) There's plenty of space on the Head to camp, but in the high season you'll have some neighbors.

Within sight of the hostel is the hillside bric-a-brac of **Rahinnane Castle.** While the small ruin is hardly worth a peep, the ◨**Celtic and Prehistoric Museum,** farther down the road, is a must-see. The laid-back proprietor will take you on a tour of his astounding collection, ranging from 300-million-year-old sea worm fossils, to Iron Age tools and jewelry, to an electric sheep. The museum's cafe pours cups of coffee (£1) at tables overlooking marshes and the sea. (Tel. 915 9941; www.kerryweb.ie. Museum and cafe open daily June-Sept. 10am-5pm, other times call ahead. £3, children £2.) The Slea Head Drive continues past several Iron Age and early Christian stones and ruins. **Dunbeg Fort** (£1, students 80p) and the less impressive **Fahan Group** (£1) of oratories (beehive-shaped stone huts built by early monks), cluster on hillsides over the cliffs. Slea Head looks out onto the Blasket Islands. Gaze at them from the porch of **The Enchanted Forest** (tel. 915 6234). Within the bright yellow house lies the "fairytale museum." Though the cynical may scoff at dioramas with teddy-bear figures, others will delight in the precious presentations of the four seasons and Celtic pagan holidays. (Open daily mid-Mar.-Sept. 11:30am-6:30pm. £2.50, students £2.)

North of Slea Head, the scattered settlement of **Dunquin** (Dún Chaoin) offers stone houses, a pub, and Irish speakers, but no grocery store. Stock up in Dingle or in Ballyferriter if you're going to stay here or on Great Blasket. **Kruger's** (tel. 915 6127), purportedly the westernmost pub in Europe, features pub grub, spontaneous music sessions, and fantastic views. (Entrees around £5.) Its adjacent **B&B** has comfortable rooms. (£16.) Along the road to Ballyferriter, **An Óige Hostel (HI)** (tel. 915 6121) provides adequate bunk rooms and a window-walled dining room that looks out onto the sea. (June-Sept. dorms £6.50-7.50, twins £9 per person; Oct.-May £5.50-6.50, £8. Showers closed 9am-5:30pm. Breakfast £2. Sheets £1. Lockout 10:15am-5pm. Midnight curfew.)

Outstanding exhibits are contained within the **Blasket Centre** (tel. 915 6444), just outside of Dunquin on the road to Ballyferriter. Writings and photographs of the Great Blasket authors recreate the lost era of the islands. The museum also shows a 20min. film on the islanders and presents exhibits on the past richness and current status of the Irish language. (Open daily July-Aug. 10am-7pm, Easter-June and Sept.-Nov. 10am-6pm; last admission 45min. before closing. £2.50, students £1.)

BLASKET ISLANDS (NA BLASCAODAÍ)

Six islands comprise the Blaskets: Beginish, Tearaght, Inishnabro, Inishvickillane, Inishtooskert, and Great Blasket. Evacuated in 1953, the Blasket Islands were once inhabited by proud but impoverished villagers, poet-fishermen, and memoirists. At the beginning of the 20th century, the Blaskets were idealized as the bastion of unadulterated Irish culture, and scholar George Thompson compared the isolated *gaeltacht* culture to Homeric Greece. Mainlanders sponsored Blasket storytellers in publishing their autobiographies. The resulting memoirs bemoaned the decline of the *gaeltacht* culture; among them were Maurice O'Sullivan's *Twenty Years A-Growing*, Thomas O'Crohan's *The Islander*, and Peig Sayers's *Peig*. The titles are obscure outside Ireland, but still required reading for Irish secondary school students. One author reluctantly warned that "after us, there will be no more." Mists, seals, and occasional fishing boats may continue to pass the Blaskets, but the unique way of life that once took place there is extinct.

Days on Great Blasket allow for uninterrupted rumination. Wander through the mist down to the white strand, follow the grass paths along the island's 4 mi. length, explore the silent stone skeletons of former houses clustered in the village, and observe the puffins and seals that populate the island. Have a homebaked scone in the small **cafe** near the old village. (Open irregularly 10am-6pm.) **Campers** can pitch their tents anywhere for free. Rumor has it that by the summer of 2000, there should be a hostel on the island. If you plan to stay, stock up on supplies in Dingle or Ballyferriter—there's no hot water, food (other than the cafe's small snacks), or electricity on the island. Keep in mind that if the weather is bad, the boats don't run; people have been stuck here for three weeks during gales. **Boats** (tel. 915 6422) for the Blaskets depart from Dunquin (daily May-Sept. every 30min. from 10am to 3pm, £10 return). A shuttle runs from Dingle to the Blasket ferry and back (2 per day, £6; ask at the Mountain Man for details). The ferry company also runs 2-3hr. **cruises** that circle the islands without landing (2 per day, £16).

BALLYFERRITER (BAILE AN FHEIRTÉARAIGH)

Ballyferriter is West Dingle's closest approximation to a town center. The surrounding settlement is an unpolluted *gaeltacht*—even the Guinness signs are in Irish. Many visitors land in Ballyferriter and head straight for **Tigh Pheig** (Peig's Pub), Main St. (tel. 915 6433), where prosaic voices discuss life all day long. Frequent evening trad sessions and two pool tables have the locals stopping in. Peig's makes a welcoming spot for an appetizing meal. (Daily specials £5.50.) Across the street, **Tigh Uí Mhurchú** (Murphy's; tel. 915 6224) competes for the bargain lunch-hunters, and pours pints to the rhythm of nightly music. The largest grocery in town is **O Shcilleaghán Market** (tel. 915 6157) in the town center. (Open daily May-Sept. 9am-9pm, winter 9am-8pm.) 5min. outside town on Dunquin Rd., the very simple **An Cat Dubh** (Black Cat Hostel; tel. 915 6286) crosses your path in a tacky but friendly sort of way. Don't worry, black cats are a sign of good luck in Ireland. (Dorms £7. **Camping** £3 per person. Open May-Sept.) The B&B next door, **An Spéice** (tel. 915 6254), provides quiet rest. (£15, with bath £17.)

The **Chorca Dhuibhne Museum** (tel. 915 6100), in the center of town, brims with photos and text relating to the area's wildlife, archaeology, and folklore. (Open daily 9:30am-6pm. £1.50, students £1.) The museum is a noble attempt at making the area's history accessible, and a good starting point for visiting nearby ancient sites. From the hostel at Ballyferriter, follow the signs to the Iron Age **Dún An Óir** (Fort of Gold), where, in 1580, the English massacred over 600 Spanish, Italian, and Irish soldiers who participated in a rebellion against Queen Elizabeth. From the main road, sign-posted roads branch to **Riasc,** a puzzling monastic site with an engraved standing slab. Heading eastward, **Gallarus Oratory** (tel. 915 5333) is a well-marked detour on the road back to Dingle Town. The small, carefully crafted church is a masterpiece of 8th century stonework. The adjacent **visitor center** presents a 15min. video tour of Dingle's ancient places. (Oratory always open. Visitor center open daily Apr. -mid-Oct. 9:30am-8pm. £1.50, students £1.)

NORTH DINGLE

Both hikers and beach loafers can get their fix on the peninsula's northern shore. Jaw-dropping views from the mountains motivate casual hikers to make the day-trip from Dingle Town. While the seaside villages hold little of enduring interest, they're all pleasant places to get a meal, a pint, or a night's rest.

From Dingle Town, a winding cliff-side road runs north by way of the 1500 ft. **Connor Pass.** Buses won't fit on the narrow road, but cars can squeeze through, and bikers and walkers are sustained by valley views on the 3 mi. of mild incline. As the road crests the **Brandon Ridge,** your labors are rewarded with one of Ireland's best views. On a clear day, visitors can gaze awe-struck at lakes thousands of feet below, and see as far as Valentia Island off the south coast across the peninsula to the Maharee Islands to the north. As the road twists downhill, a small waterfall and a few picnic tables mark the base of **Pedlars Lake.** Be careful on the slippery slope that leads up to the lake, named in honor of a traveling tradesman who lost his wares (and his life) to brigands nearby. These days one is more likely to encounter a geologist than a bandit—the glacier-sliced lakes and boulder-pocked landscape are evidence of the Ice Age.

Beyond the lake, the road heads downhill to the coast. Signs point out the westward fork to **Cloghane.** The quiet hamlet is a good starting point for hikes up the 3127 ft. **Mt. Brandon.** The devout head up the "Saint's Road" to the summit each July 25, in honor of St. Brendan, who allegedly carved the trail. Back in Cloghane, the **Tigh Tomsi Hostel** (tel. 713 8299) offers unglamorous but welcome beds. (Dorms £8. Sheets £1. Wash and dry £4.)

Back toward Tralee in **Stradbally,** the friendly **Connor Pass Hostel (IHH)** (tel. 713 9179) has welcoming beds. (Dorms £7. Open mid-Mar.-Nov.) The hostel makes a good base for hikes in the **Slieve Mish Mountains** to the east. The 2713 ft. ascent to **Cáherconree** culminates with views of the peninsula, the ocean, and the Shannon Estuary. Stradbally is also an excellent place from which to embark on the **Loch a'Duín** nature and archaeology walk. Inquire at the friendly, multi-faceted **Tomásin's Pub** (tel. 713 9179) across the street from the hostel for info packets (£3). The pub also serves mean grub. (Warm lunch £3.50-7, served noon-4:30pm; dinners £7-11, served 6-9pm.) A trip to Stradbally is incomplete without walking the quarter-mile to the beach. The strand beyond the dune is especially magnificent at low tide.

Castlegregory, with a tourist office and a grocery store, may make the best home base for exploring north Dingle. From Castlegregory, head north up the sandy **Maharees Peninsula** where you can swim at numerous strands, or rent sailboards from **Focus Windsurfing** (tel. 713 9411; from £5 per hour). The **Maharees Regatta** hits the waves in early July, and a week or two later Castlegory's **Summer Festival** wakes up the town a bit. A **bus** to **Tralee** runs on Fridays (£3.80). The **tourist information center** (tel. 713 9422) is small but informative. (Open M-F 9:30am-5pm.) **Spar Market** (tel. 713 9433) offers edible caloric matter. (Open daily 8:30am-10pm.) The quiet **Lynch's Hostel** (tel. 713 9777) is the better of the two hostels in town. (Dorms £8, doubles £9 per person. **Bike rental** £6 per day.) If you're stuck, try **Fitzgerald's Euro-Hostel** (tel. 713 9133), above the pub. (Dorms £7.) In a restored stone cottage, ☒**Milesian Restaurant,** Main. St., hosts frequent music and poetry readings and an ever-changing menu with vegetarian options. (Dinners £5.95-7.95. Open Easter-Nov. and winter weekends 1-11:30pm.) Across the street, **O'Donnell's Pub** (tel. 713 9560) plays frequent trad in a setting based on Western saloons. **Ned Natterjack's** (tel. 713 9491), named for the rare and quite vocal Natterjack toad that resides in this area, presents various styles of music and a glorious beer garden.

TRALEE

While tourists tend to identify Killarney as the core of Kerry, Tralee (pop. 20,000) is the county's residential and economic capital. Though traffic and industrial development render some neighborhoods a bit dreary, multi-million pound projects have added new, splashy tourist attractions to the cosmopolitan city center. No tourist development, however, could possibly top Tralee's famed gardens. The annual **Rose of Tralee** festival is a centuries-old pageant that has Irish eyes glued to their TV sets every August.

▐ TRANSPORTATION

Airport: Kerry Airport (tel. 64644), off N22 halfway between Tralee and Killarney. **Ryanair** (tel. (01) 609 7999) flies to London.

Trains: Edward St. and John Joe Sheehy Rd. (tel. 712 3522). Ticket office opens daily during sporadic hours. Trains tie Tralee to **Killarney** (40min.; M-Sa 5 per day, Su 4 per day; £5.50), **Cork** (2½hr.; M-Sa 5 per day, Su 3 per day; £17), **Galway** (3 per day, £33.50), **Dublin** (4hr.; M-Sa 4 per day, Su 3 per day; £33.50), **Waterford** (4hr., M-Sa 1 per day, £33.50), and **Rosslare Harbour** (5½hr., M-Sa 2 per day, £33.50).

Buses: Edward St. and John Joe Sheehy Rd. (tel. 712 3566). Station open in summer M-Sa 8:30am-6pm, Su 9am-3:30pm; in winter M-Sa 9am-5:15pm. Buses rumble off to **Killarney** (40min.; June-Sept. M-Sa 14 per day, Su 8 per day; Oct.-May M-Sa 5 per day, Su 6 per day; £4.40), **Dingle** (1¼hr.; July-Aug. M-Sa 8 per day, Su 4 per day; Sept.-June M-Sa 4 per day, Su 2 per day; £5.90), **Limerick** (2¼hr.; M-Sa 7 per day, Su 7 per day; £9), **Cork** (2½hr.; M-Sa 6 per day, Su 3 per day; £9.70), and **Galway** (M-Sa 6 per day, Su 4 per day; £13).

Taxi: Call-A-Cab (tel. 712 0333). **EuroCabs** (te. 712 7111). Cabs park at the intersection of Denny St. and The Mall. £1 per mile, less for longer distances.

Bike Rental: O'Halloran, 83 Boherboy (tel. 712 2820). Sometimes, you've just got to ride. £6 per day, £30 per week; helmet included. Open M-Sa 9:30am-6pm.

▐ ORIENTATION AND PRACTICAL INFORMATION

Tralee's streets are hopelessly knotted; it's wise to arm yourself with a free map from the tourist office. The main street in town—variously called **The Mall, Castle St.,** and **Boherboy**—holds many stores and restaurants along its roughly east-west path. **Edward St.** connects this main thoroughfare to the train and bus stations. Wide **Denny St.** runs south to the tourist office and park.

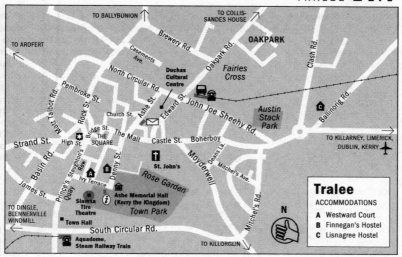

Tralee
ACCOMMODATIONS
A Westward Court
B Finnegan's Hostel
C Lisnagree Hostel

Tourist Office: Ashe Memorial Hall (tel. 712 1288), at the end of Denny St. From the station, go into town on Edward St., turn right on Castle St., and then left onto Denny St. The staff provides free maps. Open July-Aug. M-Sa 9am-7pm; Su 9am-6pm; May-June and Oct. M-Sa 9am-6pm; Oct.-Apr. M-F 9am-5pm.

Banks: Bank of Ireland, Castle St. Open M 10am-5pm, Tu-F 10am-4pm. **AIB,** corner of Denny and Castle St. Open M 10am-5pm, Tu-F 10am-4pm. Both have **ATMs.**

Camping Equipment: Landers, Courthouse Ln. (tel. 712 6644), has an extensive selection. No tent rental. Open M-Sa 9am-6pm, Su 9:30am-1pm and 2-6pm.

Laundry: Kate's Launderette, Boherboy (tel. 712 7173). Large loads £5-6; 10% student discount. Open M-Sa 8:45am-6pm.

Pharmacy: Kelly's Chemist, The Mall (tel. 712 1302). Open M-F 9am-8pm, Sa 9am-6pm.

Emergency: Dial 999; no coins required. **Garda:** High St. (tel. 712 2022).

Counseling and Support: Samaritans, 44 Moyderwell (tel. 712 2566). 24hr. hotline.

Hospital: Tralee County General Hospital, off Killarney Rd. (tel. 712 6222).

Post Office: Edward St. (tel. 712 1013), off Castle St. Open M and W-Sa 9am-5:30pm, Tu 9:30am-5:30pm.

Internet Access: Cyberpost, 26 Castle St. (tel. 718 1284). £2 per 10min., £1 for each additional 20min. Open July-Sept. M-Sa 10am-10pm, Oct.-June 10am-6pm.

PHONE CODE:	By any other name would still be 066.

▟ ACCOMMODATIONS

Tralee has several scattered but reasonable hostels, that can barely contain festival-goers in late August. Rows of pleasant B&Bs line Edward St. as it becomes Oakpark Rd.; others can be found along Princes Quay, close to the Park.

Collis-Sandes House (IHH) (tel. 712 8658; email colsands@indigo.ie; www.colsands.com). Near-perfect, but far from town. Follow Edward St./Oakpark Rd. 1 mi. from town, take the first left after Halloran's Foodstore, and follow signs another ½ mi. to the right, or save yourself and call for pick up. Magnificent high ceilings and impressive Moorish arches lend grandeur to this stone mansion. Free lifts to town and pub-runs. 4- to 6-bed dorms £8, doubles from £10 per person. **Camping** £4 per person. Continental breakfast £1. Laundry £3. Wheelchair accessible.

Finnegan's Hostel (IHH), 17 Denny St. (tel. 712 7610). At the end of the city's most dignified street, this majestic 19th century townhouse contains part of the old town castle. A great location and a plush common room, but the mattresses can be a bit lumpy. Wood-floored bunk rooms are named after Ireland's literary heroes. Dorms £9, twins and doubles with bath £10 per person. Laundry £3.

Lisnagree Hostel (IHH), Ballinorig Rd. (tel. 712 7133). On the left fork just after the traffic circle before the Maxol garage (follow Boherboy away from town), 1 mi. from town center and close to the bus/train station. A small, pretty, relaxed hostel perfect for families or couples, but a bit remote for anyone who wants to hit the pubs at night. Bike and walking tours. 4-bed dorms with bath from £8.50, doubles £18-20, singles £12.

Westward Court (IHH), Mary St. (tel. 718 0041). Follow Denny St. to the park, then turn right, and right again at the Ivy Terrace Diner. A spotless and uniform series of dorms. 4-bed dorms £11, doubles £16 per person, singles £17.50. Continental breakfast included. Laundry £5. Wheelchair accessible. 3am curfew.

Dowling's Leeside, Oakpark Rd. (tel. 712 6475). About ½ mi. from town center on Edward St./Oakpark Rd. Pamper yourself at this cheerful B&B, decorated with gorgeous Irish pine antique furniture, cushy chairs, and fresh flowers. The lovely hostess and friendly dog will make you want to move in. All rooms have shower and TV. Singles £19, doubles £17 per person.

Castle House, 27 Upper Castle St. (tel. 712 5167). Watch TV and listen to the traffic go by in your well equipped room. Singles £22-25, doubles and twins £18-20 per person.

Woodlands Park, Dingle Rd. (tel. 712 1235), ¼ mi. past the Aquadome. Decent camping. Free showers, game room. Tent £4-4.25 without car. Open Mar. 15 to Oct.

FOOD

True gourmands may be disappointed with the culinary landscape of Tralee, but pub grub and fast food are readily available. If they don't sell it at the massive **Tesco** (tel. 712 2788) in The Square, you probably shouldn't be eating it. (Open M-W and Sa 8:30am-8pm, Th-F 8:30am-10pm, Su 10am-6pm.) Across the street, **Seancra** (tel. 712 2644), peddles health food and organic produce. (Open M-W and Sa 9am-6pm, Th 9am-8pm, F 9am-9pm.)

Mozart's, 4 Ashe St. (tel. 712 7977). A range of well-prepared delights, from stuffed baguettes (£2.95-3.95) in the afternoon to stir-fries and steaks in the evening (£6.95-11.95). Open mid-May-Sept. M-Sa 9am-9:30pm; Oct. to mid-May 9am-7pm.

The Skillet, Barrack Ln. (tel. 712 4561), off The Mall. A traditional decor is matched with stew and other Irish specialties. Lunch runs from £4-7, but dinner is pricier. Open M-Sa 9am-10pm, Su noon-10pm.

Brat's Place, 18 Milk Market Ln., a pedestrian walkway off The Mall. Tasty, conscientiously prepared vegetarian food with mostly local and organic ingredients. Soup £1.50; warm entrees £4.50. Open M-Sa 12:30-2:30pm, later if food lasts.

Hob Knobs, The Square (tel. 712 1846). Low-key cafeteria-style cafe with tasty breakfasts and decent lunches. Most meals £3-5. Open M-Sa 8am-5pm.

Roots, 76 Boherboy (tel. 712 2665). An ever-changing though limited menu of vegetarian food with gargantuan portions (£3-4). Open M-F 11am-3:30pm.

Pizza Time, The Square (tel. 712 6317). No pretense, just high quality food at low prices. Pizza, pasta, and burgers. Open M-Th noon-midnight, F-Sa noon-3am.

PUBS

Baily's Corner Pub (tel. 712 3230), at Ashe and Castle St. Kerry's Gaelic football legacy hangs on the walls while real-life players join an older crowd at the bar. Frequent trad.

Paddy Mac's, The Mall (tel. 712 1572). A Tralee favorite with trad two nights a week.

SOUTHWEST IRELAND

Abbey Inn, The Square (tel. 712 3390). Tough crowd comes to hear live rock most weekends. Bono swept here! When U2 played here in the late 70s, the manager made them sweep the floors to pay for their drinks because he thought they were so bad. Meatloaf, however, drank for free. Open Su-F until 1am.

Seán Óg's (tel. 712 8822). With its impressive fireplace (hand-built by the owner) and lots of trad, year-old Seán Óg's has already generated a lively following.

McDades, Edward St. (tel. 712 1877). This immense, polished wood pub attracts the younger set with discos and live rock on weekends.

👁 SIGHTS

Tralee is home to Ireland's second-largest museum, ▧ **Kerry the Kingdom,** Ashe Memorial Hall, Denny St. Perennially a contender for museum awards, the Kingdom marshals all the resources of display technology to tell the story of Co. Kerry from 8000 BC to the present. Vivid dioramas and videos of everything from Kerry's castles to her greatest Gaelic football victories keep your attention rapt. "Geraldine Tralee" downstairs takes you through a superbly assembled recreation of medieval city streets, as seen from a small moving cart. You can even sample the old city's stench! (Tel. 712 7777. Open Mar.-Oct. daily 10am-6pm; Nov.-Dec. noon-4:30pm. ₤5.50, students ₤4.75.)

Across from the museum, the **Roses of Tralee** bloom each summer in Ireland's second-largest town park. The gardens were designed in 1987 to convert floraphobes into rose-sniffers. The gray carpeting in **St. John's Church,** Castle St., dampens the echo and the Gothic mood, but the stained glass is worth a look. The building on the Prince's Quay traffic circle looks like a cross between a Gothic castle and a space-age solarium, but it's actually Tralee's ₤4.5-million **Aquadome,** complete with whirlpools, steam room, sauna, and gym. (Tel. 712 8899. Open daily 10am-10pm. ₤6, students ₤4.)

Just down Dingle Rd., the **Blenneville Windmill and Visitor Centre** is the largest operating windmill in the British Isles. Recalling Blenneville's status as Kerry's main port of emigration during the Famine, a small **museum** focuses on the "coffin ships" that sailed from Ireland during the Famine. (Tel. 712 1064. Open Apr.-Oct. daily 10am-6pm. ₤2.75, students ₤2.25.) The nearby **Jeanie Johnston Visitor Shipyard** builds in 19th century style. (Tel. 712 9999.) The restored **Tralee & Dingle Railway** runs the 2 mi. between the aquadome and the Blennerville complex. (Tel. 712 1064. Trains leave the aquadome every hour on the hour and leave the windmill on the half-hour. July-Aug. 10:30am-5:30pm; May-June and Sept. 11am-4pm; closed on occasional service days. ₤2.75, students ₤2.25.)

🎵 ENTERTAINMENT

The **Siamsa Tíre Theatre** (tel. 712 3055), next to the museum at the end of Denny St., is Ireland's national folk theater. It mounts brilliant summer programs depicting traditional Irish life through mime, music, and dance. (Productions July-Aug. M-Sa; May-June and Sept. M-Th and Sa. Shows start at 8:30pm. Box office open M-Sa 9am-8:30pm. ₤10, students ₤8.) The **Dúchas Cultural Centre,** Edward St., produces dance and musical performances. (July-Aug. Tu 8:30pm. Tickets ₤4.) Less culturally elite entertainment is available in Tralee's two nightclubs. The Brandon Hotel's club **Spirals,** Prince's Quay (tel. 712 3333), dances the disco (W and F-Su), while **The Courthouse** (tel. 712 1877), behind McDades Pub on Edward St., keeps an over-23 crowd groovin'. Both stay open until 1:45am. (Cover ₤4-5.) For other local goings-on, get a copy of *The Kerryman* (85p) at most newsagents.

Lovely, marriageable Irish lasses from around the world come to town during the last week of August for the nationally beloved **Rose of Tralee Festival.** A maelstrom of entertainment surrounds the main event, a personality competition to earn the coveted title "Rose of Tralee." Rose-hopefuls or spectators can call the Rose office, in Ashe Memorial Hall (tel. 712 1322).

SOUTHWEST IRELAND

TARBERT

A tiny and peaceful seaside spot on the N69, Tarbert is home to an incredible hostel and a convenient ferry service running between Counties Kerry and Clare. The boat ride will save you an 85 mi. coastal drive through Limerick. **Bus Éireann** stops outside the hostel on its way from **Tralee** to **Doolin** and **Galway** (mid-June-Sept. M-Sa 3 per day, Su 2 per day; Galway to Tralee £15). During the rest of the year, the nearest stop to Tarbert is in **Kilrush**. Despite lacking *Let's Go* endorsement, hitchers report mid-afternoon success from Killimer, the ferry port 1 mi. from Tarbert, to Kilrush (see p. 289). **Shannon Ferry Ltd.** (tel. (065) 53124) makes the 20min. ferry trip across the Shannon between Tarbert and Killimer (June-Aug. every 30min. from both sides, Apr.-Sept. 7:30am-9:30pm and Oct.-Mar. 7am-7:30pm every hr. on the half-hour from Tarbert and on the hour from Killimer; Su year round from 9am; £8 per carload, £2 per pedestrian or biker). Tarbert's **tourist office** (tel. (068) 36500), in the carefully restored **1831 Bridewell Jail and Courthouse,** offers a surprisingly interesting tour concerning Irish prison history. (Open Apr.-Oct. daily 10am-6pm. £3, students £2.) Be sure to get cash before you come; the nearest **ATM** is 15 mi. away in Listowel. The ◪**Ferry House Hostel** (tel. (068) 36555) is the three-year-old occupant of a 200-year-old building in the center of town. Before opening, the friendly owners spent a year traveling and taking detailed notes on the best and worst of the world's hostels. The success of their study is evident in comfy, wide mattresses, stone hallways wide enough for a truck to pass through, hot showers with strong water pressure, and a great coffeeshop. (Dorms £7, doubles £18. Laundry £1-4. Open May-Sept. 8am-7pm.) Recently revamped **Coolahan's** is the most notable of Tarbert's five pubs, a cozy little establishment that takes great pride in its own old age. A few hundred meters from the ferry stands **Tarbert House,** the home of the family of Signeur Leslie of Tarbert since 1690. The recently restored exterior rivals the period pieces and priceless art it protects. (Tel. (068) 36198. Open daily 10am-noon and 2-4pm. £2. Tours given by Mrs. Leslie herself.) The hour-long **Tarbert House Woodland Walk** takes ramblers through Leslie's Wood, with views of the River Shannon, Tarbert Old Pier, and Tarbert Bay. (Pamphlets with map available at the tourist office.)

WESTERN IRELAND

Even Dubliners will tell you that the west is the "most Irish" part of Ireland. Yeats agreed: "For me," he said, "Ireland is Connacht." For less privileged Irish in recent centuries, Connacht mostly meant poor soil and emigration. When Cromwell uprooted the native Irish landowners in Leinster and Munster and resettled them west of the Shannon, the popular phraseology for their plight became "To hell or to Connacht." The potato famine (see p. 12) that plagued the entire island was most devastating in the west—entire villages emigrated or died. Today, every western county has less than half of its 1841 population. Though miserable for farming, the land from Connemara north to Ballina is a boon for hikers, cyclists, and hitchhikers, as they enjoy the isolation of boggy, rocky, or brilliantly mountainous landscapes. Western Ireland's gorgeous desolation and enclaves of traditional culture are now its biggest attractions.

The city Galway is a different story: long a successful port, in the 20th century it grew into a boom town for the young. Farther south, the barren moonscape of the Burren, the Cliffs of Moher, and a reputation as the center of the trad music scene attracts travelers to Co. Clare. The Shannon River has provided subsistence and tourism to the West for generations. It flows through the city of Limerick, the latest in Ireland's growing list of hip, youthful cities.

HIGHLIGHTS OF WESTERN IRELAND

■ The pubs of **Galway** (p. 306) spawn musical brilliance and copious *craic*.
■ Glimpse at life on the **Aran Islands** (p. 300), from the ring forts of pre-Christian settlers to the *curraghs* of today's fishermen.
■ See all you can of haunting, windswept **Connemara** (p. 317): ride in on the **Coast Road** (p. 320), spend a night in the pubs of **Clifden** (p. 320), and pass through **Inishbofin** (p. 323) and **Connemara National Park** (p. 324) on the way back.
■ The village of **Doolin** fiddles while the nearby **Cliffs of Moher** (p. 293), **Burren** (p. 295), and **Pounalbrane Dolmen** (p. 297) stun with their natural wonders.
■ Explore the cliffs and beaches of **Achille Island** (p. 331), imagining the days when Pirate Queen Grace O'Malley controlled the surrounding waters from her home on **Clare Island** (p. 331).

LIMERICK AND CLARE

Limerick City is an urban speck beside the long expanse of weird geology and unique flora that line the Clare Coast. Convenient to Shannon Airport and a host of quintessential Irish attractions, Limerick is attracting tourists like flies to fruit-cake. The economy of Limerick has ridden the tide of the recent EU boom, and made a distant memory out of the city's historic poverty. Geology defines Co. Clare: fine sands glisten on the beaches of Kilkee, skyscraper-high limestone slabs mark the Cliffs of Moher, and 100 sq. mi. of exposed limestone form Ireland's most peculiarly alluring landscape, the Burren.

LIMERICK CITY

Despite a thriving trade in off-color poems, Limerick City has long suffered from a bad reputation. The Vikings settled around Limerick in 922, presaging a millennium of turbulence. During the English Civil War, Limerick was the last stronghold of Royalist support against Cromwell's army. Three times besieged and conquered, Limerick's citizens thought they had won a measure of peace with the Treaty of Limerick in 1691, agreed upon after the Jacobites were defeated in their last stand against King William's armies. The treaty's vague promise of Catholic protection was soon violated, and the treaty remained a sore point in Anglo-Irish relations for the next 150 years (see **The Protestant Ascendancy**, p. 10).

Though its 18th century Georgian streets and parks remain regal and elegant, later industrial and commercial developments gave the city a dull and urban feel. During much of the 20th century, hard economic times spawned poverty and crime. What little attention was paid to Limerick seemed to celebrate squalor, as exemplified by the Irish-American author Frank McCourt's internationally successful memoir *Angela's Ashes*. Yet, the mayor of Limerick raised a spirited protest against McCourt's characterization of his city: whether or not outsiders have noticed, today's Limerick is renewed and thriving. A large student population fosters an intense arts scene, adding to a wealth of cultural treasures that have long gone unnoticed. The Republic's 3rd largest city boasts a top quality museum, a well-preserved 12th century capital and well-seasoned culture.

▣ TRANSPORTATION

Trains: Colbert Station (tel. 315 555), off Parnell St. Inquiries desk open M-F 9am-6pm, Sa 9am-5:30pm. Trains from Limerick to **Ennis** (M-Sa 2 per day, £5.50), **Dublin** (2hr.; M-Sa 9 per day, Su 8 per day; £25), **Waterford** (2hr.; M-Sa 2 per day in summer, 1 per day in winter; £12), **Cork** (2½hr.; M-Sa 7 per day, Su 6 per day; £13.50), **Killarney** (2½hr.; M-Sa 4 per day, Su 3 per day; £15), **Tralee** (3hr.; M-Sa 6 per day, Su 3 per day; £15) and **Rosslare** (3½hr., M-Sa 1 per day, £19).

Buses: Colbert Station, just off Parnell St. (tel. 313 333; 24hr. talking timetable tel. 319 911). Open June-Sept. M-F 8:10am-6pm, Su 9am-6pm; Oct.-May M-Sa 8:10am-6pm, Su 3-7pm. Limerick sends buses to **Ennis** (1hr., 7 per day, £5), **Cork** (2hr., 6 per day, £9), **Galway** (2hr., 7 per day, £9), **Tralee** (2hr., 6 per day, £9), **Waterford** (2½hr.; M-Th and Sa 5 per day, F 6 per day, Su 5 per day; £9.70), **Killarney** (2½hr.; M-Sa 6 per day, Su 3 per day; £9.30), **Dublin** (3hr.; M-Sa 8 per day, Su 5 per day; £10), **Wexford** and **Rosslare Harbour** with some departures timed to meet the ferries (4hr., 4 per day, £13), and **Sligo** (6hr., 4 per day, £14).

Taxi: Top Cabs, Wickham St. (tel. 417 417). Takes you most places in the city for under £3 and to the airport for about £15.

Bike Rental: McMahon's Cycleworld, 25 Roches St. (tel. 415 202). £7 per day, £30 per week. Open M-Sa 9am-6pm. **Emerald Cycles,** 1 Patrick St. (tel. 416 983; email emarldalp@tinet.ie). £10 per day, £40 per week; deposit £40. £12 for return at other locations. Open M-Sa 9:15am-5:30pm.

▨ ORIENTATION AND PRACTICAL INFORMATION

The N7 from Dublin lands drivers at Limerick. The city's streets form a grid pattern, bounded by the **River Shannon** to the west and by the **Abbey River** to the north. Most of the city's activity takes place on a few blocks around **O'Connell Street** (sometimes called **Patrick's St.** or **Rutland St.**). Follow O'Connell St. north and cross the Abbey River to reach **King's Island,** where St. Mary's Cathedral and King John's Castle dominate the landscape. The city itself is easily navigable by foot, but to reach the suburbs, catch a **city bus** (75p) from Boyd's or Penney's on O'Connell St. (M-Sa 7:30am-11pm, 2 per hr.; Su 10:30am-11pm, 1 per hr.). Buses #2 and 8 access the university, while bus #6 follows **Ennis Rd.** A one-week pass (£9) allowing unlimited city bus travel is available at the bus station.

Western Ireland

N

0   20 miles

0   20 kilometers

ATLANTIC OCEAN

DONEGAL

TYRONE

N. IRE.

Donegal Bay

Lower
Lough Erne

FERMANAGH

Enniskillen

Belmullet

Ballycastle

*Killala
Bay*

Easky

Inishcrone

Sligo Bay

Sligo

Drumclif

Manor
hamilton

Dromahair

Bangor

Ballina

S L I G O

Tober-
curry

Collooney

Riverstown

*Blacksod
Bay*

*Lough
Conn*

Ballysadare

Ballymote

C A V A N

Keel
*Achill
Island*

M A Y O

Boyle

Drumshanbo

*Lough
Allen*

L E I T R I M

Carrick-
on-Shannon

*Clare
Island*

*Clew
Bay*

Castlebar

R O S C O M M O N

Castlerea

Longford

LONGFORD

Inishturk

Westport

Knock

Inishbofin

C O N N A C H T

Claremorris

Roscommon

*Lough
Ree*

WESTMEATH

*Inish-
shark*

Louisburgh

*Lough
Mask*

Ballinrose

C O N N E M A R A

Leenane

Cong

*Lough
Corrib*

Tuam

Athlone

Clifden

Oughterard

G A L W A Y

Ballinasloe

Roundstone

Galway

N6

*Aran
Islands*

Galway Bay

Loughrea

N65

OFFALY

Inishmore

Kinvara

Portumna

Birr

Inishmaan

Ballyvaughan

Gort

Inisheer

Doolin

Lisdoonvarna

LAOIS

*Cliffs of
Moher*

Corofin

*Lough
Derg*

Roscrea

Lahinch

C L A R E

Milltown Malbay

Ennis

Nenagh

Kilkee

*Shannon
Airport*

R. Shannon

T I P P E R A R Y

Thurles

Kilrush

M U N S T E R

Limerick

Cashel

*Mouth of the
Shannon*

Tarbert

Rathkeale

L I M E R I C K

Tipperary

N74

Listowel

Clonmel

Abbeyfeale

Newcastle
West

Kilmallock

*Tralee
Bay*

Tralee

WATERFORD

*Dingle
Peninsula*

Kanturk

Dungarvan

*Dingle
Bay*

Killarney

Mallow

Fermoy

K E R R Y

C O R K

Tourist Office: Arthurs Quay (tel. 317 522), in the space-age glass building. From the station, walk straight down Davis St., turn right on O'Connell St., then left just before Arthurs Quay Mall. Handy city maps (£1), and info on the entire Shannon region. Bureau de change. Open July-Aug. M-F 9am-7pm, Sa-Su 9am-6pm; May-June and Sept.-Oct. M-Sa 9:30am-5:30pm; Nov.-Apr. M-F 9:30am-5:30pm, Sa 9:30am-1pm.

Budget Travel Office: usit, O'Connell St. (tel. 415 064), across from Ulster Bank. Issues ISICs and **TravelSave** stamps. Open M-F 9:30am-5:30pm, Sa 10am-1pm. Also located at University of Limerick (tel. 332 073).

Luggage Storage: Colbert Station. Lockers £1 per day, 24hr. limit.

Laundry: Laundrette (tel. 312 712) on Mallow St. Full service £5. Open M-F 8am-6pm, Sa 8am-5pm.

Banks: Bank of Ireland (tel. 415 055), O'Connell St. **AIB** (tel. 414 388), O'Connell St. Both have **ATMs.**

Bookstore: Get a spare copy of *Let's Go* at **O'Mahoney's,** O'Connell St. (tel. 418 155).

Camping Equipment: River Deep, Mountain High, 7 Rutland St. (tel. 400 944), off O'Connell St. Open M-Th and Sa 9:30am-6pm, F 9:30am-9pm. No tent rental.

Counseling: Samaritans (tel. 412 111), for the lonely and depressed.

Pharmacy: Charlotte Quay Pharmacy, Charlotte Quay (tel. 400 722). Open daily 9am-9pm.

Emergency: Dial 999; no coins required. **Garda:** Henry St. (tel. 414 222).

Hospital: Regional (tel. 301 111), follow O'Connell Rd. past the Crescent southward.

Post Office: Main office on Lower Cecil St. (tel. 315 777), just off O'Connell St. Open M and W-Sa 9am-5:30pm, Tu 9:30am-5:30pm.

Internet Access: **Webster's,** Thomas St. (tel. 312 066). Full web and email access costs £2.50 per 30min. Bring your *Let's Go* and get 30min. free. Fruit drinks available. Open M-Sa 9am-9pm, Su 1-9pm.

There once was a **PHONE CODE** *named 061...Damn, nothing rhymes with 061.*

ACCOMMODATIONS

Limerick has two "real" hostels and several budget accommodation centers geared toward term-time university students. These dorm-like establishments are usually large and in good condition, but are slightly more expensive and less welcoming than most hostels. For those seeking refuge from the bustle of the city, Ennis St. is a B&B bonanza in the price range of £16 per person.

Clyde House, St. Alphonsus St. (tel. 314 727; email clyde@ryan-group.ie), right off Henry St. Student accommodations/hostel in a comfortable, if slightly institutional, setting. All rooms have kitchenettes. Prices include continental breakfast. 4-bed dorms £11.50, triples £37.50, twins £35, singles £20.

Finnegan's (IHH), 6 Pery Sq. (tel. 310 308). Located in a large brick building overlooking People's Park. From the bus station, cross Parnell St. and head up Daris St. for 1 long block. Take a left on Pery St. and walk 2 blocks to Harstoye St.; the hostel is on the corner. High-ceilinged common rooms and a convenient location, but somewhat crowded. 6- to 22-bed dorms £7.50, private rooms £10 per person. Laundry £3-4.

An Óige Hostel (HI), 1 Pery Sq. (tel. 314 672). Around the corner from Finnegan's. A pleasant Georgian house, a cheerful staff, and park views help ease the usual An Óige dreariness. With 2nd and 3rd floor dorms and a basement kitchen, this hotel is not for the stair-haters of the world. June-Sept. 14-bed dorms £8.50, Oct.-May £7.50; £1 less for HI members. Sheets £1. Laundry £3-4. Continental breakfast £2. Midnight curfew.

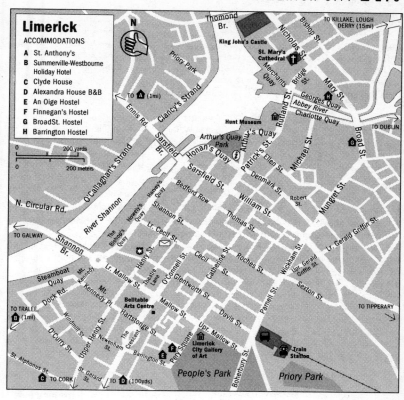

Limerick
ACCOMMODATIONS

A St. Anthony's
B Summerville-Westbourne Holiday Hotel
C Clyde House
D Alexandra House B&B
E An Oige Hostel
F Finnegan's Hostel
G BroadSt. Hostel
H Barrington Hostel

WESTERN IRELAND

Barrington Hostel (IHH), George's Quay (tel. 415 222). Far from the train and bus station, but very close to sights, restaurants, and pubs. Barrington compensates for its large size by offering relatively private dorms. 2 kitchens and a resplendent garden. 4-bed dorms £7.50, doubles with bath £12.50 per person, singles £11. Laundry £3-4.

Summerville-Westbourne Holiday Hostel (IHH), Courbrack Ave. (tel. 302 500; email info@summer-west.ie), off Dock Rd. From Colbert Station, make a left on Parnell St. then a right on Upper Mallow St. by the park. Follow Mallow St. to the traffic circle, make a left, and continue for a mile. The hostel is on the left after the Shell station. A long walk from the city center, the multiple buildings of this student housing/hostel are well equipped. No bunks. 4-bed dorms £8, twins £22, singles £13. Price includes continental breakfast. Laundry £4. Tennis court available; £1 racket rental.

Broad St. Hostel, Broad St. (tel. 317 222; email broadstreethostel@tinet.ie). Vigilant security and remarkable cleanliness are the main comforts here. 4-bed dorms £9, doubles and twins £12.50-15 per person, single £12-13. Price includes continental breakfast. Laundry £4. Wheelchair accessible.

St. Anthony's, 8 Coolraine Terr., Ennis Rd. (tel. 452 607), 1 mi. from city center; best route via Sarsfield Bridge and Ennis Rd. Pleasant rooms look out onto a flourishing garden. Homemade brown bread and jam in the morning. Doubles £17, with bath £18; singles £17.50; 50p discount with *Let's Go*.

Alexandra House, O'Connell St. (tel. 318 472), several blocks south of the Crescent. Victorian, comfortable, and pleasantly decorated. Its proximity to the city center drives prices up. Singles £20; doubles and twins £20 per person, with bath £22.50.

FOOD

Inexpensive and top-notch cafes have sprouted across the city center, presenting culinary alternatives to fast food chains. Gather groceries at **Tesco** (tel. 412 399) in Arthurs Quay Mall. (Open M-W 8:30am-8pm, Th-F 8:30am-10pm, Sa 8:30am-8pm.) **Nature's Way** (tel. 310 466), also in the mall, has a limited selection of natural foods. (Open M, W, and Sa 9am-6pm, Th 9am-7pm, F 9am-8pm.)

The Ice Cafe, Henry St. (tel. 319 790). Sandwich, salad, and coffee comprise a full meal at this hip cafe. Most meals from £3. Open M-W 9am-8pm, Th-Su 9am-midnight.

O'Grady's Cellar Restaurant, O'Connell St. (tel. 418 286). Maroon walls and faux thatch abound in this little subterranean spot. Irish meals are the substance of the menu. Most meals £5-7. Open M-F and Su noon-10pm, Sa noon-10:30pm.

The Green Onion Cafe, 3 Ellen St. (tel. 400 710), just off Patrick's St. Crimson-splashed walls etched with writing provide the setting for an elite bistro fare at egalitarian prices. Lunch £5-7. After 6pm, dinners skyrocket in price (£10-12). Open M-Sa noon-10pm.

L'Epicene, Henry St. (tel. 310 717). Fine wines and French cuisine at reasonable prices. Crepes £6; most meals £7-9.50. Open M-Sa noon-11pm.

Java's Beat Cafe, 5 Catherine St. (tel. 418 077). Flavored coffees and herbal teas keep a young crowd buzzing through the late hours. Salads, sandwiches, and bagels served to the strains of cool jazz. Open M-W 9am-1am, Th-Sa 9am-3am, Su 10:30am-1am.

Cafe Furze Bush, Catherine St. (tel. 411 733). A new cafe with a wide variety of carefully planned sandwiches. Crab meat with chive and citrus mayonnaise and side salad £5.40. Open M-Sa 10am-4pm and 6:30-10pm.

Moll Darby's, 8 Georges Quay (tel. 411 511), just across the Abbey River. Somewhat pricey, but the hearty international meals are deservedly popular. Open daily 6-11pm.

▼ PUBS

Limerick's immense student population adds spice to the pub scene, supplying a wide range of music. Trad-seekers can find their nightly dose, though the hunt may present more of a challenge than in other Irish cities. Pick up the tourist office's **Guiness Guide to Irish Music,** which covers the entire Shannon region.

Dolan's, Dock Rd. (tel. 314 483). Worth a Shannon-side walk from the city center to hear nightly trad played for rambunctious local patrons. The **Warehouse** is part of the building (see **Clubs,** below).

Nancy Blake's, Denmark St. (tel. 416 443). The best of both worlds—an older crowd huddles in the sawdust-floored interior for periodic trad, while boisterous students take in nightly rock in the open-air "outback."

Locke Bar, Georges Quay (tel. 413 733). Join the tourists and locals who drink on the quay-side patio. Inside, owner Richard Costello, former rugby player for Ireland's national team, joins in trad sessions several nights a week.

An Sibín, O'Connell St. (tel. 414 566). Dark and crowded, the underground crannies tremble with otherworldly trad most summer nights.

The Doghouse, Thomas St. (tel. 313 177). Howl your troubles away. Blues almost nightly.

Doc's, Michael St. (tel. 417 266), at the corner of Charlotte's Quay in the Granary. The spacious, arching brick interior and outdoor beer garden, complete with palm trees and a waterfall, lures festive young folks. College bands frequently play in the school year. DJs bust out chart-toppers most weekend nights.

Tom Collins, Cecil St. (tel. 415 749). A Limerick institution where the affairs of the world should be casually discussed. Unsuspecting American tourists have come here, asking for a "Tom Collins" (you know, the cocktail). The barman fetched the owner.

CLUBS

Limerick's insatiable army of students keep dozens of nightclubs thumping from 1:30pm until 2am nightly. Cover charges can be steep (£5-8), but clubs spread concession fliers good for £2-3 discounts throughout the city's pubs.

The Globe, Cecil St. (tel. 313 533). 3 floors of manic clubbery, with suggestive artwork and flashing video screens. Only club members are allowed on the top floor, where the Cranberries and U2 periodically stop by to sip £135 champagne. Cover £5.

The Warehouse (tel. 314 483), behind Dolan's on Dock Rd. Draws big-name bands and rising stars to its snazzy venue. Music Th-Sa. Cover £5-9, higher for well-known acts.

The George Hotel, O'Connell St. (tel. 414 566), hosts a variously titled and themed nightclub Th-Sa, but the circular dance floor and balcony are always packed. Cover £6.

The Works, Bedford Row (tel. 411 611). Over-23 grinders flood its 2 floors. Smooth, colored lighting lets you see who's got the funk. Cover around £6.

BPs (tel. 418 414), in Baker Place Hotel at the top of Glentworth St. A mixed crowd pulsates between the multi-colored walls. Blasts indie rock and Euro-techno beats Tu-Sa. Cover £3-5. Occasional live bands in the bar upstairs.

Temple of Sound, Glentworth St. (tel. 313 372). The young and sweaty sacrifice £4-6 to enter and hear top 40 dance hits. Open Th-Su.

SIGHTS

Gray Line (tel. 413 088) runs a thorough open-top bus tour of Limerick, departing between 10am and 4pm daily. You can hop on and off at the major sites visited. (£6.50, students and seniors £5.50.) **Walking Tours** (tel. 318 106; email smidp@iol.ie) cover either the northern, sight-filled King's Island region, or the more decrepit locations described in Frank McCourt's *Angela's Ashes*. (King's Island tour daily at 11am and 2:30pm; *Angela's Ashes* tour 2:30pm daily. Both depart from St. Mary's Action Centre, 44 Nicholas St. £4 per walker.)

English King John built a massive castle to protect the conquered city of Limerick, though he never actually visited the edifice. In fact, King John made only one trip to Ireland, during which he supposedly pulled the beards of his subjects for kicks. To reach **King John's Castle** on Nicholas St., walk across the Abbey River and take the first left after St. Mary's Cathedral. The visitor center has vivid exhibits and a video on the castle's gruesome history. The castle's history as a military fortification remains evident outside where the **mangonel** is displayed. Easily recognizable from its use in *Monty Python's Quest for the Holy Grail*, the mangonel was used to catapult pestilent animal corpses into enemy cities and castles. (Tel. 411 201. Open Mar.-Dec. daily 9:30am-6pm. Last admission 5pm. £4.20, students £3.20.) The rough exterior of nearby **St. Mary's Cathedral** was built in 1172 on the site of a Viking meeting place. Fold-down seats, built into the wall on the side of the altar, display elaborate carvings that depict the struggle between good and evil. They are called *misericordia*, Latin for "acts of mercy," and used in long services during which sitting was prohibited. (Tel. 416 238. Open daily 9:15am-5pm.)

The fascinating **Hunt Museum,** Custom House, Rutland St., houses the largest collection of medieval, Stone Age, and Iron Age artifacts outside the national museum in Dublin, as well as what may be one of Leonardo da Vinci's four "Rearing Horses" sculptures. The eclectic collection includes one of the world's smallest jade monkeys, a gold crucifix given by Mary Queen of Scots to her executioner, and a coin reputed to be one of the infamous 30 pieces of silver paid to Judas by the Romans. The impressive collection is appreciably enhanced by an excellent guided tour. (Tel. 312 833. Open M-Sa 10am-5pm, Su 2-5pm. £4, seniors and students £3.) **Limerick City Gallery of Art,** Pery Sq., contains a densely packed collection of Irish paintings as well as international exhibits. (Tel. 310 633. Open M-F 10am-6pm, Sa 10am-1pm. Free.) Abstract and experimental pieces fill the small **Belltable Arts Centre,** O'Connell St. (Tel. 319 866. Open M-Sa 9am-7pm. Free.)

♫ ENTERTAINMENT

The **Belltable Arts Centre,** 69 O'Connell St. (tel. 319 866; www.commerce.ie/belltable), stages excellent, big-name productions year-round. (Box office open M-S 9am-5:30pm and prior to performances. Tickets £5-10, student discounts.) The **Theatre Royal,** Upper Cecil St. (tel. 414 224), hosts the town's largest contests. The **University Concert Hall** (tel. 331 549), on the university campus, showcases opera dance, and music. (Tickets £6-17.50.) The free *Calendar of Events and Entertainment* is available at the tourist office.

NEAR LIMERICK: ADARE

Adare's well-preserved medieval architecture and meticulous rows of thatched cottages have earned it a reputation as one of the prettiest towns in Ireland. With that distinction come bus loads of tourists, who patronize the town's pricey restaurants and fancy hotels. While the monastic buildings and castle ruins may be worth a daytrip, there's little to hold the interest of a budget traveler.

Buses travel to Adare from **Limerick** (20min., 7 per day, £3.50) and **Tralee** (1¾hr. 7 per day). The **tourist office** (tel. 396 255) is located on Main St. in the Heritage Center complex. (Open June-Oct. M-F 9am-7pm, Sa-Su 9am-6pm; Nov.-Dec. and Mar.-May M-Sa 9am-5pm.) The **AIB,** just off Main St., has an **ATM. Bike rental** is available from **Eddie Daly** (tel. 396 091); try to call 24 hours in advance. (£10 per day. 061 is a **phone code** for all seasons.

Although there is no hostel here, Adare is B&B central. Many people touring the Shannon region or awaiting flights at the airport prefer to stay here rather than in Limerick. Good choices include the clean, modern rooms at **Riversdale** Manorcourt, Station Rd. (tel. 396 751; doubles £16 per person, £18 with bath) and the friendly **Ardmore** (tel. 396 167) about ¾ mi. outside of town on Tralee Killarney Rd. (doubles and twins £15 per person; open Mar.-Oct.; call ahead. Food is generally expensive in Adare. The best budget food option is to stock up at **Centra** on Main St. and picnic in Town Park. (Open M-Sa 9am-7pm, Su 9am-1pm.) **The Blue Door** (tel. 396 481), a 200-year-old thatched cottage with roses blooming outside, offers reasonable lunches (around £5) and pricey dinners. (Open M-F 10am-4pm and 6:30-9:30pm, Sa-Su noon-9:30pm.) A similar lunchtime value can be found at **The Arches Restaurant** (tel. 396 246), where main course and coffee hovers around £7. (Open M-Sa 11am-9:30pm, Su 11am-3:30pm.) Downtown Adare sports two pubs named "Collin's": **Pat Collin's Bar** (tel. 396 143) next to the post office on Main St., and **Shean Collin's Bar** around the corner. Each has one night of trad a week.

The medieval Fitzgerald family endowed Adare with several thriving monasteries of three different orders. The **Trinitarian Abbey,** which survives on Main St., was established in the 13th century by an order of monks devoted primarily to liberating Christian prisoners during the Crusades. Renovated in the 19th century, the priory now serves as the town's Catholic Church. Farther down Main St. toward Limerick stands the 14th century **Augustinian Priory.** The quiet cloister preserves a sense of serenity, though the grounds are now home to a basketball court. The **Franciscan Friary** is accessible only by crossing the fairways of the Adare Manor golf course, on Limerick Rd. On the banks of the River Maigue towards Limerick lies the 13th century **Desmond Castle.** For now the castle is under renovations and closed to visitors; it may be open by the fall of 2000. **Walking tours** of the town start from the tourist office on request. (£3. Back in the village, the **Adare Heritage Centre,** in the same building as the tourist office, uses models and videos in an engaging attempt to prove that the town is "a place of consequence." (Tel. 396 666. Open daily Mar.-Oct. 9am-6pm £3, students and seniors £2.) Nature trails wind through the 600-acre **Currachase Forest Park,** 5 mi. from Adare. The **Adare Jazz Festival** kicks off in mid March. **Horse trials** and **country fairs** are scheduled in the surrounding area in March, May, and October.

LOUGH DERG

Northeast of Limerick, the river Shannon widens into the lake region of Lough Derg. Affluent middle-aged tourists powerboat between the small towns of Killaloe, Mountshannon, and Portumna. Younger and vehicle-free travelers are rarer here than they are in regions to the south and west. Lough Derg's tourist activities provide a good workout, but little sightseeing; there are plenty of fishing, boating, and swimming opportunities, but archaeological attractions are few and far between. The Lough Derg Way walking path starts in Limerick, follows the western bank of the Shannon up to Killaloe, then crosses over to Ballina; it passes Arra Mountain on the way. The Neolithic tombs known as the "Graves of the Leinstermen" mark the refuge of Fintan the White, legendary consort of Cesair.

Commuter **buses** run along Lough Derg Drive to and from **Limerick** (June-Aug. M-F 1 per day, Sept.-May M-F 2 per day), but the thrice-weekly bus (Tu, F, and Sa) will be more conveniently timed for sightseers based in the city. Really lucky hitchhikers may be able to score a lift from Limerick. *Let's Go* does not approve of hitchhikers or their craft.

BUNRATTY

Eight miles northwest of Limerick along Ennis Rd., **Bunratty Castle** and **Bunratty Folk Park** bring together a jumbled but unforgettable collection of historical attractions from all over Ireland. Bunratty Castle is allegedly Ireland's most complete medieval castle, with superbly restored furniture, tapestries, and stained-glass windows. During summer months, crowds of visitors clog its narrow stairways, making for frustrating tours of the chambers and battlements. (Tel. (061) 361 511. Open daily June-Aug. 9am-6:30pm; Sept.-May 9:30am-5:30pm. Last admission 1hr. before closing. £5.25, students £3.80.) The castle derives much of its popularity from the medieval feasts that it hosts nightly for deep-pocketed tourists. Local damsels dressed in period costume serve wine and meat to would-be chieftains accompanied by music. (5-course meal with wine £32. Book ahead.)

The folk park originated in the 60s, when builders at Shannon Airport couldn't bear to destroy a quaint cottage for a new runway. Instead, they moved the cottage to Bunratty. Since then, reconstructions of turn-of-the-century houses and stores from all over Ireland have been added. Peat fires are lit in the cottages each morning by "inhabitants" dressed in period costume. The Bunratty complex also claims one heavily touristed pub. The first proprietress at **Durty Nelly's,** founded in 1620, earned her name by serving Bunratty soldiers more than just beer. **Buses** between **Limerick** and **Shannon Airport** pass Bunratty.

KILLALOE AND BALLINA

The pleasant hills and lakeside orientation of Killaloe (KILL-a-loo), Co. Clare, 15 mi. outside of Limerick along the Lough Derg Drive and just south of the lake, offer a respite from the throbbing city. Old churches testify to the town's role as a 7th century religious center, though mushrooming condo developments infringe on its tranquility. Across a narrow medieval bridge is tiny Ballina, Co. Limerick.

■ PRACTICAL INFORMATION. The **tourist office** (tel. 376 866), in the former Lock House on the Killaloe side of the bridge, provides free maps of the area and information on several rural walks around Killaloe. (Open daily May-Sept. 10am-6pm.) An **ATM**-blessed **AIB** (tel. 376 115) sits on Main St. (Open M and W-F 10am-4pm, Tu 10am-5pm.) The **post office** (tel. 376 111) is farther uphill. (Open M-F 9:30am-12:30pm and 1:30-5:30pm, Sa 9:30am-12:30pm.) The **phone code** is 061, subduer of the Vikings and progenitor of the O'Briens.

■■■ ACCOMMODATIONS, FOOD, AND PUBS. Killaloe is a manageable daytrip from Limerick, but several nice B&Bs near town make it a pleasant stopover. The very hospitable **Kincora House,** Main St. (tel. 376 149; email koncorahouse@tinet.ie), across from Crotty's Pub, is filled with well-maintained antiques and serves a healthy breakfast on request. (Doubles and twins £22 per person.) The best place to stock up for a luau is **McKeogh's** (tel. 376 249), on Main St. in Ballina. (Open M-W 9am-7:30pm, Th-F 9am-9pm, Sa 9am-8:30pm, Su 9:30am-1pm.) Super-fresh seafood makes **Dalcassian,** Main St. (tel. 376 762), near the cathedral, a local favorite. (Dinner entrees £7-9; cheaper bar menu until 5pm. Open daily 11am-11pm.) The immensely popular **Crotty's Courtyard Bar** (tel. 376 965) serves up hearty grub on a patio decorated with antique ads. (Most meals £5-8; food served noon-3pm and 5-10pm.) Next to the bridge in Ballina, **Molly's** (tel. 376 632) serves pub grub with vegetarian options and waterside views. *Al fresco* pints are served if the weather allows. (Most meals £4.50-5.50; food served from 12:30-9:30pm.) Periodic trad echoes across the bridge at the **Anchor Inn** (tel. 376 108).

🎫 **SIGHTS.** At the base of the town on Royal Parade lies **St. Flannan's Cathedral,** built between 1195 and 1225 and still in use. Inside the cathedral, the Thorgrim Stone is inscribed in both Scandinavian characters and the monks' *ogham* script, with a prayer for the conversion of the Viking Thorgrim to Christianity. Market Sq. may have once held the Kincora palace of High King Brian Ború, who lived here from 1002 to 1014. The other candidate for the site of Ború's palace is the abandoned fort known as **Beal Ború,** 1½ mi. out of town toward Mountshannon, now a subtle circular mound in a quiet forest glade. The legends of Ború continue at the **Heritage Center,** where interactive displays document the days when steamboats chugged across the lake. (Open daily 10am-5:30pm. £1.50, students £1.) In late July, the **Irish Chamber Orchestra** forms the foundation of the **Killaloe Music Festival** (tel. 202 620). In August, Killaloe celebrates **Féile Brian Ború,** four days of music, watersports, and various Ború-based activities.

Lough related activities abound in Killaloe. The **Derg Princess** (tel. 376 364) leaves from across the bridge in **Ballina** for relaxing hour-long cruises (£5). **Whelan's** (tel. 376 159) stations itself across from the tourist office and rents out **motorboats** for fishing or cruising. (£10 first hr., £5 per additional hr.) Whelan's also runs their own lake cruises aboard the **Brian Ború.** (£5 per person.) Fishing gear is rented and sold at **T.J.'s** (tel. 376 009) in Ballina. (Rod and reel £8 per day, £30 deposit. Open daily 8am-11pm.) A boat (and a bit of navigational prowess) will allow you access to the eminently picnicable **Holy Island.** A couple of miles north of Killaloe, you can indulge in an afternoon of watersports at the **University of Limerick Activity and Sailing Centre.** (Tel. 376 622. **Windsurfing** from £8 per hr., **canoeing** from £4 per hr., **sailboats** from £10 per hr.)

SHANNON AIRPORT

Fifteen miles west of Limerick off Ennis Rd. (N18), **Shannon Airport** (tel. (061) 471 444; Aer Lingus info tel. (061) 471 666) sends jets to North America and Europe. Arriving travelers descend into a blend of cottages, industrial office complexes, and housing developments. Until a few years ago, Irish law required all transatlantic flights to make an initial stop at Shannon, and many still do. **Bus Éireann** picks up passengers here on its way to **Limerick** via **Ennis** (45min.; M-Sa 22 per day, Su 13 per day; £3.50), where connections can be made to **Dublin** (4½hr., 5 per day, £10), **Waterford,** and **Tralee. Alamo** (tel. (061) 75061) is a cheap **car rental.** (£22 per day; rates vary by season.) **Thrifty** (tel. (061) 472 649) also lets automobiles. (£30 per day, £195 per week. 3 day minimum rental. 23 and older. Call ahead.)

ENNIS

Ennis (pop. 16,000), a small city 20 mi. northwest of Limerick, is a market area located near an 11th century monastic site. Ennis' pedestrian-filled cobblestone streets, make it picturesque. The city hosts makeshift produce stands along the River Fergus, pubs that shake nightly with trad, and scores of loyal hurling fans. A reputation for safe streets, city-caliber nightlife, and down-home friendliness have drawn enough migrants in the past 10 years to double the population. Its proximity to **Shannon Airport** and the **Burren** make it a common stopover for tourists, who can enjoy a day of shopping followed by a night of pub crawling.

County Clare

WESTERN IRELAND

TRANSPORTATION

Trains: The station (tel. 684 0444) is a 15min. walk from the town center on Station Rd. Open M-Sa 7am-5pm, Su 15min. before departures. Trains leave for **Dublin** via **Limerick** (M-Sa 2 per day, Su 1 per day, £17).

Buses: The station (tel. 682 4177) is next to the train station. Open M-F 7:15am-5:30pm, Sa 7:15am-4:45pm. To **Limerick** (40min., M-Sa 18 per day, Su 6 per day, £5), **Shannon Airport** (40min., M-F 13 per day, Sa 9 per day, Su 10 per day, £3.50), **Kilkee** (1hr., M-Sa 2-3 per day, Su 1-2 per day, £6.90), **Doolin** (1hr., M-Sa 3 per day, Su 1 per day, £5.50), **Galway** (1 hr., 5 per day, £7.70), **Cork** (3hr., 5 per day, £10), and **Dublin** via **Limerick** (4hr., 5 per day, £10). A **West Clare** line (7 per day) goes to various combinations of **Lisdoonvarna, Ennistymon, Lahinch, Miltown Malbay, Doolin, Kilkee,** and **Kilrush.** The crowded post bus runs from the **post office** (see **Practical Information**) to **Liscannor** and **Doolin** (M-Sa 2 per day, £2.50 to Doolin). Arrive early to get a seat.

ORIENTATION AND PRACTICAL INFORMATION

Ennis's layout can be confusing, but the city center is navigable enough that you'll eventually find what you need. The center of town is **O'Connell Square;** to reach it from the bus and train stations, head left down **Station Rd.,** turn right on **O'Connell St.,** and go down a few blocks. You'll know it by the soaring statue of Daniel O'Connell staring down at you from high atop a column. From O'Connell Sq., **Abbey St.** and **Bank St.** lead across the river to the burbs, and **High St.** runs perpendicular to O'Connell St. through the center of town. **Market Place** is between O'Connell and High St.

Tourist Offices: The brand new **Ennis Tourist Office,** O'Connell Sq. (tel. 28366), answers questions and provides bus and train information. Open June-Sept. daily 9am-9pm; Oct.-May M-Sa 9am-6pm, Su 10am-6pm.

Banks: Bank of Ireland, O'Connell Sq. (tel. 682 8615). **AIB,** Bank Pl. (tel. 682 8089). Both have **ATMs** and are open M-Tu and Th-F 10am-4pm, W 10am-5pm.

Bike Rental: Michael Tierney Cycles and Fishing, 17 Abbey St. (tel. 682 9433, after 6pm tel. 682 1293). Rentals and repair. Tierney helpfully suggests bike routes through the hilly countryside, and gives advice on fishing expeditions. Bikes £4 per afternoon, £10 per day, £40 per week; deposit £40 or credit card. Open M-Sa 9:30am-6pm.

Luggage Storage: At the bus station. Lockers 50p. Open M-Sa 7:30am-6:30pm, Su 10am-7:15pm.

Laundry: Parnell's, High St. (tel. 682 9075). Wash and dry £4-6. Open M-Sa 9am-6pm. Handy for removing the Guinness stains from your lapels.

Pharmacy: O'Connell Chemist, Abbey St. (tel. 682 0373). Open M-Sa 9am-6:30pm. **Michael McLoughlin,** O'Connell St. (tel. 682 9511), in Dunnes Supermarket. Open M-W 9am-6pm, Th-F 9am-9pm, Sa 9am-6pm.

Counseling and Support: Samaritans (tel. (850) 609 090). 24hr.

Emergency: Dial 999; no coins required. **Garda:** tel. 682 8205.

Internet Access: MacCool's Internet Cafe (tel. 682 1988), hidden in an alley just off Abbey St., near O'Connell Sq. A small but expanding cafe with five computers for the terminally addicted. £3 per 30min., £5 per hr. Open M-Sa 10am-11pm, Su 12-6pm.

Post Office: Bank Pl., off O'Connell Sq., (tel. 682 1054). Open M-F 9am-5:30pm, Sa 9:30am-2:30pm.

PHONE CODE: 065.

ACCOMMODATIONS

The **Clare Hostel** (tel. 682 9370) offers spotless rooms with bath. There's no kitchen or laundry, but other amenities, such as central heating, pool tables, and a cafe downstairs, might make up for these deficiencies. High prices include continental breakfast. Follow High St. away from O'Connell Sq., then turn left on Cornmarket St. The hostel is on the left. (Dorms £11.50, doubles £18.50 per person.) Nestled on the river across Club Bridge from Abbey St., the **Abbey Tourist Hostel (IHH)** (tel. 22620) is a 300-year-old labyrinth on Harmony Row. As is the case with most centuries-old buildings, the hostel is a bit drafty. Fortunately, it's also clean, fluorescently lit, and generally well looked-after. (Dorms July-Aug. £6.50, Sept.-June £6; private rooms £10 per person sharing. Laundry £2.50.) **Mary Conway's Greenlea B&B** (tel. 682 9049), on Station Rd. between the cathedral and the station, has sparklingly clean rooms and cheerful management. (£12-13.50. Open Mar.-Oct.) **Derrynane House** (tel. 682 8464), in O'Connell Square, will put a roof over your head right in the middle of town. Rooms are clean, cute, and quiet, even with a busy pub and restaurant downstairs. If you're not a carnivore, Derrynane offers a vegetarian alternative to the Irish breakfast prototype. (Singles £20, all with bath.)

FOOD AND PUBS

Meals in Ennis are mostly found in its pubs, but a short supply can be found elsewhere. Enormous and well-stocked **Dunnes supermarket**, O'Connell St. (tel. 684 0700), resides in the mall. (Open M-Tu and Sa 9am-6:30pm, W-F 9am-9pm, Su noon-6pm.) **Pearl City,** O'Connell St. (tel. 682 1388) serves dozens of yummy Chinese dishes. (Meals £3-10. Open daily until 1am.) **Upper Crust,** off Market Sq. (tel. 43261), sells high-class helpings for low prices. (Roast chicken £3.50. Open M-Th 8am-8pm, F-Sa 8am-6pm, Su 8:30am-2:30pm.) **Numero Uno Pizzeria** (tel. 41470) has pizzas and calzones, as well as a burger-and-fries take-away menu. The 10 in. margherita pizza (£3.70) is a heavenly respite from heavy pub fare. (Open M-Sa 12pm-12am, Su 4pm-12am; lunch specials available 12:30pm-2:30pm.) With over 60 pubs to its name, there is no shortage of nightlife in Ennis. Most all of them host sessions that help Ennis uphold Clare's reputation as a county of musical excellence. *The Clare Champion* has music listings for Ennis, and can be found in just about any shop, pub, or restaurant. ■**Cruises Pub,** Abbey St. (tel. 684 1800), next to the Friary, is a dimly lit joint. You'll find lively trad in its front section, while a high-class restaurant fills its back portion. Its 1658 birth date makes it one of the oldest buildings in Co. Clare, and much of the original interior remains intact. Over the years, Cruises has developed a strong relationship with the county's musicians. Local music stars appear nightly for cozy sessions, and international music star Maura O'Connell once lived upstairs. (Trad nightly and Su afternoons in summer.) **Brandon's Bar,** O'Connell St. (tel. 28133), serves huge plates of spuds, meat, and veggies (entrees £3.50) alongside its pints (trad W-Su). Upstairs is **The Boardwalk,** a hot spot for live trad, world, and indie music. (Cover £3 before midnight, £4 after. Open F-Sa.) **Brogan's,** O'Connell St. (tel. 29859), draws a young crowd. (Trad Tu-W.) Ennis has its fair share of dark and woody pubs serving dark and frothy pints, the darkest and woodiest being **The Usual Place,** 5 Market St. (tel. 20515). For bright lights and big-city action, **Queen's** (tel. 28963), near the Friary on Abbey St., has two swanky clubs for the mod squad. The member's bar at the back serves until 2am. (Sa rave, Su 60s-80s, charts other nights. Cover £5. Open W-Su.)

SIGHTS

Take Abbey St. northeast to the ruined and roofless 13th-century **Ennis Friary** (tel. 682 9100), Ennis' pride and joy (after the Clare hurling team, of course). Franciscans used the Friary until the 17th century at the invitation of the O'Brien family, kings of Thomond. In 1375 the seminary became one of Ireland's most important pre-Reformation theological schools. The abbey is admired for its slender panes of its east window. Inside, depictions of the Passion adorn the 15th-century **McMahon tomb.** (Open mid-May to Sept. daily 9:30am-6:30pm. £1, students 40p.) Across from the Friary, a block of sandstone inscribed with part of Yeats' "Easter 1916" remembers the Easter Rising (see p. 13). **Daniel O'Connell** watches over the town from his square. The original O'Connells were Catholic landowners dispossessed by Cromwell (see **History,** p. 7). In 1828, almost 200 years later, Ennis residents elected Catholic barrister Daniel O'Connell, soon to become "The Liberator," to represent them at Westminster (see p. 11). A 10min. walk from the town center on Mill Rd. leads to the **Maid of Erin,** a life-size statue remembering the **"Manchester Martyrs,"** three nationalists hanged in Manchester in 1867 (see also **Kilrush,** p. 289). Saturday is **Market Day** in Market Sq., where all conceivable wares are sold beneath a statue of crafty Daedalus.

COROFIN

Seven lakes and the River Fergus make the village of Corofin lush, but it's only a few miles away from the rocky Burren. Tourists eager to reach Ennis or Doolin usually overlook Corofin's quiet charm. Those in the know come to Corofin enjoy peaceful walks through beautifully pastoral scenes, and perhaps to trace their roots. **Buses** travel to **Ennis** (M-Sa 1 per day, £6) and **Lahinch** (M-Sa 1 per day, £4.20). The **tourist office,** Church St. (tel. 37955), is in the **Clare Heritage Centre.** (Open June-Sept. daily 10am-6pm.) The **post office** is on Main St. (Open M-F 9am-1pm and 2-5:30pm, Sa 9am-1pm.) The **phone code** is 065.

The **Corofin Village Hostel and Camping Park,** Main St. (tel. 37683), offers clean, modern facilities, internet access (£1 per hr.), and bureau de change. Superhelpful Jude and Marie can arrange bird watching trips and know quite a bit about the area's archeological hot spots. The hostel has hot showers and great water pressure. (Dorms £7.50, private rooms £9. **Camping** £4, £10 per family; less in off season. Laundry £5. Wheelchair accessible.) **Spar Market,** Main St., sells fruits, vegs, and staples. (Open daily 9am-8pm.) **Curtin's,** Mian St. (tel. 37525), has a front room with trad in one corner and thick pints in the other, and a back room with a well-stocked jukebox, huge screen TV, pool tables, and youngsters. The **Corofin Arms** (tel. 37373) serves up good pub grub at reasonable prices, garnished with trad and folk four nights a week. (Jumbo sandwiches with salad and fries £3.95.) On Thursday evenings from June to August, the **Teác Celide,** Main St., near the post office, organizes music, song, set dancing, poetry, and tea. (Starts at 9pm; £3.)

If you have more than a sneaking suspicion that your ancestors emigrated from County Clare, the **Clare Heritage and Genealogical Research Centre,** Church St. (tel. 37955), can probably help you trace your roots through birth, marriage, and death certificates. The hum-drum **Heritage Museum** across the street houses artifacts from the potato famine, emigration, and landowner days in a decaying Protestant church. (£2, students £1.50.) A history trail that stays within 2 mi. of the village center leads you to Corofin's sights. The trail visits well-preserved 12th-century **St. Tola's Cross** and the battlefield where, in 1318, Conor O'Dea's victory put off English domination for another two centuries. Three miles south of Corofin, **Dysert O'Dea Castle and Archaeology Centre** (tel. 37722), housed in a restored 15th century tower, uncovers the more distant past and explains the archaeological features of the surrounding lands. (Open May-Sept. daily 10am-6pm. £2.50). The **Dromore National Nature Reserve** and its peaceful, swan-inhabited lakes are about 8 mi. west of Corofin. Follow signs to Ruan Village; the reserve is signposted from there. Guided tours are available, but the trails allow you to ramble. Those eager to try the luck at nabbing one of the fish in Corofin's lakes and rivers can call **Burke's** (tel. 37677) and hire a boat (£10) with a day's notice.

Travel helps you remember who you forgot to be.....

Council *Travel*

CLARE COAST

Those traveling between Co. Clare and Co. Kerry should take the 20-minute **Tarbert-Killimer car ferry** across the Shannon estuary, avoiding an 85 mi. drive by way of Limerick ($8 per carload, $2 for pedestrians and bikers; see **Tarbert**, p. 274).

KILRUSH

The route to the Clare Coast from either Tarbert or Limerick passes through Kilrush (pop. 2900), a market town with the coast's only marina and a strong sense of Clare's history. The town's name derives from the gaelic "Cill Rois," meaning "church of the meadow." A permanent settlement landed in Kilrush in the 12th century when monks from nearby Scattery Island built a church on the mainland. By 1600, Kilrush was a significant harbor on the Shannon. In the Famine era, the town was a political hot-bed. Kilrush tenants banded together to withhold rent from their absentee landlords. Their actions led to the coining of the term "boycott"; the word's namesake is the debt collector who was the first to be refused. In the 20th century, Kilrush gained fame as the home of the folk musicians who rekindled national interest in traditional music. The music endures there today.

⚑ PRACTICAL INFORMATION. Bus Éireann (tel. (065) 682 4177 in Ennis) stops in Market Sq. on its way to **Ennis** (M-Sa 3-5 per day, Su 2-3 per day) and **Kilkee** (M-Sa 2-4 per day, Su 1-2 per day). The tourist information office is in the **Kilrush Heritage Centre,** Town Hall (tel. 905 1577), on Market Sq. If your appetite is still whet for Kilrush's history, pick up Paul Gleeson's *Kilrush: A Walking Tour* ($2.50). (Open May-Sept. M-Sa 10am-12:30pm and 2-5:30pm, Su noon-3:30 pm.) A bureau de change is in the tourist office. **AIB,** Frances St. (tel. 905 1012), has an **ATM.** (Open M 10am-5pm, Tu-F 10am-4pm.) **Bike rental** is available at **Gleesons,** Henry St. (tel. 905 1127), which is affiliated with Raleigh Rent-A-Bike. ($8 per day, $35 per week, $50 deposit.) Anthony Malone's **pharmacy** Frances St. (tel. 52552), has all you need. (Open M-Sa 9am-6pm, Su 11am-1pm.) The **Internet Bureau** (tel. 905 1061), beside the marina, provides access to the web and helpful, highly knowledgeable management. ($3 per half-hour. Open early to late daily, call for hours.) The **post office** (tel. 905 1077) is on Frances Street. (Open M-F 9am-5:30pm, Sa 10-4.) The **phone code** squeezes out 065 on its trusty concertina.

▗▚☑ ACCOMMODATIONS, FOOD, AND PUBS. Katie O'Connor's Holiday Hostel, Frances St. (tel. 905 1133), next to the AIB, provides clean and comfortable quarters in rooms that date back to 1797. Hostelers enjoy an open hearth. (Dorms $7, doubles $18, quads $25.) The **Kilrush Creek Lodge** (tel. 905 2855), in the cyan and red building across from the marina, is a large, clean, group-oriented accommodation with an affiliated adventure center next door. (Dorms $13, doubles $30. Full Irish breakfast included. Laundry $4.) B&Bs in Kilrush are plentiful and expensive. The **Iveragh House** (tel. 905 1176) on Frances St. boasts beautiful garden views for a reasonable $18-$20.

You can stock up on goodies at the **Mace Supermarket** (tel. 905 1885), on the first floor of the hostel. The **Central Restaurant** (tel. 905 2477), on Market Sq., prepares light fare at the right price. Sandwiches, pastries, quiche—everything but the Coca Cola is made on the premises. (Open M-Sa 9am-6pm, Su 11am-3pm.) Across the street from the hostel, **Cosidines** (tel. 905 1095) is a 150-year-old bakery that's been in the same family for 5 generations; it still uses the same ovens and mixers it did in the 1850s. Another remnant of the bakery's 19th century history are the bars on its windows; they kept out hungry, penniless types during Famine times. (Open M-Sa 8am-6pm.) Of Kilrush's 15 or so pubs, at least one is sure to have music on summer nights. **Crotty's Pub,** Market Sq. (tel. 905 2470), is the legendary spot where concertina player Lizzy Crotty helped repopularize trad in the 1950s. (Trad Tu-Th, Sa-Su.) Crotty's also cooks up pub grub and offers a beautifully restored **B&B.** The rooms are spacious, and come with fireplaces for toasty evenings. ($20.)

■ **SIGHTS.** At the **Kilrush Heritage Centre,** you can hear the town's memories of the Great Famine on "Kilrush in Landlord Times," a self-guided cassette tour (£2). A permanent exhibition describes Kilrush in the times of Napoleon, and the Famine. Audio-visuals disturbingly recreate the scene of an 1888 eviction. In town, a monument facing the Town Hall remembers the Manchester Martyrs of 1867 (see **Ennis,** p. 287). Just outside town on the ferry road, the dirt paths of 420 acre **Kilrush Forest Park** promise adventure, romance, and ultimately return to town. Kilrush's real attraction, however, lies offshore at **Scattery Island,** the site of a 6th century Monastic settlement. St. Senan reputedly once banned women from stepping foot on the island. His words hold little weight today, as mixed boatloads of tourists visit daily. The island has been uninhabited since the 1970s, leaving behind the rubble of monastic ruins, churchyards, and a circular tower. Boats depart regularly in summer (June-Sept. 4-5 per day, £4.50 return) and irregularly in other seasons. The tourist office books tours, and transportation can be arranged with Gerald Griffins (tel. 905 1327). The island sits in the Shannon estuary, home to Ireland's only known resident population of bottlenose dolphins. On the mainland, the **Scattery Island Centre,** Merchant's Quay (tel. 905 2139), can tell you more about the island's history and ecology. (Open mid-June to mid-Sept. daily 9:30am-6:30pm. Free.) Get up close and personal with the ecology at the **Kilrush Creek Adventure Centre** (tel. 905 2855), next to the Kilrush Lodge, on the water. The centre allows experts and novices alike to design their own land- or sea-based adventure. **Windsurfing, kayaking, sailing, orienteering,** and a variety of activities are instructed by a fully certified staff. (£15 for a half day, includes instruction and equipment. Call ahead.) The **Éigse Mrs. Crotty** ("Rise up Mrs. Crotty!") festival celebrates the glory of the concertina (see **Music,** p. 26) with lessons, lectures, and non-stop trad for a weekend in mid-August.

KILKEE

These days, Kilkee is where the Irish come to holiday. Four years ago, it was a quiet, small-time beach resort on the southwest tip of Co. Clare. A few rows of isolated, stately Victorian houses overlooked a perfect crescent of white sand. Nearby, gorgeous cliffs cut islands out of the craggy coast. The picture has changed since the institution of curious government tax incentives produced a massive building spree in the area. The number of homes tripled, as did prices. Overnight, dozens of cinder block housing units were packed into the formerly grand old estates. Nature still reigns triumphant, however, in the surrounding cliff scenery, and the human touch has done some good when it comes to Kilkee's lively pub scene.

■ **PRACTICAL INFORMATION.** Bus Éireann (tel. (065) 682 4177 in Ennis) leaves from Neville's Bar (the sign reads Kett's), around the corner from the tourist office by the central square. Buses head to **Limerick** (2hr., 3-4 per day) via **Ennis** (1hr.), and for **Galway** with an hour-long stop at the **Cliffs of Moher** (4hr., 2-3 per day). The **tourist office** (tel. 56112) is next to the Stella Maris Hotel in the central square. (Open daily June-Sept. 10am-6pm.) The **ATM** at the **Bank of Ireland,** O'Curry St. (tel. 56053), hands out cash. (Open M 10am-12:30pm and 1:30-5pm, Tu-F 10am-12:30pm and 1:30-4pm.) **Williams** (tel. 56041), opposite the post office on Circular Rd., **rents bikes.** (£6 per day; deposit £30.) The **post office** (tel. 56001) is on Circular Rd. (Open M-F 9am-5:30pm, Sa 9am-12:30pm.) Kilkee's **phone code** is camping out at 065.

■ **ACCOMMODATIONS, FOOD, AND PUBS.** The family-run **Kilkee Hostel (IHH),** O'Curry St. (tel. 56209), creates an atmosphere of fellowship among the travelers and itinerant geology students who gather in its large living room. Rooms are sunny, clean, and fill up fast; call ahead. (Dorms £7. Sheets 50p. Laundry £4.) **Dunearn House B&B** (tel. 56545) sits atop high cliffs on the coastal road. Gorgeous rooms with incredible bay-views play pleasant tricks on the eyes. (Singles £23.50, doubles £34.) At **Cunningham's** (tel. 56430), a neatly arranged battalion of well-maintained caravans provide a view for canvas-covered campers. Turn left onto the coast road and take the first turn-off behind the pink building. (Tents £7-8. Open Easter-Sept.)

A **Central Stores supermarket** (tel. 56249) vends victuals on the corner of O'Curry St. and Circular Rd. (Open summer M-Th 9am-8:30pm, F-Su 9am-9pm; winter daily 9am-8pm.) **The Pantry,** O'Curry St. (tel. 56576), is a culinary oasis in a desert of fast food. "Life's too short to drink bad wine," so the Pantry stocks up a large selection, with gourmet offerings to further please you palette. (Lunches £4-5, dinners £8-10. Open daily June-Sept. 9:30am-noon, 12:30-5pm, and 6:30-9:30pm). In the alley behind The Pantry, the **Country Cooking Shop** makes desserts for the decadent traveler. **Eats & Treats** (tel. 56866) also serves snacks to hungry beach bums. (Open June-Oct. daily 9am-7pm.) **Purtills,** O'Curry St. (tel. 56900), is a full restaurant—a rare and pricey breed in these parts. Home-spun delicacies and generous portions go well with the comforting farmhouse decor. (Salmon £9.95. Open Easter-Sept. daily 6-10pm, Oct.-Mar. Sa-Su 6-10pm.)

After a day spent frolicking, or simply snoring on the beach, you can happily fritter away even more time by drinking your way through the dense strip of pubs along O'Curry Street. **Richie's** (tel. 56597) informal setting and friendly staff make it a good place to start. The **Central Bar** (tel. 56103) has plenty of seating, pool tables, and dark red wood to go with the dark pints. The **Old Bistro** (tel. 56898) is a rough-hewn gem rebuilt four years ago by a handy Limerick chef and his wife. The upstairs restaurant offers candlelit romance, and the downstairs pub—decorated with choice farm tools—promises good old-fashioned *craic*. Look for acoustic entertainment and the handsome barman Jack. The **Myles Creek Pub** (tel. 56670) has pints to set your mind adrift. **O'Mara's** (tel. 56286) is a traditional Irish bar: old men with little pints of Guinness for teeth. Kilkee has a happening after-hours scene that occasionally sees last call come precariously close to the next first call. If you would rather see the stars and sunrise from the sand, the palatial bar and large stage of the **Strand Bar** (tel. 56177) is a great place to end your crawl. A high-heel's throw from the beach, the Strand has live music and dancing on most nights in the summer, from trad and rock, to all out cabaret.

⬛ SIGHTS. The spectacular **Westend Cliff Walk** begins at the end of the road to the left of the seacoast and makes a gentle climb up to the top of the cliffs. Aspiring poets should bring their notebooks and attempt in vain to capture this sea-battered beauty. Plus, not much rhymes with "cliff." Two sets of **Diamond Rocks** lie on the coast. The original is a slippery, kelp-coated mussel bed next to the harbour where locals bring nets at low tide. A gravel path from the car park leads to them. The "new" Diamond Rocks are quartz rocks farther up the coast. Four **Pollock Holes** provide natural rock pools for swimming. Modest types beware: the fourth is known as a men's nudist bathing spot, although a far more popular one is **Burns' Cove,** past the golf course on the other side of the coast. The path out to the new Diamond Rocks leads into **Loop Head Drive,** where the John Wayne classic *Ryan's Daughter* was filmed. The photogenic drive runs through small villages, ruined farmhouses, and plenty of pasture to the **Loop Head Lighthouse,** at the very tip of Co. Clare. On the way, it passes through **Carrigaholt,** a village 7 mi. south of Kilkee on the Shannon Estuary. The **Kilkee Pony Trekking & Riding Center** (tel. 906 0071) will saddle you up and guide you through Kilkee's splendid beach and past some of Ireland's greenest fields. (Early morning rides £25.)

MILLTOWN MALBAY

Milltown Malbay, 20 mi. north of Kilkee, is what Doolin was in the early 80s: the cutting edge of traditional music. While Doolin moved from impromptu sessions to paid concerts long ago, Milltown is keeping it real. As superb musicians continue to move here from all over the country, things are only getting better. The high point of the year is a large music festival hosted by the Willie Clancy School of Traditional Music (tel. 84148). During **Willie Week,** thousands of musicians, instrument-makers, fans, tourists, and *craic* addicts will flock here from all corners of the globe to celebrate the famous Irish piper who was born here. Participants pay £50 for the week's lectures, lessons, and recitals, while the musically-challenged are given a wide variety of set-dancing classes. Incessant trad sessions in the town's packed pubs are free, but

WESTERN IRELAND

range in quality (beware). Accommodations are booked months in advance, but the notice board at the community center in town can provide some leads. The **Lahinch Hostel** (see p. 292), ten miles to the north, is your best bet if there's just no room for you in Milltown. Since it has no hostels and scant transportation, Milltown doesn't get many tourists during the rest of the year. However, **The International Darlin' Girl from Clare Festival**, modeled after the Rose of Tralee Festival (see p. 270), is gathering steam in its 10th year. The pageant, accompanied by open air ceilis on the main square, sees the streets filled to the brim with locals and aspiring darlin' each August.

The **Bank of Ireland** (tel. 708 4018) is next to O'Friels. (Open M-W and F 10am-12:30pm and 1:30-4pm, Th 10am-12:30pm and 1:30-5pm.) **Byrne's** on Ennis Rd. (tel. 708 4079) **rents bikes,** and has a limited supply of camping equipment. (Bikes £7 per day, £35 per week. Open M-Sa 9:30am-6:30pm.) Marie Kelly's **pharmacy** (tel. 84440) is on Main St. (Open M-Tu and Th-Sa 9:30am-6pm, W 9:30am-7pm.) Miltown Mal-bay's **phone code** bangs 065 on its *bodhrán*.

The affordable **Station House** (tel. 84008) at the old railway station, five minutes down the road from Cleary's (below), is run by darlin' twins. The sprawling build-ing has huge beds, clean rooms, and a good driveway to hitch to Lahinch from. (£17.) Right in the center of town, **O'Loughlin's Ocean View B&B** (tel. 708 4249) has clean rooms and a staircase built by Willie Clancy himself. (High-season £18, low-season £15.) **Campers** take refuge above the **Spanish Point Beach**. **Spar Supermarket & Bakery**, Main St. (tel. 708 4093), sells super groceries. (Open M-Sa 9am-9pm, Su 9am-1:30pm.) Its name means "potato skins", but when **An Sceallain** (tel. 708 4498) Main St., fires up the ovens, out come delicious pizzas (£2-7).

Milltown squeezes 15 pubs into two blocks; on any given night, several of them host sessions. At ◪**Cleary's** (tel. 708 4201), an easy-going, busy bar just off the main street on the Ennistymon Road, musicians often outnumber listeners. It's locally known as "The Blond's" after a former proprietor. Bridie is no longer a blond, but she's still got it. **Clancy's** (tel. 708 4077) also has excellent trad, and the occasional blues session. The sign above **O'Friel's** (tel. 708 4275) still says "Lynch's" after all these years; "a local favorite with decent grub" would be more accurate. Willie, of Willie Week fame, once lived here. (Trad on weekends.)

LAHINCH

Once a resort town, always a resort town. The small holiday spot of Lahinch devel-oped in the 1880s as a haven for the well-to-do and its popularity as a seaside resort has scarcely waned in the subsequent years. Nestled in a corner of a mile-wide strand of smooth sand deposited by the Inagh River, Lahinch is the surfing capital of Ireland. Natural attractions aside, those seeking the arcades, bars, and discos won't be disappointed.

Buses (tel. 682 4177) roll in two to three times a day during the summer from **Doolin, Ennis, Galway, Limerick,** and **Cork** to the edge of town near the golf courses. There's a **bank** and **ATM** in Ennistymon, about 2 mi. east of town. A **bureau de change** (tel. 708 1743) rests at the top of Main St. (Open M-Su 9am-10pm.) The **post office**, Main St. (tel. 708 1001), will also change your money. (Open M-F 9am-1pm and 2-5:30pm, Sa 9am-1pm.) The brand-new **Lahinch Fáilte** (tel. 708 2082) at the bot-tom of Main St., organizes tours, sells ferry and bus tickets and **rents bikes**. **Internet Access** is there for the taking at **Raphael's Internet & Ice Cream Cafe** (tel. 708 1020) on Main St. (£3 per hr.) The **phone code** is 065.

Clean, comfortable bunk rooms and a waterfront location score a birdie at the **Lahinch Hostel (IHH)** (tel. 708 1040), on Church St. in the town center. (Dorms £7.50, doubles £24. Laundry £2. **Bike rental** £7 per day.) **The Village Hostel (IHH)** (tel. 708 1550), a 2 mi. bus ride west into Liscannor, features a huge, echoing kitchen, locally mined stone floors, and a laid-back way of life. (Dorms £7; private rooms £9, with packed lunch and dinner £15. Sheets 50p. **Camping** £4 per person.) The **Cliff Walk B&B** (tel. 708 1602) on N67, has comfortable and clean rooms. You'll break-fast in a sunny dining area with a view of the bay. (£18-£20.) The **Lahinch Caravan & Camping Park**, also on N67 (tel. 708 1424) provides space for camping. (£5 per tent. Open Easter-Sept. **Bike rental** £7 per day; open daily 9am-9pm.)

Mrs. O'Brien's Kitchen, Main St. (tel. 708 1020), serves stomach-soothing breakfasts all day in addition to a diverse lunch and dinner menu. An airy alternative to the usual pub scene, it hosts a wine bar from 9pm to 1am. Be sure to check out the canary with the great legs. (Veggie lasagna ₤7.35. Open Mar.-Sept. daily 8am-1am.) **Kenny's Bar,** Main St. (tel. 708 1433), resounds most nights with ballads, trad, and rock. Candles glow from whiskey-bottles, and the back patio is a nice spot from which to people-watch. The tasty Irish stew (₤5) was once written up in the *New York Times*. **O'Looneys Bar & Restaurant** (tel. 708 1414), has decent grub and a view of the crashing waves. The **Nineteenth Bar** (tel. 708 1440), is the place to swap golf stories and hear trad, folk, and rock nightly at 9:30pm. The disco ball spins in this tiny town at the **Claremont Hotel** (tel. 708 1007) on Main St. (Cover ₤4. Open F-Su.)

Arcades, rides, and general amusements along the beach provide entertainment during the day or evening. Those curious about the creatures swimming in the Atlantic can have their questions answered at **Seaworld.** (Tel. 708 1901. Open 10am-8pm. ₤3.80, students ₤3). Visit **Kenny Woolen Mills,** Main St. (tel. 81400), for excellent deals on locally knitted sweaters. The **Cliffs of Moher** are a mere 15min. away by bus, and ferries leave from nearby Liscannor (Lahinch-Doolin bus route) for the Aran Islands (see p. 300).

CLIFFS OF MOHER

The Cliffs of Moher are justifiably one of Ireland's most famous sights. The stunning view from the edge leads 700 ft. straight down into the open sea. American poet Wallace Stevens based his poem "The Irish Cliffs of Moher" on photographs, as he'd never been here. Don't make his mistake. These cliffs are so high you can actually see gulls whirling below you. On a clear day, the majestic cliffs afford views of Loop Head, the Kerry Mountains, the Twelve Pins of Connemara, and the Aran Islands. Close to the car park sits **O'Brien's Tower;** don't fall for its illusions of medieval grandeur—it was built in 1835 as a viewing tower by Cornelius O'Brien, an early tourism-promoter. You'll do just as well to stick to the ground view. (Open daily Apr.-Oct. 9am-7:30pm. ₤2, students 60p.) Most tour groups cluster around the tower, but better views await a bit farther along the coast. Occasionally marked paths wander along the cliffs, but most tourists drop away after the first curve.

Three miles south of Doolin, the Cliffs brush against R478; cars pay ₤1 for use of the parking lot. **Bus Éireann** clangs by on the summer-only Galway-Cork route (M-Sa 3 per day). The 26 mi. **Burren Way** and several trails weave more elusively through raised limestone and beds of wildflowers from Doolin (3hr.) and Liscannor (3½hr.). Those who shun the advice of *Let's Go* and **hitch** report mixed success in finding rides here. The **tourist office** (tel. (065) 81171), beside the parking lot, houses a bureau de change; a tea shop in the same building rejuvenates wind-blown travelers. (Open daily Apr.-Oct. 9:30am-5:30pm.) **Aran Ferries** (tel. 81368) operates a fantastic cruise that leaves from the pier in nearby Liscannor and sails along directly under the cliffs (55min., 1 per day, ₤10).

DOOLIN

Something of a national shrine to Irish traditional music, the little village of Doolin draws thousands of visitors every year to its three pubs, a fact that speaks volumes for both the pubs and the music. Most of Doolin's two hundred or so permanent residents run its four hostels, countless B&Bs, and pubs. The remaining residents farm the land and, in their spare time, wonder how so many backpackers end up in their small corner of the word. But not even bus-loads of tourists and raucous trad can dent the pervasive sense of peace in what is essentially a sleepy little town.

The 8 mi. paved and bicycle-friendly segment of the **Burren Way** links Doolin to the **Cliffs of Moher.** The steep climb along the road from Doolin to the Cliffs lets bicyclists coast the whole way back, reserving energy for another night of foot-stomping fun at the pubs. Pedestrians will find the route an exhausting but do-able half-day trip. Boats leave the pier on the other end of town for the **Aran Islands,** but boats from Galway and Rossaveal are cheaper under almost any circumstances (see **Galway,** p. 306).

🔒 ORIENTATION AND PRACTICAL INFORMATION

Doolin is shaped like a barbell, made up of two villages about a mile apart from each other. Close to the shore is the **Lower Village** with **Fisher St.** running through it. Fisher St. passes through a stretch of farmland on its way to the **Upper Village,** where it turns into **Roadford.** A traveling **bank** comes to Lower Village every Thursday from 11am to 2pm, but there's a permanent bureau de change at the **post office,** across from the Rainbow Hostel. The nearest **ATM** is in Ennistymon, 5 mi. to the southeast. The **Doolin Bike Store** (tel. 707 4282), outside the Aille River Hostel, **rents bikes** (£7 per day; open M-Su 9am-8pm), as does **Simply Cycling** (tel. 707 4429; £5 per day; deposit £40; open Apr.-Oct. daily 9:30am-9:30pm; call Nov.-Mar.). The **post office** (tel. 74209) operates from the Upper Village. (Open M-F 9am-1pm and 2-5:30pm, Sa 9am-1pm.) Doolin's **phone code** retired at 065.

🏠 ACCOMMODATIONS

Tourists pack Doolin in the summer, so book ahead for hostels. B&Bs are common, but those along the main road tend to be expensive.

Aille River Hostel (IHH) (tel. 707 4260), halfway between the villages, in a cute cottage by the river. Small, relaxed hostel with groovy ambience and clean, well-maintained rooms. Local musicians often stop by the Aille to warm up before gigs in the pubs. Free laundry. No phone. Dorms July-Aug. £7.50, Sept.-May £7; doubles £16; triples £24. **Camping** £3.50. Open mid-Mar. to mid-Nov.

Flanaghan's Village Hostel (tel. 74564), a half-mile up the road from the Upper Village. This brand-new and still-expanding hostel boasts spacious sunny rooms, mammoth leather couches, and a back garden with farm animals. Plus, you'll have plenty of time to sober up on the long walk home. Dorms £7, off season £6.50. Laundry £1.50.

Rainbow Hostel (IHH) (tel. 707 4415), Upper Village. Just a few steps from those pubs of legend, McGann's and McDermott's. Small, with pastel rooms and a casual atmosphere. Free 1½hr. guided walking tours of the Burren for hostelers. Dorms July-Aug. £7.50, Sept.-June £8; doubles July-Aug. £16. Laundry £3.

Doolin Hostel (IHH) (tel.707 4006), Lower Village. Geared towards large groups, the Doolin is a rambling old hostel with clean, comfortable rooms. Run by "Paddy," as he is affectionately known to visitors, the hostel offers more than the average budget accommodation: a shop, a bureau de change, tennis courts and rackets, and bus ticket sales. Buses stop outside the door daily. Dorms £7.50, doubles £18. Sheets 50p. Laundry £3. Reception 8am-9pm. **Bike rental** £6 per day for hostelers.

Westwind B&B (tel. 707 4227), Upper Village, behind McGann's, in the same driveway as the Lazy Lobster. The rooms are sunny and immaculately clean. The breakfasts please, with great omelettes. Quentin Tarantino stayed here in '95, but nobody really noticed because Co. Clare had just won the All-Ireland Hurling Championship. The owners give helpful advice to spelunkers and other Burren explorers. £15.

Doolin Cottage (tel. 707 4762), one door down from the Aille. The friendly, young proprietors keeps their rooms spotless and brightly decorated. The full breakfast menu is hearty with vegetarian-friendly choices. Doubles £22, with bath £24. Open Mar.-Nov.

Campsite (tel. 707 4458), near the harbor, has a kitchen, laundry facilities, a view of the Cliffs of Moher, and no apparent name. £4 per tent plus £1.50 per person. Showers 50p. Laundry £3.

🍴📺 FOOD AND PUBS

Doolin's few restaurants are pushing pricey, but all three pubs serve up excellent grub at moderate prices. The 🐸**Doolin Cafe** (tel. 707 4795), Upper Village, is a gem, emitting positive karma, and pampering meat lovers, vegetarians, and vegans alike. Talented chefs use local produce and seafood for an inventive menu. (Sandwiches £2-4, dinners £6-10. Open daily Apr.-Oct. 10am-10pm.) The **Doolin Deli** (tel. 707 4633), near O'Connor's in the Lower Village, packs overstuffed sandwiches (£1.30) and stocks groceries. (Open June-Sept. M-Sa 8:30am-9pm, Su 9:30am-9pm.) **Bruach na hAille** (tel. 74120) has a working antique phonograph player and delicious, creative home-grown dishes. The three-course early-bird special is a budget-friendly luxury with huge portions and gourmet flavor. (£10 early-bird special until 7:30. Open daily St. Patrick's day-Oct. 6-9:30pm.)

If Doolin looks like a ghost-town at first glance, have no fear: the people are all in the pubs. The pint-pouring threesome keep the crowds loyal with their musical brilliance. Both O'Connor's and McGann's have won awards for the best trad music in Ireland. The underdog and unofficial favorite of many a local is **McDermott's** (tel. 707 4328). Most summer standing-room-only sessions start at 9:30pm nightly in the summer, and on the weekends in winter. **McGann's** (tel. 707 4133), Upper Village, has music nightly at 9pm in the summer, on winter weekends at 9pm. **O'Connor's** (tel. 74168), Lower Village, is the busiest, most touristed of the three, with drink, song, and music nightly and Sunday afternoons all year.

THE BURREN

If there were wild orchids, cantankerous cows, and B&Bs on the moon, it would probably look a lot like the Burren. The area comprises nearly 100 sq. mi. and almost one third of Co. Clare's coastline. The lunar beauty of the Burren includes jagged gray hills resembling skyscrapers turned to rubble, hidden depressions that open up into a labyrinth of caves, and wildflowers found nowhere else. As Oliver Cromwell complained, "There is not wood enough to hang a man, nor water enough to drown him in, nor earth enough to bury him in." He shouldn't have worried, though; there are more than enough rocks to bash a man's skull and plenty of cliffs to throw him off.

The best way to see the Burren is to walk or cycle it, but be warned that the dramatic landscape makes for exhausting climbs. George Cunningham's *Burren Journey* series is worth a look (£4.50), as are Tim Robinson's meticulous maps (£5). *The Burren Rambler* maps (£2) are also extremely detailed. All of the surrounding tourist offices (at Kilfenora, Ennis, Corofin, the Cliffs of Moher, or Kinvara) are bound to stock these maps and any other information on the Burren that you might need.

Bus service in the Burren is as confused as the geography. Bus Éireann (tel. (065) 682 4177) connects Galway to towns in and near the Burren a few times a day during summer but infrequently during winter. Every summer weekday (June-Oct.) some of those buses continue from Killimer on the Shannon Car Ferry to Killarney and Cork. Bus stops are the Doolin Hostel in Doolin (p. 295), Burke's Garage in Lisdoonvarna (p. 296), Linnane's in Ballyvaughan (p. 297), and Winkles in Kinvara (p. 298). Other infrequent but year-round buses run from some individual Burren towns to Ennis. Full-day bus tours from **Galway** are another popular way to see the Burren (see p. 295). Hitching requires patience. *Let's Go* does not recommend hitchhiking.

KILFENORA

The village of Kilfenora lies 5 mi. southeast of Lisdoonvarna on R478; its Burren Heritage Center and several grocers make it an ideal departure point for bicyclists and trekkers heading into the Burren. Visitors are wise not to overlook Kilfenora's several non-geological sights: seven high crosses, numerous wedge tombs, and a castle. Kilfenora also has its store of trad musicians, making it a less advertised participant in the Clare coast's brilliant music scene.

The **post office** (tel. (065) 88001) is across from the grocery store on Main St. (Open M-F 9am-1pm and 2-5:30pm, Sa 10am-1pm.) In the yellow house across the street from the Burren Centre, **Ms. Mary Murphy**, Main St. (tel. (065) 88040), greets arriving guests with tea and coffee. Clean and comfortable rooms are all en suite, and you'll get the full fry in the morning. (Single £17, doubles £30. Open June-Sept.) **Bridgid and Tony's B&B** (tel. (065) 88148) has clean and airy rooms, hearty breakfasts, and smart kids. (£14 per person.) Kilfenora has only three pubs, but enough music and dancing to make you miss your bus in the morning. **Vaughan's** (tel. 88004) offers set dancing in the adjacent thatched cottage on Thursday and Sunday nights, trad sessions on Fridays, and open-air dancing on Sunday afternoons. (Meals £5; served 7-9pm.) Kitty Linnane and her ceili band of '54 put Kilfenora on the musical map; **Linnane's** (tel. (065) 88157) still hosts trad sessions. (Nightly in summer, weekends in winter, year-round W supersession.) At **Nagle's** (tel. 708813) the plush crimson upholstery and woodwork lend a deceptively upscale feel to a friendly, down-to-earth local haunt. (Music F-Su.)

The **Burren Interpretive Centre** presents a lecture on the natural history of the region and shows an excellent film on Burren biology. It's the most popular of its kind in the region. (Tel. (065) 88030. Open daily June-Sept. 9am-5pm; Mar.-May and Oct. 9am-5pm. Lecture and film £2.50, students £2.) Next to the Centre, Church of Ireland services are still held in the nave of the **Kilfenora Cathedral.** (1st and 3rd Su of the month, 9:45am.) The rest of the Cathedral and its graveyard stand open to the sky. Although the structure itself dates from 1190, the site has held churches since the 6th century. (Tours July-Aug. £2.50, students £2. Ask at the tourist office.) West of the church is the elaborate 12th century **Doorty Cross,** one of the "seven crosses of Kilfenora." Although time and erosion have taken their toll, carved scenes of three bishops and Christ's entry into Jerusalem are still identifiable. Odd birds and menacing heads cover its sides.

LISDOONVARNA

The locals call it "Lis-doon," but for everyone else in Ireland, its name is synonymous with its Match Making Festival. The month-long *craic*-and-snogging fest has drawn the likes of Jackson Browne and Van Morrison to its all-day music stages. Amidst the hullabaloo, farm boys and girls of all ages—their crops safely harvested, but with wild oats yet to sow—gather together to pick their mates. Local celebrity and professional matchmaker Willie Daley from Ennistymon presides over the event. No one is really saying how successful the festival is in making matches that last longer than a 6-pint hangover, but as one Lisdoon local puts it, "Everything works if you want it to." Before the days of match making, people flocked to Lisdoonvarna for its mineral springs. In the 1700s, Lisdoonvarna saw carriage upon carriage of therapy-seekers rolling in to try the curative wonders of sulphur, iron, magnesia, and copper. You can still give it a whirl at the **Spa Wells Health Centre,** Sulfur Hill Rd. (tel. 74023), at the bottom of the hill south of town. If you can't stay for a bath, at least savor their aromatic sulfur water. (30p per glass; sulphur bath £10, full massage £18, sauna £5. Open June-Oct. daily 10am-6pm.) **Buses** travel 4 mi. to **Doolin,** and on to **Lahinch** daily from the main square during summer (1-3 per day). Lisdoonvarna's **phone code,** 065, is a sagittarius who enjoys watersports and foot massages.

There are no hostels in Lisdoonvarna. To find a decent B&B for £15-16, close your eyes, point your finger, spin around until confused, open your eyes, et voilá! Dermot of ▓**Dooley's Caherleigh House** (tel. 707 453) makes every guest feel pampered with tea & cookies, crackling fires, and superb breakfasts. His rooms are huge and decadently pink. (£18 per person.) Or you can dream of that special someone under the foot-high comforters at **Mrs. O'Connor's Roncalli House** (tel. 707 4115). It's a 7min. walk from the town center, just keep walking past the Esso station and then another filling station. (Singles £16, doubles £25; all with bath.) The **Roadside Tavern,** Doolin Rd. (tel. 74494), is dimly lit and decorated with shellacked postcards from around the world. Ghostly old photos of sessions past form a backdrop to their living version. (Mar.-Sept. nightly at 9:30pm, Oct.-Feb. Sa only.) The tavern also cooks up yummies. (Food served daily noon-8:45pm.)

CARRON

A pub, a hostel, and a mile-wide, 5 yd. deep puddle in the midst of a limestone landscape is the sum total of Carron. Sure enough, it's a mind-boggling figure. The village lies off a small road connecting Bellharbor to Killnaboy; to get there, drive (8min.) or hike (1½hr.) south from Bell Harbor. Hitching odds approach zero, which is how much *Let's Go* recommends that form of transportation.

A single magnificent hostel overlooks Europe's largest disappearing lake. **Clare's Rock Hostel** (tel. (065) 89129) houses half the town's population. It opened in 1998 with comfortable dorms with bath, tastefully decorated interior spaces, and a cheerful management. (Dorms £7, private rooms £10. Laundry £5. Open May-Oct.) Just across the way, Carron's pub **Croide Na Boirne** (tel. (065) 89109) offers gorgeous views, a crackling fire, and filling meals. The building was once a jail, and the pub still has the iron bars to prove it. Don't worry, the guns are purely decorative. (Burger £3.75. Food served Apr.-Dec. noon-9:30pm.) Four miles northwest of Carron is the **Poulnabrane Dolmen,** a well-known, photogenic group of Irish rocks. About 5000 years ago, over 25 people were put to rest with their pots and jewels under the five ton capstone, only to be dug up by curious archaeologists in 1989. Two miles east of Carron, Ireland's only perfumery (tel. (065) 89102) creates scents from the Burren's wildflowers. (Open daily June-Sept. daily 9am-7pm; Oct., Nov., Mar-May 9am-5pm.)

BALLYVAUGHAN

Along the jagged edge of Galway Bay, 8 mi. west of Kinvara on N67, the Burren's desolation is suddenly interrupted by the little oasis of Ballyvaughan. Its harbor shimmers by day, while its pubs shimmy nightly with lively trad sessions. The town center is just minutes from caves and castles, making it a frequent stop-over for spelunkers and archeology fiends. The **phone code** is 065.

There's no hostel in Ballyvaughan, but the **Bridge Hostel** (tel. 76134) is an 8 mi. bus ride west to Fanore. Isolated in the fingers of the Burren, the Bridge pampers visitors with peat fires and home-cooked meals. (Dorms £6, doubles £17. **Camping** £4 per person. Breakfast £3, dinner £4. Wash £2. **Bike rental** £5 per day. Open Mar.-Oct.) In town, **Seaside Oceanville** (tel. 77051), next door to Monk's on the pier, has gorgeous views and is only a short distance from the pub. (£18-19 per person, singles rarely available. Open May-Oct.) **Gentian Villa B&B** (tel. 77042) has clean, comfortable rooms and friendly chat on the Main Rd. towards Kinvara. (£16 with bath. Open Easter-Oct.) **O'Briens B&B,** above the pub and restaurant on Main Street, (tel. 77003) has pleasing rooms, a magic fireplace, and a breakfast buffet. (Singles £25; double £40, £35 in off-season.)

Spar (tel. 77077) sells various food stuffs. (Open daily 9am-8pm.) At **An Féar Gorta** ("the hungry grass"; tel. 77023), tea, tasty little cakes and a garden setting enchant. You can read *The Legend of the Hag of Loughrask* while you wait for your food. (Sandwiches from £2. Open June-Sept. M-Sa 11am-5:30pm.) The sunny little **Tea Junction Cafe** (tel. 77289) has sandwiches and veggie entrees, but tempts you to ruin your appetite with their famous rhubarb pie. (Open daily 9am-6pm.) At **Monk's Pub** (tel. 77059), fishermen unload their catch right into the kitchen. The tourists crowd around the huge stone fireplace for the trad and ballad sessions, while locals gravitate towards the bar. (Fish cakes with salad £6.95. Music three nights a week in summer, five nights in winter.) Back in town, **Greene's** (tel. 77147) is a small, card-playing locals' pub with an older crowd that knows where the Guinness runs best. Huge helpings of their daily special (around £5) are hot from noon to midnight. Go early if you value your elbow room.

A mile out of Ballyvaughan on N67 is the turnoff for **Newtown Castle and Trail,** where you can find the restored 16th century home of the O'Loghlens, the princes of the Burren. The hour-long tour includes ancient Clare manuscripts and Bardic Poetry recitals. Another hour-long guided tour covers about a half-mile of beautiful hillside terrain, discusses the geology of the Burren, and visits a Victorian folly "gazebo" (a miniature children's castle), as well as an 18th century military water-

WESTERN IRELAND

works system. (Tel. 77216. Open Easter-early Oct. daily 10am-6pm. Castle or trail tour ₤2, both ₤3.50.) Prehistoric bears once inhabited the two million-year-old **Aill-wee Cave** (EYEL-wee), 2 mi. south of Ballyvaughan and almost 1 mi. into the mountain. The tour's fancy lighting tricks don't significantly harm the natural wonder of the myriad waterfalls. Anyone scared of the dark should avoid the caves, as should serious spelunkers. (Tel. 77036. Open daily July-Aug. 10am-6:30pm; mid-Mar. to June and Sept. to early-Nov. 10am-5:30pm. ₤4.25, students ₤3.50.)

KINVARA

Despite the lines of cars that plow right through it every day on their way from Galway to the Burren, Kinvara (pop. 2300 and growing rapidly) is a fairly well-kept secret. This fishing village has an excellent music scene, a vibrant artistic community, and a well-preserved medieval castle. Bus Éireann connects Kinvara to Galway (₤3.80) and Doolin (June-Sept. M-Sa 4 per day, Su 2 per day; ₤5.50). Would-be poets on their way to Yeats' summer homes (see **Coole Park and Thoor Ballylee,** p. 299) can **rent bikes** at McMahon's (tel. 637 577), just up the street from the hostel on the Ballyvaughan Rd. (₤5 per day, ₤ 35 per week; ID deposit.) **Kinvara Pharmacy,** Main St. (tel. 637 397), soothes your blisters. (Open M-Sa 9:30am-6pm.) The **post office** (tel. 637101) sends postcards. (Open M-F 9am-1pm and 2-5:30pm, Sa 9am-1pm.) The **phone code** is 091.

📍 **ACCOMMODATIONS. Johnston's Hostel (IHH),** Main St. (tel. 37164), uphill from the Quay, is a relaxing, if fortuitous, retreat. Cupid seems to have pitched a tent on the roof: the owner, his sisters, and over a dozen others have met their mates here, as did many others back when the gigantic common room was a dance hall. (Dorms ₤7.50. **Camping** ₤4.50. Sheets ₤1. Showers 50p. Laundry ₤4. Open June-Sept.) Right in town, the fabulous **Fallons B&B** (tel. 637 483) is an excellent abode above the Spar market. It's run with the help of their seven fantastic kids. (₤20 per person sharing.) The gardens of **Mary Walsh's Cois Cuain B&B,** on the Quay (tel. 637 119), inspire a cheerful interior. (₤18 per person sharing. Open Apr.-Nov.)

📷 **FOOD AND PUBS.** The **Londis Supermarket** (tel. 637 250) does its grocery thing on the main road. (Open M-Sa 9am-9pm, Su 9am-8pm.) **Rosaleen's** (tel. 637 503) stuffs you up with sandwiches, all-day breakfast, and delicious desserts. For pub grub with a creative flair, **Keogh's** is a good choice. The dinner menu, served until 9:30pm, is a bit pricey, but daily specials suit a low budget. (Chicken breast ₤5.95.) The whimsical **Cafe on the Quay** (tel 637 654) whips up sandwiches and seafood right by the water. (Salmon fish cakes ₤5.95. Open 9am-7pm daily.)

Kinvara has many more pubs of note than most towns twice its size. Across the street from the hostel is **Tully's** (tel. 637 146), where a grocery and bar keep company in smoky surroundings; U.S. license plates, of all things, provide the atmosphere for the best impromptu trad sessions in Kinvara. **Winkle's** (tel. 637 137) has music and set dancing Wednesday through Saturday nights. Dizzyingly huge amounts of liquor line the wall at **Greene's** (tel. 637 110). The night-time view of the bay from the candle-lit **Pierhead** (tel. 638 188) is enough to set your heart aflutter. If that doesn't work, perhaps the lively trad will. (Music Tu, Th, and Sa.) **Ould Plaid Shawls** (tel. 637 400) has a puzzling name considering the youth of its clientele; they enjoy occasional spontaneous trad sessions, and championship darts Tuesday at 10:30pm (₤2 to play). Pots, pans, and pictures of Kinvara's yesteryear hang on **Connolly's** (tel. 637 131) walls, while a wall of flowers obscures the entrance. The small, intimate interior will nurture your relationship with your pint.

🏰 **SIGHTS. Dunguaire Castle,** 10min. from town on Galway Rd., is really a tower house—a popular type of dwelling for country gentlemen of the 16th century. The narrow, winding staircase weaves its way to the battlements, which provide an expansive view of the town, sea, and countryside. From May to September, medieval banquets are held at 5:30pm and 8:45pm, at which lords and ladies sup as they are entertained with music and a literary pageant. (Tel. 37108. Open May-Sept. daily 9:30am-5pm. £2.75, students £1.90.) The first weekend in May, the town loses its marbles at the **Cuckoo Fleadh,** which brings over 200 musicians into town. The **Cruinniu Na Mbad Festival** (Gathering of the Boats) draws Galway hookers to Kinvara for a racy weekend in August.

DOORUS PENINSULA

Beside Kinvara, the Doorus Peninsula reaches out into Galway Bay. The house that Yeats and Lady Augusta Gregory inhabited while planning the Abbey Theatre (see p. 120) and collaborating on plays is now the isolated **Doorus House Hostel (An Óige/HI)** (tel. 637512). Originally the country seat of an expatriate French aristocrat, this well-appointed hostel sits gracefully among old oak trees and peers out on the great expanse of a tidal estuary. (June-Sept. dorms £7, Oct.-May £5.50. Sheets 80p. Reception 5-10:30pm.) For those not enamored of nature, it's probably best to stay in Kinvara, but for families with cars, hikers, and bikers, Doorus is righteous. Three castles, several holy wells, a handful of ring forts, a cave, winged critters, panoramic views, and boggy islands await the rambler; most are detailed in *Kinvara: A Rambler's Map and Guide*, available in town for £2. A 10 mi. round trip west from the hostel to the **Aughinish Peninsula** offers views of the Burren across the bay. The more convenient blue-flag **Traught Strand** is just a 5min. walk from the hostel. **Campers** can pitch a tent in the field nearby and wake to the slosh of surf. After a hike, the **Traveller's Inn** (tel. 637116) pub and grocery at Knockgarra, in the middle of the peninsula, is a great place to relax over a pint. (Open for groceries daily 9am-10pm). The **Galway-Doolin bus** does not pass through Doorus but will stop on request at the turnoff on Ballyvaughan Rd. (June-Sept. M-Sa 4 per day, Su 2 per day; Oct.-May M-Sa 1 per day). From there the hostel is 2 mi. (follow the signs toward the beach).

COOLE PARK AND THOOR BALLYLEE

W. B. Yeats eulogized his two retreats that lie about 20 mi. south of Galway near **Gort**, where N18 meets N66. One is now a ruin and national park; the other has been restored to appear as it did when Yeats lived there. Neither is accessible by bus; biking from Kinvara is the best option.

The **Coole Park** nature reserve was once the estate of Lady Augusta Gregory, a friend and collaborator of Yeats (see **The Irish Literary Revival**, p. 23). To Yeats, the estate represented the aristocratic order that crass industrialists and wars of the 1920s were destroying: "ancestral trees/ Or gardens rich in memory glorified/ Marriages, alliances and families/ And every bride's ambition satisfied." Although the house was destroyed in the 1922 Civil War (see **Independence and Civil War**, p. 14), the yew walk and garden survived. In the picnic area, the famous "autograph tree", a great copper beach, bears the initials of some important Irish figures: George Bernard Shaw, Sean O'Casey, Douglas Hyde (first president of Ireland), and Yeats himself. The **Coole Park Visitors Centre** eschews talk of Yeats in favor of local rocks, trees, and wildlife. (Tel. (091) 631 804. Open mid-Apr.-mid-June Tu-Su 10am-5pm; mid-June-Aug. daily 9:30am-6:30pm; Sept. daily 10am-5pm. Last admission 45min. before closing. £2, students £1.) A mile from the garden, **Coole Lake** is where Yeats watched "nine-and-fifty swans... all suddenly mount/ And scatter wheeling in great broken rings/ Upon their clamorous wings." Swans still gather here in winter.

Three miles north of Coole Park, a road turns off Galway Rd. and runs a mile further to **Thoor Ballylee,** a tower built in the 13th and 14th centuries. In 1916, Yeats bought it for £35, renovated it, and lived here with his family off and on from 1922 to 1928. While he was cloistered here writing "Meditations in Time of Civil War," Republican forces blew up the bridge by the tower. In Yeats's account, they "forbade us to leave the house, but were otherwise polite, even saying at last 'Goodnight, thank you.'" A film on Yeats's life plays at the **Visitors Centre,** where a coffee shop sells cakes and toasties. (Tel. (091) 631 436. Open Easter-Sept. daily 10am-6pm. £3, students £2.50.)

ARAN ISLANDS (OILEÁIN ÁRANN)

The three Aran Islands—Inishmore, Inishmaan, and Inisheer—rest in Galway Bay 15 mi. southwest of Galway City. Sections of the islands are covered with slabs of limestone that resemble the stark landscape of the Burren in Co. Clare (see p. 295). The green fields that compose the rest of the islands' surface are the result of centuries-worth of farmers' piling acres of stones into the walls that create a maze across the island. Their masonry is based on a mixture of thin seaweed, soil, sand, and manure. The harshness of this secluded existence resulted in the survival of only a tiny population on the islands today. Yet the Arans have been inhabited for thousands of centuries. Iron Age peoples appreciated the isolation and built awe-inspiring ring-forts on the edges of precipices to ensure it. Early Christians flocked to the trio seeking spiritual seclusion; the ruins of their ancient churches and monasteries now litter the island. During medieval times, clans fought for control of the Arans. Elizabeth I set up a garrison here. Their position at the mouth of the Galway Bay gave the islands periodic military and commercial importance, but fishing and farming have lasted as the islanders' primary occupations.

The islands' cultural isolation has drawn artistic attention since the start of the 20th century. In 1894, Dublin-born writer John Millington Synge asked W.B. Yeats for creative criticism. Yeats told him to go to the Arans, learn Irish, and write plays about the islanders. Synge followed his advice, and received international attention (see **The Irish Literary Revival**, p. 23). In the 1930s, Robert Flaherty's ground-breaking film *Man of Aran* added to the islands' fame. Helped by this artistic attention, the islands' reputation for harboring traditional ways of life has stimulated a small tourist industry.

During July and August, crowds of curious visitors surround every monument and fill every pub on Inishmore. The stretches of land between the sights, however, remain deserted. Visitors are rarer on Inishmaan and Inisheer, the two smaller islands, but their numbers are rising as the inter-island ferries become larger and more frequent. The scenery remains breathtaking, regardless of the number of people who see it. The lifestyle also remains traditional—locals still make *curraghs* (small boats made from curved wicker rods tied with string and covered with cowskin and black tar). Some retain local styles of dress, footwear, and fishing, and almost all speak Irish. Many foreign visitors express a sense of "invading" the island, and there is certainly a tangible difference in attitude toward natives from that generally experienced on the mainland. The **phone code** would like to thank the class of 099.

▶ GETTING THERE

Three ferry companies—**Island Ferries, O'Brien Shipping/Doolin Ferries,** and **Liscannor Ferries**—operate boats to the Aran Islands. They reach the islands from four points of departure: **Rossaveal** several miles west of Galway (30min. to Inishmore), **Doolin** (30min. to Inisheer), **Liscannor** (30min. to Inisheer), and **Galway** (1½hr. to Inishmore). Ferries serving Inishmore are reliable and leave daily. Even in the summer, ferries to the smaller islands are less certain. There is no charge to bring bicycles on board. If the ferry leaves from Rossaveal, the company making the trip will provide a shuttle bus from Galway City to Rossaveal, usually for £3. Flying with **Aer Árann** is double the cost, double the fun, and a fraction of the time.

> **Island Ferries** (tel. (091) 561 767, after hours 72273), based in the Galway Tourist Office. The Aran Sea Bird serves all 3 islands year-round from Rossaveal (35min., £15 return). A bus connects the tourist office in Galway with the ferry port (departs 1½hr. before sailing time, £4 return). The Sea Sprinter connects Inishmore with Inisheer via Inishmaan (£10 return per island). They also offer a package deal: the bus from Galway, return ferry to Inishmore, and one night's accommodation at the Mainistir House Hostel with breakfast for £21, with B&B instead for £24.

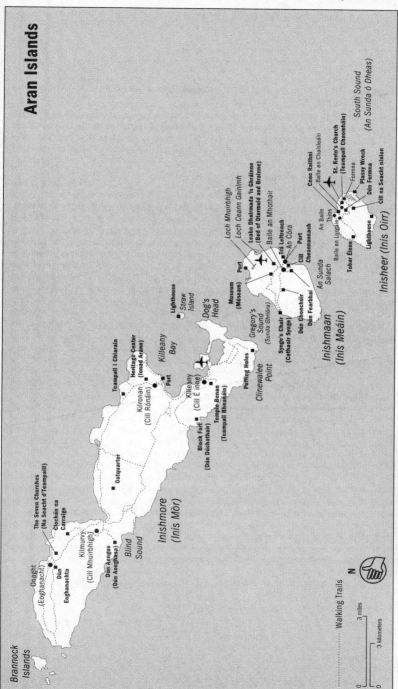

Aran Islands

Brannock Islands

Inishmore (Inis Mór)

Blind Sound

Onaght (Eoghanacht)
The Seven Churches (Na Seacht dTeampaill)
Clochán na Carraige
Dún Eoghanachta
Kilmurvy (Cill Mhuirbhigh)
Dún Aengus (Dún Aonghasa)

Oatquarter

Teampall I Chiaráin
Heritage Center (Ionad Árann)
Kironan (Cill Rónáin)
Port
Killeany Bay
Killeany (Cill Éinne)
Black Fort (Dún Dúchathair)
Temple Benan (Teampall Bheanáin)

Lighthouse
Straw Island

Dog's Head

Killeany

Puffing Holes
Clinewalee Point

Gregory's Sound (Sunda Ghréóir)
Synge's Chair (Cathaoir Synge)

Museum (Múseam)

Port
Loch Murbhigh
Loch Ceann Gainimh
Leaba Dhiarmada 'is Ghráinne (Bed of Diarmuid and Grainne)
Baile an Mhothair
Trá Leitreach
An Córa
Cill
Cill Port
Cheannanach
Dún Chonchúir
Dún Fearbhaí

An Sunda Salach

Inishmaan (Inis Meáin)

An Baile Thíos
An Baile
Baile an Lurgáin
Baile an Lurgáin
Cnoc Raithní
Baile an Chaisleáin
St. Kevin's Church (Teampall Chaomháin)
Formna
Plassy Wreck
Dún Formna
Cill na Seacht nInion
Tobar Éinne
Lighthouse

Inisheer (Inis Oírr)

South Sound (An Sunda ó Dheas)

N

Walking Trails

0   3 miles
0   3 kilometers

O'Brien Shipping/Doolin Ferries (tel. (065) 74455 in Doolin, (091) 567 283 in Galway, after hours (065) 71710). Year-round service connects Doolin and Galway to the Aran Islands. Galway to any island £12 return. Doolin to Inishmore £20 return, to Inishmaan £18 return, and to Inisheer £15 return. ISIC discount £3. Galway-Aran-Doolin £25. All trips from Doolin include inter-island travel; otherwise, inter-island trips £5 return. Cars always £100.

Liscannor Aran Ferries (tel. 065) 81368). Ferries depart twice a day from Liscannor and stop at Inishmaan and Inisheer. £17 return.

Aer Árann (tel. (091) 593 034), 19 mi. west of Galway at Inverin, flies to all three islands. Reservations are accepted over the phone or in person at the Galway Tourist Office. 10min. to Inishmore. In summer 20-25 per day; in winter 4 per day. £18, £35 return. Bus from Galway tourist office leaves 1hr. before departure (£2.50).

INISHMORE (INIS MÓR)

The archaeological sites of Inishmore (pop. 900), the largest of the Aran Islands, are among the most impressive in Ireland. Of the dozens of ruins, forts, churches, and "minor sites" (holy wells and kelp kilns), the most amazing is the Dún Aengus ring fort, where a small semicircular wall surrounds a sheer 300 ft. drop off the craggy cliffs of the island's southern edge. Inishmore is by far the most touristed of the three islands. Crowds disembark at Kilronan Pier on the center of the island, spread out to lose themselves amid the stone walls and stark cliffs, then coalesce again around major sights. Minivans and "pony traps" traverse the island, encouraging anyone on foot to climb aboard and pay up. Exactly 437 kinds of wildflowers rise from the stony terrain and over 7000 mi. of stone walls divide the land. Kilronan (Cill Rónáin), above the pier on the north shore, is the only place to buy supplies. The airstrip is on Inishmore's east end, while Kilmurvy and most of the major sites are on the west.

⚠ PRACTICAL INFORMATION

Ferries land in **Kilronan,** a cluster of buildings that make up the island's only village. **Minibuses** roaming the island can be flagged down for a ride (£5 return to Dún Aengus). The buses also organize 2hr. tours of the island (about £5). The tourist office in Kilronan (tel. 61263) changes money, holds bags during the day (75p), and sells the *Inis Món Way* (£1.50) and several other maps. (Open Feb.-Nov. daily 10am-6:15pm.) Anyone spending a few days on the Arans should invest in the Richardson map (£5), which meticulously documents virtually every rock on all three islands. **Aran Bicycle Hire** (tel. 61132) rents bikes. (£5 per day, £21 per week; deposit £9. Open Mar.-Nov. daily 9am-5pm.) Strangely enough, bike theft here is a problem—lock it up, or don't ever leave it. **Internet access** is available at the heritage center. The **post office** (tel. 61101), up the hill from the pier, past the Spar Market, has a bureau de change. (Open M-F 9am-5pm, Sa 9am-1pm.)

⚑ ACCOMMODATIONS

A free bus to the hostels meets all the ferries at the pier.

The Kilronan Hostel (tel. 61255). Huge, sunny, and spotless, with an ocean view from the dining room. Its location is just seconds from the pier and directly upstairs from the *craic* at Joe Mac's pub. Dorms July-Aug. £9, Sept.-June £8.

Mainistir House (IHH) (tel. 61169). It's earned a reputation as a haven for writers, musicians, and yuppies, but regular backpackers are sort of welcome too. If you don't mind the distance from the pubs, you'll be in mauve heaven. Esthete Joël dishes up creative, organic, all-you-can-eat buffet dinners (£7). He also gets up at 6:30am to make porridge and fresh scones for all. Book ahead, especially during July and August. Dorms £8, singles £15, doubles £ 20. Laundry £5. **Bike rental** £5 per day.

Dún Aengus Hostel (tel. 61318). Hides 4 mi. west in Kilmurvey; take the first turnoff to the right from the beach. This hostel, a 10min. walk from Dún Aengus, is a great outpost for outdoorsy types. Dorms £7. Laundry £2.

An Aharla (tel. 61305). Take the turnoff across from Joe Watt's on the main road; it's the first building on the left. Wile away the night before an open peat fire. The family-home-turned-hostel is a bit ragged, but loyal fans are smitten with its ultra laid back atmosphere and quiet location. Dorms £6.

Hostel Lodge (tel. 61457), across the road from An Aharla. A new hostel with incredible sea views and a price that includes tea and toast for breakfast. 8-bed dorm £7.

St. Kevin's (tel. 61485), behind Kilronan Hostel. The air's a bit stale, but this 40-bed hostel has clean rooms, high ceilings, and proximity to the pubs. Dorms £7.50.

St. Brendan's House (tel. 61149). An ivy-covered house across the street from the ocean. Apr.-Oct. £13, with continental breakfast £11; Nov.-Mar. £10, £8.

Beach View House (tel. 61141), 3 mi. west of Kilronan. Some rooms have views of Dún Aengus and framed versions of the Alps. Singles £23, doubles £34. Open May-Sept.

FOOD AND PUBS

Spar Market (tel. 61203), past the hostel in Kilronan, seems to be the island's social center. (Open M-Sa 9am-8pm, Su 10am-6pm.) The **Ould Pier** (tel. 61228), up the hill from the town center, serves up great, cheap grub. Eat inside or outside on sturdy picnic benches adorned with fresh flowers. (Fish and chips £4.95.) **Tigh Nan Phaidt** (tel. 61330), in a thatched building at the turnoff to Dún Aengus, specializes in home-cooked bread with home-smoked fish. (Smoked salmon sandwich £4.50. Open daily July-Aug. 10am-9pm, Mar.-June and Sept.-Dec. 10am-5pm.) For wonderful organic lunches in a historic setting, try **The Man of Aran Restaurant** (tel. 61301), located just past Kilmurvey Beach to the right. (Toasties £2. Lunch daily 12:30-3:30pm.) Traditional musicians occasionally strum on the terrace at **Tí Joe Mac** (tel. 61248), overlooking the pier. West of the harbor on the main road, **Joe Watty's** offers food, music, and conversation to accompany thick pints. **The American Bar** (tel. 61303) attracts younger islanders and droves of tourists with music most summer nights. On Friday, Saturday, and Sunday nights in the summer, the first steps of a **céilí** begin at midnight at the dance hall. (Cover £3.) *Man of Aran* is still screened daily at the community center. (£3.)

SIGHTS

The sights themselves are crowded, but the paths between them are desolate and unmarked, especially since too many visitors do the minibus tour. Cycling or walking makes for a day-long, hugely rewarding excursion. The tourist office's £3 maps correspond to yellow arrows that mark the trails, but the markings are frustratingly infrequent and can vanish in fog. The island's most famous monument, dating from the first century BC, is magnificent **Dún Aengus**, 4 mi. west of the pier at Kilronan. The fort's walls are 18 ft. thick and form a semi-circle around the sheer drop of Inishmore's northwest corner. One of the best-preserved prehistoric forts in Europe, Dún Aengus commands a sublime view of the ocean from its hill. Controversy continues as to whether it was built for defensive or ritual reasons. **Be very careful:** strong winds have blown tourists off the edge and to their deaths.

Many visitors are fooled by the occasional appearance of an island on the horizon. The vision is so realistic that it appeared on maps until the 20th century. Down the side of the cliff, the **Worm Hole** is a saltwater lake filled from the limestone aquifer below the ground. The bases of the surrounding cliffs have been hollowed by mighty waves to look like pirate caves. If you follow the cliffs to the left of Dún Aengus for about a mile, you can actually climb down to the level of the Worm Hole. The sound of the waves crashing under the rock is worth the 30min. walk. Two roads lead to the fort from Kilronan, an inland one and a quieter coastal one. Left off the main road a half-mile past Kilmurvey is **Dun Eoghanachta,** a huge circular fort with 16 ft. walls. To the right past Eoghanachta are the **Seven Churches.** Both are evidence of the island's earliest inhabitants. The island's best beach is at **Kilmurvey.**

Uphill from the pier in Kilronan, the new, expertly designed **Aran Islands Heritage Centre** (Ionad Árann; tel. 61355) beckons inquisitive tourists. (Open Apr.-Oct. daily 10am-7pm. ₤2, students ₤1.50.) Soil and wildlife exhibits, old Aran clothes, a cliff rescue cart, and *curraghs* combine for a surprisingly fascinating introduction to the natural and human life of the island. The **Black Fort** (Dún Dúchathair), a mile south of Kilronan over eerie terrain, is larger than Dún Aengus, a millennium older, and the unappreciated beauty of the two.

INISHMAAN (INIS MEÁIN)

Seagulls circle the cliffs while goats chew their cud, but there's little human activity to observe in the limestone fields of Inishmaan (pop. 300). For those who find beauty in solitude, a walk along the rocky cliff top is bliss. With the rapid and dramatic changes on the other two islands over the last three years, Inishmaan remains a fortress, quietly avoiding the hordes of barbarians invading from the east via Doolin and Galway. The ferry runs to the island almost regularly, but it is difficult to find a budget bed for the night.

For **tourist information,** as well as a chance to buy a variety of local crafts, try the **Inishmaan Co-op** (tel. 73010). Take the turn-off for the knitwear factory, continue straight, and then make a right turn after the factory. The **post office** (tel. 73001) is in Inishmaan's tiny village, which spreads out along the road west of the pier and divides the island in half. **Mrs. Faherty** (tel. 73012) also runs a B&B, signposted from the pier, and will fill you up with an enormous dinner. (Doubles ₤28. Dinner ₤11. Open mid-Mar.-Nov.) **Tig Congaile** (tel. 73085), on the right-hand side of the first steep hill from the pier, is a gorgeous B&B. (₤18.) Its restaurant concentrates on perfecting seafood. (Lunch under ₤5, dinner from ₤8.50. Open June-Sept. daily 9am-9pm.) The **An Dún Shop** (tel. 73067) sells some food at the entrance to Dún Chonchúir. **Padraic Faherty's** thatched pub is the center of life on the island, and serves a small selection of grub until 6:30pm.

Beyond the thoughts rolling around in your head, there's little to speak of or do on Inishmaan. All the same, the scenery's a feast for the eyes. The *Inishmaan Way* brochure (₤1.50) describes a 5 mi. walking route to all of the island's sights. The thatched cottage where Synge wrote much of his Aran-inspired work from 1898 to 1902 is a mile into the island on the main road. Across the road and a bit farther down is **Dún Chonchúir** (Connor Fort), an impressive 7th century ring fort. At the western end of the road is **Synge's Chair,** where the writer came to think and compose. The view of splashing waves and open seas is remarkable, but an even more dramatic landscape awaits a bit farther down the path where the coastline comes into view. To the left of the pier, the 8th century **Cill Cheannannach** church left its remains on the shore. Islanders were buried here until the mid-20th century under simple stone slabs. A mile north of the pier is Inishmaan's safest beach, **Trá Leitreach.** Entering the **Knitwear factory** (tel. 63009) is uncannily like stepping into a Madison Ave. boutique. The company sells its sweaters internationally to all sorts of upscale clothiers, but visitors can get them here right off of the sheep's back at nearly half the price. (Open M-Sa 10am-5pm, Su 10am-4pm.)

INISHEER (INIS OÍRR)

The Arans have been described as "quietness without loneliness," but Inishmaan can get damn lonely, and Inishmore isn't always quiet. Inisheer (pop. 300), the smallest Aran, is a compromise that lives up to the famous phrase. Islanders and stray donkeys seem to be present in even proportions on this island that is less than 2 mi. in diameter

Inisheer's town **tourist information** (tel. 75008) is cheerfully given in English or Irish from the small wooden hut on the beach near the main pier. (Open July-Aug. daily 10am-6pm.) **Rothair Inis Oírr** (tel. 75033) **rents bikes.** (₤5 per day, ₤25 per week.)

The **post office** (tel. 75001) is farther up the island to the left of the pier in the cream house with turquoise trim. (Open M-F 9am-1pm and 2-5:30pm, Sa 9am-1pm.)

The ▓**Brú Hostel (IHH)** (tel. 75024), visible from the pier, is clean and spacious. Upper-level rooms have skylights for stargazing. Call ahead in July and August. (4- to 6-bed dorms £7.50; private rooms £10 per person, with bath £11. Continental breakfast £2, Irish breakfast £4. Sheets £1. Laundry £4.) A list of Inisheer's 19 B&Bs hangs on the window of the small tourist office. **Bríd Póil's B&B** (tel. 75019) is booked all summer six months in advance due to the reputation of its beautiful view and amazing gourmet meals. It is worthwhile to call in case there's been a last-minute cancellation. (£16, with bath £17. Meals £12.) **Sharry's** B&B (tel. 75024), behind the Brú Hostel, has views and high ceilings. (£16.) The **Ionad Campála Campground** (tel. 75008) stretches its tarps near the beach for campers who don't mind chilly ocean winds. (£2 per tent, £10 per week. Showers 50p. Open May-Sept.)

Tigh Ruairí (tel. 75002), an unmarked pub and shop in a white building just up the road, is your best bet for groceries on the island. (Shop open July-Aug. daily 9am-8:30pm; Sept.-June M-Sa 9am-7:30pm, Su 10:45am-12:30pm.) **Marb Gané** (tel. 75049) serves coffee and treats by the pier. (Open June-Sept. daily 10am-6pm.) Monkfish leap from the sea into the kitchen of **Fisherman's Cottage** (tel. 75703), 350 yd. to the right of the pier. They are then killed, expertly cooked, and served. (Catch of the day £7. Open daily 11am-9:30pm.) **Tigh Ned's** pub lies next to the hostel and caters to a younger crowd, while the pub at the **Ostan Hotel** (tel. 75020), just up from the pier, is exceptionally crowded and dark. (Food served daily 11am-9:30pm.)

You can see the sights of the island on foot or from a pony cart tour (tel. 75092). The **Inis Oírr Way** covers the island's major attractions on a 4 mi. path. The first stop is in town at **Cnoc Raithní**, a bronze-age tumulus (stone burial mound), which is 2000 years older than Christianity. Walking along the **An Trá** shore leads to the romantic overgrown graveyard of **St. Kevin's Church** (Teampall Chaomhain). This St. Kevin, patron saint of Inisheer, is believed to be a brother of St. Kevin of Glendalough (see p. 139). On June 14, islanders hold mass in the church's ruins in memory of St. Kevin; lately, a festival has been tacked on. St. Kevin's nearby grave is said to have great healing powers. Below the church, a pristine, sandy beach stretches back to the edge of town. Farther east along the beach, a grassy track leads to **An Loch Mór,** a 16 acre inland lake where wildfowl prevail. The stone ring fort **Dún Formna** is above the lake. Continuing past the lake and back onto the seashore is the **Plassy wreck,** a ship that sank offshore and washed up on Inisheer in 1960. The Inisheer lighthouse is nicely visible from the wreck. The walk back to the island's center leads through **Formna Village** and on out to **Cill na Seacht nIníon,** a small monastery with a stone fort. The remains of the 14th century **O'Brien Castle,** razed by Cromwell in 1652, sit atop a nearby knoll. On the west side of the island, **Tobar Einne,** St. Enda's Holy Well, is believed to have curative powers.

COUNTY GALWAY

Small County Galway manages to contain a panorama of attractions in its 6000 square kilometers. Galway City is the world headquarters of *craic*, especially during its many festivals. The area to the west of Galway, on the other hand, offers peaceful, rugged scenery for terrific hiking and biking opportunities. Clifden has a thriving nightlife, while Inishbofin is an intense dose of nothingness. Connemara is a largely Irish-speaking region lined with exquisite beaches. Cong, a popular hamlet just over the Mayo border (listed in Co. Galway), boasts grassy boglands and long-abandoned ruins.

GALWAY

In the past few years, the city's reputation as Ireland's cultural capital has brought young Celtophiles flocking to Galway (pop. 60,000). Mix over 13,000 students at Galway's two major universities, a large transient population of twenty-something Europeans, and waves of international backpackers, and you have a small college town on *craic*.

Legacies of the 14 tribes who rebuilt and ruled Galway after a conflagration in 1490 dot the town. Later, the city became a commercial hub: Galway hookers harvested the ocean for fish and trade, bringing in Spanish and English goods and exporting produce from fertile inland sections of the county. Today, Galway's energy is spent on its cultural endeavors: numerous theater companies, and the promotion of the Irish language. Galway's arts, film, and horse-racing festivals follow one another in rapid succession during the summers, drawing still larger crowds. Sightseers find Galway a convenient base for trips along the Clare coast or to Connemara. Backpackers appreciate the disproportionate number of fine hostels. Pub-crawlers find inspiration in its wondrous variety of drinking establishments. Most of all, young people come here for each other, in huge numbers, making vibrant, cosmopolitan Galway Europe's fastest-growing city.

■ ORIENTATION

Bus or rail to Galway will deposit you in **Eyre Square,** a central block of lawn and monuments with the train and bus station on its east side. To the northeast of the square along **Prospect Hill,** a string of B&Bs begs for business. The town's commercial zone spreads out to the south and west. West of the square, **Woodquay** is an area of quiet commercial and residential activity. Williamsgate St. descends southwest into the lively medieval area around **High St., Shop St., Cross St.,** and **Quay St.** Flashy pubs, restaurants, shops, and dominate this area, which was recently pedestrianized. Fewer tourists venture over the bridges into the more bohemian **left bank** of the Corrib, where those in the know enjoy fantastic music in Galway's best pubs. Just south of the left bank is the **Claddagh,** Galway's original fishing village. A road stretches west past the quays to **Salthill,** a tacky beachfront resort with row houses and skyrocketing property values. To the north of the west bank are the university areas of **Newcastle** and **Shantallow,** quiet suburbs where students and families live. Galway's Regional Technical College is a mile east of the city center in suburban **Renmare,** which dozes peacefully by its bird sanctuary.

■ TRANSPORTATION

Airport: Carnmore (tel. 755 569). 3 small Aer Lingus planes jet to Dublin daily.

Trains: Eyre Sq. (tel. 561 444). Open M-Sa 7:40am-6pm. Trains to Dublin (3hr.; M-F 5 per day, Sa-Su 3-4 per day; M-Th and Sa £15, F and Su £21) stop in Athlone (M-Th and Sa £7.50, F and Su £13.50); transfer at Athlone to all other lines.

Buses: Eyre Sq. (tel. 562 000). Open July-Aug. M-Sa 8:30am-7pm, Su 8:30am-6pm; Sept.-June M-Sa 8:30am-6pm, Su 8:30am-noon and 1:40-6pm. Private bus companies specialize in the run to **Dublin. P. Nestor Coaches** (tel. 797 144) leaves from Imperial Hotel, Eyre Sq. (M-Th and Su 2 per day, F 7 per day, Sa 5 per day; £5 single or day return, £8 open return). **Citylink** (tel. 564 163) leaves from Supermac's, Eyre Sq. (5 per day, last bus at 5:45pm; same prices as Nestor's). A west Clare **shuttle** to **Doolin, Lisdoonvarna,** and **Fanore** leaves various Galway hostels on request (June-Sept. 1 per day, £5). **Michael Nee Coaches** (tel. 51082) drives from Forester St. through **Clifden** to **Cleggan,** meeting the **Inishbofin** ferry (M-Sa 2-4 per day; £5 single, £7 return). **Bus Éireann** heads to **Belfast** (M-Sa 2-3 per day, Su 1 per day; £17), **Cork** (5 per day, £12), **Dublin** (M-Sa 8-9 per day, Su 7-8 per day; £8), and the **Cliffs of Moher** (May 24-Sept. 19 M-Sa 3-4 per day, Su 1-2 per day; £8.60) by way of **Ballyvaughan** (£5.90).

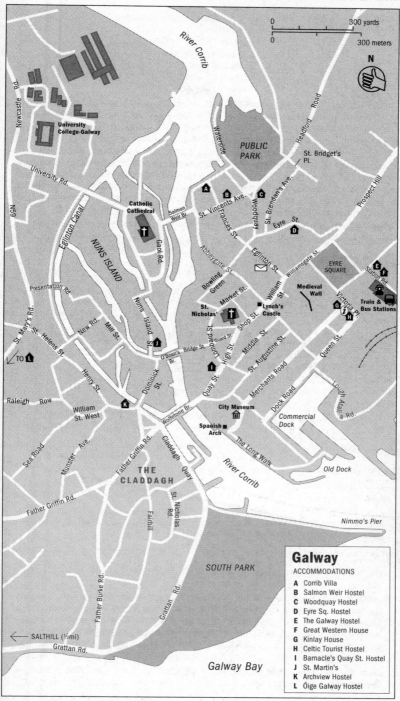

Galway

ACCOMMODATIONS

A Corrib Villa
B Salmon Weir Hostel
C Woodquay Hostel
D Eyre Sq. Hostel
E The Galway Hostel
F Great Western House
G Kinlay House
H Celtic Tourist Hostel
I Barnacle's Quay St. Hostel
J St. Martin's
K Archview Hostel
L Óige Galway Hostel

Ferries: Two companies ferry folks to the **Aran Islands;** both have ticket and information booths in the tourist office. **Island Ferries** (tel. 568 903) go from Rossaveal, west of Galway on the R336, to Inishmore (Apr.-Oct. 3 per day, May-Sept. 1 per day), Inisheer (2 per day), and Inishmaan (1 per day; all routes £14 return). A bus runs to Rossaveal (£4, £2 discount at Mainistir House hostel on Inishmore). **O'Brian Shipping** (tel. 567 283) leaves from the Galway docks with possible connection to **Doolin** (daily June-Sept., Oct.-May 3 per week, £14 return). See **Aran Islands,** p. 300.

Local Transportation: City buses (tel. 562 000) leave Eyre Sq. for all parts (every 20min., 70p). Buses go to each area of the city: #1 to **Salthill,** #2 to **Knocknacarra** (west) or **Renmare** (east), #3 to **Castlepark,** and #4 to **Newcastle** and **Rahoon.** Service M-Sa 8am-9pm, Su 11am-9pm. Commuter tickets £8 per week, £29 per month.

Taxis: Big O Taxis, 21 Upper Dominick St. (tel. 585 858). **Galway Taxis,** 7 Mainguard St. (tel. 561 111), around the corner from McSwiggan's Pub. 24hr. service. Taxis can usually be found around Eyre Sq. **Hackneys** are considerably cheaper than taxis due to differences in licensing and fixed-price service; they are run by **MGM** (tel. 757 888), **Claddagh** (tel. 589 000), and **Eyre Square** (tel. 569 444). There's a waiting station 3 doors down from the tourist office.

Car Rental: Budget Rent-a-Car, Eyre Sq. (tel. 566 376). Call for rates and restrictions.

Bike Rental: Europa Cycles, Hunter Buildings, Earls Island (tel. 563 355), opposite the cathedral. £3 per day, £5 per 24hr., £25 per week; deposit £30. Open M-F 9am-6pm. **Celtic Cycles,** Queen St., Victoria Pl. (tel. 566 606), next to the Celtic Hostel. £7 per day, £30 per week; deposit £40 or ID; drop-off charge £12. Open daily 9am-6pm.

Hitching: Dozens of hitchers wait on Dublin Rd. (N6) scouting rides to Dublin, Limerick, or Kinvara. Most catch bus #2, 5, or 6 from Eyre Sq. to this main thumb-stop. University Rd. leads drivers to Connemara via N59. *Let's Go* does not recommend hitchhiking.

⁊ PRACTICAL INFORMATION

TOURIST AND FINANCIAL SERVICES

Tourist Office: Victoria Pl. (tel. 563 081). A block southeast of Eyre Sq. The industrious staff and Aran Islands info booth make the pamphlet mania more exciting than ever. Open July-Aug. daily 8:30am-7:45pm; May-June and Sept. daily 8:30am-5:45pm; Oct.-Apr. M-F and Su 9am-5:45pm, Sa 9am-12:45pm. The **Salthill** office (tel. 520 500) is in an odd round metallic building visible from the main beach. Open daily 9am-5:45pm.

Travel Agency: USIT, Kinlay House, Victoria Pl., Eyre Sq. (tel. 565 177) is moving at some point in 2000 to Mary St. TravelSave stamps £8. Open May-Sept. M-F 9:30am-5:30pm, Sa 10am-3pm; Oct.-Apr. M-F 9:30am-5:30pm, Sa 10am-1pm.

Banks: Bank of Ireland, 19 Eyre Sq. (tel. 563 181). Open M-W and F 10am-4pm, Th 10am-5pm. **AIB,** Lynch's Castle, Shop St. (tel. 567 041). Exactly the same hours, but much more attractive. Both have **ATMs.**

American Express: 7 Eyre Sq. (tel. 562 316). Open May-Sept. M-F 9am-9pm, Sa 9am-7pm, Su 10am-7pm; Oct.-Apr. M-Sa 9am-5pm.

LOCAL SERVICES

Camping Equipment: River Deep Mountain High, Middle St. (tel. 563 968). Open M-Th and Sa 9:30am-6pm, F 9:30am-9pm.

Bookstores: Eason, 33 Shop St. (tel. 562 284), has a huge selection of books and international periodicals. Open M-Th and Sa 9am-6:15pm, F 9:30am-9pm. **Kenny's** (tel. 562 739), between High and Middle St., has an enormous collection of Irish interest books. Open M-Sa 9am-6pm. **Charlie Byrne's Bookshop,** Middle St. (tel. 562 776), has a massive stock of secondhand, discounted, and remaindered books. Open July-Aug. M-Sa 9am-8pm, Su noon-6pm; Sept.-June M-Th and Sa 9am-6pm, F 9am-8pm.

Library: St. Augustine St. (tel. 561 666). Open Tu-Th 11am-8pm, M and F-Sa 11am-5pm. Overrun with small, loud children.

Bisexual, Gay, and Lesbian Information: P.O. Box 45 (tel. 566 134). Recorded information on meetings and events. Gay line Tu and Th 8-10pm. Lesbian line W 8-10pm. The *Gay Community News* is available at Charlie Byrne's Bookshop (above).

Laundry: The Bubbles Inn, 18 Mary St. (tel. 563 434). Wash and dry £4. Open M-Sa 9am-6:15pm. **Prospect Hill Launderette,** Prospect Hill (tel. 568 343). Wash and dry £4. Open M-Sa 8:30am-6pm; last wash 4:45pm.

Pharmacies: Flanagan's, Shop St. (tel. 562 924). Open M-Sa 9am-6pm. **McGoldrick's,** Upper Salthill (tel. 562 332). Open daily July-Aug. 9am-9pm, Sept.-June 9am-7pm.

EMERGENCY AND COMMUNICATIONS

Emergency: Dial 999; no coins required. **Garda:** Mill St. (tel. 563 161).

Counseling and Support: Samaritans, 14 Nuns Island (tel. 561 222). 24hr. phones. **Rape Crisis Centre,** 3 St. Augustine St. (tel. (850) 355 355). Limited hours.

Hospital: University College Hospital, Newcastle Rd. (tel. 524 222).

Post Office: Eglinton St. (tel. 562 051). Open M and W-Sa 9am-5:30pm, Tu 9:30am-5:30pm.

Internet Access: Net Access, The Old Malte Arcade, High St., (tel. 569 772). £5 per hr., £4 with student ID. Free coffee when you log in. **Cyberzone:** Eyre Square. (tel. 561 415), above Supermac's. £2 per 30min., £3 per hr. Open daily 7am-midnight.

PHONE CODE:	091 has fetching boats.

▌ ACCOMMODATIONS

In the last few years, the number of hostel beds in Galway has tripled to approach one thousand. Nevertheless, you'll need to make reservations in July and August. Large, custom-built hostels gather around Eyre Square near the bus and train station. Smaller, friendlier ones clump a 5min. walk westwards at Woodquay, or across the river around Dominick Street. Rates are 10-20% higher in the summer.

HOSTELS AND CAMPING

Salmon Weir Hostel, St. Vincent's Ave., Woodquay (tel. 561 133). In a town where the hostels seem to get bigger and more impersonal by the minute, this homey hostel is easy to love. Guests congregate in the living room, then bound off to the pubs together. Rooms are scrupulously cleaned daily, and the showers are hot. Free tea, coffee, washing powder, and peace of mind. No smoking. June-Aug. 4-bed dorms £9, 6-bed dorm 8.50, 10-bed dorms £8, doubles £22. Laundry £3. Curfew 2am, in summer 3am.

Great Western House (IHH), Eyre Sq. (tel. 561 150 or (800) 425 929), in a mammoth building across from the station. Approaches hostel heaven with sauna, pool room, video games, and extra-wide bunks. Clean and modern with cheap full Irish breakfasts available. Bureau de change. July-Aug. and bank holidays 8- to 12-bed dorms £10, 4- to 6-bed dorms with bath £12.50, doubles with bath £32, singles £18. Off-season £1.50-3 cheaper. Small breakfast included, full breakfast £1. Laundry £5. **Bike rental** £6 per day. Internet access £2 per 20min. 24hr. reception. Wheelchair accessible.

Woodquay Hostel, 23-24 Woodquay (tel. 562 618). Cute exterior, better inside. Loungers love the huge living room with potted plants and comfy couches. The roomy candlelit dining area makes even the skimpiest of budget-conscious meals romantic. Clean and close to the pubs. Dorms £7.50, 4-bed suite £10, twin £10, single £12.

Kinlay House (IHH), Merchants Rd. (tel. 565 244), across from the tourist office. Megalithic, and a bit sedate. Rooms come with washcloths and closet space. Gigantic security monitors at reception remind you they're watching. July-Sept. 8-bed dorms £8.50; 6-bed dorms with bath £11; 4-bed dorms £11.50, with bath £12.50; doubles £14 per person, with bath £16; singles £20; Oct.-June dorms 50p-£1 cheaper, private rooms £2 cheaper. Small breakfast included. Laundry £3.50. 24hr. internet access £5 per hr. Bureau de change. Co-ed dorms. Wheelchair accessible.

WESTERN IRELAND

Barnacle's Quay Street Hostel (IHH), Quay St. (tel. 568 644). Shop St. becomes Quay St. Tidy dorms and a peerless location in the city center make this hostel the place to be, especially for professional pub-crawlers. Excellent security. Challenging floorplans. Big dorms £7-8.50, 8-bed dorms £7.50-9, 6-bed dorms £8-9.50, 4-bed dorms with bath £9.50-12, doubles with bath £24-29. Laundry £3.50.

Eyre Sq. Hostel, 35 Eyre St. (tel. 568 432). A small, laid-back hostel with giant windows. Tiny kitchen and living room nearly force coziness in this quiet, yet central, location. High-season big dorms £8, 4-bed dorms £10, doubles £24; off-season £7, £9, £22.

Corrib Villa (IHH), 4 Waterside (tel. 562 892), just past the courthouse, about 4 blocks down Eglinton St. from Eyre Sq. This Georgian townhouse has high ceilings and clean rooms. Its interior is freshly painted in patriotic hues. July to mid-Sept. dorms £8.50, mid-Sept. to June £7.50.

The Galway Hostel, Eyre Sq. (tel. 566 959), across from the station. Burren Shale tiles lead up past the soft yellow walls to poorly ventilated dorms with super-clean bathrooms. The small kitchen fills fast in this 80-bed hostel. June-Sept. 14-bed dorms £8; 8-bed dorms £8.50; 4-bed dorms £11, with bath £13; doubles £28; Sept.-May dorms £1 cheaper, doubles £2 cheaper.

Celtic Tourist Hostel, Queen St., Victoria Pl. (tel. 586 606; night 521 559), around the corner from the tourist office. Large dorms can get crowded. July-Aug. dorms £8.50, private rooms £11 per person; Sept.-June £7.50, £10. Sheets £1. **Bike rental** £7 per day.

Archview Hostel, Dominick St. (tel. 586 661). The cheapest, most laid-back accommodations in town, in the heart of Galway's bohemian district. This place has seen some wear and tear over the years, but it's comfortable, and a short stumble home from your big night on Dominick St. Dorms £6, off-season £5.

An Óige Galway Hostel (tel. 527 411). Follow Dominick St. to the west and turn left onto St. Mary's Rd. When school lets out for the summer, St. Mary's school for boys, an imposing building surrounded by playing fields, puts bunks in its classrooms and gyms to form a 180-bed hostel. Close to Galway's best bars, but far from the station. Big dorms £9, 4-bed dorms £10, twins £11. Breakfast included. Open late June to Aug.

BED AND BREAKFASTS

St. Martin's, 2 Nuns' Island (tel. 568 286), on the west bank of the river at the end of Dominick St. (visible from the Bridge St. bridge). Gorgeous riverside location with a grassy lawn. Singles £20, doubles £36.

Mrs. Ruth Armstrong, 14 Glenard Ave. (tel. 522 069), close to Salthill. Full Irish breakfast and friendly chatter. £15, off-season £12-13.

Mrs. E. O'Connolly, 24 Glenard Ave. (tel. 522 147), Salthill, off Dr. Mannix Rd. Bus #1 from Eyre Sq. Excellent B&B for super-cheap prices. £10 with continental breakfast, £12 with full Irish breakfast.

CAMPING

Camping: Salthill Caravan and Camping Park (tel. 523 972 or 522 479). On the bay, a half-mile west of Salthill. Crowded in summer. £3 per hiker or cyclist. Open May-Oct.

LONG-TERM STAYS

Galway has a large population of young, transient foreigners who visit, fall in love, find jobs, stay for a few months, and move on. Most share apartments in and around the city, where rents run from $30 to $50 per week. The best place to look is the *Galway Advertiser*. Apartment hunters line up outside the *Advertiser*'s office on Church St. (the small alley off Shop St. behind Eason) on Wednesdays at around 2pm; when the classified section is released at 3pm, they dash to the nearest phone box (one block up on Shop St.). An ideal time to start looking for jobs or apartments is the third week of May, when the university lets out. **Corrib Village** (tel. 527 112), in Newcastle, offers housing for the summer. Some hostels have cheap weekly rates ($30-35) in winter. Jobs aren't too hard to come by in Galway either. The Thursday morning *Galway Advertiser* is the place to look. Others find service jobs simply by asking. A four month student visa or other work permit helps a great deal, although the situation isn't hopeless without them (see p. 45). The **Galway Chamber of Commerce** (tel. 563 536), on Merchant's Rd. near the docks, will put those seeking more permanent jobs in touch with recruiters.

☐ FOOD

The large student population in Galway guarantees plenty of cheap, satisfying eats. The east bank has the greatest concentration of restaurants; the short blocks around Quay, High, and Shop St. are filled with good values.

The **Supervalu** (tel. 567 833), in the Eyre Square mall, is a chef's playground. (Open M-W and Sa 9am-6:30pm, Th-F 9am-9pm.) **Evergreen Health Food,** 1 Mainguard St. (tel. 564 215), has just the healthy stuff. (Open M-Th and Sa 9am-6:30pm, F 9am-8pm.) **Healthwise,** Abbeygate St. (tel. 568 761), promises better living through conscientious consumption. (Open M-F 9:30am-6pm, Sa 9:30am-5:30pm.) On Saturday mornings, an **open market** sets up in front of St. Nicholas Church on Market St. with seafood, pastries, and fresh fruit. (Open daily 8am-1pm.) Fishermen sell cups of mussels fresh from the bay (about £1).

▧ **Apostasy,** Dominick St. (tel. 561 478). A hip coffeeshop with an unbelievable after-hours scene. New-age regulars fill the place pretending to talk art until 4am each morning. Pub crawlers halfheartedly try to sober up with cups of strong coffee. Garlic bread with olives and mozzarella £2.20. Cappuccino £1.

▧ **The Home Plate,** Mary St. (tel. 561 475). Checkered tablecloths welcome you to take a seat in this little gem. Between noon and 3pm, it can get even cozier as the whole city pours in for huge sandwiches, veggie entrees, and mexican dishes. Entrees £4-6, large sandwiches £2.50. Open M-Sa noon-9:30pm.

The Long Walk (tel. 561 114), next to the Spanish Arch and a lot more intriguing. The first floor of a medieval battlement is transformed into a relaxed cafe and wine bar with live jazz on most afternoons. Food served M-Sa 12:30-3pm and 6-10pm, Su 6-10pm.

McDonagh's, 22 Quay St. (tel. 565 809). Locals and tourists flock here for world-class fish & chips. Certificates, newspaper clippings, and magazine articles line the wall to prove its popularity. Especially crowded after the pubs close. Cod fillet and chips £3.50. Take-away is cheaper than the restaurant. Restaurant open daily noon-11pm; take-away open M-Sa noon-midnight, Su noon-11pm.

Café Du Journal, Quay St. (tel. 568 428). Enter and instantly relax. Over-stuffed bookshelves and chilled-out regulars line the dark, multi-colored walls. Grab a newspaper, a powerful coffee, and a huge sandwich. Open M-Sa 9am-10pm.

Fat Freddy's, Quay St. (tel. 567 279). Galway's youth give high marks to the large pies rolling down the pipe at this pizza joint, although the wait can be a drag. Large pizza £5. Students 10% off M-F 3-6pm. Open daily 9am-11:30pm.

Anton's (tel. 582 067). A bit off the beaten path: a 3min. walk up Father Griffin Rd. over the bridge near the Spanish Arch. Meals are culled from a cornucopia of vegetables, fruits, and meats. Prepared by Anton himself right before your eyes. Salad and bread £3; creative sandwiches £2.50. Open Tu-Sa 11am-6pm.

Pierre's, Quay St. (tel. 566 066). 3-course meal £12. If you're going to break the bank (or at least a tenner) it ought to happen at this Quay St. favorite. Delicious lunches under £5; pre-theater special served 6-7pm, £8.90.

Food for Thought, Lower Abbeygate St. (tel. 565 854). This busy coffeeshop and wholefood restaurant serves an interesting variety of vegetarian dishes (£2.50) and mind-bogglingly large baps (from £2.50). At peak times, the queue can deteriorate into a contact sport. Open M-Sa 8am-6pm.

The Couch Potatas, Upper Abbeygate St. (tel. 561 664). Visitors to Ireland really should experience the potatoes. Huge stuffed spuds covered in various sauces and toppings, all served with side salads. "Hawaii 5-0" is a baked potato with ham, cheese, pineapple, and onion (£4.85). Crowded at lunchtime. Open M-Sa noon-10pm, Su 1-10pm.

WESTERN IRELAND

◪ PUBS

Galway's pub scene is centuries old and still brilliantly creative. They come in all flavors, from the fantastical to the traditional, so shop around. Trad blazes across town nightly, but Dominick St. is the best place to hear it. Good and bad versions of rock, folk, country, and blues, also rear their heads. Very broadly speaking, Quay St. pubs cater more to tourists, while locals stick to Dominick St. pubs. Only big gigs have cover charges. For schedules check *The List*, free and available at most pubs and newsstands.

DOMINICK STREET

◪ **Roisín Dubh** ("The Black Rose"), Dominick St. (tel. 586 540; www.RoisinDubh.net). Big-name Irish and international musicians light up the stage and electrify the audience. Primarily rock, but folk, blues, and trad as well. Irish record labels, including the pub's own, promote new artists here, and music enthusiasts of all ages turn out in numbers. Occasional M and Tu cover £5-10.

◪ **The Crane,** 2 Sea Rd. (tel. 587 419), a bit beyond the Blue Note. Well known as the place to hear trad in Galway. Enter through the side door and hop up to the 2nd floor loft. 2 musicians quickly become 6, 6 become 10, 10 become 20. Trad "whenever."

La Graal, 38 Lower Dominick St. (tel. 567 614). A candlelit wine bar and restaurant, La Graal draws a crowd of continentals and other sophisticates. Exquisite staff. Salsa dancing Th, gay-friendly disco Su. Open until 1am.

The Blue Note, William St. West (tel. 589 116). With its finger firmly on the pulse of the European dance scene, the Blue Note throbs every night of the week with guest DJs.

Aras Na nGael, Dominick St. (tel. 526 509). A bar for Irish speakers, this club nonetheless welcomes all sorts (kind of). Absorb the rhythms of the Irish language as you quietly nurse your Guinness.

Taylor's, Dominick St. (tel. 589 385). A holdover from another era, Taylor's is overlooked by tourists seeking flashier new entertainment venues. The locals who proclaim it the best pint in town don't mind much. Trad nights M, W, Sa, and Su.

THE QUAY

◪ **The King's Head,** High St. (tel. 566 630). Medieval decorations allow pub-goers to sit on thrones and talk to suits of armor. Huge stage area and funky lighting host live bands every night. Several bars make the wait for a pint non-existent. Occasional trad. Lunchtime theater M-Sa 1-2pm, £2. Popular jazz brunch Su noon-1:45pm.

The Quays, Quay St. (tel. 568 347). Popular with the younger crowd and scamming yuppies. The massive, multi-floored interior was built with carved wood and stained glass from an old church. Worth a visit to see the interior. Cover bands electrify the equally impressive upstairs extension nightly 10pm-1:30am. £5 cover.

Seaghan Ua Neachtain (called **Knockton's**), Quay St. (tel. 568 820). One of the oldest and most genuine pubs in the county. A mixed crowd trades in personal space for warmth and energy. Trad nightly.

Buskar Browne's/The Slate House (tel. 563 377), between Cross St. and Kirwin's Ln. Guilty drinkers should head to this former nunnery. Its fantastic 3rd floor "Hall of the Tribes" is the most spectacular lounge in Galway. Blaring techno and charts accompany videos being beamed onto the walls.

The Front Door, Cross St. (tel. 563 757). Beams of light criss-cross the dark interior of this deceivingly small pub. As it gets busier, more rooms open, moving up 3 stories and sprouting appendages all over the block. Get lost with that special someone.

Taaffe's, Shop St. (tel. 564 066). Everyone from tweed-capped men to platform-shoed mods comes here for daily quality trad at 5 and 9pm. As the bartender explains, there is "no useless bric-a-brac to distract from the job of drinking here."

The Lisheen, 5 Bridge St. (tel. 563 804). Outstanding and ceaseless trad nightly and Su morning. A musicians' and pool-shooters' haven.

Padraig's, (tel. 563 696), at the docks. Opens at 7:30am daily for fishermen, and plain ol' die-hards. You know who you are.

EYRE SQUARE

▨ **The Hole in the Wall.** This surprisingly large pub fills up fast with lots of singles and the occasional high-profile celebrity. An ideal meet-market with huge booths for intimate groups, three bars for mingling, and tables to dance on.

McSwiggin's, Eyre St. (tel. 568 917), near Eglinton St. A sprawling mess of small rooms and stairwells spanning 3 stories, McSwiggin's holds hundreds of tourists at a time. The *craic* is good, though, and so is the food.

Skeffington Arms (tel. 563 173). A splendidly decorated, multi-storied hotel with 6 different bars. The Skeff is a well-touristed pub crawl unto itself.

▤ CLUBS

Between 11pm and midnight, the pubs empty out, and the tireless go dancing. Unfortunately, Galway's clubs lag far behind its pubs. On the other hand, those who arrive at the clubs between 11:30pm and 12:15am are legally assured of a free meal with their entrance fee. **Monroe's Tavern,** Dominick St. (tel. 583 397), has Irish set dancing on Tuesdays, while **Le Graal** nearby has salsa on Thursdays. **GPO,** Eglinton St. (tel. 563 073), doesn't look good, but it draws a high-energy crowd nonetheless. Bank holiday Mondays are "Sheight Night"—dress your worst and listen to Abba's greatest hits. **The Alley,** behind the Skeff, draws a young local crowd with its unimaginative music and decor. (Cover £3-6.) The more adventurous and mobile head out to the **Liquid Club,** King's Hill (tel. 522 715), in Salthill. Expect a provocative dance mix that should fuel your engine until well into morning. A hackney service is the best way to get there and back. (Open Th-Su. Cover £6.)

◉ TOURS

Half- or full-day group tours are often the best way to see the sights of Galway, the Burren, and Connemara if you don't have much time. Some offer excellent values, with lower prices than bus tickets. For hour-long tours in and around the city, hop on one of the many buses that line up outside the tourist office (most £5, students £4). Several lines depart from the tourist office once a day for both Connemara and the Burren (about £10, students £8), including **O'Neachtain Tours** (tel. 553 88), **Gaeltacht Tours** (tel. 593 322), **Connemara Tours** (tel. 562 905), **Bus Éireann** (tel. 562 000), and **Healy Tours** (tel. 770 066). **Western Cultural and Heritage Tours** (tel. 521 699) leave from the tourist office at 2:30pm daily June through August. **Arch Heritage Tours** (tel. 844 133) explore the flora, fauna, and archaeology of the Burren. The **Corrib Princess** (tel. 592 447) sails from Galway's Woodquay on a tour of Lough Corrib to the north (1½hr., June-Aug. daily 2:30pm and 4:30pm, £5).

◉ SIGHTS

Present-day Galway is far more interesting than it was in days of yore, but those digging for interesting sights usually find enough to last an afternoon.

EYRE SQUARE. The park was rededicated to receive the official name John F. Kennedy Park. Around its grassy common, a small collection of monuments speak for various interests. A rusty sculpture celebrates the Galway Hooker. Another is a life-size portrait of the Irish-speaking poet Pádraig Ó'Cónaire. The sidewalk outside the Great Southern Hotel on the square's east side hides two foot-scrapers, small cast iron implements once used by Galway's gentry to scrape the muck off their feet. On the south side of the square is the Eyre Square Shopping Center, a large indoor mall that encloses a major section of Galway's medieval town wall. The wall was originally built in the 13th century and stood unnoticed until the construction of the shopping development nine years ago.

CLADDAGH. Until the 1930s, this area was an Irish-speaking, thatched-cottage fishing village. Stone bungalows replaced the cottages, but a bit of the small-town appeal and atmosphere still persists. The famous Claddagh rings, traditionally used as wedding bands, are mass-produced today. The rings depict the thumb and forefingers of two hands holding up a crown-topped heart. The ring should be turned around upon marriage; once the point of the heart faces inward, the wearer's heart is no longer available. *(Across the river south of Dominick St.)*

NORA BARNACLE HOUSE. The home of James Joyce's life-long companion. The table where he composed a few lines to Nora draws the admiration of Joyce addicts. Also on display are their love letters. *(8 Bowling Green. Tel. 564 743. Open mid-May to mid-Sept. M-Sa 10am-1pm and 2-5pm. £1.)*

LYNCH'S CASTLE. The elegant 1320 mansion now houses the Allied Irish Bank. The Lynch family ruled Galway from the 13th to the 18th century. The bank's displays relate a dubious family legend. In the late 1400s, Lynch Jr. killed a Spaniard whom he suspected of liking his girlfriend. The son, sentenced to hang, was so beloved by the populace that no one would agree to be the hangman. Lynch Sr., the lord of the castle, was so determined to administer justice that he hanged his own son. The window behind St. Nicholas Church is supposedly the one from which Lynch Sr. lynched Lynch Jr. A skull and crossbones engraved in the glass remembers the deed. *(Exhibit room open M-W and F 10am-4pm, Th 10am-5pm. Free.)*

CHURCH OF ST. NICHOLAS. The church is replete with oddities from unpredictable sources. A stone marks the spot where Columbus supposedly stopped to pray before hitting the New World. Note the three-faced clock on the exterior; local folklore claims that the residents on the fourth side failed to pay their church taxes. Glorious stained glass and relics from the Connacht Rangers provide more distractions. *(Market St., behind the castle. Open May-Sept. daily 9am-5:45pm. Free. Unnecessary tour £1, students 50p.)*

CATHEDRAL OF OUR LADY ASSUMED INTO HEAVEN AND ST. NICHOLAS. The boring exterior of Galway's Catholic cathedral provides no hint of the controversy that assailed its eclectic design 25 years ago: the interior consists of enormous bare walls of Connemara stone decorated with elaborate mosaics. *(Beside the Salmon Weir Bridge at the intersection of Gaol and University Rd. Excellent tours M-F 9:30am-4:30pm. Organ practice M-F 3:30-5:30pm. Open Su for mass.)*

GALWAY CITY MUSEUM. Old photographs of the Claddagh, a knife-sharpener by a peat fire, and some fishy statistics are the main contents of this small museum. *(In the tower house next to the Spanish Arch. Tel. 567 641. Open May-Oct. daily 10am-1pm and 2:15-5:15pm; check at the tourist office for Nov.-Apr. opening times. £1, students 50p.)*

SALTHILL. From the Claddagh, the waterfront road leads west, where the coast alternates between pebbles and sand; when the ocean sunset turns red, it's time for some serious beach frolicking. Two casinos, a swimming pool, and an amusement park join the ugly new hotels that dominate the esplanade.

MENLO CASTLE. Depending on your energy level, hire a boat and drift, row, or zoom up Lough Corrib to visit the ruins of the seat of the Blake family. Frank Dolan's fleet of rowboats will take you away from the maddening crowd and up Galway's gorgeous stretch. *(13 Riverside, Woodquay. Tel. 565 841. £1.50-3 per hr.)*

OTHER SITES. Across the University Rd. bridge from the cathedral is the **National University of Ireland at Galway,** founded 159 years ago during the Great Famine. Today the university enrolls some 6,000 students a year. By the river, the **Long Walk** makes a pleasant stroll, bringing you to the **Spanish Arch.** Built in 1584 as a defensive bastion for the port, this worn, one-story stone curve is revered by townspeople despite its unimpressive stature.

♫ ENTERTAINMENT

ARTS, THEATER, AND FILM

The *Advertiser* and *Galway Guide* (both free) provide listings of events, and are available at most pubs and newsagents.

SIAMSA NA GAILLIMHE. Dancers, singers, musicians, and actors routinely stun audiences with their showcase of traditional Irish art. *(The Galway Folk Theatre, at University College. Tel 755 479. Performances June 22-Aug. 28 M-F 8:45 pm. Tickets from £7.)*

THE GALWAY ARTS CENTRE. The center hosts rotating art and photography exhibits and frequent workshops on dance, writing, and painting. *(47 Dominick St. Tel. 565 886. Open M-Sa 10am-5:30pm.)*

THE TOWN HALL THEATRE. This Courthouse Sq. theater hosts everything from the Druid Theatre Company's Irish-themed plays and original Irish films to international hit musicals. *(Tel. 569 777. Programming daily in summer; most performances 8pm. Tickets £5-15, student discounts most shows.)*

AN TAIBHDHEARC. (An TIVE-yark.) Founded in 1928 by a group of academics from Galway University, the mostly Irish-language theater has launched quite a few Irish actors into the limelight. Poetry readings, musicals, and other events alternate with full-blown plays. *(Middle St. Tel. 562 024. 7 performances per year. Box office open M-F 10am-6pm, Sa 1-6pm. Tickets £6-9.)*

EVENTS

Festivals rotate through Galway all year long, with the greatest concentration during the summer months. Reservations during these weeks are necessary.

GALWAY ARTS FESTIVAL. For two crazed weeks in mid-July, the largest arts festival in Ireland reels in famous trad musicians, rock groups, theater troupes, and filmmakers. The highlight of the festival is the Big Day Out, held on the first Saturday, when big-name pop groups come to town for a massive concert. *(Tel. 583 800.)*

GALWAY RACES. The gates go up at the end of July. Those attending the races celebrate horses, money, and stout, not necessarily in that order. The grandstand bar at the 23,000 capacity Ballybrit track holds the world record for the longest bar in Europe, measuring over 70 yd. from end to end. The major social event is Ladies' Day, when those with the best hats and overall dress are officially recognized. Competition is notoriously stiff. *(Tel. 753 870. Race tickets £8-10 at the gate.)*

GALWAY INTERNATIONAL OYSTER FESTIVAL. Galway's last big festival of the year takes place in late September. Street theater, parades, and free concerts surround this 45-year-old Galway tradition, which culminates in the Guinness World Oyster Opening Championship. *(Tel. 566 490.)*

GALWAY POETRY AND LITERATURE FESTIVAL. Also known as the Cúirt, this festival gathers the very highest of the nation's brows in the last week of April. Past guests have included Nobel Prize-winner and Caribbean poet Derek Walcott and reggae star Linton Johnston. *(Tel. 565 886.)*

GALWAY FILM FLEADH. Ireland's biggest film festival, which features independent Irish and international filmmakers, screens its stuff in early July.

GALWAY HOOKER FESTIVAL AND TRADITIONAL BOAT REGATTA. Hookers can be seen in Galway all year round, but the fourth weekend in June, they race off to Portaferry, Northern Ireland (see p. 426). Fish nets, not fishnets, characterize these boating beauties with heavy, black hulls and billowing sails.

WESTERN IRELAND

LOUGH CORRIB

Three hundred and sixty-five islands dot Lough Corrib, one for every day of the year. The eastern shores of Lough Corrib and Lough Mask stretch quietly into fertile farmland. The western shores slip into bog, quartzite scree, and the famously rough Connemara country. The island of Inchagoill, in the middle of the lough, contains the site of the second-oldest existing Christian monuments in Europe.

OUGHTERARD

Little more than a small population center along the N59 between Galway and Clifden, Oughterard (OOK-ter-rard) sees most tour buses and rental cars blink briefly in its direction before they head off to bigger, better-known attractions. Still, Oughterard has a number of worthwhile outdoor activities: a relaxing canoe trip on Lough Corrib or a hike into the Maam Turk Mountains. The ruins on Inchagoill Island and Cong's *Quiet Man* mania are only a ferry ride away.

7 PRACTICAL INFORMATION. Bus Éireann coaches on their way from **Galway** to **Clifden** stop in Oughterard (30min. to Galway, 1½hr. to Clifden; July-Aug. M-Sa 4-6 per day, Su 1-2 per day; Sept.-June 1 per day). **Hitchers** report easy going, at least in summer, between Galway and anywhere west or northwest. *Let's Go* does not recommend hitchhiking. An independent **tourist office** (tel. 552 808) sells the useful *Oughterard Walking & Cycling Routes* handbook for £2. (Open May-Aug. M-Sa 9am-5:30pm, Su 10am-2pm; Sept.-Apr. M-F 9am-5:30pm.) The **Bank of Ireland,** Main St. (tel. 552 123), has an **ATM.** (Open M-W and F 10am-4pm, Th 10am-5pm.) **Geoghegan's Pharmacy,** Main St. (tel. 552 348), fills prescriptions. (Open M-Tu and Th-Sa 9:30am-1:30pm and 2:15-6pm, W 9:30am-1pm.) The **post office** (tel. 552 201) is also on Main St. (Open M-F 9am-1pm and 2-5:30pm, Sa 9am-1pm.) The **phone code,** 091, croons: "Thanks for the memories, Oughterard."

▄▐█▌ ACCOMMODATIONS, FOOD, AND PUBS. Friendships are quickly forged at the **Lough Corrib Hostel (IHH),** Camp St. (tel. 552 866). Its walls are lined with snapshots of backpackers who have come, gone, and left their mark. Ed and his merry pranksters look after each hosteler, introducing them to the comedy and intrigue of Oughterard nightlife. (Dorms £7, private rooms £8. **Camping** £4. Sheets 50p. Bike rental £7.50. Open Apr.-Nov.) **Cranrawer House (IHH),** a 10min. walk down Station Rd. (tel. 552 388), is a beautiful hostel with superior facilities in a quiet spot. The owner is a professional angler and will guide day expeditions onto the lough. (May-Sept. 8- to 10-bed dorms £7.50, 5-bed dorms with bath £8.50, private rooms with bath £9; Oct.-Apr. £6.50-£8.50. Laundry £4.50.) **Cregg Lodge B&B,** Station Rd. (tel. (095) 552 493), knows how to lodge. (£14, with bath £16. Open Apr.-Sept.) At **Wild Wood B&B,** Main St. (tel. 552 231), wild roses peek through the windows into fluffy, spacious rooms. (£16-17.)

Keogh's Grocery, The Square (tel. 552 583), sells food, fishing tackle, and hardware. The photo of a bewildered Bob Hope trying to buy some snacks is not for sale. (Open summer M-Sa 8am-10pm; winter M-Sa 8am-8pm, Su 9am-9pm.) A sunny restaurant with a sweet staff, **The Village Inn,** Main St. (tel. 552 088), is your best bet for a budget lunch. (Chicken baguette with fries £4.95.) Cheap sandwiches, all-day breakfasts, and tasty desserts morph into pricier entrees after 6pm. Good pub grub and brilliant *craic* dock at **The Boat Inn,** The Square. (Tel. 552 196. Irish stew £4.95. Food served 10:30am-10pm.) Thatched **Power's Bar** (tel. 552 712), a few doors down, is a local favorite. (Music F-Su.) Across the street, **Keogh's Bar** (tel. 552 222) encourages people to eat, drink, and be merry. (Music Tu-Su in summer, F-Su in winter.) **The Mayfly** (tel. 552 179) is an essential stop on the teenybopper pub crawl. (Disco F-Sa.)

◉ SIGHTS. A mile south of town, a turn-off from N59 leads to 16th century **Aughnanure Castle** (tel. 82214), where a river, red with peat, curves around a fortified tower. (Open daily mid-June to mid-Sept. 9:30am-6:30pm. £2, students £1.) The secret chamber, feasting hall, and murder hole are highlights of the quality tour. The view from the castle roof is tremendous. (Key available at the ticket booth.) Glann Rd. covers the 9 mi. from Oughterard to the infamous **Hill of Doon**, where the pre-Celtic Glann people annually sacrificed a virgin to the panther goddess Taryn. It is said that the practice continued in secret until the 1960s, when they ran out of virgins. The 16 mi. **Western Way Walk** begins where Glann Rd. ends and passes along the lake shore to Maam at the base of the Maam Turk mountain range.

Competitors from all over Ireland assemble in June for the **Currach Racing Championships.** The tourist office sells tickets for **Corrib Cruises** (tel. 82644), with two to three boats running daily between Cong, Oughterard, Ashford Castle, and Inchagoill (£6-12, additional £3 per bike). Equestrian hopefuls can start their careers by **pony trekking** (tel. 55212).

NEAR OUGHTERARD: INCHAGOILL

Inchagoill (INCH-a-gill), reputed to mean "the Island of the Stranger," has been uninhabited since the 1950s. There is little to see on the island other than a few ancient monastic ruins and toppled gravestones. Yet, at the right time of day, Inchagoill's eerie beauty makes it as captivating as any of its more touristed island cousins. Two churches, about which very little is known, hide quietly down the right-hand path from the pier. **St. Patrick's Church,** built in the 5th century, is now only a stack of crumbling stone. The famous **Stone of Lugna,** supposedly the tombstone of St. Patrick's nephew and navigator, stands 3 ft. high among the stones surrounding the church. The inscription on the stone translates to mean "stone of Luguaedon the son of Menueh." It is the earliest known example of the Irish language written in Roman script, and the second-oldest known inscribed Christian monument in Europe (the oldest are the catacombs of Rome). **The Church of the Saint** dates back to the 12th century. On the south side of the island is a now-defunct coffee house built by the Guinnesses. Ed Hickey at Lough Corrib Hostel in Oughterard can take you out to Inchagoill or bring you back "any time" (4-person min., £6 return). Several other hostels in Oughterard also run boats out to the island (see Oughterard). The **Corrib Queen** (tel. (092) 46029) sails daily from Lisloughrea Quay on the Quay Rd. in Cong, and from the Quay Road in Oughterard, and offers a brief but enlightening tour of the island (1½hr., June-Aug. 4 per day, £10 return). Those interested in more extensive exploration should take a morning ferry out and return in the afternoon.

CONNEMARA

Connemara is composed of a lacy net of inlets and islands, a rough gang of inland mountains, and some bogs in between. This thinly populated and geographically erratic western arm of Co. Galway harbors some of Ireland's most desolate yet breathtaking scenery. The jagged southern coastline of Connemara teems with safe beaches ideal for camping, sinuous estuaries, and tidal causeways connecting to rocky offshore islands. The relatively uninteresting developed strip from Galway to Rossaveal soon gives way to pretty fishing villages such as Roundstone and Kilkieran. Ireland's largest gaeltacht stretches along the coast; Connemara-based Irish-language radio, Radio na Gaeltachta, broadcasts from Costelloe. English-speaking Clifden, Connemara's largest town, also hosts its largest crowds. Squishy bogs spread between the coast and two major mountain ranges, the Twelve Bens and the Maamturks, which rise up like little green hills that just forgot to stop growing. Northeast of the Maamturks is Joyce Country, named for the the predominance of that surname in the area. Tom Joyce, the original Welsh settler of the region, was said to be 7 ft. tall, and many of his descendents share his uncommonly high vertical elevation.

WESTERN IRELAND

Counties Galway, Mayo, and Sligo

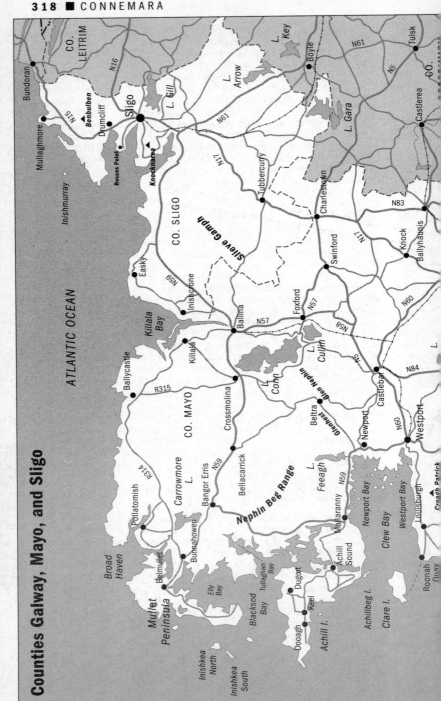

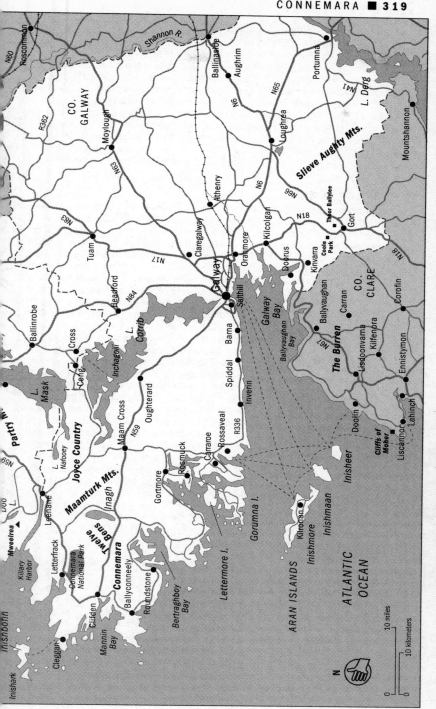

Cycling is a particularly rewarding way to absorb Connemara. The 60 mi. rides from Galway to Clifden via Cong or to Letterfrack are common routes, although the roads become a bit difficult toward the end. The seaside route through Inverin and Roundstone to Galway is another option, and each of the dozens of loops and backroads in north Connemara is as spectacular as the next. **Hiking** through the boglands and along the coastal routes is popular. The **Western Way** footpath offers dazzling views as it winds 31 mi. from Oughterard to Leenane through the Maamturks. **Buses** regularly service the main road from Galway to Westport, with stops in Clifden, Oughterard, Cong, and Leenane. N59 from Galway to Clifden is the main thoroughfare; R336, R340, and R341 make more elaborate coastal loops. **Hitchers** report that locals are likely to stop; *Let's Go* does not recommend hitchhiking. Watching Connemara fly by through the tinted windows of a **bus tour** (see **Galway,** p. 306), is better than missing it altogether.

SOUTH CONNEMARA

N59, the direct route from Galway to Clifden, passes through bare mountainous scenery, while the coastal route weaves in and out of the peninsulas and islands of South Connemara. A barren, boggy, lake-ridden frontier with few roads spans the large distance between the two highways. Drive-through territory runs straight along the Galway coast through the Irish-speaking suburbs of **Barna, Spiddal,** and **Inverin;** although Spiddal does have a small beach, far better ones await farther west. Boats leave for the Aran Islands from nearby **Rossaveal** (see **Aran Islands,** p. 300), west of which the landscape morphs into a lively and complicated mesh of intertwined estuaries, peninsulas, and islands. When the tides fall, bays become ponds, islands become peninsulas, and beaches grow wider. The first turnoff after Rossaveal leads to **Carraroe,** an Irish-speaking hamlet notable for its coral beaches.

At Gortmore, a detour through Rosmuck leads to **Padraig Pearse's Cottage,** which squats in a small hillock overlooking the northern mountains. Pearse and his brother spent their summers here learning Irish and dreaming of an Irish Republic (see **Easter Rising,** p. 13). The Republic-come-true declared the cottage a national monument. (Tel. (091) 570 4292. Open mid-June to mid-Sept. daily 9:30am-6:30pm. £1, students 40p.) Farther along the coast, the little fishing village of **Roundstone** curves along a colorful harbor. From the bay, one can see a few striking Bens rising in the distance. Errisbeg Mountain overlooks Roundstone's main street, and the 2hr. hike up culminates in a panoramic view of Connemara. **Roundstone Musical Instruments** (tel. (095) 35875) is the only full-time *bodhrán* (see **Traditional Music,** p. 26) maker in the world (Open daily June-Sept. 9:30am-7:30pm, Oct.-May 9:30am-5:30pm.) Where there are musical instruments, there is music, and **An galún Taoscta** is where you're likely to find it. (W trad, Su lunch session.) Afterwards, bang your *bodhrán* in the direction of **Wits End B&B** (tel. (095) 35951; July-Aug. £18 with bath, lower prices in the off-season). Two miles along the coast from Roundstone, the beaches between Dog's Bay and Gorteen Bay fan out to a small knobby island. On a bog near Ballyconneely, the last town before Clifden, John Alcock and Arthur Brown landed the first nonstop transatlantic flight in 1919.

CLIFDEN (AN CLOCHÁN)

Clifden is called the capital of Connemara because of its size, not its cultural membership in the *gaeltacht*; this busy English-speaking town has more amenities and modernities than its old-world, Irish-speaking neighbors. Clifden's proximity to the scenic bogs and mountains of the region attracts crowds of tourists, who enjoy the frenzied pub scene that starts up in the town at nightfall. Two high spires overlook its central wad of hotels, pubs, and souvenir shops. Clifden slumbers in the winter but explodes in the peak season as rental cars jockey for parking spaces, tour buses bring traffic to a standstill, and crowds of international visitors fill its five hostels. Yuppie shoppers check out the arts-and-crafts studios, and youths scope the liveliest pub scene this side of Galway.

⊡ TRANSPORTATION

Buses: Bus Éireann rolls from the library on Market St. to **Westport** via **Leenane** (1½hr., late June to Aug. 1-2 per day), and **Galway** via **Oughterard** (2hr.; June-Aug. M-Sa 5 per day, Su 2 per day; Sept.-May 1 per day; £6.50). **Michael Nee** (tel. 51082) runs a private bus from the courthouse to **Galway** (June-Sept. 3 per day, £5) and **Cleggan** (June-Sept. 1-2 per day, Oct.-May 2 per week; £3).

Taxi: Joyce's (tel. 21076).

Bike Rental: Mannion's, Bridge St. (tel. 21160, after hours 21155). £7 per day, £40 per week; deposit £10. Open M-Sa 9:30am-6:30pm, Su 10am-1pm and 5-7pm.

Boat Rental: John Ryan, Sky Rd. (tel. 21069). Prices negotiable.

⚡ ORIENTATION AND PRACTICAL INFORMATION

Market St. meets **Main St.** and **Church Hill** at **The Square.** The buildings on the south side of Market St. hide a surprising cliff drop. N59 makes a U-turn at Clifden; most traffic is from Galway, 1½hr. southeast, but the road continues northeast to Letterfrack and Connemara National Park. Hitchers ignore *Let's Go's* discouragement and usually wait at the Esso station on N59.

Tourist Office: Market St. (tel. 21163). Info on all of Connemara. Open July-Aug. M-Sa 9:45am-5:45pm and Su noon-4pm; May-June and Sept. M-Sa 9:30am-5:30am.

Banks: AIB, The Square (tel. 21129). Open M-Tu and Th-F 10am-12:30pm and 1:30-4pm, W 10am-5pm. **ATM. Bank of Ireland,** Sea View (tel. 21111). Open M-F 10am-12:30pm and 1:30-5pm.

Laundry: The Shamrock Washeteria, The Square (tel. 21348). Wash and dry £4. Open M-Sa 9:30am-6pm.

Pharmacy: Clifden Pharmacy (tel. 21821). Open M-F 9:30am-6:30pm, Sa 9:30am-6pm.

Emergency: Dial 999; no coins required. **Garda:** tel. 21021.

Hospital: Tel. 21301 or 21302.

Post Office: Main St. (tel. 21156). Open M-F 9:30am-5:30pm, Sa 9:30am-1:30pm.

PHONE CODE:	095, locally known as a náid a naoi a cúig.

⚞ ACCOMMODATIONS

B&Bs litter the streets; the going rate is £18-20 per person. Reservations are necessary in July and August.

The Clifden Town Hostel (IHH), Market St. (tel. 21076). Great facilities, spotless rooms, and a quiet atmosphere close to the pubs. Despite the modern decor, old stone walls remind you that the house is 180-years-old. Sean has lived on this street his whole life and will cheerfully divulge its deepest secrets. Dorms £8, triples £10 per person, quads £9 per person, doubles £12 per person; off-season private room £1-2 cheaper.

Brookside Hostel, Hulk St. (tel. 21812), head straight at the bottom of Market St. Clean, roomy dorms look over innocuous, fat sheep loitering in the backyard. Owner will painstakingly plot a hiking route for you. Dorms £7-8, private rooms £8-9. Laundry £4.

Ard Rí Bay View, Market St. (tel. 21866), behind King's Garage. Small, comfortable hostel with nice views and a central location. July-Aug. dorms £5-6, private rooms £8.

Blue Hostel, Sea View (tel. 21835), Market St. This slightly tattered family home provides little elbow room, but prioritizes cleanliness. Dorms £6, private rooms £8. Free laundry.

Leo's Hostel (IHH), Sea View (tel. 21429), straight on Market St. past The Square. This big old house is showing its age, but the turf fire, location, and astounding "loo with a view" still delight. Dorms £8, private rooms £9. Laundry £3. **Bike rental** £5 per day.

White Heather House, The Square (tel. 21655). Great location and panoramic views from most rooms, all with bath and TV. £16-18.

Kingston House, Mrs. King, Bridge St. (tel. 21470). Friendly staff, huge breakfasts, and spiffy rooms with a partial view of the church. Singles £20, doubles £34-36.

Shanaheever Campsite, (tel. 21018), a little over 1 mi. outside Clifden on Westport Rd. The tranquility of this spot compensates for its distance from the pubs. Game room, hot showers, and kitchen. £8 per 2-person tent, £3 per additional person. Laundry £4.50.

FOOD

Finding a good restaurant or cafe in Clifden requires little effort; justifying the prices for a tight budget is more difficult. **O'Connor's SuperValu,** Market St., might be the best place to score some cheap eats. (Open M-F 8:30am-8pm, Su 9am-7pm.)

An Tulan, Westport Rd. (tel. 21942). Offers home-cooked meals at compassionate prices. Sandwiches from £1.20, entrees around £4. Open daily 10am-10:30pm.

Mitchell's Restaurant, The Square (tel. 21867). A cozy, candlelit restaurant serving hearty plates for all palates. Burgers £5.95. Open daily noon-10:30pm.

Derryclare Restaurant, The Square (tel. 21440). Lunch specials quell pangs of shopper's guilt. 6 oysters £4.50. Pasta around £7. Open daily 8am-10:30pm.

Walsh's, The Square (tel. 21283). A busy bakery that looks tiny but actually has quite a large seating area. Soups, salads, and baps each around £2. Open Sept.-June M-F 8am-9pm, Sa 8am-6:30pm, Su 9am-6:30pm; later hours in summer.

E.J. King's, The Square (tel. 21330). Crowded bar serves excellent food on exceptionally old wood furniture. Fish and chips £4.95. Food served daily noon-9pm. The official restaurant upstairs serves the same food at higher prices.

PUBS

Mannion's, Market St. (tel. 21780). Bring your own instrument, or just pick up some spoons when you get there. Music nightly in summer, F-Sa in winter.

King's, The Square (tel. 21800). The town's best pint by consensus.

Malarkey's, on Church Hill. Perpetually packed and jiggity jammin' on Thursdays.

E.J. King's, The Square (tel. 21330). Talk, laugh, shout, or sing in this touristy pub.

Its name is **Humpty's** (tel. 21511). On weekends, there's no stopping Humpty's from getting busy, from the panoramic back window seats to the bathrooms.

Clifden House (tel. 21187), in Smuggler's Lodge at the bottom of Market St. The place to be for booty-shaking disco. High-season Th-Su, off-peak Sa. Cover £4-5.

SIGHTS

There are no cliffs in Clifden itself, but 10 mi. long Sky Rd. loops around the head of land to the west of town, and paves the way to some dizzying ones. It's best covered by bicycle, but involves several strenuous climbs. A mile down Sky Rd. stand the ruins of **Clifden Castle,** once home to Clifden's founder, John D'Arcy. Farther out, a peek at the bay reveals the spot where U.S. pilots Alcock and Brown landed after crossing the ocean in a biplane. One of the nicer ways to acquaint yourself with Connemara is by hiking south to the Alcock and Brown monument, situated just off the Ballyconnelly road 3 mi. past Salt Lake and Lough Fadda.

In all honesty, bogs are hard to appreciate. Open yourself up to their secrets by joining the inspiring tours of a critically acclaimed archaeologist-raconteur from the **Connemara Walking Center,** Market St. The tours explore the history, folklore, geology, and archaeology of the region. (Tel. 21379. Open Mar.-Oct. M-Sa 10am-6pm. One full-day or two half-day tours daily from Easter to Oct.; call for a schedule. £8-20.) Walks investigate the bogs, mountains, and Inishbofin and Omey islands. The office sells wonderful maps and guidebooks.

Clifden Town Hall erupts with performances of traditional music, dance, and song every Tuesday in July and August at 9pm. Clifden's artsy pretensions multiply in late September during the annual **Clifden Arts Week** (tel. 21295), featuring dozens of free concerts, poetry readings, and storytellings. On the third Thursday of August, attractive, talented contenders come to Clifden from miles around to compete for top awards at the **Connemara Pony Show.**

INISHBOFIN

Inishbofin has all the rugged beauty and serenity of the Aran Islands with half the stone walls and three times the sheep. 7 mi. from the western tip of Connemara, the island of Inishbofin (pop. 200) keeps time according to the ferry, the tides, and the sun; visitors can easily adapt to their system. There's little to do on the island other than scramble up the craggy hills, sunbathe on the sand, commune with the seals, watch birds fishing among the coves, and sleep under a blanket of bright stars. The smattering of tourists suggests that the island isn't completely removed from the universe, but Inishbofin seems to be part of another world.

7 **PRACTICAL INFORMATION.** **Ferries** leave for Inishbofin from **Cleggan,** a tiny village with stunning beaches 10 mi. northwest of Clifden. Two ferries serve the island. The **Island Discovery** (tel. 44642) is the larger, steadier, faster, and more expensive of the two (30min.; July-Aug. 3 per day, Apr.-June and Sept.-Oct. 2 per day; £12). The **M.V. Dun Aengus** (Paddy O'Halloran, tel. 45806) runs year-round (45min.; July-Aug. 3 per day, Apr.-June and Sept.-Oct. 2 per day, Nov.-Apr. 1 per day; £10). Both ferries carry bikes for free. Tickets are most conveniently purchased on the ferry itself. Drivers can leave cars parked free of charge at the Cleggan Pier. Stock up at the **Spar** (tel. 44750) before you go, especially if you're taking a later ferry. (Open daily 9am-10pm.) **Bike rental** is available at the Inishbofin pier (tel. 45833) for £5-7.50 per day. Four-legged contraptions can be hired from **Inishbofin Pony Trekking** (tel. 45853) for £12 per hr., but the island's steep hills and narrow roads are best explored on foot. The **phone code** is Day's 095.

♦♦♦ **ACCOMMODATIONS, FOOD, AND PUBS.** Kieran Day's excellent **Inishbofin Island Hostel (IHH)** (tel. 45855) is a 10min. walk from the ferry landing; take a right at the pier and head up the hill. Visitors are blessed with a large conservatory and swell views. (Dorms £6.50, private rooms £9-10 per person. **Camping** £4 per person. Sheets £1. Laundry £4.) The very remote **Horseshoe B&B** (tel. 45812) sets itself apart on the east end of the island. (£13.) The **Emerald Cottage** (tel. 45865), a 10min. walk west from the pier, welcomes guests with home-baked goodies. (£13.) There is no camping allowed on the beach or the adjacent dunes. Close to the pier, **Day's Pub** (tel. 45829) serves food from noon to 5pm. In back of the pub, **Olive's Bistro** delights wind-blown diners with huge, delicious servings. (Omelette with fries and salad £6. Open nightly 7:30-9:30pm.) **Day's Shop** (tel. 45829) is behind the pub and sells picnic-applicable items. (Open M-Sa 11:30am-1:30pm and 3-5pm, Su 11:30am-12:30pm.) The island's nightlife is surprisingly vibrant, with frequent trad performances in the summer. The smaller, more sedate **Murray's Pub,** a hotel-bar 15min. west of the pier, is the perfect place for conversation, slurred or otherwise.

♦ **SIGHTS.** Days on Inishbofin are best spent meandering through the rocks and wildflowers of the island's four peninsulas. Paths are scarce; each peninsula usually warrants about a 3hr. walk. Most items of historical interest are on the southeast peninsula. East of the hostel lie the ruins of a 15th century **Augustinian Abbey,** built on the site of a monastery founded by St. Colman in 667. A well and a few gravestones remain from the 7th century structure. East past the abbey, a conservation area encompasses long pristine beaches and a picturesque village. Swimming in the clear waters is permitted, but, please, no eroding the dunes. The most spectacular views of the island reward those who scramble up nearby **Knock Hill. Bishop's Rock,** a short distance off the mainland, becomes visible at low tide. Cromwell supposedly once tied a recalcitrant priest to the rock and forced his comrades to watch as the tide drowned him. On the other side of the island, to the west of the pier, is the imposing **Cromwellian fort,** which was built for defense but in practice used to hold prisoners before transporting them to the West Indies.

The ragged northeast peninsula is fantastic for bird watchers: gulls, cornets, shags, and a pair of peregrine falcons fish among the cliffs and coves. Nearby, gannets wet their nests. Inishbofin provides a perfect climate for vegetation hospitable to the corncrake, a bird that's near extinction everywhere other than Seamus Heaney's poems; two pairs of corncrakes presently call Inishbofin home. Fish swim in the clear water of two massive blowholes, while small land masses called **The Stags** tower offshore. The tidal causeway that connects The Stags to the mainland during low tide is extremely dangerous—do not venture out onto it. **Trá Gheal** (meaning "Silvery Beach") stretches along the northwest peninsula, but swimming here is dangerous. Off to the west is Inishark, an island inhabited by sheep and gray seals; the seals are most visible during mating season in September and early October. Inspirational archaeologist Michael Gibbons, at **Connemara Walking Center** in Clifden, offers tours focusing on Inishbofin's history, archaeology, and ecology. Leo Hallissey's fantastic **Connemara Summer School** (tel. 41034), held during the first week in July, studies the island's archaeology and ecology.

INISHTURK

Inishturk (pop. 90) is where Inishbofiners go to get away from the stress of modern life. A small, rounded peak rising 600 ft. out of the ocean between Inishbofin and Clare Island, Inishturk has more spectacular walks and views than either. You would never guess it now, but before the famine, the island teemed with a population of nearly 800. Nowadays, Inishturk seems virtually undiscovered. Those attempting an expedition to Inishturk should treat it as such: bring adequate supplies and a good book. There are no budget restaurants on the island, but the three excellent B&Bs serve home-cooked meals of epic proportions. **Concannon's B&B** (tel. (098) 45610) is just above a fish restaurant on the pier, and boasts enormous rooms with views. (£15, with bath £18. Dinner £12.) **Paddy O'Toole's B&B** (tel. 45510), about a mile from the harbor on the west village road, comes with an in-house accordion player and occasional ceilis in the dining room. (Single £18, double £30. Dinner £12.) Guests at the Heanue's **Ocean View** (tel. 45520), up the road from Concannon's, heartily applaud the fantastic meals and decadent rooms. (Single £17, with bath £19; doubles £32, with bath £34; off-season prices £2-3 less.) Above the pier to the left, the community center serves beer and light snacks, and hosts traditional dancing, singing, and music sessions. **John Heanue's Caher Star** (tel. (098) 45541) discovers the island twice a day (leaves from Cleggan Tu-Th, from Roonah F-M; £15 return). Anything can happen in this brave new world, but nothing ever really does—that's part of it's charm.

CLIFDEN TO WESTPORT

The area to the east and northeast of Clifden hunches up into high hills and then collapses into grass-curtained bogs occasionally interrupted by startling rocks. The landscape of Connemara National Park conceals a number of curiosities, including hare runs, orchids, and roseroot.

CONNEMARA NATIONAL PARK

Outside Letterfrack, Connemara National Park occupies 7¾ sq. mi. of mountainous countryside, which thousands of birds call home. The far-from-solid terrain of the park is composed of bogs thinly covered by a screen of grass and flowers. Be prepared to muddy your shoes and pants, and raise your pulse. Guides lead free 2hr. walks over the hills and through the bogs (July-Aug. M, W, and F at 10:30am) and give lectures on the region's history and ecology (July-Aug. W 8:30pm; free). The **visitors center** excels at explaining blanket bogs, raised bogs, turf, and heathland. (Tel. (095) 41054. Open daily June 10am-6:30pm; July-Aug. 9:30am-6:30pm; May and Sept. 10am-5:30pm. £2, students £1.)

The **Snuffaunboy Nature Trail** and the **Ellis Wood Trail** are easy hikes. The Snuffaunboy features alpine views while the Ellis wood submerges walkers in an ancient forest; both teem with wildflowers. A guidebook mapping out 30min. walks (50p) is available at the visitors center, where the staff helps plan longer hikes. More experienced hikers often head for the **Twelve Bens** (*Na Benna Beola*, a.k.a. the Twelve Pins), a rugged range that reaches 2400 ft. heights and is not recommended for single or beginning hikers. There are no proper trails, but Jos Lynam's guidebook (£5) meticulously plots out 18 fantastic hikes through the Twelve Bens and the Maamturks. Hikers often base themselves at the **Ben Lettery Hostel (An Óige/HI)** (tel. (095) 51136), which overlooks sheep and postcard-quality stretches of scenery in Ballinafad. The turn-off from N59 is 8 mi. east of Clifden. (June-Aug. £6; Easter-May and Sept. £5.50.) A hike from this remote but friendly hostel through the park to the Letterfrack hostel can be done in a day. A tour of all 12 Bens takes experienced walkers about 10hr. Biking the 40 mi. circle through Clifden, Letterfrack, and the Inagh valley is breathtaking, but only appropriate for fit bikers.

LETTERFRACK

Although it claims three pubs and a legendary hostel, Letterfrack, located at the crossroads of Connemara National Park, hasn't quite achieved town status. The **Galway-Clifden** bus (M-Sa; mid-June-Aug. 11 per week, Sept. to mid-June 4 per week) and the summertime **Clifden-Westport** bus (M and Th 2 per day, Tu-W and F-Sa 1 per day) stop at Letterfrack. Hitchers report medium-length waits on N59. *Let's Go* does not recommend hitchhiking. The **phone code** is 095.

Uphill from the intersection, the **Old Monastery Hostel** (tel. 41132) is one of Ireland's finest. Sturdy pine bunks, desks, and couches fill the spacious high-ceilinged rooms, a peat fire burns in the lounge, and framed photos of jazz greats hang in the cozy basement cafe. Steve, the owner, cooks mostly organic vegetarian buffet dinners in the summer (buffet £7, plate £4) and fresh scones for breakfast. (8-bed dorms £8, 6-bed dorms £9, 4-bed dorms £10. Breakfast included. Laundry £4. **Bike rental** £7 per day. Internet access £3 per hr.) Good pub grub, groceries, pints, and friendly locals are available at **Veldon's** (tel. 41046), which fills at 10:30am and empties late, sometimes after a trad session. (Shop open daily June-Aug. 9:30am-9pm, Sept.-May 9:30am-7pm.) **The Bard's Den** (tel. 41042), across the intersection, hopes for tourists with its skylight and large open fire. Photos of long-gone local characters dignify the walls of **Paddy Coyne's**, a few miles north of Letterfrack in Tully Cross. Jackie Coyne's Wednesday night lessons in the Irish broom dance dignify nothing at all, but they sure are fun.

Ocean's Alive is a new tourist magnet at Derryinver, 1½ mi. north of Letterfrack. Its touch tank aquarium lets you fondle the crabs, but hands off the old fishing artifacts and cottage replica. The sunny coffee shop sells cheap eats (sandwiches £1-2), and hosts Sunday trad sessions in the afternoon or evening. (Tel. 43473. Open May-Sept. 9:30am-7pm, Oct.-Apr. 10am-4:30pm. £3.50, students £2.50.) A cruise on the **Connemara Queen** runs from the center daily in the summer, and carries live bands with it two nights a week. (£10 per person.) Letterfrack hosts two environmentally oriented festivals a year. During **Bog Week,** the last week in October, and **Sea Week,** the first week in May, world-famous environmentalists gather to discuss bog- and sea-related issues while musicians jam amongst the peat.

The road from Letterfrack to Leenane passes **Kylemore Abbey,** a castle dramatically set in the shadow of a rocky outcrop. Built in 1867 by an English industrialist, the castle has been occupied since 1920 by a group of Benedictine nuns, who cheerfully chat with interested tourists. There's more to see at the small neo-Gothic church a few hundred feet down from the abbey. A rocky path winds up above the castle to a ledge with a view of the lake that you'll be loath to leave. A statue with arms aloft marks the end of your 30min. climb. (Tel. (095) 41146.

Abbey open Apr.-Oct. 9am-6pm, Nov.-Mar. 10am-4pm. £3, students £2.) The newly restored six-acre **Victorian Walled Garden** is worth a gander for those enamoured of banana plants and other horticultural anomalies in the hardly tropical country. (Open Easter-Nov. £3, students £2.50; garden and abbey £5, £4.)

LEENANE

Farther east along N59, **Killary Harbour,** Ireland's only fjord, breaks through the mountains to the wilderness outpost of Leenane (pop. 47). Wrapped in the skirts of the **Devilsmother Mountains,** this once populous region was reduced to a barren hinterland during the famine; today, the crumbled remnants of farms cover the surrounding hills. *The Field* was filmed here in 1989, and no one in town will ever forget it. The murder scene was shot at Aasleagh Falls. At **Leenane Cultural Centre** (tel. (095) 42323), on the Clifden-Westport Rd., spinning and weaving demonstrations reveal the final fate of wool. (Open daily Apr.-Oct. 10am-7pm. £2, students £1.50.) The coffee shop in the Centre is your best bet for a cheap lunch in town. (Sandwiches and sweets £1.25-4.) **Killary Harbour Hostel (An Óige/HI)** (tel. (095) 43417) perches on the very edge of the shore, 7 mi. west of Leenane. This remote hostel has staked out an unbeatable waterfront location. An in-house shop stocks the necessities, but the hostel interior looks much like a 70s college dorm. (Dorms £7, off-season £6. Open Jan.-Nov.) You can have your breakfast with Jesus, or at least a stained-glass likeness of him, at **The Convent B&B** (tel. (095) 42240), on the northern side of town along N59. The dining room was once a chapel; the rooms connected to it come with great views of the bay. (Singles £20-24, doubles £29.) Catching a lift from Leenane feels like winning the lottery, except for the money part. *Let's Go* does not see the incentive to hitchhike.

COUNTY MAYO

Co. Mayo fills northwestern Ireland with a large expanse of remarkable emptiness consisting of bog and beach. Towns and cities sporadically pop up out of nowhere: Westport is somewhat upscale and popular, Ballina is best known for its Moy fisheries, and old sea resorts such as Achill Island and Enniscrone line the seaboard. Mayo's fifteen minutes of fame occurred in 1798, "The Year of the French," when General Humbert landed at Kilcummin. Combining French soldiers, Irish revolutionaries, and rural secret societies into an army, Humbert launched an attack. The English retaliated and won at Ballina and Ballinamuck.

CONG

Just over the border from County Galway is cozy little Cong (pop. 300). Bubbling streams and shady footpaths criss-cross the surrounding forests, at the edge of which crumbles a ruined abbey. Nearby, a majestic castle towers over the choppy waters of Lough Corrib. Cong was once the busy market center of a more densely populated region, and Cong's abbey was a tower of learning with 3,000 students. In the past century, however, main roads were built to bypass the hamlet; were it not for two recent events, Cong might have slumbered into obscurity. In 1939, Ashford Castle was turned into a £500 per night luxury hotel, bringing the rich and famous to Cong from around the world. In 1951, John Wayne and Maureen O'Hara shot *The Quiet Man* here. Thousands of fans come each year to find the location of every shot while providing locals with amazement and profit.

🖪 **PRACTICAL INFORMATION. Buses** leave for **Westport** (M-Sa 1 per day) from Ashford gates, **Clifden** (M-Sa 1 per day) from Ryan's Hotel, and **Galway** (M-Sa 1-2 per day) from both (all £6). The town's **tourist office,** Abbey St. (tel. 46542), will point you toward Cong's wonders, listed in *The Cong Heritage Trail* (£1.50). *Cong: Walks, Sights, Stories* (£2.80) describes good hiking and biking routes. (Open daily Mar.-Oct. 9:30am-6pm.) **O'Connor's Garage,** Main St. (tel. 46008), **rents bikes.** (£7 per day, students £5 per day; £30 per week; ID or £40 deposit. Open daily

8am-9pm.) Get your fix at **Daly's Pharmacy** (tel. 46119) on Abbey St. (Open M-F 10am-6pm.) The **post office** (tel. 46001) is on Main St. (Open M-Tu and Th-Sa 9am-1pm and 2-5:30pm, W 9am-1pm.) The **phone code** 092 is rarely used by quiet men.

▮▮▮ ACCOMMODATIONS, FOOD, AND PUBS. The **Quiet Man Hostel** and the **Cong Hostel**, owned by the same charming family, are perfect if you're in the mood for a bit of company. Both screen the "legendary" film nightly in mini-theaters, have a bureau de change and laundry service (£5), **rent bikes** (£6 per day, £4 per ½-day), and will lend fishing rods, guidebooks, and rowboats free of charge. The **Quiet Man Hostel (IHH)**, Abbey St. (tel. 46511, reservations 46089), across the street from Cong Abbey, is central, spotless, and sociable. For those who just can't shake Quiet Man fever, the rooms are all named after film's characters. (Dorms £6. Continental breakfast £2.50.) **Cong Hostel (IHH)**, Quay Rd. (tel. 46089), a mile down the Galway Rd., is clean, and comfortable, with skylights in every room. The playground, picnic area, game room, and piano are sure to keep you entertained. The **camping** area is tremendous, and sprouts its own little village every summer. (Dorms £6, doubles with bath £18. Continental breakfast £2.50, full Irish breakfast £4. Extensive camping facilities £4.) The **Courtyard Hostel (IHH)**, Cross St. (tel. 46203), provides peace of mind several miles off the beaten track, east of Cong. Buses from Galway stop here, or call ahead for pick-up from Cong. This gem is worth the trek; stables have been beautifully transformed into dorms, and the former barn now sports an elegant gourmet restaurant where you can have lunch without breaking the bank. (Dorms £7, private rooms £8.50. **Bike rental** £5 per day. **Camping** £3.) As usual, B&Bs are everywhere. Smothered in geraniums and ivy, **White House B&B**, Abbey St. (tel. 46358), across the street from Danagher's Hotel, offers TV and bath in every room. (£17, off-season £16; £20 for singles.) Not even the ghosts can stop you from **camping** on **Inchagoill Island.**

Cooks can go crazy at **O'Connor's Supermarket**, Main St. (Tel. 46008. Open daily 8am-9pm.) Just across the street from the White House B&B, young locals and Ashford Castle staffers down mammoth meals and countless pints at **Danagher's Hotel and Restaurant.** (Tel. 46494. Roast of the day, vegetables, and potatoes £6. Live music.) **Lydon's**, on Main St. across from the supermarket, has the most trad. The **Quiet Man Coffee Shop**, Main St. (tel. 46034), is obviously obsessed. A bright, cheery street-front counter rides in tandem with a dark dining room overlooking a river; both are freckled with black and white memorabilia from the film. (Soup and sandwich £2.70. Open mid-Mar. to Oct. daily 10am-6:30pm.) The nearest nightclub, **The Valkenburg**, is in Ballinrobe; a bus picks groups up outside Danagher's weekend nights at around 11:30pm and drops them back at 3am. (Cover £5, bus £3.)

◘ SIGHTS. The heirs to the Guinness fortune, Lord and Lady Ardilaun, lived in **Ashford Castle** from 1852-1939, a structure as impressive as the lake itself. Today, big-deal diplomatic visitors use government funds to spend nights in the castle. *The Quiet Man* was shot on its grounds. The castle is closed to non-guests, but you can see the **gardens** for £3. Oscar Wilde once informed Lady Ardilaun that she could improve them by planting petunias in the shape of a pig, the family crest. Though his clever design was never brought to fruition, the grounds do hold exotic floral delights. A walk from the castle along Lough Corrib leads to a monument bearing Lady Ardilaun's alarming message to her lost Lord: "Nothing remains for me/What does remain is nothing."

The sculpted head of its last abbot keeps watches over the ruins of the 12th century **Royal Abbey of Cong**, near Danagher's Hotel in the village. (Always open. Free.) The last High King of a united Ireland, Ruairi ("Rory") O'Connor, retired to the abbey for his final 15 years of life, after multiple losses to Norman troops. Across the abbey grounds, a footbridge spans the **River Cong.** Past the **Monk's Fishing House** and to the right, the path leads to **Pigeon Hole, Teach Aille, Ballymaglancy caves** and finally to a 4000-year-old burial chamber, **Giant's Grave.** (Hostels lend out detailed cave maps.) Spelunkers have access to the caves, but **Kelly's Cave** is locked; the key

WATER, WATER, EVERYWHERE... Clonbur, where Mount Gable rises up above the flatness, was the site of a 19th century engineering disaster. The Dry Canal is a deep 4 mi. groove in the earth just east of Cong off the Galway road, near the Cong Hostel. Locks punctuate the useless canal as if water were flowing through it. While there is water aplenty in Ireland, not even fairies could make it stay in the porous chalk bed. The canal-opening ceremony in the 1840s was a surprising failure, as water that was let into the canal from Lough Mask promptly vanished into the absorbent walls. The canal could have been sealed and made useful, but by the 1850s trains had already replaced canals as the most efficient means of commercial transport, leaving the canal as hapless as its engineers.

is held at the Quiet Man Coffee Shop. Safe spelunking requires a friend who knows when to expect you back, two flashlights, waterproof gear, and caution. Spelunking with a partner is always safer and more fun; never enter a dark cave alone.

The Quiet Man Heritage Cottage (tel. 46089), a replica of a set from the film tries to make up for the fact that most of the film was actually shot on a Hollywood lot. "The quiet man will never die," the center's video promises. (£2.50, students £2. Open daily 10am-6pm.) Contestants come from all over Ireland for the extraordinary John Wayne and Maureen O'Hara look-alike contest, at the annual **Cong Midsummer Ball.** Gentlemen: practice your swagger.

WESTPORT

One of the few planned towns in the country, Westport (pop. 4300) still looks marvelous in the Georgian-period costumes of her designer. In the summer, Westport doesn't know quite how to accessorize the droves of visitors that traipse the tree-lined mall, central Octagon, and shop-encrusted Bridge Street. There's a range of activities to occupy tourists in town: savor its thriving pub life, drink tea at dapper cafes, shop for commemorative snow-globes, and admire the fresh coats of paint on the newest rash of B&Bs. Book ahead in July and August and go to the pubs early if you want to beat the crowds—beds, pint glasses, and bar stools fill up faster than you can say "no vacancy".

⌨ TRANSPORTATION

Trains: Trains arrive at the Altamont St. Station (tel. 25253 or 25329 for inquiries), a 5min. walk up on North Mall. Open M-Sa 9:30am-6pm, Su 2:15-6pm. The train goes to **Dublin** via **Athlone** (M-Th and Sa 3 per day, F and Su 2 per day; £15).

Buses: For bus info, call the tourist office. Buses leave from the Octagon on Mill St. and travel to **Ballina** (M-Sa 1-3 per day, Su 1 per day; £6.70), **Castlebar** (M-Sa 6 per day, £2.50), **Louisburgh** (M-Sa 3 per day, £3.20), **Galway** (M-F 6 per day, £8.80), and **Knock** (M-Sa 3 per day, Su 1 per day; £8.80).

Taxis: Brendan McGing, Lower Peter St. (tel. 25529). 50p per mi.

Bike Rental: Breheny & Sons, Castlebar St. (tel. 25020). £5 per day, £7 per 24hr., £35 per week; £30 deposit. Bikes can be dropped off in Galway.

🛈 ORIENTATION AND PRACTICAL INFORMATION

The tiny **Carrowbeg River** runs through **Westport's Mall** with **Bridge St.** and **James St.** extending south. **Shop St.** connects **Bridge St.** to **James St.** on the other end. Westport House and ferries to Clare Island are on **Westport Quay,** a 45min. walk west of town. The N60 passes through Clifden, Galway, and Sligo on its way to Westport. Hitchers proclaim it to be an easy route, but *Let's Go* still refuses to recommend hitchhiking.

Tourist Office: North Mall (tel. 25711). Open Apr.-Oct. M-Sa 9am-12:45pm and 2-5:45pm, July-Aug. also Su 10am-6pm.

Travel Agency: Westport Travel, 4 Shop St. (tel. 25511). Student discounts; Western Union Money Transfer point. Open M-Sa 9:30am-6pm.

Banks: Bank of Ireland, North Mall (tel. 25522), and **AIB,** Shop St. (tel. 25466), have **ATMs** and are both open M-W and F 10am-4pm, Th 10am-5pm.

Laundry: Westport Washeteria, Mill St. (tel. 25261), near the clock tower. Full service £4, self-service £2.50, powder 40p.

Pharmacy: O'Donnell's, Bridge St. (tel. 25163). Open M-Sa 9am-6:30pm. Rotating Su openings (12:30-2pm) are posted on the door.

Emergency: Dial 999; no coins required. **Garda:** Fair Green (tel. 25555).

Post Office: North Mall (tel. 25475). Open M-Sa 9am-noon and 2-5:30pm.

Internet Access: Dunning's Cyberpub, The Octagon (tel. 25161). A Guinness with your email? £5 per 30min. Open daily 9am-11:30pm.

PHONE CODE:	098.

▟ ACCOMMODATIONS

Westport's hostels are exceptional. Its B&Bs are easily spotted on the Castlebar and Altamont Rd. off North Mall. Most charge £18-20.

The Granary Hostel (tel. 25903), 1 mi. from town on Louisburgh Rd., near the main entrance to Westport House. The converted granary is flanked by a peacegarden and conservatory. Dorms £6. Open Jan.-Nov.

Old Mill Holiday Hostel (IHH), James St. (tel. 27045), between The Octagon and the tourist office. Character and comfort in a renovated mill and brewery. Kitchen and common room lockout 11pm-8am. Dorms £7. Sheets £1. Laundry £3.

Slí na h-Óige (HYI), North Mall. (tel. 28751). Appropriately named "the way of the young," this small, family-run hostel has comfortable beds, frequent trad, and Gaelic lessons upon request. Internet access £2 per 30min. Dorms £7. Open June-Sept.

Club Atlantic (IHH), Altamont St. (tel. 26644 or 26717), a 5min. walk up from the mall across from the train station. Popular with huge youth organizations, this massive 140-bed complex has recreational facilities, a shop, an elephantine kitchen, and an educational exhibition on Croagh Patrick. Dorms are quiet and comfortable. Guests can use sauna and swimming pool facilities at the nearby Westport Hotel for £4. June-Sept. dorms £6.50, doubles £13.80, singles £9; mid-Mar.-May and Oct. dorms £5.50, doubles £11.80, singles £9. **Camping** £4. Sheets £1. Laundry £2.

Dunning's Pub, The Octagon (tel. 25161). Centrally yet quietly located above a bustling pub and convenient internet cafe. Guests lounge with their pints and pizzas at sidewalk tables out front, surveying all the action. £17.

Altamont House, Altamont St. (tel. 25226). Enthusiastic guests wax poetic in the guest book. Roses peep in the windows wishing they could book a room—even though the garden is a modern Eden in itself. £17 per person, £19 with bath, £2-3 extra for singles.

◖ FOOD

The **country market** by the Town Hall at The Octagon vends farm-fresh vegetables, eggs, and milk. (Open Th 10:30am-1:30pm.) Processed foods are abundant at the **SuperValu** supermarket (tel. 27000) on Shop St. (Open M-W and Sa 8:30am-7:30pm, Th-F 8:30am-9pm, Su 10am-6pm.)

WESTERN IRELAND

McCormack's, Bridge St. (tel. 25619). Locals praise this teahouse's exemplary teas and pastries. Ravenous tourists devour huge sandwiches, salads, and hot dishes. Hot bacon bap £2.60, pasta salad £3.75. Open M-Tu and Th-Sa 10am-6pm.

Kinara Cafe (tel. 26029), in an alley off Bridge St. Trendy bistro serving inventive sandwiches, salads, and mouth-watering desserts. Thai chicken curry £6.95. Eat before 8pm and pay less. M-W 10am-6pm, Th-Sa 10am-10pm, Su 10am-4pm.

The Continental Health Food Shop and Cafe, High St. (tel. 26679). Enjoy succulent sandwiches (under £3) by the fireplace. Open Tu-Sa 10am-6pm.

The Urchin, Bridge St. (tel. 27532). A menu full of old favorites. Lunch is inexpensive (sandwiches about £3); dinner isn't, but does offer some good vegetarian options (spinach roulade £8.50). Open daily 10am-10pm; lunch served noon-3pm.

Cafolla, Bridge St. (tel. 25168). Incredibly cheap. 7 in. cheese pizza £1.75. Open June-Sept. M-Sa 11am-1am, Su noon-11pm; Oct.-May M-Sa 11am-11pm, Su 5-11pm.

PUBS

Search Bridge St. to find a *craic* dealer that suits you.

 Matt Molloy's, Bridge St. (tel. 26655). Owned by the flautist of the Chieftains. All the cool people, including his friends, go here. Officially, the trad sessions occur nightly at 9:30pm, but really anytime of the day is deemed appropriate. Go early and don't flout the back room if you like yours sitting down.

Henehan's Bar, Bridge St. (tel. 25561). A run-down exterior hides a vibrant pub. The beer garden in the back is ripe for people-watching; 20-somethings fight 80-somethings for space at the bar. Music nightly in summer, on weekends in winter.

The West (tel. 25886), at Bridge St. and South Mall, on the river. Choose between the light and creamy outside and the dark and woody inside. The teenage crowd is firmly in control of both. Live rock most summer nights.

O'Malley's Pub, Bridge St. (tel. 27308), across from Matt Molloy's. Smoke billows and Guinness flows. A winding, dark, and intriguing old-style pub. There's a big TV for the sports fans in the house and 80s music for everyone else. DJs F-Su.

Pete McCarthy's, Quay St. (tel. 27050), uphill from The Octagon. Old, dark, and smoky pub attracts regulars. Trad on weekends in summer.

The Towers, The Quay (tel. 26534), 1 mi. from town center. Fishing nets and excellent grub hook lots of customers. Beef in Guinness. Meals £5-10. Music F-Su in summer, F-Sa in winter.

The only disco in town is in the **Castlecourt Hotel,** Castlebar St. The guitars on the walls give an uninspired nod to the Hard Rock Cafe, but the computerized lighting effects are unique. (Cover £5. Open F-Su. 18 and older.)

▧ SIGHTS

The current commercial uses of **Westport House** must be a bitter pill to swallow for its elite inhabitant, Lord Altamont, the 13th great-grandson of Grace O'Malley (see **Amazing Grace**, p. 127). The zoo and train ride may entertain children, but the carnival and terrifying bog butter in the museum are hardly worth the entrance fee. (Tel. 25430. Open May and early Sept. daily 2-5pm; June to late Aug. M-Sa 11:30am-6pm, Su 1:30-7; July to mid-Aug. M-Sa 10:30am-6pm, Su 2-6pm. May-June and Sept. £5, July-Aug. £6. £4 discount 2-6pm.) The grounds, on the other hand, are beautiful and free. To get there, take James St. above The Octagon, bear right, and follow the signs to the Quay (45min.). More interesting is the **Clew Bay Heritage Centre** at the end of the Quay. The narrow interior crams together a pair of James Connolly's gloves, a sash belonging to John MacBride, and a stunning original photograph of Maud Gonne. A genealogical service is also available. (Tel. 26852. Open July-Sept. M-F 10am-5pm, Su 2-5pm; Oct.-June M-F noon-3pm. £1.)

Conical **Croagh Patrick** rises 2510 ft. over Clew Bay. The summit has been revered as a holy site for thousands of years. Perhaps because of its height, it was sacred to Lug, Sun God, God of Arts and Crafts, and one-time ruler of the Túatha de Danann (see **Legends and Folktales**, p. 20). St. Patrick worked it here in 441, praying and fasting for 40 days and nights, arguing with angels, and then banishing snakes from Ireland. The deeply religious climb Croagh Patrick barefoot on Lughnasa, the last Sunday in July, Lug's holy night. Others climb the mountain just for the exhilaration and the view. It takes about four hours total to climb and descend the mountain. Be warned that the ascent can be quite steep and the footing unsure. Well-shod climbers start their excursion from the 15th century **Murrisk Abbey**, several miles west of Westport on R395 toward Louisburgh. Buses go to Murrisk (July-Aug. M-F 3 per day, Sept.-Sa 2 per day), but a cab (tel. 27171) is cheaper for three people and more convenient. Pilgrims and hikers also set out for Croagh Patrick along the Tóchar Phádraiga path from **Ballintubber Abbey** (tel. (094) 30709), several miles south of Castlebar and 22 mi. from Croagh Patrick. Founded in 1216 by King of Connacht Cathal O'Connor, the abbey still functions as a religious center. In late September, Westport celebrates its annual **Westport Arts Festival** (tel. 28833) with a week of free concerts, poetry readings, and plays.

CLARE ISLAND

An isolated, scenic dot in the Atlantic, Clare Island (pop. 170) feels like a contemporary rural village that just happens to be out in the ocean. The school, church, and grocer are 1½ mi. straight along the harbor road. Grace O'Malley, known locally as Granuaile, ruled the 16th century seas west of Ireland from her castle above the beach. Her notorious fleet swiftly and brutally exacted tolls from all ships entering and leaving Galway Bay (see **Amazing Grace,** p. 127). Granuaile died in 1603 and was supposedly laid to rest here under the ruins of the **Clare Island Abbey,** near the shop. Her descendants make sure that no new surnames make it onto the island. Hiking around the deserted island is fun when it's clear; a leaflet with five walks is available at the hotel or souvenir shop. You can search for buried treasure on the west coast of the island, where the cliffs of **Knockmore Mountain** (1550 ft.) rise from the sea. **Ozzy** (tel. 45120) runs off-road tours of the island out of his dockside souvenir shop (2hr., £5, 4-person min.). Charlie O'Malley's **Ocean Star Ferry** (tel. 25045) and the **Clare Island Ferry** (tel. 26307) leave from **Roonah Point,** (25min.; July-Aug. 5 per day, May-June and Sept. 3-5 per day; Oct.-Apr. call to schedule; £10 return; bikes free). The **phone code** is 098.

O'Leary's Bike Hire is near the harbor (£5 per day); if no one's there, knock at **Beachside B&B** (tel. 25640). Their clean en suite rooms and warm hospitality are yours for £15. Just past the beach, the **Sea Breeze B&B** (tel. 26746) offers similar comforts for the same price. **O'Malley's Cois Abhain** (tel. 26216) is 3 mi. from the harbor, but the proprietor will pick you up. She also whips up huge evening meals and packs lunches for island explorers. (Singles £18, doubles £30. Packed lunch £3, dinner £12.) **O'Malley's store** (tel. 26987) has the island's staples. (Open daily 11am-6pm.) **McCabe's Coffeeshop** (tel. 26250), by the pier, serves snacks, soups, and rolls for under £3 each. Clare's only pub, in the **Bay View Hotel** (tel. 26307), to the right along the coast from the harbor, pours pints until 2am.

ACHILL ISLAND

Two decades ago, Achill (AK-ill) Island was Co. Mayo's most popular holiday refuge. Its popularity has inexplicably dwindled, but Ireland's biggest little island is still one of its most beautiful and personable. Ringed by glorious beaches and cliffs, Achill's interior consists of acres of bog and a few mountains. The town of Achill Sound, the gateway to the island, has the nicest hostel and the most amenities, while Keel has more promising nightlife. Connecting to Keel and forming a flat strip along Achill's longest beaches, the seaside resorts of Pollagh and Dooagh serve as brief stopovers for bikers, hillwalkers, and motorists. Dugort, in the north, is less busy, but its hostel, pub, and restaurant can sustain any backpacker. Achill's most potent vistas are farther west in Keem Bay and at Croaghaun Mountain. During the first two weeks of August, the island hosts the **Scoil Acla** (tel. 45284), a festival of traditional music and art.

Buses run infrequently over the bridge from Achill Sound, Dugort, Keel, and Dooagh to **Westport, Galway,** and **Cork** (summer M-Sa 5 per day, winter M-Sa 2 per day), and to **Sligo, Enniskillen,** and **Belfast** (summer M-Sa 3 per day, winter 2 per day). Hitchers report relative success during July and August, but cycling is more reliable and preferred by *Let's Go*. The island's **tourist office** (tel. 47353) is next to Ted Lavelle's Esso station in Cashel, on the main road from Achill Sound to Keel. (Open daily 10am-5pm.) True island explorers will pay £3.35 for Bob Kingston's map and guide, but there's a freebie for the rest. There's no bank on the island, so change money on the mainland or suffer rates worthy of Grace O'Malley. The **phone code** is 098.

ACHILL SOUND

Achill Sound's convenient location at the island's entrance warrants the high concentration of shops and services in its center. Practicality isn't the only reason to stop in Achill Sound: an internationally famous stigmatic and faith healer sets up her House of Prayer here. She draws thousands to the attention-starved town each year. Townspeople are divided between utter skepticism and complete awe of her powers, but universally grateful for the business. About 6 mi. south of Achill Sound and left at the first crossroads, two sets of ruins stand near each other. The ancient **Church of Kildavnet** was founded by St. Dympna when she fled to Achill Island to escape her father's incestuous desires. The remains of **Kildavnet Castle,** really a fortified tower house dating from the 1500s, proudly crumble nearby. Grace O'Malley, the swaggering, seafaring pirate of medieval Ireland, once owned the castle. The spectacular Atlantic Drive, which roams along the craggy south coast past beautiful beaches to Dooagh, makes a fantastic bike ride.

The town has a **post office** with a bureau de change (tel. 45141; open M-F 9am-12:30pm and 1:30-5:30pm, Sa 9am-1pm), a **SuperValu supermarket** (open daily 9am-7pm), and a **pharmacy** (tel. 45248; open July-Aug. M-Sa 9:30am-6pm, Sept.-June Tu-Sa 9:30am-6pm). **Achill Sound Hotel** (tel. 45245) **rents bikes.** (£6 per day, £30 per week; deposit £40. Open daily 9am-9pm.) **The Wild Haven Hostel** (tel. 45392), a block left past the church, glows with polished floors and antique furniture. The sunny, conservatory doubles as a swanky dining room. (Dorms £7.50, private rooms £10 per person. **Camping** £4. Breakfast £3.50; candle-lit dinner £12.50. Sheets £1. Laundry £5. Lockout 11am-3:30pm, except on rainy days.) The **Railway Hostel,** just before the bridge to town, is a simple affair in the old station (the last train arrived in the 1930s). The proprietors can be found at **Mace Supermarket** (tel. 45187) in town. They have the keys to the place, and a massive volume with all the info you could possibly need for any length stay. (Dorms £6, private rooms with bath £7 per person. Sheets £1. Laundry £1.50.) Opposite the Railway Hostel, **Alice's Harbour Bar** (tel. 45138) flaunts gorgeous views, a stonework homage to the deserted village, and a boat-shaped bar. (Bar food £4-6. Served noon-6pm. Music on weekends.)

KEEL

Keel is a pleasantly outdated resort at the bottom of a flat, wide valley. The sandy **Trawmore Strand** sweeps three miles eastward, flanked by cliffs. Encouraged by a government tax scheme, hundreds of holiday developments have sprung up like dandelions across the valley in the past three years. Two miles north of Keel on the road looping back to Dugort, the self-explanatory **Deserted Village** is populated only by stone houses that were used until the late 1930s by cattle ranchers. Resist the temptation to crawl up and around the existing structures: not only are many of them dangerously unstable, but doing so will incur the wrath of the bloodthirsty archeologists who rove the site in the summer months when the **Archaeological Summer School** hits town. (Call Theresa McDonald, tel. (0506) 21627.)

O'Malley's Island Sports center (tel. 43125) **rents bikes.** (£7 per day, £40 per week. Open daily 9am-6pm). The common areas of the **Wayfarer Hostel (IHH)** (tel. 43266) are almost as expansive as the views. (Dorms £6, private rooms £6.50 per person. Sheets 50p. Laundry £2.50. Open mid-Mar. to mid-Oct.) Keel is home to at least two prayer-answering B&Bs. Mrs. Joyce's **Marian Villa** (tel. 43134), is a 20-room hotel/ B&B with thoughtfully decorated rooms, and a veranda that looks onto the sea. The panoramic breakfast buffet will keep you going all day, and then some. (Rooms with bath start at £20.) **Roskeel House** (tel. 43537) has newly refurnished, spacious suites. Its sea views can be enjoyed a block behind the Annexe Inn. (£18- 25. Open Easter-Oct.) Cowering in the shadow of impressive cliffs, the **Keel Sandy- banks Caravan and Camping Park** (tel. 43211) provides a sandy spot to drive your tent stakes into. (July-Aug. £6.50 per tent, late May-June and Sept. £5.)

Spar market sells crisps and biscuits. (Open M-Sa 9:30am-9pm, Su 9am-6pm.) Although Keel has numerous chippers, more nutritious food and sweaters are available at **Beehive Handcrafts and Coffee Shop** (tel. 43134). Salads, sandwiches, and home-baked goodies delight; the apple-rhubarb pie is orgasmic. (Open daily 10am-6:30pm.) **Calvey's** (tel. 43158), next to Spar market, whips up hearty meals. (Catch of the day £6. Open daily 10am-10pm.) Inspired drinking is encouraged at the very vinyl **Annexe Inn** (tel. 43268); music is applauded at nightly sessions during July and August, and Saturdays other months.

DOOAGH

Corrymore House, 2 mi. up the road from Keel in Dooagh (DOO-ah), was one of sev- eral Co. Mayo estates owned by Captain Boycott, whose mid-19th century tenants went on an extended rent strike that verbed his surname. **The Pub** (tel. 43120), Main St., is managed by the beloved mistress of the house. A grueling bike ride over the cliffs to the west of Dooagh leads to the blue-flag **Keem Bay** beach, the most beautiful spot on the island, wedged between the seas and great green walls of weed, rock, and sheep. Basking sharks, earth's second-largest fish, were once fished off Keem Bay, but bathers who don't look like plankton have nothing to fear. A river of amethyst runs through the Atlantic and comes up in **Croaghaun Mountain,** west of Keem Bay. Most of the accessible crystals have been plundered, but Frank Macnamara, an old local, still digs out the deeper veins with a pick and a shovel, and sells them from his store in Dooagh. The mountains, climbable from Keem Bay, provide bone-chilling views of the **Croaghaun Cliffs,** contenders in the Irish contest to be the highest sea cliffs in Europe.

DUGORT

A right turn after Cashel leads to the northern part of the island, where Dugort, a tiny hamlet perched atop a sea cliff, has slept through the 20th century and will likely sleep through the 21st. Mist-shrouded **Slievemore Mountain** looms to its east. Curious Germans come here to see the former cottage of Heinrich Böll, now a retreat for artists-in-residence. His favorite pub, **The Valley,** serves pints to literary pilgrims. Cemeteries and abandoned buildings west of Dugort are the result of a futile mid-1800s effort to convert the islanders to Protestantism by sending in Irish-speaking missionaries. On the other side of Slievemore Mountain lives **Giant's Grave,** a chambered tomb easily accessible from Dugort. Other megalithic tombs lurk nearby. The main tomb, a mile past McDowell's Hotel, up the main road past Keel, is sign-posted and the easiest to find. Boats leave for the **seal caves** from the pier at Dugort up the road from the Strand Hotel daily at 11am and 6pm.

A soft pillow for your head awaits at **Valley House Hostel** (tel. 47204). The 100- year-old house is a fading beauty, where sturdy bunks keep company with antique furniture, massive windows, and stately views. An in-house pub is the most luxuri- ous amenity. (Dorms £7. Open Easter-Oct.) The brutal maiming of the woman who once owned the house was the basis of Synge's play *Playboy of the Western World* (see **Irish Literary Revival,** p. 23). The road to the hostel turns left off the main road 2 mi. east of Dugort at the valley crossroads. Nearby, self-proclaimed seafood specialist **Atoka Restaurant** (tel. 47229) feeds hearty portions to local fans. (Entrees £6-12. Open daily May to late Sept. 8:30am-11pm.) Those who stay for B&B get a bed and breakfast. (£15, with bath £16.) **Seal Caves Caravan and Camping Park** (tel. 43262) lies between Dugort Beach and Slievemore Mountain. Check in up the road at the blue house/shop. (July-Aug. £3 per person, Apr.-June and Sept. £2.50.)

MULLET PENINSULA

Other than anglers ogling the 38 varieties of fish swimming off the west coast, few visitors make it out to the Mullet Peninsula. The blue-flag beaches are therefore empty, and outsiders are welcomed with genuine Irish hospitality. Cold Atlantic winds rip into the barren western half; soggy moorland covers the middle. Budget accommodations are scarce. Remote Belmullet, with the most amenities, occupies the isthmus between Broad Haven and Blacksod Bay. Irish is spoken farther down, where farms and small white cottages dot the bogland.

7 PRACTICAL INFORMATION. An infrequent **bus** service runs the length of the peninsula from **Ballina** (M-Sa July-Aug. 2 per day, Sept.-June 1 per day; £7.50). The **Erris Tourist Information Centre**, in the Haven Shop on Barrack St. (tel. 81500), is amazingly helpful. (Open June-Sept. daily 9:30am-7:30pm, Oct.-May M-Sa 9am-5:30pm.) **Lavelle's Bar** (tel. 81372) provides solid, unofficial info to everyone else. The **Bank of Ireland** (tel. 81311) has an **ATM**. (Open M-W and F 10am-12:30pm and 1:30-4pm, Th 10am-12:30pm and 1:30-5pm.) **Belmullet Cycle Centre,** American St. (tel. (086) 237 7069), **rents bikes.** (£7 per day. Open M-Sa 10:30am-6pm.) **Centra Supermarket** is on Main St. (Open M-Sa 9am-9:30pm.) The **post office** (tel. 81032) is at the end of Main St. (Open M and W-Sa 9am-2pm and 3-5:30pm, Tu 9:30am-5:30pm). The **phone code** is a late-night 097.

█▐█ ACCOMMODATIONS, FOOD, AND PUBS. The relaxing **Kilcommon Lodge Hostel** (tel. 84621) is in Pollatomish, 10 mi. northeast of Belmullet. The rooms are clean, the common rooms cozy, and evening meals prepared with love. Bunnies, ducks, and other woodland characters are live lawn-ornaments. Owners advise on hiking routes. (Dorms £6, private rooms £7 per person.) Just after the hostel, the new **Cuan na Farraige** dive center (tel. 87800) provides B&B (£18), dinner, and water sports. **Mairín Murphy** (tel. 81195) runs Belmullet's nicest B&B from her turquoise house 350 yd. up the hill from Padden's; a studio apartment suite and meals available. (Singles £23.50, doubles £34.) Half a block down from the square, the good ol' fashioned **Mill House B&B,** American St. (tel. 81181), near the bridge, has cute rooms and cheery conversation. (Singles £13, doubles £26.) The **Western Strands Hotel** (tel. 91096), Main St., is close to the pubs and provides breakfast and bath for all. (Singles £17, doubles £30.)

   The Appetizer (tel. 82222) sells sandwiches and desserts. (Open daily 9am-3pm.) Belmullet's pub scene is purely *craic* and locals. **Lavelle's** (tel. 81372) provides expensive, hearty dinners and just-as-filling but half-as-expensive pub fare (£4-6). At night, the crowds come to Lavelle's for Belmullet's best pints. Portraits of Mayo hurlers adorn the walls of **Lenehan's** (tel. 81098), the first and last stop on the old men's gossip circuit. **Clan Lir,** Main St., popular with the young, gets packed during football games. Knock if the doors are closed. Birdwatchers flock to the **Anchor Bar,** Barrack St. (tel. 81007), which records ornithological sightings; the nightclub out back opens on weekends. (Cover £5.)

◎ SIGHTS. The **Ionad Deirbhle Heritage Centre,** in Aughleam at the end of the peninsula, explores items of local interest, including the history of the whaling industry and the Inishkey (Inis Gé) islands. (Tel. 85728. Open Easter-Oct. 10am-6pm. £2.) **Josephine and Matt Geraghty** (tel. 85741) run boat trips to the islands, which were inhabited until a disastrous fishing accident in 1935 (1 per day in summer, 3 per week in winter; £12 per person, 6 person minimum). Fly fishing abounds from both shore and boat in nearby **Cross Lake**; contact **George Geraghty** (tel. 81492). The **Belmullet Sea Angling Competition** (tel. 81076), in mid-July, awards £2 per pound for the heaviest halibut. The **Feille Iorras** peninsula-wide music festival (tel. 81147) will be held the last weekend in July.

BALLINA

What Knock is to the Marian cult, Ballina (bah-lin-AH) is to the religion of bait and tackle. Hordes in olive green waders invade the town each year during the salmon season (Feb.-Sept.). Ballina, however, has non-ichthyological attractions as well, including lovely vistas, river walks, and a raging weekend pub scene. Almost everyone in a 50 mi. radius, from sheep farmers to students, packs into town on Saturday nights. Former Irish President Mary Robinson grew up in Ballina and refined her political skills in the town's 40-odd pubs (see **Current Issues,** p. 17).

TRANSPORTATION

Trains: Station Rd. (tel. 71818), near the bus station. Open M-F 7:30am-6pm, Sa 9am-1pm and 3:15-6pm. Service to **Dublin** via **Athlone** (M-Sa 3 per day, £15). From the station, go left, bear right and walk 4 blocks to reach the town center.

Buses: Station Rd. (tel. 71800 or 71825). Open M-Sa 9:30am-6pm. Buses to **Westport** (1½hr.; M-Sa 3 per day, Su 1 per day; £10), **Sligo** (2hr., M-Sa 3-4 per day, £7.30), **Galway** (3hr.; M-Sa 9 per day, Su 5 per day; £9.70), **Athlone** (1 per day, £11), and **Dublin** via **Mullingar** (4hr., 3 per day, £8). From the bus station, turn right and take the first left; the city center is a 5min. walk.

Taxis: Mulherin Taxi Service, The Brook (tel. 22583 or 21783).

Bike Rental: Gerry's Cycle Centre, 6 Lord Edward St. (tel. 70455). £7 per day, £30 per week. Collection service available. Open M-Sa 9am-7pm.

ORIENTATION AND PRACTICAL INFORMATION

Ballina's commercial center is on the west bank of the **River Moy**. A bridge crosses over to the cathedral and tourist office on the east bank. The bridge connects to **Tone St.**, which turns into **Tolan St.** This strip intersects **Pearse St.** and **O'Rahilly St.**, which run parallel to the river, to form Ballina's center.

Tourist Office: Cathedral Rd. (tel. 70848), on the river by St. Muredach's Cathedral. Open June-Aug. M-Sa 10am-1pm and 2-5:30pm.

Banks: Bank of Ireland, Pearse St. (tel. 21144). Open M-W and F 10am-4pm, Th 10am-5pm. **Irish Permanent Building Society,** Pearse St. (tel. 22777). Open M-F 9:30am-5pm. Both have an **ATM.**

Bookstore: Keohane's, Arran St. (tel. 21475), stocks the best regional guidebooks. Open M-Sa 8am-6:30pm, Su 8am-1:30pm.

Laundry: Moy Laundrette, Cathedral Rd. (tel. 22358). Wash and dry £4.50. Open M-Sa. 9am-6pm.

Pharmacy: S. Quinn and Sons, Pearse St. (tel. 21365). Open M-Sa 9am-6pm.

Emergency: Dial 999; no coins required. **Garda:** Walsh St. (tel. 21422).

Post Office: Casement St. (tel. 21498). Open M-Sa 9am-5:30pm.

Internet Access: Moy Valley Resources, 7-0905 in the same building as the tourist office. Open Easter-Sept. M-Sa 10am-1pm and 2-5:30pm.

PHONE CODE:	096 sings "super pub grub, super pub grub."

ACCOMMODATIONS

Hogan's American House (tel. 70582), a restful, family-run place with a dated but dignified interior, has a convenient location just up from the bus station. (Singles £15, doubles £25 for *Let's Go* readers. Breakfast £5.) Dozens of nearly identical B&Bs line the main approach roads into town. The river, the lake, and sea fishing are just a cast away from Ms. Corrigan's **Greenhill** (tel. 22767), on Cathedral Close behind the tourist office. (£18, with bath £20; £5.50 extra for single.) Two doors down, Breda Walsh's **Suncraft** (tel. 21573) is a another good option. (Doubles with bath £34.) A few miles from town on the road to Enniscrone, the luxurious **Red River B&B** offers clean, huge rooms and breakfasts whipped up by the friendly family that runs it. **Belleek Camping and Caravan Park** (tel. 71533) is 2 mi. from Ballina toward Killala on R314, behind the Belleek Woods. (£4 per person with tent. Laundry and kitchen available. Open Mar.-Oct.)

◖▲ FOOD AND PUBS

Aspiring gourmets can prepare for a feast at the **Quinnsworth** supermarket (tel. 21056) on Market Rd. (Open M-W 9am-7pm, Th-F 9am-9pm, Sa 9am-6pm.) Pubs and restaurants tend to go hand in hand in Ballina; get the same food for half the price by sitting in the pub. **Cafolla's** (tel. 21029), just up from the bridge, is fast, cheap, and almost Italian. (Open M-Sa 10am-12:30pm.) **Tullio's,** Pearse St. (tel. 70815), exudes elegance and has pleasantly surprising prices. Gourmet pizzas, burgers, and pasta dishes around £5-7. (Restaurant open daily noon-3pm and 6-10pm; bar food served noon-10pm.) **Humbert's Restaurant,** Pearse St. (tel. 71520), is a local coffee and tea shop that provides cheap eats. (£2-5.)

Gaughan's has been pulling the best pint in town since 1936. No music or TV—just conversation, snugs, great grub, and homemade snuff. Jolly, musical drinkers are fixtures of **The Parting Glass** (tel. 72714) on Tolan St. (Weekly trad sessions.) Down by the river on Clare St., the **Murphy Bros.** (tel. 22702) serve pints to twentysomethings amongst dark wood furnishings. They also dish out superb pub grub. The restaurant upstairs is Ballina's best (and priced accordingly). The rest of the town's youngsters crowd the **Broken Jug** (tel. 72379) on O'Rahilly St., and **The Loft** (tel. 21881), a dark, intimate cellar bar on Pearse St. (Music Tu-F and Su.) **Doherty's** (tel. 21150), by the bridge, revels in the angling lifestyle. (Trad Th and Sa.) **An Bolg Bui** (tel. 22561) next door is Irish for "the yellow belly." The pub calls itself a "young fisherperson's pub" and sells tackle and licenses along with pints. Belleek Castle is an expensive hotel, but its **Armada Bar,** built from an actual 500-year-old Spanish wreck, is accessible and affordable. Downstairs, another bar occupies a medieval banquet hall. Of Ballina's four clubs, **Longneck's** (tel. 22702), behind Murphy's, is the most popular. (Cover £3-5. Open July-Aug. Tu-Su. 21 and over.) **The Pulse,** behind the Broken Jug, is a close second. (Cover £3-5. Open W and F-Su.)

░ SIGHTS

The bird-rich **Belleek Woods** (bah-LEEK) around Belleek Castle are a fairytale forest with an astonishing bird-to-tree-to-stream ratio. To reach the Belleek Woods entrance, cross the lower bridge near the cathedral on Pearse St. and keep Ballina House on your right. At the back of the railway station is the **Dolmen of the Four Maols,** locally called "Table of the Giants." The dolmen, which dates back to 2000 BC, is said to be the burial site of four Maols who murdered Ceallach, a 7th century bishop. They were hanged at Ardaree, then commemorated with a big rock. The lonely **Ox Mountains** east of Ballina are cyclable. Dirt and asphalt trails criss-cross their way up the slopes. The 44 mi. **Ox Mountain Drive** traces the scenic perimeter of the mountains and is well sign-posted from Tobercurry (21 mi. south of Sligo on the N17). The **Western Way** footpath begins in the Ox mountains and winds its way past Ballina through Newport and Westport, ending up in Connemara. Tourist offices sell complete guides. Equestrian enthusiasts can ride at the **Ardchuan Lodge** (tel. 45084), 5 mi. north of Ballina on the Sligo road. (Pony trekking £10 per hr.)

The annual, week-long **Ballina Street Festival** (tel. 70905) has been swinging mid-July since 1964. All of Co. Mayo turns up for the festival's **Heritage Day,** when the streets are closed off and life reverts to the year 1910. All the flashier aspects of traditional Irish life are staged, including greasy pig contests.

NEAR BALLINA

N59 and N26 puncture Ballina; R297 off N59 northwest runs to Enniscrone, a quintessential Irish sea spot. Cute Killala, boggy Ballycastle, and the archaeological extravaganza of Ceide Fields are threaded onto R314 north. The remote and seemingly innocuous stone bridge, known as the ▨**Musical Bridge,** fords the Owenmore River. Curious marks run the length of the stone walls on either side, and a pile of small stones sits on each end. To play a tune on the bridge, run full speed from end to end, dragging a stone across the top of the handrail.

ENNISCRONE (INISHCRONE)

Eight miles northeast of Ballina on scenic Quay Rd. (R297), the gorgeous Enniscrone Strand stretches along the east shore of Killala Bay. On sunny summer days Irish weekenders vie for towel space. Most days, however, the miles of sand are unpopulated. Zillions of new holiday homes sprawl around the town and behind the beach. Across from the beach, the family-run **Kilcullen's Bath House** (tel. 36238) simmers. Steam baths in cedar wood cabinets and cool seaweed baths relax even the most tense of travelers. (Steam bath ₤10 per 30min. Seaweed bath ₤8, with steam bath. Massage ₤15. Towels supplied.) A tea room with views of the strand awaits post-soak. (Open daily July-Aug. 10am-10pm; May-June and Sept.-Oct. 10am-9pm; Nov.-Apr. 11am-8pm.) **Fishing** enthusiasts should contact John McDonagh (tel. 45332) for guidance and equipment. An unofficial **tourist office** hides off Pier Rd. (Open M-F 11am-7pm.) The **phone code,** 096, skips the light fantastic.

 Gowan House B&B, Pier Rd. (tel. 36396), is set just back from the sea. The big bedrooms are decorated in bright colors and finished off with Baltic Pine. (₤17 with bath.) Maura O'Dowd's **Point View House,** Main St. (tel. 36312), serves a home-style dinner (₤9) before sending you to a comfortable night's sleep. (₤15 with bath.) **The Atlantic Caravan Park** (tel. 36132) puts some grass under your tent. (₤5 per tent. Laundry facilities.) **Walsh's Pub,** Main St. (tel. 36110), serves great pub grub all day and hosts weekly music sessions. **Harnett's Bar,** Main St. (tel. 36137), cooks good but pricey food amid matchbox-covered walls. (Food served 1-2:30pm and 6-8pm.)

BALLYCASTLE, CEIDE FIELDS, AND KILLALA

Ballycastle is a strip of houses, shops, and pubs bordered by rich farmland and holiday cottages on one side and bog on the other. By offering housing and studio space, the Ballinglen Arts Foundation has brought several prominent and emerging artists to Ballycastle. Bus Éireann has a service to **Killala** and **Ballina** (M-Sa 1 per day, ₤5). **Ulster Bank** opens its mini-office Tuesdays from 10am to noon.

 Palatial digs (with bath), huge meals, and potpourri under the pillow grace **Mrs. Chambers' Suantai B&B** (tel. 43040), on the Killala road. (Singles ₤20, doubles ₤32.) **Ceide House Restaurant** (tel. 43105), has Mayo cuisine. (Entrees ₤5-7. Open daily 9am-9pm.) They also offer comfortable lodgings in the center of town. (₤13 per person, with bath ₤15.) **Mary's Bakery** (tel. 43361), whips up baked goods and scrumptious lunch specials. (Open daily 10am-6pm.) **McNamee's Supermarket** (tel. 43057) sells peanut butter, jelly, and more. (Open daily 9am-10pm.) Dark, low-ceilinged **Katie Mac's** (tel. 43031) wears its blackened floorboards and ancient walls with pride. (Trad on weekends; sing-alongs known to happen.)

 A small brochure from the tourist office (20p) outlines three walks around the area. One follows a bucolic path to the ocean, the **Dun Briste** seastack, and stoic **Downpatrick Head.** The multi-layered rock formation supposedly broke off from the mainland during a dispute between St. Patrick and a pagan king; St. Patrick used the geological disturbance to prove God's power. The **North Mayo Sculpture Trail** follows the R314 from Ballina to Belmullet. Fifteen modern sculptors have created site-specific installations of earth and stone to celebrate the rugged wilderness of north Mayo; brown "Tír Sáile" signs mark the trail.

Five miles west toward the Mullet Peninsula, the **Ceide** (KAYJ-uh) **Fields** are open to visitors through an **interpretive center,** which offers exhibits, films, and guided tours of the largest excavated neolithic landscape in the world. The center itself is particularly interesting: a tall, incongruous pyramid of peat and glass, constructed around a 5000-year-old Scotch pine that had been dug out of the bog. If all the muck gets you down, the 350 million-year-old **Ceide Cliffs** rise high nearby. (Tel. 43325. Tours every hr., film every 30min. £2.50, students £1. Open daily June-Sept. 9:30am-6:30pm, mid-March to May and Oct. 10am-5pm, Nov. 10am-4:30pm.)

Eight miles south of Ballycastle along the Ballina road is **Killala,** a charming seaport best known as the site of the French Invasion of 1798 (see **Rebellion, Union, and Reaction,** p. 10). 1067 French soldiers landed at Killala to join the United Irishmen under Wolfe Tone in a revolt against the British. Instead of finding a well-armed band of revolutionaries, the French found a smattering of poor, Irish-speaking peasants. Undeterred, they pressed on with the revolution, winning a significant victory at Castlebar before being soundly hammered by British forces at Ballnamuck.

KNOCK

At 8pm on August 21, 1879, St. Joseph, St. John, and the Virgin Mary appeared at Knock with a cross, a lamb, an altar, and a host of angels. The vision materialized before at least 15 witnesses, who stood in the rain for two hours watching the apparitions and chanting the Rosary. The Catholic hierarchy endorsed the miracle, and Knock quickly developed into a major pilgrimage site, with over 1.5 million pilgrims visiting each year. The streets overflow with entrepreneurs hawking anything and everything emblazoned with the Knock label, while the churches fill with serious prayer.

■ **PRACTICAL INFORMATION.** Knock lies between Galway and Sligo on N17. The **Horan Cutríl Airport** (tel. 67222), 11 mi. north of town near Charlestown, is the subject of a tune by Christy Moore, and attracts pilgrim cash with direct flights to the U.K. **Bus Éireann** stops at Coleman's and Lennon's; buses depart for **Westport** (Su 1 per day, £9), **Sligo** (Su 3 per day, £7.70), and **Dublin** (2 per day, Su 1 per day; £10). Knock's **tourist office** (tel. 88193) is suitably central. (Open daily May-Sept. 10am-5pm.) Inside the office is **Bank of Ireland.** (Open May-Oct. M and Th 10:15am-12:15pm, Nov.-Apr. M 10:15am-12:15pm.) The **shrine office** (tel. 88100), across the street, sells Knock literature, official calendars, and the *Knock Pilgrim's Guide* (10p), which has prayers and a useful map. (Open daily June-Oct. 9am-8:30pm, Nov. 10am-6pm.) The **post office** (tel. 88209) is in the Spar by the traffic circle. (Open Tu-Sa 9am-5:30pm, M 9am-1pm.) **Phone code** 094, is on a religious tour.

■■■ **ACCOMMODATIONS, FOOD, AND PUBS.** "Hostels" in town are for the sick or elderly, but B&Bs line the roads into town. Mrs. Kelly's **Cara** (tel. 88315), on Kiltamagh Rd., is particularly welcoming, if ascetic. (Singles £15, doubles £30.) **Knock Caravan and Camping** (tel. 88223) is 5min. from the church on the Claremorris side. (July-Aug. £6 per tent, plus 25p per person; single backpacker £4; Mar.-June and Sept.-Oct. £5.50 per tent, 25p per person; single backpacker £3.50. Laundry £3.50.) The **Knock International Hotel,** Main St. (tel. 88466) has clean, centrally located rooms; in July and August they're as scarce as atheists. (Rooms from £12, B&B from £16.) **Beirne's Restaurant** (tel. 88161), on the main road offers a set 3-course lunch and enough tables to seat bus loads of worshippers. (£6.75. Lunch served noon-3pm. Open daily noon-6pm.) **Ard Mhuire's** (tel. 88459) is a split-level restaurant on Main St. that serves buffet style food. (All entrees under £4. Open Apr.-Oct. 10am-7:30pm.)

SIGHTS. Knock's religious sights cluster around the shrine built on the site of the Apparition. Numerous healings are believed to have occurred in the courtyard. The monumental **Church of Our Lady** holds 20,000 people for mass. (Services M-Sa at 8, 9, 11am, noon, 3, and 7:30pm; Su 8, 9:30, 11am, noon, 3, and 7pm.) Free holy water is dispensed near the shrine. **The Knock Folk Museum,** to the right of the basilica, portrays rural 19th century life. (Tel. 88100. Open daily July-Aug. 10am-7pm, May-June and Sept.-Oct. 10am-6pm. £2, students £1.50.) The thatched-cottage and the old photographs of Irish life are the best reasons to visit. Knock's biggest festival, the **Feast of Our Lady of Knock,** is on August 21.

WESTERN IRELAND

NORTHWEST IRELAND

The farmland of the upper Shannon spans northward into Co. Sligo's mountains, lakes, and ancient monuments. A mere sliver of land connects Co. Sligo to Co. Donegal, the second-largest and most remote of the Republic's counties, with its most spectacular scenery. Donegal's *gaeltacht* is a storehouse of genuine, unadulterated Irish tradition. Hitchhikers report that the upper Shannon region is difficult to thumb through; drivers in Donegal provide the most rides in all of Ireland. Easy or hard, *Let's Go* does not recommend hitchhiking.

HIGHLIGHTS OF NORTHWEST IRELAND

■ **Sligo** (p. 340) is surrounded by **Benbulben, Drumcliffe,** and other sites made famous by W.B. Yeats's poetry.

■ Start your trek up the **Slieve League Peninsula** (p. 359) at the boisterous pubs of **Donegal Town** (p. 356). **Kilcar** (p. 361) and **Glencolmcille** (p. 362) provide an excellent night's rest before your hike up the tallest seacliffs in Europe at the peninsula's tip.

■ **Gweedore** (p. 370) is Ireland's largest *gaeltacht*, and the verdent setting of **Glenveagh National Park** (p. 375), myth-bedecked **Bunbeg** (p. 371), and the **Poison Glen** (p. 370).

■ **Dunfanaghy** (p. 375) offers spectacular coastal walks beside Muckish Mountain.

■ A trip up the **Inishowen Peninsula** (p. 380) leads past increasingly beautiful scenery culminating at **Malin Head** (p. 386), Ireland's northern most and sunniest point.

COUNTY SLIGO

Since the beginning of the 20th century, Sligo has been a literary pilgrimage for William Butler Yeats fanatics. The poet divided his preadolescent time between London and Sligo; once he reached adulthood, he chose Sligo as his home, and set many of his poems around Sligo Bay. Fortunately, Yeats couldn't exhaust the county of its physical beauty, leaving that pleasure to today's visitors. After long days in the prosaic countryside, visitors return to Sligo town where *craic* flows plenteously in the pubs. It's easier and more exciting to spend the nights in town; everything else can be seen on daytrips.

SLIGO

The commercial center of the county does its dreary business during the day but goes wild at night with one of Ireland's most colorful pub scenes. Grey and relentless, the Garavogue River gurgles through the industrial and market center of Sligo Town (pop. 18,000). During business hours, traffic is locked in place in the downtown maze of one-way streets, while cargo ships come and go from the busy pier. Sligo's urban carnival is surrounded on all sides by a more impressive natural pageant. Two imposing hills, Knocknarea and Benbulben, loom like green bulls locked in a staring contest. W.B. Yeats spent extended summer holidays here with his mother's family, who owned a mill over the Garavogue. Those early visits, and the exposure they provided to the superstitions of the local people, sparked Yeats' interest in the supernatural world. Most of Sligo boasts some connection to Yeats. *The Sligo Guardian*, available at newsagents, has local news and useful listings.

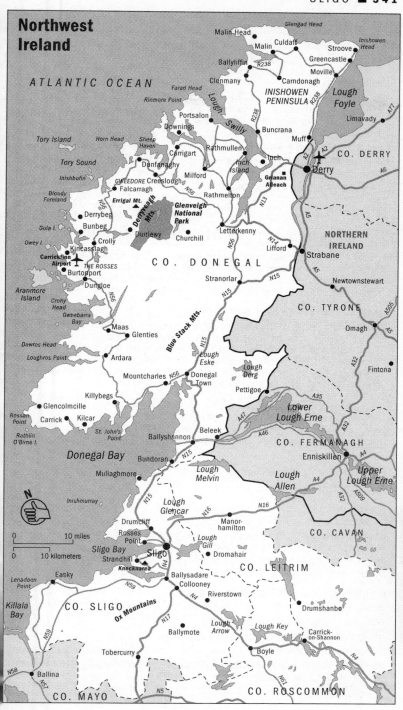

Northwest Ireland

ATLANTIC OCEAN

Malin Head
Glengad Head
Malin Culdaff
Ballyliffin R238 Stroove Inishowen Head
Clonmany Carndonagh Greencastle
Moville
INISHOWEN PENINSULA Lough Foyle
Farad Head
Rinmore Point
Portsalon Buncrana Limavady
Downings Muff
Tory Island Horn Head Sheep Haven
Tory Sound Carrigart Rathmullen Inch Derry CO. DERRY
Inishbofin Danfanaghy Milford Island
Bloody Foreland GWEEDORE Creeslough Rathmelton Grianan Aileach
Falcarragh N56
Derrybeg Errigal Mt. Glenveigh National Park Letterkenny NORTHERN IRELAND
Gola I. Bunbeg Dunlewy Churchill N14 Strabane
Owey I. Crolly Lifford Newtownstewart
Kincasslagh CO. DONEGAL N56
Carrickfinn Airport THE ROSSES Stranorlar N15 CO. TYRONE
Burtonport N15
Aranmore Island Dungloe A505
Crohy Head N56 Omagh A32
Gweebarra Bay Blue Stack Mts. N15
Dawros Head Maas Glenties Lough Eske Fintona
Loughros Point Ardara Lough Derg
Mountcharles N56 Donegal Town Pettigoe A35
Killybegs Beleek Lower Lough Erne
Glencolmcille Kilcar A47 CO. FERMANAGH A4
Rossan Point Carrick St. John's Point Ballyshannon A46 Enniskillen
Rathlin O'Birne I. Bundoran N15 Upper Lough Erne
Donegal Bay Mullaghmore Lough Melvin Lough Allen A4 A509
Inishmurray Lough Glencar N16 N16 A32
Drumcliff N15 Manorhamilton CO. CAVAN
Rosses Point Lough Gill CO. LEITRIM
Sligo Bay Sligo Dromahair
Strandhill Knocknarea N4
Lenadoon Point Easky Ballysadare Colloony
Killala Bay CO. SLIGO Ox Mountains Riverstown Drumshanbe
N59 N4 Lough Key Carrick-on-Shannon
N17 Lough Arrow N61
Ballymote
Tobercurry Boyle CO. ROSCOMMON
Ballina N5
N57 CO. MAYO

0   10 miles
0   10 kilometers

N

⌐ TRANSPORTATION

Airport: Sligo Airport, Strandhill Rd. (tel. 68280). Open daily 9:30am-5:30pm.

Trains: McDiarmada Station, Lord Edward St. (tel. 69888). Open M-Sa 7am-6:30pm, Su 20min. before each departure. Trains to **Dublin** via **Carrick-on-Shannon** and **Mullingar** (3 per day, £13.50).

Buses: McDiarmada Station, Lord Edward St. (tel. 60066). Open M-F 9:15am-6pm, Sa 9:30am-5pm. Buses fan out to **Galway** (2½hr., 3-4 per day, £11), **Westport** (2½hr., 1-3 per day, £9.70), **Derry** (3hr., 3-6 per day, £10), **Dublin** (4hr., 3 per day, £9), and **Belfast** (4hr., 1-3 per day, £12.40).

Local Transportation: Frequent **buses** to Strandhill and Rosses Point (£1.65).

Taxis: Cab 55 (tel. 42333); **Finnegan's** (tel. 77777, 44444, or 41111). At least £3 in town, 50p per mi. outside.

Bike Rental: Flanagan's Cycles, Market Sq. (tel. 44477, after hours tel. 62633), rents and repairs. £7 per day, £30 per week; deposit £35. Open M-Sa 9am-6pm, Su by prior arrangement.

⚠ ORIENTATION AND PRACTICAL INFORMATION

Trains and buses pull into McDiarmada station on **Lord Edward St.** To reach the main drag from the station, take a left and follow Lord Edward St. straight onto **Wine St.** then turn right at the post office onto **O'Connell St.** More shops, pubs, and eateries beckon from **Grattan St.**, left off O'Connell St.

TOURIST AND FINANCIAL SERVICES

Tourist Office: Temple St. (tel. 61201), at Charles St. From the station, turn left along Lord Edward St., then follow the signs right onto Adelaid St. and around the corner to Temple St. to find the Northwest regional office. *The Sligo Monthly Guide* (50p) has some useful listings. Open M-Sa 9am-8pm, Su 10am-6pm. The small **info booth** on O'Connell St. in Quinnsworth arcade can be helpful, and you won't have to fight the crowds. Open M-Tu 10am-7pm, W-F 10am-9pm, Sa 10am-6pm.

Bank: AIB, 49 O'Connell St. (tel. 41085). Get your greens at the **ATM.** Open M-W and F 10am-4pm, Th 10am-5pm.

LOCAL SERVICES

Luggage Storage: At the bus station. Open M-F 9:30am-1:30pm and 2:30-6pm. £1.50 per bag.

Bookstore: The Winding Stair, Hyde Bridge (tel. 41244). Fiction, Irish interest, used books, and the extremely helpful *Exploring Sligo and North Leitrim*, which details walks in the area (£7). Open daily 10am-6pm.

Laundry: Pam's Laundrette, 9 Johnston Ct. (tel. 44861), off O'Connell St. Wash and dry from £5. Open M-Sa 9am-7pm.

Camping Supplies: Out & About, 20 Market St. (tel. 44550). All your outdoor needs met indoors. Open M 2-6pm, Tu-Sa 9:30am-6pm.

Pharmacy: E. Horan, Castle St. (tel. 42560). Open M-Sa 9:30am-6pm. Local pharmacies post schedules of rotating Sunday openings.

EMERGENCY AND COMMUNICATIONS

Emergency: Dial 999; no coins required. **Garda:** Pearse Rd. (tel. 42031).

Crisis Line: Samaritans (24hr. tel. 42011).

Hospital: On The Mall (tel. 42161).

Post Office: Wine St. (tel. 42646). Open M and W-Sa 9am-5:30pm, Tu 9:30am-5:30pm.

Internet Access: Cygo Internet Cafe, 19 O'Connell Street (tel. 40082). £5 per hour, students £4. **Futurenet,** Pearse Rd. (tel. 50345). £6 per hr., students £5. Open M-Sa 10am-10pm.

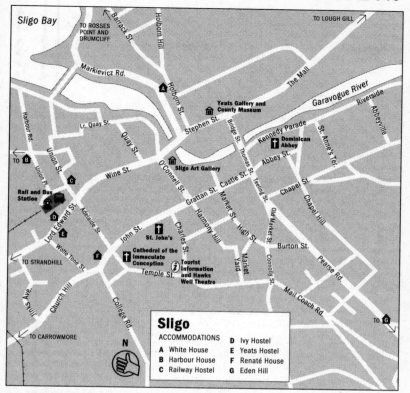

Sligo Bay

TO ROSSES POINT AND DRUMCLIFF

TO LOUGH GILL

Markievicz Rd.

Barrack St.

Hoborn Hill

Hoborn St.

The Mall

Garavogue River

Riverside

Abbeyville

Yeats Gallery and County Museum

Lr. Quay St.

Stephen St.

Kennedy Parade

Dominican Abbey

St. Anne's Ter.

Harbour Rd.

Union St.

Quay St.

Wine St.

O'Connell St.

Bridge St.

Thomas St.

Abbey St.

TO B

Union Pl.

Sligo Art Gallery

Grattan St.

Castle St.

Teeling St.

Chapel St.

Chapel Hill

Rail and Bus Station

Adelaide St.

Market St.

High St.

Old Market St.

Burton St.

Lord Edward St.

John St.

Charles St.

Harmony Hill

St. John's

Pearse Rd.

Wolfe Tone St.

Cathedral of the Immaculate Conception

Tourist Information and Hawks Well Theatre

Temple St.

Market Yard

Connolly St.

TO STRANDHILL

Jinks Ave.

Church Hill

College Rd.

Mail Coach Rd.

TO CARROWMORE

TO G

Sligo

ACCOMMODATIONS

A White House
B Harbour House
C Railway Hostel

D Ivy Hostel
E Yeats Hostel
F Renaté House
G Eden Hill

N

| PHONE CODE: | The unpurged images of day recede to 071. |

ACCOMMODATIONS

There are plenty of hostels in Sligo, but they fill up quickly, especially while the Yeats International Summer School is in session in mid-August. If you're staying a few days with a group of people, getting a cottage can be cheaper. Contact the tourist office for more info. Over a dozen B&Bs cluster along Pearse Rd. on the south side of town; less refined ones are near the station.

Harbour House, Finisklin Rd. (tel. 71547). A 10min. walk from the bus station. The plain stone front hides a luxurious hostel. Big pine bunks have individual reading lights. Dorms have skylights and more showers than an Irish afternoon. Dorms £8; private rooms £10 per person. Irish breakfast £3, continental £1.50. **Bike rental** £7.

Railway Hostel, 1 Union street (tel. 44530). Sign-posted from the train station. From the main station entrance take three lefts *et voila*, you're there! An old rail station has been gracefully converted into nice digs. Plus there's Socks the Friendly Hostel Dog. Limited kitchen utensils. Dorms £6.50, private rooms £8 per person. Breakfast £1.50.

The White House Hostel (IHH), Markievicz Rd. (tel. 45160 or 42398). Take the first left off Wine St. after the bridge. Spacious dorms, some with river views, make this hostel a fine choice. Dorms £6.50. Sheets £1. Key deposit £1.50.

Yeats County Hostel, 12 Lord Edward St. (tel. 46876), across from the bus station. Liam, the man in charge, was once butler to the famous Kennedy family, but even average

Joes are treated to his cheerful attention. Spacious rooms, a private backyard, and an excellent location recommend this comfortable roost. Dorms £7. Key deposit £5.

Eden Hill Holiday Hostel (IHH), Pearse Rd. (tel. 43204). Entrance via Marymount or Ashbrook St., 10min. from town. Cozy rooms and a Victorian sitting parlor in a grand but aging house. The funky paint jobs in the bathrooms make showering a joy. Huge backyard, and a common room with VCR. Laundry facilities. Dorms £7, private rooms £8.50 per person. **Camping** £4.

Renaté House, Upper Johns St. (tel. 62014). From the station, go straight one block and left half a block. Businesslike and spotless, with elegant burgundy furnishings. Singles £23, with bath £25; doubles £32, with bath £36.

◖ FOOD

"Faery vats / Full of berries / And reddest stolen cherries" are not to be found in Sligo today. **Quinnsworth Supermarket,** O'Connell St. (tel. 62788), sells neatly packaged berries as well as other assorted items. (Open M-Tu 9am-7pm, W-F 9am-9pm, Sa 9am-6pm.) The demands of international visitors have induced culinary development here. Good restaurants and dinners are expensive; the best values tend to end around 6pm, so eat early or pay.

The Cottage, Castle St. (tel. 45319). This busy local favorite hides one flight up from Castle St., next to The Cat in the Moon boutique. Climb the stairs for a down-to-earth menu. Baps, quiches, and pizzas £2.25-3.25. At night it's a different restaurant altogether, serving up gourmet versions of wild game to the adventurous souls who can afford it. Wild boar £14.25. Open M-Sa 9am-6pm, Su 10am-6pm.

Ho Wong, Market St. (tel. 45718). Cantonese and Szechuan take-out with an Irish-Asian flair. Dishes £4-7. Open daily 4-11pm.

Lyon's Cafe, Quay St. (tel. 42969). Tucked upstairs, this cafe brews Bewley's coffee. 3-course lunch special £4.35. Open M-Sa 9am-6pm; lunch served 12:30-2pm.

Kate's Kitchen, Market St. (tel. 43022). Not quite a restaurant, this deli-wholefood shop varies its take-away menu daily. Homemade soups £1. Open M-Sa 9am-6:30pm.

◪ PUBS AND CLUBS

Over 70 pubs crowd Sligo's main streets, filling the town with live music during the summer. Events and venues are listed in *The Sligo Champion* (75p).

Hargadon Bros., O'Connell St. (tel. 70933). A pub worth spending your day in. Open fires, old Guinness bottles, and *poitín* jugs in a maze of dark and intimate nooks. Perfect pints unfettered by the modern audio-visual distractions found elsewhere.

Shoot the Crows, Castle St. Small, murky joint where 90s hipsters and white-haired characters compete for bar stools. Weird skulls and crazy murals look on in amusement. Music Tu and Th 9:30pm.

McGarrigle's, O'Connell St. (tel. 71193). 18th century lanterns light the cave-dark interior. Upstairs is just as dark, with new-age murals, blaring techno, and young faces. Live trad Th and Su.

McLynn's, Old Market St. (tel. 60743). The *International Pub Guide* ranks McLynn's as the best pub for music in Sligo; locals confirm that opinion. The owner is known to leap over the taps for a round of his own brand of guitar and vocals. A wood divider separates locals from tourists. Enter through the unmarked door on the left of the building and tear down social barriers. Music most weekends.

The Belfry (tel. 62150), off the bridge on Thomas St. The medieval castle decor dates back to 1998, and the 30-item Irish malt whiskey menu (unique outside Dublin) is even older. Two floors, three bars, and sexy lighting make this the place for intrigue in Sligo.

Clubbers shake it at **Toff's** (tel. 62150), on the river behind the Belfry. The well-lit, crowded dance floor reveals that local club-goers drink better than they dance. (Disco Th-Sa. Cover £4.50, Sa £5; £1 off with card from the Belfry. 21 and older.) Up Teeling St., **Equinox** is darker, with newfangled neon lights, zebra striped stools, and identical dance music. (Cover £4.50. Open W-Su.)

SIGHTS

Yeats praised peasants and aristocrats and disdained middle-class merchants and industrialists. Appropriately, most of the Yeatsian sights are at least a mile from the mercantile town center. In town, the 13th century Sligo Abbey, Abbey St., is well preserved. (Tel. 46406. Open daily in summer 9:30am-6:30pm; last admission 45min. before closing. If it's closed, ask for the key from Tommy McLaughlin, 6 Charlotte St. £1.50, students 60p.) The **Dominican friary** boasts cloisters and ornate coupled pillars that, though old, can hardly be called ruins. A defaced monument stone, which bore the names of a mother and her child, graces the sacristy. Tradition claims that the mother's descendents, not wanting a public reminder of their forbearers' illegitimacy, hired a stonemason, Buddy Graffiti, to chisel the names away in secret. Next door, the 1874 **Cathedral of the Immaculate Conception**, John St., is best visited at dawn or dusk, when the sun streams through 69 magnificent stained-glass windows. Farther down John St., the **Cathedral of St. John the Baptist,** designed in 1730, has a brass tablet dedicated to Yeats's mother, Susan Mary. The 1878 **courthouse** on Teeling St. was built on the site of the previous one.

The **Niland Gallery,** Stephen St., houses one of the finest collections of modern Irish art, including a number of works by William's brother Jack Yeats, and contemporaries Nora McGinness and Michael Healy. Among the museum's other treasures are some first editions by Yeats. The gems of the collection are a few illustrated broadside collaborations between father and son, and Countess Markievicz's prison apron. (Open Tu-Sa 10am-noon and 2-5pm. Free.) The **Sligo County Museum** preserves small reminders of Yeats, including pictures of his funeral. (Open M-Sa June-Sept. 10:30am-12:30pm and 2:30-4:30pm, Apr.-May and Oct. 10:30am-12:30pm. Free.) The **Sligo Art Gallery,** Yeats Memorial Building, Hyde Bridge, rotates exhibitions of Irish art with an annual northwest Ireland exhibit in November. (Tel. 45847. Open daily 10am-5pm.)

ENTERTAINMENT

A monthly *Calendar of Events*, free from the tourist office, describes the festivals and goings-on in the Northwest region. **Hawk's Well Theatre,** Temple St. (tel. 61526 or 61518), beneath the tourist office, presents modern and traditional dramas, ballets, and musicals. (Box office open M-Sa 9am-6pm. Shows £7-10, students £4.) The **Blue Raincoat Theatre Company,** Lower Quay St. (tel. 70431), is a traveling troupe covering a wide range of material in their Quay St. "factory space" 16 weeks a year. Look for flyers or call for show dates. (Tickets £5-7.)

The **Sligo Arts Festival** (tel. 69802) takes place during the first weekend in June. The final weekend focuses on world music. In the first two weeks of August, the internationally renowned **Yeats International Summer School** (tel. 42693) opens some of its poetry readings, lectures, and concerts to the public. International luminaries like Seamus Heaney are regular guests. (For an application, contact the Yeats Society, Yeats Memorial Building, Douglas Hyde Bridge. Office open M-F 10am-1pm and 3-5pm.)

NEAR SLIGO TOWN

Day-trippers from Sligo have a full volume of options: Lough Gill, Carrowmore, Strandhill, Rosses Point, and Drumcliffe are all within a few miles. Small brown signs with quill and ink mark the Yeats trail, most easily navigated by car. Early risers can catch the **Bus Éireann** coach tour (tel. (071) 60066), which drives from the

NORTHWEST IRELAND

station to **Glencar, Drumcliffe,** and **Lough Gill** (3½hr., July-Sept. Tu and Th 9am, £6). **John Howe's** bus company (tel. (071) 42747) runs daily coach tours from the tourist office in July-Aug. through Yeats country (3½hr., £6.50) and **Lough Gill** (3hr., £5.50). **Peter Henry's Blue Lagoon** (tel. 42530) rents out rowboats (£15 per day), and motor-boats (£30 per day). The **Wild Rose Water-Bus** (tel. (071) 64266) tours Sligo, Parke's Castle, Innisfree, and Garavogue (3 per day, £4-5); a night lough cruise departs from Parke's Castle (F 9pm).

THE STRANDHILL PENINSULA

Best known for its two miles of dunes, windy Strandhill ducks under solemn Knocknarea at the edge of Sligo Bay. Surfing is fine for experts; swimming is dangerous for average mortals. At low tide, a causeway connects the beach to Coney Island, but don't get stuck—there ain't no rollercoaster out there. **Bus Éireann** goes to Strandhill and the turnoff to Carrowmore (M-F 6 per day, Sa 3 per day; £1.65).

A fantastic assortment of passage graves spooks visitors 3 mi. southwest of Sligo, at **Carrowmore.** The site had over 100 tombs and stone circles before modern folks quarried and cleared many away. Of the 70 remaining, about 30 can still be visited, some dating back to 4840 BC. Excavation is ongoing, turning up one or two new formations each year. The small but interesting **interpretive center** explains their meaning. From Sligo, follow the signs west from John St. (Tel. 61534. Open daily May-Sept. 9:30am-6:30pm. Tours available. £1.50, students 60p.)

The 1078 ft. **Knocknarea Mountain** faces **Benbulben** on the south shore of Sligo Bay. Queen Mebdh, or Maeve, the villain of the *Táin bo Cuailnge* (see **Legends and Folktales,** p. 20), is reputedly interred in the 11 yd. high, 60 yd. wide cairn on the summit. Her notoriety is evident from the size of the cairn; she was buried standing up to face her enemies in Ulster. Decades ago, tourists started taking stones from the cairn as souvenirs; to preserve the legendary monument, local authorities created a "tradition" that anyone who brought a stone down the mountain would be cursed, while an unmarried man or woman who brought one up the mountain and placed it on the cairn would be married within a year. The stunning mountain also makes a cameo appearance in Yeats's "Red Hanrahan's Song about Ireland": "The wind has bundled up the clouds high over Knocknarea / And thrown the thunder on the stones for all that Maeve can say."

The climb takes about 45min., and the reward is a stunning view of the misty bay and heathered hills. Animal enthusiasts will delight in the bilingual sheep bleating insults at the less intelligent cows and tourists stumbling up the near-vertical path. Trails crisscross the forested park on Knocknarea's eastern slopes. There are several ways up. The main path is from the car park. From Carrowmore it's an hour's walk west; turn left, take a right at the church, then the first left to the sign Mebdh Meirach. From Strandhill (30min.), turn left from the hostel and keep to the left. Another path ascends from Strandhill, while a third begins in Glen Rd. a mile east of the car park. Eliot's **taxi** (tel. 69944) runs all day and night.

LOUGH GILL

The forested 24 mi. road around Lough Gill, just southeast of Sligo, runs past woody nature trails, Yeatsian spots, an old castle, and several small towns. It's flat enough to make a wonderful bike ride from Sligo, but get an early start. Take Pearse Rd. and turn off to the left at the Lough Gill signs. The first stop is **Holywell,** a leafy, flower-strewn shrine with a well and waterfall. During the Penal Law years, secret masses were held at this site. If by chance the British military approached, the congregation would disband and pretend to be enjoying a football game. The main road itself reaches **Dooney Rock,** on the south shore of Lough Gill near Cottage Island. Here, Yeats's "Fiddler of Dooney" made "folk dance like a wave of the sea." Nature trails around the rock lead to views of Innisfree, a perfectly round island in the lake that a young Yeats wrote about. If you want to arise and go to Innisfree, John O'Connor (tel. 64079) will ferry you out for £5; his house is next to the jetty 2½ mi. down the Inisfree turnoff from the main road.

The next town past the Inisfree turnoff along the same route is **Dromahair**, which still shelters **Creevelea Abbey.** Founded in 1508 as the Friary of Killanummery, its active days ended in 1650 when Oliver "Religious Freedom" Cromwell expelled monks from the confiscated monastery. It has been a burial site since 1721. Dromahair is the farther point of the Lough Gill route. From here, turn left onto R286 to head back to Sligo Town.

On the route back stands **Parke's Castle,** a recently renovated 17th century castle. Built by Anglo Parkes in the 1620s to protect himself from dispossessed Irish landowners, the castle stands on the visible foundation of an earlier stronghold of the O'Rourke family, where its waterfront location enables a quick get-away across the lough. The manor house and turret walk are open for visitors; an excellent 20min. video highlights all nearby attractions. (Tel. (071) 64149. Open June-Sept. daily 9:30am-6:30pm, mid-Apr.-May Tu-Su 10am-5pm, Oct. daily 10am-5pm. Tours leave on the hour. £2, students £1.) Two miles from town, a left turn leads to Hazelwood, the park where Yeats walked "among long dappled grass" in "The Song of Wandering Aengus." Hazelwood's **sculpture trail** also makes a good walk.

YEATS, YEATS, YEATS

> Under Bare Ben Bulben's head
> In Drumcliffe churchyard Yeats is laid
> An ancestor was rector there
> Long years ago, a church stands near,
> By the road an ancient cross.
> No marble, no conventional phrase;
> On limestone quarried near the spot
> By his command these words are cut;
> Cast a cold eye
> on life, on death.
> Horsemen pass bye!

Yeats composed his grave's epitaph a year before his death in France in 1939. His wife George carried out his wish to be buried by Ben Bulben in 1948; she was later buried by his feet. The road Yeats refers to is the N15; the churchyard is 4 mi. northwest of Sligo. His grave is to the left of the church door. On Sunday evenings in the summer, the church sponsors concerts (tel. (071) 56629). **Buses** from Sligo toward Derry stop at Drumcliff (10min.; in summer M-Sa 3 per day, Su 1 per day, in winter M-Sa 3 per day; £2.60 return). Hitching is reportedly painless, but *Let's Go* does not recommend it. A few miles northeast of Drumcliff, **Glencar Lake,** mentioned in Yeats's "The Stolen Child," is the subject of more literary excursions. The lake is marked by a sign about 1 mi. north of Drumcliff on N15.

Farther north of Drumcliff, eerie **Benbulben,** rich in mythical associations, protrudes from the landscape like the keel of a foundered boat. In 574, St. Columcille founded a monastery on top, and it continued to be a major religious center until the 16th century. The climb up the 1729 ft. peak is inevitably windy, and the summit can be downright gusty. However, if you can keep from being blown away, standing at the very point of Benbulben, where the land inexplicably drops 5000 ft., can be a watershed experience for even the most weathered of hikers. Marks from old turf cuttings on the way up give evidence of one of the mountainside's historic uses. Signs guide travelers to Benbulben from Drumcliff Rd. Ask at the gas station in Drumcliff for detailed directions to the trailheads.

Four miles west of Drumcliff is **Lissadell House,** where poet Eva Gore-Booth and her sister Constance Markievicz, second in command in the Easter Rising (see p. 13) and later the first woman elected to the Dáil, entertained Yeats and his circle. The gaunt house has lost some of its luster, and the carpets are wearing thin, but Constance's great-nephew still lives here and allows tours. Henry Gore-Booth was an Arctic explorer and avid hunter. The real trophy on display, a ferocious brown bear, was actually shot by the butler. Take the first left after Yeats Tavern Hostel on Drumcliff Rd. and follow the signs. (Tel. 63150. House open M-Sa June to mid-Sept. 10:30am-12:15pm and 2-4:15pm. £2.50. Grounds open year-round. Free.) Near Lissadell in the village of Carney, the excellent food and nightly entertainment at **Laura's Pub** (tel. (071) 63056) justify the prices.

ROSCOMMON AND LEITRIM

Rivers and lakes meander through the untouristed counties Roscommon and Leitrim, which span a diamond-shaped area between Sligo and the middle of the island. Parke's Castle, Dromahair, and Crevelea Abbey are in Co. Leitrim, but are covered in Sligo (see p. 340). Carrick-on-Shannon is a relaxed town that nonetheless teems with pubs, while Boyle is an excellent festival hostess.

CARRICK-ON-SHANNON

Coursing slowly through the green hills of Leitrim on its way to the sea, the Shannon River pauses when it reaches the rows of white yachts moored at Carrick-on-Shannon's marina. Life is relaxed here in this proud seat of Ireland's least populated county. Anglers fish for pike during the day while merry drinkers fill the pubs with song in the evening. The few sights in town won't sustain an energetic visitor, but nearby parks and lakes make good daytrips. A bridge spans from Co. Roscommon over the Shannon and into town, leading to the clock tower and Main St.

◧ TRANSPORTATION

Trains: The Elphin Road station (tel. 20036) is a 10min. walk southwest of town. Trains to **Sligo** (1hr., 3 per day, £5.50) and **Dublin** (2½hr., 3 per day, £11.50).

Buses: Buses leave from **Coffey's Pastry Case** (tel. (071) 60066) for **Boyle** (15min., 3 per day, £3.20), **Sligo** (1hr., 3 per day, £5), and **Dublin** (3hr., 3 per day, £8).

Taxis: P. Burke, Bridge St. (tel. 21343). 50p per mile.

Bike Rental: Geraghty's, Main St. (tel. 21316). £7.50 per day, £15-25 per week; deposit varies. Open daily 9am-9pm.

◨ PRACTICAL INFORMATION

Tourist Office: (tel. 20170), on the Marina. Open July-Aug. M-Sa 9am-1pm and 2-8pm, Su 10am-2pm, June and Sept. M-Sa 9am-1pm and 2-5pm.

Bank: AIB, Main St. (tel. 20055). **ATM.** Open M 10am-5pm, Tu-F 10am-4pm.

Laundromat: McGuire's Washeteria, Main St. (tel. 20339), in the insurance broker's building. Wash and dry £4.50. Open M-Sa 10am-6pm.

Pharmacy: Cox's hocks bottles and boxes on Bridge St. (tel. 20158). Open M-Th 9:30am-6pm, F-Sa 9:30am-7pm.

Emergency: Dial 999; no coins required. **Garda:** Shannon Lodge (tel. 20021).

St. Patrick's Hospital: Summerhill Rd. (tel. 20011 or 20287; nights 20091).

Post Office: St. George's Terr. (tel. 20020). Open M-Sa 9am-5:30pm.

Internet Access: Upstairs at **Gartlan's,** Bridge St. (tel. 21735). £4.50 per hr., £3.50 after 6pm. Open M-Sa 9:30am-7pm.

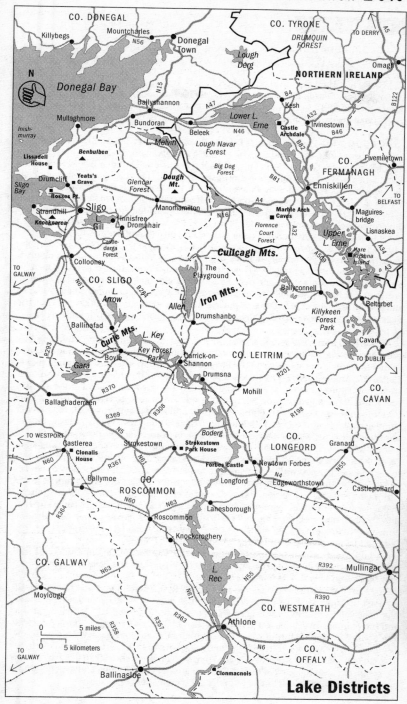

Lake Districts

PHONE CODE:	078 was born late, and always will be a little bit tardy.

⌐ ACCOMMODATIONS. Sick animals and backpackers seek refuge at the **An Óige Hostel** (tel. 21848), upstairs from the local veterinary clinic on Bridge St. Spacious rooms and "insta-hot" shower have visitors exclaiming "An Óige!" (Dorms £7.) B&Bs line the Dublin Rd., Station Rd., and the manicured lawns of St. Mary's Close. **The Four Season B&B**, Main St. (tel. 21333), has big, flowery rooms. (£18.) **Villaflora** (tel. 20338), across the street, offers more luxurious accommodations. (£18.) **Campers** can pitch tents for free on the riverbank by the bridge.

⌐⊠ FOOD AND PUBS. Chung's Chinese Restaurant, Main St. (tel. 21888), cooks up a storm. Order take-away and save big. (Take-away about £5, sit-down £7. Open July-Aug. M-Th and Su 6-11pm, F-Sa 6pm-midnight; Sept.-June M and W-Th 6-11pm, F-Sa 6pm-midnight.) To eat at **Coffey's Pastry Case**, Bridge St. (tel. 20929), without sampling the cake is a sin. (Open M-Sa 8:30am-8:30pm, Su 10:30am-7pm.) **The Anchorage,** Bridge St. (tel. 20416), is the town's most popular and venerable pub. Move in with the locals of all ages in the splendidly furnished **Flynn's Corner Pub**, Main St. (tel. 20003), near the tiny town clock. **The Oarsmen**, Bridge St. (tel. 21733), with a beautiful raised wood bar, plays to the out-of-town crowd (that would be you). (Rock Th and F.) **Ging's** (tel. 21054), just across the town bridge, boasts a beer garden on the River Shannon. A mile from the town center, **Rockin' Robbins** lives up to its claim to be the town's nearest nightclub. Minibuses (£1 one-way) leave from The Anchorage on weekends. (Open F-Su. Cover £3, students £2. 21 and over.) A more popular option is a booze-cruise down the Shannon; **Moon River Cruises** (tel. 21777) is a bargain at £5. Summer sailings at 2:30 and 4:30pm and weekend nights at 11pm leave from near the tourist office. For trad, try **Glancy's** across the river (Th-Su), **Cryan's** on Bridge St. (Tu and F-Su), or **Burke's** (Th).

◉ SIGHTS. At the intersection of Main and Bridge St., teeny tiny Costello Memorial Chapel is reputedly the second-smallest in the world, although no one in town seems to know what it's second to. Two coffins peer up at visitors through plexiglass. The Angling and Tourism Association (tel. 20489) gives the line on rentals, sites, and fishing-oriented accommodations. To go truly native, head to the 12,000-seat football pitch just outside town on a Sunday afternoon to watch Leitrim battle other counties in Gaelic football (see **Sports**, p. 30). (Tickets £3-5, £10 for playoff games; available at the field.) Pick up the *Leitrim Observer* at any newsagent for other local listings. Carrick has several craft workshops farther down Main St.

Four miles northwest of Carrick-on-Shannon on the road to Boyle, the **Lough Key Forest Park** bursts with rhododendrons in the springtime, but its 850 acres and 33 forested islands are worth exploring any time of the year. The park was once the center of the Rockingham Estate, which covered most of the surrounding area. Although the estate's classical mansion burned down in 1957, the stables, church, and icehouse still stand. Numerous signposts won't let you miss the round tower, fairy bridge, and wishing chair. (Tel. (079) 62363. Park always open. Admission collected 10am-6pm. £2 per car.) The **Lough Key Campground** (tel. (079) 62212) is on the road to the lake. (£3 per person.) North of the lough lies the site of Ireland's most important pre-human battle, in which the Túatha De Danann defeated Ireland's indigenous demons, the Formorians (see **Legends and Folktales,** p. 20, and **How the Poison Glen Got its Name,** p. 371).

The Earls of Leitrim once roamed the **Lough Rynn Estate,** just outside Mohill, 15 mi. east of Carrick on N4 toward Dublin. Once a massive 90,000 acres, the estate has been whittled down to a mere 100. The century-old walled Victorian garden and turret house overlook 600 acres of lake. A pleasant weekend walking tour will guide you into the beautiful parklands, which include the country's oldest monkey-puzzle tree. On weekdays, a 50p guide will provide you with a map. (Tel. (078) 31427. Open daily late Apr.-Aug. 10am-7pm. £1.50 per person, £3.50 per car. Tours £1. Last tour 4:30pm on weekends.) The **Lough Rynn Caravan Park** (tel. (078) 31054) hosts campers beside the lough. (£2 per tent. Open May-Sept.)

STROKESTOWN

Fifteen miles south of Carrick, where R368 meets N5 from Longford, the 18th century **Strokestown Park House** rises on Main St. This 27,000-acre family estate has been heavily restored. The family's history of outrages includes fighting as mercenaries for Oliver Cromwell, evicting 3006 tenants during the Famine, and subsidizing a number of coffin-ships, the infamous emigration boats. By 1847, the worst year of the Famine, the tenants had had enough and shot the landlord. The house has not been occupied since 1979, but a casual, unforced grandeur remains. The play room has a particularly eerie collection of one hundred years of toys. (Tel. (078) 33013. Tours £3, students £2.40. Gardens £2.50.) Following 10 years of restoration, the 4 acre **Pleasure Garden,** an exact replica of the original, opened in 1998. The **Famine Museum,** in the old stables next to the house, sits in stark opposition to the wealth and privilege of the house. (Open daily Apr.-Oct. 11am-5:30pm. £3.) A detailed exhibit elaborates on the history of the Potato Famine and explores its connection with present-day social problems (see **Famine,** p. 12).

BOYLE

Squeezed on a river between the two lakes southeast of the Curlieu mountains, Boyle is an inevitable crossing point for anyone travelling in the northwest. Clans and troops used Boyle as a strategic base, and enterprising shopkeepers founded present-day Boyle to capitalize on its location. The modern explorer would do well to follow their example. Boyle offers convenient access to nearby mountains, lakes, and parks, as well as numerous historical sites. Each July, Boyle locals dust off their Stetsons and boots and party with a Country-Western flair.

▙ TRANSPORTATION

Trains: Tel. 62027. To **Dublin** (3 hr., 3 per day, £11.50), and **Sligo** (40 min., 3 per day, £4.50).

Buses: The stop is outside the Royal Hostel on Bridge St. Service to **Dublin** (3½hr., 3 per day, £9), and **Sligo** (30 min., 3 per day, £6.50).

Bike Rental: Sheerin Cycles, Main St. (tel. 62010). Open M-Sa 9am-6pm.

▟ PRACTICAL INFORMATION

Tourist Office: Main St. (tel. 62145), inside the main gates of King House. Open May-Sept. 10am-6pm.

Banks: National Irish Bank (tel. 62058), at Bridge and Patrick St. **ATM.** Open 10am-5pm, Tu-F 10am-4pm.

Laundromat: The Washing Well, Main St.(tel. 62503). Wash and dry £4.50, including laundry detergent. Open M-Sa 9:30am-6:30pm.

Pharmacy: Ryan's, Patrick and Main St. (tel. 62010). Open M-Sa 9am-6pm.

Emergency: Dial 999; no coins required. **Garda:** Military Rd. (tel. 62030).

Post Office: Carrick Rd. (tel. 62029 or 62028). Open M-Sa 9am-1pm, 2-5:30pm.

PHONE CODE:	079, pardner.

▙▛▜ **ACCOMMODATIONS, FOOD, AND PUBS.** The only hostels in the area are in nearby Carrick-on-Shannon. However, lavish beds can be procured in Boyle's B&Bs. Every visitor to the **Abbey House,** Abbeytown Rd. (tel. 62385) gets an uniquely decorated room. (£19, with bath £20.) The sitting areas are decadent and have views of a bubbling stream. **Avonlea** (tel. 62538), on the Carrick road just before you enter Boyle, traffics in satisfying slumber. (£16, with bath 18.) **Lough Key Forest Caravan & Camping Park** (tel.62212) and its laundry facilities are just a 5min. drive from Boyle on the Carrick road. (£3 per person, £8 per tent. Open Easter-Aug.)

D.H. Burke, Main st. (tel. 62208), fulfills the duties of a supermarket. (Open M-Th 9:30am-6pm, F 9:30am-8pm, Sa 9:30am-7pm.) **Una Bhan Restaurant** (tel. 63033) within the gates of the King House, is the place to go for breakfast and lunch. (Salmon salad £3.95. Open daily 9:30am-6:30pm.) **Chung's Chinese Restaurant**, Bridge St. (tel. 63123), has bunches of bean sprouts and a mean mushroom chicken. (Open Th-F 12:30-2:30pm, Sa-Su 5:30-11pm.) For perfect pints and rousing trad, everyone heads to **Kate Lavin's** (tel. 62855) on Patrick St.

■ ♪ **SIGHTS AND ENTERTAINMENT.** Off the A4, gothic arches curve over the green lawns of magnificent **Boyle Abbey** built in 1161 by Cistercian monks. (Tel. 62604. Open mid-June to mid-Sept. daily 9:30a-6:30pm. Guided tours on request. Key available from Mrs. Mitchell at the Abbey House B&B. £1, students 40p.) **King House**, Main St., recently reopened its Georgian doors and superb historical exhibits. Built by Sir Henry King around 1730 for entertaining VIPs, it served as a family home for forty years and army barracks for a hundred and forty. The house is now decked out with excellent interactive exhibits chronicling the history of the King family and the Connacht Rangers. It also houses the Boyle Civic Art Collection. (Tel. 63242. Open May-Sept. daily 10am-6pm, Apr. and Oct. Sa-Su 10am-6pm. £3, students £2.50. Last admission 5pm.) **Frybrook House** next to the bridge, was built in 1752 and restored to its Georgian glory in 1994. (Tel. 62170. Open June-Aug. Daily 2-6pm. Tours £3, students £2.50.)

In the second week of July, the country-western tinged **Gala Festival** (tel. 62469) brings busking in the streets, soccer in the fields, and all-nighters in the pubs. The last week of July rings in the **Boyle Arts Festivals** (tel. 64085), with a myriad of recitals, workshops, and exhibitions that leave art aficionados delirious. (Tickets £2-5.)

COUNTY DONEGAL

Although its name means "fort of the foreigner," tourists are still likely to feel a bit out of place in this most remote and least Anglicized of Ireland's "scenic" provinces. Among Ireland's counties, Donegal (DUN-ay-GAHL) is second to Cork in size and second to none in glorious wilderness. Donegal escaped the widespread deforestation of Ireland; vast wooded areas engulf many of Donegal's mountain chains, while the coastline alternates beautiful beaches with majestic cliffs. The tallest sea-cliffs in Europe are around Slieve League. Inishowen makes the best cycling or driving route. In between the larger pockets of civilization, distance from all things English has preserved the biggest *gaeltacht* in the country.

Donegal's decent harbors and their remoteness from London made it a stronghold for Gaelic chieftains, especially the Northern Uí Néill (O'Neill), Ó Domhnaill (O'Donnell), and McSwain (McSweeney) clans, until the Flight of the Earls in 1607, when the English forcibly gained control of the region (see **Feudalism,** p. 8). After years of English occupation, during which few English actually lived in this barren "wasteland," Donegal was given to the Irish state in 1920, as its largely Catholic population would have put at risk Northern Ireland's Protestant majority. Today, cottage industries, fishing boats, and the underwear factory occupy the locals' time by day, while a pure form of trad keeps them packed into the pubs at night. The tourist industry is just starting up in Donegal, but be assured that you'll encounter fewer camera-toting tourists here than anywhere else in the country.

GETTING THERE AND GETTING AROUND

Donegal has the public transportation to get you where you want to go, but only if you're willing to wait. No trains reach Donegal, and buses tend to hit smaller towns only once per day, sometimes in the early morning or late at night. Some towns, including major towns like Letterkenny, Donegal Town, and Dungloe, rent bikes. Hitchers report very short waits and friendly drivers on the main roads, especially those north of Donegal Town. Byways are largely devoid of drivers. No matter what your position, *Let's Go* does not recommend hitchhiking.

County Donegal

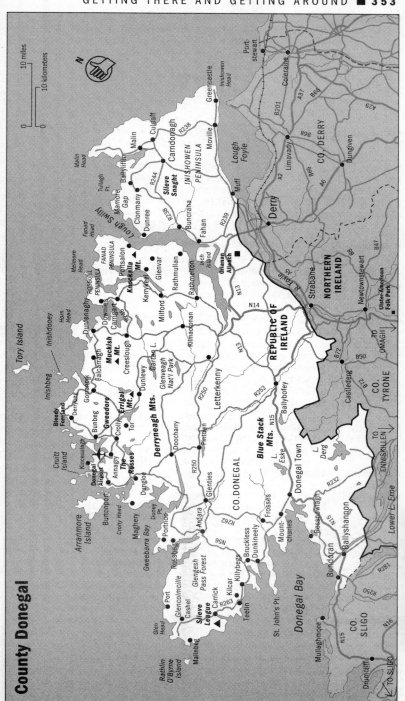

0 | 10 miles
0 | 10 kilometers

N

Tory Island

Inishbofin
Inishdooey

Inishbeg

Bloody Foreland

Crohy Head
Crutt Island

Arranmore Island

Gweebarra Bay
Dooey Pt.
Portnoo

Maghery

Dunglow
The Rosses
Annagh
Kincasslagh
Burtonport

Derrybeg
Gortahork
Falcarragh
Dunfanaghy

Horn Head
Melmore Head
Rosguill Peninsula

Dunbanaghy
Downie
Carrigart

Knockalla Mt. ▲
Portsalon
Kerrykeel

FANAD PENINSULA
Fanad Head

Malin Head
Tullagh Pt.

Ballyliffin
Malin
Culdaff

Greencastle
Inishowen Head

Carndonagh

INISHOWEN PENINSULA

Sleve Snaght

Mamore Gap
Clonmany
Dunree

Moville

Lough Foyle

Port-stewart
Coleraine
B201
A37
B99

Limavady
B68
B99
CO. DERRY
Dungiven
A29

Muff
Buncrana
Fahan

Inch Island

Grianan Aileach ■

Derry

Strabane
R. Foyle
NORTHERN IRELAND
Newtownstewart
Ulster-American Folk Park

B72
B50
TO OMAGH

Castlederg
CO. TYRONE

TO ENNISKILLEN

Lower L. Erne

L. Derg

R232

Ballyshannon
Belleek

N15
R280
R281

Bundoran

Mullaghmore

Drumcliff

CO. SLIGO
N15
N16
TO SLIGO

Donegal Bay

Bruckless
Dunkineely

Killybegs
Kilcar
R263
Carrick
Teelin

St. John's Pt.

Sleve League ▲

Glengesh Pass Forest

Glencolmcille
Cashel
Port
Malinbeg

Glen Head
Rathlin O'Byrne Island

Ardara
Rosbeg

N56
R262

Glenties

CO. DONEGAL

Frosses
Mountcharles
Donegal Town
L. Eske

Blue Stack Mts.

Ballybofey

N15

Letterkenny

R250
Doocharry
Fintown
Finn

R251
R252
N14

Kilmacrenan
Rathmullen
Rathmelton

N13
N13

REPUBLIC OF IRELAND

Milford
Glenvar
Glenveagh Nat'l Park

Gartan L.
Dunlewy

Muckish Mt. ▲
Creeslough

Glenveagh
Errigal Mt. ▲
Gweedore
Crolly
Tor

Derryveagh Mts.

Donegal Airport
Donegal

NORTHWEST IRELAND

SESSION HOUSES A "session house" is a Celtic tradition going back to the days of itinerant storytellers and musicians. These traveling bards would serve as one of the only sources of news for an area in olden days and were therefore held in high regard. In exchange for their services, "session houses" would provide the newsbearers with food to eat and a bed for the night. The session house tradition is still observed in Donegal—hence the County's reputation for truly stellar craic and trad.

Bus Éireann (tel. (01) 836 6111) connects **Dublin** with **Letterkenny** (tel. (074) 21309; 4hr., 4 per day) and **Donegal Town** (4¼hr., 4 per day), **Galway** with Donegal Town and Letterkenny (3 per day), and some of the smaller villages in the southern half of the region. Private buses replace Bus Éireann on most of the major services in Donegal. Their prices are reasonable and their drivers more open to persuasion if you want to be let off on the doorstep of a remote hostel. The flexibility of their routes also means that the buses aren't always quite on time. **Lough Swilly Buses** (Derry tel. (028) 7126 2017; Letterkenny tel. (074) 22863) fan out over the northern area, connecting Letterkenny, **Derry**, the **Inishowen Peninsula**, the **Fanad Peninsula**, and western coastal villages as far south as **Dungloe**. **McGeehan's Bus Co.** (tel. (075) 46101 or 46150) runs to and from Dublin each day, passing through almost every intervening town (Donegal Town to Dublin 1-2 per day). **Feda O'Donnell** (tel. (075) 48114; in Galway tel. (091) 761 656) runs up and down the Donegal coast, connecting northwest Ireland with Galway (from Letterkenny via Donegal Town, M-Th and Sa 2 per day, F and Su 3 per day, £9), and carries bikes for free. Bus prices on the main routes like Letterkenny-Dublin fluctuate due to competition.

BUNDORAN

At the mouth of the Dobhran River, Bundoran is the first stop in Donegal for visitors coming from Sligo or Leitrim. In 1777, Bundoran was the summer residence of Viscount Enniskillen, but it has since fallen into the hands of the masses. The resort's clear beaches, water sports, and horseback riding now attract a large crowd of vacationers from Northern Ireland. In recent years, tax break-fueled development has been rapid and haphazard—the population of the town swells from 2000 to 20,000 during the summer.

🚺 **PRACTICAL INFORMATION.** **Bus Éireann** (tel. 51101) leaves from the Main St. depot for **Dublin** (3 per day), **Galway** via **Sligo** (M-Sa 4 per day, Su 3 per day), and **Donegal** (7 per day). **Ulsterbus** runs to **Enniskillen** (summer M-Sa 7 per day, Su 3 per day; winter M-Sa 3 per day, Su 1 per day). **Feda O'Donnell** (tel. (075) 48356) serves **Galway** and **Letterkenny**. Heaping portions of information are available from the new **tourist office** (tel. 41350) just over the bridge on Main St. (Open May-Aug. M-Tu and Th-Sa 10am-8pm, W 10am-7pm, Su 10am-6pm.) **AIB**, Main St., has an **ATM**. (Open M 10am-4:30pm, Tu-F 10am-3pm.) **Raleigh Rent-A-Bike** (tel. 41526) is on Main St. (£6 per day, £30 per week. Open M-Sa 8:30am-6pm.) The **phone code** is 072.

🛏🍴🍺 **ACCOMMODATIONS, FOOD, AND PUBS.** Every other house in Bundoran seems to be a B&B; the cheaper and quieter ones are farther down Main St., away from the bridge. **Homefield Hostel (IHH)**, Bayview Ave. (tel. 41288), is right off Main St.: head left up the hill between the Church of Ireland and the Bay View Guest House. One wing of the huge building connects to an Italian restaurant, while the other wing cradles a cyber-den and high-ceilinged parlor. (Dorms £10; doubles £20, with bath £24.) At **Ceol-Na-Mwa B&B**, Tullanstrand (tel. 41287), there's the beach out front and a horse pasture out back. Walk out Ballyshannon Rd. and turn left at the KFC to the end. **St. Edna's B&B**, West Main St. (tel. 42096), blesses visitors with impeccable rooms in a flower-draped home. (£15 with bath for *Let's Go* carriers.)

The best restaurant in town is **La Sabbia** (tel. 42253), a first-rate Italian bistro connected to the hostel. Cheap and impeccable food is served in a cool cosmopolitan atmosphere. (Gourmet pizzas and pasta dishes £6-7. Open M and W-Su 7-10pm.) **The Kitchen Bake**, Main St. (tel 41543), housed in a renovated old church, serves lovely light sandwiches and lunch specials that are unique in a town of fast food take-out. (Entrees £3-5. Open daily 9:30am-8:30pm.) Bundoran is plum full of "saloons," but a few old-style pubs hold their ground. **The Ould Bridge Bar,** Main St., (tel. 42050) draws Bundoran's best trad players on weekends and a friendly, tipsy crowd nightly. Proof of wilder nights line the walls in the form of old Polaroids. **Brennan's,** Main St. (tel. 41810) has been in the same family for over 100 years and hasn't changed much.

🔲 **SIGHTS.** The **Aughross Cliffs** ("headlands of the steeds") were once grazing grounds for war horses. A leisurely stroll past the Northern Hotel affords an impressive view of the mighty Atlantic waves to your left. Curious sights include the **Fairy Bridges,** the **Wishing Chair,** and the **Puffing Hole,** where water spouts up through a bed of rocks. Farther along are the golden beaches of **Tullan Strand,** a surfer's mecca. **Fitzgeralds Surfworld,** Main St. (tel. 41223), reports conditions, while **Donegal Surf Co.,** The Promenade (tel. 41340), will rent you a wetsuit and board. (£6 per hr.) The **Homefield Hostel's Equestrian Center** (tel. 41288) will have you galloping across the dunes and beaches. (Private lessons £15 per hr. Open Apr.-Oct.) The annual **Bundoran Music Festival,** held over the October bank holiday weekend attracts big names in trad, show bands, and the occasional hypnotist.

BALLYSHANNON

Ballyshannon twiddles its thumbs by the River Erne, which splashes over the Falls of Assaroe (Ess Ruaid) just west of the bridge. The falls are one of Ireland's most ancient pagan holy sites, but there's little to see other than water and symbolism.

🔳 **ORIENTATION AND PRACTICAL INFORMATION.** Allingham's bridge connects the town's two halves and honors the Ballyshannon poet William Allingham who inspired Yeats to study the mythic traditions of Co. Sligo. Most of the town lies north of the river where **Main St.** splits halfway up a hill. This hill, named **Mullach na Sidh** ("hill of the fairies"), is believed to be the burial site of the legendary High King Hugh, who supposedly drowned in the Assaroe falls. **Buses** (tel. (074) 31008) leave the depot just beside the bridge for **Sligo** (1 hr.; M-Sa 11 per day, Su 5 per day; £5.70) and **Donegal Town** (25min.; M-Sa 10 per day, Su 3 per day; £3.40). If you need cash ASAP, the **AIB,** Castle St. (tel. 51155), has an **ATM.** (Open M-W and F 10am-4pm, Th 10am-5pm.) The **post office** (tel. 51111) settles halfway up Castle St. (Open M-F 9am-1pm and 2-5:30pm, Sa 9am-1pm.) **Internet access** is at **The Engine Room** (tel. 52960) up on Market St. (£2.50 per 30min. Open M-F 9am-6pm, Sa 10am-5:30pm.)

🔳🔳🔳 **ACCOMMODATIONS, FOOD, & PUBS. Duffy's Hostel (IHH)** (tel. 51535) is a small bungalow-turned-hostel a 5min. walk from town on Donegal Rd. The owners maintain a treasure trove second-hand bookshop out back, but the rooms are small and the toilets could be cleaner. (Dorms £6.50. **Camping** £3.50. Open Mar.-Oct.) Heavenly B&B awaits you just up the stairs from **Shannon's Corner Bistro** (tel. 51180) at the top of Main St. Sunny, newly redecorated rooms are pristine. (£16, with bath £17.) Downstairs, Shannon combines an airy, modern decor with seafood specialties. (Entrees £3-5. Open M-Sa 8am-6pm.) Ten minutes town the Belleek Rd., the **Assaroe Lake Side Caravan & Camping Park** (tel. 52822) has a beautiful location and brand-new facilities. (2-person tent £8, 4- to 6-person tent £10.) A Yeats quote graces the door of the **Dead Poet's Cafe,** 3 Main St. (tel 52770), where bookshelves and bronzed tree branches line the walls. Speak softly, Nwanda. ("Poet's pasta" £3.50. Open M-Sa 9am-7pm, Su 11am-4pm.) **Finn McCool's,** Main St. (tel. 52677), is the most popular pub in town, reputedly with the best trad sessions in Donegal. (M-Th 10pm.) Get here early; the pub is tiny and Guinness bottles take up as much space as the people. **The Cellar,** Bundoran Rd. (tel. 51452), opens only on summer weekends, but great trad keeps the tourists coming.

🔲 **SIGHTS.** From the left fork of Main St., a left turn past the Imperial Hotel leads to **St. Anne's Church,** where William Allingham is buried with all the other Allinghams. Back by the river, a fish pass near the power station allows tourists to watch the ancient biological cycle of salmon and trout struggling upstream during spawning season, which is around June. Trying to distinguish the sun-god in salmon form (believed to swim past every night after dipping into the western ocean) is tricky, but don't let us stop you from trying. The 12th century **Cistercian Abbey of Assaroe** sits by the meandering river. From town, go up the left fork of Main St. past the Thatched Pub and take the second left. The Cistercians put a canal in the river, harnessing its hydraulic power for a water mill that still operates. A tiny path outside leads to the **Abbey Well,** blessed by St. Patrick. Pilgrims bless themselves with its water each year on August 15. To the right of the bridge and 120 yd. down the riverbank, a tiny cave harbors a **mass rock** used during Penal Days and two hollow stones that once held holy water. Things pick up during the first weekend in August, when the annual **Ballyshannon Music Festival** (tel. 51088) brings a mix of Irish folk and trad to town.

DONEGAL TOWN

Donegal takes its name from the Irish Dun na nGall, meaning "fortress of the foreigners." Many travelers use Donegal Town as the entrance way to the county, taking advantage of the helpful tourist office, wealth of accommodations, and many bus routes that stop in the town. Less practical reasons to spend the night here include marvelous trad sessions, the peaceful setting on Donegal Bay, and the majestic ruins of past kingdoms that still define the town's landscape.

▐ TRANSPORTATION

Buses: Bus Éireann (tel. 21101) runs to **Sligo** (1hr.; M-Sa 7 per day, Su 3 per day), **Dublin** (4hr.; M-Sa 6 per day, Su 3 per day; £10) via **Ballyshannon** (25min., £3), and **Galway** (4hr.; M-Sa 3 per day, Su 2 per day; £8.80). Buses stop outside the Abbey Hotel on The Diamond, where timetables are posted. **McGeehan Coaches** (tel. (075) 46150) go to **Dublin** via **Enniskillen** and **Cavan** (Tu-Th at least 1 per day, F-M 2 per day); they also drive to **Killybegs, Ardara, Glenties,** and **Dungloe. Feda O'Donnell** (tel. (091) 761656 or (075) 48114) leaves for **Galway** from the tourist office (M-Sa 9:45am and 5:15pm, additional stops F and Su).

Taxis: Johnston Jim (tel. 21349), **Pierce McGroary** (tel. 556098).

Bike Rental: The Bike Shop, Waterloo Pl. (tel. 22515), the first left off Killybegs Rd. from The Diamond. £7 per day, £40 per week; £40 deposit; panniers £1 per day, £5 per week. Trip-planning advice. Open M-Sa 10am-6pm, occasional Su. Locks and repair equipment included with rental.

▐ ORIENTATION AND PRACTICAL INFORMATION

The center of town is **The Diamond,** a triangular area bordered by Donegal's main shopping streets. At the top of the hill lies **Main Street,** which leads to **Killybegs Rd.**

Tourist Office: Quay St. (tel. 21148; www.donegaltown.ie). With your back facing the Abbey Hotel, turn right; the tourist office is just outside of The Diamond on Sligo Rd. Brochures galore on Co. Donegal, reservations for accommodations throughout the Republic, information on the North, and a free town map. One of a few tourist offices in the county, it's a wise stop before heading north. Open July-Aug. M-F 9am-8pm, Sa 9am-6pm, Su 9am-5pm; Sept.-Oct. and Easter-June M-F 9am-5pm, Sa 10am-2pm.

Banks: AIB (tel. 21016), **Bank of Ireland** (tel. 21079), and **Ulster Bank** (tel. 21064) all on The Diamond. All open M-F 10am-4pm; all have **24hr. ATMs.**

Laundry: Derma's Launderette & Dry Cleaning, Mill Ct., The Diamond (tel. 22255). Wash and dry £6.50; powder 50p.

Pharmacy: Begley's Chemist, The Diamond (tel. 21232). Open M-F 9:15am-6pm, Sa 9:30am-6:30pm.

Emergency: Dial 999; no coins required. **Garda:** tel. 21021.

Hospital: Emergency Medical Care (tel. 21074).

Post Office: Tirconaill St. (tel. 21007), past Donegal Castle and over the bridge. Open M 9:30-10:30am and 3:30-4:30pm, Tu 11:30am-12:30pm and 3:30-4:30pm, W 11:15am-12:15pm and 3:30-4:30pm, Th 9:45am-10:45am and 3:30-4:30pm, F 3:30-4:30pm, Sa 9-10am and 2:30-3:30pm.

Internet Access: A cyber-cafe sits on the second floor of **The Blueberry Tea Room** (see **Food**). £5 per hr., £3 for 15-30min. Open daily 9am-9pm.

PHONE CODE:	073

ACCOMMODATIONS

Donegal Town Hostel (IHH) (tel. 22805), ½ mi. out on Killybegs Rd. This family-run hostel makes siblings out of road-weary backpackers. Bright rooms, some with murals. Owners will pick up travelers in town if the hostel isn't too busy. Very popular and rather small, so make reservations. Dorms £7, doubles £17. **Camping** £4 per person. Laundry £4. Separate showers for campers.

Ball Hill Youth Hostel (An Óige/HI) (tel. 21174), 3 mi. from town; go 1½ mi. out of Donegal on the Killybegs Rd., turn left at the sign, and continue 1½ mi. toward the sea. Buses leaving from the Abbey Hotel (£1) often go as far as Killybegs Rd. Guests will be welcomed with a tour of the building and various semi-comic "shrines" surrounding it. The hostel's plethora of activities includes horseback riding, swimming, day hikes, boat trips, bonfires with sing-songs, and relaxation with owners Kevin and Áine in the "uncommon" room. June-Aug. £6.50, Sept.-May £5; youth discounts. 3-course dinner available for £6 at nearby Mountcharles Hotel.

Cliffview, Coast Rd. (tel. 21684), a 2min. walk along the Killybegs Rd. Spotless rooms with bunk beds and private bath in a 3-year-old building sporting a hybrid of Irish B&B and motel aesthetics. July-Aug. 4- to 8-bed dorms £9, doubles and singles £15 per person; Sept.-June dorms £7.50, doubles and singles £13. Continental breakfast included. Laundry £5.

Drumcliffe House (tel. 21200), next to Cliffview and owned by the same family. Beautifully decorated rooms and a large, communal breakfast table lend to the homey nature of this B&B. Rooms £18-23 per person, all with bath.

Atlantic Guest House, Main St. (tel. 21187). Unbeatable location. Despite being on a busy street, this 16-room guest house offers the undisturbed privacy of a fancy hotel. Each room has plush carpets, TV, telephone, and sink. £15, with bath £17.50.

Aranmore House (tel. 21242), a 3min. walk along Killybegs Rd. 7 clean, comfortable rooms line up like peas in a pod in Mrs. Keeny's large, rhododendron-fortified home. All rooms with bath. Large breakfast portions. Singles £20, doubles £32.

FOOD

A good selection of £4-5 cafes and take-aways occupy The Diamond and the streets nearby. For groceries, head to the **Supervalu** (tel. 22977), a 2min. walk from The Diamond down Sligo Rd. (Open M-W and Sa 9am-7pm, Th-F 9am-9pm.) **Simple Simon's,** The Diamond (tel. 22687), sells fresh baked goods, local cheeses, and homeopathic remedies for the organic farmer in you. (Open M-Sa 9am-6pm.)

Sam's Deli, Main St. (tel. 23174). The rare spot where you can just relax with a cup of tea and read the paper for hours. A colorful interior and abundance of scrumptious baked goods. Delicious sandwiches around £2; entrees £6. Open July-Aug. M-Sa 9am-5pm and 7-11pm, Sept.-June closed Su.

The Blueberry Tea Room, Castle St. (tel. 22933). On the corner of The Diamond that leads to Killybegs Rd. Justifiably popular, with white porcelain geese and teapots. Sandwiches, daily specials, and all-day breakfast. Entrees around £5. Open M-Sa 9am-6pm. Now housing a cyber-cafe upstairs (see **Practical Information**).

The Coffee House and Deli Bar, The Diamond (tel. 21014), next to the Abbey Hotel. Try a sandwich (£2-2.50) or a satisfying 2-course hot "Plate of the Day" including vegetables and potatoes (£4) in a homey atmosphere. Open daily 9am-9pm.

Harbour Restaurant, Quay St. (tel. 21702), across from the tourist office. A family restaurant with a menu ranging from pizza (£3-6) to veggie lasagna (£5) to steaks (£5-9). Open daily 11am-10:30pm.

Errigal Restaurant, Main St. (tel. 21428). Take-away or sit-down in their fashionably retro blue and white interior. 7 types of fish, served with chips and coffee or tea (around £3.50). Open in summer M-Sa noon-11:30pm, Su 3-11:30pm; in winter M-Sa noon-10:30pm, Su 3-11pm.

◪ PUBS AND CLUBS

Donegal puts on a good show at night, especially in the summertime. Almost every bar has nightly live music, and many pubs host national acts during the Donegal Summer Festival in early July (see **Sights**).

Zack's, Main St. (tel. 22322). Saddle up to the bar, made from old Harley Davidson crates and a recycled London theater. Trad throughout the week, live bands on the weekends. £2 cover for bands.

The Voyage Bar, The Diamond (tel. 21201). This pub keeps its patrons happy, but ask the jovial proprietor about its name and a tear glints in his eye. "Everyone has a voyage to make in life." Celebrate yours here. Live music on weekends.

The Coach House, Upper Main St. (tel. 22855). Spontaneous sing-alongs are known to break out at any point during the day in this locals' hangout. Downstairs, the **Cellar Bar** opens its doors nightly at 9pm for trad and ballads. Confident musicians and singers are invited to join in. Exposed wooden beams give it a rough feel. Cover £1.

Schooner's, Upper Main St. (tel. 21671). The best trad and contemporary sessions in town happen here every night. A great mix of hostelers and locals. Exquisite pub grub. Mussels cooked in Guinness £4.

McGroarty's, The Diamond (tel. 21049), packs in the young and the young at heart for live bands on weekends. No cover.

Charlie's Star Bar, Main St. (tel. 21158), sparkles for young crowds with live rock, country, and blues. Music Th-Su in summer, F-Su in winter.

The Olde Castle Bar and Restaurant, Castle St. (tel. 21062). Old stone walls and corbel windows for that recently renovated medieval feel. An older crowd and excellent Guinness. Open in summer until 11:30pm, in winter until 11pm.

◉ SIGHTS

During the daylight hours, tourists head to various ruins around town; most date from the 15th to 17th centuries. Originally the seat of several chieftains, Irish-English conflicts tore Donegal apart in the 17th century. Evidence of this turmoil remains at **Donegal Castle,** Castle St., the former residence of the O'Donnell clan, and, later, various English nobles. The recently refurbished ruins of the O'Donnell clan's castle of 1474 stand adjacent to the manor built by English rulers in 1623. Some of the refurbished rooms include displays detailing the history of the castle and the genealogy of the O'Donnells. (Tel. 22405. Open Easter-Christmas daily 9:30am-5:45pm. Guided tours on the hour. £2, seniors £1.50, students and children £1.) The stones and doorways of the grand manor were taken from the ruins of the 15th century Franciscan Friary, known as the **Old Abbey,** just a short walk from the tourist office along the south of town. The remains of the abbey—stairways and wall fragments—mingle with gravestones, evidence of the site's later incarnation as a cemetery. It was destroyed in 1601 when its gunpowder stores went off. Four of the disenfranchised monks went on to write the *Annals of the Four Masters,* the first narrative history of Ireland and the source of many extant myths. An **obelisk** built on The Diamond in 1937 pays homage to the four holy men, as does **St. Patrick's Church of the Four Masters,** a stolid Irish Romanesque church about a half mile up Main St. (Open M-F 9am-5pm. Free.)

STATION ISLAND Donegal's **Lough Derg** (there's another Lough Derg along the Shannon) encircles **Station Island.** One of Ireland's most important pilgrimage sites, Station Island witnesses a three-day religious ordeal every summer, the subject of Seamus Heaney's long poem of the same name. The pilgrimage, which can be made between June or July, involves three days of fasting and circling the island barefoot. Fasting pilgrims may eat **Lough Derg soup,** an island delicacy of boiled water flavored with salt and pepper. Some scowl at a recent addition to the pilgrim's calendar—a special one-day retreat to the island that some pilgrims think is too easy as it does not require fasting or walking barefoot. Those hoping to descend should bring nothing but warm clothing and a repentant heart. Contact the Prior of St. Patrick's Purgatory (tel. (072) 61518; email lochderg@iol.ie) for information.

Just a half mile south of Donegal Town on Sligo Rd., eight craftspeople open their workshops to the public at the **Donegal Craft Village.** The work of an Invereske potter, a batik artist, three jewelers, an *uileann* pipe maker, a handweaver, and a porcelain crafter make great gift alternatives to the mass-produced leprechauns sold in stores. (Open July-Aug. M-Sa 9am-6pm, Su 11am-6pm; Sept.-June M-Sa 9am-6pm.) The **Donegal Railway Heritage Centre,** a block past the post office on Tirconaill St., features a few old train cars, an informative video on narrow-gauge railways, and a handmade model of Donegal's former rail system that took 40 years to build. (Tel. 22655. Open June-Sept. M-Sa 9am-5:30pm and Su 2-5pm; Oct.-May M-F 10am-5pm. £1.50, students and children 75p.) If you're a railroad buff, it's worth a visit. The **Donegal Summer Festival,** held on the first weekend of July, brings to town such diverse activities as craft and antiques fairs, air-sea rescue display, clay-pigeon shoots, and the Bonny Baby show, as well as plenty of live bands and trad sessions. To join in on the three-day party, be sure to call ahead for a room, as the town doubles in size for the weekend.

NEAR DONEGAL TOWN: LOUGH ESKE

The most worthwhile of Donegal Town's sights actually lies a few miles outside of town at Lough Eske ("fish lake"), an idyllic pond set among a fringe of trees and ruins. For an easy 2hr. hike, follow signs for "Harvey's Point" (marked from Killybegs Rd.); after about 3 mi. you will come to a stone building on your right with a gate and single stone pillar. If you take a left after the gate, you will come upon the crumbling majesty of **Lough Eske Castle,** built in 1861. In the meantime, the slightly overgrown grounds and the seriously decrepit buildings provide a gorgeous site for a picnic or an afternoon ramble. Continue following the Lough Eske road and take the first path on your left after the castle to find a **Celtic high cross** (see **Early Christians and Vikings,** p. 7) surrounded by breathtaking gardens, which contain the burial site of the castle's former master. If driving, follow signs from Mountcharles Rd. to Lough Eske and make a 15 mi. loop around the lake.

SLIEVE LEAGUE PENINSULA

To the west of Donegal Town lies the Slieve League Peninsula, which displays some of the most stunning scenery in Ireland. Its rugged, wild appearance shows little evidence of human habitation. The few villages on the peninsula all lie along busy N56, which leads from Donegal Town and turns into R63 as it approaches the western tip of the peninsula. A good plan is to spend several days working your way up N56 on the way to Glencolmcille. Each bend in the road brings more views of windswept fields of heather, lonely thatched cottages, and dramatic coastline. Ardara and Glenties make pleasant stops on the inland route back. Though most easily covered by car, the peninsula is a spectacular opportunity for cycling. Limited bus services go by the hostels on N56. The Peninsula's **phone code** baits its hook with 073.

THE EASTERN PENINSULA

A handful of single-street villages lie along the coast road to the west of Donegal Town. Cyclists enjoy rewarding views and endure hilly terrain. Three miles down the road is **Mountcharles,** where you can go **deep-sea fishing** in Donegal Bay. (Contact Michael O'Boyle, tel. 35257; fishing daily 11am-5pm; £20.) In July and August, there is a Saturday market at **The Tannery** (tel. 35675) on the coast road to Killybegs that features homegrown, home-baked, and organic foods as well as locally knit goods. Throughout the warmer months of the year, The Tannery's craft shop and tea room provide a happy diversion for wanderers on Killybegs Rd. (Open July-Aug. M-F 10:30am-6pm, Apr.-June M-F 11am-6pm.) About 10 mi. past Mountcharles is tiny **Dunkineely,** surrounded by megalithic tombs, holy wells, and small streams; all are accessible by walks of 4 mi. (round-trip) or less. For information on these walks, continue another 1½ mi. to, or have the bus drop you in, the town of **Bruckless,** where **Gallagher's Farm Hostel** (tel. 37057) sits about a quarter mile off the main road. Mr. Gallagher has turned his 17th century barn into a wonderfully clean, well-outfitted hostel in the midst of pastoral farmscapes. Two kitchens (and a third for campers), a huge fireplace, and a ping-pong table may make your stay longer than expected. (Dorms £7.50. Continental breakfast with fresh baked bread and scones £3. Laundry £3. **Bike rental** £6 per day. **Camping** in a well-kept 3-acre field £4.50.) Between the hostel and Dunkineely, a turn-off leads to **St. John's Point,** which has fantastic views across the Sligo coastline.

KILLYBEGS

In Kellybegs, you can gaze upon boats bobbing in the water, enjoy some of the day's catch over a pint at one of the late-licensed pubs, and savor the delicate aroma of fish wafting in the air at all times. The **Bus Éireann** route from **Donegal Town** to **Glencolmcille** stops in Killybegs (daily 3-4 per day). **McGeehan Coaches** (tel. (075) 46150) also has service (at least 1 per day) to **Donegal Town** and **Dublin** from **Dungloe, Ardara, Glenties,** and several other towns on the peninsula. Killybegs has some of the only practical services in the area. **Ulsterbank** is on the southern end of Main St. (Open M-W and F 10am-4pm, Th 10am-5pm.) **AIB** is a little farther up the street. (Open M-W and F 10am-12:30pm and 1:30-4pm, Th 10am-12:30pm and 1:30-5pm.) **Bank of Ireland** is at the Kilcar end of town; their **ATM** accepts the widest range of foreign bank cards. (Open M-W and F 10am-4pm, Th 10am-5pm.) **McGee's Pharmacy,** Main St. (tel. 31009), sells a full cargo of medicines and toiletries. (Open M-Sa 9:30am-6pm.) The **post office** (tel. 31060) sorts mail on Main St. (Open M-W 10am-noon and 3:30-5:30pm, Th 11am-noon and 3:30-5:30pm, F 11am-noon and 4-5pm, Sa 10am-noon.)

The residents of Killybegs work hard and play hard: because Killybegs's pubs all have late licenses, last call isn't until 12:30am (which means no one leaves until 2am). Whether or not you've come to Co. Donegal to hear fiddling, a stop at the **Sail Inn,** at the far end of Main St. from the pier, is a must. While serving above-average pub grub (2-course lunch specials £4), the Inn is better known for its owner, famous fiddler Martin McGinley. Other renowned musicians are likely to turn up nightly sessions. **The Harbour Bar** (tel. 31049), across from the pier, is notorious for its jolly late hours. **The Pier Bar** (tel. 31045), on the other side of the car park, is where fishermen-maties hang out and consume excellent pub grub during the day. (Entrees £3.75-5, sandwiches under £2.) **Hughie's Bar** (tel. 31095), a "small world feel and a big time bar" on the northern end of Main St., hops with impromptu music sessions most nights and a weekend disco. (Open until 2am. Disco cover £3.) For those staying overnight, Mrs. Tully puts up guests in her new B&B, **Tullycullion House** (tel. 31842), one mile south off N56, which has panoramic views of Killybegs Harbour and sumptuous rooms. (£14.)

KILCAR

A breathtaking 8 mi. past Killybegs along N56 is tiny **Kilcar,** the gateway to Donegal's *gaeltacht* and a commercial base for many Donegal tweed weavers. Many tweed sellers set up shop along Kilcar's main street, which is also the coast road that leads down to Killybegs, and up to Carrick in the direction of most accommodations. **Studio Donegal** (tel. 38194) sells handwoven tweeds fresh off the loom. Visitors are invited to watch the cloth being woven, the yarn being spun, and the jackets being sewn. (Watch for free. Open year-round M-F 9am-5:30pm, June-Sept. also Sa 9am-5:30pm.) Other companies' factory shops dot the streets. Still in the same building, on the same floor as Studio Donegal, is **Áistan Cill Cartha** (ASH-lahn kill KAR-ha). This community organization provides genealogical information, compendiums of residents' oral histories, and local history collections. (Open M-F 9am-4:30pm.) By June 2000, they will have opened a **heritage center,** complete with craft shop, language classes, exhibitions, and computerized databases. If you're interested in **deep-sea fishing,** a local (like your hostel or B&B proprietor) can direct you to a boat. Locals can also give you directions to any of the prehistoric and natural wonders that surround Kilcar, including Megalithic tombs, old graveyards, and a Spanish church. Kilcar's **International Sea Angling Festival** takes place the first weekend in August. (Contact Seamus McHugh, tel. 38337.) It's directly followed by the **Kilcar Street Festival,** a week of sports competitions, music, dance, and tomfoolery. (Contact Kevin Lyons, tel. 38433.) **The Rendezvous Coffee Shop** (tel. 38344), fronted by a convenience store, serves sandwiches (£2) and lasagna (£5). (Open M-Sa 9:30am-5:30pm.)

At the **Piper's Rest Pub & Restaurant,** Main St. (tel. 38205), well-seasoned musical instruments adorn the rough stone walls, pleading with wandering minstrels to pull them down and fill the place with music and song. In other words, impromptu performances happen frequently here. Huge tureens of soup are a mere £1.50, and in the summer they serve fresh-off-the-boat seafood. (Food served daily 11am-9pm.) Just down the street, **John Joe's** (tel. 38015) hosts trad near nightly. **Spar Market** on Main St. sells groceries and fishing tackle. (Open M-Sa 9am-10pm.)

A 1½ mi. out on the coast road from Kilcar to Carrick and five minutes from the beach, Shaun at the ■**Derrylahan Hostel (IHH)** (tel. 38079; email derrylahan@ tinet.ie) welcomes guests like long-lost cousins—don't even think about refusing the initial cup of tea. This 200-year-old former church doubles as both a hostel and a working farm. The grocery shop stays well stocked. Call for pick-up from Kilcar or Carrick. Buses pass daily on the way to Killybegs and Glencolmcille. Calling ahead to book a bed in July and August is a good idea, but coming in the spring during lambing season is an even better one. (Dorms £7, private rooms £10. Laundry £4.50. **Camping** £4, with separate showers and kitchen.) On the way to Derrylahan, just under 1 mi. from Killybegs, **Dun Ulun House** (tel. 38137) is a luxurious alternative to hostel life at virtually the same price. The flowery beds, hardwood floors, and gorgeous views in the 2- to 4-bed rooms are turned into small dorms, if you're willing to share. Guests also have the option of self-catering; the house provides a well-outfitted kitchen. (Doubles and twins £12.50 per person, rooms with 3 or more beds £9.50 per person; B&B prices higher. All rooms with bath. Rooms in cottage across road £5 per person, with linens £6.50. Laundry £5. **Camping** £3, with separate facilities.)

CARRICK, TEELIN, AND SLIEVE LEAGUE

Slieve League claims the hotly contested (in Ireland) title of being the highest sea cliffs in Europe. Undoubtedly, the sheer face of its 2000 ft. drop into the Atlantic is spectacular. Most Slieve League hikers stay in Kilcar, from which they can comfortably drive, bike, or walk (about 6hr. return) to the mountain. From Kilcar, the coast road passes the tiny village of **Carrick.** For most of the year Carrick is but a brief stopping point for travelers seeking refreshment. The village scene is transformed during the last bank holiday weekend in October, when Carrick hosts the annual **Carrick Fleadh,** with barrels of creamy, foaming refreshment accompanied by trad. **Fishing** is rewarding around Teelin Bay, particularly in an area called **Salmon Leap.** (Remember that salmon fishing is illegal without a license.) The **Glen River** is best for trout. Tackle can be bought at the Spar Market in Kilcar. The Carrick area also offers several practical amenities for the local explorer. **Little Acorn Farm** (tel. 39386), located off the main Kilcar-Carrick road approximately 1 mi. before Carrick, offers **horses** for guided trail rides or (for the experienced rider) self-guided rides. (About £12 per hour.) About 1 mi. past Carrick is the even smaller village of **Teelin,** where Mrs. Maloney at **Teelin Bay House** (tel. 39043), the third B&B on the road to Teelin, is deservedly famous for the care she bestows upon her guests. It's a bit of a hike, but the view just keeps getting better. Book well ahead. (Singles £15, doubles £26.)

In clear weather it'd be unconscionable *not* to visit **Slieve League,** a mountain set along a precipitous, beautiful coastline rimmed with 1000 ft. cliffs. To reach the mountain, turn left halfway down Carrick's main street and follow signs for Teelin. At the **Rusty Mackerel Pub** (tel. 39101), you can turn left for the inland route to Slieve League. Alternatively, a turn to the right (the most popular decision) leads along the sea cliffs on the way up to Bunglass. At the end of the road at Bunglass sits a carpark. From here, a cliff path heads west along the coast. It should take 1½hr. to walk from Carrick to the car park. About a half-hour along the path continuing from the car park, the mountain top narrows to 2 ft. On one side of this pass—called **One Man's Pass**—the cliffs drop 1800 ft. to the sea. On the other side, the cliffs drop a measly 1000 ft. to a rocky floor. There are no railings, and the phobic sometimes slide across the 30m pass on their butts or hands and knees. (You can still enjoy a steep climb by walking along the inland face of the mountain.) The path then continues all the way along the cliffs to **Rossarrel Point,** near Glencolmcille. The entire Slieve League Way usually takes six to seven hours to walk. **Never go to Slieve League in poor weather.** Use extreme caution if you plan to cross the pass; it is not a necessary part of the hike across Slieve League. People have died here under poor conditions; several hikers have been blown off the pass by the strong winds. It's always a good idea to ask a local expert for advice. In non-ideal weather, the cliffs at Bunglass are safer option.

GLENCOLMCILLE (GLEANN CHOLM CILLE)

The parish on the western top of the Slieve League peninsula, Glencolmcille (glen-kaul-um-KEEL), is the base of several tiny towns and huge natural wonders; its land consists of rolling hills and sandy coves that lie between two huge sea cliffs. Named after St. Columcille, who founded a monastery here, this Irish-speaking area and pilgrimage site centers around the street-long village of Cashel, which lies just off N56 on, unsurprisingly, Cashel St. The road leads past the village's several storefronts and down to the coast, where most of the area's accommodations and attractions are located. Buses of tourists head for the Folk Village (see **Sights**), but few venture beyond it to the desolate, wind-swept cliffs. Though less dramatic than the mountain paths, N56 is the convenient route to most of Glencolmcille. **McGeehan's buses** leave from Biddy's Bar for **Kilcar, Killybegs, Ardara, Glenties,** and **Letterkenny** once a day, twice from July to mid-September. **Bus Éireann** has services to **Kilcar** and **Killybegs.** (Ask at the hostel or tourist office for details.) Glencolmcille's tiny **tourist office** (tel. 30116) is on Cashel St. (Open July-Aug. M-Sa 9:30am-9pm, Su noon-6pm; Apr.-June and Sept. to mid-Nov. M-Sa 10am-6pm, Su 1-5pm.) A bureau de change can be found at the Folk Village and the **post office,** east of the village center. (Post office open M-F 7:30am-1pm and 2-5:30pm, Sa 9am-1pm.) The nearest banks and **ATMs** are in Kilcar and Ardara.

■■■ **ACCOMMODATIONS, FOOD, AND PUBS.** A trip to Donegal wouldn't be complete without a visit to Mary and her "favorite" son, Leo, at the ■**Dooey Hostel (IHO),** the oldest independent hostel in Ireland. To get there, turn left at the end of the village and follow the signs ¾ mi. uphill. The hostel is built into the hillside overlooking the sea, and a wide spectrum of flowers grows into the rocky face that is the hostel's corridor. The colorfulness of this atrium is matched only by that of its owners' personalities. (Dorms £6.50, doubles £14. **Camping** £3.50. Wheelchair accessible. Campers share hostelers' facilities.) Mrs. Ann Ward's **Atlantic Scene** (tel. 30186), the next house after the hostel, lives up to its name. The beds are soft, but you'll stay up just to admire the view longer. (£14.90. Open May-Sept.) More B&Bs surround the Folk Village.

The **Lace House Restaurant and Cafe**, above the tourist office on Cashel St., is a chipper with a large menu of fried foods and a second-story view of sea cliffs. (Entrees £3-4. Open Easter-Sept. daily 10am-9pm.) **An Chistan** (AHN KEESHT-ahn, "the kitchen"; tel. 30213), at the Foras Cultúir Uladh (see **Sights**), is especially affordable at lunch. (Sandwiches £2; entrees £5. Open M-Sa 10am-6pm, Su noon-6pm.) The **teashop** in the Folk Village tempts with delicious sandwiches (£1.50) and Guinness cake (80p). **Byrne and Sons Food Store,** Cashel St., supplies the basics in solids, liquids, and printed matter. (Open M-Sa 9:30am-10pm, Su 9:30am-1pm and 7-9pm.) Cashel's pubs have a dark, dusty 1950s Ireland feel to them: imagine spare rooms with plastic-covered snugs, and, for once, a minimal amount of wood paneling. Although the pubs are primarily a haven for locals, they develop an affinity for visitors during July and August. Most famous among them is the unassuming 120-year-old **Biddy's** (tel. 30016), at the mouth of Carrick Rd. Since it's the favorite of the older crowd, you'll meet lots of Irish speakers. (Trad at least 3 times a week during the summer.) **Roarty's** (tel. 30273), the next pub down Cashel St., welcomes guests with trad several times a week. Last on the road is **Glen Head Tavern** (tel. 30008), the largest and youngest of the three pubs. Practically the whole village could fit into its recently redone lounge, which hosts legendary impromptu trad sessions.

⚄ SIGHTS. Glencolmcille's craft movement began in the 1950s under the direction of the omnipresent **Father James McDyer,** who was also responsible for getting electricity in Glencolmcille, founding the Folk Village, and building the local football field. Today, the town is renowned for its handmade products, particularly sweaters, which are on sale at numerous "jumper shops" on the roads surrounding the town. Close to town is the **Foras Cultúir Uladh** (FOHR-us KULT-er UH-lah; "The Ulster Cultural Institute"), which runs the Oideas Gael institute for the preservation of the Irish language and culture. The Foras offers regular courses on such varied pursuits as hill walking, painting, pottery, local archaeology, traditional music, and Gaelic. It also has frequently changing exhibitions on local history and concerts and performances on a regular basis. (Tel. 30248. Open daily 9am-6pm.)

A bit past the village center is Father McDyer's **Folk Village Museum and Heritage Centre,** the town's attraction for non-hiking, non-Irish speaking tourists. The museum is housed in stone cottages with immaculately thatched roofs, which date from 1700, 1850, and 1900. The 1850s schoolhouse is open to the general public. The guided tours describe the furniture and tools from each of these eras in Irish history. A short nature trail from the village leads up a hill past various reconstructed remains, including a Mass rock, a sweat house, and a lime kiln. The **craft shop** stocks a good assortment of sweaters, books, and postcards and is possibly the only place in the world where you can buy rosary beads made from seaweed. The **sheeben** (the old name for an illegal drinking establishment) sells homemade heather, fuchsia, and seaweed wines (free samples with tour) and whiskey marmalade. (Tel. 30017. Open Easter-Sept. M-Sa 10am-6pm, Su noon-6pm. Tours July-Aug. every 30min., Apr.-June and Sept. every hr. £2; students, seniors, and children £1.25.) The beginning of July brings the two-day **Glencolmcille Folk Festival,** a lively and occasionally raucous celebration.

Fine beaches and cliffs make for excellent hiking in all directions. A 5 mi. walk southwest from Cashel leads to **Malinbeg**, a winsome hamlet at the edge of a sandy cove. This coastal area was once notorious for smuggling *poitín* through tunnels, some of which may still be in use. When a sunny day happens to grace Donegal, a trip to the **Silver Strand** will be well rewarded with stunning views of the gorgeous

---

ALONE IN THE HUSK OF MAN'S HOME Many a poetic, brooding type has felt compelled to isolate him or herself in the far reaches of Co. Donegal. The valley next to Port has provided refuge to poet Dylan Thomas, as well as artist Rockwell Kent. Only two cottages stand in this valley, and no roads touch it. Dylan Thomas' self-imposed isolation was meant to clean the alcoholism out of his system, although the area's *poitín* smuggling foiled that plan. The locals are sure to break out into grins if you ask them about Rockwell Kent, who supposedly came to Port to hide from the American CIA, and never left his cottage after dark.

---

beach and surrounding rocky cliffs. From the strand, you can start the long-distance trek along the Slieve League coastline (see **Carrick, Teelin, and Slieve League,** p. 361). A sandy beach links the cliffs on the south and north sides of Glencolmcille. North of Glencolmcille, **Glen Head,** easily identifiable by the Martello tower at its peak, is an hour's walk from town through land laden with prehistoric ruins, including St. Colmcille's stations of the cross. The tourist office and hostel in town each have a map that shows the locations of major sites. A third walk from town begins at the Protestant church and climbs over a hill to the ruins of the ghostly "famine village" of **Port** in the valley on the other side (3hr. walk). Supposedly haunted by crying babies, this eerie village has been empty since its inhabitants emigrated during the Famine. The only current resident, according to local rumor, is an eccentric artist who lives by the isolated bay without electricity or water. The gargantuan phallic rock sticking out of the sea is just what it appears to be: the only part of the Devil still visible after St. Colmcille banished him to the ocean.

The road east from Glencolmcille to Ardara passes through the spectacular **Glengesh Pass.** Nine hundred feet above sea level, the road tackles the surrounding mountains with hairpin turns. Biking is common in these parts, but be warned that the steep and winding pass offers a challenging ride suitable to only the most intrepid cyclists. Hitching is a tough task along this unfrequented road. *Let's Go* does not recommend hitchhiking.

ARDARA

The historic center of the Donegal tweed industry, Ardara (ar-DRAH) now attracts mostly tweed-fiends with high credit limits. Other towns have replaced Ardara as the cheapest sources of locally knit and woven articles; better deals can often be found at small "craft centres" in surrounding villages. Today, Ardara's Heritage Centre plays an important role in the movement to revive traditional hand-weaving techniques. On the first weekend of June during the **Weavers' Fair,** weavers from all over Donegal congregate in Ardara to show their weft; musicians add further festivity to the weekend.

⚐ PRACTICAL INFORMATION. **Bus Éireann** stops in Adara on its **Killybegs-Portnoo** route (2 per day) in front of **Spar Market** (tel. 41107) on Main St. (Open M-F 8:30am-8pm, Sa 8:30am-9pm, Su 8:30am-1pm.) **McGeehan's** halts on The Diamond at least once a day in the summer as part of its **Dublin-Donegal Town-Dungloe** trip. The **Ardara Heritage Centre** (tel. 41704) has tourist information. (Open Jan.-Nov. daily 9:30am-6pm.) **Ulster Bank,** The Diamond (tel. 41121) has a **24hr. ATM. Rent bikes** at **Don Byrne's** (tel. 41156), past town on Killybegs Rd. (Open M-W and F 10am-12:30pm and 1:30-4pm, Th 10am-12:30pm and 1:30-5pm.) The **Ardara Medical Hall,** Front St., next to the Heritage Centre, is just a **pharmacy.** (Open M-Sa 9am-1pm and 2-6pm.) The **post office** (tel. 41101) is opposite the Heritage Centre. (Open M-F 9am-1pm and 2-5:30pm, Sa 9am-1pm.) The **phone code** is 075 rows from completion.

⚐🍴🍺 ACCOMMODATIONS, FOOD, AND PUBS. The **Drumbarron Hostel (IHO)** (tel. 41200) offers clean, sunny rooms directly on The Diamond. Travelers can get keys at the house across the way from the hostel's side entrance. (Dorms £7, doubles £16. Flexible curfew 1am.) The hostel's owners offer far more aesthetically appealing accommodations across the street at the **Drumbarron B&B.** The rooms have hardwood floors and walls decked with the owner's semi-abstract paintings. (Doubles ₤30, with bath ₤36.) **Charlie's West End Cafe** (tel. 41656) lacks the trendy atmosphere its name suggests. The service is quick and the prices are low for a tourist town—probably because Charlie's is frequented primarily by locals. (Enormous lunch specials ₤3.75, sandwiches ₤1.50. Open M-Sa 10am-10:30pm, Su 2-10:30pm.) Decked out in bright copper kettles and warm woolen mittens, **Nancy's Bar,** Front St., just might become one of your favorite things. Come for the seafood, or the weekend trad sessions. (Steamed mussels ₤4.) **Peter Oliver's Central Bar,** Main St. (tel. 41311), has trad every single night June through September. Arrive early if you want breathing space. For a quieter pint, head two doors down to the **Corner Bar** (tel. 41726). It rumbles with trad twice a week.

■ **SIGHTS.** The **Ardara Heritage Centre,** The Diamond, tells the story of the centuries-old Donegal tweed industry. Live weaving demonstrations show the full-bodied dexterity required of hand-loom weavers in creating the richly varied textiles that, these days, are sold in mass quantities throughout the world. Donegal tweeds incorporate dyes made from four natural elements: lichen, blackberries, heather, and soot. On-site hand-weavers will gladly answer your most burning questions about the craft. (Tel. 41704. Open Jan.-Nov. daily 9:30am-6pm. Free.) The **tea room** serves food when the center is open. (Entrees ₤1-3.)

Beautiful walks are there for the taking along the peninsula located east of Ardara. From town, head south toward Glencolmcille and turn right at the "Castle View" horse-riding sign toward **Loughros Point** (LOW-crus). At the next horse-riding sign, either turn right for a beautiful view of Ardara Bay, or continue straight to reach stupendous views of the sea at the Point (1hr. walk). Five miles out from town, the **Maghera Caves** once sheltered shipwrecked sailors from the Spanish Armada (1½hr. walk). The six caves vary in size and depth; all require a flashlight. At low tide you can enter the Dark Cave, once the refuge of *poitín* makers. Be warned that a rising tide could trap you inside; for daily tide times, check the *The Irish Independent.* To reach the caves, follow the main road south past the Loughros turnoff, then follow the signs several miles west on small roads. The road that passes the caves continues across a mountain pass to Dungloe. Independent and guided **horse rides** start from **Castle View Ranch** (tel. 41212), 2½ well-posted miles from the town center off Glencolmcille Rd. (₤10 per hr., ₤45 per day.)

GLENTIES

Glenties is best known for being a five-time winner of "Ireland's Tidiest Town" and—rather incongruously—for hosting one of the area's largest discos each Saturday. Dusting and dancing create a spirited beauty in this village; Brian Friel's play *Dancing at Lughnasa,* written about his aunts, captures Glenties beautifully. Several pleasant walks nearby also recommend the town. It makes a good stop along Bus Éireann or McGeehan's routes through northwest Donegal.

■ **PRACTICAL INFORMATION.** In town, the **Bank of Ireland,** Main St., has one of the area's few **24hr. ATMs.** (Open M-W and F 10am-12:30pm and 1:30-4pm, Th 10am-12:30pm and 1:30-5pm). **Glentie's Medical Hall,** Main St., provides pharmaceutical goodies. (Open M-Tu and Th-F 9:30am-1pm and 2-6pm, W 9:30am-1pm.) The **post office** (tel. 51101), is destined to appear on a postcard. (Open M-F 9am-1pm and 2-5:30pm, Sa 9am-1pm.) The **phone code** is a tidy twist at 075.

■■■ **ACCOMMODATIONS, FOOD, AND PUBS.** **Campbell's Holiday Hostel (IHH)** (tel. 51491), just around the bend at the far end of Main St. toward Ardara, provides cheap and clean rooms decorated in primary colors. The common space has a fireplace, satellite TV, and two fully equipped kitchens. (Dorms July-Aug. ₤8, private rooms ₤10 per person; Sept.-June ₤6, ₤8. Sheets ₤1. Wash and dry ₤3. Wheelchair accessible.) The most convenient and best-priced B&Bs in the area are at the opposite end of Main St. **Andros B&B** (tel. 51234) has rooms and suites for up to four with plush carpeting. (£16 per person, all with bath.) Her daughter-in-law runs **Marguerite's B&B,** (tel. 51699) next door in a nearly identical house, although Marguerite's rooms have hardwood floors and TVs. (£17 per person, all with bath.)

Thomas Beecht's **organic farm** (tel. 51286) is reached by heading down Main St. toward Columcille and turning left at a sign for the farm, located 2 mi. down Meenahall Rd. There is also a wholefood shop called **Good Earth** (tel. 51794; open M-Sa 9:30am-6pm), and a large **Spar Market** (open M-Th 8am-8pm, F-Sa 8am-9pm, Su 8am-1:30pm). For a sit-down meal, the bar in the **Highlands Hotel** (tel. 51111) is a tasty option. (2-course lunch £4, chowder £3, sandwiches under £2.) **Jim McGuinness's** offers standard chipper fare to young kids and late-night dancers. (Open M-Th noon-midnight, F noon-2am, Sa noon-4am, Su 5pm-midnight.)

Like everything else, the pubs in town are on Main St. **Paddy's Bar** (tel. 51158), though somewhat packaged, has great music performances every night during the summer. (Trad W.) At **John Joe's** (tel. 51333), on the opposite side of Main St., you'll hear the Irish tongue and live music bouncing off low ceilings at least twice a week. At the far end of town toward Dungloe, the **Limelight** (tel. 51118) has a ballroom's worth of space, and attracts dancers from all over Donegal to its five bars and splendid discos. (Friday alcohol-free for ages 14-18, cover 10pm-1am £3; Saturday 18 and older, £4. Open 10pm-2am.)

■ **SIGHTS.** Next to the hostel, **St. Connell's Museum and Heritage Centre** is a good starting point for exploration of the surrounding countryside. Its informed staff will introduce you to local history and nearby sites of interest. An assortment of exhibitions and videos mostly concern St. Connell and the remaining markers of his 6th century missionary; it also has a "study room" for genealogy. (Open Apr.-Sept. M-F 10am-12:30pm and 2-4:30pm. £2, students 50p.)

Good walks in the surrounding countryside are sign-posted from the crossroads next to the Heritage Centre, and the staff inside offer advice. Among the more satisfying walks is one that takes you to **Inniskeel Island,** 8 mi. past Glenties toward Dungloe; signs point the way from Narin Beach, where drivers can park. The island, where the ruins of **St. Connell's** 6th century church lie, is accessible only when the tide is out; check the *Irish Independent* for times. An hour's walk brings you to **Lough Anney,** the reservoir for Glenties and Ardara; follow the directions to the organic farm (see **Food**), and the reservoir is a bit farther ahead to your right in the hills. A 2½ mi. walk along the **Owenrea River** leads to **Mullantayboyne;** follow the directions to the organic farm, but turn right off the main road at the Meenahalla sign instead of left. The river lies ahead on this side road.

The 12th of September brings the **Harvest Fair** to Glenties, an annual celebration of local agriculture, industry, and beer drinking. On the first weekend in October, fiddlers from all over the world descend upon Glenties for **Fiddler's Weekend.** Call the hostel for information on either.

THE DONEGAL GAELTACHT

In this part of Ireland, Irish culture—language, music, dance—is lived, not practiced. Most visitors, whether well-traveled backpackers, students of the Irish language, or the rare tour-bus passenger, come to Donegal with a purist's appetite for Irish culture and leave well satiated. The Donegal dialect of Irish is distinct from other dialects (like Connemara and Munster). The Donegal style of music is bred most successfully around the *gaeltacht.* Buses run infrequently, so be sure to plan your schedule—or not, because you may decide to stay. The **phone code** for the whole area is 075.

THE ROSSES

N56 bumps and bounces along the spectacularly beautiful midwest coast from Glenties to Dungloe. Expansive, sandy beaches are isolated by the eerie stillness of the Derryveagh Mountains. To the north and west of Burtonport stretch the Rosses, a stretch of land that's largely untouched and a bog ecologist's paradise. Stony soil dotted with tiny ponds covers the glacially crumpled ground of this headland. The Rosses is referred to as the broken *gaeltacht*, for its Irish-speaking community also uses some English. The corruptive influence of the English language is hardly to be feared in these parts, for locals are likely to tell you that this is the "real" Donegal, where peat cutting and salmon fishing keep the economy and old customs alive.

DUNGLOE (AN CLOCHAN LIATH) AND CROHY HEAD

Dungloe (dun-LO), known locally as the capital of the Rosses, is a busy market town near spectacular Crohy Head where travelers stock up before hurrying on to the Gweedore and the mountains.

⛰ PRACTICAL INFORMATION. Dungloe is a stopping point for **Bus Éireann** (tel. (073) 21101) on its way to Donegal town thrice daily in July and August. The following private lines also service Dungloe: **McGeehan's** (tel. 46150) to **Dublin; Swilly** (tel. 21380) to **Derry; Doherty's** (tel. 21105) to Glasgow via **Letterkenny** and **Belfast; Jim O'Donnell** (tel. 48356) to **Belfast** via **Letterkenny** and **Derry;** and **Feda O'Donnell** (tel. 48114) to **Galway.** The Dungloe **tourist office** (tel. 21297), on a well-marked side street off Main St. toward the shore, has free maps of the town, and it's a good idea to stop in here before heading into the Rosses and Gweedore since it's the last Bord Fáilte you'll find in the area. (Open June-Sept. M-Sa 10am-1pm and 2-6pm.) Main St. sports a **Bank of Ireland** (tel. 21077) with a **24hr. ATM,** and an **AIB** (tel. 21179). (Both open M-W and F 10am-12:30pm and 1:30-4pm, Th 10am-12:30pm and 1:30-5pm.) **Dennis Brennan** (tel. 22633) provides **taxi** services. Pharmaceuticals proliferate at **O'Donnell's Pharmacy,** Main St. (tel. 21386; open M-Sa 9am-6pm), like philatelists at the teeny **post office,** Quay Rd. (tel. 21067), off Main St. (open M-F 9am-1pm and 2-5:30pm, Sa 9am-1pm).

⛰⛺☰ ACCOMMODATIONS, FOOD, AND PUBS. **Greene's Independent Holiday Hostel (IHH),** Carnmore Rd. (tel. 21943), is right off Main St. away from the waterfront. Mr. Green's basic hostel offers a well upholstered common room and enormous kitchen. (6- to 9-bed dorms £7, doubles £18, singles £8. Laundry £3 flexible. Curfew Tu-Th 1am, F-M 2am. **Bike rental** £5 per day.) **Park House,** Carnmore Rd. (tel. 21351), across from the Supervalu, has huge, fluffy beds and an open kitchen. (Singles £20, doubles £3; all with bath.) **Hillcrest B&B,** Barrack Brae (tel. 21484), is at the top of the hill on the Burtonport end of town, about 100 m. past the end of Main St. It has views of the water and pretty rooms with bath. (£15.) There is also a two-bedroom flat, with bath and kitchen. (£40 per night.) **Dungloe Camping and Caravan Park** (tel. 21943) is right behind the hostel. (£4 per tent with 1 person, £2 for each additional person; £2 per car.)

If you're cooking, stop by the **Cope Supermarket,** Main St. (Open M-Th 9am-6pm, F 9am-7pm.) **SuperValu** is about a half-mile down Carnmore Rd. (Open M-Th 9am-6:30pm, F 9am-8pm, Sa 9am-7pm.) The posh **Riverside Bistro** has vegetarian entrees for just £6, but carnivores pay £8-12 for meat or fish. (Open daily June-Aug. noon-10pm, Sept.-May noon-3pm and 6-10pm.) Weekend trad sessions at **Beedy's,** Main St. (tel. 21219), bring in seasonal musicians from all over Donegal. During the week, a local crowd hangs out here. **Bridge Inn** (tel. 21036) hosts a disco on weekend nights. (Cover £5.) When the nightclub isn't open, idle youngsters congregate at the **Atlantic Bar** (tel. 22166), across the street. At the other end of town, the **Tirconnail Bar,** Main St. (tel. 21479), has beautiful ocean views that inspire contemplative musing over slow pints.

☒ **SIGHTS.** Hundreds of party-lovers flock to Dungloe in the last week of July for the **Mary from Dungloe Festival,** named after a popular folk song about the tragic love affair between Mary and a callous American. The population swells to 80,000 during this 10 day celebration. The highlight of the festival, of course, is the selection of the annual Donegal ambassador, Mary from Dungloe, although most attendees would say that it's the three concerts that Daniel O'Donnell is guaranteed to perform during the week. For festival info and ticket bookings, call the **Festival Booking Office** (tel. 21254), next to the tourist office. (Open M-Sa 10am-6pm.)

Crohy Head, the peninsula 6 mi. southwest of Dungloe, collects strangely shaped rock formations around a jagged coast. **Crohy Head Youth Hostel (An Óige/HI)** (tel. 21950), in an old coast guard station, offers stupendous views over the Atlantic. (Easter-June £5.50, under 18 £4.50; July-Sept. £6.50, under 18 £5. Call ahead.) To reach the peninsula and the hostel from Dungloe, turn onto Quay Rd. toward Maghery halfway down Main St. and follow the bumpy road along the sea. The hostel is about a mile past the village of Maghery.

BURTONPORT

About 5 mi. north of Dungloe, the fishing village of Burtonport is less a town than a few pubs clustered around a pier. The ferry to Arranmore Island docks here, and the village is also a good base for fishing and boat trips to the many uninhabited islands in the area. More salmon land here than in any other spot in Ireland or Britain. Intense sea angling competitions take place during July and August (call the Dungloe tourist office for details). The **Burtonport Festival** rouses up locals the week preceding the Mary of Dungloe Festival in July with a similar program of endemic trad, dance, and sport. **Sea anglers** are booked from the shop on Burtonport Pier (tel. 42077); be sure to call ahead. (Open daily 10am-5pm or so. Fishing trips £15, rod rental £4.50.) The **post office** (tel. 42001) is at the start of town, about 200 yd. from the pier. (Open M-F 9am-1pm and 2-5:30pm, Sa 9am-1pm.)

The **Cope** (tel. 42004), at the top of the town, is the largest **grocery** on either side of the water, so stock up before boarding the ferry to Arranmore Island. (Open M-Sa 9am-6pm.) All Burtonport's pubs squat around the harbour, and most sport a maritime theme. Beside the harbor, the bar of **Skipper's Tavern** (tel. 42234) teems with nets, skippers' hats, and nautical knots. (Trad most summer nights.) Nearby, the **Lobster Pot,** Main St. (tel. 42012), won the James Joyce award for authentic Irish pubs. The wall hangings include Irish soccer jerseys, and Jaws's head bursting from the wall and clutching a nail-polished hand. (Sandwiches £2, entrees £5-7. Restaurant open daily 6-10pm; bar open daily 1-10pm.) The **Harbor Bar and Takeaway** (tel. 42321), next to the pier, has food and drink. (Soup £1.20, entrees £3-4.) Across the street at **O'Donnell's Bar** (tel. 42255), landlubbers can escape the salt air at Burtonport's oldest pub. (Trad on weekends.)

Five miles north of Burtonport on the Coast Road dwells the little village of **Kincasslagh,** birthplace of the sweetheart singer Daniel O'Donnell and the site of his **Viking House Hotel** (tel. 43295); the hotel, though beyond the means of the budget traveler, is mecca for countless members of the blue-rinse gang on O'Donnell pilgrimages. A minor road heads west to **Cruit Island,** not really an island at all, but rather a peninsula with nice beaches and a host of thatched cottages. Farther north, the magnificent stretch of sand known as **Carrickfinn Strand** is marred only by the presence of tiny **Donegal Airport** (tel. 48284; flights to **Dublin** and other domestic airports, connections to international destinations).

ARRANMORE ISLAND

On **Arranmore Island** ("Arainn," "Aran," or "Arran Island" on some maps), a rocky, boulder-covered landscape makes for knee-scraping day-hikes and spooky midnight prowling. The ferry ride out is scenic, passing smaller, mostly abandoned rocky islands. About 600 people live in the sheltered southeast corner of the island, where most accommodations and amenities lie. The smaller population on the other side of the island speaks Irish and feels less influence from the mainland.

⚑ PRACTICAL INFORMATION. The **ferry** office (tel. 20532) is open daily 8:30am to 7:30pm, and sends boats to Burtonport (20min.; July-Aug. M-Sa 8 per day, Su 7 per day, Sept.-June 4-6 per day; £6 return, students £5, seniors free with ID, children £3, bicycles £1.50). A tourist establishment of note is **Bonner's Restaurant** (tel. 20532), which serves as ferry booking office, B&B, and take-out shop. (Meals £4-5. Open daily 8:30am-8:30pm.) Uphill behind Bonner's, the small **Tourist Information Center** welcomes visitors and sells decorative maps of the island (£2). (Open M-Sa noon-6pm, Su 3-6pm.)

▉▉▉ ACCOMMODATIONS, FOOD, AND PUBS. Along the shore to the left of the ferry port stretches a string of pubs and houses. The house closest to the ferry is the **Boat House** (tel. 20511), where life-long residents offer clean rooms and expert advice on exploring the island. (£18.) One of the island's greatest traditions is its grand summertime nightlife. With 24hr. licenses to serve fishermen returning from sea, some pubs serve "refreshments" into the morning. Accordingly, the list of pubs is a long one for such a small island. To the left of the ferry dock as you step off the boat is **Phil Bàn's** (tel. 20908). The ocean laps against its foundation at high tide, but it's well established on the island, as is the attached grocery store. (Open M-Sa 9am-6pm, Su noon-2pm.) **Pally's** (tel. 20584) is a mile past the ferry dock; turn left off the main road toward the sea, and take the first left. Just take the advice of the enormous signpost that reads "have a jar at Pally's Bar." **Neilly's** (tel. 20509), a half mile down the main road, has an intimate, local feel. **O'Donnell's Atlantic Bay** (tel. 20918) offers sessions most weekends during the summer and a breathtaking view of the bay. Up the hill to the right of the ferry terminal, **Boyle's Night Club** (tel. 20512) hosts a Saturday night dance party. (Cover £2.) Just above the ferry docks, **Early's Pub** (tel. 20515), is where Daniel O'Donnell earned his first gig, but the tiny space wouldn't fit an umpteenth of O'Donnell's present following. As a token of thanks to Arranmore's early support, O'Donnell gives an annual concert on the island and brings teary-eyed hordes with him.

▉ SIGHTS. Four priceless pearls were a gift to Red Hugh O'Donnell from Philip II for Red Hugh's help in saving Spanish sailors when Armada ships went down off the coast. The pearls were last seen on Arranmore Island in 1905, and people are still searching. Locals can also tell you a less romantic version of the story: hungry Spanish sailors exchanged the pearls for food, tobacco, and booze. The last inheritor put them in Lloyd's Bank in London, where they sit today in their not-so-priceless splendor. The pearls make a great story, but more impressive is the island's landscape and hiking opportunities. **The Arranmore Way**, a well-marked footpath, runs the circumference of the island and will lead you along three possible paths; the longest trail goes to the lighthouse at the far tip of the island, high above impressive cliffs and rushing water. A map of trails (£2) is available from the tourist center. A full perambulation of Arranmore Way takes a good six hours.

RANNAFAST

In the heart of the Donegal *gaeltacht*, the village of **Annagry** marks the beginning of the **Rannafast** area, famous for its storytelling tradition. *Seanachies*, or storytellers, prolong the life of the Irish language and narrative tradition. In the summer, Annagry hosts total-immersion Irish-language camps that draw teenagers from all over the Republic. About 500 yd. south of the village, on top of a hill to the left of the road, is **Teàc Jack's** pub and restaurant (tel. 48113). Local musicians congregate here on weekend nights in the summer. (Soup and bread £1.30, sandwich £1.20, entrees £2-4.) About 3 mi. farther down the road is **Leo's Tavern.** Leo is the father of multi-layered voice guru Enya and the family group Clannad, whose silver, gold, and platinum records decorate the walls of this otherwise modest music hall. Leo plays his enormous electric piano-accordion on stage and leads a sing-along for a typically international audience nightly, while his son Bartely runs the pub. On Wednesday nights in July and August a large company of musicians gather at Leo's for trad sessions; trad takes on unpredictable nights during the year. For a more predictable music experience, head to **Teach Tessie,** across the street, where locals gather for fine trad on Sunday nights.

GWEEDORE

Gweedore, the Irish-speaking coastal region northeast of the Rosses, is one of the most remote and wonderful parts of Ireland. Quilted with sheep and stone fences, the ragged, grassy mountains welcome walking enthusiasts. Cyclists are enthralled with the challenging but quiet roads. Crolly is the gateway to this, the most beautiful part of Donegal. Beyond Crolly, the road leads to exquisite beaches and the legendary Poison Glen. Errigal Mountain's sheer face and Bloody Foreland's oceanfront appear otherworldly; Tory Island *is* a world apart from Ireland, with its own elected king and freedom from Irish taxes, as well as a demonic past.

CROLLY AND TOR

The N56 intersects with the coastal road at a small bridge. The coastal road twists and bends along the jagged edges where Donegal meets the sea, leading you through spectacular scenery dotted with small Irish-speaking villages. Smart travelers stop at **Crolly,** just past the bridge at N56, for a pint and groceries. Several bus lines stops in front of Paddy Oig's pub. **Feda O'Donnell** (tel. 48114) provides a daily coach service to and from **Galway** and **Donegal Town** via **Letterkenny; Swilly** (tel. 21380) passes on its **Dungloe-Derry** route; **John McGinley Coaches** (tel. (074) 35201) makes Crolly its starting point for a **Dublin** journey; and **O'Donnell Trans-Ulster Express** (tel. 48356) goes by on its way to **Belfast.** The postmistress at the Crolly **post office** (tel. 48120) is a good source of information on the area and can point you toward accommodations. (Open M-F 9am-5:30pm, Sa 9am-1pm.) The **Crolly Filling Station,** next to the post office, provides everything from groceries and gasoline to bike repairs and car rental. (Open M-Sa 9am-11pm, Su 9am-10pm.)

Paddy Oig's pub (tel. 31306) has everything a body could need: **camping,** pub grub (sandwiches £1), and Tuesday and Thursday night trad sessions in the summer. **Coillín Darach Caravan & Camping Park** (tel. 32000), just behind the pub, has modern facilities, a convenience store with the basic commodities (open daily 9am-10pm), and the odd tennis court. (July-Aug. £6 tent, Sept.-June £4. Electricity £1. Laundry £2.) Just past Paddy Oig's, a weather-beaten sign will point you toward ■Screagan an Iolair Hill Hostel (SCRAG an UH-ler; tel. 48593), which lies 4 mi. up a mountain road at **Tor** in **Glenveagh National Park.** Turn left off the coastal road at the sign and follow Tor Road past breathtaking scenery and climbs; when you pass Lough Keel, the road divides. Hostel-seekers should continue straight ahead to reach one of the best hostels in Ireland, with a great book collection, ever-changing views of the surrounding crags, and a "meditation room". The hostel is remote, but most visitors come here for at least several days; kind owners Eamon and Mireilla will share a wealth of information on local hikes and points of interest, and the stellar common room stores a fine library of pamphlets and books on regional events, sites, and transportation. (Dorms £7.50, private rooms £9. Laundry £3. Open all year, but call ahead Nov.-Feb.)

Tor Rd. continues past Ashardan Waterfall and Lake, and finally into Glen Tor. Crolly and the hostel nearby make a good base for exploring the pristine heath lands of the **Derryveagh Mountains,** inhabited by red deer. Trails for hikers of varying abilities, clearly shown on the *Ordnance Survey Discovery Series I,* begin at the hostel in Tor. As the trails are often hard to follow, hikers should always inform the hostel warden of their plans.

ERRIGAL MOUNTAIN AND DUNLEWEY

One mile north of Crolly, N56 and the coastal road diverge. N56 turns inland and reaches R251 after about 5 mi. This road leads east through **Dunlewey** past the foot of conical **Errigal Mountain,** Ireland's second highest mountain, and eventually to Glenveagh National Park. The drive is studded with stunning views. A mile from the foot of Errigal Mountain in Dunlewy village, the spruce-sheltered 46-bed **Errigal Youth Hostel (An Óige/HI)** (tel. 31180) is a clean, no frills, hiker's haven with a warm proprietress. (Dorms July-Sept. £7, Oct.-June £6.) A few minutes up the road is a turn-off to **Dunlewey Lake** and the **Poison Glen** (see **How Poison Glen Got its Name,**

HOW POISON GLEN GOT ITS NAME According to the Ulster Cycle of Irish mythology, the coast of Donegal was originally inhabited by the Fomorian race of evil tempered devils. The leader of the Fomorians was the giant Balor, a demon famed for his single "evil eye" that would turn the beholder to dust when the eyelid was lifted by two assistants tugging on its chains. Balor ruled the country from his fort on Tory Island until the fateful day when the young Lugh (later to be the god of light) challenged him to battle. Balor accepted the challenge and met Lugh at Dún Lughaidh ("Lugh's Fort," pronounced Dun-LEW-y). Intelligent Lugh took aim for Balor's eye before the eyelid was lifted, then closed his own eyes and let his arrow fly; it struck Balor directly in the Evil Eye and killed him. The poison from Balor's eye supposedly spread across the ground of the battlesite, making it unfit for even animals to graze on. The poisonous plant that today covers the valley is called "spurge" (Latin name *euphorbia*), although where that name comes from is anyone's guess. Another theory states that Poison Glen is a mistranslation of the Irish for "Beautiful Glen."

above). Within the wooded area of the glen is the former manor of the English aristocracy. In an open spot next to the lake stands their abandoned church; its decaying, roofless exterior makes a spooky addition to the myth-laden glen. If you continue along the paved road around a few curves, you will eventually reach an unmarked car park that signals the beginning of the trail up Errigal Mountain (2466 ft.). You must follow this trail in order to scramble through the loose scree to the summit. Expect the climb to take two to three hours total. A dangerous, narrow ridge must be traversed to reach the summit. Be sure to keep an eye on the clouds—they've been known to congregate suddenly around the mountaintop. The summit is the smallest in Ireland, and the sheer face of the mountain could shorten your journey from one hour to one minute.

Back at the bottom, just before the hostel, the **Ionad Cois Locha Dunlewey**, or **Dunlewey Lakeside Center** (tel. 31699), offers boat tours, weaving demos, a craft shop, roaming local animals, enough info on the area to count as a tourist office, and a fire-warmed cafe. (Open Easter-Oct. M-Sa 10:30am-6pm, Su 11am-7pm. Boat trips $2.70, students $2. Thatched weaving cottage town $2.50, students $2. Combined ticket $4.) The center also offers a stunning series of trad concerts during the summer (tickets $3-10, usually $5) and music workshops all year.

BUNBEG AND BLOODY FORELAND

Where N56 moves inland, R257 continues along the coast to **Bunbeg**. The coastal road traverses a strip of continuously stunning scenery; this stretch is perfect for cyclists, since there's little traffic. Hitchers tend to stay on N56, where cars are more common. *Let's Go* does not recommend hitchhiking. Bunbeg Harbour, the smallest enclosed harbor in Ireland, was a main of exit and entry at the height of Britain's imperialism. Relics from that period line the harbor: military barracks, grain stones, and look-out towers. Bunbeg's harbor is one of two docking places for **Donegal Coastal Cruises** (a.k.a. **Turasmara**; tel. 31991), ferry service for Tory Island; in the summer, it makes a morning and an afternoon trip daily, weather permitting ($15 return, students $13). Halfway from the town to the harbor, a single stone pillar marks a rough path that leads to the banks of the Clady River, where salmon fishermen do their craft. The **Bunbeg House** (tel. 31305), on the waterfront, serves sandwiches ($2.50) and seafood (from $5).

If you continue past the Bunbeg turnoff, you will immediately see the irresistible ⬛**Hudi Beag's** pub (tel. 31016). On Monday nights, only the truly unmusically-inclined could walk past the intense session taking place within this pub. A stone's throw away is **An Chisteanach** (an KEESH-nach), a cozy sit-down deli with stomach-stretching portions for about $5. (Open M-Sa 8:30am-7pm.)

On the streets of nearby **Derrybeg** are several banks, but only the **AIB** has both a buruea de change and an **ATM**. (Open M-F 10am-1pm and 2-4:30pm.) **Teach Thomais** (tel. 31054), the oldest shop in the parish, sells a delightful collection of English and Gaelic books and crafts (if the shop's locked, knock at the kitchen door to its right). **Gweedore Chemists** (tel. 31254) is housed in a green building across the street from Hudi Beag's. The **post office** is also on the main street. (Open M-F 9am-1pm and 2-5:30pm.)

About 7 mi. north of Bunbeg, **Bloody Foreland,** a short length of rough scarlet rock, juts into the sea. At sunset, the sea reflects the deep red hue of the sky and rocks. An old legend holds that the sea is colored with the blood of sailors who perished in the wrecks of Spanish galleons. Farther west, the headland at **Magheraroarty** offers miles of unspoiled beaches. A holy well remains full of fresh water despite tidal rushes twice a day. **Ferries** to Tory Island (tel. (074) 35061) travel from Magheraroarty, but the pier is much more isolated than that at Bunbeg.

TORY ISLAND

Visible from the Bloody Foreland, barren Tory Island, named for its *tors* (hills), sits 8 mi. off the coast. The weather-beaten cottages and people of Tory fulfill many visitors' imaginative visions of what old Ireland looked like, but that characterization underestimates the weirdness of Tory's landscape and people. The island has a mythical status as the home of the demonic Fomorians. The Fomorians were the original Tory Island pirates who regularly invaded the mainland under the leadership of Balor of the Evil Eye (see **How the Poison Glen Got Its Name,** p. 371). Its age-old reputation as a haven for pirates prompted people to equate the word "Tory" with "pirate" or "rascal." The use of "Tory" to mean "Conservative" derives from this Irish slang. (A Whig was originally a Scottish horse thief.) Tory's pirateering reputation was accurate as recently as the last century, when the island thrived off its *poitín* production—the inaccessibility of the island thwarted British efforts to control its trade. The present-day island is completely exhausted of turf, all six layers of which were burned in *poitín* production, and its soil appears more sandy and grassy than that on the mainland. Only one tree survives in the harsh conditions of the small island's sea-exposed area. The eastern end of the island breaks apart into a series of jagged sea cliffs.

This small Irish-speaking community has managed to maintain a strong sense of independence. Islanders refer to the mainland as "the country," and still elect a **"Rí na nOileán"** (king of the island) to a lifetime position, which mainly involves serving as the island's PR man—he'll greet you when you get off the boat and can tell stories of the island's past. Many of the island's unusual traditions remain intact, including the superstition that deters fishermen from rescuing drowning boatsmen. Another tradition claims that a stone on one of the island's hills has the power to fulfill wishes. This stone sits on the east end of the island on an unapproachable perch; if you throw three stones onto it, your wish will come true. In addition to the wishing stone, the island offers a cursing stone. The location of the latter has been concealed by local elders to prevent its misuse. The cursing stone has been credited with the 1884 shipwreck of a Dublin gunboat coming to collect taxes. The islanders still pay no taxes.

The only way to get out to the island is via the **ferry,** also known as Donegal Coastline Cruises or Turasmara (tel. 31320). The ferry runs boats from **Bunbeg** (tel. 31991; 1½hr., June-Sept. 1 per day, fewer Oct.-May); **Magheraroarty** (tel. (074) 35061; 40min., June-Aug. 2 per day), and **Portnablagh** (departs July-Aug. W 2pm). All crossings are £15 return (students £13; bicycles free). Be sure to call ahead to check departure times as they depend on tides and weather; storms have stranded travelers here for days in summer or even weeks in winter.

Club Thoraighe (tel. (074) 65121) features Tory Island trad, which beats out a slightly stronger rhythmic emphasis than the mainland music, and *ceìlis,* with mandatory attendance for all islanders. The island's 160 people support a surprising number of businesses, all located along a quarter of a mile stretch of the island's one street: store, hotel and restaurant, craft shop, chipper, and **Gailearai Dixon** (Dixon Gallery). The gallery showcases the work of the Tory Primitives, a group of local artists promoted by Derrick Hall of Glebe Gallery fame (see p. 373). The "primitive" moniker derives from the fact that the first Tory artist, James

SAINT—OR PIED PIPER? Saint Columcille (also known as Columba) landed on Tory Island 1400 years ago. Since that time, nary a rat has been seen on the isle. Locals say the land remains vermin-free because Columcille blessed its clay, banishing the rodents. Today, rat-plagued individuals journey here from hither and yon to collect a lump of Tory's holy clay. The owner of a house a bit past the gallery dispenses the mud, always free of charge, since you can't sell Saintliness.

Dixon, began painting with the materials available to him: house paint and a brush made from his donkey's tail. Their work usually depicts the natural scenery of the island in color-drenched pigments, evoking the living fury of the sea around Tory or the shadowy ruins of the island's medieval religious past. The island's interesting historical sights include the ruins of the **monastery** that St. Colmcille founded in the 6th century and the **Tau Cross** close to the town center.

FINNTOWN AND DENYBEG

Two tiny villages provide further accommodations for travelers meandering about the Donegal *gaeltacht*. Barely living up to its second syllable, **Fintown** is a miniscule settlement within easy reach of good hiking and fishing. At **Glenleighan House (IHO)** (tel. 46141), Bríd (Breege) McGill welcomes guests with open arms. (4-bed dorms £6; private rooms £7; B&B doubles £24, with bath £30.) To get there, take the R250 from Glenties. Near the intersection with R250, you'll see a phone booth on the right. Turn left there, and the hostel is the third house on the left. Located about 1 mi. off the main road in **Denybeg**, toward the coast, **Backpacker's Hostel** (tel. 32244) offers guests beds, views of the beach, and the sound of sheep bleating under your window. (8-bed dorms £7, private rooms £10 each.)

GLENVEAGH NATIONAL PARK

On the eastern side of the Derryveagh Mountains, **Glenveagh National Park** is 37 sq. mi. of forest glens, bogs, and mountains. One of the largest herds of red deer in Europe roams the park; deer-watching is best done at dusk and in the winter months after October, when the deer come down to the valley to forage. Despite Glenveagh's being the second most popular national park in Ireland, you probably won't be aware of any other human presence within the enormous pristine area—make sure to hold on to the free map handed out at the visitor's center. The hostels in **Crolly** (p. 370) and **Dunlewy** (p. 370) are most convenient to the park. (Tel. (074) 37090 or 37262. Open daily 10am-6:30pm. £2, students £1, seniors £1.50.)

Summertime tourists can take the free minibus from the park's entrance to **Glenveagh Castle**, 2½ mi. away (departs every 10-15min., last trip 1½hr. before closing). The castle was built in 1870 by the founder of the Glenveagh Estate, John Adair, shortly after he was married. Despite its relative youth, Glenveagh Castle looks like a medieval keep with its thick walls, battle-ready rampart, turrets, and round tower. Adair had a nasty reputation that doesn't suit the beauty of the land; in the cold April of 1861, he evicted 244 tenants on trumped-up charges. Many of them decided to emigrate to Australia while others were forced into the workhouse. (Same hours as park. Last tour 1¼hr. before closing. £2, students and children £1, seniors £1.50.) The surrounding **gardens** brighten up the bleak aspect of Adair's lonely castle; they are the design of a later owner, the American Henry McIlhenry. (Tours of the garden leave from Castle Courtyard July-Aug. Tu and Th 2pm.) He planted the gardens around the estate and left it to the government at his death. The areas around the castle are posh and highly cultivated; plots farther away are named after the area of the world to which their species belong (the Dutch garden, for example) and appear almost unkept. Marked nature trails begin at the castle. A mile up the incline behind the castle is **View Point**, which provides a glimpse of the park's vast expanse. Park rangers lead guided nature walks and more strenuous hill walks. (Call for information or to schedule a walk.) The **visitor's center** has more information about these or self-guided hikes. (Open Mar.-Nov. same hours as park.) The center can also prepare you for your hike with a 10min. video on the park's wildlife and history, several exhibits, and a meal at its cafeteria-style restaurant. (Most entrees £4-5.)

Five miles away from the visitor's center in Churchill is the **Glebe Gallery,** the display space of artist Derek Hill. He sponsored the Tory Island school of painters, and their work makes up the majority of the gallery's collection, supplemented by the work by mainland Donegal artists, and several pieces by internationally renowned European masters, including Louis de Brocquay and Picasso. (Tel. (074) 37071. Open Easter week and late-May to late-Sept. Sa-Th 11am-6:30pm, last tour 5:30pm. £2, students £1.) On the other side of the lake at the **Glebe House,** a centuries-old family home, the newly opened **St. Colmcille Heritage Center** has a permanent display on the life and times of the saint who brought Christianity to Donegal. (Hours and admission same as the Glebe Gallery.) Nearby is St. Colmcille's **Bed of Loneliness,** an enormous horizontal stone slab on which the saint spent the night before entering exile. Many emigrants have since performed the night of lying on the stone to prevent future loneliness.

FALCARRAGH

Northeast of the Bloody Foreland, white beaches stretch along the coast. Inland a bit, in the midst of a continuously irregular area of rocky hills and fertile valleys, sits Falcarragh. This Irish-speaking town is remarkably busy, considering its language preference. It's a colorful rest stop for those heading to beach beyond Dunfanaghy. While *Let's Go* does not recommend hitching, it is reportedly easy here.

Falcarragh provides many of the region's basic services. The **Bank of Ireland** (tel. 35484) provides an **ATM.** (Open M-W, F 10am-12:30pm and 1:30-4pm, Th 10am-12:30pm and 1:30-5pm.) **Flynn's Pharmacy** (tel. 35778) has medical goods and more. (Open M-Sa 9am-6pm.) **McGinley's** supermarket (tel. 35126) provides an amazing array of whole-grain bread, skimmed milk, and veggies as well as the ordinary groceries. (Open daily 9:30am-10pm.) Falcarragh's **post office,** Main St. (tel. 35110), delivers mail. (Open M-F 9am-1pm and 2-5:30pm, Sa 9am-1pm.) The **phone code** wears daisies in its hair when going to 074.

Overnighters in Falcarragh might choose to hit the pub, then retire upstairs to the **Shamrock Lodge Hostel (IHH)** (tel. 35859) on Main St. (Dorms £6, doubles £16.) Next to the post office, **Patricia McGroddy** (tel. 35145) offers B&B in a modern abode. (£15.) You can eat huge portions in sun-kissed wooden booths at **John's Restaurant** at the top of Main St. (Steaks £8-8.90, seafood and meat entrees £2.30-5, salads £3-5, sandwiches £1.20. Open M-Sa 10am-9pm, Su 2-9pm.) Alternatively, head to **Mighty Mac's** (tel. 65386), next to the post office, for cheaper fare in a "take-away/cafe." The shop is a chipper with a unique pop-inspired decor. (Burgers £1. Open daily 9am-1:30am.) The **Gweedore Bar,** Main St. (tel. (074) 35293), curries the local businessmen's favor with a reasonable lunch menu. (Lunch specials £3.75, served 12:30-2:30pm.)

Falcarragh lives pub life to the fullest. The **Shamrock Lodge,** or **Lóistín na Seamróige,** in the center of town, is by far the most distinctive. It buzzes with human activity well into the night. The "young room," as owner Mary calls it, has a jukebox, pool table, and comfy leather seats; old folks congregate in the poster-bedecked front bar. Trad sessions here display the local talent—and remember that most of Ireland's best trad bands have come out of Northern Donegal. (W, Sa trad, F rhythm and blues.) On Ballyconnell Rd., just off Main St. at the northern end of town, **The Loft Bar** (tel. 35992) presents a collection of old mugs and flowery upholstery in a cave-dark space, with folk music on summer weekends. The **Anchor Bar** offers lively trad on Wednesday nights.

About three miles outside of Falcarragh, colossal sand dunes squat on the beaches of **Back Strand** and **Ballyness.** To reach them follow the signs for "Trà," meaning beach, from the southern end of town. The **New Lake**—so called because it was formed in 1912 after a massive storm blocked up this former estuary—features a world-famous ecosystem and lots of frisky otters.

DUNFANAGHY

Seven miles north of Falcarragh, Dunfanaghy still has an Anglo-Irish feel from its days as the administrative center of the region. Today it's home to one of Donegal's finest hostels, the **Corcreggan Mill Hostel (IHH)** (tel. (075) 36409). Nearly six miles north of Falcarragh and 1½ mi. south of Dunfanaghy, Corcreggan sits by the side of the road in a complex that consists of a kiln house, a railway car, and an organic garden. Owner Brendan has converted an old wooden railway car into comfortable 4-bed dorms and private doubles with mahogany floors and walls. The railway car is sheltered underneath the roof of a house and has exceedingly comfortable common rooms laden with fascinating railroad memorabilia and furniture. In addition, 10-bed dorms and doubles are available in the former kiln house. Three kitchens—two for hostelers, one for campers—have been redone using recycled materials to keep the traditional atmosphere. A Swilly **bus** stops right at the door. (Kiln house dorms £7 in summer, £6 in winter; loft doubles £9, £8. Railway car dorms £9 in summer, £8 in winter; doubles £11, £10. **Camping** £4.) Hostelers team up at night to hire a local minibus to travel to and from the pubs (about £2 per person return).

Danny Collins' bar (tel. 36205) stays open from 10:30am until whenever it shuts down. The pub serves food from 1 to 9:30pm. (Soup £1.20, meat and vegetarian entrees £4-6.) Across the street, the Carrig Rua Hotel houses the **Red Rock Cafe,** which offers substantial, well-made lunches for £5. (Lunch served 12:30-2:30pm.) The **Village Shop** sells groceries. (Open 9am-11pm.) Also on Main St., **An Chistin Bistro** dishes out home-cooked meals for around £5 and sandwiches for £1.50 in a diner-like setting.

The **Dunfanaghy Workhouse Heritage Center** has created an excellent exhibit on the effects of famine in northwest Donegal, including a series of life-size dioramas following the life of a local woman named Hannah (1834?-1926), who survived the famine and at one point lived in the workhouse. This former poorhouse has undergone a miraculous transformation from the days of the famine, when it gave minimal shelter and rations to the destitute under prison-like conditions. (Tel. 36540. Open Mar.-Oct. M-F 10am-5pm, Sa-Su noon-5pm. £2, children £1.)

Between Dunfanaghy and Falcarragh is a maze of small roads and boggy hills. One can easily walk, cycle, drive, or hitch to any of the natural attractions within a 5 mi. radius of either town. **Horn Head,** sign-posted on the way into Dunfanaghy, invites long rambles around its pristine beaches, megalithic tombs, and gorse-covered hills. Those tireless hikers who make the 3½hr. trek to the far north tip of Horn Head from Dunfanaghy will experience some of the most spectacularly high sea cliffs in Ireland. **Ards Forest,** a couple of miles past Dunfanaghy, features a number of nature trails ranging from 1½ to 8 mi. Adjacent to the forest are pristine beaches accessible only on foot. (Open July-Aug. daily 10:30am-9pm, Easter-June and Sept. Sa-Su 10:30am-4pm.) **Marble Hill Windsurfing** (tel. 36231) lets you experience the water's strength firsthand. (Instruction session £20; board hire £8 per hr., £12 per 2hr.) Turning your back to the sea anywhere in Dunfanaghy will bring the expanse of the Muckish Mountain into view.

FANAD PENINSULA

The Fanad Peninsula juts into the Atlantic between Lough Swilly and Mulroy Bay. Lush greenery makes a striking complement to the peninsula's sandy beaches. The eastern edge, outlined by the villages of **Rathmelton, Rathmullan,** and **Portsalon,** is by far the nicest part of the peninsula, with colorful old houses and sweeping views across Lough Swilly. Rathmelton and **Milford** (on the western edge of the Lough) offer the most services and nightlife. The pretty **Knockalla Mountains** are easy to climb. The lucky few who get to the far reaches of the peninsula will find their efforts rewarded with a bounty of beaches. The peninsula favors drivers with beautiful views from remote roads, but the Swilly bus makes two circular trips out to the end of the peninsula per day. The broad, relatively flat stretches of road from Rathmelton to Rathmullan are kind to cyclists; after that, sharp inclines become frequent as the road narrows and grows unkempt. The **phone code** for the entire peninsula is 074.

RATHMELTON

A river flanked by stone walls and trees runs through the venerable, 17th century town of Rathmelton (ra-MEL-ton) at the mouth of the Leannan Estuary, the eastern gateway to the peninsula.

⚑ ORIENTATION AND PRACTICAL INFORMATION. The Mall runs along the river and contains most of the town's handful of goods and services. The **National Irish Bank,** The Mall (tel. 51028), has a bureau de change but no ATM. (Open M-W and F 10am-12:30pm and 1:30-3pm, Th 10am-12:30pm and 1:30-5pm.) **Bridge Launderette,** The Mall (tel. 51333), takes its name from its location. (Laundry £3.50-4.50. Open M-Sa 9am-6pm.) **O'Donnell's Pharmacy** (tel. 51080) is also on The Mall. (Open M-Tu and Th-Sa 9am-1pm and 2-6pm, W 9am-1pm.) The **post office** resides on Castle St. (tel. 51001), off The Mall. (Open M-F 9am-5:30pm, Sa 9am-1pm.)

⚑⛌⛉ ACCOMMODATIONS, FOOD, AND PUBS. Just off The Mall and right on the Swilly bus route, **Crammond House,** Market Sq. (tel. 51055), has expansive rooms with high ceilings in a 1760s townhouse. (£15, with bath £17. Open Easter-Oct.) Just around the corner, **Lennon Lodge** (tel. 51228) houses guests in tidy 2- to 5-bed rooms. (£10 per person, with bath £12. Breakfast £3.) At Mrs. Rena McCrea's **B&B** (tel. 51010), The Mall, you'll find fluffy beds. (£14, with bath £17.)

Whoriskey's/Spar Supermarket (tel. 51006) sells DIY meals. (Open M-Sa 8:30am-10pm, Su 8:30am-9pm.) Rathmelton's eateries offer sandwiches and fine dining, but little middle ground. **The Fish House Craft Gallery** (tel. 51316), where salmon were once smoked in the town's fishing heyday, now sells tea and sandwiches along with sweaters and local pottery. (Open May-Sept. daily 10am-7pm.) Take your sandwich outside and you can dine with the swans along the river. For affordable feasts in a more refined, candlelit setting, cross the street to the posh but reasonably priced **Mirabeau Steak House** (tel. 51138) on The Mall. (Steak from £7, fish from £6.) At the top of town on the road to Milford, well-established **Bridge Bar** (tel. 51119) knows how to please its customers with music at least three nights a week. **Conway's** (tel. 51297), an old thatched cottage at the bottom of the hill down Church St., pours proper pints in an intimate atmosphere.

◉ SIGHTS. To discover the area's heritage, turn off The Mall and go uphill past Market Sq.; a right at Mary's Bar after Crammond House will bring you to Back Lane and the old **Presbyterian Meetinghouse.** Francis Makemie, who founded the first American Presbytery in 1706, grew up in Rathmelton and worshipped here. The building now houses the town library and the paper-pushing **Donegal Ancestry Centre** (tel. 51266). The center, part of Irish Genealogical Project Centres, will help you trace your Donegal ancestors for a fee. (Open M-Th 9am-4:30pm, F 9am-4pm.) Crowds flock to the **Lennon Festival** in mid-July for a carnival and parade.

RATHMULLAN

Five miles north along the main coastal road, the coastal town of Rathmullan boasts historical, mythical, and logistical significance. In 1607, the last powerful Gaelic chieftains, Hugh O'Neill and Red Hugh O'Donnell, fled from Ireland after suffering numerous defeats to British invaders. They and 99 of their retinue set sail from Rathmullan for Spain to gather military support from the Catholic King Phillip II. Their ship blew off course and they landed in France. Eventually, they died in Rome while still soliciting foreign aid. Their departure is known as the Flight of the Earls (see **Feudalism,** p. 8). In more recent Anglo-Irish struggles, Wolfe Tone, the famous champion of Irish independence, was arrested in Rathmullan in 1798 (see **Rebellion, Reunion, Reaction,** p. 7). The town's tales are very much alive and present at the **"Flight of the Earls" Heritage**

Centre, at the town center. A helpful staff uses artwork, literature, and wax models to recount Rathmullan's history in detail. The building, a particularly foreboding Martello tower, is a historic monument of the British Admiralty. (Tel. 58229. Open Apr.-Sept. daily 10am-12:30pm and 1:30-5pm. ₤1.50, students and seniors ₤1, children 75p.) Around the corner, the remains of the **Rathmullan Priory,** a 14th century Carmelite monastery, lie shrouded in ivy.

Tourist information is gladly dispensed at the Heritage Centre (see below). **Mace Supermarket** (tel. 58148), on the coast road into town, supplies basic gastronomic needs. (Open daily 9am-9pm.) Quiet **Pier Hotel** (tel. 58178) has multiple personalities: its **B&B** offers very clean, sunny rooms in an old Georgian home (₤15, with bath ₤25); it serves pub grub (entrees ₤4-5; food served 12:30-9:30pm); and it's a popular **pub,** with a good mixture of young and old around the simple bar, midweek trad sessions, and live contemporary music Friday and Saturday. Next door to the Heritage Center, the **Beachcomber Bar** (tel. 58125) offers beach access. One wall is taken up by a gigantic view of the water, and a sandy beer garden opens out back in the summer. The **Water's Edge Inn** (tel. 58182), with funky orange walls, is set on the very spot where the Earls set sail, a 10min. walk south of the town. (Lunch served 12:30-5pm, ₤4-6; dinner served 6-10pm, ₤10-15.)

THE NORTHERN AND WESTERN PENINSULA

North of Rathmullan, the road narrows and winds and dips to accommodate the increasingly wild landscape. These remote roads are discouraging to pedestrians and all but the most fit bikers, and hitchhiking is nearly impossible; *Let's Go* does not recommend hitchhiking. As the road continues, it hits a series of clustered buildings, called "towns" only because each has a church and a post office. A little over halfway from Rathmullan to Portsalon, a signposted lane leads from the main road to remote **Bunnaton Hostel (IHO),** Glenvar (tel. 50122), high on a hill above the lough. The hostel lodges in the Captain's Quarters of a former Coast Guard Station, built in 1813. (Dorms ₤7, private rooms ₤9. Breakfast ₤2-4.) Continuing north, the main road becomes both mind-bogglingly steep and breathtakingly beautiful. Just before Portsalon, the road crests a hill, where **Knockalla Strand** (rated the second best in the world by a British "beach expert") and the tip of the northern peninsula suddenly appear. **Camping** facilities are available next to Knockalla Strand at the **Knockalla Holiday Centre** (tel. 59108), 3 mi. south of Portsalon. (₤7 per 2-person tent, ₤10 per 3- to 4-person tent. Open Easter-Sept.)

Portsalon (port-SAL-un), on the descent, consists of three shops and a series of homes along the water. It was once a resort town, but the resort hotel burned down three years ago, leaving just a beach that needs nothing to recommend it. The **Portsalon House B&B** (tel. 59395), next to the post office on the main road, has wonderful rooms perfumed by the rosebushes outside. (Singles ₤20; doubles ₤30, with bath ₤35.) About one hour north of Portsalon by bike, the **Great Arch of Doaghbeg** keeps the **Fanad Lighthouse** company. The arch, a mass of rock over 80 ft. wide detached from seaside cliffs, is visible from above, though not from the main road. It is best reached through the 6 acre **Ballydaheen Gardens,** a seaside array of Japanese and English gardens that blends into the natural landscape amazingly well. (Open May-Sept. M, Th, and Sa 10am-3pm. ₤3, children ₤1.) From Fanad Head, the route down the western side of the peninsula winds in and out of the inlets of **Mulroy Bay.** Mrs. Borland's **Avalon Farmhouse** (tel. 59031), on Main St. in tiny **Tamney**—also reachable by a road that cuts across the peninsula from Portsalon—has homemade jam and attractive decor. (₤15, with bath ₤17. Open Apr.-Sept.) In **Kerrykeel,** farther south at the foot of the Knockalla Hills, you can **camp** right on Mulroy Bay in **Rockhill Park** (tel. 50012). About 1½ mi. out of Kerrykeel along Glenvar Rd. is a signpost to the **Gortnavern Dolmen,** a spectacular megalithic tombs.

NORTHWEST IRELAND

LETTERKENNY (LEITIR CEANNAN)

Letterkenny is the center of action in Donegal, but that's not saying much. Several years ago, residents lamented the arrival of a traffic light at the intersection of Main St. and Port Rd., the first in Co. Donegal. Today, the commercial, academic, and ecclesiastical center has several traffic lights; cars in the rest of the county still roam freely. Most tourists arrive in Letterkenny to make bus connections to the rest of Donegal, the Republic, and Northern Ireland. Letterkenny's relative urbanity also brings in pub-goers for weekend revelry.

■ TRANSPORTATION

Buses: At the junction of Port and Derry Rd. in front of the Quinnsworth Supermarket. **Bus Éireann** (tel. 21309) runs a "Hills of Donegal" tour, including **Dungloe, Glenveigh National Park,** and **Gweedore** (M-Sa 11am, £10), and regular service to **Derry** (40min.; M-Sa 12 per day, Su 3 per day; £4), **Sligo** (2hr., 3 per day, £9), **Donegal Town** (50min., £4.80) on the way to **Galway** (5 hr., 3 per day, £12), and **Dublin** (5hr., 4 per day, £10). **Feda O'Donnell Coaches** (tel. (075) 48114 or (091) 761 656) drives to **Galway** (£9) via **Donegal Town** (M-Th and Sa 2 per day, F and Su 3 per day; £4) and to **Crolly** (£4) via **Dunfanaghy** (2 per day, more F and Su). **Lough Swilly Buses** (tel. 22863) head north toward the **Fanad Peninsula** (M-Sa 2 per day, £6) to **Derry** (M-Sa 9 per day, £4), and south to **Dungloe** (M-Sa 3 per day, £8). **John McGinley Coaches** (tel. 35201) sends a bus twice a day to **Gweedore** via **Dunfanaghy** and to **Dublin** (£9). **McGeehan's Bus** (tel. (075) 46101) goes twice a day to **Killybegs** (£6) and **Glencolmcille** (£8). **Northwest Busways** (tel. (077) 82619) sends buses around Inishowen (M-F 4 per day, Sa 3 per day), making stops in **Buncrana** (£2.60), **Carndonagh** (£3.20), and **Moville** (£3.50). **Doherty's Travel** (tel. (075) 21105) has buses that leave for **Dungloe** and **Burtonport** from Dunnes at 5pm daily (£4).

Local Transportation: Letterkenny Bus Service (**Handy Bus;** tel. (087) 414 714). Extensive city routes (70p).

Bike Rental: Church St. Cycles (tel. 26204), by the cathedral. £40 per week; deposit £40. Open M-Sa 10am-6pm. **Starlight Garage** (tel. 22248). £7 per day, £35 per week, deposit £10. Open M-Sa 9am-6pm.

■ PRACTICAL INFORMATION

Tourist Offices: Bord Fáilte (tel. 21160), ¾ mi. past the bus station and out of town on Derry Rd. Info on Co. Donegal and accommodations bookings. Open July-Aug. M-Sa 9am-8pm, Su 10am-2pm; Sept.-June M-F 9am-5pm. **Chamber of Commerce Visitors Information Centre,** 40 Port Rd. (tel. 24866 or 25505), is closer with a slightly smaller selection of info on Letterkenny and the rest of Co. Donegal. Open M-F 9am-5pm.

Banks: AIB, 61 Upper Main St. (tel. 22877 or 22807). **Bank of Ireland,** Lower Main St. (tel. 22122). **Ulster Bank,** Main St. (tel. 24016). All are open M-W and F 10am-4pm, Th 10am-5pm. AIB and Bank of Ireland both have **24hr. ATMs.**

Laundry: Masterclean, High Rd. (tel. 26880), across from the hostel. Wash and dry £6. Dry cleaning. **Duds 'n' Suds** (tel. 28303). Open M-F 8am-9pm, Sa 8am-8pm. Wash and dry about £5.

Hospital: Letterkenny General (tel. 25888).

Pharmacy: Magee's Pharmacy, Main St. (tel. 21419). Open M-W 9am-6:30pm, Th-F 9am-8pm, Sa 9am-6:30pm.

Counseling and Support: Samaritans, 20 Port Rd. (24hr. phone-line tel. 27200). Drop in for one-on-one counseling Th-Su 7-10pm. **Letterkenny Women's Refuge,** Pearse Rd (tel. 26267). Open M-F 9am-5pm. **Boots,** Main St. (tel. 25499). Open M-W and Sa 9am-6pm, Th-F 9am-8pm. **Letterkenny's Women's Center,** Port Rd. (tel. 24985). Open M-F 9am-1pm and 2-5pm.

Post Office: Halfway down Main St. (tel. 22287). Open M and W-F 9am-5:30pm, Tu 9:30am-5pm, Sa 9am-5:30pm.

Internet Access: Cyberworld, Main St. (tel. 20440), in the Courtyard Shopping Center. £5 per hr., students £3.50 per hr. **Letterkenny Central Library and Arts Center,** Main St. (tel. 24950 or 21968).

PHONE CODE:	Numberkenny 074.

ACCOMMODATIONS

The Manse Hostel (IHH), High Rd. (tel. 25238). From the bus station, head up Port Rd. toward town and turn right up the lane marked "Covehill House B&B." Continue past the playground, through the parking lot, and 50 yd. up the road. The hostel is across the street. Dated decor, but the bunked beds are as comfy as you can imagine. 3-,4-, and 6-bed dorms £7, private doubles and twins £16. Sheets 50p in dorms.

The Arhc Hostel (IHO), Upper Corkey (tel. 57255). This hostel is located 6 mi. out of town in Pluck; to get there, take the Derwy (Littort) Rd. from the roundabout near the bus station. Continue straight at the next roundabout onto the divided carriageway. At the first break in the median, turn right across the carriageway and then head left, following the signs for Pluck. Stay on the same road until it passes under a small archway, then fork right. The hostel is on the right. Better yet, call from town for pick-up. The Gallagher family welcomes hostelers to the 6 beds in a refinished loft above their stable. £7.50. Open May-Oct.

White Gables, Mrs. McConnellogue, Lower Dromore (tel. 22583). Lower Dromore is the 3rd exit from the roundabout 1 mi. out on Derry Rd.; the house is ½ mi. along Lower Dromore, around a bend. Call for pick-up from town. Clean and cheery rooms. The upstairs balcony has great views of Letterkenny's green fields. £16, with bath £17.

Riverside B&B (tel. 24907), off Derry Rd. 1 mi. past Letterkenny. Turn left after the Clan Ree Hotel; signs point the way. Huge rooms with views of the quiet countryside. Full-sized snooker table. £14, with bath £16.

FOOD

Letterkenny offers a fair share of cheap meals in pleasant—even quirky—cafe settings. **Quinnsworth** (tel. 22555), in the Letterkenny Shopping Center behind the bus station, has all you could ask for in a grocery store. (Open M-W 9am-7pm, Th-F 9am-9pm, Sa 9am-6pm, Su noon-6pm.) **SuperValu** (tel. 27053), on the lower level of the Courtyard Shopping Centre, is well stocked and central. (Open M-W and Sa 9am-6:15pm, Th-F 9am-9pm, Su 2-6pm.) **The Natural Way,** 55 Port Rd. (tel. 25738), sells wholefood and herbal remedies. (Open M-Sa 9am-6pm, F 9am-8pm.)

The Beanery, Main St., Market Shopping Centre. 2 floors of dining, include outdoor balcony seating. 4-course meals £3-4, sandwiches around £2. Open M-Sa 9am-6:30pm, Su 9am-6pm. Hot food served until 4pm, sandwiches until 6pm.

Cafe Rico, Oliver-Plunkett Rd. (tel. 29808), at the end of Main St. away from the bus station. Full breakfasts and heaping sandwiches (£2-4) in a hip coffee shop.

Galfees, Main St. (tel. 27173), in the basement of the Courtyard Shopping Centre. It's a carvery 12:15-3pm, a fresh food bar 8:30am-5pm, and a bar/restaurant 5-10pm. Irish illustrations bedeck its dark wood walls and transcend the shopping mall. Most evening entrees £4-5. Cheaper evening menu served 5-8pm; dinner served until 10pm.

Pat's Too, Main St. (tel. 21761). Hearty take-away meals for the budget traveler. Sit-in option in its tiled interior. Always crowded at night. 9 in. pizza about £4, kebab special £3.75. Delivery available. Open M-Th 1pm-12:30am, F and Su 1pm-1am, Sa 1pm-3:30am.

PUBS

McGinley's, 25 Main St. (tel. 21106). A hugely popular student bar in the chapel-like upstairs; a more adult population on the Victorian ground floor. Live rock, pop, and blues W-Su.

McClafferty's, 54 Main St. (tel. 21581). In the daytime its patrons are an older, contemplative set; at night they're young and frisky. Modern ballads and rock Su.

Cottage Bar, 42 Main St. (tel. 21338). A kettle on the hearth, animated conversation around the bar, and nuns drinking Guinness in the corner. Trad Tu and Th.

The Old Orchard Inn, High Rd. (tel. 21615). A 5min. walk past Manse Hostel in a secluded parking lot. The 3 floors of logwood furniture and leafery are always packed. The cellar bar on the bottom floor hosts occasional trad; the disco on the top floor is a local magnet. Disco open W and F-Sa until 2am. Cover £4-5.

 SIGHTS

Neo-Gothic **St. Eunan's Cathedral,** perched high above town on Church Ln., looks like the heavenly kingdom when it's floodlit at night. Church Ln. is on your right up Main St. away from the bus station. Proposed as a "resurrection of the fallen shrines of Donegal," the cathedral's construction took 11 years—all years of economic hardship and depression. The story of St. Columb is beautifully carved in the arch at the junction of the nave and transcript. (Open daily 8am-5pm, except during Sunday masses at 8, 9, 10, and 11:15am, and 12:30pm. Free.) Opposite St. Eunan's, the smaller **Parish Church of Conwal** (Church of Ireland) shelters a number of tombstones, some of which date from the 17th century. (Sunday services 8 and 10:30am.)

Renovated during the summer of 1999, the **Donegal County Museum,** High Rd. (tel. 24613), should be opened for the 2000 season with exhibits of anything and everything having to do with Co. Donegal. (Expected to be open M-F 10am-12:30pm and 1-4:30pm, Sa 1-4:30pm. Free.)

INISHOWEN PENINSULA

It would be a shame to leave Ireland without seeing the Inishowen Peninsula, an untouristed mosaic of pristine mountains, forests, meadows, and white sand beaches that reaches farther north than "the North." The peninsula is dotted with villages and two towns, Buncrana and Cardonagh. The winding road that connects them affords views of continually sublime scenery. It takes two to three days to see the entire peninsula properly without a car, and even with a car one would hardly want to spend less time.

The nearest commercial center to Inishowen is Derry, whose residents often vacation here. **Lough Swilly** (head office tel. (01504) 262 017; Buncrana depot tel. (077) 61340) runs buses from Derry to points on the Inishowen: **Buncrana** (35min.; M-F 10 per day, Sa 12 per day, Su 3 per day), **Moville** (50min., 5 per day), **Carndonagh** (1hr., M-F 6 per day, Sa 4 per day), **Malin** (1¼hr.; M, W, and F 1 per day, Sa 3 per day), and **Malin Head** (1½hr.; M, W, and F 1 per day, Sa 3 per day). Swilly also connects **Buncrana** directly to **Carndonagh** (50min., M-Sa 3 per day). Swilly Buses offers an eight day "rambler ticket" (£18, students £12) and student rates on all individual trips; their return fares are considerably cheaper than two single tickets. **Northwest Buses** (tel. (077) 82619) runs from **Moville** through **Culdaff, Carndonagh, Ballyliffen, Clonmany, Buncrana, Fahan,** and on to **Letterkenny** (M-F 4 per day, Sa 3 per day); from **Shrove** to **Derry** via **Moville** (1hr., M-Sa 3 per day); from **Buncrana** to **Derry** (M-Sa 5 per day); and from **Malin Head** to **Derry** via **Culdaff** and **Muff** (M-Sa 2 per day).

Inishowen's unusual inland landscape is outdone only by its striking northern and western shores. The clearly posted **Inish Eoghin 100** road takes exactly 100 mi. to navigate the peninsula's perimeter. Drivers will find this the best route for

Inishowen
Peninsula

seeing Inishowen. *Let's Go* does not recommend hitchhiking, but hitchers report having an easy time on this road. Cycling can be difficult in places, particularly near the Gap of Mamore, due to ferocious northwesterly winds and hilly terrain. Cyclists may resort to using the roads that crisscross the peninsula to shorten long distances between sights. The map published by the Inishowen Tourism Society, available at the Cardonagh tourist office, is the most comprehensive. The **phone code,** 077, was born in the year of the serpent.

GRIANÁN AILIGH

Ten miles south of Buncrana at the bottom of the peninsula and 3 mi. west of Derry (see Northern Ireland, p. 458), the hilltop ringfort Grianán Ailigh (GREEN-in ALL-ya) is an excellent place to start or finish your tour of Inishowen. This site has been a cultural center for at least 4000 years: first as a Druidic temple at the grave site of Aedh, the son of The Dagda, divine king of the Túatha De Dannan of pre-Christian Ireland; then as a seat of power for the northern branch of the Uí Néill clan, who ruled Ulster and moved here after their chieftain married Princess Aileach of Scotland; and finally as a Mass rock where Catholics worshipped in secret during the time of the Penal Laws (see **Protestant Ascendancy,** p. 10). Much of the present stone structure is a 19th century reconstruction, but the bottom section of the circular wall is original. Beyond the fort, a cross marks the site of a healing well holy since pre-Christian times and supposedly blessed by St. Patrick.

The fort figures into many legends and tales, including the naming of Inishowen (the Island of Owen). Owen was the son of **Niall of the Nine Hostages,** the semi-legendary ancestor of the Uí Néill (O'Neill) clan. One story claims that Niall slept with an old hag to gain sovereignty over Ireland. Once in charge, he captured young St. Patrick and brought him to Ireland as a slave. Having escaped captivity and begun his missionary work, St. Patrick baptized Niall's son Owen at this very same hillfort, consecrating the Uí Néill fortress as a Christian holy site. The prominence of Grianán Ailigh as the home of rulers ended in the 11th century when Donal McLaughlin, the Prince of Inishowen, was defeated by Brian Ború's grandson, Murtagh O'Brien. Each of O'Brien's men was ordered to carry away one stone from the royal palace of Aileach so that it could never be an outsider's seat of power. The symbolic identity of the fort survived past its physical destruction, and after the Flight of the Earls in 1607 (see **Feudalism,** p. 8, and **Rathmullan,** p. 376), Red Hugh O'Neill swore he'd return to Grianán Ailigh as high ruler of Ireland. Legend has it that Red Hugh's soldiers still lie slumbering in a cave near the fort, each with one hand on the hilt of his sword and the other on the reins of his also-sleeping horse. When the new ruler of Ireland lands on the island, they will awake.

To reach the fort from Derry, turn off Derry Rd. at Bridgend onto N13, which leads to Letterkenny. From Letterkenny, follow N13 past the turnoff for R265 and R237. Signs before Burt point the way. Two miles down N13 from Bridgend is the Catholic **Burt Circular Chapel,** a modern-day replica of the ancient fort. Just past the Circular Chapel on the N13 is the **Grianán Ailigh Heritage Center** (tel. 68000), inside a former Church of Ireland. The center can prepare you for the 2 mi. journey with informative displays and stomach-bending meals. (Open 10am-10pm. Admission £1; students, seniors, and children 75p. Lunch specials £4-5; served noon-3pm.) Grianán Ailigh is on top of the hill, on a path behind the Circular Chapel. The 300 year old Burt Woods are next to the fort. No public transport comes near the fort, so the carless will have to cycle or walk. Travelers who choose to hitch say drivers are particularly nice on the 2 mi. incline; hill or no hill, *Let's Go* does not recommend hitching. A 2½ mi. route begins at the Burt Circular Chapel, offering cyclist a gentler alternative. (Directions available at the tourist office.) A pleasant 9 mi. shortcut returns to Buncrana; take the first left after Burt Circular Chapel heading towards Bridgend.

BUNCRANA

Long Slieve Snaght looms over Buncranca, north of Fahan. While not terribly exciting in itself, the town offers beds and conveniences to Inishowen explorers.

⚠ PRACTICAL INFORMATION. A temporary **tourist office** (tel. 20020) resides in the Chamber of Commerce building on St. Oran's Rd. To get there, proceed down Main St. away from the bus depot. Halfway down the hill, turn right on St. Oran's Rd.; the tourist office is one block away on the right. It offers maps and brochures for Buncrana and the entire peninsula and books accommodations. (Open June-Aug. M-Sa 9am-5pm.) **AIB,** 8 Market Sq. (tel. 61087; open M-W and F 10am-12:30pm and 1:30-4pm, Th 10am-12:30pm and 1:30-5pm), and **Bank of Ireland,** Main St. (tel. 61795; open M-W and F 10am-4pm, Th 10am-5pm), both have **24hr. ATMs. Valu-Clean,** Lower Main St. (tel. 62570), is a clean value. (Laundry £4.50. Open M-Sa 9am-6pm). **E. Tierney Chemist's,** Lower Main St. (tel. 62412), is the local pharmacy. (Open M-F 9:30am-6:30pm, Sa 9:30am-6pm.) The **post office,** Main St. (tel. 61010), is also a newsagent. (Open M-F 9am-1:15pm and 2:15-5:30pm, Sa 9am-1pm.)

⚑ ACCOMMODATIONS, FOOD, AND PUBS. Waterfront House, Swilly Terr. (tel. 61222), has huge, comfortable rooms, a great view of Swilly Lough, and an inexhaustibly hospitable owner. To get there, take Derry Rd. toward the town center, turn onto Swilly Rd. just before the shorefront, then turn left onto Swilly Terr. All rooms have baths; a kitchen, coffee, and tea are always accessible. (£16.) **Golan View B&B**, Ardaravan Rd. (tel. 62644), is closer to Main St. Take Maginn Ave. uphill; the hostel is on the right. Sunny halls complement the cheery proprietor. (Singles £20, doubles £32. All rooms with bath.)

O'Donnell's Supermarket (tel. 61719), past the bus depot away from the waterfront, sells staples behind a stunning storefront with two cheery murals. (Open M-Sa 8am-10:45pm, Su 8am-10pm.) Banks, bars, and bikes bump elbows on Main St. The blue and orange interior of **Cranberrys**, 49 Upper Main St. (tel. 63900), serves sandwiches (£2-4) and 2-course lunch specials (£4-5) during the day; the swank dinner menu is dearer. (Entrees about £8. Open daily 9am-10pm.) In the middle of Main St., the **Town Clock Restaurant** (tel. 62146) covers the middle ground, with local favorites from toasties to kebabs. (Most dishes £3-4. Open M-Sa 9am-9pm, Su 10:30am-9pm.) The **West End Bar**, Upper Main St. (tel. 61067), has a copper bar that shines like a lucky penny. (Live music some weekends.) **O'Flaitbeartais** (o-FLAH-her-tees), Main St. (tel. 61305), has a hunting aesthetic, but locals of all trades flock here nightly. **The Millennium Music Box** (tel. 61564), in Market Sq. on Main St., is a den of youth pop culture that glows with violet light.

◙ SIGHTS. The town's most widely promoted attraction—aside from its shore—is the community owned and operated **Tullyarvan Mill**, half a mile north of town on Dunree Rd. (a continuation of Main St.). This renovated corn mill presents a mixture of exhibitions on textile history, tracing Buncrana's transition from hand-weaving in 1739 to Fruit-of-the-Looming in 1999. The mill also houses a craft shop and coffee shop. (Tel. 61613. Open June-Sept. M-F 9am-6pm, Sa-Su 2-5pm.) Two castles overlook peaceful, pretty **Swan Park**: the stately Queen Anne-era **Buncrana Castle**, in which Wolfe Tone was imprisoned after the French "invasion" of 1798 failed (see **Rebellion, Union, and Reaction**, p. 10); and the 1430 **O'Doherty Keep**, a not quite Arthurian castle that looks more like a derelict mansion. Both are closed to the public. To reach the park, walk up Main St. toward the shorefront. Follow Castle Ave. from the roundabout next to the West End Bar and Cinema. The park is beyond the Castle Bridge, which arcs 100 yd. to the right. A **coastal walk** begins at Castle Bridge, goes past the keep, turns left at the castle, and then ascends the hill. **Ned's Point Fort**, also along the coast, was built in 1812 but is surprisingly (and not very pleasantly) modern-looking. The path passes Porthaw Bay and culminates in sandy **Sragill Strand. Friar Hegarty's Rock**, beyond the beach, witnessed the friar's murder during the Penal Times (see **Protestant Ascendancy**, p. 10).

WEST INISHOWEN

From Buncrana, the Inish Eoghin 100 runs through Dunree Head and the Mamore Gap, while R238 cuts through the interior directly to Clonmany and Ballyliffen.

DUNREE HEAD AND THE MAMORE GAP

Fort Dunree and Mamore Gap were the last area of the Republic occupied by the British, who passed the fort to the Irish army in 1938. **Dunree Head** pokes out into Lough Swilly 6 mi. northwest of Buncrana. Salt-and-peppered peaks rise up against the ocean buffered by the occasional bend of sandy, smooth beach. At the tip of the head, **Fort Dunree** hides in the jagged sea cliffs. Today the fort holds a military museum and is a superb vantage point for admiring the sea-carved landscape of the Inishowen and Fanad peninsulas. An example of the Guns of Dunree, one of six built during the 1798 Presbyterian Uprising to defend Lough Swilly against hypothetical Napoleonic invaders, is among the museum's displayed weaponry. The museum's exhibits also include copies of German Intelligence maps of the Inishowen Peninsula from World War II. The fort's location overlooking Lough Swilly is a boon for birdwatchers. (Open June-Sept. M-Sa 10am-6pm, Su 1-6pm. Fort and walks £2, students, seniors, and children £1.)

NORTHWEST IRELAND

Farther north along Inish Eoghin 100 toward Clonmany, a sign points left to the edge of the **Mamore Gap.** This breathtaking pass teeters 800 ft. above sea level between Mamore Hill and Urris. Otherworldly views over the mountains to the Atlantic can be seen from the eastern face of the pass. The steep road through the pass proves difficult, though worthwhile, for hikers and cyclists. It's only a 30min. climb uphill; most bikers will be forced to walk up this incline. It's easier to drive, although the hairpin turns over the sea are sometimes frightening. Queen Mebdh of Connacht, Cú Chulainn's archenemy in the Táin (see **Legends and Folktales,** p. 20), is supposedly buried here (and at Knocknarea, Co. Sligo, and a few other places).

The road descends from the gap onto wave-scoured northern beaches. The Inish Eoghin 100 proceeds to Urris, Lenan Head, and inviting Lenan Strand. Once, known for its prodigious (even for Donegal) *poitín* production, Urris was the last area in Inishowen to relinquish spoken Gaelic. The subdivided flat-bed farms along the road reveal the continued influence of Famine-era farming practices. Heading north, the road passes over Dunaff Head, through Rockstown Harbour, and past Tullagh Bay. 2mi. from Clonmany, the road arrives at the **Tullagh Bay Caravan and Camping Park** (tel. 76289) between the mountains and sea. One of the choicest beaches on the peninsula is just outside your tent. (£5 per 2-person tent; 50p per additional person. Showers 20p. Wash £1; dry 50p per 30min. Shop open daily mid-June-Aug. 9:30am-9:30pm. Park open Easter-mid-Sept. Call ahead; they may be changing professions.)

CLONMANY, BALLYLIFFEN, AND DOAGH ISLAND

North of the Gap, two tiny villages, **Clonmany** and **Ballyliffen,** are separated by one mile. Their combined forces make a restful spot to spend the night on a leisurely exploration of the Inishowen peninsula: Clonmany provides the pubs and food, while Ballyliffen has plenty of accommodations and long stretches of sandy beach tackled by crystal-clear ocean water.

In Clonmany, grab a big bite to eat at the **Glasbody Center,** Main St. (tel. 76915), which has a friendly staff and home-cooked meals. (Full entrees £3-4. Open daily 9am-midnight.) **Briney's Bar** (tel. 76415), at the far end of Main St., is your last chance for a pint before hitting the coast road, which offers only incomparable beaches and mountains. Live music on weekends ranges from country to Irish ballads. (Bar food about £3.) More country music and occasional trad fills the weekend air in and around **McFeeley's** (tel. 76122), across the street at Corner House. Both pubs are saturated with trad during the **Clonmany Festival** in the first full week of August. **McEleney's Cycles** (tel. 76541), halfway between Clonmany and Ballyliffen, **rents bikes.** (£7 per day, £30 per week; deposit £40. Open M and Sa 10am-5pm, Tu-F 10am-7pm.)

Ballyliffen's highlights are a famous golf course and three long miles of golden sands on Pollan Strand. Grassy dunes connect Ballyliffen with **Doagh Island,** where **Carricksbrahy Castle,** a former seat of the MacFaul and O'Donnell clans, now exists in wave-crashed ruins at the end of a 2½ mi. beach walk. Wanderers can stay in spacious, well furnished rooms at the **Castlelawn House** (tel. 76600 or 76977), just behind the Strand Hotel. (Doubles £18 with bath, singles £19.)

Doagh Visitor's Centre (tel. 76493) can be reached by turning left off the road from Ballyliffen to Cardonagh. The way is well sign-posted along the only road on the land strip. The center is a large reconstruction of famine life, with real sod houses and a fascinating display of the local plants used for sustenance and medicinal purposes. Check out the bogbine, a plant that grows in mossy wetland areas; its juice is still used as a last-resort cure for acne. (Open daily 10am-5pm. £2.50, children, students, and seniors £1.50.) Guided **pony-trekking** (tel. (086) 873 0197) is also available at the center (£6 per 30min., £10 per hr.).

NORTH INISHOWEN

From the southeastern coast, R240 cuts straight up the middle of the peninsula to commercial Carndonagh, a good stop for amenities. North of Carndonagh, R238 veers east to Culdaff. Going north on R242 leads to Malin Head, the northernmost tip of the island.

CARNDONAGH

Two miles south of Trawbreaga Bay, "Carn" is Inishowen's main market town, where the peninsula's farmers swarm on alternate Mondays to sell sheep and cattle. Northern explorers conveniently hit all the necessary commodities and services in this busy hub of the northern peninsula. **Inishowen Tourism,** Chapel St. (tel. 74933), just off The Diamond, is non-Bord Fáilte and remarkably helpful with info on the entire peninsula and accommodations bookings. (Open June-Aug. M-F 9:30am-7pm, Sa 10am-6pm, Su noon-6pm; Sept.-May M-F 9:30am-5:30pm.) **AIB,** The Diamond (tel. 74388), is the only bank in town with a **24hr. ATM**. (Open M 10am-12:30pm and 1:30-5pm, Tu-F 10am-12:30pm and 1:30-4pm.) **Carn Cabs,** The Diamond (tel. 74580), provides taxis for late-night jaunts. **McCallion's Cycle Hire** (tel. 74084), 3 mi. from town on Ballyliffen Rd. Mr. McCallion will collect and deliver cycles anywhere on the peninsula. (£6 per day, £25 per week.) **ValuClean,** Bridge St. (tel. 74150), washes and dries for £4.60. (Open M-Sa 9am-6pm.) **McAteer's,** The Diamond (tel. 74120), is the local pharmacy. (Open M-Sa 10am-6pm.) **G&S Supersave** (tel. 74124), in the Carnfair Shopping Centre on Bridge St., sells a full array of foods. (Open M-F 9am-9pm, Sa 9am-10pm, Su 11am-9pm.) Also in the Carnfair Shopping Centre is **The Book Shop** (tel. 74389), which offers second-hand books to read on the beach and a huge selection for Irish history enthusiasts. (Open M-Sa 11am-7pm, Su 2-7pm.) The **post office** (tel. 74101) meters mail on Bridge St. (Open M-F 9:30am-1:30pm and 2:30-5:30pm, Sa 9:30am-1pm.)

Less than half a mile from The Diamond, Chapel St. turns into Millbrae when it hits **Dunshenny House** (tel. 74292), where dainty flowered wallpaper sets the mood. (£15 with full breakfast, all with bath. Book in advance.) One mile out of town on Malin Rd., **Ashdale Farmhouse B&B** (tel. 74017) has a peaceful rural setting and an atmosphere that guests rave about; the owners are friendly, the beds are marvelous, and the breakfasts are grand. (Singles £18, with bath £19; doubles £32, with bath £34.) **The Coffee Shop,** The Diamond, is a modest but hugely popular spot where the owner is sure to give a proper welcome to new faces in Carndonagh. (Sandwiches £1.20. Open M-Sa 9am-5pm.) **The Quiet Lady,** Main Rd. (tel. 74777), gets noisy at night when she plays modern beats for a dancing local crowd. (Live music W and Sa-Su. DJ Fridays.) During the day she offers quiet but filling 2-course meals, including roasted meats and vegetables (about £3). Tiny **Bradley's Bar,** Bridge St. (tel. 74526), is best known as the local "men's pub." Queen Victoria supposedly used the toilet in the men's room, although the place shows no hint of having been graced by her requisite frills.

Commercial Carn has but one sight to offer, the old Church of Ireland that hulks half a mile down Bridge St. Outside its walls, **Donagh Cross,** a 7th century Celtic cross, is all that remains of the monastery founded by St. Patrick when he brought Christianity to the peninsula. Two shorter pillars flank the cross. One depicts David playing his harp; the other stands in the graveyard of the church and displays Christ's crucifixion. The church's bell supposedly came from the Spanish Armada ship *Trinidad de Valoencera*, which went down in Kinnagoe Bay.

CULDAFF

The area around Culdaff on the eastern side of the peninsula holds a variety of ancient monuments. The "Bronze Age triangle" above the Bocan Parochial House, one mile from Culdaff toward Moville, includes the **Bocan Stone Circle,** the **Temple of Deen,** and **Kindroyhead,** where there is evidence of a prehistoric field and fort system. A 4 yd. tall **high cross** stands next to the **Cloncha Church,** which is sign-posted 1½ mi. from Culdaff toward Moville. Culdaff hosts the annual **Charles Macklin Festival** (tel. 79104) in the second weekend in October, with performances of the 17th century playwright's plays, poetry competitions, and a slew of trad sessions.

The brand-spanking-new **Pines Hostel,** Bunagee Rd. (tel. 79060), houses guests in a spiffy owner-built house with a hearth-warmed common room. (£6.50, doubles £20. Sheets £1.) Anyone on a trad pilgrimage should stop in at ▓**McGrory's** (tel. 79104), where sessions sometimes last until dawn and the fresh food attracts half the town at dinnertime. (Meat and vegetarian entrees £3-6.) Attached to McGrory's is possibly the best live music venue in the northwest, Mac's Backroom Bar, which has attracted the likes of Altan and Sharon Shannon. Chummy owners Neil and John McGrory play regularly in sessions. Wednesday nights are the wildly popular "country jam" (£4), where you're likely to hear tongue-in-cheek covers of anything from Al Green to Prince. (Trad Tu and Sa, in summer Th as well. Cover £5 on Sa.) **Culdaff Strand,** best seen at daybreak or dusk, is a short walk from McGrory's.

MALIN HEAD

Inishowen's most popular attraction is Malin Head, the northernmost tip of Ireland. Aside from its latitude, the stretch is remarkable for its rocky, wave-tattered coast and sky-high sand dunes. Inish Eoghin 100 continues east from Cardonagh to Malin Head, passing through the tiny, tidy town of Malin on its way. Five miles from Culdaff, R242 coincides with the Inish Eoghin 100 and winds toward Lagg, where the five standing rocks of **Five Fingers Strand** jut into the ocean. The water looks tempting but is icy cold and dangerous for swimming. The sand dunes here are reputedly the highest in Europe, towering over 100 ft. high in some places. Turn left above the little white church (near the Inish Eoghin 100 signs) to get to this worthwhile detour. High above the beach, **Knockamany Bens** provide fantastic views of the whole peninsula and even Tory Island on a clear day. Most amazingly, meteorologists have repeatedly recorded Malin Head as the sunniest spot in Ireland.

The scattered town of **Malin Head** includes **Bamba's Crown,** the northernmost tip of Ireland, a tooth of dark rock rising up from the ocean spray. Until the 19th century, Malin Head was the site of an annual pilgrimage in which young men and women "frisked and played in the water all stark naked" to celebrate the sea god's affair with the goddess of the land (see **The Wee of all Flesh,** p. 387). On a clear day, the Head offers a view of Scotland, and perhaps an opportunity to hear the call of the corncrake, a nearly extinct bird. A Lloyds' of London signal tower, built in 1805 by the British Admiralty to catalogue the ships sailing to and from North America, still stands sentry over the point. Written in white-washed stones on a nearby lower cliff and readable from thousands of feet above, "S. S. EIRE" (*Saor Stát Éire;* "Irish Free State") identified Ireland as neutral territory to Nazi would-be bombers. People have removed many of the stones to spell out their own names nearby. A path to the left of the carpark leads to **Hell's Hole,** a 250 ft. chasm that roars devilishly with the incoming tide. Farther down the coast arcs around the naturally formed **Devil's Bridge.** The bridge is no longer safe to walk on, so the Devil is stuck down in the hole. The raised beaches around Malin Head (the result of glaciers' passage through the region millions of years ago) are covered with semi-precious stones; walkers sifting through the sands may find jasper, quartz, small opals, or amethysts. The **Atlantic Circle** is a 5 mi. circuit of the Inish Eoghin 100 that tours the tip of the peninsula.

The area around Malin Head teems with affordable accommodations; choosing a hostel will be difficult but inevitably rewarding. To reach the ▓**Sandrock Holiday Hostel (IHO),** Port Ronan Pier (tel. 70289), take the left fork

THE WEE OF ALL FLESH Just past Bree along the right-hand fork of R242 is the "Wee House of Malin" (Teach na Maiohann). This unassuming collection of cave, well, and ruined stone church in a seaside cove exemplifies the melding of pagan and Christian ritual. The well was once the site of Druidic festivals, but after its blessing by medieval St. Muirdhealach, it became the object of devout Christians' annual pilgrimages on August 15. The pilgrims' behavior, however, might not accord with usual expectations: a 17th century observer commented that upon reaching the well, male and female bathers would wash the sins off each others' naked flesh. The famed "wee house" (actually a cave behind the church) was said to fit an infinite number of people inside. In reality, the cave contains a copper mine; experts speculate that this ancient story developed from the ease with which copper was removed and the cave expanded. The young people of Malin Head still celebrate August 15, but in these more modest days they call it "Sports Day" and participate in only fully-clothed athletic events in broad daylight.

off the Inish Eoghin 100, just before the Crossroads Inn (also a bus stop). This hostel is right on the water with huge views and potential glimpses of seals, dolphins, and puffins. (10-bed dorms £6.50. Sheets £1. Wash £3, dry £1.50. **Bike rental** £5 per day for guests, £7 per day for non-guests.) On the Inish Eoghin 100, after the phone booth and across from the post office, the **Malin Head Hostel (IHO, IHH)** (tel. 70309) welcomes guests with an open fire, reflexology, homemade elderflower cordial, and carraigan moss jam (made from a local seaweed). The rooms are impeccably clean, and Mary's garden yields fresh, cheap veggies for hostelers' consumption. (5-bed dorms £6.50; twins and doubles £17. Sheets £1. Wash £2, dry £1.50. **Bike rental** £6 per day.) Half a mile south of the Crossroads Inn, across the street from the phone box, Mrs. Doyle at **Barraicín** (tel. 70184) keeps a friendly, comfortable B&B and tends a beautiful garden. A bulletin board with maps and photos of local sights helps plan the day's agenda. If you're traveling by bus, get off at Malin Head's only phone booth, which stands a bit before the post office. (Singles £18; doubles £30, with bath £32.) Five miles past Malin on the way into Malin Head, the **Druin Doo B&B** (tel. 70287), has a wonderful loft for weary travelers. (£15.) A broader view recommends Mrs. Anne Hawes' **Highview B&B** (tel. 70283). After passing the Bree Inn, look for the signposts, and turn right at the second one. Coming from Malin, the turn-off is before the phone booth (ask the bus driver to stop at the Parkhouse). (Singles £19, doubles £32; all with bath.)

All of Malin Head's pubs have licensed fisherman's late hours and sell groceries. Trad sessions, fishing tackle, and revitalizing brew are all sold at **Farren's,** Ireland's northernmost pub. (Music nightly July-Aug.). **Seaview Bar and Restaurant,** commonly referred to as "Vera Dock's," pours your pint in its 12 ft. by 12 ft. space beneath shelves full of corn flakes and motor oil. It opens at 8am and closes (supposedly) at 1am. The restaurant next door serves tasty local seafood. (£5-7. Open daily 9am-10pm.) **The Cottage** (tel. 70257), located along the Atlantic Circle near Bamba's Crown, provides tea, scones, crafts, and the closest thing to a tourist trap at Malin Head. (Open June-Aug. daily 11am-6pm. Sessions 9:30pm F mid-July to mid-August. £2; bring in your own alcohol.) The **Curiosity Shop** (tel. 70236), farther along the Inish Eoghin 100 next to Eskie Bay, sells funky flea market goods that make Malin Head a whole lot hipper than one would think, and is truly a unique experience. (Always open.) Back toward Malin along R242, **Bree Inn** (tel. 70161) delivers heaping plates of food in front of an open fire. (Food served daily Easter-Aug. noon-10pm, Sept.-Easter 4-10pm.) Back in Malin, lift a pint at **McCleans'** (tel. 70607), a pub/market combination popular with the Gaelic Football Association boys. (Shop open M-Sa 9am-10pm, Su 4-10pm.)

NORTHWEST IRELAND

EAST INISHOWEN

Though overshadowed by its northern neighbor Malin Head, **Inishowen Head** draws beach-bathers to the natural beauty of Shroove Strand. The most northern beaches, which look over Lough Foyle, gather small crowds on the handful of hot days in an Irish summer. A delightful "shore walk" runs about 6 mi. between the small thumb of Inishowen Head and Moville. Any local can direct you to **Port a Doris**, a delightful little cove accessible only at low tide, and littered with semi-precious Shroove pebbles. **Tunn's Bank**, a huge sandbank a few hundred yards offshore, is reputedly the resting place of *Manannan McLir*, the Irish sea god whose children were turned into swans.

GREENCASTLE AND MOVILLE

Small Moville is located at the intersection of R239 (from Derry) and R238 (from Culdaff). Smaller Greencastle hides 3 mi. north along R239.

In the grassy, forested seaside promenade of Moville, **Peter Bush** at the Coast Guard Station (tel. 82402) 1 mi. out along Derry Rd. **rents boats.** (Open M-F 9am-5pm.) **Inishowen Adventures** (tel. 82460), at the Moville Boat Club on Front Shore, offers **sailing, windsurfing,** and **snorkeling.** (Open from 2pm F-Su or by appointment; instruction available.) An **AIB** (tel. 82050) with a **24hr. ATM** is on Main St. (Open M-W and F 10am-12:30pm and 1:30-4pm, Th 10am-12:30pm and 1:30-5pm.) **Ulster Bank**, Main St., also has a **24hr. ATM. Hannon's Pharmacy**, Main St. (tel. 82649), cures ills. (Open M-Sa 9:30am-6pm.) The **post office** (tel. 82016) is on Malin Rd., which intersects Main St. (Open M-F 9am-1pm and 2-5:30pm, Sa 9am-1pm.)

The **Moville Holiday Hostel (IHH)** (tel. 82378), off Malin Rd. about 350 yd. past Main St., was lovingly converted from old stone-walled farm buildings. A walk around the hostel's forested grounds will reveal the oldest bridge in Ireland and a mystical Italian ground sculpture. Inside are large 4- and 8-bed dorms, two private rooms with bath, and a hearth-warmed kitchen. Hostelers get a 50% discount on the standard fare for NorthWest Busways; owners will organize cheap transportation to and from McGrory's Pub in Culdaff. (Dorms £6.50; private rooms £11 per person. Key deposit £1. Sheets £1. Towels 50p.) Next door and under the same ownership, **Gulladuff House** (tel. 82378) provides sweet, spacious, and well-antiqued rooms in the 18th century farmhouse that once housed the tillers of the hostel's land. (£15, with bath £18.) At Mrs. McGuinness's **Dunroman B&B** (tel. 82234), off Derry Rd. across from the football field, breakfast is served in a sunny conservatory overlooking the River Foyle. Green plants and murals painted by the eldest daughter complete the splendid setting. (£16, with bath £17.50.) **Eamon Gillen & Sons,** Main St., will sell you all the groceries you require. (Open daily 10am-6pm.) The local budget traveler's haven is at the **Barron's Cafe**, Main St. (tel. 82472), which serves heaps of food cooked in the kitchen of the family house behind the storefront. (All-day breakfast £4, burgers around £2, entrees £4-6. Open daily 9:30am-9:30pm.) There is also a plethora of chippers and tea-shops scattered along the streets leading to the shore. Fishermen and bikers keep company at the **Hair o' the Dog Saloon** (tel. 82600), at the Lower Pier behind Main St. Not so common pub grub includes juicy, American-style hamburgers on homemade kaiser buns (£2-4), and pizza (£3-5). (Live music weekends. Food is served noon-9pm.) Patrons are welcome to bring along their tent or caravan and spend the night overlooking the lough. **McGuire's Bar,** The Square (tel. 60363), has a DJ three times a week and live music weekly. (No cover.) **Terry's Tavern** (tel. 82183), on Main St., gathers an older local crowd in its front rooms, and a younger set in the back room. (Open M-F 5pm-1am, Sa-Su 2pm-1:30am.) Thirteen other pubs also grace the streets of tiny Moville, making for a pleasant pub crawl.

From Inishowen Head, the road leads south to **Greencastle**, a village that throws some spice (or sea salt, at least) into the one-street Irish-village mix. Institutions associated with a sophisticated fishing industry line its coast, including fishermen's schools, a net-weaving factory, a maritime museum, and a fish factory. Greencastle's **castle**, built by the Red Earl of Ulsteris now an ivy-covered ruin. The Irish government maintains a center for training professional fishing boats next to the ruins. Relics of life on the seas are in the spotlight at the **Greencastle Maritime Museum** (tel. 81363) on the shorefront. Housed in an old coast guard station, the museum's impressive collection includes a traditional but newly-built Fanad *curragh*, an Armada room, a 19th century rocket cart for rescuing passengers of wrecked ships, ship models, and photographs. (Open June-Sept. daily 10am-6pm, by appointment during the rest of the year. £2; students, seniors, and children £1.)

In a secluded mansion overlooking Lough Foyle, Mrs. Anna Wright warmly welcomes guests to the high-ceilinged, aristocratic **Manor House** (tel. 81011). From Main St., head out of town in the direction of the castle. Turn right at the first road after the town, following the sign to the castle and the fort. Pass bank and fork right at the bottom of the hill, following the signs to the B&B. Also on the road from Derry is the **Brooklyn Cottage** (tel. 81087), a modest whitewashed house with all the conveniences of a modern urban apartment. You'll further appreciate its view of Lough Foyle after a conversation with its owner, Peter Smith, chairman of the Maritime Museum. (Singles £20, doubles £36; all with bath and TV. Open Feb.-Nov.) In a spic 'n' span kitchen behind an inviting neo-Georgian storefront, **Seamy's Fish and Chips** (tel. 81379) does justice to the work of Greencastle's seamen. (All meals under £2.25. Open M-F noon-1am, Sa-Su 2pm-1am.) Next door at **Kealy's Bar** (tel. 81105), stacked gleaming bottles line the walls. While Kealy's has enough liquor to keep a trawler's worth of fishermen happy, there's only enough seating for Greencastle's tiny population. The **Greencastle Fort** (tel. 81044), next to the castle, was once a Napoleonic sea fort that housed 160 redcoats and 30 bluecoats to man nine cannons, and it has served the likes of Kaiser Wilhelm and the emperor of Japan. Today it protects an inn and a pub with affordable grub. (Meals £6-8; served daily in summer noon-9:30pm. Spontaneous trad sessions most summer weekend nights.) **The Drunken Duck** (tel. 81362), a few miles north of Greencastle, is a friendly pub so-called because of a local woman whose beer leaked into her ducks' feeding troughs.

NORTHERN IRELAND

Northern Ireland's natural beauty includes the Glens of Antrim's pockets of green; Giant's Causeway, one of the world's strangest geological sights; and the Fermanagh Lake District. The ceasefires of recent years have allowed Belfast and Derry to develop into hip, pub-loving destination for travelers and students. Pub culture, urban neighborhoods, and tiny villages show everyday life in a divided society of mostly peaceful citizens.

The predominantly calm tenor of life in the North has also been overshadowed overseas by media headlines concerning politics and bombs. Although the North maintains a strong education system and a progressive health insurance policy, unemployment and poor housing are pressing problems. Some writers describe the North's conflicts in terms of class. According to these essayists, the moderate middle class wants peace, but the working classes have less to lose and therefore have historically supported the reactionary extremists. Violent fringe groups on both sides are less visible than the huge division in civil society that sends Protestants and Catholics to separate neighborhoods, separate stores, separate pubs, and often separate schools, with separate, though similar, traditional songs and slang. Oftentimes the split is hard for an outsider to discern, especially in rural vacation spots. On the other hand, it would be near impossible for a visitor to leave Northern Ireland without seeing streetcurbs in both cities and villages painted the official colors of their residents' sectarian identity. The widespread support of the 1998 Peace Agreement raises hopes for a resolution to the struggles that have divided the island for centuries, but the events of 1999 show that the success of the Agreement hangs in the balance.

HIGHLIGHTS OF NORTHERN IRELAND

■ Take in **Belfast's** (p. 399) murals, Golden Mile, Donegall Square, and Docklands on a black cab tour.

■ The **Glens of Antrim** (p. 441) harbour tiny villages between glorious mountains, forests, and coastal paths.

■ Sixty million-year-old volcanic rock formations at **Giant's Causeway** (p. 453) are the stuff of Irish myth and legend.

■ **Derry's** (p. 458) Tower Museum, St. Columb's Cathedral, and the murals of the Bogside neighborhood illuminate this city's complex past.

■ The Ulster Way weaves a hiking path through 560 mi. of Northern Ireland, passing through the spectacular but underexplored **Sperrin Mountains** (p. 475).

ESSENTIALS

MONEY

AUS$1 = £0.40	UK£1 = AUS$2.48
CDN$1 =£0.42	= CDN$2.39
EUR1= £0.66	= EUR1.51
IR£1 = UK£0.83	= IR£1.20
NZ$1 = £0.33	= NZ$3.03
SAR1=£0.10	= SAR9.83
US$1 = £0.62	= US$1.61

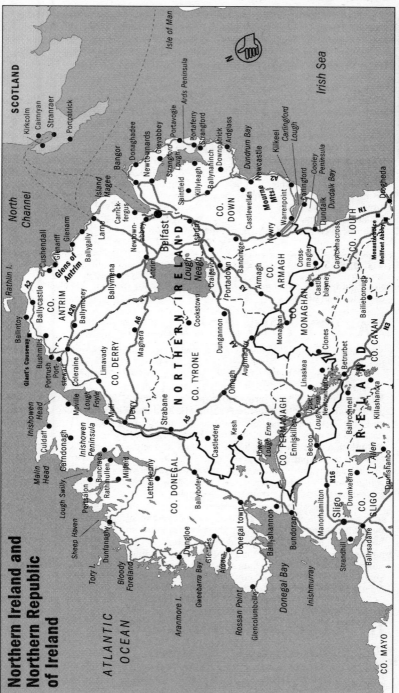

Northern Ireland and
Northern Republic
of Ireland

The information in this book was researched during the summer of 1999. Inflation and the Invisible Hand may raise or lower the listed prices by as much as 20%. The European Union's Echo Service posts daily exchange rates on the web (www.dna.lth.se/cgi-bin/kurt/rates?).

Legal tender in Northern Ireland is the British pound. Northern Ireland has its own bank notes, which are identical in value to English and Scottish notes of the same denominations but not accepted outside Northern Ireland. Both English and Scottish notes, however, are accepted in the North. The Republic of Ireland's pounds are generally not accepted in the North, with the exception of some border towns which will calculate the exchange rate and add an additional surcharge. U.K. coins now come in logical denominations of 1p, 2p, 5p, 10p, 20p, 50p, and £1. Most banks are closed on Saturday, Sunday, and all public holidays. On "bank holidays," occurring several times a year in both countries (see p. 490), most businesses shut down. Usual weekday bank hours in Northern Ireland are Monday to Friday 9:30am to 4:30pm.

For more comprehensive travel information, see p. 35.

TELEPHONES

Northern Ireland is reached by using the U.K. **country code** 44. The **phone code** for every town in the North is 028.

SAFETY AND SECURITY

Although sectarian violence is dramatically less common than in the height of the Troubles, some neighborhoods and towns still experience turmoil during sensitive political times. It's best to avoid traveling in Northern Ireland during **Marching Season,** from July 4 to July 12 (**Orange Day;** see p. 393). The twelfth of August, when the Apprentice Boys (see p. 10) march in Derry, is also a testy period during which urban areas should be avoided. The most common form of violence is property damage, and tourists are unlikely targets, but transportation and services may shut down if there are problems—you don't want to be stranded. Vacation areas like the Glens and the Causeway Coast are less affected by the parades. In general, use common sense in conversation, and, as in dealing with any issues of a culture not your own, be respectful of locals' religious and political perspectives. Overall, Northern Ireland has one of the lowest tourist-related crime rates in the world.

Border checkpoints have been removed, and armed soldiers and vehicles are less visible in Belfast and Derry. Do not take **photographs** of soldiers, military installations, or vehicles; if you do, your film will be confiscated and you may be detained for questioning. Taking pictures of political murals is not a crime, although many people feel uncomfortable snapping pictures in the residential neighborhoods where the murals sit. Unattended luggage is always considered suspicious and worthy of confiscation. It is still generally unsafe to hitch in Northern Ireland. *Let's Go* never recommends hitchhiking.

HISTORY AND POLITICS

Northern Ireland is a region that lacks a collective cultural identity. Its citizens still recognize themselves by their political allegiances rather than geographic lines—as Unionists and Nationalists. The 950,000 Protestants are generally Unionists, who want the six counties of Northern Ireland to remain in the U.K.;

the 650,000 Catholics tend to identify with the Republic of Ireland, not Britain, and many are Nationalists, who want the six counties to be part of the Republic. Extremists bring violence into the argument; they are referred to as Loyalists and Republicans, respectively. The conflict between them has seemed intractable. In 1998, the world felt a tentative optimism descend upon the North when its two communities collectively voted into being the monumental Peace Agreement, but the passage of 1999 has proven that internal challenges are far from over.

For more information about the geographic region of Northern Ireland before the formation of the Republic, see **Life and Times,** p. 7.

BRITISH RULE
AND THE DIVISION OF IRELAND

The 17th century's **Ulster Plantation** systematically set up English and Scottish settlers on what had been Gaelic-Irish land and gave Derry to the City of London—hence the name "Londonderry" (see p. 9). Protestants fleeing France in the late 17th century sought refuge in Ulster, bringing commercial skills to the small linen-manufacturing industry. Over the following two centuries, merchants and working-class immigrants from nearby Scotland settled in northeast Ulster. Institutionalized religious discrimination that limited Catholic access to land ownership and other basic rights made it profitable for Scottish Protestants to settle here. The British developed an industrial economy in Cos. Antrim and Down while the rest of the island remained agricultural. By the end of the 19th century, Belfast was a booming industrial center with thriving textile and ship-building industries, but most refused to hire Catholic workers.

As the Republican movement gained fervor in the South in the late 19th century, the picture looked much different in the Northeast. The Ulster Plantation and Scottish settlement, over the course of 300 years, had created a working-and middle-class population in Ulster who identified with the British Empire and did not support Irish Home Rule. The **Orange Order,** named after King William of Orange, who had won victories over Catholic James II in the 1690s (see p. 10), organized the Ulster Protestants in local lodges, with ritualistic behaviors resembling those of the masonic order. They ordained July 12th as an annual holiday on which to hold parades to celebrate William's defeat of James at the Battle of the Boyne. The Order's constituency continued to grow long after the Act of Union in 1801 (see p. 10) made its original mission obsolete. In the 1830s, the government attempted to dissolve the Order. It quietly gained momentum, however, culminating in its explosive opposition to the first Home Rule Bill in 1886 (see p. 12).

Lawyer and politician **Edward Carson** and his ally **James Craig** translated Ulster Unionism into terms the British elite understood. When Home Rule looked likely in 1911, Carson held a mass meeting, and Unionists signed the Ulster Covenant of Resistance to Home Rule (1912). In 1914, when Home Rule appeared imminent, the Unionist **Ulster Volunteer Force (UVF)** (see p. 12) armed itself by smuggling guns in through Larne—an act that prompted fearful Nationalists to smuggle their own guns in through Howth. World War I gave Unionists more time to organize and gave British leaders time to see that the imposition of Home Rule on all of Ulster would mean havoc: the UVF intended to fight the **Irish Republican Army (IRA)** (see p. 14) who in turn would fight the police. The **1920 Government of Ireland Act** created two parliaments for North and South. The Act of Union went nowhere in the south and was quickly superseded by the Anglo-Irish Treaty and Civil War (see p. 14), but the measure—intended as a temporary one—became the basis of Northern Ireland's government until 1973. The new Parliament met at **Stormont,** near Belfast.

The new statelet included only six of the nine counties in the province of Ulster, excluding Donegal, Monaghan, and Cavan, which had Catholic majorities. This arrangement suited the one million Protestants in the six counties, yet it threatened the several hundred thousand Protestant Unionists living elsewhere on the island and the half-million Catholic Nationalists living within the new Ulster. Carson and Craig had approved these odd borders, hoping to create the largest possible area with a permanent Protestant majority. Craig, as the North's first Prime Minister, his successor **Sir Basil Brooke,** and most of their Cabinet ministers thought in terms, as Brooke put it, of "a Protestant state for a Protestant people." Orange lodges and other strongly Protestant groups continued to control politics, and the Catholic minority boycotted elections. Anti-Catholic discrimination was widespread. The **Royal Ulster Constabulary (RUC),** the new and Protestant police force in the North, filled its ranks with part-time policemen called Bs and **B-Specials,** a major source of Catholic casualties. The IRA continued sporadic campaigns in the North through the 20s and 30s with little result. In the Irish State, the IRA was gradually suppressed.

The 1930s sent the Northern economy into the dumps, requiring more and more British subsidies, while the Stormont Cabinet aged and withered. **World War II** gave Unionists a chance to show their loyalty. The Republic of Ireland stayed neutral and stayed out, but the North welcomed Allied troops, ships, and air force bases. The need to build and repair warships raised employment in Belfast and allowed Catholics to enter the industrial workforce for the first time. The Luftwaffe firebombed Belfast toward the end of the war, making it one of the U.K.'s most damaged cities. In May 1945, Churchill thanked the North and attacked Éire's neutrality in a famous speech.

Over the following two decades, a grateful British Parliament poured money into Northern Ireland. The North's standard of living stayed higher than the Republic's, but discrimination and joblessness persisted. The government at Stormont neglected to institute social reform, and parliamentary districts were painfully and unequally drawn to favor Protestants. Large towns were segregated by religion, perpetuating the cultural separation. After a brief, unsuccessful try at school desegregation, Stormont ended up granting subsidies to Catholic schools. As the Republic gained a sure footing, violence receded on the island and, barring the occasional border skirmish, the IRA was seen as finished by 1962 when the *New York Times* bid it a formal, eulogy-like farewell. **Capt. Terence O'Neill,** who became the third Stormont Prime Minister in 1963, tried to enlarge the economy and soften discrimination, meeting in 1965 with the Republic's Prime Minister, Sean Lemass. O'Neill may have epitomized the liberal Unionist attitude when he said, "If you treat Roman Catholics with due kindness and consideration, they will live like Protestants."

THE TROUBLES

The economy grew, but the bigotry festered, as did the Nationalist community's resentment at being left unemployed and unrepresented. The American civil rights movement inspired the 1967 founding of the **Northern Ireland Civil Rights Association (NICRA),** which worked to end anti-Catholic discrimination in public housing. NICRA leaders tried to distance the movement from constitutional concerns, although many of their followers didn't get the message: the Republican song "A Nation Once Again" often drowned out "We Shall Overcome" in demonstrations. Protestant extremists included the acerbic **Dr. Ian Paisley,** whose **Ulster Protestant Volunteers (UPV)** overlapped in membership with the illegal, resurrected, paramilitary UVF. The first NICRA march was raucous but nonviolent. The second, in Derry in 1968, was a bloody mess disrupted by Unionists and then by the RUC's water cannons. This incident is thought of as the culmination of the Troubles.

Catholic **John Hume** and Protestant **Ivan Cooper** formed a new civil rights committee in Derry but were overshadowed by Bernadette Devlin's student-led, radical **People's Democracy (PD).** The PD encouraged, and NICRA opposed, a four-day peaceful march from Belfast to Derry starting on New Year's Day, 1969. Paisleyite harassment along the way was nothing compared to the RUC's physical assault on Derry's Catholic Bogside once the marchers arrived. After that, Derry authorities agreed to keep the RUC out of the Bogside, and this area became **Free Derry.** O'Neill, granting more civil rights concessions in hopes of calming everyone down, was deserted by more of his hardline Unionist allies. On August 12, 1969, Catholics based in Free Derry threw rocks at the annual Apprentice Boys parade along the city walls. The RUC attacked the Bogside residents, and a two-day siege ensued. Free Derry retained its independence, but the violence showed that the RUC could not maintain order alone. The British Army arrived—and hasn't left yet.

O'Neill resigned in 1969. Between 1970 and 1972, Stormont leaders alternated concessions and crackdowns to little effect. The rejuvenated IRA split in two, with the Socialist "Official" faction practically fading into insignificance as the new **Provisional IRA,** or **Provos** (the IRA we primarily hear about today), took over with less ideology and more arms. British troops became the IRA's main target. In 1970, John Hume founded the **Social Democratic and Labor Party (SDLP),** with the intension of bringing about social change through the support of both Catholics and Protestants; by 1973, it had become the moderate political voice of Northern Catholics. British policies of **internment without trial** outraged Catholics and led the SDLP to withdraw from government. The pattern was clear: any concessions to the Catholic community might provoke Protestant violence, while anything that seemed to favor the Unionists risked an explosive IRA response.

On January 30, 1972, British troops fired into a crowd of non-violent protesters in Derry; the famous event, called **Bloody Sunday,** and the ensuing reluctance of the British government to investigate, increased Catholic outrage. Fourteen Catholics were killed: the soldiers claimed they had not fired the first shot, while Catholics said the soldiers shot at the backs of unarmed, fleeing marchers. Only in 1999 did official re-examination of the event begin. On February 2, 1972, the British embassy in Dublin was burned down. Soon thereafter, the IRA bombed a British army barracks. After further bombings in 1973, Stormont was dissolved and replaced by the **Sunningdale executive,** which split power between Catholics and Protestants. This policy was immediately crippled by a massive Unionist work stoppage, and a policy of **direct British rule** from Westminster began. A referendum that year, asking if voters wanted Northern Ireland to remain part of the United Kingdom, showed that voters supported the Union at a rate of 90 to 1—Catholics had boycotted the polls. The verdict didn't stop the violence, which brought an average of 275 deaths per year between 1970 and 1976.

In 1978, 300 Nationalist prisoners in the Maze Prison in Northern Ireland began a campaign to have their special category as political prisoners restored. The campaign's climax was the 10-man H-Block **hunger strike** of 1981. The leader, **Bobby Sands,** was the first to go on hunger strike. He was elected to Parliament from a Catholic district in Tyrone and Fermanagh even as he starved to death. Sands died after 66 days and became a martyr; his face is still seen on murals in the Falls section of Belfast (see p. 417). The remaining prisoners officially ended the strike on October 3.

Sands's election was no anomaly. The hunger strikes galvanized Nationalists, and support for **Sinn Fein,** the political arm of the IRA, surged in the early 80s. British Prime Minister Margaret Thatcher and Taoiseach Garret FitzGerald signed the **Anglo-Irish Agreement** at Hillsborough Castle in November 1985. The Agreement granted the Republic of Ireland a "consultative role" but no legal authority in the governance of Northern Ireland. It improved relations between London and Dublin but infuriated extremists on both sides. Protestant paramilitaries began to attack the British Army, while the IRA continued its bombing campaigns in England. In 1991 and 92, the Brooke Initiative led to the first multi-party talks in the North in over a decade, but they did not include Sinn Fein. In December 1993, the **Downing Street Declaration,** issued by Prime Minister John Major and Taoiseach Albert Reynolds, invited the IRA to participate in talks if they refrained from violence for three months.

THE 1994 CEASEFIRE

On August 31, 1994, the IRA announced a complete cessation of violence. While Loyalist guerillas cooperated by announcing their own ceasefire, Unionist leaders bickered over the meaning of the IRA's statement; in their opinion, it did not go far enough—only the IRA's disarmament could signify a commitment to peace. Nonetheless, **Gerry Adams,** Sinn Fein's leader, defended the statement and called for direct talks with the British government. The peace held for over a year.

In February 1995, John Major and Irish Prime Minister John Bruton issued the **joint framework** proposal. The document suggested the possibility of a new Northern Ireland Assembly that would include the "harmonizing powers" of the Irish and British governments and the right of the people of Northern Ireland to choose their own destiny. Subsequently, the British government began talks with both Loyalists and, for the first time, Sinn Fein. Disarmament was the most prominent problem in the 1995 talks—both Republican and Loyalist groups refused to give up their weapons.

A flurry of tragic events left the future of Northern Ireland as tenuous as ever. The IRA ended their ceasefire on February 9, 1996, with the bombing of an office building in London's Docklands. Despite this setback, the stalled peace talks, to be chaired by U.S. diplomat **George Mitchell,** were slated for June 10, 1996. Ian Paisley, now leader of the extreme **Democratic Unionist Party (DUP),** objected to Mitchell's appointment, calling it a "dastardly deed," but did not boycott the talks. The talks proceeded sluggishly and precariously. Sinn Fein did not participate in these talks because it did not agree to the **Mitchell Principles,** which included the total disarmament of all paramilitary organizations. Despite this exclusion, Sinn Fein's popularity grew in Northern Ireland: in the May elections, they gathered 15% of the vote. The credibility of Sinn Fein was seriously jeopardized on June 15, 1996, when a blast in a Manchester shopping district injured more than 200 people.

As the peace process continued, the Orangemen's July and August marches grew increasingly contentious. Parades through Catholic neighborhoods incited violence on the part of both residents and marchers. The government created a **Parades Commission** to oversee the rerouting of parades and encourage the participation of both sides in negotiations. Protestants see the Commission's decisions as infringing on their rights to practice their culture. Catholics argue that the marches are a form of harassment and intimidation from which they deserve protection. Violence flared around **Orange Day, 1996,** when the Parades Commission banned an Orange Order march through the Catholic Garvaghy Rd. in Portadown, a staunchly Protestant town. Unionists reacted by throwing petrol bombs, bricks, and bottles at police, who answered with plastic bullets. After four days of violence, police allowed the marchers to go through, but this time Catholics responded with a hail of debris. Nightly rioting by both sides also took place in Belfast, where RUC policemen were wounded, and in Derry, where Catholic Dermot McShane died after being run over by a jeep.

On October 7, the IRA bombed British army headquarters in Belfast, killing one soldier and injuring thirty in the first bombing in Northern Ireland in two years. In early 1997, the IRA tried to make Northern Ireland an issue in the upcoming elections in Great Britain by making several bomb threats, including one that postponed the Grand National horse race. No one was injured, but public ire was aroused and John Major condemned Sinn Fein.

In May of 1997, the Labour party swept the British elections and **Tony Blair** became Prime Minister, bringing hope for peaceful change. Sinn Fein made its most impressive showing yet: Gerry Adams and member Martin McGuinness won seats in Parliament but were barred from taking their seats by their refusal to swear allegiance to the Queen. Despite this act, the government ended its ban on talks with Sinn Fein. Sinn Fein, however, refused to join the talks. Hopes for a ceasefire were dashed when the car of a prominent Irish republican was bombed; in retaliation, the IRA shot two members of the RUC.

GOOD FRIDAY AGREEMENT AND RECENT EVENTS

The British government's Northern Ireland Secretary **Mo Mowlam** had a rough introduction to her new job: **marching season** in 1997 was the most violent in recent years. The Orange Order held a large march through Portadown a week before Orange Day. More than 80 people were hurt in the ensuing rioting and looting, and Mowlam came under scrutiny for allowing the parade to go on without considering the consequences. On July 10, the Orange Order called off and re-routed a number of contentious parades, offering hope for peace. The marches that were held were mostly peaceful; police fired plastic bullets at rioters in Derry and Belfast, but there were no casualties. On July 19, the IRA announced an "unequivocal" **ceasefire** to start the following day.

In September 1997, Sinn Fein joined the peace talks. Members of the **Ulster Unionist Party (UUP),** the voice of moderate Protestants, joined shortly thereafter and were attacked by Ian Paisley and the DUP for sitting with terrorists. **David Trimble,** leader of the UUP, assured Protestants that he wouldn't negotiate directly with Sinn Fein. Co-founders of the recently formed, religiously mixed **Northern Ireland Women's Coalition,** Catholic Monica McWilliams and Protestant Pearl Sagar brought a human rights agenda and a strong commitment to peace to the talks, where they were subjects of derision by Ian Paisley.

Some groups still opposed the peace process. In January 1998, another 12 people were killed by sectarian violence, mostly committed by extremist Loyalists against Catholic civilians. After two Protestants were killed by Catholic extremists in early February, Unionist leaders charged Sinn Fein with breaking its pledge to support only peaceful actions toward political change and tried to oust party leaders from the talks. Mitchell, Mowlam, Blair, and Irish Prime Minister Bertie Ahern continued to push for progress, holding the group to a strict deadline in April. Mowlam made the unprecedented move of visiting Republican and Loyalist prisoners in the maximum-security Maze prison to encourage their participation in the peace process.

After an interminable week of late-night negotiations, the delegates approved a draft of the **1998 Northern Ireland Peace Agreement** in the early morning after April 10, Good Friday. The Agreement above all emphasized that change in Northern Ireland could come only with the consent of the majority of its people. It declared that the "birthright" of the people is the right to choose whether to personally identify as Irish, British, or both; even as the status of Northern Ireland changes, the Agreement says, residents retain the right to hold Irish or British citizenship.

On Friday, May 22, in the first island-wide vote since 1918, residents of both the North and the Republic voted the Agreement into law. A resounding 71% of the North and 94% of the Republic voted yes to the Agreement, meaning that a majority of Protestants voted in favor of the Peace Agreement, which divided governing responsibilities of Northern Ireland into three strands. The main body, a new 108-member **Northern Ireland Assembly,** assigns committee posts and chairs proportionately to the parties' representation. Catholics see this body as an opportunity for reclaiming the political power they were long denied. On June 25, the UUP and the SDLP won the most seats, and Sinn Fein garnered more support than ever before, winning 18 assembly seats and two in the executive. David Trimble of the UUP and Seamus Mallon of the SDLP were elected First Minister and Deputy First Minister, respectively, by the assembly. The second strand, a **North-South Ministerial Council,** serves as the cross-border authority. At least 12 possible areas of focus were under consideration by them in 1998, including social welfare issues such as education, transportation, urban planning, tourism, and EU programs. The final strand, the **British-Irish Council,** approaches issues similar to those considered by the North-South Council, but operates on a broader scale, concerning itself with the entire British Isles.

While most felt that Northern Ireland was finally on the verge of lasting peace, a few controversial issues remained unresolved. Sinn Fein called for disbanding the still very largely Protestant RUC, which was cited in an April 1998 United Nations report for its systematic intimidation and harassment of lawyers representing those accused of paramilitary crimes. Blair declared that the RUC would continue to exist, but in June appointed Chris Patten, the former governor of Hong Kong, to head a small one-year commission to review the RUC's recruiting, hiring, and training practices, as well as its culture and symbols.

The 1998 marching season brought challenges and tragedy to the newly arrived peace. In the end of May, just a week after the Agreement was voted in, a march by the Junior Orange Order provoked violence on Garvaghy Rd., the Catholic zone in largely Protestant Portadown, where violence had erupted in 1996. In light of this disturbance, the Parades Commission hesitated in granting the Orange Day marching permits. On June 15, the Parades Commission rerouted the Tour of the North, banning it from entering the Catholic Cliftonville Rd.-Antrim Rd. areas in Belfast. Aside from two short stand-offs with the RUC, the parade proceeded without conflict. The day after the assembly elections, however, violence broke out between Nationalists and policemen at a parade in West Belfast. The beginning of July saw a wave of violence that included hundreds of bombings and attacks on security forces as well as a slew of arson attacks on Catholic churches.

Other parades passed peacefully, but a stand-off began over the fate of the **Drumcree** parade. The parade, which occurs July 4, was not given permission to march down the Catholic section of Garvaghy Rd. in Portadown. Angered by the decision but encouraged by a history of indecision by the British government, thousands of people participated in a week-long standoff with the RUC that affected the whole country. Rioting occurred there and elsewhere, and Protestant marchers were angered by what they saw as the disloyalty of their own police force. Neither the Orangemen nor the Parade Commission would budge, and the country looked with anxiety toward Orange Day, July 12, which would be the climax of the tense situation. On July 11, however, a Catholic home in almost entirely Protestant Ballymoney was firebombed in the middle of the night by local hooligans, and three young boys, Richard, Mark, and Jason Quinn, were killed. Marches still took place the following day; but instead of rioting against the Orangeman who passed though their neighborhoods, Catholics looked on at the marches in silence, holding black balloons and carrying signs that read "for shame." The seemingly intractable Drumcree stand-off gradually lost it numbers, and the Church of Ireland publicly called for its end. Although some tried to distance the boys' deaths from the events at Drumcree, the murders led to a reassessment of the Orange Order and to a new sobriety about the peace process.

On August 15, 1998, a bombing in the religiously mixed town of **Omagh,** County Tyrone, left 29 dead and 382 injured. A tiny splinter group calling itself the "Real IRA" claimed responsibility for the attack. The terrorists' obvious motive for the worst atrocity of the Troubles was to undermine the Agreement. Sinn Fein's Gerry Adams unreservedly condemned the attack. However, the terrible act only underlined the fact that the majority of people in Northern Ireland, both Catholic and Protestant, had voted in favor of the agreement.

In October of 1998, Catholic John Hume and Protestant David Trimble received the Nobel Peace Prize for their participation in the peace process. The coming year, however, evidenced the failure to form the Northern Ireland Assembly, the fundamental premise of the Agreement. Two major provisions of the pact became the source of irreconcilable difference between Catholic and Protestant politicians: the gradual decommissioning of all paramilitary groups' arms, and the early release of political prisoners. Tensions rose out of the **Northern Ireland (Sentences) Bill,** voted against by members of the UUP, the DUP, and the British Conservative Party, splitting the U.K. Parliament for the first time during the talks. The bill will release all political prisoners, including those convicted of murder, by May 2000; dissenters feared that the bill did not sufficiently link the release of prisoners to their organizations' full disarmament. Of greatest concern for most Unionists was the issue of decommissioning: the military wings of political parties, most notably Sinn Fein, were expected to disarm themselves in time for the June elections. Difficulties arose due to the Agreement's lack of a time frame for decommissioning. During the summer of 1999, the deadline for the Assembly's inauguration was pushed farther and farther back as Unionists refused to take seats with Sinn Fein; Blair, Mowland, and Ahern spent long nights attempting to negotiate between sides. In July of 1999, Prime Minister Trimble failed to appear on the day that he was due to appoint the newly elected Assembly. Many interpreted Trimble's behavior as following the prerogatives of his own Unionist political party, rather than the democratic will of the voters who approved the Peace Agreement. Trimble's nationalist Deputy Prime-Minister Seamus Mallon resigned the following day.

The 1999 marching season started well, with little trouble around the twelfth of July. Violence began on August 12 as the Apprentice Boys marched through Derry and Belfast. Catholics in Belfast staged a sit-down protest in the path of the marchers, only to be forcefully removed by the RUC. In Derry, the streets fell prey to petrol bombs and riot gear. The North's long history of turmoil remains unresolved at the start of the new millennium.

BELFAST

The second-largest city on the island, Belfast (pop. 330,000) is the center of the North's cultural, commercial, and political activity. Acclaimed writers and the annual arts festival in November maintain Belfast's reputation as a thriving artistic center. West Belfast's famous sectarian murals are perhaps the most informative source on the effects of the Troubles on the city. The bar scene—a mix of Irish and British pub culture, and less traditional international trends—entertains locals, foreigners, and a lively student population. Despite Belfast's reputation as a terrorist-riddled metropolis, the city feels more neighborly than most international—and even Irish—visitors expect.

Belfast was founded as the capital of the "Scots-Irish" Presbyterian settlement in the 17th century, and was William of Orange's base during his battles against King James II in 1690 (see **The Protestant Ascendancy,** p. 10). In the 19th century, Belfast became the most industrial part of Ireland, with world-famous factories and shipyards. By 1900, Belfast had gathered enough slums, smoke, flax mills, Victorian architecture, and social theorists to look more British than Irish. The ship-building industry regularly drew Scottish laborers across the channel for jobs, securing the region's allegiance to the U.K. During the Troubles, armed British soldiers patrolled the streets, frequent military checkpoints slowed auto and pedestrian traffic, and stores advertised "Bomb

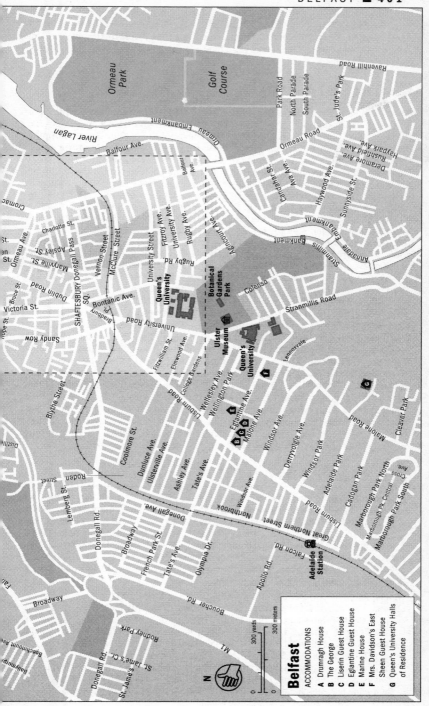

Belfast

ACCOMMODATIONS
A Drumragh House
B The George
C Liserin Guest House
D Eglantine Guest House
E Marine House
F Mrs. Davidson's East
G Sheen Guest House
   Queen's University Halls
   of Residence

300 yards
300 meters

N

Damage Sales." Since the days of the Peace Agreement (see **The Good Friday Agreement,** p. 397), foreign and domestic investors flock to the city on the Lough. Today's visitors will discover a bustling urban center peppered with hip pubs, clubs, and cafes.

✈ ORIENTATION

Buses arrive at the Europa bus station on **Great Victoria St.** near several landmarks: the Europa hotel, the Crown Liquor Saloon, and the Opera House. To the northeast is the City Hall in **Donegall Square.** A busy pedestrian shopping district extends north for four blocks between City Hall and the enormous Castlecourt Shopping Centre. Donegall Pl. becomes **Royal Ave.,** and runs from Donegall Square through the shopping area. In the eastern part of the shopping district is the **Cornmarket** area, where several centuries of characteristically Belfast architecture hold their ground amongst modern establishments. South of the bus station, Great Victoria St. meets **Dublin Rd.** at **Shaftesbury Sq.** The stretch of Great Victoria St. between the bus station and Shaftesbury Sq. is known as the **Golden Mile** for its highbrow establishments and Victorian architecture. **Botanic Ave.** and **Bradbury Pl.** (which becomes University Rd.) extend south from Shaftesbury Sq. into the **Queen's University area,** where cafes, student pubs, and budget accommodations await. In this southern area of the city, the busiest neighborhoods center around **Stranmillis, Malone,** and **Lisburn Rd.** The city center, Golden Mile, and the university area are quite safe; Belfast in general is safer than most American and European cities.

Divided from the rest of Belfast by the Westlink Motorway, working class **West Belfast** is more politically volatile than the city center. There remains a sharp division between sectarian neighborhoods. The Protestant neighborhood stretches along **Shankill Rd.,** just north of the Catholic neighborhood, centered around **Falls Rd.** The two are separated by the **peace line.** The **River Lagan** divides industrial **East Belfast** from the rest of the city. The shipyards and docks that brought Belfast fame and fortune extend north on both sides of the river as it grows into **Belfast Lough.**

M1 and M2 motorways join to form a backwards "C" through Belfast. A1 branches off from M1 around **Lisburn** and heads south to Newry, where it changes to N1 before continuing through **Dundalk** and **Drogheda** to **Dublin.** M2 merges into A6 then heads northwest to **Derry. Larne** is connected to Belfast by the A8.

⊏ TRANSPORTATION

Airports: Belfast International Airport (tel. 9042 2888) in Aldergrove. **Aer Lingus** (tel. (0645) 737 747), **British Airways** (tel. (0345) 222 111), **Jersey European** (tel. 9045 7200), **British Midlands** (tel. (0870) 607 0555), and **Air U.K.** land here. **Airbus** (tel. 9033 3000) runs to Belfast's Europa (Glengall St.) bus station in the city center (M-Sa every 30min. 5:45am-9:30pm, Su about every hr. 7am-8:45pm; £5, £8 return). **Belfast City Airport,** at the harbor, is the destination of **Manx Airlines** (tel. (0345) 256 256) and **Jersey European. Trains** run from the airport to Central Station (M-F 31 per day, Sa 26 per day, Su 2 per day; 90p).

Trains: All trains arrive at Belfast's **Central Station,** East Bridge St. (tel. 9089 9411). Some also stop at **Botanic Station,** on Botanic Ave. in the center of the University area, or the **Great Victoria Station** (tel. 9043 4424), next to the Europa Hotel. Trains roll in from **Derry** (2½hr.; M-F 7 per day, Sa 6 per day, Su 3 per day; £6.70) and **Dublin** (2½hr.; M-F 8 per day, Sa 8 per day, Su 5 per day; £17). Call for info on other destinations. To get to Donegall Sq. from Central Station, turn left and walk down East Bridge St. Turn right on Victoria St. then left after 2 blocks onto May St., which runs into Donegall Sq. South. A better option for those disoriented or encumbered with luggage is the **Centrelink** bus service, free with rail tickets (see **Local Transportation,** below).

Buses: There are two main stations in Belfast. Buses traveling to and from the west and the Republic operate out of the **Europa (Glengall St.) Station** (tel. 9033 3000; inquiries M-Sa 7:30am-8:30pm, Su 9am-7:30pm). Buses to **Dublin** (M-Sa 8 per day, Su 3 per day; £10.50) and **Derry** (M-Sa 15 per day, Su 6 per day; £6.50). Call for other route info. Buses to and from Northern Ireland's east coast operate out of **Laganside Station** (same tel. and hours as Europa).

Ferries: To reach the city center from the **Belfast SeaCat terminal** (tel. (01345) 523 523), you have two options. If you're arriving late at night or early in the morning, a **taxi** is your best bet; the docks can be somewhat unsafe at night. If on foot, take a left when you exit the terminal onto Donegall Quay. Turn right onto Albert Sq. about 2 blocks down at the Customs House (a large Victorian stone building). After 2 more short blocks, turn left on Victoria St. (not Great Victoria St.). Turn right again at the clock tower onto High St., which runs into Donegall Pl. Here, a left will lead you to the City Hall and Donegall Sq. (at the end of the street), where you can catch a **Centrelink** bus (see **Local Transportation,** below). **Larne ferry terminals** are easily accessible by bus or train from the Belfast city center. (Buses 1hr.; M-F 17 per day, Sa 15 per day, Su 3 per day; £2.60.) For information on ferries and hovercraft to Belfast from **England** and **Scotland,** see **By Ferry,** p. 33.

Local Transportation: The red **Citybus Network** (24hr. recorded info tel. 9024 6485), is supplemented by **Ulsterbus's** "blue buses" to the suburbs. Travel within the city center 50p, seniors and children under 16 free. Citybuses going south and west leave from Donegall Sq. East; those going north and east leave from Donegall Sq. West (80p). Money-saving 4-journey tickets £2.70, seniors and children £1.35. 7-day **"gold cards"** allow unlimited travel in the city (£11.50). 7-day **"silver cards"** permit unlimited travel in either North Belfast, West/South Belfast, or East Belfast (£7.50). All transport cards and tickets can be bought from kiosks in Donegall Sq. and around the city. Open M-Sa 8am-6pm. The **Centrelink** green bus connects all the major areas of Belfast in the course of its cloverleaf-shaped route: Donegall Sq., Castlecourt Shopping Centre, Europa and Langanside Bus Stations, Northern Ireland Rail Station, and Shaftesbury Sq. The buses can be caught at any of 12 designated stops (every 15min.; M-F 7:15am-8:30pm, Sa 8:35am-8:30pm; 50p, free with bus or rail ticket). Late **Nightline** buses cover 5 extensive routes from Shaftesbury Sq. to various parts of the city. Tickets (£2.50) must be bought in advance from ticket units in Shaftesbury Sq.

Taxis: 24hr. metered cabs abound: **City Cab** (tel. 9024 2000; wheelchair accessible), **Diamond Taxi Service** (tel. 9064 6666), **Fon a Cab** (tel. 9023 3333), and **Jet Taxi** (tel. 9032 3278). Residents of West and North Belfast utilize the huge **black cabs** you'll see in the city center. They follow set routes, collecting and discharging passengers along the way (standard 60p charge).

Car Rental: McCausland's, 21-31 Grosvenor Rd. (tel. 9033 3777), is Northern Ireland's largest car rental company. £40 per day, £180 per week; £11.75 surcharge to drive in the Republic. Ages 21-70. Open M-Th 8:30am-6:30pm, F 8:30am-7:30pm, Sa 8:30am-5pm, Su 8:30am-1pm. 24hr. car return at all offices. Other offices at **Belfast International Airport** (tel. 9442 2022) and **Belfast City Airport** (tel. 9045 4141). **Budget,** 96-102 Great Victoria St. (tel. 9023 0700). £39-59 per day, £155-250 per week. Ages 23-70. Open M-F 9am-5pm, Sa 9am-12pm. **Belfast International Airport Office** (tel. 9423 332). Open daily 7:30am-11:30pm; **Belfast City Airport Office** (tel. 9054 1111). Open M-Sa 8am-9:30pm, Su 10am-9:30pm.

Bike Rental: McConvey Cycles, 10 Pottingers Entry (tel. 9033 0322) and 467 Ormeau Rd. (tel. 9049 1163). £7 per day, £40 per week; deposit £30; panniers £5 per week. Locks supplied. Open M-Sa 9am-5:30pm. **ReCycle Bicycle Hire,** 1-5 Albert Sq. (tel. 9031 3113), will pick up cycles M-F from Belfast hostels. £6.50 per day; £30 per week; £50 or passport deposit; locks and helmets supplied. Open M-F 9am-5pm, Sa 10am-5pm.

Hitching: Notoriously hard in and out of Belfast—most people take the bus out as far as Bangor or Larne before they stick out a thumb. *Let's Go* doesn't recommend hitchhiking.

🔢 PRACTICAL INFORMATION

TOURIST AND FINANCIAL SERVICES

Tourist Office: 59 North St., St. Anne's Court (tel. 9024 6609). Supplies a great booklet on Belfast, the usual info on the surrounding areas, and an excellent map of the city with bus schedules (free). Formulate specific questions for the hurried staff. 24hr. computerized info kiosk outside. Open July-Aug. M-F 9am-7pm, Sa 9am-5:15pm, Su noon-4pm; Sept.-June M 9:30am-5:15pm, Tu-Sa 9am-5:15pm.

Irish Tourist Board (Bord Fáilte), 53 Castle St. (tel. 9032 7888). Provides info on the Republic and makes reservations for accommodations "south of the border." Open Apr.-Sept. M-F 9am-5pm, Sa 9am-12:30pm; Oct.-Mar. M-F 9am-5pm.

Travel Agency: USIT, College St., 13b The Fountain Centre (tel. 9032 4073), near Royal Ave. Sells ISICs, European Youth Cards, **TravelSave** stamps (£7), and virtually every kind of bus or rail pass imaginable. Books ferries and planes, and compiles round-the-world itineraries. Open M and W-F 9:30am-5:30pm, Tu 10am-5:30pm, Sa 10am-4pm. **Additional office** at Queen's University Student Union (tel. 9024 1830). Open M-Tu and Th-F 9:30am-5:30pm, W 10am-5:30pm.

Youth Hostel Association of Northern Ireland (YHANI): 22 Donegall Rd. (tel. 9032 4733). Books YHANI hostels free, international hostels for £2.80. Sells HI membership cards to NI residents (£8, under 18 £5). Open M-F 7am-11pm.

Consulates: U.S. Consulate General, Queens House, Queen St. (tel. 9032 8239). Open M-F 1-4pm. **Canada, Australia, Republic of Ireland, South Africa,** and **New Zealand** not represented.

Banks: Banks and **ATMs** are a dime a dozen in Belfast, virtually one on every corner. The major offices are **Ulster Bank,** Donegall Square West (tel. 9027 6000); **First Trust,** 1-15 Donegall Sq. North (tel. 9031 0909); **Bank of Ireland,** 54 Donegal Pl. (tel. 9024 4901); and **Northern Bank,** 14 Donegall Sq. West (tel. 9024 5277). Most banks open 9am-4:30pm.

Currency Exchange: Thomas Cook, 22-24 Lombard St. (tel. 9088 3800). Cashes Thomas Cook traveler's checks with no commission, others with 2% commission. Open M-Sa 9am-5:30pm. **Belfast International Airport office** (tel. 9444 7500). Open May-Oct. M 5:30am-11pm, Tu-Th 5am-10pm, F-Su 5:30am-midnight; Nov.-Apr. Sa-Th 5:30am-7pm, F 5:30am-8pm. **American Express** is accepted at Lloyds, which has an agreement with Bank of Ireland, and Bank Link. Most banks, the YHANI on Donegall Rd., and post offices provide bureaus de change and traveler's check cashing services for a small fee.

LOCAL SERVICES

Luggage Storage: For security reasons there is no luggage storage at airports, bus stations, or train stations. All four **hostels** will hold bags during the day for those staying there, and the Ark will also hold bags during extended trips if you've stayed there (see **Accommodations**).

Bookstore: Eason's, Royal Ave., Castlecourt Shopping Centre (tel. 9023 5070). Large Irish section; lots of travel guides. Open M-W and F-Sa 9am-6pm, Th 9am-9pm, Su 1-6pm. **Dillon's,** 44-46 Fountain St. (tel. 9024 0159), has a huge selection of everything from chess to chemistry. Open M-W and F-Sa 9am-5:30pm, Th 9am-9pm. **Queen's University Bookshop,** 91 University Rd. (tel. 9066 6302), offers Irish history textbooks and a renowned collection of Beat generation authors and manuscripts. Open M-F 9am-5:30pm, Sa 9am-5pm. There are dozens of second-hand bookstores around; a quick walk in the university area is sure to turn up several.

Libraries: Linen Hall Library, 17 Donegall Sq. North (tel. 9032 1707). See **Sights,** p. 412. Extensive genealogy and information on the Troubles. Free Irish language courses

Sept.-May. To get a visitor's pass, you must have a photo ID. Open M-F 9:30am-5:30pm, Sa 9:30am-4pm. **Belfast Central Library,** Royal Ave. (tel. 9024 3233). Open M and Th 9:30am-8pm, Tu-W and F 9:30am-5:30pm, Sa 9:30am-1pm.

Women's Resources: Ardoyne Women's Centre, Butler St. (tel. 9074 3536).

Bisexual, Gay, and Lesbian Information: Rainbow Project N.I. (tel. 9031 9030). Open M-F 10am-4pm. **Lesbian Line** (tel. 9023 8668). Open Th 7:30-10pm.

Counseling and Support: Samaritans (tel. 9066 4422). 24hr. line for depression. **Rape Crisis Centre,** 29 Donegall St. (tel. 9022 3470). Open M-F 10am-6pm, Sa 11am-5pm. **Contact Youth,** 2A Ribble St. offers a counseling hotline M-F 10am-midnight (tel. 9045 6654) and one-on-one counseling appointments (tel. 9045 7848). Toll-free number available M-F 4pm-9pm and varied weekend hours (tel. 0808 808 8000).

Disability Resources: NI Council on Disability (tel. 9049 1011). Open M-F 9am-5pm.

Laundry: Student's Union, Queen's University, University Rd. Wash £1, dry 20p per 5min. Open M-F 9am-9pm, Sa 10am-9pm, Su 2-9pm. Students only. **Duds & Suds,** Botanic Ave. (tel. 9024 3956). TV for the wait. Wash £1.95, dry £1.95; £1.80 each for students and seniors. Open M-F 8am-9pm, Sa 8am-6pm, Su noon-6pm. Last load 1½hr. before closing. **YHANI,** 22 Donegall Rd. £3 for powder, wash, and dry (see **Hostels,** p. 405).

Camping Equipment: The Scout Shop and Camp Centre, 12-14 College Sq. East (tel. 9032 0580). Ring bell for entry. Vast selection. Open M-Sa 9am-5pm. **Graham Tiso of Scotland,** 12-14 Cornmarket (tel. 9023 1230), offers 3 floors of everything you could possibly need to survive in the great outdoors. Also has notice boards and flyers for people trying to coordinate hiking, climbing, and water-related trips. Open M-W and F-Sa 9:30am-5:30pm, Th 9am-8pm.

Pharmacy: Boot's, 35-47 Donegall Pl. (tel. 9024 2332), next to the Europa Bus Station. Open M-W and F-Sa 8:30am-6pm, Th 8:30am-9pm, Su 1-5pm.

EMERGENCY AND COMMUNICATIONS

Emergency: Dial 999; no coins required. **Police:** 65 Knock Rd. (tel. 9065 0222).

Hospitals: Belfast City Hospital, 9 Lisburn Rd. (tel. 329 241). From Shaftesbury Sq. follow Bradbury Pl. and take a right at the fork. **Royal Victoria Hospital,** 12 Grosvenor Rd. (tel. 240 503). From Donegall Sq., take Howard St. west to Grosvenor Rd.

Post Office: Central Post Office, 25 Castle Pl. (tel. 9032 3740). Open M-Sa 9am-5:30pm. **Poste Restante** mail comes here. **Postal code:** BT1 1NB hopes to have a future in comedy. Two **branch offices** are: **Botanic Garden,** 95 University Rd. (tel. 9038 1309), across from the university (**postal code:** BT7 1NG), and **Shaftesbury Square,** 7-9 Shaftesbury Sq. (tel. 9032 6177; **postal code:** BT2 7DA). Both open M-F 8:45am-5:30pm, Sa 10am-12:30pm.

Internet Access: Belfast Central Library (see **Local Services**). £2 per hour. **Revelations Internet Cafe,** 27 Shaftesbury Sq. £5 per hr. Open M-F 10am-10pm, Sa 10am-8pm, Su noon-10pm. Some accommodations also have net access.

■ ACCOMMODATIONS

Nearly all of Belfast's budget accommodations are located near Queen's University, south of the city center. Convenient to pubs and restaurants, this area is by far the best place to stay in the city. If you have a lot of baggage you may want to catch a **Centrelink** bus to Shaftesbury Sq., or bus #59, 69, 70, 71, 84, or 85 from Donegall Sq. East to areas to the south. A walk to these accommodations takes 10 to 20 minutes from the bus or train station. Hostels and B&Bs are busy in the summer; reservations are recommended.

HOSTELS AND UNIVERSITY HOUSING

Arnie's Backpackers (IHH), 63 Fitzwilliam St. (tel. 9024 2867). A 15min. walk from Europa bus station on Great Victoria St. Take a right to head away from the Grand Opera House; at Shaftesbury Sq., take the right fork on Bradbury Pl. then fork left onto University Rd. Fitzwilliam St. is on your right across from the university. Relaxed atmosphere. If people bore you, find companionship in Rosy and Snowy, the Jack Russell proprietors. 4- to 6-bed dorms £7.50. Key deposit £2. Luggage storage during the day.

The Ark, 18 University St. (tel. 9032 9626). Follow the directions to Arnie's above; University St. is the third left off University Rd. The Ark's guests find it difficult to leave, often becoming resident staff members. 6-bed dorms £6.50, 4-bed dorms £7.50, doubles £28. Weekend luggage storage. Internet access £3.50 per hr. Sony playstation £3 per hr. Laundry £2.50. 2am curfew.

The Linen House Youth Hostel (IHH), 18-20 Kent St. (tel. 9058 6400; email info@belfasthostel.com; www.belfasthostel.com). From Europa Bus Station turn left on Great Victoria St. for two blocks, then right onto Howard St. for two more. Across from the main entrance to City Hall, turn left onto Donegall Place, which becomes Royal Ave. Take the next left onto Kent St.; the hostel is on the left. This converted 19th-century linen factory now houses scores of weary travellers. 18-bed dorms £6.50, 6- to 10-bed dorms £7.50, 8-bed dorms with bathroom £8.50, singles £12, doubles and twins £20. About 130 beds total. Internet access £5 per hr. Laundry £3. £5 key deposit.

Macpackers, 1 Cameron St. (tel. 9022 0485), just off Botanic Ave. A social atmosphere in a basic setting. 4- to 6-bed dorms £7.50 per night.

Belfast Hostel (YHANI/HI), 22 Donegall Rd. (tel. 9032 4733). Clean, modern rooms with 2 to 6 beds, some with bath. Located near Sandy Row, a Loyalist area that has seen violence during the July marching season. No kitchen. Dorms £8-10. Breakfast £2. Laundry £3. 24hr. reception. Book ahead for weekends. Wheelchair accessible.

Queen's University Accommodations, 78 Malone Rd. (tel. 9038 1608). Bus #71 from Donegall Sq. East or a 25min. walk from Europa. University Rd. runs into Malone Rd.; the residence halls are on your left. An undecorated, institutional dorm provides spacious singles or twin rooms with sinks and desks. Strong, reliable showers. Singles and doubles £8 per person for UK students, £9.40 for international students, £11.75 for non-students. Open mid-June to mid-Sept. and Christmas and Easter vacations.

YWCA, Queen Mary's Hall, 70 Fitzwilliam St. (tel. 9024 0439). From the bus station, see Arnie's, above. Co-ed and always full during the school year. Spic 'n' span doubles and singles with sinks. Limited self-service kitchen open 7am-11pm. 3-bed dorms £9.50, with linen £11, with linen in Aug. £12. B&B £15. Breakfast £3, dinner £6. Laundry £3.

BED AND BREAKFASTS

B&Bs occupy every other house between Malone and Lisburn Rd., just south of Queen's University. They tend to be surprisingly similar in price, quality, and decor, and their competitive standards work in the traveler's favor. Calling ahead is generally a good idea; most owners, however, will refer you to other accommodations if necessary.

The George, 9 Eglantine Ave. (tel. 9068 3212). Immaculately clean rooms, all with shower and TV. More stained-glass windows than your average Victorian row-house, and saloon-appropriate leather couches in the common room. Singles £20; doubles £40, with bath £44. 3% service charge for Visa and MC.

Marine House, 30 Eglantine Ave. (tel. 9066 2828). This mansion defies the stereotypes of B&B architecture and overcomes the alienating hotel-like implications of its size. Hospitality and housekeeping standards as high as the ceilings. Singles £22; doubles £40, with bath £42; triples £57.

Peter's Hill

Westlink

Kent St.

North St.

St. Anne's Cathedral

Talbot St.

Gordon St.

Dunbar St.

Toms St.

River Lagan

Brown St.

Gardiner St.

Boyd St.

Samuel St.

Royal Ave.

Donegall St.

Hill St.

Albert Sq.

Custom House

Brown St.

Gresham St.

Tourist Board

North St. Arcade

Waring St.

Victoria St.

Queen's Sq.

Millfield

Francis St.

Garfield

First Presbyterian Church

Rosemary St.

Bridge St.

High St.

Church St.

Ann St.

Divis St.

Berry St.

Royal Ave.

Lombard St.

RUC Station

Oxford St.

Hamill St.

Bank St.

Castle Place

Cornmarket

Ann St.

NO-CAR ZONE

Marquis St.

Castle St.

Bury St.

College Ct.

Queen St.

Fountain St.

Castle Lane

Callender St.

Arthur St.

Victoria Square

Town Hall

Old Museum

College Square E.

College St.

Linenhall Library

Donegall Pl.

Chinchester St.

Durham St.

College Square N.

Wellington Place

Donegall Sq. N.

City Hall

Donegall Sq. E.

Montgomery St.

Gloucester St.

Athol St.

Donegall Sq. W.

Donegall Sq. S.

May St.

Little May St.

E. Bridge St.

Grosvenor Rd.

Opera House

Howard St.

St. South

Glengall St.

Great Victoria St.

James St.

Franklin St.

Adelaide St.

Alfred St.

Jo Hamilton St.

Europa Hotel

Europa Bus Station

Crown Liquor Saloon

Bedford St.

Linen St.

Russell St.

Grace St.

McAuley St.

Great Victoria St. Rail Station

Clarence St.

Linen Hall St.

Cronac St.

Sandy Row

Bruce St.

Ormeau Ave.

Linfield Rd.

Bankmore St.

Wellwood St.

Dublin Rd.

Maryville St.

Apsley St.

Lindsay St.

Howard St. South

Charlotte St.

Ormeau Rd.

Albion St.

Sandy Row

Blythe St.

Donegall Pass

SHAFTESBURY SQ.

Elm St.

N

Donegall Rd.

B

Bradbury Pl.

Botanic Ave.

Botanic Rail Station

Vernon St.

Cooke St.

City Hospital Rail Station

Lower Crescent

McClure St.

Shaftesbury Ave.

Lisburn Rd.

Claremont St.

Upper Crescent

Cameron St.

C

Wolseley St.

Cromwell Rd.

Mount Charles

D

University St.

Camden St.

Fitzwilliam St.

E

F

University Square

College Park

Fitzroy Ave.

Rugby Rd.

University Ave.

Elmwood Ave.

Visitor's Center

Queen's University

Rugby Ave.

College Gdn.

G

Botanic Gardens

College Park Ave.

0   100 yards

0   100 meters

Central Belfast

ACCOMMODATIONS

A Linen House
B EYHANI
C Macpackers
D The Ark
E Arnie's Hostel
F YWCA
G Queen's Univ. Housing

Avenue Guest House, 23 Eglantine Ave. (tel. 9066 5904). Though dearer than some of its neighbors, this B&B justifies the cost with fluffy beds, a modern decor, and plentiful accoutrements. All rooms with bath. Singles £35, doubles £45.

Liserin Guest House, 17 Eglantine Ave. (tel. 9066 0769). Comfy beds and a huge velvet-covered lounge make the Liserin an inviting abode. All rooms have TV and showers; rooms on the top floor have sky lights. Coffee, tea, and biscuits available all day in the dining room. Singles £20, doubles £38, triples £57.

Eglantine Guest House, 21 Eglantine Ave. (tel. 9066 7585). The owner is the sister of the Liserin's proprietor, and treats her guests with equal hospitality. Small but comfortable. Singles £20, doubles £38, triples £54.

Botanic Lodge, 87 Botanic Ave. (tel. 9032 7682), on the corner of Mt. Charles Ave. B&B comfort with as short a walk to the city center as possible. Singles £22; doubles £40.

Drumragh House, 647 Antrim Rd. (tel. 9077 3063), several miles north of city center, close to Belfast Castle. Citybuses #123 and 45 stop in front. A quiet neighborhood. At the foot of Cave Hill with pretty gardens and spacious rooms. Call ahead; only three rooms. £18.

Mrs. Davidson's East-Sheen Guest House, 81 Eglantine Ave. (tel. 9066 7149). The best deal in Belfast if you can get one of their large rooms. Enormous breakfasts. Rooms are bright and clean. £19.50.

🍴 FOOD

Belfast's eateries assume a cosmopolitan character, with flavors from around the globe. Dublin Rd., Botanic Rd., and the Golden Mile have the highest concentration of restaurants. Bakeries and cafes dot the shopping areas; nearly all close by 5:30pm. On Thursdays, however, most of the city center stays open until 8:45pm. Most convenience stores offer a full supply of groceries, although their prices are high. **Tesco Supermarket** at 2 Royal Ave. (tel. 9032 3270) and 369 Lisburn Rd. (tel. 9066 3531) sells slightly cheaper food. (Open M-W and Sa 8am-7pm, Th 8am-9pm, F 8am-8pm, Su 1-5pm.) The **Spar Market** at the top of Botanic Rd. is open nearly 24 hours. (Open M 6am-Su 3am.) For fruits and vegetables, plunder the lively **St. George's Market,** East Bridge St., in the enormous warehouse between May and Oxford St. (Open Tu and F 6am-3pm.) **The Nutmeg,** 9A Lombard St. (tel. 9024 9984), supplies healthy foods, baked goods, and raw ingredients. (Open M-Sa 9:30am-5:30pm.) So does **Canterbury Dyke's,** 66-68 Botanic Ave. (Open M-F 7:30am-7pm, Sa-Su 8am-6:30pm.) **Lower Lisburn Rd.,** which runs parallel to University Rd., has a good selection of inexpensive bakeries and fruit stands.

QUEEN'S UNIVERSITY AREA

The Other Place. It's anybody's guess where this place is, but the others are located at 79 Botanic Ave. (tel. 9020 7200), 133 Stranmillis Rd., and 537 Lisburn Rd. They share a menu featuring an array of ethnic foods, from Thai to Cajun, and play a correspondingly eclectic soundtrack. Open M-Sa 8am-11pm.

Bookfinders, 47 University Rd. (tel. 9032 8269). Super-cool smoky bookstore/cafe with mismatched dishes and retro counter-culture paraphernalia. Its beauty is more than skin-deep—the relaxed atmosphere would make anyone feel at home. Soup and bread £2-3. Sandwiches around £2. Art gallery upstairs. Open M-Sa 10am-5:30pm.

Maggie May's Belfast Cafe, 50 Botanic Ave. (tel. 9032 2622). The walls look like brown newsprint sketched with the Belfast of yesteryear. Relax with a cup of tea and a free newspaper; order food when you feel like it. Sandwiches £2-3. 3-course meals £4-5. Open M-Sa 8am-10:30pm, Su 10am-10:30pm.

The Ground Floor, 159 Stranmillis Rd. (tel. 9020 1201). Students and business people relax on the funky chairs and sofas of this excellent, if somewhat pricey, coffeeshop. Coffee (£1-2) and tea (£1.20) from the ordinary to the exotic. Hip sandwiches £4. £3 minimum from 12:30-2:30pm during the week.

Cafe Clementine, 245 Lisburn Rd. (tel. 9038 2211), 3 blocks south of Eglantine St. Excellent food in this hot hangout for 20-somethings. Jazz concerts on weekend nights. Creative sandwiches on croissants or baguettes around £3, entrees about £4. Open M-Tu 9am-4:30pm, W-F 9:30am-10pm, Sa 9:30am-10:30pm, Su 10am-5pm.

Cloisters Bistro, 1 Elmwood Ave. (tel. 9032 4803), in the Queen's University Student Union. Cafeteria-style food and atmosphere efficiently satiate hunger with a few frills as well. A hearty meal for about £3. Open M-F 8:30am-4pm in summer, M-F 8:30am-6:30pm during the school year.

Taj Mahal, 96 Botanic Ave. (tel. 9031 3999), serves classic Indian dishes in a refined atmosphere. Try the 3-course business lunch for £4.95, served daily 11:30am-3pm.

THE GOLDEN MILE AND DUBLIN ROAD

Pizza Express, 25-27 Bedford Rd. (tel. 9032 9050). One of the few places in town that serves real pizza, but the grandeur of its spiral staircase and Hollywood-esque decorations make it more exotic than your typical pizza chain. 1- to 2-person pizzas £4-6. Open M-Th 11:30am-11:30pm, F-Sa noon-midnight.

Spuds, 23 Bradbury Pl. (tel. 9033 1541). Meat and potatoes—in fast-food form. Get your spud stuffed with anything from bacon and cheese to chicken curry. Most spuds around £2. Open M-W 9am-2am, Th-Sa 9am-3am, Su 9am-1am.

Feasts, 39 Dublin Rd. (tel. 9033 2787). Serves a variety of Irish and international farmhouse cheeses in sandwiches (£3) and other dishes (£5-7).

Revelations Internet Cafe, 27 Shaftesbury Sq. (tel. 9032 0337). Get connected to cool music and ultra sci-fi art in the area's only privately run internet center. Internet access £5 per hr., students and hostelers £4 per hr. Sandwiches £2-3; lots of veggie options. Open M-F 10am-10pm, Sa 10am-8pm, Su noon-8pm.

Cafe Mozart, 67 Dublin Rd. (tel. 9031 5200). Serves freshly made sandwiches and entrees for £3-4. Open M-Sa 10am-5pm, Su 10am-4pm.

Cafe Booth, 40 Dublin Rd. (tel. 9031 0854), in the Salvation Army building. Huge portions of food for the hungry, weary traveler in a flowery, yellow setting. Most entrees around £2.50. Open M-Sa 8am-3:30pm.

NORTH OF DONEGALL SQUARE

Azzura, 8 Church Ln. (tel. 9024 3503). This tiny cafe dishes out pizzas and gourmet sandwiches for £2-3, and mountains of pasta for about £4. Open M-Sa 9am-5pm.

Roscoff Bakery & Cafe, 27-29 Fountain St. (tel. 9031 5090). The fast-food cousin of the world-famous Roscoff's Restaurant, this cafe serves a more affordable feast. Soup or sandwich £2.40. Divine breads. Open M-W and F-Sa 7:30am-5:30pm, Th 7:30am-8:30pm.

Cafe Deauville, 58 Wellington Pl. (tel. 9032 6601), at the corner of College Sq. Intricate mosaic exterior; interior's not bad either. Breakfast or lunch £2-3. Open M-Sa 8am-4:30pm.

Caffe Casa, 12-14 College St. (tel. 9031 9900). Claims to serve the best coffee in Belfast. Munch a sandwich (£3), entree (£4), or sumptuous dessert in a swank wood and metallic setting. Open M-W, F-Sa 8:30am-5:30pm, Th 8:30am-7pm.

Espresso Bar Company, 11 Chichester St. (tel. 9043 9400). This ultra-modern take on a Tuscan countryside cafe greets patrons with an upscale and truly innovative daily menu. Wild boar foccaccia £3.75; Jamaican jerk salmon £5.25. Wine and beer available. Open M-F 8am-5:30pm, Sa 9am-5:30pm.

Bewley's, Rosemary St. (tel. 9023 4955), just inside of the Donegall Arcade. For those missing Dublin, this Bewley's is a good replica of the original Japanese tea room (see p. 104). Sandwiches £2.45; entrees £4.75. Newspapers and magazines upstairs. Open M-W and F-Su 8am-5:30pm, Th 8am-9pm.

Windsor Dairy & Home Bakery, 46 College St. (tel. 9032 7157), has a mouth-watering selection of fresh baked goods, sandwiches (£1.60), and entrees (£2). Seating not available, but the food is well worth taking out. Open M-Sa 8:30am-5:30pm.

✓ PUBS AND CLUBS

Pubs were prime targets for sectarian violence at the height of the Troubles in the 60s and 70s. As a result, most of the popular pubs in Belfast are new or restored. The *Bushmills Irish Pub Guide*, by Sybil Taylor, relates the history of Belfast's pubs (£7.95; available at the tourist office or local book stores). Ask the staff at the Queen's University Student Centre or the workers at the hostels about the latest hip night spots. Once again, *Let's Go* proudly presents the Belfast Pub Crawl and Pub Crawl Map. Since the city center closes early and can feel pretty deserted late at night, we recommend beginning early in Cornmarket's historic entries, visiting the traditional downtown, then partying until closing time in the university area.

CORNMARKET

Morning Star Pub, Pottinger's Entry (tel. 9022 3976), between Ann and High St. A glorious Victorian wrought-iron bracket draws all eyes to the sign hanging above its door.

White's Tavern, Winecellar Entry, off Lombard and Bridge St. Belfast's oldest pub has been serving drinks since 1630. An excellent stop for an afternoon pint.

NORTH OF DONEGALL SQUARE

Kelly's Cellars, 30 Bank St. (tel. 9032 4835), off Royal Ave. just after the Fountain St. pedestrian area. The oldest pub in Belfast that hasn't been renovated, and it doesn't need to be. Become a regular. Frequent Trad downstairs (free); live bands, including folk and rock upstairs (£3 cover).

Kavanagh's Bar, 24 Bank St. (tel. 9024 9080), next to Kelly's. Kelly's younger sister has slightly higher ceilings. Blues, folk, trad, and rock bands W-Sa. No cover.

Madden's Bar, 74 Berry St. (tel. 9024 4114). Old wooden bar with musical instruments on the walls. Attracts good-sized crowds with its traditional Irish bands (Th-Sa) and traditional blues and folk (Su). £2-3 cover for live bands.

The Hercules Bar, 61-63 Castle St. (tel. 9032 4587). This recently rejuvenated bar pulls in the best musicians that the local soil produces. Trad jam sessions F-Sa, blues and jazz other nights. Owners will direct you to other good live music venues. Open until 2am on weekends. No cover.

Queen's Bar, 4 Queen's Arcade (tel. 9032 1347), off Fountain St. Friendly, low-pressure atmosphere in a tiny alley off Donegall Pl. attracts a mix of people, gay and straight.

THE GOLDEN MILE AND THE DUBLIN ROAD

Katie Daly's and **The Limelight,** 17 Ormeau Ave. (tel. 9032 5942). A truly hip bar/nightclub complex. Live music at Katie Daly's most nights. Tu and F-Sa are student disco nights at the Limelight. Cover £3. One of Belfast's best music venues with a knack for hiring bands before their time.

Lavery's Gin Palace, 12 Bradbury Pl. (tel. 9032 7159). It doesn't look it, but this is the place to be for all kinds of (cool) people, from people who try too hard to those who don't try hard enough. Open until 1am. Dancing upstairs on weekends. Cover £2.50.

Crown Liquor Saloon, 46 Great Victoria St. The only National Trust-owned pub has been bombed 32 times, but you'd never know it. Gilt ceilings, gas lamps, and Victorian snugs make for a very special drink.

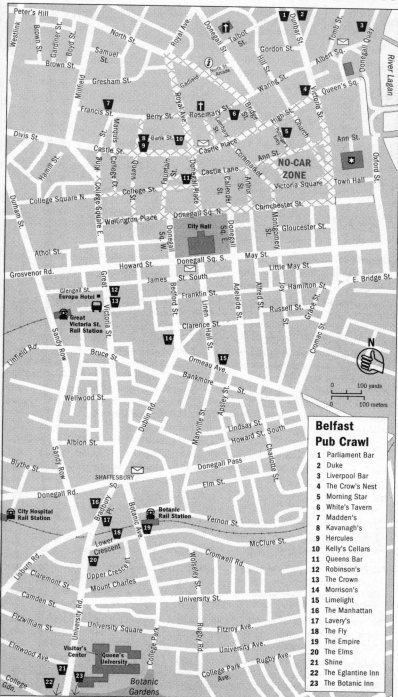

**Belfast
Pub Crawl**

1 Parliament Bar
2 Duke
3 Liverpool Bar
4 The Crow's Nest
5 Morning Star
6 White's Tavern
7 Madden's
8 Kavanagh's
9 Hercules
10 Kelly's Cellars
11 Queens Bar
12 Robinson's
13 The Crown
14 Morrison's
15 Limelight
16 The Manhattan
17 Lavery's
18 The Fly
19 The Empire
20 The Elms
21 Shine
22 The Eglantine Inn
23 The Botanic Inn

Robinson's, 38-40 Great Victoria St. (tel. 9024 7447). Incredibly lively. 4 floors of theme bars including a Fibber McGees, an Irish Pub hosting nightly trad sessions (no cover); top two floors form a swingin' club W-F (cover £5-7).

Morrisons, 21 Bedford St. (tel. 9024 8458). Painstakingly reconstructed "traditional" atmosphere, modeled after a bar of the same name in the Republic. It's comforting to think that 2 such places exist in the world. Live bands F and Sa. Cover around £4.

The Manhattan, 23-31 Bradbury Pl. (tel. 9023 3131). Huge 3-story nightclub that's packed with a younger crowd clad in Brit-pop fashions. No cover for first-floor bar; nightclub cover (£4-6). Dress to impress.

The Fly, 5-6 Lower Crescent (tel. 9023 5666). This swank 3-story nightclub with an entomological bent relates all its decorations to its pesky namesake. Bono probably wouldn't buy it, but Belfast's masses are dressing up and swarming to it. Live DJs nightly. No cover.

QUEEN'S UNIVERSITY AREA

The Eglantine Inn (the "Egg"), 32 Malone Rd. (tel. 9038 1994). Almost an official extracurricular, this pub keeps students from their studies. Open until 1am. The Egg is also a great place for a filling meal. Entrees £2-4.

The Botanic Inn (the "Bot"), 23 Malone Rd. (tel. 9066 0460). Huge and hugely popular student bar. Trad on Tu. No cover. "Record club" (60s, 70s, and 80s music) Th-Sa. Cover £2. 21 and older. Open until 1am.

The Empire, 42 Botanic Ave. (tel. 9024 9276). This 120-year old building was once a church, but its 2 stories have been entirely revamped to resemble Belfast's Victorian music halls. Each floor's stage is likely to have a performer, hired or not. Sept.-June comedy Tu, trad Th, live bands Th-Sa. Cover £4.

Shine, Queen's University Student Union (tel. 9032 4803). A convenient, expensive spot to play hooky. Live DJs make the Union the place to learn about cutting edge trends in youth culture. Cover £7-12.

THE BEST OF THE REST

These pubs lie outside the city center, Donegal Road, and Queen's circuit. At night, one should take a cab to the pubs near the docklands.

The Liverpool Bar, Donegall Quay (tel. 9032 4796), opposite the SeaCat terminal. This 150-year-old building has also been a lodging house and a brothel. Today it boasts the best trad in the city. Music M, W, F, and Su. Occasional cover.

The Front Page, 9 Ballymoney St. (tel. 9032 4924). The tiny box of a building sits alone among vast and vacant docks, but it's the center of the universe to the locals who pack it nightly. Live music on weekends ranges from fine to amazing.

The Rotterdam Bar, Pilot St. (tel. 9075 3275) behind the SeaCat terminal, to the right, on the waterfront. Hosts frequent trad sessions and an outdoor summer concert series.

The Parliament Bar, 2-6 Dunbar St. (tel. 9023 4520), around the corner from the Duke. Considers itself the premier gay bar in Northern Ireland. A formerly traditional bar that now looks like it's been transplanted to the Greek Islands. Disco Tu and F-Su; cover £2-7. Live bands Th; cover £2. Bingo on M.

The Duke of York, 11 Commercial Ct. (tel. 9024 1062). A student crowd hangs out at this bar and club near the Arts College. The collection of beer advertisements shows discriminating aesthetic taste. F-Sa nightclub upstairs, live bands downstairs. £3 cover.

The Crow's Nest, 26 Skipper St. (tel. 9032 5491), off High St. across from the Albert Memorial Clock. The interior is proud to be loud with live music, discos at Flave's 70s Revival Bar upstairs, and karaoke on weekends. Cover varies.

▣ TOURS

BLACK CAB TOURS. Residents of West Belfast provide the best introduction to the city's sectarian neighborhoods. Cab tours provide a fascinating, if biased commentary that highlights the murals, paraphenalia, and sights on both sides of the peace wall. Backpackers and locals alike arrange tours through the hostels; these are your best bet for a good tour at a fair price. *(£6-7per person.)*

BELFAST: A LIVING HISTORY. Citybus (see p. 403) provides several tours that hit the city's major sights, both glitzy and gritty. The tourist office can provide brochures on Citybus's choice routes. *(Leaves from Castle Place, in front of the post office. Tel. 9045 8484. 2½hr. June-Sept. tours every Tu, Th, and Su at 10am and 2pm. £8, students £7, seniors and children £5.50.)*

▣ SIGHTS

DONEGALL SQUARE

BELFAST CITY HALL. The administrative and geographic center of Belfast is distanced from the crowded downtown streets by a grassy square. Its green copper dome (173 ft.) is visible from any point in the city. After Queen Victoria granted Belfast's cityhood in 1888, this symbol of civic pride was built on the site of demolished linen warehouses. Neoclassical marble columns and arches figure prominently in A. Brunwell Thomas's 1906 design. Inside, a grand marble staircase ascends to the second floor. Portraits of the city's lord mayors somberly line the halls, and glass and marble shimmer in three elaborate reception rooms. The **City Council's** oak-paneled chambers, used only once a month, are deceptively austere considering the Council's reputation for rowdy meetings that sometimes devolve into fist fights. If you want to see the council in action, a councillor can sign you into the otherwise inaccessible debates with 48hr. notice. Directly in front of the main entrance, an enormous marble **Queen Victoria statue** stares down at visitors with a formidable grimace, while bronze figures representing shipbuilding and spinning writhe at her feet. A more sympathetic sculpted figure of womanhood stands on the eastern side of the garden, commemorating the fate of the *Titanic* and its passengers. An inconspicuous pale gray stone column commemorates the 1942 arrival of the U.S. Expeditionary Force, whose soldiers were stationed here to defend the North from Germany; it was rededicated after President Clinton's visit to Belfast in 1996. The interior of City Hall is accessible only by guided tour. *(Tel. 9032 0202, ext. 2346. 1hr. tours June-Sept. M-F 10:30am, 11:30am, and 2:30pm; Sa 2:30pm. Oct.-May M-Tu and Th-F 2:30pm, W 11:30am. Free.)*

OTHER SIGHTS. One of Belfast's oldest establishments is the **Linen Hall Library.** The library was originally located across the street in the linen hall that became present-day City Hall; it was moved to its present location in 1894. The red hand of Ulster decorates the top of its street entrance. The library contains a famous collection of political documents relating to Northern Ireland. Devoted librarians scramble for every Christmas card, poster, hand bill, and newspaper article related to the Troubles that they can get their hands on. *(17 Donegall Sq. St. Tel. 9032 1707. Open M-W and F 9:30am-5:30pm, Th 9:30am-8:30pm, Sa 9:30am-4pm.)* Nearby, the **Scottish Provident Institution,** built in 1902, displays a decadent facade that glorifies virtually every profession that has contributed to industrial Belfast. *(Across the street from City Hall, on the corner of Donegall Sq. North and East Bedford St.)*

CORNMARKET AND ST. ANNE'S CATHEDRAL

Just north of the city center, a shopping district envelops eight blocks around Castle St. and Royal Ave. This area, known as Cornmarket after one of its original commodities, has been a marketplace since Belfast's early days. In the

17th century, it was surrounded by city walls. A McDonald's stands on the site of the old city castle (hence Castle St.). Although the Cornmarket area is dominated by modern buildings, relics of old Belfast remain in the tiny alleys, or **entries,** that connect some of the major streets. A drink at any of the pubs along these alleys will have your imagination swimming in nostalgic reverie.

ST. ANNE'S CATHEDRAL. Belfast's newspapers all set up shop around St. Anne's, also known as the **Belfast Cathedral.** This Church of Ireland cathedral was begun in 1899. To keep from disturbing regular worship, it was built around a smaller church already on the site. Upon completion of the cathedral's exterior, builders extracted the earlier church brick by brick. Each of the cathedral's 10 interior pillars name somebody's idea of Belfast's 10 fields of professionalism: Science, Industry, Healing, Agriculture, Music, Theology, Shipbuilding, Freemasonry, Art, and Womanhood (a nice enough profession, but the pay is lousy). In a small enclave called the Chapel of Peace, the cathedral asks visitors to pray for international peace between 1 and 2pm. (Donegall St., located near the Tourist Office, a few blocks from the city center. Open daily 9am-5pm. Su services: communion 10am, Eucharist 11am, evensong 3:30pm.)

ENTRIES. Between Ann and High St. runs **Pottinger's Entry,** which contains the **Morning Star Pub** (see **Pubs,** p. 410) in all its old-world splendor. (Open daily 11:30am-1am.) **Joy's Entry,** farther down Ann St., is the alley where the *Belfast News Letter* was printed for over 100 years. The only establishment still in the entry, Globe Tavern, is disappointingly modern inside. Off Lombard and Bridge St., **Winecellar Entry** is the site of Belfast's oldest pub, **White's Tavern** (see **Pubs,** p. 410), serving drinks since 1630. (Open daily 11:30am-11:30pm.)

OTHER SIGHTS. The city's oldest public building, **The Old Stock Exchange,** sits on the corner of North and Waring St. Tireless Charles Lanyon designed a new facade for the building in 1845 when the original was deemed not grand enough. The **First Presbyterian Church of Belfast,** the city's oldest church, still stands just a block to the west, on Rosemary St. (Open W 10:30am-12:30pm.)

THE DOCKS AND EAST BELFAST

Although the docks area was once the activity hub of old Belfast, continued commercial development has made the area more suitable for industrial machinery, than people. Reminders of the city's ship-building glory days, however, remain in the East Belfast shipyards, surrounded by former employee housing. The most famous of the shipyards is Harland & Wolff. Unfortunately, the builders' most famous creation was the *Titanic.* The shipyards figure in numerous poems and novels set in Belfast, notably at the end of Paul Muldoon's "7, Middagh St." Today, the twin cranes nicknamed **"Samson and Goliath"** tower over the Harland & Wolff shipyard and are visible from all points across the river.

LAGAN LOOKOUT AND LAGAN WEIR. The £14-million weir was built to eliminate the Lagan's drastic tides, which used to expose stinking mud flats during ebb. The Lookout offers an interesting room full of displays on the history of Belfast, and the purpose and mechanism of the weir. Both structures are part of a huge development project that includes the **Laganside Trail** along the far side of the river and **Waterfront Hall,** a recently opened concert hall with an uncanny resemblance to a sponge cake. (Donegall Quay, across from the Laganside bus station. Tel. 9031 5444. Lookout open Mar.-Sept. M-F 11am-5pm, Sa noon-5pm, Su 2-5pm; Oct.-Feb. Tu-F 11am-3:30pm, Sa 1-4:30pm, Su 2-4:30pm. £1.50, children 75p, concession £1.)

ONE OXFORD STREET GALLERY. Contemporary Belfast artists exhibit their work here. (Western side of the Lagan. Tel. 9031 0400. Open M-F 10am-4pm. Free.)

SINCLAIR SEAMEN'S CHURCH. The Presbyterian minister delivers his sermons from a pulpit carved in the shape of a ship's prow, collections are taken in miniature lifeboats, and an organ with port and starboard lights taken from a Guinness barge carries the tune. The exterior was designed by prolific

Charles Lanyon, who also designed the Custom House, the Queen's campus, and almost every other notable 19th century building in Belfast. (except the Albert Memorial Clock Tower and he was angry about that). *(Corporation St., just down the street from the SeaCat terminal. Su services 11:30am and 7pm. Tours W 2-4pm.)*

OTHER SIGHTS. The stately **Custom House,** built by Charles Lanyon in 1857, stands between Queen Sq. and Albert Sq. on the approach to the river from the clock tower. Designed in an imaginative E-shape, it rests on an elaborate pediment of Britannia, Neptune, and Mercury, the god of trade. Belfast also has its own version of the leaning tower of Pisa and Big Ben in one: the **Albert Memorial Clock Tower.** Designed in 1865 by W. J. Barre, the 115 ft. tower leans precariously at the entrance to the docks area, where Oxford St. runs beside the Lagan. The name refers to Prince Albert, Queen Victoria's consort.

THE GOLDEN MILE

"The Golden Mile" refers to a strip along Great Victoria St. containing many of the jewels in the crown of Belfast's establishment.

GRAND OPERA HOUSE. Belfast's pride and joy, the opera house was cyclically bombed by the IRA, restored to its original splendor at enormous cost, and then bombed again. Ask at the stage door on Glengall St. if there's a rehearsal going on; if not, they'll give you a tour. *(Tel. 9024 0411. Booking office open M-Sa 9:45am-5:30pm.)* The **Grand Opera House Ticket Shop** sells tickets for performances including musicals, operas, ballets, and concerts. *(2-4 Great Victoria St. Tel. 241 919, 24hr. info line tel. 249 129. Open M-W 8:30am-8pm, Th 8:30am-9pm, F 8:30am-6:30pm, Sa 8:30am-5:30pm.)*

THE CROWN LIQUOR SALOON. The National Trust has restored this highly frequented pub to make it a showcase of carved wood, gilded ceilings, and stained glass. Box-like snugs fit groups of two to 10 comfortably. Just ring the buzzer when you want another round (see **Pubs,** p. 412).

EUROPA HOTEL. Damaged by 32 bombs in its history, the Europa has the dubious distinction of being "Europe's most bombed hotel." In March of 1993, the hotel installed shatterproof windows, which seem to have deterred would-be bombers.

QUEEN'S UNIVERSITY AREA

QUEEN'S UNIVERSITY BELFAST. Charles Lanyon designed the Tudor-revival brick campus in 1849, modeling it after Magdalen College, Oxford. The **Visitors Centre,** in the Lanyon Room to the left of the main entrance, offers Queen's-related exhibits and merchandise. *(University Road. Visitors Center tel. 9033 5252. Open Apr.-Sept. M-Sa 10am-4pm, Oct-Mar. M-F 10am-4pm.)*

BOTANIC GARDENS. Birds do it; bees do it; and on warm days, the majority of the student population does it. You, too, can bask in Belfast's occasional sun behind the university. Meticulously groomed, the gardens offer a welcome green respite from the traffic-laden city streets. Inside the gardens lie two 19th-century greenhouses, the toasty **Tropical Ravine House** and the more temperate Lanyon-designed **Palm House.** Don't forget to stop and smell the rose gardens, featuring Europe's most fragrant bloomers. *(Tel. 9032 4902. Open daily 8am-dusk. Tropical House and Palm House open Apr.-Sept. M-F 9am-noon and 1-5pm, Sa-Su 1-5pm; Oct.-Mar. M-F 10am-noon and 1-4pm, Sa-Su 1-4pm. Free.)*

ULSTER MUSEUM. This national-caliber museum has developed a variety of exhibits to fill its huge display halls. Irish and modern art, local history, antiquities, and the Mummy of Takabuti are all subjects for investigation. The treasure salvaged from the *Girone*, a Spanish Armada ship that sank off the Causeway Coast in 1588, is also on display here. *(In the Botanic Gardens, off Stranmillis Rd. Tel. 9038 1251. Open M-F 10am-5pm, Sa 1-5pm, Su 2-5pm. Free, except for some traveling exhibitions.)*

THE RAPE OF THE FALLS The area stretching from Divis Tower to Cavendish Sq. is known as the **Lower Falls**. This area was sealed off by the British Army for 35 hours in July, 1970, in an episode known as the **Rape of the Falls.** Soldiers, acting on a tip that arms were hidden in some of the houses, searched homes at random while residents were forbidden to leave the area, even for milk or bread. It is estimated that before this event, there were only 50 Republicans in the area. After the incident, however, over 2000 people turned to the IRA. Many regard this raid to be the biggest tactical mistake ever made by the British army in Northern Ireland.

SOUTH BELFAST

Riverside trails, ancient ruins, and idyllic parks south of Belfast make it hard to believe that you're only a few minutes from the city center. The area can be reached by buses #70 and 71 from Donegall Sq. East. The **Belfast Parks Department** (tel. 9032 0202) and the **N.I. Tourist Board** (tel. 246 609) can provide maps.

SIR THOMAS AND LADY DIXON PARK. The most stunning of the parks, Upper Malone Rd., boasts over 20,000 rose bushes. The gardens were founded in 1836 and include the stud China roses, imported between 1792 and 1824, which provided the foundation for present-day British roses.

OTHER SIGHTS. Four miles north along the tow path near Shaw's Bridge lies Giant's Ring, a 4500-year-old earthen ring with a dolmen in the middle. Little is known about the 600 ft. wide circle, but experts speculate that it was built for the same reasons as England's Stonehenge. *(Always open. Free.)* Those hoping to track down long-lost relatives should head to the Public Record Office. *(66 Balmoral Ave. Tel. 9066 1621. Open M-F 9:15am-4:15pm.)*

NORTH BELFAST

BELFAST CASTLE. In 1934, the Earl of Shaftesbury presented this relatively new building to the city. The castle sits on top of cave hill, long the seat of Ulster rulers. The ancient King Matudan had his McArt's Fort here, where the more modern United Irishmen plotted rebellion in 1795. The summit is nicknamed "Napoleon's Nose." Marked trails lead north from the fort to five caves in the area, thought by historians to be ancient mines; only the lowest is accessible. *(Open M-Sa 9am-10:30pm, Su 9am-6pm. Free.)*

WEST BELFAST AND THE MURALS

Separated from the rest of the city by the Westlink motorway, the neighborhoods of West Belfast have historically been at the heart of the political tensions in the North. The Catholic area (centered on **Falls Rd.**) and the Protestant neighborhood (centered on the **Shankill**) are grimly separated by the **peace line,** a gray and seemingly impenetrable wall. Along the wall, abandoned houses with blocked-up or broken windows point to a troubled past and an uncertain future. These two neighborhoods embody both the raw sentiment that drives the Northern Irish conflict and the casual calm with which those closest to the Troubles approach daily life. The most dominant feature of the neighborhoods is their family community. West Belfast is not a center of consumer tourism or a "sight" in the traditional sense. The streets display political murals, which you will soon come across as you wander among the houses. Be discreet when photographing murals. As the murals in the Falls and Shankill change constantly, the sections below describe only a few. We provide a glossary of some common symbols (see **A Primer of Symbols,** p. 418).

It is best to visit the Falls and Shankill during the day, when the murals can be seen. The Protestant Orangemen's marching season, around July 12, is a risky time to visit the area, since the parades are underscored by mutual antagonisms that can lead to political violence (see **History and Politics,** p. 393). To see both the Falls and Shankill, the best plan is to visit one then return to the

Worldwide Calling Made Easy

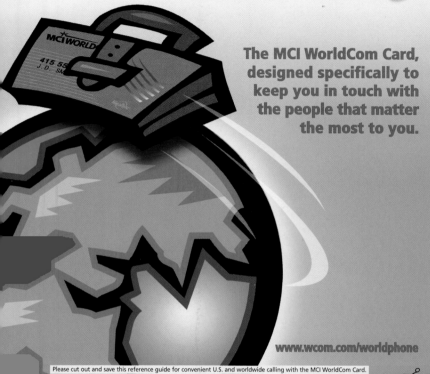

The MCI WorldCom Card, designed specifically to keep you in touch with the people that matter the most to you.

www.wcom.com/worldphone

Please cut out and save this reference guide for convenient U.S. and worldwide calling with the MCI WorldCom Card.

And, it's simple to call home or to other countires.

Dial the WorldPhone toll-free access number of the country you're calling from (listed inside).

Follow the easy voice instructions or hold for a WorldPhone operator. Enter or give the operator your MCI WorldCom Card number or call collect.

Enter or give the WorldPhone operator your home number.

Share your adventures with your family!

COUNTRY		WORLDPHONE TOLL-FREE ACCESS #
St. Lucia ÷		1-800-888-8000
Sweden (CC) ◆		020-795-922
Switzerland (CC) ◆		0800-89-0222
Taiwan (CC) ◆		0080-13-4567
Thailand ★		001-999-1-2001
Turkey (CC) ◆		00-8001-1177
United Kingdom	(CC) To call using BT ■	0800-89-0222
	To call using CWC ■	0500-89-0222
United States (CC)		1-800-888-8000
U.S. Virgin Islands (CC)		1-800-888-8000
Vatican City (CC)		172-1022
Venezuela (CC) ÷ ◆		800-1114-0
Vietnam ●		1201-1022

(CC)	Country-to-country calling available to/from most international locations.
÷	Limited availability.
▼	Wait for second dial tone.
▲	When calling from public phones, use phones marked LADATEL.
■	International communications carrier.
★	Not available from public pay phones.
◆	Public phones may require deposit of coin or phone card for dial tone.
●	Local service fee in U.S. currency required to complete call.
▶	Regulation does not permit Intra-Japan calls.
✣	Available from most major cities

MCI WorldCom Worldphone Access Numbers

MCI WORLDCOM℠

The MCI WorldCom Card.

The easy way to call when traveling worldwide.

The MCI WorldCom Card gives you…

- Access to the US and other countries worldwide.
- Customer Service 24 hours a day
- Operators who speak your language
- Great MCI WorldCom rates and no sign-up fees

For more information or to apply for a Card call:
1-800-955-0925

Outside the U.S., call MCI WorldCom collect (reverse charge) at:
1-712-943-6839

COUNTRY	WORLDPHONE TOLL-FREE ACCESS #
Argentina (CC)	
To call using Telefonica ■	0800-222-6249
To call using Telecom ■	0800-555-1002
Australia (CC) ◆	
To call using AAPT ■	1-800-730-014
To call using OPTUS ■	1-800-551-111
To call using TELSTRA ■	1-800-881-100
Austria (CC) ◆	0800-200-235
Bahamas	1-800-888-8000
Belgium (CC) ◆	0800-10012
Bermuda ÷	1-800-888-8000
Bolivia (CC) ◆	0-800-2222
Brazil (CC)	000-8012
British Virgin Islands ÷	1-800-888-8000
Canada (CC)	1-800-888-8000
Cayman Islands	1-800-888-8000
Chile (CC)	
To call using CTC ■	800-207-300
To call using ENTEL ■	800-360-180
China ÷	108-12
For a Mandarin-speaking Operator	108-17
Colombia (CC) ◆	980-9-16-0001
Collect Access in Spanish	980-9-16-1111
Costa Rica ◆	0800-012-2222
Czech Republic (CC) ◆	00-42-000112
Denmark (CC) ◆	8001-0022
Dominican Republic	
Collect Access	1-800-888-8000
Collect Access in Spanish	1121
Ecuador (CC) ÷	999-170
El Salvador	800-1767

COUNTRY	WORLDPHONE TOLL-FREE ACCESS #
Finland (CC) ◆	08001-102-80
France (CC) ◆	0800-99-0019
French Guiana (CC)	0-800-99-0019
Guatemala (CC) ◆	99-99-189
Germany (CC)	0-800-888-8000
Greece (CC) ◆	00-800-1211
Guam (CC)	1-800-888-8000
Haiti ÷	193
Collect Access in French/Creole	190
Honduras ÷	8000-122
Hong Kong (CC)	800-96-1121
Hungary (CC) ◆	00▼800-01411
India (CC) ÷	000-127
Collect Access	000-126
Ireland (CC) ◆	1-800-55-1001
Israel (CC)	
BEZEQ International	1-800-940-2727
BARAK	1-800-930-2727
Italy (CC) ◆	172-1022
Jamaica ÷	Collect Access 1-800-888-8000
(From Special Hotels only)	873
(From public phones)	#2
Japan (CC) ◆	To call using KDD ■ 00539-121▶
To call using IDC ■	0066-55-121
To call using JT ■	0044-11-121
Korea (CC)	To call using KT ■ 00729-14
To call using DACOM ■	00309-12
To call using ONSE	00369-14
Phone Booths÷	Press red button, 03, then ✳
Military Bases	550-2255
Lebanon	Collect Access 600-MCI (600-624)

COUNTRY	WORLDPHONE TOLL-FREE ACCE
Luxembourg (CC)	0800-(
Malaysia (CC) ◆	1-800-80-(
To call using Time Telekom ■	1-800-18-(
Mexico (CC)	Avantel 01-800-021-(
Telmex ▲	001-800-674-(
Collect Access in Spanish	01-800-021-(
Monaco (CC) ◆	800-9(
Netherlands (CC) ◆	0800-022-(
New Zealand (CC)	00(
Nicaragua (CC)	Collect Access in Spanish
(Outside of Managua, dial 02	
Norway (CC) ◆	800-1(
Panama	
Military Bases	2810
Philippines (CC) ◆	To call using PLDT ■ 10(
To call using PHILCOM ■	102
To call using Bayantel ■	123
To call using ETPI ■	106
Poland (CC) ÷	00-800-111-2
Portugal (CC) ÷	800-800
Puerto Rico (CC)	1-800-888-8
Romania (CC) ÷	01-800-
Russia (CC) ◆ ÷	
To call using ROSTELCOM ■	747-
(For Russian speaking operator)	747-
To call using SOVINTEL ■	960-
Saudi Arabia (CC) ÷	1-8(
Singapore	8000-112
Slovak Republic	(CC) 00421-0(
South Africa (CC)	0800-99-
Spain (CC)	900-99-

city center before heading to the other, as the area around the peace line is still desolate. The most comprehensive and convenient tour of Belfast's sectarian neighborhoods is offered by **black cabs,** community shuttles that whisk residents to the city center, picking up and dropping off passengers along their set routes. For the standard fare (60p), you can ask to be let off anywhere along the route. Select black cabs can also reasonably be hired by groups for **tours** of the Falls or Shankill (see **Tours,** p. 413).

THE FALLS. This Catholic neighborhood is much larger than Shankill and houses a younger, rapidly multiplying population. On **Divis St.,** a high-rise apartment building marks the site of the **Divis Tower,** an ill-fated housing development built by optimistic social planners in the 1960s. This project soon became an IRA stronghold and saw some of the worst of Belfast's Troubles in the 1970s. The British army still occupies the top three floors, and Shankill residents refer to it as "Little Beirut."

Continuing west, Divis St. turns into the **Falls Rd.** The **Sinn Fein** office is easily spotted: one side of it is covered with an enormous portrait of Bobby Sands (see **The Troubles,** p. 394) and an advertisement for the Sinn Fein newspaper, *An Phoblacht.* Continuing down the Falls you will see a number of murals characterized by Celtic art and the Irish language. They display scenes of traditional music and dance, or grimmer portraits of Famine victims. One particularly moving mural, on the corner of the Falls and RPG Ave., shows the 10 hunger strikers who died in 1981-82 above a quote from Bobby Sands: "Our revenge will be the laughter of our children." Murals in the Falls, unlike those of the Shankill, are becoming less militant in nature, though there are a few left in the Lower Falls that refer to specific acts of violence. One shows women banging bin lids on the ground to warn neighbors of British paratroopers. The grim slogan reads: "25 years of resistance—25 more if needs be." Other political graffiti, concerning Sinn Fein, the RUC, and Protestant paramilitary groups, is everywhere.

The Falls Rd. soon splits into **Andersontown Rd.** and **Glen Rd.,** the site of Ireland's only urban *gaeltacht.* On the left are the Celtic crosses of **Milltown Cemetery,** the resting place of many Republican dead. Inside the entrance, a memorial to Republican casualties is bordered by a low green fence on the right. The grave of Bobby Sands rests here. Another mile along the Andersontown Rd. lies the road's namesake—a housing project (formerly a wealthy Catholic neighborhood)—and more murals. The Springfield Rd. RUC station is the most-attacked police station in Ireland and the U.K.; its charred defenses are formidable, as are the directional video cameras and microphones that deck its eight-story radio tower.

SHANKILL. North St., to the left of the tourist office, turns into **Shankill Rd.** as it crosses the **Westlink** and then arrives in Protestant Shankill, once a thriving shopping district. Current housing preferences have led to a generational gap between the residents of Shankill and the Falls. Turning left (coming from the direction of North St.) onto most side roads leads to the **peace line.** At Canmore St., a mural on the left depicts the Apprentice Boys "Shutting the Gates of Derry—1688" as the Catholic invaders try to get through (see **Rebellion, Reunion, Reaction,** p. 10). Some murals in Shankill seem to glorify the UVF and UFF rather than celebrate any aspect of Orange culture. A little farther, also on the left and across a small park, a big, faded mural labeled "UVF—then and now" depicts a modern, black-garbed Protestant paramilitary man and a historical "B-Specials" soldier side-by-side (see **British rule and the Division of Ireland,** p. 350). The densely decorated **Orange Hall** sits on the left at Brookmount St. McClean's Wallpaper, on the right, was formerly Fizzel's Fish Shop, where 10 people died in an October 1993 bomb attack. The side streets on the right guide you to the **Shankill Estate** and more murals. Through the estate, **Crumlin Road** heads back to the city center past an army base, the courthouse, and the jail, which are on opposite sides of the road but linked by a tunnel. The oldest Loyalist murals are found here.

A PRIMER OF SYMBOLS IN THE MURALS OF WEST BELFAST

PROTESTANT MURALS

Blue, White, and Red: The colors of the British flag; often painted on curbs, signposts, etc., to demarcate Unionist murals and neighborhoods.

The Red Hand: The symbol of Ulster (found on Ulster's crest), usually used by Unionists to emphasize the separateness of Ulster from the rest of Ireland. Symbolizes the hand of the first Norse King, which he supposedly cut off and threw on a Northern beach to establish his primacy.

King Billy/William of Orange: Sometimes depicted on a white horse, crossing the Boyne to defeat the Catholic King James II at the 1690 Battle of the Boyne. The Orange Order was later founded in his honor.

The Apprentice Boys: A group of young men who shut the gates of Derry to keep out the troops of James II, beginning the great siege of 1689. They have become Protestant folk heroes, inspiring a sect of the Orange order in their name. The slogan **"No Surrender,"** also from the siege, has been appropriated by radical Unionists, most notably Rev. Ian Paisley (see **The Troubles**, p. 394).

Lundy: The Derry leader who advocated surrender during the siege; now a term for anyone who wants to give in to Catholic demands.

Taig: Phonetic spelling of the Irish given name Teague; Protestant slang for a Catholic.

Scottish Flag: Blue with a white cross; recalls the Scotch-Presbyterian roots of many Protestants whose ancestors were part of the Ulster Plantation (see p. 9).

CATHOLIC MURALS

Orange and Green: Colors of the Irish Republic's flag; often painted on curbs and signposts in Republican neighborhoods.

Landscapes: Usually imply Republican territorial claims to the North.

The Irish Volunteers: Republican tie to the earlier (nonsectarian) Nationalists.

Saiorsche: "Freedom"; the most common Irish term found on murals.

Éireann go bráth: "Ireland forever"; a popular IRA slogan.

Tiocfaidh ár lá: (CHOCK-ee-ar-LA) "Our day will come."

Slan Abnaile: (slang NA-fail) "Leave our streets"; directed at the primarily Protestant RUC police force.

Phoenix: Symbolizes united Ireland rising from the ashes of British persecution.

Lug: Celtic god, seen as the protector of the "native Irish" (Catholics).

Green ribbon: IRA symbol for "free POWs."

Bulldog: Britain.

Bowler Hats: A symbol for Orangemen.

SANDY ROW AND NEWTOWNARDS ROAD. The Shankill area is shrinking as middle-class Protestants leave it, but a growing Protestant population lives on **Sandy Row.** This stretch is a turn off of **Donegall Rd.** at **Shaftesbury Sq.** An orange Arch topped with King William marks its start. Nearby murals show the Red Hand of Ulster, a bulldog, and King William crossing the Boyne.

While murals in the Falls and Shankill are often defaced or damaged, better-preserved and more elaborate murals adorn the secure Protestant enclave of **East Belfast,** across the Lagan. A number line **Newtownards Rd.** One mural likens the UVF to the ancient hero, Cuchulainn—Ulster's defender. In so doing, it unintentionally illustrates the overlap in the two sides' cultural authorship.

⚐ ARTS AND ENTERTAINMENT

Belfast's many cultural events and performances are covered in the monthly *Arts Council Artslink*, which is free at the tourist office. Daily listings appear in the daily *Belfast Telegraph* (which also has a Friday arts supplement) as well as in Thursday's issue of the *Irish News*. For more extensive information on pub entertainment, pick up the free, biweekly, two-page news bulletin *That's Entertainment*, available at the tourist office, hostels, and most pubs. The **Crescent Arts Centre,** 2 University Rd. (tel. 9024 2338), supplies general arts info, but mostly specific news about their own exhibits and concerts, which take place September through May. They also host eight-week courses in yoga, trapeze, writing, trad, ballet, and drawing. **Fenderesky Gallery,** 2 University Rd. (tel. 9023 5245), inside the Crescent Arts Centre building, hosts contemporary shows all year. (Open M-Sa 11:30am-5:30pm.) The **Old Museum,** 7 College Sq. North (tel. 9023 5053; 9023 3332 for tickets), is Belfast's largest venue for new contemporary artwork. (Open M-Sa 10am-5:30pm. Free.) Besides art exhibits, it features a large variety of dance, theater, and live music performances as well as workshops. (Most performance tickets around £6, students and concessions £3.) A word of warning to the summer traveler: July and August are slow months for Belfast arts; around July 12 the whole city shuts down.

THEATER

Belfast's theater season runs from September to June. The truly **Grand Opera House,** Great Victoria St. (tel. 9024 0411), shows off a mix of opera, ballet, musicals, and drama. Tickets for most shows can be purchased either by phone or in person at the box office, 2-4 Great Victoria St. (Tel. 9024 1919 for reservations; 24hr. info line tel. 249 129. Open M-W 8:30am-8pm, Th 8:30am-9pm, F 8:30am-6:30pm, Sa 8:30am-5:30pm. Tickets £8 and up. 50% student rush tickets available after noon for M-Th performances. Wheelchair accessible.) **The Arts Theatre,** 41 Botanic Ave. (general inquiries tel. 316 901; box office tel. 9031 6900), houses its own company but hosts a wide array of touring troupes and individual performers. (Open Aug.-June; box office at 23 Botanic Ave. open M-Sa 10am-7pm. Tickets £3-10.) **The Lyric Theatre,** 55 Ridgeway St. (tel. 9038 1081), mixes Irish plays with international theater. (Tickets about £8.50 M-Th, £11 F-Su; student discounts M-F.) **The Group Theatre,** Bedford St. (tel. 9032 9685), produces comedies and farces in the Ulster Hall from September to May. (Box office open M-F noon-3pm. Tickets £2-6.) The **Old Museum Art Centre,** 1 College Sq. North (tel. 9023 3332 for tickets), presents avant-garde contemporary works. (Tickets usually £6, students and seniors £3.)

MUSIC

Ulster Hall, Bedford St. (tel. 9032 3900), brings Belfast everything from classical to pop. Try the independent box offices for tickets: **Our Price** (tel. 9031 3131) or the **Ticket Shop** at Virgin (tel. 9032 3744). **The Grand Opera House** (see **Theater**) resounds with classical vocal music. **Waterfront Hall,** 2 Lanyon Pl. (tel. 9033 4400), is Belfast's newest concert center, hosting a series of performances throughout the year. (Tickets £5-35, average £10-12; student discounts available.) The **Ulster Orchestra** (tel. 9023 3240) plays concerts at Waterfront Hall and Ulster Hall. (Tickets £5-23.)

FILM

There are two major movie theaters in Belfast. Commercial films are shown at **Virgin Cinemas,** 14 Dublin Rd. (tel. 9024 5700 for 24hr. info; (0541) 555 176 for credit card bookings); most movies come here three to seven months after their U.S. release. (£4.25, students and children £3; £3 all day Tu and M-F before 5pm.) **Queen's Film Theatre** (tel. 9024 4857), in a back alley off Botanic Ave., draws a more artsy crowd. (£2-3.80. "Meal and movie" discounts for certain restaurants.)

EVENTS

QUEENS UNIVERSITY BELFAST FESTIVAL. Belfast reigns supreme in the art world for three weeks each November during the university's annual festival. Over 300 separate performances of opera, ballet, film, and comedy invade venues across the city, drawing groups of international acclaim. Tickets for the most popular events sell out months ahead of time, although there's almost always something to see if you haven't planned ahead. *(Tel. 9066 7687. For advance tickets and schedules, write to: Mailing List, Festival House, 25 College Gardens, Belfast BT9 6BS. Ticket sales by mail begin September 15. From October 15 through the festival's end, tickets are available by phone. Prices range from £2.50 to £25.)*

WEST BELFAST ARTS FESTIVAL. This week-long series of events is the high point of Falls residents' year. The nationalist festival celebrates Irish traditional culture, hosting both big name trad groups and indebted rockers. It will convince you, if nothing else can, that West Belfast is more proud and friendly than most neighborhoods. *(First Week in August. Tel. 9032 4363; www.irish-culture.com.)*

NEAR BELFAST: ULSTER FOLK AND TRANSPORT MUSEUM

In **Holywood,** the Ulster Folk Museum and Transport Museum stretches over 176 acres. To reach it, take the Bangor Rd. 7 mi. east of Belfast on A2. Both buses and trains stop here on their way to Bangor. Half a day is just long enough to see the museums here, although spending fewer than two hours would be foolish. Established by Act of Parliament in the 1950s, the ■**Folk Museum** aims to preserve the way of life of Ulster's farmers, weavers, and craftspeople. The Folk Museum contains over 30 buildings from the past three centuries and all nine Ulster counties, including Monaghan, Cavan, and Donegal in the Republic. All but two of the buildings are transplanted originals, painstakingly moved and reconstructed stone by stone. All have been successfully placed in the museum's natural landscape to create an amazing air of authenticity. While attendants unobtrusively stand nearby to answer questions, there are no cheesy historical scenes or written explanations to interrupt the visitor's own imaginative role-play. The printer's shop on "Main Street" contains a working original 1844 newspaper press from the *Armagh Guardian*—ask the attendant for a demonstration. The museum also hosts special events, including trad music, dance performances and workshops, storytelling festivals, and textile exhibitions.

The Transport Museum and the Railway Museum are across the road from the Folk Museum. Inside the **Transport Museum,** horse-drawn coaches, cars, bicycles, and trains display the history of moving vehicles. Their motorcycle exhibition is extensive, following the evolution of the genre from the ABC Skootamota, a 1919 gem, to Harley mania with a life-size 1950s diner installation. A *Titanic* exhibit that includes original blueprints traces the Belfast-built ship and its fate. The hangar-shaped **Railway Museum** stuffs in 25 old railway engines, including the largest locomotive built in Ireland. (Tel. 9042 8428. Open July-Aug. M-Sa 10:30am-6pm, Su noon-6pm; Apr.-June and Sept. M-F 9:30am-5pm, Sa 10:30am-6pm, Su noon-6pm; Oct.-Mar. M-F 9:30am-4pm, Sa-Su 12:30-4:30pm. £4, students and seniors £2.50. Partially wheelchair accessible.)

DOWN AND ARMAGH

Locals flock to this sleepy but scenic area to take advantage of the seaside. The coast of Down and the Ards Peninsula is covered with fishing villages, holiday resorts, and 17th-century ruins. The Mourne Mountains, almost directly south of Belfast and just a lough away from the Republic, rise above the town of Newcastle, the largest seaside resort in Down. An inland county surrounded by rivers and lakes, Armagh is set on the rolling hills of Northern Ireland's drumlin belt. The best time to visit Co. Armagh is during apple blossom season in May, when the countryside, known as the "Orchard of Ireland," is covered in pink. Armagh town is an ecclesiastical center of great historical interest; traces of human habitation at Navan Fort date back to 5500 BC. Co. Armagh's other population centers, Craigavon and Portadown near Lough Neagh, are industrial centers of less interest to tourists, although Craigavon does host the Lough Neagh Discovery Centre. The **Ring of Gullion** in South Armagh is a circle of hills containing Slieve Gullion and some astounding volcanic rock formations. Much of the area is privately owned, but visitors can enjoy its amenities at Slieve Gullion Forest Park, which has trails up the mountain as well as an 8 mi. road for cars or bikes. Call the Slieve Gullion tourist office (tel. (01693) 848 084) for information.

BANGOR

Bangor found a place on early medieval maps of Ireland with its famous Abbey, a center of missionary activity, but this pious era in Bangor's history ended in the 9th century with the Viking raids. By the Victorian era, Bangor had become eminent again, this time as *the* seaside resort for Belfast residents. Today, Bangor caters to families and older vacationers during the week and hosts busloads of twenty-somethings on the weekends. Its location makes it both an inevitable and an enjoyable stop on the way down the Ards Peninsula.

▐▀ TRANSPORTATION

Trains: Abbey St. (tel. 270 141), next to the bus station. Trains chug to **Belfast** (30min.; M-F 38 per day, Sa 26 per day, Su 9 per day; £2.60).

Buses: Abbey St. (tel. 271 143). Buses run to **Belfast** (45min., M-Sa 33 per day, Su 8 per day, £2.20) and all **Ards Peninsula** towns, including **Donaghadee** (30min., M-F 17 per day, Sa 14 per day, Su 6 per day, £1.10).

▐ ORIENTATION AND PRACTICAL INFORMATION

The train and bus stations are next to each other at the top of Main St., which runs past the tourist office on its way to the marina. Most sights are near the waterfront.

Tourist Office: Tower House, 34 Quay St. (tel. 270 069). Great brochures on the Down coast. Will book accommodations. Open July-Aug. M 10am-7pm, Tu-F 9am-7pm, Sa 10am-7pm, Su noon-6pm; Sept.-June M 10am-7pm, Tu-F 9am-5pm, Sa 10:30am-4:30pm.

Banks: First Trust, 85 Main St. (tel. 270 628). Open M-Tu and Th-F 9:30am-4:30pm, W 10am-4:30pm. **Northern Bank,** 77 Main St. (tel. 271 211). Open M 10am-5pm, Tu-F 10am-3:30pm, Sa 9:30am-12:30pm. **Ulster Bank,** Main St. (tel. 270 924), open M-F 9:30am-4pm. All have 24hr. **ATMs.**

Pharmacy: Boots Pharmacy, 79-83 Main St. (tel. 271 134). Open M-Sa 9am-5:30pm.

Emergency: Dial 999; no coins required. **Police:** Castle Park Ave. (tel. 454 444).

Counseling and Support: Samaritans, 92 Dufferin Ave. (tel. 464 646). Open 24 hrs.

Post Office: 143 Main St. (tel. 450 150). Open M-Sa 9am-5:30pm. **Postal Code:** BT20 482.

▐ ACCOMMODATIONS.

Although Bangor is without hostel or campground, it teems with B&Bs in the £15-20 range; all of them are listed in the tourist office window. Along coastal Seacliff Rd. (Quay St., which runs by the tourist office, becomes Seacliff) and inland Princetown Rd. (from the train station, take a left on Dufferin Ave., which becomes Princetown), B&Bs are within spitting distance of each other. The **Lisnacree,** 53 Princetown Rd. (tel. 462 571), offers sunny colors and tips about Bangor attractions (£16). Next door, **Tara Guesthouse,** 51 Princetown Rd. (tel. 468 924), pampers guests with spacious rooms, all with bath, TV, and telephone (singles £25; doubles £40). On the other side of town, **Pierview House,** 28 Seacliff Rd. (tel. 463 381), offers hospitality comparable to the charm of its original

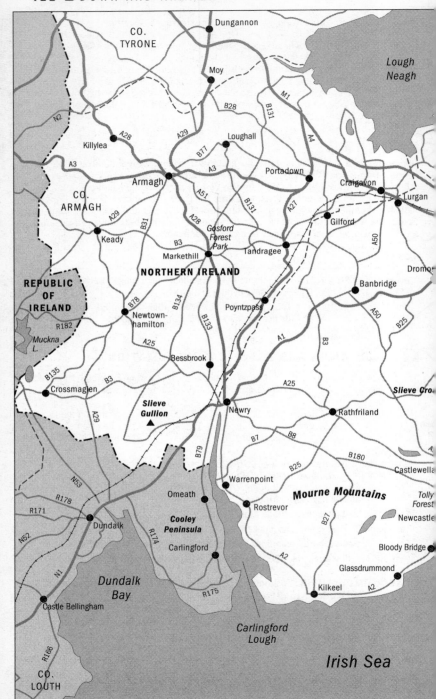

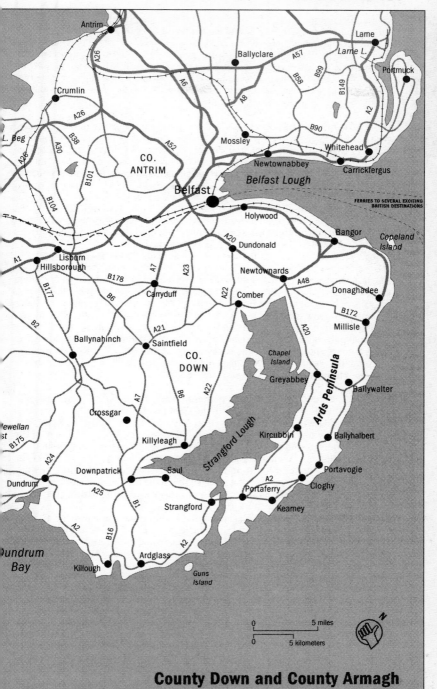

County Down and County Armagh

Victorian decorations (£16). B&Bs on Seacliff Road are highly recommended for their spectacular views of the sea. **Ramelton House B&B**, 55 Princeton St. (tel. 271 813) has rooms with hot pot, TV, bath. (1 twin, 2 doubles, £20 per person). **Ashley House**, 50 Queens Parade (tel. 473 918) has good views (singles £18; doubles £35). **Bethany House**, 58 Queens Parade (tel. 274 178) is further down the street (singles £16; doubles £32). The **Hebron House** next door is owned by the same proprietors. Nicer, but more expensive of course, it has sunny, flowery rooms with good beds and great views. (Singles £20; doubles £36).

📷🍴 **FOOD AND PUBS.** A resort town, Bangor has no shortage of places to eat. Every third shop on Main St. sells baked goods and sandwiches, and every pub in town serves grub during lunch and dinner. **The Diner,** 8 Dufferin Ave., provides good, filling and quite cheap food. (3-course "diner meal" £3.25; open M-Sa 8:30am-6:30pm, Su 10am-4pm). A few yards farther along the avenue, the **Ratz Continental Restaurant and Café**, 32 Dufferin Ave., serves sandwiches (£2), stuffed potatoes (£3) and lunch specials (£5) in a homey and inviting atmosphere, complete with stone walls and a fireplace. **The Cosy Teapot,** 28 Dufferin Ave. (tel. 466 572), has home-cooked food and a fetish for figurative teapots—the enormous collection competes with customers for seating space (sandwiches around £2, entrees around £4; open M-Th 10am-4:30pm, F-Sa 10am-7pm).

Pubs gather along High St. and the waterfront. **Jenny Watts,** 41 High St. (tel. 270 401), is a former Bushmill's "bar of the year." It looks but doesn't feel the part; an older crowd sips pints slowly and sniffs at the debauchery of those with a liking for hard liquor (21+). Just down the street at **Wolseys,** 24 High St. (tel. 460 495), regulars enjoy cheap meals (£4-5 from noon on) in green velvet and mahogany snugs with music for the younger crowd upstairs on weekends (for live folk and jazz bands and disco cover £2-3). The windows to **Donegan's,** 44 High St. (tel. 270 362), traditional-pub soul are stained with a Fauvist's color palette. Live music daily (no cover), 2-course lunch (£5.25). **The Windsor,** 24 Quay St. (tel. 473 943), has pints on the ground floor and DJs above. Check out the marine outside and the great drinks inside the **Steamer Bar,** 30-32 Quay St. (tel. 467 699).

🏛 **SIGHTS. North Down Visitors and Heritage Centre,** Town Hall, Castle Park, is in the "Elizabethan Revival" style house of the Hamilton family, once the owner of all the land around Bangor. (Tel. 271 200. Open July-Aug. Tu-Sa 10:30am-5:30pm, Su 2-5:30pm; Sept.-June Tu-Sa 10:30am-4:30pm, Su 2-4:30pm. Free.) The rest of the Hamilton Estate around the center consists of 129 sometimes wooded, sometimes grassy acres that now compose the public **Castle Park.** Nearby, 37 acre **Ward Park,** up Castle St. or Hamilton Rd. from Main St., entices with tennis courts, bowling greens, and a cricket pitch. A string of lakes down the middle also harbors a wildlife sanctuary. The **North Down Coastal Path** forays for 15 mi. from Holywood through Bangor and Groomsport to Orlock Point. Along the way are abandoned World War II lookouts; Helen's Bay, a popular bathing spot; Crawfordsburn Country Park; **Greypoint Fort**, an old fort with a massive gun; and a giant redwood. Bicycles are banned from the path. The region is recognized for its colonies of black guillemots, which look like penguins. The most striking Bangor-Holywood portion begins at the Pickie Fun Park, near the Marina, and takes 2-3 hr. to walk (7mi. northwest of Bangor along A2).

The path also passes through the picturesque village of Crawfordsburn, 3mi. from Bangor, the home of Ireland's oldest hotel. **The Old Inn,** Main St. (tel. 853 255), dates back to 1614 and still maintains many of its original wood decorations. The Inn has been visited by luminaries ranging from Peter the Great of Russia to C.S. Lewis and serves up affordable food in its "Parlour Bar" (goat cheese tart £2.95; serving food M-Sa noon-7pm, Su noon-9:30pm). The **Crawfordsburn Country Park,** off B20 at Helen's Bay, is another of Northern Ireland's popular forest parks. It offers both coastal paths and green forests. (Park open daily 8:30am-dark. Center open daily Apr.-Sept. 10am-6pm; Oct.-Mar. 10am-5pm. Free.) The **Visitors Centre** (tel.

853621) provides plentiful information about the park's natural history and trails. The Bangor **bus** and **train** both run through Crawfordsburn. Bangor claims to be the festival capital of Northern Ireland, hosting numerous events throughout the year (contact the Bangor tourist office for details).

ARDS PENINSULA

The Ards Peninsula is bounded on the west by tranquil Strangford Lough; to its east lies the agitated Irish Sea. The shore of Strangford Lough from Newtownards to Portaferry is crowded with wildlife preserves, historic houses, crumbling ruins, spectacular lake views, and tourists. On the Irish Sea side of the Ards, each fishing village seems tinier and twice as nice as the one before.

Ulsterbus leaves Laganside Station in **Belfast** to traverse the peninsula, stopping in almost every town. **Trains** roll no farther than **Bangor**. From the south, a **ferry** crosses frequently between **Strangford** and **Portaferry** (see p. 426). The Ards Peninsula can also be seen efficiently by bike.

DONAGHADEE

The fishing villages that line the coast south of Bangor consist of little more than one harbor and a few pubs each. The largest is Donaghadee, famous for its lifeboat and lighthouse. Donaghadee was Ulster's most important passenger port from the 17th century until 1849, when Larne replaced it. Composer Franz Liszt spent several days here waiting for a ship to bring him and his piano to England.

A well-spent morning would include a stroll to the still-operational first electrical lighthouse in Ireland. Past the lighthouse, the **town commons,** formerly communal potato fields, spread along the shore. At the other end of town, an old ruined *motte* (MOTE) towers above the village on Donaghadee's single hill. The former castle's most recent use was holding ammunition used to blast stone from the hill to build the harbor. Down at Lemons Wharf is the spruced-up and well-loved **RNLB Sir Samuel Kelly.** In 1953, the *Samuel Kelly* rescued scores of passengers when the ferryboat *Princess Victoria* sank just offshore on its way from Scotland to Belfast. Quinton Nelson (tel. 9188 3403) at the marina skips passenger boats out to the **Copeland Islands,** a wildlife sanctuary just offshore, from June to September. (Frequency dependent upon demand. £4, children £2.)

A restful night in Donaghadee can be spent at **The Deans,** 52 Northfield Rd. (tel. 9188 2204), across from the school playground. (Singles £19, doubles £33.) A handful of pubs and eateries are scattered along High St. Most notable is **Grace Neill's Pub and Bistro,** 35 High St. (tel. 9188 2553), the oldest pub in Ireland according to the *Guinness Book of World Records.* During its 388-year lifespan, Grace Neill's has supposedly catered to the likes of Peter the Great and Oliver Cromwell. It boasts a world-class chef and lunch specialties ranging from Thai to Italian dishes. (Meals around £5.) A few doors to the left, **Boswell's,** 7 High St. (tel. 9188 8001), provides nightly entertainment for the town. In the summer, you can barbecue in the backyard beer garden. If you're not in the mood for pub grub, head to **Alfie's** on High St. Combine Alfie's three counters—ice cream, baked goods, and bistro—to make a multi-course meal for about £4.

Ulsterbus drives to Donaghadee from **Bangor** (25min.; M-F 26 per day, Sa 15 per day, Su 5 per day; £1.40) and **Belfast** (1hr.; M-F 24 per day, Sa 17 per day, Su 7 per day; £2.30). South of Donaghadee, gnat-sized fishing villages buzz along the eastern shoreline. **Millisle, Ballywalter, Ballyhalbert, Portavogie, Cloughey,** and **Kearney** make good stops on an afternoon's drive, but none merit a special visit. **Portavogie** is charming, and **Millisle** is home to the **Ballycopeland Windmill.** A2 runs the length of the shore, where hitching is reportedly easy, but *Let's Go* doesn't recommend it.

MOUNTSTEWART AND GREY ABBEY

Fifteen miles southeast of Belfast on A20, roving pheasants greet you at **Mountstewart House and Gardens.** To reach Mountstewart from Belfast, take the Portaferry bus from Laganside Station and ask the driver to let you off at Mountstewart (45min.; M-F 20 per day, Sa 15 per day, Su 8 per day; £2.15). Held by a string of Marquesses of Londonderry, both house and garden are now National Trust property. They are worth a detour to see and provide a truly striking contrast to the many plebeian homes found at the Ulster Folk Museum (see **Near Belfast,** p. 420). Many of the trappings of the stately 18th-century **Mountstewart House** are faded and tattered, but the regal portraits, gilded ceilings, chandeliers, and china still manage to give the place an air of grandeur. The 22 chairs in the formal dining room once held the arses of Europe's greatest diplomats at the 1814 Congress of Vienna, where they divvied up the post-Napoleonic continent. Lady Edith had each seat embroidered with the arms of its occupant and of his country. (Tel. 4278 8387 or 4278 8487. Open May-Sept. W-M, including bank holidays, 1-6pm; Apr. and Oct. Sa-Su 1-6pm. Last tour 5pm. Admission for house and garden £3.50, children £1.75.)

The **gardens,** covering 85 acres, are a more enticing attraction than the house. The estate comprises seven gardens and several woodsy walks, all designed by Edith, Lady Londonderry in the early part of this century. Taking advantage of Ireland's temperate climate, Lady Edith imported flowers, trees and shrubs from as far afield as Australia. She created a doozy of a **Dodo Terrace,** which contains a menagerie of animal statues meant to display the many rare species that Noah put in his ark. The **Shamrock Garden,** whose name belies its shape, contains a Red Hand of Ulster made of begonias and a topiary Irish Harp; the surrounding foliage depicts the story of the hunt of a stag who was saved by the devil. An afternoon could easily be spent strolling through the gardens; more ambitious ramblers, however, might choose to explore the surrounding estate, including the Lake Walk, Rock Walk, and Rhododendron Hill. (Open Apr.-Sept. daily 11am-6pm; Oct. Sa-Su 11am-6pm; Mar. Su 2-5pm. Admission to the garden £3, children £1.50.)

The neoclassical **Temple of the Winds,** used by Mountstewart's inhabitants for "frivolity and jollity," sits atop a hill with a super view of Strangford Lough. (To reach the temple from Mountstewart House, turn left on the main road and go about a quarter mile. Open May-Sept. W-M 2-5pm, Apr. and Oct. Sa-Su 2-5pm. Admission to the temple £1.)

PORTAFERRY

Portaferry lies on the southern tip of the Ards Peninsula and peers across the teeming, critter-filled depths of Strangford Lough at Strangford town. Tourists stop in at this quiet seaside village to check out its aquatic offerings, including a recently built aquarium and an annual sailing regatta.

⁊ ORIENTATION AND PRACTICAL INFORMATION. To reach the Lough from the bus stop, follow **Church St.,** which turns into **Castle St.,** downhill for about 200m, passing several eateries and the Exploris aquarium on the way. **Ulsterbuses** from Belfast drop visitors at **the Square** in the center of town (1½hr.; M-F 18 per day, Sa 16 per day, Su 8 per day; £3.30). **Ferries** (tel. 4488 1637) leave Portaferry's waterfront at 15 and 45 minutes past the hour for a 10-minute chug to Strangford, returning on the hour and half-hour (M-F 7:45am-10:45pm, Sa 8:15am-11:15pm, Su 9:45am-10:45pm; 85p, seniors and children ages 5-16 50p, cars £4). The effusive Portaferry **tourist office** (tel. 4272 9882) is just behind the castle (follow signs from The Square toward the docks). Besides the usual plethora of brochures, and **bureau de change,** it also offers an exhibit on the maritime features of Strangford Lough, and a 12-minute video on the medieval "tower houses" of Co. Down. (Open July-Aug. M-Sa 10am-5:30pm, Su noon-6pm; Easter-June and Sept. M-Sa 10am-5pm, Su 2-6pm.) **Northern Bank,** 1 The Square (tel. 4272 8208; open M 10am-5pm, Tu-W and F 10am-3:30pm, Th 9:30am-3:30pm; **24hr. ATM**) and the **post office,** 28 The Square (tel. 4272 8201; open M-W and F 9am-5:30pm, Th 9am-1pm, Sa 9am-12:30pm) are both within spitting distance of the bus stop. The **postal code** is BT22 1LN.

ACCOMMODATIONS, FOOD, AND PUBS. A peaceful stay awaits at the **Portaferry Barholm Youth Hostel,** 11 The Strand (tel. 4272 9598), at the bottom of Castle St. The hostel looks out onto the pretty villagescape with its miniature ferry port. Defying hostel stereotypes, Barholm is practically luxurious, with several singles and many doubles, semi-private bathrooms, a greenhouse-like dining room, and great views. Because a Queens University Belfast marine biology lab is nearby, the hostel often hosts groups of students and lecturers; reservations are necessary on weekends. (Dorms £10.95. Laundry £3. Wheelchair accessible.)

The Shambles Bistro and Coffee Shop disperses quick bites on Castle St. (Soup and sandwich £1.95.) For a pricier, more substantial meal, wander down to the **Cornstore,** Castle St. (tel. 4272 9779), just before Exploris and the Portaferry castle. Decked in sailing splendor, this small restaurant specializes in tasty traditional food and seafood on weekends. (Most meals £6-8.) The **Ferry Grill,** on High St. across from Spar Market, stays open for a late-night bite on weekends, and serves variations on a burger-and-fries for less than £2. There are also numerous fresh fruit and veggie **markets** and convenience stores scattered around High St. and the Square. At night, everyone stumbles into the **Fiddler's Green,** Church St., where publican Frank leads rowdy traditional sing-alongs and welcomes live folk bands many evenings. The pub's instrument-covered walls are a testament to its first love. Doubting Thomases will enjoy the green grass of the beer garden out back. John Wayne paraphernalia covers the walls of **The Quiet Man** across the street. On weekends, the pub plays music, from disco to live bands, and throws a Saturday night happy hour from 9-10pm. **M.E. Dunnigan's,** Ferry St., is a tiny pub just up from the waterfront so crammed with locals that *craic* is guaranteed.

SIGHTS. Portaferry's claim to fame is **Exploris,** The Ropewalk. Located near the dock next to the ruins of **Portaferry Castle,** Exploris houses first-rate exhibits on local ocean and seashore ecology; it is Northern Ireland's only public aquarium and heralded as one of the U.K.'s best. The aquarium takes you on a journey beginning in the shallow waters of Strangford Lough and ending in the depths of the Irish Sea. Within its spooky, cavernous corridors, open tanks teem with sea-rays and nurse sharks, a "touch tank," and interactive displays for children. Exploris recently added a seal sanctuary to welcome injured seals. (Tel. 4272 8062. Open Mar.-Aug. M-F 10am-6pm, Sa 11am-6pm, Su 1-6pm; Sept.-Feb. M-F 10am-5pm, Sa 11am-5pm, Su 1-5pm. £3.85, students, seniors, and children £2.70.)

Another big tourist attraction in Portaferry, the **Galway Hooker Festival and Traditional Boat Regatta** (see p. 315) sails to town each year during the fourth weekend in June. Hookers are traditional fishing boats with thick, black hulls and billowing sails made in the west of Ireland. Hookers are not the only oddly named sailing ships on display: the regatta also includes Nobbies, Prawners, Luggers, and East Coast Smacks. Besides the regatta itself, the festivities include live trad, country, bluegrass, folk, and pipe band music. For general info, call the **Ards Borough Council** (tel. 9181 2215; email tourism@ards-council.gov.uk) in Newtownyards. Peter Killen (tel. 9182 4000) provides sailing information. Book B&Bs months in advance. From Easter through the end of September, the Market House in the square welcomes a **country market** every Saturday 10am-1pm.

LECALE

Called by some "The Island of Lecale," the region spans along the west coast of Strangford Lough from the village of Strangford and to the market town Downpatrick, and then continues inland to Ballynahinch to the north and Dundrum to the west. It was once bound entirely by bodies of water, including the Irish Sea, Strangford Lough, and a series of streams and ponds. Industrialization passed Lecale by, even as it hit the surrounding areas of County Down, leaving Lecale culturally isolated. Today, agricultural industries still support the area.

STRANGFORD

This tiny harbor village lies just across the Lough from Portaferry, northeast of Downpatrick on A25 and north of Ardglass on A2. It's convenient to the Castleward House and Estate, a glorious homestead that the National Trust protects. accommodations, food, pubs

▆▆▆ ACCOMMODATIONS, FOOD, AND PUBS. Buses for Downpatrick leave from the ferry dock (30min.; M-F 9 per day, Sa 5 per day; £1.60). **Ferries** leave for Portaferry every 30min. (M-F 7:30am-10:30pm, Sa 8am-11pm, Su 9:30am-10:30pm; 85p). The **Castle Ward Caravan Park** (tel. 4488 1680), lies on the Castle Ward National Trust property. (£5 per small tent. Free showers. Open mid-Mar. to Sept.) **The Strangford Caravan Park** (tel. 4488 1888) resides at 87 Shore Rd. Turn left from the ferry dock and take the Ardglass Rd. from town for about 2 mi. (£5 per tent, £6 with electricity. Laundry £3.) **Mary Breen** runs a B&B at 46 Downpatrick Rd. (tel. 4488 1563). Book months in advance during opera season. Chatty locals nurse their pints at **The Lobster Pot,** 11 The Square. Make sure to check out the daily specials for excellent food at low prices. (Specials £5-6.) There's a warm welcome for you at the **Cuan Bar and Restaurant,** The Square (tel. 4488 1222), with pub grub throughout the day. (Most meals £5-8.) Duck into **The Hole in the Wall Public House** (tel. 4488 1301), on the road to Downpatrick, run by a golf buff and decorated with leaded glass. Both the Cuan and the Hole in the Wall offer live music on weekends.

▆ SIGHTS. Strangford's tourist appeal lies in its proximity to the ▆**Castle Ward House and Estate.** This 18th-century estate, once owned by the couple Lady Anne and Lord Bangor and now the property of the National Trust, lies atop a hill approximately 2 mi. from Strangford. One wing of the house, built in 1768, is classical, which satisfied Lord Bangor; the other is Gothic, to suit Lady Anne's fancy. Alas, even exorbitant compromise was not enough, and they split up soon after the house was built. The 700-acre estate features a rectangular lake, a tower house, a restored corn mill, and a "Victorian pastimes center" for children. (Tel. 4488 1204. House open May-Aug. M-W and F-Su 10am-5:15pm, Apr. and Sept.-Oct. Sa 1-6pm, Easter week daily 1-6pm. £2.60, children £1.30. Grounds open year-round dawn to dusk. £1 in winter, free during the rest of the year.) In the summer, the **Castle Ward Opera** performs here (tel. 9066 1090 for tickets and info). To get to the estate by car from Strangford, take A25 toward Downpatrick. The entrance to the grounds is about 2 mi. up the road on the right (£3.50 per car). Pedestrians seeking a safe shortcut should follow the Castleward Rd. to the caravan park. From there a wide path leads through the woods and to the entrance of the grounds.

The **Strangford Lough Wildlife Centre** is located on the estate and provides information on the natural environment of the lough. If you are walking, you could also follow A25, but turn off the main road at the entrance to the Castle Ward Caravan Park. Follow the driveway to the right fork, and go through the brown gate on your right. This takes you to the **Loughside Walk,** a 30min. stroll along the coastline to the Centre, during which you can accumulate scores of observations on the local wildlife. (Open July-Aug. M-W and F-Su 2-6pm; Apr.-June and Sept. Sa-Su 2-6pm.) In town, a small 16th-century tower house optimistically called **Strangford Castle** stands to the right of the ferry dock as you disembark. Wander into its dark, spooky interior and find a spectacular view from the third floor. (Key to gate available from Mr. Seed, 39 Castle St., across from the tower house's gate, 10am-7pm.)

DOWNPATRICK

Downpatrick's name highlights its two defining characteristics: it's the Down county seat, and the supposed burial place of St. Patrick. The town's streets are filled with shoppers, loitering school children, and heavy traffic by day, when young and old flock to town from nearby villages to do a day's shopping or learning. The surrounding countryside, dotted with St. Patrick-related religious and archaeological sites, is best seen in a day-trip by bike or car. Many visitors spend the night in the hostels at Portaferry (see p. 426) and Newcastle (see p. 431).

⌐ TRANSPORTATION

Buses: 83 Market St. (tel. 4461 2384). Buses to **Strangford** (25min.; M-F 9 per day, Sa 4 per day; £1.85), **Newcastle** (20min.; M-F 19 per day, Sa 11 per day, Su 6 per day; £2.20), and **Belfast** (45min.; M-F 28 per day, Sa 15 per day, Su 6 per day; £3.30).

Local Transportation: Buses run M-Sa 9:55am-4:45pm, 7 per day.

Taxis: 96 Market St. (tel. 4461 4515), run M-Th 10am-1:45am, F-Su 10am-3:30am.

Bicycles: Down Discount Cycles, 45b Church St. (tel. 4461 4990), next to the Texaco station. Open M-Sa 9:30am-5:30pm. Rentals £5 per day.

☑ ORIENTATION AND PRACTICAL INFORMATION

Market St., the main street in town, is flanked by the bus station at one end and connections to all other significant streets at the opposite. From the station, the first of these streets on the right is **St. Patrick's Ave.** Further on, Market St. meets **Irish St.** on the right, **English St.** on the left, and **Church St.** straight ahead. **Scotch St.** lies between Church and Irish St.

Tourist Office: 74 Market St. (tel. 4461 2233), across from the Supervalu shopping center (moving to the Heritage Center on Market St. in the fall of 2000). Open July-mid-Sept. M-F 9am-6pm, Sa 10am-6pm, Su 2-6pm, bank holidays 11am-6pm; mid-Sept.-June M-F 9am-5pm, Sa 10am-5pm, bank holidays 11am-6pm.

Banks: Northern Banks, 58-60 Market St. (tel. 4461 4011). Open M 9:30am-5pm, Tu-F 10am-3:30pm, Sa 9:30am-12:30pm. **24hr. ATM. Bank of Ireland**, 80-82 Market St. (tel. 4461 2911). Open M-Tu and Th-F 9:30am-4:30pm, W 10am-4:30pm.

Pharmacy: Foy's Chemist, 16 Irish St. (tel. 4461 2032). Open M-F 9am-5:30pm. **Deeny Pharmacy**, 30A St. Patrick's Ave. (tel. 4461 3807). Open M-Sa 9am-5:30pm.

Emergency: Dial 999; no coins required. **Police:** Irish St. (tel. 4461 5011).

Hospital: Downe Hospital (tel. 4461 3311).

Post Office: 65 Market St. (tel. 4461 2061), inside the shopping center. Open M-F 9am-5:30pm, Sa 9am-12:30pm. **Postal code:** BT30 6LZ.

⌐☐☑ ACCOMMODATIONS, FOOD, AND PUBS.

B&Bs in Downpatrick tend to be pricey, and many visitors opt to spend the night at one of the hostels in Portaferry or Newcastle, or camp at one of the caravan parks near Strangford. The closest campground is **Castle Ward**, near Strangford (see p. 428). Within Downpatrick, **Dunleath House**, 33 St. Patrick's Dr. (tel. 4461 3221), has luxurious accommodations and a friendly proprietress. (Single £20, double £36.)

Downpatrick's eateries surpass those of many nearby towns in both quality and quantity. The ▨**Daily Grind Coffee Shop**, 21A St. Patrick's Ave. (tel. 4461 5949), offers a wide selection of scrumptious gourmet sandwiches (£2-3), specialty salads (£3-4), and rich desserts. (Open M-Sa 10am-4:30pm.) The **Iniscora Tea Room**, 2-6 Irish St. (tel. 4461 5283), is inside the Down Civic Arts Centre (see **Sights**). The profits from its simple, economical lunches go to the Down Residential Project for the Disabled. **Oakley Fayre's** bakery and sit-down cafe, 52 Market St. (tel. 4461 2500), provides full meals, like lasagna and cottage pie (each £4) in a diner-esque seating area behind their traditional bakery. (Open M-Sa 9am-5:15pm.) For picnic food from mom-and-pop shops, try **Quinn's Home Bakery**, 10-12 Scotch St. (tel. 4461 2432; open M-Sa 8:30am-5:30pm) or the deli in **Hanlon's Fruit and Veg**, 26 Market St. (open M-Sa 8am-5:45pm).

For a heavy meal, at a more substantial price, **Denvir's**, 14 English St. (tel. 4461 2012), is an excellent choice. The pub dates from 1642, and has housed the likes of Daniel O'Connell and Jonathan Swift. The United Irishmen who fought for home rule in the Rebellion of 1798 met here under the pretext of being a literary society (see **Rebellion, Union, and Reaction**, p. 10). When the rebellion failed, the Denvir family was forced to flee to America, where the next generation became the founders of Denver, Colorado. Today Denvir's restaurant serves meals made with wild herbs, plants, and mushrooms gathered by the friendly proprietress. (Lunch

£3-5, served M-Sa noon-2:30pm; dinner £5-9, served Su-Th 6-8pm, F-Sa 7-9pm.) The pub serves bar snacks and hosts live music. A little out of the way, good *craic* and trad make it worth the few minutes walk to **Mullans,** 48 Church St. (tel. 4461 2227). **The Russell,** 7 Church St. (tel. 4461 4170), claims to serve the best Guinness in town due to its double-cooled tap. Thomas Russell, one of the leaders of the 1803 Presbyterian rebellion for home rule, supposedly haunts the building.

■ **SIGHTS. Down County Museum and Heritage Centre,** at the end of English St. (walk down Market St. away from the bus station and then follow the signs), does regional history with unusual flair. Housed in the jail where Thomas Russell was hanged, the museum introduces you to St. Patrick, a wax gang of 19th-century prisoners, and the story of Co. Down. (Tel. 4461 5218. Open June-Aug. M-F 10am-5pm, Sa-Su 2-5pm; Sept.-May Tu-F and bank holidays 10am-5pm, Sa 2-5pm. Free.) The **Down Civic Arts Centre,** 2-6 Irish St., in the old town hall, hosts traveling exhibitions (free) and stages musical performances in autumn. (Tel. 4461 5283. Open M and F-Sa 10am-4:30pm, Tu and Th 10am-10pm. Ticket prices vary.)

Next to the museum is the Church of Ireland **Down Cathedral** (tel. 4461 4922). A Celtic monastery until the 12th century, the cathedral became a Benedictine monastery under the Norman conqueror John de Courcey and then proceeded to fall into ruin. Rebuilt in 1818, the present cathedral incorporates stone carvings from its medieval predecessor into its walls and houses the only private pew boxes still in use in Ireland. The entrance of the church proclaims that it proudly represents 1500 years of Christianity, beginning with St. Patrick's settlement in nearby Saul (see **Near Downpatrick**). In the graveyard, a stone commemorates the **grave of St. Patrick;** he is joined by the remains of **St. Brigid** and **St. Colmcille** (also known as St. Columba). Although it is uncertain whether the gravestone marks the correct site, it does bring visitors to a beautiful view above Downpatrick and its surroundings.

A similar view is afforded atop the **Mound of Down.** This Bronze Age hill fort was once known as Dunlethglaise, or "fort on the green hill." Later, in the Iron Age, an early Christian town flourished on the mound until Anglo-Norman invaders under John de Courcy defeated the Irish chief Macdunleavy and his troops. Today, visitors will be hard pressed to find signs of the fort or the city, but the green hill remains a lovely spot for a walk on the outskirts of town.

NEAR DOWNPATRICK: SAUL

All sights touched by St. Patrick are revered in County Down, but most beloved is Saul. Follow the signs on Saul Rd. for 2 mi. past Downpatrick to reach **Saul Church,** located on the site where St. Patrick is believed to have landed in the 5th century. After being converted to Christianity, the local chieftain Dichu gave Patrick a barn *(sabhal)* which later became the first parish church in Ireland. (Tel. 4461 4922. Open daily until 6pm, Sunday services at 10am.) 1933 replicas of an early Christian church and round tower commemorate the landing. A little more than a mile further along Saul Rd., on the summit of Slieve Patrick, stands **St. Patrick's Shrine.** The monument consists of a huge granite statue of the saint, bronze panels depicting his life, and an open-air temple. Even nonbelievers will appreciate the 360° view of the lough, the mountains, and, on a clear day, the Isle of Man. The **Struell Wells,** on the Ardglass road to the southeast of Downpatrick, are also linked to St. Patrick. Water runs through underground channels from one well to the next, finally flowing into 200-year-old bath houses. Belief in their curative powers originated long before Christianity arrived on the scene.

One mile from Downpatrick on the Belfast road (A7) lie the ruins of the **Cistercian Inch Abbey,** the earliest standing Gothic ruins in Ireland. The abbey was founded in 1180 by the Norman conqueror John de Courcy to make up for his destruction of the Eneragh monastery a few years earlier. The site, located on an island in the Quoile River, makes an excellent backdrop for a picnic. (Open Apr.-Sept. Tu-Sa 10am-7pm, Su 2-7pm. £1.) One mile from Downpatrick off Strangford Rd., the **Quoile Pondage Nature Reserve** offers hiking trails and birdwatching around a lake created in 1957 when a tidal barrier was erected to prevent the flooding of Downpatrick. The barrier allowed an unusual assortment of vegetation, fish, and insect life to grow. The **Quoile Countryside Centre** provides a surplus of information. (Tel. 4461 5520. Open Apr.-Sept. daily 11am-5pm, Oct.-Mar. Sa and Su 1-5pm.)

NEWCASTLE AND THE MOURNES

The plastic arcades, joke shops, and waterslide parks of Newcastle's waterfront provide dramatic contrast to the majestic Mourne Mountains at the south end of town. On summer weekends, children crowd the streets and vacationers scramble for places in carnival lines and spots on the beach. The town is also an inexpensive place to stay and eat while hiking in the surrounding wilderness.

The 15 rounded peaks of the Mourne Mountains sprawl across the southeastern corner of Northern Ireland. Volcanic activity pushed up five different kinds of granite beneath a shale crust 50 million years ago. Several million more years of rain and ice created the gray, spotted face of hard acidic granite on the mountains today. No road penetrates the center of the mountains, so hikers are left in welcome solitude. Due to the glaciers of the last Ice Age, the peaks form a skewed figure-eight with two large valleys in the middle. The larger of these valleys holds **Ben Crom** and **Silent Valley,** reservoirs built early this century to supply water to Belfast. Outdoorsy types spending the night in Newcastle would do well to use up an afternoon checking out the untrammeled dunes to the north of town.

▐ TRANSPORTATION

Buses: Ulsterbus, 5-7 Railway St. (tel. 4372 2296), at the end of Main St., away from the mountains. Buses run to: **Downpatrick** (20min.; M-F 20 per day, Sa 12 per day, Su 5 per day; £2.15), **Belfast** (1hr.; M-F 20 per day, Sa 20 per day, Su 10 per day; £4.40), **Newry** (1¾hr.; M-F 8 per day, Sa 5 per day; £3.50), and **Dublin** (3hr.; M-Sa 4 per day, Su 2 per day; £9.70).

Taxi: Donard Cabs (tel. 4372 4100 or 4372 2823); **Shimna Taxis** (tel. 4372 3030).

Bike Rental: Wiki Wiki Wheels, 10B Donard St. (tel. 4372 3973). Beside the Xtra-Vision building (left from the bus station). Offers full accessories. £6.50 per day, £30 per week; children £5 per day. Driver's license, passport, or credit card deposit. Open M-Sa 9am-6pm, Su 2-6pm.

Hitching: Those thumbing a ride should stand at either end of the main road. *Let's Go* does not recommend hitchhiking.

▐ ORIENTATION AND PRACTICAL INFORMATION

Newcastle's main road stretches along the waterfront, changing from **Main St.** (where it intersects with **Railway St.,** the site of the Ulsterbus stop) to **Central Promenade** to **South Promenade.**

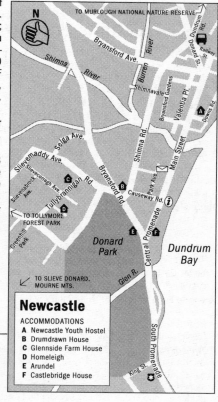

Newcastle

ACCOMMODATIONS
A Newcastle Youth Hostel
B Drumdrawn House
C Glennside Farm House
D Homeleigh
E Arundel
F Castlebridge House

Tourist Office: 10-14 Central Promenade (tel. 4372 2222), in a blue and white building 10min. down the main street from the bus station. Free map and visitor's guide. Open July-Aug. M-Sa 9:30am-7pm, Su 1-7pm; Sept.-June M-Sa 10am-5pm, Su 2-6pm.

Banks: First Trust Bank, 28-32 Main St. (tel. 4372 3476). Open M-Tu and Th-F 9:30am-4:30pm, W 10am-4:30pm. **24hr. ATM. Northern Bank,** 60 Main St. Open M 9:30am-5pm, Tu-F 10am-3:30pm. **24hr. ATM.**

Laundry: Craftsman, in the shopping center on Main St. (tel. 4372 3863), will wash, dry, and fold a 10lb. bag of laundry for £3.80. Open M-Sa 8am-5:30pm. **Dirty Duds,** 58A Valentia Pl. (tel. 4372 6190). £2.50 self-service wash, £2 dry. Open M-Sa 9am-6pm.

Camping Equipment: Hill Trekker, 115 Central Promenade (tel. 4372 3842). Mourne trail maps, hiking tips, info about guided tours, and hiking boots (£1.50 per day, £10 per week, deposit £10). Owned, though not always staffed, by knowledgeable hiking enthusiasts. Open Tu-W and Sa-Su 10am-5:30pm, Th 10am-4:45pm, F 10am-6:15pm.

Pharmacy: G. Maginn, 9 Main St. (tel. 4372 2923). Open M-Sa 9am-6pm. **Thornton's Chemist,** 49 Central Promenade (tel. 4372 3248). Open M-Sa 9am-6pm. **Emergency:** Dial 999 (including **Mountain Rescue**).

Police: South Promenade (tel. 4372 3583).

Post Office: 33-35 Central Promenade (tel. 4372 2418). Open M-W and F 9am-5:30pm, Th and Sa 9am-12:30pm. **Postal Code:** BT33 OAA.

Internet Access: The East Down Institute (tel. 4372 2451). From the bus station, 1 block inland, left onto Castlewellan Rd. Computers in the library. £3 per 30min., £5 per hour. Open M-F 8:30am-4:30pm.

▚ ACCOMMODATIONS AND CAMPING

B&Bs in this summer resort town range in price from affordable to sky high; fortunately, there is a hostel. Of the area's campsites, Tollymore Forest Park is probably the most scenic, but the Mournes themselves are a free and legal alternative.

Newcastle Youth Hostel (YHANI/HI), 30 Downs Rd. (tel. 4372 2133). Follow Railway St. toward the water and take a right onto Downs Rd. at the Percival Arms. The best bet for the budget traveler—central, on the waterfront, and cheap. Quarters are tight even for a hostel, but such discomforts are appeased by the prime location and the hospitality of the proprietress. Well-furnished kitchen. Dorms £8.25, under 18 £7.25; 6-person family apartment £35. Prices £1 higher for non-HI members. Lockers 50p. Laundry £2. Check-in 5pm-11:30pm.

Castlebridge House, 2 Central Promenade (tel. 4372 3209). Understandably popular, with cozy rooms and an ideal location overlooking the bay. £15.

Homeleigh, 7 Slievemoyne Park (tel. 4372 2305), the second left off Tullybrannigan Rd. A strangely pleasing mix of 1970s and Victorian decor greets you in Mrs. McBride's home. Guests rave about generous breakfasts. £14.

Drumrawn House, 139 Central Promenade (tel. 4372 6847), about a 15min. walk from the bus station. This Georgian townhouse has a marvelous sea view. £21.50.

Arundel, 23 Bryansford Rd. (tel. 4372 2232). Just off the southern end of Central Promenade (after the Anchor Bar). Comfy beds, a huge lounge, and a mountain view. £18.

Glenside Farm House, 136 Tullybrannigan Rd. (tel. 4372 2628). A standard B&B where you can fall asleep to the sound of bleating sheep. It's a long, if lovely, 1½ mi. walk from town (take Bryansford Rd. and follow signs for Tullybrannigan—or take a taxi). Clean, simple rooms. Small single £12; doubles £22.

Tollymore Forest Park, 176 Tullybrannigan Rd. (tel. 4372 2428), a 2 mi. walk along A2. Or take the "Busybus" which leaves the Newcastle Ulsterbus station at 10am and noon, more often during the high season (10min., 75p). Excellent **camping** facilities include showers, a cafe with delicious doughnuts, and 584 hectares of well-marked walks and gardens. Good Friday to Sept. £10 per tent or caravan; Oct. to Th before Easter £6.50. £1.50 for electricity.

FOOD

The nougat-like density of take-aways, candy stores, and ice cream shops on the waterfront could keep you on a permanent grease and sugar high. Well-rounded meals, however, can be found at reasonable prices.

Toscana, 47 Central Promenade. Leans towards things Italian. Individual pizzas £3-5, dinners £4-6. Bar snacks served 11am-11pm, pizza and dinner after 6pm.

The Strand, 53-55 Central Promenade. Satiates even ravenous diners with filling dinners (£5-6), each served with a generous basket of scones and tea.

Seasalt, 51 Central Promenade. The frugal gourmet will enjoy a variety of sandwiches (£2-3) made with Irish farmhouse cheeses, ready made salads, fine desserts, and other sundry delicacies.

The Cookie Jar, Main St. Sandwiches made to order and a wide selection of breads and baked goods. Open M-Sa 9am-5:30pm.

The Cygnet Coffee Shop, Savoy Ln. (tel. 4372 4758), just off Main St. near the bus station. A better-than-usual selection of light fare at less-than-usual prices. Sandwiches £1.50, entrees £3-4. Open daily Mar.-Nov. 10am-5:30pm.

PUBS

There are pubs-a-plenty in Newcastle. Most all of them lie on the waterfront.

Quinn's, 62 Main St. (tel. 4372 6400). This recently restored pub now sports a 50s-era interior. Live jazz, blues, and trad on weekends.

Anchor Bar, 9 Bryansford Rd. (tel. 4372 3344). A century-old pub, with stain glass windows depicting the ferocious Irish sea. Lunch £2-4, served noon-2:30pm.

Percy French, (tel. 4372 3175), in the Slieve Donard Hotel at the northern end of the beach. Boasts a classier drink. Mr. French was a popular Irish songwriter in the last century whose flowery lyrics still appeal to sentimentalists.

Donard Bar, in the Donard Hotel on Main Street. An older crowd convenes here to enjoy conversation, pints, and cushy couches.

The Central Park Nite Club, (tel. 4372 2487), on the south end of Central Promenade. Live bands in the lounge on weekends. Disco in the nightclub F-Su. Cover around £2.

THE MOURNE MOUNTAINS

Before heading for the hills, stop at the **Mourne Countryside Centre,** 91 Central Promenade (tel. 4372 4059), and the **Mourne Heritage Trust** just two doors down. A friendly and knowledgeable staff leads hikes and offers a broad selection of guides and maps of the mountains. Those planning short excursions can purchase *Mourne Mountain Walks* (£6), which describes 10 one-day hikes. Those planning to stay in the Mournes overnight should buy the *Mourne Country Outdoor Pursuits Map* (£5), a detailed topographical map. (Center open July-Aug. M-F 9am-5pm; winter hours vary.) If the center is closed, ask for maps at the tourist office and advice at Hill Trekker (see **Practical Information**). Seasoned hikers looking for company might want to join the **Mourne Rambling Group** (tel. 4372 4315), which sends groups into the Mournes each Sunday. Shuttlebuses run between Silent Valley and Ben Crom (June Sa-Su 1 per day, July-Aug. 3 daily; £2.15).

The **Mourne Wall,** built between 1904 and 1923, encircles 12 of the mountains just below their peaks. Following the length of the 22 mi. wall takes a strenuous eight hours; many people break it up with a night under the stars. The Mourne's highest peak, **Slieve Donard** (850 m.), towers above Newcastle. The trail to it is wide and well maintained, and paved in many places with flag and cobblestones (5hr. return). The record for running up and down is fabled to be 98 minutes. **Donard Park** provides the most direct access to the Mournes from Newcastle; it's convenient to both Slieve Donard and nearby **Slieve Commedagh** ("the mountain of watching"). The park lies on the corner of Central Promenade and Bryansford Rd. Follow the dirt path at the back of the carpark carefully (it crosses two bridges). It eventually joins the Glen River Path for about 1½ mi. to reach the Mourne Wall. At the wall, turn left for Slieve Donard, right for Slieve Commedagh. Those seeking a more remote trek might try **Slieve Bernagh** (739 m.) or **Slieve Binnian** (747 m.), most easily accessed from **Hare's Gap** and **Silent Valley,** respectively. The two craggy peaks, both with tremendous views, can be combined into a half-day, 12 mi. hike. A comprehensive walk will combine highlands, lowlands, mountains, and the coastal area to the south of town, or rolling farmland to the north. Most of the land in and around the Mournes is privately owned. Visitors should bear this in mind and treat the environs with respect (close those sheep gates!).

Wilderness **camping** is legal and popular. Common spots include the **Annalong Valley,** the shores of **Lough Shannagh,** and near the **Trassey River. Hare's Gap** and the shore of **Blue Lough** at the foot of Slievelamagan are also good places to pitch a tent. While camping around the Mourne Wall is allowed, camping in the forest itself is strictly prohibited because of the risk of forest fires. Remember to bring warm clothing since the mountains get cold and windy at night and Irish weather conditions are known to change suddenly. A local volunteer **Mountain Rescue** team (tel. 999) is available in case of emergencies.

◪ NEARBY FOREST PARKS

Three parks managed by the Department of Agriculture are just a hop, skip, and a jump from Newcastle. **Tollymore Forest Park** lies just 2 mi. west of town at 176 Tullybrannigan Rd. Within the park, ancient stone bridges, rushing waters, and very well-marked trails delight all ages. The Shimna River cuts the park in half from east to west. Four main trails, ranging from one to eight miles in length, afford glimpses of diverse wildlife including deer, foxes, badgers, and, if you're particularly quiet, otters. The "Rivers Trail" hike (3 mi.) encompasses most of the park and is highly recommended, as is the hike to the **viewpoint** (3½ mi.). (Tel. 4372 2428. Open daily 10am-10pm. £2, under 17 50p; £3.50 car.) The park is amply equipped with a campground (see p. 432), visitors center, cafe, and impressive outdoor arboretum. If you're not up for the rambling walk to Tollymore, take one of Ulsterbus's "Tollymore" shuttles from the Newcastle bus station (15min.; departs 10am, noon, and 4:30pm year-round, more frequently in July and Aug.; 75p).

Castlewellan Forest Park spreads itself out in the hills just north and east of the Mournes. Its entrance is at the top of the main street in Castlewellan. From the Newcastle bus station take Castlewellan Rd. into town. Turn left on Main St. at the roundabout and continue for 400m. (Tel. 4377 8664. Open M-F 10am-sunset, Sa-Su 10am-5pm. £3 per car. Call M-F 8:30am-4:30pm for info and site booking. **Camping** Easter-Sept. £10 per large tent, £6.50 small tent; Oct.-Easter £6.50; additional £1.50 for electricity.) The campground is opposite the library. The park contains easily accessible attractions: a Scottish baronial castle (now a Christian Conference Centre, not open to the public), an impressive **Sculpture Trail** (with sculptures made of natural materials), and the North's **National Arboretum.** The park's lake overflows with trout; single-day or seasonal fishing permits are available from the ranger station April to mid-October. Buses run from Newcastle to Castlewellan (10min.; M-F 26 per day, Sa 20 per day, Su 6 per day; 95p).

At the opposite end of town you'll find the **Murlough National Nature Reserve,** on Dundrum Rd. (A24) to Belfast. Home to sand dunes, heath, and woodlands, Murlough boasts marvelous swimming, as well as seal-watching during the fall moulting season. Plenty of critters can be observed throughout the year, including badgers, foxes, skylark, meadow pipits, and the endangered European insect species of marsh fritillary. To get there, take the Downpatrick or Belfast bus from Newcastle and get off at Murlough. (Tel. 4375 1467. Beach and walks open in daytime. £2 per car in high season; free other times.)

WARRENPOINT

A few miles down the coast from Newcastle, on the north side of Carlingford Lough, is the pretty harbor town of Warrenpoint. It first gained fame as a resort town in the 1800s, when having just a pretty beach was enough to satisfy tourists. Today, nearby Rostrevor is a large part of Warrenpoint's appeal. Rostrevor draws annual crowds to the area for the Fiddler's Green Festival, making Warrenpoint a hospitable source of accommodations. During the rest of the year, you can sit on the sea wall for hours and watch colorful spinnakers float across the water against the backdrop of the Mourne Mountains.

7 ORIENTATION AND PRACTICAL INFORMATION. The **bus station** is on **The Square,** with **Church St.** to the left and the waterfront to the right as you leave the station; **ferries** land at the other end of the waterfront. Pick up tourist info and free maps at the **tourist office,** 41 Church St. (tel. 4175 2256), just beyond The Square. (Open Sept.-June M-F 9am-5pm; July-Aug. M-F 9am-5pm, Sa noon-6pm.) **Ulster Bank,** 2 Charlotte St., **Northern Bank** on Queen St., and **First Trust** at The Square all have **24hr. ATMs.** The **Red Star Passenger Ferry** (tel. 4177 3070), runs a sporadic service across the Lough to Omeath, a town in the Republic (May-Aug., weather and tides permitting; £2 return). **Rent bicycles** at **Stewart's Cycles,** 14 Havelock Pl. (tel. 4177 3565), beside the Surgery Clinic on Marine Parade. (Also does repairs. £6 per day, £25 per week. Open M-Tu and Th-F 2-6pm.) **Ace Taxis** (tel. 4175 2666) will pick you up at any hour. **Walsh's Pharmacy,** 25 Church St. (tel. 4175 3661), is open M-Sa 9am-6pm, W 9am-1pm. In an **emergency** dial 999, no coins required. The **post office** (tel. 4175 2225) is at 9 Church St. (Open M-Tu and Th 8:30am-5:30pm, W 8:30am-1pm, F 9am-5:30pm, Sa 9am-12:30pm.) The local **postal code** is BT34 3HN.

▌◖▨ ACCOMMODATIONS, FOOD, AND PUBS. If you want a single and insist on luxury close to town, stay at the **Whistledown Inn,** 6 Seaview (tel. 4175 2697). This B&B is directly on the waterfront at the end of Church St., on the second floor of an enormous Victorian townhouse. (£25.) **The Mournes,** 16 Seaview, offers basic rooms with hot pot and TV. (£17.50.) Because B&Bs are a bit pricey here, those with cars might opt to stay in Newcastle.

Warrenpoint has eateries a plenty, and most have a take-out option ideal for beach picnics. **Diamonds Restaurant,** The Square (tel. 4175 2053), is always packed with happy locals devouring burgers (£3), pasta (£4-5), seafood (£4-5), and desserts. (Open M-Th 10am-7:30pm, F-Su noon-10pm.) The **Genoa Cafe,** next door, boasts about having served fish and chips to Warrenpoint since 1910. Today the restaurant sports a thoroughly modern decor, but the fish and chips (£1.80 and less) are deep-fried in tradition. Opened in 1854, **Bennetts,** 21 Church St. (tel. 4175 2314), is a local favorite for lunch and a pint. (Lunch daily 12:30-3pm, dinner and bar snacks 5-9:30pm.) For a quick bite, try the **Central Cafe,** 32 Church St. (tel. 4175 2693), across from the tourist office, the closest you'll get to a diner atmosphere. (Sandwiches under £2.)

Pubs fill in the gaps between restaurants around the Square. The **Crown Entertainment Complex,** The Square (tel. 4175 2917), has two floors of fun: an old-style bar on the first that stages music Wednesday through Sunday, a DJed "fun club" in back, and "Mingles' Nightclub" with disco on the second floor Friday and Saturday. (Cover £2-4.) **Jack Ryan's** offers live music Thursday to Sunday, and pub grub. (Most dishes £4-5; served 12:30-2:30pm, 5:30pm till closing.) Facing the Crown is **Cearnógs** ("the square"), 14 The Square (tel. 4177 4077), where young crowds pour in on weekends for good *craic.*

NEAR WARRENPOINT: ROSTREVOR

The village of Rostrevor lies 3 mi. from Warrenpoint along A2, and hosts several lively festivals during the summer. Thousands of people gather here each August to witness the **Maiden of the Mournes Festival;** maidens from Ireland, Europe, and some parts of the U.S. gather to display their personalities and talents. This event is preceded by the **Fiddler's Green Festival.** During this late-July extravaganza, fans (and performers) of traditional Irish music, storytelling, and art gather to share good *craic.* (Contact Tommy or Sam Sands, tel. 38577.) Rostrevor is also known for **Kilbroney Park** which contains Rostrevor Forest, one of the few remaining virgin Irish Oak forests in Ireland, as well as the usual assortment of wildlife, wild walks, and wild picnic facilities. (Open daily dawn-dusk. Free.)

ARMAGH

The pagan worshippers who built huge ceremonial mounds at Navan Fort named their city Ard Macha (Macha's Height) after the legendary Queen Macha. According to tradition, St. Patrick came to Armagh (arm-AH) in the 5th century to convert the pagan hot-spot. Since then, Armagh has become Ireland's ecclesiastical capital for both the Catholic Church and the Church of Ireland, amassing cathedrals and monuments along the way.

⬕ TRANSPORTATION

Buses: Buses stop at the station on Lonsdale Rd. To **Belfast** (1hr.; M-F 20 per day, Sa 15 per day, Su 8 per day; £5) and **Enniskillen** (2hr., M-Sa 3 per day, £5.50).

Local Transportation: Intercity **buses** (tel. 3752 2266) stop at The Mall West. Two refurbished 40s-style **coaches** cart tourists from sight to sight in summer. Schedules available at the tourist office.

Bike Rental: Brown's Bikes, 21A Scotch St. (tel. 3752 2782). £7 per day, £30 per week. Helmets £1 per day. Open M-Sa 9am-5:30pm.

⚋ ORIENTATION AND PRACTICAL INFORMATION

English St., Thomas St., and **Scotch St.** comprise Armagh's city center. Just to the east lies **The Mall,** a former race course that was converted into a grassy park when betting was deemed inappropriate to the city's sanctity. Just west of the city center, two cathedrals sit on neighboring hills: the Catholic Cathedral lifts two neo-Gothic spires, while a medieval-looking tower represents the Church of Ireland.

Tourist Office: Old Bank Building, 40 English St. (tel. 3752 1800). From the bus drop facing The Mall, turn left, walk past The Mall, and turn left up the hill onto College St. The tourist office is 15 yd. down the first street on the left. Pick up the *Armagh Visitor Magazine* (free), with a map of all the major sites. Open M-Sa 9am-5pm, Su 1-5pm.

Bank: Northern Bank, 78 Scotch St. (tel. 3752 2004). **ATM.** Open M 9:30am-5pm, Tu-F 10am-3:30pm.

Pharmacy: J. W. Gray, corner of Russell and English St. Open M-Sa 9am-6pm. Rotating Sunday schedule printed in the Thursday paper.

Emergency: Dial 999; no coins required. **Police:** Newry Rd. (tel. 3752 3311).

Hospital: Tower Hill (tel. 3752 2341), off College Hill.

Internet Access: Armagh Computer World, 43 Scotch Street (tel. 3751 0002). Open M-Sa 9am-6pm. £3 per half-hour.

Post Office: 31 Upper English St. (tel. 3751 0313). *Poste Restante* mail held across the street at 46 Upper English St. (tel. 522 856). Open M-F 9am-5:30pm, Sa 9am-12:30pm. **Postal code:** BT617AA.

⬕ ACCOMMODATIONS

Armagh's **hostel (YHANI/HI),** behind the old health clinic, (tel. 3751 1800) is sparklingly clean and huge. From the tourist office, turn left twice and follow Abbey St. for two blocks until the hostel appears on your right. All rooms have TV and bath. Dinner and breakfast are available. (6- and 4-bed dorms £10.75, doubles £11.50; £1 off for members. Laundry £3. Reception 7:30am-midnight; daytime lockout in winter.) The **Padua Guest House,** 63 Cathedral Rd. (tel. 3752 2039), is just past the Catholic Cathedral. Mrs. O'Hagen and her large doll collection greet guests with a cup of tea. (£16.) Make a right on Desart Rd., and turn left 50 yd. down to reach **Desart Guest House,** 99 Cathedral Rd. (tel. 3752 2387). It's a formidable mansion, but the rooms are sunny, clean, and plush. (£15.) **Gosford Forest Park** (tel. 3755 1277; ranger tel. 3755 2169), off A28, offers **camping** 7 mi. southeast of Armagh. Take the #40 bus to Market Hill. (Easter-Sept. £8.50 per 2-person tent, Oct.-Easter £5.50.)

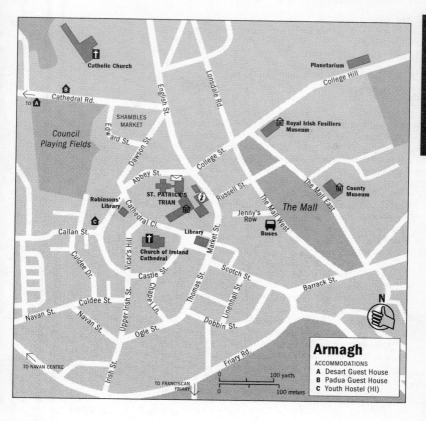

FOOD AND PUBS

Weekdays it's hard to find a restaurant in Armagh that stays open after 6pm. Armagh's few eateries are scattered across English and Scotch St. Your best bet may be to pick up groceries at **Emerson's** (tel. 3752 2846) on Scotch St. (Open M-W 8:45am-5:30pm, Th-F 9am-9pm, Sa 8:45am-6pm.) The **Basement Cafe** (tel. 3752 4311) sits under the Armagh Film House on English St. next to the library and serves cheap meals to cool cats. (Sandwiches ₤1.85. Open M-Sa 9am-5:30pm.) The **Rainbow Restaurant,** 13 Upper English St. (tel. 3752 5391), serves standard lunch fare buffet style. (4-course lunch special ₤3.50; lunch served noon-2pm. Open M-Sa 8:30am-5:30pm.) **Our Ma's Cafe,** 2 Lower English St. (tel. 3751 1289), is clever, cheap, and delicious. (3-course lunch ₤3.75. Open M-Sa 9am-5:30pm, Su 9am-3:30pm.) When the fruits fall from Armagh's apple trees, **Johnston's Bakery,** 9 Scotch St. (tel. 522 995), turns them into delicious treats. (Apple turnovers 30p. Open M-Sa 9am-6pm.) **The Station Bar,** 3 Lower English St. (tel. 3752 3731), looks like a dive, but is one of the most popular pubs in town, with trad two nights a week in winter and good conversation year-round. **Harry Hoots,** Railway St. (tel. 522 103), sounds and is fun. **The Northern Bar** (tel. 3752 7315) across the street provides live entertainment and dancing three nights a week at 9:30pm.

👁 SIGHTS

Armagh's twin cathedrals preside impressively over the city. The **Church of Ireland Cathedral of St. Patrick** is a 19th century restoration of a 13th century structure that enlarged upon the 5th century original attributed to Patrick himself. The cathedral is the final resting place of the great Irish King Brian Ború (see **Early Christians and Vikings,** p. 7). It also contains an Iron Age sculpture of a king with a prosthetic arm. (Tel. 3752 3142. Open daily Apr.-Sept. 10:30am-5pm; Oct.-Mar. 10:30am-4pm. Tours June-Aug. M-Sa 11:30am and 2:30pm. Free.) Across town, the **Catholic Church of St. Patrick** raises its spires from Cathedral Rd. Opened in 1873, the cathedral's imposing exterior and exquisite mosaic interior are marred only by the ultra-modern granite sanctuary, which appears to be a combination of pagan and Martian design. Dark water stains on lower sections of the cathedral walls are legacies of the Famine, when work on the cathedral halted and the half-completed building was left exposed to the elements. (Open daily 9am-6pm. Free.)

In the center of town, **St. Patrick's Trian** shares a building with the tourist office. Most of the exhibits emphasize St. Patrick's role in Armagh, although his link to the town is historically ambiguous. The **Armagh Story** is a walk-through display and audio-visual presentation in which plaster Vikings, priests, and pagan warriors relate the lengthy history of the town. A smaller, fanciful display geared for children recreates Swift's Land of Lilliput. (Tel. 3752 1801. Open July-Aug. M-Sa 10am-5:30pm, Su 1-6pm; Sept.-June M-Sa 10am-5pm, Su 2-5pm. £3.35, students £2.50.) Up College Hill north of The Mall is the **Armagh Observatory,** founded in 1790 by Archbishop Robinson (see below). Would-be astronomers can observe the modern weather station and a refractory telescope dating from 1885. The **Robinson Dome** provides self-guided tours. (Tel. 3752 2928.) Celestial wonders await in the **Planetarium,** College Hill, where a 3cm chunk of Mars is on display. Booking ahead is strongly recommended, as seating is limited. (Tel. 523 689. £3.50, students £2.50.)

At the **Armagh County Museum,** on the east side of The Mall, undiscriminating historians have crammed a panoply of 18th century objects—old wedding dresses, pictures, stuffed birds, jewelry, and militia uniforms—into huge wooden cabinets. (Tel. 3752 3070. Open M-Sa 10am-5pm. Free.) The **Royal Irish Fusiliers Museum,** The Mall East, houses the treasure of over 150 years of the business of war. (Tel. 522 911. Open M-F 10am-12:30pm and 1:30-4pm. £1.50, students £1.) On Friary Rd., south of the town center, the ruins of the 13th century **Franciscan Friary,** the longest-standing friary in Ireland, occupy a peaceful green corner of the **Palace Demesne.** The palace and its chapel and stables were built by the 18th century Archbishop of Armagh, Richard Robinson, in an effort to rebuild the entire city. Although the palace itself is closed to the public, the **Palace Stables Heritage Centre** puts on a slick multi-media show about "A Day in the Life" of the closed palace. (Tel. 3752 9629. Open Apr.-Sept. M-Sa 10am-7pm, Su 1-7pm; Oct.-Mar. M-Sa 10am-5pm, Su 2-5pm. £2.80, students £2.20.) Peek at a first edition of *Gulliver's Travels,* covered with Swift's own scrawled comments, at the **Armagh Public Library,** built on Abbey St. in 1771. (Tel. 3752 3142. Open M-F 10am-12:30pm and 2-4pm.) One might prefer to spend a nice day at **Gosford Forest Park,** 7 mi. southeast of Armagh, which includes a castle, old walled garden, poultry sheds, and miles of nature trails. (Open daily 10am-sunset. £2 per car, £1 per person.)

Armagh holds an annual **Comhaltas Ceoltori Traditional Music Festival** around the first week of June and an arts festival in October. In mid-August, the Ulster **Road Bowls Finals** are held throughout Armagh. In this popular local game, contestants compete to see who can throw an 8 oz. solid ball 4km in the fewest throws. Negotiating the bumps and turns in the road can be difficult, injecting an element of brain into this contest of brawn. **The Apple Blossom Festival** (tel. 3752 9600), in the second week of May, brings a number of events to the city and culminates in a lavish May Ball. On March 17, people come from far and near to celebrate the feast of the city's patron on **St. Patrick's Day.**

THE BUCKFAST CURE Buckfast tonic wines, produced by the Benedictine monks of the Buckfast Abbey, are sold in two places: Devon and Co. Armagh. While the government warning on the orange label informs the would-be drinker that "Tonic wine does not imply health-giving or medicinal properties," "Bo," as it is popularly termed, has gained near-mythic stature with a certain section of the Armagh community. Though some might pass it off as Bacchus' gift to the wino, those who make the drink a part of their lives know better. Swearing that it's an experience as much like drunkenness as Budweiser is like Guinness, aficionados advise restrained consumption for first-time Buckfast drinkers. Evidence of its effects appears on Sunday mornings, when broken green Buckfast bottles are strewn across Armagh's streets. It's made of, among other things, .009% vanillin, .05% caffeine, .65% sodium glycerophosphate (to keep the drinker very regular), and 15% alcohol. At £5 for .75 liters, it's dirt cheap.

NEAR ARMAGH: NAVAN FORT (EMAIN MACHA)

On the outskirts of Armagh, the mysterious Navan Fort, also called Emain Macha (AHM-win maka), was the capital of the Kings of Ulster for 800 years. It may look like a grassy mound of dirt but with a little imagination and a lot of historical knowledge, you might see extensive defensive fortifications and elaborate religious paraphernalia on the site. Where the mound now stands, a huge wooden structure 40 yd. in diameter was constructed in 94 BC, filled with stones, promptly burnt to the ground in a religious rite, and covered with soil. In legend, Queen Macha founded the fort, although it is also associated with St. Patrick, who probably chose Ard Macha as a base for Christianity because of its relative proximity to this pagan stronghold. (Always open. Free.) **Navan Centre,** built deep into a nearby hill, presents a fascinating hour-long program of films and interactive exhibits on the archaeological evidence of the hills and the legends associated with the site. The center is on Killylea Rd. (A28), 2 mi. west of Armagh; the fort is a 10min. walk from the center. (Tel. (01861) 525 550. Open M-Sa 10am-6pm. £3.95, students £3.)

LOUGH NEAGH AND OXFORD ISLAND

A giant once scooped a heap of prime Ulster real estate out of the ground and hurled it into the Irish sea, creating the Isle of Man and Lough Neagh. The U.K.'s largest lake sits smack in the center of Northern Ireland, touching five of the North's six counties. Though not yet appreciated in Ireland, the Lough Neagh eel is considered a great delicacy on the continent. Birdwatching, water-skiing, and various aquatic activities are just about the only amusements in the towns around the Lough; its shores are best seen as daytrips from Belfast or Armagh.

On the southeast shore of the Lough, the **Lough Neagh Discovery Centre,** Oxford Island National Nature Reserve, Craigavon, contains acres of wooded parkland for exploration, with or without a guided tour. The lakeshore hosts hundreds of bird species. Audio-visual displays inside the center detail the lake's ecosystem and wildlife. Boat rides to the islands run irregularly on Sundays. (Tel. (01762) 322 205. Open Apr.-Sept. daily 10am-7pm; Oct.-Mar. W-Su 10am-5pm. Last admission 1hr. before closing. Audio-visual displays £2.) The **Kinnego Caravan Park,** Kinnego Marina, Lurgan (tel. (01762) 327 573), greets campers. (£6 per 2-person tent.)

Just off M1, 10 mi. north of Armagh, **Peatlands Park** contains nature reserves, an interpretive center with interactive displays on the natural and human history of peat bogs, and a small railroad that was originally used to carry turf out of the bogs. Turf-cutting demonstrations take place on busy days. (Tel. (01762) 851 102. Park open daily Easter-Sept. 9am-9pm; Oct.-Easter 9am-5pm. Visitor center open June-Sept. daily 2-6pm. Both free; railroad £1, seniors 50p.)

ANTRIM AND DERRY

A coastal road skirts the northern edge of Co. Antrim and Derry, traveling across a long distance of rapidly changing geological, commercial, and cultural phenomena. As the road meanders west from Belfast, stodgy and industrial Larne gives way to lovely little seaside towns. The nine wooded glens of Antrim, stomping grounds of the Ancient Ulaid dynasty, squat in valleys between tame mountains. Near the midpoint of the island's northern coast, fantastic Giant's Causeway spills out into the ocean. This moderately trafficked middle section of the coast road is a cyclist's paradise. Industrialization resumes past the Causeway when the road hits Portrush and Portstewart, where carnival lights create stunning scenery. The road finally arrives at Derry, the North's second largest city, where a turbulent history and recent redevelopment projects contribute to a fascinating cityscape.

LARNE

The **ferries** that depart for Scotland from the harbor are the only worthwhile reason to pass through industrial Larne. This route is less frequented since the institution of the more convenient Hoverspeed SeaCat service to Belfast (see **By Ferry**, p. 33). **P&O Ferries** (tel. (0990) 980777) operates passages from Larne to Cairnryan, Scotland. Travelers should book ahead and arrive 45min. early, as there are always standby passengers waiting for your seat. The center of Larne Town is 15min. inland from the harbor.

🛈 PRACTICAL INFORMATION. The bus and train stations lie adjacent to a roundabout, two minutes from the town center; the tourist office and town center are well sign-posted from the roundabout. To reach town, take the first right outside of the ferry port. As the road curves left, it becomes **Curran Rd.** and then **Main St. Trains** (Belfast office tel. 9089 9411 or 9023 0671, Larne office tel. 2826 0604) chug from Central Station in **Belfast** to Larne Town and Larne Harbour (50min.; M-F 20 per day, Sa 16 per day, Su 6 per day; £3.20.) **Buses** (tel. 2827 2345) leave frequently from Station Rd. for Laganside Station in **Belfast** (1½hr., express 50min.; M-F 14 per day, Sa 15 per day, Su 2 per day). Those departing on a ferry from Larne should ensure that their train or bus terminates in Larne Harbour rather than in Larne Town, a 15min. walk away. The **tourist office,** Narrow Gauge Rd. (tel. 2826 0088), has loads of info, a free town map, and **internet access.** If you're just off the boat, the 20min. video overview of the sights of Northern Ireland is worth a view. The staff books accommodations in the North, the Republic, and Scotland. (Open July-Aug. M-F 9am-6pm, Sa 9am-5pm; Sept.-Oct. and Mar. M-F 9am-5pm; Easter-June M-Sa 9am-5pm.) Info available 24hr. from the computer on the building exterior. **Northern Bank,** 19 Main St. (tel. 2827 6311), has a **24hr. ATM.** (Open M and W-F 9:30am-5pm, Tu 10am-3:30pm, Sa 9:30am-12:30pm.) **Ulsterbank,** 9 Upper Cross St. (tel. 2827 5757), also has a **24hr. ATM.** (Open M-F 9:30am-4:30pm.) Larne's **post office,** 98 Main St. (tel. 2826 0489), feels an affinity for the **postal code** BT4 01RE. (Open M-F 9am-5:30pm, Sa noon-5:30pm.)

▮▩▨ ACCOMMODATIONS, FOOD, AND PUBS. Larne's not really the sort of town that people want to stay in. But if you're too weary to move on, there's no shortage of beds. B&Bs most convenient to both the harbor and the bus and train stations and adjacent streets are along Curran Rd. The clean rooms in Mrs. McKane's **Killyneedan,** 52 Bay Rd. (tel. 2827 4943), are stocked with TVs, hotpots, and decorative mugs. (£15, with bath £16.) Bay Rd. intersects Curran Rd. just before the ferry terminal. **The Curran Caravan Park,** 131 Curran Rd. (tel. 2827 5505), midway between the harbor and town, has congested caravan and tent grounds. Be sure to pause reflectively before Larne's Ulster-American Memorial Statue just outside the park gates. (£4.50 per 2-person tent, £1.50 per extra person.)

The giant **Co-op Superstore**, Station Rd. (tel. 2826 0737), next to the bus station, has an enormous selection. (Open M-W 9am-9pm, Th-F 9am-10pm, Sa 9am-8pm, Su 1-6pm.) The main street of town is littered with cheap sandwich shops, all basically equivalent in value and quality. **Chekker's Wine Bar**, 33 Lower Cross St. (tel. 2827 5305), serves a broad selection of bistro food in a take-your-time atmosphere. (Most meals ₤3-5; food served daily noon-9pm.) The cozy, lamp-lit **Bailie**, 111-113 Main St. (tel. 2827 3947), serves congratulatory pints to brave sea travelers. (Entrees ₤4-5; food served 12:30-8pm. Open 11:30am until closing.)

GLENS OF ANTRIM

North of Larne, nine lush green valleys, or "glens," slither from the hills and high moors of Co. Antrim down to the seashore. The villages along the coast provide beds and basic sustenance for glen-wanderers, as well as a glimpse into the cultural traditions of rural Northern Ireland. A2 connects the small towns at the foot of each glen. The glens and the mountains and waterfalls within them can best be seen by making daytrips inland from one of the coastal villages. The area's only hostel is in Cushendall (see p. 445).

Bus service in the glens exists on a limited scale. Two **Ulsterbus** routes serve the area year-round (Belfast tel. 9032 0011, Larne tel. 2827 2345). Bus #162 from **Belfast** stops in **Larne, Ballygally, Glenarm,** and **Carnlough** (M-F 7 per day, Sa 6 per day, Su 3 per day) and sometimes continues to **Waterfoot, Cushendall,** and **Cushendun** (M-F 5 per day, Sa 3 per day). Bus #150 runs between **Ballymena** and **Glenariff** (M-Sa 4 per day) then **Waterfoot, Cushendall,** and **Cushendun** (M-F 5 per day, Sa 3 per day). #150 also connects to **Belfast** via **Cushendun, Cushendall, Waterfoot,** and **Glenariff** (M-Sa 3 per day). The summertime Antrim Coaster follows the coast road from **Belfast** to **Coleraine,** stopping at every town along the way (late May to early July M-Sa 2 per day, early July-late Sept. daily 2 per day). Cycling is fabulous. The coast road from Ballygally to Cushendun is both scenic and flat; once the road leaves Cushendun, however, it becomes hilly enough to make even motorists groan. The Cushendall hostel **rents bikes.** Hitching is difficult, and the winding, narrow road between the cliffs and the sea wall make drivers feel less guilty about not stopping. Crossroads are the best places to try one's luck, but *Let's Go* sees hitchhiking as the wrong path to follow in life.

GLENARM

Six flat, winding, coastal miles lead through gradually less polluted and populated skylines to arrive at pristine Glenarm. Glenarm ("glen of the army") was once the chief dwelling place of the MacDonnell clan. The village is comprised of several centuries-old houses, a couple of pubs, and a wealth of short walks. The **madman's window** appears on the right just before you enter town. The natural formation earned its name when an artist jumped to his death from it. A huge arch at the top of Altmore St. is the entrance to **Glenarm Forest,** where trails trace the river's path for miles. (Open daily 9am to dusk.) **Glenarm Castle,** nestled just off the main street behind the trees north of the river, is the current residence of the 13th Earl of Antrim. Its 17th century gate is visible from Castle St. and open to the public annually on July 14 and 15; the castle's gardens are open year-round and entered by way of the left fork off the Ballymena road past town towards Cushendall. The town also boasts both a heritage trail and a walk along a former water-duct; brochures on both are available at the tourist office or from B&B proprietors. The **Ulster Way** trail passes through town, if you're up for the hike (see p. 73). The **Glenarm Festival** brings this sleepy town to life during the first week of July with events ranging from an eating competition to the multi-categoried Best-Kept Garden/Basket/Window-box/Tub Contest.

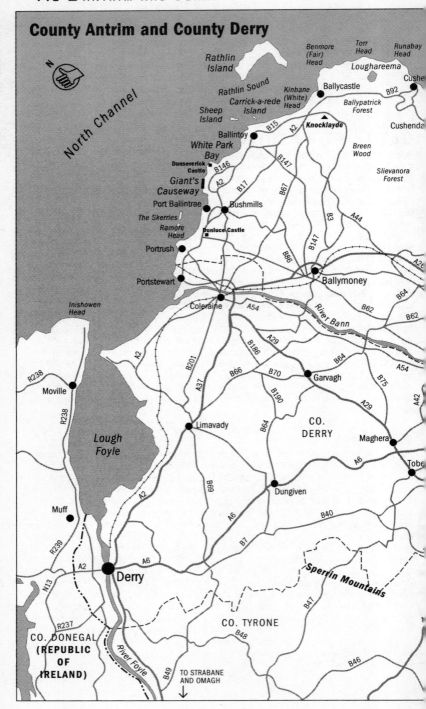

County Antrim and County Derry

N

North Channel

Rathlin Island

Rathlin Sound

Carrick-a-rede Island

Sheep Island

Kinbane (White) Head

Benmore (Fair) Head

Torr Head

Runabay Head

Cushe

Loughareema

Ballycastle

B92

Ballypatrick Forest

Cushenda

Ballintoy

B15

A2

Knocklayde

Breen Wood

Slievanora Forest

White Park Bay

Dunseverick Castle

B146

Giant's Causeway

A2

B17

B147

B67

B3

A44

Port Ballintrae

Bushmills

B147

The Skerries

Ramore Head

Dunluce Castle

Portrush

B86

A2

Portstewart

Ballymoney

B62

B64

B62

Coleraine

A54

River Bann

A54

A29

B186

B64

A42

B201

B66

B70

Garvagh

B75

Inishowen Head

A2

B190

A29

R238

A37

B64

CO. DERRY

Maghera

Moville

R238

Limavady

Tobe

Lough Foyle

B69

Dungiven

A6

Muff

A6

B40

R239

B7

Sperrin Mountains

Derry

A6

A2

N13

R237

CO. TYRONE

B47

CO. DONEGAL (REPUBLIC OF IRELAND)

River Foyle

B49

B48

B46

TO STRABANE AND OMAGH

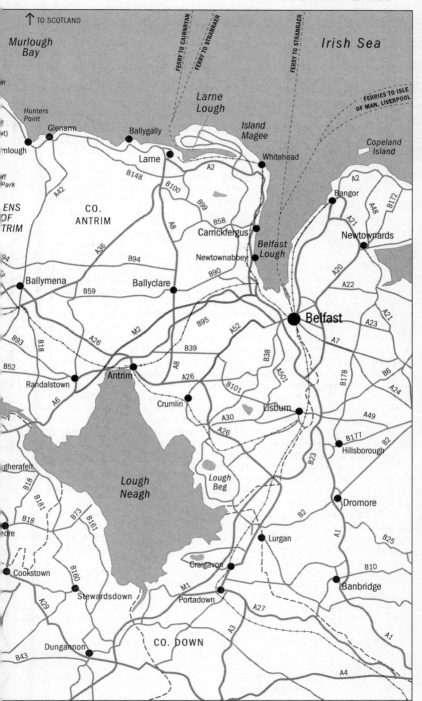

The **tourist office** (tel. 2884 1087), in the town council building beside the Bridge, provides friendly advice on the attractions of the area. (Open by demand, but summer hours generally run Tu 9am-3pm, W noon-3pm, Th-F 9am-noon.) Glenarm's **post office** (tel. 2884 1218) is halfway down Toberwine St. (Open M-Tu and Th-F 9am-1pm and 2-5:30pm, W and Sa 9am-12:30pm.) The **postal code** is BT44 0AP.

The period furniture and exposed wooden beams at **Nine Glens B&B,** 18 Toberwine St. (tel. 2884 1590), have aged as well as Glenarm itself. The bedrooms, however, are completely modern. Fresh fruit and tea available all day. (£15 with bath.) **Margaret's B&B,** 10 Altmore St. (tel. 2884 1307), provides comfortable rooms with 1950s decor. (£14.) The **Spar Market,** 4 Toberwine St. (tel. 2884 1219), supplies your picnic needs. (Open M-Tu and Th-Sa 9am-6pm, W 9am-5pm.) Across the street, the **Gallery Coffee Shop,** 7 Toberwine St., is a showcase of country home cooking. (Most meals £3-4. Open daily 10:30am-9pm.) **Poacher's Pocket,** 1 New Rd. (tel. 2884 1221), serves meaty-heavy plates. (Entrees £6-7, burgers £3.50; food served daily noon-8pm.) **The Coast Road Inn,** 3-5 Toberwine St. (tel. 2884 1207), draws a more mature and sedate clientele. The **Bridge End Tavern,** 1-3 Toberwine St., is nothing fancy, just drinks and good company.

WATERFOOT AND GLENARIFF

Nine miles farther up the coast, the village of Waterfoot guards Antrim's broadest glen, Glenariff, often deemed the most beautiful of the nine. Thackeray dubbed Glenariff "Switzerland in miniature," presumably because of its steep and rugged landscape; numbered bank accounts and trilingual skiers are rare. The glen is contained within the very large **Glenariff Forest Park,** 4 mi. south of the village along Glenariff Rd. (A43 toward Ballymena). The **bus** between **Cushendun** and **Ballymena** (#150) stops at the official park entrance (M-F 5 per day, Sa 3 per day). If you're walking from Waterfoot, however, you can enter the park 1½ mi. downhill of the official entrance by taking the road that branches left toward the Manor Lodge Restaurant. Cars can park in either the official car park or the Manor Lodge's parking lot, but you'll have to pay pedestrian admission charges if you enter Glenariff from Manor Lodge. (Tel. 2175 8769 or 2175 8232. Open daily 10am-8pm. £3 per car or £1.50 per adult pedestrian, 50p per child pedestrian.)

Once inside the park, you are confronted with a wealth of trails ranging from a half-mile to five miles round-trip; all trails pass the Glenariff and Inver Rivers and the three waterfalls that supply them. The most stunning walk is the **Waterfall Trail,** marked by blue triangles: it follows the cascading, fern-lined Glenariff River from the park entrance to the Manor Lodge (1 mi. from entrance to lodge, 3 mi. round-trip). Other trails lead to more subtle and less frequented beauty. All of the walks officially begin and end at the car park, where you will also find the **Glenariff Tea House** (tel. 2565 8769). This bay-windowed restaurant offers fresh snacks (sandwiches £1.75), exotically seasoned meals (£5-6), and free **maps** of the park's trails. (Open daily Easter-Sept. 11am-6pm.) The entrance to the **Moyle Way,** a 17 mi. hike from Glenariff to Ballycastle, is directly across from the official park entrance. Ask a ranger for details.

Glenariff Forest Park Camping, 98 Glenariff Rd. (tel. 2175 8232), encourages travelers to pitch a tent. (Tents £9, off-season £6.) In Waterfoot, closer to the comfort of civilization, **Lurig View B&B,** 4 Lurig View, Glen Rd. (tel. 2177 1618), off Garron Rd. about a half-mile past town on the waterfront, provides big, comfy beds and tasty, enormous breakfasts. (£16, off-season £15.)

Waterfoot is a one-street town, with two charismatic pubs. **The Mariners' Bar,** 7 Main St. (tel. 2177 1330), has live music of various sorts on Friday and Saturday nights. Across the street, **Bar-a-Hooley,** 4-6 Main St. (tel. 2177 2906), has indoor and outdoor *craic* with a bar and a beer garden. The **Cellar Bar,** downstairs, has live music ranging from country to trad on weekends. **Angela's Restaurant and Bakery,** 32 Main St. (tel. 2177 1700), run out of a family home, serves home-cooked meals with cheeky names like Kiss the Blarney Cake. (Most meals £3-4.) The back patio has grand views of Lurigethan Hill, to the left, and Garron Point, to the right. (Open daily 9am-5pm, takeaway 6pm-midnight.) **Kearney's Cost Cutter,** 21 Main St. (tel. 2177 1213), is the place to stock up before your hike through Glenariff. (Open M-Sa 8am-10:30pm, Su 8am-9pm.)

The road from Waterfoot to Cushendall may scarcely be a mile, but it's jam-packed. The **coastal caves** that line the Coast Rd. have served as everything from a school to a blacksmith's shop. Their most famous inhabitant was "Nanny of the Caves," a 19th century *poitín* brewer who lived in her two-compartment cave-home for 50 years. The lucrative business kept Nun Marry, as she was legally known, alive to the ripe old age of 100. Just beyond the caves is the unmistakable **Red Arch,** carved out of sandstone by wind and water. On top of the arch lie the ruined walls of Red Bay Castle, built by Scottish exiles in the 13th century and currently being renovated. The arch's underside has been reinforced with concrete.

CUSHENDALL

Cushendall is nicknamed the capital of the Glens, most likely because its village center consists of *four* streets instead of just one. The additional storefronts house a surplus of goods, services, and pubs. Moors and hills border the town. Cushendall is the closest human settlement to three of the nine glens: Glenballyeamon, Glenaan, and Glencorp.

▆ TRANSPORTATION

Buses: Ulsterbus #150 runs to **Ballymena** via **Waterfoot** and **Glenariff** (M-F 5 per day, Sa 3 per day). Ulsterbus #162 goes to **Larne** via **Waterfoot, Glenarm,** and **Ballygally** (M-F 3 per day, Sa-Su 2 per day). July-Aug., the **Antrim Coaster** (#252) runs through Cushendall toward **Portrush, Larne,** and **Belfast** (2 per day).

Bike Rental: Ardclinis Activity Centre, 11 High St. (tel. 2177 1340). Mountain bikes £10 per day; deposit £50. Wetsuits £5 per day. They also provide advice on hill-walking, canoeing, and gorge-walking.

▇ ORIENTATION AND PRACTICAL INFORMATION

The busiest section of Cushendall is its crossroads. From the center of town, **Mill St.** turns into **Chapel Rd.** and heads toward Ballycastle; **Shore Rd.** extends in the other direction toward Glenarm and Larne. **Hill St.** leads uphill from **Bridge Rd.,** a section of the **Coast Rd.** that continues towards the sea at Waterfoot.

Tourist Office: 25 Mill St. (tel. 2177 1180), near the bus stop at the Cushendun end of town, has a wealth of info. Open July-Sept. M-F 10am-1pm and 2:30-5pm, Sa 10am-1pm; Oct. to mid.-Sept. and Mar.-June Tu-Sa 10am-1pm.

Banks: Northern Bank, 5 Shore St. (tel. 2177 1243). Open M 9:30am-12:30pm and 1:30-5pm, Tu-F 10am-12:30pm and 1:30-3:30pm. **24hr. ATM** accepts Visa, Master-Card, and Cirrus.

Camping Equipment: O'Neill's Country Sports, 25 Mill St. (tel. 2177 2009). Fishing tackle, tents, and maps. Open Apr.-Sept. M-Sa 9:30am-6pm, Su 12:30pm-4:30pm; Oct.-Mar. M-Sa 9:30am-6pm.

Pharmacy: E.L. Gillan Pharmacy, 8 Mill St. (tel. 2177 1523). Open M-Sa 9am-6pm.

Post Office: Mill St. (tel. 2177 1201). Open M and W-F 9am-1pm and 2-5:30pm, Tu and Sa 9am-12:30pm. **Postal code:** BT44 0RR.

▙ ACCOMMODATIONS

Cushendall Youth Hostel (YHANI/HI), 42 Layde Rd. (tel. 2177 1344). This YHANI hostel occupies a lovely spot just ½ mi. from town. Layde Rd. is the left-hand (uphill) fork from Shore Rd. A recent architectural tune-up generated a gargantuan kitchen and dining area. 10- to 14-bed dorms £8.25, under 18 £7.25. Continental breakfast £2. Sheets included. Laundry £2. **Bike rental** £6 per day, £4 per half-day. Reception open 7:30am-10:30am and 5-11pm.

■ **Glendale,** Mrs. Mary O'Neill's, 46 Coast Rd. (tel. 2177 1495). It's hard to imagine a warmer welcome. Rooms are huge and as soothing to the weary traveler as is the proprietress's colorful company. Tea, coffee, biscuits, and bath in each room. £16.

Cushendall Caravan Park, 62 Coast Rd. (tel. 2177 1699), adjacent to Red Bay Boatyard. Free showers but no kitchen. 2-person tent £5; family tent £8.50. Wash £1, dry £1.50 per 15min.

Glenville Caravan Park, 22 Layde Rd. (tel. 2177 1520), 1 mi. out of town. Showers, toilets, and a splendid view of the ocean. £4 per tent.

■■ FOOD AND PUBS

Spar Market, 2 Coast Rd. (tel. 2177 1763), just past Bridge Rd., has a plentiful fruit and veggie selection. (Open daily 7:30am-10pm.)

Harry's, 10-12 Mill St. (tel. 2177 2022). Bar snacks break the boundaries of their nomenclature with everything from orange to cointreau sauces on their meats; vegetarian entrees on request. Bar snacks around £5, restaurant meals £2-3 more; food served daily noon-9:30pm.

Gillan's Home Bakery and Coffee Shop, 6 Mill St. (tel. 2177 1404). Simple food that you could cook yourself for only a few pence less. Sandwiches (£1.35) can be polished off with baked goods that you probably couldn't cook yourself. Most meals around £2. Open M and W-Sa 9am-6pm, Tu 9am-3pm.

The Half Door, 6 Bridge St. (tel. 2177 1300). Take-away pizzas with inexplicable North American names. Medium £2.70, large £3.70; toppings 50-70p. Open daily from 5pm until the pubs close.

■ **Joe McCollam's,** 23 Mill St., a.k.a. "Johnny Joe's." One of the best pubs on the island. Features impromptu ballads, fiddling, and slurred limericks. Exciting most nights of the week, but musicians are guaranteed to gather F-Su nights.

Lurig Inn, 5 Bridge St. (tel. 2177 1527), in an inconspicuous off-white building across the street from the Half Door. Rough and ready.

■ SIGHTS

The sandstone **Curfew Tower** in the center of town on the corner of Mill and High St. was built in 1817 by the eccentric Francis Turley. This landlord of Cushendall made his fortune in China. Upon his return, he built the tower with features that include openings for pouring boiling oil on non-existent attackers, and a bell rung every night at "quiet time" for the town (hence the tower's name). Today it is privately owned and closed to the public. The extensive remnants of **Layde Church,** a medieval friary, lie a quarter-mile past the hostel along Layde Rd. The church was established in 1306, at which time it was valued at 20 shillings for tax purposes. Today its ruins are noteworthy for their surrounding graveyard and spectacular seaviews. (Always open. Free.) Pretty cliffside walks begin at its carpark. The graveyard includes Cross Na Nagan, a pagan holestone used for marriage ceremonies and Christianized into a Celtic cross by four strokes carved into the hole. **Tieveragh Hill,** a half-mile up High St., is known locally as Fairy Hill, with a gate that leads to the Otherworld inhabited by ancient "little people." Locals still refuse to cut the hedgerows in which the little people supposedly dwell. **Lurigethan Hill** (1153 ft.) would soar above town if its summit weren't flattened on the way up. A climb to the top rewards with up-close access to a virtually intact Iron Age promontory fort. Locals race up the hill for a yearly "Lurigethan Run."

Ossian's Grave rests a few miles away on the lower slopes of **Tievebulliagh Mountain.** Actually a neolithic burial cairn dating from around 4000 BC, it is linked by tradition with the Ulster warrior-bard Ossian who was supposedly buried here in about AD 300 (see **Literary Traditions,** p. 20). Ossian, while relaying his family's adventures to St. Patrick, allegedly tried to convince the saint that Christianity was far too restrictive for the boisterous Gaels. Young Yeats's first long poem is based on this episode. A2 leads north from Cushendall toward Ballymoney to the lower slopes of Tievebulliagh, where a sign points the way to the grave. The steep walk up the southern slope of **Glenaan** rewards with views of the lush valley.

The Glens of Antrim **Rambling Club** has a series of short and long walks planned throughout the year. Contact the chairman (Liam Murphy, tel. 2565 6079) or the Cushendall tourist office for details. In the third week of July, the annual **Guinness Relay** pits neighbor against neighbor in a race across the Dunn Bridge (all of 100 ft.) with a tray of Guinness.

NEAR CUSHENDALL: CUSHENDUN

In 1954, the National Trust bought the miniscule, picturesque seaside village of Cushendun, 5 mi. north of Cushendall on A2. Since then, Big Brother has protected the town's "olde," squeaky-clean image. This white-washed and black-shuttered set of buildings lies by a vast beach perforated by wonderful, murky **caves** carved within red sea cliffs. The largest cave, located just past the Bay Hotel, serves as the only entrance to **Cave House,** which was built in 1820 and is currently occupied by the Mercy religious order and closed to the public. From behind the hotel, an excruciatingly steep path leads to the clifftop. Other, less painful walks meander around historical monuments in the town and nearby **Glendun** (free map of walks available at the Cushendun Tea Room), a preserved village that is a fine example of Cornish architecture. The relatively unimpressive "Maud Cottages" that line the main street were built by Lord Cushendun for his wife in 1925. Tourist information postings in town warn you against mistaking them for almshouses.

Buses pause at Cushendun's one grocery shop on the coast road on their way to **Waterfoot** via **Cushendall** (June-Sept. M-F 9 per day, Sa 5 per day, Su 3 per day; Oct.-May M-F 7 per day, Sa 3 per day, Su 1 per day) and to **Portrush** (June-Sept. M-F 2 per day, Sa 2 per day, Su 2 per day; Oct.-May M-F 3 per day, Sa 2 per day).

The town's most popular attraction is also its only real pub. **Mary McBride's,** 2 Main St. (tel. 2176 1511), used to be the *Guinness Book of World Records's* "smallest bar in Europe." Today the original bar is still there, but it has been vigorously expanded to create a lounge. Cushendun's characters leave the smallest bar only when trad musicians arrive and start a session in the lounge, usually on Thursday nights in the summer. McBride's also offers pub grub. (Steak and Guinness pie £5; food served daily noon-9pm.) **Cushendun Tea Room** (tel. 2176 1506), across the street, serves less exciting and less expensive food. It also passes out some tourist brochures on the town's sights, but you're best off consulting the Cushendall Tourist Office for such information before you hit Cushendun itself. (Burgers and sandwiches £1.50-2, full entrees around £4. Open July-Aug. daily 11:30am-7pm; Sept.-June weekends only, noon-6:30pm.) One mile toward Cushendall, **Sleepy Hollow B&B,** 107 Knocknacarry Rd. (tel. 2177 61513), is to your right off the coast road and has flowery, well-kept rooms and a sweet proprietress. (Singles £20, doubles £36; all with bath.) **Camping** at **Cushendun Caravan Site,** 14 Glendun Rd. 50 yds. from the end of the beach (tel. 2177 61254), is cheap, with a TV/game room and showers but no kitchen. (Tents £5.50 per tent. Laundry £2. Open Mar.-Sept.)

CAUSEWAY COAST

Past Cushendun, the northern coast shifts from lyrical to dramatic mode. Six-hundred foot sea-battered cliffs tower over white wave-lapped beaches and then give way to spectacular Giant's Causeway, for which the region is named. Lying among colossally beautiful scenery, the Causeway itself is a spillage of 40,000 black and red hexagonal stone columns formed by volcanic eruptions 65 million years ago. Thousands of visitors swarm the site today, but few venture beyond the Visitors Center to miles of stunning coastline.

A2, which is suitable for cycling, is the major thoroughfare between the main towns along the Causeway. **Ulsterbus #172** runs between **Ballycastle** and **Portrush** along the coast (1hr.; M-F 7 per day, Sa 5 per day, Su 4 per day) and makes frequent connections to **Portstewart.** In good summer weather, the open-topped orange **Bushmills Bus** (Coleraine bus station; tel. (01265) 7043 3334) outlines the coast between **Coleraine,** 5 mi. south of Portrush, and **Giant's Causeway** (July-Aug. 5 per day). The summertime Antrim Coaster bus (Belfast Bus Station, tel. 9033 3000) runs up the coast from **Belfast** to **Portstewart** via just about every town in *Let's Go* (late June to early July M-Sa 2 per day; early July to late Sept. daily 2 per day). Ulsterbus also runs package **tours** in the area that leave from **Belfast, Portrush,** and **Portstewart** (£3-9). Those hitching along A2 or the marginally quicker inland roads find that the lack of cars and high ratio of tourists slows them down. *Let's Go* does not recommend hitchhiking.

CUSHENDUN TO BALLYCASTLE

There are two popular ways to travel this stretch of land, and both have their merit. The quick route follows the relatively straight A2. The other is twisty and more scenic, beginning just outside of Cushendall. It passes the relatively unexplored **Murlough Bay,** protected by the National Trust, where a stunning landscape hides the remains of the medieval church of **Drumnakill,** once a pagan holy site. Farther west is **Torr Head,** a long peninsula that is the closest Ireland physically gets to Scotland. The road then bumps and grinds on to **Fair Head,** 7 mi. north of Cushendun and 3 mi. south of Ballycastle. This headland of heather-covered rocks attracts international hikers and winds past lakes, including **Lough na Cranagh.** In the middle of this lake sits a *crannog,* a man-made island built by the Celts in the Bronze Age as a well-fortified while recreationally equipped dwelling-place for the ruling elite. Bikes should be left at the hostel: the hills are so horrific that cyclists will spend more time walking than wheeling, and it's only a 1½hr. hike from Ballycastle. Although drivers should head straight for this splendid stretch of road, they seldom do. The lack of autos translates into poor hitching conditions, though *Let's Go* believes that's always the case. Taking A2 straight from Cushendun to Ballycastle also has its advantages. It is more manageable for cyclists, with one long climb, but an even longer descent from a boggy plain. A2, the official bus route, also leads past its own set of attractions. A few miles northeast of Cushendun, a high hollow contains a vanishing lake, called **Loughareema,** that in the summer can appear and disappear into the bog in less than a day. When the lake is full, it has fish in it, but where do they go when it empties? Answer: into the caverns beneath the porous limestone on which the lake lies. The lake stays full only when silt is blocking the pores. The lake is more commonly called Fairy Lough, but there's no scientific explanation for that. Farther along, part of the high plain has been drained and planted with evergreens. The result is secluded **Ballypatrick Forest,** which includes a forest drive and several pleasant, pine-scented walks. **Camping** is allowed with a permit from the ranger or the **Forest Office,** 155 Cushendall Rd. (tel. 2076 2301 or 2563 1860), 2 mi. toward Ballycastle on A2. (Tents £4.50. Basic facilities. Park open daily 10am to sunset.) Just before Ballycastle is **Ballycastle Forest,** significant for harboring **Knocklayde Mountain** (1695 ft.) in its midst. The mountain is eminently climbable. Its base is approximately 1 mi. into the forest.

BALLYCASTLE

The Causeway Coast leaves the sleepy Glens behind when it hits Ballycastle, a bubbly seaside town that shelters Giant's Causeway-bound tourists. Warm summer weekends bring carloads of locals to its beaches; music-lovers flock to its pubs every summer weekend. Although Ballycastle means "town of the castle," don't look for one here: the castle met its demise in 1856.

⌐ TRANSPORTATION

Buses: Stop at the Marine Hotel. **Ulsterbus** rides to **Portrush** (50min.; M-F 7 per day, Sa 5 per day, Su 4 per day), **Cushendall** via **Cushendun** (50min., M-F 1 per day), and **Belfast** via **Ballymena** (3hr.; M-F 6 per day, Sa 4 per day). In summer, Ulsterbus's **Antrim Coaster** runs through the **Glens of Antrim** and **Larne** to **Belfast** (full trip 3½-4hr.; late May to early July M-Sa 2 per day, early July-late Sept. 2 daily). **McGinn's** (tel. 2076 3451) also runs trips to **Belfast** (1½hr., F 4pm and Su 8pm, £3.50).

Ferries: **Argyll and Antrim Steam Packet Co.** (tel. (08705) 523 523) runs ferries between **Campbeltown, Scotland** (on the Kintyre Peninsula) and Ballycastle (3hr.; July-Oct. 19 2 per day in each direction; £20-25, cars and caravans accepted, vehicles and driver £80-105). See **Rathlin Island,** p. 451, for info. on the service to it.

Bike Rental: Northern Auto Factors, 41 Castle St. (tel. 2076 3748). Perfect for a trip to Rathlin. £6 per day, £30 per week.

Taxis: Tel. 2076 2822 or 2076 3697.

⁊ ORIENTATION AND PRACTICAL INFORMATION

Ballycastle's main street runs perpendicular to the waterfront. It starts at the ocean as **Quay Rd.**, becomes **Ann St.**, and then turns into **Castle St.** as its passes **The Diamond.** Most restaurants and shops are found along Ann and Castle St. As Quay Rd. meets the water, the road takes a sharp left onto **North St.**, where more stores and food await; a right from Quay puts you on **Mary Rd.**, where the tourist office rests. A park sits on the harbor; to its west is the ferry service, and to its east is the town's beach. B&Bs nest on Quay Rd.

Tourist Office: Sheskburn House, 7 Mary St. (tel. 2076 2024). Information on the entire Antrim coast. Books accommodations. 24hr. computerized information outside. Open July-Aug. M-F 9:30am-7pm, Sa 10am-6pm, Su 2-6pm; Sept.-June M-F 9:30am-5pm.

Banks: First Trust Bank, Ann St. (tel. 2076 3326). Open M-Tu and Th-F 9:30am-4:30pm, W 10am-4:30pm. **Northern Bank,** Ann St. (tel. 2076 2238). Open M 9:30am-12:30pm and 1:30-5pm, Tu-F 10am-12:30pm and 1:30-3:30pm. Both have **ATMs.**

Pharmacy: McMichael's, 10 Ann St. (tel. 2076 3342). Open M-Sa 9am-1pm and 2-6pm.

Emergency: Tel. 999. **Police:** Ramoan Rd. (tel. 2076 2312 or 2076 3125).

Hospital: Dalriada Hospital, Coleraine Rd. (tel. 2076 2666).

Post Office: 3 Ann St. (tel. 2076 2519). Open M-Tu and Th-F 9am-1pm and 2-5:30pm, W 9am-1pm, Sa 9am-12:30pm. **Postal code:** BT54 6AA.

⌐ ACCOMMODATIONS

Watch out for the Ould Lammas Fair on the last Monday and Tuesday in August. B&Bs fill almost a year in advance, and hostel beds fill weeks before the big event.

Castle Hostel (IHH), 62 Quay Rd. (tel. 2076 2337), centrally located between the promenade and the town center. This 40-bed hostel has a relaxed and welcoming atmosphere. Dorms £6, private rooms £7.50 per person. Wash £1.

Ballycastle Backpackers Hostel, 4 North St. (tel. 7026 3612 or 7026 9458), next to the Marine Hotel. Provides basic budget accommodations. Try to get a room with a sea view. Dorms £6, private rooms £7.50.

Cuchulainn House, 56 Quay Rd. (tel. 7026 2252). Breakfast on fresh fruit and local baked goods. Mrs. McMahon outdoes herself with home-made pamphlets on the Ulster myth cycle and immaculate rooms. Singles £16.50, doubles with bath £39.

Fragrens, 34 Quay Rd. (tel. 2076 2168). Mrs. Greene offers a fruit bowl at breakfast in her 17th century home, one of Ballycastle's oldest. £15, with bath £17.

Hilsea, 28 North St. (tel. 2076 2385). A large guest house offering bright rooms decorated with watercolors; some have beautiful views of gorgeous Fair Head. Snack on tea and scones in the dining room. Singles £17.50; doubles £35, with bath £37.

FOOD AND PUBS

Brady's Supermarket, 54 Castle St. (tel. 2076 2268), is a 10min. walk from the hostels. (Open daily 8am-10pm.) Closer to the harbor, the **Fruit Shop,** The Diamond (tel. 2076 3348), sells greens and other colors. (Open M-Sa 8am-6pm.) **Herald's,** 22 Ann St. (tel. 2076 9064), serves huge portions at cheap prices. The kind staff is the icing on the cake. (Entrees £2-3.) **Wysner's,** 16-18 Ann St. (tel. 2076 2372), sets its sights on healthy meals. (Lunch around £5, dinner special around £8. Open July-Aug. M-Sa 8am-9pm; Sept.-June M-Th 8am-5pm, F-Sa 8am-10pm. Only coffee and snacks served 3:30-5pm.) **Donnelly's Home Bakery and Restaurant,** Ann St., offers a selection of home-cooked meals for under £3 and is a great spot for tea and cookies. **The Strand Restaurant,** North St., next to the sea, has a large menu that includes several vegetarian dishes and dandy desserts. (Cold platters less than £6, burgers around £4. Open daily July-Aug. 11am-10pm, Sept.-June 11am-9:30pm.) At the other end of the food spectrum is **Flash-in-the-Pan,** 74 Castle St. (tel. 2076 2251); stained-glass window walls decorate this chipper. (Meals £1.50-2. Open Su-Th 11am-midnight, F-Sa 11am-1am.)

Trad is in vogue year-round in Ballycastle, but summer nights promise several venues nightly. Tourists head for tiny, fire-warmed **House of McDonnell,** Castle St. (tel. 2076 2975), for trad on Fridays; it also features folk on Saturday and spontaneous trad other days of the week. Guinness guzzlers fill the **Boyd Arms,** 4 The Diamond (tel. 2076 2364), to enjoy trad on Friday nights. **McCarroll's Bar,** a.k.a. "Pat's," 7 Ann St. (tel. 2076 2123), is the place to be on Thursdays, when it hosts terrific traditional reels and jigs. The trad-bursting **Central Bar,** 12 Ann St. (tel. 2076 3877), has an ebullient owner who can't contain the crowds. (Music W.) **The Harbour Bar,** 6 North St. (tel. 2076 2387), is the least self-conscious of pubs; locals come here for strong drinks and *craic.* **Legends Nightclub,** in the Marine Hotel, has a disco on Saturdays and Sundays. (Cover £5.)

SIGHTS

Just off The Diamond, the Holy Trinity Church of Ireland—better known as the **Boyd Church**—raises an octagonal spire over its plain interior. This edifice, like most of Ballycastle, was built by the 18th century landlord Hugh Boyd, who industrialized the area and created the town center, including Quay Rd., Ann Rd. (named after his wife), and the docks where the tennis courts now are. Most of his improvements fell to ruin when his grandsons took over in the days when industry-derived incomes fell out of fashion. Perhaps the town's most impressive sight is the 15th century **Bonamargy Friary,** which stands relatively intact in the middle of the golf course a half-mile out of town on Cushendall Rd. You can clamber around some of the rooms in the priory and read the fascinating gravestones surrounding the church. The cemetery's most notable resident is "the black nun," a 17th century recluse who had her grave placed where people would step on her, as a posthumous self-punishment for having turned away her unmarried pregnant sister.

Those who want to get up close and personal with the Irish Sea should contact **Moyle Outdoor Pursuits** (tel. 2076 9521) for fishing and sightseeing tours. If you're lacking in sea legs, you could just **fish** off the pier, where pollock, mackerel, colefish, plaice, and cod abound. The Town Council sells fishing licenses in the same building as the tourist office. (£11, 8-day £23.50. Open M-F 9:30am-1pm, 2-5pm.) You can always throw on your toggins and go for a swim by the beach.

The **Ould Lammas Fair,** Northern Ireland's oldest and most famous fair, has taken place in Ballycastle in the last week of August for 412 years. Originally a week-long fiesta, the festival is now crammed into two frenzied days. Continuing the traditions of the ancient Celtic harvest festival, the fair jams Ballycastle's streets with vendors selling cows, sheep, crafts, and baked goods. Trad musicians have the pubs packed. *Dulse* (nutritious seaweed dried on local roofs, reputedly good for the brain) and *yellow-man* (sticky toffee made from a secret recipe) are two curiosities that originated with the fair.

RATHLIN ISLAND

Just off the coast at Ballycastle, bumpy, boomerang-shaped Rathlin Island ("Fort of the Sea") is the ultimate in escapism for 20,000 puffins, the odd golden eagle, 100 human beings, and four daily ferries of tourists. Its windy surface supports few trees, but it's an ecological paradise of orchids, purple heather, and seabirds. The contrast between the white chalk and black basalt cliffs that encircle the island caused the novelist Charles Kingsley to compare Rathlin to a "drowned magpie." Before the Famine ravaged Ireland, more than 1000 people inhabited the island; in just twenty years, the population dwindled to half of that. Most of Rathlin's emigrants set sail for America and created their own community in Maine. Despite the fact that electricity only arrived in Rathlin in 1992, Rathlin has a unique place in the history of science and technology; in 1898, the Italian scientist Marconi sent the first wireless telegraph message from Rathlin to Ballycastle.

Rathlin makes a beautiful daytrip, but there is absolutely nothing to do on the island in bad weather. **Caledonian MacBrayne** runs a ferry service from Ballycastle to the island. The **Ballycastle tourist office** (tel. 2076 2024) is your best source of information on schedules, since the ferry service is based in Scotland. In the summer, the ferry runs to the island four times daily from the pier at Ballycastle, up the hill from Quay Rd. on North St. (45min.; June-Sept. 4 per day, Oct.-May 2 per day; £7.80 return). The small MacBrayne office at the Ballycastle pier (tel. 2076 2024), open before each departure, sells tickets. A leaflet available at the Ballycastle tourist office contains a decent map and description of the island's walks and sights. For a more complete presentation of the island's intricately intertwined history and myths, visit the island's own **Boat House Heritage Center** (tel. 2076 3951) at the opposite end of the harbor from the ferry. Showcasing a wealth of photographs and documents that relay Rathlin's history, the center sells pamphlets on the birds of Rathlin (50p) and the lighthouses (10p each). (Open May-Aug. daily 11:30am-4:30pm, other months by arrangement. 50p, children free.)

There are three different **minibus** services which leave from the ferry docks to drive to the **Kebble Bird Sanctuary** at the western tip of the island, 4½ mi. from the harbor. Call Gusty McCurdy (tel. 2076 3909), Irene McFaul (tel. 2076 3949), or Johnny Curry (tel. 2076 3905) (20 min.; every 20-30min.; £2 single, £3 return). The **lighthouse** is the best place to view birds, but it's accessible only with the warden's supervision; call Liam McFaul (tel. 2076 3948) in advance. Peak bird-watching season lasts from May to mid-July. The minibuses will also make trips to **Rue Point,** 2½ mi. from the harbor (£3 return). Here, visitors marvel at the crumbled remains of **Smuggler's House,** with wall cavities that hid contraband in the days when pirates and smugglers fueled Rathlin's economy. Ironically, the official tax house is just yards away. The feud between the hated coast guards and the Rathlin residents reached boiling point when the former filled in the smuggler-frequented harbor at Usher Point, at the south end of the island. **Fair Head,** where seals frolic freely, looms a few miles away from Rue Point.

If you need a break from civilization, spend the night at tiny **Soernog View Hostel** (tel. 2076 3954; SIR-nock). Take a right from the dock and turn left at the side road before the pub. At the top of the road, turn right; the hostel is a quarter-mile ahead on the left. Call ahead for pick-up. This tiny hostel has six beds, so be sure to call from the mainland to make sure there's one left for you. Most importantly, bring groceries with you. (Dorms £8. Laundry £2.) **McCuaig's Bar** (tel. 2076 3974) sometimes allows free **camping** on its grounds. The bar is the single entertainment center for the entire island, and a food source. (Sandwiches and toasties £1.50-2, burgers £1.50-2, a limited selection of entrees £3-4.) The head of Duncan, Rathlin's last Highland bull who went crazy and had to be shot in 1880, is the showpiece of the pub's otherwise plain interior.

I AM A CERTIFIED HERO

I, _____, *Let's Go: Ireland 2000* reader, am hereby to be referred to as a hero because I crossed the treacherous rope-bridge to Carrick-a-rede Island. Possession of this certificate entitles me to hero-worship.

Witness: _____

Date: _____

BALLINTOY AND CARRICK-A-REDE ISLAND

Five miles west of Ballycastle, the modest village of Ballintoy consists of a church, a tiny harbor, several pubs, a hostel, and a fisherman's bridge that's one of the most frequented tourist destinations in Northern Ireland. Two remarkable islands put Ballintoy's name on the map: Sheep Island and Carrick-a-rede Island, both of which are so small in size that they might more aptly be described as giant grass-covered rocks. Visible from Ballintoy village, Sheep Island is home to puffins, razor bills, shag, kittiwakes, and the largest cormorant colony in Ireland. The miniscule island was once used to graze sheep—11 sheep, to be exact. Ten were thought to be too few (they would get fat) and 12 too many (they would starve). Smaller and better-known **Carrick-a-rede Island** lies offshore to the east of Ballintoy. Meaning "rock in the road," Carrick-a-rede presents a barrier to migrating salmon returning to their home rivers. Fishermen have set up their nets for over 250 years at the point off the island by which salmon have to pass in their migration westward. To reach the nets, the fishermen annually string a rope bridge between the mainland and the island, where it hangs from April to September. Crossing the shaky, 48 in. wide, 67 ft. long bridge over the dizzying 100 ft. drop to rocks and sea below is now the business of thousands of tourists every year. Be **extremely careful** in windy weather, as the bridge has been known to flip over. Wardens are on site during opening hours to insure visitors' safety, and the bridge is certainly a lot safer than the days when it only had one handrail to cling to. A sign a half-mile east of Ballintoy marks the turnoff for the bridge from the coast road; the car park is a quarter-mile farther, and the bridge is three quarters of a mile past the car park.

The walk out to the bridge takes you along the heights of the Larrybane sea cliffs. You'll likely notice at least one of several species of unusual birds, including cliff-nesting, black-and-white razor bills, brown-and-white-bellied guillemots, and lots of mundane gulls. Tiny Carrick-a-rede is as generous to birdwatchers as it is to salmon fishermen. Ask the wardens for the **National Trust's** leaflet on the site, which provides a map of the area's geological notables. A fishing hut totters on the east side of the island, from which salmon nets stretch out into the sea. On a clear day, you can see the Hebrides. The **tea room** by the parking lot (tel. 2076 2178) sells snacks, posts information on the site, and offers a bit of local advice. For 50p, they'll give you a certificate stating that you successfully crossed the bridge; you can save your money and use ours instead (see **I am a certified Hero,** above). (Tea room open Apr.-Sept. daily 11am-7pm.) The **center** is open while the rope-bridge is up. (Open daily July-Aug. 10am-8pm; Apr.-June and Sept. 10am-6pm. £2 per car, £1 per motorcycle, pedestrians free.) Free **camping** can be arranged with the wardens (tel. 2076 2178). The cliff walks are always open.

Quiet Ballintoy provides beds and grub to Carrick-a-rede's thrillseekers. The aptly titled **Sheep Island View Hostel (IHH)**, 42A Main St. (tel. 2076 9391 or 2076 2470), has one of the biggest kitchens you'll ever see. (Dorms with bath £9. Continental breakfast £2.50; Ulster fry £4. Wash £1, dry £1. Barbecue facilities available. Wheelchair accessible.) The two surrounding **camping** greens are as pristine as the hostel, with separate facilities and views of Sheep's Island. (£3 per person.) Call the hostel for pick-up from anywhere between Cushendall and Portrush. A shop at the entrance to the hostel provides basic groceries. (Open daily 8:30am-10pm.) In town, the frosted-glass-windowed **Fullerton Arms** (tel. 2076 9613) and the come-as-you-are **Carrick-a-rede** (tel. 2076 2241) compete from across the street for locals' business. Both offer standard pub grub daily from 12:30 to 8:30pm in the £3-5 range and music almost every summer night.

Three miles west along the coast road from Ballintoy is **Whitepark Bay Youth Hostel (YHANI)** (tel. 2073 1745). Its out-of-the-way setting, overlooking one of the most famous—though unswimmable—beaches on the Antrim Coast is either a blessing or a boon, depending on whether or not you have a car. The Portrush-Ballycastle bus (#172) or the Antrim coaster (#252) will drop you off 200 yd. from the hostel, but there are no shops or pubs for miles around. Once there, few of the visitors spend their precious time complaining and save their energy for the beach. Impeccably clean, this hostel is the YHANI of the 21st century. A restaurant sells the most basic food stuffs. (Breakfast £2.50, dinner £4.50. 4-bed dorms £9.75, twin room £11.75. Oct.-Mar. lockout 11am-5pm. **Bike rental** £6 per day.) There is a splendid 1 mi. **nature trail** along the bay.

GIANT'S CAUSEWAY

Advertised as the eighth natural wonder of the world, Giant's Causeway is Northern Ireland's most famous sight. Be warned that 2000 visitors arrive each day in July and August. A spillage of 40,000 hexagonal columns of basalt form a 60-million-year-old honeycomb path from the foot of the cliffs far into the sea. Geologists have decided that the Causeway resulted from an unusually steady cooling of lava that stimulated crystallization.

The Causeway is always open and free to pedestrians. **Giant's Causeway Visitors Center** sits at the pedestrian entranceway to the Causeway from the carpark. Besides offering the usual tourist information, a bureau de change, and a post office, it sells an excellent leaflet of walks (75p) that will guide you the 8 mi. back to Whitepark Bay or along several shorter circular walks. Every 15min., it runs Causeway Coaster minibuses the half-mile to the columns (60p, £1 return). An audio-visual show (£1) informs about the facts and fictions of the Causeway. (Tel. 2073 1855. Center open daily June 10am-6pm; July-Aug. 10am-7pm; Mar.-May and Sept. 10am-5pm; Nov.-Feb. 10am-4:30pm. Parking £3 per car.) A tea room offers refreshment in the center. (Tea room closes 30min. before the visitors center.)

Many paths loop to and from the Causeway. Two begin at the Visitors Center, one passing along the high cliffs and another along the low coast close to the Causeway. The paths meet after 1 mi., and you can return by the road not taken. Taking the low road provides more instant gratification, while the high road affords spectacular sea views. The low road also allows something of a downhill walk for a portion of the trail. At the end of this walk, 4½ mi. east of the Causeway's center, you will see the scanty though overwhelmingly romantic ruins of **Dunsverick Castle,** the Iron Age fort of Sobhairce, high above you on a sea cliff. Bus #172 and the Antrim Coaster stop in front of the castle, from where it's 4½ mi. far-

THE REAL MCCOOL Irish legend states that the warrior giant Finn McCool fell in love with a female giant named Una on Staffa Island, off the Scottish coast. The devoted lover built the Causeway to bring her across to Ulster, which explains the existence of similar beehive-esque rock formations on Staffa. The Scottish giant Benandonner followed them to Ireland to defeat Finn and take Una back home with him. When McCool realized how big his Scottish rival was, he realized the folly of his physical confidence and decided to rely on the strength of his wit. The wily Irishman, with the help of his wife Una, disguised himself as an infant. When the Scottish giant saw the size of this Irish "baby," he was terrified by the anticipated proportions of the father. Benandonner quickly fled back to Scotland, destroying the Causeway on his return trip in order to ensure that the huge father McCool would never be able to cross the sea to challenge him.

ther to Ballintoy. The well-tended track winds through naturally sculpted amphitheaters and inlets studded with creatively named formations (such as the "organ"). Although not essential, the center's trail leaflet contains a helpful map and basic geological descriptions.

BUSHMILLS

The ardently Protestant town of Bushmills, 2 mi. west of Giant's Causeway, has been the home of **Bushmills Irish Whiskey** since 1608, making it the oldest functioning whiskey producer in the world. The Bushmills distills their whiskey three times, a process that your tour guide happily expounds upon. Irish monks invented whiskey in the 6th century and called it *uisce beatha* (is-CAH BAHN-a), "water of life." Travelers have been stopping at Bushmills for some stimulation since ancient days when it was on the route from the castles of Dunluce and Dunseverick to Tara. When the distillery is operating, you get to see whiskey being made. Production stops for three weeks in July for maintenance, but (less interesting) tours are still held; around Christmas, neither distilling nor tours occur. (Tel. 2073 1521. Open M-Sa 9:30am-5:30pm; last tour 4pm. Tours, with free sample, Apr.-Oct. every 15-20min.; Nov.-Mar. M-F at 10, 11am, noon, 1:30, 2:30, 3:30pm. £3.50, students and seniors £3.) An abandoned **Electric Tramway line,** the first of a few hydroelectric-powered tram rails, runs from Bushmills to the Causeway Visitors Center via Portrush. For information, contact Giant's Causeway Visitors Center or the Portrush Tourist Office.

PORTRUSH

By day, the merry-go-rounds, water slides, and arcades of Portrush go full-throttle as bushels of Northern vacationers roam the streets and its two beaches. By night, young mobs party at nightclubs along the chilly seafront. Giant's Causeway and Portstewart are within easy cycling distance.

▐ TRANSPORTATION

Trains: Eglinton St. (tel. 7082 2395), in the center of town. Trains to **Belfast** (2hr.; M-F 9 per day, Sa 7 per day, Su 4 per day; £5.15) and **Derry** (1hr.; M-F 7 per day, Sa 6 per day, Su 4 per day; £4.95).

Buses: Leave from Dunluce St. Regular buses to **Portstewart** (13min.; M-F 23 per day, Sa 18 per day, Su 9 per day; £1). Ulsterbus #172 (M-F 7 per day, Sa 6 per day, Su 4 per day) runs along the coast to **Bushmills** (20min.), **Giant's Causeway** (25min.), **Ballintoy** (40min.), and **Ballycastle** (1hr.). The open-topped **Bushmills Bus** (#177) goes to **Portstewart, Bushmills,** and **Giant's Causeway** in good weather (daily 5 per day). The Ulsterbus **Portrush Puffer** runs circles around the town (July-Aug. M-Sa 11am-7pm, Su 2-7pm; Apr.-June and Sept. M-Sa 10am-6pm, Su 2-6pm; £1.40).

Taxis: Tel. 7082 3483, 7082 2223, or 7082 5013.

Bike Rental: Bicycle Doctor, 104 Lower Main St. (tel. 7082 4340). £7 per day, £30 per week; deposit £40 or passport. Open daily 9am-6pm; bikes can be returned after closing with advance notice. **Woody's Surf-Skate-Snow** (see **Surfing Equipment,** below).

▐ PRACTICAL INFORMATION

Tourist Office: Dunluce Centre (tel. 7082 3333), off Sandhill Dr., just south of the town center. Brochures galore, bureau de change, and accommodation bookings. Ulsterbus representative on hand to arrange day tours. Open mid-June to Aug. daily 9am-7pm, Apr.-June and Sept. M-F 9am-5pm, Sa-Su 12-5pm, Mar. and Oct. Sa-Su 12-5pm.

Banks: First Trust, 25 Eglinton St. (tel. 7082 2726). Open M-Tu and Th-F 9:30am-4:30pm, W 10am-4:30pm. **Northern Bank,** 60 Main St. (tel. 7082 2327). Open M 9:30am-5pm, Tu-F 10am-3:30pm; closed daily 12:30-1:30pm except July-Aug. Bureau de change. **Ulster Bank,** 33 Eglinton St. (tel. 7082 3730). Open M-F 9:30am-12:30pm and 1:30-4:30pm. All have **24hr. ATMs.**

Pharmacy: Heron Chemist, 5-9 Main St. (tel. 7082 2324). Open July-Aug. daily 9am-10:30pm, Sept.-June M-Sa 9am-6pm, Su 2-6pm.

Surfing Equipment: Troggs Surf Shop, 88 Main St. (tel. 7082 5476). Surfboards £5 per day, bodyboards £3 per day, wetsuits £5 per day; deposit credit card or driver's license. 2hr. lesson with equipment £15. Open daily July-Aug. 10am-10pm, Sept.-June 10am-6pm. **Woodie's Surf-Skate-Snow,** 102 Main St. (tel. 7082 3273). Surfboards £5 per day, wetsuits £4 per day; deposit credit card. Bicycle rental £7 per day. Open daily 10am-6pm.

Emergency: Dial 999; no coins required. **Police:** Tel. 7082 2721.

Post Office: 23 Eglinton St. (tel. 7082 3700). Open M-Tu and Th-F 9am-12:30pm and 1:30-5:30pm, W 9am-1pm, Sa 9am-12:30pm. **Postal code:** BT56 8DX.

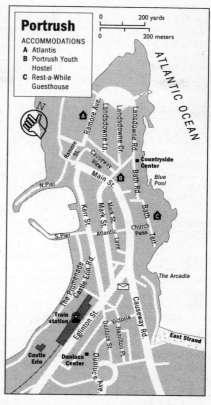

Portrush

ACCOMMODATIONS
A Atlantis
B Portrush Youth Hostel
C Rest-a-While Guesthouse

ACCOMMODATIONS

Portrush is a convenient place to begin or end a tour of Giant's Causeway, since most buses that serve the Causeway stop here. When the university at Coleraine sets students free for the summer, plenty of student housing becomes holiday accommodations. Almost every other townhouse along Mark St., Kerr St., and Raymore Ave. is a B&B. Most are indistinguishable in character and price (£15-20).

Portrush Youth Hostel, 5 Causeway View Terr. (tel. 7082 4845). A 10min. walk from the bus stop; turn left onto Dunluce St. and follow it toward the harbor. When you come to a three-pronged fork, take the middle road, which is Mark St. The hostel is a few yards past the intersection of Mark St. and Main St., on Causeway View Terr. From the train station, Mark St. is the second left after turning left out of the station. Relax in the homey common room that's filled with carpeted furniture. Free tea and coffee. Dorms £7. Laundry £3. Cycles £5 per day. Internet access £4 per hour.

A-Rest-a-While Guesthouse, 6 Bath Terr. (tel. 7082 2827). Mismatched neo-Victorian decorations endear guests to this huge B&B. Some rooms overlook the beach. £15.

Atlantis, 10 Ramore Ave. (tel. 7082 4583). An ocean view. Free tea and coffee. Evening meal £5. Singles £16; doubles £30, with bath £35.

FOOD

The proliferation of fast food in Portrush may overwhelm, but a few good restaurants hide amid the neon. If you're not up to the search, stock up on groceries at **Mace,** 58 Main St. (Open daily 9am-10pm.)

The Singing Kettle, 3-5 Atlantic Ave. (tel. 7082 4254). Soothing, lace-curtained relief for weary travelers. While in any other town it might seem boring, such wholesomeness is appreciated in Portrush. Vegetarian options. Afternoon dinner £4-5, served noon-5pm; slightly more exotic evening meals (£5-8) served 6-10pm. Open daily July-Aug. noon-5pm and 6-10pm, Sept.-June 11am-5pm.

Donovans, Main St. (tel. 7082 2063), looks and sounds like a trad pub but doesn't taste like pub grub. Irish meals are made zesty by worldly seasonings. Most lunches £5-8. Dinners £8-11. Music nightly. Open M-Sa noon-2:30pm and 5-10pm, Su noon-9:30pm.

Don Giovanni's, 9-13 Causeway St. (tel. 7082 5516). Authentic Italian food and owners. Impeccable interior. Pizza £4-7, pasta £6-7. Open daily 5:30-11pm.

The Alamo, Eglinton St. (tel. 7082 2000). Celebrate Ulster-American imperialism with American-style pizza. Free delivery. Ten inch pizza £4-6. Open M-Th 5pm-2am, F-Sa 5pm-3am, Su 5pm-1am.

■ PUBS AND ENTERTAINMENT

The **Harbour Bar,** 5 Harbour Rd. (tel. 7082 2430), wants to be a sailors' pub. The hippest complex in town swallows up one whole corner block on Main St. with the **Atlantic Bar** and the **Trocado Lounge** (tel. 7082 3693). At the Trocado Lounge, DJs and live bands do their thing while customers sample 35 different flavors of vodka. **Shunter's,** in the railway station, powers its engines with live music most summer nights. (Cover £1-5.) Partiers head to techno-heavy **Traks Nightclub** (tel. 7082 2112) at the railway station. Facing the Harbor, **The Rogues,** 54 Kerr St. (tel. 7082 2946), is another wiggle-silly night spot. (Cover varies.) Finish your evening (or begin your morning) at a Portrush institution: **Beetles Bar and Disco** (everyone calls it **Kelly's;** tel. 7082 3539), just outside Portrush on Bushmills Rd. Kelly's has 11 bars and four discos, including **Lush!** (tel. 7082 2027), voted one of the top-ten U.K. clubs by *DJ Magazine*. Excessive and occasionally tacky, the club has a niche for every imaginable type of teenager.

Higher art forms reach this non-stop party when Northern Irish theater companies travel to Portrush to perform on the **Summer Theatre** stage (tel. 7082 2500).

■ SIGHTS

The most widely advertised attraction in Portrush is the kiddie-ride of a heritage site, **Dunluce Center,** Dunluce Arcade. Technologically vivid displays about anything from zoo creatures to mythical heroes keep kids wide awake. Moving seats in the Turbo Tours theater make wide-screen "adventure" films that much more real. For 50p you can climb a squat tower to look at the view. (Tel. 7082 4444. Open July-Aug. daily 10:30am-7:30pm; Sept. daily noon-5pm; Oct. Sa-Su noon-5pm; Apr.-June M-F noon-5pm, Sa-Su 10am-6pm. Turbo Tours £2.50, myths and legends £2.30; whole center £5.) In refreshing contrast, the understated **Countryside Centre,** 8 Bath Rd., next to East Strand, is small but enthusiastically attended. The assortment of displays includes wildlife exhibits, a tide pool with sea urchins and starfish, a fossil and crystal exhibit, and a display of a sea-wreck. A viewing platform outside can help identify the many land masses in the distance. A governmentally protected fossil bed sits outside. (Tel. 7082 3600. Open June-Sept. W-M noon-8pm. Viewing platform always open. Free.)

Luckily, it is not difficult to escape Portrush's amusement-park atmosphere. The **East Strand Beach** stretches out for 1½ mi. toward Giant's Causeway. At the far end of the beach is a car park; from here, it is another 1½ mi. along the main road to **Dunluce Castle,** a surprisingly intact 16th century fort. The castle has been partially restored and houses an information center, complete with a 15min. video. A walk around the peripheral castle grounds is almost as interesting, and it's free. The castle was built close to the cliff's edge; so close, in fact, that one day the kitchen fell into the sea. (Open June-Aug. Tu-Sa 10am-6pm, Su noon-6pm; April-May and Sept. Tu-Sa 10am-6pm, Su 2-6pm; Oct.-Mar. Tu-Sa 10am-4pm, Su 2-4pm. Last admission 30min. before closing. £1.50, students and seniors 75p.) The best surfing on the North Antrim coast is at **Portballintree Beach,** where the waves majestically soar almost as high as the nearby castle. Inside Portrush proper are a series of short walks on Ramore Head, next to the harbor.

PORTSTEWART

Although it's as crowded as its neighbor Portrush, Portstewart feels more like a friendly small town. A friendly rivalry between the two manifests itself in the different characteristics of their beachbathers: while Portrush's techno beat draws in swarms of young slicksters, Portstewart is geared towards beachbathing family-types. A good beach and an oceanfront lined with ice cream parlors are the main attractions for the locals that swarm Portstewart.

🚹 PRACTICAL INFORMATION. **Buses** stop in the middle of **The Promenade.** Portstewart's tiny **tourist office,** Town Hall (tel. 7083 2286), is in the red brick building that sits on the crescent at the far end of The Promenade. (Open July-Aug. M-Sa 10am-1pm and 1:30-4pm.) **First Trust,** 13 The Promenade (tel. 7083 3273), offers financial services inside and out with a **24hr. ATM.** (Open M-F 9:30am-4:30pm.) **McElhone's Numark Pharmacy,** 22A The Promenade (tel. 7083 2014), distributes prescriptions and advice. (Open M-Sa 9am-5:30pm.) The **post office,** 90 The Promenade (tel. 7083 2001), does the usual. (Open M-Tu and Th-F 9am-1pm and 2-5:30pm, W 9am-1pm, Sa 9am-12:30pm.) The **postal code** is BT55 7AG.

📷🏠🍴 ACCOMMODATIONS, FOOD, AND PUBS. The Victoria Terr. area, on the left as you head out of town on the Portrush Rd., has beds galore. From the bus stop, face the sea, turn right, and follow Main St. around the corner. Victoria Terr. juts out to the left. **Rick's Causeway Coast Independent Hostel (IHH),** 4 Victoria Terr. (tel. 7083 3789), is friendly and comfortable. The walls are lined with maps and stunning mountain photographs. The staff will take as good care of you as they do of the healthy plants that make something of a conservatory out of the common room. (Dorms £6, doubles and twins £15. Free barbecue. £2 key deposit. Laundry £2, free if you stay for more than one night.) **Wanderin' Heights,** 12 High Rd. (tel. 7083 3250), parallel to the Portrush road near Victoria Terr., provides B&B in blue floral rooms. (£16, with bath £20; off-season £15, £18.)

Portstewart cultivates both good cooks and a tradition of superb ice cream. **Mace Supermarket,** (tel. 7083 3203) on The Promenade, has an impressive selection of groceries and cheeses. (Open M-Su 8am-midnight.) **Good Food and Company,** 44 The Promenade (tel. 7083 6386), serves sandwiches (£1.50-1.70), breads, and baked goods. (Open M-Sa 9am-10pm; Sept.-June M-Sa 9am-6pm.) **Ashiana Indian Kitchen,** 12 The Diamond (tel. 834455), has take-away options, which come with rice or bread and are slightly cheaper than eating at the restaurant. (Entrees around £7. Open M-Sa 5pm-midnight, Su 5-10pm; take-away open M-F 5pm-midnight, Sa 5pm-2am, Su 5-11pm.) The more adventurous diner might try the **Montagu Arms** (tel. 7093 4146), on The Promenade, which offers a "Beat the Clock" special: a 10 oz. sirloin steak with chips and sauteed onions for £5 if you order at 5pm. The price goes up 25p every 15 minutes. The really early bird can enjoy a 2-course lunch for £5 from 12:30-2:30pm. **Morelli's Sundae Garden,** The Promenade (tel. 7083 2150), is infamous for its superbly sugary concoctions. (Sundaes about £3. Open July-Aug. daily 9am-11pm; hours vary during the rest of the year.) Most of the town, and all of its students, head for the **Anchor Pub,** 87 The Promenade (tel. 7083 2003), to put back some pints by the fire while studying the intricate handiwork of the framed sailor's knots on the walls. (Disco upstairs M-Tu and Th-Sa. Cover £2 or free.) Across the street, **Stafford's,** 28 The Promenade (tel. 7083 6000), dark green and mahogany bar draws a mixed crowd, while its upstairs nightclub, **Chaines** packs in dancing youngsters. (Disco M-Tu, Th-Sa. Cover £3 on Sa.) **Skipper's Wine Bar** (tel. 7083 4401), next door in the Anchorage Inn, serves upscale pub grub in the shinier version of the Anchor Pub. (Lunch about £5, bigger dinner portions for about £6-8; food served noon-2:30pm and 5-9:30pm.)

🔆 SIGHTS. Beachcombers have a full day ahead of them on the 6½ mi. coastal path that leads from **Portstewart Strand** on the west side of town east toward Portrush. The path takes you past sea cliffs, blow holes, an ancient hermit's house, and plenty of other odd sights that a free map from the tourist office will help you recognize. Portstewart Strand, half a mile west of town, is owned and preserved in all its beauty by the National Trust. (Visitors facilities open daily May-Aug. 10am-6pm. £2.50 per car.) The **Port-na-happle rock pool,** located between town and the beach, is ideal for bathing. A small but dedicated group of surfers call these waters home. For those who dare to try out the Irish waves, there are two surf shops in town. **Troggs,** 20 The Diamond (tel. 7083 3361), rents wetsuits, surfboards, and bodyboards. (Equipment £3-10 per day. Open July-Aug. daily 10am-7pm; Apr.-June

Sa-Su 10am-6pm.) **Ocean Warriors** (tel. 7083 6500), located at both 80 The Promenade and on the Strand, rents wetsuits and bodyboards (each £2 per hr., £5 per day) and surfboards (£10 per day). According to locals, the best waves hit the shore from September to March and reach five to six feet. The **Flowerfield Arts Center,** 185 Coleraine Rd. (tel. 7083 3959), shelters traveling art exhibitions and holds frequent lectures on subjects ranging from local history and folklore to the royal family. (Open M-F 10am-1pm and 2-5pm.)

DOWNHILL

Farther out along the A2 coast road toward Derry is Downhill, home to a pub, a beach, and the still glorious remnants of a royal estate. The village's greatest attraction, however, might be the ▨**Downhill Hostel** (tel. 7084 9077). The hostel has a beach out front, is backed by cliffs, and is bordered by a rocky stream. High bunks, hand-sewn quilts, and a luxurious shower provide more reason to stay for a couple of nights. (Dorms £6, private rooms £9 per person. Laundry £3.50.) The closest food source other than Downhill's pub is the grocery store 2 mi. away in Castlerock, so do your shopping before you arrive. **Bus** #134 from Coleraine to Limavady swings by (7-8 per day); ask the driver to stop at the hostel and it's a 2min. walk straight ahead. The train stops 2 mi. from Downhill at Castlerock on its way from Belfast to Derry; from there, call the hostel for free pick-up.

The land between Castlerock and Downhill once belonged to the Earl Bishop Frederick Hervy, Earl of Bristol and Derry, who will long be remembered as one of the wackiest members of British aristocracy ever to tamper with the Irish landscape. Challenging the coast's stoic, irreproachable seacliffs with a heavy handy of human decadence, he built **Downhill Castle** in the late 18th century. His house was once one of Europe's greatest treasure troves, but it suffered from a disastrous fire and was completely abandoned after World War II. The residence was later bought by an American businessman who gutted it and sold the windows, chandeliers, and furnishings abroad, leaving behind only the stone shell of the former palace. On the cliffs in front of the castle, **Musendun Temple** all but teeters before a precipitous drop to the sea. This circular library was based on the Temples of Vesta in Italy and was named after the niece with whom locals speculated the Earl Bishop had an affair. Behind the castle sit the remains of another of Hervey's architectural frivolities, the mausoleum he built for his brother. Ignoring warnings that the windy clifftop would not long support a structure, he erected a monument twice the height of the one that now stands. A second tier and the statue atop it both toppled in a windstorm. The decapitated statue now stands in the National Trust-administered gardens further inland on the property. (Temple open July-Aug. daily noon-6pm; Apr.-June and Sept. Sa-Su noon-6pm. Grounds open year-round. Free.) Hervey's estate peers down at **Downhill Beach,** one of the most gorgeous on the Northern coast and great for surfing.

DERRY (LONDONDERRY)

Derry competes with Dublin for the most long-lasting contributions to Irish political history. The past is remarkably present in the landmarks and districts that comprise Derry's physical appearance, from the administrative centers within its city walls to the Bogside neighborhood that sits outside them. Derry has been a center of culture and politics for thousands of years. Once a Celtic holy place, the arrival of Christianity converted it into a monastic center in the 6th century. Derry became a major commercial port under the Ulster Plantation of the 17th century (see p. 9); under the English feudal system, the city became the outpost of London's authority, who renamed it Londonderry. (Although phonebooks and other such bureaucratic traps use this official title, most Northerners refer to the city as Derry.) The city's troubled history spans from the siege of Derry in 1689, when the now-legendary Apprentice Boys closed the city gates on the advancing armies of the Catholic King James II (see p. 10), spawning antagonisms that continued into the civil rights turmoil of the 1960s, when protests against religious discrimination against Catholics exploded into violence publicized world-wide. In 1972, the Troubles reached their pinnacle on Bloody Sunday, a tragic public massacre during which British soldiers shot into a crowd of peaceful protesters. The nationalist population is still seeking redress from the British government for the event (see **The Troubles,** p. 394). The past three centuries of Derry's history have given rise to the iconography used by both sides of the sectarian conflict.

Modern Derry is in the middle of a determined and largely successful effort to cast off the legacy of the Troubles. While the political turmoil that lasted until the mid-1980s flattened the city, today the city's skyline displays both medieval and modern architectural feats. Despite occasional unrest in the staunchly sectarian areas of the city, it seems that many Derry residents believe consensus is possible. Construction and commerce are booming, and most parts of the city, especially the downtown area, show evidence of Derry's rapid development. The city council is starting new programs to promote peace, improve morale, and attract more tourists. Derry's controversial history and its depiction in murals make for fascinating sights, as do less contentious aspects of the city, including its brilliant music scene, thriving artistic community, and irrepressible pub life.

⌐ TRANSPORTATION

Airport: Eglinton/Derry Airport, Eglinton (tel. 7181 0784). 7 mi. from Derry. Flights to points within the British Isles.

Trains: Duke St., Waterside (tel. 7134 2228), on the east bank. A free **Rail-Link bus** connects the bus station to the train station. Trains from Derry go east to **Belfast** via **Coleraine, Ballymena,** and **Lisburn** (2½hr.; M-F 7 per day, Sa 6 per day, Su 3 per day; £6.40). Connections may be made from Coleraine to **Portrush.**

Buses: Most stop on Foyle St. between the walled city and the river. **Ulsterbus** (tel. 7126 2261) serves all destinations in the North and some in the Republic. To **Belfast** (1½-3hr.; M-F 15 per day, Sa 14 per day, Su 8 per day; £6.80), **Omagh** (M-F 14 per day, Su 9 per day, Su 6 per day; £4.70), **Dublin** (M-Sa 5 per day, Su 2 per day; £10.50). **Lough Swilly** bus service (tel. 7126 2017) heads to **Letterkenny,** the **Fanad Peninsula,** and the **Inishowen Peninsula.** Buses to **Malin Head** (1½hr.; M-F 2 per day, Sa 3 per day; £6), **Letterkenny** (1hr., M-Sa 9 per day, £4), **Buncrana** (35min.; M-F 12 per day, Sa 12 per day, Su 3 per day; £2.40). **Northwest Busways** (tel. (077) 82619 in the Republic) heads to **Inishowen** from Patrick St. opposite the Multiplex Cinema; to **Malin Head** (2 per day, £4.20) and **Cardonagh** (5 per day, £3), and to **Buncrana** (8 per day, £2.20).

Taxi: City Cabs, William St. (tel. 7126 4466). **Foyle Taxis,** 10a Newmarket St. (tel. 7126 3905 or 7137 0007).

Car Rental: Ford Rent-a-Car, Desmond Motors Ltd., 173 Strand Rd. (tel. 7136 0420). £37 per day, £184 per week; weekend package F-M 4pm-9am £73.50; deposit £180. 25 and over. Open July-Aug. M-F 9am-5:30pm, Sa 9am-4pm; Sept.-June M-F 9am-5:30pm, Sa 9am-1pm.

Bike Rental: Rent-A-Bike, Lone Moor Rd. (tel. 7128 7128). Sells a range of accessories and offers a pick-up service. £7 per day, £30 per week; deposit passport or £50.

✚ ORIENTATION

Derry straddles the **River Foyle** just east of the border of Co. Donegal in the Republic. The **city center** and the **university area** both lie on the Foyle's western banks. The old city within the medieval walls is now Derry's downtown with a pedestrianized shopping district around Waterloo St. In the center of the old city lies The Diamond, from which radiate four main streets: **Shipquay St.** to the northeast, **Butcher St.** to the northwest, **Bishop St.** to the southwest, and **Ferryquay** to the southeast. **Magee University** is to the north on **Strand Rd.** The famous Catholic **Bogside** neighborhood that became Free Derry in the 70s (see **The Troubles,** p. 394) is west of the city walls. On the south side of the walls is the tiny Protestant enclave of the **Fountain.** The residential areas of the Foyle's western bank are primarily Catholic, while most of Derry's Protestant population lives on the eastern bank, where the housing estates commonly known as the **Waterside** are located. The train station is on the east side of the river and can be reached from the city center by way of the **Craigavon Bridge.**

◪ PRACTICAL INFORMATION

TOURIST AND FINANCIAL SERVICES

Tourist Office: 44 Foyle St. (tel. 7126 7284), inside the Derry Visitor and Convention Bureau. Be sure to ask for the truly useful *Derry Tourist Guide, Visitor's Guide,* and free maps of the town. Books accommodations throughout the island. **Bord Fáilte** (tel. 7136 9501) keeps a desk here, too. Open July-Sept. M-F 9am-7pm, Sa 10am-6pm, Su 10am-5pm; Oct.-Easter M-Th 9am-5:15pm, F 9am-5pm; Easter-June M-Th 9am-5:15pm, F 9am-5pm, Sa 10am-5pm. They also keep a computer info point at the bus station.

Budget Travel: usit, Ferryquay St. (tel. 7137 1888). ISICs, TravelSave stamps, and other discount cards. Sells bus and plane tickets and rail passes. Books accommodations world-wide. Open M-F 9:30am-5:30pm, Sa 10am-1pm.

Banks: First Trust, Shipquay St. (tel. 7136 3921). Open M-Tu and Th-F 9:30am-4:30pm, W 10am-4:30pm. **Bank of Ireland,** Straud Rd. (tel. 7126 4141). Open M-F 9:30am-4:30pm. **Northern Bank,** Guildhall Sq. (tel. 7126 5333). Open M-W and F 9:30am-3:30pm, Th 9:30am-5pm, Sa 9:30am-12:30pm. **Ulster Bank,** Guildhall Sq. (tel. 7126 1882). Open M-F 9:30am-4:30pm. All have **24hr. ATMs.**

LOCAL SERVICES

Laundry: Duds 'n' Suds, 141 Strand Rd. (tel. 7126 6006). Pool table and TV. Wash and dry £3.60. Open M-F 8am-9pm, Sa 8am-6pm. Last wash 90min. before closing.

Women's Center: 32 Great James St. (tel. 7126 7672). Girls club. Open M-Th 9:30am-5pm, F 9am-2pm.

Gay, Lesbian, and Bisexual Information: 37 Clarendon St. (tel. 7126 4400). Information for the whole of the North. Open Th 7:30-10pm.

Disability Resources: Foyle Disability Action, 52-58 Strand Rd. (tel. 7136 0811), serves the physically or mentally disabled. Open M-F 9am-1pm and 2-5pm. **P.H.A.B.,** 6 Pump St. (tel. 7137 1030), gives advice. Open M-F 9am-5pm.

Pharmacy: Boots, 3a-b Strand Rd. (tel. 7126 4502). Open M-Th 9am-5:30pm, F 9am-9pm, Sa 9am-6pm.

EMERGENCY AND COMMUNICATIONS

Emergency: Dial 999; no coins required. **Police:** Strand Rd. (tel. 7136 7337).

Hospital: Altnagelvin Hospital, Glenshane Rd. (tel. 7134 5171).

Counseling and Support: Samaritans, 16 Clarendon St. (tel. 7126 5511). Open daily 10am-10pm. 24hr. phone service.

Post Office: 3 Custom House St. (tel. 7136 2563). Open M 8:30am-5:30pm, Tu-F 9am-5:30pm, Sa 9am-12:30pm. **Postal code:** BT48 6AA. Unless addressed to 3 Custom House St., *Poste Restante* letters will go to the Postal Sorting Office (tel. 7136 2577) on the corner of Great James and Little James St.

Internet Access: Central Library, Foyle St. (tel. 7127 2300). Open to all. £2.50 per hr. Open M-W and F 9:15am-5:30pm, Th 9:15am-8pm, Sa 9:15am-5pm.

◤ ACCOMMODATIONS

Derry is home to two hostels, but budget travelers do well to indulge in beautiful and well-priced B&Bs. Most accommodations are just outside the city walls.

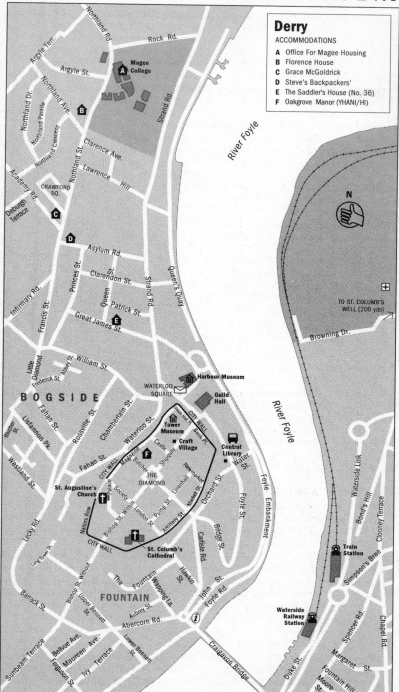

Derry

ACCOMMODATIONS

A Office For Magee Housing
B Florence House
C Grace McGoldrick
D Steve's Backpackers'
E The Saddler's House (No. 36)
F Oakgrove Manor (YHANI/HI)

Derry City Independent Hostel (Steve's Backpackers), 4 Asylum Rd. (tel. 7137 7989 or 7137 0011). Down Strand Rd. 7min. from the city center; Asylum Rd. is on the left just before the RUC station. This relaxed, friendly 16-bed hostel offers earfuls of advice on Derry's history and nightlife. Dorms £7.50. £2 key deposit. Laundry £3. Internet access £3 per hr. 6pm-8am, £4 per hr. 8am-6pm. Stay four days here or at Macpackers in Belfast and the fifth night is free.

Oakgrove Manor (YHANI/HI), Magazine St. (tel. 7128 4100). A sky-high mural on the side of the building identifies this large and institutional hostel located within the city walls. 24hr. access with night watchman. 8- to 10-bed dorms £7.50, 3- to 10-bed dorms with bath £8.50; B&B with bath £15. Ulster fry £2.50, continental breakfast £1.50. Towels 50p. Laundry £3.50. Checkout 10am. Wheelchair accessible.

Magee College (tel. 575283 or 375218), on corner of Rock and Northland Rd. Walk a quarter mile up Strand Rd and turn left onto Rock Rd; Magee College is at the top of the hill on the left. The Housing Office is on the ground floor of Woodburn House, a red brick building just after the main building. Singles in 5-bedroom flats £14.10, students £11.75. Free laundry. Available during Easter week and mid-May to Sept. Mandatory reservations M-F 9am-5pm. Ask for dishes and linens. Wheelchair accessible.

■ **The Saddler's House (No. 36),** 36 Great James St. (tel. 7126 9691). Friendly, historically knowledgeable owners make their Victorian house into your ultimate comfort zone. French press coffee, fresh fruit and cheese, and homemade jam at breakfast. The same couple also run **The Old Rectory,** an award-winning, restored Georgian Townhouse at 16 Queen St. Both houses £18, with bath £20.

Florence House, 16 Northland Rd. (tel. 7126 8093; email ray@mcginley.in2home.co.uk). Large, sunny bedrooms in a Georgian house that looks onto the university. Home to two grand pianos, three uprights, and an astonishingly musical family. £17.

Grace McGoldrick, 10 Crawford Sq. (tel. 7126 5000), off Northland Rd, near Strand Rd. and the university. A 5min. walk to city center. Soothing rooms with high ceilings. Singles £20, doubles £35; all with bath.

◪ FOOD

Excellent take-aways and cafes abound in Derry, but restaurants, mostly located around the walled city, tend to be expensive. **Tesco** supermarket, in the Quayside Shopping Center, is a few minutes walk from the walled city along Strand Rd. (Open M-Sa 8:30am-9pm, Su 1-6pm.) Various convenience stores with later hours are scattered around Strand Rd. and Williams St.

■ **Rhubarb and Custard** Custom House St. (tel. 7137 7977), near the Guild Hall. This colorfully rustic cafe sells sandwiches (£2) and a filling two-course lunch special (£3). Lots of vegetarian options. Open M-Sa 9am-5:30pm.

Piemonte Pizzeria (tel. 7126 6828), at the corner of Claredon St. and Strand Rd. Pizza to please all palates. Lots of happy families and favorably impressed dates. Individual pizzas £4-6. The take-away next door is 50p-£1 cheaper and open 30min. later. Restaurant open Su-Th 5-11:30pm, F and Sa 5pm-12am.

Indigo (tel. 7127 1011), 27 Shipquay St., serves flavorful, internationally-inspired foods in a stylish interior. Entrees £6-8, two-course special £6. Open daily 11am-11pm.

Fitzroy's, 2-4 Bridge St. (tel. 7126 6211), next to Bishops' Gate. Cafe culture and filling meals ranging from a simple chicken breast to mussels cooked in champagne. Most meals around £5. Open M-W and Sa 9am-6pm, Th-F 9am-9pm, Su noon-6pm.

The Sandwich Co., The Diamond (tel. 7137 2500) and 61 Strand Rd. (tel. 7126 6771), corner of Ferryquay and Bishop St. Big baguettes stuffed with a wide range of tasty fillings. Sandwiches £1.50-2.50. Open M-Th 8am-5:15pm, F 8am-5:30pm, Sa 8am-5pm.

Boston Tea Party, 13-15 Craft Village (tel. 7126 9667). Delicious cakes and incredibly inexpensive food. Outside seating is a relief in the anti-urban though cramped setting of the craft village. Full meal £2-3. Tea and scone £1. Open daily 9am-5:30pm.

⚓ PUBS AND CLUBS

Derry's nightlife has the city center buzzing like a 24hr. generator. Plenty of pubs lie within spitting distance of each other, and pub crawls are a mode of transport after nightfall. Trad and rock can be found any night of the week, and all age groups keep the pubs lively until the 1am closing time. Most bars have cheap drink promotions during the week.

Peadar O'Donnell's, 53 Waterloo St. (tel. 7137 2318). Named for the famous Donegal Socialist who organized the Irish Transport and General Workers Union and took an active role in the 1921 Irish Civil War. Banners and sashes of all nationalities and orders cover the ceiling, while *craic* covers the ground level. Live trad nightly.

The Gweedore Bar, 59-61 Waterloo St. (tel. 7126 3513). The back door has connected to Peadar's since Famine times. The Gweedore hosts rock, bluegrass, and funk while maintaining a traditional bar aesthetic.

The Townsman Bar, 33 Shipquay St. (tel. 7126 0820). Attracts a young and colorful crowd to its surreal decorative scheme. 20 purple pool tables and an open ceiling (in nice weather) over the bar. DJs nightly. Weekend cover £5-6.

Squire's Night Club, 33 Shipquay St. (tel. 7126 6017). The Townsman's sweaty cousin where big-name DJs drop in the last Sunday of every month. Dry ice and an alternative music room distinguish this disco. Live bands M, 2 DJs Th-Su. Cover £1-10; usually around £2 until 11pm, £3 after.

The Strand Bar, 35-38 Strand Rd. (tel. 7126 0494). 4 floors of decadently decorated space. The downstairs has live Irish music Tu-Th; the middle bar plays 70s and 80s; and the top floor is a hip nightclub with theme nights and promotions. Cover £3-6.

The Dungloe, 41-43 Waterloo St. (tel. 7126 7716). Three huge floors with a 1950s feel. Live music weekly every Tu-Sa at 11pm, including trad, blues, and rock.

The Carraig Bar (a.k.a. The Rock), 113-119 Strand Rd. (tel. 7126 7529), in the university area. Destroyed by a bomb in 1973, this Victorian bar with stained glass has recovered wonderfully. Sleek second floor hosts discos Tu and Th. Occasional cover.

👁 TOURS

Walking tours provide an introduction to the city's history-laden geography. These tours let you walk on top of the city walls in order to show how what lies within them has shaped what lies without.

DERRY VISITOR AND CONVENTION BUREAU GUIDED WALKING TOURS. The tourist office sponsors several well-prepared guided walks. *(Leaves from the tourist office. Tel. 7126 7284. July-Oct. M-F 11:15am and 3:15pm, Nov.-May M-F 2:30pm. £3.25; students, seniors and children £2.)*

NORTHERN IRELAND TOURS AND GUIDES LIMITED. Stephen McPhilemy intelligently describes Derry's history with vim and vigor. *(Tours depart from the tourist office. Tel. 7128 9051. May-Sept. daily 10:30am and 2:30pm. Call to schedule other times. £3.)*

FOYLE CIVIC BUS TOURS. This Ulsterbus tour suits non-walkers and makes six stops, including the university, Guild Hall, and St. Eugene's Cathedral. *(Leaves from the Foyle St. depot. Tel. 7126 7284. July-Aug. Tu 2pm. £3.)*

👁 SIGHTS

Derry began as a Celtic holy place and later became the site of a monastery founded by St. Columcille in the 6th century. The city itself was built at the beginning of the 17th century as the crowning achievement of the Ulster Plantations (see **Plantation and Cromwell,** p. 9). After the "Flight of the Earls" in 1607 (see **Rathmullan,** p. 376), much of Ulster was left without local leaders. The

English seized the moment to take land from native Catholic residents for redistribution to Protestant settlers from England and Scotland. Derry itself was granted to the London guilds and renamed on the maps as "Londonderry" to assert its new Anglo-Irish identity. The displaced local Catholics rebelled several times with no success, while sectarian antagonism grew. When King James II approached the city in 1689 with several thousand French troops behind him, the Protestant inhabitants of the city rallied around the cause of his opponent, King William of Orange; the ensuing **Siege of Derry** lasted 105 days (see **The Protestant Ascendancy,** p. 7). The siege created Loyalist heroes in the **Apprentice Boys,** who closed the city gates on James. They did so against the will of **Robert Lundy,** the city leader who advocated surrender during the siege and has been hated by Loyalists ever since. His effigy is still burnt annually at the **August 12th** ceremony commemorating the event, when hundreds of present-day Apprentice Boys gather from around the world and march around the city's walls.

Always a major port, Derry became an industrial center by the 19th century. The city was also the main emigration point in Ireland, and massive numbers of Ulster-Irish Catholics as well as Presbyterians fled the area's religious discrimination. Around the time of the Famine, many Catholics gave up on emigration and formed the **Bogside** neighborhood outside the city walls. The creation of the Republic made Derry a border city, and a Catholic majority made it a headache for Unionist leaders; it became the locus of some of the most blatant civil rights violations, including gerrymandering and religious discrimination. The civil rights marches that sparked the Troubles originated here in 1968. **Free Derry,** the western, Catholic part of the city, controlled by the IRA and a "no-go area" for the army from 1969-72; **Bloody Sunday,** January 30, 1972, when British troops fired on demonstrators and killed 14; and **Operation Motorman** (the July 1972 army effort to penetrate the "no-go" area and arrest IRA leaders), became powerful logos for Catholics in Derry and Nationalists everywhere. Although the Derry landscape was once razed by years of bombings, today the city has been rebuilt and looks sparklingly new. Violence still erupts occasionally in Derry during the July marching season and other contentious sectarian events, but, on the whole, recent years have seen the relatively peaceful coexistence of Derry's Catholic and Protestant populations. Moves to mix religions in the Derry school system may someday unify civil society.

THE OLD CITY

THE WALLS. Derry's city walls, 18 ft. high and 20 ft. thick, were erected between 1614 and 1619. They have never been breached, hence Derry's nickname "the Maiden City." A walk along the top of this mile-long perimeter takes about 20min. and affords a far-reaching view of Derry from its self-contained early days to its present urban sprawl. Seven **cannons** perch along the northeast wall between Magazine and Shipquay Gates. They were donated by Queen Elizabeth I and the London Guilds who "acquired" the city during the Ulster Plantation. A plaque on the outside of this section of wall marks the water level in the days when the Foyle ran right along the walls (it's now 300 ft. away). The stone tower along the southeast wall past New Gate was built to protect **St. Columb's Cathedral,** the symbolic focus of the city's Protestant defenders. Stuck in the center of the southwest wall, **Bishop's Gate** was remodeled in 1789 into an ornate triumphal gate in honor of William of Orange, the Protestant victor of the battles of 1689. The northwest wall supports **Roaring Meg,** a massive cannon donated by London fishmongers in 1642 and used in the 1689 siege. The sound of the cannon alone was rumored to strike fear into the hearts of enemies. The huge marble platform that now stands here was built to hold a marble statue of the Rev. George Walker, joint-governor of Derry during the siege. The first statue placed here, blown up in 1973, showed him waving a fist in the direction of the site of the Battle of the Boyne and the Bogside. Its replacement was ready in 1992, but hours before its unveiling, an anonymous phone call threatened to blow the new one up if it overlooked the Bogside. The authorities backed down, and the quite defaced marble Rev. Walker II now stands in a churchyard within the city walls.

MEMORIAL HALL. The Apprentice Boys have had their headquarters here for centuries. Inside, there is supposedly a museum's worth of historical items dating back to the Apprentices who shut the 1689 city gates. Admission is strictly regulated and highly unlikely. Membership today is open only to Protestant men, although they allow women in to cook and clean. *(Between Royal Bastion and Butcher's Gate. Closed to non-members.)*

ST. COLUMB'S CATHEDRAL. The tall spire of the cathedral in the southwest corner of the walled city is visible from almost anywhere in Derry. Built between 1628 and 1633, St. Columb's Cathedral was the first Protestant cathedral in Britain or Ireland (all the older ones were confiscated Catholic cathedrals). The original spire of wood coated with lead was in disrepair at the time of the Great Siege, so the city's defenders removed its lead and smelted it into bullets and cannonballs. Today's steeple is the church's third. The interior is fashioned of roughly hewn stone and holds an exquisite Killybegs altar carpet, a bishop's chair dating from 1630, and 214 hand-carved Derry-oak pews, of which no two are the same. The entrance room of the church displays a large mortar ball on a stand. Look in the top and you'll notice a deep well in the ball. During the siege of Derry, hundreds of such mortars were packed with gun power and fired upon the city, exploding on impact. This one, however, was packed with the surrender note from King James' forces, and fired onto church grounds. Given the infrequency with which those under siege inspected the cannon balls that fell on their city, it probably took a considerable amount of time before the note was discovered. Like many Protestant churches in the North, St. Columb's is bedecked with war banners, including flags from a Napoleonic battle, the Crimean War, the first and second World Wars, and the two yellow flags captured from the French at the Great Siege. A tiny, museum-like **chapterhouse** at the back of the church displays the original locks and keys of the four main city gates, part of Macaulay's *History of England*, and relics from the 1689 siege. The tombstones flat on the ground in the graveyard outside were leveled during the siege to protect the graves from Jacobite cannonballs. *(Off Bishop St. in the Southwest corner of the city. Tel. 267313. Open Apr.-Oct. M-Sa 9am-5pm, Nov.-Mar. M-Sa 9am-4pm. £1 donation suggested for cathedral; chapterhouse 50p.)*

GUILDHALL. This neo-Gothic building was formerly home to the City Council. First built in 1887, wrecked by fire in 1908, and destroyed by bombs in 1972, today's structure contains replicas of the original stained-glass windows. Among the bountiful rarities is the mayor's chain of office, which was officially presented to the city by William of Orange. Upstairs, the hall houses an enormous organ with over three thousand pipes. The ghost of Sam Mackay, a former superintendent, now haunts the Guildhall. The hall also sponsors various concerts, plays, and exhibitions throughout the year. *(Shipquay Gate. Tel. 7137 7335. Open M-F 8:30am-5:30pm. Free tours every hour on the hour. 9:30am-4:30pm.)*

TOWER MUSEUM. Engaging walk-through dioramas and audiovisual displays relay Derry's long history. A series of short videos illustrate Derry's economic, political, and cultural past. The whole museum deserves at least 2hr. *(Union Hall Place, just inside Magazine Gate. Tel. 7137 2411. Open July-Aug. M-Sa 10am-5pm, Su 2pm-5pm; Sept.-June Tu-Sa 10am-5pm. Last entrance 4:30pm. £3.75, students and seniors £1.25.)*

OTHER SIGHTS. Maritime buffs should head to the **Harbour Museum**, Guildhall St., which features paintings and artifacts related to Derry's harbor history. *(Tel. 7137 7331. Open M-F 10am-1pm and 2-4:30pm. Free.)* The **Calgach Center**, 4-22 Butcher St., helps trace Donegal and Derry roots with an extensive heritage library and a helpful genealogy center. *(Tel. 7137 3177. Open M-F 9am-5pm. Free*

PARIS, NEW YORK, DERRY In the last century, the opulent homes of local statesmen and merchants were located within Derry's city walls. In those days, the wealthy wives of the city would order their fashionable dresses from London. When the dresses arrived, the ladies donned their new garb and met to stroll about all day long on the city walls in their new frilly frocks. The poverty-stricken residents of the Bogside looked up at the ladies on the wall above their neighborhood and were enraged at the decadent lifestyle on display. On one occasion, several Bogside residents took it upon themselves to write a letter of complaint about the parading "cats" to the London papers. The press in London were so amused by the nickname for Derry's finest ladies that it stuck, and the phrase "cat walk" fell into common usage.

admission. Database search usually costs over £20.) Also in the center is **The Fifth Province**, a flashy multimedia display of the history of Celtic Ulster. (Open M-F 10am-4:30pm. £3, students and seniors £1.) The **Derry Craft Village**, Shipquay St., was built from cast-away building materials by entrepreneurial youth in an abandoned lot in the Bogside. The village encompasses a pleasant courtyard surrounded by cafes, kitschy craft shops, and **Bridie's Cottage**, the summertime host to Derry's award-winning **Teach Ceoil (Music House)**. Between July 10 and September 30, the Cottage offers lunchtime performances of Irish music, reading, and dance (M-F 1-2pm; free) and Thursday night "Irish suppers" (8:30pm; £6 includes supper, *ceílí* dancing, and trad sessions). Stop by **The Irish Shop** in the Craft Village for information. (Open M-Sa 9am-5:30pm.)

OUTSIDE THE WALLS

Much has been preserved in the "walled city" of Derry, providing visitors with a sense of the city as it stood during the days of the Great Siege. Everything outside the walls, on the other hand, hails a new age of onrushing modernity with multiple commercial, political, and religious interests.

ST. COLUMBA'S CHURCH. Its builders intended to construct the edifice on the site of St. Columba's first monastery. Recent scholarship, however, suggests that it is on the site of the holyman's visions of Christ. Current thought places St. Columba's first monastery at the site where St. Augustine's Church now stands, on Palace St., inside the walled city. Even so, St. Columba's Church, which houses a rough copy of the Book of Kells, is worth a visit. (Tel. 262301. Church open daily July-Aug. 9am-9pm, Sept.-June 9am-8:30pm. Free.)

MAGEE COLLEGE. The university has changed its affiliation several times: originally a member of the Royal University of Ireland in 1879, by 1909 it had become part of Trinity College Dublin. It has been part of the University of Ulster since 1984. The neo-Gothic building shines among its clumsy neighbors. (10min. east of city center. Tel. 7137 1371.)

WORKHOUSE MUSEUM. This original building displays the history of its use during the Famine. (Glendermot Rd. Tel. 7131 8328. Open M-Sa 10am-4:30pm.)

RESIDENTIAL NEIGHBORHOODS AND MURALS

Near the city walls, Derry's residential neighborhoods, both Catholic and Protestant, display brilliant murals; most pay tribute to past historical events, such as the civil rights movements of the 1970s, and are less immediately inflammatory than some of those in Belfast. Many of the murals can be seen from the viewpoints on the city wall. For a key to their iconography, see p. 418.

WATERSIDE AND THE FOUNTAIN ESTATE. These two neighborhoods are home to Derry's Protestant population. The Waterside is nearly split in its percentage of Catholics and Protestants, but the Fountain is almost entirely Protestant. The Fountain is reached from the walled city by exiting through the left side of Bishop's Gate; it is contained by Bishop, Upper Bennett, Abercorn, and

Hawkin St. This small area of only 600 residents holds the more interesting Protestant murals. The few Loyalist murals in the Waterside lie along Bond and Irish St.

THE BOGSIDE. This famous Catholic neighborhood is easily recognizable. A huge sign just west of the city walls at the junction of Fahan St. and Rossville Sq. declares "You Are Now Entering Free Derry." It was originally painted in 1969 on the end of a row-house; the houses of the block have since been knocked down, but this end-wall remains with a frequently repainted but never reworded message. This powerful mural is surrounded by other, equally striking, nationalist artistic creations, and the spot is referred to as **Free Derry Corner.** Nearby, a stone monument commemorates the 14 protesters shot dead on Bloody Sunday. In both Belfast and Derry, peace groups have recently organized children of all religions to paint large non-sectarian murals. "The Auld Days," at the junction of William and Rossville St. across from Pilot's Row Community Centre in the Bogside, is one of several such works. Another piece of public art, a sculpture at the city-side end of Craigavon Bridge, shows two men reaching out to each other across a divide.

▣ ENTERTAINMENT

Derry has a full-blooded arts scene. **Orchard Gallery,** Orchard St. (tel. 7126 9675), is one of the best spots on the island for viewing well-conceived exhibitions of contemporary Irish and international artists' works. (Open Tu-Sa 10am-6pm. Free.) The **Foyle Arts Centre** (tel. 7126 6657), on Lawrence Hill off Strand Rd., offers classes in a broad range of arts, including music, drama, and dance; they also have a darkroom and occasional exhibitions and concerts. (Open M-Th 9am-10pm, F-Sa 9am-6pm.) The **Rialto Entertainment Center,** 5 Market St. (box office tel. 7126 0516), looks like a tacky multiplex but is actually Derry's most prestigious and largest venue for plays, concerts, and musicals, as well as the occasional photography show. (Box office open M-Sa 9:30am-5pm. Tickets £2-20, student rates available.) **The Playhouse,** 5-7 Artillery St. (tel. 7126 8027), specializes in the work of young playwrights and performers. (Tickets £3-7.) St. Columb's Hall, Orchard St. (tel. 7126 2845), houses the **Orchard Cinema** (tel. 7126 7789), an intimate theater that screens a mix of art house, cult, classic, and foreign films. (Tickets £3.50, students £2.50.) The **Guildhall** (tel. 7137 7335) combines government and artistic functions to produce a range of shows, including jazz concerts and dance championships. Checking the local paper is ultimately the most successful means of scoping out the local arts scenes.

Feís Doirecdmcill, during Easter week, is a festival of Irish dancing, verse speaking, and music in the Guildhall with three sessions daily (£1 each). In late February, **Feís Londonderry,** also held in the Guildhall, features Irish music and a drama competition; three daily sessions cost £1 each.

FERMANAGH

Fermanagh is Northern Ireland's lake district; Upper and Lower Lough Erne extend on either side of Enniskillen, connecting to the Shannon River through a canal to the south. The northern section of Lower Lough extends to Donegal, while the Upper Lough, a labyrinth of connected pools and rivers concealed by trees, extends south into Co. Cavan. Islands surface in both lakes. Vacationers, mostly Northerners, crowd the caravan parks and the walking paths in July and August. Hiking, biking, boating, canoeing, and orienteering provide the area's excursions. The well-marked **Kingfisher Bike Trail** (tel. 6632 0121), inaugurated in 1998, connects the towns in the lake district, circling from Belleek through Enniskillen, Belturbet, Leitrim, and back up through Belcoo and Kittycloguer. A free tourist office pamphlet outlines several itineraries. Serious hik-

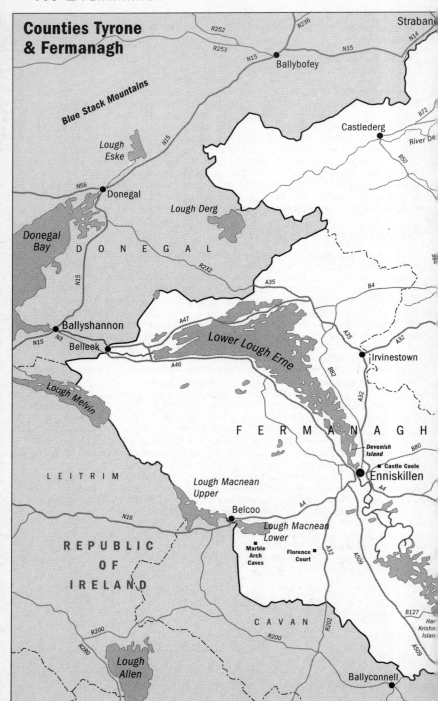

Counties Tyrone & Fermanagh

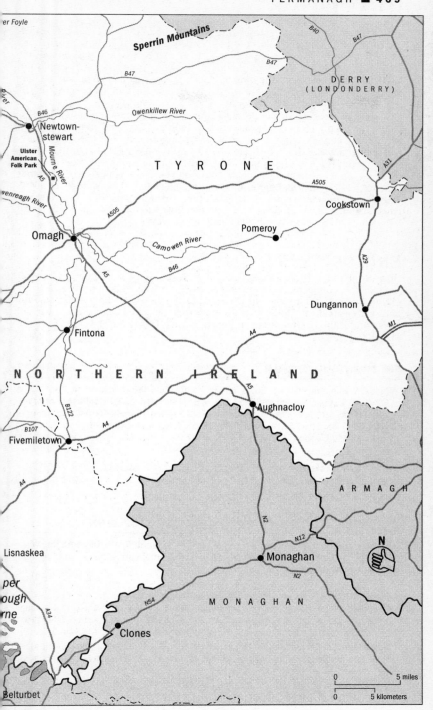

ers might consider tackling the Fermanagh stretch of the Ulster Way. These 23 mi. of forested paths are marked by wooden posts with yellow arrows and stenciled hikers. Leading from Belcoo to Lough Navar, the path is neither smooth nor level, so bicyclists should think again. Take a detailed map; food and transport are scarce. The tourist office's Ulster Way pamphlet and the Fermanagh section of *The Ulster Way* (both 75p) contain detailed descriptions of the route, its sights, and its history.

A week of boating on the **Shannon-Erne waterway** is another option to consider. The original Shannon-Erne link was built in 1846, abandoned in 1869 in favor of the steam engine, and restored for tourism in 1994 as the longest navigable inland waterway in Europe. Boats cost £15-40 per person per night for a week's cruise on a 2- to 8-person boat; most marinas along the lakes are free, there are kitchenettes on the boats, and no experience is necessary. **Aghinver** (tel. 6663 1400), **Belleek Charter Cruising** (tel. 6665 8027), **Carrybridge** (tel. 6638 7034), and **Erne Marine** (tel. 6634 8267) rent boats by the week; prices range from £380-675 per week for a 2- to 4-person boat to £700-1450 per week for an 8-person boat. Services are available along the way.

ENNISKILLEN

Busy Enniskillen (pop. 14,000) lies on an island between Upper and Lower Lough Erne, connected to the mainland by five traffic-choked bridges. A lively city in the midst of a large but declining farming district, Enniskillen's shops and services make it a good base for exploring the Lake District. The town will never forget the IRA bombing on Remembrance Day, 1987, that killed 11 people and injured 61.

▐▀ TRANSPORTATION

Buses: Wellington Rd. (tel. 6632 2633), across from the tourist office. Open M-Sa 8:45am-5:30pm. Service to **Sligo** (1hr., M-Sa 3 per day, £7.30), **Belfast** (2½hr.; M-F 10 per day, Sa 8 per day, Su 5 per day; £6.50), **Derry** (3hr.; M-F 7 per day, Sa 4 per day, Su 3 per day; £6.30), **Dublin** (3hr.; M-Sa 4 per day, Sa 5 per day, Su 3 per day; £9.70), and **Galway** (5hr., M-Sa 1 per day, £13).

Taxis: Call-a-Cab (tel. 6632 4848).

Bike Rental: Lakeland Canoe Center (tel. 6632 4250, evenings 6632 2411), just upstream from the bridge. Ring the bell at the dock on the river bank and someone will row over. £9 per day, £50 per week.

▐ ORIENTATION AND PRACTICAL INFORMATION

Enniskillen's main streets run laterally across the island: **Queen Elizabeth Rd.** to the north, the five segments that compose the island's main street in the middle tiers, and **Wellington Rd.** to the south.

Tourist Office: Fermanagh Tourist Information Centre, Wellington Rd. (tel. 6632 3110), across from the bus station. Free giant maps. Open July-Aug. M-F 9am-7pm, Sa 10am-6pm, Su 11am-5pm; May-June and Sept. M-F 9am-5:30pm, Sa 10am-6pm, Su 11am-5pm; Oct.-Mar. M-F 9am-5pm; Apr. M-F 9am-5pm, Sa 10am-6pm, Su 11am-5pm.

Banks: First Trust Savings Bank, 8 East Bridge St. (tel. 6632 2464). Open M-F 9:30am-4:30pm. **Halifax Building Society,** 20 High St. (tel. 327 072). Open M-F 9am-5pm, Sa 9am-noon. Both have **ATMs.**

Luggage Storage: Ulsterbus Parcel-link (tel. 6632 2633), at the bus station. 50p per bag. Open daily 9am-5:30pm.

Laundry: Paragon Cleaners, 12 East St. (tel. 6632 5230). £5-7 per load. Open daily 9am-1pm and 1:30-5:30pm.

Pharmacy: P.F. McGovern, High St. (tel. 6632 2393), passes out pills. Open M-Sa 9am-5:30pm. Rotating Su hours.

Emergency: Dial 999; no coins required. **Police:** Tel. 6632 2823.

Hospital: Erne Hospital, Cornagrade (tel. 6632 4711).

Post Office: East Bridge St. (tel. 6632 4525). Open M-F 9am-5:30pm, Sa 9am-12:30pm. **Postal code:** BT74.

ACCOMMODATIONS

Backpackers choose between the pseudo-island a stone's throw from the downtown and the solace of a renovated stable in a country park 11 mi. from town. Have the foresight to call ahead to either and all else.

Lakeland Canoe Centre, Castle Island (tel. 6632 4250, evenings 6632 2411). Walk down from the tourist office to the river, ring the bell for a ferry, and be prepared to wait. The hostel is on 3 interlocking pagodas on the island. Dorms £9; B&B £11. **Camping** £4 per person, includes ferry fee and use of hostel facilities. Sports equipment rental.

Castle Archdale Youth Hostel (YHANI/HI) (tel. 6862 8118), 11 mi. from town. Take the Pettigoe bus to Lisarrick, head 1 mi. left down Kesh-Enniskillen Rd., turn right into the park at a small church, and walk 1 mi. The hostel occupies the stables of a now demolished but once stately home. The park's extensive grounds have a marina, tea room, deer pen, bog garden, and miles of forested nature walks. Peacocks roam the yard. Dorms £8.50. **Camping** (tel. 6862 1333) at the caravan park down the hill. £6 per 2-person tent, £10 per 4-person tent. Open Mar.-Oct.

Rossole House, 85 Sligo Rd. (tel. 6632 3462). An expensive, spiffy option. Located in a gorgeous stone Georgian house on Rossole Lough. Singles £22, doubles £36.

Abbeyville, 1 Willoughby Ct. (tel. 6632 7033). A well-marked 10min. walk down the A46 Belleek Rd. Mrs. McMahon's flowery rooms are stocked with tourist info. Singles £25; doubles £36, with bath £36.

FOOD AND PUBS

Barbizon Cafe, 5 East Bridge St. (tel. 6632 4556). Both a coffeeshop and a gallery for the Swiss artists who run it. Bouncy benches welded from tractor seats make the crispy falafel (£3) taste that much better. Open M-Sa 8:30am-6pm.

Kamal Mahal, Water St. (tel. 6632 5045). Bowls of rice round out already large portions of awe-inspiring Indian food. Take-away or sit-down. Open daily noon-midnight.

Franco's, Queen Elizabeth Rd. (tel. 6632 4424). Cozy nooks, wooden tables, and red napkins hide behind the wall of plants that fronts this popular bistro. Pizza from £4.75, pasta from £6.65. Opens noon-late. Live music weekends in July-Aug.

The Crowe's Nest, High St. (tel. 6632 5252). Gas masks, swords, and other digestive aids are exhibited around this central pub and grill that serves a number of health-conscious meals. Huge all-day breakfast £4. Lasagne £5. Live music nightly at 10pm ranges from country to trad. Nightclub out back on weekends. Cover £3-5.

Bush Bar, 26 Townhall St. (tel. 6632 5210). The middle room glows with orange lightbulbs while the back room has a clubby atmosphere. Trad M at 9:30pm.

Blakes of the Hollow, 6 Church St. (tel. 6632 2143). Reads "William Blake" out front. So old and red they put it on a postcard. Brightly lit for golden youths. Tu and Th trad.

👁 SIGHTS

Enniskillen Castle was home in the 15th century to the fearsome Gaelic Maguire chieftains and became Elizabethan barracks in the middle ages; these days it houses two separate museums. The **Heritage Center** presents a comprehensive look at rural Fermanagh, beginning with a pottery display and culminating in a large-scale tableau of an 1830s kitchen. The **Museum of the Royal Inniskilling Fusiliers and Dragoons** is a military buff's playground. (Tel. 6632 5000. Open M 2-5pm, Tu-F 10am-5pm; May-Aug. also Sa 2-5pm; July-Aug. also Su 2-5pm. ₤2, students ₤1.50.)

A mile and a half south of Enniskillen on A4, **Castle Coole** rears up in neoclassical hauteur. The National Trust spent ₤7 million restoring it for tourists. The acres of landscaped grounds are covered by buttercups, wild daisies, and the occasional golf ball. Don't miss the addition of the servant's tunnel tour on how the other nine-tenths lived. The castle grounds are 10min. along on Dublin Rd.; the castle itself appears at the end of a 20min. hike up the driveway. (Tel. 6632 2690. Open May-Aug. F-W 1-6pm, Apr. and Sept. Sa-Su 1-6pm. Last tour 5:15pm. Tours ₤2.80. Parking ₤2.) Diagonally across the street from the castle entrance, the **Ardhowen Theatre** (tel. 6632 5440) poses by the lake shore, satisfying dance, drama, music, and film enthusiasts. (Box office open M-Sa 10am-4:30pm, and until 8:30pm on the night of a performance. Tickets ₤5-8.)

LOWER LOUGH ERNE: BELLEEK

Tiny Belleek, 25 mi. from Enniskillen on A46 at the northern tip of Lower Lough Erne, is famous for its delicate, lace-like china. Tours of the **Belleek Pottery Factory** feature the tradesmen in action. The visitors' center has new goods for sale and old goods for show, such as "Crouching Venus." Nothing's at discount prices, however, since all flawed pieces are destroyed. (Tel. 6865 8501. Open Mar.-Oct. Sa 10am-6pm, Su 2pm-6pm; Nov.-Feb. M-F 9am-6pm. 3 tours per hr. ₤2.) **ExplorErne,** also in Belleek, provides tourist info and chronicles the history and heritage of the Lough Erne region. (Tel. 6865 8866. Open daily mid-Mar.-Oct. 10am-6pm. ₤1.)

DEVENISH ISLAND

The ruins on tiny Devenish Island are a worthwhile destination for those interested in Irish medieval history and archaeology. St. Molaise founded a monastic center here in the 6th century. Viking raids and later Plantation reforms hurt monastic life; by the 17th century, the whole congregation moved to Monea, on the mainland. Today all that remain are **St. Molaise's House,** an oratory; an 81 ft. round tower dating from the 12th century; and a 15th century Augustinian priory. The round tower is completely intact—you can even climb to the top. **MV Kestrel** tours (tel. 6632 2882) cruise to Devenish Island and Lower Lough Erne from the Round 'O' Jetty in Brook Park, just down A46 (Belleek Rd.) from Enniskillen (May-June 1 per week, July-Aug. 1-2 per day, Sept. 3 per week; ₤4-5). If you want to see only the island, the **Devenish Ferry** leaves from Trory Point, 4 mi. from Enniskillen on Irvinestown Rd. or a mile walk to the left from the Trory ferry bus stop on the Pettigoe route (Apr.-Sept. Tu-Sa 10am-7pm, Su 2-7pm; ₤2.25, includes ticket to small museum on island). Dress warmly, as strong winds howl across the lake.

For more monastic ruins, try **Boa Island** and **White Island,** a few miles from Devenish. The dashing duo are also of interest for their many brilliant examples of both pagan and Christian carvings. You can drive across Boa Island on the Kesh-Belleek Rd., and a ferry service based at the **Castle Archdale Marina** (tel. 6663 1850) runs an hourly boat to White Island (July-Aug. daily 11am-6pm on the hour, Easter-June and Sept. on weekends; ₤3).

SOUTH OF ENNISKILLEN

Ten miles southwest of Enniskillen, Florence Court and the Marble Arch Caves can be combined into a daytrip. **Florence Court** is an 18th century Georgian mansion. The building is surrounded by the **Florence Court Forest Park,** which includes an impressive walled garden. The Rococo Court once housed the Earls of Enniskillen; the third Earl left behind his fossil collection for visitors' delectation. Aside from this remnant, however, few of the original contents of the house remain. To reach the estate, take Sligo Rd. out of Enniskillen, then turn left onto the A32 (Swanlinbar Rd.) and follow the signs. (Tel. 6634 8249. Estate open year-round 10am to 1hr. before dusk. Florence Court open June-Aug. W-M noon-6pm, Apr.-May and Sept. Sa-Su noon-6pm; last tour 5:15pm. £2.80.)

Four miles farther on the road from Florence Court to Belcoo are the **Marble Arch Caves,** a subterranean labyrinth of hidden rivers and weirdly sculpted limestone. Take the Sligo bus to Belcoo and follow the signposts for 3 mi.; this route uses backroads that make it a fairly difficult hitch. *Let's Go* does not recommend hitchhiking. An underground boat trip begins the 75min. tour, which leads to impressive creations sculpted by nature's weird hand over thousands of years. The reflections of stalactites in the river are not to be missed. (Tel. 6634 8855. Open daily July-Aug. 10am-5pm, Mar.-Sept. 10am-4:30pm. Tours every 15min. £5, students £3. Spelunkers should book a day ahead in summer.)

BELTURBET

The sleepy little town of Belturbet, Co. Cavan in the Republic, sits on a hill that overlooks the River Erne. Much to its surprise, recreational anglers and Shannon-Erne boaters recently put Belturbet on the tourist map, so the town went ahead and opened a little **tourist office** (tel. (049) 22044) on Bridge St. (Open daily 10am-8pm.) A pleasant walk meanders down the river and across **Turbet Island,** where a 12th century Norman fortification deteriorates gracefully. West of Belturbet, the ■**Sandville House Hostel** (tel. (049) 22591) offers nature-lovers a veritable orgy and quiet-lovers a feast of solitude. Lose yourself in a morning of canoeing through the thousand fingers of the Upper Erne; find yourself in the evening by the roaring fireplace of the converted barn. Call from Belturbet or Ballyconnell for pick-up by one of the friendly staff. (Dorms £6. **Canoe rental** £5 per day. Laundry £1. Open Mar.-Nov.) **Mrs. McGreevy's Erne View House,** Bridge St. (tel. (049) 22289), provides a quiet night's sleep. (Singles £15-18, doubles £18-22.) Stop in at **The Seven Horseshoes,** Main St. (tel. (049) 22166), for a pint of the blonde in the black skirt among wagon-wheel chandeliers, furry hides, and stuffed pheasants. A few drinks at **The Mad Ass** (tel. (049) 22595) and you'll bet yours on just about anything. Belturbet rouses itself a bit the first week of August during the **Festival of the Erne** (tel. (049) 22044), when women seek the title "Huzzar Lady of the Erne," and men compete to see which man can pull the largest live fish out of the water.

TYRONE

What lakes are to Fermanagh, trees are to Tyrone. In a country where trees are as rare as sunshine, Tyrone has something to boast about. This forested expanse of parks and mountains stretches from Lough Neagh to Donegal. Omagh is a quiet, pretty town with a fantastic hostel. The international-tourist hungry Ulster History Park and Ulster American Folk park provide distraction nearby.

OMAGH

On August 15, 1998, a bomb ripped through Omagh's busy downtown area, killing 29 innocent people and injuring hundreds more. Later, "The Real IRA", a splinter group of the Provisional IRA, took responsibility for the act. The bombing cast a tragic spotlight on the formerly obscure town. Yet the grotesquely violent act did not quash the friendliness of this resilient market town. Omagh is a short drive away from two major tourist attractions: the elaborate Ulster American Folk Park and the informative Ulster History Park. It sits in view of a mist-shrouded mountain range with a pine-scented forest spread across it. In the town itself, Georgian townhouses slope up the main street and abut a classical courthouse.

▐ TRANSPORTATION

Buses: Ulsterbus runs from the station on Mountjoy Rd. (tel. 8224 2711) to **Derry** (1hr.; M-Sa 11 per day, Su 4 per day; £4.50), **Belfast** (2hr.; M-Sa 8-9 per day, Su 4 per day; £5.90), **Dublin** (3hr.; M-Sa 6 per day, Su 4 per day; £9.50), and **Enniskillen** (1hr., 1 per day, £4.20). **Luggage storage:** 50p. Open M-F 9am-5:45pm.

Taxis: Tel. 8210 5050. At the bus depot, with 2 drivers per cab for evening company. £4 to hostel, £6 to Folk Park (see **Sights**).

▌ ORIENTATION AND PRACTICAL INFORMATION

Omagh clusters around the south side of the **River Strule.** Cross the bridge from the bus depot to get downtown; to the right of the bridge, **High St.** splits into **John St.** and **George St.,** which are lined with pubs.

Tourist office: Tel. 8224 7831. Town maps and warm welcomes are free, but that detailed geological survey of the Sperrin Mountains with all the hiking trails and roads marked on it in all sorts of colors will cost you (£4). Open Apr.-Sept. M-Sa 9am-5pm, Oct.-Mar. M-F 9am-5pm.

Banks: First Trust (tel. 8224 7133). **ATM.** Open M-Tu and Th-F 9:30am-4:30pm, W 10am-4:30pm.

Pharmacy: Boots, 47 High St. (tel. 8224 5455). Open M-Sa 9am-5:30pm.

Hospital: Tyrone County ER (tel. 8224 5211).

Post office: 7 High St. (tel. 8224 2970). Open M-F 9am-5:30pm, Sa 10am-12:30pm.

Postal code: BT78 1AB.

▐ ACCOMMODATIONS

Commune with the sheep at the **Glenhordial Hostel,** 9a Waterworks Rd. (tel. 8224 1973). The white building peers down on the distant lights of Omagh through a thick veil of boxed, potted, and hung flowers. The attached conservatory provides the perfect setting for an early evening chat. Call the owners for pick-up or directions for the 45min. walk. (Dorms £6.50. Laundry £1.50. **Bike rental** £7.50 per day.) A 10min. walk from town, the **4 Winds,** 63 Dromore Rd. (tel. 8224 3554), defines comfortable accommodation. Mr. Thomas, a former professional chef, provides tea, coffee, and a filling Irish breakfast, and packs lunches on request. Call for pick-up or directions. (£15, with bath £17.) Pitch a tent 8 mi. north of Omagh at Gortin. **Glen Caravan and Camping Park,** Gortin Rd. (tel. 8164 8108), provides plots in the forest. (£4 per 2-person tent.)

◖▛ FOOD AND PUBS

Watch huge, made-to-order sandwiches materialize before your eyes at **Central Perk** (tel. 8224 6236). Fresh coats of bright paint, and a stellar coffee menu attract friends and enemies to this hip little sandwich cafe. (Sandwiches £1.25-

2.50. Open M-Sa 9am-5pm.) **Grant's,** 29 George St. (tel. 8225 0900), serves a wide range of pastas, steaks, and seafood to earn scrumptious success. Dinner is pricey, while lunch fits most budgets. (Entrees about £5. Open M-Th noon-10pm, F-Sa noon-10:30pm, Su 5-10pm.) **Mickey Disco's,** 39 John St. (tel. 8224 4868), fires up tasty pizzas from £4. (Open daily 5-11pm; takeout until 1am.) High atop High Street, **Chinese Castle** (tel. 8224 5208) dishes out affordable yummy food. Take away dishes £5-6, eating in will cost a wee bit more. (M-Sa noon-2pm and 5-11:45pm, Su 5pm-11:45pm.) **Sally O'Brien's** (tel. 8224 2521), down the street, started as a tea merchant back in the 1880s but has since moved on to stronger brews. The old tea boxes are still on display. On weekend nights, clubbers swarm the disco upstairs. (Cover £3-5.) They drift to **McElroy's** (tel. 8224 4441), 100 yd. past George St., on Saturday nights, to join the suits of armor and a wooden tiger on the dance floor. (Cover £4-6.)

◆ SIGHTS

Five miles north of Omagh on Strabane Rd., the **Ulster American Folk Park** eagerly chronicles the experiences of the two million folk who emigrated from Ulster in the 18th and 19th centuries. Full-scale tableaux of a famine cottage, a New York City Irish tenement, and a non-cuddly bear are included in the indoor museum's exhibits. Most of the outdoor buildings are originals, including the dockside brick buildings and the 100 ft. brig in the Ship and Dockside Gallery. Live "19th century" people are on display in the 19th century Ulster town, American seaside town, and Pennsylvania back-country village, where they answer questions, pose for pictures, and ply their trades. July 4th celebrations, farming demonstrations, craft workshops, and historical reenactments are among the frequent special events. Admission includes access to the **Emigration Database,** an extensive collection of books about Irish-Americana and emigration. (Tel. 8224 3292. Park open Easter-Oct. M-Sa 11am-6:30pm, Su 11:30am-7pm; Oct.-Easter M-F 10:30am-5pm. Last admission 1½hr. before closing. £3.50, students £1.70. Database open M-F 9:30am-4:30pm. Wheelchair accessible.) The bus from Omagh to Strabane can leave you at the park (M-Sa 5-7 per day, Su 2 per day; £1.20).

The **Ulster History Park,** 7 mi. out of town on Gortin Rd., is a sort of theme park for historical Irish structures. The many replicas include a dolmen, an early monastery, a *crannog*, and a Plantation settlement (see **History,** p. 7). An indoor museum shows you the way. Special events, such as the St. Patrick's Day festivities and early August craft fair, mark the calendar. The Gorkin bus will stop here (M-Sa 5 per day, £1.30). (Tel. 8164 8188. Open Apr.-Sept. M-Sa 10:30am-6:30pm, Su 11:30am-7pm; Oct.-Mar. M-F 10:30am-5pm. Last admission 90min. before closing. £3.50, students £2; joint ticket with folk park £5.75, £3.) The deer-infested, "purely coniferous" **Gortin Glen Forest Park** is just a 3min. walk left from the History Park. Nature trails and breathtaking views abound. (Open daily 10am-sunset. Cars £3.) Archaeology enthusiasts should check out Ireland's answer to Stonehenge; situated on the A505 between Omagh and Cookstown, **An Creagán** overflows with 44 well-preserved monuments dating from the Neolithic Period. (Tel. 80761 1112. Open daily during summer and M-F during winter.) During the first weekend in May, born-again Celts descend on **Creggan** to re-enact the ancient **Bealtaine Festival,** a seasonal rite at which ancient livestock paraded through rings of fire.

⛰ SPERRIN MOUNTAINS

A little more than 20 mi. northeast of Omagh sprout the petite but striking Sperrin Mountains. Fortunately for nature, but not for tourists, only narrow and poorly marked roads make their way into the area. Walkers and cyclists can pick up the **Ulster Way** 3½ mi. east of Sperrin (see **By Foot,** p. 73). This section of the trail is over 25 mi. long: it weaves through the heart of the mountains and then meets A6 4 mi.

south of Dungiven. Omagh's **tourist office** (see p. 473) sells the *Ordnance Geological Map* (£4), *The Ulster Way: Accommodation for Walkers* (30p), and *The Ulster Way* (£1); the latter details the best trails through the mountains (5 trails 10-36 mi. long). The **Sperrin Heritage Centre,** on the Plumbridge-Draperstown Rd. a mile east of Cranagh, presents a state-of-the-art multimedia presentation featuring storytelling ghost bartenders, glaciation, bootlegging in the Poteen Mountains, and the discovery of gold. Try your own luck with a pan for 65p. (Tel. (6621) 48142. Open May-Oct. M-F 11am-6pm, Sa 11:30am-6pm, Su 2-7pm. £1.80.)

Just north of the Sperrins in Dungiven on A6, the ■Flax Mill Hostel (IHH) (tel. (015047) 42655) charms visitors with gas lamps, a sit-down bath, and beds covered with homemade quilts. Visitors should take advantage of the cheap, wholesome organic food available on site: the owners grow their own vegetables, make their own breads and jams, and collect eggs from their free-range chickens. Owner Herman provides history lessons and hill-walking routes. Call for pick-up, or take Derry Rd. from Dungiven, turn right after the bridge toward Limavady, and follow the signs for 2 mi. (Dorms £5. **Camping** £3. Continental breakfast £1.70.)

LONDON

Cheap flights to Ireland often involve stop-overs in London. Long-term visitors to Ireland might take advantage of the inexpensive tickets to London from Dublin and Belfast. The center of flashy young Britpop culture, London also has Big Ben, Buckingham Palace and the Tower of London looming in the backround. Its arts scene shines, and its shops and clubs are world renowned (though beware that London's pubs close at a puritanical 11pm). In between the hostel, the airport, and the ferry, you should find time to experience a dab of London's pulsing urbanity.

For an absolutely smashing little book packed with first-rate information on this city, grab a copy of *Let's Go: London 2000* or its trusty glossy, mappy sidekick, *Let's Go Map Guide: London.*

 Many area codes in the U.K. are changing. For long-distance phone calls to London (any call where you have to dial the area code), both new (020) and old numbers (0171 or 0181) will work until Autumn 2000, after which only the new number will work. For local calls (calls made without an area code), you must use the old number before April 22, 2000, and you must use the new number from April 22, 2000. *Let's Go* has listed London numbers as they will be after the change: if you are making a local phone call within London before April 22, 2000, then drop the first digit of the 8 digit number. For more information, call the helpline toll-free at (0808) 224 2000 or check www.numberchange.org.

✈ ORIENTATION

London is divided into boroughs, postal code areas, and districts. Both the borough name and postal code prefix appear at the bottom of most street signs.

Central London, on the north side of the Thames and roughly bounded by the Underground's Circle Line, contains most of the major sights. Within central London, the vaguely defined **West End** incorporates Mayfair, the shopping streets around Oxford Circus, the theaters and tourist traps of Piccadilly Circus and Leicester Sq., Soho, chic Covent Garden, and London's unofficial center, **Trafalgar Square.** East of the West End lies **Holborn,** center of legal activity, and **Fleet Street.**

Around the southeastern corner of the Circle Line is **The City:** London's financial district. Farther east is the ethnically diverse and working-class **East End** and the epic construction site of **Docklands.** Back west along the river and the southern part of the Circle Line is the district of **Westminster,** the royal, political, and ecclesiastical center of England. In the southwest corner of the Circle Line, below the expanse of **Hyde Park,** are gracious **Chelsea,** embassy-laden **Belgravia,** and posh **Kensington.** Around the northwest corner of the Circle Line, tidy terraces border **Regent's Park;** nearby are **Paddington** and **Notting Hill Gate,** home to large Indian and West Indian communities. The Circle Line's northeast corner leads to **Bloomsbury,** which harbors the British Museum.

Trying to reach a **specific destination** in London can be frustrating. Numbers often go up one side of a street and down the other. **Postal code prefixes,** which often appear on London street signs and in street addresses, may help you find your way. The letters stand for compass directions, with reference to the central district (itself divided into WC and EC, for West Central and East Central). A **good map** is key. Visitors staying longer ought to buy a London street index such as *London A to Z* or *Nicholson's Streetfinder* (from £2).

For the most part, London is a tourist-friendly city. It's hard to wander unwittingly into unnerving neighborhoods; these areas, in parts of Hackney, Tottenham, and South London, lie well away from central London. The areas around King's Cross/St. Pancras and Notting Hill Gate Tube stations are bit seedy at night.

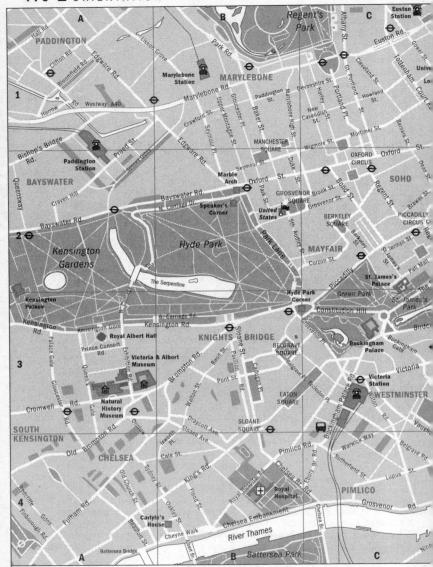

Central London: Major Street Finder

◨ TRANSPORTATION

Airports: Heathrow Airport (tel. 8759 4321; www.baa.co.uk) is the world's busiest airport. The **Heathrow Express** (www.heathrowexpress.com) travels between Heathrow and Paddington Station every 15 minutes (5:10am-11:40pm, £10); the express train departs from Heathrow terminals #1, 2, 3, and 4. London Transport's **Airbus** (tel. 7222 1234) zips from Heathrow to central points, including hotels (1hr., £6). From **Gatwick Airport** (tel. (01293) 535 353), take the BR Gatwick Express train to Victoria Station (35min., daily 5am-midnight every 15min., midnight-5am every 30min.; £8.50). **National Express** (tel. (08705) 808 080) buses run from Victoria Station to Gatwick (1hr., departs every hr. 5:05am-8:20pm, £8.50). **Taxis** take twice as long and cost 5 times as much.

Trains: 8 major stations: Charing Cross, Euston, King's Cross, Liverpool St., Paddington, St. Pancras, Victoria, and Waterloo. All stations linked by Underground. Info at station ticket offices, any LTB or BTA tourist office, or from **British Rail** (24hr. tel. (0345) 484 950; www.britrail.com).

Buses: Victoria Coach Station (Tube: Victoria), located on Buckingham Palace Rd., is the hub of Britain's denationalized coaches. **National Express** (tel. (08705) 808 080) services an expansive network. Greater London area served by **Green Line** (tel. 8668 7261; www.greenline.co.uk), which leaves frequently from Eccleston Bridge behind Victoria Station. Buy tickets from the driver. Deals include the one-day **Rover** ticket (£7, valid on Green Line coaches and London County buses M-F after 9am, Sa-Su all day).

Public Transportation: London is divided into 6 concentric transport zones; fares depend on the distance of the journey and the number of zones crossed. Call the **24hr. help line** (tel. 7222 1234) for help planning subway and bus travel. The **Underground** (or **Tube**) is fast, efficient, and crowded. Opens 6am-midnight. Buy your ticket before you board and pass it through automatic gates at both ends of your journey. The **Travelcard** is a must for budget travelers. Travelcards can be used on the Underground, regular buses, British Rail (Network SouthEast), and the Docklands Light Railway. Available in one-day, one-week, and one-month increments from any station; some restrictions apply. The **bus** network is divided into 4 zones. In and around central London, one-way fares range from 50p to £1.20, depending on the number of zones you cross. **Night buses** (the "N" routes) run frequently throughout London 11:30pm-6am. All pass through Trafalgar Sq. Pick up free maps and guides at **London Transport's Information Centres** (look for the lower-case "i" logo on signs) at the following Tube stations: Euston, Victoria, King's Cross, Liverpool St., Oxford Circus, Piccadilly, St. James's Park, and at Heathrow Terminals 1, 2, and 4.

Taxis: A light signifies that they're empty. Fares are steep, and 10% tip is standard.

◪ PRACTICAL INFORMATION

TOURIST AND LOCAL SERVICES

Tourist Offices: London Tourist Board Information Centre, Victoria Station Forecourt, SW1 (tel. (0839) 123 432; recorded message only; 39-49p per min.). Tube: Victoria. Info and accommodations booking (£5 booking fee, plus 15% refundable deposit). Open Apr.-Nov. daily 8am-7pm; Dec.-Mar. M-Sa 8am-6pm, Su 8am-5pm. Additional offices: **Heathrow Airport,** open daily Apr.-Nov. 9am-6pm; Dec.-Mar. 9am-5pm, and **"Liverpool St." Underground Station** open M 8:15am-7pm, Tu-Sa 8:15am-6pm, Su 8:30am-4:45pm. **City of London Information Centre,** St. Paul's Churchyard, EC4 (tel. 7606 3030). Tube: St. Paul's. Open daily 9:30am-5pm.

Embassies and High Commissions: Australia, Australia House, The Strand, WC2 (tel. 7379 4334). Tube: Aldwych or Temple. Open M-F 9:30am-3:30pm. **Canada,** MacDonald House, 1 Grosvenor Sq., W1 (tel. 7258 6600). Tube: Bond St. or Oxford Circus.

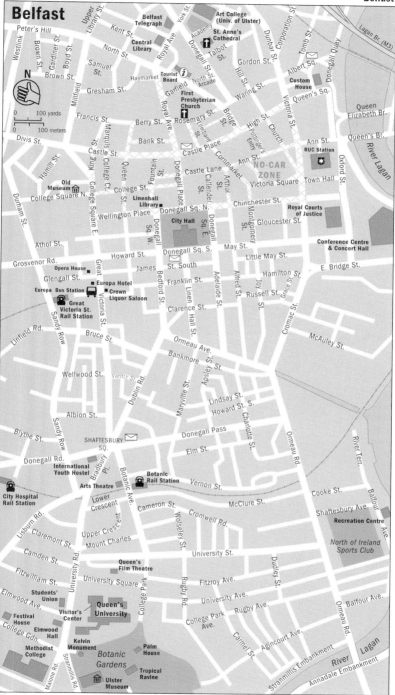

Belfast

Belfast

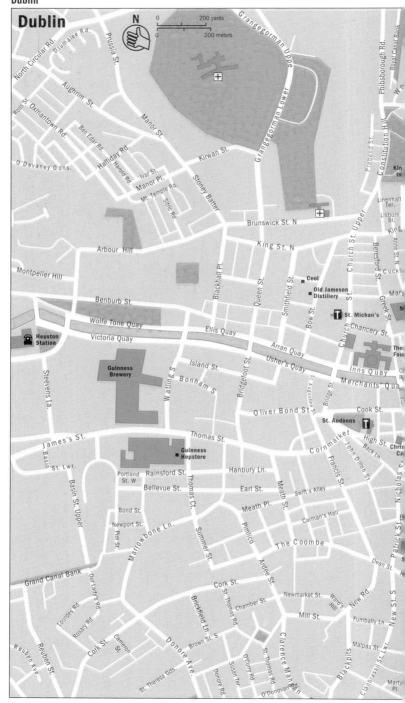

Dublin

N

0   200 yards
0   200 meters

Cork and Galway

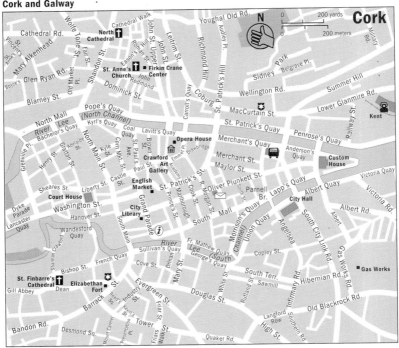

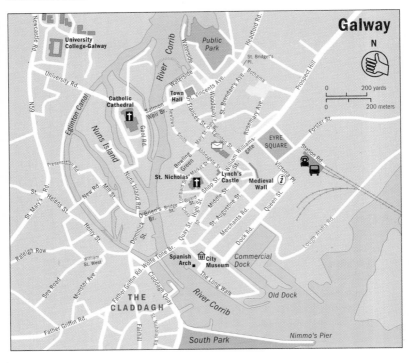